D0435974

DATE DUE

POWERSHIFT

ALVIN TOFFLER

POWER SHIFT

KNOWLEDGE, WEALTH, AND VIOLENCE

AT THE EDGE OF THE 21st CENTURY

BANTAM BOOKS

NEW YORK • TORONTO • LONDON • SYDNEY • AUCKLAND

POWERSHIFT:
KNOWLEDGE, WEALTH, AND VIOLENCE AT THE EDGE OF THE 21ST CENTURY
A Bantam Book / November 1990

Library of Congress Cataloging-in-Publication Data

Toffler, Alvin.
  Powershift : knowledge, wealth, and violence at
the edge of the 21st century.

  Includes bibliographical references.
  1. Social history—1945–   . 2. Economic
history—1945–   . 3. Power (Social sciences)
4. Social change. I. Title.
HN17.5.T6417 1990   303.4   90-1068
ISBN 0-553-05776-6

Published simultaneously in the United States and Canada

Foreign Editions of Powershift *(a partial list)*

Dutch	*Veen Publishers*
Finnish	*Otava Oy*
French	*Librairie Artheme Fayard*
German	*Econ Verlag*
Italian	*Sperling & Kupfer Editore*
Japanese	*Fuso Sha*
Korean	*Korea Economic Daily*
Portuguese	*Distribuidora Record (Brazil)*
Norwegian	*J. W. Cappelens Forlag*
Spanish	*Plaza y Janes*
Swedish	*Bokforlaget Bra Bocker*

PRINTED IN THE UNITED STATES OF AMERICA

BVG 0 9 8 7 6 5 4 3 2

For Karen
with love
from both of us

CONTENTS

A PERSONAL PREFACE   xvii

PART ONE: THE NEW MEANING OF POWER   1

1 THE POWERSHIFT ERA   3

    The End of Empire   4
    God-in-a-White-Coat   7
    Bombarded by the Future   9
    The Making of a Shabby Gentility   10

2 MUSCLE, MONEY, AND MIND   12

    High-Quality Power   15
    One Million Inferences   17
    Facts, Lies, and Truth   18
    The Democratic Difference   19

PART TWO: LIFE IN THE SUPER-SYMBOLIC ECONOMY   23

3 BEYOND THE AGE OF GLITZ   25

    The Business Commandos   27
    Dale Carnegie and Attila the Hun   31
    The Consultant's Hidden Mission   33

4 FORCE: THE YAKUZA COMPONENT   35

    Blood and Snow-Money   36

On Zeks and Goons   37
A Monopoly of Force   40
The Hidden Gun   40
The Trajectory of Power   42

5 WEALTH: MORGAN, MILKEN . . . AND AFTER   45

The X-Shaped Desk   46
Milken versus Morgan   47
Opening the Gates   48
The Counterattack   51
Tampons and Car Rentals   52
The Post–Wall Street Era   53
The Zigzag of Power   56
The Looming Fight for Global Control   58

6 KNOWLEDGE: A WEALTH OF SYMBOLS   60

Inside the Skull   61
An Epitaph for Paper   62
Designer Currencies and Para-Money   64
Power Failures   66
21st-Century Money   68

7 MATERIAL-ISMO!   69

The New Meaning of Joblessness   71
The Spectrum of Mind-Work   74
Lowbrows versus Highbrows   76
Lowbrow Ideology   79
Highbrow Ideology   80

8 THE ULTIMATE SUBSTITUTE   84

The Alchemy of Information   86
Knowledge versus Capital   88

PART THREE: THE INFORMATION WARS   93

9 THE CHECKOUT BATTLE   95

Behind the Shoot-outs   96
The Scent of Miss America   97
The "Push-Money" Ploy   98
Beyond the Supermarket   100
The Double Payment   102
The Intelligent Supermarket   104
A Threat to the "Shoguns"   105

10 EXTRA-INTELLIGENCE   107

Bach, Beethoven, and Wang   107
The Telephone Fad   109
Secrets and Secret-aries   110
Electronic Highways   111
The Self-Aware Network   113
Messing with the Message   115

11 NET POWER   119

The Search for Denim   120
The Bingo-ed Wholesaler   121
Real Estate and Rails   123
Mobilizing for Electronic War   124
The Customer Loop   125
Business Blitzkrieg   127
The Rise of Info-Monopolies?   128

12 THE WIDENING WAR   130

The Half-Trillion Dollar Stake   131
Strategic Standards   133
The Main Bout   135
Computer Democracy   137
The Paradox of Norms   138
The Beer and Sausage Minuet   139

13 THE EXECUTIVE THOUGHT POLICE 141

Levels of Combat 142
The Two-Party Campaign 143
Strategic Retreat 145
The Giant Brain Era 147
The Ethics of Information 150
The Paradox Bomb 151

14 TOTAL INFORMATION WAR 153

Rusty Tracks and Hotel Love-Sounds 154
INs and OUTs 157
Wholistic Espionage 159
A 75-Cent Error 160

PART FOUR: POWER IN THE FLEX-FIRM **163**

15 THE CUBBYHOLE CRASH 165

The Bureaucracy-Busters 165
An Infinity of Cubbyholes 166
Power versus Reason 167
"Camelephants" and Hot Potatoes 169
Choked Channels 171
Free-Flow Knowledge 174
Knowledge Is Power Is Knowledge 178

16 THE FLEX-FIRM 180

The End of the Cookie-Cut Company 183
The De-colonization of Business 184
Dancing on Tables 184
Fam-Firms of the Future 187

17 TRIBAL CHIEFS AND CORPORATE COMMISSARS 190

A Diversity of Powers 198
The Missing Panacea 200
The Limits of Control 202

18 THE AUTONOMOUS EMPLOYEE 204

Unblocking Minds 205
The Feckless Farmer 206
The New Chains 207
The Electronic Proletariat 209
Tomorrow's Work Regimen 210
The Non-interchangeable Person 212
Two Imperatives 213
The Demand for Access 214

19 THE POWER-MOSAIC 218

From Monoliths to Mosaics 220
Meat-Cleaver Management 221
The Monopolists Inside 224
In the Belly of the Behemoth 226
Relational Wealth 227
Power in Mosaics 228
Beyond the Corporation 230

CODA: THE NEW SYSTEM FOR WEALTH CREATION 233

The New Economic Metabolism 233
A Hailstorm of Pleas 235
Tomorrow's Wealth 238

PART FIVE: POWERSHIFT POLITICS 241

20 THE DECISIVE DECADES 243

Dynasties and Democracies 244
Shifting Levels 245
Earth Politics 248
An Explosion of Ethnics 249
Mosaic Democracy 250
Pivotal Minorities 252

21 THE INVISIBLE PARTY 256

The Ministry of the 21st Century 257
The Global Buzzword 258
Stripping for Action 259
Disappearance of the Hierarchs 261
Secret Teams and Plumbers 262

22 INFO-TACTICS 265

Alfalfa Secrets and Guided Leaks 266
The Masked Source 268
Back-stabbers and Back-Channels 270
The Double-Channel Ploy 272
On the Receiving End 273
Massaging the Message 274
In-fighters and Savvy Staffers 276

23 META-TACTICS 278

Eskimos and Mind-Workers 279
Truth versus Power 280
The Kidnapped Finger 282
Chernobyl in the Ballot Box 284
Gimme a Number! 285
Data Base Deception 287
Phantom People 290

24 A MARKET FOR SPIES 295

Butterflies and Bombs 296
The Kremlin's Limousines 298
The Main Competitors 300
Swapping Secrets 301
The Looming Giants 304
Warplanes and "Watch Lists" 305
Line X versus James Bond 308
The Coming Eco-Wars 311
The Privatization of Spying 312
The New Meaning of "Private Eye" 315
Contradictions at the Core 317

25 THE INFO-AGENDA 320

A Hunger for Knowing 321
Terrorist Bombs and AIDS Victims 324
The New Global Feedback 326
The Indiana Jones Code 328

26 THE IMAGE MAKERS 332

The Multi-channel Society 334
The Arrival of Choice 336
The Coming Eurovision 337
The Global Sell 339
The New Barons 341
The Forging of Global Opinion 343

27 SUBVERSIVE MEDIA 347

The Nasty Little Man on TV 348
Three Media Modes 351
Media-fusion 352
Valleys of Ignorance 353
The Revolutionists' Media Strategy 354
The China Syndrome 356

28 THE "SCREENIE" GENERATION 359

The Slave Golfer 360
A Decadent Luxury 361
More than Compassion 363
Electronic Activism 364
The Information Divide 366
The New Alliance 368

CODA: YEARNINGS FOR A NEW DARK AGE 372

Holy Frenzy 372
Eco-theocracy 377
The New Xenophobes 382

PART SIX: PLANETARY POWERSHIFT   **389**

29 THE GLOBAL "K-FACTOR"   391

Pyramids and Moonshots   392
Hand-me-down Economics   393

30 THE FAST AND THE SLOW   397

Coming Home   399
Strategic Real Estate   402
Beyond Raw Materials   404
Expensive Cheap Labor   405
Hyper-speeds   406
Electronic Gaps and Dynamic Minorities   408

31 SOCIALISM'S COLLISION WITH THE FUTURE   413

The Breaking Point   413
The Pre-cybernetic Machine   415
The Property Paradox   417
How Many "Left-handed" Screws?   419
The Dustbin of History   420

32 THE POWER OF BALANCE   423

The Democratization of Death   424
The Ocean of Capital   425
The New Architecture of Knowledge   426
The One-Legged Soviet   428

33 TRIADS: TOKYO . . . BERLIN . . . WASHINGTON   430

The Japanese Gun   430
The Economic Godzilla   431
The *Juku* Race   433
The New *Ost-Strategie*   437
Europe's Morning After   440
From Leftism to Semiology   443
The Wounded Giant   445

The Declining Twins   446
The Woody Allen Impact   448
A Choice of Partners   452

34 THE GLOBAL GLADIATORS   456

The Resurrection of Religion   456
The Empire of Cocaine   459
The Dispersed "Oppressor"   460
The Corporate Condottieri   462
The U.N.-Plus   462
New-Style Global Organizations   463

CODA: FREEDOM, ORDER, AND CHANCE   467

Assumptions   **473**

Bibliography   **477**

Notes   **507**

Acknowledgments   **552**

Index   **555**

A PERSONAL PREFACE

Powershift is the culmination of a twenty-five-year effort to make sense of the astonishing changes propelling us into the 21st century. It is the third and final volume of a trilogy that opened with *Future Shock,* continued with *The Third Wave,* and is now complete.

Each of these three books can be read by itself as an independent work. But together they form an intellectually consistent whole. Their central subject is change—what happens to people when their entire society abruptly transforms itself into something new and unexpected. *Powershift* carries forward the earlier analysis and focuses on the rise of a new power system replacing that of the industrial past.

In describing today's accelerating changes, the media fire blips of unrelated information at us. Experts bury us under mountains of narrowly specialized monographs. Popular forecasters present lists of unrelated trends, without any model to show us their interconnections or the forces likely to reverse them. As a result, change itself comes to be seen as anarchic, even lunatic.

By contrast, this trilogy starts from the premise that today's high-speed changes are not as chaotic or random as we are conditioned to believe. It contends that there are not only distinct patterns behind the headlines, but identifiable forces that shape them. Once we understand these patterns and forces, it becomes possible to cope with them strategically, rather than haphazardly on a one-by-one basis.

However, to make sense of today's great changes, to think strategically, we need more than bits, blips, and lists. We need to see how different changes relate to one another. Thus *Powershift,* like its two predecessors, sets out a clear and comprehensive synthesis—an overarching image of the new civilization now spreading across the planet.

It then zeros in on tomorrow's flashpoints, the conflicts we face as the new civilization collides with the entrenched forces of the old. *Powershift* contends that the corporate takeovers and restructurings seen so far are only the first salvos in far larger, quite novel business battles to come. More important, it holds that the recent upheavals seen in Eastern Europe and the Soviet Union are mere skirmishes compared with the global power struggles that lie ahead. Nor has the rivalry among the United States, Europe, and Japan reached its full intensity.

In short, *Powershift* is about the crescendoing struggles for power that still face us as the industrial civilization loses world dominance and new forces arise to tower over the earth.

For me, *Powershift* is a high point reached after a fascinating journey. Before continuing, however, a personal note is required. For I did not make this journey alone. This entire trilogy, from inception to completion, has had an uncredited co-author. It is the combined work of two minds, not just one, although I have done the actual writing and have accepted the plaudits and criticisms for both of us.

My co-author, as many already know, is my best friend, spouse, and partner, my love for forty years: Heidi Toffler. Whatever the faults of this trilogy, they would have been far more serious without her skeptical intelligence, her intellectual insight, keen editorial sense, and general good judgment about ideas and people alike. She has contributed not merely to after-the-fact polishing but to the formulation of the underlying models on which the works are based.

While the intensity of her involvement varied from time to time, depending on her other commitments, these books required travel, research, interviews with hundreds of people around the world, careful organization, and drafting, followed by endless updating and revision, and Heidi took part at every stage.

Nevertheless, for reasons that were partly private, partly social, partly economic—and that varied at different times over the past two decades—the decision was made to credit only the actual writer.

Even now Heidi refuses to lend her name to a book jacket, out of integrity, modesty, and love—reasons that seem sufficient to her, though not to me. I can only redress this shortcoming with these personal, prefatory words: I feel that the trilogy is as much hers as mine.

All three books probe a single lifetime—the period beginning, say, in the mid-1950s and ending approximately seventy-five years later, in 2025. This span can be called the hinge of history, the period in which smokestack civilization, having dominated the earth for centuries, is finally replaced by another, far different one following a period of world-shaking power struggles.

But, while focused on the same period, each of the three books uses a different lens with which to probe beneath the surface of reality, and it may be useful for readers to define the differences among them.

Thus *Future Shock* looks at the *process* of change—how change affects people and organizations. *The Third Wave* focuses on the *directions* of change—where today's changes are taking us. *Powershift* deals with the *control* of changes still to come—who will shape them and how.

Future Shock—which we defined as the disorientation and stress brought on by trying to cope with too many changes in too short a time—argued that the acceleration of history carries consequences of its own, independent of the actual directions of change. The simple speed-up of events and reaction times produces its own effects, whether the changes are perceived as good or bad.

It also held that individuals, organizations, and even nations can be overloaded with too much change too soon, leading to disorientation and a breakdown in their capacity to make intelligent adaptive decisions. They could, in short, suffer from future shock.

Against the then-current opinion, *Future Shock* declared that the nuclear family was soon to be "fractured." It also foreshadowed the genetic revolution, the rise of a throwaway society, and the revolution in education that may now, at long last, be beginning.

First published in the United States in 1970, and subsequently all over the world, the book touched an unsheathed nerve, became a surprise international best-seller, and generated avalanches of commentary. It became one of the most cited works in social science literature, according to the Institute for Scientific Information. The phrase *future shock* entered the daily language, turned up in many dictionaries, and today constantly appears in headlines.

The Third Wave, which followed in 1980, had a different focus. Describing the latest revolutionary changes in technology and society, it placed them in historical perspective and sketched the future they might bring.

Terming the agricultural revolution of 10,000 years ago the First Wave of transforming change in human history, and the industrial revolution the Second Wave, it described the major technological and social changes beginning in the mid-1950s as a great Third Wave of human change—the start of the new, post-smokestack civilization.

Among other things, it pointed at new industries to come— based on computers, electronics, information, biotechnology, and the like, terming these the "new commanding heights" of the economy. It foreshadowed such things as flexible manufacturing, niche markets, the spread of part-time work, and the de-massification of the media. It described the new fusion of producer and consumer and introduced the term *prosumer.* It discussed the coming shift of some work back into the home, and other changes in politics and the nation-state system.

Banned in some countries, *The Third Wave* became a best-seller in others, and for a time was the "bible" of the reform intellectuals in China. First accused of spreading Western "spiritual pollution," then released and published in vast quantities, it became the best-selling book in the world's most populous nation, second only to the speeches of Deng Xiaoping. The then–Prime Minister, Zhao Ziyang, convened conferences about it and urged policymakers to study it.

In Poland, after a legitimately abridged version was published, students and Solidarity supporters were so outraged at the cuts, they published an "underground" edition and also distributed pamphlets containing the missing chapters. Like *Future Shock, The Third Wave* inspired many responses among its readers, leading among other things to new products, companies, symphonies, and even sculptures.

Now, twenty years after *Future Shock* and ten years after *The Third Wave, Powershift* is at last ready. Picking up where its predecessors left off, it focuses on the crucially changed role of knowledge in relationship to power. It presents a new theory of social power, and explores the coming shifts in business, the economy, politics, and global affairs.

It seems hardly necessary to add that the future is not "knowable" in the sense of exact prediction. Life is filled with surrealistic surprise. Even the seemingly "hardest" models and data are frequently based on "soft" assumptions, especially where these concern human affairs. Moreover, the very subject of these books —accelerant change—makes the details in them subject to obsolescence. Statistics change. New technologies supplant older ones. Political leaders rise and fall. Nevertheless, as we advance into the terra incognita of tomorrow, it is better to have a general and incomplete map, subject to revision and correction, than to have no map at all.

While each of the works in the trilogy is built on a model different from, but compatible with, the others, all the books draw on documentation, research, and reportage from many disparate fields and many different countries. Thus, for example, in preparing this work, we attempted to study power at the pinnacle and in the depths of society.

We have had the opportunity to meet for hours with Mikhail Gorbachev, Ronald Reagan, George Bush, several Japanese Prime Ministers, and others whom most would count as among the most powerful men in the world.

At the opposite end of the spectrum, one or both of us also visited squatters in a South American "city of misery" and women prisoners under life sentence—both groups thought to be among the most powerless on earth.

In addition, we discussed power with bankers, labor unionists, business leaders, computer experts, generals, Nobel Prize–winning scientists, oil tycoons, journalists, and the top managers of many of the world's biggest companies.

We met with the staff people who shape decisions in the White House, in the Élysée Palace in Paris, in the Prime Minister's office in Tokyo, and even in the offices of the Central Committee of the Communist Party in Moscow. There a conversation with Anatoly Lukyanov (then on the staff of the Central Committee, later the second-highest official of the U.S.S.R. after Gorbachev) was interrupted by an unexpected call for a meeting of the Politburo.

Once, I found myself in a sunlit room surrounded by books in a small town in California. Had I been led into that room blindfolded, I might never have guessed that the intelligent young woman in T-shirt and jeans who faced me across an oak library table was a murderer. Or that she had been convicted of participation in a grisly sexual crime. Or that we were in a prison—a place where the realities of power are laid bare. From her I came to understand that even prisoners are by no means powerless. Some know how to use information for power purposes with all the manipulative finesse of Cardinal Richelieu in the court of Louis XIII, a point directly relevant to the theme of this book. (This experience led my wife and me, on two occasions, to teach a seminar for a class consisting mainly of murderers—from whom we learned much.)

Experiences like these, supplementing exhaustive reading and analysis of written source materials from around the world, made the preparation of *Powershift* an unforgettable time in our lives.

We hope that readers will find *Powershift* as useful, pleasurable, and enlightening as, we are told, they found *The Third Wave* and *Future Shock*. The sweeping synthesis started a quarter century ago is now complete.

—ALVIN TOFFLER

PART ONE

THE NEW MEANING OF POWER

Power grows out of
the barrel of a gun.
—MAO TSE-TUNG

Money talks.
—ANONYMOUS

Knowledge itself is power.
—FRANCIS BACON

1

THE POWERSHIFT ERA

This is a book about power at the edge of the 21st century. It deals with violence, wealth, and knowledge and the roles they play in our lives. It is about the new paths to power opened by a world in upheaval.

Despite the bad odor that clings to the very notion of power because of the misuses to which it has been put, power in itself is neither good nor bad. It is an inescapable aspect of every human relationship, and it influences everything from our sexual relations to the jobs we hold, the cars we drive, the television we watch, the hopes we pursue. To a greater degree than most imagine, we are the products of power.

Yet of all the aspects of our lives, power remains one of the least understood and most important—especially for our generation.

For this is the dawn of the Powershift Era. We live at a moment when the entire structure of power that held the world together is now disintegrating. A radically different structure of power is taking form. And this is happening at every level of human society.

In the office, in the supermarket, at the bank, in the executive suite, in our churches, hospitals, schools, and homes, old patterns of power are fracturing along strange new lines. Campuses are stirring from Berkeley to Rome and Taipei, preparing to explode. Ethnic and racial clashes are multiplying.

In the business world we see giant corporations taken apart and put back together, their CEOs often dumped, along with thousands of their employees. A "golden parachute" or goodbye package of money and benefits may soften the shock of landing for a top manager, but gone are the appurtenances of power: the corporate jet, the limousine, the conferences at glamorous golf

3

resorts, and above all, the secret thrill that many feel in the sheer exercise of power.

Power isn't just shifting at the pinnacle of corporate life. The office manager and the supervisor on the plant floor are both discovering that workers no longer take orders blindly, as many once did. They ask questions and demand answers. Military officers are learning the same thing about their troops. Police chiefs about their cops. Teachers, increasingly, about their students.

This crackup of old-style authority and power in business and daily life is accelerating at the very moment when global power structures are disintegrating as well.

Ever since the end of World War II, two superpowers have straddled the earth like colossi. Each had its allies, satellites, and cheering section. Each balanced the other, missile for missile, tank for tank, spy for spy. Today, of course, that balancing act is over.

As a result, "black holes" are already opening up in the world system: great sucking power vacuums, in Eastern Europe for example, that could sweep nations and peoples into strange new—or, for that matter, ancient—alliances and collisions. Power is shifting at so astonishing a rate that world leaders are being swept along by events, rather than imposing order on them.

There is strong reason to believe that the forces now shaking power at every level of the human system will become more intense and pervasive in the years immediately ahead.

Out of this massive restructuring of power relationships, like the shifting and grinding of tectonic plates in advance of an earthquake, will come one of the rarest events in human history: a revolution in the very nature of power.

A "powershift" does not merely transfer power. It transforms it.

THE END OF EMPIRE

The entire world watched awestruck as a half-century-old empire based on Soviet power in Eastern Europe suddenly came unglued in 1989. Desperate for the Western technology needed to energize its rust-belt economy, the Soviet Union itself plunged into a period of near-chaotic change.

Slower and less dramatically, the world's other superpower also went into relative decline. So much has been written about America's loss of global power that it bears no repetition here. Even more striking, however, have been the many shifts of power away from its once-dominant domestic institutions.

Twenty years ago General Motors was regarded as the world's premier manufacturing company, a gleaming model for managers in countries around the world and a political powerhouse in Washington. Today, says a high GM official, "We are running for our lives." We may well see, in the years ahead, the actual breakup of GM.

Twenty years ago IBM had only the feeblest competition and the United States probably had more computers than the rest of the world combined. Today computer power has spread rapidly around the world, the U.S. share has sagged, and IBM faces stiff competition from companies like NEC, Hitachi, and Fujitsu in Japan; Groupe Bull in France; ICL in Britain, and many others. Industry analysts speculate about the post-IBM era.

Nor is all this a result of foreign competition. Twenty years ago three television networks, ABC, CBS, and NBC, dominated the American airwaves. They faced no foreign competition at all. Yet today they are shrinking so fast, their very survival is in doubt.

Twenty years ago, to choose a different kind of example, medical doctors in the United States were white-coated gods. Patients typically accepted their word as law. Physicians virtually controlled the entire American health system. Their political clout was enormous.

Today, by contrast, American doctors are under siege. Patients talk back. They sue for malpractice. Nurses demand responsibility and respect. Pharmaceutical companies are less deferential. And it is insurance companies, "managed care groups," and government, not doctors, who now control the American health system.

Across the board, then, some of the most powerful institutions and professions inside the most powerful of nations saw their dominance decline in the same twenty-year period that saw America's external power, relative to other nations, sink.

Lest these immense shake-ups in the distribution of power seem a disease of the aging superpowers, a look elsewhere proves otherwise.

While U.S. economic power faded, Japan's skyrocketed. But success, too, can trigger significant power shifts. Just as in the

United States, Japan's most powerful Second Wave or rust-belt industries declined in importance as new Third Wave industries rose. Even as Japan's economic heft increased, however, the three institutions perhaps most responsible for its growth saw their own power plummet. The first was the governing Liberal-Democratic Party. The second was the Ministry of International Trade and Industry (MITI), arguably the brain behind the Japanese economic miracle. The third was Keidanren, Japan's most politically potent business federation.

Today the LDP is in retreat, its elderly male leaders embarrassed by financial and sexual scandals. It is faced, for the first time, by outraged and increasingly active women voters, by consumers, taxpayers, and farmers who formerly supported it. To retain the power it has held since 1955, it will be compelled to shift its base from rural to urban voters, and deal with a far more heterogeneous population than ever before. For Japan, like all the high-tech nations, is becoming a de-massified society, with many more actors arriving on the political scene. Whether the LDP can make this long-term switch is at issue. What is not at issue is that significant power has shifted away from the LDP.

As for MITI, even now many American academics and politicians urge the United States to adopt MITI-style planning as a model. Yet today, MITI itself is in trouble. Japan's biggest corporations once danced attendance on its bureaucrats and, willingly or not, usually followed its "guidelines." Today MITI is a fast-fading power as the corporations themselves have grown strong enough to thumb their noses at it. Japan remains economically powerful in the outside world but politically weak at home. Immense economic weight pivots around a shaky political base.

Even more pronounced has been the decline in the strength of Keidanren, still dominated by the hierarchs of the fast-fading smokestack industries.

Even those dreadnoughts of Japanese fiscal power, the Bank of Japan and the Ministry of Finance, whose controls guided Japan through the high-growth period, the oil shock, the stock market crash, and the yen rise, now find themselves impotent against the turbulent market forces destabilizing the economy.

Still more striking shifts of power are changing the face of Western Europe. Thus power has shifted away from London, Paris, and Rome as the German economy has outstripped all the rest. Today, as East and West Germany progressively fuse their economies, all Europe once more fears German domination of the continent.

To protect themselves, France and other West European nations, with the exception of Britain, are hastily trying to integrate the European community politically as well as economically. But the more successful they become, the more of their national power is transfused into the veins of the Brussels-based European Community, which has progressively stripped away bigger and bigger chunks of their sovereignty.

The nations of Western Europe thus are caught between Bonn or Berlin on the one side and Brussels on the other. Here, too, power is shifting rapidly away from its established centers.

The list of such global and domestic power shifts could be extended indefinitely. They represent a remarkable series of changes for so brief a peacetime period. Of course, some power shifting is normal at any time.

Yet only rarely does an entire globe-girdling *system* of power fly apart in this fashion. It is an even rarer moment in history when all the rules of the power game change at once, and the very nature of power is revolutionized.

Yet that is exactly what is happening today. Power, which to a large extent defines us as individuals and as nations, is itself being redefined.

GOD-IN-A-WHITE-COAT

A clue to this redefinition emerges when we look more closely at the above list of apparently unrelated changes. For we discover that they are not as random as they seem. Whether it is Japan's meteoric rise, GM's embarrassing decline, or the American doctor's fall from grace, a single common thread unites them.

Take the punctured power of the god-in-a-white-coat.

Throughout the heyday of doctor-dominance in America, physicians kept a tight choke-hold on medical knowledge. Prescriptions were written in Latin, providing the profession with a semi-secret code, as it were, which kept most patients in ignorance. Medical journals and texts were restricted to professional readers. Medical conferences were closed to the laity. Doctors controlled medical-school curricula and enrollments.

Contrast this with the situation today, when patients have astonishing access to medical knowledge. With a personal computer and a modem, anyone from home can access data bases like Index Medicus, and obtain scientific papers on everything from Addison's disease to zygomycosis, and, in fact, collect more information about a specific ailment or treatment than the ordinary doctor has time to read.

Copies of the 2,354-page book known as the PDR or *Physicians' Desk Reference* are also readily available to anyone. Once a week on the Lifetime cable network, any televiewer can watch twelve uninterrupted hours of highly technical television programming designed specifically to educate doctors. Many of these programs carry a disclaimer to the effect that "some of this material may not be suited to a general audience." But that is for the viewer to decide.

The rest of the week, hardly a single newscast is aired in America without a medical story or segment. A video version of material from the *Journal of the American Medical Association* is now broadcast by three hundred stations on Thursday nights. The press reports on medical malpractice cases. Inexpensive paperbacks tell ordinary readers what drug side effects to watch for, what drugs not to mix, how to raise or lower cholesterol levels through diet. In addition, major medical breakthroughs, even if first published in medical journals, are reported on the evening television news almost before the M.D. has even taken his subscription copy of the journal out of the in-box.

In short, the knowledge monopoly of the medical profession has been thoroughly smashed. And the doctor is no longer a god.

This case of the dethroned doctor is, however, only one small example of a more general process changing the entire relationship of knowledge to power in the high-tech nations.

In many other fields, too, closely held specialists' knowledge is slipping out of control and reaching ordinary citizens. Similarly, inside major corporations, employees are winning access to knowledge once monopolized by management. And as knowledge is redistributed, so, too, is the power based on it.

BOMBARDED BY THE FUTURE

There is, however, a much larger sense in which changes in knowledge are causing or contributing to enormous power shifts. The most important economic development of our lifetime has been the rise of a new system for creating wealth, based no longer on muscle but on mind. Labor in the advanced economy no longer consists of working on "things," writes historian Mark Poster of the University of California (Irvine), but of "men and women acting on other men and women, or . . . people acting on information and information acting on people."

The substitution of information or knowledge for brute labor, in fact, lies behind the troubles of General Motors and the rise of Japan as well. For while GM still thought the earth was flat, Japan was exploring its edges and discovering otherwise.

As early as 1970, when American business leaders still thought their smokestack world secure, Japan's business leaders, and even the general public, were being bombarded by books, newspaper articles, and television programs heralding the arrival of the "information age" and focusing on the 21st century. While the end-of-industrialism concept was dismissed with a shrug in the United States, it was welcomed and embraced by Japanese decision-makers in business, politics, and the media. Knowledge, they concluded, was the key to economic growth in the 21st century.

It was hardly surprising, therefore, that even though the United States started computerizing earlier, Japan moved more quickly to substitute the knowledge-based technologies of the Third Wave for the brute muscle technologies of the Second Wave past.

Robots proliferated. Sophisticated manufacturing methods, heavily dependent on computers and information, began turning out products whose quality could not be easily matched in world markets. Moreover, recognizing that its old smokestack technologies were ultimately doomed, Japan took steps to facilitate the transition to the new and to buffer itself against the dislocations entailed in such a strategy. The contrast with General Motors—and American policy in general—could not have been sharper.

If we also look closely at many of the other power shifts cited above, it will become apparent that in these cases, too, the changed role of knowledge—the rise of the new wealth-creation system—either caused or contributed to major shifts of power.

The spread of this new knowledge economy is, in fact, the explosive new force that has hurled the advanced economies into bitter global competition, confronted the socialist nations with their hopeless obsolescence, forced many "developing nations" to scrap their traditional economic strategies, and is now profoundly dislocating power relationships in both personal and public spheres.

In a prescient remark, Winston Churchill once said that "empires of the future are empires of the mind." Today that observation has come true. What has not yet been appreciated is the degree to which raw, elemental power—at the level of private life as well as at the level of empire—will be transformed in the decades ahead as a result of the new role of "mind."

THE MAKING OF A SHABBY GENTILITY

A revolutionary new system for creating wealth cannot spread without triggering personal, political, and international conflict. Change the way wealth is made and you immediately collide with all the entrenched interests whose power arose from the prior wealth-system. Bitter conflicts erupt as each side fights for control of the future.

It is this conflict, spreading around the world today, that helps explain the present power shake-up. To anticipate what might lie ahead for us, therefore, it is helpful to glance briefly backward at the last such global conflict.

Three hundred years ago the industrial revolution also brought a new system of wealth creation into being. Smokestacks speared the skies where fields once were cultivated. Factories proliferated. These "dark Satanic mills" brought with them a totally new way of life—and a new system of power.

Peasants freed from near-servitude on the land turned into urban workers subordinated to private or public employers. With this change came changes in power relations in the home as well. Agrarian families, several generations under a single roof, all ruled by a bearded patriarch, gave way to stripped-down nuclear families from which the elderly were soon extruded or reduced in prestige and influence. The family itself, as an institution, lost much of its social power as many of its functions were transferred to other institutions—education to the school, for example.

Sooner or later, too, wherever steam engines and smokestacks multiplied, vast political changes followed. Monarchies collapsed or shriveled into tourist attractions. New political forms were introduced.

If they were clever and farsighted enough, rural landowners, once dominant in their regions, moved into the cities to ride the wave of industrial expansion, their sons becoming stockbrokers or captains of industry. Most of the landed gentry who clung to their rural way of life wound up as shabby gentility, their mansions eventually turned into museums or into money-raising lion parks.

Against their fading power, however, new elites arose: corporate chieftains, bureaucrats, media moguls. Mass production, mass distribution, mass education, and mass communication were accompanied by mass democracy, or dictatorships claiming to be democratic.

These internal changes were matched by gigantic shifts in global power, too, as the industrialized nations colonized, conquered, or dominated much of the rest of the world, creating a hierarchy of world power that still exists in some regions.

In short, the appearance of a new system for creating wealth undermined every pillar of the old power system, ultimately transforming family life, business, politics, the nation-state, and the structure of the global power itself.

Those who fought for control of the future made use of violence, wealth, and knowledge. Today a similar, though far more accelerated, upheaval has started. The changes we have recently seen in business, the economy, politics, and at the global level are only the first skirmishes of far bigger power struggles to come. For we stand at the edge of the deepest powershift in human history.

2

MUSCLE, MONEY, AND MIND

An ultramarine sky. Mountains in the distance. The clatter of hoofbeats. A solitary rider draws closer, sun glinting from his spurs. . . .

Anyone who sat in a darkened theater enraptured by cowboy movies as a child knows that power springs from the barrel of a six-shooter. In film after Hollywood film, a lone cowboy rides in from nowhere, fights a duel with the villain, returns his revolver to its holster, and rides off once more into the hazy distance. Power, we children learned, came from violence.

A background figure in many of these movies, however, was a well-dressed, paunchy personage who sat behind a big wooden desk. Typically depicted as effete and greedy, this man also exerted power. It was he who financed the railroad, or the land-grabbing cattlemen, or other evil forces. And if the cowboy hero represented the power of violence, this figure—typically the banker—symbolized the power of money.

In many westerns there was also a third important character: a crusading newspaper editor, a teacher, a minister, or an educated woman from the "East." In a world of gruff men who shoot first and question later, this character represented not merely moral Good in combat with Evil, but also the power of culture and sophisticated knowledge about the outside world. While this person often won a victory in the end, it was usually because of an alliance with the gun-toting hero or because of a sudden lucky strike—finding gold in the river or inheriting an unexpected legacy.

Knowledge, as Francis Bacon advised us, is power—but for knowledge to win in a western, it usually had to ally itself with force or money.

Of course, cash, culture, and violence are not the only sources of power in everyday life, and power is neither good nor bad. It is a dimension of virtually all human relationships. It is, in fact, the reciprocal of desire, and, since human desires are infinitely varied, anything that can fulfill someone else's desire is a potential source of power. The drug dealer who can withhold a "fix" has power over the addict. If a politician desires votes, those who can deliver them have power.

Yet among the numberless possibilities, the three sources of power symbolized in the western movie—violence, wealth, and knowledge—turn out to be most important. Each takes many different forms in power play. Violence, for example, need not be actual; the threat of its use is often enough to bring compliance. The threat of violence can also lurk behind the law. (We use the term *violence* in these pages in a figurative, rather than literal, sense—to include force as well as physical coercion.)

Indeed, not only modern movies but also ancient myths support the view that violence, wealth, and knowledge are the ultimate sources of social power. Thus Japanese legend tells of *sanshu no jingi*—the three sacred objects given to the great sun goddess, Amaterasu-omi-kami—which to this day are still the symbols of imperial power. These are the sword, the jewel, and the mirror.

The power implications of sword and jewel are clear enough; the mirror's, a bit less so. But the mirror, in which Amaterasu-omi-kami's saw her own visage—or gained knowledge of herself—also reflects power. It came to symbolize her divinity, but it is not unreasonable to regard it as a symbol of imagination, consciousness, and knowledge as well.

Furthermore, the sword or muscle, the jewel or money, and the mirror or mind together form a single interactive system. Under certain conditions each can be converted into the other. A gun can get you money or can force secret information from the lips of a victim. Money can buy you information—or a gun. Information can be used to increase either the money available to you (as Ivan Boesky knew) or to multiply the force at your command (which is why Klaus Fuchs stole nuclear secrets).

What's more, all three can be used at almost every level of social life, from the intimacy of home to the political arena.

In the private sphere, a parent can slap a child (use force), cut an allowance or bribe with a dollar (use money or its equivalent), or—most effective of all—mold a child's values so the child *wishes* to obey. In politics, a government can imprison or torture a dissident, financially punish its critics and pay off its supporters, and it can manipulate truth to create consent.

Like machine tools (which can create more machines), force, wealth, or knowledge, properly used, can give one command over many additional, more varied sources of power. Thus, whatever other tools of power may be exploited by a ruling elite or by individuals in their private relationships, force, wealth, and knowledge are the ultimate levers. They form the power triad.

It is true that not all shifts or transfers of power are a result of the use of these tools. Power changes hands as a result of many natural events. The Black Death that swept Europe in the 14th century sent the powerful to the grave along with the powerless, creating many vacancies among the elite in the surviving communities.

Chance also affects the distribution of power in society. But as soon as we focus on purposeful human acts, and ask what makes people and whole societies acquiesce to the wishes of the "powerful," we find ourselves once more facing the trinity of muscle, money, and mind.

To stick as closely to plain-speak as possible, we will use the term *power* in these pages to mean purposeful power over people. This definition rules out power used against nature or things, but is broad enough to include the power exerted by a mother to prevent a baby from running in front of an onrushing car; or by IBM to increase its profits; or by a dictator like Marcos or Noriega to enrich his family and cronies; or by the Catholic Church to line up political opposition to contraception; or by the Chinese military to crush a student rebellion.

In its most naked form, power involves the use of violence, wealth, and knowledge (in the broadest sense) to make people perform in a given way.

Zeroing in on this trinity and defining power in this manner permit us to analyze power in a completely fresh way, revealing perhaps more clearly than before exactly how power is used to control our behavior from cradle to cremation. Only when this is understood can we identify and transform those obsolete power structures that threaten our future.

HIGH-QUALITY POWER

Most conventional assumptions about power, in Western culture at least, imply that power is a matter of quantity. But, while some of us clearly have less power than others, this approach ignores what may now be the most important factor of all: the *quality* of power.

Power comes in varying grades, and some power is decidedly low in octane. In the fierce struggles soon to sweep through our schools, hospitals, businesses, trade unions, and governments, those who understand "quality" will gain a strategic edge.

No one doubts that violence—embodied in a mugger's switchblade or a nuclear missile—can yield awesome results. The shadow of violence or force, embedded in the law, stands behind every act of government, and in the end every government relies on soldiers and police to en*force* its will. This ever-present and necessary threat of official violence in society helps keep the system operating, making ordinary business contracts enforceable, reducing crime, providing machinery for the peaceful settlement of disputes. In this paradoxical sense, it is the veiled threat of violence that helps make daily life nonviolent.

But violence in general suffers from important drawbacks. To begin with, it encourages us to carry a can of Mace, or to crank up an arms race that increases risks to everyone. Even when it "works," violence produces resistance. Its victims or their survivors look for the first chance to strike back.

The main weakness of brute force or violence, however, is its sheer inflexibility. It can only be used to punish. It is, in short, low-quality power.

Wealth, by contrast, is a far better tool of power. A fat wallet is much more versatile. Instead of just threatening or delivering punishment, it can also offer finely graded rewards—payments and payoffs, in cash or kind. Wealth can be used in either a positive or a negative way. It is, therefore, much more flexible than force. Wealth yields medium-quality power.

The highest-quality power, however, comes from the application of knowledge. Actor Sean Connery, in a movie set in Cuba during the reign of the dictator Batista, plays a British mercenary. In one memorable scene the tyrant's military chief says: "Major, tell what your favorite weapon is, and I'll get it for you." To which Connery replies: "Brains."

High-quality power is not simply clout. Not merely the ability to get one's way, to make others do what you want, though they might prefer otherwise. High quality implies much more. It implies efficiency—using up the fewest power resources to achieve a goal. Knowledge can often be used to make the other party *like* your agenda for action. It can even persuade the person that she or he originated it.

Of the three root sources of social control, therefore, it is knowledge, the most versatile, that produces what Pentagon brass like to call "the biggest bang for the buck." It can be used to punish, reward, persuade, and even transform. It can transform enemy into ally. Best of all, with the right knowledge one can circumvent nasty situations in the first place, so as to avoid wasting force or wealth altogether.

Knowledge also serves as a wealth and force multiplier. It can be used to augment the available force or wealth or, alternatively, to reduce the amount needed to achieve any given purpose. In either case, it increases efficiency, permitting one to spend fewer power "chips" in any showdown.

Of course, maximum power is available to those in a position to use all three of these tools in clever conjunction with one another, alternating the threat of punishment, the promise of reward, along with persuasion and intelligence. The truly skilled power players know intuitively—or through training—how to use and interrelate their power resources.

To assess the different contenders in a power conflict—whether a negotiation or a war—therefore, it helps to figure out who commands access to which of the basic tools of power.

Knowledge, violence, and wealth, and the relationships among them, define power in society. Francis Bacon equated knowledge with power, but he did not focus on its quality or on its crucial links to the other main sources of social power. Nor could anyone until now foresee today's revolutionary changes in the relationships among these three.

ONE MILLION INFERENCES

A revolution is sweeping today's post-Bacon world. No genius in the past—not Sun-Tzu, not Machiavelli, not Bacon himself—could have imagined today's deepest *powershift:* the astounding degree to which today both force and wealth themselves have come to depend on knowledge.*

Military might until not long ago was basically an extension of the mindless fist. Today it relies almost totally on "congealed mind"—knowledge embedded in weapons and surveillance technologies. From satellites to submarines, modern weapons are constructed of information-rich electronic components. Today's fighter plane is a flying computer. Even "dumb" weapons today are manufactured with the help of supersmart computers or electronic chips.

The military, to choose a single example, uses computerized knowledge—"expert systems"—in missile defense. Since subsonic missiles speed along at about 1,000 feet a second, effective defense systems need to react in, say, 10 milliseconds. But expert systems may embody as many as 10,000 to 100,000 rules elicited from human specialists. The computer must scan, weigh, and interrelate these rules before arriving at a decision as to how to respond to a threat. Thus the Pentagon's Defense Advanced Research Projects Agency (DARPA), according to *Defense Science* magazine, has set as a long-range goal the design of a system that can make "one million logical inferences per second." Logic, inference, epistemology—in short, brain work, human and machine—is today's precondition for military power.

Similarly, it has become a business cliché to say that wealth is increasingly dependent on brainpower. The advanced economy could not run for thirty seconds without computers, and the new complexities of production, the integration of many diverse (and constantly changing) technologies, the de-massification of markets, continue to increase, by vast leaps, the amount and quality of information needed to make the system produce wealth. Furthermore, we are barely at the beginning of this "informationalization" process. Our best computers and CAD-CAM systems are still stone-ax primitive.

---

*A power shift is a transfer of power. A "powershift" is a deep-level change in the very nature of power.

Knowledge itself, therefore, turns out to be not only the source of the highest-quality power, but also the most important ingredient of force and wealth. Put differently, knowledge has gone from being an adjunct of money power and muscle power, to being their very essence. It is, in fact, the ultimate amplifier. This is the key to the *powershift* that lies ahead, and it explains why the battle for control of knowledge and the means of communication is heating up all over the world.

FACTS, LIES, AND TRUTH

Knowledge and communication systems are not antiseptic or power-neutral. Virtually every "fact" used in business, political life, and everyday human relations is derived from other "facts" or assumptions that have been shaped, deliberately or not, by the preexisting power structure. Every "fact" thus has a power-history and what might be called a power-future—an impact, large or small, on the future distribution of power.

Nonfacts and disputed facts are equally products of, and weapons in, power conflict in society. False facts and lies, as well as "true" facts, scientific "laws," and accepted religious "truths" are all ammunition in ongoing power-play and are themselves a form of knowledge, as the term will be used here.

There are, of course, as many definitions of knowledge as there are people who regard themselves as knowledgeable. Matters grow worse when words like *signs, symbols,* or *imagery* are given highly technical meanings. And the confusion is heightened when we discover that the famous definition of *information* by Claude Shannon and Warren Weaver, who helped found information science, while useful for technological purposes, has no bearing on semantic meaning or the "content" of communication.

In general, in the pages ahead, *data* will mean more or less unconnected "facts"; *information* will refer to data that have been fitted into categories and classification schemes or other patterns; and *knowledge* will mean information that has been further refined into more general statements. But to avoid tedious repetition, all three terms may sometimes be used interchangeably.

To make things simple and escape from these definitional

quicksands, even at the expense of rigor, in the pages ahead the term *knowledge* will be given an expanded meaning. It will embrace or subsume information, data, images, and imagery, as well as attitudes, values, and other symbolic products of society, whether "true," "approximate," or even "false."

All of these are used or manipulated by power-seekers, and always have been. So, too, are the media for conveying knowledge: the means of communication, which, in turn, shape the messages that flow through them. The term *knowledge,* therefore, will be used to encompass all of these.

THE DEMOCRATIC DIFFERENCE

Besides its great flexibility, knowledge has other important characteristics that make it fundamentally different from lesser sources of power in tomorrow's world.

Thus force, for all practical concerns, is finite. There is a limit to how much force can be employed before we destroy what we wish to capture or defend. The same is true for wealth. Money cannot buy everything, and at some point even the fattest wallet empties out.

By contrast, knowledge does not. We can always generate more.

The Greek philosopher Zeno of Elea pointed out that if a traveler goes halfway to his destination each day, he can never reach his final destination, since there is always another halfway to go. In the same manner, we may never reach ultimate knowledge about anything, but we *can* always take one step closer to a rounded understanding of any phenomenon. Knowledge, in principle at least, is infinitely expandable.

Knowledge is also inherently different from both muscle and money, because, as a rule, if I use a gun, you cannot simultaneously use the same gun. If you use a dollar, I can't use the same dollar at the same time.

By contrast, both of us can use the same knowledge either for or against each other—and in that very process we may even produce still more knowledge. Unlike bullets or budgets, knowledge itself doesn't get used up. This alone tells us that the rules of the knowledge-power game are sharply different from the precepts relied on by those who use force or money to accomplish their will.

But a last, even more crucial difference sets violence and wealth apart from knowledge as we race into what has been called an information age: By definition, both force and wealth are the property of the strong and the rich. It is the truly revolutionary characteristic of knowledge that it can be grasped by the weak and the poor as well.

Knowledge is the most democratic source of power.

Which makes it a continuing threat to the powerful, even as they use it to enhance their own power. It also explains why every power-holder—from the patriarch of a family to the president of a company or the Prime Minister of a nation—wants to control the quantity, quality, and distribution of knowledge within his or her domain.

The concept of the power triad leads to a remarkable irony.

For at least the past three hundred years, the most basic political struggle within all the industrialized nations has been over the distribution of wealth: Who gets what? Terms like *left* and *right,* or *capitalist* and *socialist* have pivoted on this fundamental question.

Yet, despite the vast maldistribution of wealth in a world painfully divided between rich and poor, it turns out that, compared with the other two sources of worldly power, wealth has been, and is, the *least* maldistributed. Whatever gulf separates the rich from the poor, an even greater chasm separates the armed from the unarmed and the ignorant from the educated.

Today, in the fast-changing, affluent nations, despite all inequities of income and wealth, the coming struggle for power will increasingly turn into a struggle over the distribution of and access to knowledge.

This is why, unless we understand how and to whom knowledge flows, we can neither protect ourselves against the abuse of power nor create the better, more democratic society that tomorrow's technologies promise.

The control of knowledge is the crux of tomorrow's worldwide struggle for power in every human institution.

In the chapters immediately ahead we shall see how these changes in the nature of power itself are revolutionizing relationships in the world of business. From the transformation of capital to the growing conflict between "highbrow" and "lowbrow" businesses, from the electronic supermarket to the rise of family business and the emergence of startling new organizational forms, we will trace the new trajectory of power. These deep changes in business and the economy are paralleled by significant changes in politics, the media, and the global espionage industry. Finally, we will see how today's tremendous, wrenching powershift will impact on the impoverished nations, the remaining socialist nations, and the future of the United States, Europe, and Japan. For today's powershift will transform them all.

PART TWO

LIFE IN THE SUPER-SYMBOLIC ECONOMY

3

BEYOND THE AGE OF GLITZ

Business may be turning out products and profits. But it is hard to resist the suspicion that it is also becoming a popular form of theater. Like theater, it has heroes, villains, drama, and—increasingly—it has stars.

The names of business tycoons ricochet through the media like those of Hollywood celebrities. Surrounded by publicists, trained in all the arts of self-promotion, characters like Donald Trump or Lee Iacocca have become living symbols of corporate power. They are satirized in the comics. They (and their writers) crank out best sellers. Both men have even been mentioned—or perhaps arranged to have themselves mentioned—as potential candidates for the presidency of the United States. Business has arrived in the Age of Glitz.

Business had its stars in the past, too, but the very context of stardom is different today. The tinselly new glamour acquired by business is a superficial facet of the new economy, in which information (including everything from scientific research to advertising hype) plays a growing role. What is happening is the rise of an entirely new "system for wealth creation," which brings with it dramatic changes in the distribution of power.

This new system for making wealth is totally dependent on the instant communication and dissemination of data, ideas, symbols, and symbolism. It is, as we will discover, a super-symbolic economy in the exact sense of that term.

Its arrival is transformational. It is not, as some still belatedly insist, a sign of "de-industrialization," "hollowing out," or economic decay, but a leap toward a revolutionary new system of production. This new system takes us a giant step beyond mass production toward increasing customization, beyond mass marketing and distribution toward niches and micro-marketing, beyond the monolithic corporation to new forms of organization, beyond the nation-state to operations that are both local and global, and beyond the proletariat to a new "cognitariat."

The collision between forces favoring this new system of wealth creation and defenders of the old smokestack system is the dominant economic conflict of our time, exceeding in historical importance the conflict between capitalism and communism or among the United States, Europe, and Japan.

Moving from an economy based on smokestacks to one based on computers requires massive transfers of power, and it largely explains the wave of financial and industrial restructuring that has been ripping through the corporate world, throwing up new leaders, as companies desperately seek to adapt to fresh imperatives.

Takeovers, raids, acquisitions, leveraged buy-outs, corporate buy-backs, all made financial headlines throughout the 1980s, and involved not only U.S. firms but many foreign companies as well, despite legal and other restrictions that limit "unfriendly" takeovers in countries like West Germany, Italy, or Holland.

It would be an exaggeration to say that all these wild doings on Wall Street and the thrashing about in companies around the world are direct manifestations of the shift to a new kind of economy. Tax considerations, the integration of Europe, financial liberalization, old-fashioned greed, and other factors all play a role. Indeed, men like Trump and Iacocca represent, if anything, men of the past rather than heralds of the new. Successfully lobbying Washington to bail out a failing auto maker, Iacocca's chief claim to fame, or putting one's name on flashy skyscrapers and gambling casinos hardly make one a business revolutionary.

In a revolutionary period, however, all sorts of strange flora and fauna appear—atavists, eccentrics, publicity hounds, saints, and crooks, along with visionaries and genuine revolutionaries.

Beneath all the razzle-dazzle, the refinancings and reorganizations, there is an emerging pattern. For what we are seeing is a change in the structure of business and the beginnings of a shift of power from "smokestack money" to what might be called "super-symbolic money"—a process we will explore in more detail later.

This broad restructuring is necessary as the entire wealth-creation system, driven by competitive pressures, steps up to a more advanced level. Thus, to picture the takeover frenzy of the late eighties as nothing more than an expression of me-first greed is to miss its larger dimensions.

Nevertheless, the new economy has rewarded well those who first saw it coming. In the smokestack era any list of the richest people in the world would have been dominated by car makers, steel barons, rail magnates, oil moguls, and financiers, whose collective wealth ultimately came from the organization of cheap labor, raw materials, and the manufacture of hardware.

By contrast, *Forbes* magazine's latest list of the ten richest American billionaires includes fully seven whose fortunes were based on media, communications, or computers—software and services rather than hardware and manufacturing. They reflect what the Japanese call the new "softnomics."

The spasm of mergers, takeovers, divestitures, and financial reshufflings is, however, only one aspect of the transition to the new economy. At the same time that they are trying to fend off raiders or to make acquisitions, companies are also frantically striving to cope with an info-technological revolution, a restructuring of markets, and a host of other related changes. It adds up to the biggest shake-up the business world has known since the industrial revolution.

THE BUSINESS COMMANDOS

So deep a restructuring doesn't happen without anguish and confrontation. As happened at the start of the industrial revolution, millions find their incomes threatened, their ways of work made obsolete, their futures uncertain, their power slashed.

Investors, managers, and workers alike are thrown into conflict and confusion. Strange alliances spring up. New forms of judo are invented. In the past, labor unions exerted power by striking or threatening to do so. Today, in addition, they hire investment bankers, lawyers, and tax experts—purveyors of specialized knowledge—hoping to become part of a restructuring deal rather than its victim. Managers seeking to head off a takeover, or to buy out their own firm, along with investors seeking to profit from such upheavals, are increasingly dependent on timely, pinpointed information. Knowledge is a key weapon in the power struggles that accompany the emergence of the super-symbolic economy.

So is the ability to influence the media—thereby shaping what others know (or think they know). In this volatile environment, flashy personalities skilled at manipulating symbols have a distinct advantage. In France the epitome of the entrepreneur is Bernard Tapie, who claims to have built a privately held business with annual revenues of $1 billion. Tapie hosts his own TV show. In Britain, Richard Branson, who founded the Virgin Group, breaks speedboat records and, in the words of *Fortune,* enjoys "the sort of celebrity once reserved for rock stars or royalty."

As an old system cracks, the faceless bureaucrat-managers who run it are blown away by a guerrilla army of risk-taking investors, promoters, organizers, and managers, many of them antibureaucratic individualists, all of them skilled at either acquiring knowledge (sometimes illegally) or controlling its dissemination.

The arrival of the new super-symbolic system for creating wealth not only shifts power but changes its style as well. One need only compare the temperaments of, say, John DeButts, the slow, solemn man who ran the American Telephone and Telegraph Company in the 1970s before it was broken up, with that of William McGowan, who cracked AT&T's monopoly and created MCI Communications Corporation to compete with it. Impatient and irreverent, the son of a railroad unionist, McGowan began by peddling alligator purses, wound up raising funds for Hollywood producers Mike Todd and George Skouras when they made the wide-screen version of *Oklahoma,* and then founded a small defense contracting firm before zeroing in on AT&T.

Or compare the cautious "business statesmen" who ran General Electric for a decade or two, with Jack Welch, who gained the nickname "Neutron Jack" as he tore up the giant and reshaped it.

The stylistic shift reflects changed needs. For the task of restructuring companies and whole industries to survive in the super-symbolic economy is not a job for nit-picking, face-saving, bean-counting bureaucrats. It is, in fact, a job for individualists, radicals, gut-fighters, even eccentrics—business commandos, as it were, ready to storm any beach to seize power.

It has been said that today's risk-taking entrepreneurs and deal-makers resemble the "robber barons" who originally built the smokestack economy. Today's Age of Glitz, indeed, does bear a resemblance to the so-called Gilded Age, just after the American Civil War. That, too, was a time of fundamental economic restructure, following the defeat of agrarian slavery by the rising forces of the industrializing North. It was the era of conspicuous consumption, political corruption, wild spending, financial peculation and speculation, peopled by larger-than-life characters like "Commodore" Vanderbilt, "Diamond Jim" Brady, and "Bet a Million" Gates. Out of that era, marked by anti-unionism and contempt for the poor, came the decisive burst of economic development that thrust America into the modern industrial age.

But if today's new breed are more buccaneer than bureaucrat, they could be termed "electronic pirates." The power they seize is dependent on sophisticated data, information, and know-how, not just bags of capital.

Says California financier Robert I. Weingarten, describing the corporate takeover process, "The first thing you do is create a computer screen which lists your criteria. Then you search for a target company that meets them by running these criteria against various data bases until you identify the target. And the last thing you do? The last thing you do is call a press conference. You start with the computer and end with the media.

"In between," he adds, "you call in a host of highly specialized knowledge workers—tax lawyers, proxy war strategists, mathematical modelers, investment advisers, and PR experts—most of whom are also very dependent on computers, facsimile machines, telecommunications, and the media.

"Nowadays the ability to make a deal happen very often depends more on knowledge than on the dollars you bring to the table. At a certain level it's easier to obtain the money than the relevant know-how. Knowledge is the real power lever."

Because takeovers and restructure challenge power, they produce high drama, hence heroes and villains. Names like Carl Icahn and T. Boone Pickens become household words around the world. Feuds break out. Steve Jobs, co-founder of Apple Computer and once the boy wonder of American industry, resigns after a corporate *coup d'état* by John Sculley, despite Jobs's vast holdings in the company. Iacocca continues his interminable vendetta against Henry Ford II. Roger Smith of General Motors is satirized in a movie, *Roger & Me,* and savaged in public by Ross Perot, the computer millionaire whose company Smith acquired. The list lengthens each day.

To imagine that takeovers are peculiarly American, an artifact of inadequate regulation of Wall Street, is to miss their deeper significance. In Britain, Roland "Tiny" Rowland battles bitterly for control of Harrods department store and Sir James Goldsmith, the burly, brash financier launches a $21 billion raid on BAT Industries PLC. Carlo de Benedetti, head of Olivetti, battles with Gianni Agnelli of the Fiat empire and *il salòtto buono*—the inner circle of entrenched industrial power in Italy—and shocks all of Europe with a sudden bid for control of Société Générale de Belgique of Brussels, a group that controls a third of the entire Belgian economy.

Groupe Bull, the French computer firm, eyes the computer operation of Zenith in the United States. Groupe Victoire takes over Germany's second-largest insurer, Colonia Versicherung A.G., while the Dresdner Bank buys out the French Banque Internationale de Placement.

In Spain, where drama often turns into melodrama, the public has been treated to what the *Financial Times* has called "probably the most riveting and, ultimately, tasteless, display in decades," an explosive battle between "los beautiful people" and "los successful people"—old and new money.

Focused on control of the nation's three largest banks and their related industrial empires, the battle pitted Alberto Cortina and his cousin Alberto Alcocer against Mario Conde, a brilliant, Jesuit-trained lawyer who captured control of Banco Español de Crédito and tried to merge it with Banco Central, already the largest bank in the country. The battle hit the pages of the soft-porn press when one of "los Albertos" fell in love with a twenty-eight-year-old marquesa who was photographed in a nightclub wearing a miniskirt sans undies.

In the end the grand merger, touted by the Spanish Prime Minister as "possibly the economic event of the century," broke apart like shattered glass, leaving Conde fighting to survive in his own bank.

All this is exciting fodder for the media mills, but the international character of the phenomenon tells us that something more is involved than glitz, greed, and local regulatory failures. As we'll see, something more serious *is* happening. Power is shifting on a hundred fronts at once. The very nature of power—the mix of force, wealth, and knowledge—is changing as we make the transition to the super-symbolic economy.

DALE CARNEGIE AND ATTILA THE HUN

It is hardly surprising that even smart executives seem confused. Some rush out and read how-to books with silly titles like *Leadership Secrets of Attila the Hun*. Others peruse mystical tracts. Some take Dale Carnegie courses on how to influence people, while others attend seminars on the tactics of negotiation, as though power were purely a matter of psychology or tactical maneuver.

Still others privately bewail the presence of power in their firms, complaining that power-play is bad for the bottom line—a wasteful diversion from the push for profit. They point to energy dissipated in personal power squabbles and unnecessary people added to the payroll of power-hungry empire-builders. Confusion is redoubled when many of the most effective power wielders smoothly deny having any.

The bewilderment is understandable. Free-marketeer economists like Milton Friedman tend to picture the economy as an impersonal supply-and-demand machine and ignore the role of power in the creation of wealth and profit. Or they blandly assume that all the power struggles cancel one another out and thus leave the economy unaffected.

This tendency to overlook the profit-making importance of power is not limited to conservative ideologues. One of the most influential texts in U.S. universities is *Economics* by Paul A. Samuelson and William D. Nordhaus. Its latest edition carries an index that runs to twenty-eight pages of eye-straining fine print. Nowhere in that index is the word *power* listed.

(An important exception to this power-blindness or purblindness among celebrated American economists has been J. K. Galbraith, who, regardless of whether one agrees with his other views, has consistently tried to factor power into the economic equation.)

Radical economists do a lot of talking about such things as business's undue power to mold consumer wants, or about the power of monopolies and oligopolies to fix prices. They attack corporate lobbying, campaign contributions, and the less savory methods sometimes used by corporate interests to oppose regulation of worker health and safety, environment, progressive taxation, and the like.

But at a deeper level, even activists obsessed with limiting business power mistake (and underestimate) the role of power in the economy, including its positive and generative role, and seem unaware that power itself is going through a startling transformation.

Behind many of their criticisms lurks the unstated idea that power is somehow extrinsic to production and profits. Or that the abuse of power by economic enterprises is a capitalist phenomenon. A close look at today's powershift phenomenon will tell us, instead, that power is intrinsic to all economies.

Not only excessive or ill-gotten profits, but all profits are partly (sometimes largely) determined by power rather than by efficiency. (Even the most inefficient firm can make a profit if it has the power to impose its own terms on workers, suppliers, distributors, or customers.) At virtually every step, power is an inescapable part of the very process of production—and this is true for all economic systems, capitalist, socialist, or whatever.

Even in normal times, production requires the frequent making and breaking of power relationships, or their constant readjustment. But today's times are not "normal." Heightened competition and accelerated change require constant innovation. Each attempt to innovate sparks resistance and new power conflicts. But in today's revolutionary environment, when different systems of wealth creation collide, minor adjustments often no longer suffice. Power conflicts take on new intensity, and because companies are more and more interdependent, a power upheaval in one firm frequently produces reverberating shifts of power elsewhere.

As we push further into a competitive global economy heavily based on knowledge, these conflicts and confrontations escalate. The result is that the power factor in business is growing more and more important, not just for individuals but for each business as a whole, bringing power shifts that often have a greater impact on the level of profit than cheap labor, new technology, or rational economic calculation.

From budget-allocation battles to bureaucratic empire-building, business organizations are already increasingly driven by power imperatives. Fast-multiplying conflicts over promotions and hiring, the relocation of plants, the introduction of new machines or products, transfer pricing, reporting requirements, cost accounting, and the definition of accounting terms—all will trigger new power battles and shifts.

THE CONSULTANT'S HIDDEN MISSION

The Italian psychologist Mara Selvini Palazzoli, whose group studies large organizations, reports a case in which two men together owned a group of factories. The president hired a consulting psychologist, ostensibly to boost efficiency. Telling him that morale was low, he encouraged the consultant to interview widely to find out why the work force seemed riddled with ulcer-producing levels of anger and envy.

The vice-president and co-owner (30 percent, versus 70 percent owned by the president) expressed skepticism about the project. Hiring a consultant, the president shrugged, was merely "the thing to do" nowadays.

Analysis by Palazzoli's group revealed a snake pit of power relationships gone awry. The consultant's overt agenda was to increase efficiency. But his real task was different. In actuality, the president and vice-president were at dagger-points and the president wanted an ally.

Palazzoli and her group write: "The president's secret agenda was an attempt to gain control, through the psychologist, of the whole company, including manufacturing and sales [which were largely under the control of his vice-president and partner]. . . . The vice-president's secret agenda was to prove himself superior to his partner and to show that his authority derived from his greater technical competence [i.e., better knowledge] and more commanding personality."

The case is typical of many. The fact is that all businesses, large and small, operate in a "power field" in which the three basic tools of power—force, wealth, and knowledge—are constantly used in conjunction with one another to adjust or revolutionize relationships.

But what the above case chronicles is merely "normal" power conflict. In the decades just ahead, as two great systems of wealth creation come into violent collision, as globalization spreads and the stakes rise, these normal contests will take place in the midst of far greater, more destabilizing power battles than any we have yet seen.

This doesn't mean that power is the only goal, or that power is a fixed pie that companies and individuals fight to divide, or that mutually fair relationships are impossible, or that so-called "win-

win" deals (in which both sides gain) are out of the question, or that all human relations are necessarily reduced to a "power nexus," rather than to Marx's famous "cash nexus."

But it strongly suggests that the immense shifts of power that face us will make today's takeovers and upheavals seem small by comparison, and will affect every aspect of business, from employee relations and the power of different functional units—such as marketing, engineering, and finance—to the web of power relations between manufacturers and retailers, investors and managers.

Men and women will make those changes. But the instruments of change will be force, wealth, and knowledge and the things they convert into. For inside the world of business, as in the larger world outside, force, wealth, and knowledge—like the ancient sword, jewel, and mirror of the sun goddess Amaterasu-omi-kami—remain the primary tools of power. Failure to understand how they are changing is a ticket to economic oblivion.

If that were all, business-men and -women would face a time of excruciating personal and organizational pressure. But it is not all. For a powershift, in the full sense, is more than a transfer of power. It is a sudden, sharp change in the nature of power—a change in the mix of knowledge, wealth, and force.

To anticipate the deep changes soon to strike, therefore, we must look at the role of all three. Thus, before we can appreciate what is happening to power based on wealth and knowledge, we must be prepared to take an unsettling look at the role of violence in the business world.

4

FORCE: THE YAKUZA COMPONENT

He is a celebrity. The business world's equivalent of a star. His marriages make the gossip pages. His name induces fear and fascination in the financial community. Still in his forties, he is a cocky man, by turns charming and choleric. He is a rabid reader whose Sunday afternoons may be spent wandering the Upper East Side of Manhattan, unrecognized in a turtleneck sweater, in search of a bookstore to browse in. He has butted heads with some of the mightiest corporate chieftains, made front-page business news, and built a personal fortune estimated at nearly half a billion dollars.

He is also a lawbreaker.

What's more, the law he has broken is not some wimpy law against stock market shenanigans or white-collar crime. It is the most macho of laws—that which prohibits violence.

Paraphrased for brevity's sake, here is his story.

> After flames broke out in one of my company's computer centers in a nearby city, our investigators came to the conclusion the fire was set by a pissed-off employee. Trouble is, we didn't have evidence that would stand up in court, and we couldn't get the local cops interested. Even if we could, we knew it would take forever to get anything done about it.
>
> So we wired up another employee with a hidden tape recorder and sent him to a bar, where he sidled up to the guy we suspected. He admitted it. Even bragged about it. When he did that, I wasn't going to take any chances. So our security men had a little talk with him and threatened

to break his legs (or more) if he didn't quit his job in my company and get the hell out of town—fast!

Was that against the law? Sure. Would I do it again? You bet! The next fire he set could have killed some of my employees. Am I going to wait around for the cops and the courts to see what would happen?

This story reminds us that in every society there is what might be called a "secondary enforcement system," which operates around the edges of the formal, official law-enforcement system. But it also tells us that, under the smooth surface of business, things happen that few wish to speak about.

We seldom stop to think about force as a factor in business. Most of the trillions of business transactions carried out each day are so free of anything suggesting violence, so peaceful on the surface, that we seldom lift the lid to see what may be seething below.

Yet the same three sources of power we find in family life, government, or any other social institution operate in business as well, and much as we might prefer to think otherwise, violence has always been part of the economy.

BLOOD AND SNOW-MONEY

From the day the first paleolithic warrior smashed a rock into a small animal, violence has been used to produce wealth.

Taking preceded making.

It may be just a fluke, but *Roget's Thesaurus,* which devotes 26 lines to synonyms of the word *borrowing* and 29 lines to *lending,* devotes fully 157 lines to alternative descriptions of *taking*—including "capture," "colonize," "conquer," and "kidnap," not to mention "rape," "shanghai," and "abduct."

The agricultural revolution, starting some 10,000 years ago, represented a dramatic shift from taking—through fishing, foraging, or hunting—to making wealth. But even agriculture was steeped in violence.

Knout and knife, club and quirt were as much a part of the agricultural economy as the sickle, the scythe, or the spade.

Before the smokestack revolution, when our great-grandparents slaved away on the soil, the whole world was as economically underdeveloped as the poorest, most capital-starved countries today. There were no "developed" economies to turn to for billion-dollar loans or foreign aid. Where, then, did the first fortunes come from that financed the earliest smokestack industries?

Many of them flowed, directly or indirectly, from pillage, plunder, and piracy . . . from the slavemaster's whip . . . from the conquest of land . . . brigandage . . . extortion . . . terrorization of the peasant by the lord . . . forced Indian labor in gold and silver mines . . . from the vast tracts of land granted by grateful monarchs to their warriors and generals.

These pools of red-stained wealth turned pink and later snowflake-white as they passed from father to son and grandson, over the generations. Eventually they funded those first iron foundries, textile mills, shipping lines, and clock factories that came alive in the late 1600s and early 1700s.

Violence continued to play a role in the production of wealth in those early factories and mills, as children were shackled to machines and beaten, women miners brutalized or raped, men cudgeled into resignation.

ON ZEKS AND GOONS

The use of force to extract wealth did not end with the age of the steam engine. In the 20th century, violence was used on a truly grand scale.

In the Soviet Union's infamous camps, like Vorkuta, millions of "zeks" and other prisoners provided dirt-cheap labor for logging and mining. At first, writes the Soviet economist Vasily Selyunin, these were used to suppress political opposition to the 1917 revolution; later they "became a means of solving purely economic tasks." Hitler's factories during World War II, using slave labor from all over Europe, turned out munitions, chemicals—and corpses. And South Africa's brutal treatment of its black majority has been a form of labor control based on police dogs, truncheons, and tear gas.

The history of the labor movement in the United States, as in many other nations, is steeped in repressive violence and occasional terrorism. From the Molly Maguires, who tried to organize the Pennsylvania coal fields in the 1870s, to the Knights of Labor; from the Haymarket massacre in 1886 at the start of the campaign for an eight-hour workday, to the great textile strike in Gastonia, North Carolina, in 1929 and the Memorial Day massacre at Republic Steel in Chicago in 1937, employers and police attempted to prevent the organization of unions.

As recently as the late 1930s in the United States, companies hired strong-arm men to break strikes or to intimidate union organizers and their followers. Harry Bennett and his infamous "goon squads" were routinely called out to bust heads when Ford Motor Company employees asked for raises or threatened to organize. Not infrequently the Mafia helped employers "deal with" militant workers. In South Korea today many companies have set up "Save the Company" squads to break strikes and prevent unionization. At the Motorola plant in Seoul, violence reached the point at which two workers doused themselves with gasoline and set themselves on fire to protest the company's refusal to recognize a union.

Japanese employers in the early postwar period called on the Mafia-like Yakuza to intimidate union activists. And in Japan, even today, despite its advanced stage of economic development, the Yakuza factor has not completely vanished.

Yakuza-linked *sokaiya*—pointy-shoed hooligans and thugs—often turn up at stockholder meetings of Japanese corporations, either to embarrass or to protect the management. In 1987 the first meeting of shareholders following the privatization of the Nippon Telegraph and Telephone Company (NTT) was marked by disruption when a garishly dressed *sokaiya* accused a director of pinching his secretary. Dozens of others leaped to their feet to drag out the discussion. One demanded to know why he had to queue up for the toilets in the building. When an officer apologized, the man asked why an NTT employee had committed an indecent act. To groans from the audience, he hit his stride with questions about missing promissory notes worth a few thousand dollars and about telephone bugging.

The *sokaiya* did not stop this harassment, intended to embarrass rather than reform the company, until suddenly, as though from nowhere, a large number of husky young men surrounded the room—at which point the *sokaiya* quietly made their exit.

Not all business crime ends so peacefully, as Japan discovered when Kazuo Kengaku, a well-known investment fund manager with links to the Yakuza, was found encased in concrete in Osaka. The Yakuza are also involved deeply in real estate speculation and supply strong-arm men to frighten residents or small shop-owners reluctant to move out of the way of high-rise developments. So well known are these tactics that they provided the substance for Juzo Itami's 1989 movie, *A Taxing Woman's Return*.

Valuable real estate also lay behind a recent case in which the collapse of a financial deal led to fraud litigation. An American lawyer in Tokyo, Charles Stevens of Coudert Brothers, representing a U.S. firm, received threatening calls and wound up keeping a baseball bat at his desk.

Violence in the business demimonde takes on bizarre forms on occasion—especially on the fringes of the entertainment business. In South Korea local film distributors have tried to frighten customers away from theaters showing U.S. films by releasing snakes in the theaters. In France, when Saudi Arabian investors, together with the French government, built Mirapolis, a $100 million amusement park, carnival workers, fearing competition, poured sand in the gears of thrill rides. (The park turned out to be a disaster for other reasons.)

Similarly, Japanese *sarakin*, like loan sharks the world over, sometimes rely on physical "persuasion" to coerce borrowers into repaying usurious debts—the money from these activities flowing smoothly into major banks and other financial institutions.

In the United States, as in many other countries, force is sometimes used to shut the mouths of corporate "whistle blowers" —employees who call attention to the questionable practices of their bosses.

This was the role Karen Silkwood chose for herself. Silkwood was killed in a car crash after protesting her employer's handling of nuclear materials, and there are those who still, years after the event, question whether the crash was accidental. They will never stop believing that her company had her killed.

Of course, all these cases are dramatic precisely because they are exceptions in the advanced economies. The daily experience of an American executive with a sheaf of printout in hand, the Japanese salaryman on his telephone, or the salesperson spreading a sample on a counter is so remote from any hint of violence that even to mention it is to draw skeptical looks.

Yet just because most transactions in business involve no direct violence does not mean that violence has vanished.

The reality is that violence has been contained, transmuted into another form—and hidden.

A MONOPOLY OF FORCE

One reason that overt corporate or business violence is now so rare is that over the years it has been increasingly "contracted out." Instead of businesses producing their own violence, they have, in effect, bought the services of government. In all industrial nations, state violence replaces private violence.

The first thing any government tries to do, from the moment it is formed, is to monopolize violence. Its soldiers and police are the only ones legally permitted to exert violence.

In some cases the state is politically controlled by the corporations, so that the line between the exercise of private and public power is hair-thin. But the old Marxist idea—that the state is nothing more than the "executive committee" of the ruling corporate power—ignores what we all know: that politicians more often act on their own behalf than on the behalf of others.

Moreover, the Marxist assumed that only capitalist corporations or governments would ever use force against unarmed workers. That was before communist police, armed with tear gas, fire hoses, and more ominous equipment, tried to stamp out Poland's Solidarity union movement in the early 1980s, and China massacred its students and workers near Tiananmen Square, behaving exactly like the soldiers and police of Pinochet's Chile or any number of other vehemently anticommunist countries.

By seizing into its own mailed fist the technologies of violence, and attempting to eliminate or control all violence, the state reduces the independent manufacture of violence by the corporation and other institutions.

THE HIDDEN GUN

A second reason why direct physical aggression seems to have almost vanished from ordinary business life is that violence has been sublimated into law.

All business, capitalist and socialist alike, depends upon law. Every contract, every promissory note, every stock and bond, every mortgage, every collective bargaining contract, every insurance policy, every debit and credit is ultimately backed by the law.

And behind every law, good or evil, we find the barrel of a gun. As tersely put by former French President Charles de Gaulle, "The law must have force on its side." Law *is* sublimated violence.

Thus when one company sues another, it asks the government to bring the *force* of law to bear. It wants the government's guns (concealed behind obscuring layers of bureaucratic and judicial rigmarole) stuck into the ribs of its adversary to compel certain actions.

It is not entirely accidental that corporate lawyers in the United States are often called "hired guns."

The very frequency of recourse to law (as distinct from other ways of resolving business disputes) is a fair measure of force in the economy. By this criterion, the United States has a "force-full" economy. Today there are 5.7 million business establishments in the United States and 655,000 lawyers—i.e., approximately one for every nine businesses. More than a thousand civil lawsuits are painfully processed by the clogged district court systems every business day of the year.

U.S. businessmen complain loudly about the allegedly unfair intimacy between Japanese business and government. Yet ironically, when it comes to settling disputes, it is the Americans, not the Japanese, who rush to litigate, thereupon calling upon the power of the state to intervene on their behalf.

From the smallest commercial litigation to the multibillion-dollar lawsuit involving a dispute between Pennzoil and Texaco over a takeover bid, law masks force—which, in the end, implies the potential application of violence.

Corporate campaign contributions can be seen as another camouflaged way of getting a government to pull a gun out of its holster in the interest of a company or industry.

In Japan, when Hiromasa Ezoe, chairman of the Recruit company, passed out huge amounts of stock at below-market price to top politicians in the ruling Liberal Democratic Party, his attempt to curry favor was so blatant it outraged the press and public and led to the resignation of Prime Minister Noboru Takeshita. The scandal bore some resemblance to the earlier case of the Flick empire in West Germany, whose executives channeled illegal funds to various political parties.

The Japanese also spend over $60 billion a year—more than they spend for their automobiles—in 14,500 garishly lit "pachinko parlors," where they play a game that involves guiding a stainless-steel ball downward past obstacles into an appropriate slot. Winners receive prizes, some of which they can exchange for money. Like game arcades in the United States, pachinko is a cash business, made to order for tax evasion and money laundering. Criminal gangs siphon off protection money from the parlors and sometimes war with one another for control of the most lucrative one. To ward off legislation aimed at opening their books to the police, parlor operators have made large contributions to both leading parties.

Whenever business funds are passed to candidates or political parties, the presumption is that a quid pro quo is expected. In the United States, despite repeated reforms and changes in the laws governing campaign contributions, every important industry pipes funds to one or both of the parties to buy, at a minimum, a hearing for its special point of view; and ingenious methods— inflated speaking fees, the purchase of otherwise unsalable books, the "loan" of real estate, the granting of low-interest loans—are constantly invented to avoid or evade the legal restrictions.

The mere existence of government creates a set of indirect, often hidden, and unintentional cross-subsidies and cross-penalties in the economy. To the extent that government actions are ultimately backed by force—by guns and soldiers and police—the notion of power-free or violence-free economics is puerile.

But the last, and most important, reason why corporations— and even governments—resort to open violence less often than in the preindustrial past is that they have found a better instrument with which to control people.

That instrument is money.

THE TRAJECTORY OF POWER

That power, and even violence, remain part of the world of business should not surprise us. What should raise our eyebrows is the remarkable change in the *way* force is applied.

A slavemaster or feudal lord transplanted from antiquity into today's world would find it hard to believe, even astonishing, that we beat workers less—and they produce more.

A ship's captain would be amazed that sailors are not physically abused and shanghaied into service.

Even a journeyman carpenter or tanner from the 18th century would be nonplussed at the idea that he could not legally bash his fist into a sassy apprentice's mouth. See, for example, William Hogarth's color engraving entitled "Industry and Idleness," printed in England in 1796. In it we see two " 'prentices"—one working happily at his loom, the other dozing. At the right, the boss approaches angrily brandishing a stick with which to beat the idler.

Both custom and law now restrain this open use of force in the modern world. This vestigialization of violence in the economy, however, did not spring from Christian charity or gentle altruism.

What happened is that, during the industrial revolution, the elites in society shifted from a primary reliance on the low-quality power produced by violence, to the mid-quality power produced by money.

Money may not produce the immediate results of a fist in the face or a gun in the ribs. But, because it can be used both to reward *and* punish, it is a far more versatile, flexible tool of power—especially when the ultimate threat of violence remains in place.

Money could not become the main tool of social control earlier, because the vast majority of humans were not part of the money system. Peasants in the preindustrial ages basically grew their own food, made their own shelter and clothing. But as soon as factories replaced farms, people no longer grew their own food and they became desperately dependent on money for survival. This total dependence on the money system, as distinct from self-production, transformed all power relationships.

Violence, as we've just seen, did not disappear. But its form and function changed as money became the prime motivator of the work force and the main tool of social control during the three industrial centuries.

It is this which explains why smokestack societies, capitalist and socialist alike, have proved more grasping and acquisitive, more money-obsessed than far poorer, preindustrial cultures. Greed no doubt goes back to Paleozoic times. But it was industrialism that made money into the prime tool of power.

In sum, the rise of the industrial nation-state brought the systematic monopolization of violence, the sublimation of violence into law, and the growing dependence of the population on money. These three changes made it possible for the elites of industrial societies increasingly to make use of wealth rather than overt force to impose their will on history.

This is the true meaning of powershift. Not simply a transfer of power from one person or group to another, but a fundamental change in the mix of violence, wealth, and knowledge employed by elites to maintain control.

Today, just as the industrial revolution transmuted violence into law, so we are transmuting money—indeed, wealth in general—into something new. And just as the smokestack age saw money assume a primary role in gaining or maintaining power, so today, at the edge of the 21st century, we face another twist in the history of power. We are on the brink of a new powershift.

5

WEALTH: MORGAN, MILKEN . . . AND AFTER

When a man has got vast power, such as you have—you admit you have, do you not?"

"I do not know it, sir."

The man in the witness chair, who "did not know" he held power, was a bull-necked, bristle-browed banker with a fierce mustache and an outsized nose. The congressional committee investigator pressed him: "You do not feel [powerful] at all?"

"No," he replied smoothly, "I do not feel it at all."

The time was 1912. The witness, in a dark suit and wing collar, with a gold watch chain draped across his generous paunch, dominated three or four giant banks, three trust companies, an equal number of life insurance companies, ten railroad systems, plus, among a few other odds and ends, United States Steel, General Electric, AT&T, Western Union, and International Harvester.

John Pierpont Morgan was the quintessential financial capitalist of the industrial era, the very symbol of turn-of-the-century money power.

A womanizing churchgoer and moralizer, he lived in conspicuous opulence and gluttony, holding business meetings amid damask and tapestries from the palaces of Europe, next to vaults containing Leonardo da Vinci notebooks and Shakespeare folios. Morgan looked down his monumental nose at Jews and other minorities, hated trade unions, sneered at new money, and fought ceaselessly with the other "robber barons" of his era.

Born enormously rich in an era of capital scarcity, he was imperious and driven, savagely repressing competition, sometimes relying on methods that would probably now have landed him in jail.

Morgan assembled huge sums and poured them into the great smokestack industries of his time—into Bessemer furnaces and Pullman cars and Edison generators and into tangible resources like oil, nitrates, copper, and coal.

But he did more than simply seize targets of opportunity. He planned strategically and helped shape the smokestack age in the United States, accelerating the shift of political and economic power from agricultural to industrial interests, and from manufacturing to finance.

Furthermore, he was said to have "Morganized" industry in the United States, creating a hierarchically ordered, finance-driven system and, according to his critics, a "money trust," which essentially controlled the main flows of capital in the country.

When Morgan blandly denied having any power, the cartoonists had a field day, one picturing him sitting astride a mountain of coins marked "Control over $25,000,000,000"; another as a dour emperor in crown and robes, with a mace in one hand and a purse in the other.

While to Pope Pius X he was a "great and good man," to the *Boston Commercial Bulletin* he was a "financial bully, drunk with wealth and power, who bawls his orders to stock markets, directors, courts, governments and nations."

Morgan concentrated capital. He consolidated small companies into ever larger and more monopolistic corporations. He centralized. He regarded top-down command as sacred and vertical integration as efficient. He understood that mass production was the coming thing. He wanted his investments to be protected by "hard" assets—plants, equipment, raw materials.

In all this he was a near-perfect reflection of the early smokestack age he helped to create. And whether Morgan "felt powerful" or not, his control of vast sums in a period of capital scarcity gave him immense opportunities to reward and punish others and to make change on a grand scale.

THE X-SHAPED DESK

When his name first exploded into the headlines, Michael Milken was an intensely private, work-obsessed man in his early forties, nominally a senior vice-president of Drexel Burnham Lambert, an investment banking firm actually co-founded by Morgan in 1871. Despite this deceptive title, Milken was more than just another senior vice-president. He was the architect of a whole new order in American finance. He was, as many soon recognized, the J. P. Morgan of our time.

In the 1980s, Drexel became one of Wall Street's hottest investment banking firms. And because Milken's hard-driving efforts were mainly responsible for its spectacular growth, he was allowed to run his own largely independent shop, three thousand miles from the firm's headquarters in the East. His office was just across from the Beverly Wilshire Hotel in Beverly Hills, California.

Milken would arrive at his office as early as 4:30 or 5:00 A.M., in time to squeeze in a few meetings before the opening of the New York Stock Exchange, three time zones away. CEOs of major corporations, trekking in from New York or Chicago, would drag themselves red-eyed to these conferences, hat in hand, seeking financing for their companies. One might want to build a new plant; another might wish to expand into new markets; a third might wish to make an acquisition. They were there because they knew Milken could find the capital for them.

Throughout the day Milken would sit at the center of a huge X-shaped trading desk, whispering, wheeling, dealing, shouting, surrounded by a frenzy of employees working the telephones and computer screens. It was from this desk that he and his team reshaped modern American industry, as Morgan had done in an earlier day.

A comparison of how each did it tells a lot about how the control of capital—and hence the power of money in society—is changing today. And it begins with the personal.

MILKEN VERSUS MORGAN

While J. P. Morgan was paunchy, fierce-looking, and imposing, Milken is tall, slender, clean-shaven, with curly black hair and the look of a startled doe. While Morgan was born with the proverbial silver spoon in his baby mouth, Milken, son of a CPA, collected soiled spoons off tables at the coffee shop where he worked for a time as a busboy.

Morgan commuted between Wall Street, mid-Manhattan, an estate on the Hudson, and palatial residences in Europe. Milken still lives in a far-from-palatial wood and brick home in Encino, in the not-quite-fashionable San Fernando Valley of Los Angeles. Seldom far from the Pacific Ocean, he keeps his eyes focused on Japan, Mexico, and the developing economies to the south.

Morgan surrounded himself with compliant young ladies and left his wife and family to languish in his absence; Milken is, by all accounts, a family man. Morgan disliked Jews. Milken is Jewish.

Morgan despised trade unions; Milken has served as a financial consultant for rail, airline, and maritime unions. The idea that employees might own their own firms would have struck Morgan as arrant communism. Milken favors worker-ownership and believes it is going to play a major role in American industry in the years to come.

Both men accumulated vast power for themselves, became notorious in the press, came under government investigation for real and/or alleged wrongdoing. But, far more important, they shifted the *structure* of power in America in remarkably different ways.

OPENING THE GATES

When Milken was born on July 4, 1946, the American economy was still dominated by huge companies formed, for the most part, in the Morgan era. These were the General Motors and Goodyear Tires, the Burlington Mills and Bethlehem Steels of the world. These smokestack firms, the so-called Blue Chips, along with their lobbyists, political fund-raisers, and trade associations, plus organizations like the National Association of Manufacturers, had enormous political, as well as economic, clout. Collectively, they sometimes acted as though the country belonged to them.

This corporate power was magnified by their influence on the media through the control of immense advertising budgets, and their ability, at least in theory, to shut down a plant in a recalcitrant congressman's district, and shift the investments and jobs to another where the political climate was more favorable. Often they were able to induce the labor unions representing their blue-collar workers to join them in a lobbying effort.

This "smokestack power," moreover, was further protected by a financial industry that made it difficult for competitors to challenge Blue Chip dominance. As a result, the basic structure of industrial power remained largely unchanged through mid-century in the United States.

Then something happened.

Milken was still in elementary school in 1956, when, for the first time, service and white-collar workers came to outnumber blue-collar workers in the United States. And by the time he began his career as a young investment banker the economy had already begun its rapid transition to a new system of wealth creation.

Computers, satellites, vastly varied services, globalization, were creating a totally new, change-filled business environment. But the financial industry, hidebound and protected by legislation, formed a major barrier to change.

Until the 1970s, long-term capital was readily available for Blue Chip dinosaurs, but much more difficult for smaller, innovative and entrepreneurial firms to obtain.

Wall Street was the financial Vatican of the world, and in the United States two "rating services"—Moody's and Standard & Poor's—guarded the gates of capital. These two private firms assigned risk ratings to bonds, and only some 5 percent of American companies were considered by them to be of "investment grade." This locked thousands of companies out of the long-term debt market or sent them to banks and insurance companies for loans rather than to investors in the bond market.

A student, first at the University of California in Berkeley and later at the Wharton School of the University of Pennsylvania, Milken studied investor risk. He discovered that many of the smaller firms frozen out of Wall Street had good records for paying their debts. They seldom defaulted and were prepared to pay higher than usual interest if anyone would buy bonds from them.

From this counterintuitive insight came the so-called high-yield or "junk" bond, and Milken, now a young underling at Drexel, proceeded to sell them to investors with missionary zeal.

The details of the story are not important for our purposes. What matters is that Milken succeeded beyond anyone's wildest expectations. The result was that he almost single-handedly broke the financial isolation that had hitherto been imposed on this secondary tier of companies. It was like a dam bursting. Capital poured into these companies, passing through Drexel on its way. By 1989 the junk-bond market reached an astronomical $180 billion.

Rather than creating a "money trust," therefore, as Morgan had done, Milken made finance more competitive and less monopolistic, opening the gates, as it were, and freeing thousands of companies from dependence on banks and insurance companies. They also bypassed the snooty Wall Street firms that existed to serve the Blue Chips. Milken's bonds permitted managers to go directly to the public and to institutional lenders like pension funds for the capital with which to build new plants, to expand markets, to do research and development—or to take over other firms.

Roughly 75 percent of junk bonds were quietly used for investment in new technology, or to open new markets, and for other noncontroversial purposes. Drexel's advertising made much of the fact that while employment in the Blue Chips, the old giants, was not keeping pace with the economy's expansion, jobs in the smaller firms they financed multiplied more rapidly than in the economy at large. But some of the capital Milken supplied was used in pitched takeover battles.

These dramatic financial showdowns filled the headlines and kept the stock market and the nation itself spellbound. Stock prices soared and plunged on rumors of more, and still more, takeovers and raids affecting some of the nation's best-known companies. Deals were made that no longer provided a reasonable balance of risk and reward for the investor. Debt was pyramided on top of unrealistic debt in an orgy of speculation. Taxi drivers and waitresses knowingly discussed the latest news and called their stockbrokers, hoping to cash in on the killings to be made as competing raiders bid up the stock of corporations marked for takeover. As other Wall Street firms entered the junk-bond market, the money machine created by Milken and Drexel, no longer in their hands alone, became a runaway juggernaut.

Such violent upheavals, often involving highly personal power struggles, led to a slaughter of the innocents. Companies were "downsized," workers ruthlessly laid off, executive ranks decimated. Not surprisingly, a massive counterattack was launched with Milken as the principal target.

THE COUNTERATTACK

By forcing open the sluice gates of capital, Milken had rattled the entire structure of smokestack power in America. While enriching Drexel Burnham (and feathering his own nest to the amazing tune of $550 million in 1987 alone), he also made bitter enemies of two extremely powerful groups. One consisted of the old-line Wall Street firms who previously had had a stranglehold on the flow of capital to American corporations; the other consisted of the top managers of many of the largest firms. Both had every reason to destroy him if they could. Both also had powerful allies in government and the media.

First savaged in the press, which pictured him as the very embodiment of capitalist excess, Milken was then hit with a ninety-eight-count federal indictment charging him with securities fraud, market manipulation, and "parking" (illegally holding stock that belonged to Ivan Boesky, the arbitrageur who was jailed for insider trading). Threatening to use sweeping legal powers designed to deal with the Mafia, rather than with stock market wrongdoing, the federal government forced Drexel to sever its relationship with Milken and pay a crushing $650 million fine to Uncle Sam.

At the same time, some of the worst-case buy-outs began to come apart, panicking investors and pushing down the value of most junk bonds, safe and unsafe alike. Soon Drexel, struggling to stabilize itself after the $650 million fine, and itself holding $1 billion in junk bonds, found itself driven to the wall. Drexel collapsed with a thunderous crash. Milken, already tried and convicted in the press, ultimately pled guilty to six violations in a complex deal that erased all other criminal charges.

However, as in the case of Morgan, the question of whether or not he broke the law is far less important for the country than his net impact on American business. For while finance was restructuring other industries, Milken was restructuring finance.

The conflict between those, like Morgan, who wanted to restrict access to capital so that they could themselves control it, and those like Milken, who fought to widen access, has a long history in every country.

"There has been a long struggle," writes Professor Glenn Yago of the State University of New York (Stony Brook), "to innovate U.S. capital markets to make them more accessible. Farmers fought for credit in the 19th century, and agricultural productivity increases . . . were the outcome. In the '30s, small businessmen got relief from being squeezed out from bank credit windows. After World War II, workers and consumers sought credit for home ownership and college education. In spite of resistance by those who would restrict popular access to credit, financial markets responded to demand and the country flourished."

While an excess of credit can unleash inflation, there is a difference between excess and access. By broadening access, Milken's firm could, as Connie Bruck, one of his most savage critics, admits, "reasonably sustain the claim . . . that it had furthered the 'democratization of capital,' " which is why some trade unionists and African-Americans rallied to his defense in his time of trouble.

Morgan and Milken, in short, changed American finance in contrary ways.

TAMPONS AND CAR RENTALS

Furthermore, while Morgan was the ultimate centralizer and concentrator, operating on the assumption that the whole was worth more than its parts, Milken and the people he financed often started from the opposite assumption. Thus the 1960s and 1970s had seen the formation of gigantic, unwieldy, unfocused "conglomerates"—huge companies built on bureaucratic management and a blind belief in "economies of scale" and "synergy." The bonds Milken sold financed takeovers designed to bust up these behemoths and create slimmer, more maneuverable and more strategically focused firms.

Virtually every Milken-funded takeover resulted in the sell-off of divisions or units, because, in fact, the parts *were* worth more than the whole; the synergy, less than imagined.

A striking case in point was the breakup of the Beatrice Companies, an ungainly agglomeration that combined, with little logic, Avis car rentals, Coca-Cola bottling, Playtex brassieres, the manufacture of tampons, along with the food processing that had once formed its core business. After its parts were sold to other companies, Beatrice was a much smaller firm operating more sensibly in the food, cheese, and meat business. Borg-Warner, an industrial firm, sold off its financial operations. Revlon, after take-over, sold off its medical business and other units unrelated to its central skills—the cosmetic industry.

Milken's easing of access to capital also helped nourish upstart firms in the new service and information sectors that are key to the advanced economy.

Surely this was not Milken's primary purpose. He was more than willing to fund rust-belt industries as well. But, operating at a moment when the entire economy was in transit out of the smoke-stack era, he was certainly aware of this fundamental change and, in some ways, helped spur it on. Thus at one point he told *Forbes* magazine that much of the restructuring going on had to do with the country's transition out of the industrial age, adding that "in an industrial society, capital is a scarce resource, but in today's information society, there's plenty of capital."

Since Milken's high-yield or junk bonds worked to the advantage of newer, less established companies rather than the Blue Chips, all of whom had easy access to conventional financing, it is not surprising that many of his beneficiaries were in the fast-expanding service and information sectors where newer companies were likely to be found.

Thus Milken helped reorganize or channeled capital into cellular telephones, cable television, computers, health services, day care, and other advanced business sectors—whose growing power challenged the dominance of the old smokestack barons.

In short, Morgan and Milken alike, but in almost diametrically different ways, shook the established power structure in their time and for this reason, quite apart from legal issues, called down upon themselves hailstorms of controversy and calumniation. For good or ill, legally or not, each changed finance in ways that corresponded to the emerging needs of the economy in their time.

THE POST–WALL STREET ERA

Dramatic as they seemed at the time, the upheavals wrought by Milken were only part of a much larger revolution. For today's changes in the control and channeling of capital—still one of the primary sources of power in society—parallel even deeper changes in the entire economy.

In Morgan's time, and throughout the heyday of Wall Street power, the mass production of millions of identical products was symbolic of "modern times." Today, exactly as first suggested in *Future Shock* in 1970 and elaborated in *The Third Wave* in 1980, we are standing the principle of mass production on its head.

Computer-driven technologies are making it possible to turn out small runs of increasingly customized goods aimed at niche markets. Smart companies are moving from the production of long runs of commodity products to short runs of "higher value added products" like specialty steels and chemicals. Meanwhile, constant innovation shortens product life cycles.

We find precisely parallel changes in the financial service industry, which is also diversifying product lines and shortening product life cycles. It, too, is spewing out a stream of niche products—new types of securities, mortgages, insurance policies, credit instruments, mutual funds, and endless permutations and combinations of these. Power over capital flows toward firms capable of customization and constant innovation.

In the new Third Wave economy, a car or a computer may be built in four countries and assembled in a fifth. Markets, too, expand beyond national boundaries. In the current jargon, business is becoming global. Once more, in direct parallel, we find the financial services—banking, insurance, securities—all racing to "globalize" in order to serve their corporate clients.

The Third Wave economy operates at super-high speeds. To keep pace, financial firms are pouring billions into new technologies. New computers and communications networks not only make possible the variation and customization of existing products, and the invention of new ones, but also drive transaction speeds toward instantaneity.

As new-style factories shift from "batch processing" to round-the-clock or "continuous flow" operations, finance follows suit, and shifts from "banker's hours" to twenty-four-hour services. Financial centers crop up in multiple time zones. Stocks, bonds, commodities, and currencies trade nonstop. Electronic networks make it possible to assemble and disassemble billions in what seems like nanoseconds.

Speed itself—the ability to keep pace or stay ahead—affects

the distribution of profit and power. A good example is the shrink-age of the "float" once enjoyed by banks. "Float" is the money in customers' accounts on which a bank can earn interest while cus-tomer checks are waiting to clear. As computers accelerate the clearing process, banks gain less advantage from these funds and are forced to find alternative sources of revenue—which leads them into frontal competition with other sectors of the financial industry.

As capital markets expand and interlink, from Hong Kong and Tokyo to Toronto and Paris, crossing time zones, money runs faster. Velocity and volatility both rise, and financial power in society shifts from hand to hand at faster and faster speeds.

Taken together, all these changes add up to the deepest re-structure of world finance since the early days of the industrial era. They reflect the rise of a new system of wealth creation, and even the most powerful firms, once controlling vast flows of capital, are tossed about like matchsticks in a gale.

In 1985, America's largest investment banker, Salomon Broth-ers, committed itself to build an impressive $455 million headquar-ters on Manhattan's Columbus Circle. By spring of 1987 Salomon became the target of a possible takeover; in October it had to shut down the municipal bond business it had dominated for twenty years; its commercial paper department went, too; 800 of its 6,500 employees were laid off; the October 1987 stock market crash slammed into the firm, and by December it was ignomini-ously forced to back out of the big headquarters deal at a cost of $51 million.

As profits plummeted and its own stock price fell, internal schisms rent the firm apart. One faction favored sticking to its traditional role as a capital supplier to the Blue Chips. Another sought to enter the high-yield or junk bond business that Milken had pioneered and reach out to second-tier firms. Defections and chaos followed. "The world changed in some fundamental ways," rued its chairman, John Gutfreund, "and most of us were not on top of it. We were dragged into the modern world."

The "modern world," however, is a volatile, hostile place for the old dragons. Not only individuals and companies, but whole sectors of the financial industry totter. The collapse of more than five hundred savings-and-loans banks in the United States, requiring the government to pump hundreds of billions into an emergency rescue plan, reflects the rising instability. Government regulatory agencies designed for a simpler, slower smokestack world proved unable to anticipate and avert the looming disaster, as hundreds of these "thrift institutions," caught off guard and crushed by rapidly shifting interest rates, went down in a welter of corruption and stupidity.

THE ZIGZAG OF POWER

As the global economy grows, the financial marketplace itself becomes so vast that it dwarfs any single institution, company, or individual—even a Milken. Tremendous currents rip through the system causing eruptions and perturbations on a global scale.

From the dawn of the industrial era, money power was centered in Europe. By the end of World War II it had shifted decisively to North America, and more specifically to the southern tip of Manhattan island. U.S. economic dominance went unchallenged for nearly three decades. From then on, money—and the power that flows from it—has been zigzagging unsteadily across the planet like a pachinko ball gone mad.

In the mid-seventies, seemingly overnight, the OPEC cartel sucked billions out of Europe, North America (and the rest of the world), and sent them zigging into the Middle East. Immediately, these petrodollars were zagged into bank accounts in New York or Zurich, zigged out once more in the form of gigantic loans to Argentina, Mexico, or Brazil, shot right back to U.S. and Swiss banks. As the value of the dollar fell and trade patterns shifted, capital zagged again to Tokyo, and zigged back into real estate, government bonds, and other holdings in the United States—all at speeds that stagger the experts struggling to understand what is happening.

With each such lurch of capital comes a corresponding redistribution of power at the global and local levels. As oil money fire-hosed into the Middle East, Arab nations began to wield a huge cudgel in international politics. Israel found herself increasingly isolated in the U.N. African countries, needing oil and eager for foreign aid from the Arabs, broke off diplomatic relations with Jerusalem. Petrodollars began to influence the media in various parts of the world. And the lobbies of hotels in Riyadh, Abu Dhabi, and Kuwait were jammed with attaché-case-carrying supplicants—salesmen, bankers, executives, and wheeler-dealers from around the world, pleading ignominiously with this or that spurious relative of a royal family for contacts and contracts.

However, by the early 1980s, as OPEC unity fell apart and oil prices collapsed, the frenzy waned, and so did Arab political power. Today the horde of supplicants, often representing the largest banks and corporations in the world, mill about the lobbies of hotels like the Okura or the Imperial in Tokyo.

The growing volatility of the world capital market, dramatized by such huge swings and punctuated by stock market crashes and recoveries, as in the "Two Octobers"—October 1987 and October 1989—are a sign that the old system is increasingly going out of control. Old safety mechanisms, designed to maintain financial stability in a world of relatively closed national economies, are as obsolete as the rust-belt world they were designed to protect.

Globalized production and marketing require capital to flow easily across national boundaries. This, in turn, demands the dismantling of old financial regulations and barriers erected by nations to protect their economies. But the step-by-step relaxation or removal of these barriers in Japan and in Europe has negative consequences as well.

The result is a larger and larger pool of capital instantly available anywhere. But if this makes the financial system more flexible and helps it overcome localized crises, it also raises the ante, escalating the risk of massive collapse.

Modern ships are built with watertight compartments so that a leak in one part of the hull can't flood and sink the entire vessel. Liberalization of capital so that it can flow freely is the equivalent of eliminating these fail-safe compartments. Essential for the advance of the economy, it increases the danger that a serious collapse in one country will spread to others. It also threatens the power of one of the most important economic institutions of the industrial age: the central bank.

THE LOOMING FIGHT FOR GLOBAL CONTROL

Until a decade or so ago, a relative handful of central bankers and government officials could decisively affect the price of everything from Danish hams to Datsun cars by manipulating interest rates and intervening in foreign currency markets.

Today this is becoming harder for them to do. Witness the explosive growth of the "forex," or foreign exchange, markets and the electronic networks that facilitate them.

Only a few years ago the Bank of Japan could influence the yen–dollar ratio by buying or selling 16 billions' worth of dollars. Today such sums are laughable. An estimated 200 billion dollars' worth of currencies are traded every day in London, New York, and Tokyo alone—more than a trillion a week. (Of this, no more than 10 percent is associated with world trade; the remaining 90 percent is speculation.)

Against this background the role of individual central banks, and even of the major ones acting in concert, is limited at best.

Because power is rapidly shifting out of the hands of central bankers and the governments they nominally represent, we hear urgent calls for new, more centralized regulation at a supra-national level. These are attempts to control a post-smokestack financial system by using essentially the same tools used during the smokestack age—merely raised to a higher power.

In Europe some political leaders call for the elimination of national currencies and the creation of a single all-European central bank. France's former finance minister Édouard Balladour and West Germany's foreign minister Hans Dietrich Genscher are joined by many French, Belgian, and Italian officials in pushing for this higher level of centralization. Though still some time off in the future, says economist Liane Launhardt of Commerzbank A.G. in Frankfurt: "We will eventually have to have a European central bank."

Against this supra-nationalism, Prime Minister Margaret Thatcher of Britain has waged a rear-guard action in defense of national sovereignty. But even at the world level we begin to see increasing attempts by the G-7, the group of seven largest industrial economies, to synchronize and coordinate their policies with respect to currencies, interest rates, and other variables. And academics and some financial experts argue for a "world central bank."

If the globalizers win, it will mean further weakening of the power of existing central banks—the key regulators of capital in the noncommunist world since the dawn of the smokestack age.

The decades to come will therefore see a titanic power struggle between the globalizers and the nationalists over the nature of new regulatory institutions in the world capital markets. This struggle reflects the collision between a moribund industrial order and the new global system of wealth creation that is replacing it.

Ironically, however, these proposals to centralize control of global finance at a higher level run counter to developments at the actual level of economic production and distribution, both of which are becoming more dispersed, diverse, and decentralized. This suggests that the outcome of this historic power struggle may satisfy neither nationalists nor globalists. History, full of surprises, could force us to reframe the issues in novel ways and to invent wholly new institutions.

One thing seems clear. When the battle to reshape global finance reaches its climax in the decades ahead, many of the greatest "powers that be" will be overthrown.

Yet even these upheavals in the distribution of world money-power reveal less than the whole story. They will be dwarfed in history by a revolution in the nature of wealth itself. For something odd, almost eerie, is happening to money itself—and all the power that flows from it.

6

KNOWLEDGE: A WEALTH OF SYMBOLS

Once upon a time, wealth was elemental. You had it or you didn't have it. It was solid. It was material. And it was easy to understand that wealth gave power, and power wealth.

It was simple because both were based on the land.

Land was the most important capital of all. Land was finite—meaning that if you used it, no one else could use it at the same time. Better yet, it was eminently touchable. You could measure it, dig it, turn it, plant your feet on it, feel it between your toes, and run it through your fingers. Generations of our ancestors either had it or (literally) hungered for it.

Wealth was transformed when smokestacks began to stab the skies. Machines and materials for industrial production, rather than land, now became the most critically needed form of capital: steel furnaces, textile looms and assembly lines, spot welders and sewing machines, bauxite, copper, and nickel.

This industrial capital was still finite. If you used a furnace in a steel foundry making cast-iron engine blocks, no one else could use that furnace at the same time.

Capital was still material as well. When J. P. Morgan or other bankers invested in a company, they looked for "hard assets" on its balance sheet. When bankers considered a loan, they wanted "underlying" physical, tangible collateral. Hardware.

However, unlike most landowners who knew their wealth intimately, who knew each hill, each field, each spring and orchard, few industrial-age investors ever saw, let alone touched, the machines and minerals on which their wealth was based. An investor received paper instead, a mere symbol, a bond or stock certificate representing some fraction of the value of the corporation using the capital.

Marx spoke of the alienation of the worker from his or her product. But one might also have spoken of the alienation of the investor from the source of his or her wealth.

Today, at a pace that would have blinded Marx and/or Morgan, capital is being transformed again.

INSIDE THE SKULL

As service and information sectors grow in the advanced economies, as manufacturing itself is computerized, the nature of wealth necessarily changes. While investors in backward sectors of industry still regard the traditional "hard assets"—plant, equipment, and inventories—as critical, investors in the fastest growing, most advanced sectors rely on radically different factors to back their investments.

No one buys a share of Apple Computer or IBM stock because of the firm's material assets. What counts are not the company's buildings or machines, but the contacts and power of its marketing and sales force, the organizational capacity of its management, and the ideas crackling inside the heads of its employees. The same is of course true throughout the Third Wave sectors of the economy—in companies like Fujitsu or NEC in Japan, Siemens of West Germany, France's Groupe Bull, in firms like Digital Equipment, Genentech, or Federal Express. The symbolic share of stock represents, to a startling degree, nothing more than other symbols.

The shift to this new form of capital explodes the assumptions that underpin both Marxist ideology and classical economics, premised alike on the finite character of traditional capital. For unlike land or machines, which can be used by only one person or firm at a time, the same knowledge can be applied by many different users at the same time—and if used cleverly by them, it can generate even more knowledge. It is inherently inexhaustible and nonexclusive.

Even this, however, only hints at the full scope of the revolution in capital. For if the shift toward knowledge-capital is real, then capital itself is increasingly "unreal"—it consists largely of symbols that represent nothing more than other symbols inside the memories and thoughtware of people and computers.

Capital has therefore gone from its tangible form, to a paper form that symbolized tangible assets, to paper symbolizing symbols in the skulls of a continually changing work force. And, finally, to electronic blips symbolizing the paper.

At the very same time that capital increasingly comes to rest on intangibles (a relentless process temporarily disguised by obsolete accounting rules and tax regulations), the instruments traded in the financial markets are similarly growing ever more remote from tangibility.

In Chicago, London, Sydney, Singapore, and Osaka, billions are traded in the form of so-called "derivative" instruments—such as securities based not on the stock of individual companies but on various indices of the market. A step even further removed from "fundamentals" are options based on these indices. And beyond that, in a kind of shadow world, are so-called "synthetics," which, through a series of complex transactions, offer an investor results that simulate or mirror those of an existing bond, stock, index, or option.

We are speeding toward even more rarified investments based on indices of indices of indices, derivatives of derivatives, synthetics mirroring synthetics.

Capital is fast becoming "super-symbolic."

Just as much of the power of modern science lies in longer and longer chains of reasoning, just as mathematicians build more and more extended structures, piling theorem upon theorem to yield a body of knowledge that yields still more abstract theorems, precisely as artificial intelligencers and "knowledge engineers" construct dizzying architectures of inference, so, too, we are creating a capital of progressive derivation, or—some might say—of infinitely receding mirrors.

AN EPITAPH FOR PAPER

If this were all, it would be revolutionary. But the process is pushed even further by parallel changes in the nature of money.

Most of us hear the rustle of paper when we think of dollars, francs, yen, rubles, or deutsche marks. Yet nothing would have seemed odder to one of our great-great-grandparents who miraculously time-traveled into the present. He or she would never have accepted "useless" paper for a bolt of wearable calico or a bushel of edible corn.

Throughout the agricultural age or First Wave civilization, money consisted of some material substance that had a built-in value. Gold and silver, of course. But also salt, tobacco, coral, cotton cloth, copper, and cowrie shells. An endless list of other useful things also served, at one time or another, as money. (Paper, ironically, had only limited use in daily life prior to the spread of mass literacy, and was therefore seldom—if ever—used as money.)

At the dawn of the industrial era, however, strange new ideas began to circulate about money. In 1650, for example, a man named William Potter published a prescient tract in England suggesting something previously unthinkable—that "symbolic wealth was to take the place of real wealth."

Forty years later, when people like Thomas Savery were tinkering with early steam engines, the idea was actually tried out.

It was the American colonists, forbidden by the British to mint gold or silver coins, who for the first time—in the Western world at least—began printing money.

This switch, from an inherently valuable commodity like gold or tobacco or furs to virtually worthless paper, required a tremendous leap of faith on the part of users. For unless a person believed that others would accept paper, and deliver goods for it, it had no value at all. Paper money was based almost entirely on trust. And paper money dominated the industrial society—the civilization of the Second Wave.

Today, as a more advanced Third Wave economy emerges, paper money faces near-total obsolescence. It is now clear that paper money, like assembly lines and smokestacks, is an artifact of the dying industrial era. Except for economically backward countries and quite secondary uses, paper money will go the way of the coral shell and copper bracelet currency.

DESIGNER CURRENCIES AND PARA-MONEY

There are today some 187 million Visa credit card holders in the world, using their cards at some 6.5 million retail stores, gas stations, restaurants, hotels, and other businesses, and running up bills at the rate of $570 million per day, 365 days a year. Visa is only one credit card firm.

When a restaurant owner transmits your card number to Visa or American Express, the credit card company's computers credit the restaurant account with the appropriate amount, deduct an amount from its own books, and increase the amount you owe to it. This, however, is still primitive card play.

With what is called a "smart card," the very act of handing it to a cashier who runs it through an electronic device would result in the price of the dinner being instantly debited from your bank account. You don't pay at the end of the month. Your bank account pays right away. It is like a check that clears instantaneously. Patented by Roland Moreno, a French inventor, the smart card has been pushed by French banks, along with the French postal and telecommunications services. The card, made by the Bull group, has a microchip embedded in it, and is claimed to be virtually fraud-proof. Some 61 million are already in use in Europe and Japan.

Eventually, as electronic record keeping and banking become more integrated, the store's cashless cash register will link directly to the store's bank. As charges are deducted from the customer they will instantly be credited to the retailer's account and start earning interest immediately—reducing the bank's "float" to zero.

Simultaneously, instead of customers paying bills at fixed intervals—say once a month—rents, charge accounts, and similar regular expenses may be paid, bit by bit, bleeding electronically from one's bank account in tiny droplets, as it were, on a minute-by-minute basis. Paralleling developments in the manufacturing sector, such changes promise to move the financial system further from batch processing to continuous-flow operation and toward the ultimate goal of real-time or instantaneity.

Someday, with the even smarter cards to come, you may, if you so wish, deduct the price of a meal or a new car not from your bank account but from the equity in your home—or even, in theory, from the value of jewelry or Japanese prints you may own.

Coming down the pike is the "super-smart card," otherwise called the "electronic bank-in-your-wallet." Made experimentally by Toshiba for Visa International, the plastic card contains a microchip that allows the user to check his or her bank balances, buy and sell shares, make airline reservations, and perform a variety of other tasks.

The new technologies also make possible a dialectical return to a condition that existed before the industrial revolution—the coexistence of multiple currencies in a single economy. Money, like breakfast foods and a thousand other artifacts of daily life, is becoming more diversified. We may be approaching the age of "designer currencies."

"Suppose," writes *The Economist,* "a country had privately issued money alongside the official stuff. . . . Consumers in some countries already have this parallel money—otherwise known as the pre-paid magnetic card, whose store of value runs down as it is used."

Japan is awash in this para-money. Customers buy 10 million cards a month from NTT, the phone company. They pay a sum in advance, then use the cards for making telephone calls. NTT loves it because it gets money in advance—and thus enjoys a "float" of the kind that banks used to enjoy before the speedup of check clearing began shrinking it. As of 1988, NTT had sold 330 million cards for some 214 billion yen. Consumers can also get cards for all sorts of other things, such as rail tickets and video games.

One can imagine many highly specialized types of para-money. The U.S. Department of Agriculture is piloting a program that would ultimately replace food stamps issued to the poor with a smart card programmed with one month's worth of benefits and a personal identification number. The user would run it through the supermarket checkout terminal, which would verify identification before deducting the purchase from the user's remaining balance. The system is aimed at providing better accounting while reducing fraudulent use, black marketing, and counterfeiting. This is only a step away from what might be called a "Basics Card" for all welfare recipients, which would be usable only for food, rent, and public transit.

Another example of para-money is as close as the nearest school cafeteria. Thirty-five U.S. school districts are already preparing to launch a school lunch card system designed by Prepaid Card Services, Inc., of Pearl River, New York. Paid for weekly or monthly in advance by the parent, the kiddie-card is linked to a school computer, which keeps a running account of purchases at the lunch counter.

(By stretching the imagination only a little, one can also picture a programmable card, for example, that would permit parents to customize diet. One child's card might be invalid, say, for soft drinks. If a child had a milk allergy, the card would be invalid for foods containing dairy products, and so forth.)

One can also picture special cards issued to children that could be used in movie theaters or video stores but would be electronically unacceptable for X-rated films. All kinds of custom currencies are possible, including what might be called "programmable money."

In short, once a symbol of middle-class arrival, cards are becoming ubiquitous. Millions of elderly Americans who for years received a monthly Social Security check (a piece of paper worth a certain number of paper dollars) have stopped getting it. Instead, the government sends an electronic blip to each recipient's bank, which then credits his or her account with the amount of the Social Security payment.

U.S. federal agencies also use credit cards for both buying and collecting funds. In fact, according to Joseph Wright, deputy director of the White House Office of Management and Budget, Uncle Sam is "the largest credit card user in the world."

Nowhere in any of these transactions does anything remotely like "money" in the traditional sense change hands. Not a single coin or piece of paper money is exchanged. The "money" here consists of nothing more than a string of zeros and ones transmitted by wire, microwave, or satellite.

All this is now so routine, and accepted with such confidence, that we hardly stop to doubt it. On the contrary, it is when we see large sums of paper money change hands that we suspect something is fishy. We assume that cash payment is intended to cheat the tax collector or that someone is in the drug racket.

POWER FAILURES

Such deep changes in the money system cannot occur without threatening entrenched institutions that have, until now, enjoyed positions of extraordinary power.

At one level the substitution of electronic money for paper money is a direct threat, for example, to the very existence of banks as we know them. "Banking," according to Dee Hock, former chairman of Visa International, "will not retain its position as the primary operator of payment systems." Banks have had a government-protected monopoly in check-clearing services. Electronic money threatens to supplant this system.

In self-defense, some banks have entered into the credit card business themselves. More important, they have extended their reach with automatic teller machines. If banks issue debit cards and put ATMs at millions of retail locations, they may repel the attack of the credit card companies. Since debit cards make it possible for the shopkeeper to receive payment instantly, instead of waiting for Diner's Club or American Express or Visa to remit payment, store owners may not wish to continue paying them a percentage of each sale.

On another front, banks face attack from a wide variety of nonbanks. In Japan, for example, the Ministry of Finance has qualms about the idea that private companies like NTT can issue value-bearing plastic "notes"—a kind of currency—and operate outside the banking system and its rules. If a company can take in money for a prepaid card, it is accepting a "deposit," exactly like a bank. When the user spends, he or she is making the equivalent of a "withdrawal." And when the card company pays the vendor, it is operating a "payment system." These are functions that once only banks could perform.

Moreover, if card companies can issue credit to users, as they and the cardholders see fit, unconstrained by the kind of limits and reserves that govern banks, central banks risk losing their grip on monetary policy. In South Korea, plastic money has expanded so rapidly that the government fears it is feeding inflation.

In brief, the rise of electronic money in the world economy threatens to shake up many long-entrenched power relationships. At the vortex of this power struggle is knowledge embedded in technology. It is a battle that will redefine money itself.

21ST-CENTURY MONEY

Of course, money, whether in the form of metal or paper (or paper backed by metal), is unlikely to vanish completely. But barring nuclear holocaust or technological cataclysm, electronic money will proliferate and drive out most alternatives, precisely because it combines exchange with real-time record-keeping, thus eliminating many of the costly inefficiencies that came with the traditional money system.

If we put this all together now, a rather striking pattern becomes plain. Capital—by which we mean wealth put to work to increase production—changes in parallel with money, and both take on new forms each time society undergoes a major transformation.

As they do so, their knowledge content changes. Thus agricultural-era money, consisting of metal (or some other commodity), had a knowledge content close to zero. Indeed, this First Wave money was not only tangible and durable, it was also *pre-literate*—in the sense that its value depended on its weight, not on the words imprinted on it.

Today's Second Wave money consists of printed paper with or without commodity backing. What's printed on the paper matters. The money is symbolic but still tangible. This form of money comes along with mass literacy.

Third Wave money increasingly consists of electronic pulses. It is evanescent . . . instantaneously transferred . . . monitored on the video screen. It is, in fact, virtually a video phenomenon itself. Blinking, flashing, whizzing across the planet, Third Wave money *is* information—the basis of knowledge.

Increasingly detached from material embodiments, capital and money alike change through history, moving by stages from totally tangible to symbolic and ultimately today to its "super-symbolic" form.

This vast sequence of transformations is accompanied by a deep shift of belief, almost a religious conversion—from a trust in permanent, tangible things like gold or paper to a belief that even the most intangible, ephemeral electronic blips can be swapped for goods or services.

Our wealth is a wealth of symbols. And so also, to a startling degree, is the power based on it.

7

MATERIAL-ISMO!

One day while Ronald Reagan was still in the White House a small group assembled around the table in the Family Dining Room to discuss the long-range future of America. The group consisted of eight well-known futurists and was joined by the Vice President and three of Reagan's top advisers, among them Donald Regan, the President's newly appointed chief of staff.

The meeting had been convened by the author at the request of the White House, and opened with the statement that while futurists differed on many technological, social, and political issues, there was common agreement that the economy was going through a deep transformation.

The words were hardly voiced when Donald Regan snapped, "So you all think we're going to go around cutting each other's hair and flipping hamburgers! Aren't we going to be a great manufacturing power anymore?"

Remembered more for his "kiss and tell" memoirs than his performance in office, Regan subsequently was sacked after a nasty fight with Nancy Reagan, the First Lady. But this was his very first day on the job, and he hurled the gauntlet onto the highly polished table amid the dishes.

The President and Vice President looked around expectantly for a reply. Most of the males at the table seemed taken aback by the brusqueness and immediacy of his attack. It was Heidi Toffler, co-author of *Future Shock, The Third Wave,* and this book as well, who took Regan on. "No, Mr. Regan," she replied patiently. "The United States will continue to be a great manufacturing power. There just won't be as high a percentage of people working in factories."

Explaining the difference between traditional manufacturing

methods and the way Macintosh computers are produced, she pointed out that the United States was surely one of the great food producers in the world—with fewer than 2 percent of the work force engaged in agriculture. In fact, throughout the past century, the more its farm labor force shrank relative to other sectors, the stronger, not weaker, the United States became as an agricultural power. Why couldn't the same be true of manufacture?

The startling fact remains that after many ups and downs, manufacturing employment in the United States in 1988 was almost exactly the same as it was in 1968: slightly over 19 million. Manufacturing contributed the same percentage of national output as it did thirty years earlier. But it was doing all this with a smaller fraction of the total work force.

Moreover, the handwriting is clear: Because American population and the labor force are both likely to expand, and because many American manufacturers automated and reorganized in the 1980s, the shrinkage of factory employment relative to the total must continue. While the United States, according to some estimates, is likely to generate 10,000 new jobs a day for the next decade, few if any will be in the manufacturing sector. A similar process has been transforming the European and Japanese economies as well.

Nevertheless, even now Donald Regan's words are still occasionally echoed by captains of badly run American industries, union leaders with dwindling membership rolls, and economists or historians who beat the drum for the importance of manufacture—as though anyone had suggested the reverse.

The self-perpetuated myth that America is going to lose its manufacturing base has led to loony proposals like those in a recent business magazine which called for the United States to impose a 20 percent tariff on "all imports" and to prohibit the foreign purchase of any American company.

Behind much of this hysteria is the notion that the shift of employment from manual work to service and mental-sector jobs is somehow bad for the economy and that a small manufacturing sector (in terms of jobs) leaves the economy "hollowed out." Such arguments recall the views of the French physiocrats of the 18th century who, unable to imagine an industrial economy, regarded agriculture as the only "productive" activity.

THE NEW MEANING OF JOBLESSNESS

Much of the lamentation over the "decline" of manufacture is fed by self-interest and based on obsolete concepts of wealth, production, and unemployment.

As early as 1962, a seminal work called *The Production and Distribution of Knowledge in the United States* by the Princeton economist Fritz Machlup laid the foundation for an avalanche of statistics documenting the fact that more workers now handle symbols than handle things. Throughout the late fifties and early sixties, in books, articles, reviews, monographs, and in at least one internal white paper prepared for IBM, a small band of futurists in the United States and Europe forecast the transition from muscle work to mental work or work requiring psychological and human skills. At the time, these early warnings were largely written off as too "visionary."

Since then, the shift away from manual labor toward service work and super-symbolic activity has become widespread, dramatic, and irreversible. In the United States today these activities account for fully three quarters of the work force. The great transition is reflected globally in the surprising fact that world exports of services and "intellectual property" are now equal to that of electronics and autos combined, or of the combined exports in food and fuels.

Because the early signals were ignored, the transition has been unnecessarily rocky. Mass layoffs, bankruptcies, and other upheavals swept through the economy as old rust-belt industries, late to install computers, robots, electronic information systems, and slow to restructure, found themselves gutted by more fleet-footed competition. Many blamed their troubles on foreign competition, high or low interest rates, overregulation, and a thousand other factors.

Some of these, no doubt, played a role. But equally to blame was the arrogance of the most powerful smokestack companies—auto makers, steel mills, shipyards, textile firms—who had for so long dominated the economy. Their managerial myopia punished those in the society least responsible for industrial backwardness and least able to protect themselves—their workers. Even middle managers felt the hot scorch of joblessness and saw their bank accounts, egos, and sometimes their marriages collapse as a result. Washington did little to cushion the shocks.

The fact that aggregate manufacturing employment in 1988 was at the same level as 1968 doesn't mean that the workers laid off in between simply returned to their old jobs. On the contrary, with more advanced technologies in place, companies needed a radically different kind of work force as well.

The old Second Wave factories needed essentially interchangeable workers. By contrast, Third Wave operations require diverse and continually evolving skills—which means that workers become less and less interchangeable. And this turns the entire problem of unemployment upside down.

In Second Wave or smokestack societies, an injection of capital spending or consumer purchasing power could stimulate the economy and generate jobs. Given one million jobless, one could, in principle, prime the economy and create one million jobs. Since the jobs were either interchangeable or required so little skill that they could be learned in less than an hour, virtually any unemployed worker could fill almost any job. Presto! The problem evaporates.

In today's super-symbolic economy this is less true—which is why a lot of unemployment seems intractable, and neither the traditional Keynesian or monetarist remedies work well. To cope with the Great Depression, John Maynard Keynes, we recall, urged deficit spending by government to put money into consumer pockets. Once consumers had the money, they would rush out and buy things. This, in turn, would lead manufacturers to expand their plants and hire more workers. Goodbye, unemployment. Monetarists urged manipulation of interest rates or money supply instead, to increase or decrease purchasing power as needed.

In today's global economy, pumping money into the consumer's pocket may simply send it flowing overseas, without doing anything to help the domestic economy. An American buying a new TV set or compact-disc player merely sends dollars to Japan, Korea, Malaysia, or elsewhere. The purchase doesn't necessarily add jobs at home.

But there is a far more basic flaw in the old strategies: They still focus on the circulation of money rather than knowledge. Yet it is no longer possible to reduce joblessness simply by increasing the number of jobs, because the problem is no longer merely numbers. Unemployment has gone from quantitative to qualitative.

Thus, even if there were ten new want ads for every jobless worker, if there are 10 million vacancies and only one million unemployed, the one million will not be able to perform the available jobs unless they have skills—knowledge—matched to the skill requirements of those new jobs. These skills are now so varied and fast-changing that workers can't be interchanged as easily or cheaply as in the past. Money and numbers no longer solve the problem.

The jobless desperately need money if they and their families are to survive, and it is both necessary and morally right to provide them with decent levels of public assistance. But any effective strategy for reducing joblessness in a super-symbolic economy must depend less on the allocation of wealth and more on the allocation of knowledge.

Furthermore, as these new jobs are not likely to be found in what we still think of as manufacture, what will be needed is not just a question of mechanical skills—or, for that matter, algebra, as some manufacturers contend—but a vast array of cultural and interpersonal skills as well. We will need to prepare people, through schooling, apprenticeships, and on-the-job learning, for work in such fields as the human services—helping to care, for example, for our fast-growing population of the elderly, providing child care, health services, personal security, training services, leisure and recreation services, tourism, and the like.

We will also have to begin according human-service jobs the same respect previously reserved for manufacture, rather than snidely denigrating the entire service sector as "hamburger flipping." McDonald's cannot stand as the symbol for a range of activities that includes everything from teaching to working at a dating service or in a hospital radiology center.

What's more, if, as often charged, wages are low in the service sector, then the solution is not to bewail the relative decline of manufacturing jobs, but to increase service productivity and to invent new forms of work-force organization and collective bargaining. Unions—primarily designed for the crafts or for mass manufacturing—need to be totally transformed or else replaced by new-style organizations more appropriate to the super-symbolic economy. To survive they will have to stop treating employees en masse and start thinking of them as individuals, supporting, rather than resisting, such things as work-at-home programs, flextime, and job-sharing.

In brief, the rise of the super-symbolic economy compels us to reconceptualize the entire problem of unemployment from the ground up. To challenge outworn assumptions, however, is also to challenge those who benefit from them. The Third Wave system of wealth creation thus threatens long-entrenched power relationships in corporations, unions, and governments.

THE SPECTRUM OF MIND-WORK

The super-symbolic economy makes obsolete not only our concepts of unemployment, but our concepts of work as well. To understand it, and the power struggles that it triggers, we will even need a fresh vocabulary.

Thus, the division of the economy into such sectors as "agriculture," "manufacturing," and "services" today obscures, rather than clarifies. Today's high-speed changes blur the once-neat distinctions. It might surprise Mr. Regan, who is concerned about too many Americans cutting each other's hair, that the founder of one of Europe's largest computer manufacturers has repeatedly said, "We are a service company—just like a barbershop!"

Instead of clinging to the old classifications, we need to look behind the labels and ask what people in these companies actually have to do to create added value. Once we pose this question, we find that more and more of the work in all three sectors consists of symbolic processing, or "mind-work."

Farmers now use computers to calculate grain feeds; steelworkers monitor consoles and video screens; investment bankers switch on their laptops as they model financial markets. It matters little whether economists choose to label these as "agricultural," "manufacturing," or "service" activities.

Even occupational categories are breaking down. To label someone a stockroom attendant, a machine operator, or a sales representative conceals rather than reveals. The labels may stay the same, but the actual jobs don't.

It is a lot more useful today to group workers by the amount of symbolic processing or mind-work they do as part of their jobs, regardless of the label they wear or whether they happen to work in a store, a truck, a factory, a hospital, or an office.

At the top end of what might be called the "mind-work spectrum" we have the research scientist, the financial analyst, the computer programmer, or for that matter, the ordinary file clerk. Why, one might ask, include file clerks and scientists in the same group? The answer is that, while their functions obviously differ and they work at vastly different levels of abstraction, both—and millions like them—do nothing but move information around or generate more information. Their work is totally symbolic.

In the middle of the mind-work spectrum we find a broad range of "mixed" jobs—tasks requiring the worker to perform physical labor, but also to handle information. The Federal Express or United Parcel Service driver handles boxes and packages, drives a van, but now also operates a computer at his or her side. In advanced factories the machine operator is a highly trained information worker. The hotel clerk, the nurse, and many others have to deal with people—but spend a considerable fraction of their time generating, getting, or giving out information.

Auto mechanics at Ford dealers, for example, may still have greasy hands, but they will soon be using a computer system designed by Hewlett-Packard that provides them with an "expert system" to help them in trouble-shooting, along with instant access to one hundred megabytes of technical drawings and data stored on CD-ROM. The system asks them for more data about the car they are fixing; it permits them to search through the masses of technical material intuitively; it makes inferences and then guides them through the repair steps.

When they are interacting with this system are they "mechanics" or "mind-workers"?

It is the purely manual jobs at the bottom end of the spectrum that are disappearing. With fewer manual jobs in the economy, the "proletariat" is now a minority, replaced increasingly by a "cognitariat." More accurately, as the super-symbolic economy unfolds, the proletariat *becomes* a cognitariat.

The key questions about a person's work today have to do with how much of the job entails information processing, how routine or programmable it is, what level of abstractions is involved, what access the person has to the central data bank and management information system, and how much autonomy and responsibility the individual enjoys.

To describe all this as "hollowing out" or to write it off as "hamburger slinging" is ridiculous. Such catch phrases devalue exactly that part of the economy that is growing fastest and generating the most new jobs. They ignore the crucial new role of knowledge in the production of wealth. And they fail to notice that the transformation of human labor corresponds precisely to the rise of super-symbolic capital and money, sketched in the previous chapter. It is part of the total restructure of society as we race into the 21st century.

LOWBROWS VERSUS HIGHBROWS

Such immense changes cannot come without power conflict, and to anticipate who will gain and who will lose, it may help to think of companies on a similar mind-work spectrum.

We need to classify companies not by whether they are nominally in manufacturing or services—who really cares?—but by what their people actually do. CSX, for example, is a firm that operates railroads throughout the eastern half of the United States, along with one of the world's biggest oceangoing containerization businesses (CSX brings Honda auto parts to the United States). But CSX increasingly sees itself as in the information business.

Says Alex Mandl of CSX: "The information component of our service package is growing bigger and bigger. It's not just enough to deliver products. Customers want information. Where their products will be consolidated and de-consolidated, what time each item will be where, prices, customs information, and much more. We are an information-driven business." Which means that the proportion of CSX employees in the middle and higher ranges of the mind-work spectrum is increasing.

What this suggests is that companies can be roughly classified as "highbrow," "midbrow," or "lowbrow," depending on how knowledge-intensive they are. Some firms and industries need to process more information than others, in order to produce wealth. Like individual jobs, they can be positioned on the mind-work spectrum according to the amount and complexity of the mind-work they do.

Psychiatrist Donald F. Klein, director of research of the New York State Psychiatric Institute, carries this idea one step further and insists that these differences, in turn, are reflected in the general levels of intelligence required of workers. "Do you really think that the average worker at Apple is not smarter than the average worker at McDonald's?" he asks. "The top management at McDonald's may be just as smart as the top management at Apple (although I doubt it), but the proportion of the staff of these corporations who require high IQ and symbolic skills surely differs considerably."

According to this reasoning, one should be able to arrive at a collective IQ score for each company. Are Chrysler workers inherently smarter than those at Ford or Toyota? (Not are they better educated, but are they natively more intelligent?) What about IQ rankings, say, for Apple versus Compaq, or General Foods versus Pillsbury? Carried to absurdity, one might imagine a new ranking for the Fortune 500—according to collective IQ.

But do high-IQ firms necessarily produce more wealth than low-IQ firms? Are they more profitable? Surely, other qualities, like motivation and drive or, for that matter, the intensity of competition, may have more to do with corporate success. And how should one measure intelligence in any case? There are strong reasons to believe that conventional IQ tests are culturally biased and take too few aspects of intelligence into account.

We don't need to entertain fanciful scenarios, however, to notice that, quite apart from the intelligence level of individual employees, highbrow firms behave differently from firms that are less knowledge-dependent.

Lowbrow firms typically concentrate mind-work in a few people at the top, leaving muscle work or mindless work to everyone else. Their operating assumption is that workers are ignorant or that, in any case, their knowledge is irrelevant to production.

Even in the highbrow sector today one may find examples of "de-skilling"—simplifying jobs, reducing them to their smallest components, monitoring output stroke by stroke. These attempts to apply methods designed by Frederick Taylor for use in factories at the beginning of the 20th century are, however, the wave of the lowbrow past, not the highbrow future. For any task that is so repetitive and simple that it can be done without thought is, eventually, a candidate for robotization.

In contrast, as the economy moves more toward super-symbolic production all firms are being compelled to rethink the role of knowledge. The smartest firms in the highbrow sector are the first to rethink the role of knowledge and to redesign work itself. They operate on the assumption that productivity and profits will both skyrocket if mindless work is reduced to a minimum or transferred to advanced technology, and the full potential of the worker is tapped. The goal is a better-paid but smaller, smarter work force.

Even midbrow operations that still require physical manipulation of things are becoming more knowledge-intensive, moving up the mind-work spectrum.

At GenCorp Automotive in Shelbyville, Indiana, a spanking-new $65 million plant soon to employ five hundred workers making plastic body panels for Chevrolets, Pontiacs, and Oldsmobiles is being completed. Each worker, not just supervisors and managers, will receive $8,000–$10,000 worth of training. In addition to learning the physical tasks required, they will be trained in problem solving, leadership skills, role playing, and organization processes. Workers are to be divided into teams. Supported by computer, they will learn statistical process control methods. Each team will learn many different tasks, so that they can switch jobs and minimize boredom. Team leaders receive a full year's training, including visits abroad.

GenCorp is not investing so heavily for altruistic reasons. It expects payback in the form of quick start-up at the plant, as well as better quality, less waste, and more output per worker.

Highbrow firms, in general, are not charitable institutions. Although the work in them tends to be less physically onerous than in lowbrow operations, and the surroundings more agreeable, these firms typically demand *more* of their employees than lowbrow firms do. Employees are encouraged to use not only their rational minds, but to pour their emotions, intuitions, and imagination into the job. This is why Marcusian critics see in this an even more sinister "exploitation" of the employee.

LOWBROW IDEOLOGY

In lowbrow industrial economies, wealth was typically measured by the possession of goods. The production of goods was regarded as central to the economy. Conversely, symbolic and service activities, while unavoidable, were stigmatized as nonproductive. (They sometimes still are by economists applying routine measures of productivity designed for the manufacturing sector and inapplicable to the services, which are, by their very nature, harder to measure.)

The manufacture of goods—autos, radios, tractors, TV sets—was seen as "male" or macho, and words like *practical, realistic,* or *hardheaded* were associated with it. By contrast, the production of knowledge or the exchange of information was typically disparaged as mere "paper pushing" and seen as wimpy or—worse yet—effeminate.

A flood of corollaries flowed from these attitudes. For example, that "production" is the combination of material resources, machines, and muscle . . . that the most important assets of a firm are tangibles . . . that national wealth flows from a surplus of the trade in goods . . . that trade in services is significant only because it facilitates trade in goods . . . that most education is a waste unless it is narrowly vocational . . . that research is airy-fairy . . . and that the liberal arts are irrelevant or, worse yet, inimical to business success.

What mattered, in short, was matter.

Incidentally, ideas like these were by no means limited to the Babbitts of capitalism. They had their analogs in the communist world as well. Marxist economists, if anything, have had a harder time trying to integrate highbrow work into their schema, and "socialist realism" in the arts produced thousands of portrayals of happy workers, their Schwarzenegger-like muscles straining against a background of cogwheels, smokestacks, steam locomotives. The glorification of the proletariat, and the theory that it was the vanguard of change, reflected the principles of a lowbrow economy.

What all this added up to was more than a welter of isolated opinions, assumptions, and attitudes. Rather it formed a self-reinforcing, self-justifying ideology based on a kind of macho materialism—a brash, triumphant "material-ismo!"

Material-ismo, in fact, was the ideology of mass manufacture.

Whether voiced by captains of capitalism or by conventional economists, it reflects, as the *Financial Times* wryly commented, "a view of the primacy of material product that would be appreciated by Soviet planners." It is a cudgel used in the power struggle between the vested interests of the smokestack economy and those of the fast-emerging super-symbolic economy.

There was a time when material-ismo may have made sense. Today, when the real value of most products lies in the knowledge embedded in them, it is both reactionary and imbecile. Any country that, out of choice, pursues policies based on material-ismo condemns itself to becoming the Bangladesh of the 21st century.

HIGHBROW IDEOLOGY

The companies, institutions, and people with a strong stake in the super-symbolic economy haven't yet fashioned a coherent counter-rationale. But some of the underlying ideas are falling into place.

The first fragmentary foundations of this new economics can be glimpsed in the still-unrecognized writings of people like the late Eugen Loebl, who during eleven years in a communist prison in Czechoslovakia, deeply rethought the assumptions of both Marxist and Western economics; Henry K. H. Woo of Hong Kong, who has analyzed "the unseen dimensions of wealth"; Orio Giarini in Geneva, who applies the concepts of risk and indeterminacy in his analysis of services of the future; and the American Walter Weisskopf, who writes on the role of non-equilibrium conditions in economic development.

Scientists today are asking how systems behave in turbulence, how order evolves out of chaotic conditions, and how developing systems leap to higher levels of diversity. Such questions are extremely pertinent to business and the economy. Management books speak of "thriving on chaos." Economists rediscover the work of Joseph Schumpeter, who spoke of "creative destruction" as necessary to advance. In a storm of takeovers, divestitures, reorganizations, bankruptcies, start-ups, joint ventures, and internal reorganizations, the entire economy is taking on a new structure that is light-years more diverse, fast-changing, and complex than the old smokestack economy.

This "leap" to a higher level of diversity, speed, and complexity requires a corresponding leap to higher, more sophisticated forms of integration. In turn, this demands radically higher levels of knowledge processing.

Without this higher coordination, and the mind-work it requires, no value can be added, no wealth created by the economy. Value, therefore, is dependent on more than the mixture of land, labor, and capital. All the land, labor, and capital in the world won't meet consumer needs if they cannot be integrated at a far higher level than ever before. And this changes the entire notion of value.

A recent report by Prométhée, an independent think tank in Paris, put it this way: "Value is in fact 'extracted' throughout the production/provision of a product/service. So-called service economies . . . are not characterized by the fact that people have suddenly begun to fulfill their lives through non-tangible consumption but rather by the fact that activities pertaining to the economic realm are increasingly integrated."

Drawing heavily on the 17th-century writings of René Descartes, the culture of industrialism rewarded people who could break problems and processes down into smaller and smaller constituent parts. This disintegrative or analytic approach, when transferred to economics, led us to think of production as a series of disconnected steps.

Raising capital, acquiring raw materials, recruiting workers, deploying technology, advertising, selling, and distributing the product were all seen as either sequential or as isolated from one another.

The new model of production that springs from the super-symbolic economy is dramatically different. Based on a systemic or integrative view, it sees production as increasingly simultaneous and synthesized. The parts of the process are not the whole, and they cannot be isolated from one another.

Information gained by the sales and marketing people feeds the engineers, whose innovations need to be understood by the financial people, whose ability to raise capital depends on how well satisfied the customers are, which depends on how well scheduled the company's trucks are, which depends in part on employee motivation, which depends on a paycheck plus a sense of achievement, which depends . . . et cetera, et cetera.

Connectivity rather than disconnectedness, integration rather than disintegration, real-time simultaneity rather than sequential stages—these are the assumptions that underlie the new production paradigm.

We are, in fact, discovering that "production" neither begins nor ends in the factory. Thus, the latest models of economic production extend the process both upstream and downstream—forward into aftercare or "support" for the product even after it is sold, as in auto-repair warrantees or the support expected from the retailer when a person buys a computer. Before long, the conception of production will reach even beyond that to ecologically safe disposal of the product after use. Companies will have to provide for post-use cleanup, forcing them to alter design specs, cost calculations, production methods, and much else besides. In so doing they will be performing more service, relative to manufacture, and they will be adding value. "Production" will be seen to include all these functions.

Similarly, they may extend the definition backward to include such functions as training of the employee, provision of day care, and other services. An unhappy muscle-worker could be compelled to be "productive." In high-symbolic activities, happy workers produce more. Hence, productivity begins even before the worker arrives at the office. To old-timers, such an expanded definition of production may seem fuzzy or nonsensical. To the new generation of super-symbolic leaders, conditioned to think systemically rather than in terms of isolated steps, it will seem natural.

In brief, production is reconceptualized as a far more encompassing process than the economists and ideologists of lowbrow economics imagined. And at every step from today on, it is knowledge, not cheap labor; symbols, not raw materials, that embody and add value.

This deep reconceptualization of the sources of added value is fraught with consequence. It smashes the assumptions of both free-marketism and Marxism alike, and of the material-ismo that gave rise to both. Thus, the ideas that value is sweated from the back of the worker alone, and that value is produced by the glorious capitalist entrepreneur, both implied in material-ismo, are revealed to be false and misleading politically as well as economically.

In the new economy the receptionist and the investment banker who assembles the capital, the keypunch operator and the salesperson, as well as the systems designer and telecommunications specialist, all add value. Even more significantly, so does the customer. Value results from a total effort, rather than from one isolated step in the process.

The rising importance of mind-work will not go away, no matter how many scare stories are published warning about the dire consequences of a "vanishing" manufacturing base or deriding the concept of the "information economy." Neither will the new conception of how wealth is created.

For what we are watching is a mighty convergence of change—the transformation of production coming together with the transformation of capital and money itself. Together they form a revolutionary new system for wealth creation on the planet.

8

THE ULTIMATE SUBSTITUTE

Anyone reading this page has an amazing skill called literacy. It comes as a shock sometimes to remember that all of us had ancestors who were illiterate. Not stupid or ignorant, but invincibly illiterate.

Simply to read was a fantastic achievement in the ancient world. Saint Augustine, writing in the 5th century, refers to his mentor, Saint Ambrose, the Bishop of Milan, who was so learned that he could actually read without moving his lips. For this astonishing feat he was regarded as the brainiest person in the world.

Not only were most of our ancestors illiterate, they were also "innumerate," meaning they couldn't do the simplest arithmetic. Those few who could were deemed downright dangerous. A marvelous warning attributed to Augustine holds that Christians should stay away from people who could add or subtract. It was obvious they had "made a covenant with the Devil to darken the spirit and to confine man in the bonds of Hell"—a sentiment with which many a fourth-grade math student today might agree.

It wasn't until a thousand years later that we find "reckoning masters" teaching pupils bound for commercial careers.

What this underscores is that many of the simplest skills taken for granted in business today are the product of centuries and millennia of cumulative cultural development. Knowledge from China, from India, from the Arabs, from Phoenician traders, as well as from the West, is an unrecognized part of the heritage relied on today by business executives all over the world. Successive generations have learned these skills, adapted them, transmitted them, and then slowly built on the result.

All economic systems sit upon a "knowledge base." All business enterprises depend on the preexistence of this socially constructed resource. Unlike capital, labor, and land, it is usually neglected by economists and business executives when calculating the "inputs" needed for production. Yet this resource—partly paid for, partly exploited free of charge—is now the most important of all.

At rare moments in history the advance of knowledge has smashed through old barriers. The most important of these breakthroughs has been the invention of new tools for thinking and communication, like the ideogram . . . the alphabet . . . the zero . . . and in our century, the computer.

Thirty years ago anyone with the slenderest ability to use a computer was described in the popular press as a "mathematical wizard" or a "giant brain," exactly as Saint Ambrose was in the age of moving lips.

Today we are living through one of those exclamation points in history when the entire structure of human knowledge is once again trembling with change as old barriers fall. We are not just accumulating more "facts"—whatever *they* may be. Just as we are now restructuring companies and whole economies, we are totally reorganizing the production and distribution of knowledge and the symbols used to communicate it.

What does this mean?

It means that we are creating new networks of knowledge . . . linking concepts to one another in startling ways . . . building up amazing hierarchies of inference . . . spawning new theories, hypotheses, and images, based on novel assumptions, new languages, codes, and logics. Businesses, governments, and individuals are collecting and storing more sheer data than any previous generation in history (creating a massive, confusing gold mine for tomorrow's historians).

But more important, we are interrelating data in more ways, giving them context, and thus forming them into information; and we are assembling chunks of information into larger and larger models and architectures of knowledge.

None of this implies that the data are correct; information, true; and knowledge, wise. But it does imply vast changes in the way we see the world, create wealth, and exercise power.

Not all this new knowledge is factual or even explicit. Much knowledge, as the term is used here, is unspoken, consisting of assumptions piled atop assumptions, of fragmentary models, of unnoticed analogies, and it includes not simply logical and seemingly unemotional information data, but values, the products of passion and emotion, not to mention imagination and intuition.

It is today's gigantic upheaval in the knowledge base of society—not computer hype or mere financial manipulation—that explains the rise of a super-symbolic economy.

THE ALCHEMY OF INFORMATION

Many changes in the society's knowledge system translate directly into business operations. This knowledge system is an even more pervasive part of every firm's environment than the banking system, the political system, or the energy system.

Apart from the fact that no business could open its doors if there were no language, culture, data, information, and know-how, there is the deeper fact that of all the resources needed to create wealth, none is more versatile than these. In fact, knowledge (sometimes just information and data) can be used as a replacement for other resources.

Knowledge—in principle inexhaustible—is the ultimate substitute.

Take technology.

In most smokestack factories it was inordinately expensive to change any product. It required highly paid tool-and-die makers, jig-setters, and other specialists, and resulted in extended "downtime" during which the machines were idle and ate up capital, interest, and overhead. That's why cost per unit went down if you could make longer and longer runs of identical products.

Instead of these long runs, the latest computer-driven manufacturing technologies make endless variety possible. Philips, the giant Dutch-based electronics firm, manufactured one hundred different models of color TV in 1972. Today the variety has grown to five hundred different models. Bridgestone Cycle Company in Japan is promoting the "Radac Tailor-Made" bike, Matsushita offers a semicustomized line of heated carpets, and the Washington Shoe Company offers semicustomized women's shoes—thirty-two designs for each size—depending on the individual customer's feet as measured by computer in the shoe store.

Standing the economics of mass production on their head, the new information technologies push the cost of diversity toward zero. Knowledge thus substitutes for the once-high cost of *change* in the production process.

Or take materials.

A smart computer program hitched to a lathe can cut more pieces out of the same amount of steel than most human operators. Making miniaturization possible, new knowledge leads to smaller, lighter products, which, in turn, cuts down on warehousing and transportation. And as we saw in the case of CSX, the rail and shipping firm, up-to-the-minute tracking of shipments—i.e., better information—means further transportation savings.

New knowledge also leads to the creation of totally new materials, ranging from aircraft composites to biologicals, and increases our ability to substitute one material for another. Everything, from tennis rackets to jet engines, is incorporating new plastics, alloys, and complex composites. Allied-Signal, Inc., of Morristown, New Jersey, makes something called Metglas, which combines features of both metal and glass and is used to make transformers far more energy-efficient. New optical materials point to much faster computers. New forms of tank armor are made of a combination of steel, ceramics, and uranium. Deeper knowledge permits us to customize materials at the molecular level to produce desired thermal, electrical, or mechanical characteristics.

The only reason we now ship huge amounts of raw materials like bauxite or nickel or copper across the planet is that we lack the knowledge to convert local materials into usable substitutes. Once we acquire that know-how, further drastic savings in transportation will result. In short, knowledge is a substitute for both resources and shipping.

The same goes for energy. Nothing illustrates the substitutability of knowledge for other resources than the recent breakthroughs in superconductivity, which at a minimum will drive down the amount of energy that now must be transmitted for each unit of output. At present, according to the American Public Power Association, up to 15 percent of electricity generated in the United States is lost in the process of moving it to where it is needed, because copper wires are inefficient carriers. This transmission loss is the equivalent of the output of fifty generating plants. Superconductivity can slash that loss.

Similarly, Bechtel National, Inc., in San Francisco, along with Ebasco Services, Inc., of New York, is working on what amounts to a giant, football-field-sized "battery" for storing energy. Down the road such storage systems can help eliminate the power plants that are there to provide extra electricity in peak periods.

In addition to substituting for materials, transportation, and energy, knowledge also saves time. Time itself is one of the most important of economic resources, even though it shows up no-where on a company's balance sheet. Time remains, in effect, a hidden input. Especially when change accelerates, the ability to shorten time—for instance, by communicating swiftly or by bringing new products to market fast—can be the difference between profit and loss.

New knowledge speeds things up, drives us toward a real-time, instantaneous economy, and substitutes for time expenditure.

Space, too, is conserved and conquered by knowledge. GE's Transportation Systems division builds locomotives. When it began using advanced information-processing and communications to link up with its suppliers, it was able to turn over its inventory twelve times faster than before, and to save a full acre of warehouse space.

Not only miniaturized products and reduced warehousing, but other savings are possible. In one year the United States turns out 1.3 trillion documents—sufficient, according to some calculations, to "wallpaper" the Grand Canyon 107 times. All but 5 percent of this is still stored on paper. Advanced information technologies, including document scanning, promise to compress at least some of this. More important, the new telecommunications capacity, based on computers and advanced knowledge, makes it possible to disperse production out of high-cost urban centers, and to reduce energy and transport costs even further.

KNOWLEDGE VERSUS CAPITAL

So much is written about the substitution of computerized equipment for human labor that we often ignore the ways in which it also substitutes for capital. Yet all the above also translate into financial savings.

Indeed, in a sense, knowledge is a far greater long-term threat to the power of finance than are organized labor or anticapitalist political parties. For, relatively speaking, the information revolution is reducing the need for capital per unit of output. In a "capital-ist" economy, nothing could be more significant.

Vittorio Merloni is a fifty-seven-year-old Italian businessman whose family owns 75 percent of a company called Merloni Elettrodomestici. In a small side room at the education center of the Banca Nazionale del Lavoro in Rome, he converses candidly about his firm. Ten percent of all the washing machines, refrigerators, and other major household appliances sold in Europe are made by Merloni's company. His main competitors are Electrolux of Sweden and Philips of Holland. For four turbulent years Merloni served as head of Confindustria, the Italian confederation of employers.

According to Merloni, Italy's recent economic advances are a result of the fact that "we need less capital now to do the same thing" that required more capital in the past. "This means that a poor country can be much better off today with the same amount of capital than five or ten years ago."

The reason, he says, is that knowledge-based technologies are reducing the capital needed to produce, say, dishwashers, stoves, or vacuum cleaners.

To begin with, information substitutes for high-cost inventory, according to Merloni, who uses computer-aided design and shoots data back and forth via satellite between his plants in Italy and Portugal.

By speeding the responsiveness of the factory to the market and making short runs economical, better and more instantaneous information makes it possible to reduce the amount of components and finished goods sitting in warehouses or railroad sidings.

Merloni has cut a startling 60 percent from his inventory costs. Until recently, his plants needed an inventory of 200,000 pieces for 800,000 units of output. Today they turn out 3 million units a year with only 300,000 in the pipeline. He attributes this massive saving to better information.

Merloni's case is not unique. In the United States, textile

manufacturers, apparel makers and retailers—organized into a Voluntary Inter-Industry Communications Standards (VICS) committee—are looking forward to squeezing $12 billion worth of excess inventory out of their system by using a shared industry-wide electronic data network. In Japan, NHK Spring Company, which sells seats and springs to most of the Japanese carmakers, is aiming to synchronize its production lines to those of its customers so perfectly as to virtually eliminate buffer stocks.

Says one NHK official: "If this system can be implemented, we can theoretically reduce our inventories to nil."

Cuts in inventory, of course, not only translate back into the smaller space and real estate costs mentioned earlier, but also into reduced taxes, insurance, and overhead. Similarly, Merloni points out, he is able to transfer funds from London or Paris to Milan or Madrid in minutes, saving significant interest charges.

Even though the initial cost of computers, software, information, and telecommunications may itself be high, he says, the overall savings mean that his company needs less capital to do the same job it did in the past.

These ideas about capital are spreading around the globe. In the words of Dr. Haruo Shimada of Keio University in Tokyo, we are seeing a shift from corporations that "require vast capital assets and a large accumulation of human capital to carry out production" to what he calls "flow-type" corporations that use "much less extensive capital assets."

As though to underscore this shift and the importance of knowledge in the economy of tomorrow, the major Japanese corporations are now, for the first time, pouring more funds into research and development than into capital investment.

Michael Milken, who, for better or worse, knows a thing or two about investment, has summed it up in six words: "Human capital has replaced dollar capital."

Knowledge has become the ultimate resource of business because it is the ultimate substitute.

What we've seen so far, therefore, is that in any economy, production and profits depend inescapably on the three main sources of power—violence, wealth, and knowledge. Violence is progressively converted into law. In turn, capital and money alike are now being transmuted into knowledge. Work changes in parallel, becoming more and more dependent on the manipulation of symbols. With capital, money, and work all moving in the same direction, the entire basis of the economy is revolutionized. It becomes a super-symbolic economy, which operates according to rules radically different from those that prevailed during the smoke-stack era.

Because it reduces the need for raw materials, labor, time, space, and capital, knowledge becomes the central resource of the advanced economy. And as this happens, its value soars. For this reason, as we'll see next, "info-wars"—struggles for the control of knowledge—are breaking out everywhere.

PART THREE

THE INFORMATION WARS

9

THE CHECKOUT BATTLE

Not long ago it was announced that the Smithsonian Institution of Washington, D.C., one of the most prestigious museums in the world, was considering the purchase of a small diner in New Jersey. It was the plan of the Smithsonian to move this little restaurant to Washington, make it part of the museum, perhaps even operate it, to illustrate the synthetic materials used during a certain period in American life. The plan was never carried out.

For many Americans the roadside diner exercises a nostalgic fascination. Many a 1930s Hollywood scene took place in a diner. Hemingway's famous story "The Killers" is set in a diner. So, quite beyond illustrating the uses of vinyl and Formica, there was a certain logic to the Smithsonian's surprising idea.

But if the Smithsonian ever wishes to show what America meant to the outside world in the 1950s, the dead center of the 20th century, it should buy and relocate not a diner but a supermarket.

Pushing a cart down a brightly lit supermarket aisle was a weekly ritual for a majority of American families. The supermarket with its glistening, packed shelves became a symbol of plenty in a hungry world. It was a marvel of American business and was soon emulated the world over.

Today the supermarket is still there, but, largely unnoticed by the public, it has become a battlefield in the information wars—one of many raging throughout the business world today.

BEHIND THE SHOOT-OUTS

From one end of the United States to the other, a multibillion-dollar tug-of-war today pits giant manufacturers like Nabisco, Revlon, Procter & Gamble, General Foods, and Gillette, once at the top of the industrial heap, against the lowly retail stores that put their products into the customer's shopping bag. Fought at the checkout counter, this battle gives a glimpse of things to come in the super-symbolic economy.

In the early days of the supermarket the big food processors and manufacturers would send their thousands of salespeople across the country to call on these stores and push their various lines of food, cosmetics, soft drinks, cleaning supplies, and the like. Every day, thousands of negotiations occurred.

In this day-to-day dickering, sellers had the edge. They carried with them the clout of their giant firms, which even the largest supermarket chains could not match. Each of these mega-firms was a commanding presence in its chosen markets.

The Gillette Company, for instance, until the late 1970s sold six out of every ten razor blades used in the United States. When the French firm Bic, the world's largest maker of ballpoint pens and disposable cigarette lighters, challenged Gillette on its home turf with a line of disposable razor blades, Gillette fought back and wound up with 40 to 50 percent of the U.S. disposable market. Bic was left with under 10 percent. Gillette operated outside its own country too. Today, Gillette has company locations in forty-six countries and manufacturing plants in twenty-seven, spread across the globe from Germany and France to the Philippines.

When a Gillette salesperson came to call, the supermarket listened hard—or else.

From the 1950s into the 1980s, the balance of power, with the giant manufacturers at the top and the wholesalers and retailers at the bottom, remained essentially unchanged. One of the reasons for manufacturer-power was control of information.

THE SCENT OF MISS AMERICA

At the peak of this dominance, these manufacturers were among the heaviest mass advertisers in America. This gave them effective command of the information reaching the consumer.

Gillette was particularly astute. It spent heavily to advertise razor blades or shaving cream on TV broadcasts of baseball's World Series. It plugged its perfumes on the televised Miss America Pageant.

Gillette typically ran six "marketing cycles" in the course of a year, each with a big backup ad campaign. This was called "pull-through" marketing—designed to "pull" customers into the store aisles and wipe the shelves clean in no time. These campaigns were so effective, supermarkets could hardly afford *not* to carry the Gillette products.

In turn, success at the cash register meant that Gillette, like the other big firms, could order its own supplies in bulk, at reduced prices. In this way, by coordinating production and distribution with the mass media, manufacturers by and large came to dominate all the other players in the production cycle—farmers and raw material suppliers as well as retailers.

In fact, the Gillette man (rarely a woman) could often dictate to the store how many blades it would buy, what types, how they would be displayed, when they would be delivered, and, not infrequently, what the price would be.

This was economic power in action, and it could not have existed without the pivotal control of information. It was Gillette, after all, not the retailer, who touted the advantages of Foamy shaving cream on television, or showed stubble-faced athletes using Gillette blades to get a clean shave. What the world knew about these products it learned from Gillette.

Moreover, if Gillette controlled the information going *to* the consumer, it also collected information *from* the consumer. At every stage, Gillette simply knew more than any of its retailers about how, when, and to whom its products would sell.

Gillette knew when its advertising would appear on television, when new products were to be launched, what price promotions it would offer, and it was able to control the release of all this information. In short, Gillette and the other mass manufacturers stood *between* the retailer and the customer, feeding information under their exclusive control, to both.

This control played a critical, though largely overlooked, role in maintaining the traditional dominance of the manufacturer vis-à-vis the store. And it paid off.

There was a time when Campbell Soup didn't even take the trouble to list a phone number on its salespeople's calling cards. "No use calling them," a vice-president of the Grand Union supermarket chain points out. "They never made deals."

Similarly, when Gillette's salesman came to the store to sell, he knew what he was talking about. The buyer did the listening.

THE "PUSH-MONEY" PLOY

The weapon used by retailers to hurl the big manufacturers back on their heels is a small black-and-white symbol.

Ever since the mid-sixties a little noticed committee of retailers, wholesalers, and grocery manufacturers had been meeting with companies like IBM, National Cash Register, and Sweda to discuss two common supermarket problems: long checkout lines and errors in accounting.

Couldn't technology be used to overcome these difficulties?

It could—if products could somehow be coded, and if computers could automatically "read" the codes. Optical scanning technology was still in its infancy, but the computer companies, sensing a major new market, gladly worked with the retailers.

On April 3, 1973, the "symbol selection committee" agreed on a single standard code for their industry. The result was the now familiar "Universal Product Code" or "bar code"—the shimmery black lines and numbers that appear on everything from detergent to cake mix—and the swift spread of optical scanning equipment to read them.

Today, bar coding is becoming near universal in the United States, with fully 95 percent of all food items marked with the UPC. And the system is fast spreading abroad. By 1988 there were 3,470 supermarkets and specialty and department stores in France using it. In West Germany, at least 1,500 food stores and nearly 200 department stores employed scanners. All told, not counting the United States, there were 78,000 scanners at work from Brazil to Czechoslovakia and Papua New Guinea.

In Japan, where the new retail technologies spread like fire in a high wind, 47 percent of all supermarkets and 72 percent of all convenience stores were already equipped by 1987.

The bar code did more, however, than speed the checkout line for millions of customers or reduce errors in accounting. It transferred power.

The average U.S. supermarket now stocks 22,000 different items, and with thousands of new products continually replacing old ones, power has shifted to the retailer who can keep track of all these items—along with their sales, their profitability, the timing of advertising, costs, prices, discounts, location, special promotions, traffic flow, and so on.

"Now," says Pat Collins, president of the 127 Ralph's stores in southern California, "we know as much, if not more than, the manufacturer about his product." Ralph's scanners scoop up vast volumes of data, which then helps its managers decide how much shelf space to devote to what products, when.

This is a crucial decision for competing manufacturers who are hammering at the doors, pleading for every available inch of shelf on which to display their products. Instead of the manufacturer telling the store how much to take, the store now compels manufacturers to pay what is known as "push money" for space, and staggering sums for particularly desirable locations.

Says *USA Today:* "The result [of such changes] is a war over turf: product makers battling grocers—and fighting each other—to win and keep their spots in supermarkets."

And it is clear who is winning—at the moment.

Says Kavin Moody, formerly corporate director of Management Information Systems at Gillette: "We want to control our own destiny . . . but the trade is getting more powerful. . . . They're looking for smarter deals and cooperative relationships. They're looking for better prices, which squeezes our margins. . . . The buyer used to be the flunky. Now he's backed up by all kinds of sophisticated tools."

Retail data become a more potent weapon when computer-analyzed and run through models that permit one to manipulate different variables. Thus, buyers use "direct product profitability" models to determine just how much they actually make on each product. These models examine such factors as how much shelf space is occupied by a square package as against a round one, what colors in the packaging work best for which products.

A version of this software is provided to retailers, in fact, by Procter & Gamble, one of the biggest manufacturers, in the hope of ingratiating itself with them. Armed with this software, P&G's sales force offers to help the store analyze its profitability if it, in turn, will share consumer information with P&G.

Retailers also use "shelf management" software and "space models" to help them decide which manufacturer's lines or goods to carry and which to reject, which to display in prime eye-catching space and which to put elsewhere. "Plan-a-Grams" printed out by computer give shelf-by-shelf guidance.

Having seized control of the main flow of data coming *from* the customer, retailers are also beginning to influence, if not control, the information going *to* the customer.

According to Moody, "The buyer can control the fate of a promotion. . . . To a large extent, they dictate what the consumer is going to see."

At both ends, therefore, the big food and package-goods companies have lost control of the information that once gave them power.

BEYOND THE SUPERMARKET

Beginning in the supermarket, the high-tech battle for control of information has caught fire elsewhere too. Scanners, lasers, hand-held computers, and other new technologies are pouring into drugstores, department stores, discount stores, bookstores, electrical appliance stores, hardware stores, clothing stores, specialty shops, and boutiques of all kinds. In these markets, too, manufacturers suddenly face antagonists who are keener, more confident, sometimes just short of arrogant.

"If you don't have Universal Product Codes on your goods, don't sit down, because we're not going to write the order," declares a peremptory sign in the buying office of Toys-R-Us, the 313-store chain.

As power shifts, retailer demands grow more aggressive. Bypassing the country's 100,000 independent manufacturers' representatives, dealing direct with its suppliers, Wal-Mart, the United States' fourth-biggest chain, insists that companies like Gillette change how they ship. Once more accommodating, Wal-Mart now demands that all its orders be filled 100 percent accurately—down to the numbers, sizes, and models of the products—and that deliveries be made to *its* schedule, not the supplier's. Failure to fill the order or deliver precisely on time could result in a supplier's payments being held ransom or a "handling cost" being deducted.

This puts manufacturers up against the wall: Either they increase inventories or they install new, more advanced technologies for de-massifying their factory output, moving to shorter rather than longer factory runs and faster turnaround times. Both are costly options. At the same time, retailers are imposing tighter quality standards—right down to the quality of the print on the packaging.

This seemingly trivial matter is in fact critical, since much of the information on which retail power now increasingly depends is found in the bar code, and bad printing means that the scanners may not be able to read the code accurately. Some retailers are threatening to hold the supplier responsible if the bar code on the package cannot be read properly by their scanning equipment.

Millions of customers have waited at checkout lines while clerks have passed the same package over the electronic scanner again and again before the scanner picked up the print message properly. All too often the clerk is forced to ring the product price up manually on the cash register.

Some storekeepers, in effect, are now threatening, "If my scanner can't read your code, it's your problem. I'm not telling my clerk to try again and again, and keep the customer waiting. If it doesn't scan, and we have to enter it manually, we're going to toss the product into the customer's bag and not charge for it. We'll give the product away and stop payment to you!"

Nobody ever talked back to the big companies that way. But then, nobody had the information that retailers now have.

So vital is this information that some manufacturers are now paying the retailers for it—either directly, or in exchange for services, or through intermediary firms who buy the data from retailers and sell them to manufacturers.

THE DOUBLE PAYMENT

This contest at the checkout counter has important implications for the consumer as well—and for the economy generally. Among other things it should help us rethink our obsolete assumptions about the respective roles of producers and consumers.

For example, in a world in which money is "informationalized" and information "monetized," the consumer pays for every purchase twice over: first with money and a second time by providing information that is worth money.

The customer typically gives this away for nothing. It is this valuable information that the retailers, manufacturers, banks, credit card issuers (and a lot of other people) are now fighting to control. In Florida and California, retail chains have fought blistering legal battles with banks over this issue. The central question their lawyers are asking one another is: "Who owns the customer data?"

The legal answers are not yet in. But one thing is certain: No one is asking the customer.

In theory, the customers' reward for providing data will be lower prices deriving from greater efficiency in the system. But it is by no means guaranteed that any part of this saving will be passed on, and, to the degree that the customer is the source of this crucial information, it is like giving the retailer an interest-free "information loan" in the hopes of future payback.

Since data originating with the customer are increasingly needed for the design and production (as well as distribution) of goods and services, the customer is in fact becoming a contributor to, if not an actual part of, the production process. The consumer, in a sense, is a co-producer of his or her own purchases.

But does the customer in fact "own" this information? Or does it acquire value only after it is collected and processed?

We lack the vocabulary, let alone laws and economic concepts, with which to deal with these unfamiliar questions arising from the information wars. But the issues involve the transfer of billions of dollars—and a subtle shift of economic and social bargaining power.

What does a customer give away free to the store, the manufacturer, or his or her credit card company?

Take the simplest of cases: A mother, home from work, in haste to make dinner, discovers she is out of margarine.

Dashing into the nearest store, she snatches a pound of

Fleischmann's sweet unsalted margarine made by Nabisco off the shelf. Hurrying to the checkout counter, she waits her turn, grabbing a copy of *TV Guide* from the rack near the register, and hands her purchases to the clerk, who passes them over the scanner.

In principle, she has communicated the following to the store computer: (1) a type of product she uses; (2) its brand; (3) its size or amount; (4) the fact that she preferred unsalted margarine to the regular; (5) the time of the purchase; (6) what other items, brands, sizes, etc., she bought at the same time; (7) the size of her total bill; (8) the kind of magazine in which an advertiser might reach her; (9) information about where additional shelf space is now available; and much more besides.

If a customer buys several bagfuls of different products, the same data become available for each item, and it becomes theoretically possible to *interrelate* these items to one another, in order to infer a *pattern* of purchasing—a consumption "signature" of each individual or group of customers.

If the shopper pays with a credit card, of course, much more is revealed.

Now the customer is also providing: (1) name; (2) address and postal code (important for segmenting markets); (3) credit information; (4) a basis for inferring the family income; and, potentially, much more besides.

By combining all this, it will soon become possible to construct a surprisingly detailed picture of the individual's life style, including driving habits, travel, entertainment and reading preferences, the frequency of meals outside the home, purchases of alcohol, condoms or other contraceptives, and a list of favored charities.

Marui, a leading Japanese general-goods retailer which issues its own credit card, uses a system called M-TOPS. This permits Marui to zero in on families who have just changed residence. It does this by identifying purchases that usually go with furnishing a new home. On the assumption that a family buying air conditioners or kitchen cabinetry might be in the market for new beds as well, Marui has been able to achieve astonishingly high direct-mail responses.

Leaving aside for a time the unsettling issues this raises about privacy in a super-symbolic economy, much of this information, once in the hands of any commercial enterprise—supermarket chain, bank, manufacturer—can also be sold for a price or bartered for a discount on services. The market for such information is huge.

"Data protection" laws in many countries now seek to regulate the uses of computerized information, but the data banks are filling up, the possibilities of integration are increasing, and the economic value of the information is soaring.

All this, however, is only a primitive first approximation of the future.

THE INTELLIGENT SUPERMARKET

Consumers may soon find themselves in supermarkets lined with so-called "electronic shelves." Instead of paper tags indicating the prices of canned goods or paper towels, the edge of the shelf itself will be a blinking liquid crystal display with digital readouts of the prices. The magic of this new technology is that it permits the store to change the price of thousands of products automatically and instantaneously as data streak in from the scanners at the front of the store.

Prices might plummet for slow-selling goods, climb for the hot items, rising and falling continuously in real-time response to supply and demand. Telepanel, Inc., a Toronto firm, estimates that such a system, capable of pricing 8,000 to 12,000 items, would cost the store in the range of $150,000 to $200,000 and pay for itself within two years.

Carried only a short step further, the electronic shelf might also provide shoppers with nutritional and price information at the touch of a button. Nor are such systems contemplated only for supermarkets. Says *Business Week:* "Drug chains, convenience stores, and even department stores already are planning their own versions of the system."

Down the line are even "smarter" shelves that would not merely send information to the customer, but elicit information from him or her. Hidden sensors, for example, make it possible to know when a customer passes a hand over a particular shelf or item, or when traffic exceeds or falls below expectation at a particular display.

Soon the customer will hardly be able to blink in the store, or move his or her arms, without providing the storekeeper with more and yet more usable or salable data.

The moral and economic implications of all this have hardly been explored by business or by consumer advocates. (Those interested in organizing consumer power had better start thinking about all this quickly, before the systems have been laid in place.) For now, it is only necessary to understand that profit margins today increasingly depend on information judo.

A THREAT TO THE "SHOGUNS"

Many of these same forces are changing power relationships in Japan as well. According to Alex Stewart, author of a definitive report on the Japanese distribution system, "retailers are now the dominant force within the distribution industry," while "manufacturers have to rely increasingly on retailers to interpret the needs of the marketplace."

George Fields is chairman and CEO of ASI Market Research (Japan). According to Fields, in Japan "distribution no longer means putting something on the shelf. It is now essentially an information system." Distribution anywhere, he notes, "will no longer be a chain of inventory points, passing goods along the line, but an information link between the manufacturer and the consumer."

What Fields is perhaps too polite to say, and what the Japanese in particular feel uncomfortable in making explicit, is that this transformation will dethrone many of the "shoguns" of industry in Japan. In Japan, too, power will shift toward those firms or industrial sectors that know best how to win the info-wars.

But the battle between manufacturers and retailers is only beginning, and it is not a two-sided struggle. The real-life tug-of-war has drawn many others into the battle zone—everyone from banks and computer manufacturers to truckers and telephone companies.

Squeezed between manufacturers and retailers are wholesalers, warehousers, transport firms, and others, each engaging in a fiercely competitive war-against-all, wielding advanced information and communications technologies as the main weapons.

Moreover, what we've seen so far is only the opening skirmish, and manufacturers themselves are mounting important counter-offensives—selling through alternative channels outside the store (direct mail, for example), using computers and telecommunications to set up their own vertically integrated distribution systems, buying up retail stores, and attempting to leapfrog technologically, to get ahead of the retailers.

Information flowing from these technologies will transform all our production and distribution systems, creating vast power vacuums that completely new groups and institutions are already racing to fill.

10

EXTRA-INTELLIGENCE

In 1839 a down-at-heels artist who gave lessons in drawing was asked by a pupil whether payment of a ten-dollar fee would be helpful. The art teacher—a sometime dabbler in the mysteries of electromagnetism—replied, "It would save my life, that's all."

Samuel F. B. Morse had already proved that he could send coded messages along an electric wire. But it wasn't until four years later, by dint of strenuous lobbying, that Morse managed to persuade the U.S. Congress to appropriate $30,000 to build a telegraph line between Washington and Baltimore. It was on the opening of that earliest line that Morse sent his historic telegram— "What hath God wrought!" With that Morse opened the age of telecommunications and triggered one of the most dramatic commercial confrontations of the 19th century. He started a powerful process that is still unfolding in our time.

Today, even as the battle of the supermarket checkout counters intensifies, a larger conflict is shaping up, centered on control of what might be called the electronic highways of tomorrow.

BACH, BEETHOVEN, AND WANG

Because so much of business now depends on getting and sending information, companies around the world have been rushing to link their employees through electronic networks. These networks form the key infrastructure of the 21st century, as critical to business success and national economic development as the railroads were in Morse's era.

Some of these are "local area networks," or LANs, which merely hook up computers in a single building or complex. Others are globe-girdling nets that connect Citibank people the world over, or help Hilton reserve its hotel rooms and Hertz its cars.

Every time McDonald's sells a Big Mac or a McMuffin, electronic data are generated. With 9,400 restaurants in 46 countries, McDonald's operates no fewer than 20 different networks to collect, assemble, and distribute this information. Du Pont's medical sales force plugs laptops into its electronic mail network, and Sara Lee depends on its nets to put L'eggs hosiery onto the shelves. Volvo links 20,000 terminals around the world to swap market data. DEC's engineers exchange design information electronically worldwide.

IBM alone connects 355,000 terminals around the world through a system called VNET, which in 1987 handled an estimated 5 trillion characters of data. By itself, a single part of that system—called PROFS—saved IBM the purchase of 7.5 million envelopes, and IBM estimates that without PROFS it would need nearly 40,000 additional employees to perform the same work.

Networking has spread down to the smallest businesses. With some 50 million PCs in use in the United States, Wang now advertises its networking equipment over the radio, sandwiching its commercials about "connectability" between Bach suites and Beethoven symphonies.

Companies daily grow more dependent on their electronic nets for billing, ordering, tracking, and trading; for the exchange of design specifications, engineering drawings, and schedules; and for actually controlling production lines remotely. Once regarded as purely administrative tools, networked information systems are increasingly seen as strategic weapons, helping companies protect established markets and attack new ones.

The race to build these networks has taken on some of the urgency that accompanied the great age of railroad construction in the 19th century, when nations became aware that their fate might be tied to the extensiveness of their rail systems.

Yet the power-shifting implications of this phenomenon are only dimly perceived by the public. To appreciate their significance, it helps to glance back at what happened after Samuel Morse strung the first telegraph network.

THE TELEPHONE FAD

By the mid-19th century Morse franchises had built thousands of miles of telegraph lines. Competing companies sprang up, networks grew, and an intense race began to connect major cities to one another across the continent. Stringing its wires along railroad rights of way, a company called Western Union began gobbling up smaller companies. Within eleven years its lines reached from one end of America to the other, and its capital had shot up from $500,000 to $41 million—a bank-boggling amount in those days.

Soon its subsidiary, the Gold & Stock Telegraph Company, was providing high-speed information for investors and gold speculators—paving the way for today's Dow Jones or Nikkei.

At a time when most messages were still carried across the continent in saddlebags or railway cars, Western Union had a stranglehold on the means of advanced communication.

Success, as usual, bred corporate arrogance. Thus, in 1876, when a voice teacher named Alexander Graham Bell patented the first telephone, Western Union tried to laugh it off as a joke and a fad. But as public demand for telephone service soared, Western Union made it clear it was not about to surrender its monopoly. A knockdown conflict ensued, and Western Union did everything possible to kill or capture the newer technology.

It hired Thomas Edison to invent alternatives to the Bell technology. Its lawyers fought Bell in court.

"At another level," writes Joseph C. Goulden, author of *Monopoly*, "Western Union barred Bell from the right-of-way monopolies it owned for its wires along highways and railroads. Western Union had its instruments in every major hotel, railway station, and newspaper office in the nation, under terms which forbade installations of telephones. A Bell manager in Philadelphia was forbidden to erect lines anywhere in the city; his workers frequently were jailed on complaints sworn by Western Union. The telegraph company's political influence in Washington kept Bell phones from federal offices."

Despite all this, Western Union failed, swept aside not so much by its smaller antagonist as by the business world's desperate hunger for better communications. In turn, the winner of that corporate power struggle grew into the biggest privately owned

business the world had ever seen—the American Telephone &
Telegraph Company (AT&T).

SECRETS AND SECRET-ARIES

The benefits of communication—whether Morse's telegraph,
Bell's telephone, or today's high-speed data networks—are relative.
If no one has them, all competing firms operate, as it were, at the
same neural transmission rate. But when some do and others
don't, the competitive arena is sharply tilted. So companies rushed
to adopt Bell's new invention.

Telephones changed almost everything about business. They
permitted operations over a greater geographical area. Top executives could now speak directly with branch managers or salesmen
in distant regional offices to find out, in detail, what was going on.
Voice communication conveyed far more information, through
intonation, inflection, and accent, than the emotionless dah-dits of
Morse code ever could.

The phones made big companies bigger. They made centralized bureaucracies more efficient. Switchboards and operators proliferated. Secretaries overheard calls and learned when to keep
mum. They learned to screen calls, thereby partially controlling
access to power.

At first the phone also abetted secrecy. A lot of business could
now be transacted without the incriminating evidence of a piece of
paper. (Later came technologies for wiretapping and bugging,
tipping the scales in the never-ending battle between those who
have business secrets and those who want to penetrate them.)

The indirect benefits of this advanced communications system
were even greater. Phones helped integrate the industrializing
economy. Capital markets became more fluid; commerce, easier.
Deals could be made swiftly, with a confirming letter as follow-up.

Phones accelerated the pace of business activity—which, in
turn, stepped up the rate of economic development in the more
technically advanced nations. In this way, one might argue that
telephones, over the long term, even affected the international
balance of power. (This claim is less outrageous than it might seem
at first glance. National power flows from multiple sources, but

one can crudely track the rise of America to a position of global dominance by looking at its communications system relative to other nations. As late as 1956, half of all the telephones in the world were in the United States. Today, as America's relative dominance declines, that percentage has slipped to about one third.)

ELECTRONIC HIGHWAYS

As more and more of the economy came to depend on phones, the companies or government agencies that provided or regulated them became enormously powerful too. In the United States, AT&T, otherwise known as the Bell System or Ma Bell, became the dominant supplier of telecommunications services.

It is hard for those accustomed to decent telephone service to imagine operating an economy or a business without it, or to function in a country where the telephone company (usually the government) can deny even basic phone service or delay its installation for years. This bureaucratic power gives rise to political favoritism, payoffs, and corruption, slows down national economic development, and frequently determines which enterprises have a chance to grow and which must fail. Yet such is the situation still prevailing in many of the formerly socialist and nonindustrial nations.

Even in the technologically advanced nations, phone service suppliers and regulators can control the fate of entire industrial sectors, by providing or refusing specialized services, setting differential prices, and through other means.

Sometimes angry or frustrated users strike back. In fact, the biggest corporate restructuring in history, the court-ordered breakup of AT&T in 1984, can illustrate the point.

The U.S. government had been trying without success to dismantle AT&T since the 1940s on grounds that it was charging customers too much. Government attorneys hauled the company into court, cases dragged on interminably, but nothing fundamental changed. Warning shots were fired across the corporation's bow, but even during Democratic administrations pledged to strong antitrust action, nothing cracked the AT&T grip on the U.S. communications system.

What ultimately shifted the power balance was a combination of new technology and the irrepressible demand of business phone users for more and better service.

Starting in the 1960s, a large number of American businesses had begun installing computers. Simultaneously, satellites and many other new technologies erupted from the laboratories—some of them out of AT&T's own Bell Labs. Soon corporate computer users began demanding a great variety of new data network services. They wanted computers to be able to talk to one another. They knew the necessary technology was feasible. But the diverse data services they desperately needed represented, at the time, too small a market to whet Ma Bell's appetite.

As a protected monopoly the phone company had no competition, and was therefore slow to respond to these new needs. As computers and satellites spread, however, and more companies needed to link them up, business disgruntlement with AT&T intensified. IBM, the prime supplier of mainframes, presumably lost business because AT&T was dragging its feet, and had other reasons for wishing to see AT&T's monopoly cracked. All these unhappy corporations were politically savvy.

Gradually anti-AT&T sentiment in Washington mounted. Ultimately, it was the combination of new technologies and rising hostility to Ma Bell that provided the political climate for the climactic bust-up that occurred. Breaking AT&T into pieces, the court, for the first time since the early decades of the century, opened telecommunications in the United States to competition. There were, in other words, structural forces, not merely legal reasons, behind the massive breakup.

Just as an overwhelming business demand for better communications had defeated Western Union a century earlier, so again, new technologies and an overwhelming unmet demand for new services ultimately defeated AT&T. By now the rate of technological change has become white-hot and companies are far more dependent on telecommunications than ever in history.

The result is that airlines, car makers, and oil companies are all engaged in a many-sided war for control of the emerging communications systems. Indeed, as we'll shortly see, truckers, warehousers, stores, factories—the entire chain of production and distribution—are being shaken.

Moreover, as money becomes more like information, and information more like money, both are increasingly reduced to (and moved around by) electronic impulses. As this historic fusion of telecommunications and finance deepens, the power inherent in the control of networks increases exponentially.

All this explains the fierce urgency with which companies and governments alike are hurling themselves into the war to control the electronic highways of tomorrow. Amazingly, however, few top business leaders actually understand the stakes, let alone the fantastic changes restructuring the very nature of communications in our time.

THE SELF-AWARE NETWORK

Anyone can see and touch the telephone or computer on the nearest desk. This is not true of the networks that connect them to the world. Thus we remain, for the most part, ignorant about the high-speed advances that are fashioning them into something resembling the nervous system of our society.

The networks that Morse, Western Union, Bell, and others set up when they first began stringing wires were unintelligent, if not downright stupid. Common sense taught that a straight line is the shortest distance between two points. So engineers sought this straight line, and messages sent from one city to another were always sent over this pathway.

As these first-stage networks expanded, however, it was discovered that in the world of the network, a straight line is not necessarily the best way to get a message from one place to another. In fact, more messages could flow faster if, instead of always sending a call, say, from Tallahassee to Atlanta via the same route, the network could count the calls in each leg of the system and then shunt the Atlanta-bound call onto available lines, sending it as far away as New Orleans or even St. Louis, rather than delaying it because the shortest straight-line route happened to be busy.

Primitive though it was, this was an early injection of "intelligence" or "smarts" into the system, and it meant, in effect, that the network was beginning to monitor its own performance. With this the entire system leaped to a second stage of development. This breakthrough led to many additional innovations, often of marvelous ingenuity, that eventually allowed the telephone network to monitor many more things about itself, to check its components and anticipate and even diagnose breakdowns.

It was as though a once-dead or inert organism suddenly began checking its own blood pressure, pulse, and breathing rate. The network was becoming self-aware.

Crisscrossing the entire planet, with wires running into hundreds of millions of homes, with whole copper mines of cable snaking under the streets of cities, with complex switching systems and transmission technologies in them, these second-stage networks, constantly refined, improved, extended, and given more and more intelligence, were among the true marvels of the industrial age.

Because they are largely invisible to the ordinary user, our civilization has radically underestimated the congealed brilliance and conceptual beauty of these hidden networks as well as their evolutionary significance.

For while some human populations still lack even the most rudimentary telephone service, researchers are already hard at work on another revolutionary leap in telecommunications—the creation of even more sophisticated third-stage networks.

Nowadays, as millions of computers are plugged into them, from giant Crays to tiny laptops, as new networks continually spring up, as they are linked to form a denser and denser interconnected mesh, a still higher level of intelligence or "self-awareness" is needed to handle the incredibly vast volumes of information pulsing through them.

As a result, researchers are racing to make networks even more self-aware. Their goal is so-called neural networks. These will not only route and reroute messages, but actually learn from their own past experience, forecast where and when heavy loads will be, and then automatically expand or contract sections of the network to match the requirements. This is as though the San Diego Freeway or a German *Autobahn* were clever enough to widen and narrow itself according to how many cars it expected at any moment.

Yet even before this major effort is complete, another even more gigantic leap is being taken. We are moving not into a fourth-stage system, but to another kind of intelligence altogether.

MESSING WITH THE MESSAGE

Until now, even the smartest networks, including the new neural networks, had only what might be called "intra-intelligence." All their "smarts" were aimed inward.

Intra-intelligence is like the intelligence embedded in our own autonomic nervous system, which regulates the involuntary operations of the body, such as heartbeat and hormonal secretions—the functions we seldom think about, but which are necessary to sustain life.

Intra-intelligent networks deliver the message precisely as sent. Scientists and engineers struggle to maintain the purity of the message, fighting to eliminate any "noise" that might garble or alter the message. They may scramble it or digitize it or packetize it (i.e., break it into short spurts) to get it from here to there. But they reconstitute it again at the receiving end. And the message content remains the same.

Today we are reaching beyond intra-intelligence toward networks that might be called "extra-intelligent." They do not just transfer data. They analyze, combine, repackage, or otherwise alter messages, sometimes creating new information along the way. Thus massaged or enhanced, what comes out the other end is different from what is fed in—changed by software embedded in the networks. These are the so-called "Value Added Networks," or VANs. They are extra-intelligent.

At present most VANs merely scramble and rescramble messages to adapt them to different media. For example, in France the Atlas 400 service of France Telecom accepts data from a mainframe computer, say, then repackages it in a form that can be received by a PC, a fax machine, or a videotex terminal.

Not very exciting, it would appear. But the concept of adding value to a message doesn't stop with altering its technical characteristics. The French Minitel network, which links 5 million homes and businesses, offers Gatrad, Mitrad, Dilo, and other services that can accept a message in French and automatically deliver it in English, Arabic, Spanish, German, Italian, or Dutch—and vice versa. While the translations are still rough, they are workable, and some services also have the specialized vocabularies needed for subjects involving, say, aerospace, nuclear, or political topics.

Other networks receive data from a sender, run them through a computerized model, and deliver an "enhanced" message to the end-user.

A simple hypothetical example illustrates the point.

Imagine that a trucking firm based in the outskirts of Paris must regularly dispatch its trucks to forty different European distributors, restocking their shelves with a product. Road conditions and weather differ in various parts of Europe, as do currency exchange rates, gasoline prices, and other factors. In the past each driver calculated the best route, or else phoned the transport company each day for instructions.

But imagine instead that an independent VAN operator—a common carrier—not only can send signals to truck drivers all over Europe, but also collects current information on road conditions, traffic, weather, currencies, and gas prices. The Paris trucker can now load its daily messages and routing instructions onto the VAN for distribution to its drivers. But the messages, before reaching the drivers, are run through the network's software program, which automatically adjusts routes to minimize driving time, mileage, gas costs, and currency expenses in light of the latest data.

In this case, the instructions sent by the transport firm to its drivers are altered en route and "enhanced" before reaching them. The telecommunications carrier firm—the operator of the Value Added Network—has added value by integrating the customer's message with fresh information, transforming it, and then distributing it.

This, however, suggests only the simplest use of an extra-intelligent net. As the networks come to offer more complex services—collecting, integrating, and evaluating data, drawing automatic inferences, and running input through sophisticated models—their potential value soars.

In short, we are now looking toward networks whose "smarts" are no longer aimed at changing or improving the network itself but which, in effect, act on the outside world, adding "extra-intelligence" to the messages flowing through them.

Still largely a gleam in their architects' eyes, extra-intelligent nets represent an evolutionary leap to a new level of communication. They also raise to a higher level the sophistication required of their users. For a company to load its messages on a VAN and permit them to be altered without a deep understanding of the assumptions buried in the VAN's software is to operate on blind faith, rather than rational decision. For hidden biases built into the software can cost a user dearly.

Foreign airlines, for example, have complained to the U.S. Department of Transportation that they are discriminated against in the electronic network that thousands of U.S. travel agents use in choosing flights for their clients. Called Sabre, the computerized reservation system is run by AMR Corp., which also owns American Airlines. The system, which monitors reservations on many airlines, has extra-intelligence embedded in it in the form of a software model that tells the travel agent the best available flights. At issue in the complaint were the assumptions built right into this software.

Thus, when a travel agent searches, say, for a flight from Frankfurt to St. Louis, Missouri, her computer screen displays the flights in order depending upon the length of time they take. The shorter the flight the better. But the Sabre software automatically assumed that changing planes and transferring from one airline to another takes ninety minutes, irrespective of the actual time required. Since many of their flights to the United States required a change of plane and transfer to a domestic American airline, the foreign carriers charged that the hidden premises of the software unfairly penalized those whose interline transfers require less than ninety minutes. For this reason, they argued, their flights were less likely to be chosen by travel agents. In short, the extra-intelligence was biased.

Imagine, soon, not a handful of such disputes and networks, but thousands of VANs with tens of thousands of built-in programs and models, continually altering and manipulating millions of messages as they whiz through the economy along these self-aware electronic highways. Britain alone already boasts eight hundred VANs, West Germany seven hundred, and more than five hundred companies in Japan have registered with the Ministry of Posts and Telecommunications to operate VANs.

The existence of VANs promises to squeeze untold billions of dollars out of today's costs of production and distribution by slashing red tape, cutting inventory, speeding up response time. But the injection of extra-intelligence into these fast-proliferating and interlinked nets has a larger significance. It is like the sudden, blinding addition of a cerebral cortex to an organism that never had one. Combined with the autonomic nervous system, it begins to give the organism not merely self-awareness and the ability to change itself, but the ability to intervene directly in our lives, beginning first with our businesses.

Because of this, networks will take on revolutionary new roles in business and society. And even though, so far as we know, no one has yet used extra-intelligence for pernicious or even criminal purposes, the spread of extra-intelligent networks is still in its infancy, with rules and safeguards yet to be defined.

Who knows what will follow? By creating a self-aware electronic neural system that is extra-intelligent, we change the rules of culture as well as business.

E-I, as we may call it, will raise perplexing questions about the relationships of data to information and knowledge, about language, about ethics and the abstruse models concealed in software. Rights of redress, responsibility for error or bias, issues of privacy and fairness will all cascade into executive suites and the courts in the years to come as society tries to adapt to the existence of extra-intelligence.

As the implications of E-I will someday reach far beyond mere business matters, they should cause deep social, political, and even philosophical reflection. For prodigies of labor, intellect, and scientific imagination that dwarf anything involved in constructing Egyptian pyramids, medieval cathedrals, or Stonehenge are now being poured into the construction of the electronic infrastructure of tomorrow's super-symbolic society.

E-I, as we shall see next, is already upsetting power relationships in whole sectors of the emerging economy.

11

NET POWER

Japan worries. To the outside world it often seems economically invincible. But things look different from inside. It has no energy supplies of its own, grows little food, and is highly sensitive to trade restrictions. If the yen goes down, it worries. If the yen goes up, it worries. But individual Japanese do not just worry about the economy in general. They also worry about their own future. So they are among the world's biggest savers. And they buy massive amounts of insurance.

For a long time the chief beneficiaries of all this anxiety were the giant insurance companies. Today, however, it is the insurers who are doing the worrying.

The government is opening the door that once kept out competition from Japan's aggressive securities brokers. Tough, world-class companies like Nomura and Daiwa, the Merrill Lynches or Shearsons of Japan, are preparing to move in on the insurance industry's turf.

Topping that off, the entire insurance field is in an uproar of change. Customers are demanding all sorts of newfangled policies and financial services which these venerable giants—Nippon Life is over one hundred years old—find hard to create and manage.

To deal with threats like these, the big insurance firms have begun laying down an electronic line of defense. Nippon Life is betting nearly half a billion dollars on a new information system that adds 5,000 PCs, 1,500 larger computers for its satellite offices, mega-machines for branches and headquarters, plus optical scanners and other equipment, all plugged together in a single network.

Rival Dai-Ichi Mutual is also running hard, building a network that will allow agents in the field to dial up central data banks, respond to synthesized voice commands on the phone, and get facsimile printouts of the data they need about customers or policies. Meanwhile, Meiji Mutual, with its 38,000 field agents, mainly women, is also racing to arm itself with the weaponry of communications.

Nor are the insurance companies alone. All of Japan, it would seem, is going electronic. Writes *Datamation:* "Major service companies are installing networks with 5,000 or more PCs and workstations in every corner of Japan." Says Meiji's Toshiyuki Nakamura: "If we don't . . . we might lose everything."

Nakamura is right. For as electronic networks spread, power is beginning to shift. And not just in Japan. The United States and Europe, too, are wiring up as never before. It is the electronic race of the century.

THE SEARCH FOR DENIM

Consider a pair of jeans. The denim in them may well have come from Burlington Industries. This giant American textile firm sends its customers free software that allows them to communicate directly with Burlington's mainframe, to paw through its stock of denims electronically, to find the particular batch of fabric they want, and to order it—all at instantaneous speeds.

Manufacturers like Burlington hope such services will distinguish them from their competitors, make life easier for customers— and simultaneously lock those customers into the new "electronic data interchange" (EDI) systems so tightly that it will become hard for them to escape.

At their simplest, EDI systems simply permit the electronic exchange of documents between companies or business units— invoices, specifications, inventory data, and the like. But leaving it at that is rather like calling Mozart a tunesmith. For by wedding one another's data bases and electronic systems, companies are able to form highly intimate partnerships.

For example, while Burlington opens its inventory files to its customers, Digital Equipment, the computer maker, opens its design secrets to its suppliers. When DEC places an order for components, it may electronically transfer its entire Computer-Aided-Design file to the supplier firm, so that both buyer and seller can work more closely together, step by step. The object is intimacy.

The big auto companies now virtually refuse to do business with suppliers who are not equipped for electronic interaction. At Ford, fifty-seven parts plants have been told they must electronically exchange shipping schedules, material requisitions, releases, and receipts with both customers and suppliers.

The benefits of EDI are not only a reduction in paperwork and inventory, but quicker, more flexible response to customer needs. Together these can amount to massive savings.

But the worldwide shift to electronic interchange also implies radical changes in the business system. Companies are forming into what might be called "information-sharing groups." More communication is crossing—and sometimes blurring—organizational boundaries.

Whether in a Japanese insurance company or an American automaker, EDI forces major changes in accounting and other control systems. When a company goes electronic, jobs change; people move around; some departments gain clout, others lose. The entire relationship of the firm to its suppliers and customers is shaken up.

Such power shifts, however, are not merely limited to individual firms. Whole sectors of the economy are already feeling the impact of EDI. For EDI can be used as a weapon to wipe out go-betweens and intermediaries.

THE BINGO-ED WHOLESALER

Shiseido, Japan's top cosmetics firm, for example, uses its networks to sidestep the traditional distribution chain. Shiseido's powders, creams, eye shadows, lotions, and what-have-you are everywhere in Japan and are beginning to make a splash in U.S. and European markets as well.

By connecting its computers directly to those of its customers, Shiseido end-runs wholesalers and warehousers, delivering from its own distribution centers directly to the stores. If Shiseido and other manufacturers can "talk" directly with their retailers, and retailers can electronically access information in the manufacturer's own computers, who needs an intermediary?

"The wholesaler? Bingo! Bypassed," says Monroe Greenstein,

a retail industry analyst at the Bear, Stearns securities firm in New York. To avoid that fate, wholesalers, too, are turning to electronic weaponry.

The most publicized, by now classic case of a wholesaler taking the offensive—and capturing new power in the marketplace—involves American Hospital Supply, now a part of Baxter Health Care Corporation. Starting as early as 1978, AHS began placing terminals inside hospitals and allowing them to dial directly, through a network, to its computers. It was much simpler for hospitals to order supplies from AHS by pushing a button than to deal with other, less sophisticated suppliers.

In turn, AHS used the network to zap all sorts of useful information about products, usage, costs, inventory control, etc., to its customers. Because AHS's system was so responsive and reliable, hospitals were able to cut back on their own inventories, saving them substantial money. And if a hospital placed all its business with AHS, the company provided an entire management information system for the hospital. AHS's business skyrocketed.

Consultant Peter Keen, from whose study, *Competing in Time,* some of these data are drawn, describes how Foremost McKesson, a pharmaceutical wholesaler, applied the AHS strategy to its own field.

As customer orders flow into Foremost McKesson's computers electronically from hand-held terminals placed in 15,000 stores, they are instantly sorted and consolidated. This generates Foremost McKesson's own orders, fully half of which are then, in turn, instantly and automatically transmitted to *its* supplier firms.

Such high-speed systems allow AHS, Foremost, and many other firms to wire themselves so snugly into their customers' daily operations that it becomes costly and complex for them to shift their business elsewhere. In return, the systems save their customers significant sums and help them manage more smartly all around. All this pays off in negotiating power.

But AHS and McKesson are still exceptions. Most wholesalers could face an electronic squeeze play, caught between manufacturers and increasingly sophisticated retailers.

REAL ESTATE AND RAILS

Warehouse companies are next in line for trouble as extra-intelligence spreads through the economy.

The increasing customization and flexible manufacture made possible by computers, means, among other things, a shift from a few big orders for uniform products to many smaller orders for diversified products. Simultaneously, the speedup of business encouraged by electronic networking increases pressures for just-in-time delivery to factories and stores.

All this implies fewer bulk shipments, shorter storage times, faster turnaround, and more insistence on precise information about the whereabouts of every stored item—less space, more information.

This substitution reduces the clout of the space merchant and pushes smart warehousers into a search for alternative functions. Some are using networks and computers to sell customers data software services, transportation management, packing, sorting, inspecting, knockdown and assembly services, and the like. Still others—Sumitomo Warehouse in Japan, for instance—are moving into real estate development as the traditional functions of the warehouser dry up.

The super-symbolic economy and the spread of extra-intelligence also shake up the transportation sector—railroads, shippers, and truckers. Like warehousers, many truckers are also turning to electronic networks to save themselves.

In Japan the move toward short-run factory production and the push for just-in-time delivery means a big surge in short-haul work. And instead of delivering big loads on a once-a-week schedule, the pressure is toward smaller but far more frequent dropoffs. The most rapid growth is seen in door-to-door delivery.

What we see, therefore, are all the traditional sectors of the production and distribution system wielding extra-intelligence to stay alive, or as an offensive weapon to extend their power.

MOBILIZING FOR ELECTRONIC WAR

The scale of the electronic war rises when whole industries mobilize to do battle.

Rather than individual firms, industry-wide groups are taking collective action. Such industry-wide networks are especially notable in Japan, where their formation is strongly encouraged by the ubiquitous Ministry of International Trade and Industry. Thus MITI is prodding the petroleum industry to complete a net that will link refiners, oil tank facilities, and retailers. Industry-wide Value Added Networks have already appeared in fields as disparate as frozen foods, eyeglasses, and sporting goods.

Similar industry-wide nets are springing up elsewhere. In Australia two competing Value Added Networks, Woolcom and a service offered by Talman Pty., Ltd., for wool brokers and exporters, are vying for business and looking ahead to link-ups with Tradegate, an international trade net, and EXIT, an export clearance system.

In the United States a major drive is under way to complete a network that will tie together not only textile manufacturers like Burlington, but apparel makers and the giant retailers like Wal-Mart and K Mart. To stoke up support for this effort, business leaders like Roger Millikin, chairman of Millikin & Company, make speeches, hold seminars, fund studies, and preach the network gospel.

A key problem in the industry has been slow response time. Clothing fashions change swiftly, so the industry wants to compress the time between order and delivery from weeks to days by installing an electronic network that runs from the textile mill to the retail checkout counter. By speeding response, huge cuts in inventory become possible.

The electronic system allows retailers to order smaller batches and replace the fast-sellers more frequently as styles and consumer tastes change, instead of sitting on slow-moving merchandise. Milliken cites the experience of one department store chain that was able to sell 25 percent more slacks while, at the same time, carrying 25 percent fewer slacks in its inventory. Indeed, with the system only partly in place, results have been dramatic. The campaign began in 1986. By 1989, according to Arthur Andersen & Company, more than seventy-five retailers had invested an estimated $3.6 billion in the system, called Quick Response, and had already benefited to the tune of $9.6 billion.

In fact, Millikin and many others believe so many more billions can be saved that electronic intelligence can serve as a weapon in international trade wars. If efficiency can be raised enough, and rapidly enough, the reasoning goes, the American textile and apparel industries would be able to compete more effectively against cheap labor imports.

As individual companies and entire industries race to position themselves for the future by building their own special-purpose networks, other giants are racing to lay in place global multipurpose networks that will carry messages for anyone.

What we are seeing, therefore, is the emergence of several types or layers of electronic networks: private nets primarily designed for the employees of a single firm; EDI hookups between individual companies and their customers and/or vendors; and industry-wide networks. To these, however, must now be added generic networks—so-called common carriers—which are needed to connect these lower-level networks to one another and to transport messages for everyone else.

The volume of messages and data now surging through this neural system is so huge that an even larger-scale battle has erupted among big companies who wish to dominate this common carrier service. Giants like British Telecom, AT&T, and Japan's KDD are racing to expand their capacity and speed up data flows. To complicate matters, large companies that have their own global nets sell services to outsiders and compete with the common carriers. Thus Toyota, for example, and IBM fight for business that might otherwise go to one of the old telephone companies. General Electric operates a network in seventy countries, and Benetton, based in Italy, relies on GE to connect 90 percent of its employees.

What is forming under our eyes, therefore, is an entirely new, multilayered system, the economy's infrastructure for the 21st century.

THE CUSTOMER LOOP

Its growth is causing new struggles for the control of knowledge and communication, struggles that are shifting power among people, companies, industries, sectors, and countries. Yet the "neuralization" of the economy has scarcely begun and new players enter the power game every day. They include credit card companies, the great Japanese trading houses, equipment manufacturers, and many others.

Crucial to this emerging system is the plastic card in the consumer's wallet. Whether it is an automatic teller machine card, a conventional credit card, or a "smart" debit card, the card is a network's link to the individual. That link can, in principle, be expanded vastly.

As everyone from banks and oil companies to local merchants moves more deeply into the electronic age . . . as the cards themselves become smarter, carrying and conveying vast amounts of information . . . and as money itself becomes "super-symbolic," no longer pegged to either metal or paper . . . the card provides the missing link in the emerging neural system.

Whoever controls the card—bankers or their rivals—has a priceless channel into the home and daily life. Thus we see a push to link individual customers to the specialized networks. In Japan, JCB Co., a credit card firm, together with NTT Data Communications, is launching a card women can use at their hairdressers'. It hopes to connect 35,000 hairdressers with 10 million card-carrying customers in a two-year period.

The long-range dream of the world's network builders is a single integrated loop, running from the customer (who will electronically tell business what goods or services to make) . . . to the producer . . . through what remains of distribution intermediary firms . . . to the retailer or the electronic home shopping service . . . to the ATM or the credit card payment system . . . and ultimately back into the home of the consumer.

Any company or industrial group that can seize control of the main steps in this cycle will wield decisive economic power—and hence considerable political power as well. But seizing it will depend less on capital than on brains—intelligence embedded in computers, software, and electronic networks.

BUSINESS BLITZKRIEG

Economies of the past, whether agricultural or industrial, were built around long-lasting structures.

In place of these, we are laying the electronic basis for an accelerative kaleidoscopic economy capable of instantly reshuffling itself into new patterns without blowing itself apart. The new extra-intelligence is part of the necessary adaptive equipment.

In the confusing new flux, businesses can use extra-intelligence to launch surprise attacks on entirely fresh territory, which means that companies can no longer be sure where the next competitive push will come from.

The classic blitzkrieg—much analyzed in the network literature—was Merrill Lynch's launch of its Cash Management Account in 1977, an early use of information technology for a strategic, as distinct from merely administrative, purpose.

The Cash Management Account, or CMA, was a new financial product that combined four previously separate services for the customer: a checking account, a deposit account, a credit card, and a securities account. The customer could move money back and forth among these at will. There was no float and the checking account paid interest.

The integration of these previously disparate products into a single offering was made possible only by Merrill Lynch's sophisticated computer technology and electronic networks. In twelve months, Merrill sucked in $5 billion of customer funds and by 1984, according to consultant Peter Keen, $70 billion had flooded into Merrill Lynch's hands. Keen calls it a "preemptive strike" against the banks, which saw vast sums withdrawn by customers who preferred the CMA to an ordinary bank checking account. A securities house, not subject to bank regulation and not regarded as a bank, devastated the banks.

Since then, many banks and other financial institutions have offered similar packages, but Merrill had a several-year head start on them.

The strange new hybrid patterns of competition—which reflect a restructuring of markets as a result of extra-intelligence—are seen in the move of retailers like Japan's Seibu Saison group into the financial services business. A Seibu subsidiary is planning to install electronic cash dispensers in railroad stations. British

Petroleum, having set up its own internal bank, sells banking services to outsiders.

Extra-intelligent networks help explain the widespread push for deregulation of industry, and they suggest that existing government regulations will prove less and less effective. For existing regulations are based on categories and divisions among industries that no longer exist in the age of extra-intelligence. Should banking regulations apply to nonbanks? What, after all, is a bank these days?

By linking actual operations across company lines, by making it possible for companies to compete in fields once regarded as alien, extra-intelligent networks break up the old specializations, the old institutional division of labor.

In their place come new constellations and clusters of companies, densely interrelated not merely by money but by shared information.

Ironically, it is the disruption caused by this drastic restructuring of the economy around knowledge that explains many of today's breakdowns and inefficiencies—the misplaced bills, the computer errors, the inadequate service, the sense that nothing works properly. The old smokestack economy is disintegrating; the new super-symbolic economy is still being built, and the electronic infrastructure on which it depends is still in a primitive stage of development.

Information is the most fluid of resources, and fluidity is the hallmark of an economy in which the production and distribution of food, energy, goods, and services increasingly depend on symbolic exchange.

What emerges is an economy that itself looks more like a nervous system than anything else, and which runs according to rules no one has as yet formulated coherently.

Indeed, the unprecedented rise of extra-intelligence raises profound, sometimes chilling questions for society as a whole, quite different from those raised by earlier communications revolutions.

THE RISE OF INFO-MONOPOLIES?

Extra-intelligence can squeeze untold billions of fat and waste out of the economy. It potentially represents an enormous leap forward—the substitution of brainpower and imagination not merely for capital, energy, and resources, but for brutalizing labor as well.

But whether extra-intelligence produces a "better" way of life will depend partly on the social and political intelligence that guides its overall development.

The more automated and extra-intelligent our networks become, the more human decision-making is hidden from view, and the more dependent we all become on preprogrammed events based on concepts and assumptions that few understand and that are sometimes not even willingly disclosed.

Before long the power of computers will leap forward because of parallel processing, artificial intelligence, and other stunning innovations. Speech recognition and automatic translation will, no doubt, come into wide use, along with high-definition visual displays and concert-class sound. The same networks will routinely carry voice, data, images, and information in other forms. All this raises profound philosophical questions.

Some see in all this the coming monopolization of knowledge. "The moment of truth," wrote Professor Frederic Jameson of Duke University at an earlier stage in the rise of the symbolic economy, ". . . comes when the matter of the ownership and control of the new information banks . . . [strikes] with a vengeance." Jameson raises the specter of a "global private monopoly of information."

That fear is now far too simple. The issue is not whether one giant global private monopoly will control all information—which seems highly unlikely—but who will control the endless *conversions and reconversions* of it made possible by extra-intelligence, as data, information, and knowledge flow through the nervous system of the super-symbolic economy.

Baffling new issues about the uses and misuses of knowledge will arise to confront business and society as a whole. They will no longer simply reflect Bacon's truth that knowledge is power, but the higher level truth that, in the super-symbolic economy, it is knowledge *about* knowledge that counts most.

12

THE WIDENING WAR

Umbrellas and automobiles are different. Not just because of size, function, and cost. But for a reason we seldom stop to consider. A person can use an umbrella without buying another product. An automobile, by contrast, is useless without fuel, oil, repair services, spare parts, not to mention streets and roads. The humble umbrella, therefore, is a rugged individual, so to speak, delivering value to its user irrespective of any other product.

The mighty auto, by contrast, is a team player completely dependent on other products. So is a razor blade, a tape recorder, a refrigerator, and thousands of other products that work only when combined with others. The television set would stare blankly into the living room if someone somewhere were not transmitting images to it. Even the lowly closet hanger presupposes a rack or bar to hang it on.

Each of these is part of a product *system*. It is precisely their systemic nature that is their main source of economic value. And just as "team players" must play by certain agreed-on rules, systemic products need standards to work. A three-pronged electrical plug doesn't help much if all the wall sockets have only two slots.

This distinction between stand-alone and systemic products throws revealing light on an issue that is widening today's information wars all around the world. The French call it *la guerre des normes*—"the war over standards." Battles over standards are raging in industries as diverse as medical technology, industrial pressure vessels, and cameras.

Some of the most explosive—and public—disputes are directly related to the ways in which data, information, knowledge, images, and entertainment are created and distributed.

In essence a global battle over dollars and political power, its outcome will reach into millions of homes. It will radically shift power among the industrial giants of the world: companies like IBM, AT&T, Sony, and Siemens. And it will affect national economies.

Nowhere is this battle more public than in the three-way fight to determine what kind of television the world will watch in the decades to come.

THE HALF-TRILLION-DOLLAR STAKE

Three basic television standards are in use in different parts of the world at present: NTSC, PAL, and SECAM, each slightly different but incompatible. Because of this, an American program like *The Cosby Show* usually has to be converted from one system to another before it can be telecast abroad. But the images produced by all three systems are fuzzy by contrast with what is known as HDTV—the television of tomorrow.

"High-definition TV" is to today's home video screens what the compact disc is to the scratchy platter played on great-grandma's gramophone. High definition can put pictures on the TV screen that match the quality of the best big-screen movies. It can make an image blast off the computer monitor looking as bright and sharp as the finest printed page.

Congressman Mel Levine has pointed out in testimony before the telecommunications subcommittee of the U.S. House of Representatives that, despite its name, more is involved than just TV. HDTV, he said, "represents a new generation of consumer electronics, one that will drive technological developments in dozens of areas, from chip to fiber-optic to battery to camera technology."

Because HD image quality is so good, it could even make it possible for cinemas all over the world to receive their movies via satellite, rather than on film as at present, which would open an additional immense market for satellite receivers and other equipment.

In total, therefore, the decision as to which HDTV standard(s) to use will shape a world market estimated to be worth half a trillion dollars.

Japanese engineers have worked on HDTV for nearly twenty years. Now high definition is about to burst on the world economic scene. And when it does, writes Bernard Cassen in *Le Monde Diplomatique*, "the Japanese and the Americans threaten to render all European television sets obsolete—and to be the only ones with the power to replace them."

The Japanese hoped the world would adopt a single standard for HDTV. This would have simplified matters and saved them a lot of money. With their head start, had they been able to sell this basic international standard, the way would have been open for a massive expansion of the Japanese consumer electronics industry.

To head off this onslaught, however, European governments and TV networks (in many cases one and the same) have agreed to stick with broadcast standards that are incompatible with the Japanese system. This, they hope, will give European manufacturers a chance to play technological catch-up. High definition could then be introduced in stages by the Europeans themselves.

Thirty-two European broadcasters, universities, and manufacturers hastily formed themselves into the Eureka 95 project and began developing a complete set of high-definition technologies, covering everything from studio and transmission equipment to television sets. Thomson, S.A., of France coordinated the team working on technical standards for TV production; Robert Bosch GmbH of West Germany focused on studio equipment; Thorn/EMI of Britain, on TV receivers.

The Europeans, meanwhile, also began courting the United States. West Germany's minister of posts and telecommunications, Christian Schwarz-Schilling, flew to Washington and proposed a formal alliance, arguing that "we should not permit Japan to get supremacy in the next generation of standards."

By now the Japanese began to worry that the Europeans might steal a march on them, actually launching a counterattack on both the U.S. and Japanese domestic markets with their Euro-version of HDTV. To block this, Japanese manufacturers have lobbied strongly in the United States against the European system.

Given all this uncertainty, the Japanese are also quietly preparing to market different sets for different parts of the world, as a fallback in the event they cannot impose a single standard.

Economic paranoia is rampant in the United States as well, where the entire HDTV issue is bogged down in hairsplitting technical debate, political controversy, and commercial rivalry.

The three big U.S. broadcast networks want to slow down HDTV. They argue for a single U.S. standard that could carry current signals as well as the new HDTV pictures. By contrast, the U.S. cable industry and direct satellite broadcasters argue that this single standard would paralyze research into better cable and satellite transmission.

Congress, in the meantime, wants to make sure that when new sets start pouring into American homes, they will come from American plants. "Right now," says Congressman Edward J. Markey, "Japanese and European companies are far out in front . . . while our domestic consumer electronics industry is moribund."

Amid charges of "techno-nationalism," the TV tug-of-war will wax hotter for years to come. But even as the battle for the future of television heats up, a parallel struggle is under way to shape the future of the computer.

STRATEGIC STANDARDS

Today's blistering pace of innovation forces manufacturers to choose a strategy: either invent and impose a standard on your industry, or piggyback on someone else's standard—or be driven into a commercial Siberia in which your products have limited uses and markets.

IBM has been the dominant force in the computer industry since its inception. It was IBM's blue-suited and buttoned-down salespeople who first put mainframes into government offices and corporations. And for nearly two decades IBM faced only weak and disorganized competition.

Much of IBM's monumental success could be traced to its early ability to set—and enforce—a standard for what goes on inside computers.

At first it was the hardware that counted most. But gradually it became clear that software is the most important element in any computer system. So-called "applications programs" were sets of instructions to the machine to perform tasks like accounting or word-processing, printing, displaying graphics, and communicating. But every computer has built into it a kind of meta-program called an "operating system," which determines what other kinds of programs it can or cannot run.

The key to dominating the computer industry lies in software—

without which the machines are inert and useless. But the key to dominating software is the operating system. And the ultimate lever of control—the key to dominating operating systems—lies in the standards to which they, in turn, are held. It was IBM's control of these that made it the superpower of the computing world.

Despite IBM's efforts, however, other operating systems have sprung up over the years, from Ada, which is promoted by the U.S. Department of Defense, to Unix, originally offered by AT&T, plus many variations of these. When Apple Computer started the microcomputer revolution in the mid-seventies, it specifically opted to create non-IBM-compatible machines, choosing a different operating system.

Today an all-out battle is being fought internationally between IBM and its chief competitors to set the operating systems standard for the future. The struggle is highly technical, with experts arguing with other experts. But the implications reach far beyond the computer industry itself, and governments see it as directly related to their economic development plans for tomorrow.

Because IBM still dominates the field, and because its operating systems constrain users and competitors alike, a London-based organization called X/Open has been set up to create a standard for the operating systems of mini-computers, workstations, and PCs—the newer fields in which IBM is most vulnerable. Originally set up by AT&T, Digital Equipment, and the German Siemens, it now includes Fujitsu as well, all demanding a new standard that is "open," rather than a barrier to non-IBM equipment.

Since then the pressure on IBM has become so strong, it has been compelled to join the group and to pledge, cross its heart, that it will in the future commit itself to "open" policies.

Even before this setback had fully sunk in, IBM faced another challenge, this time pitting it directly against Ma Bell, the American Telephone & Telegraph Company. As long ago as the 1960s, AT&T software engineers had developed an operating system called Unix for their own use. It had certain characteristics that made it attractive to universities and to some of the smaller computer makers. Not yet in the computer business itself, AT&T let them use Unix for pennies. They, in turn, produced their own customized variations of Unix. Since then Unix has become increasingly popular, with Sun Microsystems selling Unix-based machines to the fast-growing workstation market.

In a shrewd strategic stroke, AT&T promptly bought into Sun

and formed an alliance with Xerox, Unisys, Motorola, and other companies to create a single Unix standard under AT&T's leadership.

Backed by AT&T and these allies, Unix's growing popularity presented a direct threat to the dominance of IBM and other computer manufacturers with proprietary operating systems. Thus IBM, the new convert to operating-system glasnost, or openness, counterattacked.

Faced with the danger that a unified version of Unix would be available on AT&T machines before anyone else's, IBM now formed its own alliance to fight back. Called the Open Software Foundation, this group now includes DEC, Groupe Bull from France, Siemens and Nixdorf from West Germany, and many others. It is working to formulate its own alternate standard for Unix.

Charges and countercharges blare from full-page ads in *The Wall Street Journal* or the *Financial Times* as the battle over computer operating-system standards heats up. Once more the fate of giant corporations and whole industries hinges on a war over standards.

THE MAIN BOUT

One of the most important things computers do today is talk to one another. In fact, computers and communication are so closely fused today as to be inseparable.

This means that computer companies must defend not only their operating systems, but also their access to, or control of, telecommunications networks. If operating systems control what goes on *inside* computers, telecommunications standards control what goes on *between* computers. (The distinction, in reality, is not so neat, but good enough for our purposes here.) And here again we find companies and countries locked in a bitter struggle over the main systems that process our information.

Because more data, information, and knowledge now flow across national boundaries, the info-war over telecommunications is, if anything, even more politically fraught than the war over operating systems.

General Motors, for example, in trying to tie together its

global production, has devised its own standard to allow its machines to communicate with one another even though they come from different makers. It calls this standard MAP (for Manufacturing Automation Protocol) and has tried to promote its worldwide adoption by other manufacturers and its own suppliers.

To block GM, the European Community has talked thirteen giant manufacturing companies, including BMW, Olivetti, British Aerospace, and Nixdorf, into supporting a counter-standard called CNMA. If European machines are going to talk to one another, the EC seems to be saying, it will not be on terms defined by General Motors—or the United States.

This toe-to-toe over electronic communication in the factories of the planet, however, is only part of the even larger battle for control of the world's extra-intelligent networks.

As Japanese firms began to connect up electronically with plants and offices around the world a host of companies rushed to sell them the necessary computers and telecommunications links. This is a field in which U.S. technology still outstrips that of Japan; and IBM, once again, was a major player. But the Japanese Ministry of Posts and Telecommunications announced that any networks linking Japan with the outside world would have to conform to a technical standard set by an obscure United Nations consultative committee on telecom policy. This ruling would have kept IBM in Japan from using equipment and systems designed to its own proprietary standard. The result was a massive lobbying effort in Washington and Tokyo, negotiations between the two governments, and ultimately, a back-off by Japan.

When each country's telephone system was controlled by a single company or ministry, national standards were set and international standards were then decided by the International Telecommunications Union.

Life was simple—until computers wanted to talk to one another.

By the 1980s, as new technologies avalanched into the market, businesses and individuals alike were using machines built by different manufacturers, using different operating systems, running programs written by different software houses, and trying to send messages around the world through a patchwork of cables, microwaves, and satellites belonging to different countries.

The result today is the much-bewailed electronic Tower of Babel, and it explains why desperate cries for "connectivity" and "interoperability" echo around the business world. And here yet again the main struggle has shaped up as IBM versus The World.

IBM has long promoted a standard called System Network Architecture. The problem with SNA is that while it allows (some, not all) IBM machines to talk to other IBM machines, it is decidedly deaf to a great many non-IBM computers.

As *The Wall Street Journal* once put it: "Hooking any non-SNA computers into those networks is a programmer's nightmare. Rivals wanting to sell their computers to IBM's legion of customers must mimic SNA in their own machines." This indirect control of access to information may have been tolerable when most computers *were* IBMs, but not today. Hence the cry has gone up for computer democracy.

COMPUTER DEMOCRACY

No longer ready to accept IBM's dominance, competitors have searched for a weapon with which to strike down Goliath. And they found one.

That mighty slingshot is a counter-standard called OSI (Open System Interconnection), which is intended to permit all kinds of computers to talk freely to one another. Heavily promoted by the European computer makers, OSI has forced IBM to retreat from its restrictive policies.

The conflict heated up when a dozen European computer manufacturers, appalled by IBM domination, reached agreement in 1983 that they would jointly undertake the incredibly complex work needed to design the specifications for an open system. Sensing the implications, European governments leaped to support them.

On the other side, Uncle Sam, watching this gang-up of forces against IBM, cried foul. Charging the Europeans with discrimination in their decisions, Donald Abelson of the Office of U.S. Trade Representative, stated that "Americans suspect . . . that we are the subject of a conspiracy."

Since then the anti-IBM campaign has expanded. Support for it has come from Esprit, the Common Market's program for the support of science and technology. At the end of 1986 the Council of Ministers of the European Community ruled that a subset of OSI options would be the standard for computer sales to governments in the community.

IBM responded to this attack with an offering confusingly called System Applications Architecture, or SAA, which included a version of SNA, and by offering customers a choice of either SNA or OSI products.

Then faced with this formidable opposition, IBM once more followed the principle "If you can't lick 'em, join 'em." Joining these various groupings, IBM pledged on scout's honor that it will henceforth support the open standard. It was, as in the case of operating systems, a last-minute religious conversion called into question by IBM's critics and competitors.

Like General Motors and many other giants of the industrial age, IBM expanded to fill every available inch of its ecological niche, adapted itself all too comfortably to it, and now finds itself in an increasingly hostile, fast-changing environment in which sheer size, once an advantage, is now often a handicap. To some it appears that the battle over telecommunications standards is the beginning of the post-IBM era.

On the surface, IBM's main rivals, American and foreign, have won. It might also appear that Europe has won. The war, however, is not yet over. The battle over standards is never won.

THE PARADOX OF NORMS

There is a hidden paradox in these power struggles. As business produces more diversified products, there is, in addition to a mounting pressure for more standards, a countereffort to make products more and more versatile by accommodating multiple standards. (This is why some portable TV sets provide a button that allows the user to switch back and forth among the European PAL and SECAM standards and the American NTSC standard.)

Another technique used to make products more versatile is to break them down into smaller and more numerous modular components. This reduces the importance of the external standard. But at the same time, it increases the number of "micro-standards" embedded *inside* the product and needed to make the components work together.

However, no sooner is one standard established—OSI, for example—than new technologies drive it into obsolescence or irrelevancy. And as soon as we have arrived at standards for networks, or for software, the battleground shifts to a still higher and more complex plane. Thus, where two or more standards compete, new equipment appears that permits a user to convert from one system to another. But the appearance of adaptors gives rise to a need for standards for adaptors. Today, therefore, we are even seeing attempts to create what might be termed "standards for standards"—a group called the Information Technology Requirements Council was established not long ago for precisely this purpose in the field of communications.

The fight to control standards, in other words, shifts from higher to lower levels and back up again. But it does not go away. For the battle is part of the larger, continuing war for the control, routing, and regulation of information. It is a key front in the struggle for power based on knowledge, and it is raging not just in the technical thickets of television, computers, and communication, but in the nearest *bierstube* and, indeed, in the kitchen itself.

THE BEER AND SAUSAGE MINUET

Standards have long been set by industries or governments to assure the safety or quality of products and, more recently, to safeguard the environment. But they are also designed by protectionist governments to keep competitive foreign products out or to advance an industrial policy. West Germany, for instance, conveniently enough for local industry, effectively barred foreign beer on grounds that it was "impure."

And what good is beer without sausage? So Italian canned luncheon meats were also excluded, as were many other imported foods that happened to contain an additive widely used to improve the consistency of the jelly in canned ham and beef.

It took a minuet of negotiations and ultimately the threat of legal action by the European Community to make the Germans back down. By now it should come as no surprise that GATT, the General Agreement on Tariffs and Trade, has devised yet another standard—this one intended to reduce the use of standards for unfair trade purposes.

But even beyond their competitive purpose and their use as

weapons in today's blistering trade wars, there is another, deeper reason why *la guerre de normes* is heating up.

A provocative article by the French writer Philippe Messine has suggested that fights over standards must multiply, because in advanced economies the ratio of systemic products to stand-alone products rises, putting standards "at the center of great industrial battles."

This important insight is underlined by the fact that computer-based manufacture leads to a tremendous increase in the variety of products, which means that systems must link more products into wholes or gestalts, and that, in turn, explains why demands for standards *must* skyrocket.

It also helps us understand Messine's remark that the new systemic products increasingly include "an important non-material component, gray matter." For the manufacture of many goods in small runs aimed at segments or niches of the market increases the amount of information needed to coordinate the economy, making the entire cycle of production and distribution more knowledge-dependent.

Then, too, as science and technology advance, technical standards themselves reflect our deeper knowledge. The tests and technologies employed to measure standards become more precise; tolerances, narrower. More information and ever-deeper knowledge are embedded in the standards.

Finally, as competitive innovations drive more new products into the marketplace, filling (and simultaneously creating) new consumer needs, the push for the definition of standards itself propels research forward.

Thus, on every front—scientific, political, economic, and technological—the battle over standards can be expected to intensify as the new system for wealth creation replaces the fast-fading smokestack world of the past.

Victors in the widening wars over standards will wield immense, high-quality power in the fast-arriving world of tomorrow.

13

THE EXECUTIVE THOUGHT POLICE

Tom Varnum is forty-eight years old and still married to his first wife. He works nearly sixty hours a week, in return for which he receives $162,000 a year. He also has some stock options and extra life insurance, but travels tourist or business class when he flies. He's been with his company for more than ten years and in his present job for nearly five. Just below the top rank in his firm, he dreams of someday becoming a Chief Executive Officer, but knows his chances are remote. In the meantime, he wants parity with his company's Chief Financial Officer.

The problem is that Tom is a specialist and his superiors think he doesn't know enough about general management. So he feels trapped in his specialty, and he reads enviously about colleagues who have left the profession behind and broken into the mainstream of corporate management at the highest levels—people like Art Ryan, who is now vice-chairman of Chase Manhattan Bank, or Ed Schefer, a vice-president and group manager at General Foods USA, or Josephine Johnson, executive vice-president at Equicor, a joint venture of Equitable Life and Hospital Corporation of America.

Tom is sharp, bright, clean-cut, and articulate, but he tends to lapse into a jaw-breaking jargon that leaves co-workers and superiors suitably puzzled and instantly brands him a "techie."

While Ryan, Schefer, and Johnson are real people who began as computer specialists and "migrated" outward from Information Systems, or "IS," and upward into senior management, Tom is a fictional composite whose traits, according to a recent survey, match those of an increasingly restive and assertive group of executives known as "chief information officers." In the United States today more than two hundred big corporations use the title "Chief Information Officer" or some close approximation of it. Not many years ago there was no such thing. Nomenclature varies, but in many firms the CIO title is a notch or two up from such related designations as "Manager of Data Processing," "Vice-President of Information Systems," or "Director, Management Information Systems."

CIOs are the men—only a few, so far, are women—who are responsible for spending the huge budgets corporations now allocate for computers, data processing, and information services. Because of this they find themselves at the hot center of the info-wars.

LEVELS OF COMBAT

Eavesdrop on a group of CIOs at a conference, and chances are that before long you will hear their standard complaints: That they are misunderstood by top management. Bosses view them as budget-busting cost centers, whereas they believe that effective high-tech Information Systems can actually cut costs and bring in a profit. Bosses are too uninformed—*ignorant* is the *mot juste*—about computers and communications to make intelligent judgments. And they aren't patient enough to learn. In fact, only one CIO in thirteen actually gets to report directly to his president or chief executive officer.

But while CIOs may grumble, they are far from powerless. As the super-symbolic economy expands, business expenditures for knowledge-processing soar. Only a fraction of these are for computers and related information systems. But that fraction represents enormous amounts of money.

By 1988 sales of the world's top one hundred information technology firms, according to *Datamation* magazine, topped the $243 billion mark. A conservative projection shows this rising to $500 billion within a decade. Anyone who helps direct these purchases and allocate these funds is hardly bereft of clout. What CIOs scarcely mention, however, is that they also allocate information—the source of power for others and, not incidentally, for themselves.

As soon as a company budgets mega-dollars for information technology, struggles break out as different factions try to bite a chunk off the budget. But in addition to traditional turf and money conflicts, CIOs also find themselves smack in the middle of fights over information itself. Who gets what kinds of information? Who has access to the main data bases? Who can *add* to that data base? What assumptions are built into the accounting? Which department or division "owns" what data? And even more important, who dictates the assumptions or models built into the software? The conflicts over such questions, while seemingly technical, clearly affect the money, status, and power of individuals and businesses.

Moreover, these conflicts escalate. As the CIO and his staff redirect flows of information, they shake existing power relations. To use the expensive new computers and networks effectively, most companies are compelled to reorganize. Major restructurings are thus set in motion—and these trigger repercussive power struggles throughout the firm.

Before long, smart management, prodded by the CIO, discovers that new information technology isn't just a way to cut paperwork or speed service. It can sometimes be used strategically to capture new markets, create new products, and enter entirely new fields. We've already seen Citibank selling software to travel agents in the United States, or Seino Transport in Japan peddling software to truckers. Such forays into new businesses begin to change the shape and mission of the organization. This, however, triggers even more dangerous power struggles in the executive suite.

To complicate matters, as computers and communications fuse and networks proliferate, a new power group begins to poke its head under the managerial tent: the telecommunications managers and their staff, who often jockey with the IS people for resources and control. Should communications be subordinate to Information Systems or independent?

Chief information officers thus find themselves at the vortex of many disputes, some of which lead to, or become part of, revolutions at the highest level.

THE TWO-PARTY CAMPAIGN

This is what happened several years ago inside Merrill Lynch, the best known American securities firm and one with a staggering budget for information services.

In 1976, Merrill Lynch's total revenues, after ninety-one years of doing business, reached the magic billion-dollar mark. Ten years later, information and information technology had become so important that DuWayne Peterson, Merrill's head of Systems Operations and Telecommunications, by himself presided over an annual budget of $800 million—and that was only part of the total spent on information services and systems.

Merrill Lynch was basically divided into two parts. Its Capital Markets people created "products"—specialized funds, underwritings, stock and bond offerings—a dizzying profusion of investment vehicles. They also disbursed the capital raised by the firm. Its Retail people, by contrast—some 11,000 securities brokers in 500 branches—sold the products to investors.

These two sides of the house were almost like two different political parties or tribes. Each had its own culture, leaders, and specialized needs. Each placed different demands on Merrill's information systems.

In the words of Gerald Ely, a Merrill vice-president: "On the Capital Markets side, it's all real-time. . . . It all happens now, the profit and loss, the inventories, the prices . . . everything has to be there, real time. . . . I thought it was bad on the Retail side. When I got to the Capital Markets side I walked into a whole different world . . . different people . . . with different attitudes. The data center runs differently, obviously. The programmers and the people who manage them are different. The talents they need, the knowledge of the business, the understanding of the products, the integration of product and technology—I've never seen it quite as intense."

Not surprisingly, there was a fundamental tension between the two sides of the house, and they wanted quite different things from the huge budget for information services and technology. Capital Markets was constantly demanding instantaneous, highly analyzed and sophisticated data, while Retail needed more transactional data, but less refined and complex information.

A similar tension is found in many of the other big financial firms. Thus, those mostly concerned with assembling and providing capital—the Salomon Brothers, First Bostons, Morgan Stanleys, and Goldman, Sachses—invest more heavily in information and communications systems, as a rule, than those firms, like Merrill, Shearson, or Hutton, that are still primarily oriented toward retail securities.

At Merrill the collision between the two sides of the house ended with a political battle royal and the departure of the CEO, a man regarded as sympathetic to the Capital Markets people and their informational needs.

While the budget for information systems was not the critical factor in the Merrill case, it is likely to become more and more central to corporate politics as computers and communication begin to change strategies and missions at the very highest levels.

STRATEGIC RETREAT

An exact illustration of this was provided by Bank of America when it decided on a strategic expansion of its trust business.

In 1982, BofA had assets of $122 billion, employed 82,000 people in more than 1,200 branches and offices from Sacramento to Singapore. Its trust department alone managed $38 billion in funds for some 800 large institutional investors and pension funds. Among its trust customers were the Walt Disney Company, AT&T, Kaiser Aluminum, and other industrial heavyweights. But the bank had fallen behind technologically. At that point it decided to expand its beachhead in the trust business, in competition with Bankers Trust, State Street of Boston, and the other East Coast financial giants.

BofA's head of trust operations, Clyde R. Claus, realized he would need a state-of-the-art computer system. The old system, though recently given a botched $6 million face-lift, would be hopelessly inadequate.

The day of the proverbial "widows and orphans," who went to the bank's trust department, timidly asked the bank to invest their funds, and were satisfied with terse semiannual or annual reports— that day was long past. Trust customers now were far more sophisticated. Some had huge accounts. They wanted detailed information broken down every which way. The big ones had their own powerful computers, telecommunications nets, and sophisticated financial analysis software, and they demanded complex up-to-the-instant data.

So Claus and BofA's information systems group hired consultants and contractors to build the most advanced information system in the trust field. Some 3.5 million lines of programming code were written; and 13,000 hours of training were devoted to preparing employees to use the new information system.

Despite this crash effort, the new system lagged behind its deadlines. Endless bugs plagued the project. Worse yet, the existing system was falling further and further behind, too. Customers were muttering. The pressures rose.

In 1986 the trust department's in-house newsletter, *Turtle Talk,* received an anonymous letter warning Claus not to implement the new system. It was, the letter writer claimed, not ready. If Claus thought so, it was because someone had "pulled the wool" over his eyes.

But Claus couldn't wait. Customers were already three months behind on their statements. Things had got so bad that BofA officials were paying out huge sums to customers on the "honor" system, because they couldn't locate the records needed to verify the amounts. Crisis followed crisis. Battle followed battle. Upheavals in the bank's top management, sudden changes in policy, layoffs, staff relocations, all took a disastrous toll on the trust division. By 1988, having poured an estimated $80 million down the sump, the entire project collapsed. Bank of America backed ignominiously out of the trust business.

The rout was complete.

Heads rolled down the carpeted corridors in the months that followed. Out went Claus. Out went several senior VPs. (Out, too, went 320 of the 400 employees of the main software and system design contractor.)

Out went customers—taking with them about $4 billion worth of assets. Out went parts of the trust operation, one piece having previously been sold off to Wells Fargo, another turned over to State Street of Boston, one of the industry leaders that BofA had intended to challenge.

It was Napoleon's retreat from Moscow all over again.

Systems experts, whether called CIOs or directors of systems engineering or managers of management information systems, are point men in the info-wars, vulnerable to bullets from any direction. A brief look at their rise, fall, and resurrection provides a keen insight into how power shifts as the control of information changes hands.

THE GIANT BRAIN ERA

When computers first arrived in corporate offices about three decades ago, the press was filled with speculation about the coming of the "giant brain." This electronic mega-brain would contain all the information needed to manage a firm.

(This first-phase fantasy of a total, all-inclusive data bank and decision system led, in the Soviet Union, to an even more extended version. There, it was thought, a few giant electronic brains controlled by Gosplan, the state planning agency, would direct not a single enterprise but the entire national economy.)

Order would once and for all replace informational disorder or chaos. No more sloppiness. No more bursting file cases. No more lost memos. No more uncertainty.

Such megalomaniac fantasies vastly underestimated the increased diversity and complexity in a super-symbolic economy. They arrogantly underrated the role of chance, intuition, and creativity in business. Most important, they also assumed that the people on top of a business knew enough to specify what information was, or was not, needed by the people working below them in the hierarchy.

The title of Chief Information Officer did not yet exist in American firms, but there was a small "Data Priesthood"—the data-processing professionals. Because no one else could make the "giant brain" do anything, these few professionals essentially "owned" the firm's mainframes, and anyone who wanted information processed had to come to them. The priests enjoyed the blessings of an info-monopoly.

Then came the micros.

Desktop computers arrived with the force of a whirlwind in the late 1970s. Immediately sensing that these cheap new machines would erode their power, many data professionals threw everything they had into a campaign to keep them out of their companies. The DP priests sneered at the microcomputers' limited capacity and small size. They fought against budgeting funds for them.

But just as an entrenched monopoly, Western Union, could not keep telephones out of the hands of Americans in the 19th century, the business community's voracious hunger for information swept aside all opposition from the data professionals. Soon thousands of executives were end-running the data priests, buying their own machines and programs, beginning to network with one another.

It became clear that companies would need dispersed computer power, not just a few centrally controlled mainframes. The "giant brain" fantasy was dead, and with it the concentrated power of the DP staff. Today, in many big firms more than half of all computer processing power is outside the Information Systems department, and, as a senior manager of Deloitte & Touche puts it, the computer professionals still have "worlds more to lose."

Executives no longer came, tugging their forelocks and shuffling their feet, to beg for a few minutes of computer time. Many, no longer under the control of the DP priesthood, had their own sizable departmental budgets for computers.

The priests now faced a situation not unlike that of the medical doctors, who lost their godlike status as more and more medical knowledge seeped into the lay press and the media. Instead of dealing with computer illiterates, the DP professionals now confronted a large number of "end-users" who knew some of the basics of simple computing, read computer magazines, bought machines for their kids at home, and were no longer awestruck by anyone who rattled on about RAM and ROM.

The "micro revolution" demonopolized computer information and shifted power out of the hands of the priesthood.

The micro revolution, however, was soon followed by the connectivity revolution—and power shifted once again.

Like most revolutions, the micro revolution was a messy affair. With individuals and their departments rushing out to buy whatever kind of machines, software, and services they wanted, the result was an electronic Tower of Babel. So long as these were mainly stand-alone systems, it didn't matter much. But once it became necessary for these machines to talk to the mainframes or to one another and the outside world, the drawbacks of unrestrained liberty became starkly apparent.

Computer professionals carried a grave warning to their bosses. Computer democracy could end by shrinking the power of top management itself. How could anyone responsibly run a company when its entire computerized information system was out of control? Different machines, different programs, different data bases, everyone "doing his own thing" raised the specter of anarchy in the office. It was time to clamp down.

In every revolution there is a period of upheaval and extremism, followed by a period of consolidation. Thus the DP staff, backed by senior management, now set about institutionalizing the revolution and, in the process, recouping some of the priesthood's erstwhile influence.

To impose order on computers and communications, the new CIOs were handed far greater resources and responsibilities than ever before. They were told to integrate systems, connect them up, and formulate what might be called "rules of the electronic road." Having originally been hoarders of centralized information, and later having lost control of the system for a time, the new information systems people and the CIOs who lead them have now re-emerged as data police, enforcing new rules that, together, define the firm's information system.

These rules, which cover technical standards and types of equipment, also usually govern access to central data banks, priorities, and many other matters. Ironically, the latest surprising twist of the screw finds many CIOs singing the virtues of the very microcomputers they once despised.

The reasons are clear. Micros are no longer the 98-pound weaklings they once were. Together with minis and workstations, they are now so powerful they can actually take over many of the old functions of the mainframe. Hence, many CIOs are calling for "downsizing" and further decentralization.

"Downsizing is a phenomenal trend," reports Theodore Klein of the Boston Systems Group, Inc. "I was recently at a conference of sixty MIS directors and just about every one was doing this in some form." In the words of *CIO* magazine, the journal of the CIOs, "Downsizing puts control in the hands of business-unit managers." But that control is now firmly governed by rules set by computer professionals. Many CIOs, in fact, with support from above, are attempting to recentralize control under the flag of "network management."

Says Bill Gassman, a marketing specialist for DEC: "Network management is more than a technical issue; it's political." His view is shared by others who believe, in the words of *Datamation* magazine, that "the argument for centralized network management . . . frequently masks a desire by some within MIS organizations to regain personal operational control lost during the past few years."

In short, while info-wars rage in the corporation's external environment—pitting, as we saw, retailers versus manufacturers, or industries and even nations against one another—info-wars on a smaller scale are raging internally as well.

CIOs and their staffs become, whether they mean to or not, info-warriors. For though they may not conceive of their function in these terms, their largely unrecognized task is to redistribute power (while trying, not surprisingly, to expand their own).

Functioning as both highway engineers and state troopers on our fast-growing electronic highways—they build as well as attempt to manage the systems—they are put in the distasteful position of being, in a sense, the corporation's "executive thought police."

THE ETHICS OF INFORMATION

As such, they earn their paychecks. Their jobs are filled with stress and difficulty. Indeed, it is hard to exaggerate the staggering complexity of the rules needed in engineering and integrating a large-scale corporate information system that delivers information to those who need it . . . that prevents fraud, sabotage, or invasion of personal privacy . . . that regulates access to various networks and data banks by employees, customers, and suppliers . . . that sets priorities among them . . . that produces numberless special-ized reports . . . that allows users to customize their software . . . that meets dozens of other requirements, does it all within budget-ary constraints—and then does it over and again as new technolo-gies, competitors, and products appear.

Devising rules to guide such a system requires such high-level technical expertise that CIOs and their staffs often lose sight of the human implications of their decisions. Who gets access is, in fact, a political issue. Privacy is a political issue. Designing a system so that it serves one department better than another is a political act. Even timing is political, if one unit gets a lower communications priority than another, so that it must wait for service. The allocation of cost is always a power issue.

Thus, as soon as we begin to speak of policing information, all sorts of disquieting "para-political" questions pop up.

Two employees are caught up in a bitter personal feud. One of them learns the appropriate computer passwords, enters the personnel files, and puts damaging material into an adversary's records. None of this comes to light until the victim has already left and gone to work for another firm, where discovery of the damaging information leads to dismissal. What happens? Who is responsible? The first company?

Are a worker's chances for promotion unfairly reduced if he or she lacks or loses access to an important data base?

With only a trace of imagination, it is possible to multiply scores of such questions. In the absence of comprehensive public policies, it is left to private firms to think through the personal and political implications of all the rules governing their information systems. But should such questions, with their human rights implications, be left entirely to private companies? And if so, who in any particular firm should write the rules? The chief information officer?

We are, here, on thin and alien ice. Few have much experience with the ethical, legal, and ultimately political questions arising from the need to impose constraints on the flow of business information. Top management, as a rule, delegates the task. But to whom?

Should the rule-writing power be shared? And with whom? Should companies establish internal "information councils" or even "legislatures," to write the laws governing information rights, responsibilities, and access? Should unions share in this decision-making? Do we need "corporate courts" to settle disputes over security and access? Do we need "information ethicists" to define a new informational morality?

Will the rules regulating information in industry condition public attitudes toward freedom of information in the larger society? Might they accustom us to censorship and secrecy? Will we eventually need an explicit Bill of Electronic Information Rights?

Every one of these is a power issue, and the decisions about them will shift power within the firm and, ultimately, in society at large.

THE PARADOX BOMB

The more turbulent, unstable, and non-equilibrial tomorrow's business environment becomes, the more unpredictable the needs of users.

Rapid change means chance. It means uncertainty. It means competition from the least-expected quarter. It means big projects that collapse and small ones that stun one with their success. It means new technologies, new kinds of skills and workers, and wholly unprecedented economic conditions.

All this is amplified when the competition is blistering hot and comes, very often, from countries or cultures that are drastically different from the one the business was designed to serve.

How, in this kind of world, can even the cleverest CIO accurately pre-specify what information will be needed by whom? Or for how long?

In today's high-turbulence environment, business survival requires a stream of innovative products or services. Creativity requires a kind of corporate glasnost—an openness to imagination, a tolerance for deviance, for individuality, and the serendipity that has historically accounted for many creative discoveries, from nylon and latex paint to products like the NutraSweet fat substitute.

There is, therefore, a profound contradiction between the need for careful channeling and close control of information, on the one hand, and the need for innovation on the other.

The safer and surer a business information system, and the better it is protected, pre-defined, pre-structured, and policed, the more it will constrain creativity and constipate the organization.

What we learn, therefore, is that the information wars now raging in the outside world—over everything from supermarket scanners and standards to television sets and technonationalism—are mirrored inside the corporation as well.

Power, in the business of tomorrow, will flow to those who have the best information about the limits of information. But before it does, the info-wars now intensifying will alter the very shape of business. To know how, we need to take a closer look at this crucial resource—knowledge—whose pursuit will shake the powers-that-be from New York to Tokyo, from Moscow to Montevideo.

14

TOTAL INFORMATION WAR

A new concept of business is taking shape in response to the info-wars now raging across the world economy. As knowledge becomes more central to the creation of wealth, we begin to think of the corporation as an enhancer of knowledge.

We speak of adding value by upgrading information. We talk about improving the firm's human resources. And we begin poking our noses into information that doesn't belong to us. All, it would seem, is fair in love and info-war.

On April 25, 1985, the telephone rang at the offices of Texas Instruments in Dallas, Texas. A voice with a foreign accent asked for a meeting with a company security executive. A Syrian electrical engineer who sought political asylum in the United States, Sam Kuzbary had once worked at TI before being fired as a security risk. Rumor had it that the CIA had helped him get out of Syria, where he had once worked for the Syrian military. Kuzbary carried a gun in his car. Now, he said, he wanted to ingratiate himself with TI and get his job back. He had information, he said, about important secrets that had been stolen from TI.

That call led to an early morning raid by Dallas police on the offices of a small high-tech firm called Voice Control Systems, Inc., founded originally by a real estate developer who wound up in jail for drug smuggling. Now owned by a different investment group and headed by a former president of U.S. Telephone, VCS, it turned out, employed numerous former TI researchers, including Kuzbary.

What the police found were 7,985 files copied from the computers at TI's advanced research project on speech recognition. A scorching race was (and still is) under way among major computer firms, including IBM and Texas Instruments, to find a way for computers to understand human speech. (They can already, but

153

only in limited and costly ways.) Everyone knows that whoever wins this race will have the potential for fabulous profits. In fact, at the time, Michael Dertouzos, head of computer science at the Massachussetts Institute of Technology, considered that "whoever breaks the logjam to make machines understand spoken words will gain control over the information revolution."

Were the engineers who jumped ship at TI and joined VCS really guilty of stealing research worth $20 million, as TI charged?

In the trial that followed, Dallas prosecutors Ted Steinke and Jane Jackson insisted a crime had been committed. Lawyers for defendants Tom Schalk and Gary Leonard, however, pointed out that none of the material taken was marked with the words TI— STRICTLY PRIVATE which were supposed to be on all secret material. What's more, the lab in which the work was done was headed by Dr. George Doddington, a brilliant maverick who often described his lab as "free and open" and argued that major breakthroughs would come only if researchers from different companies and universities shared their knowledge. Even more to the point, VCS didn't seem to be using any of the TI material.

Schalk insisted to the jury that at no time during his work at TI had he regarded any of this material as secret. Leonard said he merely wanted to keep a historical record of research he had done, and that he had copied a TI computer directory because it contained a list of the people in his Sunday-school class.

To all of which Steinke, the prosecutor, replied: "One thing they can't change. They snuck these programs out without telling anyone."

The Dallas jury, some of its members crying as the verdict was read, found the men guilty. They were sentenced and fined, then placed on probation. Both appealed the ruling and immediately went back to work, trying to make computers understand speech.

RUSTY TRACKS AND HOTEL LOVE-SOUNDS

It is hard to know if industrial espionage is actually on the rise, because, in the words of Brian Hollstein of the American Society for Industrial Security's committee on the protection of information, "Being a victim of industrial espionage is a lot like getting venereal disease. Many may have it, but nobody wants to talk about it." On the other hand, more lawsuits are being filed against information thieves and pirates.

Hollstein has thought about the value of information more than most. "Many corporations," he said a few years ago, "really don't understand. . . . They still think in terms mainly of moving around men and materials," as though still locked into the smokestack economy. "What it amounts to," he has said, "is a failure to recognize that information has value."

That attitude is changing swiftly. As wars for the control of information heat up, many companies have decided they need more information about the plans, products, and profits of their adversaries. Thus the dramatic rise of what is known as "competitive intelligence."

Smart companies, of course, have always kept an eye cocked at their competitors, but today adversarial knowledge is prime ammunition in the info-wars.

Several factors account for the changed attitude. The speed with which any market can now be invaded from outside, the long lead times needed for research (in contrast with shorter product life-cycles), and stiffer competition all have contributed to the much-publicized systematization and professionalization of business spying.

The pressure for continual innovation means more resources are flowing into new products, some requiring extremely heavy research expense. "Designing a chip can take hundreds of labor-years and millions of dollars. Simply copying the competition is both faster and cheaper," writes John D. Halamka in *Espionage in Silicon Valley*, explaining why companies now engage in reverse engineering—taking apart a rival product to learn its secrets. Xerox reverse-engineers competitive copiers. Companies reverse-engineer services to find out what makes them profitable.

Yet another factor promoting the rise of competitive intelligence has been the widespread reorganization of strategic planning. Once a highly centralized activity carried out by staff personnel reporting to top management, planning has been pushed down into the operating units, where it is often carried out by practical line managers geared to rough-and-tumble competition. Knowing what competitors are up to has immediate tactical advantage as well as possible strategic use.

All this helps explain why 80 percent of the thousand largest

U.S. firms now have their own full-time sleuths and why the Society of Competitor Intelligence Professionals alone claims members from at least three hundred companies in six nations. Their companies keep them busy.

Before the Marriott Corporation committed itself to launching the Fairfield Inn chain of low-cost hotels, reports *Fortune*, it sent a team of snoops into nearly four hundred rival hotels to check on what soaps and towels they supplied, how good the front desk was in dealing with special problems, and whether the sounds of lovemaking could be heard in adjoining rooms. (The sounds were simulated by one of Marriott's CI agents while another in the next room listened for them.)

Marriott also hired executive headhunters to interview (and pump) the regional managers of rival chains, to find out how much its competitors were paying, what training they offered, and whether their managers were happy.

When the Sheller-Globe Corporation, maker of heavy truck cabs, wanted to design a new cab, it systematically called on potential customers, asking them to rank the opposition on seven scales covering gasoline mileage, comfort, windshield visibility, ease of steering, seating, accessibility of controls, and durability. The information set targets for the Sheller-Globe design team to beat.

Like real spies, business intelligence agents begin their hunt with a careful scan of "open" sources. They pore over trade journals, newsletters, and the general press for clues to a competing firm's plans. They read speeches, study recruiting ads, attend meetings and seminars. They interview former employees, many of whom are eager to talk about their old companies.

But CI snoops—among them, paid outside consultants—have also been known to fly a helicopter over a plant for clues to a competitor's capacity, to scour trash baskets for discarded memos, and to employ more aggressive measures as well. A look at a rival's internal phone directory can help one construct a detailed map of its organization, from which it is possible to estimate its budget. One Japanese company sent experts to look at the rail tracks leaving the plant of an American competitor. The thickness of the rust layer—presumably indicating how often or how recently the tracks were used—was a clue to the factory's production.

On occasion, zealous practitioners bug hotel rooms or offices where rivals are negotiating a deal. Even less savory are the U.S. defense contractors who paid "consultants" to learn in advance how much their competitors were bidding on a Pentagon project, thus permitting them to underbid. In turn, some of the consultants reportedly bribed military personnel to get the facts.

Of course, competitive intelligence professionals define CI as the *legal* pursuit of information. But a recent Conference Board survey of senior managers suggests that 60 percent of them think anything goes when it comes to corporate spying.

The hotting-up of today's info-wars is part of a growing recognition that knowledge, while central to the new economy, violates all the rules that apply to other resources. It is, for example, inexhaustible. We know how to add value to ingots of steel or bolts of cloth. But how to add value to a good idea is much more problematic. We lack the new accounting and management theories needed to grapple with super-symbolic realities.

We do not yet know how to manage a resource that is salable, but much of which is supplied (often at no charge) by customers themselves. Or, for that matter, either willingly or unwittingly, by competitors. Nor have we yet come to understand how the corporation as a whole engages in knowledge enhancement.

INS AND OUTS

The info-wars cast the corporation—and the work that goes on in it—into a new light.

Forget, for a moment, all conventional job descriptions; forget ranks; forget departmental functions. Think of the firm, instead, as a beehive of knowledge processing.

In the day of the smokestack it was assumed that workers knew little of importance and that relevant information or intelligence could be gathered by top management or a tiny staff. The proportion of the work force engaged in knowledge processing was tiny.

Today, by contrast, we are finding that much of what happens inside a firm is aimed at replenishing its continually decaying knowledge inventory, generating new knowledge to add to it, and upgrading simple data into information and knowledge. To accomplish this, employees constantly "import," "export," and "transfer" data and information.

Some employees are essentially importers. These "OUT-IN" people gather information from outside the company and deliver it to their co-workers inside. Market researchers, for example, are OUT-INers. Studying consumer preferences in the external world, they add value by interpreting what they learn, and then deliver new, higher-order information to the firm.

Public relations people do the reverse. They market the firm to the world by collecting information internally and disseminating or exporting it to the outside world. They are IN-OUTers.

House accountants are basically IN-IN people, gathering most of their information from inside the firm and transferring it internally as well.

Good salespeople are two-way RELAYS. They disseminate information, but also collect it from outside and then report it back to the firm.

These functions relate to *flows* of data, information, or knowledge. Cutting across them is a set of functions that have to do with upgrading the *stock* of data, information, and knowledge that the firm and its people already possess.

Some mind-workers are creators, capable of finding new, surprising juxtapositions of ideas, or putting a fresh spin on an old idea; others "edit" new ideas by matching them against strategic requirements and practical considerations, then deleting those that are irrelevant.

In reality, we all do all these things at various times. But while different functions emphasize one or another, no conventional job descriptions or management texts deal with such distinctions—or their implications for power.

At almost every step in this knowledge processing, some people or organizations gain, and others lose, an edge. Thus, conflicts—tiny, sometimes highly personal info-wars—are fought over things like who will or will not be invited to a meeting, whose names appear on the routing slip, who reports information to a superior directly and who, by contrast, is asked to leave it with a secretary, and so forth. These organizational battles—"micro info-wars," so to speak—are hardly novel. They are a feature of all organizational life. They take on new significance, however, as the super-symbolic economy spreads.

Since the value added through smart knowledge-processing is critical in the new system of wealth creation, 21st-century accountants will find ways to assess the net economic value added by various informational activities. The performance ratings of individuals and units may well take into account their contribution to knowledge enhancement.

Today, a geologist who finds a huge oil strike is likely to be well rewarded by the company for adding to its reserves. Tomorrow, when knowledge resources are recognized as the most important of all, employee remuneration may well come to hinge, at least in part, on the success of each individual in adding value to the corporate knowledge reserve. In turn, we can expect even more sophisticated power struggles for the control of knowledge assets and the processes that generate them.

WHOLISTIC ESPIONAGE

We are already witnessing the beginnings of a change in management assumptions about the functions of the work force. Thus, all employees are increasingly expected to add not merely to the firm's knowledge assets in general, but to its competitive intelligence arsenal as well.

According to Mindy Kotler, president of Search Associates, a company that does CI work for both U.S. and Japanese firms, the Japanese take a far more wholistic view of intelligence than do the Americans. While Japanese executives regard information collection as a routine part of their job, she says, "If you ask a typical Harvard M.B.A., he says it's the company librarian's job."

That narrow assumption, however, is fading. At General Mills every employee is expected to engage in competitive intelligence gathering. Even janitors when buying supplies are supposed to ask vendors what competing firms are buying and what they are doing.

Telephone companies in the United States run seminars and distribute literature explaining the methods and benefits of CI to their executives. Bayer even rotates executives through its CI staff to teach them the importance of this kind of information collection. GE links CI directly into its strategic planning.

Pushed to extremes, such measures inch us toward the notion of the corporation as a total info-war fighting machine.

A 75-CENT ERROR

While the business press has paid superficial attention to the rise of business spying, little has been said about the relationship of CI to the spread of information systems and the rise of the chief information officer.

Yet the connection is not hard to find.

It is easy enough to picture the espionage branch of a business requesting cooperation from the chief information officer in gathering information about a competitor. The CIO is increasingly responsible not merely for information systems inside the firm, but for electronic links into the data bases of other companies. This means he controls systems that penetrate, at least to some limited degree, the electronic perimeter of suppliers, customers, or others, and information from or about a competitor may be no more than one electronic synapse away.

For more than a year three West German computer spies were able to access data relating to nuclear weapons and the strategic defense initiative (SDI) by breaking into 430 computers. They rifled at will through more than 30 of them linked in a network set up by the Pentagon's Defense Advanced Research Projects Agency. They were spotted only after Clifford Stoll, an ex-hippie computer system manager at the Lawrence Berkeley Laboratory, noticed a 75-cent discrepancy between two files.

Many business networks are still highly vulnerable to penetration by determined thieves or spies, including disgruntled current or former employees suborned by a competing firm. According to *Spectrum,* the journal of the Institute of Electrical and Electronics Engineers, "Members of most [local area networks] can add modems to their personal computers, creating new passageways in the system unbeknownst to system administrators."

With customers able to access a manufacturer's inventory records electronically, with suppliers made privy to their customers' design secrets, the possibilities for the diversion of information to a competitor are real, despite access limits and passwords.

This access, moreover, can be direct or through intermediaries—including intermediaries who are unaware of what they are doing. In CIA jargon, some informants are "witting" and others not. Business spies, too, can make use of third parties to gain access to information useful as ammunition in the info-wars.

If, say, two retailers like Wal-Mart and K Mart are both electronically plugged into the computers of the same supplier, how long will it be before an overzealous CI unit, or one of a growing horde of CI consultants, proposes breaking through the ID numbers and passwords on the manufacturer's mainframe, or tapping into the telecommunications lines and foraging through its data banks? If a U.S. government's defense research network could be compromised by Soviet intelligence, relying on a few spies armed with personal computers and working from their homes in West Germany, how secure are the commercial networks and corporate data bases on which our economy now depends?

The example is purely hypothetical, with no implication that either Wal-Mart or K Mart has actually done this or would even consider it. But there are now thousands of electronic data interchange systems, and new technologies open stunning opportunities for both licit and illicit data collection.

With only a little imagination, one can picture a competitive intelligence firm planting equipment across the street from a major store and tapping into the signals sent by optical scanners to its cash registers, thus supplying rich, real-time data to a competitor or manufacturer. As discoveries in the U.S. Embassy in Moscow have shown, it is already technologically possible for one firm to rig devices that will literally print out a duplicate of every letter typed by the CEO's secretary in a rival firm.

But total information war might not end with passive information collection. The temptation to engage in "commercial covert action" is growing. Consultant Joseph Coates of J. F. Coates, Inc., has suggested the day may come when a hard-pressed competitor feeds false orders into a rival firm's computers, causing it to overproduce the wrong models and undersupply those that are directly competitive.

Revolutions in video, optics, and acoustics open the way to spy on or interfere with human-to-human communication as well. Speech synthesis may make it possible to fake the voice of a manager and use it to give misleading telephone instructions to a subordinate. The imaginative possibilities are endless.

All this, of course, has led to a race to develop counterintelligence technologies. Some networks now require users to have a card that generates passwords in synchronization with those demanded by a host computer. Other systems rely on fingerprints or other physical and behavioral traits to confirm the identity of a user before allowing access. One system shoots a beam of low-intensity infrared light into a person's eye and scans the unique blood vessel patterns in the back of the retina to confirm identity. Another identifies a user by the rhythm of his or her key-strokes.

Because of its cost, sophisticated encryption or coding is largely limited today to the defense industries and financial institutions—banks, for example, making electronic funds–transfers. But GM already codes information moving on its electronic interchange links, and the toy-maker Mattel encodes certain data when they are down-loaded to a customer's computers or when they are physically transported from place to place.

Seesaw battles between offense and defense are a reflection of the info-war.

At every level of business, therefore—at the level of global standards for television and telecommunications . . . at the level of the retailer's checkout counter . . . at the level of the automatic teller machine and the credit card . . . at the level of extra-intelligent electronic networks . . . at the level of competitive intelligence and counterintelligence—we are surrounded by info-war and info-warriors fighting to control the most crucial resource of the Powershift Era.

PART FOUR

POWER IN THE FLEX-FIRM

15

THE CUBBYHOLE CRASH

The war for economic supremacy in the 21st century has already begun. The main tactical weapons in this global power struggle are traditional. We read about them in the daily headlines—currency manipulation, protectionist trade policies, financial regulations, and the like. But, as in the case of military competition, the truly strategic weapons today are knowledge-based.

What counts for each nation in the long run are products of mind-work: scientific and technological research . . . the education of the work force . . . sophisticated software . . . smarter management . . . advanced communications . . . electronic finance. These are key sources of tomorrow's power, and among these strategic weapons none is more important than superior organization—especially the organization of knowledge itself.

This, as we shall see next, is what today's attack on bureaucracy is mainly about.

THE BUREAUCRACY-BUSTERS

Everyone hates a bureaucrat.

For a long time businessmen maintained the myth that bureaucracy was a disease of government. Civil servants were called lazy, parasitic, and surly, while business executives were pictured as dynamic, productive, and eager to please the customer. Yet bureaucracy is just as rampant in business as in the public sector. Indeed, many of the world's largest corporations are as arthritic and arrogant as any Soviet ministry.

Today a search is on for new ways to organize. In the Soviet

Union and Eastern Europe the political leadership is at war with elements of its own bureaucracy. Other governments are selling off public enterprises, experimenting with things like merit pay and other innovations in the civil service.

But it is in business that the drive for new organizational formats is most advanced. Hardly a day passes without some new article, book, or speech decrying the old top-down forms of pyramidal power.

Management gurus publish case histories of companies experimenting with new organizational approaches, from "underground research" at Toshiba to the antihierarchical structure of Tandem Computers. Managers are advised to take advantage of "chaos," and a thousand formulas and fads are tried and discarded as fast as new buzz-phrases can be coined.

Of course, no one expects bureaucratic organization to disappear. It remains appropriate for some purposes. But it is now accepted that companies will wither under competitive fire if they cling to the old centralized bureaucratic structures that flourished during the smokestack age.

In smokestack societies, even when ultimate power is in the hands of charismatic and even antibureaucratic leaders, it is typically exercised on their behalf by bureaucrats. The police, the army, the corporation, the hospital, the schools, all are organized into bureaucracies, irrespective of the personality or style of their top officers.

The revolt against bureaucracy is, in fact, an attack on the dominant form of smokestack power. It coincides with the transition to the super-symbolic economy of the 21st century, and it explains why those who create "post-bureaucratic" organizations are truly revolutionary, whether they are in business, government, or the civil society.

AN INFINITY OF CUBBYHOLES

Any bureaucracy has two key features, which can be called "cubbyholes" and "channels." Because of this, everyday power—routine control—is in the hands of two types of executive: specialists and managers.

Specialized executives gain their power from control of information in the cubbyholes. Managers gain theirs through their control of information flowing through the channels. It is this power system, the backbone of bureaucracy, which is now coming under fire in large companies everywhere.

We think of bureaucracy as a way of grouping people. But it is also a way of grouping "facts." A firm neatly cut into departments according to function, market, region, or product is after all a collection of cubbyholes in which specialized information and personal experience are stored. Engineering data go to the engineers; sales data to the sales department.

Until the arrival of computers, this "cubbyholism" was the main way in which knowledge was organized for wealth production. And the wondrous beauty of the system was that, at first, it appeared to be endlessly expandable. In theory, one could have an infinity of cubbyholes.

In practice, however, companies and governments are now discovering that there are strict limits to this kind of specialization. The limits first became apparent in the public sector as government agencies grew to monstrous proportions, reaching a point of no return. Listen, for example, to the lament of John F. Lehman, Jr., a recent U.S. Navy Secretary.

In the Pentagon, Lehman confessed to his colleagues, so many specialized cubbyhole-units had sprung up that it is "impossible for me or anyone at this table to accurately describe ... the system with which, and within which, we must operate."

As private companies grew to gargantuan size they, too, began to smack up against the limits of organizational specialization. Today, in company after company, the cubbyhole system is crashing under its own weight. Nor is it just bigness that makes it unworkable.

POWER VERSUS REASON

As we leave the industrial era behind, we are becoming a more diverse society. The old smokestack economy serviced a mass society. The super-symbolic economy services a de-massified society. Everything from life styles and products to technologies and the media is growing more heterogeneous.

This new diversity brings with it more complexity, which, in turn, means that businesses need more and more data, information, and know-how to function. Thus, huge volumes of the stuff are being crammed into more and more cubbyholes—multiplying them beyond comprehension and stretching them to the bursting point.

Today's changes also come at a faster pace than bureaucracies can handle. An uptick of the yen in Tokyo causes instantaneous purchases and sales in Zurich or London. A televised press conference in Tehran triggers an immediate reply in Washington. A politician's off-the-cuff remark about taxes sends investors and accountants instantly scurrying to reevaluate a takeover deal.

This speedup of change makes our knowledge—about technology, markets, suppliers, distributors, currencies, interest rates, consumer preferences, and all the other business variables—perishable.

A firm's entire inventory of data, skills, and knowledge is thus in a constant state of decay and regeneration, turning over faster and faster. In turn, this means that some of the old bins or cubbyholes into which knowledge has been stuffed begin to break into parts. Others are crammed to overload. Still others become useless as the information in them becomes obsolete or irrelevant. The relationships of all these departments, branches, or units to one another constantly change too.

In short, the cubbyhole scheme designed for Year One becomes inappropriate for Year Two. It is easy to reclassify or sort information stored in a computer. Just copy a file into a new directory. But try to change organizational cubbyholes! Since people and budgets reflect the scheme, any attempt to redesign the structure triggers explosive power struggles. The faster things change in the outside world, therefore, the greater the stress placed on bureaucracy's underlying framework and the more friction and infighting.

The real trouble starts, however, when turbulence in the marketplace, the economy, or society stirs up completely new kinds of problems or opportunities for the firm. Suddenly decision-makers confront situations for which no cubbyholed information exists. The more accelerated the rate of change in business—and it is speeding up daily—the more such one-of-a-kind situations crop up.

On December 3, 1984, the executives of Union Carbide awoke

to discover that their pesticide plant in Bhopal, India, had released a toxic cloud and caused the single worst accident in industrial history. The disaster killed more than 3,000 and injured another 200,000. Decisions had to be made instantly, rather than through the usual tortuous processes.

Equally unique, though far less disastrous, events are hitting business executives like hailstones. In Japan, the managers at Morinaga Chocolate learn that a mysterious killer is poisoning their product . . . Guinness in Britain is struck by a stock manipulation scandal . . . Pennzoil and Texaco are flung into a titanic legal struggle . . . the Manville Corporation is forced to bankrupt itself in dealing with lawsuits arising from having exposed its workers to asbestos . . . CBS has to fend off a blitzkrieg raid by Ted Turner . . . United Airlines faces an unprecedented buy-out bid from its own pilots, which then falls apart and triggers a crash on Wall Street. Such events—and many that are smaller and less publicized—hurl managers into situations for which nothing has adequately prepared them, or their bureaucracies.

When situations arise that can't easily be assigned to pre-designated informational cubbyholes, bureaucrats get nasty. They begin to fight over turf, money, people—and the control of information. This unleashes tremendous amounts of energy and raw emotion. Instead of solving problems, however, all this human output is burned up in the *Sturm und Drang*. What's still worse, these fratricidal battles make the firm behave irrationally. The vaunted "rationality" of bureaucracy goes out the window. Power, always a factor, now replaces reason as the basis for decision.

"CAMELEPHANTS" AND HOT POTATOES

When a real fluke arises—something that doesn't fit naturally into anyone's informational bailiwick—the company's first instinct is to ignore it. This ostrich response is what happened the first time foreign cars began appearing in the United States. The earliest little Opels and Citroën Deux Chevaux that turned up on American streets in the late 1950s drew a shrug from Detroit's bureaucrats. Even when floods of Volkswagens began to arrive, the giant bureaucratic auto makers preferred not to think about the unthinkable. There were no units inside their companies whose task was to fight foreign competition, no cubbyholes loaded with the necessary information.

When bureaucracies are forced to deal with a problem that fits into no one's existing cubbyhole, they behave in certain stereotyped ways. After some initial fencing, someone inevitably suggests setting up a new unit (with himself or herself at its head). This is instantly recognized for what it could easily become: a budget-eating rival of the older units. Nobody wants that, so a compromise is arrived at. This compromise is that familiar bureaucratic "camelephant," the interdepartmental committee or task force. Washington is filled with them. So are big companies.

Combining the slow, lumbering gait of the elephant with the IQ of the camel, this new unit is, in effect, yet another cubbyhole, only this one is typically staffed by junior people, sent by their permanent departments not so much to solve the problem as to make sure that the new unit doesn't chip away at existing jurisdictions or budget allocations.

Sometimes the new problem is such a hot potato that nobody wants to deal with it. It is either dumped on someone young, inexperienced, and luckless, or it becomes an orphan: another problem on its way to becoming a crisis.

Faced by all this infighting, an exasperated CEO decides to "cut through the red tape." He does this by appointing a "czar," who theoretically will get the cooperation of all the relevant agencies, branches, and departments. But, lacking the information needed to cope with the problem, the czar, too, winds up depending on the pre-existing cubbyhole system.

Next the CEO decides frontal assault on the bureaucrats below will do no good. So he or she tries another standard ploy, quietly assigning the problem to a "troubleshooter" on his or her personal staff, rather than waiting for the slow, resistant bureaucratic machine to act. This attempt to end-run the existing departments only further outrages them, at which point the offended units begin working diligently to assure staff failure.

Something like this happened when Ronald Reagan assigned staff from his National Security Council, not traditionally an operational unit, to take on functions more normally carried out by the Defense, State, or CIA bureaucracies. The resulting attempt to deal with "moderates" in Iran, in the hope that they would help release American hostages, blew up in the President's face. (Afterward, the Tower Commission, investigating the Irangate fiasco, solemnly concluded that the scandal could have been avoided if the White House had "used the system"—meaning relied on the line bureaucracies rather than the White House staff. It left unsaid whether the bureaucracies, which had previously failed either to negotiate the hostage release or to rescue them with military force, would have succeeded where the staff failed.)

Similar power games are played *within* each department, as its subunits also jockey for control of money, people, and knowledge. One might think that infighting stops at moments of dire crisis. Instead, the reverse happens when executive heads are on the block. In politics and even the military, crisis frequently brings out the worst, rather than the best, in organizations.

One has only to read the history of military interservice rivalry in the heat of battle, or the life-and-death struggles between rival British intelligence and covert action agencies during World War II, to glimpse the fanaticism that purely bureaucratic struggles can generate—especially during crisis. Businesses are not exempt from this destructive game-playing and fanaticism. For the image of the "rational" bureaucracy is false. It is power, not reason, that drives the classical pyramids that still litter the business landscape.

Any hope of replacing bureaucracy, therefore, involves more than shifting people around, laying off "fat," clustering units under "group vice-presidents," or even breaking the firm into multiple "profit centers." Any serious restructure of business or government must directly attack the organization of knowledge—and the entire system of power based on it. For the cubbyhole system is in crisis.

CHOKED CHANNELS

As change speeds up, this "cubbyhole crisis" is deepened by a parallel breakdown in the "channels" of communication.

Smart business people have always known that a company succeeds only when its parts work together. If the sales force is terrific but manufacturing can't deliver on time . . . or if the ads are wonderful but not tied to the right price policy . . . if engineers have no sense of what the marketers can sell . . . if all the accountants do is count beans and the lawyers just look at the law, without asking business questions . . . the firm cannot succeed.

But smart managers also know that people in one department or unit seldom speak to their counterparts in another. In fact, this lack of cross-communication is precisely what gives mid-rank managers their power. Once more it is the control of information that counts.

Middle managers coordinate the work of several subordinate units, collecting reports from the executive-specialists who run them. Sometimes the manager receives information from one subordinate and passes it back down to another, thus serving as a formal link between cubbyholes. At other times he or she may pass information laterally to the manager heading another group of units. But a middle manager's main task is to collect the disparate information that the specialists have cut into fragments and synthesize it before passing it through channels to the next higher level in the power pyramid.

Put differently, in every bureaucracy, knowledge is broken apart horizontally and put back together vertically.

The power structure based on control of information was clear, therefore: While specialists controlled the cubbyholes, managers controlled the channels.

This system worked marvelously when business moved slowly. Today, change is so accelerated and the information needed is so complex that the channels, too, exactly like the cubbyholes, are overwhelmed, clogged with messages (many of them misrouted).

Because of this, more executives than ever are stepping outside channels to circumvent the system, withholding information from their bosses and peers, passing it sideways unofficially, communicating through "back channels," operating on "dual tracks" (one formal, the other not), adding fire and confusion to the internecine wars now tearing up even the best-managed bureaucracies.

One overlooked reason why Japanese corporations have been better so far in managing the breakdown of bureaucracy is the existence in them of a backup system lacking in American and European firms.

While Western firms are dependent on cubbyholes and channels, Japanese firms also have, overlaid on these, what is known as the *dokikai* system. The *dokikai* system is a deviation from formal bureaucracy—but one which makes it far more effective.

In a large Japanese firm all recruits hired at the same time—what might be called an "entering class" or a "cohort"—maintain contact with one another throughout their employment by the firm, rising up the ranks as they grow more senior. After a time the members of the *dokikai* are scattered through the various functions, regions, and sections of the firm. Some have risen up the grades faster than others.

But this fraternity, as it has been called, hangs out together, socializing in the evenings, swilling much beer and sake, and—most important—exchanging information from many different cubbyholes outside the formal hierarchical channels.

It is through the *dokikai* that the "real" facts or "true" facts of a situation are communicated, as distinct from the official party line. It is in the *dokikai* that men, lubricated with alcohol, speak to one another with *honto*—expressing their true feelings—rather than with *tatemae*—saying what is expected.

It is a mistake to take at face value the picture of the Japanese corporation as smoothly run, efficient, consensual, and conflict-free. Nothing is further from the truth. But the information matrix—the *dokikai* laid on top of the bureaucracy—allows know-how and know-who to flow through the company even when the formal channels and cubbyholes are overloaded. It gives the Japanese corporation an information edge.

Yet this is no longer sufficient for organizational survival, and even this system is breaking down. Thus, companies race to build electronic alternatives to the old bureaucratic communication systems, and with these come fundamental reorganization as well, not only in Japan, but in the United States, Europe, and all the advanced economies.

What we see, then, is a burgeoning crisis at the very heart of bureaucracy. High-speed change not only overwhelms its cubbyhole-and-channel structure, it attacks the very deepest assumption on which the system was based. This is the notion that it is possible to pre-specify who in the company needs to know what. It is an assumption based on the idea that organizations are essentially machines and that they operate in an orderly environment.

Today we are learning that organizations are not machinelike but human, and that in a turbulent environment filled with revolutionary reversals, surprises, and competitive upsets, it is no longer possible to specify in advance what everyone needs to know.

FREE-FLOW KNOWLEDGE

We saw in Chapter 13 how companies attempt to impose order on information by designing computerized management information systems (MIS). Some of these, it turns out, are intended to buttress the old system by employing computer and communication links merely to expand the cubbyholes and the capacity of the communication channels. Others are truly revolutionary in intent. They seek to crush the cubbyhole-and-channels system and replace it with free-flow information.

To appreciate the full significance of this development, and the power shift it implies, it helps to note the quite remarkable (though largely unremarked) parallels between bureaucracies and our early computers.

The first big mainframes ministered to by the data priests supported the existing bureaucracies in business and government. This accounts for the initial fear and loathing they aroused in the public. Ordinary people sensed that these monster machines were yet another tool of power that might be used against them. The very data bases they held resembled the bureaucracies they served.

Early business computers were used chiefly for routine purposes like keeping thousands of payroll records. John Doe's record was made up of what the computer experts called "fields." Thus his name might be the first field, his address the second, his job title the third, his base salary the fourth, and so on.

Everyone's address went into his or her second "field." Everyone's base salary figure went into his or her fourth field.

In this way, all information entered into the payroll files went to pre-specified locations in the data base—just as information in a bureaucracy was addressed to pre-specified departments or cubbyholes.

Moreover, the first computerized data systems were largely hierarchical, again like the bureaucracies they were designed for. Information was stored hierarchically in memory, and the actual hardware itself concentrated computer power at the top of the company pyramid. Brains resided in the mainframe, while at the bottom the machines were unintelligent. The jargon referred to them appropriately as "dumb terminals."

The microcomputer revolutionized all this. For the first time, it placed intelligence on thousands of desk tops, distributing data bases and processing power. But while it shook things up, it did not seriously threaten bureaucratic organization.

The reason for this was that even though there were now many computerized data banks instead of one giant central bank, the knowledge stored in them was still crammed into rigid pre-designated cubbyholes.

Today, however, we are at the edge of a further revolution in how information is organized in computerized data bases.

So-called "relational" data bases now permit users to add and subtract fields and to interrelate them in new ways. Says Martin Templeman, senior vice-president of SPC Software Services, whose products are designed for financial firms: "Taking all . . . dimensions of change into account, we realized upfront that . . . hierarchical . . . relationships between the data would be a disaster." The new data bases "had to allow new relationships to emerge."

But such systems today are still so cumbersome they cannot be easily run on microcomputers.

The next step has come with the introduction recently of "hyper-media" data bases capable of storing not merely text but also graphics, music, speech, and other sounds. More important, hyper-media combine data bases and programs to give the user far greater flexibility than earlier data base systems.

Even in the relational systems, data could be combined in only a few pre-specified ways. Hyper-media vastly multiplies the ways in which information from different fields and records can be combined, recombined, and manipulated. Information in the original data bases was structured like a tree, meaning that to go from a leaf on one branch to a leaf on another, you had to go back to the trunk. "Hyper" systems are like a web, making it possible to move easily from one piece of information to another contextually.

The ultimate goal of the hyper-media pioneers—admittedly still a distant grail—is systems in which information can be assembled, configured, and presented in an almost infinite number of ways. The goal is "free-form" and "free-flow" information.

A striking example of the genre (called "HyperCard" and popularized by Apple) was first demonstrated at a Boston computer show by its author, Bill Atkinson. What he showed stunned the audience at the time.

First to appear on his screen was a picture of a cowboy. When Atkinson indicated the cowboy's hat, other hats began to appear on the screen, one of which was the hat on a baseball player. When

Atkinson indicated the player's hat, other images associated with baseball began to appear, one after another, on the screen. He was able to extract information from the data base and detect patterns in it, in highly varied ways.

This was so different from earlier data base systems that it gave the illusion that the computer was free-associating—much like a person.

By crossing conventional categories, reaching across different collections of data, hyper-media makes it possible for, say, a designer creating a new product to let her mind weave through the stored knowledge naturally and imaginatively.

She might instantly shift, for instance, from technical data to pictures of earlier products that preceded it in the market . . . to chemical abstracts . . . to biographies of famous scientists . . . to video clips of the marketing team discussing the product . . . to transportation tariff tables . . . to clips of relevant focus groups . . . to spot prices for oil . . . or lists of the components or ingredients the new product will need . . . plus the latest study of political risk in countries from which its raw materials will have to come.

In addition to vastly increasing the sheer quantity of accessible knowledge, hyper-media also permits a "layering" of information, so that a user can first access the most or least abstract form of it, and move by stages up or down the abstraction ladder. Or, alternatively, generate innovative ideas by creating novel juxtapositions of data.

Conventional data bases are good for getting information when you know exactly what you want. Hyper systems are good for searching when you are not certain. Ford Motor Company is developing a "Service Bay Diagnostic System" for mechanics, so that they can search and browse for answers when they are not sure what's wrong with your car.

The U.S. Environmental Protection Agency makes available a "hyper-text" data base to help companies sort through and interrelate complex regulations governing 2 million underground storage tanks. Cornell University uses a hyper system for its second-year medical curriculum, permitting students to browse and search for patterns interactively. The University of Toledo is developing a hyper-text-based course in Spanish literature.

We are still far from being able to throw different kinds of data or information into a single pot and then search it entirely free of a programmer's preconceptions about what pieces are or are not related. Even in hyper systems the cross-connections a user can make are still dependent on previous programming. But the direction of research is clear. We are inching toward free (or at least freer) forms of information storage and manipulation.

Bureaucracies, with all their cubbyholes and channels pre-specified, suppress spontaneous discovery and innovation. In contrast, the new systems, by permitting intuitive as well as systematic searching, open the door to precisely the serendipity needed for innovation.

The effect is a dazzling new freedom.

The significant fact is that we are now moving toward powerful forms of knowledge processing that are profoundly antibureaucratic.

Instead of a little bureaucracy inside a machine, as it were, where everything is sequential, hierarchical, and pre-designated, we move toward free-style, open information. And instead of a single mainframe or a few giant processors having this enormous capacity, companies now have thousands of PCs, which before long will all have this capacity.

This form of information storage and processing points toward a deep revolution in the way we think, analyze, synthesize, and express information, and a forward leap in organizational creativity. But it also eventually means the breakup of the rigid little information monopolies that overspecialization created in the bureaucratic firm. And that means a painful shift of power away from the guardians of those specialized monopolies.

Even this tells only a fraction of the tale. For to these truly revolutionary ways of storing and using knowledge, we must now add the nonhierarchical communication networks that crisscross companies, crash through departmental perimeters, and link users, not merely between the specialized departments but also up and down the hierarchy.

A young employee at the very bottom of the ladder can now communicate directly with top-level executives working on the same problem; and, significantly, the CEO at the touch of a button can access any employee down below and jointly call up images, edit a proposal together, study a blueprint, or analyze a spreadsheet—all without going through the middle managers.

Is it surprising therefore that recent years have seen such savage reductions in the number of middle managers in industry?

Just as the new forms of information storage strike a blow

against specialization, the new forms of communication end-run the hierarchy. The two key sources of bureaucratic power— cubbyholes and channels—are both under attack.

KNOWLEDGE IS POWER IS KNOWLEDGE

Here then we glimpse one of the most fundamental yet neglected relationships between knowledge and power in society: the link between how a people organize their concepts and how they organize their institutions.

Put most briefly, the way we organize knowledge frequently determines the way we organize people—and vice versa.

When knowledge was conceived of as specialized and hierarchical, businesses were designed to be specialized and hierarchical.

Once a bureaucratic organization of knowledge finds concrete expression in real-life institutions—corporations, schools, or governments—political pressures, budgets, and other forces freeze the cubbyholes and channels into place. Which then tend to freeze the organization of knowledge into place, obstructing the reconceptualizations that lead to radical discovery.

Today, high-speed change requires equally high-speed decisions —but power struggles make bureaucracies notoriously slow. Competition requires continual innovation—but bureaucratic power crushes creativity. The new business environment requires intuition as well as careful analysis—but bureaucracies try to eliminate intuition and replace it with mechanical, idiot-proof rules.

Bureaucracy will not vanish, any more than the state will wither away. But the environmental conditions that permitted bureaucracies to flourish—and even made them highly efficient engines—are changing so rapidly and radically, they can no longer perform the functions for which they were designed.

Because today's business environment is convulsing with surprise, upsets, reversals, and generalized turbulence, it is impossible to know precisely and in advance who in an organization will need what information. In consequence, the information needed by both executives and workers to do their jobs well, let alone to innovate and improve the work, cannot reach the front-line managers and employees through the old official channels.

This explains why millions of intelligent, hardworking employees find they cannot carry out their tasks—they cannot open new markets, create new products, design better technology, treat customers better, or increase profits—except by going around the rules, breaking with formal procedures. How many employees today need to close their eyes to violations of formal procedure to get things done? To be a doer, a fixer, a red-tape cutter, a go-getter, they must trash the bureaucracy.

Thus, information begins to spill out of the formal channels into all those informal networks, gossip systems, and grapevines that bureaucracies seek to suppress. Simultaneously, corporations spend billions to construct electronic alternatives to the old communication structures. But all these require enormous changes in the actual organization, the way people are ranked and grouped.

For all these reasons the years ahead will see a tsunami of business restructuring that will make the recent wave of corporate shake-ups look like a placid ripple. Specialists and managers alike will see their entrenched power threatened as they lose control of their cubbyholes and channels. Power shifts will reverberate throughout companies and whole industries.

For when we change the relations between knowledge and production we shake the very foundations of economic and political life.

That is why we are on the edge of the greatest shift of power in business history. And the first signs of it are already evident in the new-style organizations fast springing up around us. We can call them the "flex-firms" of the future.

16

THE FLEX-FIRM

Meet some of today's business heroes—people like Sergio Rossi. Rossi is not some strutting bureaucrat or tycoon ensconced in a glass-sheathed skyscraper. He works instead from his home in the Val Vibrata, in eastern Italy, with three employees who use high-tech machines to turn out fine-quality purses and pocketbooks for sale in New York City department stores.

Not so far away one finds Mario D'Eustachio, who heads up Euroflex, a 200-employee firm that makes luggage for Macy's. Euroflex is a collaborative effort. Pia D'Eustachio, Mr. E.'s wife, is in charge of sales; Tito, a son, guards the finances; Tiziana, a daughter, designs the luggage; and a nephew, Paolo, runs the production side of things.

These, according to *The Christian Science Monitor,* are only 2 of the 1,650 small firms in the valley, each averaging only 15 workers, but collectively turning out over $1 billion a year in clothing, leatherware, and furniture. And Val Vibrata is only one small region—part of what is now known as the Third Italy.

Italy Numero Uno was the agricultural South. Italy Numero Due was the industrial North. Italy Numero Tre is composed of rural and semirural regions, like Val Vibrata, using high-tech and small, usually family-based enterprise to contribute to what has been called the "Italian miracle."

A similar pattern is seen in smaller cities. Modena, for example, boasts 16,000 jobs in the knitwear industry. Whereas the number of workers in firms employing more than 50 has plummeted since 1971, employment in firms with 5 or fewer workers rose. Most of these are family-run.

The virtues of family business are being discovered elsewhere too. In the United States, writes *Nation's Business,* "after years of being considered small-time, family businesses are hot." François

M. de Visscher, of the financial firm Smith Barney, says he wants his company to become "the premier investment banker to family businesses," and everyone from management consultants to marriage counselors are gearing up to sell services to what might be called "the fam-firm sector."

The smallest of these family firms are short on titles and formality; larger ones combine informality among family members at the top with formality and bureaucratic organization below.

It is glib to suggest that small is always beautiful or that an advanced economy can function without very large enterprises, especially as the global economy grows more integrated. Italian economists, for example, worry that Italy's dynamic small firms may not cut the mustard in an integrated European market, and the European Community, long an advocate of bigness, favors large-scale mergers and urges small firms to form alliances and consortia. But while consortia may make sense, the EC's infatuation with superscale may prove shortsighted—a failure to recognize the imperatives of the super-symbolic economy.

Thus, there is mounting evidence that giant firms, backbone of the smokestack economy, are too slow and maladaptive for today's high-speed business world. Not only has small business provided most of the 20 million jobs added in the U.S. economy since 1977, it has provided most of the innovation. Worse yet, the giants are increasingly lackluster as far as profits go, according to a *Business Week* study of the thousand largest firms. "The biggest companies," it reports, "are the most profitable—on the basis of return on equity—in only four out of 67 industries. . . . Well over half the time the biggest corporate player fails to attain even the industry average return on invested capital."

In many fields the savings that sheer size once made possible are fading as new technologies make customization cheap, inventories small, and capital requirements low. According to Donald Povejsil, former vice-president of corporate planning at Westinghouse, "Most of the classical justifications of large size have proved to be of minimal value, or counterproductive, or fallacious."

Small firms now can gain access to huge amounts of capital from Wall Street. They have ready access to information. And it is easier for them to use it, since they tend to be less bureaucratic.

Conversely, the "diseconomies of scale" are catching up with many of the bloated giants. It is clear, moreover, that in the economy of tomorrow huge firms will become more dependent than in the past on a vast substructure of tiny but high-powered and flexible suppliers. And many of these will be family-run.

Today's resurrection of small business and the family firm brings with it an ideology, an ethic, and an information system that is profoundly antibureaucratic.

In a family, everything is understood. By contrast, bureaucracy is based on the premise that nothing is understood. (Hence the need for everything to be spelled out in an operational manual and for employees to work "by the book.") The more things are understood, the less has to be verbalized or communicated by memo. The more shared knowledge or information, the fewer the cubbyholes and channels needed in an organization.

In a bureaucratic company, position and pay are ostensibly determined by "what you know," as though "who you know" didn't matter. Yet the reality is that "who you know" *is* important, and grows in importance as one moves up in the world. Who you know determines access to crucial knowledge—namely, information about who owes whom a favor, and who is to be trusted (which, in turn, means whose information is reliable).

In a family firm nobody kids anyone. Too much is known by all about all, and helping a son or daughter succeed by using "pull" is natural. In the bureaucratic firm, pull is called nepotism and is seen as violation of the merit system that purportedly prevails.

In a family, subjectivity, intuition, and passion govern both love and conflict. In a bureaucracy, decisions are supposed to be impersonal and objective, although, as we've seen, it is internecine power struggles that determine important decisions, rather than the cool clear rationality described in textbooks.

Finally, in a bureaucracy it is often difficult to know who has power, despite the formal hierarchy and titles. In the family enterprise, everyone knows that titles and formality don't count. Power is held by the patriarch or, occasionally, the matriarch. And when he or she passes from the scene, it is usually conferred on a hand-picked relative.

In short, wherever family relationships play a part in business, bureaucratic values and rules are subverted, and with them the power structure of the bureaucracy as well.

This is important, because today's resurgence of family business is not just a passing phenomenon. We are entering a "post-bureaucratic" era, in which the family firm is only one of many alternatives to bureaucracy and the power it embodies.

THE END OF THE COOKIE-CUT COMPANY

Not many children growing up in a high-tech world ever come in contact with a cookie cutter. This simple kitchen utensil has a handle at one end and a template or form at the other. When pressed into rolled dough, it cuts out the shape of the cookie-to-be. Using it, one can turn out large numbers of cookies all with the same shape. For an older generation, the cookie cutter was a symbol of uniformity.

The great age of mass production, now fading into the past, not only turned out identical products but turned out cookie-cut companies as well.

Glance at any Table of Organization. Chances are it consists of straight lines connecting neat little boxes, each exactly like the other. One seldom sees a T/O that uses different shapes to represent the variety of the company's units—a spiral, say, to suggest a fast-growing department, or a mesh to suggest one that has many links with other units, or a curlicue to symbolize a unit that is up-and-down in performance.

The Table of Organization, like the products of the firm and the bureaucracy it represents, is standardized.

Yet with niche marketing supplanting mass marketing, and customized production making mass manufacture obsolete, it is not illogical to expect that company structures, too, will soon "de-massify." Put differently, the day of the cookie-cut company is over. And so are the cookie-cut power structures that ran large corporations.

In *The Third Wave* we wrote about such innovations as flexible hours, flexible fringe benefits, and other "flex" arrangements that begin to treat workers as individuals and, at the same time, give the firm far greater flexibility too. Today such ideas are so commonplace that *Newsweek* headlines a story "A Glimpse of the 'Flex' Future."

What companies have not yet grasped, however, is that flexibility must cut far deeper—right to the very structure of the organization. The rigid, uniform structure of the firm must be replaced by a diversity of organizational arrangements. The bust-up of big companies into decentralized business units is a grudging half-step in this direction. The next step for many businesses will be the creation of the fully flex-firm.

THE DE-COLONIZATION OF BUSINESS

Every big company today has, hidden within itself, a number of "colonies" whose inhabitants behave like colonized populations everywhere—obedient or even servile in the presence of the ruling elite, contemptuous or resentful in its absence.

Many of us, at one time or another, have seen supposedly "big shot" managers choke back their own thoughts in the presence of their bosses, nod approval of imbecilic ideas, laugh at bad jokes, and even assume the dress, manner, and athletic interests of their superiors. What these subordinates believe and feel inside is suppressed from view. Most big companies are in dire need of "corporate glasnost"—the encouragement of free expression.

Under the smooth surface of male camaraderie and (at least in the United States) a show of equality, the "bwana" or "sahib" mentality still thrives. But the taint of colonialism in business runs even deeper.

Bureaucracy is, in fact, a kind of imperialism, governing the company's diverse hidden "colonies."

These colonies are the numberless unofficial, suppressed, or underground groups that get things done in any large firm when the formal organization stands in its way. Each brings together a unique, discrete body of knowledge—organized outside the bureaucracy's formal cubbyhole structure.

Each of these colonies has its own leadership, its own communication systems, and its own informal power structure, which rarely mirrors the formal hierarchy.

The struggle to rebuild business on post-bureaucratic lines is partly a struggle to de-colonize the organization—to liberate these suppressed groupings. In fact, one might say that the key problem facing all big companies today is how to unleash the explosive, innovative energies of these hidden colonies.

DANCING ON TABLES

When Sears, Roebuck & Company, the largest U.S. retailer, announced a major reorganization of its merchandise group not long ago, the group chairman and CEO, Michael Bozic, said it was needed because "We are competing in many diverse businesses . . . and have essentially been using one organizational format to compete in all of these businesses." This, critics implied, had made the firm sluggish and noncompetitive.

But even top managers who sense they need to "let go" or loosen the reins, in order to free up the energies of their people, drastically underestimate how far they will need to go to break the grip of bureaucracy.

Scores, if not hundreds of companies have broken themselves into numerous "profit centers," each of which, it is hoped, will act like a small, market-driven enterprise. Even some staff operations have now been designated as profit centers and must finance themselves (and thus justify their existence) by selling their in-house services. But what good is it to break a firm into profit centers if each of these is merely a cookie-cut miniature of the parent firm—a mini-bureaucracy nestling inside the mega-bureaucracy?

What is beginning now is a much more profound and revolutionary shift, which will alter the entire nature of power in business.

Most American managers still think of the organization as a "machine" whose parts can be tightened or loosened, "tuned up," or lubricated. This is the bureaucratic metaphor. By contrast, many Japanese are already using a post-bureaucratic metaphor—the corporation, they say, "is a living creature."

This implies, among other things, that it undergoes birth, maturation, aging, and death or rebirth in a new form. The Japanese term for company birth is *sogyo* and many companies today speak of experiencing a second or third or "new" *sogyo*.

It is precisely at this moment of rebirth that long-term success or failure is determined. For if the new reborn firm is still organized along bureaucratic lines, like the old one it replaces, it may have a short and unhappy second life. By contrast, if at this moment firms are permitted to reach out in new directions and to assume whatever organizational forms are most appropriate, chances for adaptation to the new, innovation-rich environment are much better.

The flex-firm concept does not imply structurelessness; it does suggest that a company, in being reborn, may cease being a mule and turn into a team consisting of a tiger, a school of piranhas, a mini-mule or two, and who knows, maybe even a swarm of information-sucking bees. The image underlines the point. The business of tomorrow may embody many different formats within a single frame. It may function as a kind of Noah's Ark.

To grasp the "flex-firm" concept, it helps to remind ourselves that bureaucracy is only one of an almost infinite variety of ways of organizing human beings and information. We actually have an immense repertoire of organizational forms to draw on—from jazz combos to espionage networks, from tribes and clans and councils of elders to monasteries and soccer teams. Each is good at some things and bad at others. Each has its own unique ways of collecting and distributing information, and ways of allocating power.

A company could conceivably have within it a monastery-style unit that writes software . . . a research team organized like an improvisational jazz combo . . . a compartmentalized spy network, with need-to-know rules, operating within the law, to scout for merger or acquisition possibilities . . . and a sales force organized as a highly motivated "tribe" complete with its own war songs and emotional membership rituals. (The author has attended the sales meeting of a major corporation where the tribal form was incipient and the members so psyched up about their jobs they quite literally danced on tabletops.)

This new way of conceiving of a company as a collection of very different organizations, many of them counterbureaucratic, reflects what already exists in some firms in a semi-smothered or embryonic form. Many businesses will find themselves moving toward this free-form model simply to stay alive in the de-massified economy of tomorrow.

The term *flex-firm* is needed because there is no handy word in the English language to describe such an entity. The French economist Hubert Landier uses the mouth-cracking term *polycellular* to describe the business of the future. Others describe it as "neural" or nervous-system-like rather than machinelike. Still others refer to the emerging business organization as a "network."

Though all these words capture some facet of the new reality, none are adequate, because the dawning business form of the future embraces them all, and more. They may *include* elements that are polycellular or neural. They may (or may not) be networked. But the organization may also include within it units that remain thoroughly bureaucratic because, for some functions, bureaucracy remains essential.

A key feature of post-bureaucratic firms is that the relationships of their parts are not closely pre-specified, like information force-fitted into an old-fashioned data base.

Instead, the units of a flex-firm may draw information, people, and money from one another and from outside organizations as needed. They may be next door to one another or continents apart. Their functions may partly overlap, like information in a hyper-media data base; for other purposes, the functions may be logically, geographically, or financially divided. Some may use many central services provided by headquarters; others may choose to use only a few.

In turn this requires freer, faster flows of information. This will mean crisscrossing, up, down, and sideways conduits—neural pathways that bust through the boxes in the table of organization so that people can trade the ideas, data, formulae, hints, insights, facts, strategies, whispers, gestures, and smiles that turn out to be essential to efficiency.

"Once you connect the right people with the right information you get the extra value added," says Charles Jepson, director of office marketing, Hewlett-Packard Company, adding that "information is the catalyst for effecting change at every level. That's what makes its power so awesome."

FAM-FIRMS OF THE FUTURE

One of the suppressed business forms struggling hardest to break free from old-style managerial bureaucracy is the mom-and-pop enterprise symbolized by people like the Rossis and D'Eustachios in Italy.

There was a time when virtually all businesses were, in fact, small family-owned firms. Beginning mainly in the 19th century, as companies grew larger, they transformed themselves into professionally managed bureaucracies.

Today, as we've seen, independent family-run units are once more multiplying. But in addition, we have witnessed the spread of franchising, which links mom-and-pop operators to the financial and promotional clout of large firms. The next logical step will come when family enterprises crop up as respected, powerful units *within* large corporations as well.

Most large firms engage in a cynical rhetoric about "family." A well-tailored chairman smiles at us from the pages of the annual report as his ghostwritten text assures us that everyone in the firm, from the chairman to the janitor, is a member of "one big family."

Yet nothing is more inimical to family forms of organization and, indeed, hostile to family life itself than the typical business bureaucracy. This accounts for the widespread corporate ban against hiring both husbands and wives.

Such rules, intended to guard against favoritism and exploitation, are now beginning to crack in the United States, as the number of highly qualified women in the work force increases and companies face difficulty in relocating one spouse when the other has a good job locally.

We can expect to see couples hired by companies—as couples. Before long we will no doubt see a wife-husband team placed in charge of a profit center and permitted—in fact, encouraged—to run it like a family business.

The same result is likely to come from the acquisition of companies like the D'Eustachios' Euroflex. If that firm were to be acquired, would it make sense to break up the family team that built it into a success in the first place? Smart acquirers would lean over backward to leave the family form intact.

Familialism, sometimes overglamorized, presents many challenges for top management.

A high-powered husband-wife team can be a formidable political force in the firm. The sublimation of expressed emotion—a corporate norm—may well give way to the shouts, tears, and seeming irrationality that often go with family life. Male-dominated companies may have to make room for women managers backed by husbands or other relatives. How in this system does one make sure important jobs are not handed off to the idiot son? How should succession be handled? None of these problems is easily solved.

On the other hand, fam-firms have great advantages. In contrast to large bureaucratic firms, they can make quick decisions. They often are willing to take daring entrepreneurial risks. Family firms can change faster, and adapt better to new market needs. Communication through constant face-to-face interaction and even pillow talk is swift and rich, conveying much with only a grunt or a grimace. Family members typically enjoy a deep sense of "ownership" in the firm, evince high motivation, are strongly loyal, and often work superhuman hours.

For all these reasons, we can expect family firms to proliferate inside as well as outside the smarter giant firms.

The Pakistani management expert Syed Mumtaz Saeed has acutely observed, "The dehumanization of the industrial era in the West has been a consequence of the relegation of the family to a purely social and non-economic role. Thus, the manager and the worker of the modern age are torn between the work-place and the home in a physical sense, and between the family and the organization in an emotional sense. . . . This conflict is central to the problems of motivation, morale and productivity in modern Western societies."

Saeed argues that Third World countries should reject bureaucratic impersonality and Western antifamilialism and build economies that are, in fact, based on family.

What he is arguing for is the retention of a classic paternalism that not only was wiped out in most big companies in the West, but is diminishing even in Japan. But this is quite different from the flex-firm, in which it is theoretically possible to have one profit center that is thoroughly paternalistic and others that are decidedly not, one unit that is run like a Marine boot camp, another like a commune. In the coming shift toward diverse organizational forms, corporate anti-colonialism, as it were, will lead to the liberation of the family business within the frame of the flex-firm.

Yet, as we see next, the family firm is only one of a host of colorful business formats that will shift power away from manager-bureaucrats in the years ahead.

17

TRIBAL CHIEFS
AND CORPORATE COMMISSARS

Every ten years the United States is invaded.
Recently an army of 400,000 fanned out from twelve beachheads and moved across the nation in a six-week campaign. At the end of that period the army withdrew, vanishing into the surrounding society along with all the logistics, telecommunications, and computers that linked its units together during its field operations.

Though seldom studied, the plans for this massive campaign hold lessons for many American businesses. For the goal of this "army" is to collect the detailed intelligence on which millions of business decisions will be based. Moreover, the very way in which the campaign is organized will provide insight to many an executive.

The organization involved is, of course, the U.S. Bureau of the Census, and its decennial operations cast revealing light on that future form of enterprise, the flex-firm. As the post-smokestack economy grows increasingly diverse, companies will be compelled to invent new, more varied business formats.

This is not just an academic theory. It has to do with survivability. Cybernetician W. Ross Ashby coined the phrase "requisite variety" many years ago to describe one of the preconditions for the survival of any system. Today's businesses simply lack the requisite variety to make it in the 21st century.

As they cast about for more adaptive ways of doing business, they will uncover—or rediscover—many arrangements now overlooked, suppressed, misunderstood, or misused by bureaucratic management. They will look for ideas everywhere: in other businesses, as well as in nonbusiness institutions like governments, political parties, universities, the military—and census bureaus.

Here is a sampling of what they will find.

The Pulsating Organization

This is an organization that expands and contracts in a regular rhythm. A good example is the U.S. Census Bureau, which swells to enormous size every ten years, then shrinks, starts planning for the next decennial count, and swells again.

Ordinarily staffed by about 7,000 regular employees, the Bureau maintains twelve regional centers around the United States. But to conduct a complete census, it sets up a parallel or "shadow" center for each of the twelve. Through them, more than 1.2 million applicants are interviewed to find the 400,000 "troops" who actually fan out and knock on every American door. These shadow centers are designed to last one year or a year and a half, and then to be dismantled. The staff then shrivels back to around 7,000. At which point planning begins for the next count ten years in the future.

Carrying this operation through successfully ought to earn the managerial equivalent of an Olympic gold medal. The 1990 census was fraught with bugs and bloopers. But the task would clearly daunt many a senior business executive. Indeed, many firms will notice that their own problems, though smaller in scale, are not entirely dissimilar. For "pulsating organizations" are present in many industries as well.

We see them in companies that gear up for annual model changes, then gear down again; in retail firms that staff up for Christmas and lay off in January; and in pickup crews used for film and television production.

In fact, one of the most rapidly proliferating formats in business today is the task force or project team, examples of what, in *Future Shock*, we termed "ad-hocracy." These, however, are only variants of the pulsating organization. While true "pulsers" grow and shrink repetitively, a project team normally carries out a single task. It therefore grows and declines once and then is dismantled. It is, in effect, a "single-pulse" organization.

Pulsing organizations have unique information and communication requirements. For its 1990 census, the Census Bureau's shadow centers, for example, were linked by some $80 million worth of computers and telecommunications equipment in a temporary network designed to be disposed of, or folded back into the permanent organization.

Executives in charge of pulsing companies or units often find their power pulsing too. Funds dry up as the unit shrinks. People disappear. The available pool of knowledge or talent diminishes. The power of rival units in the company expands relatively as the unit continues to shrink. In a pulsating power structure, the executive who commands a large project may be a "700-pound gorilla" one day—and a monkey the next. As many pulsating organizations interact, they lend a kind of rhythm to the economy.

Pulsing, however, isn't only a matter of size. Some companies pulse back and forth between centralization and decentralization. With each swing or pulse, information structures are changed— and power therefore shifts. The speedup and growing unpredictability of change point toward faster pulsing in the years ahead.

The Two-faced Organization

Another format likely to find a place in many flex-firms is a completely two-faced unit capable of operating in two modes, depending upon circumstance. The pulsating unit differs in size and organization from time to time. The Janus-like organization may remain the same in size, but shift from hierarchical to nonhierarchical command as needs demand.

A prime example is the famed British military unit, the Special Air Service, or SAS. Used for surgical antiterrorist strikes, hostage rescue, and other missions demanding surprise and deception, the SAS operates in two diametrically opposed modes. On the parade ground it is all spit, polish, and blind obedience. Regimental protocol is enforced by screaming sergeants. The privileges of rank and hierarchy are brutally upheld.

In action, however, a totally different kind of behavior is expected from the same people. SAS troops fight in tiny units, often cut off from their base, and without any officer present. There is a unit commander, but he may not hold a formal rank and is likely to be referred to simply as the "boss." The men, derisively called "sir" on the parade ground, now become "mister" or are addressed simply by first name. The same sergeant who cursed a trooper for some trivial infraction of the dress code may now tolerate jokes about those "parade ground idiots." Rank, hierarchy, and privilege are replaced under fire by a different set of ground rules.

In fact, Colonel David Stirling, who initially proposed formation of the SAS, pointed out that the smallest unit in paratroop or commando organizations consisted of eight or ten men led by a noncommissioned officer who did the thinking for the unit. Stirling insisted on something unique in military history—a four-man fighting module.

In the SAS, Stirling has written, "Each of the four men was trained to a high general level of proficiency in the whole range of the SAS capability and, additionally, each man was trained to have at least one special expertise according to his aptitude. In carrying out an operation—often in pitch-dark—each SAS man in each module was exercising his own individual perception and judgment at full stretch."

In fact, Stirling insisted on the number four to prevent orthodox leadership from arising. The danger of each person acting as a loose cannon is minimized through the selection of extremely motivated team players. The result is an organization that has been described as "a unique military democracy ... in which, if he succeeds, a man exchanges his former class and even identity for membership [in] a caste as binding as any family." It is this intense training and commitment that make it possible for the same unit to operate in both an authoritarian and a democratic mode, as the occasion demands.

Business, too, needs different behavior during normal operations and in the midst of crisis. In fact, many firms today are creating crisis centers, contingency plans, and fallback arrangements. But few actually train all their employees to operate in two contrasting modes.

The present conception of crisis management is to create a "shadow management," which waits in reserve, prepared to assume power during the emergency. Its ability to do so depends heavily on access to information and control of communications. Southern California Edison, for example, which operates the San Onofre Nuclear Generating Station, has set up a complex emergency information system that uses remote sensing, voice and video links, to tie its crisis command center to field units.

As we move further into a period of economic and political turbulence, punctuated erratically by technological breakthroughs and disasters, we can expect crises to crowd in on one another—

everything from terrorist attacks and product failures to sudden international crises. The Exxon oil spill, the collapse of the Continental Illinois bank, the wave of savings-and-loan failures, the bankruptcy of the A. H. Robins Company after the discovery of health problems related to its Dalkon Shield intrauterine contraceptive device only begin to suggest the diversity of crises that can face businesses.

Each one brings enormous power shifts with it as scapegoats are blamed, new leaders arise, and others are discredited and replaced. But the increased likelihood of crisis in a period of revolutionary change suggests we will see crisis teams and two-faced organizations spread through the business world and become a regular part of the flex-firm of tomorrow.

The Checkerboard Organization

In Austria after World War II a deal was struck between the two main political parties assuring that whichever party won the top spot would install a member of the opposition party in the second spot, and so on all the way down to the shop floor. This *proparz* system has meant that throughout the key posts in state-owned companies, banks, insurance companies, and even in schools and universities, Socialist "reds" alternated with Conservative "blacks."

Today we find an adaptation of this in, say, the Japanese bank in California that alternates Japanese and Americans at each level of the hierarchy, thus guaranteeing that Tokyo receives a flow of information seen through Japanese eyes, not simply from the top, but from many levels of the organization. Power at the pinnacle is reinforced by a constant stream of insight originating at many layers at once. As firms go global, many will no doubt try the Austrian and Japanese approach.

The Commissar Organization

Soviet Army units have traditionally had not only military commanders but political officers attached to them. While the military officer reported up the military line of command, the political officers also report to the Communist Party. The object was to keep the army subject to the party. In business, too, we often see "commissars" chosen from above and planted in subordinate units to keep an eye on things and report to the top through separate channels rather than through the normal hierarchy.

Here there are two main information channels, instead of one, violating the strict single-channel character of bureaucracy. It also reflects the deep distrust with which top management regards information flowing up through normal channels.

As change speeds up and predictability declines, CEOs will use "commissars" to end-run the bureaucracy in a desperate attempt to maintain control.

The Buro-baronial Organization

The best surviving example of feudal organization today is found in the university, where each department is a barony, professors are ranked and rule over graduate assistants, who make up the body of serfs. This feudal holdover is embedded within (and often at war with) the bureaucratic administrative structure of the university. Another example is the Congress of the United States, where 535 elected "barons" rule over a huge bureaucratic staff.

A similar combination of industrial bureaucracy and feudal barony is found in the Big Eight accounting firms, in large law offices, in brokerage houses, and in the military, where each service—army, navy, or air force—is a fiercely independent fiefdom. Generals and admirals in charge of these fiefdoms may have more real power than higher-ranked officers in staff positions who command no troops.

In "buro-baronies" the barons war with one another, often forming alliances to weaken central control. Such feudal elements are still found in business as well, along with what we might call "vestigial vassalage."

George Masters is a veteran engineer who has worked for several U.S. electronics manufacturers and now serves as the administrative aide to Philip Ames, a corporate VP in one of the world's largest computer firms. If anyone in personnel took the trouble to check, they would discover that Masters came into the company shortly after Ames arrived. And if they were to check further, they would discover the same thing happened in the company that employed both of them before they took their present jobs. And the one before that.

Hard-drinking buddies as well as workmates, Masters and Ames socialize together. They and their wives take vacations together. In fact, Masters and Ames (the people are real, the names are not) have worked together for more than fifteen years, Masters always following Ames as Ames hopped to successively higher positions.

This pattern, whether called "hitching your wagon to a star" or "riding on someone's coattails," is found in almost every large firm. Because it sharply reduces the need for communication—the two men know each other so well they can anticipate each other's reactions—it is highly efficient for some purposes, even though it violates formal personnel rules that call for "objective" selection.

The psychology of "vassalage" is extremely complex, involving everything from mentorships to the exchange of financial, sexual, or other favors. At its heart, however, the system is feudal and subjective, rather than bureaucratic and impersonal.

The power relationships are similarly complicated. At one level the "vassal," or junior, is dependent upon the "lord," or senior, who is higher up in the table of organization. Yet the top dog can be totally dependent upon his or her underling, whose chief unofficial function may be to conceal from others the weaknesses of the boss. This may be as common as fronting for the boss when he is too drunk to do his job. It may be as unusual as reading to him and making presentations for him because, unbeknownst to the company, the boss is dyslexic.

As bureaucracy weakens and its channels and cubbyholes become clogged, other neo-feudal forms and practices are likely to proliferate also, and find a place in the flex-firm.

The Skunkworks Organization

Here a team is handed a loosely specified problem or goal, given resources, and allowed to operate outside the normal company rules. The skunkworks group thus ignores both the cubbyholes and the official channels—i.e., the specialization and hierarchy of the existing corporate bureaucracy.

Tremendous energies are released; information is exchanged at high speed outside normal channels. Members develop strong emotions toward their work and one another, and very often, enormously complex projects are completed in record time.

According to Hirotaka Takeuchi and Ikujiro Nonaka of Hitotsubashi University in Japan, writing about "The New New Product Development Game," when Honda wanted to design a car that would appeal to young people, it put together a team—average age twenty-seven—and turned it loose. In the words of one young engineer: "It's incredible how the company . . . gave us the freedom to do it our way."

When Nippon Electric Company (NEC) developed its PC8000, it turned the project over to a group of former microprocessor sales engineers who had no previous experience with PCs. Says the project head: "We were given the go-ahead from top management to proceed with the project, provided we would develop the product by ourselves and also be responsible for manufacturing, selling, and servicing it on our own."

IBM's PC, which became the industry standard, was developed by a nearly autonomous group working in Boca Raton, Florida. Apart from quarterly reviews by corporate headquarters in Armonk, New York, the team was free to operate as it wished. It was also permitted to break normal corporate policy about buying from outside suppliers. Similar examples can be found at Apple, Hewlett-Packard, Xerox, and other high-tech firms.

The skunkwork format is inherently and militantly antibureaucratic.

As described by Takeuchi and Nonaka, "A project team takes on a self-organizing character as it is driven to a state of 'zero information'—where prior knowledge does not apply. . . . Left to stew, the process begins to create its own dynamic order. The project team begins to operate like a start-up company—it takes initiatives and risks, and develops an independent agenda."

Successful skunkworks develop their own leadership, based on skill and competence rather than formal rank. These newly empowered leaders often come into direct frontal conflict with the formal leader appointed by the bureaucracy to initiate and oversee the skunkwork unit.

The Self-start Team

We are also beginning to see the rise of "self-starting" teams or groups. Rather than being handed an assignment from above, they are typically drawn together by the electronic network. These "information clusters" go beyond even the skunkwork in their antihierarchical nature.

They spring up when people intensely interested in a common problem find one another electronically and begin to exchange information across departmental lines, irrespective of either geography or rank.

So long as it is compatible with a very general statement of the corporation's goals, the team sets its own objectives, often through democratic exchange.

For example, in David Stone's engineering management group at Digital Equipment Corporation, members dispersed around the world hold an electronic "conference" in which each team member puts forward her or his draft objectives.

"Each person," says Stone, "is then required by me to comment on each other's objectives with respect to whether they believe them or not, whether they are appropriate, and what support might be needed from that person that should be incorporated in their objectives. After a month and a half of this dialogue . . . we each rewrite them, based on the input, and we now have created a shared set, a team set, of objectives."

The process, antibureaucratic to its roots, can function only in an atmosphere that gives individuals considerable autonomy. The result can be a chain reaction of creativity. Because of this, such units are most common where competitive innovation is highest. As electronic nets spread and link flex-firms together, such self-start units will spring up, even across company lines.

A DIVERSITY OF POWERS

To manage the high diversity of the flex-firm will require new styles of leadership wholly alien to the bureaucrat-manager.

Senior officials will be far less homogeneous. Instead of look-alike (and think-alike) executives from central casting, the power group in the flex-firm will be heterogeneous, individualist, antibureaucratic, impatient, opinionated, and as a group, probably far more creative than today's bureaucratic committees.

Instead of neat lines of authority, the flex-firm presents a far more complex, transient, and fuzzy picture. A CEO may have to deal with what, from today's bureaucratic perspective, may appear to be a motley mixture of tribal chieftains, commissars, egotistical divas, smart and self-important barons, cheerleaders, silent technocrats, Holy Roller–style preachers, and fam-firm patriarchs or matriarchs.

Pulsing organizations, for example, need executives who can lead small organizations as well as large—or else they need an orderly system of succession that permits control to be handed off to leaders with different skills, depending upon the phase in which the organization finds itself.

In firms where the checkerboard and commissar principles are used, dual lines of communication compete. In the checkerboard, both lines terminate in the CEO's office. In the commissar arrangement, the two lines terminate in different places—one carrying reports to the CEO; the other, say, directly to the board.

All arrangements that affect the flow of information allocate or reallocate power. In baronial organizations the CEO must continually negotiate with his or her executive barons, playing them off against one another to avoid being neutered or ousted by a coalition of them.

Leadership under such conditions is less likely to be impersonal and spuriously "scientific," and more dependent, instead, on intuitive sensitivity, empathy, along with guile, guts, and plenty of old-fashioned emotion.

The flex-firm becomes increasingly political, in the sense that managing multiple constituencies is political. It is political in the sense that conscious application of power is political.

Power—the control of company money and information backed by the force of law—is shifting out from under those with legal or formal position and toward those with natural authority based on knowledge and certain psychological and political skills.

THE MISSING PANACEA

Finally, a word on networks. This form of organization has received so much attention in recent years, has been so heavily hyped, and has been defined so broadly that a touch of caution is warranted. For many, the network is a panacea.

Societies and business are riddled with networks of many kinds. We normally think of them as the informal pathways along which information and influence flow. Feminists complain that an "old boys' network" frequently operates to deprive women managers of promotion. Ex-military men often have their own network of contacts, as do former police and members of the Federal Bureau of Investigation, many of whom take jobs as corporate security officers after their retirement from government service.

Homosexuals have networks that are particularly strong in certain industries like fashion and interior design. Ethnic minorities have strong networks—the overseas Chinese throughout Southeast Asia, Jews in Europe and America, West Indians in Britain. Transplanted people in general—New Yorkers in Texas, the so-called Georgia Mafia that came to Washington when Jimmy Carter was President, the Ukrainians who came to Moscow with Leonid Brezhnev—also form their own communication networks.

In short, informal networks of many kinds crop up in virtually all complex societies. To these one must add formal networks— Masons, for example, Mormons, or members of the Catholic order Opus Dei.

For a long time the role and structure of such networks were ignored by economists and business theorists. Today they are much studied as potential models for corporate structure.

This recent interest can be traced to deep social changes. One is the previously noted breakdown of formal communication in companies. When the firm's bureaucratic channels and cubbyholes get clogged, unable to carry the heavy volumes of communication and information needed nowadays to produce wealth, the "right information" doesn't get to the "right person" as it once did, and employees fall back on the informal networks to help carry the information load.

Similarly, the de-massification of the economy compels companies and work units to interact with more numerous and varied partners than before. This means more personal and electronic contact with strangers. But when a stranger tells us something, how do we know if it is accurate? When possible, skeptical managers check in with their personal networks—people they have known or worked with for years—to supplement and verify what they learn through formal channels.

Finally, since an increasing number of business problems today require cross-discipline information, and the broken-down cubbyhole-and-channel system stands in the way, employees rely on friends and contacts in the network whose membership may be scattered across many departments and units.

These networks, formal or not, share common characteristics. They tend to be horizontal rather than vertical—meaning they have either a flat hierarchy or none at all. They are adaptive—able to reconfigure themselves quickly to meet changed conditions. Leadership in them tends to be based on competence and personality rather than on social or organizational rank. And power turns over frequently and more easily than in a bureaucracy, changing hands as new situations arise that demand new skills.

All this has popularized the notion of the corporate network among both academics and managers. Corning, Inc., which operates in four sectors—telecommunications, housewares, materials, and laboratory sciences—describes itself as a "global network." Says Chairman James R. Houghton:

"A network is an interrelated group of businesses with a wide range of ownership structures. . . . Within each sector there are a variety of business structures that range from traditional line divisions to wholly owned subsidiaries and alliances with other companies. . . .

"A network is egalitarian. There is no parent company. A corporate staff is no more, or less, important than a line organization group. And being part of a joint venture is just as important as working at the hub of the network."

Networks can be enormously useful, flexible, and antibureaucratic. But in the recent enthusiasm, elementary distinctions are often ignored.

In the 1970s one of the earliest and deepest analysts of network organization, Anthony Judge, then based in Brussels at the Union of International Associations, examined the density and response times of people networks, the structure of nets and their social functions, and the degree of connectedness they exhibit. He also compared human networks with such inanimate networks as pipelines, electric grids, railways, and transaction networks handling foreign exchange, commodity trading, and so on. Judge developed a whole little-known but useful vocabulary for the network concept.

He also brilliantly matrixed global networks against global problems, showing in a vast volume how networks of ideas or problems were linked, how networks of organizations overlapped, and how ideas and organizations were related.

More recently Netmap International, an affiliate of KPMG Peat Marwick, has developed a methodology for identifying the hidden communication networks in organizations as varied as the Republican Party and a giant accounting firm, in the course of its work for businesses and governments from Malaysia to Sweden. Says Netmap vice-president Leslie J. Berkes: "Organizations are redesigned daily by their members to get the job done. That's the real structure. It's the informal organization—the anti-organization. . . . It is the primary organization." If you cannot identify it, and track its changes, Berkes asks, "how are you going to manage it? You'll be satisfied with manipulating the formal organization with titles, hierarchies and tables of organization."

Such tracking can provide deep insight into existing organizations, but to enthuse blindly today over networks and assume that networks are "the" basic form of the future is to imply much the same uniformity that bureaucracy imposed, albeit at a higher, looser level.

Like any other type of human organization, the network has its limitations along with its virtues. Network organization is superb for fighting terrorism or a decentralized guerrilla war, not marvelous at all for the control of strategic nuclear weapons where the last thing we want is for local commanders to be free and unrestrained. The flex-firm is a broader concept, which implies an organization capable of encompassing both the formal and informal, the bureaucratic and the networked suborganizations. It implies even greater diversity.

THE LIMITS OF CONTROL

There are, however, limits to how far even a flex-firm can go toward diversity.

The spread of the "profit center"—which has seen many once-monolithic companies broken into semiautonomous, independently accounted units, each responsible for its own operations and its own profit and loss—can be seen as only a first step toward the eventual dissolution of the company altogether, atomized into a network or consortium of completely independent contractors or free entrepreneurs. In this model, every worker is a free lance, freely contracting with other free lances, to get specific jobs done.

But no social process continues forever, and the day of the total individualization of work, the ultimate dream of the theologically committed free-marketeer, is far distant. Instead, we can expect profit centers to become smaller—and more diverse—without disappearing into millions of one-person firms.

There is, after all, only so much diversity that any organization can tolerate and any managerial team manage. The argument here, therefore, is not that companies should maximize the variety of their organizational formats, but that today's companies, in their flight from the rigor mortis of bureaucracy, need to explore far more diverse options than ever before. They need, in short, to liberate their "colonies" and even to invent new formats.

In doing so, they—and we—move away from the idea that an organization is like a machine, each of its actions predictable and determinist, toward a conception of organization that is closer to the biological. Living systems are only partly deterministic, only sometimes predictable.

This is why the new electronic networks are increasingly tending toward neural rather than preplanned architectures. It is why David Stone, vice-president of international engineering at Digital Equipment, says, "You cannot tell in advance how the traffic will operate. . . . If you break a link between two places, provided that the network is still connected to those two points, it will find its own way. . . . We believe," he adds, "in the value of communication between any two individuals based on what they know rather than what their place is in the hierarchy."

Just as hyper-media, the new form of data base, permits knowledge to be arranged in extremely varied ways, the concept of the flex-firm points toward companies that can adapt in myriad ways to the twisty, quirky high-change competition that lies ahead.

The emerging flex-firm of the future, however, cannot function without basic changes in the power relationships of employees and their bosses. As we shall see next, these changes are well on their way. For power is shifting on the shop floor as well as in the executive suite.

18

THE AUTONOMOUS EMPLOYEE

During years spent working as a factory and foundry worker, we put in time on an auto assembly line. Even now, more than a third of a century later, it is impossible to forget what it felt like—especially the harrowing impact of the speedup. Every day, from the moment the bell started our shift, we workers raced to do our repetitive jobs while desperately trying to keep pace with the car bodies moving past us on the clanking, fast-jerking conveyor. The company was forever trying to accelerate the line.

Suppressed rage so filled the plant that every once in a while, for no apparent reason, an eerie wordless wail would issue from the throats of hundreds of workers, swell into a keening, ear-knifing sound as it was picked up and passed from department to department, then fade away into the clatter and roar of the machines.

As the cars sped past we were supposed to prepare them for the paint shop, hammering out dents and dings, and grinding them smooth. But the bodies flew by before we could do a good job. After they left us, they passed in front of inspectors who chalk-circled the remaining problems to be cleaned up afterward. Eight or ten hours a day of this was enough to numb us to any calls for "quality."

Somewhere there were "managers"—men in white shirts and ties. But we had almost no contact with them.

The power of these men in white shirts came not merely from our need for a paycheck, but from their superior knowledge about the factory, its goals, procedures, or plans. By contrast, we knew almost nothing about our job, except the few preprogrammed steps necessary to do it. Apart from exhortations to work harder, we received almost no information from the company. We were the last to find out if a shop or plant was to be closed down. We were given no information about the market or the competition.

We were told nothing about new products soon to be introduced, or new machines.

We were supposed to take on faith that our superiors knew what they were doing. (As the decline of the U.S. auto industry suggests, they didn't.) We were expected to show up on time, work, keep our muscles moving and our mouths shut. Even with a strong union in place, we felt powerless. A faceless "they" had us in their power. *They* were the men in white shirts. Managers. We were, during our work shift, citizens of a totalitarian state.

We are reminded of these experiences as reports arrive almost daily describing the newest plants now going up. For power is shifting in the workplace, and things will never be the same.

UNBLOCKING MINDS

General Electric makes electricity-distribution equipment in Salisbury, North Carolina. The plant is a model that GE wants to replicate at three hundred other factory locations.

In the past, if a piece of equipment broke down, a machine operator like Bob Hedenskog would have had to report it to his foreman and wait for help. Today Hedenskog makes the necessary decisions himself. He telephones a GE engineer in Plainville, Connecticut, for advice and takes responsibility for repair. On his own initiative he has ordered $40,000 worth of replacement parts, which he anticipated his machinery would need. He is part of a group of about seventy-five employees who, through committees of their own, make production, scheduling, and even some hiring decisions. Together they have cut worker-hours per unit of production by two thirds, and have slashed the time to customer delivery by 90 percent.

Some workers quit when this system was introduced, explaining that they didn't want to carry the additional responsibility it entailed. But employee turnover has fallen from 15 percent in the first year of the new system's operation to 6 percent four years later.

Similar stories are flowing in from all parts of the high-tech world. Ford Australia recently built its EA Falcon with an innovative work system that, according to the *Financial Times,* "contradicts the traditional Western way of assuring quality—namely, that management checks the output of workers who are following engineers' minutely detailed instructions."

Ford concluded that detecting defects first and correcting them later was not working. Only by allowing workers more discretion—no longer preprogramming their every move—could the goal of zero defects be approached. And this, according to the article, meant "recognizing the power of the operators right down to shop floor level."

Instead of one repetitive task, workers at the Chrysler-Mitsubishi Diamond-Star plant in Normal, Illinois, are told before being hired that they will need to handle several different jobs. They will be expected to come up with fresh ideas for improving production, and in that connection, they must be prepared to give, as well as take, constructive criticism.

At the Mazda Motor Manufacturing factory in Flat Rock, Michigan, ordinary plant workers get three weeks of training, including sessions on psychology. A small group of new hires are given six minutes to dream up twenty-five ideas on how to improve the common garden-variety bathtub, and then get only two minutes to come up with thirty more suggestions. Says Mazda's head of training, "We're trying to loosen people up and unblock them." After the initial three weeks, workers spend additional weeks on more job-specific training. Mazda estimates it spends $13,000 to hire and train the average employee.

These increasingly commonplace accounts underscore the historic shift currently taking place from "manufacture" to "mentifacture"—the progressive replacement of muscle by mind in the wealth creation process. But giving employees more say-so over the details of their work is only the tip of a more significant iceberg.

THE FECKLESS FARMER

To put this power shift into perspective, it is helpful to read the early history of the industrial revolution in England and Western Europe, and the complaints made by the earliest employers about the fecklessness, unreliability, drunkenness, and ignorance of the agrarian people from whom the early factory work force was drawn.

Every society imposes its own distinct work discipline or "regimen." Workers are supposed to obey certain rules, often unspoken. Their performance on the job is monitored, policed, and a structure of power is in place to enforce the rules.

In First Wave or agricultural societies, most peasants toiled endlessly, yet barely survived. This agrarian work force, organized into family production teams, followed a regimen set by the rhythms of season, sunrise, and sunset.

If a peasant was absent or lazy, his own relatives disciplined him. They might ostracize him, beat him, or cut his food rations. The family itself was the dominant institution in society, and, exceptions aside, it imposed the work regimen. Its dominance over the individual family member was reinforced by social pressures from the villagers.

Local elites might hold the power of life and death over the peasantry. Tradition might restrict social, sexual, and religious behavior. Peasants often suffered the cruelest hunger and poverty. And yet in their daily work lives they seemed less minutely restricted than those in the small but growing industrial labor force.

The agrarian work regimen had lasted for millennia, and until only a century or two ago, the vast majority of human beings knew no other and assumed it to be the *only* logical and eternal way of organizing work.

THE NEW CHAINS

As the first factories began to appear, a totally different work regimen came into being, at first affecting a tiny fraction of the population, then spreading as agricultural labor declined and industrial work expanded.

The urban industrial worker in a Second Wave society might be freer socially in the great, teeming anonymity of the urban slum. But in the factory itself, life was more tightly regimented.

Brute technology was designed for illiterates—which most of our ancestors were. Intended to amplify human muscle power, it was heavy, rigid, and capital-intensive. Before the invention of small electric motors, the machines were typically positioned all in a row and driven by overhead belts that set the pace for the whole factory. Later came the mechanical conveyor line that compelled armies of workers to perform motions in sync, chaining them to the production system.

It is no accident that the French term for "assembly line" is *chaine* or that everyone, from the manual laborer to the topmost managers, operated in a "chain of command."

Work was "de-skilled" or dumbed-down, standardized, broken into the simplest operations. And as white-collar work spread, offices were organized along parallel lines. Because they were not harnessed to an assembly line, clerical employees had a bit more physical freedom of movement. But the goal of management was to increase efficiency in the office by making it resemble the factory as much as humanly—or inhumanly—possible.

The smokestack factories and mills were severely criticized for their dehumanization of the worker. But even the most radical thinkers of the time regarded them as "advanced" and "scientific."

Less commented on was a change in the police function. Instead of the family policing work and pressuring its members to perform, a new power structure—hierarchical management—came into being to enforce the new rules.

This new Second Wave work regimen was at first bitterly resisted even by employers, who tried to keep the old agrarian system and to transplant it into the factory. Because families had long sweated together in the fields, early manufacturers hired whole families at once. But this system, efficient in agriculture for 10,000 years, proved totally inefficient in the factory.

Old people could not keep up with the machines. Children had to be beaten and often manacled to prevent them from running off to play. Families arrived at different times, straggling in as they had in the fields. Inevitably, the attempt to maintain a family production team in the new technological environment collapsed, and the smokestack regimen was imposed.

The lesson became clear: You couldn't organize work around a steam engine or textile loom the way you did around a hoe or a team of oxen. A new technical environment required a different discipline—and a different structure of power to police and enforce it.

THE ELECTRONIC PROLETARIAT

Today, as the super-symbolic economy develops, a new work regimen is once more supplanting an old one.

In our remaining smokestack factories and offices, conditions today are still largely the same as they were decades ago. Around the world, and especially in the newly industrializing nations, hundreds of millions of workers are still chained to a Second Wave industrial discipline.

And today, too, exactly as in the past, we still see employers underestimating the revolution taking place around them. They introduce computers and other advanced, Third Wave technologies—but attempt to retain yesterday's Second Wave work rules and power relationships.

Trying to turn their employees into "electronic proles," as George Orwell might have put it, they count keystrokes, monitor breaks, and listen in on employee phone calls. They attempt to control the most minute details of the work process. These methods, characteristic of industrial work, are especially prevalent in the processing of insurance claim forms and routine data entry in other businesses. But they can also be applied to higher-level work.

According to a report by the U.S. Congressional Office of Technology Assessment, they are "increasingly being directed to ... more skilled technical, professional and managerial positions. The jobs of commodities broker, computer programmer and bank loan officer ... could lend themselves to monitoring."

How long such methods will pay off, however, remains doubtful, for the work rules of the past contradict the new possibilities brought by advanced technology. Wherever we see radical new technology and an old work system, it is likely that the technology is misapplied and its real advantages wasted. History has shown repeatedly that truly advanced technologies require truly advanced work methods and organization.

Employers today who still think they need electronic proles resemble those reactionary ironmasters and textile-mill owners who thought they could run the new steam-driven factories with methods designed for ox power. They either quickly corrected their mistake or were driven out of business by smarter competitors who learned how to reorganize the work process itself, matching the work regimen to the most advanced technologies of the time.

Today in thousands of workplaces, from auto plants to offices, smart companies are experimenting with, or actually exploiting, the new regimen. Its key characteristic is a changed attitude toward both knowledge and power.

TOMORROW'S WORK REGIMEN

The changes now transforming work are not a result of woolly-headed altruism. They are a consequence of much heavier loads of information and communication needed for wealth production.

In the past, when most businesses were still tiny, an entrepreneur was able to know virtually all that needed to be known. But as firms grew and technology became more complicated, it was impossible for any one person to carry the entire knowledge load. Soon specialists and managers were hired and formed into the characteristic compartments and echelons of the bureaucracy. The knowledge load had to be diffused throughout the managerial ranks.

Today a parallel process is at work. Just as owners became dependent on managers for knowledge, managers are becoming dependent on their employees for knowledge.

The old smokestack division of the firm into "heads" and "hands" no longer works. In the words of Teruya Nagao, professor of information and decision sciences at the University of Tsukuba, "The separation of thinking and doing in the traditional model . . . may well be appropriate for constant technology but is hardly in keeping with rapid technological progress."

Because technologies are more complicated and turn over more frequently than in the past, workers are expected to learn more about adjacent and successive jobs. Thus, a General Motors ad proudly speaks of workers' helping to choose the lighting in their plants, selecting the sandpaper, the tools, and even "learning how the plant runs, what things cost, how customers respond to their work." In computer-integrated manufacture, says consultant David Hewitt of United Research Company, workers "need not only to know how the specific machines work, but ... how the factory works."

What is happening is that the knowledge load and, more important, the decision load are being redistributed. In a continual cycle of learning, unlearning, and relearning, workers need to master new techniques, adapt to new organizational forms, and come up with new ideas.

As a result, "submissive rule-observers, who merely follow instructions to the letter, are not good workers," says Nagao, quoting an earlier study of Sony. In fact, in today's fast-change environment, he points out, rules, too, need to be changed more frequently than in the past, and workers need to be encouraged to propose such changes.

This is so because the worker who helps frame new rules will also understand why they are necessary and how they fit into the larger picture—which means the worker can apply them more intelligently. In fact, says Reinhard Mohn, chairman of Bertelsmann A.G., one of the world's largest media conglomerates, "only regulations which are endorsed by the majority of the work force have a chance of being abided by."

But to invite workers into the rule-making process is to share power once held exclusively by their bosses. It is a power shift not all managers find easy to accept.

Workplace democracy, like political democracy, does not thrive when the population is ignorant. By contrast, the more educated a population, the more democracy it seems to demand. With advanced technology spreading, unskilled and poorly educated workers are being squeezed out of their jobs in cutting-edge companies. This leaves behind a more educated group, which cannot be managed in the traditional authoritarian, don't-ask-me-any-questions fashion. In fact, asking questions, challenging assumptions are becoming part of everyone's job.

Lowell S. Bain is the plant manager of GenCorp Automotive's new plant in Shelbyville, Indiana. Describing the role of the manager, he says, "Here the pressure comes from inside the work force—a work force that challenges management and doesn't accept its dictates or authority. Here people question objectives.... Just because you're a member of management doesn't make your ideas holy."

What we see, therefore, is a clear pattern. Workplace power is shifting, not because of fuzzy-minded do-goodism, but because the new system of wealth creation demands it.

THE NON-INTERCHANGEABLE PERSON

Another key factor shifting power on the job has to do with the concept of interchangeability. One of the most important innovations of the industrial revolution was based on the idea of interchangeable parts. But workers, too, came to be regarded as interchangeable.

Much of the relative powerlessness of the industrial working class derived precisely from this fact. So long as jobs required little skill, and workers could be trained in a few minutes to do some rote task, one worker was as good as another. Especially in periods of labor surplus, wages would drop and workers, even when unionized, had little bargaining power.

A "reserve army of the unemployed" usually was standing by to step into any available jobs. By contrast, as pointed out in Chapter 7, the jobless today cannot step into available jobs unless they happen to have the right mixture of skills at the right moment.

Moreover, as the knowledge content of work rises, jobs grow more individualized—i.e., less interchangeable. According to consultant James P. Ware, vice-president of Index Group, Inc., "Knowledge workers are less and less replaceable. The tools are used differently by each knowledge worker. One engineer uses the computer differently from the next. One market analyst analyzes things one way; the next is different."

When a worker leaves, either the company must find another with matching skills, which becomes mathematically harder (and more costly) as the variety of skills increases, or else it must train a new person, which is also expensive. Hence, the costs of replacing any one individual grow, and his or her bargaining power rises correspondingly.

The boss of a giant project team in the defense industry puts it this way: "Years ago you might have everybody doing the same thing. . . . Today it's different. Now if we lose somebody, it takes six months to train an individual to understand our system." Furthermore, because work is team-based, "When we pluck an individual out, the whole team becomes dysfunctional."

The net result of such changes is that companies tend to use fewer but better-paid workers than in the past, and in the fast-growing, leading-edge industries, the old authoritarian command structure is phasing out, replaced by a new, more egalitarian or collegial style of work.

Seen in its historical context, this represents a significant shift of power in the workplace.

TWO IMPERATIVES

The new work regimen will not wipe out all trace of the older ones. It will be a long time before the last sweatshop disappears. But two imperatives make its spread largely unstoppable.

The first is the "innovation imperative." No existing market share is safe today, no product life indefinite. Not only in computers and clothing, but in everything from insurance policies to medical care to travel packages, competition tears away niches and whole chunks of established business with the weapon of innovation. Companies shrivel and die unless they can create an endless stream of new products.

But free workers tend to be more creative than those who work under tightly supervised, totalitarian conditions. As David Stone, vice-president of international engineering at DEC, puts it, "When you're watching someone else watching your performance, you don't create much." Thus the need for innovation encourages worker autonomy.

It also implies a totally different power relationship between employer and employee. It means, for one, that intelligent error needs to be tolerated. Multitudes of bad ideas need to be floated and freely discussed, in order to harvest a single good one. And this implies a new, liberating freedom from fear.

Fear is the primary idea-assassin. Fear of ridicule, punishment, or loss of job destroys innovation. Smokestack management saw as its main task the ruthless elimination of error. Innovation, in contrast, requires experimental failure to achieve success.

A possibly apochryphal story about Tom Watson of IBM has an executive asking him if he is going to fire another executive whose $5 million project failed. "Fire him," Watson is supposed to have said. "I've just paid his tuition!" Whether true or not, it represents an attitude toward work diametrically opposed to the industrial system, and it underscores, yet again, the importance of learning.

The push toward a new work regimen is also furthered by a second imperative: speed. Advanced economies are accelerative. In the new environment, therefore, innovation is not enough. The business has to get its new products to market fast—before a competitor beats it to the punch or copies the products.

This accelerative pressure also shifts power by undermining the fixed, bureaucratic chain of command.

Not only do the new electronic networks frequently make it possible to communicate up, down, and sideways in the organization, so that an employee can skip across hierarchical levels, a similar effect is seen in personal or face-to-face communication.

In the past, a worker with a problem or a new idea got into trouble by going over the head of a superior. But acceleration forces employees to end-run the hierarchy. So employees are actually encouraged to ignore rank when necessary. At the Brother Industries headquarters in Nagoya this is routine. Says one BI personnel manager: "If a middle manager felt insulted in seeing any of his subordinates go over his head without permission, that man would immediately lose respect from both downstairs and upstairs."

Acceleration and innovation both play havoc with the power hierarchies of the smokestack past and promote the spread of the advanced, Third Wave work regimen.

THE DEMAND FOR ACCESS

For all these reasons, the new work regimen will, in time, sweep across the main sectors of the economy. And as the work force is continually ceded more autonomy, it will demand increased access to information.

During the smokestack era, arguments for the humane treatment of employees were crushed by the realities of brute technology that paid off even when workers were kept ignorant (and powerless).

Today, workers are demanding more and more access to information because they can't do their jobs effectively without it. We are thus seeing a redistribution of knowledge (and power) made necessary by new market conditions and by the new technologies themselves.

"As computer programs mimic the skills that have long set managers apart, workers in lower-level jobs can do tasks once reserved for executives," reports *The New York Times*. It quotes Charles Eberle, a former vice-president of Procter & Gamble, saying: "You suddenly have information in the hands of the people who run the machines; it's no longer reserved for people two or three rungs up the hierarchy.

"The first-level supervisors don't appreciate the power of this information until it gets into workers' hands. Then their resistance is enormous."

Clearly not all workers fit well in jobs that demand initiative, full participation, and a sharing of responsibility. Nor can all managers cope with the new-style work. But, as work units grow smaller and educational levels higher, the pressure from below mounts. The result is a fundamental shift in power relationships.

This is not the first time since the dawn of the industrial age that managers have been confronted with changing models of human relationships in the workplace. For many years the old Taylorite notions that turned the worker into an appendage of the machine were challenged by a school of "good-guy" theorists who argued that more humane treatment of employees would prove more efficient in the end.

The new regimen, increasingly espoused by management itself, is, however, more radical. In the words of Teruya Nagao: "This idea goes far beyond the assumptions of the human-relations model, where employees were made to feel important. Now they are acknowledged truly *to be* important."

It is true that the overriding power—greater than that of any individual—is that of the labor market. A shortage or surplus of some skills determines the outer parameters of the new autonomy. Many programmers or space engineers have learned that they, exactly like punch-press operators and assembly-line hands, can be pink-slipped without ceremony, while their bosses vote themselves "golden parachutes." Those cast out of work suffer a devastating decline in personal and collective power—which is a subject for a totally different book.

What is relevant here, however, is how things are changing for those *inside* the work force. And within that framework, a change of historical proportion is taking place.

In the smokestack era no individual employee had significant power in any contest with the firm. Only a collectivity of workers, massed and threatening to withhold their muscles, could force a recalcitrant management to improve the pay or status of the employee. Only group action could slow or stop production, for any individual was easily interchangeable and, hence, replaceable. This was the basis for the formation of labor unions.

If unions, with their traditional emphasis on "solidarity" and "unity," are losing membership and power in virtually all the advanced technological nations, it is precisely because workers are no longer as interchangeable as they once were.

In the world of tomorrow it will not take masses of workers to bring a company's production to a standstill, or to damage it in other ways. A "computer virus" slipped into a program, a subtle distortion of the information in a data base, the leakage of information to a competitor—these are only the most obvious of a whole range of new methods of sabotage available to the angry, the irresponsible, or the justifiably outraged individual.

The "information strike" of the future could turn out to be a one-person protest. And no laws, clever programs, and security arrangements can totally protect against this. The best defense is likely to be social pressure from one's peers. Or the simple feeling that one is treated with dignity and justice.

But far more important is the shift toward non-interchangeability. As work grows more differentiated, the bargaining position of individuals with crucial skills is enhanced. Individuals, not only organized groups, can exert clout.

Marxist revolutionists argued that power flows to those who own the "means of production." Contrasting the factory worker with the preindustrial craftsman who owned his own tools, Marx contended that workers would be powerless until they seized the "means of production" from the capitalist class that owned them.

Today we are living through the next power shift in the workplace. It is one of the grand ironies of history that a new kind of autonomous employee is emerging who, in fact, does own the means of production. The new means of production, however, are not to be found in the artisan's toolbox, or in the massive machinery of the smokestack age. They are, instead, crackling inside the employee's cranium—where society will find the single most important source of future wealth and power.

19

THE POWER-MOSAIC

In 1985, General Motors, America's largest car maker, bought control of Hughes Aircraft, the company founded by that reclusive, eccentric billionaire Howard Hughes. GM paid $4.7 billion dollars—the single largest amount ever paid for a corporate acquisition until then.

A merger mania had begun in the early 1980s, the fourth since 1900, and each year saw more corporate marriages in America, until by 1988 there were 3,487 acquisitions or mergers involving an astronomical $227 billion. Then in 1989, all the old records were smashed again when RJR-Nabisco was taken over for $25 billion.

In short, in a single four-year period the maximum size of these mergers increased more than five times. Even allowing for inflation, the growth in scale was colossal.

Of the twenty largest deals in U.S. history, all consummated between 1985 and 1989, most involved a wedding of American firms. By contrast, hardly a day now goes by without new headlines proclaiming "mixed marriages"—mergers that cross national frontiers. Thus Japan's Bridgestone acquires Firestone Tire & Rubber. Sara Lee gulps the Dutch company Akzo. England's Cadbury Schweppes swallows up France's Chocolat Poulain. France's Hachette buys up America's Grolier. Sony buys Columbia Pictures.

"The extraordinary increase in world takeover activity . . . is showing no signs of abatement," writes the *Financial Times*. "Indeed, the scramble to reorganize several key industries is likely to accelerate . . . driven by factors that go way beyond the asset-stripping moves that first sparked the U.S. merger boom."

As this suggests, while many mergers were originally based on get-rich-quick exploitation of financial or tax quirks, others were strategic. Thus, as Europe raced toward total economic integration, many of its biggest companies merged, hoping to take advantage of the pan-European market and to stave off the advances of Japanese and American giants. American and Japanese grooms looked for European brides.

Some companies were thinking on an even bigger scale, preparing themselves to operate all across the so-called "triad market" —Europe, the United States, and Japan. And beyond that, a few firms dreamed of truly conquering the "global market."

All this frenetic activity led to deep concern over the concentration of economic power in a few hands. Politicians and labor unions attacked the so-called "deal mania." Financial writers compared it to the feeding frenzy of sharks.

Looking only at the question of financial size, one might be led to believe that power in the economy of the future will eventually be controlled by a tiny handful of enormous, hierarchical monoliths, not unlike those depicted in the movies.

Yet that scenario is far too simple.

First, it is a mistake to assume all these mega-firms will stay pasted together. Previous merger manias have been followed, a few years later, by waves of divestiture. A new round of divorces looms ahead. Sometimes the anticipated market evaporates. Sometimes the cultures of the merged firms clash. Sometimes the basic strategy was wrong in the first place. Indeed, as we saw earlier, many recent buy-outs have actually been designed with divestiture in mind, so that after a gigantic merger various units are spun off from a central core, shrinking, rather than enlarging, the scale of the resultant firm.

Second, we are witnessing a growing disjuncture between the world of finance and the "real" economy in which things and services are produced and distributed. As two heart-stopping stock market crashes in the late 1980s proved, it is sometimes possible for the financial markets to collapse, at least temporarily, without significantly disrupting the actual operations of the larger economy. For capital itself is growing less, not more, important in economic wealth production.

Third, bulk doesn't necessarily add up to power. Many giant firms possess enormous power resources but cannot deploy them effectively. As the United States learned in Vietnam, and the Soviets in Afghanistan, sheer size is no guarantee of victory.

More important, however, to know how power in any industry or economy is going to be distributed, we need to look at *relation-*

ships, not just structures. And when we do, we discover a surprising paradox.

At the same time that some firms are swelling (or bloating) in size, we also see a powerful countermovement that is breaking big businesses into smaller and smaller units and simultaneously encouraging the spread of small business. Concentration of power is thus only half the story. Instead of a single pattern, we are witnessing two diametrically opposed tendencies coming together in a new synthesis.

Rising out of the explosive new role of knowledge in the economy, a novel structure of power is emerging: the power-mosaic.

FROM MONOLITHS TO MOSAICS

In the 1980s, at the very height of the merger mania, business "discovered" the profit center.

With an enthusiastic rush, companies began to break themselves into a large number of units, each of which was told to operate as though it were an independent small business. By doing so, the largest corporations began shifting from monolithic internal structures to mosaics made of scores, often hundreds of independently accounted units.

While few managers realized it, this restructure was propelled by changes in the knowledge system.

The idea of setting up separate profit centers inside the same firm was hardly new. But it was resisted in the pre-computer age because it implied a significant loss of control by top management.

Even after the mainframe computer arrived on the scene, it was difficult for companies to monitor the operations of large numbers of separately accounted "centers." It wasn't until personal computers began showing up in businesses en masse that the profit-center idea began to win serious attention in executive boardrooms. But one more precondition was needed. The micros had to be networked to mainframes. Once this began to happen in the 1980s, the profit-center concept caught fire.

At first, stand-alone microcomputers shifted power downward.

Armed with these new tools, junior executives and even rank-and-file employees tasted an unaccustomed degree of power and autonomy. But once the micros were connected to central mainframes, they also allowed top management to keep tabs on key parameters in a multiplicity of small units. It became practical to grant these units considerable freedom while still holding them financially accountable.

The information revolution thus began to widen the gulf between finance and operations, making it possible for financial concentration to go hand in hand with a considerable de-concentration of operational power.

At present, most profit centers are still only mirror images of the parent firm, baby bureaucracies hived off from the mother bureaucracy. As we advance toward the flex-firm, however, these will begin to diversify organizationally, and form themselves into mosaics of a new kind.

At S. Appolinare Nuovo in Ravenna a procession of saints is pictured on a mosaic wall. Imagine, however, a kind of kinetic mosaic, a moving mosaic composed not on a flat solid wall, but on many shifting see-through panels, one behind the other, overlapping, interconnected, the colors and shapes continually blending, contrasting, and changing.

Paralleling the new ways that knowledge is organized in data bases, this begins to suggest the future form of the enterprise and of the economy itself. Instead of a power-concentrating hierarchy, dominated by a few central organizations, we move toward a multidimensional mosaic form of power.

MEAT-CLEAVER MANAGEMENT

Indeed, inside the firm the nature of hierarchy itself is changing. For along with the creation of profit centers, the 1980s witnessed a so-called "flattening of the hierarchy," otherwise known as the massacre of the mid-ranks. Like the shift to profit centers, this change, too, was driven by the need to regain control of the knowledge system in business.

As large companies slashed their middle ranks, managers, academics, and economists who once had chorused that "bigger is better" began to sing a different tune. They suddenly discovered the "diseconomies" of scale.

These diseconomies are chiefly a result of the collapse of the old knowledge system—the bureaucratic allocation of information to departmental cubbyholes and to formal channels of communication.

As suggested earlier, much of the work of middle managers in industry consisted of collecting information from their subordinates, synthesizing it, and passing it up the line to their own superiors. As operations accelerated and became more complex, however, overloading the cubbyholes and channels, the entire reporting system began to break down.

Screw-ups and misunderstandings proliferated. Catch-22's multiplied, driving customers crazy. More people end-ran the Kafka-esque system. Transaction costs skyrocketed. Employees ran harder to accomplish less. Motivation plummeted.

Few managers understood what was happening. Show most chief executives a defective part or a broken machine on the factory floor, and they know what to do about it. Show them an obsolete, broken-down knowledge system, and they don't know what you are talking about.

What was clear was that top management couldn't wait for the step-by-step synthesis of knowledge down below, with messages slowly making their way up the chain of command. Moreover, so much knowledge fell outside the formal cubbyholes and moved outside the formal channels, and so much began moving instantaneously from computer to computer, that the masses of middle managers increasingly came to be seen as a bottleneck, rather than as a necessary aid to swift decision.

Facing competitive pressures and takeover threats, the same managers who allowed the knowledge infrastructure to become antiquated in the first place now searched desperately for ways to cut costs.

A frequent first reaction was to cut costs by padlocking plants and throwing rank-and-file workers out on the street, seldom considering that, by doing so, they were tampering with the firm's knowledge system.

Professor Harold Oaklander of Pace University, an expert on work-force reductions, points out that many "cost-cutting" layoffs are actually counterproductive for this reason.

Where union contracts call for senior workers to "bump" junior workers at layoff time, he notes, the result is a cascade of job changes. For every worker actually laid off, three or four others are transferred downward into jobs for which they lack the necessary knowledge. Long-established communication links are ruptured. The result is a fall-off, rather than the expected increase, in post-layoff productivity.

Undaunted, the top officials next zero in on the armies of middle managers they added over the years to handle the information avalanche.

American bosses who chop the payroll without regard for social consequence, or understanding of what that does to the firm's knowledge structure, are commended for "getting rid of fat." (The same is not true for managers in Japan who consider it a failure to lay people off. It is also different in many parts of Europe, where unions are represented on the board and must be persuaded that all other options have been exhausted.)

These meat-cleaver layoffs of middle managers are a belated, mostly unconscious attempt to redesign the firm's information infrastructure and speed up communication.

It turns out that many of mid-management's uncreative tasks can now be done better and faster by computers and telecommunications networks. (IBM, as we saw, estimates that just one part of its internal electronic network—the PROFS sub-net—replaces work that would otherwise have required 40,000 additional middle managers and white-collar workers.)

With new networks being laid in place daily, communications are flowing sideways, diagonally, skipping up and down the levels, ignoring rank. Thus, whatever top management may have *thought* it was doing, one result of the retrenchments has been to change the information infrastructure in the firm—and with it the structure of power.

When we create profit centers, flatten the hierarchy, and shift from mainframes to networked desktop computers, linked both to mainframes and to one another, we make power in the company less monolithic and more "mosaic."

THE MONOPOLISTS INSIDE

The information revolution pushes us still further in the direction of mosaic power by encouraging businesses, as it were, to go out shopping.

Instead of trying to do more work in-house, and thus "vertically integrating" themselves, many large firms are shifting work to outside suppliers, making it possible to scale their size down even further.

The traditional way to coordinate production was the way John D. Rockefeller did it with Standard Oil at the turn of the century—by trying to control and perform every step in the production-distribution cycle. Thus Standard, before it was broken up by the U.S. government in 1911, pumped its own oil, transported it in its own pipelines and tankers, cracked it in its own refineries, and sold it through its own distribution network.

When, to choose another example at random, Ernest T. Weir built National Steel into the most profitable U.S. steel producer in the 1930s, he started with a single ramshackle tin mill. From the start, he knew he wanted a "completely integrated" operation. Eventually, National controlled its own iron ore sources, dug its own coal, and operated its own transportation system. Weir was regarded as one of the "great organizers" of American industry.

In these companies, at each stage, a monolithic hierarchy of executives determined schedules, fixed inventories, fought over internal transfer prices, and made decisions centrally. This was command management—a style perfectly familiar to Soviet planning bureaucrats.

By contrast, today Pan American World Airways contracts out to others all "belly freight" space on its transcontinental flights. GM and Ford announce they will increase their "outsourcing" to 55 percent. An article in the American Management Association's journal, *Management Today*, is headlined "Vertical Integration of Multinationals Becomes Obsolete." Even large government agencies are increasingly farming out operations to private contractors.

The alternative to vertical integration allows competition to coordinate production. In this system, firms must negotiate with one another to win the right to carry out each successive stage of production and distribution. Decisions are decentralized. But a lot of time, energy, and money is spent on setting and monitoring specifications and in gathering and communicating the information needed in negotiation.

Each method had its pros and cons. A benefit of doing things in-house is control over supply. Thus, during a recent worldwide shortage of D-RAM semiconductor chips, IBM emerged unscathed because it made its own.

Today, however, the costs of vertical integration, in terms of money and additional bureaucracy, are both soaring, while the costs of gathering market information and negotiating are plummeting—largely because of electronic networking and the information revolution.

Better yet, the company that buys from many outside suppliers can take advantage of a breakthrough in technology without having to buy the new technology itself, retrain its workers, and make thousands of small changes in procedure, administration, and organization. In effect, it pushes much of the cost of adaptation out the front door. By contrast, doing things in-house produces dangerous rigidity.

Often, doing it inside is also more expensive. Unless forced to compete against outside suppliers, the in-house provider of components or services becomes, in effect, an "internal monopoly" able to foist higher prices on its own in-house customers.

To keep this monopoly going, inside suppliers typically hoard the knowledge they control, making it difficult to compare their performance objectively against outside competitors. This control of technical and accounting information makes it politically difficult to break the internal monopoly.

But here again we find information technology driving change by undermining these knowledge-monopolies.

A recent M.I.T. study in companies like Xerox and General Electric points out that "computerized inventory control systems and other forms of electronic integration allow some of the advantages" of vertical integration to be retained when work is shifted outside.

The plummeting cost per unit of computerized information also improves the position of small outside suppliers, which means that, increasingly, goods or services become the product not of a single monolithic firm but of a mosaic of firms. The mosaic created by profit centers inside the firm is paralleled by the creation of a larger mosaic without.

IN THE BELLY OF THE BEHEMOTH

The same forces help account for today's surprising population explosion of small business in general, which moves us still further from an economy of monoliths.

Small and medium-sized firms have won recognition as the new centers of employment, innovation, and economic dynamism. The small business entrepreneur is the new hero (and often heroine) of the economy.

In France, reports the *Financial Times,* "big business support schemes have been jettisoned for programmes more likely to help the small business." The United Kingdom provides subsidized management consulting services to increase small business organizational efficiency. In the United States, *Inc.* magazine, which measures the activity of the one hundred top small businesses, reports an average five-year growth rate that "approaches the incomprehensible—high enough to astonish (us) and to stagger (the companies that experience it)."

In place of an economy dominated by a handful of giant monoliths, therefore, we are creating a super-symbolic economy made up of small operating units, some of which may, for accounting and financial reasons, be encapsuled inside large businesses. An economy built of boutiques, rather than behemoths (though some of the boutiques remain inside the belly of a behemoth).

This many-shaped, multi-mosaic economy requires entirely new forms of coordination, which explains the ceaseless split-up and formation of so-called strategic alliances and other new arrangements.

Kenichi Ohmae, brilliant head of the McKinsey office in Tokyo, has called attention to the growth of triangular joint ventures involving companies or parts of companies in all three—Japan, the United States, and Europe. Such "trilateral consortia," he writes, "are being formed in nearly every area of leading edge industry including biotechnology, computers, robots, semiconductors, jet engines, nuclear power, carbon fibers, and other new materials." These are manufacturing mosaics, and they are redrawing business boundaries in ways that will redefine national boundaries as well.

In Italy, Bruno Lamborghini, vice-president for corporate economic research, Olivetti, speaks of the "networking of companies" based on "alliances, partnerships, agreements, research and technical cooperation." Olivetti alone has entered into fifty such arrangements.

Competitive position, says Lamborghini, "will no longer depend solely on ... internal resources," but on the pattern of relationships with outside units. Like data bases, success is increasingly "relational."

And, significantly, the new relations of production are not fixed, rigid, and prespecified—like the position of names and addresses in an old-fashioned data base. They are fluid and free-form as in hyper-media. The new mosaic organization of companies and the economy thus begins to reflect (and promote) changes in the organization of knowledge itself.

To understand power in the business world of tomorrow, therefore, forget fantasies of near-total concentration, a world dominated by a few mega-firms. Think, instead, about power-mosaics.

RELATIONAL WEALTH

In the bustling city of Atlanta, Georgia, the single largest enterprise employs some 37,000 workers. This mainstay of the economy has a payroll of over $1.5 billion a year. Its key facilities occupy 2.2 million square feet of space.

This massive service enterprise is not, however, a company or corporation. It is the Atlanta airport.

It is a giant mosaic consisting of scores of separate organizations —everything from airlines, caterers, cargo handlers, and car rental firms to government agencies like the Federal Aviation Administration, the Post Office, and the Customs Service. Employees belong to many different unions, from the Air Line Pilots Association to the Machinists and Teamsters.

That the Atlanta airport creates wealth is not doubted by hotelkeepers, restaurants, real estate interests, auto dealers, and others in the city, not to mention the 56,000 other employees in Atlanta whose jobs are indirectly generated by the airport operations.

Little of this wealth results from the effort of any individual firm or agency. The wealth flowing from this meta-mosaic is precisely a function of *relationships*—the interdependence and coordination of all of them. Like advanced computerized data bases, the Atlanta airport is "relational."

Though relationships have always been important in the creation of wealth—being implied in the very concept of the division of labor—they become far more important as the number and diversity of "players" in the mosaic system increase.

As this number rises arithmetically, relationships increase combinatorially. Moreover, these relationships can no longer be based on simple command, in which one participant imposes behavior on the others. Because of interdependence, the players increasingly rely on consensus, explicit or otherwise, which takes account of the interests of many.

As knowledge itself is organized relationally or in hyper-media form—meaning that it can be constantly reconfigured—organization, too, must become hyper-flexible. This is why an economy of small, interacting firms forming themselves into temporary mosaics is more adaptive and ultimately more productive than one built around a few rigid monoliths.

POWER IN MOSAICS

A generation ago, mosaics had a different structure. Typically, they looked like pyramids or wheel-and-spoke arrangements. A big company was surrounded by a ring of suppliers and distributors. The giant dominated the other firms in its grouping, dealers and suppliers alike serving essentially as its satellites. Customers and labor unions were also weak in comparison with the jumbo company.

It goes without saying that large firms today still carry tremendous clout. But things are rapidly changing.

First, suppliers today are no longer just selling goods or services. They are also supplying critical information and, conversely, sucking information out of the buyer's data bases. They are, as the buzzword has it, "partnering" with their clients.

At Apple Computer, says CEO John Sculley, "We're able to . . . rely on an independent network of third-party business partners—independent software developers, makers of peripheral equipment, dealers and retailers. . . . Some critics wrongly assert that such arrangements have led to the emergence of the 'hollow corporation,' a vulnerable shell whose survival is dependent on outside companies."

Sculley challenges this view, pointing out that this mosaic arrangement permits Apple itself to be lean, fleet, and adaptive, and that especially in times of crisis it was the "partners" who helped Apple pull through. In fact, he contends, "for every dollar of revenue in the catalyst company, the external infrastructure may generate three to four additional dollars of sales. . . . Of far greater import is the enhanced flexibility to turn change and chaos into opportunity."

In the past, companies often mouthed the rhetoric of partnership. Today they are finding themselves thrust into it.

By tracing information patterns in a power-mosaic, we gain a clue to where real power and productivity lie. For example, communication flows might be densest between a parts supplier and a manufacturer (or more accurately between a specific unit of each). The shipping operation of one and the stock-intake operation of the other form, in effect, a single organic unit—a key relationship. The fact that for accounting purposes, or for financial reasons, one is part of Company A and the other a part of Company B is increasingly divorced from the productive reality. In fact, the people in each of these departments may have more common interest in and loyalty to this relationship than to their own companies.

At Matsushita in Japan the partnering process has been formalized into something called "high productivity through investment of total wisdom."

Matsushita meets with its subcontractors at an early stage of a product's design and asks them to help improve it, in order to shorten time lags and get the product to market faster.

Kozaburo Sikata, chairman of Kyoei-kai, the association of Matsushita subcontractors, expects this system to become standard practice. Sharing previously unshared information at the start is not something Matsushita does out of the goodness of its heart, but because competition demands it. And one can be sure that, as big as Matsushita is, its executives listen carefully when its 324 organized suppliers speak.

Beyond this, suppliers these days aren't just linked electronically to the big company, like spokes to a wheel-hub; they are, and increasingly will be, linked to one another as well, which means they are in a far stronger position to form coalitions when necessary to apply pressure on the big firm.

There is still another reason why the emerging mosaics no longer necessarily consist of dominators and dominated. With the breakup of the monolithic corporation into profit centers, many supplier or customer firms find themselves dealing not with the full force and power of a giant, but with a profit center smaller and often weaker than themselves. The size of the parent firm, once a major factor, is increasingly irrelevant.

It is, therefore, no longer sensible, as power shifts from monoliths to mosaics, to take for granted that giant firms dominate the mosaics of which they are a part.

Indeed, the large firm is also pressured from the other side, by customers who are increasingly organized into "users councils." Ostensibly these groups are in business to exchange technical data. In reality, they are a new form of consumer lobby.

Proliferating rapidly and arming themselves with high-powered legal, technical, and other expertise, users' organizations represent countervailing power, and can often compel their supplier firms, regardless of size, to meet their demands.

Such groups are especially active in the computer field, where, for example, users of VAX and Lotus software are organized. IBM customers are organized into many groups, joined in a single international council that represents some 10,000 companies, including some of the biggest in the world. IBM now boasts that it listens to its users. It better.

Members of these groups may at one and the same time be customers, competitors, and joint venturers. Business life is becoming confusingly poly-relational.

The idea, therefore, that a few monolithic giants will command the economy of the future is simple-minded.

BEYOND THE CORPORATION

Such largely unnoticed changes will also force us to rethink the very functions of the firm. If much of the value added derives from *relationships* in the mosaic system, then the value a firm produces and its own value comes, in part, from its continually changing *position* in the super-symbolic economy.

Accountants and managers who attempt to quantify added value and assign it to specific subsidiaries or profit centers are compelled to make arbitrary, often quite subjective judgments, since conventional accounting typically ignores the value-generating importance of "organizational capital" and all these complex, ever-changing relationships. Accounting categories like "good will" only crudely and inadequately reflect the mounting importance of such assets.

Management theorists are belatedly beginning to speak of "organizational capital." But there is also what might be called "positional capital"—the strategic location of the firm in the overall web-work of mosaics and meta-mosaics.

In any given industry, a crucial position in one of these wealth-producing systems is money in the bank—and power in the pocket. To be frozen out or forced to the periphery can be disastrous.

All this suggests that the big corporation or company is no longer necessarily the central institution for the production of material wealth in the capitalist world and the advanced economies generally.

What we are seeing is the divorce of the big corporation from the key material processes of wealth creation. These are performed by small and medium-sized business or by the subcorporations called profit centers. With so much of the hands-on work done in these units, the functions of top management in the large corporation have less and less to do with ensuring production and more to do with setting very general strategic guidelines; organizing and accounting for capital; litigating and lobbying; and substituting information for all the other factors of production.

This delegation or contracting-out of many of the functions of the large corporation—once the central production institution in the economy—has a historical precedent.

The industrial revolution stripped away many of the functions from the traditional family—that other key institution of society. Education went to the schools, care of the elderly went to the state, work was transferred to the factory, and so forth. Today, since many of its former functions can be carried out by small units armed with high-powered information technology, the large business firm is being similarly stripped of some of its traditional reasons for being.

The family did not disappear after the industrial revolution. But it became smaller, took on more limited responsibility, and lost much of its power vis-à-vis other institutions in the society.

The same is happening to the large corporation as we transit out of the smokestack era dominated by Brobdingnagian business.

In short, even as big corporations expand, the significance of the corporation, as an institution, contracts.

It is still too early for any of us fully to understand the power-mosaics that are now rapidly taking form and the long-term destiny of the corporation. But one thing is certain: The notion that a tiny handful of giant companies will dominate tomorrow's economy is a comic-book caricature of reality.

CODA:

THE NEW SYSTEM
FOR WEALTH CREATION

Not long ago Wendy's International, whose 3,700 fast-food restaurants stretch from the United States and Japan to Greece and Guam, introduced an "Express Pak" order for drive-in customers. It consists of a hamburger, French fries, and a Coke. But the customer has to utter only the words *Express Pak* instead of specifying each item separately. The idea was to accelerate service. In the words of one Wendy's spokesperson, "We may be talking three seconds. But the cumulative effect can be significant."

This seemingly trivial business innovation tells us a lot about the future of power. For the speed with which we exchange information—even seemingly insignificant information—is related to the rise of a completely new system for wealth creation. And that lies behind the most important power shifts in our time.

THE NEW ECONOMIC METABOLISM

In itself, of course, how quickly Wendy's sells hamburgers is not exactly a matter of earth-shaking significance. But one of the most important things to know about any system, and particularly any economic system, is its "clock-time," the speed with which it operates.

Every system—from the human body's circulatory system to the society's wealth creation system—can operate only at certain speeds. Too slow and it breaks down; too fast and it flies apart. All systems consist of subsystems, which likewise function only within a certain speed range. The "pace" of the whole system can be thought of as the average of the rates of change in its various parts.

Each national economy and each system of wealth creation operates at its own characteristic pace. Each has, as it were, a unique metabolic rate.

We can measure the speed of a wealth-making system in many ways: in terms of machine processes, business transactions, communication flows, the speed with which laboratory knowledge is translated into commercial products, or the length of time needed to make certain decisions, lead times for delivery, and so on.

When we compare the overall pace of First Wave or agrarian systems of wealth creation with that of Second Wave or industrial systems, it becomes clear that smokestack economies run faster than traditional agricultural economies. Wherever the industrial revolution passed, it shifted economic processes into a higher gear.

By the same token, the new system of wealth creation described in these pages operates at speeds unimaginable even a generation or two ago. Today's economic metabolism would have broken the system in an earlier day. A new "heterojunction" microchip that switches on and off in two trillionths of a second symbolizes the new pace.

In *Future Shock*, first published in 1970, we argued that the acceleration of change would transform society, and showed what happens to systems when speeds exceed their adaptive capabilities. We demonstrated that acceleration itself has effects independent of the nature of the change involved. Hidden within this finding is an economic insight that goes beyond the old "time is money" cliché. The acceleration effect, indeed, implies a powerful new law of economics.

This law can be stated simply: When the pace of economic activity speeds up, each unit of time comes to be worth *more* money.

This powerful law, as we shall see, holds profound implications not just for individual businesses, but for whole economies and for global relations *among* economies. It has special meaning for the relations between the world's rich and poor.

A HAILSTORM OF PLEAS

Returning from broad economic theory to the practicalities of everyday life makes it clear that Wendy's managers, in speeding up their business, are reacting to customers who demand instant responses. They want fast service, and they want products that save time in their lives. For in the emerging culture, time itself becomes a valuable product.

Beyond this, in today's increasingly competitive world economy, the ability to bring products to market fast is essential. The blistering speed with which fax machines or VCRs or other consumer electronic items sweep the market astonishes makers and customers alike.

In small numbers, facsimile machines existed for decades. As long ago as 1961, Xerox research laboratories demonstrated what was called an LDX machine—for long-distance xerography—which did much of what today's faxes do.

Several things blocked its commercialization. Thus, postal systems still functioned with reasonable efficiency, while telephone systems were still comparatively backward and long-distance services expensive.

Suddenly, in the late 1980s, several things came together. Fax machines could be produced at low cost. Telecommunications technologies vastly improved. AT&T was broken up, helping to cut the relative cost of long-distance services in the United States. Meanwhile, postal services decayed (slowing transaction times at a moment when the economy was accelerating). In addition, the acceleration effect raised the economic value of each second potentially saved by a fax machine. Together these converging factors opened a market that then expanded with explosive speed.

In the spring of 1988, as though overnight, Americans received a hailstorm of phone calls from friends and business associates pleading with them to install a fax. Within a few months, millions of fax machines were buzzing and bleeping all over America.

Under today's competitive conditions, the rate of product innovation is so swift that almost before one product is launched the next generation of better ones appears. Having recently bought twenty megabytes of hard disc storage for a personal computer,

should one now buy forty, seventy—or just twenty more, in anticipation of the fact that CD-ROM storage will soon be available? (By
the time these figures reach print, they may look primitive.)

In terminology reminiscent of space flight or nuclear war,
marketers now speak of the "launch window"—the all-too-brief
interval after which a new product is likely to fail because of
competition from more advanced models.

These accelerative pressures lead to new production methods.
Thus one way to move faster is to do simultaneously what you
used to do sequentially. Hence the recent appearance of the term
simultaneous engineering.

In the past a new product was designed first, manufacturing
methods worked out later. Today, says David W. Clark, vice-president
of engineering for the Jervis B. Webb Company, a maker of
materials-handling equipment, "You're defining and designing
the manufacturing process concurrently with designing the end
product."

"S.E.," as it is known, requires unprecedented precision and
coordination. Says Jerry Robertson of Automation Technology
Products: "The concept of simultaneous engineering . . . has been
around for over fifteen years." Only recently, however, has "progress in computing power and data base capability" begun to make
it feasible.

Another accelerative step is to eliminate or redesign parts—to
make products with fewer components and to modularize them.
This requires more exquisite tolerances and higher levels of information and knowledge. IBM redesigned one component of its
4720 printer and not only cut its cost from $5.95 per unit to $1.81
but also reduced manufacture time from three minutes to seconds.
As at Wendy's, seconds count.

Still another accelerative step is the introduction of "just-in-
time" delivery of components, pioneered by the Japanese. Instead
of suppliers' making long runs of a part and delivering them in big
batches at infrequent intervals, the system requires the frequent
delivery of small numbers of each part, precisely when they are
required for assembly. The effect of this innovation is to speed
production and slash the capital tied up in inventory. Britain's
Rolls-Royce, for example, reports that its just-in-time system has
cut lead times and inventory by 75 percent.

Speed of response to customer demand has become a critical

factor differentiating one company's product or service from that of another. Travel agents, banks, financial services, fast-food franchisees, all vie with one another to provide instant information and gratification.

In the past, employers sought to accelerate production through the speedup of the workers. One of the great humanizing contributions of the old trade union movement was its battle to limit the speedup. In thousands of backward factories and offices, this battle has not yet been won.

Under the new system of wealth creation, however, hands-on labor costs plummet as a percentage of overall cost, and speed is gained not by sweating the work force but through intelligent reorganization and sophisticated electronic information exchange. Knowledge substitutes for sweat as the entire system picks up speed.

In June 1986, Motorola, Inc., formed a twenty-four-member team—code-named Team Bandit—and gave it a seemingly impossible assignment. Its goal was to design a new radio-pager and a world-class computer-integrated manufacturing facility for producing it. The new plant would have to meet super-high quality requirements, defined as a 99.9997 percent probability that each unit of output would be perfect.

The time limit: eighteen months.

Today at Boynton Beach, Florida, the plant turns out customized radio pagers in production runs as small as one of a kind. Twenty-seven robots do the physical work. Of forty employees, only one actually touches the product. The Team Bandit operation succeeded—with seventeen days to spare.

Even the automotive industry, a slow-paced dinosaur by comparison with the camera industry or electronics, is struggling to shorten time frames.

The success of Japan's car industry is partly a reflection of the fact that Japanese manufacturers can design and introduce an entirely new model in half the time it takes European and American car makers.

At Toyota, which Joseph L. Bower and Thomas M. Hout in the *Harvard Business Review* characterize as a "fast-cycle company," simultaneous engineering, advanced information systems, self-organizing teams, and the sharing of information with suppliers at an early stage, result, according to Hout and Bower, in "an ever-faster development cycle . . . frequent new product introductions, and a constant flow of major and minor innovations on existing models."

Similarly, they cite the case of a bank that cut the time needed to make a decision on a loan from several days to thirty minutes, by presenting the necessary information to a group of loan specialists simultaneously, rather than routing it in sequence from one specialist to the next.

So powerful is the "accelerative effect," according to consultant Howard M. Anderson, founder of the Yankee Group, that companies must now have "one overriding goal: speed. Speed at all costs . . . hyper-speed."

What is emerging is a radical new economic system running at far faster speeds than any in history.

TOMORROW'S WEALTH

In earlier pages we sketched elements of this new wealth-creation system. It is now possible to put all the pieces together into a single coherent frame. Doing so makes clear how revolutionary this new way of making wealth really is—and how starkly different it is from the ways wealth was produced in the past.

1. The new accelerated system for wealth creation is increasingly dependent on the exchange of data, information, and knowledge. It is "super-symbolic." No knowledge exchanged, no new wealth created.

2. The new system goes beyond mass production to flexible, customized, or "de-massified" production. Because of the new information technologies, it is able to turn out short runs of highly varied, even customized products at costs approaching those of mass production.

3. Conventional factors of production—land, labor, raw materials, and capital—become less important as symbolic knowledge is substituted for them.

4. Instead of metal or paper money, electronic information becomes the true medium of exchange. Capital becomes extremely

fluid, so that huge pools of it can be assembled and dispersed overnight. Despite today's huge concentrations, the number of sources of capital multiply.

5. Goods and services are modularized and configured into systems, which require a multiplication and constant revision of standards. This leads to wars for control of the information on which standards are based.

6. Slow-moving bureaucracies are replaced by small (de-massified) work units, temporary or "ad-hocratic" teams, increasingly complex business alliances and consortia. Hierarchy is flattened or eliminated to speed decision-making. The bureaucratic organization of knowledge is replaced by free-flow information systems.

7. The number and variety of organizational units multiply. The more such units, the more transactions among them, and the more information must be generated and communicated.

8. Workers become less and less interchangeable. Industrial workers owned few of the tools of production. Today the most powerful wealth-amplifying tools are the symbols inside workers' heads. Workers, therefore, own a critical, often irreplaceable, share of the "means of production."

9. The new hero is no longer a blue-collar worker, a financier, or a manager, but the innovator (whether inside or outside a large organization) who combines imaginative knowledge with action.

10. Wealth creation is increasingly recognized to be a circular process, with wastes recycled into inputs for the next cycle of production. This method presupposes computerized monitoring and ever-deeper levels of scientific and environmental knowledge.

11. Producer and consumer, divorced by the industrial revolution, are reunited in the cycle of wealth creation, with the customer contributing not just money but market and design information vital for the production process. Buyer and supplier share data, information, and knowledge. Someday, customers may also push buttons that activate remote production processes. Consumer and producer fuse into a "prosumer."

12. The new wealth creation system is both local and global. Powerful microtechnologies make it possible to do locally what previously could be done economically only on a national scale.

Simultaneously, many functions spill over national boundaries, integrating activities in many nations into a single productive effort.

These twelve elements of the accelerative economy are inter-related, and mutually reinforce the role of data, information, and knowledge throughout the economy. They define the revolution-ary new system of high-tech wealth creation. As pieces of this system come together, they undermine power structures designed to support the wealth-making system of the industrial age.

The new system of wealth creation as summarized here helps explain the tremendous upheavals now spreading across the planet—premonitory shudders that herald a collision of wealth creation systems on a scale never before seen.

PART FIVE

POWERSHIFT POLITICS

20

THE DECISIVE DECADES

In Bluefield, West Virginia, on November 9, 1989, a schoolteacher wept. All across the world, millions shared her moment of joy. Glued to their television screens, they saw the Berlin Wall brought down. For an entire generation, East Germans had been imprisoned, maimed, or shot for trying to get past that twenty-eight-mile wall. Now they were pouring through it into West Germany, eyes gleaming, faces registering everything from exhilaration to culture shock. Soon the hammers went to work. And today remnants of the wall that once bisected Berlin, and indeed all of Germany, are souvenirs of stone and cement gathering dust on countless mantelpieces.

Because it concretized, one might say, the end of Soviet-imposed totalitarianism throughout Central and Eastern Europe, the downfall of the wall drew an elated response in the West. Shortsighted intellectuals and politicians joined in an ode to joy that would have done Beethoven proud. With Marxism on the ropes, they chorused, the future of democracy was now assured. We had reached the very end of ideology itself.

Today Eastern Europe seethes with instability. Poland faces total economic breakdown. Romanian crowds clash in the streets. And Yugoslavia's president warns that "extremist right parties" and "revanchist forces" could ignite "civil war and the possibility of foreign armed intevention." Anti-Semitism and ancient ethnic hatreds run rampant. Post-war borders are called into question. The collapse of Soviet power over Eastern Europe, far from assuring democracy, has opened a combustive vacuum into which fools and firebrands seem ready to rush. Western Europe's drive toward integration has been thrown into confusion.

Looming over this vast continental spectacle are threats of

a Soviet split-up that could easily trigger a generation of wars, raising anew nuclear dangers that were supposed to have been relaxed.

Ironically, even as millions who have never had it grope for freedom, the established democracies in North America, Western Europe, and Japan themselves face an expected internal crisis. Democracy is entering its decisive decades. For we are at the end of the age of mass democracy—and that is the only kind the industrial world has ever known.

DYNASTIES AND DEMOCRACIES

In any system, democratic or not, there needs to be some congruence between the way a people make wealth and the way they govern themselves. If the political and economic systems are wildly dissimilar, one will eventually destroy the other.

Only twice before in history have we humans invented a wholly novel way of creating wealth. Each time we invented new forms of government to go with it.

The spread of agriculture wiped out tribal groupings, hunting bands, and other social and political arrangements, replacing them with city-states, dynastic kingdoms, and feudal empires. The industrial revolution, in turn, wiped out many of these. With mass production, mass consumption, and mass media there arose in many countries a counterpart system: "mass democracy."

Mass democracy, however, met bitter resistance. The old forces of feudal agrarianism—the landed gentry, the hierarchical church, and their intellectual and cultural apologists—resisted, co-opted, and battled the rising industrialism and the mass democracy it often brought with it.

Indeed, in all smokestack societies the central political struggle has not been, as many imagine, between left and right. It has been between admirers of First Wave agrarianism and "traditionalism" on the one side and the forces of Second Wave industrialism or "modernism" on the other.

Such power struggles are frequently fought under other banners—nationalism, for example, or religion, or civil rights. They run through family life, gender relations, schools, the professions, the arts, as well as politics. Today that historic conflict, still raging, is being overshadowed by a new one—the struggle of a Third Wave, postmodern civilization against both modernism and traditionalism.

And if it is true that a new knowledge-based economy is superseding smokestack production, then we should expect a historic struggle to remake our political institutions, bringing them into congruence with the revolutionary post-mass-production economy.

All the industrial societies already face convergent crises—crises in all their most basic systems: urban systems, health systems, welfare systems, transport systems, ecological systems. Smokestack politicians continue to respond to these crises one at a time, with variations of the old approaches. But they may be insoluble given existing institutions, designed for the mass society.

In addition, the rising economy hurls totally new problems and crises at us that shatter the conventional assumptions and alliances of the mass democratic era.

SHIFTING LEVELS

The age of mass democracy was also the age of immense concentrations of power at the level of the nation. This concentration reflected the rise of mass-production technology and national markets. Today's short-run technologies change things.

Take a loaf of bread.

Baked goods originally came from local bakeries. But with industrialization, mom-and-pop bakeries were overwhelmed by supermarkets that bought baked goods from giant national companies like Nabisco in the United States. Today, surprisingly, many U.S. supermarkets, in addition to selling the national brands, have begun to bake on their own premises. We are coming full circle— but on the basis of more sophisticated technology.

Photos, once sent to Rochester, New York, to be centrally processed by Kodak, can now be developed and printed on every street corner. Commercial printing, which once required heavy investment and complex machinery, can now be done using small, advanced copying equipment in shops in every neighborhood. New technologies are thus making local production competitive again.

Simultaneously, however, the advanced economy transfers other forms of production to the global level. Cars, computers, and many other products are now no longer made in a single country, but require components and assembly in many nations. These twin changes, one driving production down and the other up, have direct political parallels.

Together they explain why we see pressures for political decentralization in all the high-tech nations, from Japan and the United States, across Europe—along with simultaneous attempts to shift power upward to supra-national agencies.

The most significant of the latter is the European Community's drive to re-centralize power at a higher level by creating a single integrated market, along with a single currency and a single central bank.

But even as the EC steamroller attempts to flatten differences and concentrate political and economic decision-making, various regions are taking advantage of its attack on national power from above to launch a parallel attack from below. "The single European market," says Jean Chemain, head of the economic development agency for the area around Lyon in France, "offers us a great opportunity to break the centralization of Paris." In fact, the entire Rhône-Alpes region, of which Lyon is a part, is hooking up with regions outside France—Catalonia, Lombardy, and Baden-Württemberg—in pursuit of mutual interests.

As the super-symbolic economy spreads, it will create constituencies for radical shifts of power among local, regional, national, and global levels. The "politics of levels" can be expected to split voters into four distinct groupings: "globalists," "nationalists," "regionalists," and "localists." Each will defend its perceived identity (and its economic interests) with ferocity. Each will seek allies.

Each group will attract different financial and industrial supporters, depending on self-interest, but each will also attract talented artists, writers, and intellectuals who will manufacture appropriate ideological rationales for them.

What's more—contrary to conventional opinion—regions and localities, instead of becoming more uniform, are destined to grow more diverse. "You make a serious error if you look at the U.S. as an entity. Different parts of the United States are as different as night and day," says James Crupi, president of the Dallas-based International Leadership Center.

One might not go as far as Crupi, who suggests "The U.S. is

on its way to becoming a nation of city-states." But a close look at statistics for the 1980s already shows widening differences between the two coasts, the Midwest, and the oil patch, and between the big urban centers and the suburbs. Whether measured in housing starts, rates of growth, employment levels, investment, or social conditions, these differences are likely to widen further, rather than narrow, under the impact of a new economy that runs counter to the homogenization of the smokestack era.

As regions and localities take on their own cultural, technological, and political character, it will be harder for governments to manage economies with the traditional tools of central bank regulation, taxation, and financial controls. Raising or lowering interest rates or setting a new tax rate will produce radically different consequences in different parts of the same country.

And as these disparities widen, they may well trigger an explosion of extremist movements demanding regional or local autonomy or actual secession. The bombs are present, waiting to be detonated in all the advanced economies.

In every nation some regions already regard themselves as economically cheated by the central authorities. Promises to reduce regional differences have delivered little, as any resident of Glasgow will tell you. (The renewal of secessionist sentiment in Scotland, according to press reports, has worried the Queen enough for her to express private fears about the breakup of the United Kingdom.) Canada hangs together by a thread.

Apart from economic inequalities, moreover, there are also long-festering linguistic and ethnic cells of secession in places like South Tyrol, Brittany, Alsace, Flanders, Catalonia. A united Western Europe will have to grant increasing regional and local autonomy—or smash all these movements with a steel fist.

In Central Europe, so long as the Hapsburgs ruled, in the 19th and early 20th centuries, hostilities among their German, Italian, Polish, Magyar, Slovak, and Austrian subjects were suppressed (barely) by the central power. Once Hapsburg power disintegrated after World War I, these groups hurled themselves at one another's throats with a vengeance. The collapse of Soviet power in Central Europe has raised age-old ghosts. Already we see a sharp intensification of the conflict over the Hungarian minority in Romania and the Turks in Bulgaria.

Farther south, Yugoslavia could break apart as its Serbs, Albanians, Croats, and other nationalities war with one another.

And all this ignores the gigantic centrifugal forces that threaten to splinter the Soviet Union itself.

The smokestack era was the great age of nation-building, which led to central control over small communities, city-states, regions, and provinces. It was this consolidation that made national capitals the centers of enormous state power. The decline of the smokestack era will set loose bone-deep resentments, vast and violent emotional tides, as the locus of power is transferred. In many parts of the world it will multiply extremist groups for whom democracy is a bothersome obstacle, to be destroyed if it stands in the way of their fanatic passions.

EARTH POLITICS

During the period of mass democracy, people, parties, and policies were typically categorized as either left-wing or right-wing. Issues were usually "domestic" or "foreign." They fit into a neat framework.

The new system of wealth creation makes these political tags, and the coalitions that went with them, obsolete. Ecological catastrophes are neither right-wing nor left-wing, and some are both domestic *and* international.

Many of our most serious environmental problems—from air pollution to toxic waste—are by-products of the old, industrial methods of creating wealth. By contrast, the new system, with its substitution of knowledge for material resources, its dispersal, rather than concentration, of production, its increasing energy efficiency, and its potential for dramatic advances in recycling technologies, holds out the hope of combining ecological sanity with economic advance.

It is unlikely, however, that the next decade or two will pass without new Chernobyls, Bhopals, and Alaska oil spills, legacies of the smokestack era. These, in turn, will lead to bitter conflicts over new technologies and their possible consequences. Social groups inside each country (and, indeed, whole countries) will demand "ecological indemnification" from one another and fight over the allocation of clean-up costs. Others will demand "ecological blackmail" or "ransom" to abstain from actions that could send fallout,

acid rain, weather changes, toxic wastes, or other dangerous products across their neighbors' borders.

Will the advanced economies wind up making "ecological welfare payments" to the Brazils and Indias of the world to deter
them from destroying rain forests, jungles, or other environmental
resources? What about natural disasters in a newly networked
world economy? An earthquake in Tokyo can now send Wall
Street reeling into chaos. Should Wall Street contribute to Tokyo's
earthquake-preparedness programs? Are such issues left-wing or
right-wing? Domestic or foreign?

The attempt to deal politically with such problems will not
only fragment old alliances, but breed more zealots—world savers
for whom environmental requirements (as they define them) supersede the niceties of democracy.

AN EXPLOSION OF ETHNICS

As the super-symbolic economy develops, it is accompanied by
population shifts and migrations. Immigration politics—fiercely
controversial at any time—will be fought against a background
marked by atavistic nationalism and ethnicism, not merely in remote places like Armenia and Azerbaijan, or in Albania and Serbia,
but in New York and Nagoya, Liverpool and Lyon.

In industrial mass societies, racism typically took the form of a
majority persecuting a minority. This form of social pathology is
still a threat to democracy. White street toughs, skinheads, admirers of the Nazis, says Morris Dees of the Southern Poverty Law
Center, "are on their way to becoming . . . domestic terrorists."

But the new system for creating wealth brings with it economic de-massification and much higher levels of social diversity.
Thus, in addition to traditional conflict between majority and minorities, democratic governments must now cope with open warfare *between* rival minority groups, as happened in Miami, for
example, between Cuban and Haitian immigrants, and elsewhere
in the United States between African-Americans and Hispanics. In
Los Angeles, Mexican-Americans fight for jobs held by Cuban-
Americans. In affluent Great Neck, on Long Island, near New
York City, tensions rise between American-born Jews and Iranian

Jewish immigrants who refuse to surrender their old life-ways. African-American rap groups sell anti-Semitic records. Korean shopkeepers and African-Americans collide in the inner cities.

Under the impact of the new production system, resistance to the "melting pot" is rising everywhere. Instead, racial, ethnic, and religious groups demand the right to be—and to remain—proudly different. Assimilation was the ideal of industrial society, corresponding to its need for a homogeneous work force. Diversity is the new ideal, corresponding to the heterogeneity of the new system of wealth creation.

Governments may, in an atmosphere of hostility, have to accommodate certain groups who insist on preserving their cultural identity—everyone from Turks in Germany, or Koreans, Filipinos, and South Sea Islanders in Japan, to North Africans in France. At the same time, governments will also have to mediate among them.

This will become progressively harder to do, because the ideal of homogeneity (in Japan, for example) or of the "melting pot" (in the United States) is being replaced by that of the "salad bowl"—a dish in which diverse ingredients keep their identity.

Los Angeles with its Koreatown, its Vietnamese suburbs, its heavy Chicano population, its roughly seventy-five ethnically oriented publications, not to mention its Jews, African-Americans, Japanese, Chinese, and its large Iranian population, provides an example of the new diversity. But the salad-bowl ideal means that governments will need new legal and social tools they now lack, if they are to referee increasingly complex, potentially violent disputes. The potential for antidemocratic extremism and violence rises even as regions, nations, and supra-national forces battle for power.

MOSAIC DEMOCRACY

Mass democracy implies the existence of "masses." It is based on mass movements, mass political parties, and mass media. But what happens when the mass society begins to de-massify—when movements, parties, and media all splinter? As we move to an economy based on noninterchangeable labor, in what sense can we continue to speak of the "masses"?

If technology permits the customization of products, if markets are being broken into niches, if the media multiply and serve continually narrowing audiences, if even family structure and culture are becoming increasingly heterogeneous, why should politics still presume the existence of homogeneous masses?

All these changes—whether rising localism, resistance to globalization, ecological activism, or heightened ethnic and racial consciousness—reflect the increased social diversity of advanced economies. They point to the end of the mass society.

But with de-massification, people's needs, and therefore their political demands, diversify. Just as market researchers in business are finding more and more differentiated segments and "micro-markets" for products, reflecting the rising variety of life styles, so politicians are bombarded by more and more diverse demands from their constituencies.

While mass movements may fill Tiananmen Square in Beijing or Wenceslas Square in Prague, in the high-technology nations mass movements, while still a factor, increasingly tend to fragment. Mass consensus (on all but a handful of high-priority issues) becomes harder to find.

The initial result, therefore, of the breakup of the mass society is a tremendous jump in the sheer complexity of politics. In terms of winning elections, the great leaders of the industrial era faced a comparatively simple task. In 1932, Franklin D. Roosevelt could assemble a coalition of half a dozen groups—urban workers, poor farmers, the foreign-born, the intellectuals. With it, his Democratic Party was able to command power in Washington for a third of a century.

Today an American presidential candidate must piece together a coalition composed not of four or six major blocs, but of hundreds of groupings, each with its own agenda, each changing constantly, many surviving only a matter of months or weeks. (This, not just the cost of television advertising, helps explain the rising cost of American elections.)

What is emerging, as we'll see, is no longer a mass democracy but a highly charged, fast-moving "mosaic democracy" that corresponds to the rise of mosaics in the economy, and operates according to its own rules. These will force us to redefine even the most fundamental of democratic assumptions.

Mass democracies are designed to respond mainly to mass input—mass movements, mass political parties, mass media. They do not yet know how to cope with mosaics. This leaves them doubly vulnerable to attack by what we might call "pivotal minorities."

PIVOTAL MINORITIES

Scientists exploring turbulence, instability, and chaos in nature and society know that the same system—whether it is a chemical system or a country—behaves differently depending on whether it is in an equilibrial or a non-equilibrial condition. Push any system—a digestive system, a computer system, an urban traffic system, or a political system—too far, and it violates its traditional rules and acts bizarrely.

When the environment becomes too turbulent, systems become non-linear, and this creates vast opportunities for tiny groups. We are, in fact, rapidly moving into a new stage of politics that might be called "opportunity time" for the pivotal minorities.

As politics becomes increasingly de-massified, leaders who once dealt with a few big, more or less predictable political constituencies are seeing these splinter into countless small, temporary, single-issue grouplets, continually forming, breaking, and re-forming alliances—all at high speeds.

Any one of these, finding itself at a strategic political intersection at just the right moment, can leverage its clout. In 1919 a railroad machinist named Anton Drexler headed a tiny political group in Munich—a group so small it was no more than a fringe of the fringe. At its first public meeting it managed to attract only 111 listeners. The speaker at that meeting held the floor for thirty minutes. His name was Adolf Hitler.

There are many explanations for Hitler's rise, but one can be found in the new science of non-equilibrial systems. This new science teaches us that in moments of extreme instability of the kind found in Germany at the time, three things happen. Sheer chance plays an enlarged role. Pressures from the outside world carry more weight. And positive feedback creates gigantic snowball effects.

An example of the snowball effect as it operates in today's world is provided by the media. By focusing a hand-held camera, a reporter can instantly project even the tiniest group of political cranks or terrorists onto the world's consciousness, and give it far more importance than it could garner on its own. Once this happens, the group becomes "news," and other media cover its activities, which, in turn, makes it still bigger news. A "positive feedback loop" is set up.

Snowballing can also come about in other ways. In a globally linked economy, a foreign political or commercial interest can pump money and resources into a tiny group, which suddenly explodes in size and, in turn, attracts more resources.

Chance, outside help, and the snowballing process help explain why—throughout the history of mass democracy—extremist cults, revolutionary cabals, juntas, and conspiracies have flourished in times of seething turmoil, and why a once-insignificant group can suddenly become "pivotal." The difference for mosaic democracies is that, in the past, a majority could sometimes restrain or overwhelm dangerous extremists. But what if there is no coherent majority?

Some pivotal minorities may, of course, be good. But many are toxic to democracy. They vary. The P-2 Masonic lodge in Italy sought to take power in the country. The Jewish Defense League, with support from U.S. citizens, seeks power in Israel. Nazi-esque groups, some of them heavily armed, spew anti-Semitic and racist hate, and dream of taking over Washington. Some of their members have engaged in gun battles with the Federal Bureau of Investigation. An African-American organization in the United States, headed by an admirer of Hitler, saw its ranks swell with the aid of a $5 million interest-free loan from Libya's Qaddafi. Add to this witch's brew the megalomaniac LaRouchite movement with its "intelligence operations," its branches and front groups reaching from the United States to West Germany and Mexico.

In the United States, hate groups will proliferate as social unrest grows in the decade ahead, according to Dr. William Tafoya, the FBI's outstanding expert on the future. These groups will attempt to infiltrate U.S. police agencies to facilitate acts of domestic terrorism. "If I were a racist, what better place to initiate my hidden agenda than behind the shield of a badge?" Tafoya asks.

Citing unemployment, poverty, homelessness, and illiteracy as breeding grounds of social unrest, Tafoya has catalogued the rising frequency of race-related crimes, riots, and beatings and warns that the framework for social justice has become "loose dry straw" waiting for a spark to ignite it.

Nor are domestic social conditions the only ones that matter. Emigré groups, like the Kurds in Sweden or the Sikhs in Canada, carry their political passions and sense of injustice from the "old country" into the new. In the past, emigrants were largely cut off from their original homelands. Today, with instant communication and jet travel, the old culture retains its grip and its political movements live on abroad. Such groups want to seize power, too, not in the host country but in the homeland, creating complex, strained international relations.

Insignificant in normal times, such groups reach a "takeoff" stage when the cultural and social soil is right and when the mainstream political parties are paralyzed or so evenly matched that a tiny coalition partner can tip the power balance.

Healthy democracies should tolerate the widest possible diversity, and there is nothing unusual or particularly frightening about the existence of such grouplets—so long as the political system remains equilibrial. But will it?

We already live in a world of barely contained fanaticisms. Groups seek to impose totalitarian dogma not merely on one nation, but on the entire world. Ayatollahs incite murder, calling for the assassination of Salman Rushdie, a writer whose words offend them. Anti-abortion protesters bomb clinics. Separatist movements leave a trail of car bombs and blood in defense of their national identity. And religio-political terrorists think nothing of hurling a grenade into a café or downing a 747, as if the death of a vacationing secretary or a salesman with his case full of catalogues would somehow win points from God.

Because of an out-of-date conception of progress, many in the West assume that fanatic, irrational, hate-mongering ideologies will vanish from the earth as societies become more "civilized." Nothing, says Professor Yehezkel Dror of Hebrew University in Jerusalem, is more misleadingly smug. An internationally respected policy analyst and futurist, Dror contends that "confessional conflicts, 'holy wars,' committed crusaders and martyrdom-seeking warriors" are not merely relics of the past. They are portents of the future.

His study of "high-intensity aggressive ideologies" analyzes the international threat posed by them. But for the democracies, the threat is domestic as well, for as culture and economics are fused in the new economy, and new emotionally charged issues arise, the dangers of pivotal minorities and global fanaticism escalate in tandem.

The rise of a new kind of economy, never before known, threatening to many, demanding rapid changes in work, life style, and habits, hurls large populations—terrified of the future—into spasms of diehard reaction. It opens cleavages that fanatics rush to fill. It arms all those dangerous minorities who live for crisis in the hopes of catapulting themselves onto the national or global stage and transporting us all into a new Dark Age.

Instead of the much-touted "end of ideology," we may, in both global and domestic affairs, see a multiplicity of new ideologies spring up, each inflaming adherents with its single vision of reality. Instead of President Bush's famous "thousand points of light," we may well face a "thousand fires of fury."

While we are busy celebrating the supposed end of ideology, history, and the Cold War, we may find ourselves facing the end of democracy as we have known it—mass democracy. The advanced economy, based on computers, information, knowledge, and deep communication, calls into question all the traditional defenses of democracy, challenging us to redefine them in 21st-century terms.

To do that, we need a clearer picture of how the system works and how it is already changing.

21

THE INVISIBLE PARTY

Shortly after Ronald Reagan was elected to the American presidency, Lee Atwater, one of his chief aides (later successively George Bush's campaign manager and chairman of the Republican National Committee), met with friends for lunch at the White House. His candor at that table was remarkable.

"You will hear a lot in the coming months about the Reagan Revolution," he said. "The headlines will be full of the tremendous changes Reagan plans to introduce. Don't believe them.

"Reagan does want to make a lot of changes. But the reality is, he won't be able to. Jimmy Carter pushed the 'system' five degrees in one direction. If we here work very hard and are extremely lucky, Reagan may be able to push it five degrees in the opposite direction. That's what the Reagan Revolution is really about."

Despite a media focus on individual politicians, Atwater's remark underlines the degree to which even the most popular and highly placed leader is a captive of the "system." This system, of course, is not capitalism or socialism, but bureaucratism. For bureaucracy is the most prevalent form of power in all smokestack states.

Bureaucrats, not democratically elected officials, essentially run all governments on an everyday basis, and make the overwhelming majority of decisions publicly credited to Presidents and Prime Ministers.

"All Japanese politicians . . ." writes Yoshi Tsurumi, head of the Pacific Basin Center Foundation, "have become totally dependent on the central bureaucrats for drafting and passing bills. They stage Kabuki plays of 'debates' on bills according to scenarios created by the elite bureaucrats of each ministry."

Similar descriptions apply with varying degrees of force to the civil services of France, Britain, West Germany, and the other countries routinely described as democratic. Political leaders regularly bemoan the difficulty they face in getting their bureaucracies to carry out their wishes. The fact is that, no matter how many parties run against one another in elections, and no matter who gets the most votes, a single party always wins. It is the Invisible Party of bureaucracy.

THE MINISTRY OF THE 21ST CENTURY

The revolutionary new economy will transform not only business but government. It will do this by altering the basic relationship between politicians and bureaucrats, and by dramatically restructuring the bureaucracy itself.

It is already causing power to shift *among* the various bureaucracies.

A prime example is the rise of the Japanese Ministry of Posts and Telecommunications (MPT). From 1949 on this ministry had three basic functions. It handled the mail and, like many European postal services, offered customers insurance and savings accounts. (These were originally set up to serve people living in remote rural regions largely ignored by the banks and insurance companies.) In power-conscious Tokyo, the Teishin-sho, as it was called, was regarded as a minor ministry.

Today the renamed MPT is one of the giants, often hailed as the "Ministry of the 21st Century." It achieved this new status after 1985, when—in what must have been a knockdown *nawabari-arasoi,* or turf battle—it won responsibility for the development of the entire Japanese telecommunications industry, from radio and television broadcasting to data communication.

It thus combines in a single agency financial functions (which are increasingly dependent on advanced telecommunications) and the telecommunications functions themselves. No organizational intersection is likely to be more strategic.

Explaining MPT's rise to power, the *Journal of Japanese Trade and Industry* writes:

"A sophisticated information-oriented society in which information circulates smoothly thanks to telecommunications is not complete in itself. When information flows, people, goods and

money also flow. When information about a product is disseminated, as in advertising, people go and buy it. The flow of information is accompanied by 'physical flow' and 'cash flow.' The MPT
alone among the ministries has a direct interest in all three of these
phenomena."

Other governments, of course, divide the functions of their
ministries and departments differently, but it hardly needs a wizard to anticipate that power will flow toward those agencies that
regulate information in the super-symbolic economy and win jurisdiction over expanding functions.

As education and training become central to economic effectiveness, as scientific research and development become more significant, as environmental issues gain importance, agencies with
jurisdiction in those fields will gain clout relative to those that deal
with declining functions.

But these inter-bureaucratic power shifts are only a minor
part of the unfolding story.

THE GLOBAL BUZZWORD

After half a century in which governments continually took on
more tasks, the decades since the start of the super-symbolic economy have seen a truly remarkable development.

In the advanced economies, leaders as different as Republican
Ronald Reagan and Socialist François Mitterand began to systematically strip away governmental operations or functions. They
have been emulated by Carlos Salinas de Gortari in Mexico, Saddam
Hussein in Iraq, by dozens of other leaders around the world, and
most important by reformers throughout Eastern Europe, all of
whom suddenly began calling for key government enterprises to
be denationalized or their tasks contracted out to be performed by
others. *Privatization* became a global buzzword.

This is widely taken to be a sign of the triumph of capitalism
over socialism. But the push toward privatization cannot be simply
written off as a "capitalist" or "reactionary" policy, as it so often is.
Opposition to privatization and similar measures is not "progressive." Whether recognized or not, it is a defense of the unelected
Invisible Party, which holds massive power over people's lives,

irrespective of whether their governments are "liberal" or "conservative," "right-wing" or "left-wing," "communist" or "capitalist."

Moreover, few observers have noticed the hidden parallels between the privatization push in the public sector and today's restructuring of business in the private sector.

We've already seen big firms splitting themselves into small profit centers, flattening their pyramids, and installing free-form information systems that break up bureaucratic cubbyholes and channels.

Few seem to have considered that if we change the structure of business and leave government unchanged, we create a gaping organizational mismatch that could damage both. An advanced economy requires constant interaction between the two. Thus, like a long-married couple, government and business eventually must take on some of each other's characteristics. If one is restructured, we should expect corresponding changes in the other.

STRIPPING FOR ACTION

In 1986, when Allen Murray took over as chairman, the Mobil Corporation was America's third-largest company. Like other oil companies, Mobil had, during the early eighties, launched a major drive to diversify. It bought Montgomery Ward, the giant retail firm, and Container Corporation, the packager.

No sooner did Murray take charge than the axe began to chop. In less than two years he had sold off $4.6 billion in assets, including both Montgomery Ward and Container Corp. "We have gotten back to basics at Mobil," declared Murray. "We're in the businesses we know how to run." Petroleum engineers, it turned out, were not terrific marketers of women's clothing or paperboard boxes.

The same questioning of functions has now begun in government as well. What business calls "divestiture," politicians the world over now call "privatization."

Thus, Japan's government decided it didn't need to be in the railroad business. When it announced plans to sell off the Japan National Railways, the employees struck. In a coordinated campaign of sabotage widely attributed to the Chukaku-ha, or "Middle

Core," radical group, signaling equipment was damaged in twenty-four places in seven regions, and travel in the Tokyo area was paralyzed. Fire broke out in a station. The railway union denounced the sabotage. Some 10 million commuters were inconvenienced. But the plan went through, and the rail lines are now privately owned.

The Japanese government also decided it didn't need to be in the telephone business. This led to the sell-off of Nippon Telephone and Telegraph, Japan's biggest single employer (with some 290,000 jobs). When ownership of NTT was shifted from the public to the private sector, it swiftly became, for a time, one of the world's most highly valued corporations.

Headlines outside Japan tell a similar story: Argentina privatizes thirty companies ... West Germany sells off Volkswagen ... France divests itself of Matra, a defense manufacturer, along with such giant state enterprises as St.-Gobain, Paribas, Compagnie Générale d'Électricité, and even Havas, an advertising agency.

Britain sells shares in British Aerospace and British Telecom. ... Heathrow, Gatwick, and other airports are now run by a privatized BAA (once the government-owned airport authority), and the government-operated bus services are now private. Canada sells stock in Air Canada to the public.

Seen in perspective, the privatizations to date amount to no more than a fleabite on a dinosaur's hide, and even recently privatized firms could be renationalized in the event of a sudden change in political fortunes or a world-scale economic collapse.

Nevertheless, a deep reconceptualization is under way—a first nervous step toward slimming down and restructuring governments in ways that roughly parallel organizational changes in the private economy.

None of this is to say that privatization is the panacea claimed by Margaret Thatcher and free-market purists. It often carries its own long list of shortcomings. Yet, at a time when all governments face a kaleidoscopic, bewildering world environment, privatization helps leaders focus on strategic priorities rather than dissipating the taxpayers' resources on a hodgepodge of distracting sidelines.

Still more significant, it speeds up response times in both the divested and the retained operations. It helps bring government back into sync with the rising pace of life and of business in the symbolic economy.

Privatization, however, is not the only way in which governments are, consciously or not, trying to cope with the new realities.

DISAPPEARANCE OF THE HIERARCHS

We saw earlier that many corporations, from auto makers to airlines, are struggling to cut down on the degree of "vertical integration"—the reliance on their own people, keeping everything in-house, rather than contracting tasks to outside supplier firms.

Many governments, too, are clearly reexamining their "make or buy" decisions and questioning whether they should actually be running laboratories and laundries and performing thousands of other tasks that could be shifted to outside contractors. Governments are moving toward the principle that their task is to assure the delivery of services, not to perform them.

Whether the specific function is, or is not, appropriate for private-sector contractors to perform, the drive toward contracting out is the mirror image of industry's reappraisal of vertical integration.

Again, exactly like businesses, governments are also beginning to bypass their hierarchies—further subverting bureaucratic power. "There are fewer hierarchies in Washington today than in Roosevelt's time," says political scientist Samuel Popkin of the University of California at San Diego. There are "fewer leaders with whom a President can cut a deal and reasonably expect them to be able to enforce it in their agency or committee."

Power has shifted away from the old hierarchs, creating a far more fluid, confusing system, with continually shifting centers of power.

New communications technologies also undermine hierarchies in government by making it possible to bypass them entirely. "When a crisis occurs anywhere in the world," states Samuel Kernell, a colleague of Popkin's at UCSD, "the White House can instantaneously communicate with persons who are on the spot. . . . These instantaneous relays to the President from on-the-spot observers and commanders disrupt the traditional channels of information and the chain of command."

Kernell adds: "Specialists who do not yet have access to the last-minute information cannot address the President's concerns."

However, despite such changes, as complexity grows, change accelerates, and bureaucratic responses lag as more and more problems pile up that bureaucracies cannot handle.

SECRET TEAMS AND PLUMBERS

Under normal circumstances, much of the work of, let us say, Presidents of the United States or Prime Ministers of Japan has been

• to make choices among options (prepared in advance for them by their respective bureaucracies),
• about issues they understand only superficially,
• and then only when the different parts of their bureaucracy are unable to reach agreement.

There are, of course, decisions that only top leaders can take—crash decisions that cannot wait for the bureaucratic mills to grind, turning-point decisions, war and peace decisions, or decisions that require extraordinary secrecy. These are non-programmable, as it were, decisions that come directly from the leader's viscera. But these are comparatively rare when things are running "normally."

When, however, we enter a revolutionary period, and a new wealth system clashes with the power structures built around an old one, "normalcy" is shattered. Each day's headlines report some new unpredicted crisis or breakthrough. Global and domestic affairs alike are destabilized. Events accelerate beyond any reasonable capacity to stay on top of them.

In conditions like these, even the best bureaucracies break down, and serious problems are allowed to fester into crises. The "homeless problem," in the United States, for example, is not a problem of inadequate housing alone, but of several interlinked problems—alcoholism, drug abuse, unemployment, mental illness, high land prices. Each is the concern of a different bureaucracy, none of which can deal effectively with the problem on its own, and none of which wants to cede its budget, authority, or jurisdiction to another. It is not merely the people who are homeless, but the problem.

Drug abuse, too, requires integrated action by many bureaucracies simultaneously: police, health authorities, the schools, the foreign ministry, banking, transportation, and more. But getting all these to act effectively in concert is almost impossible.

Today's high-speed technological and social changes generate precisely this kind of "cross-cutting" problem. More and more of them wind up in limbo, and more turf wars break out to consume government resources and delay action.

In this environment, political leaders have the opportunity to seize power from their own bureaucrats. Conversely, as they see problems escalating into crises, political leaders are often tempted to take extreme measures, setting up all kinds of task forces, "czars," "plumber's groups," and "secret teams" to get things done.

Driven by frustration, some political leaders come to despise their bickering civil servants, and rely ever more heavily on intimates, on secrecy, informal orders, and arrangements that end-run and actually subvert the bureaucracy.

This is, of course, exactly what the Reagan White House did so disastrously in the Irangate case, when it set up its own secret "enterprise" to sell arms to Iran and pipe the profits to the contra forces in Nicaragua, even at the risk of violating the law.

Less dramatically, when George Bush asked the State Department and the Pentagon to prepare proposals for him to present to NATO, in mid-1989, the usual hordes of mid- and senior-level bureaucrats put on their green eyeshades and masticated the ends of their pencils. But what ultimately came up the line from them were a series of warmed-over, trivial proposals.

Bush was under political pressure, at home and abroad, to come up with something more dramatic—something that would steal the thunder from the latest proposals made by Soviet leader Gorbachev. To get it, he threw away the bureaucratic script, called in Cabinet members and a handful of senior aides, and drew up a plan to withdraw some U.S. troops from Europe. It won instant approval from the allies and the American public.

Similarly, West German Chancellor Helmut Kohl simply ignored his foreign ministry when he first outlined his list of ten conditions for uniting the two Germanys.

Whenever a leader end-runs the bureaucracy in this way, dire warnings that disaster looms rise from its ranks. This is often followed by leaks to the press designed to undermine the new policy.

Nevertheless, in times of rapid change, requiring instant or imaginative responses, cutting ministries or departments out of the loop comes to be seen as the only way to get anything done, which accounts for the proliferation of *ad hoc* and informal units that increasingly honeycomb governments, competing with and sapping the formal bureaucracy.

All this, when combined with privatization and the looming redistribution of power to local, regional, and supra-national levels, points to basic changes in the size and shape of government tomorrow. It suggests that, as we move deeper into the super-symbolic economy, mounting pressures will force governments, like corporations before them, into a process of painful restructure.

This organizational agony will come even as politicians attempt to cope with a wildly unstable world system, plus all the dangers outlined in the previous chapter, from unprecedented environmental crises to explosive ethnic hatreds and multiplying fanaticisms.

What we can expect to see, therefore, is sharpened struggle between politicians and bureaucrats for control of the system as we make the perilous passage from a mass to a mosaic democracy.

22

INFO-TACTICS

Today we live in the age of instant media, a bombardment of contending images, symbols, and "facts." Yet the more data, information, and knowledge are used in governing as we penetrate deeper into the "information society," the more difficult it may become for anyone—political leaders included—to know what is really going on.

Much has been written about how TV and the press distort our image of reality through conscious bias, censorship, and even in inadvertent ways. Intelligent citizens question the political objectivity of both print and electronic media. Yet there is a deeper level of distortion that has been little studied, analyzed, or understood.

In the coming political crises that face the high-tech democracies, all sides—politicians and bureaucrats, as well as the military, the corporate lobbies, and the swelling tide of citizens groups—will use "info-tactics." These are power plays and ploys based on the manipulation of information—for the most part before it ever gets to the media.

With knowledge in all its forms becoming more central to power, with data, information, and knowledge piling up and pouring out of our computers, info-tactics will become ever more significant in political life.

Before we can understand the sophisticated techniques that will shape political power in the future, we need to look at the methods used by today's most successful power players. These "classic" techniques are not taught in any school. Shrewd players of the political power game know them intuitively. The rules have not been formalized or set down systematically.

Until this is done, talk about "open government," an "informed citizenry," or "the public's right to know" remains rhetorical. For these info-tactics call into question some of our most basic democratic assumptions.

ALFALFA SECRETS AND GUIDED LEAKS

On July 4, 1967, in the White House, President Lyndon Johnson signed a measure called the Freedom of Information Act. At the signing ceremony he declared, "Freedom of information is so vital that only the national security, not the desire of public officials or private citizens, should determine when it must be restricted."

No sooner had Johnson spoken than a reporter asked if he could obtain a copy of the original draft of these remarks. It was the first request made in the full radiant flush of the new freedoms guaranteed by the act.

Johnson turned him down cold.

The "Secrecy Tactic" is the first, probably oldest, and most pervasive info-tactic. Today the U.S. government classifies as secret some 20 million documents a year. Most of these pertain either to military and diplomatic affairs—or to matters that might embarrass officialdom. But if that seems undemocratic and even hypocritical, most other countries are far more secretive, defining everything from alfalfa yields to population statistics as state secrets. Some governments are positively paranoid. Virtually everything they do is secret unless specifically declared otherwise.

Secrecy is one of the familiar tools of repressive power and corruption. But it also has its virtues. In a world filled with bizarre generalissimos, narco-politicians, and killer-theologians, secrets are necessary to protect military security. Moreover, secrecy makes it possible for officials to say things they would not dare utter in front of a TV camera—including things that need saying. They can criticize their bosses' policies without embarrassing them publicly. They can compromise with adversaries. Knowing how and when to use a secret is a cardinal skill of the politician and bureaucrat.

Secrets give rise to the second most common info-tactic, another classic tool of power: the "Guided Leak Tactic."

Some secrets are kept; others leak. When the leak is inadvertent it is merely an ineffectually kept secret. Such leaks drive officials into deep dementia. "Why," one CIA official is supposed to have asked, "do we have to send the China estimate to U.S. military commands overseas just because that's where the action is? That's where the leaking is, too." In short, better to keep information secret than to send it to those who need it.

By contrast, "guided leaks" are informational missiles, consciously launched and precision-targeted.

In Japan targeted leaks have produced spectacular effects. The Recruit-Cosmos financial scandal, which led to the ouster of Prime Minister Noboru Takeshita in 1989, offered a field day for leakers mainlining inside information from the office of the chief prosecutor, Yusuke Yoshinaga, to the daily press. "Without these press leaks," says Takashi Kakuma, author of books on corruption in Japan, "I'm sure their investigation would have been stopped. . . ."

Reporters received carefully timed spurts of information, which were moves in an exquisite power ballet. By releasing details to the press, the prosecutors prevented higher-ups in the Ministry of Justice from emasculating the investigation and protecting the upper reaches of the Takeshita government and the Liberal Democratic Party. Without these guided leaks, the government might have survived.

In France, too, leaks have historically played a major political role. Recounting France's difficulties in disentangling from the Indochina War, a White House document states: "Leak and counter leak was [sic] an accepted domestic political tactic. . . . Even highly classified reports or orders pertaining to the war were often published verbatim in the pages of political journals."

So prevalent are leaks in London that, according to Geoffrey Pattie, a minister of state for trade and industry, they have created a pall of suspicion inimical to innovation. Officials hesitate to voice a new idea, he charges, for fear it will be leaked instantly and its author made to look ridiculous before the idea has had a chance to be considered.

"But unless someone thinks," said Pattie, "which sooner rather than later entails thinking aloud, no new thinking will be done and no old thinking will be brought up to date."

In Washington, where guided leaks from a still unidentified source called Deep Throat forced Richard Nixon to resign the presidency, and where guided leaks are still a daily phenomenon, leak-phobia is rampant. Says Dave Gergen, a former director of communications in the White House:

"Fifteen years ago presidential aides felt free to write candid memos and have serious, far-reaching disagreements with each other—and the President. Watergate put a stop to that. One quickly learned never to write anything on paper that you would be unhappy to see on page one of *The Washington Post.* . . . Never say anything controversial in a conversation where more than one other person was present."

The ironic consequence, he pointed out, is that "when the really inconsequential issues come along, an army of bureaucrats moves in to consider it [*sic*]. But the more important the issue, the fewer the numbers involved—almost solely because of the fear of leaks."

Of course, the same officials who excoriate leakers are themselves very often the best source of guided leaks. While serving in the White House as national security adviser, Henry Kissinger once wanted the telephones of his staffers wiretapped to find out whether they were leaking embarrassing information to the press and Congress. But Kissinger himself was—and remains—a "leakmaster."

Secrets and guided leaks, however, are only the two most familiar info-tactics used in political and bureaucratic war. They may not be the most important.

THE MASKED SOURCE

Any data, information, or knowledge that is communicated requires (1) a source or sender; (2) a set of channels or media through which the message flows; (3) a receiver; and of course (4) a message. Power players intervene at each of these points.

Take the Sender.

When a letter arrives in the mail, the first thing we usually want to know is who sent it. The identity of the Sender is, in fact, a crucial part of any message. Among other things, it helps us decide how much credence to give the message.

This is why the "Masked Source Tactic" is so frequently used. An ostensibly nonpartisan citizens group that sends out millions of fund-raising letters may actually be financed and controlled covertly by a political party. A political action committee with a fine-sounding name may be run by the lobbyist for a rapacious industry. A patriotic-sounding organization may be controlled by a foreign country. Both the KGB and the CIA covertly channel funds into publications, labor unions, and other institutions in targeted countries and help set up friendly organizations. The "Masked Source Tactic" is the basis for front groups of all political stripes.

But masking the message-sender can take many forms, in many different settings, from business boardrooms to prison cells.

An imprisoned murderer once described how she could bring power to bear on a jail guard who was harassing her. She could, she said, write a letter of complaint to the prison warden. However, if the guard found out, life would be made even more miserable for her. She could also, she said, go over the warden's head and write to a politician complaining of brutal treatment, and pleading with him to put pressure on the warden to call off his guard. But this was even more risky.

"Fortunately," she observed in a memorable phrase, "prisons are filled with idealists. And so," she said, "I could get another inmate to write to the politician for me," thus concealing the real source of the message.

Officials throughout business and government play variations of this game. When an underling "pulls rank," using a superior's name (often without authorization) to gain an advantage, he or she is using the Masked Source Tactic.

A classic twist on the Masked Source Tactic influenced U.S. policy during the Vietnam War. It was used in 1963, when a report prepared by Robert McNamara and General Maxwell Taylor advised the President and the nation that "it should be possible to withdraw the bulk of U.S. personnel" by the end of 1965.

This forecast was bolstered by data supposedly originating in Saigon. What readers of the report were not told is that much of what was datelined Saigon had been prepared in Washington, then transmitted to Saigon so it could be sent back to Washington looking as though the data actually came from the field. The source was disguised to lend the data greater authenticity.

A special class of Masked Source messages are outright forgeries.

Seldom used in everyday bureaucratic warfare, it is well known in international affairs where strange forgeries have on occasion changed history—like the Zimmermann Telegram that helped propel the United States into World War I.

In 1986 the U.S. State Department publicly exposed as forged a document that described a "confidential" meeting at the Pentagon. It quoted then Secretary of Defense Caspar Weinberger as saying that SDI, the Strategic Defense Initiative, would "give the United States . . . the ability to threaten the Soviet Union with a knockout blow." If true, the quotation would have bolstered Soviet arguments against the SDI program.

But the document was a fake circulated in West Germany (presumably by the Soviets) as part of the public campaign drumming up sentiment against SDI. Another forged document about SDI turned up in the Nigerian press.

More recently an anti-Japanese forgery turned up in Washington when Congressman Tom McMillen rose in the House of Representatives to read what he called an "internal, high-level Japanese government memo."

Ostensibly addressed to the Prime Minister from his "Special Assistant for Policy Coordination," the memo called for Japanese investments in the United States to be planted in congressional districts where they could be used to influence U.S. politics.

Nothing could have been better calculated to intensify Japan-bashing in the United States. But rather than a Japanese government document, it turned out to be an embarrassing fiction traced to Ronald A. Morse, an official of the Asian program of the Woodrow Wilson Center for Scholars. Morse said he had written it merely to illustrate, in a dramatic way, what he believed to be current Japanese attitudes. He claimed he had told its recipients the document was bogus.

BACK-STABBERS AND BACK-CHANNELS

All messages move through channels. But some channels are more equal than others.

All executives know that the "routing slip" which determines who gets to see a memo is a tool of power. Keeping someone "out of the loop" is a way of clipping his or her wings. Sometimes the person kept out of the loop is the person on top.

When John H. Kelly was the U.S. ambassador in Beirut, he sent messages direct to the White House National Security Council, using the facilities of the CIA, rather than through the normal

State Department chain of command. This meant he was end-running his own boss, Secretary of State George P. Shultz.

Kelly, while in Washington, also met numerous times with Oliver North and other NSC officials in connection with their plan to trade arms to Iran in return for hostages—a plan Shultz had advised against.

Shultz was so furious when he learned about the Beirut incident that he blasted Kelly publicly, and formally prohibited State Department personnel from communicating outside departmental channels without express instructions from either himself or from the President. It is unlikely, however, that any such order will ever wipe out the practice. Back-channels are too useful to power-shifters.

On hearing of this case, Congressman Lee Hamilton, chairman of the House Intelligence Committee, blurted, "I don't think I have ever heard of that happening before—totally bypassing an American Secretary of State."

Irritation may have fogged his memory. A precisely parallel case of back-channeling took place when the American ambassador to Pakistan communicated secretly with the White House National Security Council, again bypassing a Secretary of State. In this earlier case, the back channel was set up by Henry Kissinger, then serving as head of the NSC. Kissinger used it in arranging President Nixon's secret mission to China, which resulted in restoring relations between the two countries.

Kissinger was an enthusiastic back-channeler, eager to keep information out of the official bureaucratic system and in his own hands. Claiming he had the President's approval, he once invited William J. Porter, the U.S. ambassador to South Korea, to communicate directly with him without going through Porter's boss, William Rogers, then Secretary of State.

Porter's diary notes his reaction: "Here's the Nixon-Kissinger secret diplomatic service shaping up, secret codes and all. . . . If the President agreed to create a super-net of ambassadors under his security adviser without the knowledge of the Secretary of State something new was happening in American history. . . . I concluded that I was just a country boy and I'd keep my head down."

When the SALT treaty was being negotiated with the Soviets, the American team in Geneva was headed by Gerard C. Smith. But Kissinger and the Pentagon's Joint Chiefs of Staff set up a private channel so that certain staff people could communicate with them directly without Smith's knowledge.

Kissinger also maintained a back-channel to Moscow, again bypassing the State Department, sending messages to the Politburo through Anatoli Dobrynin, rather than through the appropriate State Department specialists or their counterparts in the Soviet Foreign Ministry. Only a few people in Moscow—in the Politburo, the secretariat, and the Soviet diplomatic corps—were ever aware that messages were being passed back and forth this way.

The most celebrated—and perhaps most fateful—use of the Back-Channel Tactic helped prevent World War III.

This occurred during the Cuban missile standoff. Formal messages ricocheted back and forth between President Kennedy and Soviet leader Khrushchev while the world held its breath. Russian missiles in Cuba were pointed at American soil. Kennedy ordered a naval blockade. It was at that moment of high tension that Khrushchev sent Aleksandr Fomin, his KGB chief in Washington, to call on an American newsman, John Scali, whom Fomin had earlier met.

On the fourth day of the crisis, with danger escalating by the moment, Fomin asked Scali whether he thought the United States would agree not to invade Cuba if the Soviets pulled out their missiles and bombers. That message, relayed by the journalist to the White House, proved to be a key turning point in the crisis.

THE DOUBLE-CHANNEL PLOY

But even such uses of the Back-Channel Tactic are simple by comparison with the more sophisticated method that might be called the Double-Channel Tactic—the sending of alternative or contradictory messages through two different channels to test reactions or to sow confusion and conflict among the recipients.

Twice during negotiations over the antiballistic missile system, Kissinger and Soviet Foreign Minister Alexei Gromyko each relied on a back-channel to bypass their own normal chain of command. During these talks, in May 1971 and April 1972, Kissinger had reason to suspect that the Russians were using the Double-Channel Tactic against him.

Years later Arkady Shevchenko, a former Gromyko assistant, defected to the United States and wrote in his autobiography that

Kissinger's suspicion had been unwarranted. It was not a deliberate ploy but confusion, arising because one of the Soviets had been "operating on outdated instructions from Moscow, knowing no better." Whether or not this is correct is irrelevant here. What is clear is that Back- and Double-Channeling are much-used techniques to shift power.

ON THE RECEIVING END

There is also a dazzling variety of games played at the receiving end of the communication process.

The most familiar of these is the Access Tactic—meaning the attempt to control access to one's superior, and thereby to control the information he or she receives. Top executives and lowly secretaries alike know this game well. Access conflicts are so common they hardly merit further comment.

Then there is the Need-to-Know Tactic, much favored by intelligence agencies, terrorists, and underground political movements, by means of which data, information, and knowledge are compartmentalized and carefully kept away from all but specified receivers with a validated "need to know."

The exact converse of this is the Need-Not-to-Know Tactic. A former Cabinet Secretary in the White House explains it this way:

"Should I, as a White House official, know something? Does knowing it mean I have to take action? Can the person telling me then go to someone else and say, 'I've already discussed this with the White House'? That could put me in a pissing contest between two other players I don't know anything about and have nothing to do with. . . . There was a lot I didn't *want* to know about."

The Need-Not-to-Know Tactic is also used by subordinates to protect a superior, leaving the leader in a position to claim ignorance if things go sour. During the Irangate investigation a joke that went the rounds in Washington made the point.

QUESTION: How many White House aides does it take to screw in a light bulb?
ANSWER: None. They like to keep Reagan in the dark.

By the same token, there is also a Forced-to-Know Tactic,

more popularly known as the CYA, or "cover your ass," memo. Here the power player makes sure that another player has been notified of something, so that if things fall apart, the recipient can share the blame.

Variations are numerous, but for every game played with sources, channels, and receivers, there is a multitude of ploys and stratagems directed at the message itself.

MASSAGING THE MESSAGE

Infinite varieties of deception (and self-deception) are found in the masses of data, information, and knowledge that flow through the government's mind-work mill every day. Space constraints make it impossible to continue illustrating and classifying them here. Instead, we will list just a few more in abbreviated form.

• THE OMISSION TACTIC. Because politics is so intensely adversarial, political messages are even more consciously selective than most. Typically, they have gaping holes where someone applied the Omission Tactic and ripped relevant or balancing facts out of them.
• THE GENERALITY TACTIC. Here details that might lead to bureaucratic or political opposition are glossed over with airy abstraction. Diplomatic communiqués are rife with examples—which accounts for their frequently brain-numbing style.
• TIMING TACTICS. Here the most common approach is to delay sending a message until it is too late for the receiver to do anything about it. Thick budget documents are dumped in the laps of legislators who are supposed to respond to them in a few days—well before they can intelligently digest and analyze them. White House speechwriters are known to deliver their drafts of a presidential speech at the latest possible moment, allowing other staffers minimum time to monkey with the text.
• THE DRIBBLE TACTIC. Here, data, information, and knowledge are doled out in tiny takes at different times, rather than compiled into a single document. In this way the pattern of events is broken up and made less visible to the receiver.

• THE TIDAL WAVE TACTIC. When someone complains about being kept uninformed, the shrewd player ships him or her so much paper that the recipient is drowned and cannot find the essential facts in all the froth.

• THE VAPOR TACTIC. Here a host of vaporous rumors are released, along with some true facts, so that receivers cannot distinguish the latter from the former.

• THE BLOW-BACK TACTIC. Here a false story is planted overseas so that it will be picked up and reprinted by the domestic press. This tactic is employed by intelligence and propaganda agencies. But sometimes the blow-back is inadvertent—or seems to be.

The CIA once planted a story in the Italian press about the terrorist Red Brigade. This account was picked up and incorporated in a book published in the United States, the galley proofs of which were read by then-Secretary of State Al Haig. When Haig commented on the story in a press conference, his remarks were then, in turn, incorporated in the finished version of the book. This self-referential process is more common than imagined.

• THE BIG LIE TACTIC. Made famous by Hitler's propaganda minister, Josef Goebbels, it is based on the idea that if a lie is macro enough it will be believed more readily than any number of mere micro-lies. In this category was the 1987 report spread by Moscow claiming that the world AIDS epidemic was launched by the CIA in the course of experiments with biological warfare agents in Maryland. Widely disseminated around the world, the story is utterly repudiated by Soviet scientists.

• THE REVERSAL TACTIC. Few examples of tampering with, or massaging, the facts require as much chutzpah as the Reversal Tactic. This simply turns a given message inside out. An example occurred not long ago in Israel, where no love was lost between Prime Minister Yitzhak Shamir and Foreign Minister Shimon Peres. At one point Shamir instructed the Foreign Ministry to notify its embassies around the world that Peres had no authority to promote an international conference aimed at resolving the Arab-Israeli problem.

Peres's staff at the Foreign Ministry received the Prime Minister's message, but simply scrapped it and sent out cables saying the exact opposite. When a senior official was later asked how that could happen, he replied: "How can you ask me such a question? This is a war."

IN-FIGHTERS AND SAVVY STAFFERS

Given this lengthy list of techniques widely used for doctoring the messages that flow through government offices, it becomes apparent that few statements, messages, or "facts" in political or governmental life can be taken at face value. Almost nothing is power-neutral. Most data, information, and knowledge circulating in government are so politically processed that even if we ask, *Cui bono?*—whose interest is served?—and even if we think we've got the answer, we may still not be able to cut through the "spin" to the reality beneath it.

And all this occurs before the media further reprocesses reality to fit its own requirements. Media massage merely further denatures the "facts."

The implications of what we have just seen go to the crux of the relationship between democracy and knowledge. An informed public is held to be a precondition for democracy. But what do we mean by "informed"?

Restricting government secrecy and gaining public access to documents are necessary in any democracy. But these are only feeble first steps. For to understand those documents we need to know how they have been doctored along the way as they passed from hand to hand, level to level, and agency to agency in the bureaucratic bowels of government.

The full "content" of any message does not appear on the page or the computer screen. In fact, the most important political content of the document may be the history of its processing.

At a still deeper level, the ubiquity of these most commonly exploited info-tactics casts doubt on any lingering notion that governing is a "rational" activity or that leaders are capable of "objectively based" decision.

Winston Churchill was right when he refused to read "sifted and digested" intelligence analyses, insisting instead on seeing the "authentic documents . . . in their original form," so he could draw his own conclusions. But it is obviously impossible for any decision-maker to read all the raw data, all the information, and grapple with all the knowledge needed for decision.

What we have seen here are just a few of the tricks of the trade exploited by streetwise political in-fighters and savvy staffers in world capitals from Seoul to Stockholm or Bonn to Beijing.

Smart politicians and bureaucrats know in their bellies that data, information, and knowledge are adversarial weapons—loaded and ready to be fired—in the power struggles that constitute political life.

What most of them do *not* yet know, however, is that all these Machiavellian ploys and devices must now be regarded as kindergarten stuff. For the struggle for power changes when knowledge *about* knowledge becomes the prime source of power.

As we see next, we are about to enter the era of "meta-tactics" in the mind-work mills we call government, moving the entire power game to an even higher level.

23

META-TACTICS

An unnoticed "first" in politics was marked in 1989. That was the year John Sununu moved into the White House as its chief of staff, making him in all likelihood the world's most highly placed "computernik." In a world bristling with microchips, he was the first computer-literate person ever to occupy one of the pinnacles of political power.

A mechanical engineer by training, Sununu had done doctoral work at the Massachusetts Institute of Technology and was known as a whiz who could spot and correct programming errors and question the mathematical model underlying an environmental impact statement. Whatever one may think of his political views, Sununu undeniably understood the power-potential of computerized information.

Before arriving in Washington, Sununu had served as governor of New Hampshire. When Sununu installed an electronic fiscal and financial control system for the state, members of the legislature demanded access to the data stored in the IBM mainframe. Sununu sidetracked their proposals, declaring, "They'll get what we think they need."

According to *Time* magazine, Sununu "seemed to be trying to shift the balance of political power" by "holding the state's computerized financial data close to his chest."

In the end, the governor was forced to give one legislative official a password providing access to some (but not all) of the disputed data. Similarly, though a state court had held that citizens had a right to see and copy public documents, Sununu insisted that this did not apply to computerized data. Sununu, as governor, fully understood the power of knowledge about knowledge.

ESKIMOS AND MIND-WORKERS

Sununu's action in New Hampshire was hardly subtle. Stamping something *confidential* or withholding access is an age-old tactic. New, more potent tools—many of them computer-based—are now available to those who wish to control data, information, and knowledge.

In fact, we are witnessing a shift to a higher—and less visible—level of power struggle that reflects the rising level of abstraction and complexity in society generally as the super-symbolic economy spreads.

Take, for example, computers. We now use computers to build computers. We are also developing CASE—computer-assisted software engineering. This is based on what might be termed "meta-software"—software designed to produce software. One can imagine a future in which CASE is used to produce the meta-software, itself, in a kind of infinite regress, as the process moves to higher and higher levels of abstraction.

Similarly, in the early 1980s, "spreadsheet software" spread rapidly through the business world. These computer programs permitted hundreds of thousands of users to put numbers into columns and rows, as in a ledger book, and to manipulate them easily. Because they could automatically show how a change in one number or variable would affect all the others, they accustomed a whole generation of users to think in terms of "what if" scenarios. What would happen if we raised the price of a product by 2 percent? What if interest rates fell by half a point? What if we could get the new product to market a month sooner? But spreadsheets, like traditional ledgers, were two-dimensional, flat as a chessboard.

In 1989, Lotus Development Corporation, the main spreadsheet supplier, introduced its 1-2-3 Release 3.0. This program can be used to create three-dimensional spreadsheets—the accounting equivalent of moving chess pieces up and down as well as backward and forward on the conventional board. It permits users to simulate change in a business or a process in far more complex and revealing ways. It leads users to ask much smarter what-if questions at a much higher level.

The new system of wealth creation requires a symbol-drenched work force. Constant exposure to the data deluge—to media, computers, paperwork, fax machines, telephones, movies, posters, advertisements, memos, bills, invoices, and a thousand other symbolic stimuli, with millions spending their time attending meetings, presenting ideas, persuading, negotiating, and otherwise exchanging images—makes for an increasingly "info-savvy" population.

Just as Eskimos develop high sensitivity to differences in the properties of snow, and farmers can almost intuitively sense weather and soil changes, mind-workers become attuned to this informational environment.

This rising sophistication compels those in power to seek new, higher-level instruments of persuasion and/or social control.

Satellites, videocassettes, narrow-casting, niche-identification, cluster-targeting, extra-intelligent networks, instant polling, simulation, mathematical modeling, and other such technologies are becoming a taken-for-granted part of the political environment in the affluent nations. And along with these come new ways of manipulating computerized information that make all the conventional info-tactics of the politician or bureaucrat look crude and klutzy by comparison.

Along with changes in the general population, therefore, fed by the shift to the new wealth-creation system, comes a parallel upgrading of the tools of manipulation used by politicians and government officialdom to hold on to their power. That is what meta-tactics are all about.

TRUTH VERSUS POWER

To grasp what is meant here by "meta-tactics," think for a moment about business. Naïve investors look at a company's "bottom line" to assess its soundness and profitability. But, as *Fortune* magazine put it, "profits, like sausages . . . are esteemed most by those who know least about what goes into them." Sophisticated investors, therefore, study not merely the bottom line but what lies behind it—the so-called "quality of earnings."

They look at the numbers that make up the numbers; at the assumptions that underlie them; and even at the accounting and computer models that manipulate them. This is analysis at a higher level. It is, we might say, an example of simple meta-analysis.

When GM can legally add nearly $2 billion to its (ostensible) profits in one year by changing the length of time over which it depreciates its plants, altering the way it reports on its pension plan, monkeying with the value assigned to its inventories, and changing the supposed worth of the cars it leases, think of what governments or their agencies can do with their accounting.

Governments, of course, have been "cooking their books" at least since the invention of double-entry ledgers by the Venetians in the 14th century. They have been "cooking" all sorts of data, information, and knowledge, not just budgetary or financial, since Day One. What's new is the ability to fry, broil, or microwave the stuff with the help of computers.

Computers do good things. They vastly increase the know-how potentially available to decision-makers. They improve the efficiency of many services. They help integrate complex processes.

The computer revolution makes it possible to model—and therefore better understand—various social problems, from unemployment to rising health costs and environmental threats, in ways never before possible. We can apply multiple models to the same phenomenon. We can examine the interplay of many more factors. We can create data bases on an unprecedented scale, and analyze the data in extremely sophisticated ways.

Wherever the new system of wealth creation takes root, governments cannot run without computers any more than businesses can. Nor should we want them to. Governments were less, not more, democratic before the arrival of computers and other advanced information technologies.

But politics is about power, not truth. Decisions are not based on "objective" findings or profound understanding, but on the conflict of forces, each pursuing its perceived self-interest. Computers cannot eliminate this necessary (and useful) parry, thrust, and cut of power struggle. They raise it, instead, to a higher level.

Political leaders and senior bureaucrats themselves underestimate how dependent they have become on computers—and how vulnerable, therefore, to those who know how to manipulate them for power purposes. The reason for this is that most governmental computer processing typically occurs at the lowest rather than highest levels of the mind-work hierarchy. We don't see Presidents or party chiefs punching keyboards or gazing at screens. Yet the people on top make scarcely a decision, from the choice of a warplane to the determination of tax policy, that does not rest on "facts" that have at some point been manipulated by specialists using computers.

Whether it has to do with hospital beds, import controls, or meat inspection, by the time any problem or policy comes up for a vote or a decision, it has been described (and counter-described) in terms that are quantified, aggregated, abstracted, and pre-formatted for the computer.

And at every point in this process, from the creation of a data base to the way information in it is classified, to the software used to analyze it, the information is open to manipulation so subtle and frequently invisible it makes such standard political info-tactics as secrecy or leaks look crude by comparison.

When we add the distortions produced by meta-tactics to all those deliberately introduced by officials and politicians who play the conventional "info-games" described in the last chapter, we can reach only one conclusion:

Political knowledge reaches the decision-maker only after passing through a maze of distorting mirrors. Tomorrow the mirrors themselves will reflect still other mirrors.

THE KIDNAPPED FINGER

A rapidly accumulating international literature tells lurid stories about computer crime—about bank swindles, espionage, viruses sent from one computer to destroy the contents of others. Movies like *WarGames* have dramatized the dangers from unauthorized entry to the computer and communication systems that control nuclear weapons. According to a published report in France, the Mafia has kidnapped an IBM executive and cut off his finger because it needed his fingerprint to breach a computer security system.

The U.S. Department of Justice has defined a dozen different methods used in computer-based criminal activity. They range from switching or altering data as they enter the computer, to putting self-concealing instructions into the software, to tapping the computers. Widely publicized cases of "computer viruses" have illustrated the potential for sabotage of military and political communications and computation.

But relatively little thought has been given so far to the ways in which similar techniques might alter political life.

One day in 1986, Jennifer Kuiper, a staff aide of Congressman Ed Zschau, saw her computer screen go blank. When she got her machine up and running again, two hundred letters had disappeared. Four days later hundreds of letters and addresses disappeared from the computer of Congressman John McCain. Capitol Hill police, claiming to have eliminated the likelihood of staff error, launched a criminal investigation.

According to Zschau, himself the founder of a computer software firm before entering politics, "Every office on Capitol Hill can be broken into in this way. . . . It can bring the work that a member of Congress does to a complete halt."

Writing in the *Information Executive,* specialist J. A. Tujo pointed out that, with 250,000 word processors used in the offices of American lawyers, it "becomes feasible for a lawyer's unscrupulous opposing counsel to glean compromising information by illegal access" to his or her computer—and that this can be accomplished with cheap electronic equipment purchasable in the corner Radio Shack.

Politicians and officials, however, may be even more vulnerable. Thousands of computers, many of them linked in networks, are now found in congressional offices, the homes of elected officials and lobbyists, as well as on the desk tops of hundreds of thousands of civil servants who regulate everything from soybean quotas to air travel safety standards. Unauthorized and secret entry could cause endless troubles and shift power in unexpected ways.

Computers also increasingly populate election campaign headquarters. Thus new, virtually undetectable games can be played in the ballot box itself.

CHERNOBYL IN THE BALLOT BOX

In Seoul, South Korea, in December 1987, after sixteen years of military rule, a general election took place. The results of this bitterly fought three-way contest were ultimately accepted and the country got on with its business. But in the immediate aftermath, political observers noted certain peculiarities in the balloting.

The winner's percentage of margin, established in the earliest returns, remained strangely unchanged throughout the night and across regions. A highly popular opposition candidate cast doubt on the size of his own victory in Kwangju Province, saying he couldn't believe that he had actually garnered 94 percent of the votes. At best, he claimed, he should have won a maximum of 80 percent. The suspicion grew that someone was tampering not with the ballot boxes, but with the computers that compiled the results.

This suspicion was never confirmed, so far as we know, but Maggie Ford, the *Financial Times* correspondent in Seoul, citing a Washington political analyst, pointed out that "it would be extremely easy to draw up a computer model of an acceptable decision result. This could be adjusted for people's perceptions of voter choice, regional, class, and age background, and events during the campaign. Such a model could design the size of a majority."

Such a model could also, presumably, be used to tailor the results so subtly in key districts as to provide a victory without leaving an overt trail. This is possible if a sophisticated programmer, gaining access to the right password, instructs the computer to credit some percentage of the votes of one candidate to another and then to spring a "trapdoor"—which, in effect, erases any record of what has been done.

The Election Watch project of the Urban Policy Research Institute, basing itself in part on work done by two Princeton University computer scientists, Jon R. Edwards and Howard Jay Strauss, concludes that "the advent of computerized vote counting over the past two decades has created the potential for election fraud and error on a scale previously unimagined."

Many current election officials disagree, but Election Watch gains support from Willis H. Ware, a senior researcher at the Rand Corporation. Ware puts it even more dramatically: The vulnerability of electronic voting systems is such that "there is probably a Chernobyl or a TMI [Three Mile Island] waiting to happen in some election, just as a Richter-8 earthquake is waiting to happen in California."

Give these admittedly speculative scenarios a further twist. Imagine what might be done if the computer were "fixed" by technicians, programmers, or systems integrators working for a multinational corporation that wants a particular senator, say, driven from office. Or imagine that the electronic ballot box is under the indirect, secret control not of a party or corporation but of a foreign power. An election could be swung by adding or subtracting a tiny—unnoticed—number of votes from each precinct. No one might ever know.

Caveat candidate!

GIMME A NUMBER!

The vulnerability isn't just inside the computers, or at election times, but in the way computer-generated data, information, and knowledge are used and misused.

Smart politicians and officials, of course, do what smart people in general have always done when presented with new information. They demand to know more about its sources and the reliability of the data behind it; they ask how samples were drawn in polls and what the response rates were; they note whether there are inconsistencies or gaps; they question statistics that are too "pat"; they evaluate the logic, and so forth.

Smarter power players also take into account the channels through which the information arrived and intuitively review in their minds the various interests who might have "massaged" the information in transit.

The smartest people—a minority of a tiny minority—do all the above, but also question assumptions and even the deeper assumptions on which the more superficial assumptions are based.

Finally, imaginative people—perhaps the fewest of all—question the entire frame of reference.

Government officials are found in all four categories. However, in all the high-tech countries they are so harried, so pressured, that they typically lack the time and attention span, if not the brains, to think past the surface "facts" on which they are pressed to make decisions. Worse yet, all bureaucracies discourage out-of-frame thinking and the examination of root premises. Power-players take advantage of this fact.

When David Stockman, who headed the U.S. Office of Management and Budget, proposed budget cuts to the President and White House staff, he carefully chose the reductions from programs accounting for only 12 percent of the total budget. In discussing these cuts with his higher-ups, he never provided context.

Telling tales out of school, he later wrote:

"What they didn't realize—because I never made it clear—was that we were working in only a small corner of the total budget. . . . We hadn't even looked at three giant programs that accounted for over *half* of the domestic budget: Social Security, veterans' benefits, and Medicare. Those three alone cost $250 billion per year. The programs we had cut saved $25 billion. The President and White House staff were seeing the tip of the budget iceberg; they weren't finding out about the huge mass which lurked below the waterline. . . .

"No one raised any questions about what *wasn't* being reviewed."

Were they willfully ignorant, too much in a hurry to ask, or blinded by Stockman, a master of statistical legerdemain? Or were they just "snowed" by all the computer-generated numbers?

A political speech is barely worth making these days unless it is stuffed with computer-derived statistics. Yet most decision-makers seldom question the numbers that have been crunched for them.

Thus Sidney Jones, a former Under Secretary of Commerce, once proposed setting up a Council of Statistical Advisers to serve the President. Presumably they would have been able to tell the President how the notorious "body count" statistics during the Vietnam War were being massaged. Or why the CIA and the Pentagon couldn't agree on how powerful Soviet nuclear tests were, and therefore on whether or not the U.S.S.R. was violating the Threshold Test Ban Treaty of 1975. Or why the Commerce Department figures on gross national output were wildly exaggerated at one time, then corrected down to show the economy in a near-recession.

The reasons in every case were highly technical—but they were also, inevitably, political. Even the most objective-seeming numbers have been hammered into shape by the push and pull of political power struggle.

The U.S. Census Bureau takes more pains than most agencies

to make public its definitions and statistical procedures so that users can form their own judgments about the validity of its figures. Its top experts readily admit, however, that such reservations and footnotes are routinely ignored in Washington.

According to one Census staffer: "The politicians and the press don't care. All they say is 'Gimme a number!' "

There are two reasons for this. One is mere naïveté. Despite all we have learned in the past generation about the spurious quality of much seemingly hard computer data, according to the Census official responsible for automatic data processing and planning, "Computer output is still regarded as Gospel."

But there is a deeper reason. For political tacticians are not in search of scholarly "truth" or even simple accuracy. They are looking for ammunition to use in the info-wars. Data, information, and knowledge do not have to be "accurate" or "true" to blast an opponent out of the water.

DATA BASE DECEPTION

Governments rely increasingly on computer-stored data bases. While Sununu's withholding of access to data is an example of ordinary info-tactics at work, subtle tampering with the data base is an example of meta-tactics.

Meta-tacticians attack the data base not by controlling access to it, but by determining what may or may not be included in it in the first place.

The ten-year census questionnaire used in the United States must be approved by Congress. Says a senior Census official: "Congress puts various pressures on us. We do a sample survey on farm finance. We've been directed by Congress *not* to collect that data because it might have been used to cut federal support for farmers." Companies in every industry also pressure the Census Bureau to ask, or to avoid asking, certain questions. For example, it has been asked to include a question about mobile homes in its housing survey to supply data needed by a company in that business. Since the number of questions that can be included in the questionnaire is always limited, lobbyists fight one another and apply fierce pressure on the Bureau.

No matter how computerized and seemingly "objective," data bases thus reflect the values and power relationships of society.

Controlling what goes into today's endlessly multiplying data bases is, however, only the simplest of meta-tactics. Far more subtle are attempts to control the way data are broken into categories or classes.

Well before the computer era, at a time when the U.S. government was concerned about overconcentration in the auto industry, General Motors employed a lobbyist who sat in a little-known body, the Federal Statistics Users Council. His job was to assure that figures for the industry were lumped together so they could never be publicly disaggregated—thus, the degree of economic concentration might be given in terms of how large a share of the industry was controlled by the "top three" companies, but never by the top company alone—General Motors.

Today, advanced systems are used to index, classify, and categorize the data flowing into computer data bases. With the help of computers the same data can be "cut" or recategorized many different ways. Thus, intense political battles are waged over more and more obscure, abstract, seemingly technical questions.

Many power struggles take place over the indicators used in data bases and the relative importance assigned to them. If you want to know how many angels can dance on the tip of a warhead, do you count their haloes or their harps? Hospital beds, which are easily counted, are sometimes presumed to be an indicator of the level of health services in a community. But would the number of doctors per thousand residents be a better measure? And what do either of these reveal about the actual health of local residents? The number of beds may reflect government subsidy programs that reward or penalize hospitals based on bed-count, rather than on the provision of real services to the community.

To get a true picture of the population's health needs, should one count patients? Cures? Life expectancy? Infant mortality? The choice of an indicator or group of indicators will heavily affect the output.

Meta-tacticians know the WYMIWYG Principle—What You Measure Is What You Get.

Panels of experts, teams of government specialists, lobbyists, and others wrestle frequently with such questions. While some participants are not clever enough to ask deep-probing questions or to understand the hidden significance, others can and do. In so doing, they typically fight for their own commercial or departmental interests. While couched in highly technical jargon, the conflicts are often, in fact, strongly political.

Most of this skirmishing takes place out of sight of the public, and well below the level of senior officials and Cabinet members, who rarely have the time or inclination to understand the hidden issues in any case. Lacking these and the training needed to cut through the barrage of facts and pseudo-facts themselves, decision-makers are forced to rely more on technical specialists.

The monitoring of more variables, plus the enormous jump in data processing capacity made possible by computers, changes the problem facing political decision-makers from information under-load to information overload.

This overload also means that interpretation becomes more important than simple collection. Data (of varying quality) are plentiful. Understanding is rare. But shifting the emphasis to interpretation means more processing at higher levels in the mind-work hierarchy. This alters power relationships among the experts themselves. It also shifts the info-tacticians' playing field to a much higher, meta-level.

A perfect example has to do with the latest satellite observation systems used to monitor U.S.-Soviet arms control agreements. Recently launched satellites deliver such a deluge of data—from their locations in space they can detect objects as small as a few inches—that interpreters drown in the flood. Says Thomas Rona, deputy director of the White House Science Office, "In the past the problems have been mostly connected with sensing the data. Now, they are more in filtering and interpreting it."

The sheer volume, reports *Science* magazine, threatens "to overwhelm even armies of analysts," leading to pressures to auto-mate the interpretation function.

This, in turn, encourages a reliance on artificial intelligence and other "knowledge engineering" tools. But their use raises the level of abstraction still further, and buries the critical assumptions of the system under still heavier layers of inference.

In business, according to *Datamation* magazine, "corporations are looking to embed the inferencing capabilities" of expert systems into their existing computer systems. Some 2,200 such expert systems are already operating in North America, doing everything from diagnosing factory tools that malfunction to analyzing chemical spills and evaluating applications for life insurance. Expert systems are spreading in government, too, where they have even been used by the FBI to help investigate serial murders.

What this implies is a dependence on complex rules elicited from experts of various kinds, weighted, systematized, and installed in computers to support the making of decisions. We can expect the spread of similar technologies throughout government—including in political life itself, where decisions often have to be taken on the basis of a mass of complex, imprecise, cross-related, ambiguous facts, ideas, images, and proposals, and just plain deceits intended to produce power shifts.

What these tools mean, however, is that the logic driving decisions is further "embedded" and, so to speak, invisibilized. Paradoxically, the very system that delivers clarifying information itself becomes more opaque to most of its end-users.

This is no reason to avoid artificial intelligence and expert systems. But it points to a deep process with important ramifications for democracy.

Politics were no purer in some earlier Golden Age. From China's Lord Shang to the Borgias of Italy, those in power have always manipulated the truth to serve their needs. What is changing dramatically today is the level at which these mind-games are played.

The world will face staggering new problems in the decades ahead—dangers of global ecological catastrophe, the breakup of longstanding military balances, economic upheavals, technological revolutions. Every one of these requires intelligent political action based on a clear apprehension of the threats and potentials.

But how accurate are the images of reality on which governments base their survival decisions? How accurate can they be when all the data and information on which they are based are vulnerable to repeated and invisible "meta-massage"?

PHANTOM PEOPLE

In the spring of 1989, when Dr. James T. Hansen, chief of NASA's Goddard Institute for Space Studies, prepared to testify before the U.S. Congress on the "greenhouse effect"—the overheating of the global climate—he submitted his text for clearance to the White House Office of Management and Budget. Hansen firmly believed that the time had come for the U.S. government to take significant action to prevent drought and other severe effects of climatic warming.

When he got his text back, however, he discovered that the OMB had added a paragraph throwing doubt on the scientific evidence about planetary warming, and considerably softening his position. He protested, lost the internal battle, and then made his personal views public through the press.

Behind this collision between the administration and one of the government's top scientists lay a little-noticed bureaucratic battle. The U.S. State Department and the Environmental Protection Agency both wanted the United States to take the international lead in combating the greenhouse problem. By contrast, the OMB and the Department of Energy backed a go-slow approach.

When Hansen took his protest to the media, Senator Al Gore, one of the few technologically sophisticated members of the U.S. Congress, demanded that the OMB "testify about the basis for their conclusions. I want to determine . . . the climatic models they have used."

This reference to "models" is a sure tip-off that the struggle would be waged at the meta-tactical level. For more and more government programs and policies are shaped by the assumptions and sub-assumptions buried inside complex computer models.

Thus while Gore in the Senate was questioning the models relied on by the go-slow camp, Sununu in the White House was challenging the reliability of the models that provided ammunition for the other side. Wrote *Insight* magazine: "He is on top of the scientific literature and thinks the computer models predicting significant warming are too primitive to form a reliable basis for action."

Today, whether dealing with the economy, health costs, strategic arms, budget deficits, toxic waste, or tax policy, behind almost every major political issue we find teams of modelers and counter-modelers supplying the raw materials for this kind of political controversy.

A systematic model can help us visualize complex phenomena. It consists of a list of variables, each of which is assigned a weight based on its presumed significance. Computers make it possible to build models with much larger numbers of variables than the unaided intellect alone. They also help us to study what happens when the variables are given different weights or are interrelated in alternative ways.

But no matter how "hard" the final output may appear, all models are ultimately, and inescapably, based on "soft" assumptions. Moreover, decisions about how much importance to assign to any given variable, or its weighting, are frequently "soft," intuitive or arbitrary.

As a result, political in-fighters, skilled at meta-tactics, battle fiercely over weights, variables, and the way they are linked. Despite the political pressures that tilt and bias the outcome, the results of such conflicts normally come packaged in impressive, seemingly neutral and value-free computer printout.

Models are used in developing and choosing policies, in evaluating program effectiveness, and in asking "what if . . ." questions. However, as we learn from *Data Wars,* a recent study of government modeling, they can also be used to "obscure an issue or to lend credence to a previously made policy position . . . to delay decision-making; to give symbolic rather than real attention to a decision; to confuse or obfuscate decision-making," and so on.

The authors conclude: "Model use occurs as much for political and ideological need as for technical [substantive decision] need." This, they note, is necessarily so because "computer models influence 'who gets what.' "

A study by the U.S. Congressional Research Service, for example, pointed out that government cuts in social programs during the 1980s threw at least 557,000 Americans into poverty. The number provided ammunition to politicians who opposed such cuts. But this figure was not based on counting the poor. Instead, like an increasing number of other statistics, it was a result of politically contentious premises built into a model that attempted to show what might have happened had the budget cuts not taken place.

Just how rarefied meta-tactics become as computer data spreads in government is illustrated by the controversy that broke out over missing people and what the Census Bureau technicians call "hot deck imputation."

In November 1988 the cities of New York, Houston, Chicago, and Los Angeles filed a lawsuit against the U.S. Bureau of the Census to force a change in the way it counts. They were joined by civil rights groups, the Conference of Mayors, and other organizations.

In any census, some groups are undercounted. Poor, transient, and homeless groups are harder to count. Undocumented aliens may not wish to be counted. Others escape the information net for other reasons. Whatever its reason, undercounting can have potent political consequences.

Because Washington sends billions of tax dollars back to the cities and states, cities can be deprived of federal funds to which they might otherwise be entitled. Since seats in the House of Representatives are apportioned on the basis of population, states with large uncounted populations may be cheated of full representation. This, in turn, can cost them many other benefits. Inadequate information can thus shift power.

To compensate for undercounting, the Census Bureau's computers, on finding a house for which information is lacking, are now programmed to assume that the unaccounted-for people have characteristics similar to people who live nearby. The computers then fill in the missing data, as though it had been provided by the missing people.

The result is that millions of persons, presumed to exist, are really a phantom population whose characteristics we are guessing at. Hot deck imputing may be a better way of compensating for the unknown than previously used statistical methods, but, as with all such techniques, its assumptions are open to challenge. On the strength of these assumptions—informed as they might be—voters in Indiana lost one member in Congress whose seat was reassigned to Florida instead. "Hot deck imputation" shifted political power.

In sum, therefore, a new stage of political conflict is developing—a battle over the assumptions that lie behind assumptions that lie behind still other assumptions, often embedded in complex computer software. It is a conflict over meta-questions. It reflects the rise of the super-symbolic economy. This new economy could not run for a second without human contact, imagination, intuition, care, compassion, psychological sensitivity, and other qualities we still identify with people rather than machines. But it also requires ever more complex and abstract knowledge, based on vast avalanches of data and information—all of which is subject to increasingly refined political manipulation.

What this look at info-tactics, and especially the new meta-tactics, teaches us is that laws that set limits on governmental secrecy only touch the outermost skin of democracy's knowledge problem. The new economy, by its very nature, requires a free exchange of ideas, innovative theories, and a questioning of authority. And yet . . .

Despite glasnost, despite "freedom of information" legislation, despite leaks and the difficulty today's governments face in keeping things secret—despite all these and more—the actual operations of those who hold power may well be growing more, not less, opaque.

That is the "meta-secret" of power.

24

A MARKET FOR SPIES

One of America's funniest humorists, Art Buchwald, once imagined a meeting of spies in the Café Mozart in East Berlin, including George Smiley, John le Carré's famous fictional character. "Does anyone know who'd like to buy the plans for the Warsaw Pact defense of the northern corridor?" Buchwald has Smiley ask.

"Forget it, Smiley," comes the reply. "There's no market for defense secrets anymore. The Cold War is over and Moscow is giving away Warsaw Pact plans, not buying them."

The Buchwald column was amusing, as usual. But the loudest laugh must have come from the world's real, as distinct from fictional, spies. For among the boom businesses of the decades ahead, espionage will be one of the biggest. Spies are not only here to stay, we are about to see their entire industry revolutionized.

As the entire society shifts toward a new system of wealth creation based on knowledge, informational functions of governments mushroom, and certain types of stolen knowledge, secret knowledge, are worth more, not less, to those who need them.

In turn, this will challenge all conventional ideas about democracy and information. For even if we leave aside covert action and domestic surveillance, and focus instead on the "pure" work of the spy—the collection and interpretation of foreign intelligence—we find a system emerging that goes beyond anything we have previously known as espionage.

Just how far beyond becomes clear when we glance briefly backward.

BUTTERFLIES AND BOMBS

Spies have been busily at work at least since the Egyptian *Book of the Dead* termed espionage a soul-endangering sin. But from the Pharaohs to the end of World War II the technologies available for espionage remained primitive, and early spies, like early scientists, were largely untrained amateurs.

In the first years of the 20th century, Robert Baden-Powell, later the founder of the Boy Scout movement, masqueraded as a dotty butterfly collector when he hiked through the Balkans, sketching fortifications and hiding their outlines in drawings of complicated butterfly wings. (Baden-Powell insisted that enthusiastic amateurs, who regarded spying as sport, would do the best work.)

Another self-taught spy was the Japanese Captain Giichi Tanaka. After serving on the staff of the Japanese military attaché in Moscow, learning to speak Russian and claiming adherence to the Russian Orthodox church, Tanaka took a leisurely two-month trip back to Tokyo so he could reconnoiter the Trans-Siberian and Chinese Eastern railroads, bringing back with him intelligence used by Tokyo in planning for the Russo-Japanese war of 1905. Much spy literature today still focuses on the derring-do of intrepid individuals pursuing military secrets.

The industrial revolution, however, transformed war. The conscripted mass army, the mechanization of transport, the machine gun, mass-produced tanks and airplanes, and the concept of total war were all products of the Second Wave or smokestack era. The potential for mass destruction grew, right along with the rise of mass production, reaching its final point of no return in the U.S.-Soviet nuclear stalemate.

The industrialization of intelligence followed that of war. In the early 20th century, spying became more systematic and bureaucratic, with the Tsar's fearsome Okhrana, forerunner of the KGB, leading the way. Espionage schools were set up. Spies began to be trained as professionals.

But a handful of even well-trained spies could no longer satisfy the growing market for intelligence. Thus, just as individual craft took a back seat to assembly-line production in the factory, attempts were made to mass-manufacture intelligence.

By early in the 20th century, the Japanese were no longer relying exclusively on a handful of full-timers like Tanaka but on thousands of foot-soldier spies, as it were—emigrants settled in China or Siberia, cooks, servants, and factory workers who reported on their host countries. Japanese intelligence, following the factory production model, used unskilled "espionage workers" to mass-produce information, then built a growing bureaucracy to process the "take."

After the 1917 revolution in Russia, Lenin promoted the idea of "rabcors" or "people's journalists"—thousands of ordinary workers were encouraged to write to the newspapers denouncing supposedly antirevolutionary saboteurs and traitors. The idea of masses of amateur correspondents was applied to foreign intelligence, too, and by 1929 there were three thousand so-called "rabcors" in France, including workers in state arsenals and the defense industries who were told to write to the Communist press to expose their poor working conditions. These contributions, however, provided useful insights into war production, and the most revealing letters were not published, but sent on to Moscow. It was another attempt at mass collection of low-level intelligence by amateurs.

High-level espionage, however, was entrusted to carefully trained professionals. Richard Sorge, born in Baku and raised in Berlin, became one of the most brilliant Soviet agents in history. Because of his German boyhood, Sorge was able to penetrate the Nazi Party and get himself sent to Japan posing as the enthusiastically pro-Hitler correspondent for the *Frankfurter Zeitung*—a cover that won him access to top German and Japanese officials and diplomats in Tokyo.

The Soviets were terrified of a Japanese surprise attack on Siberia. Sorge correctly told them it would never happen, but that the Soviet Union would be attacked by Germany instead. In 1941, Sorge actually sent Moscow advance news of the coming Nazi invasion of the U.S.S.R., warning that 150 German divisions were concentrating in preparation. He even pinpointed the date—22 June 1941. But his information was ignored by Stalin.

Sorge was about to tip off Moscow about the coming Japanese attack on Pearl Harbor—once again naming the exact date—when he was captured and later executed by the Japanese. Sorge was subsequently described by General Douglas MacArthur as "a devastating example of a brilliant success of espionage." Sorge's career surely underscored the continuing value of the courageous and resourceful individual spy and spymaster.

But World War II also saw remarkable breakthroughs in every-

thing from coding and deciphering equipment to reconnaissance aircraft, radio, and radar—technologies that laid the basis for
true mass production of intelligence, some of it high-level stuff
indeed.

THE KREMLIN'S LIMOUSINES

Since then, fantastic technical advances have filled the sky with
eyes and ears automating the collection of mass data. Satellites,
advanced optics, and other imaging equipment constantly monitor
the earth. Acoustical sensors blanket strategic sea lanes. Listening
stations, giant radars, and other electronic devices dot the planet
from Australia to Norway.

Technological intelligence, or "Techint," now includes: Signals
Intelligence, or "Sigint" (which, in turn, embraces communications,
electronics, and telemetry); "Radint" (which sweeps up signals sent
by or to radars); and "Imaging intelligence" (which includes photography, infrared, and other detection tools). All use the biggest
and most advanced computers on earth. So vast, costly, and powerful are these systems that they have shoved intelligence gathered
by humans, or "Humint," into a second-class position.

William E. Burrows, author of a study of space espionage, has
summed up these high-tech systems in the following terms:

"The remote sensing systems with which each side monitors
the other and most of the rest of the world are so many, so
redundant, and so diffuse that no preparation for an all-out attack
could take place without triggering multiple alarms. . . . Orders
for armies to march, planes to fly, and civilians to hide must be
communicated relatively quickly over vast areas, and what is communicated can be intercepted; everything necessary to wage the
war must be moved, and what is moved can be photographed."

The big eavesdroppers in the sky can monitor all military,
diplomatic, and commercial messages sent by phone, telex, radio,
teletype, or other means via satellites or microwave systems. They
have even been able to listen in on Kremlin bigwigs in their
limousines and Chinese scientists at the Lop Nor nuclear weapons
site. (The Chinese subsequently quit using over-the-air communications and installed secure below-ground lines.)

There are serious limits on all this. Despite its vaunted "spy-in-the-sky" capabilities, the United States was red-faced to discover that the Soviets, who were supposed to have destroyed 239 SS-23 missiles, had secretly transferred 24 of them to East Germany. There are other failings too. An increasing number of codes can no longer be cracked because of computer advances in coding. Weather still interferes with some photoreconnaissance. Adversaries can use their own electronic countermeasures to blind or deceive the collection systems. Nevertheless, factory-style mass collection of data has been spectacularly achieved.

Naturally, not all intelligence involves either high technology or trench-coated snoops. A vast amount is derived from "open sources"—careful reading of the press, monitoring of foreign broadcasts, study of officially released statistics, attendance at scientific and commercial conferences—all of which, when added to the secret materials, becomes raw material for the intelligence mill.

To handle all these data, from both human and technical sources, a dizzying bureaucracy has grown up which applies the factory principle of the division of labor, breaking production into a sequence of steps. The process begins with the identification of client needs, the collection of raw material from both open and secret sources, translation, decoding, and other preparation, followed by analysis and its packaging into reports which are then disseminated to clients.

Many corporations today are learning that this form of sequential production is inadequate. As we saw, in the new economy steps are eliminated or made simultaneous. Bureaucratic organization is too slow and cumbersome. Markets change rapidly. Mass production itself is giving way to "flexible production" of more and more customized products. The result for many industries has been a profound crisis.

Not surprisingly, intelligence, too, finds itself at a crisis point. The new collection technologies have been so effective, they now vacuum up so much computerized imagery and listen in on so many phone calls, they deluge intelligence agencies with so much information it can no longer be processed adequately. They now increasingly cause "analysis paralysis."

Finding the right piece of information, analyzing it correctly, and getting it to the right customer in time are turning out to be bigger problems than collecting it in the first place.

Today, therefore, as the world moves toward a new system of

producing wealth, superseding the smokestack system, intelligence operations face a crisis of restructure paralleling that which has overtaken the economy itself.

THE MAIN COMPETITORS

It helps to think of spying as a gigantic business. In fact, it is not inappropriate that the U.S. Central Intelligence Agency is nicknamed The Company.

As in any industry, there are a few giant firms and many smaller ones. In the global espionage industry, U.S. producers are dominant. These include, apart from the CIA, the Pentagon's Defense Intelligence Agency and, above all, the National Security Agency and the National Reconnaissance Office, which together are responsible for most of the "techint" data collection. In addition there are specialized military intelligence units attached to various military commands. Less known are the small intelligence units, frequently staffed by CIA people on loan, in the State Department, the Energy Department, the Treasury, the Commerce Department, and sprinkled throughout the government. Together they form the U.S. "intelligence community."

The Soviets, on their side, rely on part of the KGB (the other part has domestic security functions) to collect foreign intelligence, and on the GRU, which specializes in military and technological espionage. The Soviets, too, possess a vast system of satellites, ground stations, giant radar, reconnaissance aircraft, and other means to monitor international communications and nuclear activities around the world.

The British—famed for excellent analytic skills and for the number of Soviet moles who succeeded in worming their way into their intelligence agencies—depend on their Secret Intelligence Service, known as MI6, and their own NSA counterpart, called Government Communications Headquarters, or GCHQ.

The French CIA is the DGSE, also known as La Piscine or "the swimming pool," and is supplemented by the GCR, or Groupement de Contrôles Radioélectrique. Frequently on the outs with other Western services, it is rising in prestige, despite its Keystone Kops performance in the so-called Greenpeace incident, which led to the sinking of the *Rainbow Warrior,* a ship belonging to anti-nuke protesters.

The highly rated Israeli Mossad, often called "The Institute," and the West German Bundesnachrichtendienst are also important producers, as are the three main Japanese services. The first of these is the Naicho, or Cabinet Research Office, a small organization that reports directly to the Japanese Prime Minister. The Naicho pulls together information from military intelligence; from private organizations and news media like Kyodo News Service and Jiji Press; and from the Chosa Besshitsu, or "Chobetsu," which handles electronic and aerial reconnaissance, focusing mainly on North Korea, China, and the U.S.S.R. (In 1986, eighty-four years after Giichi Tanaka's firsthand look-see at the Trans-Siberian Railroad, the Soviets discovered an odd Japanese container on the railroad. Techint had supplanted Humint.)

In short, virtually every nation has some semblance of an agency for the collection of foreign intelligence. Additionally, certain nongovernmental institutions, from giant oil companies to the Vatican, conduct extensive intelligence operations. In aggregate, these organizations form one of the world's greatest "service" industries.

SWAPPING SECRETS

All these "companies" are part of a massive information marketplace. Part of any industrial economy consists of sales of goods or services, not to "end consumers" but from one business to another. In the same way, spies have long traded with one another.

Edward Gleichen, a British spy at the turn of the 20th century, surveyed Moroccan fortifications, sometimes with the good-natured help of local populations who, he reported, "assisted me in 'shooting' angles and slopes." This intelligence was later handed over to the French, who were busy "pacifying the natives." What the British received in exchange is not recorded, but this kind of truck and barter, as Adam Smith might have termed it, is not only rampant behind the scenes, but growing.

Much like today's global corporations, spy agencies are linked in consortia and alliances. Ever since 1947, a secret pact known as the UKUSA Security Agreement has linked the NSA, the British GCHQ, and their Canadian, Australian, and New Zealand counterparts. Later, the NATO organization joined the pact. (Since 1986, however, New Zealand has been excluded from the intelligence-sharing arrangement because it prohibited nuclear-armed American vessels from entering its ports.) Members of such consortia maintain uneasy links, sharing information and misinformation, accusing one another of leaking secrets or having been penetrated by an adversary, or of holding out some secrets.

The modern world's second great intelligence consortium, from the end of World War II until the 1990s, was, of course, controlled from Moscow and included most of the East European nations plus Cuba and North Vietnam.

One case that illustrates their relationships involved James D. Harper, a retired electrical engineer in California whose wife worked for Systems Control, a U.S. defense contractor. For $250,000, Harper sold a large number of Systems Control documents to Zdzislaw Przychodzien, supposedly an employee of the Polish Ministry of Machine Industry, but actually an agent of the Polish SB, the Sluzba Bezpieczenstwa.

The papers, dealing with U.S. ballistic missile defenses, were quickly shipped to Warsaw, sorted, copied, and then picked up by case officers of the Soviet KGB. The KGB is said to have routinely "tasked" the satellite services with specific assignments.

The Harper story was repeated many times with the agencies of East Germany, Bulgaria, Hungary, and Romania when Eastern Europe was under Soviet domination. While all these countries also pursued their own perceived self-interests, they were so organically linked to the Soviets, they even continued collaborating with the Soviets for a time after the overthrow of their communist governments.

But not everyone was a member of the two big intelligence camps. Nor did members trade only with one another. Many other buyer-seller relationships exist. In many nations when a new regime or different party takes over the government, one of its most important decisions (never discussed publicly) is the choice of an "intelligence vendor" or "wholesaler."

A good example was the case of President Raul Alfonsin, who headed the first democratic government of Argentina after the military junta fell. In 1985 insiders in his civilian government were debating the problem. The main suppliers that Argentina could hook up with were the CIA, the French, the British, or the Israeli Mossad. Under the deal, Argentina's spies would feed its supplier with information about certain countries, in return for a stream of information about countries that Argentinian intelligence could not afford to cover or couldn't penetrate.

The British were out, because of the then still-fresh Falklands/ Malvinas war, which pitted them against the Argentinians. The CIA? It had had relations with the previous regime in Buenos Aires, and anyway it might be best to avoid both the superpowers. The French were a possibility, but while strong in Africa, they were weak on the ground in South America, where, after all, Argentina's main interests lie. "Alas," said one Argentine official, "the problem is that in intelligence matters, one never knows with whom one is dealing."

Similar questions are, no doubt, being debated in all the Eastern European nations that have loosened their ties with Moscow and are even now searching for new spy-partnerships in Western Europe and elsewhere.

Even in the United States, intelligence-sharing practices change with the arrival of a new administration. South Africa, lacking satellites of its own, has received intelligence about neighboring black nations from both the United States and the British. This included information about the African National Congress, the main black opposition movement in South Africa. President Jimmy Carter banned any exchange of U.S. intelligence data with South Africa. The Reagan administration opened the pipeline again.

If the secret history of world intelligence were ever opened, all sorts of odd cross-linkages would turn up. The Australians working in Chile under CIA direction to overthrow the Allende government. The French working with the Portuguese and the Moroccans, for example, or the Romanians with the PLO. The Soviets have collected information about Israeli air and sea operations and have passed it on to Libya. The Israelis supply information to the United States.

Perhaps the most astonishing cross-linkage of all is implied in the 1989 visit of two former top KGB officials—Deputy Director Fiodor Sherbak and Valentin Zvezdenkov, chief of KGB antiterrorist operations—to the United States, where they met with former CIA Director William Colby and current officials to work out an information-sharing agreement with respect to narcotics and terrorism.

Such secret criss-cross arrangements make it possible for one nation to hide behind another and to do things that its own laws might declare illegal or questionable. The GCHQ, for example, maintains a list of Americans whose phone calls interest the NSA. The international swapping of secrets subverts all domestic restrictions on intelligence gathering.

THE LOOMING GIANTS

As the world of intelligence adapts to the emerging super-symbolic economy, this ravenous information market will demand new products, and new giants will arise to dominate it.

Looming in the not-too-distant future is the breakup or terminal enfeeblement of the UKUSA-NATO espionage alliance. As the Soviet Union's former satellites in Eastern Europe rush off, each to make its own separate deal with Western spy agencies, the world "intelligence balance" is further tilted.

In addition, as Japan and Germany take on much larger diplomatic and political (and perhaps military) roles, consonant with their enormous economic strength, they can be expected to beef up their intelligence activities, which in turn will stimulate intelligence and counter-intelligence among their neighbors, trading partners, allies, and adversaries. (We must assume, for example, that German reunification has delivered to Bonn at least some spy networks and "assets" previously run by the East Germans in the United States, France, Britain, or other nations.)

The Japanese and the Germans may themselves form the nuclei of new consortia, to which lesser powers will attach themselves. In any event, it would be surprising if both the Bundesnachrichtendienst and the Chobetsu were not enjoying substantial budget increases (no doubt disguised or hidden in the budgets of other agencies).

These power-shifting changes in the hidden world of intelligence reflect the new "correlation of forces" (to use a favorite Soviet phrase). As the new system of wealth creation intensifies competition among the high-tech nations, it will also shift the priorities of the main spy services. Three specific topics will command top-level attention from spies in the future: economics, technology, and ecology.

WARPLANES AND "WATCH LISTS"

In 1975 a Palestinian consultant to the Iraqi government was given a blunt message. Iraq, in the process of switching its political orientation from the Soviet Union to the West, was in the market for sixty military aircraft, then worth about $300 million. The consultant, Said K. Aburish, tried to negotiate the purchase with a British firm, but the government wouldn't guarantee that spare parts would be available. The Iraqis thus turned to the French, who agreed to sell them F-1 Mirages and to guarantee spare parts. But the Iraqis sensed the French were overcharging them. According to Aburish, he was then called in by the Iraqis and told: "Drop whatever you are doing, and find out what the bastards charged other countries. You have unlimited expenses—use them to bribe, buy or bully anyone."

Ironically, as he tells the story, he ultimately found the information he needed in the files of the Peace Institute in Stockholm, not exactly a friend of warplane merchants. When France's then-Prime Minister Jacques Chirac visited Baghdad shortly thereafter, Saddam Hussein, the Iraqi strongman, shoved a paper in front of him with the prices charged other countries. According to Aburish, Chirac "volunteered, on the spot, a reduction of $1,750,000 in the price of each plane." The planes went on to fly during the Iran-Iraq war that ended in 1988.

This was traditional commercial intelligence activity carried out on behalf of a government. The size of the return—i.e., $1.75 million times 60 planes, or a bit over $100 million—against the modest bribe Aburish claims he paid indicates the immense profit possibilities inherent in economic intelligence gathering. It is frequently a low-risk, high-return operation. But the Aburish case is small potatoes. It is an example of what might be termed "micro-intelligence."

Compare the potential rewards of "macro-intelligence."

When Britain negotiated its entry into the Common Market in 1973, its negotiators were armed with information from the intercepted messages of the other European countries. It is impossible to measure the bargaining edge thus gained, but it would make Iraq's $100 million look like petty cash. That was macro-intelligence.

Today the National Security Agency and the British GCHQ both maintain so-called "watch lists" of companies or organizations they monitor with more than routine interest. These include banks, petroleum companies, and commodity traders whose activities might swing the world price of, say, oil or grain.

The Soviets, too, pay a lot of attention to economic data. Says Raymond Tate, a former official of the National Security Agency, "The Soviet Union has for many years manipulated a lot of commercial markets in the world" by using its intelligence capabilities.

But it is the Japanese, according to Lionel Olmer, a former Under Secretary of Commerce in the United States, who "have the most refined and organized system of economic intelligence in the world through a network of 'operatives'—a word I do not use disparagingly—in their export trade offices. JETRO [the Japanese External Trade Organization] is the main collector. But Japanese trading companies live and die on information, and they are active everywhere, from Africa to Eastern Europe. We do not know how much of the information they collect is shared with government, but we assume almost all of it is."

When Olmer was at Commerce, he says, "We spent a year once trying to prove that the Japanese were secretly manipulating the value of the yen—in the period around 1983. We could find no hard evidence to demonstrate that the government was orchestrating up and down moves in the value of the currency. But we certainly would have liked to know." That is macro-intelligence.

In 1988–89 a major commercial tug-of-war broke out between Japan and the United States over terms for the joint production of the FSX fighter plane. In those negotiations, says Olmer, "It would have been very helpful if our government were better informed as to the Japanese government's true intentions. . . . Was it looking to the FSX project as a springboard to help Japan develop a commercial passenger jet business in competition with our own? All we got were a lot of inconsistencies." Here, too, what was at stake was not the sale of a few planes, but the fate of whole industries.

These are only the opening skirmishes, however, of an economic intelligence war that will grow more systematic, more central to government policy and corporate strategies alike in the decisive decades ahead.

The world's leading intelligence producers are being driven deeper into economic espionage by several converging factors. First, with the breakup of the Cold War, all the major agencies are searching for new missions to justify their budgets. Second, as the new wealth-creation system forces more industries to globalize, more and more companies have overseas interests to nurture or protect. These firms step up the pressure on governments for political backup and economic intelligence that may be beyond the reach of an individual firm. Whether or not public intelligence should be used for private gain, these pressures can only mount as globalization proceeds.

Beyond this, however, is a startling, largely overlooked fact. As companies, in order to operate in the new super-symbolic economy, become ever more dependent on electronics, building extensive, earth-spanning networks, transmitting data across borders, exchanging data directly between their computers and those of other companies, the entire business system becomes more vulnerable to electronic penetration by outfits like the NSA or GCHQ, Chobetsu, and their Soviet counterparts. Immense flows of fine-grained business data, once less accessible, will present a vast, irresistible target for intelligence agencies.

Finally, as the stakes rise in global trade rivalries, intelligence rivalries will heat up in parallel, leading to the intelligence equivalent of the arms race. A breakthrough by one country's spy service will immediately set all the others racing to outdo it, raising the stakes at each move.

Spying, to a greater extent than at any time in the past century, will be pressed into service in support not only of government objectives but of corporate strategy as well, on the assumption that corporate power will necessarily contribute to national power. That's why we must expect more refined monitoring of crops and mining activities in target nations, more eavesdropping on crucial trade negotiations, more stealing of engineering software, more purloined bidding data, and so on. The entire armamentarium of electronic surveillance may be pressed into commercial service, along with armies of trained human operatives determined to answer precisely the kind of questions Olmer found unanswerable during his years in the U.S. Commerce Department.

All this will lead to a boom in cryptography or coding and code-breaking, as companies and individuals seek to protect their secrets from prying eyes and ears. It will also open the door to corruption—the back-door sale of government-acquired data to private parties by agents or former agents. In the absence of enforceable international law, it will also spark bitter international conflicts.

LINE X VERSUS JAMES BOND

Like military force, economic clout is increasingly based on knowledge. High technology is congealed knowledge. As the super-symbolic economy spreads, the value of leading-edge technology soars.

In January 1985 nearly 200,000 tons of Romanian 96-inch carbon steel arrived in North America and went on sale for 40 percent less than comparable Canadian steel. The story of that shipment began thirteen years earlier, when the Romanian dicta-tor Nicolae Ceausescu placed his country's nuclear development program under the aegis of the DIE, his foreign intelligence organization.

According to Ion Pacepa, the former head of the DIE, who later defected to the West, teams of intelligence-trained engineers were provided with false papers and sent abroad to find jobs in the nuclear industry. According to Pacepa, these techno-spies actually landed positions in General Electric, Combustion Engineering, their Canadian counterparts or affiliates, as well as in Siemens, Kraftwerke Union, and AEG in West Germany and Ansaldo Nucleari Impiante in Italy. Soon technical intelligence began barreling into Bucharest.

Knowing that the Canadians were having difficulty selling their CANDU reactor, Ceausescu, through the DIE, hinted that he might buy as many as twenty CANDUs. In fact, on October 27, 1977, the Romanians signed an agreement with the Canadians under which four reactors would be entirely built by Canadians, the remainder with Romanian help. Canada thereupon laid down the welcome mat for Romanian nuclear engineers, many of them DIE agents.

The result, according to Pacepa, was that "the DIE soon ob-tained intelligence covering approximately 75 percent of CANDU-600 technology, a modern security system for nuclear plants, technol-ogy and equipment for producing heavy water, and architectural and construction plans for nuclear plants built in Canada, West Germany, and France."

Better yet, Romania was able to sweet-talk Canada into put-ting up a $1 billion loan, supposedly to be partly used as payments to Canadian firms involved in the project, the remaining Roma-nian costs to be paid to Canada in the form of countertrade or barter.

By March 1982, the entire commercial deal melted down, as it were. But Romania had already pocketed an advance tranche amounting to $320 million. Moreover, Romania also already had most of the technology it needed. All it needed to do now was send Canada goods under terms of the barter deal. Which is why Romanian steel entered Canada and began to undersell the domestic product.

The Romanian scam, combining technological espionage with an economic rip-off, is less unusual than it might appear in a world in which research costs are skyrocketing and the cost of stolen technology is dirt-cheap by comparison.

In fact, according to Count de Marenches, former chief of French intelligence: "In any intelligence service worthy of the name you would easily come across cases where the whole year's budget has been paid for in full by a single operation. Naturally, intelligence does not receive actual payment, but the country's industry profits."

This—not just military considerations—explains why spies swarm around any center of new technology, why the Soviets and others have focused on Silicon Valley, why the Russians even tried to buy three California banks, one of which made loans to many Silicon Valley companies. It is why Japan, too, is a major target today. (According to a former KGB officer stationed there, "Even the special audio equipment used by the KGB residency to monitor radio communications between Japanese National Police surveillance teams was stolen from Japan.")

The entire Romanian system was modeled after the much bigger technology espionage apparatus constructed by the Soviet Union and centered in the so-called Line X of the KGB, its Directorate T, the scientific and technological section.

A 1987 U.S. State Department report based on CIA data charged that one third of all the officials of the Soviet Chamber of Commerce and Industry are, in fact, known or suspected KGB or GRU officers. "Hosting over 200 trade exhibitions and about 100 Western business delegations annually, and inspecting thousands of goods each year give its employees extraordinary access to imported equipment. . . ." The Soviets pay special attention to robots, deep-sea marine technology, and industrial chemicals.

As the lack of hard currency makes it difficult for many nations to afford legal purchases of technology and the know-how in it, they are irresistibly drawn to illegal acquisition. This suggests a coming step-up in technological espionage by the poor countries of Africa, Asia, and South America. If they themselves cannot use the knowledge their engineers or students steal, they can at least sell it. Indeed, one of the frequently ignored aspects of technological espionage is what might be termed the "resale" market.

Furthermore, as knowledge becomes ever more central to economic, military, and political power, techno-espionage causes increasing friction among former allies.

Note the recent charges that French intelligence has intercepted IBM transatlantic communications, passed them to Groupe Bull, and also planted agents in American computer firms.

Witness, too, CoCom.

CoCom is the Paris-based Coordinating Committee on Multilateral Export Controls set up by sixteen nations to prevent the seepage of Western high technology to what was then the Soviet bloc. CoCom, the scene of escalating dissension among its members, now faces possible disintegration. Members increasingly resent its restrictions on trade, and accuse one another of using it to gain commercial advantage.

At the initiative of the Europeans and Japanese, moves are under way to shorten the list of restricted technologies and embargoed countries. But in 1983, when the United States, the main force behind CoCom, proposed that China be struck from the list, a howl arose. According to Professor Takehiko Yamamoto of Shizuoka University, Western European nations, "fearing . . . that the U.S. would take over the Chinese market . . . vehemently opposed this proposal and kept it from ever seeing the light of day."

Japan had recently been embarrassed by the Toshiba affair. This centered on a Toshiba subsidiary's illegal sale to the Soviets of highly sophisticated equipment for grinding submarine propeller blades. Under heavy U.S. pressure, Japan tightened its own domestic export controls to prevent a recurrence. One result, however, was to cut itself off from part of its Chinese market. Thus, Japanese machine tool exports to China plummeted by 65.9 percent in the single year 1987. Japan was furious, therefore, when a Cincinnati Milacron machining center turned up in Shanghai.

This kind of commercial war now threatens to explode CoCom altogether. Moreover, European economic integration means that the export controls of individual European nations are weakened, since goods can flow freely among the twelve EC nations.

The rise of the super-symbolic global economy also brings

with it, as we saw, the creation of transnational or multinational business groups, along with multiple, boundary-crossing commercial alliances and joint ventures. These increase the cross-flows of knowledge, and make it far harder to police.

For all these reasons, technology will join economics as a top-priority target for the world's spies. The spy of the future is less likely to resemble James Bond, whose chief assets were his fists, than the Line X engineer who lives quietly down the block and never does anything more violent than turn a page of a manual or flick on his microcomputer.

THE COMING ECO-WARS

A third growth business for tomorrow's spies is the environment. Environmental problems increasingly cross national boundaries, so that pollution from the Rhine affects Holland as well as Germany, acid rain ignores frontiers, and the deforestation of the Amazon has become a global concern.

Increasing environmental knowledge can help reduce such problems, but it also opens the way to sophisticated manipulation of one country's environment by another's political policy-makers. A crude example was the 1989 announcement by Turkey that it would shut off the flow of Euphrates River water to Iraq and Syria for a month. The shutdown threatened Iraqi agriculture and Syrian electrical supplies. Its purpose, according to the Turks, was to do repair work on the Ataturk Dam. But skeptics insisted there was more to the story.

Across Turkey's southern border in Iraq and Syria are the remote bases of Kurdish separatists belonging to the Marxist Kurdish Workers Party. KPW guerrillas have been slipping across into Turkey. In turn, Turkey has been demanding that Iraq and Syria guard the border and prevent such penetrations. The incursions did not stop, and were followed by the Turkish announcement of a dam shutdown. This, in turn, was followed four days later by a guerrilla raid that left twenty-eight dead in a Turkish village on the Iraqi line. The Turkish press clamored for a reprisal against the guerrilla bases in Syrian-controlled territory.

Whether the water cutoff was or was not intended to prod the

Iraqi and Syrian governments into military action against the guerrillas, it was an event with significant ecological implications, an
opening shot, one might say, in the eco-warfare that will become
more common and far more sophisticated in the decades ahead.
Someday nations may unleash genetically altered insects against
an adversary, or attempt to modify weather.

When that day comes, intelligence will provide ammunition
for the eco-wars.

On a more positive note, however, because of their satellite
remote sensing systems, intelligence agencies may be well placed to
take on the task of verifying compliance with environmental treaties, as they now verify arms control agreements.

Eco-intelligence will be integrated more closely with political
and military planning as both eco-war and eco-treaties become
part of the new global system.

The spread of the new system of wealth creation thus begins
to transform one of the universal functions of the nation-state—
the collection of foreign intelligence. What we have glimpsed so
far, however, are only the most superficial changes. Far deeper
ones lie in store.

THE PRIVATIZATION OF SPYING

We are about to see a fusion of government and private
business intelligence on a scale never before known in the capitalist
economies.

Governments and companies have long had truck with one
another. Some giant firms have long provided "cover" for government agents. For example, the Bechtel Corporation, the San
Francisco–based construction firm that had hundreds of millions of
dollars' worth of contracts in the Middle East, gave nominal jobs to
CIA operatives. In return, Bechtel received commercially valuable
intelligence from the CIA.

At one time U.S. businesses provided cover for some two
hundred intelligence agents posted abroad who pretended to be
executives. The companies were reimbursed for their costs. On the
other hand, while many countries simply "expect" their business
people to cooperate with intelligence and may apply pressure if

they refuse, the United States does not. American business executives, including those who have had contacts with high-level foreign politicians, are seldom debriefed.

The line between public and private espionage will continue to blur. As multinational corporations proliferate, many grow their own private intelligence networks—"para-CIAs," as it were. This is as true for European oil companies or banks and for Japanese trading houses as it is for American construction firms. Contact between some of these para-CIAs and the intelligence units of their own or their host countries must be assumed.

Paralleling "para-intelligence" operations abroad is the recent spread of so-called "competitive intelligence" units in domestic industry, described in Chapter 14. While designed to operate within the law, these apply, at least on a rudimentary level, many of the same methods and skills used by government intelligence operations. The possibilities for informal links with government increase as these business firms hire former spies and analysts from the ranks of government.

Such incestuous relationships will multiply as a consequence of the restructuring of world business now taking place, which is leading to complex cross-national business alliances. The company entering into a "strategic alliance" with another firm may never know that some of its partner's operations are actually espionage activities run for the benefit of some government. Or it may want to know—and demand that its own government's spies find out.

Inevitably, such changes will drag many formerly "private" business activities into the public purview, politicizing them, and firing off a succession of charges, countercharges, upheavals, and explosive scandals.

Another change that parallels recent developments in business will be a shift of emphasis from mass production to customization of intelligence. Government policy-makers are demanding more and more targeted, particularized, and precise information. This requires either customized collection of information or, at a minimum, customized analysis.

To meet this demand—especially in the fields of economics, technology, and environment—requires pinpointed tactical information about so vast a variety of matters that not even the largest intelligence producers, like the CIA, will be able to recruit, maintain, and pay for all the necessary specialists. Intelligence agencies will therefore do what companies are doing: They will contract

more work out, breaking up the vertical integration characteristic
of mass-production operations.

Espionage agencies have always done some contracting out.
The CIA and French intelligence have both hired gangsters and
Mafiosi to carry out unpleasant tasks for them. Intelligence agencies have often set up pseudo-businesses—like the famous "Foreign Excellent Trench Coat Company," used as a cover by the Red
Orchestra spy network during its work against the Nazis in World
War II, or the CIA's "proprietary" airlines used during the Vietnam War. But spies will soon be forced to rely on independent
outside suppliers and consultants to a greater extent than ever.

The basis for this "out-sourcing" is already being laid by the
proliferation of private research boutiques specializing in everything from political risk analysis to technical information searches.
Business Environment Risk Information, a Long Beach, California, firm, has made whopping mistakes on occasion, but it is also
credited with having told its business subscribers in December
1980 that Egyptian president Anwar Sadat would be assassinated.
He was, ten months later. It also correctly forecast Iraq's invasion
of Iran nine months ahead of time. As long ago as 1985, even
before the boom in such shops, there were scores of these
info-boutiques.

Many employ former senior officials or intelligence agents.
The most prominent is Kissinger Associates, which at one time or
another has employed Brent Scowcroft, national security adviser to
President Bush; Lawrence Eagleburger, the number two man in
the State Department; William Simon, a former Secretary of the
Treasury; and, of course, Henry Kissinger himself, a former national security adviser and once Secretary of State. Officials with
intelligence connections move in and out of such firms—among
them William F. Colby, former director of the CIA, who set up
his own shop in Washington after leaving the agency. Said
Colby: "The assessment business is a lot like the intelligence
business."

Private intelligence enterprises can provide "deniability" to the
governments that hire them; they can attract the best professionals
at free-market, rather than civil service, wages; they can also perform the niche tasks for which large, bureaucratic spy shops are
inherently ill-fitted.

What we may well see, therefore, is a far closer fusion or
interpenetration of business and government intelligence-seeking.

THE NEW MEANING OF "PRIVATE EYE"

However, by far the most dramatic evidence of what might be called the growing "privatization" of intelligence is occurring not on earth but in space. Five nations—the United States, France, Japan, India, and even the Soviet Union—now peddle data collected by their space satellites.

The process began in 1972, when NASA launched the first Landsat for civilian use. There are now two—Landsats 4 and 5—with a third scheduled to be launched soon. Orbiting at 438 miles above the earth's surface, the Landsats send down data that are routinely used in mineral exploration, crop forecasting, forestry operations, and similar tasks.

Landsat images are also automatically down-linked to some fifteen countries, each of which, for a fee of $600,000 per year, gets a steady stream of digitized images. Some of these have military significance. Thus, the U.S. Department of Defense is itself a purchaser of Landsat data. Landsat is also used by the Japanese military to keep an eye on Eastern Siberia. In 1984 an American scientist, Dr. John Miller at the University of Alaska, using Landsat photos, was able to detect what appeared to be Soviet tests designed to show if nuclear missiles could be launched by submarines operating under the Arctic ice.

On February 21, 1986, the French launched the SPOT satellite and went into competition with Landsat. Since then scholars, scientists, and the public have been able to study military and industrial operations anywhere on earth. The American and Soviet monopoly of space-based intelligence was cracked wide open.

While SPOT and Landsat imaging is not as good as that available to the military, it is plenty good enough. Thus, governments lacking satellites of their own are a market for SPOT's commercially available military intelligence.

More to the point, customers can now buy images and data tapes from several suppliers, then merge and manipulate the data on computers, and come up with inferential information that goes far beyond that which might be available from a single source.

Indeed, there is a thriving industry that does little but process data from one or more of these satellites. These range from the Environmental Research Institute of Michigan, to the Saudi Center for Remote Sensing in Riyadh, and the Instituto de Pesquisas

Espaçiais in São Paulo. A company in Atlanta named ERDAS, Inc., in turn, writes software for these "value added" image enhancers—two hundred of them in the world.

Perhaps the best example of the de-monopolization of intelligence data is the work of the Stockholm-based Space Media Network, which buys data from both SPOT and Landsat, crunches it through computers, and comes up with images it provides to the world press. Just so the intelligence aspect of its work is not overlooked, an SMN handout describes its work as reporting on "every part of the world where normal media access is limited or out of bounds, i.e., closed borders, critical war zones, current crises or catastrophes."

SMN has made public images showing secret Soviet preparations for a shuttle program in Tyuratam, data about a giant Soviet laser that could form part of an antimissile system, a site for Chinese missiles in Saudi Arabia, Pakistan's nuclear weapons project in Kahuta, and continuous monitoring of the Persian Gulf during the military confrontation there.

The handwriting is not on the wall, but in the sky. Space-based intelligence will continue to be de-monopolized as additional satellites and additional computer technology become available. Countries like Iraq and Brazil are deep in satellite development. Others, including Egypt and Argentina, are developing missile launch capability, and Inscom, a Brazil-China joint venture, aims to combine Brazilian satellite know-how with Chinese rocket-launch capabilities.

What was once available only to superpowers and their spies is increasingly available to lesser powers and, at some level at least, to private users and to the world media.

Indeed, with this, the media itself becomes a prime competitor to the manufacturers of intelligence. Says a former senior White House official: "When I first arrived I was a victim of the 'secrecy mystique'—if it was stamped 'secret' it was going to be really valuable. I soon found that I was often reading something I had previously read in the *Financial Times*. Even faster, instant television coverage normally beats the spies to the punch."

The continuing privatization and "media-ization" of intelligence or "para-intelligence" will force the spymasters to restructure their operations, just as many corporate CEOs have had to do. Espionage, too, will have to adapt to the new system of wealth creation on the planet. But espionage faces problems that other industries do not.

CONTRADICTIONS AT THE CORE

The clients who use intelligence—government officials and policy-makers—no longer suffer from any shortage of information. They are glutted with it.

The deluge of mass-produced data now available and the overload it causes means that, for many purposes, collection is no longer the spies' main problem. The problem is to make sense of what is collected and to get the results to the decision-makers who need it.

This is driving the spy business to rely more heavily on expert systems and artificial intelligence as computerized aids to analysis. But technology alone can't solve analysis paralysis. That requires a completely new approach to knowledge.

Since leaks of secret information can have dire consequences, including the death of informants, the CIAs and mini-CIAs of the world apply the principle of "compartmentation." Analysts working on a problem seldom get to see the whole picture, but are fed limited bits of information on a strict need-to-know basis, often with no way of evaluating the credibility of the fragments they get. In theory, the information is pieced back together and raised to a higher level as it moves up the hierarchy.

But we have seen this theory before—in bureaucratic corporations. And we have also seen that as change accelerates and the environment becomes more stormy, this system is too slow and ignores too many factors.

This is not an idle issue. Senator Sam Nunn, the leading expert on the military in the U.S. Senate, has publicly blasted the intelligence agencies for falling behind fast-moving events in Europe, making it impossible for Congress to make rational decisions about the U.S. military budget. The costs of falling behind could be calamitous.

It is precisely to overcome such problems that the smartest corporations now give employees access to more information, let them communicate freely outside channels and skip around the hierarchy at will. Such innovations, however, clash directly with the need for extreme secrecy in the espionage industry. The spies are in a double bind.

This "bind" is knotted to another. For much intelligence is not merely late, but irrelevant to the needs of the decision-makers who are the "customers."

Says Lionel Olmer, the former Under Secretary of Commerce: "We need sounder supervision by policy-level officials, so that they are not just consumers, but shapers of the process." Throughout industry, as we have seen, customers are being drawn into the design process, and users' groups are organized into networks of support for the producers. The line between production and consumption is blurring.

Olmer's suggestion that senior policy-makers help "shape" the intelligence process is logical. But the more politicians and officials help "reshape the process," the greater the danger that the estimates handed to Presidents and Prime Ministers will tell them only what they want to hear—or else reflect the narrow views of one faction or party. This would still further distort information that has already been pretzel-bent by the info-tacticians and meta-tacticians who work it over in the beginning.

If intelligence is twisted by a nation's adversary, as sometimes happens when spies are "doubled," the results can be disastrous. But the same is potentially true when it is twisted for political convenience by someone on one's own side.

The historic revolution now facing the intelligence industry, carrying it beyond mass production, places it squarely in the path of the advancing new wealth-creation system. Like other industries, the intelligence industry faces competition from unlikely quarters. Like other industries, it must form new, continually changing alliances. Like other industries, it must recast its organization. Like other industries, it must customize its products. Like other industries, it must question its deepest missions.

"A man's most open actions," wrote Joseph Conrad, "have a secret side to them." Democracies, too, no matter how open, have a secret side.

If intelligence operations, already difficult for parliaments and even Presidents to control, become so intertwined with the everyday activities of the society, so decentralized, so fused with business and other private interests as to make effective control impossible, democracy will be in mortal peril.

Conversely, so long as some nations are led by aggressive terrorists, torturers, and totalitarians, or by fanatics armed with ever more lethal weaponry, democracies cannot survive without secrets—and secret services.

How we manage those secrets—and, indeed, knowledge in general—becomes the central political issue in the Powershift Era.

25

THE INFO-AGENDA

The man with the Irish passport waited endlessly in his Tehran hotel room for the signal that never came.

Improbably armed with a chocolate cake shaped like a key, the man, as the world soon learned, was actually Robert McFarlane, former national security adviser to Ronald Reagan. Intended as a gift, the cake remained undelivered. For, as we recall, McFarlane's ill-fated attempt to free American hostages and open a back door to Iranian "moderates" exploded into the Irangate scandal, the most damaging event in the entire eight years of the Ronald Reagan presidency.

With a colorful cast of Middle Eastern arms merchants, CIA operatives, mysterious ex-generals, a handsome Marine officer and his gorgeous secretary, the congressional hearings that followed kept world television audiences spellbound.

Yet what many viewers, especially those outside the United States, missed was the crux of the case.

For the political struggle in Washington actually had little to do with terrorism, secret bank accounts, Iranian moderates, or Nicaraguan rebels. It was, rather, a showdown between the White House and an outraged U.S. Congress for control of American foreign policy. This battle for power pivoted on the refusal of the White House to inform Congress of its covert activities.

Democrats wanted to prove that the plan had been ordered by the President. The Republican White House insisted the fiasco was the work of an overzealous staff operating without presidential approval. Thus the investigations and massive media coverage focused less on foreign policy issues themselves, and more on the question of "who knew what when." Irangate became an info-war.

The lapsed memories, shredded documents, secrets, leaks, and lies still provide a rich lode of insight into the traditional tactical uses and abuses of information. But more important, the scandal offers a foretaste of the politics of the future—one in which data, information, and knowledge will become more highly politicized than ever in history. For quite apart from spies and spying, the new system of wealth creation is propelling us head-long into the era of info-politics.

A HUNGER FOR KNOWING

The power of the state has always rested on its control of force, wealth, and knowledge. What is profoundly different today is the changed relationship among these three. The new super-symbolic system of wealth creation thrusts a wide range of information-related issues onto the political agenda.

These range from privacy to product piracy, from telecommunications policy to computer security, from education and insider trading to the new role of the media. Even these touch only the tip of an emerging iceberg.

Although not yet widely noticed, this emerging info-agenda is expanding so rapidly that, in the United States, the 101st Congress saw the introduction of more than a hundred proposed laws dealing with info-issues. Twenty-six dealt with how the federal government should disseminate data and information collected at taxpayer expense. Today anyone with a personal computer and a modem can dial into a number of government data bases for information on a dizzying number of topics. But how should this dissemination work? Should the government contract with outside private firms to do the electronic distribution and sell access for a fee? Many librarians, university researchers, and civil liberties advocates argue that government information should not be sold but made available freely to the public. On the other hand, the private companies serving as intermediaries claim they provide additional services that justify charging a fee.

The info-agenda extends far beyond such concerns, however.

As we drive deeper into the new super-symbolic economy, info-issues no longer remain remote or obscure. A public whose livelihood increasingly derives from the manipulation of symbols is also increasingly sensitive to their power significance. One of the things it is already doing is asserting a wider and wider "right to know"—especially about circumstances directly related to its welfare.

In 1985 a survey by the U.S. Bureau of Labor Statistics found that more than half of 2.2 million workers involved in large-scale layoffs got less than twenty-four hours notice before being heaved out on the street. By 1987 organized labor was pushing for a law that would require large firms planning substantial layoffs to give their workers sixty days' notice, and to inform state and city authorities as well.

Employers strongly fought the proposed law, arguing that going public with this information would undermine a firm's efforts to save the plant. Who would want to invest in it, or merge with it, or contract work to it, or refinance it once the word was out that mass layoffs were about to occur?

Popular support for the measure grew, however. In the words of the Democratic Party leader in the Senate: "It's not a labor issue. It's a fairness issue."

By 1988 the battle was raging all across Washington, with the Congress lined up in favor and the White House against. Ultimately the law passed, despite the threat of presidential veto. American employees now do have a right to know in advance when they are about to lose their jobs because of a plant close-down.

Americans want more information about conditions off the job as well. Across the United States environmental groups and whole communities are clamoring for detailed data from companies and government agencies about toxic waste and other pollutants.

They were outraged not long ago to learn that at least thirty times between 1957 and 1985—more than once a year—the Savannah River nuclear weapons plant near Aiken, South Carolina, experienced what a scientist subsequently termed "reactor incidents of greatest significance." These included widespread leakage of radioactivity and a meltdown of nuclear fuel. But not one of these was reported to local residents or to the public generally. Nor was action taken when the scientist submitted an internal memorandum about these "incidents." The story did not come to light until exposed in a Congressional hearing in 1988.

The plant was operated by E. I. du Pont de Nemours & Company for the U.S. government, and Du Pont was accused of covering up the facts. The company immediately issued a denial, pointing out that it had routinely reported the accidents to the Department of Energy.

At this point, the DoE, as it is known, accepted the blame for keeping the news secret. The agency was steeped in military secrecy and the traditions of the Manhattan Project, which led to the invention of the atomic bomb in World War II. Public pressures for disclosure, however, touched off an internal struggle between Secretary of Energy John S. Herrington, fighting for higher safety standards and greater openness, and his own field managers who resisted.

But even as that conflict raged within the agency, a revolutionary new law went into effect, requiring for the first time that communities all over the United States be given explicit, detailed information about toxic wastes and other hazardous materials to which they are exposed. "For the first time," said Richard Siegel, a consultant whose firm has helped three hundred factories gear up for compliance, "the public is going to know what the plant down the street is releasing." It was another clear victory for public access.

The rising pressure for openness is not just an American phenomenon, nor is it limited to national issues.

In Osaka, Japan, citizens have formed a "Right to Know Network Kansai," which has since organized what they call "tours" of municipal and prefectural governments, for the purpose of demanding access to hitherto restricted information. Of twelve requests made at the prefectural offices, six were granted, the others quickly denied. Among these was a request for information about the governor's expense account.

The response of the Osaka city government was, so to speak, more artful. When the group demanded files relating to the city's purchase of a painting by Modigliani, now proudly hanging in the Osaka City Museum of Modern Art, officials did not say no. They just never replied. But pressures for access to public documents, local as well as national, won't go away.

The growth of what might be called info-awareness, paralleling the rise of an economy based on computers, information, and communication, has forced governments to pay more and more attention to knowledge-related issues like secrecy, public access, and privacy.

From the time the United States passed its Freedom of Information Act in 1966, broadening the right of citizens to access government documents, the concept has spread steadily through the advanced economies. Denmark and Norway followed suit in

1970; France and the Netherlands, in 1978; Canada and Australia, in 1982. This list, however, hardly tells the full story. For an even larger number of states, provinces, and cities have also passed legislation—sometimes even before the nation itself acted. This is the case in Japan, where five prefectures, five cities, two special districts, and eight towns had done so as early as 1985.

The same period has also seen the rapid diffusion of laws defining the right to privacy. Privacy laws were passed in Sweden in 1973, in the United States in 1974. In 1978, Canada, Denmark, France, and West Germany all followed suit, with Britain joining the parade in 1984. Numerous nations set up "data protection" agencies specifically designed to prevent computer abuses of privacy. The terms and methods naturally vary from nation to nation, as does their effectiveness. But the overall pattern is plain: Everywhere, as the super-symbolic economy develops, information issues became more significant politically.

TERRORIST BOMBS AND AIDS VICTIMS

Everywhere, too, there is a continuing info-war between the cult of secrecy and citizens groups fighting for even wider access. These battles cross party lines and are often so complex that they confuse the participants themselves.

For example, demands for openness get tangled when they conflict with publicly acknowledged needs for safety or security. After a terrorist bomb exploded on Pan Am Flight 103 over Lockerbie, Scotland, killing 259 passengers and crew on December 21, 1988, the press revealed that authorities had been forewarned. An outraged world demanded to know why the public at large had not been warned at the same time. Much of the anger toward the terrorists was siphoned off and directed at the authorities instead.

This anger soon led to an investigation by a subcommittee of the U.S. House of Representatives. The subcommittee made public a long list of security bulletins previously issued to airlines by the Federal Aviation Administration. In turn, this breach of secrecy angered the Secretary of Transportation, who charged that the subcommittee's action "could jeopardize lives by disclosing security methods."

Congresswoman Cardiss Collins, the subcommittee chairperson, stood by her guns, however, and labeled the Secretary's blast "misleading." In fact, she said, publicly disclosing the FAA's bulletins showed up dangerous flaws in the entire warning system and thereby served the public. But it was also clear that, with U.S. airlines alone receiving some three hundred bomb threats a year, publicizing every terrorist threat could paralyze air travel—and give the terrorists the power to upset the system at any moment for the price of a phone call.

Soon the executive branch, the legislature, the airlines, the regulatory agencies, the police, and others were all joined in a still-continuing free-for-all over control of this information.

In December 1989, just a year after the Lockerbie tragedy, Northwest Airlines received a bomb threat against its Paris-to-Detroit Flight 51. Aware of the outrage the year before, Northwest decided it would have to inform passengers ticketed on the flight. It intended to tell them at the gate before boarding. But after a Swedish newspaper broke the story, Northwest began systematically notifying passengers by telephone in advance and agreed to help them make alternate arrangements if they wished. (Not all did, and the flight was made safely.)

Demands for more open information also clash with the above-mentioned demands for privacy. Among the most emotional of all info-issues are those raised by the AIDS epidemic. As AIDS spread swiftly through many countries, carrying hysteria with it, some extremists urged that victims of the disease literally be tattooed and sequestered. Fearful parents tried to bar AIDS-infected children from the schoolroom. William Bennett, then the tough-talking U.S. Secretary of Education, called for compulsory AIDS-testing of several specified groups, including all hospital patients, couples seeking a marriage license, immigrants, and prisoners. Bennett urged further that whenever an individual's test showed positive, all spouses and past sex partners should automatically be notified.

His position provoked a storm of opposition from public health authorities, lawyers, and civil libertarians who favored voluntary testing instead. Ironically, many of those who fought for privacy in this case were among those most committed to open information in other matters.

The tests, some claimed, were indecisive. If results were made public, victims would be discriminated against on the job, in school, and mistreated in other ways. Moreover, if the tests were compulsory, many potential victims might hide or refuse to seek medical care. Bennett's position was publicly attacked by Surgeon General C. Everett Koop, the nation's top medical official.

Controversy still rages over the AIDS-testing issue, not just in Washington but in many state capitals as well. The relative rights of the individual versus those of the community, and the contradiction between privacy and openness, both remain fuzzily unresolved.

Still more cross-interests arise from the existing morass of laws governing such things as copyright, patents, trade secrets, commercial secrecy, insider trading, and the like—all part of the fast-emerging info-agenda of politics. As the super-symbolic economy continues to expand, an information ethic may emerge appropriate to the advanced economies. Today that coherent ethic is missing and political decisions are made in a bewildering moral vacuum. There are few rules that do not contradict other rules.

Many parts of the world still lack the most elementary freedom of information, and face cultural repression, brutal press censorship, and governments paranoid about secrecy. In the high-tech democracies, by contrast, where freedom of expression is moderately protected, info-politics has begun to move to a higher, more subtle level.

We are, however, only at the beginning of info-politics in the technologically advanced societies. So far we have been struggling with the easy questions.

THE NEW GLOBAL FEEDBACK

Because of the growing global character of technology, environmental problems, finance, telecommunications, and the media, new cultural feedback systems have begun to operate that make one country's information policies a matter of concern for others. The info-agenda is going global.

When Chernobyl sent radioactive clouds over parts of Europe, a great wave of anti-Soviet anger was aroused, because Soviet officials delayed notifying countries in the path of the fallout. These nations insisted that they had a *right* to know the facts, and to know them immediately.

The implication was that no nation, by itself, had the right to withhold the facts, and that an unspoken information ethic transcends national interests. By the time another disaster struck—an earthquake in Armenia—chastened Soviet authorities instantly reported it to the entire world press.

But by the terms of that implicit principle the Soviet Union was not the only transgressor. Shortly after Chernobyl, Admiral Stansfield Turner, former director of the CIA, publicly criticized the United States for failing to divulge sufficient information about the disaster gathered by its "eye-in-the-sky" satellites. Without giving away secrets, Turner declared, "Our intelligence collection capabilities . . . give us the opportunity to keep people well-informed worldwide."

In fact, as new media for dissemination of information encircle the earth, facilitating the globalization required by the new wealth-creation system, it becomes harder to contain specific information within national borders, or even to keep it out.

This is what the British government forgot during the so-called *Spycatcher* controversy in Britain. When Peter Wright wrote a book with that title, in which he made serious accusations against former officials of British counterintelligence, the Thatcher government moved to bar its publication. Wright thereupon published the book in the United States and elsewhere. The British attempt to suppress the book turned it into an international best-seller. Television and newspapers everywhere carried stories about it— thus guaranteeing that information the British government wanted to conceal would find its way back into Britain. Because of this feedback process, the British government was compelled to back down, and Wright's book went on to become a best-seller in Britain too.

The use of the media outside a country to influence political decisions inside it is also becoming more common. When the Kohl government in Bonn denied that German firms were helping Libya's strongman, Muammar el-Qaddafi, to build a chemical weapons plant fifty miles outside Tripoli, U.S. intelligence leaked its satellite and aerial reconnaissance evidence to American and European media. This led the German magazine *Stern* to undertake its own in-depth investigative report, which in turn forced a red-faced government to admit that it had known all along what it claimed not to know.

In case after case, then, we find information—who has it, how it was obtained, how it was arrived at—at the heart of both national and international political conflict. The underlying reason for the new importance of info-politics is the growing reliance of power, in all its forms, on knowledge. As this historic powershift is more widely understood, info-politics will take on added intensity.

Yet all these are mere skirmishes alongside what could turn out to be the most important info-war of the decades to come.

THE INDIANA JONES CODE

Among the most common sights in Thailand, especially in the tourist quarters, are street stalls. From these one may buy video-tapes, musical tapes, and other products at knockdown prices. One reason is that these, like all sorts of other products circulating in the world today, are pirated—meaning that the original artists, publishers, and record companies are cheated of the payments due them.

In Egypt, so-called underground publishers churn out Western books in Arabic illegally and without payment to the authors or publishers. "Book piracy in the Middle East has reached proportions second only to that in the Far East and Pakistan," according to the *Middle East* monthly published in London. In Hong Kong, police arrested 61 people after raiding 27 bookstores where they found 647 books ready to be reproduced illegally. But in many countries piracy is not merely legal but encouraged for its export potentials. New technologies make piracy cheaper and easier.

Driven by piracy that cost the American movie industry an estimated $750 million annually in the mid-1980s, Hollywood counterattacked. When *Indiana Jones and the Temple of Doom* first hit the theaters, every print of the film had subliminal coding in it that gave it a unique identifier so that, if illegal copies were made, investigators would be able to trace their origin. From then on, similar coding began to be used by many of the major studios.

Nonetheless, as late as 1989, Taiwan, for example, was home to 1,200 so-called "Movie-TV" lounges—small private rooms in which groups of teenagers could gather to watch pirated video-tapes of the latest American movies, a kind of micro-version of the drive-in movie. Teenagers formed block-long lines to patronize them. The illegal showings were so popular, they cut into ticket sales at conventional theaters. Ultimately, Hollywood pressures led to a government crackdown.

In parallel with actual piracy came the patent-wars—the refusal of various countries to pay fees or royalties, say, on a new pharmaceutical developed and tested by research scientists at enormous cost.

In addition to outright piracy, counterfeiting has become a major global industry, with cheap fakes of designer fashions and other products pouring into world markets. Ultimately even more important is the theft or illegal copying of computer software, not by individuals for their own use, but on a large scale by pirate distributors throughout the world. All these problems are heightened by the latest technologies that make copying and theft easier.

By 1989, the question of how to protect "intellectual property" —the basis of much of the new system of wealth creation—was causing political friction among nations. Intellectual property—the term itself is fraught with controversy—implies ownership of intangibles resulting from creative efforts in science, technology, the arts, literature, design, and the manipulation of knowledge in general. With the spread of the super-symbolic economy, these become more economically valuable and, hence, more political.

In Washington, political battles broke out between various trade lobbies, backed by the U.S. Trade Representative, who demanded firm U.S. action against Thailand for failing to suppress piracy and counterfeiting of U.S. creative products. They demanded that, if Thailand refused to crack down, the United States should retaliate. Specifically, this meant lifting import duty exemptions on such Thai exports as artificial flowers, tiles, dried mung beans, and telecommunications equipment.

Opposing this demand were other agencies of the U.S. government—the State Department and the National Security Council—both of which argued for leniency, placing the interests of diplomacy and military security over those of the copyright and patent owners.

On his last day as President of the United States, Ronald Reagan rejected even more stringent proposals for a crackdown, and removed the Thai exemption from import duties on the listed products.

But Thailand is hardly the worst offender against copyright and patent laws as they are understood in the advanced economies, and the minor struggle in Washington only illustrates what is happening on a hundred fronts as products of creative activity become more and more central to all the high-tech economies.

In 1989, American copyright holders, including the music industry, the computer industry, and book publishers, demanded that the U.S. government take action against twelve nations that, they claimed, were costing the American economy $1.3 billion a year in sales. The twelve included China, Saudia Arabia, India, Malaysia, Taiwan, and the Philippines.

The protection of intellectual property, though most aggressively pushed by the Americans, is also of strong concern to the European Community and Japan. The EC has called for customs authorities around the world to seize counterfeit goods and to impose criminal penalties on pirates who operate on a commercial scale.

The political battle over intellectual property is waged, among other places, in the council of the General Agreement on Tariffs and Trade, where the advanced economies face determined opposition from the nations with less developed economies, whose negotiators sometimes reflect the attitude voiced by Arab students who buy pirated books and insist that "the West's idea of copyright is elitist and designed to line the pockets of publishers."

But it is not this attitude that is most threatening to the high-tech nations. It is the gnawing philosophical question of whether intellectual property can be owned in the same sense that tangible assets are—or whether the entire concept of property needs to be reconceptualized.

Futurist and former diplomat Harlan Cleveland has written of the "folly of refusing to share something that can't be owned." Cleveland points out: "What builds a great company or a great nation is not the protection of what it already knows, but the acquisition and adaptation of new knowledge from other companies or nations. How can 'intellectual property' be 'protected'? The question contains the seeds of its own confusion: it's the wrong verb about the wrong noun."

This line of argument is often used to support the vision of a world in which all information is free and unfettered. It is a dream that dovetails neatly with the plea of the earth's poorer nations for the science and technology needed to break free of economic underdevelopment. What is not yet answered, however, is the counterquestion raised by the high-tech nations: What happens to either the poor *or* the rich if the world's stream of technological innovation runs dry? If, because of piracy, a pharmaceutical firm cannot recoup the vast sums spent in developing new drugs, it is hardly likely to invest further funds in the search. Cleveland is right that all nations will need knowledge, culture, art, and science from abroad. But if so, there must be some civilized ground rules for the exchange, and these must promote, rather than restrict, further innovation.

Arriving at these new rules, and an underlying informational ethic, in a world trisected into agrarian, smokestack, and post-smokestack economies, is already proving extremely difficult. What is obvious is that these issues can do nothing but grow in importance. The control of intangibles—ideas, culture, images, theories, scientific formulae, computer software—will consume greater and greater political attention in all countries as piracy, counterfeiting, theft, and technological espionage threaten increasingly vital private and national interests.

In the words of Abdul A. Said and Luiz R. Simmons, in *The New Sovereigns,* a study of multinational corporations: "The nature of power is undergoing a truly radical transformation. It is increasingly defined in terms of the maldistribution of information. Inequality, long associated primarily with income, is coming to be associated with technological factors and the political and economic control over knowledge."

In the 19th and early 20th centuries, nations went to war to seize control of the raw materials they needed to feed their smokestack economies. In the 21st century, the most basic of all the raw materials will be knowledge. Is that what the wars and social revolutions of the future might be about? If so, what role will the media of the future play?

26

THE IMAGE MAKERS

Benjamin Day was a twenty-three-year-old printer with wild ideas when he changed the history of what we now call the media. The year was 1833 and New York had grown to a population of 218,000. But the largest daily newspaper in the city claimed only 4,500 subscribers. At a time when the average urban worker in America earned 75 cents a day, a New York newspaper cost 6 cents, and not many people could afford them. The papers were printed on handpresses capable of turning out no more than a few hundred copies an hour.

Day took a crazy chance.

On September 3, 1833, he launched the New York *Sun* and sold it for only one penny a copy. Day unleashed a horde of newsboys into the streets to sell his paper—an innovation at the time. For $4 a week he hired another printer to go to the courthouse and cover police cases. It was one of the earliest uses of a "reporter." Within four months the *Sun* had the biggest readership in the city. In 1835 he bought the latest technology—a steam-driven press—and the *Sun* reached the unheard-of circulation of 20,000 daily. Day had invented the popular press, crime stories and all.

His innovations were paralleled at about the same time by other "wild men"—Henry Hetherington with his *Twopenny Dispatch* in England and Émile de Girardin with *La Presse* in France. The down-scale "penny paper"—called the "pauper press" in England—was more than just a commercial affair. It had lasting political effects. Along with the early trade unions and the beginnings of mass education, it helped bring the poorer classes into the political life of nations.

By the 1870s something called "opinion" had to be taken into account by politicians of every stripe. "There is, now," wrote one

French thinker, "no European government which does not reckon with opinion, which does not feel obliged to give account of its acts and to show how closely they conform to the national interest, or to put forward the interest of the people as the justification for any increase in its prerogatives."

A century and a half after Benjamin Day, another wild man came up with an idea sure to bankrupt him. Tall, gutsy, impatient, and brilliant, Ted Turner had inherited a billboard company when his father committed suicide. Turner built it, acquired radio and television stations, and was wondering what to do next when he noticed something odd. Cable television stations were springing up around the United States, but they were starving for programs and advertising. Meanwhile, up in the heavens were things called "satellites."

Turner put two and two together and turned it into five. He beamed the programming from his Atlanta station up to a satellite and down to the program-hungry cable stations. At the same time, he offered a "one-buy" national market for advertisers who wouldn't trouble to purchase time on scores of small individual cable systems. His Atlanta "superstation" became the cornerstone of a growing empire.

On June 1, 1980, Turner took the next, even loonier step. He formed what critics labeled the "Chicken Noodle Network"—for CNN, or Cable News Network. CNN became the laughingstock of every media pundit from the canyons of Manhattan to the studios in Los Angeles. Wall Street was sure it would collapse, probably taking his other businesses down with it. No one had ever even tried to create a twenty-four-hour news network.

CNN today is perhaps the most influential broadcast news source in the United States. TV monitors are constantly tuned to CNN in the White House, in the Pentagon, in foreign embassies, as well as in millions of homes all over America.

But Turner's wild dreams went far beyond the United States, and today CNN operates in eighty-six countries, making it the most global of all television networks, mesmerizing Middle East sheiks, European journalists, and Latin American politicians with its extended firsthand coverage of such events as the assassination of Egyptian President Anwar Sadat, the Chinese repression of the 1989 Tiananmen Square protests, or the American invasion of Panama. CNN is carried over the air, or over cable, into hotel rooms, offices, homes, even staterooms on the *Queen Elizabeth II*.

One of Turner's little-known prize possessions is a videotape of his private meeting with Cuba's Fidel Castro. In the course of the visit, Castro mentions that he, too, routinely watches CNN. Turner, never shy about promoting his companies, asks Castro if he would be willing to say as much on camera for a commercial. Castro puffs on his cigar and says, in effect, why not? The commercial has never run on the air, but Turner hauls it out to show to visiting friends now and then.

Turner is one of a kind. Handsome, raucous, funny, erratic, he owns a buffalo ranch, the Atlanta Braves baseball team, MGM's library of old movies, and, according to critics, the biggest mouth in the South.

A fierce exemplar of free enterprise, he was also a peace activist long before he and actress Jane Fonda began a highly-publicized romance. He launched the "Goodwill Games" in Moscow at a time when it took political, as well as financial, courage to do so. His networks also run a heavy schedule of pro-ecology programming.

Today Turner is by far the most visionary of a dozen or so hard-driving media barons who are revolutionizing the media even more deeply than Benjamin Day—and whose collective efforts will, over the long term, shift power in many countries.

THE MULTI-CHANNEL SOCIETY

The basic direction of change in the media since at least 1970, when *Future Shock* foreshadowed the coming de-massification of the airwaves, has been toward the breakup of mass audiences into segments and subgroups, each receiving a different configuration of programs and messages. Along with this has come a vast expansion of the sheer amount of imagery transmitted by television in the form of both news and entertainment.

There is a reason for this image-explosion.

Humans, of course, have always exchanged symbolic images of reality. That is what language is all about. It is what knowledge is based on. However, different societies require either more or less symbolic exchange. The transition to a knowledge-based economy sharply increases the demand for communication and swamps the old image-delivery systems.

Advanced economies require a labor force with high levels of symbolic sophistication. This work force needs instant and largely free access to all sorts of information hitherto considered irrelevant to its productivity. It needs workers who can quickly adapt to, and even anticipate, repeated changes in work methods, organization, and daily life.

The very best workers are worldly, alert to new ideas and fashions, customer preferences, economic and political changes, aware of competitive pressures, cultural shifts, and many other things previously regarded as pertinent only to managerial elites.

This wide-scan knowledge does not come out of classrooms or from technical manuals alone, but from exposure to a constant barrage of news delivered by TV, newspapers, magazines, and radio. It also comes indirectly from "entertainment"—much of which unintentionally delivers information about new life styles, interpersonal relationships, social problems, and even foreign customs and markets.

Some shows, like *Murphy Brown,* which stars the actress Candice Bergen, deliberately build drama or comedy around current news. But even when this is not the case, television shows, sometimes despite themselves, convey images of reality.

It is true that the intentional content of a television show—the plot and the behavior of the principal characters—often paints a false picture of social reality. However, there is in all television programs and commercials, as well as in movies, an additional layer of what we might call "inadvertent content."

This consists of background detail—landscape, cars, street scenes, architecture, telephones, answering machines, as well as barely noticed behavior, like the banter between a waitress and a customer as the hero seats himself at a lunch counter. In contrast with the intended content, the inadvertent detail frequently provides a quite accurate picture of quotidian reality. Moreover, even the tritest "cop shows" picture current fads and fashions, and express popular attitudes toward sex, religion, money, and politics.

None of this is ignored or forgotten by the viewer. It is filed away in the mind, forming part of a person's general bank of knowledge about the world. Thus, good and bad alike, it influences the bag of assumptions brought to the workplace. (Ironically, much of the worker's image of the world, which increasingly affects economic productivity, is thus absorbed during "leisure" hours.) For this reason, "mere entertainment" is no longer "mere."

In short, the new economy is tightly tied not only to formal knowledge and technical skills but even to popular culture and the expanding market for imagery. This seething market is not only growing, but is simultaneously being restructured. Its very categories are re-forming. For better or worse, the old lines between show business and politics, leisure and work, news and entertainment, are all crashing, and we are exposed to a hurricane of often fragmented, kaleidoscopic images.

THE ARRIVAL OF CHOICE

The main producers of this imagery until recently were the major broadcast networks. Today, in the United States, where de-massification is most advanced, their power is plummeting. Where ABC, NBC, and CBS once stood virtually alone, there are now seventy-two national services of various kinds, with more coming on line. "A new crop of networks serving 'niche' markets is the big news in cable," according to *The Hollywood Reporter*. Soon to be added are a comedy network, a consumer-business news network, and a science-fiction network. In addition, Channel One pipes programs into school classrooms, and National College Television uses satellite to target special programs to university students.

In 1970, *Future Shock* declared that "the invention of electronic video recording, the spread of cable television, the possibility of broadcasting direct from satellite . . . all point to vast increases in program variety."

Today, cable TV is available in 57 percent of American homes and is conservatively projected to reach 67 percent within the decade. The average cable user has more than twenty-seven channels to choose from, and that will soon top fifty. In a small town like Rochester, Minnesota, viewers can choose from more than forty different channels offering a wide range of material, from the Black Entertainment Network and programs in Spanish, to specialized medical training programs aimed at the larger medical community around the famed Mayo Clinic.

Cable was the first to begin fractionalizing the mass audience. Videocassette and direct broadcast satellite (delivering signals not only to cable stations but into the home itself) fractionalize the fractions. Thus videocassette offers viewers a choice of thousands of movies and programs. And recently four major companies banded together to deliver 108 channels of standard and high-definition TV to American viewers by shooting signals from the world's most powerful commercial satellite to "napkin-size" receiver dishes in the home.

Furthermore, the number of stations operating independently of the three big networks has quadrupled since the late 1970s. Many have formed themselves into syndicates or temporary groupings that compete with the majors for top-rated programming. The impact of all these de-massifying forces on the once-mighty networks has been, as *Newsweek* put it, little short of "catastrophic."

Says Robert Iger, head of ABC's entertainment division, "The key words in all of this are choice and alternatives. It's what people didn't have back in 1980. It's what they do have today." But these are precisely what the main networks were designed to prevent. For CBS, ABC, and NBC were Second Wave smokestack companies, accustomed to dealing with masses, not heterogeneous micromarkets, and are having as much difficulty adapting to the post-smokestack Third Wave economy as are General Motors and Exxon. A measure of the networks' concern was the decision of NBC to join in the direct broadcast satellite venture.

Asked what will happen to the Big Three, Al Burton, a top independent TV producer, says: "Once upon a time there were three big radio networks too. Today hardly anyone even remembers they existed."

THE COMING EUROVISION

While the de-massification of the media began earliest in the United States, Europe is now catching up.

In the United States broadcasting has been a private industry, while in most European countries radio and, especially, television were for many years either government-run or financed by special taxes paid by listeners and viewers. As a result, Europeans had even less choice of programming than Americans had when the big networks dominated.

Today's changes are remarkable. There are now more than fifty satellite TV services in Europe. British Satellite Broadcasting (BSB) plans five direct broadcast satellite services, while Sky Television, another contender, plans six distinct services.

Sky and BSB are fiercely battling, each threatening to pull the other down, each spending pots of money without any likelihood of immediate return. Both have their eye fixed on the bonanza that awaits if an estimate by Saatchi & Saatchi, Britain's biggest ad agency, proves even partly correct. According to Saatchi, within a decade more than half of Britain's homes will be equipped to receive satellite-to-home transmissions, and satellite TV will be supported by about $1.3 billion in advertising revenues. At first slow to catch on, home dishes are now selling rapidly, and number over 700,000.

British viewers, who at one time were limited to two BBC channels and who got their fourth network only in 1982, are likely to have some fifteen satellite channels available to them before long.

France, in a politically explosive move, ended its monopoly control of television in 1986, when La Cinq (Channel 5) went into service with a glitzy grand opening that featured singer-actor Charles Aznavour cutting the ribbon. In a short time France went from a country with three government-run networks to one with six networks, of which four are private. Pay-TV channels like Canal Plus in France are growing in Switzerland and the Low Countries as well.

In Italy, RAI, the state radio and television corporation, now faces competition from at least four networks. Rome boasts perhaps twenty-five channels of television.

West Germany has added two new commercial channels and has been busy cabling up since 1985, when its first private cable channel went on the air to the strains of Dvorak's *New World Symphony*. Today 6 million West German homes are already cabled. And Spain, not to be outraced, is opening three new private networks to compete with its state networks.

The situation is changing so swiftly that these estimates may be out of date by the time they see print. And no one knows for sure how many more new channels Europe will add in the years to come, doubling or perhaps tripling its total. And this is without the explosion of television and radio likely to occur in the Eastern

European countries freed of their communist governments. There, multiple networks will spring up like dandelions.

Japan, meanwhile, which has pioneered high-definition television, has been much slower, so far, to spread cable or to multiply channels. If, however, it remains true to historical precedent, when it finally makes the decision to do so, it will move with blinding speed.

Two seemingly contradictory things are happening, therefore. At the financial level: consolidation. At the actual level of what audiences get to see: increasing diversity fed by a dizzying variety of new channels and media.

THE GLOBAL SELL

The existence of a global image market has led some companies, including media companies, to a simple, linear conclusion. The time had come to "globalize," meaning they would now try doing on a global scale what they had successfully done before on a national scale.

This straight-line strategy has turned out to be a loser.

Advanced wealth creation presupposes the globalization of a good bit of manufacturing and the parallel development of global means of distribution. Thus, as manufacturing and distribution corporations began forming cross-border alliances, or merging across national frontiers, ad agencies followed suit. Taking advantage of the low dollar, Britain's WPP, for example, swallowed up both J. Walter Thompson and Ogilvy & Mather, each an American giant in its own right. In its drive to become the world's biggest agency, Saatchi & Saatchi gulped down Compton Advertising and Dancer Fitzgerald Sample, among other firms.

In theory, transnational ad agencies would be in a position to channel standardized advertising from transnational corporations into transnational media with minimum effort. The same commercials would be translated into many languages. Presto! Bigger commissions for the agency.

The rationale for the "global sell" strategy was supplied in part by marketing guru Theodore Levitt of Harvard, who preached that "the world's needs and desires have been irrevocably homogenized," and who celebrated the coming of "global" products and brands—implying that the same product, backed by the same advertising, which once sold nationally could now be sold to the whole world. The same industrial-style standardization that earlier took place on the national level would now take place on a global level.

What's wrong with the global sell theory is that it makes little distinction among the world's regions and markets. Some are still in a pre-mass-market condition; others are still at the mass-market stage; and some are already experiencing the de-massification characteristic of an advanced economy. In these last, consumers demand greater individualization and customization of products and positively shun certain homogeneous goods or services. The same marketing or advertising can hardly be expected to work in all of them.

The Levitt theory also drastically underestimates the economic impact of cultural preferences and assumptions at a time when culture is growing more, not less, important. A 1988 study by the Hill Samuel merchant bank for the Confederation of British Industry suggests that even a unified Europe cannot be regarded as uniform. According to its report, French housewives prefer washing machines that load from the top, while the British like front-loaders better. Germans regard low blood pressure as a problem needing heavy medication, while British doctors don't. The French, the Hill Samuel study notes, worry about a "heart/digestive condition known as 'spasmophilia,' the existence of which U.K. doctors don't even recognise." Are attitudes toward food, beauty, work, play, love—or, for that matter, politics—any less diverse?

In practice, the simplistic "global sell" theory proved disastrous for firms that applied it. *The Wall Street Journal*, in a front-page lead article, described the theory as a costly fiasco. The paper detailed the agonies of Parker Pen when it tried to follow the formula. (It went into the red, sacked the responsible executives, and eventually had to sell off its pen division.) When an attempt was made to peddle an Erno Laszlo skin-care brand to fair-skinned Australians and dark-skinned Italians alike, the pitch, not surprisingly, flopped. Even McDonald's, it turns out, accommodates national differences, selling beer in Germany, wine in France, and even, at one time, mutton pot pie in Australia. In the Philippines it offers McSpaghetti. If diversity is necessary in consumer products, is it likely to be less necessary in culture or political ideology? Will global media really homogenize away the differences among peoples?

The fact is that with some exceptions, cultures, too—like products—are de-massifying. And the very multiplicity of media accelerates the process. Thus it is high diversity, not uniformity, that the marketers of political candidates or ideas will be forced to confront. If products, with only rare exceptions, fail when they try to sweep the world market, why should politicians or policies succeed?

Rather than homogenizing the planet, as the old Second Wave media did, the new global media system could deepen diversity instead. Globalization, therefore, is not the same as homogeneity. Instead of a single global village, as forecast by Marshall McLuhan, the late Canadian media theorist, we are likely to see a multiplicity of quite different global villages—all wired into the new media system, but all straining to retain or enhance their cultural, ethnic, national, or political individuality.

THE NEW BARONS

The globalization of the media, necessary for the new economy, is in fact moving rapidly.

When Japan's Sony bought up Columbia Pictures Entertainment for $5 billion, acquiring Hollywood's largest library of films, including such quality products as *On the Waterfront, Lawrence of Arabia,* and *Kramer vs. Kramer,* along with 220 movie houses and 23,000 TV episodes, it shook the entertainment industry. Sony is preparing a big push to sell its 8mm video players and recorders and wanted the "software" to go with its "hardware." But the deal is only one of many that are changing the structure of the image industry.

Thus Fujisankei Communications Group has bought into Virgin Music. Britain's TV South has bought MTM Enterprises, the TV firm founded by Mary Tyler Moore. Germany's Bertelsmann Group, one of the biggest media companies of them all, owns properties in more than twenty countries. Rupert Murdoch's span reaches across three continents, and encompasses newspapers and magazines, book publishing, movies, and a TV network in the United States.

One side effect of all this activity is the rise of a colorful group of global media barons, among whom the Australian-American Murdoch was a pioneer.

Charged (sometimes unfairly) with debasing the newspapers he owns, riding roughshod over trade unions, and being a ruthless competitor, he is also a long-range thinker who systematically studies the latest technologies. Apart from the newspapers he owns or controls in Australia, the United States, and Britain, Murdoch has been carefully piecing together a vertically integrated global media empire.

He owns a significant chunk of 20th Century-Fox Broadcasting, which owns the rights to thousands of hours of films and TV programs. He owns the Fox TV network and *TV Guide* magazine in the United States. In Europe he has pioneered satellite broadcasting, and owns 90 percent of Sky Channel, a new sports network, and a twenty-four-hour news channel which draws some of its material from his London newspapers, *The Times* and *The Sunday Times*. Beyond this, he has formed a fifty-fifty joint venture with Amstrad, a British firm, to manufacture cheap satellite dishes designed to pick up broadcasts beamed into the home.

Whether this vertical integration will ultimately produce the desired "synergy" remains to be seen. Other industries, as we've seen, are moving away from vertical integration. But win or lose, Murdoch has already pumped new energy into the entire publishing and broadcast industries.

In Britain, Robert Maxwell, a swaggering bulldozer of a man—sometimes called, behind his back, the "Bouncing Czech," the "Black Hurricane," or "Captain Bob"—started out by publishing a tiny chain of obscure academic journals. Born in Czechoslovakia, Maxwell served as an officer in the British Army in World War II and later was elected to Parliament.

From his tiny scholarly publishing base, he has, in fact, built an empire made up of pieces of many existing television properties, including TF1 in France, Canal 10 in Spain, Central Television in Britain, a movie channel, and an MTV channel. His extensive operations include magazines, newspapers, and the Macmillan book publishing firm in the United States.

In sharp contrast to Maxwell and Turner, Reinhard Mohn is a modest man with a philosophical turn of mind and carefully thought-out ideas about management, employee participation, and the social responsibilities of ownership.

A German prisoner of war in Concordia, Kansas, during World War II, Mohn was impressed by American democracy and, among other things, the Book-of-the-Month Club. He returned to the small town of Guetersloh, took over the family's Bible publishing house, and proceeded to build the Bertelsmann Group into a media powerhouse. In addition to book and record clubs in Germany, Spain, Brazil, the United States, and eighteen other countries, Bertelsmann owns the Bantam Doubleday Dell Publishing Group in the United States, Plaza y Janes book publishers in Spain, as well as thirty-seven magazines in five countries, plus record labels like RCA/Ariola, and more than a few radio and television properties.

Italy's Silvio Berlusconi, meanwhile, whose TV stations account for 60 percent of all Italian ad revenues, has reached across into France, where he is part-owner of La Cinq; Germany, where he owns a major chunk of Tele-5; and into Moscow, which has named him the exclusive purveyor of advertising for the Soviet Union in Europe. Berlusconi is making eyes at Yugoslavia, Spain, and Tunisia as well.

THE FORGING OF GLOBAL OPINION

Shifts of financial power over the media always spark hot controversy. Today the sheer size of the media empires provokes anxiety. Established networks and other media are threatened. Moreover, the concentration of financial control in the hands of the Murdochs and Berlusconis conjures up memories of the great press lords of the past, such as William Randolph Hearst in the United States or Lord Northcliffe in Britain, men whose political influence was enormous and by no means universally admired.

The first and most common criticism heard today is that the new global media will homogenize the world. The failure of the "global marketing" theory, however, suggests this fear is overdrawn.

The mass media had their strongest homogenizing effects when there were only a few channels, few different media, and hence little audience choice. In the future, the reverse situation will prevail. While the content of each individual program may be good or bad, the most important new "content" of all is the existence of diversity itself. The shift from a low-choice to a high-choice media environment holds not only cultural but political implications.

High-tech governments face a future in which multiple, conflicting, custom-tailored commercial, cultural, and political messages will bombard their people, rather than a single message repeated in unison by a few giant media outlets. The old "politics of mass mobilization" and the "engineering of consent" both become far more difficult in the new media environment.

Expanded media choice is itself inherently democratic. It makes life difficult for politicians who offer their followers a choiceless environment.

A second set of complaints about the new media barons relates to their personal political views. Murdoch is charged with being too conservative. Maxwell is too close to the British Labour Party. Turner is an unpredictable maverick. This one has sold his soul to French President Mitterand, while that one is in bed with someone else. If all these charges were true, they would soon cancel one another out.

Far more important than their personal political views and alliances are the interests they hold in common. Of course, all are capitalists operating in a capitalist framework. As such, we can assume that, in general, the bottom line interests them more than any political line.

What matters most about these media lords is not whether they favor left-wing or right-wing policies and politicians. Far more significant is their support, through their actions more than their words, of the ideology of globalism. Globalism, or at least supranationalism, is a natural expression of the new economy, which must operate across national boundaries, and it is in the self-interest of the new media moguls to spread this ideology.

This self-interest, however, collides with another. For if their television and radio stations, their newspapers and magazines are to succeed financially, they will have to de-massify—which means they will have to search for niches, carry specialized material, and appeal to very local audience interests. The familiar slogan "Think global, act local" perfectly describes the new media imperatives.

The very existence, however, of powerful media of communication capable of spanning continents will shift power as between national political leaders and the global community. Thus, without necessarily intending it, the new media barons are drastically changing the role of "global opinion" in the world.

Just as in the past century national leaders were compelled to justify their actions before the court of national "public opinion," tomorrow's national leaders will confront a much-enhanced "global opinion." And just as the work of Benjamin Day or Henry Hetherington or Émile de Girardin brought the poorer classes into the political life of nations, the activities of today's media lords will bring new millions into the global decision-making process.

Today, nations flout global opinion without worrying overmuch about the consequences. World opinion did not save the victims of Auschwitz, the people of Cambodia, or, more recently, the boat people fleeing hunger and oppression in Asia. Nor did it prevent the Chinese from murdering their protesting students in Beijing.

Nevertheless, global opinion has sometimes stayed the hand of killer regimes. The history of human rights is filled with cases in which global protests have prevented the torture or murder of a domestic political prisoner. It is unlikely that Anatoly Shcharansky would have survived his encounter with Soviet prison camps had the outside world not put pressure on Moscow to release him. Andrei Sakharov's chances for survival were improved when he won the Nobel Prize and became a household word because of constant media attention around the world.

The global media system will not make nations behave like Boy Scouts. But it raises the costs of defying world opinion. In the world being constructed by the media barons, what outsiders say about a nation will carry more weight inside than it ever did before.

Governments will no doubt invent more sophisticated lies with which to rationalize their self-serving actions and manipulate the increasingly systemic media. They will also step up propaganda efforts to improve their global image. But if such efforts fail, they could suffer significant economic penalties for behavior frowned on by the rest of the world.

South Africa may deny that sanctions hurt its economy or that its pariah image also damaged the country economically. But its senior officials know better. Global opinion sets the stage for global action.

Even if an outraged world does not impose formal trade sanctions on a rogue regime, international agencies like the World

Bank may reject their pleas for multibillion loans. Private banks may shy away, foreign investors and tourists go elsewhere. Worse yet, companies and countries still willing to do business with a pariah nation are in a position to drive a harder bargain than might have been the case otherwise. Power in the negotiations shifts as a result of global imagery.

What's more, as the importance of global opinion grows in parallel with the spread of the systemic media, shrewd power-players will wield it as an unconventional weapon. It will be used not only to save some political prisoners, or to direct instant relief to disaster zones, but to spare us from some, at least, of the ecological ravages that might otherwise be inflicted on a bleeding planet.

When Armenians are attacked by Azeris in Baku, Armenians in Los Angeles know it instantly and begin mobilizing political action. When Jesuits are murdered by a death squad in El Salvador, the entire world knows it. When a trade unionist is jailed in South Africa, the word gets out. The new global media are basically in business to make a profit. But they are inadvertently raising the level of cross-national political action by a dazzling diversity of activist groups.

Without even intending it, Murdoch and Maxwell, Turner and Mohn, Berlusconi and other new media magnates are creating a powerful new tool and placing it in the hands of the global community.

But that hardly scratches the surface of what is happening. As we'll see next, the new global media system has, in fact, become the prime tool of revolution in today's fast-changing world.

27

SUBVERSIVE MEDIA

On June 30, 1988, in Victorville, California, near Los Angeles, the Sheriff's Department received a complaint. Five Mexican men were blasting loud music, drinking beer, and urinating on the lawn in a party that lasted over twelve hours. When six sheriff's deputies came to investigate and tried to quiet the men down, fists and night sticks began to fly. For the sheriff's men, it was hardly a unique event. Except for one thing.

Unknown to them, as they struggled to subdue the five, using night sticks and choke holds, a next-door neighbor pointed a videocamera out the window.

Public outrage against alleged police brutality erupted instantly after the four-minute tape was shown to the town's Latino community. Civil rights protests followed, then a lawsuit against the deputies, charging them with the use of excessive force. Said Armando Navarro, executive director of the Institute for Social Justice, a local civil rights organization, "I've dealt for twenty-one years in community activism, but I've never had something so classic, showing the violence in living color."

Lawyers for the deputies, on the other hand, contended that the tape did not tell the truth because it didn't show what happened before the camera was turned on—when, the deputies say, violence was used against *them*.

The case took on larger dimensions when the person who shot the tape disappeared and when a representative of Mexico's consulate in Los Angeles began showing up in the courtroom to monitor the trial, evidencing concern about anti-Mexican discrimination in the United States. In the end, a federal court ruled against the sheriff's men and awarded the Mexicans $1 million.

It is unlikely that the revolutionaries who overthrew the communist government in Czechoslovakia in 1989 ever heard of the case of the "Victorville Five." But in the streets of Prague, students set up TV monitors on street corners and played videotapes showing the brutality of Czech authorities trying to suppress antigovernment street rallies. The students also played tapes of speeches by dramatist Vaclav Havel, who went from being a political prisoner to the presidency. Elsewhere, in Taiwan, too, the political opposition has used videocameras and monitors to expose what they called government violence.

All across the world, new communication media, or new ways of using old ones, are being exploited to challenge—and sometimes overthrow—the power of the state. In the words of Solidarity founder Lech Walesa, describing the political upheavals in Eastern Europe, "These reforms are a result of civilization—of computers, satellite TV [and other innovations] that present alternative solutions."

THE NASTY LITTLE MAN ON TV

It is clear that the domino-wave of revolutions that swept Eastern Europe in 1989 was a consequence of three convergent forces: the long-term failure of socialism to deliver the economic wealth it promised; the announcement by the Soviet Union that it would no longer prop up communist governments with the threat of military intervention; and the avalanche of information that poured into communist countries despite all the efforts of their censors—information carried by the new means of communication.

During the quarter-century dictatorship of Nicolae Ceausescu, Romania imposed the harshest censorship of any communist regime in Eastern Europe, controlling everything that appeared in the press and especially on television. Ceausescu himself was a television fan, and especially liked episodes of *Kojak*, the American cop-show starring Telly Savalas. But for all his viewing, Ceausescu failed to understand the world media revolution and paid with his life on Christmas Day, 1989.

Had Ceausescu studied the role of the new global media system, for example, in the overthrow of Ferdinand Marcos in the Philippines, he would have known that control of the domestic media is no longer enough to keep a people in ignorance, and that domestic political events are increasingly played out on a global stage.

"What happened in the Philippines," said Professor William Adams, a media expert at George Washington University, "was an epic step toward a new kind of revolution—a revolution via the media and via symbols."

Because of historically close connections between the Philippines and the United States and the continuing presence of U.S. military bases there, Marcos and his main political opposition courted U.S. support. Both sought out foreign journalists to tell their story.

As opposition mounted, Marcos reluctantly agreed to hold an election in 1986. The ensuing campaign was given saturation coverage by the American TV cameras, drawn by the drama of Cory Aquino, widow of an assassinated hero, confronting the corrupt old dictator.

At first President Reagan supported Marcos. But as the U.S. TV coverage continued, Americans saw nice middle-class peaceful demonstrators opposed by Marcos goons, and Reagan's position began to shift. Wrote the television critic of *The Washington Post:* "It didn't look good to be allied with this nasty little man on TV."

Reagan sent an official team to Manila to monitor the elections for corruption and fraud. Led by Senator Richard Lugar, the team found ample evidence of both and disclosed its conclusions to television audiences even before reporting back officially to the President. Its reports further hurt the Marcos campaign, and what Americans saw on their TV screens instantly seeped back into the Philippines.

The TV coverage also influenced the White House, which ultimately backed an anti-Marcos military faction, and with that, the combination of force and information squeezed Marcos out of office. In the end, faced with the inevitable, Marcos fled the country and was permitted to settle in Hawaii.

Said one political analyst afterward: "If he had been one of the twentieth century's great tyrants, he would have kicked out the media and opened up with the machine guns."

Yet the reverse might well have been true for Ceausescu. Had he allowed the media in and not opened up with machine guns, he might conceivably have survived. The initial overthrow of communist regimes in other Eastern European countries in the dramatic winter of 1989 was peaceful. Only in Romania did the machine guns stutter.

One of the dictator's last acts was to order the massacre of protestors in the city of Timisoara. As Romanians swarmed into the streets of Bucharest after that, fighting broke out between the military and Ceausescu's feared security forces, the Securitate. The strife continued for days, the Securitate battling on even after Ceausescu and his wife were given a drumhead trial and shot by a firing squad.

By now the revolution was centered in Studio 4 of "Free Romanian Television." Even as snipers and commandos tried to retake the studio from them, leaders of the revolution, in control of the airwaves, played and replayed pictures of the corpses of the dictator and his wife. Only after that did the bloodshed cease.

Shortly afterward, *The New York Times* declared that his dictatorship had been replaced by a "videocracy."

Following the overthrow of communist regimes all across Eastern Europe, the *Financial Times* exulted: "The medium which George Orwell saw as the tool of enslavement has proved the liberator; not even a Ceausescu could blindfold his people."

Yet by overfocusing on television, many observers miss the larger story. For it isn't just television that is revolutionary, but the combined *interplay* of many different technologies.

Millions of computers, fax machines, printers and copying machines, VCRs, videocassettes, advanced telephones, along with cable and satellite technologies, now interact with one another and cannot be understood in isolation. Television is only a part of this much larger system, which links up at points with the intelligent electronic networks that business and finance use to exchange computerized data.

This new overarching media system is a cause of (and a reaction to) the rise of the new, knowledge-based economy, and it represents a quantum jump in the way the human race uses symbols and images. No part of this vast web is entirely cut off from the rest. And that, in turn, is what makes it potentially subversive—not just for the remaining Ceausecus of the world but for all power-holders. The new media system is a powershift accelerator.

THREE MEDIA MODES

The best way to understand its power is to place today's media revolution in historical perspective, and to distinguish clearly among three different modes of communication.

In highly oversimplified terms, we can say that in First Wave or agrarian societies, most communications passed mouth-to-ear and face-to-face within very small groups. In a world without newspapers, radio, or television, the only way for a message to reach a mass audience was by assembling a crowd. The crowd was, in fact, the first mass medium.

A crowd may "send a message" upward to its ruler. In fact, the very size of the crowd is itself a message. But whatever else the crowd may communicate, it also sends an identical message to all its participants. This message—which can be profoundly subversive—is simple: "You are not alone." The crowd, therefore, has played a crucial role in history. The problem with the crowd or mob as a communications medium, however, is that it is usually ephemeral.

The crowd was not the only pretechnological mass medium. In the West during the medieval era, the Catholic Church, because of its extensive organization, was the closest thing to a durable mass medium—and the only one able to transmit the same message to large populations *across political boundaries*. This unique capacity gave the Vatican immense power vis-à-vis Europe's feuding kings and princelings. It accounts in part for the seesaw power struggles between church and state that bloodied Europe for centuries.

The Second Wave system of wealth creation, based on factory mass production, needed more communication at a distance and gave rise to the post office, telegraph, and telephone. But the new factories also needed a homogeneous work force, and technologically based mass media were invented. Newspapers, magazines, movies, radio, and television, each capable of carrying the same message to millions simultaneously, became the prime instruments of massification in the industrial societies.

The new Third Wave system, by contrast, reflects the needs of the emerging post-mass-production economy. Like the latest "flexible manufacturing" plants, it customizes its image products and sends different images, ideas, and symbols to closely targeted population segments, markets, age categories, professions, ethnic or life-style groupings.

This new high diversity of messages and media is necessary because the new system of wealth creation requires a far more heterogeneous work force and population. The de-massification foreshadowed in *Future Shock* and elaborated in *The Third Wave* thus has become a key characteristic of the new media system. But this is only one of its aspects.

MEDIA-FUSION

Unlike the Second Wave media, each of which operated more or less independently of the other, the new media are closely interlinked and fused together, feeding data, images, and symbols back and forth to one another. Examples of this fusion abound.

A radio call-in show, which links listeners and broadcasters via the telephone lines, becomes the subject of a 1988 movie, *Talk Radio*, which in turn is shown on cable television and reviewed in the print media and then—who knows?—discussed on radio call-in shows.

Or take *Broadcast News*, a movie about television newscasters, which after being shown in many cinemas is itself shown on television and advertised in the newspapers.

Newsweek describes "the now almost commonplace spectacle of an Iowa farmer being interviewed by a print reporter who is being shot by a still photographer who is being taped by a TV crew, all of which is the subject of a magazine's media story." A still photograph of precisely that scene illustrates the *Newsweek* account.

At a deeper level, newspaper newsrooms watch TV monitors to keep abreast of the latest events. Many European correspondents in Washington watch CNN's live coverage and write their newspaper stories based on what television shows them. From serving as the medium, TV becomes the source.

TV talk-show producers get ideas for subjects and guests from the newspapers. All of them depend on fax, computers, word processors, electronic typesetters, digitized imagery, electronic networks, satellites, or other interlinked technologies.

It is this dense interpenetration that transforms the individual media into a *system*. Combined with globalization, it reduces the clout of any single medium, channel, publication, or technology relative to all the others. But it endows the media system-as-a-whole with an enormously enhanced power that permeates the planet. What is at work, therefore, is not "videocracy" but "media-fusion."

VALLEYS OF IGNORANCE

To "fusion" must be added "diffusion," for no part of the world is now completely cut off from the rest. Messages get through the most tightly guarded borders.

Despite Ceausecu's cruel censorship, many Romanians were able to pick up Bulgarian television from across the border. (Many Bulgarians, in turn, preferred Soviet television to their own.) Even before the revolution, Romanians knew the names of the anti-Ceausescu dissidents who risked imprisonment by calling for human rights. Their names were familiar from foreign broadcasts beamed into Romania.

Most East Germans were able to watch West German television stations, which told them things their Communist government would have preferred to suppress. Thus in 1989, when big anti-government demonstrations occurred in Leipzig, East Germans learned about it from West German transmissions. In the same way, they found out when Hungary opened its borders to East German refugees and where cracks were opening in the Berlin Wall. Those out of reach of these West German TV transmissions lived mainly in the Dresden region, which was spoken of as the "Valley of Ignorance." These "valleys" are getting smaller.

Cross-border television "leakage" is hardly new, nor is the fact that Voice of America and Radio Free Europe, the British Broadcasting Corporation (BBC), and others beamed shortwave programming into the communist countries. During the China democracy protests preceding the massacre near Tiananmen Square, the Voice of America broadcast eleven and a half hours a day, reaching an estimated 100 million Chinese listeners. It even broadcast simple instructions on how to avoid government attempts to "jam" the transmissions.

What is different now, however, is the subversive media strategy employed by today's revolutionaries.

THE REVOLUTIONISTS' MEDIA STRATEGY

What Ceausescu was not alone in missing were the strategic ways in which First Wave, Second Wave, and Third Wave communications can sometimes be combined or opposed to one another.

A good example is provided by religion.

One of the biggest gainers from the 1989 revolutions in Eastern Europe has been the Catholic Church, long suppressed but never destroyed by the communist regimes. The church, as suggested above, was itself a mass medium, long before today's Jim Bakkers and Jimmy Swaggerts hit the Protestant televangelical circuit, and long before Pat Robertson built so large a TV following that he was able to mount a campaign for the presidency of the United States.

The church wields power in the world today partly because of its moral influence and economic resources, but also because it continues to serve as a mass medium. Able to reach numberless millions every Sunday morning, it makes the audience for some of the world's top-rated television shows seem small indeed. Of course, it communicates with its members the other six days of the week as well, and in today's world the church makes use of newspapers, magazines, and other media in support of its face-to-face communications.

So long as the Catholic Church—or any other organized religion—can gather enormous flocks, and thus reach a mass audience, no government can ignore it. Some governments, as we know, have tried to extirpate the church (which is almost impossible). Others have tried peddling a substitute religion based on nationalism, Marxism, or some other doctrine. Still others compromise and try to co-opt the church.

In totalitarian states the existence of an unco-opted or unsuppressed mass medium in the hands of the church is a constant threat, for there is always the danger that this channel will be made available to the political opposition. This accounts for the ferocity with which communist states tried to kill off the church or to buy it off when that proved impossible.

The recognition that organized religion, whatever else it might be, is also a mass medium helps explain many recent shifts of power.

It helps explain why, so often in history, in countries as different as Iran under the Shah or South Korea under Chun Doo Hwan, economic and other popular discontents are channeled into religious movements. In Iran, of course, this canalization of protest into a religious form led to the overthrow of the Shah's secular regime. In South Korea it led to a spectacular growth of Christianity, both Catholic and Protestant. In both countries organized religion took the place of, or merged with, a political opposition.

Ironically, the more successfully a totalitarian government censors and controls all the other media of expression, the more important the church medium becomes as a potential vehicle for dissidence. It may be the only way to express opposition to a regime.

But when the church opens its "channel" and expresses popular resentment from the pulpit, the medium alters the message, and the protest, which may originate in hunger or other material grievances, is recast in religious terms. This explains why movements that start out fighting for goals having little to do with religion, per se, become transmuted into religious crusades.

In Iran, the Ayatollah Khomeini fused class resentment and nationalist rage with religious fervor. Love of Allah + hatred of imperialism + anticapitalism = a triple-charged brand of fanaticism that turned the Middle East into a tinderbox.

But Khomeini did more than combine these three elements into a single passion. He also combined First Wave media—face-to-face exhortation by his mullahs to the faithful—with Third Wave technology—audio tapes with political messages, smuggled into the mosques, where they were played and duplicated on cheap tape recorders.

To counter Khomeini, the Shah used the Second Wave media—press, radio, and television. Once Khomeini managed to overthrow the Shah and take control of the state, he also took command of these centralized Second Wave media as well.

This strategy of using First and Third Wave media to combat those who control Second Wave media is common among revolutionary movements, and was even more conspicuous in China during the pro-democracy protests of 1989. The old men in Beijing who trembled when Ceausescu fell in Bucharest, six months after they massacred students near Tiananmen Square, underestimated the power of this strategy.

THE CHINA SYNDROME

In China, too, three modes of communication clashed in the battle for control of the mind.

Wall posters were a traditional First Wave tool of protest in China. Early in 1989 posters began showing up on the walls near Beijing University, lashing out at corruption, making fun of the privileged children of the party's top leaders, urging broadened democracy, calling for the ouster of Premier Li Peng and others.

By late spring, that other First Wave communications weapon, the crowd, came into play. Using the memorial service for the late Hu Yaobang, a reformist Communist Party leader, students from Beijing universities gathered in Tiananmen Square on April 22. The protesters' initial demands were moderate, focusing mainly on freedom of expression and an end to corruption. But as the government rebuffed the student demands, the demonstrators stayed on in the square and began a hunger strike. The peaceful crowds grew.

Soon they were joined by industrial workers bearing banners that proclaimed "Here come your elder brothers." And as the government stonewalled, the momentum grew until, at its peak on May 18 and 19, more than a million still-peaceful marchers from every walk of life took to the streets. The massive size of this crowd was itself a clear message.

During this same period, a fierce struggle broke out among the Chinese authorities over how to respond. The government, headed by Li Peng, tried to turn the Second Wave media—newspapers, radio, and television—against the protesters. But the party, headed by its reformist chairman, Zhao Ziyang, controlled much of the media, including the party organ, *People's Daily*.

As this power struggle tilted back and forth, the news coverage in the Second Wave media seesawed. When Zhao's supporters gained, *People's Daily* and Chinese television showed sympathy for the strikers' demands. By contrast, when the hard-liners gained, newscasters, editors, and journalists were forced to slant news against the protesters, thus using the Second Wave media to blunt the message carried by First Wave media.

Simultaneously, however, a battle began for control of the more advanced Third Wave media: satellites, fax machines, hand-held TV cameras, computers, copiers, and global communication networks.

The hard-liners now faced a double problem. They had to win decisive control not only over the domestic media, but over foreign press coverage as well. A wild card in the situation was the presence of a vast corps of foreign journalists and broadcasters who had come to China to cover the Gorbachev-Deng summit meeting. These journalists, many relying on satellites, computers, and other advanced Third Wave tools, stayed to cover events in the streets.

Particularly important was the Cable News Network, whose round-the-clock coverage went not merely into the White House and to millions of viewers around the world but, equally important, into hotels in Beijing itself. As the political battle raged, Chinese officials cut off its satellite links to the outside world, then restored them, then told foreign broadcasters to use China TV's own up-links. Confusion reigned.

Aware that global opinion is growing more important, the hard-liners tried desperately to cut all connections between the protesters and their supporters outside China. But because China in recent years had opened extensive economic relations with the outside world, and had permitted students to study abroad, this proved very difficult.

The protesters aimed many messages directly at foreign audiences. They patiently repeated their demands for the reporters and TV crews from abroad. They translated. They painted slogans in foreign languages so television viewers outside China could instantly understand them. "Le 1789 de Chine" compared their uprising to the French Revolution. For American consumption, they sang "We Shall Overcome" and adapted the words of Patrick Henry—"Give me democracy or give me death." These efforts to reach out were rewarded by sympathy marches in Hong Kong, Taiwan, Australia, and all across the United States.

Meanwhile, at Harvard University, a Chinese student set up a Beijing-to-Boston "hot line"—an open telephone link that brought round-the-clock news from Tiananmen Square to his small apartment near Harvard. From there it went by phone, fax, and computer to Chinese students all over the United States.

In turn, students at Stanford and Berkeley created what they termed a "news-lift"—using fax machines to send back to the strikers the latest news stories appearing in the U.S. press. These were addressed to the offices of companies in Beijing and other cities, in the hope that friendly hands would deliver them to the striking students. There were an estimated 30,000 fax machines in China and 3 million phone lines into Beijing.

The Chinese students in the United States, many of them the sons and daughters of high government and party officials, also tape-recorded telephone interviews with strikers and immediately delivered these to the Voice of America, which broadcast them back into China. When the government began jamming, the VOA switched to new frequencies.

This global battle for control of knowledge and the means of communication continued even after the hard-liners, having called out troops, killed many demonstrators and smashed the strike. Again relying on the Second Wave mass media, the government now broadcast pictures of student and worker "ringleaders" and displayed telephone numbers for informers to use if they spotted the fugitives.

But the same video was broadcast outside China, and from Canada to Italy, televiewers using international direct-dial phones tried to jam the lines so Chinese informers could not reach the government. It was the first known attempt at citizen-jamming across national borders.

In China, power once more blasted out of the barrel of a gun, as Mao Tse-tung said it would. But it was clear, as the events in Eastern Europe and elsewhere underscored, that the hard-liners who seized control could not rest easy in victory. China's move into the 21st century had only just begun.

What the China story also revealed, however, with startling clarity, were the media strategies of revolution and counterrevolution. Today, the Second Wave mass media still exert enormous influence. As the world speeds deeper into the Powershift Era, however, the Second Wave tools of mind control, once so overwhelming, will themselves be overwhelmed by the subversive media of tomorrow.

28

THE "SCREENIE" GENERATION

At almost the precise midpoint of the 20th century, George Orwell published *1984*, his scorching indictment of totalitarianism. The book pictured a government in total control of the mass media. Orwell's brilliant neologisms, like *newspeak* and *doublethink*, entered the language. The book became a powerful assault weapon in the fight against censorship and mind-manipulation, which is why it was banned for decades in the Soviet Union.

While it helped rally forces opposed to dictatorship of the mind, however, the book's projection of the future turned out to be highly questionable.

Orwell correctly envisioned such technologies as two-way television screens that could be used to deliver the state's propaganda to viewers while simultaneously spying on them, and his warnings about potential invasions of privacy are, if anything, understated. But he did not foresee—nor did anyone else at the time—the most important revolution of our era: the shift from an economy based on muscle to one dependent on mind.

He did not, therefore, anticipate today's astonishing proliferation of new communication tools. The number and variety of these technologies is now so great, and changing so swiftly, that even experts are bewildered. To confront the army of technical abbreviations, from HDTV and ISDN to VAN, ESS, PABX, CPE, OCC, and CD-I, is to sink into alphabetical asphalt. Even to scan the advertisements for consumer electronics is to come away dazed.

Rise above this clutter, however, and the basic outlines of tomorrow's Third Wave media become strikingly clear.

The electronic infrastructure of the advanced economies will have six distinct features, some of which have already been foreshadowed. These half-dozen keys to the future are: interactivity, mobility, convertibility, connectivity, ubiquity, and globalization.

When combined, these six principles point to a total transformation, not merely in the way we send messages to one another, but in the way we think, how we see ourselves in the world, and, therefore, where we stand in relationship to our various governments. Put together, they will make it impossible for governments —or their revolutionary opponents—to manage ideas, imagery, data, information, or knowledge as they once did.

THE SLAVE GOLFER

In a long low building on Los Angeles's Santa Monica Boulevard, a former president of the 20th Century-Fox movie studios, Gordon Stulberg, banters with Bernard Luskin, a psychotherapist. Luskin is a former community college president and a past head of the California Educational Computing Consortium. Together they run American Interactive Media's team of educators, artists, and computer programmers who plan to launch upon the world the next advance in compact-disc technology—CD-I, as in "Interactive."

AIM plans to release discs that play on the home television screen and make it possible for the viewer to interact with the visuals. Holding a remote in the palm of the hand and using one's thumb on a tiny "joystick," the owner of a disc called "Interactive Golf" can tee off against another player, manipulating a slave golfer on the screen as he lines up his shot. You can choose his clubs and determine the power and the arc of the drive. You can make him turn to the right or left and alter his swing. You control what happens on the screen.

The "Grolier Encyclopedia" disc makes it possible to call up audiovisual information about any of its listings. The text, animation, and visuals explain, say, a car engine or a DNA molecule, and can be moved and manipulated by the user.

Other interactive AIM discs include games, Bible stories, a new kind of atlas, a course in photography developed with Time-Life, and a disk that takes you on a tour of the Smithsonian and lets you manipulate the exhibits as you stroll through.

Owned by Polygram Records, a subsidiary of N.V. Philips, the

Dutch electronics giant, AIM is just one of several firms working with interactive video technology. Their goal is to make the TV experience active, rather than passive—to put the couch potato out of business.

Meanwhile, Interactive Game Network, a Northern California firm partly funded by United Artists, Le Groupe Videotron, Ltd., and General Electronics, Ltd., is taking a different path toward the same goal. It is building a device that will allow the home viewer to participate in popular TV game shows like *Jeopardy* or *Wheel of Fortune*. Players will communicate their answers to a central computer which will check all the home scores and choose a prizewinner.

But the most radical leap toward interactivity—still a gleam in the eye—consists of a vast network of what author George Gilder has called "telecomputers": interactive TV sets that are, in effect, personal computers too.

In addition to discs or cassettes, the TV set itself will come alive in the hands of its user, according to Gilder, who has looked closely at the technological frontiers in video and computing. "The line between 'television'—a business where Japan now reigns supreme—and 'computers'—where American industry holds the best cards—is blurring every day," he reports. The coming merger of these two technologies will shift power from the old television networks to the users, allowing them "to reshape the images as they wish." This new hybrid could also shift power from Japan to the United States, Gilder claims.

Whether that is true or not, two powerful streams of technical development are both pushing toward a vast extension of video interactivity.

A DECADENT LUXURY

A second principle of the new system is mobility. The phone in the airplane cabin and, even more, the cordless phone and the mobile car phone have begun to accustom users to the idea of communication from anywhere to anywhere while in motion.

At first regarded as a decadent luxury (the earliest telephones themselves were similarly regarded in the 19th century), car phones based on cellular radio have come into widespread use in the United States.

A consortium called Phonepoint, representing the German Bundespost, France Telecom, and Nynex, the New York telephone company, as well as British Telecom, is speeding the introduction of sophisticated "pocket phones" in England as well. Nor are mobile units purely decorative status symbols. For salespeople, plumbers, physicians, and others they have become a productivity-enhancing work tool.

As people work and play on the move, the demand for even cheaper, simpler, always-there communications is soaring, which provides the basis for the coming leap to that comic-strip invention, the Dick Tracy wristwatch phone.

But the phone is only one of a host of new devices that are becoming unplugged from the wall. Sony offers a 4.6-ounce pocket-size copier. The fax machine in the car, the vest-pocket video, the laptop computer, the portable printer are all spreading fast. Mobility is a second fundamental trait of the new system.

Convertibility is next—the ability to transfer information from one medium to another. For example, we are moving toward speech-based technologies that can convert an oral message into printed form and vice versa. Machines that can take dictation from several executives at the same time and spew out typed letters are well on the way toward practicality.

Such tools may shake up everything from employment and the organization of the office, to the role of literacy in daily life. But they are trivial compared with another form of conversion: automatic translation. Automatic conversion of commercial documents from one language to another, at least in a rough-and-ready form, is already available on France's Minitel system, as we saw in Chapter 10. More sophisticated translation is the object of intense research in Japan (which regards its language as an economic barrier). Similarly, the EC, which faces the need to translate into the languages of its twelve member nations, is eager for breakthroughs.

The fourth principle of the new infrastructure, connectivity, is a buzzword among computer and telecommunications users the world over, who are demanding the ability to connect their devices to a dazzling diversity of other devices, regardless of which manufacturer made them in what country.

Despite the heated political battles over standards, immense efforts are now driving toward connectibility, so that the same mobile, interactive, video-voice telecomputer of tomorrow can tie into an IBM mainframe in Chicago, a Toshiba laptop being used in Frankfurt, a Cray supercomputer in Silicon Valley, or a house-wife's Dick Tracy phone in Seoul.

MORE THAN COMPASSION

Ubiquitization, the fifth key, is something else. By this we mean the systematic spread of the new media system around the world and down through every economic layer of society.

A potential nightmare facing high-tech governments derives from the split-up of populations into the info-rich and the info-poor. Any government that fails to take concrete action to avoid this division courts political upheaval in the future. Yet this dangerous polarization is hardly inevitable.

In fact, one can imagine considerable equality of access in the emerging society, not because of compassion or political good sense on the part of the affluent elites, but because of the workings of what might be called the Law of Ubiquity.

This law holds that strong commercial, as well as political, incentives will arise for making the new electronic infrastructure inclusive, rather than exclusive.

In its infancy the telephone was regarded as a luxury. The idea that everyone would someday have a phone was simply mystifying. Why on earth would everybody want one?

The fact that almost everyone in the high-tech nations now has a phone, rich and poor alike, did not stem from altruism but from the fact that the more people plugged into a system, the more valuable it became for all users and especially for commercial purposes.

The same proved true, as we've seen, in the early development of postal services. The industrial economy needed a way to send bills to, or advertise to, or sell newspapers and magazines to everyone, not just the rich. And today, once more, as fax machines begin to replace the industrial-era post office, similar pressures are accelerating the spread of the new technology.

There were 2.5 million fax machines in the United States in 1989, churning out billions of pages of faxed documents per year.

The fax population was doubling yearly, partly because early users were importuning friends, customers, clients, and family to buy a fax quickly, so that the early users could speed messages to them. The more faxes out there, the greater the value of the system to all concerned.

It is, therefore, in the distinct self-interest of the affluent to find ways of extending the new systems to include, rather than exclude, the less affluent.

Like phones and VCRs, faxes will begin to appear in even the humblest homes, driven by the Law of Ubiquity. And so will fiber optic cables and other advanced technologies, whether paid for by the individual, the public, or by other users whose fees will subsidize service to those who can't afford it.

The widest diffusion of communication capabilities is an inseparable part of the new system of wealth creation. The direction is almost inevitably toward what the old Bell phone company called "universal service"—i.e., ubiquity—combined with interactivity, mobility, convertibility, and connectibility.

Finally, the new infrastructure is global in scope. As capital flows electronically across national borders, zipping back and forth from Zurich to Hong Kong, Hong Kong to Norway, Norway to Tokyo, Tokyo to Wall Street in milliseconds, information traces equally complex pathways. A change in U.S. T-bill rates or the yen–deutsche mark ratio is instantly known around the world, and the morning after the big event in Los Angeles, youngsters in Ho Chi Minh City discuss the latest Grammy winners. The mental borders of the state become as permeable as its financial frontiers.

The combination of these six principles produces a revolutionary nervous system for the planet, capable of handling vastly enlarged quantities of data, information, and knowledge at much faster transmission and processing rates. It is a far more adaptable, intelligent, and complex nervous system for the human race than ever before imagined.

ELECTRONIC ACTIVISM

The rise of a new media system, corresponding in form with the requirements of a wholly new way of creating wealth, challenges those in power, giving rise to new political methods, constituencies, and alliances.

Just as people at, say, the beginning of the 18th century could not imagine the political changes that flowed from the spread of a smokestack economy, so today it is almost impossible, short of science-fiction-style speculation, to foresee the political uses to which the still emerging media system will be put.

Take, for example, interactivity.

By allowing TV viewers to use, rather than merely view, the screen, interactivity could someday change political campaigning and candidates. Interactive media make possible far more sophisticated opinion polling than ever before, not simply asking yes-no questions, but allowing respondents to make trade-offs among many options.

But the possibilities go beyond polling. Would a candidate, once elected, trade off jobs for environmental improvement—and if so, how many? How would the candidate respond to a hostage crisis, a race riot, or a nuclear disaster under differing sets of circumstances? Instead of trying to test the values and judgment of a potential President by listening to thirty-second commercials, the interactive video users of tomorrow could tune into a program, or insert a diskette, that would visually show the candidate discussing and making decisions under a variety of conditions programmed in by the voter. Political platforms could be issued in a spreadsheet format, so that the voters could manipulate their underlying budgetary assumptions and ask "what if" questions.

If large numbers can participate in a mass-appeal game show like *Jeopardy* with a computer tallying their responses, it doesn't take too much imagination to see how similar technology could be adapted to political polling or collective decision-taking—and political organizing of a new kind.

Futurists, simulation experts, and others have long speculated about the possibility of organizing very large numbers of citizens in political "games." Professor José Villegas at Cornell University developed models for such activity as far back as the late 1960s, including games that ghetto residents and squatters could engage in as a form of political education—and protest.

What was missing was the technology. The spread of networked interactivity will place the tools for political "games" in millions of living rooms. With them, citizens could, in principle at least, conduct their own polls, and form their own "electronic parties" or "electronic lobbies" and pressure groups around various issues.

One can also easily imagine electronic sabotage, not as the act of individual hackers or criminals, but for the purposes of political protest or blackmail. At 2:25 P.M. on the afternoon of January 15, 1990, engineers in Bedminster, New Jersey, noticed red lights flashing on the seventy-five screens that display the status of AT&T's long-distance telephone network in the United States. Each light indicated trouble.

"It just seemed to happen. Poof, there it was," said William Leach, manager of AT&T's network operations center. That "poof" added up to a massive breakdown in the U.S. long-distance phone system lasting for nine hours, during which an estimated 65 million calls were blocked.

AT&T investigators concluded that the breakdown resulted from a faulty computer program. But they could not "categorically rule ... out" the possibility that it resulted from sabotage. It so happened that January 15 was the national holiday celebrating the birth of Dr. Martin Luther King, Jr. It also happened to be true that some racist Americans bitterly hated King and were outraged that a national holiday should commemorate him. The AT&T "blackout" may simply have been a random occurrence. But it doesn't stretch credulity too far to imagine electronic political protests and sabotage in the future.

One needn't engage in sci-fi speculation, however, to recognize some of the profound social tensions already arising from the introduction of a new form of economy—problems related to the way knowledge is disseminated in society.

THE INFORMATION DIVIDE

Today, because the Law of Ubiquity has not yet completed its action, high-tech societies, and especially the United States, suffer from a maldistribution of information—an "information divide" as deep as the Grand Canyon.

A seemingly intractable problem in many of the high-tech nations is the existence of what has come to be called an "underclass." The presence of this underclass is not only a moral affront to affluent societies but a menace to social peace, and ultimately a threat to democracy. It is simple-minded to assume that all those in the underclass are "victims" of society or unemployment. Many, perhaps most, are there for other reasons.

What is increasingly clear, however, is that work requires higher and higher informational skills, so that even if jobs are available, most of the members of this group cannot match the knowledge requirements.

Moreover, the knowledge needed goes beyond task-specific job skills. To be truly employable a worker must share certain implicit cultural understandings about things like time, dress, courtesy, money, causality, and language. Above all, the worker must be able to get and exchange information.

These generalized cultural skills cannot come out of textbooks or training sessions alone. They presuppose a familiarity with how the world-beyond-one's-own-street functions. That kind of knowledge comes increasingly from the media environment. It is from the media that people infer both social norms and "facts" about how things work.

The nature of the media, the pictures they deliver, the groups they target, and the feedback they permit are directly related, therefore, both to employment and to the problems of the underclass. Furthermore, the cultural divide between the underclass and the mainstream society actually widens as the new media system spreads.

Jeffrey Moritz is president of National College Television, which uses satellites to distribute specialized programming to college students for forty-two hours a week. NCT claims a student audience of 700,000. Ranging in age from eighteen to thirty-four, these are citizens today and potential leaders tomorrow. They represent, if anything, the polar opposite of the young people in the underclass. (As Moritz points out, the U.S. college population of today probably includes within it two future Presidents, a hundred senators, and thousands of corporate CEOs.)

Here is how Moritz describes them:

"Today's college student of age 20 is the most 'video-sophisticated audience' in history. . . .Twenty years ago *Sesame Street* went on the air, specifically designed to educate infants and pre-school children with sophisticated television techniques including short (90-second) segments, dazzling video effects, interactive involvement, new heroes, easy daily access, etc. This audience migrated [as it grew older, to other programs like] *Electric Company, Zoom,* to *Nickelodeon,* MTV—each a move representing an inexorable progression. . . .The audience created by *Sesame Street* now reshaped all of television!"

The TV programs he cites are all either shown on the public—i.e., educational—network or on cable channels, rather than on the major Second Wave networks.

Moritz uses the term *screenie* to describe this video-drenched generation, which has digested thousands of hours of television, imbibing its "video-logic." To that must be added, for many of them, more hours of interactive video games and, even more important, of work on their own personal computers. They not only follow a different logic, but are accustomed to make the screen do things, thus making them good prospects for the interactive services and products soon to hit the market. Above all, they are accustomed to choice.

The vast divide between the youth of the underclass and the screenie, which now characterizes the United States, will widen in Europe, Japan, and other high-tech nations, too, unless steps are taken to bridge the informational Grand Canyon.

THE NEW ALLIANCE

In a knowledge-based economy the most important domestic political issue is no longer the distribution (or redistribution) of wealth, but of the information and media that produce wealth.

This is a change so revolutionary it cannot be mapped by conventional political cartography. The new wealth-creation system will compel politicians, activists, and political theorists—whether they still regard themselves as left-wing or right-wing, radical or conservative, feminist or traditionalist—to rethink all political ideas developed during the smokestack era. The very categories are now obsolete.

Social justice and freedom both now increasingly depend on how each society deals with three issues: education; information technology (including the media); and freedom of expression.

In the case of education, the reconceptualization now required is so profound, reaching so far beyond questions of budgets, class size, teacher pay, and the traditional conflicts over curriculum, that it cannot be dealt with here. Like the Second Wave TV networks (or for that matter all the smokestack industries), our mass education systems are largely obsolete. Exactly as in the case of the media, education will require a proliferation of new channels and a vast expansion of program diversity. A high-choice system will have to replace a low-choice system if schools are to prepare people for a decent life in the new Third Wave society, let alone for economically productive roles.

The links between education and the six principles of the new media system—interactivity, mobility, convertibility, connectivity, ubiquity, and globalization—have scarcely been explored. Yet to ignore the relationships between the educational system of the future and the media system of the future is to cheat the learners who will be formed by both.

Significantly, education is no longer merely a priority for parents, teachers, and a handful of education reformers, but for the advanced sectors of business as well, since its leaders increasingly recognize the connection between education and global competitiveness.

The second priority involves the speedy universalization of access to computers, information technology, and the advanced media. No nation can operate a 21st-century economy without a 21st-century electronic infrastructure, embracing computers, data communications, and the other new media. This requires a population as familiar with this informational infrastructure as it is with cars, roads, highways, trains, and the transportation infrastructure of the smokestack period.

Not everyone, of course, needs to be a telecom engineer or a computer expert, just as not everyone needs to be a car mechanic. But access to the media system, including computers, faxes, and advanced telecommunications, must be as free and easy as access is today to the transportation system. A key objective of those who want an advanced economy, therefore, should be to accelerate the workings of the Law of Ubiquity—that is, to make sure that all citizens, poor and rich alike, are guaranteed access to the widest possible range of media.

Finally, if the essence of the new economy is knowledge, the democratic ideal of freedom of expression becomes a top political priority, rather than a peripheral matter.

The state—any state—is in business to stay in power. Whatever the economic costs to the rest of us, it will seek ways to harness the latest communications revolution to its purposes, and it will set limits on the free flow of information.

Just as the state invented new forms of mind control when the industrial revolution brought mass media into being, it will search for new tools and techniques to retain at least some control over the images, ideas, symbols, and ideologies reaching its people through the new electronic infrastructure.

Enthusiasm over the way the media were used to overthrow totalitarian regimes in Eastern Europe should not blind citizens to the more sophisticated mind manipulations that governments and politicians will attempt in the future.

No society can tolerate total freedom of information. Some secrecy is necessary to all social life. Total freedom of information would mean total lack of individual privacy. There are moments of extreme crisis, moments of "clear and present danger," when absolute freedom invites arsonists to spread gasoline on a raging fire. Absolute freedom of expression is, therefore, no more possible than absolute anything else.

But the more the society advances toward a super-symbolic economy, the more important it becomes to permit an extremely wide range of dissent and free expression. The more any government chokes off or chills this rich, free flow of data, information, and knowledge—including wild ideas, innovation, and even political dissent—the more it slows down the advance of the new economy.

For the vast extension of the global neural system coincides with the most important change in the function of free expression since at least the French and American revolutions.

In the agrarian past, new ideas were often a threat to survival. In communities living on the thin edge of subsistence, using methods honed over the centuries, any deviation was dangerous to an economy that left little margin for risk. The very notion of freedom of thought was alien.

With the rise of science and the industrial revolution, a radical new notion came into being: that minds free of state or religious shackles were necessary for "progress." But the population to whom this applied was a fraction of the total.

With the revolutionary rise of the new wealth-creation system, it is not a fraction of the working population but a substantial and ever-expanding number whose productivity depends precisely on the freedom to create everything from new product designs to new computer logics, metaphors, scientific insights, and epistemologies.

Super-symbolic economies grow from cultures constantly provoked by new, often dissenting ideas, including political ideas.

The fight for free expression, once the province of intellectuals, thus becomes a matter of concern to all who favor economic advance. Like adequate education and access to the new media, freedom of expression is no longer a political nicety, but a precondition for economic competitiveness.

This discovery lays the basis for an unusual political coalition of the future—one that brings together two groups who have, since the early days of the industrial revolution, been frequent adversaries: intellectuals, scientists, artists, and civil libertarians, on the one side, and advanced managers and even shareholders and capitalists on the other, all of whom will now find that their interests depend on revolutionizing the education system, widening the access of the entire population to computers and the other new media, and protecting—even extending—freedom of expression.

Such a coalition is the best guarantee of both intellectual and economic advance in the economies of the 21st century.

For Marx, freedom was the recognition of necessity. Those who wish to build 21st-century economies could find that necessity is the mother of freedom.

CODA:

YEARNINGS FOR A NEW DARK AGE

We now face the ultimate political power shift. We can redesign democracy for the 21st century—or descend into a new Dark Age.

One path moves power from the state toward the individual. The other threatens to shrink the individual to zero.

Nothing in the foreseeable future is about to take the gun out of the hands of the state. Nothing will prevent the state from siphoning wealth into its hands and disposing of it for its own power-enhancing purposes. What *is* likely to change, as we've already begun to see, is the state's ability to control knowledge.

The new economy thrives on freer expression, better feedback between rulers and ruled, more popular participation in decision-making. It can produce a less bureaucratic, more decentralized and responsive government. It can create a greater independence for the individual, a power shift away from the state—not its "withering away" but its humanization.

Yet any new alliance of democratic groups will face three giant forces now racing toward convergence in a worldwide crusade that could, if we are not careful, sweep us into a new Dark Age.

HOLY FRENZY

Organized religion, in one form or another, had a virtual monopoly on the production and distribution of abstract knowledge in the pre-smokestack era, the time before the Enlightenment, before the birth of democracy in the West. Today, forces are at work seeking to restore that monopoly control of the mind.

The resurgence of religio-politics around the world may seem to have little to do with the rise of the computer and the new economy. But it does.

The knowledge-based wealth-creation system, of which the computer is the symbol, rings down the curtain on three centuries during which the industrial nations dominated the earth. Within the smokestack nations, this period was marked by a war for the mind between the forces of religion, aligned with the power elites of the agrarian age, and secular forces that fought for industrial "modernism" and mass democracy.

By the middle of the industrial era, these secular forces had managed to subdue organized religion, weakening its hold on the schools, on morality, and on the state itself.

By the 1960s a *Time* magazine cover was asking "Is God dead?" and a tormented Catholic Church convened the Second Vatican Council, one of its most important events in centuries. The three great religions of the West, where industrialism had triumphed, had all seen their social, moral, and political power diminish.

It was, however, precisely at this moment that the computer actually began to change the way wealth was produced. The technology that would most radically undermine the blue-collar, factory-based economy began to move more rapidly out of the laboratories and a few corporate and government installations, and into general use.

Coinciding with this revolutionary development, most advanced in the United States, there arose the hippie movement, which launched a savage attack on the cultural premises of the industrial age, including its secularism.

With the long hair came a bitter technophobia and a widespread interest in mysticism, drugs, Eastern cults, astrology, and off-brand religion. The movement looked at industrial society, hated what it saw, and urged a return to some haloed, mythical past. Its back-to-the-earthism, granny glasses, Indian beads, and headbands symbolized the hippies' rejection of the entire smokestack era and their yearning for a return to preindustrial culture. This was the seed from which sprang today's sprawling, burgeoning New Age movement, with its myriad mysticisms and its search for the sacral.

By the 1970s and 1980s, signs of crisis in the old industrial society were everywhere. Its ecological by-products threatened life itself. Its basic industries began to shrink in the face of new, high-tech goods and service production. Its urban systems, health systems, education systems, all plunged into crisis. Its greatest corporations were forced to restructure. Its labor unions declined. Its communities were torn by moral conflict, devastated by drugs, crime, family breakup, and other agonies.

Outraged by the hippies' pagan rejection of traditional Christianity, upset by the breakup of the familiar world, Christian fundamentalists also began a powerful counterattack on secularism that soon took the form of highly effective political action. Here, again, was a violent rejection of the messy, painful present and a search for the absolutist certainties of the past. Hippie and counterhippie, pagan and Christian, whatever their differences, joined in the assault on secular society.

Those launching this assault did not see themselves as enemies of democracy. Most would no doubt be offended at the very idea. Some among the hippies were, if anything, libertarians. Yet the secularism they attacked was one of the pillars of democracy in the modern era.

Meanwhile, there were signs of religious revival, followed by fundamentalist extremism, in many other parts of the world.

In the Middle East, starting at the end of World War I, leaders like Ataturk in Turkey, Reza Shah and the Shah in Iran, had come to power. These were men committed to "modernizing" their societies. They began building secular societies in which the mullahs and religious firebrands were forced to take a back seat.

These secular regimes, however, were identified with continued Western colonialism. Exploitation and corruption flourished, producing moral outrage. Ruling elites spent more time skiing in Gstaad and conferring with their private bankers in Zurich than in distributing income widely. During the Cold War, the intelligence agencies of various industrial powers, capitalist and communist alike, sometimes found it in their interest to subsidize Middle Eastern religious extremists.

All these factors kept relighting the fires of religious fundamentalism, ultimately symbolized by the holy frenzy of Khomeiniism, with its all-out attack on the modern world and the secularism it flaunted.

This fanatic attack might have carried less punch if industrial civilization, the home of secularism, were not itself in moral and social crisis, no longer offering a very attractive model for emulation by the rest of the world. Indeed, the industrial states, now torn apart internally, no longer seemed as invincible as they once had. Now hostage-takers, terrorists, and petroleum sheiks were able to jerk them around, seemingly at will.

As the smokestack era ended, therefore, its reigning secular philosophy was attacked from within and without, from many sides at once, and fundamentalism and religion in general took wing.

In the U.S.S.R., where Mikhail Gorbachev attempted to transform the economy and political system, the fires of Islamic fundamentalism began licking around the entire southern edge of the Soviet state. Soon Muslim Azeris and Christian Armenians were killing each other throughout the Caucasus, and when Soviet troops and militia were sent to restore order, the Iranian government warned Moscow not to use force against Muslims. The flames grew stronger. With Gorbachev's reforms allowing greater freedom of expression, there came signs of a revival of Christian fundamentalism as well.

Elsewhere, there were similar phenomena. In Israel, meanwhile, secular Jews were beaten and their cars stoned by Jewish fundamentalists whose ideas and social models were shaped by centuries of life in the tiny preindustrial *shtetls* of Eastern Europe and in Middle Eastern communities. In India, Muslim fundamentalism ripped across Kashmir, and Hindu fundamentalism across the rest of the subcontinent.

In Japan, where Buddhism and Shinto coexist, it is not possible to describe religion in Western terms, so the very concept of fundamentalism may be inapplicable. Nevertheless, there are evidences of a new interest in ancient forms of Shinto that the pre–World War II militarist regime exploited for its own political purposes. In 1989 the Ministry of Education issued a controversial order that pupils be taught respect for the Emperor, who is the high priest of Shinto.

What is happening is a sky-darkening attack on the ideas of the Enlightenment which helped usher in the industrial age.

While all these religious movements are, of course, different, and frequently clash with one another, and while some are extremist and others not, all of them—Christian or New Age, Judaic or Islamic—are united in one thing—their hostility to secularism, the philosophical base of mass democracy.

Today, therefore, in country after country, secularism is in retreat. What do advocates of democracy have to put in its place? So far the new, high-tech democracies have renovated neither their outdated mass democratic political structures nor the philosophical assumptions that underlie them.

Religion is not the enemy of democracy. In a secular multireligious society, with a clear separation of state and church, the very variety of beliefs and nonbeliefs adds to the vibrance and dynamism of democracy. In many countries religious movements provide the only countervailing force against state oppression. Nor is fundamentalism, as such, a threat. Yet within the giant religious revival, in every country, not just Iran, fanatics are breeding who are committed to theocratic control of the mind and behavior of the individual, and others lend them unwitting support.

Tolerance of diversity is the first commandment of the demassified society, including tolerance of the intolerant—up to a point.

Religions that are universalistic, that wish to spread all over the world and embrace every human being, may be compatible with democracy. Even religions that insist on totalitarian control over every aspect of their own members' lives, but do not try to impose their control on nonmembers, may be compatible with democracy.

What is *not* compatible are those religions (and political ideologies as well) that combine totalitarianism with universalism. Such movements are at war with any possible definition of democracy.

Yet some of the fastest-growing and most powerful religious movements in the world today exhibit precisely this lethal combination.

They are determined to seize power over the lives and minds of whole nations, continents, the planet itself. Determined to impose their own rule over every aspect of human life. Determined to seize state power wherever they can, and to roll back the freedoms that democracy makes possible.

They are the agents of a new Dark Age.

ECO-THEOCRACY

Across the world, meanwhile, a green tide is gathering momentum too. This movement for ecological sanity is essential—a positive example of ordinary people around the world leading their leaders. Propelling ecology to the top of the world agenda have been a succession of sensational catastrophes, from Three Mile Island and Chernobyl to Bhopal and the Alaska oil spill. Clearly, more lie ahead.

Industrial society has reached its outer limits, making it impossible to continue putting toxic wastes in our backyards, stripping the land of forests, dumping Styrofoam debris in our oceans, and punching holes in the ozone. The worldwide environmental movement is therefore a survival response to planetary crisis.

But this movement, too, has an antidemocratic fringe. It has its own advocates of a return to darkness. Some of them are ready to hijack the environmental movement in pursuit of their private political or religious agendas.

The issues are so complex and recalcitrant that the Green movement is likely to split into at least four parts. One part will continue to be the very model of legal, nonviolent democratic action. But, given a succession of ecological crises and tragedies, a second wing, which already exists in embryonic form, might well step up from eco-vandalism to full-scale eco-terrorism to enforce its demands.

A further split will intensify the key ideological war already dividing the environmental movement. On one side: those who favor technological and economic advance within stringent environmental constraints. Unwilling to give up on imagination and intelligence, they believe in the power of the human mind—and therefore in our ability to design technologies that will use smaller amounts of resources, emit less pollution, and recycle all wastes into reusable resources. They argue that today's crisis calls for revolutionary changes in the way the economy and technology are organized. Oriented toward tomorrow, these are the mainstream environmentalists.

Battling them for ideological control of the movement, however, are self-described "fundamentalists," who wish to plunge society into pre-technological medievalism and asceticism. They are "eco-theologues," and some of their views dovetail with the thinking of religious extremists.

The eco-theologues insist that there can be no technological relief, and that we are therefore destined to slide back into pre-industrial poverty, a prospect they regard as a blessing rather than a curse.

In a seminal series of articles in *New Perspectives Quarterly,* the main lines of debate are clearly laid out. For these reversionist thinkers, the issues are not primarily ecological but religious. They wish to restore a religion-drenched world that has not existed in the West since the Middle Ages. The environmental movement provides a convenient vehicle.

This group reduces the history of our relations with nature to biblical allegory. First there was an ecological "Golden Age," when humans lived in harmony with nature and worshipped it. The species fell from this "Eden" with the arrival of the industrial age, in which the "Devil"—technology—ruled human affairs. Now we must transit to a new "Paradise" of perfect sustainability and harmony. If not, we face "Armageddon."

This imposition of a Western, indeed Christian, parable on the far more complex history of our relations with nature is common to the "eco-theologues" who glamorize life in the medieval village.

Rudolf Bahro, an influential Green theorist now living in West Germany, explicitly holds that what is needed is "theology, not ecology—the birth of a new Golden Age which cultivates . . . the nobility in man."

He reaches back into the 13th century to quote Meister Eckhart, the founder of German mysticism, "who lived in the now despoiled Rhine River valley" and who told us that all creatures have God within them. Bahro finds the same idea in the poetic words of Mechtild of Magdeburg, another 13th-century Christian thinker, quoting her beautiful line to the effect that all creatures are "a flash of grace."

Ecological salvation thus, for him, is a matter of religion, something the secular world will never be able to offer. Bahro even approves of the Ayatollah Khomeini's remark to Gorbachev that the Soviet leader should look to Allah rather than economic reforms to solve Soviet problems.

Another theorist, Wolfgang Sachs of the University of Pennsylvania, attacks the Worldwatch Institute, a leading environmentalist research center, for its "specifically modern outlook" and dismisses Amory Lovins, the conservationist, for urging greater energy efficiency, whereas what is wanted by Sachs is "good housekeeping" in the tradition of "subsistence-oriented households."

Ivan Illich, one of our most imaginative social critics and author of several brilliant works bearing on ecological theory, is opposed to "managerial fascism" and simple-minded Ludditism. What he proposes, however, is "sustainability without development" —in short, stasis.

For Illich, poverty *is* the human condition and should be accepted as such; hence, who needs development? The new system of wealth creation, he says, has "injected new life into what would otherwise have been the exhausted logic of industrialism." He fails to see that the new knowledge-based technological system actually contradicts the old logic of industrialism at many points.

For Illich, too, the argument is ultimately theological. "God was the pattern that connected the cosmos" at a time when bare subsistence was accepted as normal and natural, a state we should return to. So long as God ruled the medieval mind, humanity and nature remained in balance. "Man, the agent of disequilibrium," upset the balance after the scientific revolution. Illich regards the concept of an "eco-system which, through multiple feedback mechanisms, can be regulated scientifically" as a snare and a delusion. Clearly, he implies, a return to a God-centered ascetic world would be preferable.

Theo-ecological rhetoric contains within it more than a hint of the Christian notion of retribution. As the writers Linda Bilmes and Mark Byford have noted, the theological Greens insist "consumption is sinful," while environmental blight is seen as "punishment for excessive consumerism, lack of spirituality, wastefulness." As in a Sunday sermon, the implication is that we should "repent, and mend our ways." Or, one might add, face fire and brimstone.

This is hardly the place to try to resolve the profound issues raised by the ecology debate—as significant a philosophical debate as that raised by the Enlightenment thinkers at the dawn of the industrial age. What is important, however, is to note the congruence between the views of the eco-theologues and the fundamentalist revival, with its deep hostility to secular democracy.

A shared emphasis on absolutes and the belief that sharp restrictions on individual choice may be required (to make people "moral," or to "protect the environment") point ultimately to a common attack on human rights. Indeed, many environmentalists themselves worry openly about the arrival of Green Ayotallahs or "eco-fascists" who impose their particular brand of salvation. Thus, Bahro cautions that "in the deep crises of humanity, charisma always plays a role. The deeper the crisis, the darker the charismatic figure who will emerge. . . . Whether or not we will have a green Adolf depends . . . on how far cultural change advances before the next Chernobyl."

One may admire the integrity and creativity of a thinker like Illich, surely no fascist himself, while recognizing the deeply anti-democratic implications of his search for the absolute, the constant, the static, and the holy. Criticizing the eco-theologues, the French sociologist Alain Touraine warns, "If we reject reason in the name of salvation from ozone depletion, we will court a Green fundamentalism, an eco-theocracy of the Ayatollah Khomeini variety."

If such anxiety sounds too extreme, it may be worth recalling the *Wandervogel* youth movement of the 1920s in Germany, where the Green movement today is most militant. The *Wandervogel* were the hippie-Greens of the Weimar Republic, roaming the countryside with their rucksacks, carrying guitars, wearing flowers, holding Woodstock-like festivals, high on spirituality and preaching a return to nature.

A decade later, Hitler was in control. Hitler also exalted pre-industrial values, picturing the Nazi utopia as one in which "the blacksmith stands again at his anvil, the farmer walks behind his plough." In the words of Professor J. P. Stern of University College, London, Hitler evoked "a pre-industrial rustic idyll." Hitler's ideologists constantly praised the "organic," urged physical fitness, and used biological analogies to justify the vilest race hate. "Hundreds of thousands of youngsters passed through the Youth Movement," writes George L. Mosse in *The Crisis of German Ideology*, "and many of them found it not very difficult to accommodate themselves to the ideological propositions of the Nazis."

Can one really imagine a Neo-Green Party, with armbands, Sam Browne belts, and jackboots, setting out to enforce its own view of nature on the rest of society?

Of course not, under normal conditions. But what if conditions are not "normal"?

Consider the consequences of another Bhopal-like eco-catastrophe set in, say, Seattle, Stuttgart, or Sheffield . . . followed by back-to-back crises elsewhere . . . followed by confusion and monstrous corruption in the disaster relief effort . . . amid fundamentalist cries that the disaster was inflicted by God as punishment for "permissiveness" and immorality. Picture all this occurring in a time of deep economic distress. Imagine an attractive, articulate "Eco-Adolf" who promises not just to solve the immediate crisis but to "purify" the society materially, morally, and politically—if only he is given extraconstitutional powers.

Some of today's eco-theological rhetoric has an absurdist flavor, as did that of the erstwhile Adolf and his ideologists. Nazi propagandists exalted the Middle Ages (especially the time when the Holy Roman Empire dominated Europe) as a period when *Kultur* reached its "highest peak."

Today, a British ecological "fundi," or fundamentalist, writes in a letter to *The Economist* that "the goals of 'fundi' Greens like myself . . . [are to] return to a Europe which existed in the distant past . . . between the fall of Rome and the rise of Charlemagne," in which the basic unit of society "was the rural holding, scarcely larger than a hamlet. . . . The only way for humans to live in harmony with nature is to live at a subsistence level."

What the eco-medievalists normally do not tell us is the political price. They seldom point out that democracy was conspicuously absent from those bucolic villages they hold up for emulation—villages ruled by the cruelest patriarchy, religious mind-control, feudal ignorance, and force. This was the *Kultur* the Nazis glamorized. Not for nothing has the period between the fall of Rome and the rise of Charlemagne become known as the Dark Ages.

By themselves the eco-theologues might be dismissed. They remain a small fringe on the far edge of the environmental movement. But it is a mistake to view them as an isolated or trivial phenomenon. The religious revival and the Green movements alike breed ultras who would be happy to jettison democracy. At their extremes, these two movements may be converging to impose new restrictions on personal and political behavior in the name of both God and Greenness. Together they are pushing for a power shift toward the past.

THE NEW XENOPHOBES

Another characteristic of the Dark Age village was extreme xenophobia—hatred for the foreigner, even for those in the very next village. With the coming of the smokestack era, individual and mass loyalties were gradually transferred from village to nation. But xenophobia, chauvinism, hatred of the outsider, the stranger, the foreigner, continued to be a tool of state power.

Today's shift to a knowledge-based economy requires more cross-national interdependence than the smokestack economy it replaces. Inevitably, this restricts the range of independent action by nations. This, in turn, leads to a xenophobic backlash in everything from commerce to culture.

Today, governments throughout Europe are bracing themselves for an onslaught of imported culture, primarily television and movies, because of the integration of the European market. They are especially jittery about the packaging of news by foreigners.

Le Monde charges that the EC's plan for *Television Without Frontiers* "risks accelerating the implantation of Anglo-Saxon producers and distributors who have taken a decisive lead in the creation of all-European networks."

Europeans are nervous about plans for a Moroccan network to begin satellite broadcasts in Arabic to Europe's 11 million or more mainly Islamic immigrants from North Africa. Concern deepened as Muslin fundamentalists scored voting successes in secular Algeria.

This, however, is only a portent of things to come. Satellite technology and other new media tools are cracking open national cultures. In the opinion of satellite expert Dan Goldin of TRW, the day may well come when home satellite receivers can be sold for a fraction of their already low price, and millions around the world will be able to pick up transmissions from abroad—a Brazilian variety show, a Nigerian newscast, a South Korean drama, a Libyan propaganda program. This cross-communication, however, threatens the "national identity" that governments seek to preserve and propagate for their own self-serving purposes.

When fears of cultural deracination are intensified by large-scale immigration, identity becomes an explosive issue.

The promoters of a European single-market, urging open

borders for capital, culture, and people, seek to displace traditional nationalist sentiments with "supra-nationalism" instead.

But precisely because the new economy is becoming more globally integrated, exporting joblessness, pollution, and culture along with products and services, we see a mounting backlash and the revival of nationalism in the high-tech world.

The Le Penist movement in France, with its viciously anti-Arab propaganda, led by a former legionnaire who terms the Nazi gas chambers "a minor point," appeals to knee-jerk xenophobic emotions. His party holds ten seats in the European Parliament.

The Republikaner Party in West Germany, formed by an ex-Waffen-SS non-com, Franz Schoenhuber, attacks not merely Turkish migrant workers but even ethnic Germans immigrating from Poland and the Soviet Union who are allegedly taking jobs, housing, and pensions away from "real Germans." With links to the Le Penists in France and extremist parties elsewhere in Europe, the Republikaner won eleven seats in the West Berlin legislature in 1989 and six in the European Parliament.

Under banners proclaiming "Germany first," Schoenhuber, like Hitler after the Versailles Treaty, portrayed Germany—now one of the world's richest countries—as a "victim" nation.

Schoenhuber, according to the respected German analyst Josef Joffe, writing in *The Wall Street Journal*, has issued a "call to arms against the rest of the world, which seeks to oppress Germany by shackling it to the past"—meaning that the world won't let Germany forget Hitler's ravages. (Schoenhuber has since quit the party, terming it too extremist.)

Any country continually cudgeled for the sins of a much earlier generation can, of course, expect an eventual backlash, a reassertion of national pride. But pride about what? Instead of urging Germany to become a world leader in developing a more advanced, 21st-century democracy, the neo-nationalists appeal to many of the anti-democratic pathologies of the German past, thus providing neighboring countries good cause for not wanting Germany to forget its crimes.

With the Berlin Wall down and the de facto reunification of Germany well advanced, what happens in Bonn and Berlin (soon, no doubt, to be the country's capital once more) has ramifications throughout Europe, and many all over the continent are watching the Republikaners carefully.

But similar nationalist movements are found all over Western

Europe, from Belgium to Italy and Spain, wherever free-flowing culture and communication and border-crossing migrants threaten the old national self-conceptions.

The resurgence of flag-waving xenophobia, however, is not limited to Europe. In the United States, too, there is a growing nationalist backlash. Fed by a fear that America is in economic and military decline, weary of being told they are too imperialist, materialist, violent, uncultured, etc., etc., even normally apolitical Americans are responding to nationalist demagogy.

Anti-immigration sentiment runs hot, encouraged by eco-extremists who claim the influx of Mexican immigration is damaging to the U.S. environment. This born-again nativism, however, is only one manifestation of a new flag-waving nationalism.

The 1990 ruling of the Supreme Court that burning a flag is a form of free political expression, protected by the U.S. Bill of Rights, led to an outpouring of high-octane emotion. Radio call-in shows were besieged by outraged callers. The White House instantly proposed changing the Constitution to ban the practice.

Another indication of the new mood is Japan-bashing, a popular sport these days among protectionists and ordinary Americans worried about the trade imbalance and the Japanese buy-up of U.S. companies and real estate.

In Japan, meanwhile, a parallel ultra-nationalism is spreading. Resurgent nationalists call for changes in the constitution to permit a more aggressive military buildup. Japan, they say, did "nothing to be ashamed of" during World War II—a view that upsets China and other nearby countries invaded by the Japanese. For suggesting that Emperor Hirohito may have shared responsibility for World War II, the mayor of Nagasaki, Hitoshi Motoshima, became the victim of an attempted assassination. A leading daily, *Asahi Shimbun,* one of whose reporters had previously been murdered, presumably by nationalists, warns that such violence "will lead to fascism."

The ultras claim, moreover, that Japan has a national "soul" and language different from and superior to that of any other nation. The cult of "Yamatoism," which promotes this concept of unique superiority, is called upon to offset a loss of national identity resulting from postwar Westernization.

Having been treated patronizingly by the United States ever since the war, and sick of being criticized by others for economic policies that have brought it tremendous success, some Japanese are willing to listen to the nationalist pitch. This patriotic hubris comes hand in hand with extraordinary financial clout on the world scene and a fast-growing military capability, and is associated with the most anti-democratic forces in Japanese society.

Finally, what makes the widespread resurgence of nationalism truly extraordinary is its reemergence as a powerful political force in the Soviet Union and the Eastern European countries. In fact, rather than democratic uprisings, the upheavals in Eastern Europe could equally well be described as nationalist uprisings among nations bent for nearly half a century to Soviet will.

Reframing the concept of "nation" is one of the most emotional and important tasks to face the world in the decisive decades before us, and maintaining national control over certain functions, rather than allowing them to be either localized or globalized, is essential. But blind tribalism and nationalism are both dangerous and regressive. And when linked to the notion of racial or God-conferred superiority, they give birth to violence or repression.

Significantly, in the U.S.S.R., where ethnic passions rocked the state itself, they are often linked to both environmentalism and religious fundamentalism. Ecological themes are exploited to arouse ethnic sentiment against Moscow. In Tashkent a movement called Birlik, which started up to block the building of an electronics plant, has taken on an Islamic fundamentalist coloration.

Even more significant than the mounting demands of ethnic minorities in the Baltic regions, Armenia, Azerbaijan, Georgia, and other parts of the U.S.S.R. for autonomy or independence is the upsurge of ethnicism in the dominant Great Russian population. Writing about Tolstoi, the historian Paul Johnson described Russian nationalism in words that could apply today. It was, Johnson says, a "chauvinist spirit, the conviction that the Russians were a special race, with unique moral qualities (personified in the peasant) and a God-ordained role to perform in the world."

This attitude is expressed in extreme form in today's anti-Semitic, anti-foreigner Pamyat organization, which claims thirty branches around the Soviet Union, 20,000 members in Moscow alone, and has strong links to both the military and KGB, as well as support from middle-level officialdom. Several of the U.S.S.R.'s best-selling authors and cultural figures are members. Pamyat, now facing criminal prosecution for spreading hate, resembles the Black Hundreds movement, which organized pogroms under the Tsar at the turn of the century.

Pamyat and similar groups portray themselves as merely interested in preserving ancient monuments, or repairing the environment, but have as their goal the re-creation of the same village-based society that the Green fundamentalists exalt. Some call for a restoration of the Tsarist monarchy, linked to religious orthodoxy.

Like Schoenhuber in Germany, who disclaims anti-Semitism but mouths Hitler-era lies about Jews, Pamyat claims innocence but issues virulent diatribes against "International Zionism and Freemasonry," and its members threaten pogroms.

A Pamyat manifesto lashes out at all who have "reduced our churches, temples, monasteries, and graves of national heroes of our Motherland" and who have "reduced the ecology of the country to a catastrophic state." It urges a massive return to the land—"Down with the giant cities!"—and a revival of the "centuries-old institution of the ploughman."

Here, then, we find xenophobic ethnicism explicitly linked to religious fundamentalism and eco-medievalism—all three in a single Dark Age package.

It is a combustible convergence of forces that could blow up in the face of democracies wherever they now exist. In its worst case, it conjures up the image of a racist or tribal, eco-fascist, theological state—a maximal recipe for the suppression of human rights, freedom of religion, and private property as well.

Such a state seems hard to imagine—except, perhaps, as a result of some immense crisis and tragedy, an eco-spasm combining ecological upheaval with vast economic crises, terror, or war.

But one need not imagine the worst-case scenario to feel a chill in the bones. It isn't necessary for such movements, or a convergence of them, to seize control of a state in order for them to savagely restrict or destroy a form of democracy that, even in the high-tech nations, is already fragile because it is increasingly out of sync with the emerging economy and society.

Governments controlled or heavily influenced by extremists who put their particular brand of religion, ecology, or nationalism ahead of democratic values do not stay democratic long.

The system of advanced wealth creation now spreading around the earth opens expanded opportunities for democracy. For the first time, as we saw, it makes freedom of expression not just a political good but an economic necessity. But as the old industrial society enters its terminal tailspin, counterforces are created that could destroy both democracy and the option of economic advance.

To save both development and democracy, political systems need to leap to a new stage, as the economy itself is doing. Whether that enormous challenge can be met will decide whether the ultimate powershift that approaches will protect or enslave the individual.

In the Powershift Era ahead, the primary ideological struggle will no longer be between capitalist democracy and communist totalitarianism, but between 21st-century democracy and 11th-century darkness.

PART SIX

PLANETARY POWERSHIFT

29

THE GLOBAL "K-FACTOR"

Few peacetime power shifts have been as dramatic as those following the swift disintegration of the once-monolithic Soviet bloc. Suddenly, immense power, centralized in Moscow for nearly half a century, shifted back to Warsaw, Prague, Budapest, Bucharest, and Berlin. In a few brief spectacular months the "East" splintered.

A second shift has accompanied the breakup of the so-called South. The LDCs, or "less developed countries",* have never been able to form a truly united front vis-à-vis the industrialized world, despite efforts beginning as long ago as the Bandung conference in Indonesia in 1955. In the 1970s the United Nations rang with rhetoric about the common needs of "the South." Programs of "South-South" technological exchange and other forms of cooperation were launched. Campaigns were begun to shift the terms of trade between the North and the South. Power did shift. But not in the way the spokesmen for a united South had hoped.

What happened instead has been the division of the LDCs into distinct groupings with very different needs. One consists of desperately poor countries still mostly dependent on First Wave peasant labor. Another group includes countries—like Brazil, India, and China—that are actually important Second Wave or industrial powers, but saddled with vast populations still scrabbling for subsistence from preindustrial agriculture. Lastly, there are nations like Singapore, Taiwan, and South Korea, which have virtually completed industrialization and are moving swiftly into Third Wave

---

*The term *less developed* is an arrogant misnomer, since many LDCs are highly developed culturally and in other ways. A more appropriate term would be "less economically developed," which is the sense in which it will be used here.

high technology. If power in the East Bloc has splintered, so, too, has power in the so-called South.

The third immense shift of power has been the emergence of Japan and Europe into rivals of the United States, leading to hyper-competition as each fights to dominate the 21st century. The so-called West, too, is now splitting apart.

While politicians, diplomats, and the press still treat these power shifts as distinctly separate phenomena, there is a deep connection among all three. The global structure that reflected the dominance of the Second Wave industrial powers has been shattered like a crystal sphere under the blow of a sledgehammer.

Naturally, such vast historical developments spring from many roots, and no single explanation can completely account for them. To reduce history to any single force or factor is to ignore complexity, chance, the role of individuals, and many other variables. But by the same token, to regard history as a succession of patternless or unrelated accidents is equally reductionist.

The future patterns of global power can only be glimpsed if, instead of looking at each major shift of power as an isolated event, we identify the common forces running through them. And, in fact, we find that all three of these epochal power shifts are closely linked to the decline of industrialism and the rise of the new knowledge-driven economy.

PYRAMIDS AND MOONSHOTS

Advances in science and technology have been so extraordinary since World War II they hardly need elaboration. If nothing had occurred but the invention of the computer and the discovery of DNA, the postwar period might still go down as the most revolutionary in scientific history. But in fact, much more has happened.

We have not only improved our technologies, we have begun to operate at deeper and deeper levels of nature, so that instead of dealing with gross chunks of matter, we can now create a layer of material so incredibly thin that, in the words of *Science*, "the electrons in it are effectively moving in only two dimensions." We can etch lines that are only 20 billionths of a meter wide. We will soon be able to assemble things one atom at a time. This is not "progress," but upheaval.

The U.S. National Academy of Engineering in 1989 listed what it considered the ten most important engineering achievements of the previous twenty-five years. It began the list with the Apollo moon landing, which it ranked in history with the building of the Egyptian pyramids. Next came the development of satellites, micro-processors, lasers, the jumbo jet, genetically engineered products, and other breakthroughs. Since the beginning of the 1950s, when the new wealth-creation system began sprouting in the United States, humans, for the first time in history, opened the pathway to the stars, identified the biological program of life, and invented intellectual tools as important as writing. This is an astonishing set of achievements in what amounts to a single generation.

Nor is it only scientific or technological knowledge that has made, or is about to make, remarkable strides. In everything from organization theory to music, from the study of ecosystems to our understanding of the brain, in linguistics and learning theory, in studies of nonequilibrium, chaos, and dissipative structures, the knowledge base is being revolutionized. And even as this occurs, competing researchers in fields like neural networks and artificial intelligence are providing new knowledge about knowledge itself.

These transformative advances, seemingly remote from the worlds of diplomacy and politics, are in fact inescapably linked to today's geopolitical eruptions. Knowledge is the "K-Factor" in global power struggles.

HAND-ME-DOWN ECONOMICS

Consider, for example, the implications of the knowledge factor for Soviet power.

Today's historic powershift, as we've seen, has made two of the most basic sources of power—violence and wealth—increasingly dependent on the third source: knowledge. Because of the spread of knowledge-based technology and the relatively free circulation of ideas, the United States, Europe, and Japan have been able to leave the socialist nations in the dust economically. But the same technology made possible a vast leap in military power as well.

A fighter airplane today is the equivalent of a computer with wings. Its effectiveness depends almost entirely on the knowledge packed into its avionics and weaponry—and into its pilot's brain. In 1982, Soviet military planners suffered a collective case of ulcers when eighty Soviet-built MiG fighters, flown by the Syrians, were destroyed by Israeli pilots, who lost not a single plane. Soviet-built tanks also did badly against Israeli armor.

Even though the U.S.S.R. had brilliant military scientists, and nukes enough to incinerate the world, it could not keep pace in the race toward super-high-technology conventional weapons or in the dash for strategic defense systems. The growing sophistication of information-based conventional weapons (which, in fact, are not conventional at all) threatened Soviet superiority on the ground in Eastern Europe.

Meanwhile, the extremely knowledge-intensive Strategic Defense Initiative (SDI) threatened to negate the value of Soviet long-range missiles. Critics of SDI complained that it would never work. But the very possibility alarmed Moscow. If SDI could, in fact, block all Soviet nuclear missiles before they hit the United States, they were useless. That would also mean that the United States could launch a first-strike nuclear attack without fear of retaliation. If, on the other hand, as is more reasonable, SDI was only fractionally effective, blocking some but not all warheads, it would leave Soviet war planners wondering which fraction of U.S. missiles would survive. In either case, SDI raised the ante, and made theoretical Soviet use of nuclear weapons, never very likely, even riskier for Moscow.

On the ground and in space, then, the Soviets confronted a double threat.

Faced with these sobering realities, plus its own economic decline, Moscow rationally concluded that it could no longer protect its Eastern European perimeter militarily, except at an unacceptable and skyrocketing cost. For both economic and military reasons, therefore, a reduction of its imperial commitments became necessary.

In the end, what did in the Soviets was not arms or economics, but the K-factor—the new knowledge on which both military strength and economic power are now increasingly dependent.

The same K-factor helps explain the fragmentation of the "developing countries" and the rise of three distinct groupings among them. For example, once the most advanced economies began to shift to computers and information-based technologies, yielding higher value-added products, they transferred many of the old muscle-based, less information-intensive operations to countries like South Korea, Taiwan, Singapore, and now to Thailand and other places. In other words, as Europe, Japan, and the United States moved to Third Wave forms of wealth-making, they passed off the old Second Wave tasks to another tier of nations. This speeded their industrialization and they left the other LDCs behind.

(Many of these "newly industrialized economies," or NIEs, in turn, are now racing to pawn off Second Wave processes on still poorer, more economically backward countries—along with the accompanying pollution and other disadvantages—while they, in turn, try to make the transition to more knowledge-intensive production.) The different speeds of economic development have separated the LDCs from one another.

And as for the inter-capitalist rivalry among Europe, Japan, and the United States, the fabulous success of U.S. postwar policy, which promoted the rebuilding of both the European and Japanese economies, helped both of them restore their shattered industrial structures. This meant the chance for a fresh start and the opportunity to replace old prewar machines with the shiniest new technology, while the United States, whose plants had not been bombed into rubble, still needed to amortize its existing industrial base.

For a variety of reasons, including a future-oriented culture and the regional economic stimulation resulting from the Vietnam War, and, of course, because of the tremendous hard work and creativity of its postwar generation, Japan leaped ahead. Its eyes always focused on the 21st century, its culture always emphasizing the importance of education, business intelligence, and knowledge in general, Japan seized on the computer and all its derivatives in electronics and information technology with an almost erotic passion.

The economic results as Japan transited from the old to the new system of wealth creation were stunning—but they threw Japan into inevitable competition with the United States. In turn, a terrified Europe launched its drive for economic and political integration, after years of dawdling.

We will return to these developments later on, but for here it is only essential to recognize that, at every step, the new knowledge-

based system of wealth creation has been either a major contributor to, or a primary cause of, the great historical shift of power
now reshaping our world. The global implications of this fact, as
we shall see next, are startling.

30

THE FAST AND THE SLOW

One of the greatest power imbalances on earth today divides the rich countries from the poor. That unequal distribution of power, which affects the lives of billions of us, will soon be transformed as the new system of wealth creation spreads.

Since the end of World War II the world has been split between capitalist and communist, North and South. Today, as these old divisions fade in significance, a new one arises.

For from now on the world will be split between the fast and the slow.

To be fast or slow is not simply a matter of metaphor. Whole economies are either fast or slow. Primitive organisms have slow neural systems. The more evolved human nervous system processes signals faster. The same is true of primitive and advanced economies. Historically, power has shifted from the slow to the fast—whether we speak of species *or* nations.

In fast economies, advanced technology speeds production. But this is the least of it. Their pace is determined by the speed of transactions, the time needed to take decisions (especially about investment), the speed with which new ideas are created in laboratories, the rate at which they are brought to market, the velocity of capital flows, and above all the speed with which data, information, and knowledge pulse through the economic system. Fast economies generate wealth—and power—faster than slow ones.

By contrast, in peasant societies economic processes move at a glacial pace. Tradition, ritual, and ignorance limit socially acceptable choices. Communications are primitive; transport, restricted. Before the market system arose as an instrument for making investment choices, tradition governed technological decisions. Tradition, in turn, relied on "rules or taboos to preserve productive techniques that were proven workable over the slow course of

397

biological and cultural evolution," according to economist Don Lavoie.

With most people living at the bare edge of subsistence, experiment was dangerous, innovators were suppressed, and advances in the methods of wealth creation came so slowly they were barely perceptible from lifetime to lifetime. Moments of innovation were followed by what seemed like centuries of stagnation.

The historical explosion we now call the industrial revolution stepped up the economic metabolism. Roads and communications improved. Profit-motivated entrepreneurs actively searched for innovations. Brute force technologies were introduced. Society had a larger surplus to fall back on, reducing the social risks of experimentation. "With technological experimentation now so much less costly," Lavoie points out, "productive methods [could] change much more rapidly."

All this, however, merely set the stage for today's super-fast symbolic economy.

The bar code on the pack of Marlboros, the computer in the Federal Express truck, the scanner at the Safeway checkout counter, the bank's automatic teller, the spread of extra-intelligent data networks across the planet, remotely operated robots, the informationalization of capital, all are preliminary steps in the formation of a 21st-century economy that will operate at nearly real-time speeds.

In due course, the entire wealth-creation cycle will be monitored *as it happens*.

Continual feedback will stream in from sensors built into intelligent technology, from optical scanners in stores, and from transmitters in trucks, planes, and ships that send signals to satellites so managers can track the changing location of every vehicle at every moment. This information will be combined with the results of continuous polling of people and information from a thousand other sources.

The acceleration effect, by making each unit of saved time *more* valuable than the last unit, thus creates a positive feedback loop that accelerates the acceleration.

The consequences of this, in turn, will be not merely evolutionary but revolutionary, because real-time work, management, and finance will be radically different from even today's most advanced methods. Even now, however, well before real-time operations are achieved, time itself has become an increasingly critical factor of production. As a result, knowledge is used to shrink time intervals.

This quickening of economic neural responses in the high-technology nations holds still-unnoticed consequences for low-technology or no-technology economies.

For the more valuable time becomes, the less valuable the traditional factors of production, like raw materials and labor. And that, for the most part, is what these countries sell.

As we shall see in a minute, the acceleration effect will transform all present strategies for economic development.

COMING HOME

The new system for making wealth consists of an expanding global network of markets, banks, production centers, and laboratories in instant communication with one another, constantly exchanging huge—and ever-increasing—flows of data, information, and knowledge.

This is the "fast" economy of tomorrow. It is this accelerative, dynamic new wealth-machine that is the source of economic advance. As such, it is the source of great power as well. To be de-coupled from it is to be excluded from the future.

Yet that is the fate facing many of today's "LDCs," or "less developed countries."

As the world's main system for producing wealth revs up, countries that wish to sell will have to operate at the pace of those in a position to buy. This means that slow economies will have to speed up their neural responses, lose contracts and investments, or drop out of the race entirely.

The earliest signs of this are already detectable.

The United States in the 1980s spent $125 billion a year on clothing. Half of that came from cheap-labor factories dotted around the world from Haiti to Hong Kong. Tomorrow much of this work will return to the United States. The reason is speed.

Of course, shifting taxes, tariffs, currency ratios, and other factors still influence businesses when overseas investment or purchasing decisions are made. But far more fundamental in the long run are changes in the structure of cost. These changes, part of the transition to the new wealth-creation system, are already sending runaway factories and contracts home again to the United States, Japan, and Europe.

The Tandy Corporation, a major manufacturer and retailer of electronic products, not long ago brought its Tandy Color Computer production back from South Korea to Texas. While the Asian plant was automated, the Texas plant operated on an "absolutely continuous" flow basis and had more sophisticated test equipment. In Virginia, Tandy set up a no-human-hands automated plant to turn out five thousand speaker enclosures a day. These supply Japanese manufacturers, who previously had them made with low-cost labor in the Caribbean.

The computer industry is, of course, extremely fast-paced. But even in a slower industry, the Arrow Company, one of the biggest U.S. shirtmakers, recently transferred 20 percent of its dress-shirt production back to the United States after fifteen years of off-shore sourcing. Frederick Atkins Inc., a buyer for U.S. department stores, has increased domestic purchases from 5 percent to 40 percent in three years.

These shifts can be traced, at least in part, to the rising importance of time in economics.

"The new technology," reports *Forbes* magazine, "is giving domestic apparel makers an important advantage over their Asian competitors. Because of fickle fashion trends and the practice of changing styles as often as six times a year, retailers want to be able to keep inventories low. This calls for quick response from apparel makers that can offer fast turnaround on smaller lots in all styles, sizes and colors. Asian suppliers, half a world away, typically require orders three months or more in advance."

By contrast, Italy's Benetton Group delivers midseason reorders within two to three weeks. Because of its electronic network, Haggar Apparel in Dallas is now able to restock its 2,500 customers with slacks every three days, instead of the seven weeks it once needed.

Compare this with the situation facing manufacturers in China who happen to need steel.

In 1988, China suffered the worst steel shortages in memory. Yet with fabricators crying out for supplies, 40 percent of the country's total annual output remained padlocked in the warehouses of the Storage and Transportation General Corporation (STGC). Why? Because this enterprise—incredible as it may seem to the citizens of fast economies—makes deliveries only twice a year.

The fact that steel prices were skyrocketing, that the shortages were creating a black market, that fraud was widespread, and that companies needing the steel faced crisis meant nothing to the managers of STGC. The organization was simply not geared to making more frequent deliveries. While this is no doubt an extreme example, it is not isolated. A "great wall" separates the fast from the slow, and that wall is rising higher with each passing day.

It is this cultural and technological great wall that explains, in part, the high rate of failures in joint projects between fast and slow countries.

Many deals collapse when a slow-country supplier fails to meet promised deadlines. The different pace of economic life in the two worlds make for cross-cultural static. Officials in the slow country typically do not appreciate how important time is to the partner from the fast country—or why it matters so much. Demands for speed seem unreasonable, arrogant. Yet for the fast-country partner, nothing is more important. Delivery delayed is almost as bad as delivery denied.

The increasing cost of unreliability, of endless negotiation, of inadequate tracking and monitoring, and of late responses to demands for up-to-instant information further diminish the competitive edge of low-wage muscle work in the slow economies.

So do expenses arising from delays, lags, irregularities, bureaucratic stalling, and slow decision-making—not to mention the corrupt payments often required to speed things up.

In the advanced economies the speed of decision is becoming a critical consideration. Some executives refer to the inventory of "decisions in process," or "DIP," as an important cost, similar to "work in progress." They are trying to replace sequential decision-making with "parallel processing," which breaks with bureaucracy. They speak of "speed to market," "quick response," "fast cycle time," and "time-based competition."

The increased precision of timing required by systems like "just-in-time delivery" mean that the seller must meet far more rigid and restrictive schedule requirements than before, so that it is easier than ever to slip up.

In turn, as buyers demand more frequent and timely deliveries from overseas, the slow-country suppliers are compelled to maintain larger inventories or buffer stocks at their own expense—with the risk that the stored parts will rapidly become obsolete or unsalable.

The new economic imperative is clear: Overseas suppliers from developing countries will either advance their own technologies to meet the world speed standards, or they will be brutally cut off from their markets—casualties of the acceleration effect.

STRATEGIC REAL ESTATE

The likelihood that many of the world's poorest countries will be isolated from the dynamic global economy and left to stagnate is enhanced by three other powerful factors that stem, directly or indirectly, from the arrival of a new system of wealth creation on the earth.

One way to think about the economic power or powerlessness of the LDCs is to ask what they have to sell to the rest of the world. We can begin with a scarce resource that only a few countries at any given moment can offer the rest of the world: strategic location.

Economists don't normally consider militarily strategic real estate a salable resource, but for many LDCs that is precisely what it has been.

Countries seeking military and political power are frequently prepared to pay for it. Like Cuba, many LDCs now have sold, leased, or lent their location or facilities to the Soviet Union, the United States, or others for military, political, and intelligence purposes. For Cuba, giving the Soviets a foothold ninety miles off the U.S. coast, and heightened political influence throughout Central America, has brought in a $5 billion annual subsidy from Moscow.

For almost half a century the Cold War has meant that even the poorest country (assuming it was strategically located) had something to sell to the highest bidder. Some, like Egypt, managed to sell their favors first to one superpower, then to the other.

But while the relaxation of U.S.-Soviet tensions may be good news for the world, it is decidedly bad news for places like the Philippines, Vietnam, Cuba, and Nicaragua under the Sandinistas, each of which has successfully peddled access to its strategic geography. From now on it is unlikely that the two biggest customers for strategic location will be bidding against each other, as they once did.

Moreover, as logistic capabilities rise, as aircraft and missile range increases, as submarines proliferate, and as military airlift operations quicken, the need for overseas bases, repair facilities, and prepositioned supplies declines.

LDCs must, therefore, anticipate the end of the seller's market for such strategic locations. Unless replaced by other forms of international support, this will choke off billions of dollars of "foreign aid" and "military assistance" funds that have until now flowed into certain LDCs.

The U.S.-Soviet thaw, as we'll see, is a Soviet response to the new system of wealth creation in the high-tech nations. The collapse of the market for strategic location is an indirect consequence.

Even if the great powers of the future (whoever they may be) do continue to locate bases, set up satellite listening posts, or build airfields and submarine facilities on foreign soil, the "leases" will be for shorter times. Today's accelerating changes make all alliances more tenuous and temporary, discouraging the great powers from making long-term investments in fixed locations.

Wars, threats, insurrections will arise at unexpected places. Thus, the military of the great powers will increasingly stress mobile, rapid-deployment forces, the projection of naval power and space operations rather than fixed installations. All this will further drive down the bargaining power of countries with locations to let or lease.

Finally, the rise of Japanese military power in the Pacific may well lead the Philippines and other Southeast Asian countries to *welcome* U.S. or other forces as a counterbalance to a perceived Japanese threat. Carried far enough, this implies even a willingness to *pay* for protection, instead of charging for it.

New outbreaks of regional war or internal violence on many continents will keep the arms business booming. But whatever happens, it will be harder to extract benefits from the United States and the Soviets. This will upset the delicate power balance among LDCs—as between India and Pakistan, for instance—and will trigger potentially violent power shifts *within* the LDCs as well, especially among the elites closely (and sometimes corruptly) linked to aid programs, military procurement, and intelligence operations.

In short, the heyday of the Cold War is over. Far more complex power shifts lie ahead. And the market for strategic locations in the LDCs will never be the same.

BEYOND RAW MATERIALS

A second blow awaits countries that base their development plans on the export of bulk raw materials such as copper or bauxite.

Here, too, power-shifting changes are just around the corner.

Mass production required vast amounts of a small number of resources. By contrast, as de-massified manufacturing methods spread, they will need many more different resources—in much smaller quantities.

Furthermore, the faster metabolism of the new global production system also means that resources regarded as crucial today may be worthless tomorrow—along with all the extractive industries, railroad sidings, mines, harbor facilities, and other installations built to move them. Conversely, today's useless junk could suddenly acquire great value.

Oil itself was regarded as useless until new technologies, and especially the internal combustion engine, made it vital. Titanium was a largely useless white powder until it became valuable in aircraft and submarine production. But the rate at which new technologies arrived was slow. That, of course, is no longer true.

Superconductivity, to choose a single example, will eventually reduce the need for energy by cutting transmission losses and, at the same time, will require new raw materials for its use. New antipollution devices for automobiles may no longer depend on platinum. New pharmaceuticals may call for organic substances that today are either unknown or unvalued. In turn, this could change poverty-stricken countries into important suppliers—while undercutting today's big bulk exporters.

What's more, in the words of Umberto Colombo, Chairman of the EC's Committee on Science and Technology, "In today's advanced and affluent societies, each successive increment in per capita income is linked to an ever-smaller rise in quantities of raw materials and energy used." Colombo cites figures from the International Monetary Fund showing that "Japan ... in 1984 consumed only 60 percent of the raw materials required for the same volume of industrial output in 1973." Advancing knowledge permits us to do more with less. As it does so, it shifts power away from the bulk producers.

Beyond this, fast-expanding scientific knowledge increases the ability to create substitutes for imported resources. Indeed, the advanced economies may soon be able to create whole arrays of new customized materials such as "nanocomposites" virtually from scratch. The smarter the high-tech nations become about micro-manipulating matter, the less dependent they become on imports of bulk raw materials from abroad.

The new wealth system is too protean, too fast-moving to be shackled to a few "vital" materials. Power will therefore flow from bulk raw material producers to those who control "eyedropper" quantities of temporarily crucial substances, and from them to those who control the knowledge necessary to create new resources *de novo*.

EXPENSIVE CHEAP LABOR

All this would be bad enough. But a third jolting blow is likely to hit the LDCs even harder and change power relations among and within them.

Ever since the smoky dawn of the industrial era, capitalist manufacturers have pursued the golden grail of cheap labor. After World War II the hunt for foreign sources of cheap labor became a stampede. Many developing countries bet their entire economic future on the theory that selling labor cheap would lead to modernization.

Some, like the "four tigers" of East Asia—South Korea, Taiwan, Hong Kong, and Singapore—even won their bet. They were helped along by a strong work ethic, cultural and other unique factors, including the fact that two bitter wars, the Korean conflict in the 1950s and Vietnam in the 1960s and early '70s, pumped billions of dollars into their region. Some Japanese referred to this dollar influx as the "divine wind."

Because of their success, it is now almost universally believed that shifting from the export of agricultural products or raw materials to the export of goods manufactured by cheap labor is the path to development. Yet nothing could be further from the long-range truth.

There is no doubt that the cheap-labor game is still being

played all over the world. Even now Japan is transferring plants and contracts from Taiwan and Hong Kong, where wages have risen, to Thailand, Malaysia, and China, where wages are still one-tenth those in Japan. No doubt many opportunities still exist for rich countries to locate pools of cheap labor in the LDCs.

But, like leasing military bases or shipping ore, the sale of cheap labor is also reaching its outer limits.

The reason for this is simple: Under the newly emerging system of wealth creation, cheap labor is increasingly expensive.

As the new system spreads, labor costs themselves become a smaller fraction of total costs of production. In some industries today, labor costs represent only 10 percent of the total cost of production. A 1 percent saving of a 10 percent cost factor is only one tenth of a percent.

By contrast, better technology, faster and better information flows, decreased inventory, or streamlined organization can yield savings far beyond any that can be squeezed out of hourly workers.

This is why it may be more profitable to run an advanced facility in Japan or the United States, with a handful of highly educated, highly paid employees, than a backward factory in China or Brazil that depends on masses of badly educated low-wage workers.

Cheap labor, in the words of Umberto Colombo, "is no longer enough to ensure market advantage to developing countries."

HYPER-SPEEDS

Looming on the horizon, therefore, is a dangerous de-coupling of the fast economies from the slow, an event that would spark enormous power shifts throughout the so-called South—with big impacts on the planet as a whole.

The new wealth-creation system holds the possibility of a far better future for vast populations who are now among the planet's poor. Unless the leaders of the LDCs anticipate these changes, however, they will condemn their people to perpetuated misery—and themselves to impotence.

For even as Chinese manufacturers wait for their steel, and traditional economies around the world crawl slowly through their paces, the United States, Japan, Europe, and in this case the Soviets, too, are pressing forward with plans to build hypersonic jets capable of moving 250 tons of people and cargo at Mach 5, meaning that cities like New York, Sydney, London, and Los Angeles will be two and a half hours from Tokyo.

Jiro Tokuyama, former head of the prestigious Nomura Research Institute, and now a senior adviser to the Mitsui Research Institute, heads a fifteen-nation study of what are called the "three T's": telecommunications, transportation, and tourism. Sponsored by the Pacific Economic Cooperation Conference, the study focuses on three key factors likely to accelerate the pace of economic processes in the region still further.

According to Tokuyama, Pacific air-passenger traffic is likely to reach 134 million . . . at the turn of the century. The Society of Japanese Aerospace Companies, Tokuyama adds, estimates that five hundred to one thousand hypersonic jets must be built. Many of these will ply Pacific routes, speeding further the economic development of the region, and promoting faster telecommunications as well. In a paper prepared for the Three T's study, Tokuyama spells out the commercial, social, and political implications of this development.

He also describes a proposal by Taisei, the Japanese construction firm, to build an artificial island five kilometers in length to serve as a "VAA," or "value added airport," capable of handling hypersonics and providing an international conference center, shops, and other facilities to be linked by high-speed linear trains to a densely populated area.

In Texas, meanwhile, billionaire H. Ross Perot is building an airport to be surrounded by advanced manufacturing facilities. As conceived by him, planes could roar in day and night bearing components for overnight processing or assembly in facilities at the airport. The next morning the jets would carry them to all parts of the world.

Simultaneously, on the telecommunications front, the advanced economies are investing billions in the electronic infrastructure essential to operations in the super-fast economy.

The spread of extra-intelligent nets is moving swiftly, and there are now proposals afoot to create special higher-speed fiber optic networks linking supercomputers all across the United States with thousands of laboratories and research groups. (Existing networks, which move 1.5 million bits of information a second, are regarded as too slow. The proposed new nets would send 3 billion bits per second streaming across the country—i.e., three "gigabits.")

The new network is needed, say its advocates, because the existing slower nets are already choked and overloaded. They argue that the project merits government backing because it would help the United States keep ahead of Europe and Japan in a field it now leads.

This, however, is only a special case of a more general clamor. In the words of Mitch Kapor, a founder of Lotus Development Corporation, the software giant, "We need to build a national infrastructure that will be the information equivalent of the national highway-building of the '50s and '60s." An even more appropriate analogy would compare today's computerized telecom infrastructures with the rail and road networks needed at the beginning of the industrial revolution.

What is happening, therefore, is the emergence of an electronic neural system for the economy—without which any nation, no matter how many smokestacks it has, will be doomed to backwardness.

ELECTRONIC GAPS AND DYNAMIC MINORITIES

For the LDCs, as for the rest of the world, power stems from the holster, the wallet, and the book—or, nowadays, the computer. Unless we want an anarchic world, with billions of poverty-stricken people, unstable governments led by unstable leaders, each with a finger on the missile launcher or chemical or bacteriological trigger, we need global strategies for preventing the de-coupling that looms before us.

A study of *Intelligence Requirements for the 1990s*, made by U.S. academic experts, warns that in the years immediately ahead the LDCs will acquire sophisticated new arms—enormous firepower will be added to their already formidable arsenals. Why?

As LDC economic power diminishes, their rulers face political opposition and instability. Under the circumstances, they are likely to do what rulers have done since the origins of the state: They reach for the most primitive form of power—military force.

But the most acute shortage facing LDCs is that of economically relevant knowledge. The 21st-century path to economic development and power is no longer through the exploitation of raw materials and human muscle but, as we've seen, through application of the human mind.

Development strategies make no sense, therefore, unless they take full account of the new role of knowledge in wealth creation, and of the accelerative imperative that goes hand in hand with it.

With knowledge (which in our definition includes such things as imagination, values, images, and motivation, along with formal technical skills) increasingly central to the economy, the Brazils and Nigerias, the Bangladeshes and Haitis must consider how they might best acquire or generate this resource.

It is clear that every wretched child in Northeast Brazil or anywhere else in the world who remains ignorant or intellectually underdeveloped because of malnutrition represents a permanent drain on the future. Revolutionary new forms of education will be needed that are not based on the old factory model.

Acquiring knowledge from elsewhere will also be necessary. This may take unconventional—and sometimes even illicit—forms. Stealing technological secrets is already a booming business around the world. We must expect shrewd LDCs to join the hunt.

Another way of obtaining wealth-making know-how is to organize a brain drain. This can be done on a small scale by bribing or attracting teams of researchers. But some clever countries will figure out that, around the world, there are certain dynamic minorities—often persecuted groups—that can energize a host economy if given the chance. The overseas Chinese in Southeast Asia, Indians in East Africa, Syrians in West Africa, Palestinians in parts of the Mideast, Jews in America, and Japanese in Brazil have all played this role at one time or another.

Transplanted into a different culture, each has brought not merely energy, drive, and commercial or technical acumen, but a pro-knowledge attitude—a ravenous hunger for the latest information, new ideas, skills. These groups have provided a kind of hybrid economic vigor. They work hard, they innovate, they educate their children, and even if they get rich in the process, they stimulate and accelerate the reflexes of the host economy. We will no doubt see various LDCs searching out such groups and inviting them to settle within their borders, in the hopes of injecting a needed adrenaline into the economy.*

Smart governments will also encourage the spread of nongovernmental associations and organizations, since such groups accelerate the spread of economically useful information through newsletters, meetings, conferences, and foreign travel. Associations of merchants, plastics engineers, employers, programmers, trade unions, bankers, journalists, etc., serve as channels for rapid exchange of information about what does and does not work in their respective fields. They are an important, often neglected communications medium.

Governments serious about economic development will also have to recognize the new economic significance of free expression. Failure to permit the circulation of new ideas—including economic and political ideas, even if unflattering to the state—is almost always prima facie proof that the state is weak at its core, and that those in power regard staying there as more important than economic improvement in the lives of their people. Governments committed to becoming part of the new world will systematically open the valves of public discussion.

Other governments will join "knowledge consortia"—partnerships with other countries or with global companies—to explore the far reaches of technology and science and, especially, the possibility of creating new materials.

Instead of pandering to obsolete nationalist notions, they will pursue the national interest passionately—but intelligently. Rather than refusing to pay royalties to foreign pharmaceutical companies on the lofty ground that health is above such grubby concerns, as Brazil has done, they will gladly pay the royalties—provided these funds stay inside the country for a fixed number of years, and are used to finance research projects carried out jointly with a local pharmaceutical firm's own experts. Profits from products that originate in this joint research can then be divided between the host country and the multinational. In this way the royalties pay for technology transfer—and for themselves. Effective nationalism thus replaces obsolete, self-destructive nationalism.

---

*During World War II the Japanese military actually drafted a plan to bring large numbers of persecuted European Jews to Manchuria, then called Manchukuo, for this purpose. However, the "Fugu Plan," as it was known, was never implemented.

Similarly, intelligent governments will welcome the latest computers, regardless of who built them, rather than trying to build a local computer industry behind tariff walls that keep out not merely products but advanced knowledge.

The computer industry is changing so fast on a world scale that no nation, not even the United States or Japan, can keep up without help from the rest of the world.

By barring certain outside computers and software, Brazil managed to build its own computer industry—but its products are backward compared with those available outside. This means that Brazilian banks, manufacturers, and other businesses have had to use technology that is inefficient compared with that of their foreign competitors. They compete with one hand tied behind them. Rather than gaining, the country loses.

Brazil violated the first rule of the new system of wealth creation. Do what you will with the slowly changing industries, but get out of the way of a fast-advancing industry. Especially one that processes the most important resource of all—knowledge.

Other LDCs will avoid these errors. Some, we may speculate, will actually invest modestly in existing venture capital funds in the United States, Europe, and Japan—on condition that their own technicians, scientists, and students accompany the capital and share in the know-how developed by the resulting start-up firms. In this way, Brazilians or Indonesians or Nigerians or Egyptians might find themselves at the front edge of tomorrow's industries. Astutely managed, the program could well pay for itself—or even make a profit.

Above all, the LDCs will take a completely fresh look at the role of agriculture, regarding it not necessarily as a "backward" sector but as a sector that potentially, with the help of computers, genetics, satellites, and other new technologies, could someday be more advanced, more progressive than all the smokestacks, steel mills, and mines in the world. Knowledge-based agriculture may be the cutting edge of economic advance tomorrow.

Moreover, agriculture will not limit itself to growing food, but will increasingly grow energy crops and feedstocks for new materials. These are but a few of the ideas likely to be tested in the years to come.

But none of these efforts will bear fruit if the country is cut off from participation in the fast-moving global economy and the telecommunications and computer networks that support it.

The maldistribution of telecommunications in today's world is even more dramatic than the maldistribution of food. There are 600 million telephones in the world—with 450 million of them in only nine countries. The lopsided distribution of computers, data bases, technical publications, research expenditures, tells us more about the future potential of nations than all the gross-national-product figures ground out by economists.

To plug into the new world economy, countries like China, Brazil, Mexico, Indonesia, India, as well as the Soviet Union and the East European nations, must find the resources needed to install their own electronic infrastructures. These must go far beyond mere telephone services to include up-to-date, high-speed data systems capable of linking into the latest global networks.

The good news is that today's slow countries may be able to skip over an entire stage of infrastructure development, leap-frogging from First to Third Wave communications without investing the vast sums needed to build Second Wave networks and systems.

The Iridium system, for example, announced by Motorola, Inc., will place 77 tiny satellites into low orbit, making it possible for millions in remote or sparsely populated regions like the Soviet Arctic, the Chinese desert, or the interior of Africa, to send and receive voice, data and digitized images through handheld telephones.

It is not necessary to lay copper or even fiber optic cable across thousands of miles of jungle, ice or sand. The portable phones will communicate directly with the nearest overhead satellite, which will pass the message along. Other advances will similarly slash the huge costs of telecommunications, bringing them within reach of today's impoverished countries. Large scale production and hyper-competition among American, European and Japanese suppliers will also drive costs down.

The new key to economic development is clear.

The "gap" that must be closed is informational and electronic. It is a gap not between the North and the South, but between the slow and the fast.

31

SOCIALISM'S COLLISION WITH THE FUTURE

The dramatic death of state socialism in Eastern Europe and its bloody anguish from Bucharest to Baku to Beijing did not happen by accident.

Socialism collided with the future.

Socialist regimes did not collapse because of CIA plots, capitalist encirclement, or economic strangulation from outside. Eastern European communist governments toppled domino-fashion as soon as Moscow sent the message that it would no longer use troops to protect them from their own people. But the crisis of socialism, as a system, in the Soviet Union, China, and elsewhere was far more deeply based.

Just as Gutenberg's invention of movable type in the mid-15th century led to the diffusion of knowledge and loosened the Catholic Church's grip on knowledge and communication in Western Europe—ultimately igniting the Protestant Reformation—so the appearance of the computer and new communications media in the mid-20th century smashed Moscow's control of the mind in the countries it ruled or held captive.

THE BREAKING POINT

As recently as 1956, Soviet leader Nikita Khrushchev could dream of "burying the West." Ironically, this was the very year when blue-collar workers in the United States were first outnumbered by knowledge and service workers—a shift that signaled the coming decline of the smokestack and the rise of the super-symbolic economy.

Equally ironic is the fact that mind-workers were typically dismissed as "nonproductive" by Marxist economists (and many classical economists as well). Yet it is these supposedly nonproductive workers who, more perhaps than any other, have given Western economies a tremendous shot of adrenaline since the mid-fifties.

Today, even with all their supposed "contradictions" unresolved, the high-tech capitalist nations have swept so far ahead of the rest of the world in economic terms as to render Khrushchev's boast merely pathetic. It was computer-based capitalism, not smokestack socialism, that made what Marxists call a "qualitative leap" forward. With the real revolution spreading in the high-tech nations, the socialist nations had become, in effect, a deeply reactionary bloc led by elderly men imbued with a 19th-century theology. Mikhail Gorbachev was the first Soviet leader to recognize this historic fact.

In a 1989 speech, some thirty years after the new system of wealth creation began to appear in the United States, Gorbachev declared, "We were nearly one of the last to realize that in the age of information science the most expensive asset is knowledge."

He rose to power not just as a remarkable individual, but as representative of a new class of better educated, largely white-collar Soviet citizens—precisely the group despised by earlier leaders. And precisely the group most closely connected with symbolic processing and production.

Marx himself had given the classic definition of a revolutionary moment. It came, he said, when the "social relations of production" (meaning the nature of ownership and control) prevent further development of the "means of production" (roughly speaking, the technology).

That formula perfectly described the socialist world crisis. Just as feudal "social relations" once hindered industrial development, now socialist "social relations" made it all but impossible for socialist countries to take advantage of the new wealth-creation system based on computers, communication, and above all, on open information. In fact, the central failure of the great state socialist experiment of the 20th century lay in its obsolete ideas about knowledge.

THE PRE-CYBERNETIC MACHINE

With minor exceptions, state socialism had led not to affluence, equality, and freedom, but to a one-party political system . . . a massive bureaucracy . . . heavy-handed secret police . . . government control of the media . . . secrecy . . . and the repression of intellectual and artistic freedom.

Setting aside the oceans of spurting blood needed to prop it up, a close look at this system reveals that every one of these elements is not just a way of organizing people, but also—and more profoundly—a particular way of organizing, channeling, and controlling knowledge.

A one-party political system is designed to control political communication. Since no other party exists, it restricts the diversity of political information flowing through the society, blocking feedback, and thus blinding those in power to the full complexity of their problems. With very narrowly defined information flowing upward through the approved channel, and commands flowing downward, it becomes very difficult for the system to detect errors and correct them.

In fact, top-down control in the socialist countries was based increasingly on lies and misinformation, since reporting bad news up the line was often risky. The decision to run a one-party system is a decision, above all, about knowledge.

The overpowering bureaucracy that socialism created in every sphere of life was also, as we saw in Chapter 15, a knowledge-restricting device, forcing knowledge into pre-defined compartments or cubbyholes and restricting communication to "official channels," while de-legitimating informal communication and organization.

The secret police apparatus, state control of the media, the intimidation of intellectuals, and the repression of artistic freedom all represent further attempts to limit and control information flows.

In fact, behind each of these elements we find a single obsolete assumption about knowledge: the arrogant belief that those in command—whether of the party or of the state—know what others should know.

These features of all the state socialist nations guaranteed economic stupidity and derived from the concept of the pre-cybernetic machine as applied to society and life itself. Second Wave machines—the kind that surrounded Marx in the 19th century—for the most part operated without any feedback. Plug in the power, start the motor, and it runs irrespective of what is happening in the outside environment.

Third Wave machines, by contrast, are intelligent. They have sensors that suck in information from the environment, detect changes, and adapt the operation of the machine accordingly. They are self-regulating. The technological difference is revolutionary.

While Marx, Engels, and Lenin all bitterly assailed the philosophy of "mechanical materialism," their own thinking, reflecting their era, remained steeped in certain analogies and assumptions based on pre-intelligent machinery.

Thus for Marxian socialists the class struggle was the "locomotive of history." A key task was to capture the "state machine." And society itself, being machine-like, could be pre-set to deliver abundance and freedom. Lenin, on capturing control of Russia in 1917, became the supreme mechanic.

A brilliant intellectual, Lenin understood the importance of ideas. But, for him, symbolic production, too—the mind itself—could be programmed. Marx wrote of freedom, but Lenin, on taking power, undertook to engineer knowledge. Thus he insisted that all art, culture, science, journalism, and symbolic activity in general be placed at the service of a master plan for society. In time the various branches of learning would be neatly organized into an "academy" with fixed bureaucratic departments and ranks, all subject to party and state control. "Cultural workers" would be employed by institutions controlled by a Ministry of Culture. Publishing and broadcasting would be monopolies of the state. Knowledge, in effect, would be made part of the state machine.

This constipated approach to knowledge blocked economic development even in low-level smokestack economies; it is diametrically opposed to the principles needed for economic advance in the age of the computer.

THE PROPERTY PARADOX

The Third Wave wealth-creation system now spreading also challenges three pillars of the socialist faith.

Take the question of property.

From the beginning, socialists traced poverty, depressions, unemployment, and the other evils of industrialism to private ownership of the means of production. The way to solve these ills was for the workers to own the factories—through the state or through collectives.

Once this was accomplished, things would be different. No more competitive waste. Completely rational planning. Production for use rather than profit. Intelligent investment to drive the economy forward. The dream of abundance for all would be realized for the first time in history.

In the 19th century, when these ideas were formulated, they seemed to reflect the most advanced scientific knowledge of the time. Marxists, in fact, claimed to have gone beyond fuzzy-headed utopianism and arrived at truly "scientific socialism." Utopians might dream of self-governing communal villages. Scientific socialists knew that in a developing smokestack society such notions were impractical. Utopians like Charles Fourier looked toward the agrarian past. Scientific socialists looked toward what was then the industrial future.

Thus, later on, while socialist regimes experimented with cooperatives, worker-management, communes, and other schemes, state socialism—state ownership of everything from banks to breweries, rolling mills to restaurants—became the dominant form of property throughout the socialist world. (So complete was this obsession with state ownership that Nicaragua, an imitative latecomer to the socialist world, even created "Lobo Jack," a state-owned disco.) Everywhere, the state, not the workers, thus became the chief beneficiary of socialist revolution.

Socialism failed to meet its promise to improve radically the material conditions of life. When living standards fell in the Soviet Union after the revolution, the decline was blamed, with some justification, on the effects of World War I and counterrevolution. Later the shortfalls were blamed on capitalist encirclement. Still later, on World War II. Yet thirty years after the war, staples like coffee and oranges were still in short supply in Moscow. In the period preceding Gorbachev's perestroika, the diet of a middle-class researcher at a state institute in Moscow was heavily based on cabbage and potatoes. In 1989, four years after the start of Gorbachev's attempt at reforms, the U.S.S.R. had to import 600 million razor blades and 40 million tubes of shaving cream from abroad.

Remarkably, though their number is declining, one still hears orthodox socialists around the world calling for the nationalization of industry and finance. From Brazil and Peru to South Africa and even in the industrialized nations of the West there remain true believers who, despite all historical evidence to the contrary, still regard "public ownership" as "progressive" and resist every effort to de-nationalize or privatize the economy.

It is true that today's increasingly liberalized global economy, uncritically hailed by the great multinational corporations, is itself unstable and could suffer a massive coronary. The distended debt balloon on which it rests could be punctured. Wars, sudden interruptions of energy or resources, and any number of other calamities could cause its collapse in the decades ahead. Under catastrophic conditions, one might well imagine the need for temporary emergency nationalizations.

Nevertheless, incontrovertible evidence proves that state-owned enterprises mistreat their employees, pollute the air, and abuse the public at least as efficiently as private enterprises. Many have become sink-holes of inefficiency, corruption, and greed. Their failures frequently encourage a vast, seething black market that undermines the very legitimacy of the state.

But worst and most ironic of all, instead of taking the lead in technological advance as promised, nationalized enterprises, as a rule, are almost uniformly reactionary—the most bureaucratic, the slowest to reorganize, the least willing to adapt to changing consumer needs, the most afraid to provide information to the citizen, the last to adopt advanced technology.

For more than a century, socialists and defenders of capitalism waged bitter war over public versus private property. Large numbers of men and women literally laid down their lives over this issue. What neither side imagined was a new wealth-creation system that would make virtually all their arguments obsolete.

Yet this is exactly what happened. For the most important form of property is now intangible. It is super-symbolic. It is knowledge. The same knowledge can be used by many people simultaneously to create wealth and to produce still more knowledge. And unlike factories and fields, knowledge is, for all intents, inexhaustible. Neither socialist regimes nor socialists in general have yet come to terms with this truly revolutionary fact.

HOW MANY "LEFT-HANDED" SCREWS?

A second pillar in the cathedral of socialist theory was central planning. Instead of allowing the "chaos" of the marketplace to determine the economy, intelligent top-down planning would be able to concentrate resources on key sectors, and accelerate technological development.

But central planning depended on knowledge, and as early as the 1920s the Austrian economist Ludwig von Mises identified its lack of knowledge or, as he termed it, its "calculation problem," as the Achilles heel of socialism.

How many shoes and what sizes should a factory in Irkutsk make? How many left-handed screws or grades of paper? What price-relationships should be set between carburetors and cucumbers? How many rubles, zlotys, or yuan should be invested in each of tens of thousands of different lines and levels of production?

To answer such questions, even in the simplest smokestack economy, requires more knowledge than central planners can collect or analyze, especially when managers, afraid of trouble, routinely lie to them about actual production. Thus, warehouses filled up with unwanted shoes. Shortages and a vast, shadowy black market became chronic features of most socialist economies.

Generations of earnest socialist planners wrestled desperately with this knowledge problem. They demanded ever more data and got ever more lies. They beefed up the bureaucracy. Lacking the supply-and-demand signals generated by a competitive market, they tried measuring the economy in terms of labor hours, or counting things in terms of kind, rather than money. Later they tried econometric modeling and input-output analysis.

Nothing worked. The more information they had, the more complex and disorganized the economy grew. Fully three quarters of a century after the Russian Revolution the real symbol of the U.S.S.R. was not the hammer and sickle, but the consumer queue.

Today, all across the socialist and ex-socialist spectrum there is a race to introduce market economics, either wholly, as in Poland, or timidly within a planned regimen, as in the Soviet Union. It is now almost universally recognized by socialist reformers that allowing supply and demand to determine prices (at least within certain ranges) provides what the central plan could not—price signals indicating what is or is not needed and wanted in the economy.

However, overlooked in the discussion among economists over the need for these signals is the fundamental change in communication pathways they imply, and the tremendous power shifts that changes in communication systems bring. The most important difference between centrally planned economies and market-driven economies is that, in the first, information flows vertically, whereas in the market, much more information flows horizontally and diagonally in the system, with buyers and sellers exchanging information at every level.

This change does not merely threaten top bureaucrats in the planning ministries and in management, but millions upon millions of mini-bureaucrats whose sole source of power depends on their control of information fed up the reporting channel.

The incapacity of the central planning system to cope with high levels of information thus set limits on the economic complexity necessary for growth.

The new wealth-creation methods require so much knowledge, so much information and communication, that they are totally out of reach of centrally planned economies. The rise of the super-symbolic economy thus collides with a second foundation of socialist orthodoxy.

THE DUSTBIN OF HISTORY

The third crashing pillar of socialism was its overweening emphasis on hardware—its total concentration on smokestack industry and its derogation of both agriculture and mind-work.

In the years after the 1917 revolution, the Soviets lacked capital to build all the steel mills, dams, and auto plants they needed. Soviet leaders seized on the theory of "socialist primitive accumulation" formulated by the economist E. A. Preobrazhensky. This theory held that the necessary capital could be squeezed out of the peasants by forcing their standard of living down to an emaciating minimum and skimming off their surpluses. These would then be used to capitalize heavy industry and subsidize the workers.

Nikolai Bukharin, a Bolshevik leader who paid for his pre-science with his life, correctly predicted that this strategy would merely guarantee agricultural collapse. Worse yet, this policy led to the murderous oppression of the peasantry by Stalin, since it was only by means of extreme force that such a program could be imposed. Millions died of starvation or persecution.

As a result of this "industry bias," as the Chinese call it today, agriculture has been a disaster area for virtually all socialist econo-mies and still is. Put differently, the socialist countries pursued a Second Wave strategy at the expense of their First Wave people.

But socialists also frequently denigrated the services and white-collar work. It was not pure coincidence that when the Soviets demanded "socialist realism" in the arts, the walls were soon cov-ered with murals of beefy workers straining muscles in steel mills and factories. Because the goal of socialism everywhere was to industrialize as rapidly as possible, it was muscle-labor that was glorified. Mind-work was for nonproductive wimps.

This widespread attitude went hand in hand with the tremen-dous concentration on production rather than consumption, on capital goods rather than consumer goods.

While some Marxists, notably Antonio Gramsci, challenged this view, and Mao Tse-tung at times insisted that ideological purity could overcome material handicaps, the fundamental thrust of Marxist regimes was to overrate material production and under-value products of the mind.

Mainline Marxists typically held the materialist view that ideas, information, art, culture, law, theories, and the other intangible products of the mind were merely part of a "superstructure" which hovered, as it were, over the economic "base" of society. While there was, admittedly, a certain feedback between the two, it was the base that determined the superstructure, rather than the reverse. Those who argued otherwise were condemned as "idealists"—at times a decidedly dangerous label to wear.

Marx, in arguing the primacy of the material base, stood Hegel on his head. The great irony of history today is that the new system of wealth creation, in turn, is standing Marx on his. Or more accurately, laying Marx and Hegel both on their sides.

For Marxists, hardware was always more important than software; the computer revolution now teaches us that the opposite is true. If anything, it is knowledge that drives the economy, not the economy that drives knowledge.

Societies, however, are not machines and they are not computers. They cannot be reduced so simply into hardware and software, base and superstructure. A more apt model would picture them as consisting of many more elements all connected in immensely complex and continually changing feedback loops. As their complexity rises, knowledge becomes more central to both their economic and ecological survival.

In brief, the rise of a new economy whose primary raw material is, in fact, soft and intangible found world socialism totally unprepared. Socialism's collision with the future was fatal.

If orthodox socialism is ready for what Lenin called the "dustbin of history," however, this does not mean that the magnificent dreams that bred it are also dead. The desire to create a world in which affluence, peace, and social justice prevail is at least as noble and widely shared as ever. Such a world cannot rise, however, on old foundations.

The most important revolution on the planet today is the rise of a new Third Wave civilization with its radical new system of wealth creation. Any movement that has not yet grasped this fact is condemned to relive its failures. Any state that makes knowledge a captive freezes its citizens in a nightmare past.

32

THE POWER OF BALANCE

The Powershift Era has only begun and already, it would appear, the future is up for grabs. With the "East" in upheaval, the "South" increasingly divided, and the leading powers of the "West"—Europe, Japan, and America—on a collision course, we face a frantic, endless round of summits, conferences, treaties, and missions as diplomats meet to construct a new global order.

No matter how much hammering, sawing, and wordsmithing they do, however, the new architecture of world power will depend less on their words than on the quantity and quality of power each brings to the table.

Are the United States and the Soviet Union both now global has-beens? If so, how many new "superpowers" will arise to take their place?

Some speak of a world organized around Europe, Japan, and the United States. Others see the world broken into six or eight regional blocs. Still others believe the bipolar world is turning into a five-sided star, with China at one of the points, India at another. Will the new Europe stretch from the Atlantic to the Soviet border—or beyond? No one can solve these puzzles with certainty. But the powershift principle can help.

It reminds us that while many other factors—from political stability to population growth—all count, violence, wealth, and knowledge are the three main rivers from which most other power resources flow, and each is now in the process of being revolutionized.

Take violence.

THE DEMOCRATIZATION OF DEATH

So much has been written about "peace breaking out" that world attention has drifted away from the menacing fact that as the two former superpowers scale down their arms, other nations are racing to fill the gap.

India, for example, despite its image as a backward, peace-loving land, has been the world's biggest arms buyer since 1986, purchasing in 1987 more weapons than warring Iran and Iraq combined. This policy has drawn fire from the Japanese and a sharp riposte from New Delhi. India already possesses nuclear weapons and is hoping to build missiles able to deliver them to a distance of 1,500 miles. Pakistan, which is also nearing nuclear capability, has a short-range missile built with Chinese help.

According to CIA Director William Webster, fully fifteen countries will be manufacturing ballistic missiles within a decade. Many are in the tense Middle East. Egypt, Iraq, and Argentina are partners in a missile-making project.

Beyond this lie a number of terrifying scenarios. Soviet nukes are located in Azerbaijan and other Muslim republics where ethnic fighting has broken out, leading some experts to speculate on the nightmarish possibility that a breakaway republic might seize some of these weapons. Asks one alarmed U.S. official: "Will the fourth-biggest nuclear power be Kazakhstan?"

So serious are the risks that Moscow has reportedly begun withdrawing nuclear arms from the tense Baltic region, and a top Soviet official, speaking privately to the author, has said: "I used to be against SDI [Washington's Strategic Defense Initiative whose goal is to intercept and destroy incoming nuclear missiles]. But now I'm *for* SDI. If the U.S.S.R. splits apart, the world could suddenly find itself confronted with ten more nuclear-armed countries."

In fact, a civil war in the Soviet Union—or any other nuclear power—raises the possibility that rebel forces might seize the weapons, or that rebel and loyalist forces might each seize part of the nuclear arsenal.

Even more ominously, some "developing countries"—Iraq and Libya are not alone—are designing plants to manufacture chemical and bacteriological weapons as well. In short, the present distribution of weapons in the world, and especially nuclear weapons, is neither fixed nor stable.

A key source of state power, therefore, the capacity for hyper-violence that was once concentrated in a few nations, is now becoming democratically but dangerously dispersed.

At the very same time, the nature of violence itself is undergoing profound change, becoming increasingly dependent on such knowledge-intensive technologies as microelectronics, advanced materials, optics, artificial intelligence, satellites, telecommunications, and advanced simulation and software. Thus, whereas the first F-16 fighters needed 135,000 lines of computer programming, the Advanced Tactical Fighter now on the drawing boards will require 1,000,000 lines. These changes in world military systems do more than merely shift power from here to there; they revolutionize the nature of the global game.

Shintaro Ishihara, a former Cabinet member in Japan, blew up a storm in Washington recently with a brief book called *The Japan That Can Say No,* which consisted of speeches he and Akio Morita, co-founder of Sony, had made on various occasions. In it Ishihara pointed out that to radically improve the accuracy of their nuclear weapons the United States and the U.S.S.R. alike would need extremely advanced Japanese-made semiconductor technology.

Referring to the United States, he said, "It has come to the point that no matter how much they continue military expansion, if Japan stopped selling them the chips, there would be nothing more they could do. If, for example, Japan sold chips to the Soviet Union and stopped selling them to the U.S., this would upset the entire military balance. Some Americans say that if Japan were thinking of doing that, it would be occupied. Certainly, this is an age where things could come to that."

Ishihara's remarks underscored the growing dependence of violence on knowledge, a reflection of today's historic powershift.

THE OCEAN OF CAPITAL

The second leg of the power triad—wealth—as previous chapters have documented, is also experiencing deep transformation as the new system for wealth creation spreads across the planet.

As corporations integrate their production and distribution across national boundaries, acquire foreign firms, and draw on brainpower from around the entire world, they inevitably need fresh sources of capital in many countries. They also need it fast. Thus we see a race to "liberalize" capital markets so that investments can flow more or less freely across national frontiers.

As noted earlier, the result is a surging ocean of capital free of restraining walls. This, however, shifts power away from central banks and individual nations, undermining sovereignty and introducing new dangers of financial fibrillation on a worldwide scale.

As we wrote in *The New York Times* shortly after the October 1987 Wall Street crash: "Building a single completely open financial system, subject to minimal regulation, is like building a supertanker without airtight compartments. With adequate dividers or safety cells, a big system can survive the breakdown of certain parts. Without them, a single hole in the hull can sink the tanker."

Since then, Alan Greenspan, chairman of the U.S. Federal Reserve Board, also has warned that the creation of multinational securities firms that buy, sell, underwrite, and invest in many nations increases the risk of large-scale breakdown. "A loss by one or more of these firms," Greenspan declared, could result in "transmitting a disturbance" from one country to another.

As finance is globalized, nations risk losing control over one of the keys to their power. The proposed all-European currency, for example, would reduce the flexibility of individual nations to cope with their own unique economic problems. Another proposal would arm the EC commissioners with far greater control over the budgets of Europe's supposedly sovereign nations than the federal government of the United States exerts over its fifty states—a centralizing power shift of massive proportions.

While this power redistribution is going on, the entire wealth system becomes, as we've seen, super-symbolic. Like violence, wealth, too, is shifting and being transformed at the same time.

THE NEW ARCHITECTURE OF KNOWLEDGE

This takes us to the third leg of the power triad: knowledge.

The wildfire spread of the computer in recent decades has been called the single most important change in the knowledge system since the invention of movable type in the 15th century or even the invention of writing. Paralleling this extraordinary change has come the equally astonishing spread of new networks and media for moving knowledge and its precursors, data and information.

Had nothing else changed, these twin developments alone would warrant the term *knowledge revolution*. But as we know, other, related changes are transforming the entire knowledge system or "info-sphere" in the high-tech world.

The hyper-speed of change today means that given "facts" become obsolete faster—knowledge built on them becomes less durable. To overcome this "transience factor," new technological and organizational tools are currently being designed to accelerate scientific research and development. Others are intended to speed up the learning process. The metabolism of knowledge is moving faster.

Equally important, the high-tech societies are beginning to reorganize their knowledge. As we've seen, the everyday know-how needed in business and politics is growing more abstract every day. Conventional disciplines are breaking down. With the help of the computer, the same data or information can now easily be clustered or "cut" in quite different ways, helping the user to view the same problem from quite different angles, and to synthesize meta-knowledge.

Meanwhile, advances in artificial intelligence and expert systems provide new ways to concentrate expertise. Because of all these changes, we see rising interest in cognitive theory, learning theory, "fuzzy logic," neurobiology, and other intellectual developments that bear on the architecture of knowledge itself.

In short, knowledge is being restructured at least as profoundly as violence and wealth, meaning that all the elements of the power triad are in simultaneous revolution. And each day the other two sources of power themselves become more knowledge-dependent.

This, then, is the turbulent background against which the rise and fall of civilizations and of individual nations needs to be seen, and it explains why most current power assessments will prove misleading.

THE ONE-LEGGED SOVIET

Diplomats like to talk about the balance of power. The powershift principle helps us gauge not only the balance of power but the "power of balance."

Nations (or alliances) can be divided into three types: those whose power is based predominantly on a single leg of the violence-wealth-knowledge stool, those whose power rests on two legs, and those whose global clout is balanced on all three of the main sources of power.

To judge how well the United States, Japan, or Europe will fare in the global power struggles to come, we need to look at all three of these sources of power, focusing special attention on the third: the knowledge base, since this will increasingly determine the value of the other two.

This knowledge base includes far more than conventional items like science and technology or education. It encompasses a nation's strategic conceptions, its foreign intelligence capabilities, its language, its general knowledge of other cultures, its cultural and ideological impact on the world, the diversity of its communication systems and the range of new ideas, information, and imagery flowing through them. All these feed or drain a nation's power and determine what quality of power it can deploy in any given conflict or crisis.

Going beyond the triad, the powershift principle introduces a further useful insight by asking about the *relationship* of violence to wealth to knowledge in any given period.

If we look at the power of balance, as distinct from the balance of power, we discover that throughout the Cold War, the power of the United States has been extremely broadly based. America not only had massive military might but supreme economic clout, and the world's best supply of power-knowledge, ranging from the finest science and technology to a popular culture much of the world wished to emulate.

By contrast, Soviet power was, and remains, totally unbalanced. Its claim to superpower status derived exclusively from its military. Its economy, a shambling wreck at home, counted for little in the world system. While its R&D was excellent in a few defense-related sectors, its general technological know-how was backward, cramped by paranoid secrecy. Its telecommunications were abominable. Its education system was mediocre, its centrally controlled media, tightly censored and backward.

Over the long run of the Cold War, it was the power-balanced United States, rather than the one-legged Soviet Union, that won the endurance race.

This insight, only half-understood by the main global players, helps explain much of what Europe, the United States, and Japan are doing as they race toward their coming collision.

33

TRIADS: TOKYO—BERLIN— WASHINGTON

Until recently Japan was a one-legged nation.

If a nation's global influence springs mainly from military potential, wealth, and knowledge, Japan's, until very recently, rested on one leg of the power triad, much like that of the Soviet Union. Instead of nuclear weapons and the equivalent of the Red Army, Japan had cash. And more cash.

But one-legged stools are notoriously unstable. And even wealth has its limitations. For this reason, Japan today is pursuing the power of balance.

THE JAPANESE GUN

At first bullied into military spending by Washington, Japan has recently needed little prodding to expand its armed forces. What has been unthinkable since Hiroshima—the notion of a nuclear-armed Japan—is no longer regarded as entirely out of the question. It has become, instead, a noticeable gleam in the eye of some Japanese hawks.

Japan's military budget is now the third-largest in the world, after that of the United States and the Soviet Union. Its hawks, according to their critics, now want to expand the military's role beyond Japan's immediate territorial waters; to write a mutual security pact with a neighboring country, giving Japan a definite role as regional policeman; and to equip the navy with an aircraft carrier so Japanese power can be projected over a much wider radius.

Japan's budding military-industrial complex is champing at the bit to build its own fighter aircraft, missiles, and other advanced weaponry. Companies like Fuji Heavy Industries, Kawasaki Heavy Industries, Nissan, Mitsubishi, and Komatso all produce military goods under U.S. license. After acrimonious negotiations with the United States, a joint project is under way to build the FSX advanced fighter plane using active phased array radar, sophisticated composite materials, and other advanced technologies. Japan is also engaged in research on missile defense.

Japan is neither aggressive nor irresponsible. Its military, since World War II, has been firmly under civilian control, and every survey shows the Japanese public to be far more peace-loving than Americans. Nevertheless, it is hard to say how long that sentiment will last as frictions rise between Washington and Tokyo. It is by no means clear what role the Japanese military might play in Southeast Asia if (1) U.S. forces were further weakened or withdrawn; and (2) war or revolution threatened Japan's huge investments in the region.

With political unrest flaring from Beijing and Hong Kong to Manila, Japan's neighbors in the region have one worried eye cocked on Japan's rearmament and the other on America's post-Vietnam retrenchment, its troop withdrawals from South Korea, and its defense cutbacks in general.

Japan is now driving toward military self-sufficiency, preliminary to suggesting, in the most courteous way, that U.S. forces are no longer needed in Japan—or in the region.

In 1988 former Prime Minister Noboru Takeshita put Japan's military buildup in sharp perspective. Japan, he told the Japanese Defense Academy, needed military power to match its enormous new economic clout. Japan is racing to balance its triad.

THE ECONOMIC GODZILLA

The second leg of Japanese power—its wealth—is already so well documented it needs little elaboration here. In 1986, Japan became the world's biggest creditor nation. In 1987 the combined value of all stocks on the Tokyo Stock Exchange shot past that of all New York Stock Exchange stocks. The world's largest banks and securities firms are now Japanese. Japanese buy-ups of prime American real estate, including landmarks like Radio City Music Hall and companies like Columbia Pictures, have ignited anti-Japanese passions in the United States. The same thing is happening in Europe and Australia. Meanwhile, the U.S. government has become dependent on Japanese investors for nearly a third of the funds needed to finance its deficit, raising fears that a sudden pullout of this support could destroy the U.S. economy.

The accumulation of such facts has given rise to predictions that Japan will become an economic Godzilla and dominate the earth for the next fifty years.

Yet Japan's economic rocket cannot orbit forever. The drive to export goods, and especially capital, will run into progressively stiffer resistance and worsened terms for trade and investment. In turn, friction will rise in the richer nations, driving more Japanese investment into the less economically developed countries, where both risks and rewards are potentially higher.

If large numbers of U.S. troops are brought home from Europe, as appears likely, the U.S. budget deficit could decline, further strengthening the dollar and lowering the yen, which in turn would slow overseas expansion. This would, among other things, drive up Japan's costs for oil, which is traded in dollars.

Japan's savings rate, already dropping, will decline further as consumers seek more amenity and leisure, and as the fast-growing older population eats into savings put aside during its working years. In turn, both these developments point toward higher interest rates and slower growth over the long term.

Worse yet, as every Japanese knows, the Japanese economy is perched atop an immense real estate bubble, waiting to explode at the slightest pinprick. When it does, the impact will send shock waves through the already unstable Tokyo Stock Exchange and radiate instantly to Wall Street, Zurich, and London.

Japan, moreover, has a long-neglected backlog of social and political problems. Its discredited political system, corrupt and cumbersome, finds both major parties out of sync with the new realities. (The Liberal Democratic Party depends too heavily on rural voters and needs a stronger urban base. The Socialists are urban, but unable to shake off their obsolete economic and political dogmas.)

The decades ahead will find a Japan far less stable than at present, for the era of linear growth is ending.

THE *JUKU* RACE

More important than either arms or wealth is the knowledge on which both are increasingly dependent. Japanese pupils often go to a *juku,* or cram school, after school hours to improve their grades. Japan, as a nation, has been enrolled in one big *juku* for decades, working overtime to expand the country's ultimate power source—its knowledge base.

Ever since 1970, Japan has thrown itself consciously and enthusiastically into the race to create an information-based economy. It started building its technological R&D capacity even earlier. In 1965 the number of scientists and engineers per 10,000 members of the work force was roughly a third that in the United States. By 1986 the ratio had surpassed that in America. The "knowledge-density" of its work force has been skyrocketing.

Japan is pushing ahead in every advanced field from biotechnology to space. It has ample capital for R&D, and for investments in high-tech start-up firms anywhere in the world. It is advancing frontiers in superconductivity, materials, and robotics. In 1990 it became the third nation, after the United States and the U.S.S.R., to send an unmanned spacecraft to the moon. Its successes in semiconductor chip manufacture have been astonishing.

But the world's scientific-technological marathon is only starting, and Japan's general technological base still lags. Japan even now spends 3.3 times more money for royalties, patents, and licenses for foreign technology than it takes in from the sale of its own. Sixty percent of that is paid to the United States. Japanese weakness is evident in fields like parallel computing architectures, computational fluid dynamics, phased array, and other advanced radar-related technologies.

Moreover, Japan, which is so advanced in the manufacture of computer chips and hardware, continues to be weak in the increasingly crucial field of software. Its much ballyhooed attempt at a great leap forward—the "fifth generation project"—has so far proved disappointing.

Financed by MITI, the Ministry of International Trade and Industry, the project was described as Japan's equivalent of sputnik, the Soviets' first space probe. Such was the advance enthusiasm that, in 1986, Dr. Akira Ishikawa of Aoyama Gakuin University in Tokyo said the Japanese saw the fifth generation project as "nothing short of a mandate for their survival, a means of . . . self-sufficiency." By 1988 it was already apparent that the project was in deep trouble, plagued by vague planning, technical problems, and a failure to produce significant commercial spinoff products. By 1989 it was reporting modest results. Even more significant, perhaps, Japan is behind in the development of "meta"-software, used for producing software itself.

In a recent survey, 98 percent of Japanese CEOs conceded U.S. supremacy in software; 92 percent agreed that the United States was still in the lead in artificial intelligence and in supercomputers; 76 percent felt the same way about computer-aided design and engineering.

In the early laps of the R&D race, therefore, the United States is slipping. Japan is gaining fast, but there are still many laps to go.

Knowledge-power, however, is not just a matter of science and technology. This is something Japan understands much better than the United States. As in chess and war, so in commercial or scientific rivalry: "Know your adversary" is still a vital rule. And here Japan is light-years ahead.

Japan knows infinitely more about the United States than the United States knows about Japan. Because Japan was militarily and politically dependent on the United States for decades, American decisions had an enormous impact on Japan. Japan *needed* to know America inside out.

For decades, therefore, Japanese have been journeying all over the United States, from Silicon Valley to Washington and Wall Street, from Harvard and MIT to Stanford, visiting thousands of businesses, government offices, laboratories, schools, and homes, consciously learning as much as possible about what makes America tick—not just commercially or politically, but culturally, psychologically, socially. This was not so much an exercise in business espionage (although some clearly took place) as an expression of Japan's deeply ingrained curiosity about the outside world and its search for a role model.

Following three hundred years of isolation from the rest of the planet, Japan, after the Meiji revolution, rushed to make up for its enforced ignorance and has become the most avid newspaper-reading nation in the world, the most inquisitive about foreign attitudes, the most eager to travel.

This intense curiosity has contrasted sharply with American provincialism. With the arrogance of the world's dominant power, with a domestic market so large it could afford to treat exports as peripheral, with the condescension of a conqueror and the unconscious racism of its primarily white skin, the United States bothered to learn little about Japan beyond some exotica in which geishas and mixed public bathing figured large. Sushi came later.

While 24,000 Japanese students hastened to study in the United States, fewer than 1,000 Americans bothered to make the reverse trip.

Japan, in fact, works harder than any other nation at expanding its general knowledge, and this helps explain why it has been so good at marketing its wares in the United States, and why U.S. firms would have double difficulty penetrating the Japanese market even if all trade barriers vanished overnight.

Yet Japan's overall knowledge base is still deficient in several dimensions. Reflecting its own racist values, it is naïve about ethnicity and fails to understand its significance in a global economy.

Japan's much-vaunted education system, which many U.S. educators and business leaders naïvely hold up as a model, is itself savagely criticized at home for its overregimentation and creativity-crushing methods. At the lower levels, teachers' unions and the educational bureaucracy snuff out any proposed innovation. Its higher education lacks the renowned quality of its manufactured goods. Japan makes better Acuras than university graduates.

Japan leads the world in spreading extra-intelligent electronic networks, and in developing high-definition television, but it lags behind both the United States and Europe in deregulating the media and allowing the full development of cable television and direct broadcast satellite, which would diversify the imagery and ideas so necessary in spurring innovation in a culture.

Where Japan is weakest of all, however, is in cultural exports. Japan today has great writers, artists, architects, choreographers, and film makers. But few are known outside Japan, and even they exercise little influence.

In pursuit of balanced power, Japan has launched a major cultural offensive—beginning in fields directly linked to the economy, like fashion and industrial design. It is now moving on to the popular arts as well, including television, movies, music, and dance, and to literature and the fine arts. The recent creation of the Praemium Imperiale awards, intended to be the Japanese equivalent of the Nobel Prize and sponsored by the Japan Art Association, indicates Japan's determination to play a significant role in world cultural affairs.

Japan faces a tremendous obstacle, however, in spreading its ideas and culture abroad. This is its language. Some nationalist Japanese scholars insist there is something mystical and untranslatable about Japanese, that it has a unique "soul." In truth, as poets and translators know, all languages are incompletely translatable, since the very categorization schemes and analogies embedded in them differ. But the fact that only 125 million people on the face of the earth speak Japanese is a significant drawback for Japan's pursuit of balanced world power. This is why Japan, more perseveringly than any other nation, presses on with research into computerized translation.

Another, even greater, challenge facing Japan is how to cope with the coming de-massification of a society that has been propagandized into believing that homogeneity is always a virtue. More than a decade ago anthropologist Kazuko Tsurumi of Sophia University pointed out that there is more diversity in Japan than its leaders acknowledge. But this was diversity within the framework of a homogenizing Second Wave society. As Japan enters the Third Wave era it will face potentially explosive heterogenizing pressures.

Its antagonism to social, economic, and cultural diversity is directly related to its greatest long-term weakness of all.

Today's Japanese are no longer the "economic animals" they were once accused of being, and their national power no longer rests on a single leg of the power triad. But in the most important power competition—the generation and diffusion of ideas, information, imagery, and knowledge—they still lag behind the United States.

With these various power resources to deploy, Japan's business and political leaders lack a clear international strategy. A consensus exists at the top about certain key domestic goals. These include expansion of the domestic economy and reduction of the need to export, improvement of the quality of life through increased leisure, and reclamation of the heavily fouled environment. But Japan's elites are deeply split over foreign economic policy, uncertain about what, if any, world role Japan should play in the future. One strategy presupposes that the world will break into regions and that Japan's role should be to dominate the East Asian/Pacific Region. This means concentrating investment and foreign aid there. It means quietly preparing for the role of regional police power. Such a policy reduces Japan's vulnerability to American and European protectionism.

A second approach suggests that Japan concentrate instead on the developing economies, wherever they may be. A variation of this approach proposes that Japan focus on creating the electronic infrastructures needed by these countries if they are to plug into the world economy. (Such a strategy fills a critical need for the "slow" countries of the world, draws on Japanese technological strengths, and helps lock these economies electronically into Japan's.)

A third strategy, perhaps the most widely held at present, sees Japan's mission as global, unconfined to any particular region. Its backers push for a "global mission," not because of some messianic vision of world domination but because they believe the Japanese economy is too big, too varied, too fast-growing to be contained within a single region or country group.

It is this "globalist" faction that urged the dispatch of navy ships to help the United States and its allies protect the Persian Gulf during the Iran-Iraq war. It is this group that favors making loans to Eastern Europe, playing a larger and larger diplomatic role on the world stage, assuming dominant positions in the International Monetary Fund, the World Bank, and other global institutions.

When Japan makes its decision among these three strategies, it will not be clear-cut. The Japanese way is frequently to split differences. Yet astute observers will be able to judge which way the bamboo stick falls. At that point, the world will first begin to feel the real impact of Japan's thrust toward tomorrow.

THE NEW *OST-STRATEGIE*

The conflict within the capitalist world will intensify as Japan's ambitions collide with those of the other main players, the United States and Europe, calling to mind these lines written on August 23, 1915:

"A United States of Europe is possible . . . but to what end? Only for the purpose of suppressing socialism in Europe, of jointly protecting . . . booty against Japan and America."

Their author was an obscure revolutionary named Vladimir Ilich Lenin, not yet the master of the Soviet Union. What would he make of today's events?

Like the crack-up of communism, the rush to European integration was triggered by the arrival of the Third Wave, with its new system of wealth creation. Says Gianni de Michelis, chairman of the EC's Council of Foreign Ministers: "Integration was the political response to the necessity of moving from an industrial to a post-industrial society." De Michelis forecasts an enormous economic boom as the market economy is extended to Eastern Europe. But the picture is not quite so rosy.

The collapse of Marxist-Leninist governments in Eastern Europe has given their people a taste of freedom and a whiff of hope. But it also changes the terms of the three-way struggle between Europe, the United States, and Japan, creates a power vacuum, and launches Western Europe on a new, unexpected strategy.

Let us assume the region stays peaceful, despite boiling ethnic hatreds in Yugoslavia, Bulgaria and Romania, and elsewhere. Assume that demagogues do not ignite border disputes among Germans, Poles, Hungarians, or Romanians, and that there will be no military repressions, civil wars, or other upheavals. Assume further that the Soviet Union does not fly into furious fragments. (A Soviet newspaper speculates that the very "concept" of a Union of Soviet Socialist Republics could "disappear from the political map of the world.")

If, against the odds, relative stability prevails, the most likely prospect for Eastern Europe is that as the Soviets withdraw, the Western Europeans will move in. And that, for all practical purposes, will mean the Germans.

Life for the East Europeans under West European tutelage could hardly be as bad as that which they suffered under the Soviets and under Hitler before them. The new velvet colonialism could even bring them much higher living standards. What it will not do, for a very long time at least, is allow Eastern Europe to move beyond the smokestack phase.

The Eastern Europeans will cherish their hard-won independence, and by uniting in some form of federation they might enhance their bargaining power vis-à-vis the West. U.S. Secretary of State James Baker proposed a Polish-Hungarian-Czech association. But not even a revived Austro-Hungarian empire and a reborn Emperor Franz Josef (some young Czechs want Vaclav Havel, the playwright-president of the new Czechoslovakia, to be named "king") or, for that matter, a "United States of Eastern Europe" can prevent this new form of satellitization from taking place.

The reason becomes obvious the moment we compare Central Europe's power triad—its military, economic, and knowledge resources—with those available to its Western neighbors.

The European Community, even without the incorporation of additional states, brings overwhelming triadic power to the Continental table.

To glimpse its enormous military potential, ignore NATO and the Warsaw Pact, and imagine the withdrawal of all but a few U.S. and Soviet troops from Europe. West Europeans are still left in command of immense military muscle.

As early as October 1988, West German Chancellor Helmut Kohl proposed the creation of an all-European army. Though he sang of partnership with the United States, the strains of "Yankee Go Home" could clearly be heard. With the Soviet threat presumably diminished, the Germans no longer think American protection necessary. It is true that a complete pullout by the Americans would double the costs of the West European military establishment. But that cost could be trimmed, spread over more countries, and made quite tolerable. The result would be a heavily muscled and armored New Europe.

If there were any doubt as to who will command tomorrow's Euro-Army, a few numbers should dispel it. Until now the French and the West Germans were almost evenly matched in conventional forces. The French military numbered 466,000; the West German Bundeswehr, 494,000. The French had twenty-one submarines; the West Germans, twenty-four. The French had nine squadrons of Mirage and Jaguar ground attack fighters; the West Germans had twenty-one squadrons of Tornados, F4-Fs, and Alphas.

However, German reunification totally skews the picture. With East and West German forces merged, Germany's military expenditures would be 40 percent greater, her army nearly 50 percent larger, and her ground attack fighter capability nearly three times greater than that of France. Reunification puts paid to the French policy voiced by former President Giscard d'Estaing, who said,

"French forces should be an equivalent of size to the other forces on our continent, that is, the German army."

Of course, France has nuclear arms—its famed *force de frappe,* and England, too, has an independent nuclear capability. But it is reasonably certain that Germany could acquire a nuclear capability overnight should it choose to—a fact fully understood by France, England, and the rest of the world.

Even more destabilizing to any intra-European military balance is the fact that, just before they were required by treaty to destroy them, the Soviets secretly transferred twenty-four SS-23 medium-range missiles to East Germany. With complete reunification, these presumably become the property of the merged German military, the last thing the Soviets had in mind.

While all the talk among European politicians is of unity, sweetness and light, therefore, generals on all sides are carefully weighing these numbers. Fighting capabilities cannot be inferred from bean-counting, and no one seriously believes in a replay of 1870, 1914, or 1939. But even this crude comparison makes it plain that, except perhaps under the direst emergency—one calling it the nuclear card into play—it is Germany that will, so to speak, call the shots in any Euro-military.

Today's Germans are not Nazi-fodder. They are steeped in affluent, middle-class democratic values, and they are anything but militaristic. Nevertheless, should Western forces ever be called upon to put down unrest in Eastern Europe, the ultimate decision will be made in Berlin, not Paris or Brussels.

For all Washington's constant carping about European reluctance to "share the burden" of defense, the New Europe is now a major military power all by itself.

EUROPE'S MORNING AFTER

Tomorrow's Euro-army will sit on a gigantic economic base, the second leg of the power triad. Gross figures for the EC, even without adding to its twelve members, are huge. With a population of 320 million it boasts a gross national product almost equal to that of the United States, and one and a half times that of Japan.

In aggregate, the EC nations account for 20 percent of world trade, more than either the United States or Japan.

As with military matters, Europe's key financial decisions will once more be made in Berlin, in the German finance ministry and the Deutschebank, a dominance reflecting economic realities. The combined German economy of $1.4 trillion is one and a half times that of the next-biggest European country, France.

Resigned to these power imbalances but fearful of them, West Europeans, led by France, urge a stronger, tighter EC federation on the assumption that it will limit Germany's freedom of action. But the stronger and more centralized the EC itself becomes as it acquires a common currency and central bank and takes on the role of environmental policeman, the stronger, not weaker, the influence of a combined Germany over the whole European apparatus.

The emergence of this Germano-centric system is, however, only part of an unfolding *Ost-Strategie* of breathtaking scope.

For the emerging economic strategy being developed by governments and corporations in the EC is to take advantage of cheap labor in Czechoslovakia, Hungary, Poland, and other East European countries and use it for low value-added mass production. The goods produced are not primarily for the East Europeans, but are intended for export to Western Europe.

In a nutshell, smokestacks in the East, computers and consumer goods in the West—with a unified Germany acting now not merely as the core of the Western community, but as manager for this entire continental system.

Execution of this broad economic strategy, which shifts hegemonic power over Eastern Europe from the Soviets to the West Europeans and Germans, will occupy the decades immediately ahead, and will be fraught with upsets and difficulties.

This fast-crystallizing *Ost-Strategie* presupposes that the Soviet Union will remain preoccupied with its own internal affairs, and that it will have to turn its military attentions to the Muslim regions on its South and to China and the Pacific, rather than toward Europe. Or that economic deals can be made with the U.S.S.R. that will soften its resistance to the Germanization of the East. This will depend on internal politics within the Soviet Union, as well as on unpredictable events in China and Asia generally.

The *Ost-Strategie* also presupposes that the EC itself can deliver on its glowing promises for Western Europe—a 4.5 to 7 percent growth rate, and 2 million to 5 million new jobs in the twelve member nations. More efficient production. Enhanced competitivity of world trade. Higher profits.

Yet EC planning is still heavily premised on obsolete notions about economies of scale, which apply far more readily to smoke-stack manufacture than to advanced economies organized around information and service activities.

Moreover, while the new system for wealth creation thrives on (and generates) heterogeneity, emphasizing customization and lo-calization of production, segmentation of markets and de-massi-fication of finance, the EC steamroller, despite rhetoric to the contrary, is intended to flatten out differences.

The Eastern end of the strategy faces major problems as well. To begin with, it takes for granted political stability in the quasi-colonies. Yet the rush toward mass democracy, with parliaments and multiple parties, does not guarantee sausages or ham on the table.

If desperate economic conditions do not significantly improve quickly, the infatuation with parliaments, parties, and voting could degenerate into chaos, charges of corruption, extraparliamentary terrorism, and a return to the kind of fascist or military regimes common in the region before World War II—perhaps with the support of foreign investors for whom stability and order is a paramount requirement.

After the initial euphoria about capital from the West, Eastern Europeans, on the morning after, will increasingly resent their new-style colonial status. Resentment will boil over into resistance. Economic scarcity will be blamed on foreign investors, "imperialists," and local scapegoats. Initial emergency loans will be followed by further emergency loans to keep the economies afloat. Down the line will come demands for loan-repayment moratoria and cancel-lations.

Even if none of this comes to pass, the root assumption of the *Ost-Strategie*, the importance of cheap labor, needs to be severely questioned. Cheap labor, as we've seen, is now increasingly expen-sive. With labor costs declining as a component of total cost, the savings will be minimal except in the most backward industries.

Similarly, as we've seen, slow economies cannot plug into fast economies easily. In Poland, until recently, it could take a month to six weeks merely to transfer funds from one bank to another. The entire Eastern metabolism is slower than that required by the

West, and its electronic infrastructure is virtually nonexistent. All this will make the *Ost-Strategie* more costly than it would appear.

Finally, if a significant amount of smokestack work *is* actually transferred to the East, West European governments can expect increased pressure from their own blue-collar trade unions, increased demands for social benefits and protectionism at home.

In Germany, in particular, this implies growing support for the political opposition. Like the neo-Nazi right, Social Democrats will sound nationalist themes in attacking the transfer of jobs to "non-Germans" who work for less than union wages. Greens, meanwhile, will oppose the transfer of pollution to a region that is already one of the most polluted on earth.

Should a Social Democratic Green coalition actually govern Germany, and thus heavily influence the rest of Europe, it would point to a slowdown in technological development on the Continent, since the Social Democrats fear its impact on employment, and the Greens are larded with Luddites and technophobes.

A European Bank for Reconstruction and Development has been created with funds supplied by many Western nations and Japan. Under the innovative leadership of Jacques Attali, the EBRD could lay down key beachheads for technological and economic advance in Eastern Europe. But it won't be easy.

Commercial and political ardor for the *Ost-Strategie* will therefore cool in the coming decade as Europe's deep problems begin to emerge. Europe has enormous wealth, but—so far—a questionable strategy for how to use it.

FROM LEFTISM TO SEMIOLOGY

Even more than in the United States and Japan, the future of European power will depend on its "third leg"—its knowledge base.

Measured by the number of Nobel Prizes and distinguished research laboratories and institutes, Western Europe has little to worry about. It has strength in nuclear energy, aerospace, and robotics, and has stuck a hesitant toe into superconductor research. The EC, which long treated science and technology as a poor relative, has stepped up its funding, especially of cross-border research projects. Science and technology are "in."

Here again, Germany leads. West German scientists enjoy the largest R&D budgets in Europe, and hold 2.5 times as many U.S. patents as either the British or the French. Since 1984, West Germans have been on the Nobel Prize science list every year, for things like the scanning-tunneling microscope or the quantum Hall effect.

Yet Europe, including Germany, trails both Japan and America in the crucial fields of computers and information technology, notably chip manufacture and supercomputers. The recent failure of Nixdorf—once West Germany's hottest computer firm—and its absorption by Siemens, along with the difficulties faced by Norsk Data in Norway and Philips in Holland, underscore Europe's embarrassing weakness in these fields.

In the related field of telecommunications, progress is suffocated by the stubborn refusal of various national PTTs—the post office and telecom ministries—to give up their monopoly control.

Meanwhile, bad as American schools are, Europe, too, has severe educational problems. Its school systems are overcentralized, formalistic, and rigid. And while Europe's cultural exports are greater and more prestigious than those of Japan, Europe lags far behind the United States as an originator of emulated life styles, art, and popular culture. One may, of course, argue that Europe's culture is aesthetically or morally superior to that of the United States, depending upon the criteria applied. But in terms of national power in today's fast-changing, video-drenched world, it is U.S. culture and popular culture that still make the running.

Ideologically and intellectually, Western Europe's prime postwar exports have been a quasi-Marxist leftism and, for a time, existentialism, followed by structuralism and, more recently, semiology. These are now waning in the world intellectual market.

In their place, however, Europe is now taking a strong lead in promoting a new political product. Europe's main ideological export in the years immediately ahead will be a green version of social democracy. This is extremely important and could find immensely receptive markets in the United States, Japan, Eastern Europe, and the Soviet Union, if it is not distorted and dominated by the ecological lunatic fringe.

Finally, whereas Japan is steeped in future-consciousness, and America focuses on the "now," Europe is still heavily past-oriented. A standing joke claims it requires five Britons to replace a burnt-out light bulb—one to screw it in, the other four to say how much better the old one was.

For all these reasons, Western Europe is unlikely to be a truly balanced Great Power until it devotes as much drive to developing its knowledge base as it does to reconfiguring its military and integrating its economy.

Europe has a grand, overarching strategy that aims at shifting regional and world power. This strategy—reborn, rather than freshly invented—is to control what the geopoliticians of the past called the planet's "heartland."

THE WOUNDED GIANT

This takes us to that wounded giant, the United States.

Of course, for the United States even more than for its global competitors, the military leg of the triad is crucial. The armed forces of Europe and Japan are both still primarily regional forces, with limited capacity for operations far from home. By contrast, those of the United States and the Soviet Union, despite cutbacks, both have global outreach.

With the U.S.S.R. troubled internally, however, and its Red Army needed to deal with threatened secessions, ethnic troubles, and potentially unstable borders from Iran all the way to China, the U.S. military has the most resources available for projecting power at a distance (for example, fourteen aircraft carriers with their assorted support ships, compared with four carriers for the Soviets, six for the Europeans). It is precisely the capacity for global projection that differentiates the American forces from all others.

America's tremendous armed might, firmly under civilian guidance and supported by able, educated officers, is, however, shackled to an obsolete strategic view of the world, still overfocused on the Soviet threat to Western Europe. The result is profound confusion about vital national interests and priorities—a form, as it were, of brain failure at the top.

Because of this, congressional pressures for cuts in defense spending, driven by local politics and largely haphazard, are unrelated to any coherent worldview.

The collapse of America's grand strategy also means that

much of its defense expenditure goes toward building the wrong weapons systems and putting them in the wrong places at the wrong time—a waste that dwarfs defense-contractor overruns or the proverbial "$700 gold-plated hammers." It also means that, apart from small ventures like the overthrow of Manuel Noriega in Panama, the United States is reacting to the great world events of our time rather than initiating them, as it once did.

The withdrawal of nearly all U.S. forces from Europe is likely. Less discussed is a possible redeployment toward the Pacific in the light of changed strategic conditions—the great uncertainties in China, the rearmament of Japan, the civil war in the Philippines, and the continued Soviet interest in the region. This shift from Europe toward a "Pacific strategy" would favor the navy and air force as against the army, whose primary focus has been Western Europe. Many of Japan's nervous neighbors would privately welcome such a redeployment.

The United States cannot police the entire tumultuous and highly dangerous world, either on its own behalf or anyone else's, but its unique capability suggests that it may, in alliance with other nations or international organizations, squelch regional conflicts that threaten world peace. In the dangerous decades ahead, many other nations may want just such a firefighter on duty.

THE DECLINING TWINS

The formulation of a new military strategy will also shape that other leg of the power triad, America's economy. Skinning the U.S. military down from a Second Wave force based on mass to a Third Wave force based on mobility, speed, and reach, the military equivalent of miniaturization, could pump new energy into the U.S. economy.

Ad hoc defense cuts, made under pork-barrel pressures from Congress, could destroy key research and development projects and slow down technological advance in the American economy, which has, until now, benefited from Pentagon contracts.

But the same troop withdrawal that could double Europe's military costs could, by the same token, help reduce the U.S. budget deficit, meaning less reliance on Japanese finance. It would create at least temporary unemployment. But it would also tend to lower interest rates and increase investment.

There is no guarantee that freed-up federal funds would necessarily be channeled to overdue social renovation, but some at least would find their way into education, day care, job training, and other uses that, intelligently planned, could help spark next-generation economic gains.

Much tooth-gnashing and wailing has taken place over America's relative economic decline—actually a measure of the success of its post–World War II strategy for putting Japan and Europe back on their feet. The fact is that, despite misconceptions, the United States still represents about the same share of Gross World Production that it did fifteen years ago.

(The big decline in this indicator came just after the war, when the destroyed European and Japanese economies came back on stream. Since the mid-1970s, the United States has roughly held its own.)

But manufacturing is no longer the most important gauge of an economy's importance. In the services and information sectors, which represent the leading edge of the super-symbolic economy, the United States outpoints not only Europe but Japan. As a result, unemployment in the United States has proved a less persistent problem than in Europe.

The trade imbalance, too, which for a time caused near panic in Washington, needs to be reconsidered in the light of the new economy. First, the widespread impression that U.S. exports have fallen is incorrect. During the 1980s, American exports to the world actually rose 61 percent. The problem was that imports rose one and a half times faster. Exports to Japan alone jumped 114 percent, but imports soared over 200 percent. That disparity is now narrowing. But far more important, an economy shifting toward domestic services may be quite healthy, even though many of its new products are not exportable—medical care, for example, or education.

More serious than America's much-lamented "twin deficits," both likely to decline, are the institutional obsolescence and social instability eroding American society and threatening to tear families, communities, and ethnic groups apart, and the spread of drugs in a society whose members are alienated from the state and from one another.

THE WOODY ALLEN IMPACT

Far more vital for U.S. power over the long run than its mass manufacturing base is its knowledge system or info-sphere.

A look at this third leg of the power triad contradicts those who would hastily write off the immense residual power of the United States. Overfocusing on arms and money, they ignore or underestimate the role of knowledge in national power.

Thus, the first enormous advantage that the United States holds at present is simply language. English is the whole world's language in international science, commerce, aviation, and scores of other fields. Until computer translation makes languages transparent to one another, the fact that hundreds of millions of human beings can understand at least some English gives American ideas, styles, inventions, and products a powerful thrust in the world.

Another strength is America's still-strong scientific and technological base. A great deal has been written about the declining percentage of patents being won by Americans, and other signs of scientific and technical infirmity.

After World War II the United States for all practical purposes was the *only* major industrial state able to engage in scientific or technical research on a large scale. Under the circumstances, it is hardly reasonable to expect the United States to continue to hold the same percentage of patents it did in the past.

The United States has lost its virtual monopoly. But its scientific and technical base still towers over that of its rivals. According to the National Science Foundation, U.S. private and public R&D spending runs about $120 billion a year, which is more than the budgets of Japan, Germany, France, and the United Kingdom combined. It is roughly three times that of Japan.

U.S. corporate R&D alone is slightly under $70 billion, much of the rest coming from the Pentagon, a great deal of whose research, despite arguments to the contrary, feeds into the civilian economy. (According to Samuel Fuller, chief of research at Digital Equipment, many product lines, from personal computers to workstations, sprang from basic science funded by the Defense Advanced Research Projects Agency.)

The United States still fields twice as many active research scientists and engineers as Japan, although the Japanese total is skyrocketing and Japanese nonacademic researchers tend to be younger.

The sheer size of America's effort does not guarantee quality. Moreover, with defense cuts likely and American corporations shifting resources from basic to more product-oriented research, the directions of change are not favorable. Still, though clearly challenged, the U.S. lead in high technology, and especially information technology, is still significant.

Japanese progress in computers and memory chips has been phenomenal, and three of its firms—Fujitsu, NEC, and Hitachi—have made dazzling progress. Today, Fujitsu nips at the heels of Digital Equipment, the world's second-largest computer manufacturer, and NEC and Hitachi are not far behind. The Japanese control 50 percent of the market for computer components and an amazing 85 percent of the market for memory chips.

When it comes to computers, as such, however, U.S. manufacturers dominated 69 percent of the world market, the other 31 percent being divided almost evenly by European and Japanese firms. The United States supplies fully 62 percent of all the world's PCs.

Among the world's top twenty computer firms in 1988, ten were American, six European, and only four Japanese. IBM alone was more than twice the combined size of Japan's Big Three together. Digital Equipment was almost as large as Europe's Big Three. In the increasingly important field of computer services, as distinct from machines, nine of the world's top ten firms are American, one European, and not a single one Japanese. (The Japanese share of the service market, only 10.6 percent in 1988, is actually projected to shrink as that of the United States grows.)

Similarly, it is true that Japan's progress in supercomputers has been remarkable, while U.S. supercomputer makers are in trouble. But once again the Japanese lead in hardware; the Americans, in systems and applications software. The race is not over.

In memory chip manufacture, Japanese mass production has decimated its American competition. But IBM was the first to announce a 16-million-bit chip, four times larger than the most advanced chips, and well ahead of the Japanese competition. Moreover, the direction of change is not so much toward mass production as toward chip customization and specialization, where design skills and sophisticated software count for more—precisely the fields of Japanese weakness. As for software itself—a $50 billion business now growing exponentially—the United States has a grip on 70 percent of the world market.

We cannot expand here on other fields, like superconductivity, telecommunications, materials, and biotechnology, but it is far too early to judge outcomes in the world's science and technology race.

Moreover, as time goes on the most important thing about a country's scientific and technological base may not be what information is in it at any given moment, but the speed with which it is continually renewed and the richness of communication carrying specialized know-how to those who need it and acquiring knowledge swiftly from all over the world. It is not the stocks but the flows that will matter.

An acknowledged disaster area for America is its factory-style school system, devastated by drugs, violence, and alienation. Unfortunately, schools are in trouble outside the United States as well, especially in the inner cities. Does one find truly good inner-city schools anywhere? Brixton? Bijlmermeer? Berlin? The education crisis is not an American monopoly.

What gives American schools an edge, despite everything, is that they are less centralized than those in Europe and Japan, and not subject to the dictates of a national ministry of education. This makes them, at least potentially, more open to experiment and innovation.

Unfortunately, the knee-jerk response of the American business and scientific communities is to call for more math and science, more lock-step learning, more Ph.D.'s. Misinformed about actual educational conditions in Japan, most would be amazed to learn that Japan's leap to the high-tech frontier, from 1975 to 1988, took place with only a small increase in the number of engineering and science Ph.D.'s.

Offsetting America's educational wasteland, however, is a key source of America's global power—its unquantified but enormous cultural impact on the planet. This is not a matter of quality—which can, of course, be passionately debated. It is simply fact that culture in one form or another flows outward from the United States. Thus, more American books are translated abroad than foreign books are translated by American publishers. From one point of view this is unfortunate, since it deprives Americans of valuable ideas and insights. But it reflects America's enormous surplus in cultural trade.

For good or ill, vast multitudes around the planet hunger to adopt Western, but also specifically American, life styles, attitudes, fashions, ideas, and innovations. It has been suggested that the global appeal of American popular culture derives from its multi-ethnic origins—fed by the Jewishness of Woody Allen, the Black-ness of Bill Cosby, the Italianness of characters like Colombo or film directors like Martin Scorsese, the Japaneseness of "Pat" Morita in *The Karate Kid,* the Cubanness of Desi Arnaz, and the WASPness of Clint Eastwood.

The surging influence of these images, along with the rich flow of science and technology rather than just economic or mili-tary power, is what makes the United States so threatening to the hard-liners who control China today or to the Ayatollahs who run Iran. American movies and television programs, not Japanese or Soviet or European, are the most watched around the world. The other major powers are simply not in the running.

Broadly speaking, the United States continues to be a rich source of innovations in science, technology, art, business, imag-ery, and knowledge in its broadest sense. This advantage may dwindle in the decades ahead, but other nations or regions will find it harder to overtake this American cultural lead than to build a new weapon system or to integrate their economies.

A review of the power triad, therefore, suggests that while the United States has severe problems, it is by no means a paper tiger. In the approaching decades it will be internally racked by social, racial, and sexual protests as the pace of power-shifting accelerates at home and abroad. But America's internal troubles will not, in all likelihood, compare with the upheavals that are to be expected in Europe, the least stable of the three great contenders for world power. Nor will Japan escape political and social turmoil as the world around it is shaken to the core.

Such quick-stroke assessments are admittedly impressionistic, and all of them are legitimately arguable, point by point. But taken together they suggest that the United States holds the most bal-anced power of any of the three great capitalist centers in the world, and that it still holds the lead in precisely that element of the power triad that is becoming most important—knowledge.

A CHOICE OF PARTNERS

Not only are most forecasts about global power based on overly simple assumptions, they misdefine power. The influential theory of Paul Kennedy, author of *The Rise and Fall of the Great Powers*, for example, which popularized the idea of American decline, essentially measures national power in terms of wealth and military capability alone. Kennedy alludes to, but undervalues, the impact of ideology, religion, and culture, all of which are becoming more important than ever. He vastly underestimates the role of knowledge—which, in fact, has now become the dominant source of both economic wealth and military strength. This is the central powershift of our time.

Moreover, power, as we've seen, is not just a matter of how much but of how good—quality of power may be as important as its quantity, and a nation's power must be related to its own goals, not merely to the power of other nations. What might be adequate for one purpose, reflecting one set of values, might be inadequate for another.

Unlike Europe, whose focus is regional, and Japan, which is hesitating between a regional and a global role, the United States is committed to a global role. Having led a global coalition for the past half-century, America can hardly imagine narrowing its ambitions to a single region. But more than psychology is involved. The U.S. economy is linked into so many parts of the world, and now depends upon so vast a variety of relationships, that to be cut off from access to any significant part of the world economy would be devastating. No American political leader can allow that to happen.

The same may turn out to be true for Japan—and perhaps for Europe as well. Thus, any serious threats of protectionism—in response, say, to an economic crisis—would totally destabilize relations among the three great capitalist centers. What's more, three is an unstable number. Parties of three frequently split into a two and a one.

Of course, many other nations and regions are already fighting for a place in the 21st-century power system. Strange new alliances and strategies will appear. Countries long relegated to the back pages of history will suddenly loom into our consciousness. But even now, European leaders are approaching Washington with what amounts to plans for a new alliance, no longer aimed at Moscow.

Some proposals are limited to specific fields, like high-definition television, or to technology generally. But broader terms are clearly in mind. The German daily the *Stuttgarter Zeitung* voices the common belief that "closer ties between Europeans and Americans can only be of mutual benefit . . . in coordinating policy . . . toward their joint competitor Japan."

But what if American long-range strategists were blind and permitted history to swing in the opposite direction—toward a tacit alliance (and economic division of the globe) between Japan and a Germanicized Europe? Japanese companies like JVC are already rushing to relocate their European headquarters in Berlin. Mitsubishi has already forged links with Messerschmitt.

The United States, even if integrated into an all–North American common market, could not for long survive this global squeeze play, the result of which might be nothing less catastrophic than World War III.

A reinvigorated U.S.-Japanese alliance, however, could produce a sharply different outcome.

U.S.-Japanese relations have never been worse since World War II. Indeed, the gap between the United States and Japan can only widen so far before dangerous sparks arc across it. Irresponsible jingos in both Tokyo and Washington, playing for easy votes and money, are deliberately stoking dangerous emotions.

If Shintaro Ishihara, a former Cabinet member, can speculate about a future in which the United States reoccupies Japan to prevent the sale of advanced chips to the Soviet, he is, by implication, speculating about outright war, voicing an incredible thought not far from consciousness in both countries. He and his American counterparts who picture Japanese and American missiles pointed at each other should remember that he who rides the tiger cannot get off.

In a world of sudden turnabouts and surprises, no fantasy can be ruled out. But the remotest risk of such confrontation should send horrors down the spine even of those who are equally weary of American superpowerdom and Japanese competition. Such a struggle could plunge the entire earth into a nightmare from which it might not recover for centuries.

The growing hostility between these two Pacific powers could only be heightened if Europe turned protectionist, forcing them into even fiercer competition in the rest of the world. Which is why the idea of a "Fortress Europe" closed to outside competition is the equivalent of a death threat to world peace.

In this highly volatile situation, America can play the coquette, allowing itself to be used as a "card" to be played by Europe or Japan in their global competition. It can play the role of mediator. Or it can forge an alliance to dominate the early decades of the 21st century. But with whom?

It is precisely here that the "power triad" analysis proves most revealing. For if we once more look at violence, wealth, and knowledge, we can glimpse the power consequences of any given lineup.

It tells us, for example, that a de facto U.S.-European alliance would weld together great military power (the old NATO, plus). It would bring together huge markets and great wealth (much of it, however, based on rust-belt manufacture and assumptions). It would merge America's science and technology with Europe's and it would assemble vast cultural power. Long cultural and ethnic ties would make this convergence natural.

Such an alliance, aimed at Japan, would call up memories of the 1930s, further accelerate Japanese rearmament, install hawks in power, and drive Japan deeper toward the developing countries as less favorable markets for its goods and capital. Militarily it could lead to a Soviet-Japanese deal and even toward some new form of Chinese adventure. For Japan to be frozen out of Europe or even, if it is imaginable, the United States, would be yet another equivalent of setting off a global time bomb.

By contrast, cold calculation also shows that a de facto alliance between the United States and Japan, despite their current tensions, would produce quite different consequences for the planet. This turnabout should not be discounted in a world in which public opinion can shift overnight and in which the United States finds itself defending Mikhail Gorbachev.

Strange as it sounds, an American-Japanese alliance to balance the power on the European "heartland" would bring together what are currently the world's first- and third-biggest military budgets; its two largest economies; and its two fastest-growing scientific and technical bases. Such a combination could form a strategic duopoly or condominium encompassing within it the fastest-growing economies in the world—those of the Pacific region, the "heart-sea" counterpart of the "heart-land."

There is, moreover, one last awesome factor differentiating the two alliances, between which the United States may find itself torn. This difference is so little discussed in Washington, Tokyo, or the European capitals that strategists in the richest and most powerful nations tend to forget it. Yet over the long run it holds potentially enormous significance in the great game of nations.

Any Euro-American alliance without Japan is basically a mono-racial, all-white power coalition in a world in which the white race is a dwindling minority. By contrast, a United States–Japan alliance, for all the racism in both those nations, is an interracial power coalition. That difference cannot but register on the rest of the planet's populations.

History does not run along railroad tracks to a pre-set future. In the Powershift Era, a period of revolutionary upheaval on the planet, many other permutations of power are possible. Europe is already worrying about the Muslim pressure on its southern flank. China could erupt in civil war. Any number of other wild-card scenarios can be imagined. Surely the rest of the world will not sit idly by as Europe, Japan, and the United States divide up the spoils. Yet strategists in Washington, Tokyo, Brussels, and Berlin may soon have to choose sides in the great triadic competition for world power.

The decision that Washington makes (consciously or by default) will shape the future of the entire rest of the planet, from China and the U.S.S.R. to the Middle East, Africa, and Latin America.

What, then, should we conclude about this inter-capitalist struggle for world power? Which of the three great contenders will triumph in history's next great powershift?

The answer, as we'll see next, is that we are asking the wrong question.

34

THE GLOBAL GLADIATORS

Asking which nations will dominate the 21st century is an exciting game. But it is, in fact, the wrong question to ask—or at least the wrong form in which to ask it—because it overlooks what could turn out to be the biggest change in global affairs since the rise of the nation-state: the coming of the Global Gladiators.

A new group of power-seekers are leaping onto the world stage and seizing sizable chunks of the clout once controlled by nations alone. Some are good; some, decidedly evil.

THE RESURRECTION OF RELIGION

When a blood-besotted Ayatollah Khomeini called for a martyr to murder Salman Rushdie, whose novel *The Satanic Verses* Khomeini denounced as blasphemous, he sent a historic message to all the world's governments. That message was instantly communicated via satellite, television, and print. The message, however, was totally misunderstood.

One may argue that Rushdie's book was in bad taste, that it deliberately offended many Muslims, that it derided an entire religion, that it violated the Koran. Indeed, Khomeini said these things. But that was not his real message.

Khomeini was telling the world that the nation-state is no longer the only, or even the most important, actor on the world stage.

Superficially, Khomeini seemed to be saying that Iran, itself a sovereign state, had the "right" to dictate what the citizens of other equally sovereign nations could or could not read. In claiming this right, and threatening to enforce it with terrorism, Khomeini suddenly catapulted censorship from a matter of domestic concern to the level of a global issue.

In a world that is witnessing the globalization of the economy and the globalization of the media, Khomeini was demanding the globalization of mind-control.

Other religions, in past eras, have asserted a similar right, and burned heretics at the stake. But in threatening cross-border assassination, Khomeini was doing more than attacking Salman Rushdie —a British citizen. He was challenging the most fundamental right of any nation-state, the right to protect its citizens at home.

What Khomeini was really telling us was that "sovereign" states are not sovereign at all, but subject to a higher Shiite sovereignty, which he alone would define—that a religion or church had rights that supersede those of mere nation-states.

He was, in fact, challenging the entire structure of "modern" international law and custom, which until then had been based on the assumption that nations are the basic units, the key players on the global stage. This assumption pictured a planet neatly divided into states, each with its flag and army, its clearly mapped territory, a seat in the U.N., and certain reasonably defined legal rights.

It is no accident that, to much of the world, Khomeini seemed a cruel throwback to the preindustrial era. He was. His assertion of the rights of religion over nation-states paralleled the doctrine medieval Popes expressed during centuries of bloody church-state conflict.

The reason this is important is that we may well be circling back to the kind of world system that existed before industrialism, before political power was packaged into clearly defined national entities.

That pre-smokestack world was a hodgepodge of city-states, pirate-held ports, feudal princedoms, religious movements, and other entities, all scrambling for power and asserting rights that we, today, assume belong only to governments. What we might now call nations were few and far between. It was a heterogeneous system.

By contrast, the nation-state system that evolved during the smokestack centuries was far more standardized and uniform.

We are now moving back to a more heterogeneous global

system again—only in a fast-changing world of high technology, instantaneous communication, nuclear missiles, and chemical warfare. This is an immense leap that carries us forward and backward at the same time, and propels religion once more to the center of the global stage. And not just Islamic extremism.

A totally different case in point is the growing global power of the Catholic Church. Papal diplomacy has figured recently in major political changes from the Philippines to Panama. In Poland, where the church won admiration for its courageous opposition to the communist regime, it has emerged as a dominant force behind the first noncommunist government. Vatican diplomats claim that the recent changes all across Eastern Europe were, in large measure, triggered by Pope John Paul II.

The Pope is no fanatic and has reached out to other religions. He has spoken out against interethnic violence. Yet echoes of a long-distant pre-secular past are heard in his call for a "Christian Europe" and his repeated criticisms of Western European democracies.

The Pope's policies call to mind a long-forgotten document that was circulated in European capitals in 1918 urging the creation of a Catholic superstate made up of Bavaria, Hungary, Austria, Croatia, Bohemia, Slovakia, and Poland. The Pope's proposed Christian (though presumably not exclusively Catholic) Europe today embraces all of Europe, from the Atlantic to the Urals, with a population of nearly 700 million people.

Such religious stirrings are part of the gathering attack on the secular assumptions that underpinned democracy in the industrial era and kept a healthy distance between church and state. (If Europe is Christian, as distinct from secular, where do nonbelievers fit in, or Hindus or Jews, or the 11 million Muslim immigrants encouraged to come to Europe to serve as cheap labor in the recent past? (Some Muslim fundamentalists actually dream of Islamicizing Europe. Says the director of the Institute of Islamic Culture in Paris: "In a few years Paris will be the capital of Islam, just as Baghdad and Cairo were in other eras.")

The emerging global power game in the decades ahead cannot be understood without taking into account the rising power of Islam, Catholicism, and other religions—or of global conflicts and holy wars among them.

THE EMPIRE OF COCAINE

Religions are not the only forces rising up to challenge the power of nation-states as such. In his massive examination of the global narcotics business, James Mills writes: ". . . the Underground Empire today has more power, wealth, and status than many nations. It flies no flag on the terrace of the United Nations, but it has larger armies, more capable intelligence agencies, more influential diplomatic services than many countries do."

The ability of a drug cartel to corrupt, terrorize, and paralyze the Colombian government for years, having first shifted its balance of trade, suggests what other outlaw groups, not necessarily narcotics traffickers, may also be able to do before long.

A measure of the cartel's menace was the enormous security provided U.S. President Bush and the leaders of Peru, Bolivia, and Colombia when they met at the so-called "drug summit" in Cartagena. The Colombians supplied a squadron of fighter-bombers, a fleet of navy ships, frogmen, antiterrorist SWAT teams, and thousands of soldiers. All this force was ranged not against a hostile nation, but against a network of families.

Governments find it increasingly difficult to deal with these new actors on the world stage. Governments are too bureaucratic. Their response times are too slow. They are linked into so many foreign relationships that require consultation and agreement with allies, and must cater to so many domestic political interest groups, that it takes them too long to react to initiatives by drug lords or religious fanatics and terrorists.

By contrast, many of the Global Gladiators, guerrillas and drug cartels in particular, are non- or even pre-bureaucratic. A single charismatic leader calls the shots quickly, and with chilling—or killing—effect. In other cases, it is unclear who the leaders really are. Governments stagger away confused from conflicts with them. With whom can one make a deal? If a deal is possible, how is one to know if the people making it can actually deliver? Can they really return hostages, stem the flow of drugs, prevent bomb attacks on embassies, or cut down on piracy?

The few international laws that have reduced global anarchy in the past are totally inadequate to deal with the new global realities.

In a world of satellites, lasers, computers, briefcase weapons, precision targeting, and a choice of viruses with which to attack people or computers, nations as we now know them may well find themselves up against potent adversaries, some no more than a millionth their size.

THE DISPERSED "OPPRESSOR"

Just as nations are proving inept in coping with terrorists or religious frenzy, they are also finding it harder to regulate global corporations capable of transferring operations, funds, pollution, and people across borders.

The liberalization of finance has encouraged the growth of some six hundred mega-firms, which used to be called "multi-nationals" and which now account for about one fifth of value added in agriculture and industrial production in the world. The term *multinational*, however, is obsolete. Mega-firms are essentially non-national.

Until the recent past, globe-girdling corporations have typically "belonged" to one nation or another even if they operated all over the world. IBM was an unquestionably American firm. Under the new system for creating wealth, with companies from several countries linked into global "alliances" and "constellations," it is harder to determine corporate nationality. IBM-Japan is, in many ways, a Japanese firm. Ford owns 25 percent of Mazda. Honda builds cars in the United States and ships them to Japan. General Motors is the largest stockholder in Isuzu. Writes management consultant Kenichi Ohmae: "It is difficult to designate the nationality of . . . global corporations. They fly the flag of their customers, not their country."

What is the "nationality" of Visa International? Its headquarters may be in the United States, but it is owned by 21,000 financial institutions in 187 countries and territories. Its governing board and regional boards are set up to prevent any one nation from having 51 percent of the votes.

With cross-national takeovers, mergers, and acquisitions on the rise, ownership of a firm could, in principle, switch from one country to another overnight. Corporations are thus becoming more truly nonnational or transnational, drawing their capital and management elites from many different nations, creating jobs and distributing their streams of profit to stockholders in many countries.

Changes like these will force us to rethink such emotionally charged concepts as economic nationalism, neocolonialism, and imperialism. For example, it is an article of faith among Latin Americans that Yankee imperialists siphon "superprofits" from their countries. But if tomorrow "superprofits" from a Mexican operation were to go to investors dispersed throughout Japan, Western Europe, and, say, Brazil (or even someday China), who exactly is the neocolonialist?

What if a transnational is nominally based in Macao or, for that matter, Curaçao, and its stock is owned by 100,000 continually changing shareholders from a dozen countries, trading in half a dozen different stock exchanges from Bombay and Sydney to Paris and Hong Kong? What if even the institutional investors are themselves transnational? What if the managers come from all over the world? What country, then, is the "imperialist oppressor"?

As they lose their strictly national identities, the entire relationship between global firms and national governments is transformed. In the past, "home" governments of such companies championed their interests in the world economy, exerted diplomatic pressure on their behalf, and often provided either the threat (or the reality) of military action to protect their investments and people when necessary.

In the early 1970s, at the behest of ITT and other American corporations, the CIA actively worked to destabilize the Allende government in Chile. Future governments may be far less ready to respond to cries for help from firms that are no longer national or multinational but truly transnational.

If so, what happens when terrorists, guerrillas, or a hostile nation threaten the people and facilities of one of the great transnationals? To whom does it turn for help? Does it meekly walk away from its investments?

THE CORPORATE CONDOTTIERI

Military might is the one thing nation-states have had that other contenders for power typically lacked. But if state or inter-governmental forces cannot impose order, the day may dawn when perfectly ordinary transnational corporations decide it is necessary to put their own brigades into the field.

Fantastic as this may sound, it is not without historical prece-dent. Sir Francis Drake waged war not merely on Spanish ships laden with silver, but on towns all along the Pacific coast of South America, Central America, and Mexico. He was financed by pri-vate investors.

Is it entirely fanciful to imagine 21st-century corporate ver-sions of the Italian condottieri?

In *The Apocalypse Brigade* the novelist Alfred Coppel has pic-tured precisely this situation—one in which a mega-oil company organizes its own army to protect oil fields from an anticipated terrorist strike. The company acts on its own because it cannot get its home government to protect its interests.

Extreme as this fictional scenario may seem, there is a certain logic to it. The inability of states to stop terrorism, despite all the armies at their command, has already forced some major corpora-tions to take matters into their own hands, hiring trained drivers, armed bodyguards, high-tech security specialists, and the like. And when Iran took some of his employees hostage, billionaire Ross Perot hired ex–Green Berets to penetrate Iran and rescue them. From here it is only a short step to mercenary troops.

THE U.N.-PLUS

Clearly we are heading for chaos if new international laws aren't written and new agencies created to enforce them—or if key Global Gladiators, like the transnational corporations, religions, and similar forces, are denied representation in them.

Proposals are coming hot and fast for all sorts of new global institutions to deal with ecology, arms control, monetary matters, tourism, telecommunications, as well as regional economic concerns. But who should control these agencies? Nation-states alone?

The less responsive to their needs governments and inter-government organizations become, the more likely it is that transnational firms will end-run governments and demand direct participation in global institutions.

It is not too hard to imagine a Global Council of Global Corporations arising to speak for these new-style firms and to provide a collective counterbalance to nation-state power. Alternatively, major corporations may demand representation in their own names, as part of a new class of membership within organizations like the United Nations, the World Bank, or GATT.

Given the growing diversity and power of Global Gladiators, the United Nations, which until now has been little more than a trade association of nation-states, may eventually be compelled to provide representation for nonstates, too (beyond the token consultative role now granted to certain nongovernmental groups, or NGOs).

Instead of one-nation–one-vote, it may well have to create additional categories of voting membership for transnational companies, religions, and other entities, which would vastly broaden its base of support in the world. On the other hand, if the nation-states who own and operate the U.N. refuse to widen representation, counterorganizations may arise as global corporations multiply and gather strength.

But whether or not such speculations prove correct in the future, the new Global Gladiators—corporate, criminal, religious, and other—already share increasing *de facto* power with nation-states.

NEW-STYLE GLOBAL ORGANIZATIONS

The question of whether some non-national "gladiators" ought to be represented in world bodies is closely related to the design of new organizations on the world scene. A key question facing the architects of the new global order is whether power should flow vertically or horizontally.

A clear example of vertical organization is the European Community, which seeks to build, in effect, a supra-government that would, according to its critics, reduce the present countries of Europe to the status of provinces rather than sovereign nations—by imposing supra-national controls over currency, central banking, educational standards, environment, agriculture, and even national budgets.

This traditional vertical model seeks to solve problems by adding another echelon to the power hierarchy. It is "high-rise" institutional architecture.

The alternative model, congruent with the emerging forms of organization in the business world and the advanced economies, flattens the hierarchy rather than extending it upward. It will be based on networks of alliances, consortia, specialized regulatory agencies, to accomplish ends too large for any single state. In this system there is no higher level of top-down control, and specialized agencies are not grouped hierarchically under a nonspecialized central body. It is the equivalent of "low-rise" architecture. It parallels the flex-firm.

Around the world today, the EC is being closely watched and, very often, taken as the only model for regional organization. Thus, the proposal to clone the EC is loudly heard, from the Maghreb and the Middle East to the Caribbean and the Pacific. A more revolutionary approach would be to lace existing organizations in each of these regions together, without imposing a new layer of control. The same might be done between nations.

Japan and the United States, for example, are so closely intertwined economically, politically, and militarily, that decisions in one have immediate high-impact consequences in the other. Under these circumstances, the day may arrive when Japan will demand actual voting seats inside the Congress of the United States. In return, the United States would no doubt demand equivalent representation in the Japanese Diet. In this way would be born the first of many potential "cross-national" parliaments or legislatures.

Democracy presupposes that those affected by a decision have a right to participate in making the decision. If this is so, then many nations should, in fact, have seats in the U.S. Congress, whose decisions have greater impact on their lives than the decisions of their own politicians.

As the world goes global, and the new system for wealth creation spreads, demands for cross-national political participation—and even cross-national voting—will bubble up from the vast populations who now feel themselves excluded from the decisions that shape their lives.

But whatever form the global organizations of tomorrow assume, they will have to pay more attention, both positive and negative, to the Global Gladiators.

To what extent should groups like religions and global corporations, as well as transnational trade unions, political parties, environmental movements, human rights organizations, and other such entities from the civil society be represented in the institutions now being planned for the world of tomorrow?

How can one keep a crucial separation between church and state at the global level to avoid the fearsome bloodshed and oppression that has so often resulted from their fusion? How might terrorists or criminals, warlords and narco-killers be quarantined? What legitimate global voice might be given to national minorities oppressed at home? What missile defense or chemical-warfare defense measures should be regional or global, rather than left to purely national responsibility?

No one can afford to be dogmatic in answering these dangerous questions of the not-so-far-off future. The questions themselves sound strange, no doubt, in a world that still conceives of itself as organized around nation-states. But at the dawn of the smokestack era, nothing sounded stranger, more radical, more dangerous than the ideas of French, English, and American revolutionaries who thought that people and parliaments should control kings, rather than the reverse, and that lack of representation was cause for rebellion.

In many countries, such ideas may provoke passionate objection on patriotic grounds. The proto-fascist French writer Charles Maurras in the 19th century expressed the traditional view that "of all human liberties, the most precious is the independence of one's country." But absolute sovereignty and independence have always been mythical.

Only countries willing to opt out of the new system of wealth creation forever can avoid plugging into the new global economy. Those who do connect with the world will necessarily be drawn into an interdependent global system populated not by nations alone, but by newly powerful Global Gladiators as well.

We are witnessing a significant shift of power from individual or groups of nation-states to the Global Gladiators. This amounts to nothing less than the next global revolution in political forms.

The shift toward hetrogeneity in the emerging world system will sharply intensify if giant nations splinter, as now seems eminently possible. The Soviet Union is fast-fracturing, with Gorbachev desperate to hold the parts together in a much-loosened framework. But some pieces will almost surely flake off and assume strange new forms in the decades to come. Whether part of the Post-Soviet Union or not, some regions will inevitably be drawn into the economic vortex of a German-dominated Europe; others into the nascent Japanese sphere of influence in Asia.

The backward republics, still dependent on agriculture and raw material extraction, may huddle together in a loosened federation. But rational economic considerations could easily be swept aside by a tidal wave of religious and ethnic strife, so that the Ukraine, the Russian republic, and Byelorussia merge into a giant mass based on Slav culture and a revivified Orthodox church. Islam could glue some of the Central Asian republics together.

China, too, could split up, with its most industrially developed regions in the South and East severing their ties with the great peasant-based China, and forming new kinds of entities with Hong Kong, Taiwan, Singapore, and perhaps a reunified Korea. The result might be a giant new Confucian Economic Community, countering the rise of Japan, while further strengthening the significance of religion as a factor in the world system.

To assume that such changes will happen without civil war and other conflicts, or that they can be contained within the obsolete frame of a nation-based world order, is both shortsighted and unimaginative. The sole certainty is that tommorrow will surprise us all.

What is brilliantly clear, then, is that as the new system of wealth creation moves across the planet it upsets all our ideas about economic development in the so-called South, explodes socialism in the "East," throws allies into killer competition, and calls into being a new, dramatically different global order—diverse and risk-filled, at once hopeful and terrifying.

New knowledge has overturned the world we knew and shaken the pillars of power that held it in place. Surveying the wreckage, ready once more to create a new civilization, we stand, all together now, at Ground Zero.

CODA:

FREEDOM, ORDER, AND CHANCE

This book has told the story of one of the most important revolutions in the history of power—a change that is now reshaping our planet. Over the past generation millions of words have been devoted to upheavals in technology, society, ecology, and culture. But relatively few have attempted to analyze the transformation in the nature of power itself—which drives many of these other changes.

We have seen how, at every level of life, from business to government and global affairs, power is shifting.

Power is among the most basic of social phenomena, and it is linked to the very nature of the universe.

For three hundred years Western science pictured the world as a giant clock or machine, in which knowable causes produced predictable effects. It is a determinist, totally ordered universe, which, once set in motion, pre-programs all subsequent actions.

If this were an accurate description of the real world, we would all be powerless. For if the initial conditions of any process determine its outcome, human intervention cannot alter it. A machine-like universe set in motion by a Prime Mover, divine or otherwise, would be one in which no one has power over anything or anyone. Only, at best, an illusion of power.

Power, in short, depends on cracks in the causal chain, events that are not all pre-programmed. Put differently, it depends on the existence of chance in the universe and in human behavior.

Yet power cannot operate in an entirely accidental universe either. If events and behavior were really random, we would be equally helpless to impose our will. Without some routine, regular-

467

ity, and predictability, life would force upon us an endless series of random choices, each with random consequences, and thus make us powerless prisoners of fortune.

Power thus implies a world that combines both chance and necessity, chaos and order.

But power is also linked to the biology of the individual and the role of government or, more generally, the state.

This is so because all of us share an irrepressible, biologically rooted craving for a modicum of order in our daily lives, along with a hunger for novelty. It is the need for order that provides the main justification for the very existence of government.

At least since Rousseau's *Social Contract* and the end of the divine right of kings, the state has been seen as party to a contract with the people—a contract to guarantee or supply the necessary order in society. Without the state's soldiers, police, and the apparatus of control, we are told, gangs or brigands would take over all our streets. Extortion, rape, robbery, and murder would rip away the last shreds of the "thin veneer of civilization."

The claim is hard to deny. Indeed, the evidence is overwhelming that in the absence of what we have earlier described as vertical power—order imposed from above—life quickly becomes a horror. Ask the residents of once-beautiful Beirut what it means to live in a place where no government has sufficient power to govern.

But if the first function of the state is to ensure order, how much is enough? And does this change as societies adopt different systems of wealth creation?

When a state imposes iron control over everyday life, silences even the mildest criticism, drives its citizens into their homes in fear, censors the news, closes the theaters, revokes passports, knocks on the door at 4:00 A.M. and drags parents from their screaming children—who is served? The citizen in need of a modicum of order—or the state itself, protecting itself from outrage?

When does order provide necessary stability for the economy—and when does it strangle needed development?

There are, in short, to analogize from Marx, two kinds of order. One might be called "socially necessary order." The other is "surplus order."

Surplus order is that excess order imposed not for the benefit of the society, but exclusively for the benefit of those who control the state. Surplus order is the antithesis of beneficial or socially necessary order. The regime that imposes surplus order on its suffering citizens deprives itself of the Rousseauian justification for existence.

States that impose surplus order lose what Confucians called the "Mandate of Heaven." Today they also lose their moral legitimacy in an interdependent world. In the new system now emerging, they invite not only the attention of global opinion but the sanctions of morally legitimate states.

The widespread opprobrium directed at the Chinese hardliners after the Beijing massacre in 1989—a wave of criticism joined in by the United States, the European Community, Japan, and most other nations of the world—was timid. Each country coolly pondered its economic interests in China before announcing a position. The U.S. President almost immediately dispatched a secret mission to smooth over ruffled relations between the two governments.

Nevertheless, despite all the opportunism and *realpolitik*, the entire world, in effect, voted on the moral legitimacy of the hardliners' regime. The world said, loud enough for Beijing to hear, that it considered the regime's murderous behavior an overreaction and an attempt to impose surplus order.

Beijing angrily replied that the rest of the world had no right to intervene in its internal affairs and that the morality of the critics could also be questioned. But the fact that so many countries were compelled to speak out—even if diffidently, and even if their private policies contradicted their public expressions—suggests that global opinion is growing more articulate, and less tolerant of surplus order.

If so, there is a hidden reason.

The revolutionary new element—a change brought about by the novel system of wealth creation—is a change in the level of socially necessary order. For the new fact is that, as nations make the transition toward the advanced, super-symbolic economy, they need more horizontal self-regulation and less top-down control. Put more simply, totalitarian control chokes economic advance.

Student pilots often fly with white knuckles tightly gripping the controls. Their instructors tell them to loosen up. Overcontrol is just as dangerous as undercontrol. Today, as the crises in the Soviet Union and other countries demonstrate, the state that attempts to overcontrol its people and economy ultimately destroys the very order it seeks. The state with the lightest touch may accomplish the most, and enhance its own power in the process.

This may—just may—be bad news for totalitarians. But enough ominous signs darken the horizon to dispel facile optimism.

Those who have read this far know that this book offers no utopian promises. The use of violence as a source of power will not soon disappear. Students and protesters will still be shot in plazas around the world. Armies will still rumble across borders. Governments will still apply force when they imagine it serves their purposes. The state will never give up the gun.

Similarly, the control of immense wealth, whether by private individuals or public officials, will continue to confer enormous power on them. Wealth will continue to be an awesome tool of power.

Nevertheless, despite exceptions and unevenness, contradictions and confusions, we are witnessing one of the most important changes in the history of power.

For it is now indisputable that knowledge, the source of the highest-quality power of all, is gaining importance with every fleeting nanosecond.

The most important powershift of all, therefore, is not from one person, party, institution, or nation to another. It is the hidden shift in the relationships between violence, wealth, and knowledge as societies speed toward their collision with tomorrow.

This is the dangerous, exhilarating secret of the Powershift Era.

ASSUMPTIONS
BIBLIOGRAPHY
NOTES
ACKNOWLEDGMENTS

ASSUMPTIONS

Because the subject is so fraught with both personal and political controversy, any book on power should be expected to lay out its main assumptions and, preferably, to make plain the underlying model of power on which it is based. No such statement can ever be complete, since it is impossible to define—or even to recognize—all one's assumptions. Nevertheless, even a partially successful effort can be useful to both writer and reader.

Here, then, are some of the assumptions from which *Powershift* springs.

1. Power is inherent in all social systems and in all human relationships. It is not a thing but an aspect of any and all relationships among people. Hence it is inescapable and neutral, intrinsically neither good nor bad.

2. The "power system" includes everyone—no one is free of it. But one person's power loss is not always another's gain.

3. The power system in any society is subdivided into smaller and smaller power subsystems nested within one another. Feedback links these subsystems to one another, and to the larger systems of which they are part. Individuals are embedded in many different, though related, power subsystems.

4. The same person may be power-rich at home and power-poor at work, and so forth.

5. Because human relationships are constantly changing, power relationships are also in constant process.

6. Because people have needs and desires, those who can fulfill them hold potential power. Social power is exercised by supplying or withholding the desired or needed items and experiences.

473

7. Because needs and desires are highly varied, the ways of meeting or denying them are also extemely varied. There are, therefore, many different "tools" or "levers" of power. Among them, however, violence, wealth, and knowledge are primary. Most other power resources derive from these.

8. Violence, which is chiefly used to punish, is the least versatile source of power. Wealth, which can be used both to reward and punish, and which can be converted into many other resources, is a far more flexible tool of power. Knowledge, however, is the most versatile and basic, since it can help one avert challenges that might require the use of violence or wealth, and can often be used to persuade others to perform in desired ways out of perceived self-interest. Knowledge yields the highest-quality power.

9. The relationships of classes, races, genders, professions, nations, and other social groupings are incessantly altered by shifts in population, ecology, technology, culture, and other factors. These changes lead to conflict and translate into redistributions of power resources.

10. Conflict is an inescapable social fact.

11. Power struggles are not necessarily bad.

12. Fluctuations caused by simultaneous shifts of power in different subsystems may converge to produce radical shifts of power at the level of the larger system of which they are a part. This principle operates at all levels. Intra-psychic conflict within an individual can tear a whole family apart; power conflict among departments can tear a company apart; power struggles among regions can tear a nation apart.

13. At any given moment some of the many power subsystems that comprise the larger system are in relative equilibrium while others are in a far-from-equilibrial condition. Equilibrium is not necessarily a virtue.

14. When power systems are far-from-equilibrial, sudden, seemingly bizarre shifts may occur. This is because when a system or subsystem is highly unstable, nonlinear effects multiply. Big power inputs may yield small results. Small events can trigger the downfall of a regime. A slice of burnt toast can lead to a divorce.

15. Chance matters. The more unstable the system, the more chance matters.

16. Equality of power is an improbable condition. Even if it is achieved, chance will immediately produce new inequalities. So will attempts to rectify old inequalities.

17. Inequalities at one level can be balanced out at another level. For this reason, it is possible for a power balance to exist between two or more entities, even when inequalities exist among their various subsystems.

18. It is virtually impossible for all social systems and subsystems to be simultaneously in perfect balance and for power to be shared equally among all groups. Radical action may be needed to overthrow an oppressive regime, but some degree of inequality is a function of change itself.

19. Perfect equality implies changelessness, and is not only impossible but undesirable. In a world in which millions starve, the idea of stopping change is not only futile but immoral.
    The existence of some degree of inequality is not, therefore, inherently immoral; what *is* immoral is a system that freezes the maldistribution of those resources that give power. It is doubly immoral when that maldistribution is based on race, gender, or other inborn traits.

20. Knowledge is even more maldistributed than arms and wealth. Hence a redistribution of knowledge (and especially knowledge about knowledge) is even more important than, and can lead to, a redistribution of the other main power resources.

21. Overconcentration of power resources is dangerous. (Examples: Stalin, Hitler, and so on. Other examples are too numerous to itemize.)

22. Underconcentration of power resources is equally dangerous. The absence of strong government in Lebanon has turned that poor nation into a synonym for anarchic violence. Scores of groups vie for power without reference to any agreed conception of law or justice or any enforceable constitutional or other restrictions.

23. If both overconcentration and underconcentration of power result in social horror, how much concentrated power is too much? Is there a moral basis for judging?

The moral basis for judging whether power is over- or under-concentrated is directly related to the difference between "socially necessary order" and "surplus order."

24. Power granted to a regime should be just sufficient to provide a degree of safety from real (not imagined) external threat, plus a modicum of internal order and civility. This degree of order is socially necessary, and hence morally justifiable.
Order imposed over and above that needed for the civil society to function, order imposed merely to perpetuate a regime, is immoral.

25. There is a moral basis for opposing or even overthrowing the state that imposes "surplus order."

BIBLIOGRAPHY

The following books have been consulted during the writing of *Powershift*. They are grouped by subject for convenience, although many deal with more than a single topic.

THE PHILOSOPHY OF POWER

[1]   Aron, Raymond. *Main Currents in Sociological Thought,* Vol. II. (New York: Basic Books, 1967.)

[2]   ———. *Politics and History.* (New Brunswick, N.J.: Transaction Books, 1984.)

[3]   Bentham, Jeremy, and John Stuart Mill. *The Utilitarians.* (New York: Anchor Books, 1973.)

[4]   Berger, Peter L., and Richard John Neuhaus. *To Empower People.* (Washington, D.C.: The American Enterprise Institute for Public Policy Research, n.d.)

[5]   Bodenheimer, Edgar. *Power, Law and Society.* (New York: Crane, Russak, n.d.)

[6]   Bogart, Ernest L., and Donald L. Kemmerer. *Economic History of the American People.* (New York: Longmans, Green, 1946.)

[7]   Bottomore, T. B. *Elites and Society.* (New York: Basic Books, 1964.)

[8]   Burnham, James. *The Machiavellians.* (New York: John Day, 1943.)

[9]   Calvert, Peter. *Politics, Power and Revolution.* (Brighton, Sussex: Wheatsheaf Books, 1983.)

[10] Canetti, Elias. *Crowds and Power.* (New York: Seabury Press, 1978.)

[11] Crozier, Brian. *A Theory of Conflict.* (London: Hamish Hamilton, 1974.)

[12] Duyvendak, J. J., ed. *The Book of Lord Shang.* (London: Arthur Probsthain, 1963.)

[13] Field, G. Lowell, and John Higley. *Elitism*. (London: Routledge & Kegan Paul, 1980.)

[14] First, Ruth. *Power in Africa*. (New York: Pantheon Books, 1970.)

[15] Galbraith, John Kenneth. *The Anatomy of Power*. (Boston: Houghton Mifflin, 1983.)

[16] Hutschnecker, A. *The Drive for Power*. (New York: M. Evans, 1974.)

[17] Janeway, Elizabeth. *Man's World, Woman's Place*. (New York: Delta Books, 1972.)

[18] ———. *Powers of the Weak*. (New York: Alfred A. Knopf, 1980.)

[19] Jouvenel, Bertrand de. *On Power*. (Boston: Beacon Press, 1969.)

[20] Keohane, Robert O., and Joseph S. Nye. *Power and Interdependence*. (Boston: Little, Brown, 1977.)

[21] Kontos, Alkis, ed. *Domination*. (Toronto: University of Toronto Press, 1975.)

[22] Kropotkin, Peter. *Kropotkin's Revolutionary Writings*. (New York: Vanguard Press, 1927.)

[23] Machiavelli, Niccolò. *The Prince*. (New York: Pocket Books, 1963.)

[24] May, Rollo. *Power and Innocence*. (New York: Delta Books, 1972.)

[25] Milgram, Stanley. *Obedience to Authority*. (New York: Harper Colophon, 1974.)

[26] Mills, C. Wright. *The Power Elite*. (New York: Oxford University Press, 1956.)

[27] More, Sir Thomas. *Utopia*. (New York: Washington Square Press, 1965.)

[28] Mudjanto, G. *The Concept of Power in Javanese Culture*. (Jakarta: Gadjah Mada University Press, 1986.)

[29] Nagel, Jack H. *The Descriptive Analysis of Power*. (New Haven: Yale University Press, 1975.)

[30] Nietzsche, Friedrich. *The Will to Power*. (New York: Vintage Books, 1968.)

[31] Osgood, Robert E., and Robert W. Tucker. *Force, Order, and Justice*. (Baltimore and London: The Johns Hopkins Press, 1967.)

[32] Pye, Lucian W., with Mary W. Pye. *Asian Power and Politics*. (Cambridge, Mass.: The Belknap Press, Harvard University Press, 1985.)

[33] Rueschemeyer, Dietrich. *Power and the Division of Labour*. (Cambridge: Polity Press, 1986.)

[34] Russell, Bertrand. *A History of Western Philosophy*. (New York: Simon and Schuster, 1972.)

[35] ———. *Power*. (London: Unwin Paperbacks, 1983.)

[36] Rustow, Alexander. *Freedom and Domination.* (Princeton: Princeton University Press, 1980.)

[37] Siu, R.G.H. *The Craft of Power.* (New York: John Wiley and Sons, 1979.)

[38] Tzu, Sun. *The Art of War.* (Oxford: Oxford University Press, 1963.)

[39] Waal, Frans de. *Chimpanzee Politics.* (New York: Harper & Row, 1982.)

[40] Wing, R. L. *The Tao of Power.* (Garden City, N.Y.: Doubleday, 1986.)

BUREAUCRACY AND SOCIAL ORGANIZATION

[41] Becker, Gary S. *A Treatise on the Family.* (Cambridge, Mass.: Harvard University Press, 1981.)

[42] Chackerian, Richard, and Gilbert Abcarian. *Bureaucratic Power in Society.* (Chicago: Nelson-Hall, 1984.)

[43] Crozier, Michel. *L'entreprise à l'écoute.* (Paris: Interéditions, 1989.)

[44] Dale, Ernest, *The Great Organizers.* (New York: McGraw-Hill, 1960.)

[45] Davis, Stanley M. *Future Perfect.* (Reading, Mass.: Addison-Wesley, 1987.)

[46] Denhart, Robert B. *In the Shadow of Organization.* (Lawrence: The Regents Press of Kansas, 1981.)

[47] Donzelot, Jacques. *The Policing of Families.* (New York: Pantheon, 1979.)

[48] Dror, Yehezkel. *Public Policymaking Reexamined.* (New Brunswick, N.J.: Transaction Books, 1983.)

[49] Galbraith, John Kenneth. *The New Industrial State.* (New York: New American Library, 1985.)

[50] Goldwin, Robert A., ed. *Bureaucrats, Policy Analysis, Statesmen: Who Leads?* (Washington, D.C.: American Enterprise Institute for Public Policy Research, 1980.)

[51] Gross, Ronald, and Paul Osterman, eds. *Individualism.* (New York: Laurel, 1971.)

[52] Heald, Tim. *Networks.* (London: Hodder & Stoughton, Coronet Books, 1983.)

[53] Heilman, Madeline E., and Harvey A. Hornstein. *Managing Human Forces in Organizations.* (Homewood, Ill.: Richard D. Irwin, 1982.)

[54] Hyneman, Charles S. *Bureaucracy in a Democracy.* (New York: Harper and Brothers, 1950.)

[55] Kahn, Robert L., and Elise Boulding, eds. *Power and Conflict in Organizations.* (New York: Basic Books, 1964.)

[56] Kennedy, Marilyn Moats. *Office Politics.* (New York: Warner Books, 1980.)

[57] ———. *Powerbase.* (New York: Macmillan, 1984.)

[58] Knight, Stephen. *The Brotherhood.* (London: Granada Books, 1985.)

[59] Le Play, Frederic. *On Family, Work, and Social Change.* (Chicago: University of Chicago Press, 1982.)

[60] Mant, Alistair. *Leaders We Deserve.* (Oxford: Martin Robertson, 1983.)

[61] Mills, C. Wright. *White Collar.* (New York: Oxford University Press, 1956.)

[62] Mintzberg, Henry. *Power In and Around Organizations.* (Englewood Cliffs, N.J.: Prentice-Hall, 1983.)

[63] Nachmias, David, and David H. Rosenbloom. *Bureaucratic Government USA.* (New York: St. Martin's, 1980.)

[64] Palazzoli, Mara Selvini, et al. *The Hidden Games of Organizations.* (New York: Pantheon Books, 1986.)

[65] Quinney, Richard. *The Social Reality of Crime.* (Boston: Little, Brown, 1970.)

[66] Rosenberg, Hans. *Bureaucracy, Aristocracy and Autocracy.* (Boston: Beacon Press, 1958.)

[67] Toffler, Alvin. *Future Shock.* (New York: Bantam Books, 1971.)

[68] ———. *Previews and Premises.* (New York: Bantam Books, 1983.)

[69] ———. *The Third Wave.* (New York: Bantam Books, 1981.)

[70] Weber, Max. *Economy and Society,* Vols. I and II. (Berkeley: University of California Press, 1978.)

[71] Welch, Mary-Scott. *Networking.* (New York: Warner Books, 1980.)

[72] Yoshino, M. Y., and Thomas B. Lifson. *The Invisible Link.* (Cambridge, Mass.: M.I.T. Press, 1986.)

BUSINESS/ECONOMICS/FINANCE

[73] Adams, Walter, and James W. Brock. *Dangerous Pursuits.* (New York: Pantheon Books, 1989.)

[74] Aguren, Stefan, et al. *Volvo Kalmar Revisited: Ten Years of Experience.* (Stockholm: Efficiency and Participation Development Council, 1984.)

[75] Aliber, Robert Z. *The International Money Game.* (New York: Basic Books, 1973.)

[76] Applebaum, Herbert. *Work in Non-Market and Transitional Societies.* (Albany: State University of New York Press, 1984.)

[77] Attali, Jacques. *Les trois mondes.* (Paris: Fayard, 1981.)

[78] Batra, Raveendra N. *The Downfall of Capitalism and Communism.* (London: Macmillan Press, 1978.)

[79] Baudrillard, Jean. *The Mirror of Production.* (St. Louis: Telos Press, 1975.)

[80] Belshaw, Cyril S. *Traditional Exchange and Modern Markets.* (London: Prentice-Hall, 1965.)

[81] Bhagwati, Jagdish. *Protectionism.* (Cambridge, Mass.: M.I.T. Press, 1988.)

[82] Brenner, Y. S. *Theories of Economic Development and Growth.* (London: George Allen & Unwin, 1966.)

[83] Bruck, Connie. *The Predators' Ball.* (New York: Simon and Schuster, 1988.)

[84] Canfield, Cass. *The Incredible Pierpont Morgan.* (New York: Harper & Row, 1974.)

[85] Casson, Mark. *Alternatives to the Multinational Enterprise.* (London: Macmillan Press, 1979.)

[86] Clough, Shepard B., Thomas Moodie, and Carol Moodie, eds. *Economic History of Europe: Twentieth Century.* (New York: Harper & Row, 1968.)

[87] Cornwell, Rupert. *God's Banker.* (New York: Dodd, Mead, 1983.)

[88] Crowther, Samuel. *America Self-Contained.* (Garden City, N.Y.: Doubleday, Doran, 1933.)

[89] Denman, D. R. *Origins of Ownership.* (London: George Allen & Unwin, 1958.)

[90] Diwan, Romesh, and Mark Lutz, eds. *Essays in Gandhian Economics.* (New Delhi: Gandhi Peace Foundation, 1985.)

[91] Dressler, Fritz R. S., and John W. Seybold. *The Entrepreneurial Age.* (Media, Pa.: Seybold Publications, 1985.)

[92] Ehrlich, Judith Ramsey, and Barry J. Rehfeld. *The New Crowd.* (Boston: Little, Brown, 1989.)

[93] Evans, Thomas G. *The Currency Carousel.* (Princeton, N.J.: Dow Jones Books, 1977.)

[94] Frank, Charles R., Jr. *Production Theory and Indivisible Commodities.* (Princeton: Princeton University Press, 1969.)

[95] Friedman, Alan. *Agnelli.* (New York: New American Library, 1989.)

[96] Galbraith, John Kenneth. *Money: Whence It Came, Where It Went.* (Boston: Houghton Mifflin, 1975.)

[97] Giarini, Orio, ed. *Cycles, Value and Employment.* (Oxford: Pergamon Press, 1984.)

[98] ———. *The Emerging Service Economy.* (Oxford: Pergamon Press, 1987.)

[99] ———, and Jean Remy Roulet, eds. *L'Europe face à la nouvelle économie de service.* (Paris: Presses Universitaires de France, 1988.)

[100] Giarini, Orio, and Walter R. Stahel. *The Limits to Certainty: Facing Risks in the New Service Economy.* (Geneva: The Risk Institute Project, n.d.)

[101] Gibb, George Sweet, and Evelyn H. Knowlton. *The Resurgent Years: 1911–1927.* (New York: Harper and Brothers, 1956.)

[102] Gregerman, Ira B. *Knowledge Worker Productivity.* (New York: A.M.A. Management Briefing, 1981.)

[103] Gurwin, Larry. *The Calvi Affair.* (London: Pan Books, 1983.)

[104] Gwynne, S. C. *Selling Money.* (New York: Weidenfeld and Nicolson, 1986.)

[105] Herman, Edward S. *Corporate Control, Corporate Power.* (New York: Cambridge University Press, 1981.)

[106] Jackson, Stanley. *J. P. Morgan.* (New York: Stein and Day, 1983.)

[107] Jones, J. P. *The Money Story.* (New York: Drake Publishers, 1973.)

[108] Josephson, Matthew. *The Robber Barons.* (New York: Harcourt, Brace & World, 1962.)

[109] Kahn, Joel S., and J. R. Llobera. *The Anthropology of Pre-Capitalist Societies.* (London: Macmillan Press, 1981.)

[110] Kamioka, Kazuyoshi. *Japanese Business Pioneers.* (Singapore: Times Books International, 1986.)

[111] Kanter, Rosabeth Moss. *Men and Women of the Corporation.* (New York: Basic Books, 1977.)

[112] Keen, Peter G. W. *Competing in Time.* (Cambridge, Mass.: Ballinger, 1986.)

[113] Kenwood, A. G., and A. L. Lougheed. *The Growth of the International Economy 1820–1960.* (London: George Allen & Unwin, 1973.)

[114] Keynes, John Maynard. *The General Theory of Employment, Interest, and Money.* (New York: Harbinger Books, 1964.)

[115] Kindleberger, Charles P. *Manias, Panics, and Crashes.* (New York: Basic Books, 1978.)

[116] Knowles, L.C.A. *The Industrial and Commercial Revolutions in Great Britain During the Nineteenth Century.* (New York: E. P. Dutton, 1922.)

[117] Kornai, Janos. *Anti-Equilibrium.* (Amsterdam: North-Holland Publishing, 1971.)

[118] Kotz, David M. *Bank Control of Large Corporations in the United States.* (Berkeley: University of California Press, 1978.)

[119] Lamarter, Richard Thomas de. *Big Blue.* (New York: Dodd, Mead, 1986.)

[120] Lavoie, Don. *National Economic Planning: What Is Left?* (Cambridge, Mass.: Ballinger, 1985.)

[121] LeClair, Edward E., Jr., and Harold K. Schneider. *Economic Anthropology.* (New York: Holt, Rinehart and Winston, 1968.)

[122] Lens, Sidney. *The Labor Wars.* (Garden City, N.Y.: Doubleday, 1973.)

[123] Levin, Doron P. *Irreconcilable Differences.* (Boston: Little, Brown, 1989.)

[124] Levinson, Harry, and Stuart Rosenthal. *CEO.* (New York: Basic Books, 1984.)

[125] Loebl, Eugen. *Humanomics.* (New York: Random House, 1976.)

[126] Maccoby, Michael. *Why Work.* (New York: Simon and Schuster, 1988.)

[127] Madrick, Jeff. *Taking America.* (New York: Bantam Books, 1987.)

[128] Mattelart, Armand. *Multinational Corporations and the Control of Culture.* (Atlantic Highlands, N.J.: Humanities Press, 1982.)

[129] Mayer, Martin. *The Bankers.* (New York: Weybright and Talley, 1974.)

[130] McCartney, Laton. *Friends in High Places: The Bechtel Story.* (New York: Simon and Schuster, 1988.)

[131] McQuaid, Kim. *Big Business and Presidential Power.* (New York: William Morrow, 1982.)

[132] Meyers, Gerald C., and John Holusha. *When It Hits the Fan.* (London: Unwin Hyman, 1986.)

[133] Mises, Ludwig von. *Human Action.* (New Haven: Yale University Press, 1959.)

[134] Mohn, Reinhard. *Success Through Partnership.* (New York: Doubleday, 1986.)

[135] Monden, Yasuhiro, et al. *Innovations in Management.* (Atlanta: Industrial Engineering and Management Press, 1985.)

[136] Moskowitz, Milton. *The Global Marketplace.* (New York: Macmillan, 1988.)

[137] Mueller, Robert K. *Corporate Networking.* (New York: Free Press, 1986.)

[138] Naniwada, Haruo. *The Crisis.* (Tokyo: The Political Economic Club, 1974.)

[139] Naylor, R. T. *Hot Money*. (New York: Simon and Schuster, 1987.)

[140] Noonan, John T., Jr. *Bribes*. (New York: Macmillan, 1984.)

[141] Nussbaum, Arthur. *A History of the Dollar*. (New York: Columbia University Press, 1957.)

[142] O'Driscoll, Gerald P., Jr., and Mario J. Rizzo. *The Economics of Time and Ignorance*. (Oxford: Basil Blackwell, 1985.)

[143] O'Toole, Patricia. *Corporate Messiah*. (New York: William Morrow, 1984.)

[144] Peacock, William P. *Corporate Combat*. (New York: Facts on File, 1984.)

[145] Polanyi, Karl. *The Great Transformation*. (Boston: Beacon Press, 1957.)

[146] Pye, Michael. *Moguls*. (New York: Holt, Rinehart and Winston, 1980.)

[147] Raymond, H. Alan. *Management in the Third Wave*. (Glenview, Ill.: Scott, Foresman, 1986.)

[148] Robertson, James. *Power, Money and Sex*. (London: Marion Boyars, 1976.)

[149] ———. *Profit or People?* (London: Calder & Boyars, 1974.)

[150] Ropke, Wilhelm. *Economics of the Free Society*. (Chicago: Henry Regnery, 1963.)

[151] Saeed, Syed Mumtaz. *The Managerial Challenge in the Third World*. (Karachi: Academy of Ideas, 1984.)

[152] Sampson, Anthony. *The Money Lenders*. (New York: Viking Press, 1981.)

[153] Schumpeter, Joseph A. *Ten Great Economists*. (New York: Oxford University Press, 1965.)

[154] Sculley, John, with John A. Byrne. *Odyssey: Pepsi to Apple*. (New York: Harper & Row, 1987.)

[155] Singer, Benjamin D. *Advertising and Society*. (Don Mills, Ontario: Addison-Wesley, 1986.)

[156] Smith, Adam. *The Wealth of Nations*. (New York: Modern Library, 1937.)

[157] Sobel, Robert. *IBM, Colossus in Transition*. (New York: Bantam Books, 1981.)

[158] ———. *The Money Manias*. (New York: Weybright and Talley, 1973.)

[159] Soule, George. *Ideas of the Great Economists*. (New York: Mentor Books, 1955.)

[160] Staaf, Robert, and Francis Tannian. *Externalities*. (New York: Dunellen, n.d.)

[161] Stadnichenko, A. *Monetary Crisis of Capitalism.* (Moscow: Progress Publishers, 1975.)

[162] Stevens, Mark. *The Accounting Wars.* (New York: Macmillan, 1985.)

[163] Stewart, Alex. *Automating Distribution: Revolution in Distribution, Retailing and Financial Services,* Japan Focus. (London: Baring Securities, 1987.)

[164] Toffler, Alvin. *The Adaptive Corporation.* (New York: Bantam Books, 1985.)

[165] Tosches, Nick. *Power on Earth.* (New York: Arbor House, 1986.)

[166] Toyoda, Eiji. *Toyota: Fifty Years in Motion.* (Tokyo: Kodansha, 1987.)

[167] Woo, Henry K. H. *The Unseen Dimensions of Wealth.* (Fremont, Cal.: Victoria Press, 1984.)

[168] Zaleznik, Abraham, and Manfred F. R. Kets de Vries. *Power and the Corporate Mind.* (Boston: Houghton Mifflin, 1975.)

[169] Zuboff, Shoshana. *In the Age of the Smart Machine—The Future of Work and Power.* (New York: Basic Books, 1988.)

MEDIA

[170] Bailey, George. *Armageddon in Prime Time.* (New York: Avon Books, 1984.)

[171] Barnouw, Erik. *Mass Communication.* (New York: Rinehart, 1956.)

[172] Biryukov, N. S. *Television in the West and Its Doctrines.* (Moscow: Progress Publishers, 1981.)

[173] Enzensberger, Hans Magnus. *The Consciousness Industry.* (New York: Seabury Press, 1974.)

[174] Freches, José. *La guerre des images.* (Paris: Éditions Denoel, 1986.)

[175] Gourevitch, Jean-Paul. *La politique et ses images.* (Paris: Edilig, 1986.)

[176] Grachev, Andrei, and N. Yermoshkin. *A New Information Order or Psychological Warfare?* (Moscow: Progress Publishers, 1984.)

[177] Orwell, George. *1984.* (New York: New American Library, 1961.)

[178] Ranney, Austin. *Channels of Power.* (New York: Basic Books, 1983.)

[179] Stephens, Mitchell. *A History of the News.* (New York: Viking Press, 1988.)

[180] Whittemore, Hank. *CNN: The Inside Story.* (Boston: Little, Brown, 1990.)

POLITICS, GOVERNMENT, AND THE STATE

[181] Allison, Graham T. *Essence of Decision.* (Boston: Little, Brown, 1971.)

[182] Bennett, James T., and Thomas J. DiLorenzo. *Underground Government.* (Washington, D.C.: Cato Institute, 1983.)

[183] Bergman, Edward F. *Modern Political Geography.* (Dubuque, Ind.: William C. Brown, 1975.)

[184] Boaz, David, ed. *Left, Right, and Babyboom.* (Washington, D.C.: Cato Institute, 1986.)

[185] Bruce-Briggs, B., ed. *The New Class?* (New York: McGraw-Hill, 1979.)

[186] Cao-Garcia, Ramon J. *Explorations Toward an Economic Theory of Political Systems.* (New York: University Press of America, 1983.)

[187] Capra, Fritjof, and Charlene Sprentnak. *Green Politics.* (New York: E. P. Dutton, 1984.)

[188] Carter, April. *Authority and Democracy.* (London: Routledge & Kegan Paul, 1979.)

[189] Chesneaux, Jean. *Secret Societies in China.* (Ann Arbor: University of Michigan Press, 1971.)

[190] Coker, F. W. *Organismic Theories of the State.* (New York: AMS Press, 1967.)

[191] Commager, Henry Steele, ed. *Documents of American History.* (New York: F. S. Crofts, 1943.)

[192] Crozier, Michel. *The Trouble With America.* (Berkeley: University of California Press, 1984.)

[193] Ford, Franklin L. *Political Murder.* (Cambridge, Mass.: Harvard University Press, 1985.)

[194] Franck, Thomas M., and Edward Weisband, eds. *Secrecy and Foreign Policy.* (New York: Oxford University Press, 1974.)

[195] Gingrich, Newt. *Window of Opportunity.* (New York: Tor Books, 1984.)

[196] Greenberger, Martin, Matthew A. Crenson, and Brian L. Crissey. *Models in the Policy Process.* (New York: Russell Sage Foundation, 1976.)

[197] Greenstein, Fred I., ed. *Leadership in the Modern Presidency.* (Cambridge, Mass.: Harvard University Press, 1988.)

[198] Henderson, Nicholas. *The Private Office*. (London: Weidenfeld and Nicolson, 1984.)

[199] Hess, Stephen. *The Government/Press Connection*. (Washington, D.C.: The Brookings Institution, 1984.)

[200] Johnson, Chalmers. *Revolutionary Change*. (Boston: Little, Brown, 1966.)

[201] Kernell, Samuel, and Samuel L. Popkin. *Chief of Staff*. (Los Angeles: University of California Press, 1986.)

[202] King, Anthony, ed. *The New American Political System*. (Washington, D.C.: American Enterprise Institute for Public Policy Research, 1979.)

[203] King, Dennis. *Lyndon LaRouche and the New American Fascism*. (New York: Doubleday, 1989.)

[204] Krader, Lawrence. *Formation of the State*. (Englewood Cliffs, N.J.: Prentice-Hall, 1968.)

[205] Kyemba, Henry. *State of Blood*. (London: Corgi Books, 1977.)

[206] Laski, Harold J. *The American Democracy*. (New York: Viking Press, 1948.)

[207] ———. *Authority in the Modern State*. (Hamden, Conn.: Archon Books, 1968.)

[208] Lebedoff, David. *The New Elite*. (New York: Franklin Watts, 1981.)

[209] Lindblom, Charles E. *Politics and Markets*. (New York: Basic Books, 1977.)

[210] Mafud, Julio. *Sociologia del peronismo*. (Buenos Aires: Editorial Americalee, 1972.)

[211] Matthews, Christopher. *Hardball*. (New York: Summit Books, 1988.)

[212] Morgan, Robin. *The Anatomy of Freedom*. (Garden City, N.Y.: Doubleday, Anchor Press, 1984.)

[213] Navarro, Peter. *The Policy Game*. (New York: John Wiley and Sons, 1984.)

[214] Nelson, Joan M. *Access to Power*. (Princeton: Princeton University Press, 1979.)

[215] Neustadt, Richard E. *Presidential Power*. (New York: John Wiley and Sons, 1960.)

[216] Oppenheimer, Franz. *The State*. (New York: Free Life Editions, 1914.)

[217] Perlmutter, Amos. *Modern Authoritarianism*. (New Haven: Yale University Press, 1981.)

[218] Perry, Roland. *Hidden Power*. (New York: Beaufort Books, 1984.)

[219] Ponting, Clive. *The Right to Know.* (London: Sphere Books, 1985.)

[220] Reed, Steven R. *Japanese Prefectures and Policymaking.* (Pittsburgh: University of Pittsburgh Press, 1986.)

[221] Regan, Donald T. *For the Record.* (San Diego: Harcourt Brace Jovanovich, 1988.)

[222] Reszler, André. *Mythes politiques modernes.* (Paris: Presses Universitaires de France, 1981.)

[223] Rubin, Barry. *Secrets of State.* (New York: Oxford University Press, 1985.)

[224] Sagan, Eli. *At the Dawn of Tyranny.* (New York: Random House, 1985.)

[225] Savas, E. S. *Privatizing the Public Sector.* (Chatham, N.J.: Chatham House, 1982.)

[226] Spencer, Herbert. *The Man vs. the State* (London: Watts, 1940.)

[227] Stockman, David A. *The Triumph of Politics.* (New York: Harper & Row, 1986.)

[228] Straussman, Jeffrey D. *The Limits of Technocratic Politics.* (New Brunswick, N.J.: Transaction Books, 1978.)

[229] Tower, John, et al. *The Tower Commission Report: President's Special Review Board.* (New York: Times Books, 1987.)

[230] Wolferen, Karl van. *The Enigma of Japanese Power.* (New York: Alfred A. Knopf, 1989.)

[231] Woronoff, Jon. *Politics the Japanese Way.* (Tokyo: Lotus Press, 1986.)

RELIGION

[232] Appel, Willa. *Cults in America.* (New York: Holt, Rinehart and Winston, 1983.)

[233] Bakunin, Michael. *God and the State.* (New York: Dover Publications, 1970.)

[234] Barthel, Manfred. *The Jesuits.* (New York: William Morrow, 1984.)

[235] Breton, Thierry. *Vatican III.* (Paris: Robert Laffont, 1985.)

[236] Chai, Ch'u, and Winberg Chai. *Confucianism.* (New York: Barron's Educational Series, 1973.)

[237] Gardner, Martin. *The New Age: Notes of a Fringe Watcher.* (New York: Prometheus Books, 1988.)

[238] Hoffer, Eric. *The True Believer.* (New York: Harper & Row, 1966.)

[239] Holtom, D. C. *The National Faith of Japan*. (London: Kegan Paul, Trench, Trubner, 1938.)

[240] Illich, Ivan. *Celebration of Awareness*. (New York: Doubleday, 1970.)

[241] Levi, Peter. *The Frontiers of Paradise*. (New York: Weidenfeld & Nicolson, 1987.)

[242] Lo Bello, Nino. *The Vatican Papers*. (London: New English Library, 1982.)

[243] Martin, Malachi. *The Jesuits*. (New York: Linden Press, 1987.)

[244] Mortimer, Edward. *Faith and Power*. (New York: Vintage Books, 1982.)

[245] Murakami, Shigeyoshi. *Japanese Religion in the Modern Century*. (Tokyo: University of Tokyo Press, 1983.)

[246] Murphy, Thomas Patrick, ed. *The Holy War*. (Columbus: Ohio State University Press, 1976.)

[247] Pipes, Daniel. *In the Path of God*. (New York: Basic Books, 1983.)

[248] Rodinson, Maxime. *Islam and Capitalism*. (New York: Pantheon Books, 1973.)

[249] Sardar, Ziauddin. *Islamic Futures*. (London: Mansell Publishing, 1985.)

[250] Schultz, Ted, ed. *The Fringes of Reason*. (New York: Harmony Books, 1989.)

[251] Swidler, Leonard, ed. *Religious Liberty and Human Rights in Nations and in Religions*. (Philadelphia: Ecumenical Press, 1986.)

[252] Thomas, Gordon, and Max Morgan-Witts. *Pontiff*. (New York: Doubleday, 1983.)

[253] Tsurumi, Kazuko. *Aspects of Endogenous Development in Modern Japan*, Part II, *Religious Beliefs: State Shintoism vs. Folk Belief*. (Tokyo: Sophia University, 1979.)

[254] Wright, Robin. *Sacred Rage*. (New York: Linden Press, 1985.)

[255] Yallop, David A. *In God's Name*. (New York: Bantam Books, 1984.)

MILITARY

[256] Aron, Raymond. *On War*. (New York: W. W. Norton, 1968.)

[257] Baynes, J.C.M. *The Soldier in Modern Society*. (London: Eyre Methuen, 1972.)

[258] Best, Geoffrey. *War and Society in Revolutionary Europe, 1770–1870*. (Bungay, U.K.: Fontana Paperbacks, 1982.)

[259] Blight, James G., and David A. Welch. *On the Brink.* (New York: Hill and Wang, 1989.)

[260] Creveld, Martin Van. *Command in War.* (Cambridge, Mass.: Harvard University Press, 1985.)

[261] Cross, James Eliot. *Conflict in the Shadows.* (Garden City, N.Y.: Doubleday, 1963.)

[262] De Gaulle, Charles. *The Edge of the Sword.* Translated by George Hopkins. (Westport, Conn.: Greenwood Press, 1975.)

[263] Dixon, Norman. *On the Psychology of Military Incompetence.* (London: Futura Publications, 1976.)

[264] Fletcher, Raymond. *£60 a Second on Defence.* (London: Macgibbon & Kee, 1963.)

[265] Ford, Daniel. *The Button.* (New York: Simon and Schuster, 1985.)

[266] Gabriel, Richard A. *Military Incompetence.* (New York: Hill and Wang, 1985.)

[267] Geraghty, Tony. *Inside the S.A.S.* (New York: Ballantine Books, 1980.)

[268] Kaplan, Fred. *The Wizards of Armageddon.* (New York: Simon and Schuster, 1983.)

[269] Levy, Jack S. *War in the Modern Great Power System 1495–1975.* (Louisville: University of Kentucky Press, 1983.)

[270] Hart, Liddell *Europe in Arms.* (London: Faber and Faber, 1957.)

[271] Mackenzie, W.J.M. *Power, Violence, Decision.* (Middlesex: Penguin Books, 1975.)

[272] Millis, Walter. *The Martial Spirit.* (Cambridge, Mass.: Literary Guild of America, 1931.)

[273] Morison, Samuel Eliot. *American Contributions to the Strategy of World War II.* (London: Oxford University Press, 1958.)

[274] Moro, Comodoro R. Ruben. *Historica del conflicto del Atlantico sur.* (Buenos Aires: Escuela Superior de Guerra Aerea, 1985.)

[275] Organski, A.F.K., and Jacek Kugler. *The War Ledger.* (Chicago: University of Chicago Press, 1980.)

[276] Pfannes, Charles E., and Victor A. Salamona. *The Great Commanders of World War II*, Vol. III, *The Americans.* (Don Mills, Ontario: General Paperbacks, 1981.)

[277] Portela, Adolfo, et al. *Malvinas su advertencia termonuclear.* (Buenos Aires: A-Z Editora, 1985.)

[278] Price, Alfred. *Air Battle Central Europe.* (New York: The Free Press, 1987.)

[279] Rivers, Gayle. *The Specialist.* (New York: Stein and Day, 1985.)

[280] Sadler, A. L., trans., *The Code of the Samurai*. (Rutland, Vt., and Tokyo: Charles E. Tuttle, 1988.)

[281] Sharp, Gene. *The Politics of Nonviolent Action*. (Boston: Porter Sargent, 1973.)

[282] Starr, Chester G. *The Influence of Sea Power on Ancient History*. (New York: Oxford University Press, 1989.)

[283] *Defense of Japan*. White Paper from the Defense Agency, Japan, translated into English by the *Japan Times*. (Tokyo: Japan Times, 1988.)

[284] *Discriminate Deterrence*. (Washington, D.C.: The Commission On Integrated Long-Term Strategy, 1988.)

[285] *The Military Balance, 1989–1990*. (London: International Institute for Strategic Studies, 1989.)

[286] *A Quest for Excellence*, Final Report to the President. (Washington, D.C.: The President's Blue Ribbon Commission on Defense Management, 1986.)

[287] *Strategic Survey, 1988–1989*. (London: International Institute for Strategic Studies, 1989.)

GLOBAL RELATIONSHIPS

[288] Adams, James. *The Financing of Terror*. (London: New English Library, 1986.)

[289] Amin, Samir. *Accumulation on a World Scale*. (New York: Monthly Review Press, 1974.)

[290] Bibo, Istvan. *The Paralysis of International Institutions and the Remedies*. (New York: John Wiley and Sons, 1976.)

[291] Blazy, Jean-Claude. *Le petit livre rouge du nationalisme*. (Paris: Nouvelles Éditions Debresse, n.d.)

[292] Booth, Ken. *Strategy and Ethnocentrism*. (London: Croom Helm, 1979.)

[293] Brown, Lester R., et al. *State of the World, 1990*. (New York: W. W. Norton, 1990.)

[294] Burnham, James. *The War We Are In*. (New Rochelle, N.Y.: Arlington House, 1967.)

[295] Burstein, Daniel. *Yen!* (New York: Simon and Schuster, 1988.)

[296] Buruma, Ian. *God's Dust*. (New York: Farrar Straus & Giroux, 1989.)

[297] Chafetz, Ze'ev. *Members of the Tribe*. (New York: Bantam Books, 1988.)

[298] Close, Upton. *Behind the Face of Japan*. (New York: D. Appleton-Century, 1934.)

[299] Colby, Charles C., ed. *Geographic Aspects of International Relations*. (Port Washington, N.Y.: Kennikat Press, 1970.)

[300] Crenshaw, Martha, ed. *Terrorism, Legitimacy, and Power*. (Middletown, Conn.: Wesleyan University Press, 1983.)

[301] Davidson, William H. *The Amazing Race*. (New York: John Wiley and Sons, 1984.)

[302] Dorpalen, Andreas. *The World of General Haushofer*. (Port Washington, N.Y.: Kennikat Press, 1942.)

[303] Elon, Amos. *The Israelis—Founders and Sons*. (New York: Holt, Rinehart and Winston, 1971.)

[304] Emmott, Bill. *The Sun Also Sets*. (New York: Times Books, 1989.)

[305] Gilpin, Robert. *U.S. Power and the Multinational Corporation*. (New York: Basic Books, 1975.)

[306] ———. *War and Change in World Politics*. (Cambridge: Cambridge University Press, 1981.)

[307] Glenn, Edmund S., and Christine Glenn. *Man and Mankind*. (Norwood, N.J.: Ablex Publishing, 1981.)

[308] Hall, Edward T., and Mildred Reed Hall. *Hidden Differences*. (New York: Anchor Press, 1987.)

[309] Harris, Marvin. *Culture, People, Nature*, 2d ed. (New York: Harper & Row, 1975.)

[310] Hofheinz, Roy, Jr., and Kent E. Calder. *The Eastasia Edge*. (New York: Basic Books, 1982.)

[311] Hoyt, Edwin P. *Japan's War*. (New York: McGraw-Hill, 1986.)

[312] Huppes, Tjerk. *The Western Edge*. (Dordrecht, the Netherlands: Kluwer Academic Publishers, 1987.)

[313] Kaplan, David E., and Alec Dubro. *Yakuza*. (Menlo Park, Cal.: Addison-Wesley, 1986.)

[314] Margiotta, Franklin D., and Ralph Sanders, eds. *Technology, Strategy, and National Security*. (Washington, D.C.: National Defense University Press, 1985.)

[315] Mende, Tibor. *From Aid to Re-colonization*. (New York: New York University Press, 1981.)

[316] Miller, Abraham H. *Terrorism and Hostage Negotiations*. (Boulder, Col.: Westview Press, 1980.)

[317] Miller, Roy Andrew. *Japan's Modern Myth*. (New York: Weatherhill, 1982.)

[318] Morita, Akio, and Shintaro Ishihara. *The Japan That Can Say "No."* (Washington, D.C.: English translation and edition attributed to the Pentagon, 1989.)

[319] Morita, Akio, Edwin M. Reingold, and Mitsuko Shimomura. *Made in Japan.* (New York: E. P. Dutton, 1986.)

[320] Nakdimon, Shlomo. *First Strike.* (New York: Summit Books, 1987.)

[321] Nixon, Richard. *No More Vietnams.* (New York: Arbor House, 1985.)

[322] Ohmae, Kenichi. *Beyond National Borders.* (Homewood, Ill.: Dow Jones–Irwin, 1987.)

[323] ———. *Triad Power.* (New York: Free Press, 1985.)

[324] Palmer, John. *Europe Without America?* (Oxford: Oxford University Press, 1987.)

[325] Park, Jae Kyu, and Jusuf Wanandi, eds. *Korea and Indonesia in the Year 2000.* (Seoul: Kyungnam University Press, 1985.)

[326] Pepper, David, and Alan Jenkins, eds. *The Geography of Peace and War.* (New York: Basil and Blackwell, 1985.)

[327] Priestland, Gerald. *The Future of Violence.* (London: Hamish Hamilton, 1974.)

[328] Pujol-Davila, José. *Sistema y poder geopolítico.* (Buenos Aires: Ediciones Corregidor, 1985.)

[329] Rangel, Carlos. *The Latin Americans: Their Love-Hate Relationship with the United States.* (New York: Harcourt Brace Jovanovich, 1979.)

[330] ———. *Third World Ideology and Western Reality.* (New Brunswick, N.J.: Transaction Books, 1986.)

[331] Rosecrance, Richard. *The Rise of the Trading State.* (New York: Basic Books, 1986.)

[332] Said, Abdul A., and Luiz R. Simmons, eds. *The New Sovereigns.* (Englewood Cliffs, N.J.: Prentice-Hall, 1975.)

[333] Sampson, Geoffrey. *An End to Allegiance.* (London: Temple Smith, 1984.)

[334] Soto, Hernando de. *The Other Path.* (New York: Harper & Row, 1989.)

[335] Sterling, Claire. *The Terror Network.* (New York: Berkley Books, 1981.)

[336] Strausz-Hupe, Robert. *Geopolitics.* (New York: G. P. Putnam's Sons, 1942.)

[337] Suter, Keith. *Reshaping the Global Agenda.* (Sydney: U.N. Association of Australia, 1986.)

[338] Talbott, Strobe. *Deadly Gambits.* (New York: Alfred A. Knopf, 1984.)

[339] Tsurumi, Shunsuke. *A Cultural History of Postwar Japan.* (London: KPI, 1987.)

[340] Walter, Ingo. *Secret Money.* (London: George Allen & Unwin, 1985.)

[341] Wanandi, Jusuf. *Security Dimensions of the Asia-Pacific Region in the 80's.* (Jakarta: Centre for Strategic and International Studies, 1979.)

[342] Wiarda, Howard J. *Ethnocentrism in Foreign Policy.* (Washington, D.C.: American Enterprise Institute for Public Policy Research, 1985.)

[343] Wyden, Peter. *Wall.* (New York: Simon and Schuster, 1989.)

[344] Young, George K. *Finance and World Power.* (London: Thomas Nelson, 1968.)

SOCIALISM AND MARXISM

[345] Aganbegyan, Abel, ed. *Perestroika 1989.* (New York: Charles Scribner's Sons, 1988.)

[346] Althusser, Louis, and Etienne Balibar. *Reading Capital.* (New York: Pantheon Books, 1970.)

[347] Amalrik, Andrei. *Will the Soviet Union Survive Until 1984?* (New York: Perennial Library, 1970.)

[348] Baldwin, Roger N., ed. *Kropotkin's Revolutionary Pamphlets: A Collection of Writings by Peter Kropotkin.* (New York: Dover Publications, 1970.)

[349] Brzezinski, Zbigniew. *The Grand Failure: The Birth and Death of Communism in the 20th Century.* (New York: Charles Scribner's Sons, 1989.)

[350] ———, and Samuel P. Huntington. *Political Power: USA/USSR.* (New York: Viking Press, 1963.)

[351] Cohen, Stephen F. *Bukharin and the Bolshevik Revolution.* (New York: Alfred A. Knopf, 1973.)

[352] ———, and Katrina Vanden Heuvel. *Voices of Glasnost.* (New York: W. W. Norton, 1989.)

[353] Daniels, Robert V. *Russia: The Roots of Confrontation.* (Cambridge, Mass.: Harvard University Press, 1985.)

[354] De Brunhoff, Suzanne. *Marx on Money.* (New York: Urizen Books, 1976.)

[355] d'Encausse, Helene Carrere. *Confiscated Power.* (New York: Harper & Row, 1982.)

[356] Fine, Ben, and Laurence Harris. *Rereading Capital.* (London: Macmillan Press, 1979.)

[357] Fletcher, Raymond. *Stalinism.* (Heanor, U.K.: Byron House Publications, n.d.)

[358] Frankel, Boris. *Beyond the State? Dominant Theories and Socialist Strategies.* (London: Macmillan Press, 1983.)

[359] Friedgut, Theodore H. *Political Participation in the USSR.* (Princeton: Princeton University Press, 1979.)

[360] Frolov, I. *Global Problems and the Future of Mankind.* (Moscow: Progress Publishers, 1982.)

[361] Gorbachev, Mikhail. *Selected Speeches and Articles.* (Moscow: Progress Publishers, 1987.)

[362] Grachev, Andrei. *In the Grip of Terror.* (Moscow: Progress Publishers, 1982.)

[363] Hamrin, Carol Lee. *China and the Challenge of the Future.* (San Francisco: Westview Press, 1990.)

[364] James, Donald. *The Fall of the Russian Empire.* (New York: Signet Books, 1982.)

[365] Kraus, Richard Curt. *Class Conflict in Chinese Socialism.* (New York: Columbia University Press, 1981.)

[366] Lichtheim, George. *The Origins of Socialism.* (New York: Frederick A. Praeger, 1969.)

[367] Loebl, Eugen. *Stalinism in Prague.* (New York: Grove Press, 1969.)

[368] Marx, Karl. *Capital,* Vol. I. (New York: International Publishers, 1939.)

[369] ———, F. Engels, and V. Lenin. *On Historical Materialism, A Collection.* (Moscow: Progress Publishers, 1972.)

[370] McMurtry, John. *The Structure of Marx's World-View.* (Princeton: Princeton University Press, 1978.)

[371] Muqiao, Xue. *China's Socialist Economy.* (Beijing: Foreign Languages Press, 1981.)

[372] Pan, Lynn. *The New Chinese Revolution.* (Chicago: Contemporary Books, 1988.)

[373] Possony, Stefan T., ed. *The Lenin Reader.* (Chicago: Henry Regnery, 1966.)

[374] Poster, Mark. *Foucault, Marxism and History.* (Oxford: Polity Press, 1984.)

[375] Rigby, T. H., Archie Brown, and Peter Reddaway, eds. *Authority, Power and Policy in the USSR.* (London: Macmillan Press, 1980.)

[376] Sassoon, Anne Showstack. *Approaches to Gramsci.* (London: Writers and Readers Publishing Cooperative Society, 1982.)

[377] Sherman, Howard. *Radical Political Economy.* (New York: Basic Books, 1972.)

[378] Sik, Ota. *The Communist Power System.* (New York: Praeger Publishers, 1981.)

[379] Starr, John Bryan. *Continuing the Revolution: The Political Thought of Mao.* (Princeton: Princeton University Press, 1979.)
[380] Wilson, Dick. *The Sun at Noon.* (London: Hamish Hamilton, 1986.)
[381] Zamoshkin, Yu. A. *Problems of Power and Management Under the Scientific Technological Revolution.* (Moscow: Soviet Sociological Association, 1974.)

FASCISM

[382] Beradt, Charlotte. *The Third Reich of Dreams.* (Wellingborough, U.K.: Aquarian Press, 1985.)
[383] Friedlander, Saul. *Reflections on Nazism.* (New York: Avon Books, 1984.)
[384] Glaser, Hermann. *The Cultural Roots of National Socialism.* (Austin: University of Texas Press, 1978.)
[385] Gregor, A. James. *The Fascist Persuasion in Radical Politics.* (Princeton: Princeton University Press, 1974.)
[386] ———. *The Ideology of Fascism.* (New York: The Free Press, 1969.)
[387] Hitler, Adolf. *Mein Kampf.* (Boston: Houghton Mifflin, 1971.)
[388] Laqueur, Walter. *Fascism: A Reader's Guide.* (Berkeley: University of California Press, 1976.)
[389] Lewin, Ronald. *Hitler's Mistakes.* (New York: William Morrow, 1984.)
[390] Mosse, George L. *The Crisis of German Ideology.* (London: Weidenfeld and Nicolson, 1964.)
[391] Reveille, Thomas. *The Spoil of Europe.* (New York: W. W. Norton, 1941.)

INTELLIGENCE AND ESPIONAGE

[392] Aburish, Said K. *Pay-Off: Wheeling and Dealing in the Arab World.* (London: Andre Deutsch, 1986.)
[393] Andrew, Christopher. *Secret Service.* (London: Heinemann, 1985.)
[394] ———, and David Dilks, eds. *The Missing Dimension.* (Chicago: University of Illinois Press, 1984.)
[395] Ball, Desmond. *Pine Gap.* (Sydney: Allen & Unwin, 1988.)
[396] ———, J. O. Langtry, and J. D. Stevenson. *Defend the North.* (Sydney: George Allen and Unwin, 1985.)

[397] Brown, Anthony Cave. *Bodyguard of Lies*. (New York: Bantam Books, 1976.)

[398] ———. *"C"*. (New York: Macmillan, 1987.)

[399] Burrows, William E. *Deep Black*. (New York: Random House, 1986.)

[400] Caroz, Yaacov. *The Arab Secret Services*. (London: Corgi Books, 1978.)

[401] Costello, John. *Mask of Treachery*. (New York: William Morrow, 1988.)

[402] Coxsedge, Joan, Ken Coldicutt, and Gerry Harant. *Rooted in Secrecy*. (Capp, Australia: Balwyn North, 1982.)

[403] Deacon, Richard. *"C": A Biography of Sir Maurice Oldfield*. (London: McDonald, 1985.)

[404] ———. *A History of the Russian Secret Service*. (London: Frederick Muller, 1972.)

[405] Donner, Frank J. *The Age of Surveillance*. (New York: Alfred A. Knopf, 1980.)

[406] Felix, Christopher. *A Short Course in the Secret War*. (New York: Dell Publishing, 1988.)

[407] Garwood, Darrell. *Undercover: Thirty-five Years of CIA Deception*. (New York: Grove Press, 1985.)

[408] Godson, Roy. *Intelligence Requirements for the 1980's*. (Lexington, Mass.: Lexington Books, 1986.)

[409] Halamka, John D. *Espionage in the Silicon Valley*. (Berkeley, Cal.: Sybex, 1984.)

[410] Henderson, Bernard R. *Pollard: The Spy's Story*. (New York: Alpha Books, 1988.)

[411] Knightley, Phillip. *The Second Oldest Profession*. (New York: W. W. Norton, 1986.)

[412] Laqueur, Walter. *A World of Secrets*. (New York: Basic Books, 1985.)

[413] Levchenko, Stanislav. *On the Wrong Side*. (Washington, D.C.: Pergamon-Brassey's, 1988.)

[414] Levite, Ariel. *Intelligence and Strategic Surprises*. (New York: Columbia University Press, 1987.)

[415] Marenches, Count de, and Christine Ockrent. *The Evil Empire*. (London: Sidgwick and Jackson, 1986.)

[416] Pacepa, Ion. *Red Horizons*. (London: Hodder and Stoughton, Coronet Books, 1989.)

[417] Perrault, Gilles. *The Red Orchestra*. (New York: Pocket Books, 1969.)

[418] Phillips, David Atlee. *Careers in Secret Operations*. (Bethesda, Md.: Stone Trail Press, 1984.)

[419] Pincher, Chapman. *Too Secret Too Long.* (New York: St. Martin's Press, 1984.)

[420] Plate, Thomas, and Andrea Darvi. *Secret Police.* (London: Robert Hale, 1981.)

[421] Prouty, Fletcher L. *The Secret Team.* (Englewood Cliffs, N.J.: Prentice-Hall, 1973.)

[422] Richelson, Jeffrey. *American Espionage and the Soviet Target.* (New York: Quill, 1987.)

[423] ———. *Foreign Intelligence Organizations.* (Cambridge, Mass.: Ballinger, 1988.)

[424] ———. *The U.S. Intelligence Community.* (Cambridge, Mass.: Ballinger, 1985.)

[425] Rositzke, Harry. *The KGB.* (New York: Doubleday, 1981.)

[426] Seth, Ronald. *Secret Servants.* (New York: Farrar, Straus and Cudahy, 1957.)

[427] Shevchenko, Arkady N. *Breaking with Moscow.* (New York: Alfred A. Knopf, 1985.)

[428] Shultz, Richard H., and Roy Godson. *Dezinformatsia.* (New York: Berkley Books, 1986.)

[429] Suvorov, Viktor. *Inside Soviet Military Intelligence.* (New York: Berkley Books, 1984.)

[430] ———. *Inside the Aquarium: The Making of a Top Spy.* (New York: Berkley Books, 1987.)

[431] Toohey, Brian, and William Pinwill. *Oyster.* (Port Melbourne, Australia: William Heinemann, 1989.)

[432] Turner, Stansfield. *Secrecy and Democracy.* (Boston: Houghton Mifflin, 1985.)

[433] West, Nigel. *The Circus.* (New York: Stein and Day, 1983.)

[434] ———. *Games of Intelligence.* (London: Weidenfeld and Nicolson, 1989.)

[435] Woodward, Bob. *Veil.* (New York: Simon and Schuster, 1987.)

[436] Wright, Peter, and Paul Greengrass. *Spycatcher.* (New York: Viking Press, 1987.)

KNOWLEDGE AND SOCIETY

[437] Afanasyev, V. *Social Information and the Regulation of Social Development.* (Moscow: Progress Publishers, 1978.)

[438] Alisjahbana, S. Takdir. *Values As Integrating Forces in Personality, Society and Culture.* (Kuala Lumpur: University of Malaya Press, 1966.)

[439] Attali, Jacques. *Noise*. (Minneapolis: University of Minnesota Press, 1985.)

[440] Bacon, Francis. *A Selection of His Works*. (Indianapolis: Bobbs-Merrill Educational Publishing, 1965.)

[441] Bok, Sissela. *Secrets*. (New York: Vintage Books, 1984.)

[442] Cherry, Kittredge. *Womansword*. (Tokyo: Kodansha International, 1989.)

[443] Cirlot, J. E. *A Dictionary of Symbols*. (New York: Philosophical Library, 1962.)

[444] Coser, Lewis A. *Men of Ideas*. (New York: Free Press, 1970.)

[445] Curtis, James E., and John W. Petras, eds. *The Sociology of Knowledge*. (New York: Praeger, 1970.)

[446] De Huszar, George B., ed. *The Intellectuals*. (Glencoe, Ill.: Free Press of Glencoe, 1960.)

[447] Doi, Takeo. *The Anatomy of Dependence*. (Tokyo: Kodansha International, 1985.)

[448] Duke, Benjamin. *The Japanese School*. (New York: Praeger, 1986.)

[449] Ekman, Paul. *Telling Lies*. (New York: W. W. Norton, 1985.)

[450] Everhart, Robert B., ed. *The Public School Monopoly*. (Cambridge, Mass.: Ballinger, 1982.)

[451] Feigenbaum, Edward, Pamela McCorduck, and H. Penny Nii. *The Rise of the Expert Company*. (New York: Times Books, 1988.)

[452] Foster, Hal. *Postmodern Culture*. (London: Pluto Press, 1985.)

[453] Foucault, Michel. *Power, Truth, Strategy*. (Sydney: Feral Publications, 1979.)

[454] Gardner, Howard. *The Mind's New Science*. (New York: Basic Books, 1985.)

[455] Gouldner, Alvin W. *The Future of Intellectuals and the Rise of the New Class*. (New York: Continuum Books, 1979.)

[456] Habermas, Jurgen. *Knowledge and Human Interests*. (Boston: Beacon Press, 1968.)

[457] Hansen, Robert H. *The Why, What and How of Decision Support*. (New York: AMA Management Briefing, 1984.)

[458] Hoffman, Lily M. *The Politics of Knowledge*. (Albany: State University of New York Press, 1989.)

[459] Keren, Michael. *Ben Gurion and the Intellectuals*. (Dekalb, Ill.: Northern Illinois University Press, 1983.)

[460] Kindaichi, Haruhiko. *The Japanese Language*. (Rutland, Vt.: Charles E. Tuttle, 1978.)

[461] Konrad, George. *Antipolitics*. (New York: Harcourt Brace Jovanovich, 1984.)

[462] Konrad, George, and Ivan Szelenyi. *The Intellectuals on the Road to Class Power.* (New York: Harcourt, Brace Jovanovich, 1976.)

[463] Kraemer, Kenneth L., et al. *Datawars.* (New York: Columbia University Press, 1987.)

[464] Lakatos, Imre, and Alan Musgrave, eds. *Criticism and the Growth of Knowledge.* (London: Cambridge University Press, 1979.)

[465] Lamberton, D. M., ed. *Economics of Information and Knowledge.* (Middlesex, U.K.: Penguin Books, 1971.)

[466] Lyotard, Jean-François. *The Post-Modern Condition.* (Minneapolis: University of Minnesota Press, 1984.)

[467] Machlup, Fritz. *Knowledge: Its Creation, Distribution, and Economic Significance,* Vol. I. (Princeton: Princeton University Press, 1980.)

[468] ———. *The Production and Distribution of Knowledge in the United States.* (Princeton: Princeton University Press, 1962.)

[469] Noer, Deliar. *Culture, Philosophy and the Future.* (Jakarta: P. T. Dian Rakyat, 1988.)

[470] Ohmae, Kenichi. *The Mind of the Strategist.* (New York: Penguin, 1983.)

[471] Ong, Walter J. *Orality and Literacy.* (London: Methuen, 1982.)

[472] ———, ed. *Knowledge and the Future of Man.* (New York: Clarion Books, 1968.)

[473] Paulos, John Allen. *Innumeracy.* (New York: Hill and Wang, 1988.)

[474] Popper, K. R. *The Open Society and Its Enemies,* Vol. I. (London: Routledge and Kegan Paul, 1962.)

[475] Powers, Richard Gid. *Secrecy and Power: The Life of J. Edgar Hoover.* (New York: Free Press, 1987.)

[476] Scott, D. R. *The Cultural Significance of Accounting.* (Columbia, Mo.: Lucas Brothers, n.d.)

[477] Singer, Kurt. *Mirror, Sword and Jewel.* (Tokyo: Kodansha International, 1973.)

[478] Sowell, Thomas. *Knowledge and Decisions.* (New York: Basic Books, 1980.)

[479] Strehlow, T.G.H. *Songs of Central Australia.* (Sydney: Angus and Robertson, 1971.)

[480] Swetz, Frank J. *Capitalism and Arithmetic.* (La Salle, Ill.: Open Court, 1987.)

[481] Taylor, Stanley. *Conceptions of Institutions and the Theory of Knowledge.* (New Brunswick, N.J.: Transaction, 1989.)

[482] Tefft, Stanton K. *Secrecy: A Cross-Cultural Perspective.* (New York: Human Sciences Press, 1980.)

[483] Van den Berg, Jan Hendrik. *Medical Power and Medical Ethics.* (New York: W. W. Norton, 1978.)

[484] Whitehead, Alfred North. *The Function of Reason.* (Boston: Beacon Press, 1958.)

COMPUTERS AND COMMUNICATIONS

[485] Acco, Alain, and Edmond Zuchelli. *La peste informatique.* (Paris: Éditions Plume, 1989.)

[486] Arnold, Erik, and Ken Guy. *Parallel Convergence: National Strategies in Information Technology.* (London: Frances Pinter, 1986.)

[487] Ashby, W. Ross. *Design for a Brain.* (London: Chapman and Hall, 1978.)

[488] Berlin, Isaiah. *Against the Current.* (New York: Viking Press, 1955.)

[489] Berlo, David K. *The Process of Communication.* (New York: Holt, Rinehart and Winston, 1960.)

[490] Cherry, Colin. *World Communication: Threat or Promise?* (London: Wiley-Interscience, 1971.)

[491] Civikly, Jean M. *Messages.* (New York: Random House, 1974.)

[492] Duncan, Hugh Dalziel. *Communication and Social Order.* (London: Oxford University Press, 1962.)

[493] Goodman, Danny. *The Complete HyperCard Handbook.* (New York: Bantam Books, 1987.)

[494] Goulden, Joseph C. *Monopoly.* (New York: Pocket Books, 1970.)

[495] Hemphill, Charles F., Jr., and Robert D. Hemphill. *Security Safeguards for the Computer.* (New York: AMA Management Briefing, 1979.)

[496] Johnson, Douglas W. *Computer Ethics.* (Elgin, Ill.: Brethren Press, 1984.)

[497] Kaligo, Al, Lou Baumbach, and Joe Garzinsky. *Telecommunications Management: A Practical Approach.* (New York: AMA Management Briefing, 1984.)

[498] Kitahara, Yasusada. *Information Network System.* (London: Heinemann Educational Books, 1983.)

[499] Landau, Robert M. *Information Resources Management.* (New York: AMA Management Briefing, 1980.)

[500] Levy, Steven. *Hackers.* (New York: Dell, 1984.)

[501] Marchand, Marie. *The Minitel Saga.* (Paris: Larousse, 1988.)

[502] McLuhan, Marshall, and Bruce R. Powers. *The Global Village.* (New York: Oxford University Press, 1989.)

[503] Mortensen, C. David. *Communication.* (New York: McGraw-Hill, 1972.)

[504] Pool, Ithiel de Sola. *Technologies of Freedom.* (Cambridge, Mass.: Belknap Press of Harvard University Press, 1983.)

[505] Poppel, Harvey L., and Bernard Goldstein. *Information Technology.* (New York: McGraw-Hill, 1987.)

[506] Shannon, Claude, and Warren Weaver. *The Mathematical Theory of Communication.* (Urbana: University of Illinois Press, 1949.)

[507] Smith, Alfred G., ed. *Communication and Culture.* (New York: Holt, Rinehart and Winston, 1966.)

[508] Spacks, Patricia Meyer. *Gossip.* (Chicago: University of Chicago Press, 1985.)

[509] Strassman, Paul A. *Information Payoff.* (New York: Free Press, 1985.)

[510] Tarde, Gabriel. *On Communication and Social Influence.* (Chicago: University of Chicago Press, 1969.)

[511] Wilcox, A. M., M. G. Slade, and P. A. Ramsdale. *Command Control and Communications.* (New York: Brassey's Defense Publishers, 1983.)

[512] Wilmot, William W., and John R. Wenburg. *Communicational Involvement: Personal Perspectives.* (New York: John Wiley and Sons, 1974.)

[513] Winograd, Terry, and Fernando Flores. *Understanding Computers and Cognition.* (Reading, Mass.: Addison-Wesley, 1986.)

SCIENCE AND TECHNOLOGY

[514] Colombo, Umberto, et al. *Science and Technology Towards the XXI Century and Their Impact Upon Society.* (Milan: The Pirelli Group, n.d.)

[515] Drexler, K. Eric. *Engines of Creation.* (New York: Anchor Press, 1986.)

[516] Dryakhlov, Nikolai. *The Scientific and Technological Revolution: Its Rss. Design for a Brain.* (London: Chapman and Hall, 1978.)

[517] Illich, Ivan. *Tools for Conviviality.* (New York: Harper & Row, 1973.)

[518]   Langone, John. *Superconductivity: The New Alchemy.* (Chicago: Contemporary Books, 1989.)

[519]   Melvern, Linda, David Hebditch, and Nick Anning. *Techno-Bandits.* (Boston: Houghton Mifflin, 1984.)

[520]   Mendelssohn, Kurt. *The Secret of Western Domination.* (New York: Praeger, 1976.)

[521]   Muroyama, Janet H., and H. Guyford Stever, eds. *Globalization of Technology.* (Washington, D.C.: National Academy Press, 1988.)

[522]   Nicolis, G., and I. Prigogine. *Self-Organization in Nonequilibrium Systems.* (New York: John Wiley and Sons, 1977.)

[523]   Prigogine, Ilya. *From Being to Becoming.* (San Francisco: W. H. Freeman, 1980.)

[524]   ———, and Isabelle Stengers. *La nouvelle alliance.* (Paris: Éditions Gallimard, 1979.)

[525]   ———. *Order Out of Chaos.* (New York: Bantam Books, 1984.)

[526]   Tuck, Jay. *High-Tech Espionage.* (London: Sidgwick and Jackson, 1986.)

[527]   *The Scientific-Technological Revolution and the Contradictions of Capitalism.* International Theoretical Conference, Moscow, May 21–23, 1979. (Moscow: Progress Publishers, 1982.)

HISTORY AND BIOGRAPHY

[528]   Allen, Frederick Lewis. *The Lords of Creation.* (New York: Harper & Brothers, 1935.)

[529]   Attali, Jacques. *A Man of Influence.* (Bethesda, Md.: Adler & Adler, 1987.)

[530]   Ayling, S. E. *Portraits of Power.* (New York: Barnes and Noble, 1963.)

[531]   Braudel, Fernand. *Afterthoughts on Material Civilization and Capitalism.* (Baltimore: Johns Hopkins University Press, 1977.)

[532]   ———. *Capitalism and Material Life 1400–1800.* (New York: Harper Colophon Books, 1973.)

[533]   ———. *The Mediterranean,* Vol. I. (New York: Harper & Row, 1972.)

[534]   ———. *The Mediterranean,* Vol. II. (New York: Harper & Row, 1972.)

[535]   ———. *On History.* (London: Weidenfeld and Nicolson, 1980.)

[536]   ———. *The Structures of Everyday Life,* Vol. I. (New York: Harper & Row, 1981.)

[537] Burke, John. *Duet in Diamonds*. (New York: G. P. Putnam's Sons, 1972.)

[538] Bury, J.P.T., ed. *The New Cambridge Modern History*. (Cambridge: Cambridge University Press, 1971.)

[539] Cashman, Sean Dennis. *America in the Gilded Age*. (New York: New York University Press, 1984.)

[540] Center for Medieval and Renaissance Studies, UCLA. *The Dawn of Modern Banking*. (New Haven: Yale University Press, 1979.)

[541] Chernow, Ron. *The House of Morgan*. (New York: Atlantic Monthly Press, 1990.)

[542] Cook, Don. *Charles De Gaulle*. (New York: G. P. Putnam's Sons, 1983.)

[543] Cooper, A. Duff. *Talleyrand*. (London: Cassell, 1987.)

[544] Corey, Lewis. *The House of Morgan*. (New York: G. Howard Watt, 1930.)

[545] Crankshaw, Edward. *The Fall of the House of Habsburg*. (New York: Penguin Books, 1983.)

[546] Crozier, Brian. *The Masters of Power*. (Boston: Little, Brown, 1969.)

[547] Curtin, Philip D. *Cross-Cultural Trade in World History*. (Cambridge: Cambridge University Press, 1984.)

[548] Custine, Marquis de. *Journey for Our Time: The Journals of the Marquis de Custine*. (London: George Prior, 1980.)

[549] Dodd, Alfred. *Francis Bacon's Personal Life-Story*, Vol. I. (London: Rider, 1949.)

[550] ———. *Francis Bacon's Personal Life Story*, Vol. II. (London: Rider, 1986.)

[551] Elias, Norbert. *Power and Civility*. (New York: Pantheon Books, 1982.)

[552] Eyck, Erich. *Bismarck and the German Empire*. (New York and London: W. W. Norton, 1950.)

[553] Febvre, Lucien, and Henri-Jean Martin. *The Coming of the Book*. (London: New Left Books, 1984.)

[554] Green, A. Wigfall. *Sir Francis Bacon*. (Denver: Alan Swallow, 1952.)

[555] Hammer, Armand, with Neil Lyndon. *Hammer*. (New York: G. P. Putnam's Sons, 1987.)

[556] Hook, Sidney. *Out of Step*. (New York: Carroll & Graf, 1987.)

[557] Isaacson, Walter, and Evan Thomas. *The Wise Men*. (New York: Simon and Schuster, 1986.)

[558] Johnson, Paul. *Intellectuals*. (New York: Harper & Row, 1988.)

[559]   Kapuscinski, Ryszard. *The Emperor*. (New York: Harcourt Brace Jovanovich, 1983.)

[560]   ———. *Shah of Shahs*. (New York: Harcourt Brace Jovanovich, 1985.)

[561]   Kennedy, Paul. *The Rise and Fall of the Great Powers*. (New York: Random House, 1987.)

[562]   Kerr, Clark, et al. *Industrialism and Industrial Man*. (Harmondsworth, U.K.: Penguin Books, 1973.)

[563]   Kula, Witold. *An Economic Theory of the Feudal System*. (London: NLB, 1976.)

[564]   Lacouture, Jean. *The Demigods*. (New York: Alfred A. Knopf, 1970.)

[565]   Markham, Felix. *Napoleon*. (New York: Mentor Books, 1963.)

[566]   Mazlish, Bruce. *James and John Stuart Mill*. (New York: Basic Books, 1975.)

[567]   McNeill, William H. *The Pursuit of Power*. (Chicago: University of Chicago Press, 1982.)

[568]   Mee, Charles L., Jr. *The End of Order*. (New York: E. P. Dutton, 1980.)

[569]   Metcalfe, Philip. *1933*. (Sag Harbor, N.Y.: Permanent Press, 1988.)

[570]   Millar, Fergus. *The Emperor in the Roman World*. (Ithaca, N.Y.: Cornell University Press, 1977.)

[571]   Myers, Gustavus. *History of the Great American Fortunes*. (New York: Modern Library, 1937.)

[572]   Nicholls, A. J. *Weimar and the Rise of Hitler*. (London: Macmillan, 1979.)

[573]   Nixon, Richard. *Leaders*. (New York: Warner Books, 1982.)

[574]   ———. *The Memoirs of Richard Nixon*. (New York: Grosset and Dunlap, 1978.)

[575]   Norwich, John Julius. *Venice: The Rise to Empire*. (London: Allen Lane, 1977.)

[576]   Nystrom, Anton. *Before, During, and After 1914*. (London: William Heinemann, 1915.)

[577]   Schevill, Ferdinand. *A History of Europe*. (New York: Harcourt Brace, 1938.)

[578]   Schlereth, Thomas J. *The Cosmopolitan Ideal in the Enlightenment Thought*. (Notre Dame, Ind.: University of Notre Dame Press, 1977.)

[579]   Schmidt-Hauer, Christian. *Gorbachev*. (Topsfield, Mass.: Salem House, 1986.)

[580]   Seward, Desmond. *Napoleon and Hitler*. (New York: Viking Press, 1988.)

[581] Stephenson, Carl. *Mediaeval Feudalism*. (Ithaca: Cornell University Press, 1967.)

[582] Stern, J. P. *Hitler*. (London: Fontana/Collins, 1975.)

[583] Tapsell, R. F. *Monarchs, Rulers, Dynasties and Kingdoms of the World*. (London: Thames and Hudson, 1983.)

[584] Thompson, E. P. *The Making of the English Working Class*. (New York: Vintage Books, 1963.)

[585] Walker, James Blaine. *The Epic of American Industry*. (New York: Harper & Brothers, 1949.)

[586] Ward, J. T. *The Factory System*, Vol. I. (Newton Abbot, U.K.: David and Charles, 1970.)

[587] Weatherford, Jack. *Indian Givers*. (New York: Crown Books, 1988.)

[588] Wendt, Lloyd, and Herman Kogan. *Bet A Million!*. (Indianapolis: Bobbs-Merrill, 1948.)

[589] Wheeler, George. *Pierpont Morgan and Friends*. (Englewood Cliffs, N.J.: Prentice-Hall, 1973.)

[590] Wilson, Derek. *Rothschild: The Wealth and Power of a Dynasty*. (New York: Charles Scribner's Sons, 1988.)

[591] Wilson, George M. *Radical Nationalist on Japan: Kita Ikki 1883–1937*. (Cambridge, Mass.: Harvard University Press, 1969.)

[592] Wittfogel, Karl A. *Oriental Despotism*. (New Haven: Yale University Press, 1964.)

NOTES

Bracketed [ ] numbers indicate items listed in the accompanying Bibliography. Thus, in the Notes, [1] will stand for the first item in the Bibliography: Aron, Raymond. *Main Currents in Sociological Thought.*

A PERSONAL PREFACE

PAGE

xix   Institute for Scientific Information, correspondence with author, January 5, 1978.

xx   Re *The Third Wave* in China, see [363]. Also "Alvin Toffler in China: Deng's Big Bang," by Andrew Mendelsohn, *New Republic*, April 4, 1988.

CHAPTER 1 THE POWERSHIFT ERA

5   "GM Is Tougher Than You Think," by Anne B. Fisher, *Fortune,* November 10, 1986.

5   Re fading U.S. computer dominance, *Datamation,* June 15, 1988.

6   "Gephardt Plans to Call for Japan-Style Trade Agency," *Los Angeles Times,* October 4, 1989.

6   For MITI, see following from *Japan Economic Journal:* "MITI Fights to Hold Influence as Japanese Firms Go Global," April 1, 1989; "Icy Welcome for MITI's Retail Law Change," October 21, 1989; "Japan Carmakers Eye Growth Despite MITI Warning," October 21, 1989; "Trade Policy Flip-Flop Puts MITI on Defensive," January 20, 1990.

7–8   Medical material based in part on interviews with staff of The Wilkerson Group, medical management consulting organization, New York; also Wendy Borow, Director of American Medical Association Division of Television, Radio and Film; and Barry Cohn, television news producer, AMA, Chicago.

9   Poster quote from [374] p. 53.

CHAPTER 2 MUSCLE, MONEY, AND MIND

On definitions: There are as many definitions of power as there are cherry blossoms in Japan, and all are fraught with difficulty. One of the most famous is Bertrand Russell's statement that "Power may be defined as the production of intended effects." Perfectly sensible, clear, and precise.

Unfortunately, even this simple sentence is spiked with hidden booby traps.

First, we need to know what is "intended" (not so easy to specify, even for the person whose intentions they are). Next, we need to understand the "effects" so we can compare these with the intentions. Yet every act itself has many second, third, and "nth" order consequences, some intended, others not. What counts as an "effect" and what doesn't?

Then, too, we need to know whether what happens was actually "produced" by the actions taken. This implies a knowledge of causality that is frequently beyond our grasp.

Finally, a rich irony pops its beady eyes out of a hole in the ground:

The more numerous and varied the intentions, the greater the odds that only a fraction of them will be realized and the more difficult it becomes to determine what actually "produced" them all. In this sense, according to Russell's perfectly plausible-sounding definition, the more limited one's intentions, the greater the range of control one may exercise.

If producing a desired effect, with minimum (identifiable) side effects, is a definition of power, then the person whose goals are most narrowly defined and whose awareness of side effects is most rudimentary will be defined as most powerful.

Despite such a cautionary example (and the knowledge that our own definition is not without conceptual difficulties) we need at least a loose working definition sufficient for our purposes. In these pages the term *power* will mean the ability to mobilize and use violence, wealth, and/or knowledge, or their many derivatives, to motivate others in ways we think will gratify our needs and desires.

13   The three legendary symbols of power still play a part in Japanese ritual. When Emporor Hirohito died in 1989, the imperial sword, jewel, and mirror, passed down from emperor to emperor, were transferred to his son, Emperor Akihito ("What Sort of Peace in Heisei?" *Economist*, January 14, 1989). For background on *san shu no jingi*, see *Encyclopedia of Japan* (Tokyo: Kodansha Publishing House) listing for "Imperial Regalia." See also [239] pp. 124–131.

13   For symbolic meanings of *mirror*, [443] p. 201.

Power is embedded not only in Japanese legend but in the language itself. Japanese, like many other languages, contains honorifics that require one to identify her or his position in the pecking order every time the lips move. It is almost impossible to speak without addressing one's words up to a superior or down to an inferior. The language thus assumes the existence of a power hierarchy. While the ideogram for a male symbolizes a rice field and strong legs, that for a woman is a submissive, kneeling figure. Such symbols reflect and perpetuate patriarchal power. *Womansword* [442], subtitled *What Japanese Words Say About Women*, is a rich source of examples. But Japanese is not the only language laden with implicit power meanings. Javanese, for example, has two "levels": *ngoko*, which is spoken to inferiors, and *krama*, to superiors. Each in turn has subtle levels within levels (*cf.* [28]).

13   Re Boesky: "Suddenly the Fish Gets Bigger," *Business Week*, March 2, 1989.
13   Re Klaus Fuchs: [411] pp. 263–264.
15–16   *Cuba* (United Artists, 1979.)
17   Military dependence on computers: "Real Time Creates 'Smart' Flight Simulators," by Richard E. Morley and Todd Leadbeater, *Defense Science*, November 1988.

CHAPTER 3 BEYOND THE AGE OF GLITZ

25   The syndicated "Doonesbury" cartoon strip by Garry Trudeau has savagely satirized real estate tycoon Donald Trump,

whose best-selling *The Art of the Deal* was produced with writer Tony Schwartz. Chrysler chairman Lee Iacocca's best-seller was written for him by William Novak. For presidential rumors, see "Iacocca for President?" *Washington Post,* December 13, 1987, and "Starwatch" (column by Jeannie Williams), *USA Today,* October 26, 1989.

26 Re the "takeover frenzy" of the 1980s, now in temporary remission, see "The World Catches Takeover Fever," *New York Times,* May 21, 1989, and "Attack on Corporate Europe," *The Times* (London), October 1, 1989. See also [73] and [127].

27 Smokestack moguls: "America's Sixty Families," *New Republic,* November 17, 1937. Contrast them with "The Forbes Four Hundred," by Harold Seneker, et al., *Forbes,* October 23, 1989.

27 Labor unions and business takeovers: "Move Over Boone, Carl, and IRV—Here Comes Labor," *Business Week,* December 14, 1987.

28–29 Re Gilded Age: [539] pp. 34–37, 50–51; also [537] pp. 70–71, 164–167, 170–171; [588] pp. 10–11; and [206] p. 64.

29 Weingarten quote: interview with author.

29 For Iacocca's feud see his mega-best-seller published by Bantam in 1984.

29 Ross Perot and GM: [123] pp. 280–289.

30 On the Italian battle between old and new money power, and the role of Carlo de Benedetti, Gianni Agnelli, and Enrico Cuccia: "The Last Emperor," *Euromoney,* October 1988. Also [95] throughout.

30 For French and German cross-border acquisitions, see "Europe's Buyout Bulge," *New York Times,* November 6, 1989. Also interview with Philippe Adhemar, Financial Minister, the French Embassy, Washington, D.C.

30 The Spanish melo-farce is reported in "A Success Story Turns Sour," *Financial Times,* February 25/26, 1989.

33 The consultant's tale is from [64] pp. 3–7.

CHAPTER 4 FORCE: THE YAKUZA COMPONENT

37 Selyunin is quoted in "Lenin Faulted on State Terror, and a Soviet Taboo Is Broken," *New York Times,* June 8, 1988.

37–38   Some accounts of labor violence in the United States will be found in [108] pp. 212–213; [122] pp. 7 and 55–63.

38   "Violence at Motorola in Korea," *Financial Times,* December 31, 1988.

38   "Firms Gang Up to Quiet Stockholder Meeting Louts," *Japan Economic Journal,* July 2, 1988; also, "Japan's Sokaiya Fail to Trap Juiciest Prey," *Financial Times,* June 27, 1989.

38–39   "Japanese Fund Manager Found Buried in Concrete," *Financial Times,* October 19, 1988.

39   Re strongarm tactics in Japanese real estate: "Shadow Syndicate," by Kai Herrman, *20/20* (London), February 1990; and "No Vacancy: Soaring Land Prices in Japan Slam Door on Housing Market," *Wall Street Journal,* October 13, 1987.

39   U.S. lawyer with baseball bat: "Nippon Steal," by Eamonn Fingleton, *Euromoney,* October 1988.

39   "Snakes Alive in Korean Cinemas," *Financial Times,* October 5, 1989.

39   Re loan sharks: [313] pp. 167–168.

39   "Silkwood: The Story Behind the Story," *New Statesman,* May 4, 1984.

41   De Gaulle is quoted in [546] p. 31.

41   Japan's Recruit scandal summarized: "Takeshita Hears the Thud of the Axes," *Economist,* February 18, 1989, and "Will the Recruit Scandal Just Go Away?" *Business Week,* June 12, 1989.

41–42   German scandal: "A Deadly Game of Dirty Tricks," *Newsweek,* October 26, 1987. Also, "A Pair of Bad Smells," *Economist,* October 17, 1987.

42   For pachinko politics: "A Pinball Bribery Scandal Rocks 2 Japanese Political Parties," *New York Times,* October 13, 1989; "Pinball Scandal Threatens Political Upsets in Japan," *Financial Times,* October 12, 1989.

CHAPTER 5   WEALTH: MORGAN, MILKEN ... AND AFTER

45–46   For Morgan, see [544] pp. 12, 49, 176–177, 191, 213–214, 236–240, 255–258, 354, 396, 403. Also, [106] pp. 13, 82, 98–99, 114, 125–127, 173, 312, front matter and Postscript; and [84] p. 99; also [541].

46–47   For Milken, Connie Bruck's *The Predator's Ball* [83] is a
         scathing portrait of Milken and the high-yield or junk
         bond business he created, but by no means adequate ana-
         lytically. The simplest and most balanced short explana-
         tion of the Milken junk bond phenomenon is "Bearing
         Down on Milken," by David Frum, *National Review,* March
         19, 1990; other important sources include "How Mike
         Milken Made a Billion Dollars and Changed the Face of
         American Capitalism," by Edward Jay Epstein, *Manhattan,
         inc.,* September 1987. See also [92] pp. 14–17, 232–233,
         236–238; "A Chat With Michael Milken," by Allan Sloan,
         Forbes, July 13, 1987; "Milken's Salary Is One for Record
         Books," *Wall Street Journal/Europe,* April 3, 1989; "Lynch
         Law," by Andrew Marton, *Regardie's,* March 1990; and
         "Caught Up in a Morality Tale," by Richard Starr, *Insight,*
         March 5, 1990.

47   Early history of Drexel: [589] pp. 124–125.

48   Milken's involvement with trade unions: "Move Over Boone,
         Carl, and IRV—Here Comes Labor," *Business Week,* De-
         cember 14, 1987; also "The Mercenary Messiah Strikes
         Again," by Mark Feinberg, *In These Times,* June 7–20, 1989.

49   U.S. shift to service-information economy: "A New Revolu-
         tion in the U.S. 'Class Structure' and Labor Force," *Fortune,*
         April 1958.

49–50   Structural impact of Milken: "How Milken Machine Financed
         Companies, Takeover Raids," *Los Angeles Times,* March 30,
         1989; also "High-Stakes Drama at Revlon," *New York Times,*
         November 11, 1985; "A Chat with Michael Milken," by
         Allan Sloan, *Forbes,* July 13, 1987; and " 'Junk Bond' Ge-
         nius Inspires Loyalty From Some, Hostility From Others,"
         Los Angeles Times, March 30, 1989.

51   Milken's indictment: " 'Junk Bond' King Milken Indicted for
         Stock Fraud," *Los Angeles Times,* March 30, 1989; also "Pred-
         ator's Fall," *Time,* February 26, 1990, on the collapse of
         Drexel; "Lynch Law," by Andrew Marton, *Regardie's,* March
         1990.

51–52   Re battle to restrict or relax credit, see "Junk Bonds—A
         Positive Force in the Market," *New York Times,* November
         23, 1987.

52   On Milken's democratizing capital: [83] p. 350.

52   Re breaking up rather than agglomerating: author interview
         with Milken; also with Dean Kehler, Managing Director,

Investment and Banking, of now-defunct Drexel Burnham Lambert. See also "The New Buy-Out Binge," *Newsweek*, August 24, 1987.

53   For remark about "information age," see "A Chat With Michael Milken," by Allan Sloan, *Forbes*, July 13, 1987. Also Milken and Kehler interviews with author.

55   Salomon's agonies: [92] pp. 351 and 356–359.

55–56   The savings and loan mess: "Can the Thrifts be Salvaged?" *Newsweek*, August 21, 1989; "Up to $100 Billion Extra Sought for S&L Rescues," *Los Angeles Times*, November 1, 1989.

56   Re foreign exchange trading: "What Moves Exchange Rates," a brilliant analysis by Kenichi Ohmae in *Japan Times*, July 29, 1987.

57   The power of central banks: "Concept of a Central Bank Gains Support in Europe," *New York Times*, June 13, 1989.

CHAPTER 6 KNOWLEDGE: A WEALTH OF SYMBOLS

63   Re early money: [536] pp. 442–443; also [141] p. 3.

On money and desire: Money is ordinarily seen as a way to fulfill need or desire. But money has also been the great liberator of desire.

In pre-money cultures the person with a chicken to spare, and a desire for a blanket, first had to find someone who had a blanket and then, among all blanket owners, had to locate the one willing to take a chicken in exchange. Desires had to match.

The invention of money changed all that. Because it is fungible, and can be converted into a virtually unlimited number of satisfactions, money unleashed the acquisitive imagination. Those who had it suddenly developed desires they never knew they had. Previously unimagined and even unimaginable possibilities suddenly loomed before one's eyes. Money fed the imaginative spirit of the human species.

Money also encouraged clever men and women to identify the desires of others, whether coarse or overrefined, and to package for sale the things, services, and experiences that would fulfill them. This made money convertible into a still wider range of desirables and therefore, in turn, made it even more useful than before. (This self-reinforcing process, once unleashed, is like a chain reaction, and explains how money became so important in human social development.)

The original invention of money also greatly increased the efficiency of wealth as a tool of power. It strengthened the hand of the rich by radically simplifying control of behavior. Thus money made it possible to reward (and punish) people without even bothering to inquire into their desires, so that a factory owner didn't need to know if the worker desired a blanket, a chicken, or a Cadillac. It didn't matter; sufficient money could buy all or any of them.

In agrarian civilizations, apart from the wealthy—whose desires ran the range from exquisitely aesthetic to perversely sensual, from metaphysical to militaristic—the range of collective desires was so small and cramped it could be summed up in two words: bread (or rice) and land.

By contrast, in smokestack societies, once the basic needs of the population were met, collective desires seemed to multiply. Desire exploded out of its ghetto and colonized new regions, as a relentless progression turned the luxuries of one generation into the "necessities" of the next.

This expansion of desire was just as evident in supposedly anti-acquisitive socialist societies as it was in the openly acquisitive capitalist nations. It was, and continues to be, the basis for the mass consumer society. And it explains why, in the industrial world, the paycheck became the most basic tool of social control.

Today, the structure of desire is in upheaval. As we move beyond smokestack culture we see not the limitation of desire, but its further extension into new, more rarefied, increasingly nonmaterial regions, along with its growing individualization.

63   For William Potter: [6] p. 154

63   On paper money: [96] p. 51.

64   Visa data from company.

64   "Smart Cards: Pocket Power," *Newsweek,* July 31, 1989; also *Economist,* April 30, 1988.

64   French work on smart cards: "A New Technology Emerges on the World Stage," *French Advances in Science and Technology* (newsletter), Summer 1986; also "Bull's Smart Cards Come Up Trumps," *Financial Times,* September 30, 1987.

64   61 million: "Smart Cards: Pocket Power," *Newsweek,* July 31, 1989.

65   NTT cards: "Putting Smart Money On Smart Cards," *Economist,* August 27, 1988.

65   U.S. Department of Agriculture project: "Smart Cards: Pocket Power," *Newsweek,* July 31, 1989.

65–66   Schools: "Debit Cards for Pupils to Use in Cafeterias," by Susan Dillingham, *Insight,* August 21, 1989.
66   Joseph Wright quote: "U.S. Plans Wide Use of Credit Cards," *New York Times,* March 1, 1989.
67   Hock quote: from interview with author.
67   Loss of central bank control: "Designer Currency Dangers," by David Kilburn, *Business Tokyo,* May 1988.
67   Plastic money in South Korea: "A State of Siege for Corporate Korea," by Michael Berger, *Billion Magazine* (Hong Kong), September 1989.

CHAPTER 7 MATERIAL-ISMO!

70   U.S. agricultural work force: *Statistical Abstract of the United States 1989* (U.S. Department of Commerce), p. 376.
70   U.S. manufacturing work force: "Flat Manufacturing Employment for 1990's," by Michael K. Evans and R. D. Norton, *Industry Week,* October 2, 1989; also "The Myth of U.S. Manufacturing," *Los Angeles Times,* October 22, 1989.
70   On xenophobic economics: "America's Destiny Is in Danger," by June-Collier Mason, *Industry Week,* June 6, 1988.
71   U.S. service work force: "End Sought to Barriers to Trade in Services," *New York Times,* October 25, 1989.
71   "Exports of Services Increase to $560 bn," *Financial Times,* September 15, 1989.
75   Expert systems and CD-ROM: "HP and Ford Motors," by John Markoff, *Windows,* vol. 1, no. 1, Fall 1987.
76   CSX: interview with Alex Mandl, Chairman, Sea-Land Service, Inc.
77   Intelligence level in different corporations: personal communication from Dr. Donald F. Klein.
78   GenCorp data: "The (New) Flat Earth Society Gathers in Shelbyville," by Brian S. Moskal, *Industry Week,* October 2, 1989.
80   Re Soviet planner mentality in West: "Is There a British Miracle?" *Financial Times,* June 16, 1988.
80   For Giarini, see [100] throughout; for Loebl, [125]; for Woo, [167]. Weisskopf's views are in Walter A. Weisskopf, "Reflections on Uncertainty in Economics," *The Geneva Papers,* vol. 9, no. 33, October 1984.

81   On Prométhée: "From Trade to Global Wealth Creation," Thinknet Commission special issue, *Project Prométhée Perspectives,* No. 4, Paris, December 1987.

CHAPTER 8   THE ULTIMATE SUBSTITUTE

84   Literacy and numeracy: [480] pp. 282–283, and 338; also "Capitalism Plus Math: It All Adds Up," *Los Angeles Times,* May 13, 1989.

86   On short-run production: "Manufacturing: The New Case for Vertical Integration," by Ted Kumpe and Piet T. Bolwijn, *Harvard Business Review,* March-April 1988. Also, "Kicking Down the Debt," *Time,* November 7, 1988, and "Customized Goods Aim at Mass Market," *Japan Economic Journal,* October 1, 1988.

87   Re new materials: "Materials Battle Heats Up," by Thomas M. Rohan, *Industry Week,* October 2, 1989; "Plastics and Ceramics Replace Steel as the Sinews of War," *New York Times,* July 18, 1989; and "Project Forecast II" in *Assault Systems,* vol 1, no. 1.

87   Superconductivity: [518] pp. 166–173.

88   Re GE: "Electronic Data Exchange: A Leap of Faith," by Neal E. Boudette, *Industry Week,* August 7, 1989.

88   1.3 trillion documents: "Throwing Away the Paper-Based System," *Financial Times,* April 26, 1989.

89   Merloni material: interview with author.

89–90   Textile and apparel industries: "EDI, Barcoding Seen the Way to Save Millions," *Daily News Record,* March 11, 1987.

90   NHK Spring Company: "Just in Time Computers," by Peter Fuchs, et al., *Business Tokyo,* May 1988.

90   Merloni on funds transfer and telecommunications: interview with author.

90   Author interview with Michael Milken.

CHAPTER 9   THE CHECKOUT BATTLE

96   For Bic-Gillette rivalry: author interviews with Tom Johnson, Director of Research, Nolan Norton & Co., consultants; Gillette Company Annual Report 1988; and [136] pp. 69–73.

96–97   On Gillette marketing: Johnson interviews; and "Marketing's New Look," *Business Week,* January 26, 1987.

98   Introduction of retail bar coding: author interview with Harold Juckett, Executive Director, Uniform Code Council, Inc. Also "UPC History," document supplied by Uniform Code Council.

98–99   International data on bar coding: mainly drawn from International Article Numbering Association.

99   Battle for retail shelf space: "Supermarkets Demand Food Firms' Payments Just to Get on the Shelf," *Wall Street Journal,* November 1, 1988; "Want Shelf Space at the Supermarket? Ante Up," *Business Week,* August 7, 1989; and "Stores Often Paid to Stock New Items," *USA Today,* August 26, 1987.

99   Gillette: Kavin W. Moody, Corporate Director, Management Information Systems, Gillette Company, interview.

99–100   Retail computer models: interviews with Tom Johnson, Director of Research, Nolan Norton & Co.; also "At Today's Supermarket, the Computer Is Doing It All," *Business Week,* August 11, 1986.

100   Plan-a-Grams: "At Today's Supermarket, the Computer Is Doing It All," *Business Week,* August 11, 1986.

100   Re Toys "R" Us: "Stores Rush to Automate for the Holidays," *New York Times,* November 28, 1987.

100–01   Wal-Mart policies: Tom Johnson interviews; also "Make That Sale, Mr. Sam," *Time,* May 18, 1987.

102   Interview with Max Hopper, Senior Vice-President, American Airlines; also [112] pp. 4–5.

103   Marui reference is drawn from [163]—i.e., "Automating Distribution: Revolution in Distribution, Retailing and Financial Services," the best, most definitive English-language report on Japanese developments in these related fields, prepared by Alex Stewart for Baring Securities Ltd., London, 1987.

104   Electronic shelves: Tom Johnson interviews; also "At Today's Supermarket, the Computer Is Doing It All," *Business Week,* August 11, 1986, and "Electronic Prices," by George Nobbe, *Omni,* November 1987.

104   Smarter shelves: Tom Johnson interviews.

105   Retailers dominant: [163].

105   Retailing as information process: "Small Stores and Those Who Service Them in Times of Structural Change," *Japan Times,* July 13, 1987.

CHAPTER 10   EXTRA-INTELLIGENCE

107   Morse material from [585] pp. 102–103.

108   Re McDonald's ISDN network, see AT&T advertisement, *Datamation*, October 1, 1987. Volvo net described in same issue.

108   Du Pont and Sara Lee: "When Strategy Meets Technology," by Therese R. Welter, *Industry Week*, December 14, 1987.

108   Figures on PCs from International Data Corporation, which defines *personal computer* to include everything that runs MS-DOS, from low-end hobby units to workstations.

109   Western Union's early days: [494]; also [585] p. 108.

109   Western Union versus AT&T: [494] pp. 34–35.

111   U.S. share of telephones: Anthony Rutkowski, Senior Counsel, International Telecommunications Union (Geneva); also "Rewiring the World," *Economist*, October 17, 1987.

111–12   Re telephone company breakup: [164] p. xxii–xxiii.

114   Neural networks: "Government Researchers Work to Nail Down Building Blocks for Neural Networks," *Defense News*, January 11, 1988.

115   Re Minitel: See *Teletel Newsletter* #5 (1989 Facts and Figures), France Telecom (Paris); and *Teletel Newsletter* #2 (International); "France Hooked on Minitel," *Financial Times*, December 13, 1989. Also, interviews with Manuel Barbero, France Telecom International (New York); Olivier Duval, Études Systèmes et Logiciels (Paris); and [501] throughout.

117   Sabre System: interview with Max Hopper, Senior Vice-President, American Airlines.

117   Numbers of Value Added Networks: "Rewiring the World," *Economist*, October 17, 1987; "Competition Endangering Small VAN Operators," *Japan Economic Journal*, April 2, 1988.

CHAPTER 11   NET POWER

119   Nippon Life: "Networking Global Finance," *Business Tokyo*, May 1988; also, "Japanese Networks Expand After Deregulation," by Robert Poe, *Datamation*, November 1, 1987.

119–20 Re Dai Ichi and Meiji Insurance: "Japanese Networks Expand After Deregulation," by Robert Poe, *Datamation*, November 1, 1987.

120 Burlington Industries: [505] p. 49.

121 Auto industry networks: "Electronic Data Interchange: A Leap of Faith," by Neal E. Boudette, *Industry Week*, August 7, 1989; and "Auto ID & EDI: Managing in the 90's," *Industry Week*, August 24, 1989.

121 Shiseido's electronic networks: [163] p. 10.

121–22 Effects on wholesalers: interview with Monroe Greenstein, Bear, Stearns and Co., Inc. (New York), and [163] pp. 10–13.

122 Hospital and drugstore networks: "Origin of the Species," by P. Gralla, *CIO* magazine. January/February 1988; also [112] pp. 46–49.

123 Japanese warehousing: [163] pp. 9, 12, 13, and 23.

124 Petroleum industry network: "MITI to Establish Oil Information Network," *Japan Economic Journal*, December 26, 1987.

124 Wool industry networks: "Woolcom Move in Paperless Trading 'Predatory Pricing' " and "Push for Closer Links," *Financial Review* (Sydney), September 4, 1989.

124–25 U.S. textile and apparel industries: "Spreading the Bar Code Gospel," *Women's Wear Daily*, September 1986; "Auto ID & EDI: Managing in the 90's," *Industry Week*, August 24, 1989; "Apparel Makers Shift Tactics," *New York Times*, September 21, 1987.

125 Battle between AT&T, KDD, and British Telecom: "A Scramble for Global Networks," *Business Week*, March 21, 1988.

125 GE's electronic services: "Messenger of the Gods," by Alyssa A. Lappen, *Forbes*, March 21, 1988. Also, "Fast Forward," by Curtis Bill Pepper, *Business Month*, February 1989.

126 Hairdresser credit card: "NTT Data to Provide Telecom VAN Service," *Japan Economic Journal*, April 1, 1989.

127 Merrill Lynch Cash Management Account: [112] p. 97.

127–28 Seibu cash dispensers: [163] p. 75.

125–28 British Petroleum: [112] p. 92.

CHAPTER 12   THE WIDENING WAR

131   High definition TV: "Consortium Set Up for New TV," *New York Times,* January 26, 1990; "Japan Tunes In While Europe Talks," *Financial Times,* April 21, 1988.

131   Levine quote: "Networks Urge Slow Shift to Sharper TV Picture System," *Los Angeles Times,* June 24, 1988.

132   European views on HDTV: "La guerre des normes," *Le Monde Diplomatique* (Paris), September 1987; and "TV Makers Take on Japanese," *Financial Times,* January 27, 1988. See also "High-Definition War," by John Boyd, *Business Tokyo,* May 1988.

132   A key roundup on the technical aspects of the HDTV contest: "Chasing Japan in the HDTV Race," by Ronald K. Jurgen, *IEEE Spectrum,* October 1989. See also "A Television System for Tomorrow," *French Advances in Technology and Science,* Winter 1987.

132   Europeans court U.S. for alliance against Japanese standards: "Bonn Calls for Joint US-Europe Effort in TV Technology Race," *Financial Times,* May 16, 1989.

132   Re different models around the world: "Firms Are Ready to Meet Any HDTV Format," *Japan Economic Journal,* October 22, 1988; and "Japan Tunes In While Europe Talks," *Financial Times,* April 21, 1988.

133   Markey quote: "Networks Urge Slow Shift to Sharper TV Picture System," *Los Angeles Times,* June 24, 1988.

133   IBM's early ability to impose order on the computer industry: "Living With Computer Anarchy," by Nawa Kotaro, *Japan Echo* (Tokyo), (special issue, 1986.)

134   Re Ada software standards: See issues of *Defense Science.*

134–35   On UNIX battle: "Computer Standards Row May Be Costly for Makers and Users," *Financial Times,* January 23, 1989; "Hopes Rise for World Computer Standard," *Financial Times,* July 12, 1988; "Standards by Fiat," by Esther Dyson, *Forbes,* July 11, 1988; and "Apollo Aims for Eclipse of the Sun," *Financial Times,* July 12, 1988. Also, "OSF à la vitesse Mach," by Patrice Aron and Guy Hervier, *01 Informatique* (Paris), November 24, 1989.

135   Open Software Foundation: "OSF à la vitesse Mach," by Patrice Aron and Guy Hervier, *01 Informatique* (Paris), November 24, 1989; "Computer Gangs Stake out Turf," *New York Times,* December 13, 1988; "Apollo Aims for

Eclipse of the Sun," *Financial Times,* July 12, 1988, and "Standards by Fiat," by Esther Dyson, *Forbes,* July 11, 1988. Also, "The Power and Potential of Computing Standards," *Financial Times,* May 26, 1988.

136 GM's standards battle: "Manufacturing Automation's Problem," by Parker Hodges, *Datamation,* November 15, 1989.

136–37 IBM's standards for computer-to-computer communication: "Japan Shifts on Computer Networks," *New York Times,* October 22, 1988; "IBM Europe Backs a Computer Language Pushed by Its Rivals," *Wall Street Journal,* May 2, 1986.

137 Open System Interconnection fight: "IBM Europe Backs a Computer Language Pushed by Its Rivals," *Wall Street Journal,* May 2, 1986; "Informatique: IBM en échec," *Le Monde Diplomatique* (Paris), September 1987.

137 U.S. protests European standards: interview with Donald S. Abelson, Director, Technical Trade Barriers, Office of the U.S. Trade Representative; also, his remarks on "The U.S. Government's View of Standards Trade Policy" before the General Assembly of the Association Française de Normalisation (AFNOR) (Paris), April 24, 1986.

139 Standards as trade barriers: "West Germany Climbs Down Over Purity of Sausages," *Financial Times,* January 18, 1988; see also Abelson speech cited above.

140 Messine's thoughtful article: "Au coeur des stratégies industrielles," *Le Monde Diplomatique* (Paris), September 1987.

CHAPTER 13   THE EXECUTIVE THOUGHT POLICE

141 Characteristics of corporate "chief information officers" drawn from survey reported in "CIOs in the Spotlight," by Lew McCreary, *CIO,* September 1989.

141 Ryan, Schefer, and Johnson: "Migration Path," by Kathleen Melymuka, *CIO,* September 1989.

142 Sales of information technology: "Charting the Champs," by Parker Hodges; and "At the Top of the IS Peak," *Datamation,* June 15, 1988.

143–45 Merrill conflict: interview with Gerald H. Ely, Vice-President, Merrill Lynch Capital Markets.

145–46 Re Bank of America: "BankAmerica Is Computing More Trouble," *American Banker,* July 16, 1987; "Bank of America's Plans for Computer Don't Add Up," *Los Angeles Times*, February 7, 1988; and "BankAmerica Asks 2 Officials to Quit, Sources Assert," *Wall Street Journal*, October 22, 1987.

148 "Worlds more to lose": Harry B. DeMaio, senior manager, Deloitte & Touche, quoted in "Security, Meet Reality," by Meghan O'Leary, *CIO* magazine, September 1989.

149 Re computer downsizing: Klein quoted from "Honey, I Shrunk the Mainframe!" by Kathleen Melymuka, *CIO* magazine, September 1989.

149 Gassman quoted from "The Politics of Network Management," by Susan Kerr, *Datamation*, September 15, 1988.

CHAPTER 14 TOTAL INFORMATION WAR

153–54 Espionage at Texas Instrument: "The Case of the Terminal Secrets," by Skip Hollandsworth, *D* magazine, November 1986.

154 Hollstein: "Telecommunications Crime," by Nat Weber, *Across the Board*, February 1986.

155 "Designing a chip . . .": [409] p. 50.

155 Xerox: "Corporate Spies Snoop to Conquer," by Brian Dumaine, *Fortune*, November 7, 1988.

155 Service products: "Reverse Engineering a Service Product," by Robert E. Schmidt, Jr., *Planning Review*, September/ October 1987.

156 On full-time sleuths: "George Smiley Joins the Firm," *Newsweek*, May 2, 1988.

156 Society of Competitor Intelligence Professionals: "Intelligence Experts for Corporations," *New York Times*, September 27, 1988.

156 Marriott's spies: "Corporate Spies Snoop to Conquer," by Brian Dumaine, *Fortune*, November 7, 1988.

156 Sheller-Globe case: "Demystifying Competitive Analysis," by Daniel C. Smith and John E. Prescott, *Planning Review*, September/ October 1987.

156–57 Defense contracting scandals: "Pentagon Fraud Inquiry: What Is Known to Date," *New York Times*, July 7, 1988; also, "Pentagon Halts Pay on $1 Billion in Contracts," *Los Angeles Times*, July 2, 1988; and "The Pentagon Up for Sale," *Time*, June 27, 1988.

157 "Anything goes" attitude: "Never Mind MIS; Consider MI5," by L.B.C., *Business Month*, February 1989.

159   GE: "Keeping Tabs on Competitors," *New York Times,* October 28, 1985.

160   On West German computer spies: "Byteman Blows the Whistle on the Sysop Cops," *Los Angeles Times Book Review,* November 19, 1989. Also "The Quest for Intruder-Proof Computer Systems," by Karen Fitzgerald, *IEEE Spectrum,* August 1989.

161   Fake orders into rival firm's computers: "Computer Crime Patterns: The Last 20 Years (1990–2010)," by Joseph F. Coates, *Datamation,* September 15, 1987.

161–62 Counterintelligence technologies: "The Quest for Intruder-Proof Computer Systems," by Karen Fitzgerald, *IEEE Spectrum,* August 1989.

CHAPTER 15 THE CUBBYHOLE CRASH

166   Toshiba's "underground research" and Tandem: "Firms Try to Make Corporate Structure Flexible," *Japan Economic Journal,* February 27, 1988.

167   On Pentagon incomprehensibility: "Entities of Democracy" (excerpts from a speech by Secretary of the Navy John F. Lehman, Jr., to the Sea-Air-Space Exposition banquet in Washington, D.C., April 3, 1985), *New York Times,* April 6, 1985.

168–69 Bhopal disaster: "Bhopal: A Tragedy in Waiting," by Gary Stix, *IEEE Spectrum,* June 1989.

169   Poisoned chocolate: "Candy with a Deadly Taste," by Peter McGill, *MacLean's* (Toronto), October 22, 1984.

169   1989 stock market crash: "The Dow Plunges 190 Points, About 7%, in a Late Selloff; Takeover Stocks Hit Hard," *New York Times,* October 14, 1989.

175   Non-hierarchical data: "Firms Seek to Gain Edge with Swift Grip on Data," by Ivy Schmerken, *Wall Street Computer Review,* July 1987.

175–76 Hyper-media: interview with Bill Atkinson, HyperCard creator. Also "A Conversation with Bill Atkinson" in [493] pp. xxi–xxxii, and pp. 1–14.

CHAPTER 16 THE FLEX-FIRM

180   Italian "miracle": "A Pattern of 'Putting Out,' " *Financial Times,* March 7, 1989, and "In Italy, an Industrial Renaissance Thrives," *Christian Science Monitor,* April 7, 1987.

180–81   New interest in family firms: "Family Business: A Hot Market," by Sharon Nelton, *Nation's Business*, September 1988. For alternative view: "The Decline of the Family Empire," *World Executive Digest* (Hong Kong), July 1987.

181   EC attitude: "Small Is No Longer Beautiful When It's Alone," *Financial Times*, July 4, 1988.

181   Dynamism of small firms: "Is Your Company Too Big?" *Business Week*, March 27, 1989. An example of how new technology helps in "The Fewer Engineers per Project, the Better," *IEEE Spectrum*, by C. Gordon Bell, February 1989.

181   Povejsil quote: "Corporate Strategy for the 1990's," by Walter Kiechel III, *Fortune*, February 29, 1988.

183   The media discover the flexible firm: "A Glimpse of the 'Flex' Future," *Newsweek*, August 1, 1988.

185   Birth and death life-cycles in business: "Changing Corporate Behavior: 1, Diversification," *Japan Economic Journal*, Summer 1988.

187   Hewlett-Packard's Jepson: "At Seatrain, the Buck Stops Here . . . and Here, Too," by William H. Miller, *Industry Week*, March 7, 1988.

189   Saeed's comment on the relationship of business organization to family life is from his thought-provoking book, [151] p. 53.

CHAPTER 17   TRIBAL CHIEFS AND CORPORATE COMMISSARS

191   Census as "pulsator": interview with Maury Cagle, U.S. Bureau of the Census; and "Census Bureau Scrambling to Fill Jobs Here," by Adam Lashinsky, *Crain's Chicago Business*, March 19, 1990.

192–93   SAS example from [279] p. 24.

193   David Stirling on the four-man module: [267] pp. 2–3 and 7–8.

193   Southern California Edison: "Information Systems for Crisis Management," by Thomas J. Housel, Omar A. El Sawy, and Paul F. Donovan, *MIS Quarterly*, vol. 10, no. 4, December 1986.

194   Continental Illinois and A. H. Robins: [132] pp. 22 and 33.

194   Checkerboard organization in Austria: "Austria's Jobs Carve-Up Keeps Bank Post Vacant," *Financial Times*, July 7, 1988.

196–97   Re "skunkworks": "The New Product Development Game," by Hirotaka Takeuchi and Ikujiro Nonaka, *Harvard Business Review*, January/February 1986.

198 Self-start teams: Interview with David Stone, Digital Equipment Corporation (Geneva).

201 Corning, Inc.: "The Age of the Hierarchy Is Over," *New York Times,* September 24, 1989.

201–02 Key thinking on networks: "The Network Alternative," proposal developed by Anthony J. N. Judge of the Union of International Associations (Brussels). Judge's matrix, showing international networks on one axis and global problems on the other, is found in *Yearbook of World Problems and Human Potential,* published by the above organization in 1976.

202 Re NETMAP: "A Business Profile," NETMAP brochure, and "Corporations Reshaped by the Computer," *New York Times,* January 7, 1987; also, remarks of Les Berkes, NETMAP vice-president at Nolan & Norton seminar, November 20, 1987, New York.

CHAPTER 18 THE AUTONOMOUS EMPLOYEE

205 General Electric plant: "Smart Machines, Smart Workers," *New York Times,* October 17, 1988.

205–206 Ford Australia: "Bringing More Brain Power to Bear," *Financial Times,* March 23, 1988.

206 Chrysler-Mitsubishi and Mazda: "How Does Japan Inc. Pick Its American Workers?" *Business Week,* October 3, 1988.

209 Misuse of computers: "Report Says Computers Spy On 7 Million Workers in U.S.," *New York Times,* September 28, 1988.

210 Re separation of thinking and doing: "Japanese Organizational Behavior" by Teruya Nagao, in [135] p. 34.

210–11 Hewitt quote from "Getting Set for Implementation," special CIM report, by Therese R. Welter, *Industry Week,* November 2, 1987.

211 Mohn quote from original English-language ms. of [134]. For European attitudes, see "La redécouverte du 'capital humain,' " *Le Monde* (Paris), October 5, 1988. Attitudes of young workers: "Jeunes: ce qu'ils croient," by Roselyne Bosch, *Le Point* (Paris), June 16, 1987, and "Families More Important," *Business Tokyo,* May 1988.

211–12 GenCorp Automotive: "The (New) Flat Earth Society Gathers in Shelbyville," by Brian Moskal, *Industry Week,* October 2, 1989.

212 Ware quote: from interview with author.

213 Stone quote: from interview with author.
214 Brother Industries: "Creativity in Japan: Some Initial Observations," by Dr. Nigel Holden, *Creativity and Innovation,* April-June 1986.
215 On shop-floor power flowing downward: "Why Managers Resist Machines," *New York Times,* February 7, 1988. See also [169] throughout, for fine-grain study of complexities introduced by new computerized technology.
215 Human-relations model: "Japanese Organizational Behavior," by Teruya Nagao, in [135] p. 27.

CHAPTER 19 THE POWER-MOSAIC

218 Takeovers and mergers: [73] pp. 11–15.
222–23 On layoffs: "General Semantics as a Diagnostic Tool in the Management of Radical Workforce Reduction," by Harold Oaklander, at 50th Anniversary Conference, Institute of General Semantics, Yale University, July 28, 1988.
223 IBM PROFS system: IBM Public Relations (Armonk, N.Y.).
224 Vertical integration in oil industry: [101] pp. 3–7.
224 Vertical integration in steel industry: [44] pp. 114–115 and 126–129.
224 Air freight operations: "Pan American World Airways to Contract Out All Belly Freight Space on Transcontinental Flights," *Journal of Commerce,* November 1, 1985.
224 Ford and GM outsourcing: "Original Auto Parts Will Grow 2–3% . . ." *Metalworking News,* August 27, 1987.
224 AMA: "Vertical Integration of Multinationals Becomes Obsolete," *Management Today,* June 1986.
225 IBM's chip manufacture: "How the Computer Companies Lost Their Memories," by George Gilder, *Forbes,* June 13, 1988.
225 M.I.T. study: "Electronic Markets and Electronic Hierarchies: Effects of Information Technology on Market Structures and Corporate Strategies," by Robert I. Benjamin, Thomas W. Malone, and Joanne Yates, Sloan School of Management, Massachusetts Institute of Technology, April 1986.
226 Small business in U.S.: "The Inc. 100," *Inc.* magazine, May 1989.
226 On trilateral consortia: [322] p. 89.
226–27 Lamborghini, from his "Technological Change and Strategic Alliances" paper at International Management Institute/

European Foundation for Management Development conference, Brussels, June 4–5, 1987.

227   Atlanta airport data from "Hartsfield Atlanta International Airport Economic Impact Report," 1987, based on data prepared by Deloitte, Haskins & Sells and Martin, Murphy, Harps and Syphoe for City of Atlanta Department of Aviation. Also "Fact Sheet" of Airport Commissioner's Office.

228–29   Sculley quotes from [154] pp. 96–97.

229   Matsushita's relations with suppliers: "Manufacturing Innovations Save 'Shitauke,' " *Japan Economic Journal*, January 16, 1988.

230   Re VAX and Lotus users groups: "The Number of User Groups Is Adding Up," by Judith A. Finn, *Digital Review*, April 18, 1988.

230   IBM users: "Council Unites Top IBM User Groups," by Paul Tate, *Datamation*, September 15, 1987.

CODA THE NEW SYSTEM FOR WEALTH CREATION

234   Two trillionths of a second: "New Chips Offer the Promise of Much Speedier Computers," *New York Times*, January 4, 1989.

236   On concurrent processing and simultaneous engineering: "Strategic Alliances Make Marketing & Manufacturing an International Game," by George Weimer, et al., *Industry Week*, November 21, 1988 ("Integrated Manufacturing" section).

236   On just-in-time: "Added Value Emanating from Acronyms," *Financial Times*, December 13, 1989.

237   Motorola's Team Bandit: "State-of-the-Art CIM in 18 Months?" by John H. Sheridan, *Industry Week*, December 5, 1988.

237–38   Japanese auto industry advantage: "Time—The Next Source of Competitive Advantage," by George Stalk, Jr., *Harvard Business Review*, July-August 1988.

237–38   Re Toyota and bank speedup: "Fast-Cycle Capability for Competitive Power," by Joseph L. Bower and Thomas M. Hout, *Harvard Business Review*, November-December 1988.

CHAPTER 20 THE DECISIVE DECADES

Governments have always manipulated information and knowledge. They have used many different tactics for inducing or compelling consent. Today, as computers and the media proliferate, the tools of control (and of popular resistance) are multiplying and becoming more subtle. To place this political development in perspective, it helps to look into the history of the state.

While certain tribal groups like the Ifugao of the Philippines, or the Nuer and Kung! Bushmen of Africa may have survived without any semblance of a state, today virtually every human on the planet is a citizen—or more bluntly a subject—of one state or another. And the state is commonly regarded as the most powerful of all social institutions.

Theories of the state abound. Alexander Rustow, the German economist, has maintained that the state arose out of the "higher hunting cultures, with their chieftancy and their strict organization for the chase and war." The historian Karl Wittfogel speculated that the need for large irrigation projects, which in turn required the mobilization and control of large masses of workers, led to the highly organized state. According to Engels's theory, elaborated in Lenin's *State and Revolution,* the state arose when people were first divided into classes. The state was an instrument used by one class to oppress another. For Marxists, therefore, the state is the "executive arm" of a ruling class.

Whatever theory one chooses to believe, it seems reasonable that a key political turning point was reached when tribal or village groups first passed the economic subsistence point. Once a community could produce and store a food surplus, some defense was needed to protect it against outside raiders and from those within the community who might try to grab it for their own use.

The first great powershift in history comes when the community chooses a "protector," usually male, from among its strongest members. It is easy to imagine this "strongman" demanding part of the community surplus in return for his protective services.

The next step in the formation of the state comes when the protector uses part of the wealth he has extracted from the population to "hire" warriors now directly beholden to him, not the community. The protector himself is now protected.

The second great powershift occurs when the task of extracting tribute or taxes is systematized, with "collectors" appointed to gather the wealth. This step, once taken, creates a self-reinforcing feedback and speeds things up, greatly increasing the power of the rulers and their supporters. The more wealth they can extract, the more soldiers they can afford, and the harder they can then squeeze the community for still more wealth.

With this added wealth, of course, the embryonic state moves to a new level. Its ruler now commands two of the three main tools of social control: violence and wealth, rather than just violence alone.

This means those in control no longer need to intimidate and dominate by force exclusively. They can now use part of the "take" extracted from the community to reward faithful followers and build political support. To the low-quality power based on violence, therefore, the ruling individual or clique now adds the far more versatile form of power based on wealth.

The next powershift occurs when clever rulers discover they can enhance their power, and actually reduce the cost of soldiers to protect them, if they can mind-wash their people. By seducing or terrorizing the population into believing an appropriate mythology, religion, or ideology, it becomes possible to persuade one's subjects that the existing power system is not only inevitable and permanent, but morally right and proper, if not actually divine. Used this way, knowledge —in the form of myth, religion, and ideology, truth as well as falsehood—becomes a key political weapon.

One might even argue that this is the moment at which the state is born—that, until this point, there are only embryonic, half-formed anticipations of the state. The state, in short, is not fully a state until it commands all three of the basic tools of social control: knowledge, as well as wealth and the potential for violence.

While this schematic is clearly speculative and grandly oversimplified, it provides a plausible explanation for the origin of the state and integrates it with the new theory of power.

246–47   Crupi quote from "Political Risk Begins at Home," *Across the Board,* January 1986.

247   Queen's worry: "Scottish Nationalism Threatens British Unity," *Los Angeles Times,* December 25, 1988.

247   Hapsburgs in Central Europe: [545] pp. 26, 27, and 422.

249   Tokyo earthquake impact: "The Japanese Earthquake Explained" (first published, September 1923), *Natural History,* April 1980; "When the Big One Hits Tokyo . . ." by Edith Terry, *World Press Review,* December 1989, and "How a Tokyo Earthquake Could Devastate Wall Street," by Michael Lewis, *Manhattan, inc.,* June 1989.

250   On growing interethnic battles in U.S.: "New Interethnic
           Conflict Replaces an L.A. History of Biracial Politics," *Los
           Angeles Times,* January 7, 1990; "Shake-Up at Latino Sta-
           tion Sparks Protest," *Los Angeles Times,* June 6, 1989; "Cu-
           bans, not Haitians, Offered Legal Status: Blacks 'Outraged,' "
           by Kathleen Kelly, *National Catholic Reporter,* February 24,
           1984; "Showdown on Middle Neck Road," by Robert Spero,
           Present Tense, May–June 1989; "Swapping Lessons," *Los
           Angeles Times,* January 11, 1990; "Rapping Solo," *Billboard,*
           January 13, 1990.
252   Hitler's first Nazi meeting: [580] p. 54.
252–53   On pivotal minorities: [103] see throughout, especially Chap-
           ter 12 on P-2 Lodge; also [95] p. 16; [165] pp. 3–4, and
           throughout, under "Gelli"; "The Roots of Kahanism," *Ha'am*
           newspaper, University of California at Los Angeles, January–
           February 1987; "Links of Anti-Semitic Band Provokes
           6-State Parley," *New York Times,* December 27, 1984; "Neo-
           Nazis Dream of Racist Territory," *New York Times,* July 5,
           1986; "The Charmer," *New York* magazine, October 7,
           1985; "Lyndon LaRouche: From Marxist Left to Well-
           Connected Right," by John Mintz, *Washington Post National
           Weekly,* February 25, 1985; "LaRouche Fringe Stirs in Ger-
           many," *New York Times,* June 30, 1986; [203] throughout.
253   On hate group proliferation: "Rioting in the Streets: Déjà
           Vu?" by William L. Tafoya, *C(riminal) J(ustice)—the Americas,*
           December 1989–January 1990.
254–55   Re the proliferation of "holy wars": "High-Intensity Aggres-
           sive Ideologies as an International Threat," by Yehezkel
           Dror, *Jerusalem Journal of International Relations,* vol. 9, no.
           1, 1987.

CHAPTER 21   THE INVISIBLE PARTY

256   Atwater's comment made to author.
256   Tsurumi article: "A Bureaucratic Hold on Japan," *Los Ange-
           les Times,* January 25, 1988.
257–58   Rival ministries in Tokyo: "Turf Battles and Telecom," by
           Kazuhisa Maeno, *Journal of Japanese Trade and Industry,* no.
           5, 1988. On intra-ministerial rivalries, see the unusually
           rich *Conflict in Japan* by Ellis S. Krauss, Thomas P. Rohlen,

and Patricia G. Steinhoff, eds. (Honolulu: University of Hawaii Press, 1984), p. 298.

258   Mexico privatization plans: "First State of the Nation Report," President Carlos Salinas de Gortari (Mexico City), November 1, 1989.

259   Mobil divestitures: "Integrated—and Determined to Stay That Way," by Toni Mack, *Forbes,* December 12, 1988, and "Less Is Less," *Forbes,* April 4, 1988.

259–60 Sabotage in Japan: "Paralysis on the Tracks," *Time,* December 9, 1985.

260   Privatization of NTT: "Hold the Phone," by Richard Phalon, *Forbes,* October 17, 1988; "Japan's Spending Spree," *World Press Review,* January 1990; see also, "Deregulation, Privatization Spur JAL to Diversify Operations," by James Ott and Eiichiro Sekigawa, *Aviation Week and Space Technology,* May 8, 1989.

260   Privatizations in many countries: "Can a Privatized Matra Do Better on Its Own?" by Jennifer L. Schenker, *Electronics,* February 18, 1988; "Why Bonn Just Can't Let Go," *Business Week,* April 4, 1988; "A Choice Menu from Jacques Chirac," by Michael McFadden, *Fortune,* January 5, 1987; "How Many Bureaucrats to Install a Phone?" by Richard C. Morais, *Forbes,* September 19, 1988; "Air Canada Comes of Age," *MacLean's* (Toronto), April 25, 1988.

261   Popkin on fewer hierarchies: [201] pp. 227–228.

263   Kohl ignores Foreign Ministry: "Ostpolitik Pays Belated Dividend for Germany's Elder Statesman," *Financial Times,* December 14, 1989.

CHAPTER 22 INFO-TACTICS

266   Johnson on freedom of information: [194] pp. 3–4.

266   20 million secret documents: "The Future of Intelligence," by Walter Laqueur, *Society,* November–December 1985.

266–67 CIA quote: [194] p. 24.

267   Recruit-Cosmos leaks: "Gentlemanly Press Gets Gloves Dirty," *Insight,* December 4, 1989.

267   Pattie quote from "Tory Thought Curbed by 'Fear of Leaks,' " *Times* (London), October 10, 1986.

267–68 Gergen on White House leaks: "Secrecy Means Big Things Get Little Thought," *Los Angeles Times,* November 27, 1986.

268   Kissinger role in telephone taps: [574] p. 388.

269   Vietnam report: [421] p. 6.

269   Re Zimmerman telegram: [397] p. 18.

270–71 Shultz-Kelly back-channel fight: "Shultz Calls Envoy Home, Saying He Dealt in Secret," *Los Angeles Times,* December 9, 1986; "Shultz Warning Envoys to Stop Bypassing Him," *New York Times,* December 18, 1986.

271   Kissinger-South Korea case is described in Seymour M. Hersh's critical volume *The Price of Power* (New York: Summit Books, 1983), pp. 42–43.

272   Kissinger-Dobrynin back-channel: [427] pp. 153 and 193.

272   Cuban missile back-channel: [407] pp. 146–147.

272–73 The Double-Channel Tactic: [427] p. 205.

275   Re Red Brigade case: [435] p. 129.

275   AIDS: See "Soviets, At Last, Face up to AIDS," *Los Angeles Times,* April 22, 1989; also "The KGB's New Muscle," *U.S. News and World Report,* September 15, 1986.

275   Reversal in Jerusalem: "Peres Office, in Israeli Infighting, Bars Shamir Message to Embassies," *New York Times,* January 15, 1987.

276   Churchill on authentic data: [398] p. 292.

CHAPTER 23   META-TACTICS

278   Sununu as computer-wise governor: "The Granite State of the Art," *Time,* January 27, 1986.

279   Computer-aided software engineering: "From CASE to Software Factories," by Herbert Weber, *Datamation,* April 1, 1989.

280   Profits like sausages and GM: "Cute Tricks on the Bottom Line," by Gary Hector, *Fortune,* April 24, 1989.

282   Mafia amputates finger: [485] p. 74.

282   U.S. Justice Department list of computer crimes: "Electronic Capers," by J. A. Tujo, *Information Executive,* vol. 2, no. 1, 1985.

283   Congressional letters vanish: "Two Cases of Computer Burglary," *New York Times,* March 21, 1986.

284   South Korean elections: "Observers Allege Computer Fraud in S. Korea Poll," *Financial Times,* December 21, 1987.

284–85 Election Watch case: "Electronic Elections Seen as Invitation to Fraud," *Los Angeles Times,* July 4, 1989.

286   Stockman: [227] p. 92.

286–87 Re Census: "Analyzing the Figures That Shape Our Daily Lives," by Richard Lipkin, *Insight,* May 22, 1989; "Political Power and Money at Stake in Census Undercount Fight," *Washington Post,* January 11, 1988; "False Signals on Inflation," *Newsweek,* July 28, 1986; "Measuring Money," by John Roberts, *National Westminster Moneycare* magazine (London), October–November 1986; also, author interview with Jack Keane, Director, U.S. Bureau of the Census, and staff.

289   Rona quote: "Spy Satellites: Entering a New Era," *Science,* March 24, 1989.

290   Inferencing capabilities and expert systems: "Car and Plane Makers Fuel Up with CAD, AI," and "Oil Companies Exploit as Much as Explore IS," both in *Datamation,* November 15, 1989. See also, "New Shells for Old Iron," by John J. Popolizio and William S. Cappelli, *Datamation,* April 15, 1989.

292   How models are used and misused: [463] pp. 9–10 and 31–32.

292   How many in poverty?: "Taking the Measure, or Mismeasure, of It All," *New York Times,* August 28, 1984.

292   Hot deck imputation: "Hide and Seek," *Atlantic,* December 1988.

292   Census lawsuit: "Accord on Census May Bring Change in Minority Data," *New York Times,* July 18, 1989.

CHAPTER 24 A MARKET FOR SPIES

296   Ancient Egyptian spies are cited in [403] p. 111.

296   Baden-Powell's butterflies: [394] pp. 7–8.

296   Captain Giichi Tanaka's tale is in [394] pp. 21–23.

296   Mass spying: [426] p. 83.

297   The use of "Rabcors" is described in [417] p. 6.

297   Richard Sorge's life story is told in [404] pp. 325–343.

298   The coverage provided by remote sensing systems: [399] p. xvi.

298   Listening to limos and Lop Nor: "Exit Smiley, Enter IBM," *The Sunday Times* (London), October 31, 1982.

300   U.S. intelligence "community": [424] and [422] throughout; [434] Chapters 1 and 2. Also, interview with Alfred Kingon, Kingon International, former White House Cabinet Secretary.

300   Re Soviet intelligence: [404] throughout; [434] Chapters 4 and 5; also, though somewhat dated, [425]. And [526] pp. 166–167 focuses on technological espionage.

300–01   French intelligence: [415] throughout; [434] Chapter 7; [423] Chapter 6.

301   German intelligence: "Smiley Without People: A Tale of Intelligence Misjudgments," *Der Tagesspiegel* (Berlin), January 6, 1990; also [434] pp. 3, 113, 127, 130, and 182; [423] pp. 127–147 and 254–257.

301   Japanese intelligence: [423] Chapter 8; see also [426] for history.

301   Trans-Siberian incident: [423] p. 255.

301–02   New Zealand's "ex-communication": "British Ban Kiwis From Intelligence Briefings," *The Sunday Times* (London), May 4, 1986.

302   The Harper espionage story is from [434] p. 165.

302–03   Argentina's dilemma: author's interviews, Buenos Aires.

303   East European collaboration with Moscow after ouster of Communist governments: "It's Still Business as Usual for Spies, Even as the Eastern Bloc Rises Up," *New York Times*, December 31, 1989.

303   U.S. intelligence to South Africa: "U.S. Is Said to Have Given Pretoria Intelligence on Rebel Organization," *New York Times*, July 23, 1986; also "Query on CIA Tie to Mandela Case Deflected," *Los Angeles Times*, June 13, 1990.

303   Australian aid to CIA in Chile: [402] pp. 24–25.

303   French-Portuguese and French-Moroccan collaboration: [415] pp. 79–80, 71–73.

303   Romanian-PLO collaboration: [416] pp. 13, 15–35, and 92–99.

303   Israeli collaboration with U.S.: [424] pp. 205–207.

303   U.S.-Soviet collaboration: "Ex-KGB Aides to Join U.S. Talks on Terrorism," *Los Angeles Times*, September 25, 1989.

304   Effect of intelligence swapping on civil liberties: [411] p. 373.

305   Iraqi warplane story: "The 300-Million-Dollar Disaster" in *The Voice of the Arab World* (London), undated; also [392] throughout.

305–06   NSA and GCHQ "watch lists": "Exit Smiley, Enter IBM," *The Sunday Times* (London), October 31, 1982.

306   Olmer quotes: interview with author.

308–09   Ceausescu's nuclear scam: [416] pp. 292–297.

309   One operation can pay the whole intelligence budget: [415] pp. 41–42.

309   KGB in Tokyo: [413] pp. 103–104.

309   Line X position in KGB Table of Organization: [434] p. 87.

310   On CoCom: "Appeal for CoCom Blacklist to be Overhauled,"
        commentary, *Frankfurter Rundschau,* November 29, 1989
        (translated in *The German Tribune,* December 10, 1989);
        "American Hypocrisy Highlighted in CoCom Rule Imple-
        mentation," *Japan Economic Journal,* July 2, 1988; "A Chal-
        lenge for High-Tech Censors," *Financial Times,* October
        19, 1988; "U.S. Set to Ease European Defence Technology
        Curbs," *Financial Times,* January 29, 1988. And [526] p. 15.

311   Eco-war: "Turkey's Stranglehold on the Euphrates Irks Its
        Neighbours," *Financial Times,* January 3, 1990.

312   Bechtel-CIA relations: [130] p. 117.

312   200 U.S. spies under "business cover": "Business Pose by
        U.S. Spies Reported," *New York Times,* February 28, 1974.

312–13 Lack of U.S. pressure on citizens to spy: [434] p. 49.

315   Five nations: author interview with Kevin Corbley, Media
        Coordinator, EOSAT (Earth Observation Satellite Company).

315   Landsat and SPOT satellites: "Space Cameras and Security
        Risks," by David Dickson, *Science,* January 27, 1989; "Civil-
        ians Use Satellite Photos for Spying on Soviet Military,"
        New York Times, April 7, 1986. Corbley interview. *Spotlight,*
        vol. 3, no. 2, June 1989 (SPOT Image Corporation); also
        SPOT Data Products and Services (catalog); and SPOT
        Surveillance brochure (which advises potential customers:
        "Before taking any decision concerning a target located
        deep inside a zone inaccessible to reconnaissance planes
        and RPVs [i.e., remotely piloted vehicles]" rely on SPOT
        images to analyze the target, the "threats" surrounding it,
        and the route leading to it. SPOT also offers "penetration
        assistance," pointing out that "passage under radar and
        missile coverage calls for in-depth study of the penetration
        route," in the form of SPOT 3-dimensional images.

315–16 The processing and enhancement of remote sensing images
        for commercial and military purposes is a growing busi-
        ness. See EOSAT "Directory of Landsat-Related Products
        and Services—United States Edition, 1988," and "Directory
        of Landsat-Related Products and Services—International
        Edition, 1989," from EOSAT, Lanham, Maryland.

316   Space Media Network: brochure from Space Media Net-
        work. Also, "Photos Prove '57 Nuclear Disaster," *Chicago
        Tribune,* December 1, 1988; "Satellite Photos Appear to
        Show Construction of Soviet Space Shuttle Base," *New York
        Times,* August 25, 1986; and Space Media Network "List of
        Media Projects."

316   Poor-country satellite and missile development: "Star Wars,"
        by Sterett Pope, *World Press Review,* December 1989.
317   Acceleration effect in intelligence: "E. European Events Out-
        run Intelligence Analysts, Panel Told," *Los Angeles Times,*
        December 13, 1989.
318   Conrad, from his *Under Western Eyes,* 1911.

CHAPTER 25   THE INFO-AGENDA

320   McFarlane in Tehran: "Iran Says McFarlane Came on Se-
        cret Mission to Tehran," *Washington Post Foreign Service,*
        November 11, 1986; "Cloak and Dagger," *Newsweek,* No-
        vember 17, 1986; "Reagan's Backdoor Hostage Deal with
        Iran," *U.S. News & World Report,* November 17, 1986;
        "Cake Delivered to Iranians Was Strictly Kosher," *Los An-
        geles Times,* February 27, 1987.
321   "Federal Information: Who Should Get It, Who Shouldn't?"
        by Diane Sherwood, *The World & I,* January 1990.
322   Layoff numbers: "Heading for an Override?" *Time,* July 18,
        1988.
322   Fairness issue: "Heading for an Override?" *Time,* July 18,
        1988; "Closing Law's Key Provisions," by Martha I. Finney,
        Nation's Business, January 1989; and "72–73 Senate Vote
        Approves Notice of Plant Closings," *New York Times,* July
        7, 1988.
323   Osaka citizens: "Group Seeks Access to City's Information,"
        Japan Times, August 29, 1989.
323–24 Freedom of information legislation: "Role of Access Coordi-
        nators Under Scrutiny," *Transnational Data and Communica-
        tions Report,* March 1989; also, "International FOI Roundup,"
        Transnational Data Report, June 1985. This journal keeps a
        running check on "FOI" developments.
324–25 Congressional inquiry: "Transportation Secretary Assails Pub-
        licizing of Terrorist Warnings," *New York Times,* April 13,
        1989.
325   Northwest case: "Northwest Planned to Disclose Bomb Threat
        at the Gate," *Los Angeles Times,* December 30, 1989; "North-
        west Warns Flight's Ticket Holders of Threat," *New York
        Times,* December 29, 1989.
325   AIDS: "AIDS: Who Should Be Tested?" *Newsweek,* May 11,
        1987; "As AIDS Spooks the Schoolroom—," *U.S. News and*

World Report, September 23, 1985; "Putting AIDS to the Test," *Time,* March 2, 1987; "Mandatory Testing for AIDS?" *Newsweek,* February 16, 1987.

326–27   Does one country have a right to know about another?: "Sweden Protests to Moscow Over Lack of Warning," *Financial Times,* April 30, 1986; "Russians Pressed to Give Full Details of Nuclear Disaster," *The Times* (London), April 29, 1986.

327   Stansfield Turner article: "The U.S. Responded Poorly to Chernobyl," *New York Times,* May 23, 1986.

327   Libya chemical weapons incident: "Libyan Plant Sparks Storm in Bonn," *Washington Post,* January 19, 1989; "West Germany in Libya Probe," *Financial Times,* January 14/15, 1989; "Senator Assails Bonn in Libya Scandal," *Los Angeles Times,* January 29, 1989; "Vigilance, Luck Expose Libya Plant," *Los Angeles Times,* January 22, 1989.

328   Tape pirates: "Thai Copyright War Divides Washington," *Financial Times,* January 27, 1989.

328   Book piracy: "Barbary Book Pirates," by Sterett Pope, *World Press Review,* June 1986; "La book connection," by Rémy Lilliet, *L'Express,* March 29, 1985; also, "Copyright Holders Name 12 Pirate Nations," *Financial Times,* April 25, 1989.

328   *Indiana Jones:* "High-Tech Tactics Slow Film Piracy," *New York Times,* January 29, 1986.

328–29   Taiwan teenagers: "Pulling the Plug on Pirate Videos," *Los Angeles Times,* January 8, 1990.

329   Stealing software: "Psst! hey, mister, want to buy some software cheap?" by Christopher Johnston, *PC Computing,* October 1988; and "Thai Copyright War Divides Washington," *Financial Times,* January 27, 1989.

330   Japanese attitude on intellectual property: "Putting a Price on Intellect," by Yuji Masuda, *Journal of Japanese Trade and Industry,* no. 5, 1988.

330   EC attitude: "Brussels Plan for IPR Control," *Financial Times,* July 4, 1989.

330   Harlan Cleveland quoted from *WFSF Newsletter* (World Future Studies Federation), July 1989.

331   Maldistribution of information quote from [332] p. v.

331   Pharmaceuticals: "Whose Idea Is It Anyway?" *Economist,* November 12, 1988.

CHAPTER 26   THE IMAGE MAKERS

332   Early newspaper history from [171] pp. 5–6, and [179] pp. 203–205.

332–33   On the rise of "public opinion": [538] p. 14.

333–34   CNN impact: "Watching Cable News Network Grow," *New York Times*, December 16, 1987; "Triumphant Ted," by Joshua Hammer, *Playboy*, January 1990; see also CNN documents: "The Growth of a Global Network," "Milestones," "Live Reporting," and [180] throughout.

333–34   Fidel Castro: Turner showed tape privately to author.

336   New TV networks and services in U.S.: "Cable," by Paula Parisi, *Hollywood Reporter*, 1989–1990 TV Preview; also " 'Channel One' Could Whittle Away at Net and Syndie Teen and Coin," by Verne Gay, *Variety*, June 14–20, 1989.

336   Number of channels available: [68] p. 281; and, "Technology Adds Choices and Programming Needs," *New York Times*, July 24, 1989.

337   Direct broadcast satellite: "One Hundred and Eight Channels by 1993? Stay Tuned, America," *International Herald Tribune*, February 22, 1990.

337   Rise of independent stations and syndicates: "The Future of Television," *Newsweek*, October 17, 1988.

337   Iger quote: "Technology Adds Choices and Programming Needs," *New York Times*, July 24, 1989.

337   "Hardly anyone remembers" quote from author interview with Al Burton, Executive Producer, Universal Television, and President, Al Burton Productions.

338   European satellite channels: "Tube Wars," by Fred V. Guterl, *Business Month*, December 1988.

338   BSB and Sky rivalry: "BSB Inks 5-Year Output Deal with Orion; Rumors of Oz' Bond Pulling Out Abound," by Elizabeth Guider, *Variety*, June 14–20, 1989; and "Activate the Death Star," *Economist*, July 8, 1989.

338   French television: "Off-Screen TV: Scandal, Sex, Money," *New York Times*, January 18, 1988; "Boost for Cable TV Industry in France," *Financial Times*, February 9, 1990; "France's New Television Order," by Adam Glenn, *Broadcasting*, August 24, 1987; "Commercial TV, Mon Dieu!" *Time*, March 17, 1986; and "Le Defi Disney," by John Marcom, Jr., *Forbes*, February 20, 1989.

338   German television: "New German TV: Idiot Culture or Breath of Air?" *New York Times*, February 11, 1985; "Tube Wars,"

by Fred V. Guterl, *Business Month,* December 1988.

339   Advertising agency mergers: "WPP, the New Giant of . . . PR?" *Business Week,* May 29, 1989; "Upbeat View at Saatchi New York," *New York Times,* June 21, 1989. Things were looking less "upbeat" by 1990.

339–40   Failure of "global sell" strategy: "Marketers Turn Sour on Global Sales Pitch Harvard Guru Makes," *Wall Street Journal,* May 12, 1988; "The Overselling of World Brands," *Financial Times,* December 21, 1988; and "Why the Single Market Is a Misnomer—and the Consequences," *Financial Times,* December 21, 1988.

341   Sony in Hollywood: "$3 Billion Bid for Columbia by Sony," *Los Angeles Times,* September 26, 1989. This initial report underestimated the actual price. Two days later, on September 28, 1989, in "Sony Has High Hopes for Columbia Pictures," the *New York Times* estimated the price at $3.4 billion. "Sony Goes to Hollywood," *The Sunday Times* (London), October 1, 1989, calculated the deal at "almost $5 billion."

341–42   Murdoch empire: "Four Titans Carve Up European TV," by William Fisher and Mark Schapiro, *Nation,* January 9/16, 1989; and "Tube Wars," by Fred V. Guterl, *Business Month,* December 1988.

342   Maxwell profiled: "Larger Than Life," *Time,* November 28, 1988; see also, "Four Titans Carve Up European TV," by William Fisher and Mark Schapiro, *Nation,* January 9/16, 1989, and "Business Goes Global," *Report on Business Magazine—The Globe and Mail* (Toronto), February 1989.

343   Mohn and Bertelsmann profiled: "Reinhard Mohn," *Nation,* June 12, 1989; see also [134] throughout; "Business Goes Global," *Report on Business Magazine—The Globe and Mail* (Toronto), February 1989; and "Bertelsmann Philosophy," Bertelsmann brochure.

CHAPTER 27 THE SUBVERSIVE MEDIA

347   Mexicans' legal victory: "Mexicans Who Sued Deputies Win $1 Million," *Los Angeles Times,* January 25, 1990; and "Videotape Is Centerpiece of 'Victorville 5' Brutality Lawsuit," *Los Angeles Times,* January 9, 1990.

347–48   Czech rebels' videos: "The Czechoslovak Pen Defies the Party Sword," *Financial Times,* November 28, 1989.

348   Political use of television and videocassettes: excellent roundup in "TV, VCRs Fan Fire of Revolution," *Los Angeles Times,* January 18, 1990.

348   Ceausescu once invited the author to "spend my vacation with me and we can watch *Kojak* together." The surprise invitation came after a long meeting between the Romanian President and the Tofflers, attended by Harry Barnes, then U.S. Ambassador to Bucharest. The year was 1976. The end of the Ceausescu story is told in "How the Ceausescus Fell: Harnessing Popular Rage," *New York Times,* January 7, 1990.

349   The role of TV in the Philippines: "Playing to the TV Cameras," *U.S. News and World Report,* March 10, 1986.

349–50   Romanian revolution: "How the Ceausescus Fell: Harnessing Popular Rage," *New York Times,* January 7, 1990; "Romanian Revolt, Live and Uncensored," *New York Times,* December 28, 1989; also, "Message of the Media," *Financial Times,* December 30, 1989.

353   Dresden out of reach of West German TV: "The Long Journey out of the Valley of the Ignorant," *Stuttgarter Zeitung,* December 19, 1989.

353   Role of Voice of America: Testimony of Richard Carlson, Director VOA, before subcommittee of House Foreign Affairs Committee, U.S. Congress, June 15, 1989; also, "Old Men Riding a Tiger and Feeling Paranoid," *Los Angeles Times,* January 8, 1990.

355   Christianity in South Korea: "Chun's $21 Million Apology," *Newsweek,* December 5, 1988; also, "Papal Nod to a Christian Boom," *Time,* May 14, 1984.

355   Khomeini's use of tape recordings: "The Ayatollah's Hit Parade," *Time,* February 12, 1979.

356   Politics of wall posters: "Peking's Posters Point Finger of Protest to the Party," *Financial Times,* June 17, 1988.

356   Summary accounts of Chinese student uprising: See [363] pp. 219–220; "State of Siege," *Time,* May 29, 1989; and, for a socialist perspective, "China's Long Winter," by Anita Chan, *Monthly Review,* January 1990. Also, "Watching China Change," by Mark Hopkins, *Columbia Journalism Review,* September/October 1989.

357–58   The new role of "meta-news" is seen in media coverage of media coverage—knowledge about knowledge again. See "The Revolution Will Not Be Televised," *Los Angeles Times,*

May 22, 1989; "China Allows Foreign Broadcasters to Resume News Transmission," *New York Times,* May 24, 1989; "China Lets World Hear but Not See," *New York Times,* May 21, 1989.

357–58 Political use of new media: ". . . As Chinese in U.S. Pierce a News Blockade," *New York Times,* May 24, 1989; also, "TV, VCRs Fan Fire of Revolution," *Los Angeles Times,* January 18, 1990; "Phones, Faxes: Students in U.S. Keep Lines of Communication Open," *Los Angeles Times,* June 6, 1989.

358 First "citizen jamming" efforts: "Chinese Students in U.S. Seeking to Foil 'Tip' Lines," *Los Angeles Times,* June 11, 1989.

CHAPTER 28 THE "SCREENIE" GENERATION

360–61 Slave golfer: author interviews with Gordon Stulberg, Chairman, and Bernard Luskin, President, American Interactive Media Corporation; also company documents.

361 Network games: "Computer Company Plans to Bring TV Viewers Into the Action," *Los Angeles Herald Examiner,* February 11, 1988.

361 Gilder: "Forget HDTV, It's Already Outmoded," *New York Times,* May 28, 1989; and "IBM-TV?" by George Gilder, *Forbes,* February 20, 1989.

363–64 Faxes and billions of pages: U.S. Congressman Edward J. Markey in "Ban Fax Attacks; They Are Costly," *USA Today,* May 31, 1989.

366 AT&T breakdown: "President Reagan Declares Martin Luther King, Jr., Day," *Jet,* January 23, 1989; AT&T Pinpoints Source of Service Disruption," *New York Times,* January 17, 1990; and "AT&T Fiasco: Tense Fight With Haywire Technology," *Los Angeles Times,* January 19, 1990.

367–68 Moritz on "screenies": Letter to author from Jeffrey M. Moritz, President, National College Television.

CODA: YEARNINGS FOR A NEW DARK AGE

373 The God-Is-Dead controversy: "Toward a Hidden God," *Time,* April 8, 1966.

375 Azerbaijan links to Muslim fundamentalism: Accounts of the 1989 uprising in Azerbaijan and the massacre of Ar-

menians in Baku differ widely as to the role of the Communist Party local leadership, Moscow's delay in using troops to restore order, and the character of the Azeri movement. "Baku: Before and After," by Igor Beliaev, *Literaturnaya Gazeta International*—"The Literary Gazette" (Moscow), March 1990; "Iran Warns Against 'Harsh' Soviet Moves in Azerbaijan," *Los Angeles Times,* January 18, 1990; "Fundamentalism Blamed for Uzbeck Rioting," *Financial Times,* June 14, 1989; "Soviets Are At Loss About Ethnic Unrest," *Wall Street Journal,* July 21, 1989; and, "Teheran Is Said to Back 'Islamic Seal' but Not Separatism in Azerbaijan," *New York Times,* January 21, 1990.

375 Fundamentalists in Israel: See "Israel's Cultural War," *The Christian Century,* July 16–23, 1986. For relationships to early German romanticism, see [303] pp. 60–63.

377 Splits in the Green Party and in Green ideology: "Greens Trade Insults at Birthday Party," *Handelsblatt* (Dusseldorf), January 15, 1990, reports on declining status of German Greens as major parties adopt some of their policies. Ideological-philosophical divide in world ecology movement is best delineated in the Spring 1989 *New Perspectives Quarterly (NPQ),* which brings together many of the leading thinkers of the ecology movement and frames the key philosophical issues. Edited by Nathan Gardels, *NPQ* is consistently among America's most challenging periodicals.

378 Bahro is from "Theology Not Ecology"; and Sachs, from "A Critique of Ecology"; both in *NPQ,* Spring 1989.

379 Illich is from "The Shadow Our Future Throws," *NPQ,* Spring 1989; [517] pp. 101–102; and [240] p. 181.

379 Bilmes and Byford are quoted from "Armageddon and the Greens," *Financial Times,* December 30–31, 1989.

380 Bahro on a "green Adolf": See "Theology Not Ecology," *NPQ,* Spring 1989.

380 Touraine's counter to ecological anti-reason: "Neo-Modern Ecology," *NPQ,* Spring 1989.

380 On German romanticism and back-to-naturism: "The Dangers of Counter-Culture," by John de Graff, *Undercurrents 21,* April/May 1977; see also [582] pp. 50–55; [384] especially Chapter 11; also [390] p. 188.

381 Nazi exaltation of the Middle Ages: [391] p. 50, and adjoining map.

381 "Green Tribe" (letter from Ron James), *Economist,* July 29, 1989.

382   Worry over Anglo-Saxon TV: "Vers un marche mondial de l'information télévisée," by Yves Eudes, *Le Monde Diplomatique* (Paris), June 1988; "Hollywood Predominance Reflects Sad State of European Industry," *Süddeutsche Zeitung* (Munich), January 6, 1990.

382   Plummeting price of satellite dishes: interview with Dan Goldin, satellite expert, TRW, Inc.

383   Le Pen on Nazis and death camps: "French Rightist Belittles Gas Chambers," *New York Times,* September 16, 1987; see also "Le Front National et le drapeau nazi dans le champ belge à Rotterdam," *Le Soir* (Brussels), November 30/December 1, 1985; and, "Europeans Showed Dissatisfaction With Ruling Parties," *Los Angeles Times,* June 24, 1989.

383   Germany's Republikaners: "Europe's Grand Parties in a Tightening Vise," *Wall Street Journal,* June 26, 1989; "Extreme Rightists Win Frankfurt Council Seats," *Los Angeles Times,* March 13, 1989; "Germany's Republikaners Start a Rumble on the Far Right," *Wall Street Journal,* July 24, 1989; and "Is Extremist or Opportunist Behind Bonn Rightist's Tempered Slogans?" *New York Times,* June 27, 1989; also "Millstone Instead of Milestone for Republicans," *Süddeutsche Zeitung* (Munich), January 15, 1990; "Former Nazi Quits as W. German Party Leader, Blaming Extremists," *Los Angeles Times,* May 26, 1990.

384   Eco-vandals and anti-immigrationists: "Saboteurs for a Better Environment," *New York Times,* July 9, 1989; see also, debate in pages of *Earth First!* (Canton, N.Y.), a publication of eco-extremists.

384–85 Japanese nationalist sentiment: "A New Japanese Nationalism," by Ian Buruma, *New York Times Magazine,* April 12, 1987; "Mayor Who Faulted Hirohito Is Shot," *New York Times,* January 19, 1990; "Attack on Nagasaki Mayor Stirs Fears of Speaking Out," *New York Times,* January 21, 1990; "Rightist Held in Shooting of Blunt Nagasaki Mayor," *Los Angeles Times,* January 19, 1990; "Japanese See a Threat to Democracy in Shooting of Nagasaki Mayor," *Los Angeles Times,* January 20, 1990.

384   "Yamato-ism" and supposed uniqueness of Japanese language: "The 'Japan as Number One' Syndrome," by Kunihiro Masao, *Japan Echo* (Tokyo), volume XI, no. 3, 1984; "A New Japanese Nationalism," by Ian Buruma, *New York Times Magazine,* April 12, 1987. See also [460] for

leading expression of Japanese linguistic uniqueness, a concept with important political and nationalist resonance, and [317], especially Chapters 7 and 12, for a refutation.

385–86   Great Russian chauvinism: [558] p. 110. See also the prescient [347] pp. 38–39 on messianic component of Slavophile nationalism and its origins, and [548] throughout.

385–86   Pamyat's green camouflage and anti-Semitism: "The Secret of Pamyat's Success," *Wall Street Journal*, April 3, 1989; "Ideological Terror" (letter), *Present Tense*, November/ December 1989; the January 18, 1990, break-in, during which thugs broke into a meeting of the Moscow Central Writers Club and shouted threatening anti-Semitic slogans, was even condemned by the Soviet Public Anti-Zionist Committee, whose "outrage" is voiced in "Statement," *Literaturnaya Gazeta International*—"The Literary Gazette" (Moscow), March 1990. More general comments and reports in "Right-Wing Russians," *Christian Science Monitor*, June 18, 1987; "Anxiety Over Anti-Semitism Spurs Soviet Warning on Hate," *New York Times*, February 2, 1990; "Yearning for an Iron Hand," *New York Times Magazine*, January 28, 1990; "Anti-Semitic Rallies Prompt Protest," *Washington Post*, August 14, 1988; and "Don't Underestimate Anti-Semitic Soviet Fringe" (letter), *New York Times*, April 3, 1989. See also [352] pp. 66 and 86.

The split between secular reformers in the Soviet Union and the messianic Russian Christian nationalists is reflected by the difference between two great and courageous dissident figures—on the one hand, the late Nobel Prize winner and human-rights campaigner, Andrei Sakharov, who was a Western-oriented small "d" democrat, and on the other, Aleksandr Solzhenitsyn, who combines Great Russian nationalism with religious mysticism and a distinct hostility to democracy.

386   Schoenhuber: "Is Extremist or Opportunist Behind Bonn Rightist's Tempered Slogans?" *New York Times*, June 27, 1989.

CHAPTER 29   THE GLOBAL "K-FACTOR"

392   Intervening at deeper levels of nature: "A Small Revolution Gets Under Way," by Robert Pool, *Science*, January 5, 1990.

393   Most important breakthroughs: "Academy Chooses 10 Top Feats," *The Institute* (Institute of Electrical and Electronics Engineers), February 1990.

394   Comment on Soviet techno-military defeat: "Dithering in Moscow," *New York Times*, December 14, 1989.

CHAPTER 30   THE FAST AND THE SLOW

397–98   On tradition as an instrument for selecting technology: [120] p. 30.

398   On reduced risk in innovation: [120] p. 35.

399–400 Fading U.S. reliance on foreign cheap labor in apparel industry: "Made in the U.S.A.," by Ralph King, Jr., *Forbes*, May 16, 1988.

400   Tandy case: author interview with John Roach, Chairman, Tandy Corporation.

400   Arrow, Atkins, and *Forbes* quote are from "Made in the U.S.A.," by Ralph King, Jr., *Forbes*, May 16, 1988.

400   Benetton turnaround time: "Fast Forward," by Curtis Bill Pepper, *Business Month*, February 1989.

400–01   Chinese steel response-time: "Bureaucracy Blights China's Steel Industry," *Financial Times*, December 16, 1988.

404   On declining energy required for each unit of output: "The Technology Revolution and the Restructuring of the Global Economy," by Umberto Colombo, in "Proceedings of the Sixth Convocation of the Council of Academies of Engineering and Technological Sciences," in [521] pp. 23–31.

405   On new composites: "A Small Revolution Gets Under Way," by Robert Pool, *Science*, January 5, 1990.

406   Japan shifting investment away from Taiwan, Hong Kong: "Political Reforms Pave Way," *Japan Economic Journal*, October 1, 1988.

406   Umberto Colombo: from [521] p. 25.

407   On faster jets and the "three T's" project: "Moving Toward a Supersonic Age," by Jiro Tokuyama, Center for Pacific Business Studies, Mitsui Research Institute (Tokyo), 1988.

407   Perot's airport: "Can Ross Perot Save America?" by Peter Elkind, *Texas Monthly*, December 1988.

408–09   On poor-country arms race: "Becoming Smarter on Intelligence," by Henrik Bering-Jebsen, *Insight*, December 26, 1988–January 2, 1989.

409–10 Re dynamic minorities: "Foreigners in Britain, New Blood," *Economist,* December 24, 1988.

410–11 Brazil on pharmaceutical royalties: "Brazil: A Practical Guide to Intellectual Property Protection," *Business America,* January 18, 1988; and "Whose Idea Is It Anyway?" *Economist,* November 12, 1988.

412 World distribution of telephones: data from Anthony Rutkowski, Senior Counsel, International Telecommunications Union (Geneva).

CHAPTER 31 SOCIALISM'S COLLISION WITH THE FUTURE

413 For Gutenberg's impact, see "A Red Square Reformation," by Robert Conot, *Los Angeles Times,* March 11, 1990.

413 Khrushchev's famous taunt to the West was made to a group of Western diplomats and reported in "We Will Bury You," *Time,* November 26, 1956.

413–14 The 1956 turning point of the U.S. economy, from its Second Wave manufacturing base toward its present Third Wave service-information base, was spotted in "A New Social Revolution," *Fortune,* April 1958, which reported 1956 figures on the work force. Figures were based on a study by Murray Wernick, an economist at the U.S. Federal Reserve Board.

414 Gorbachev on "the age of information science": from remarks by Gorbachev before the Soviet Central Committee on February 5, 1990, provided by Tass English Language service. For rise of white-collar class in U.S.S.R. see "Gorbachev Politics," by Jerry F. Hough, *Foreign Affairs,* Winter 1989–90; also, "Médias sovietiques: censure glasnost," *Le Point,* March 12, 1990.

414 On current crisis of communism as reflection of Marx's concept of the "relations of production" obstructing the "means of production": Author argued this in 1983 in [68] p. 78; also in "Future Shock in Moscow," *New Perspectives Quarterly,* Winter 1987; in "A Conversation with Mikhail Gorbachev" (series) by Heidi and Alvin Toffler, *Christian Science Monitor,* January 5, 6, 7, 1987; and, following a meeting with then-Communist Party chief Zhao Ziyang in Beijing, in "Socialism in Crisis," *World Monitor,* January 1989. The same thesis is taken up by Yegor Ligachev, a

Soviet Politburo member and rival of Gorbachev, in *World Marxist Review* (Prague), July 1987, and by Valentin Fyodorov, Vice-Rector, Moscow Institute of Economics, in "Ignorance Is Bliss," *Literaturnaya Gazeta International*—"The Literary Gazette" (Moscow), March 1990.

416   Lenin's assumptions about the role of knowledge and culture are summed up in his 1905 statement that "Literary activity must become part of the overall proletarian cause, a 'cog and screw' in the united and great social-democratic mechanism."

417   For 19th-century utopians and socialists: see [366].

418   Razor blades in U.S.S.R.: "El fracaso del marxismo-leninismo," *El Heraldo* (Mexico City), December 3, 1989.

419   Socialism's "calculation problem": see [133] Chapter 26, entitled "The Impossibility of Economic Calculation Under Socialism," especially pp. 698–699; also [120] pp. 52–65 and 241.

420   Poland's "cold turkey" shift to market economics: "East Europe Joins the Market and Gets a Preview of the Pain," *New York Times*, January 7, 1990.

420–21 Squeezing agriculture: [377] pp. 212–229; also, more detailed reconstruction of debates about Preobrazhensky's socialist primitive accumulation (sometimes translated as "primitive socialist accumulation") in [351] pp. 163–180.

422   Is the dream dead? Belatedly awakening to the rise of a new, Third Wave system of wealth creation and its social correlatives, some Western socialists and communists are trying to regroup around new themes. See: "It's the End of the Road for Communism," extract from the speech of Martin Jacques, editor of *Marxism Today*, reported in *The Sunday Times* (London), November 26, 1989. Jacques stresses ecology, gender equality, an end to central planning, the support of the "civil society." Opposing individualism, however, he sums up with: "Socialism is about interdependence, about solidarity, about equality" and a "rebirth of collectivism."

CHAPTER 32   THE POWER OF BALANCE

424   India's military muscle: "India Rejects Japanese Criticism," and "Last Indian Contingent Leaves Maldives," both in *Jane's Defence Weekly*, November 18, 1989; also, "The Awak-

ening of an Asian Power," *Time,* April 3, 1989; and, "India Is Reportedly Ready to Test Missile With Range of 1,500 Miles," *New York Times,* April 3, 1989.

424   Spread of missiles: "Third World Missile-Making Prompts Campaign by C.I.A.," *New York Times,* March 31, 1989.

424   Capture of nukes by Islamic extremists or military rebels: "U.S. Worried by Nuclear Security in Unstable Soviet Empire," *Los Angeles Times,* December 15, 1989.

425   Ishihara's famous quote about Japan's potential for tilting the world power balance by selling advanced chips to the U.S.S.R: [318] pp. 3–5. Also, "Seeing a Dependent and Declining U.S., More Japanese Adopt a Nationalistic Spirit," *New York Times,* September 1, 1989.

426   Dangers of a financial collapse: "A Post-Panic System," by Alvin Toffler, *New York Times,* October 25, 1987; Greenspan's qualms are reported in "Market Globalization Risky, Greenspan Says," *Los Angeles Times,* June 15, 1989.

426   Central controls over national budgets and fiscal policies were proposed in the Delors Report, which was approved unanimously by a committee of EC central bankers and experts in April 1989. See: "Sovereignty and Fiscal Policy," *Financial Times,* July 18, 1989.

CHAPTER 33   TRIADS: TOKYO—BERLIN—WASHINGTON

430   Japanese military spending: Pressed by Washington to "share the burden" of defense, Japan's military budget has climbed steadily, bypassing that of France and West Germany, and standing either above or just below that of the U.K., depending on currency conversions and other factors. Only the U.S. and the U.S.S.R. clearly outrank Japan—but, to put matters in perspective, they do so massively. For more detail, see [285]. Also: "The State of Japan's Military Art," by Katherine T. Chen, *IEEE Spectrum,* September 1989; "Guess Who's Carrying a Bigger Stick?" by Peter Hartcher, *World Press Review,* July 1988; and [283].

431   On rise of a new military-industrial complex in Japan: "The State of Japan's Military Art," by Katherine T. Chen, *IEEE Spectrum,* September 1989; "The Sun Also Rises Over Japan's Technology," *Economist,* April 1, 1989. Also, take

account of discussions on joint venturing in defense field between Mitsubishi and Germany's Daimler-Benz (which owns Messerschmitt and Deutsche Aerospace). These have caused misgivings among many Europeans, as in "Colossal mariage," *Le Point* (Paris), March 12, 1990.

431   Takeshita on need to balance economic power with military clout: "Japan: A Superpower Minus Military Power," *Los Angeles Times*, September 11, 1988.

432   Comparative savings rates: "Japanese Thrift? The Stereotype Suffers a Setback," *Business Week*, August 14, 1989; and "U.S. Is Getting What It Asked for in Japan," *Los Angeles Times*, February 7, 1990.

433   Rising percentage of scientists and engineers in work force: "R&D in Japan vs. the United States," *IEEE Spectrum*, February 1989.

434   Fifth generation disappointment: "What Happened to the Wonder Child?" by Stuart Dambrot, *Business Tokyo*, February 1989; and " 'Fifth Generation Computer' Makes U.S. Debut," *Los Angeles Times*, October 12, 1989.

434   Survey of Japanese CEOs: "Technology Leadership: The Votes Are In," *Information Industry Insights* (Booz-Allen Hamilton), issue 18, 1988.

435   Newspaper readership: "Millions a Day," by Annamaria Waldmueller, *World Press Review*, April 1988.

435   Numbers of foreign students: "U.S. Failing to Close Its Education Gap With Japan," *Los Angeles Times*, January 7, 1990.

437–38   Lenin on united Europe: from *Sotzial-Demokrat*, no. 44, August 23, 1915. See his collected works.

439   All-Europe army: "Kohl Praises Prospect of European Army," *Financial Times*, December 14, 1988.

439   Possible costs to Europe of a U.S. military pull-out: [287] p. 37.

439–40   French and German military figures are from [286] pp. 47–48 and 59–64; for discussion of possible budget cuts, "Changing Attitudes in a Changing Europe Leave the Bundeswehr at the Crossroads," *Die Zeit* (Hamburg), December 22, 1989.

439–40   French policy of balancing West German arms: "Return of 'The German Menace,' " by Wolfgang J. Koschnick, *Worldview*, January/February 1977.

441–42   For EC's "glowing promises," see "Social Dimension of the Internal Market," a report of the Commission of the European Communities (Brussels), September 14, 1988, especially p. 4.

443 R&D increases: "Brussels Proposes Big Rise in High-Tech Research," *Financial Times*, July 26, 1989.

444 German patents and prizes: "Ein Wissenschaftswunder?" *Economist*, November 11, 1989.

444 Nixdorf's demise and Norsk's troubles: "Siemens Takeover of Nixdorf Creates a Giant," *Die Welt* (Bonn), January 13, 1990; and "Norsk Data Suffers Further Losses," *Financial Times*, February 7, 1990.

445 For heartland theory, see [336] and [302].

445 On carriers and their battle groups, see [286].

447 U.S. imports and exports: from "U.S. Foreign Trade Highlights, 1988," U.S. Department of Commerce; also, press release of U.S. Bureau of the Census, February 16, 1990, entitled "U.S. Merchandise Trade: December, 1989." See also: "New ITA Report Shows Major Improvement in U.S. Trade Performance in 1988," in *Business America*, November 6, 1989, pp. 6 and 12.

448 Patents: U.S. patents issued to residents of foreign countries have increased steadily since 1965, when only 23 percent went to non-U.S. residents. This percentage had doubled by 1989.

448 Relative numbers of engineers and scientists: "R&D in Japan vs. the United States," *IEEE Spectrum*, February 1989.

449 Computer industry comparisons: "Chiffres clés de l'informatique mondiale," by Michel Solis and Benedicte Haquin, *01 Informatique* (Paris), November 24, 1989; and "Staying American," *Economist*, August 19, 1989.

449 IBM's 16 million-bit chip: "IBM Announces Memory Chip Breakthrough," *Los Angeles Times*, February 11, 1990.

449 Growth of software market: "Competitive Software Industry Suits Up for Global Hardball," by Jeff Shear, *Insight*, July 10, 1989.

450 Ph.D.'s: Japan found it needed to increase its number of master's degree holders instead. The figures, 1975–1988: B.A.'s up 17 percent; Ph.D.'s, up 26 percent; but M.A.'s, up fully 84 percent.

453 Re Europe/U.S. vs. Japan: "The Changing Nature of the Relationship with America," in *Stuttgarter Zeitung*, January 19, 1990, expresses a widespread European view.

CHAPTER 34   THE GLOBAL GLADIATORS

456   Rushdie case: "Unrighteous Indignation," by Christian C.
        Muck, *Christianity Today,* April 7, 1989; "Hunted by an
        Angry Faith," *Time,* February 27, 1989; "Freedom-to-Write
        Bulletin," March 1989 (PEN American Center); and "PEN
        Defends Rushdie," Spring 1989 (International PEN USA
        Center West).

458   Catholic diplomacy: "Inextricably Involved," *America,* May
        23, 1987; "No Place to Run," *Time,* January 8, 1990; "Pope
        Warns Against Divisions in the East," *New York Times,*
        January 14, 1990; "Pope Urges United Christian Europe,"
        International Herald Tribune, August 22, 1989.

458   1918 document: [234] p. 256; "Pope, Visiting France, Calls
        for a United Europe," *New York Times,* October 9, 1988.

460   600 multinationals: "Come Back Multinationals," *Economist,*
        November 26, 1988.

460   Re non-nationality of global corporations: "Borderless Econ-
        omy Calls for New Politics," by Kenichi Ohmae, *Los Angeles
        Times,* March 26, 1990; also, "Who Is Us?" by Robert
        Reich, *Harvard Business Review,* January–February 1990.

462   Sir Francis Drake: [587] pp. 28–29.

462   Perot's hostage rescue: "Ross Perot to the Rescue," by Ron
        Rosenbaum, *Esquire,* December 1980; also, "Perot's Mis-
        sion Impossible," *Newsweek,* March 5, 1979.

465   Maurras quote, from [291] p. 6.

ACKNOWLEDGMENTS

No work of this scope can be written without the support of many people—friends, sources, and numerous outside experts who patiently offered insight and clarification. Our first thanks must go to Alberto Vitale, the former chairman, and Linda Grey, president and publisher, of Bantam Books for their endless, good-humored patience and enthusiasm for the project. During all the years of preparation Alberto and Linda steadfastly refused to hurry us, insisting instead that we take all the time necessary to do the best book possible.

That patience is appreciated and, we hope, will now be rewarded. Special credit must go, too, to Bantam executive editor Toni Burbank, whose deep understanding of this book and detailed editorial suggestions have made *Powershift* more integrated and readable than it might otherwise have been.

Strong support has come, too, for more than a decade, from Perry Knowlton of Curtis Brown, Ltd., our literary agency. From the start we have always been able to count on Perry for gentle, helpful advice about the business of publishing.

A similar vote of thanks must go to one of our oldest and most erudite friends, Dr. Donald F. Klein, director of research, New York State Psychiatric Institute, for his similarly detailed—but far more tart and challenging—criticisms all along the way.

Robert I. Weingarten and Pam Weingarten helped us understand certain financial headlines as they unfolded during the writing, while Al and Sally Burton helped keep us in touch with changes in television and the media. No better guides exist.

Sociologist Benjamin D. Singer of the University of Western Ontario plied us with journal articles, suggestions and enthusiasm throughout.

Tom Johnson of Nolan, Norton, Inc., and James P. Ware of the Index Group, both outstanding business consultants, contributed insights into some of the organizational changes and "info-wars" now changing the way business works.

From start to finish, Juan Gomez has been a more-than-model aide, maintaining our extensive research collection (amazingly able to put his finger on the most obscure journal article or clipping in our files), courteously fending off intrusions during the writing, arranging our complex travel schedule, and helping us with great intelligence, responsibility, and good cheer at every step. *Para* Juan, *muchas gracias.*

Words cannot express our feelings for our daughter, Karen, who worked under high pressure during the final weeks of manuscript preparation, double-checking and updating data in several key chapters, helping to prepare the notes and bibliography, and overseeing the index—in our case a more than mechanical matter, since its categories are designed for conceptual compatibility with the indices in *Future Shock, The Third Wave,* and our other works as well.

Finally, no such list can be complete without special thanks to Deborah E. Brown, who came aboard in the final months to perform a fine-grained, final fact-check on the manuscript, assuring that it is as up-to-date and correct as possible.

In a work of such broad scope, some errors and misinterpretations are inevitable. In addition, the continually accelerating pace of change means that many details risk obsolescence in the interval between the time they are written and the time they are read. It goes without need for elaboration that ultimate responsibility for any error remains with the authors, and not with the many people who have gone out of their way to assist them.

INDEX

A. H. Robins Company, 194
ABC (American Broadcasting Companies), 5, 336–37
Abcarian, Gilbert, 479
Abelson, Donald S., 137, 521
Abstraction, 279, 289, 293
Abu Dhabi, 56
Aburish, Said K., 305, 496
Acceleration, xviii, xix, xxi, 11, 32, 54–56, 110, 117, 123, 168, 178, 195, 214, 218, 222–23, 235–36, 237–38, 262, 263, 317, 350, 397–402, 409, 419, 427; in media, 350
Acceleration effect, 238, 398–99; in economy, 234
Access Tactic, 273. See also Info-tactics
Acco, Alain, 501
Accounting, 32, 62, 157–58, 171–72, 195, 203, 226, 231, 280–81; knowledge assets, 159, 231
Activism, electronic, 364–66
Acura (automobile), 435
Ada (software), 134
Adams, James, 491
Adams, Walter, 480
Adams, William, 349
Addison's disease, 8
Adhemar, Philippe, 510
Ad-hocracy, 191, 239, 264
Advanced Tactical Fighter (aircraft), 425
Advertising, 25, 48, 50, 81, 97, 258, 260, 280, 333–34, 338–39, 340, 343, 359, 363, 365
AEG (company), 308
Aerospace industry, 17, 115, 215, 218, 260, 305, 306, 393–94, 403–4, 407, 433, 443
Afanasyev, V., 498
Afghanistan, 219
Africa, 56, 303, 306, 310, 412, 455
African National Congress, 303
African-Americans, 52, 249, 250, 253, 451. See also Ethnicity; Minorities; Race and racism
Aganbegyan, Abel, 494
Aging, 10, 231, 432
Agnelli, Gianni, 30, 510
Agrarian society (First Wave), xx, 10, 28, 36, 63, 206–7, 244–45, 391, 405, 417, 421, 466
Agriculture, 46, 52, 70, 74, 266, 307, 420, 460, 466; as advanced industry (Third Wave), 411. See also Agrarian society (First Wave); Farmers

Aguren, Stefan, 480
AIDS, 275, 325–26
Aiken, South Carolina, 322
Air Canada, 260
Air Line Pilots Association, 227
Aircraft industry. See Aerospace industry
Airlines, 48, 65, 117, 227, 260, 324–25, 407. See also names of individual carriers
Airports, 227, 260, 407
Akihito, Emperor, 509
Akzo (company), 218
Alaska, 248, 377
Albania, 247, 249
Alcocer, Alberto, 30
Alcohol and alcoholism, 103, 196, 262, 340
Alfonsin, Raul, 302
Algeria, 382
Aliber, Robert Z., 481
Alienation, 61, 450
Alisjahbana, S. Takdir, 498
Allen, Frederick Lewis, 503
Allen, Woody, 451
Allende, Salvador, 303, 461
Alliances, 452–53, 464
Allied-Signal, Inc., 87
Allison, Graham T., 486
Alpha (aircraft), 439
Alphabet, 85
Alsace-Lorraine, 247
Althusser, Louis, 494
Amalrik, Andrei, 494
Amaterasu-omi-kami, 13, 34
Amazon, 311
Ambrose, Saint, 84–85
American Airlines, 117
American Express Company, 64, 67
American Hospital Supply, 122
American Interactive Media, 360–61
American Management Association, 224
American Public Power Association, 87
American Revolution, 370
American Society for Industrial Security, 154
American Telephone & Telegraph Company (AT&T), 28, 45, 110–12, 125, 131, 134–35, 145, 235, 364, 366; divestiture, 111–12
Amin, Samir, 491
AMR Corp., 117
Amstrad (company), 342
Analogy, 85, 370, 436
Anderson, Howard M., 238

Andrew, Christopher, 496
Anglo-Saxons, 382
Anning, Nick, 503
Ansaldo Nucleari Impiante, 308
Anti-Semitism, 243, 250, 253, 383, 385–86
Anti-urbanism, 386. *See also* Back-to-nature movement; Medievalism
Aoyama Gakuin University, 434
Apocalypse Brigade, The (Coppel), 462
Apollo (spaceship), 393
Apparel industry, 90, 100, 120, 124–25, 259, 399–400
Appel, Willa, 488
Apple Computer, Inc., 29, 61, 77, 134, 175, 197, 228–29
Applebaum, Herbert, 481
Appliance industry, 89–90
Aquino, Corazon, 349
Arabs, 56–57, 84, 330, 382–83
Arctic region, 315, 412
Argentina, 56, 260, 302–3, 316, 424
Armenia, 249, 327, 346, 385
Armonk, New York, 197
Arms, 17, 37, 296, 394, 403, 424, 431, 448, 462; chemical and bacteriological, 327, 408, 424, 458, 465; nuclear, 15, 202, 244, 298, 302, 315, 322–23, 394, 424–25, 430, 440, 458; proliferation of, 424–25. *See also* Defense industry; Military
Arnaz, Desi, 451
Arnold, Erik, 501
Aron, Patrice, 520
Aron, Raymond, 477, 489
Arrow Company, 400
Arthur Andersen & Company, 124
Artificial intelligence, 129, 289–90, 393, 425, 434
Artificial islands, 407
Arts, 43, 79, 107, 175, 245, 246, 323, 328–31, 371, 415–16, 421, 435–36, 451
Asahi Shimbun, 384
Asceticism, 377–79. *See also* Poverty
Ashby, W. Ross, 190, 501
ASI Market Research (company), 105
Asia, 310, 345, 400, 441
Asia/Pacific, U.S. military withdrawal from, 446
Assembly line, 60, 63, 208. *See also* Technology
Assumptions, xxi, 18, 116–17, 129, 143, 280, 285–86, 289, 292–93, 335, 340
Assumptions (*Powershift*), 473–76
Astrology, 373
Ataturk, Kemal, 374
Ataturk Dam, 311
Atkinson, Bill, 175–76, 523
Atlanta, 113, 227, 316, 333
Atlanta Braves (team), 334
Atlanta International Airport, 227–28. *See also* Airports; Power-Mosaics
Atlas-400, 115
Attali, Jacques, 443, 481, 499, 503
Atwater, Lee, 256, 530
Audio tapes, 328, 355
Augustine, Saint, 84
Auschwitz, 345
Australia, 124, 298, 302–3, 324, 340, 342, 357, 432
Austria, 194, 247, 439, 458
Austro-Hungarian empire, 439

Auto and auto industry, 7, 27, 42, 54, 58, 71, 75, 76, 78–79, 130, 169–70, 176, 197, 204–5, 210, 218, 237, 246, 260, 281, 288, 404, 420
Auto rental industry, 52, 227
Automatic translation, 115, 129, 362, 448
Automation Technology Products (company), 236
Aviation, 17, 254, 394, 448. *See also* Aerospace industry
Avis, Inc., 52
Ayling, S. E., 503
Azerbaijan, 249, 346, 385, 424
Aznavour, Charles, 338

BAA (company), 260
Babbitt (fictional character), 79
Bach, Johann Sebastian, 108
Back-Channel Tactic, 172, 270–72. *See also* Info-tactics
Back-to-nature movement, 373, 380, 386. *See also* Environment and environmentalism; Medievalism
Bacon, Francis, 1, 12, 16–17, 129, 499
Baden-Powell, Robert, 296, 533
Baden-Württemberg, 246
Baghdad, 305, 458
Bahro, Rudolf, 378, 380, 542
Bailey, George, 485
Bain, Lowell S., 211
Baker, James, 439
Bakker, Jim, 354
Baku, 297, 346, 413
Bakunin, Michael, 488
Balance of power, 428; global, 110. *See also* Power of balance
Baldwin, Roger N., 494
Balibar, Etienne, 494
Balkan region, 296
Ball, Desmond, 496
Balladour, Édouard, 58
Baltic region, 385, 438
Baltimore, 107
Banca Nazionale del Lavoro, 89
Banco Central (Spain), 30
Banco Español de Crédito, 30
Bandung conference, Indonesia, 391
Bangladesh, 80, 409
Bank of America, 145–46
Bank of Japan, 6, 58
Bankers Trust, 145
Banking, xxi, 3, 12, 27, 30, 39, 45, 47, 49, 52, 55–57, 64–67, 74, 102, 126, 128, 145–46, 162, 194, 209, 237, 238, 263, 306, 346, 374, 398, 399, 410, 411, 417, 432, 442. *See also* Banks, central; Finance
Banks, central, 58–59, 246, 247, 426, 441. *See also* Banking; Currency
Banque Internationale de Placement, 30
Bantam Doubleday Dell Publishing Group, 343
Bar codes, 98–101
Barbero, Manuel, 518
Barnes, Harry, 540
Barnouw, Erik, 485
Barthel, Manfred, 488
Base and superstructure, 421–22
Baseball, 97, 175–76, 334
BAT Industries PLC, 30
Batch processing, 54, 64
Batista, Fulgencio, 15

Batra, Raveendra N., 481
Baudrillard, Jean, 481
Baumbach, Lou, 501
Bauxite, 60, 87
Bavaria, 458
Baxter Health Care Corporation, 122
Bayer (company), 159
Baynes, J.C.M., 489
BBC (British Broadcasting Corporation), 338, 353
Bear, Stearns and Company, Inc., 122
Beatrice Companies, 52–53
Bechtel Corporation, 312
Bechtel National, Inc., 88
Becker, Gary S., 479
Bedminster, New Jersey, 366
Beethoven, Ludwig van, 108, 243
Beijing, 251, 276, 345, 356–58, 413, 431, 469
Beijing massacre, 469
Beijing University, 356
Beirut, 270–71, 468
Belgium, 58, 384
Beliaev, Igor, 542
Bell, Alexander Graham, 109–10, 113
Bell, C. Gordon, 524
Bell Labs, 112
Bell Telephone. See American Telegraph & Telephone Company (AT&T)
Belshaw, Cyril S., 481
Benetton Group (company), 125, 400
Benjamin, Robert I., 526
Bennett, Harry, 38
Bennett, James T., 486
Bennett, William, 325–26
Bentham, Jeremy, 477
Beradt, Charlotte, 496
Bergen, Candice, 335
Berger, Michael, 515
Berger, Peter L., 477
Bergman, Edward F., 486
Bering-Jebsen, Henrik, 545
Berkes, Leslie J., 202, 525
Berlin, Isaiah, 501
Berlin, 7, 243, 297, 383, 391, 440–41, 450, 455
Berlin Wall, 243, 353, 383
Berlo, David K., 501
Berlusconi, Silvio, 343, 346
Bertelsmann Group A.G. (company), 211, 341, 343, 539
Bessemer furnaces, 46
Best, Geoffrey, 489
Bethlehem Steel, 48
Beverage industry, 96
Beverly Hills, California, 47
Beverly Wilshire Hotel, 47
Bhagwati, Jagdish, 481
Bhopal, India, 169, 248, 377, 380
Bible, the, 362. See also Religion
Bibo, Istvan, 491
Bic (company), 96
Big business, 181, 219, 226, 231
Big Eight. See Accounting
Big is beautiful. See Diseconomies of scale; Economies of scale; Scale
Big Lie Tactic, 275. See also Info-tactics
Bijlmermeer, 450
Bilmes, Linda, 379, 542
Biology, 393
Biotechnology, xx, 226, 433, 450
Birlik movement, 385

Biryukov, N. S., 485
Black Death, 14
Black Entertainment Network, 336
Black Hundreds, 385
Black market. See Underground economy
Blacks. See African-Americans
Blazy, Jean-Claude, 491
Blight, James G., 490
Blow-back Tactic, 275. See also Info-tactics
Bluefield, West Virginia, 243
BMW (company), 136
Boaz, David, 486
Boca Raton, Florida, 197
Bodenheimer, Edgar, 477
Boesky, Ivan, 13, 51, 509
Bogart, Ernest L., 477
Bohemia, 458
Bok, Sissela, 499
Bolivia, 459
Bolwijn, Piet T., 516
Bombay, 461
Bond, James (fictional character), 311
Bonn, 7, 276, 383
Book of the Dead (Egyptian), 296
Book publishing, 327, 328, 330, 341–43, 450
Bookkeeping. See Accounting
Book-of-the-Month-Club, 343
Booth, Ken, 491
Border disputes, 438
Borgia family, 290
Borg-Warner Corporation, 53
Borow, Wendy, 508
Bosch, Roselyne, 525
Boston, 357
Boston Commercial Bulletin, 46
Boston Systems Group, Inc., 149
Bottomore, T. B., 477
Boudette, Neal E., 516, 519
Boulding, Elise, 480
Boundaries, 426, 445, 460. See also Organizational boundaries
Bower, Joseph L., 237, 527
Boy Scouts, 296, 345
Boyd, John, 520
Boynton Beach, Florida, 237
Bozic, Michael, 185
Brady, "Diamond Jim," 29
Brain drain, 409
Branson, Richard, 28
Braudel, Fernand, 503
Brazil, 56, 99, 249, 316, 343, 391, 406, 409–12, 418, 461
Brenner, Y. S., 481
Breton, Thierry, 488
Brewery industry, 139, 417
Brezhnev, Leonid, 200
Bridgestone (company), 218
Bridgestone Cycle Company, 86
Britain. See Great Britain
British Aerospace (company), 136, 260
British Broadcasting Corporation. See BBC
British Petroleum (company), 127
British Satellite Broadcasting (BSB), 338
British Telecom (company), 125, 260, 362
Brittany, 247
Brixton. See London
Broadcast News (movie), 352
Broadcasting. See Media
Brock, James W., 480
Brother Industries (company), 214
Brown, Anthony Cave, 497

Brown, Archie, 495
Brown, Lester R., 491
Bruce-Briggs, B., 486
Bruck, Connie, 52, 481, 512
Brussels, 7, 30, 201, 440, 455
Brzezinski, Zbigniew, 494
BSB. *See* British Satellite Broadcasting
Bucharest, 308, 350, 356, 391, 413
Buchwald, Art, 295
Budapest, 391
Buddhism, 375. *See also* Religion
Budget, 32, 145, 178, 263, 286, 291, 304, 306, 317, 368, 426, 432
Buenos Aires, 303
Bukharin, Nikolai, 421
Bulgaria, 302, 353, 438
Bundesnachrichtendienst, 301, 304
Bundespost, 362
Bundeswehr, 439. *See also* Germany
Bureaucracy, 11, 28, 32, 52, 110, 111, 165–79, 181, 195, 196, 200, 208, 214, 225, 239, 256–64, 268, 271–72, 281, 286, 291, 299, 314, 317, 372, 415–16, 418, 419–20, 435, 459; as anti-family, 188; as imperialist, 184; as machine, 173. *See also* Info-tactics; Organization
Burke, John, 504
Burlington Industries, Inc., 120, 124
Burlington Mills (company), 48
Burnham, James, 477, 491
Buro-baronial organization. *See* Organizational forms
Burrows, William E., 298, 497
Burstein, Daniel, 491
Burton, Al, 337, 538
Buruma, Ian, 491, 543
Bury, J.P.T., 504
Bush, George, xxi, 255–56, 263, 314, 459
Business, xx, 3, 11, 15, 18, 21, 36, 107, 109, 151, 179, 269, 395, 434; alliances, 181; celebrities, 25; colonies in, 184, 203; consortia, 181; knowledge base of, 84; violence in, 35–44. *See also* Info-tactics
Business, family in. *See* Family business
Business, small. *See* Small business
Business Environment Risk Information, 314
Business espionage, 153–62. *See also* Intelligence and espionage
Business Week, 104, 181
Byelorussia, 466
Byford, Mark, 379, 542
Byrne, John A., 484

Cable News Network. *See* CNN
Cable television. *See* Television, cable
CAD-CAM, 17
Cadbury Schweppes (company), 218
Cagle, Maury, 524
Cairo, 458
Calder, Kent E., 492
California, xxi, 29, 99, 102, 194, 285, 302, 309, 361
California Educational Computing Consortium, 360
Calvert, Peter, 477
Cambodia, 345
Cameras, 130, 131, 357
Campbell Soup Company, 98
Canada, 247, 260, 302, 308–9, 324, 358
Canal Plus, 338
Canal-10, 342

CANDU (nuclear reactor), 308
Canetti, Elias, 477
Canfield, Cass, 481
Cao-Garcia, Ramon J., 486
Capital, 21, 37, 45–47, 49, 50, 51–55, 57, 60–62, 68, 72, 81, 83–84, 88–91, 110, 144, 181, 219, 231, 238, 383, 398, 411, 420–21, 425–26, 433, 442; concentration of, 46, 50–52; democratization of, 48–52; intangibility of, 61–62, 68; knowledge as substitute for, 88–89; organizational, 231; super-symbolic, 62, 68, 76; symbolic, 61–62, 68; tangibility of, 60–61, 68. *See also* Money; Wealth
Capitalism, 20, 26, 32, 41, 43, 89, 231, 256, 258, 355, 371, 387, 413–14, 417, 420, 451, 514. *See also* Inter-capitalist conflict; Intra-capitalist conflict
Cappelli, William S., 533
Capra, Fritjof, 486
Caribbean region, 400, 464
Carlson, Richard, 540
Carnegie, Dale, 31
Caroz, Yaacov, 497
Carpet industry, 86
Cartagena, Colombia, 459
Carter, April, 486
Carter, Jimmy, 256, 303
CASE (software), 279
Cashman, Sean Dennis, 504
Cassen, Bernard, 132
Casson, Mark, 481
Castro, Fidel, 334, 538
Catalonia, 246–47
Catholic Church, 14, 46, 200, 301, 351, 354, 355, 373, 413, 458; as First Wave communications medium, 351. *See also* Religion
Caucasus region, 375
Causality, 367, 392, 467
CBS (Columbia Broadcasting System), 5, 169, 336–37
CD. *See* Compact disc
CD-I, 359, 360
CD-ROM, 75, 236
Ceausescu, Nicolae, 308, 348–50, 353–54, 356, 534, 540. *See also* Romania
Celebrityhood, 25, 28, 35
Cellular telephone, 361–62. *See also* Telephone
Censorship, 254, 265, 348, 353, 358, 359, 369–71, 410, 415, 429; globalization of, 456–57
Central America, 402, 462
Central banks. *See* Banks, central
Central Europe, xviii, 4, 166, 243, 247, 258, 302–4, 306, 338–39, 348–50, 354, 358, 391, 394, 412–13, 437–38, 440–44, 458
Central Intelligence Agency (CIA), 153, 170, 266, 269–70, 275, 286, 300, 303, 312–14, 317, 320, 327, 413, 424, 461
Central Television (Great Britain), 342
Centralization, 58–59, 110, 148–49, 155, 224, 246, 248, 391, 441
Ceramics, 87
Chackerian, Richard, 479
Chafetz, Ze'ev, 491
Chai, Ch'u, 488
Chai, Winberg, 488
Chain of command. *See* Hierarchy
Chan, Anita, 540
Chance, 14, 152, 252–53, 392, 467–68, 475

Change, xvii, xix, 83, 87, 152, 178, 229, 416, 475; rates of, 234, 397–98. *See also* Acceleration
Channel One, 336
Channels. *See* Bureaucracy
Chaos, 80, 252, 392, 468
Charisma, 166
Charities, 103
Charlemagne, 381
Chase Manhattan Bank, 141
Chauvinism. *See* Nationalism
Cheap labor, 32, 37, 125, 399, 400–401, 405–6, 441, 442
Checkerboard organization. *See* Organizational forms
Chemain, Jean, 246
Chemical and bacteriological weapons. *See* Arms
Chemical industry, 37, 54
Chen, Katherine T., 548
Chernobyl, 248, 284, 326–27, 377, 380
Chernow, Ron, 504
Cherry, Colin, 501
Cherry, Kittredge, 499
Chesneaux, Jean, 486
Chevrolet (automobile), 78
Chicago, 38, 47, 62, 292, 363
Chicanos, 250
Chief information officers (CIOs), 141–52, 160
Children, 13, 37, 208
Chile, 40, 303, 461
China, xx, 40, 84, 267, 271, 290, 297–98, 301, 310, 316, 330, 333, 345, 353, 355–58, 384, 391, 400, 406–7, 412–13, 421, 424, 441, 445–46, 451, 454, 461, 466, 469
Chinese Eastern Railroad, 296
Chinese in Southeast Asia, 200, 409
Chirac, Jacques, 305, 531
Chobetsu. *See* Chosa Besshitsu
Chocolat Poulain (company), 218
Chosa Besshitsu, 301, 304, 307
Christian Armenians, 375
Christian fundamentalism, 374–76. *See also* Fundamentalism, religious
Christian Science Monitor, 180
Christianity, 355, 374, 375, 376, 378–79, 413, 458, 544. *See also* Catholic Church; Church and State; Religion; Secularism
Christmas, 191
Chrysler Corporation, 77
Chrysler-Mitsubishi Diamond-Star Plant, 206
Chukaku-ha, 259
Chun Doo Hwan, 355
Church and State, 351, 354, 376, 456–58, 465
Churchill, Winston, 10, 276, 532
CIA. *See* Central Intelligence Agency
Cincinnati Milacron, Inc., 310
CIO, 149
CIOs. *See* Chief information officers
Cirlot, J. E., 499
Citibank, 108, 143
Citizens' groups, 324, 347
Citroën (automobile), 169
City-states, 246–47
Civikly, Jean M., 501
Civil liberties, 321, 325, 371; and intelligence and espionage, 304
Civil rights, 244, 347
Civil service, 165–66, 263, 283, 314

Civil society, 322, 324, 347, 547; as part of information system, 410; representation in global institutions, 465; role in development, 410
Civil War, 28
Clark, David W., 236
Class, 355–56, 474
Claus, Clyde R., 145–46
Cleveland, Harlan, 330–31, 537
Clock factories, 37
Close, Upton, 492
Clough, Shepard B., 481
CNMA (standard), 136
CNN (Cable News Network), 333–34, 352, 357
Coates, Joseph, 161, 523
Coca-Cola Company, 52
CoCom. *See* Coordinating Committee on Multilateral Export Controls
Cognitariat, 75
Cognitive theory, 427
Cohen, Stephen F., 494
Cohn, Barry, 508
Coker, F. W., 486
Colby, Charles C., 492
Colby, William F., 303, 314
Cold War, 255, 295, 306, 374, 402, 403, 428–29
Coldicutt, Ken, 497
Collins, Cardiss, 325
Collins, Pat, 99
Colombia, 459
Colombo (fictional character), 451
Colombo, Umberto, 404, 406, 502, 545
Colonia Versicherung A.G. (company), 30
Colonialism. *See* Imperialism
Colonies, in business, 184
Columbia Pictures Entertainment, Inc., 218, 341, 432
Combustion Engineering, Inc., 308
Comic strips, 25
Commager, Henry Steele, 486
Commerzbank A.G., 58
Commissar organization. *See* Organizational forms
Communication flows, in capitalism, 420; in socialism, 420
Communication modes, 351–58
Communications, 18, 54, 85, 107, 109, 111–13, 142, 145, 150–51, 161, 165, 173–74, 188, 214, 223, 229, 254, 255, 261, 397–98, 413, 415, 420, 428, 450, 458; First Wave, 351, 354; informal, 222–23; non-verbal, 182; power content of, 276–77; Second Wave, 354; Third Wave, 354–55. *See also* Media; Networks, electronic; Telecommunications
Communism. *See* Socialism and Marxism
Communist Party (China), 356
Communist Party (U.S.S.R.), 195
Communist Party, Central Committee of (U.S.S.R.), xxi
Compact disc (CD), 360
Compagnie Générale d'Électricité (company), 260
Compaq Computer Corporation, 77
Company, The. *See* Central Intelligence Agency (CIA)
Competing in Time (Keen), 122
Competition, foreign, 5, 10, 32, 70, 71, 125, 307, 361, 369

Competition, hyper-, 412, 452–53, 466
Complexity, 168, 251, 262, 279, 293, 392
Compton Advertising, 339
Computer industry, 5, 27, 29, 30, 61, 70, 77,
    98, 113, 120, 133–38, 153–54, 197,
    330, 361, 400, 411, 444, 449; chips, 225,
    226, 234, 425, 433, 449, 453; crime,
    282; espionage, 160; services, 122, 142,
    144, 449; software, 100, 123, 133–35,
    136, 139, 146, 165, 215, 228, 278–80,
    282–83, 285, 307, 329, 331, 360, 408,
    411, 422, 425, 433–34, 449
Computer-aided design, 89, 120
Computers, xx, 9, 17, 47, 49, 54–55, 75, 78,
    82, 85, 88, 90, 106, 113–14, 123, 190,
    246, 255, 280–83, 284, 287, 291, 323–24,
    348, 350, 352, 357, 361, 369–70,
    392–93, 395, 398, 411–12, 427, 441, 460,
    528; government dependence on, 281;
    impact on organization, 141–52, 167,
    174–78, 220–21, 223; integration of,
    108, 122, 135–37, 148–50, 252; literacy,
    278; sabotage, 216, 283; types, 114,
    120, 133–34, 147–50, 174–75, 177, 197,
    220–23, 230, 235–36, 311, 321, 363,
    368, 407, 434, 444, 448–49; virus,
    282–83, 460. *See also* Data bases;
    Networks, electronic
Computers and politics, 278, 283, 284–85,
    348–50, 365, 369–70, 373, 414, 441.
    See also Meta-tactics
Concordia, Kansas, 343
Conde, Mario, 30
Conference Board, 157
Conference of Mayors, 292
Confindustria, 89
Confucian Economic Community, 466
Confucius, 469
Congressional Office of Technology Assess-
    ment, 209
Congressional Research Service, 292
Congruence: between changes in business and
    the "intelligence industry," 299–300; of
    political and economic structures, 245,
    259–60
Congruence theory. *See* Congruence
Connectivity of media. *See* Media as system
Connery, Sean, 15–16
Conot, Robert, 546
Conrad, Joseph, 318, 536
Conspiracy, 253
Consultants, 33, 145, 156–57, 181
Consumer, xx, 31, 52, 65, 72, 83, 102–5, 168,
    228, 236–37; data, 102–5, 119, 123,
    143, 158, 239; information "loan," 102–3;
    needs, 418. *See also* Prosumer
Container Corporation, 259
Continental Illinois (bank), 194
Continuous flow, 54, 64, 400
Contraception, 14, 103, 194
Contracting out, 231, 261. *See also*
    Privatization; Vertical integration
Contras, 263
Cook, Don, 504
Cooper, A. Duff, 504
Coordinating Committee on Multilateral
    Export Controls (CoCom), 310
Coppel, Alfred, 462
Copper, 60, 63, 87, 114
Copying machines, 350, 357, 362
Copyright, 326, 329, 330

Corbley, Kevin, 535
Corey, Lewis, 504
Cornell University, 176, 365
Corning, Inc., 201
Cornwell, Rupert, 481
Corporate cultures, 219
Corporation, 166, 178; divorce from wealth
    creation, 231; as knowledge enhancer,
    153, 157; non-national, 311, 460–65;
    reduced functions of, 231–32; repre-
    sentation in global institutions, 463–65.
    See also Business; Multinational
    corporations
Corruption, 14, 29, 41–42, 111, 169, 266–67,
    307, 349, 356, 374, 381, 401, 403, 418,
    442, 459
Cortina, Alberto, 30
Cosby, Bill, 451
Cosby Show, The (TV program), 131
Coser, Lewis A., 499
Cosmetics industry, 53, 96, 121
Costello, John, 497
Coudert Brothers, 39
Counterfeiting, 65, 329
Counter-intelligence, 161, 304, 327. *See also*
    Business espionage; Intelligence and
    espionage
Cowboy as symbol, 12
Coxsedge, Joan, 497
Crankshaw, Edward, 504
Cray (supercomputer), 114, 363
Creativity, 158, 213, 370
Credit cards, 64–67, 102, 126, 162. *See also*
    Money
Crenshaw, Martha, 492
Crenson, Matthew A., 486
Creveld, Martin Van, 490
Crime, xxi–xxii, 35, 38, 42, 51, 118, 169, 253,
    282, 290, 314, 332, 374, 401, 463, 465
Crisis, 168–69, 171, 193–94, 219, 245, 248,
    261–62, 290, 366, 370, 374, 377,
    380–81; management of, 193–94
Crisis of bureaucracy, 173. *See also*
    Bureaucracy
Crisis of German Ideology, The (Mosse), 380
Crissey, Brian L., 486
Croatia, 247, 458
Cross, James Eliot, 490
Cross-national political representation, 464
Cross-national research, 443
Cross-national voting, 464
Crowds, 356; as media, 351
Crowther, Samuel, 481
Crozier, Brian, 477, 504
Crozier, Michel, 479, 486
Crupi, James, 246, 529
Cryptography, 162, 299, 307
CSX Corporation, 76, 87
Cuba, 15, 302, 334, 402
Cuban missile crisis, 272
Cuban-Americans, 249
Cubbyholes. *See* Bureaucracy
Cuccia, Enrico, 510
Cultural identity, 250, 384
Cultural impact, 428
Culture, 12, 86, 118, 247, 250, 254, 326, 331,
    335, 340–41, 367, 373, 381, 382–86,
    395, 405, 416, 421, 428, 434–36, 444,
    450–51, 452, 467, 474. *See also* Arts;
    Knowledge; Popular culture
Culture, de-massified, 343–44

Culture, popular. *See* Popular culture
Culture shock, 243
Curaçao, 461
Currency, 56, 58, 63, 65–67, 116, 119, 165,
  168, 202, 246, 306, 309, 364, 399, 426,
  462. *See also* Capital; Finance; Money
Curtin, Philip D., 504
Curtis, James E., 499
Custine, Marquis de, 504
Customer data. *See* Consumer
Customization. *See* De-massification
CYA Memo. *See* Forced-to-Know Tactic
Czechoslovakia, 80, 99, 347, 439, 441

Da Vinci, Leonardo, 45
Dai-Ichi Mutual (company), 119
Daiwa (company), 119
Dale, Ernest, 479
Dalkon Shield, 194
Dallas, 153–54, 246, 400
Dambrot, Stuart, 549
Dancer Fitzgerald Sample, 339
Daniels, Robert V., 494
Dark Ages, 255, 372, 377–78, 381–82, 386,
  387. *See also* Medievalism
Darvi, Andrea, 498
Data (defined), 18
Data bases, 29, 104, 119–20, 143, 148, 150,
  174–78, 187, 203, 221, 227, 282,
  287–90, 412; government, 321
Data priesthood, 147–50. *See also* Information
  systems
Data protection legislation, 104, 323–24
Datamation, 120, 142, 149, 289
Datsun, 58
Davidson, William H., 492
Davis, Stanley M., 479
Day, Benjamin, 332–34, 345
Day care, 53, 447
De Benedetti, Carlo, 30, 510
De Brunhoff, Suzanne, 494
De Gaulle, Charles, 41, 490, 511
De Girardin, Émile, 332, 345
De Graff, John, 542
De Huszar, George B., 499
De Michelis, Gianni, 438
De Visscher, François M., 181
Deacon, Richard, 495
Debt crisis, 56
DeButts, John, 28
Decentralization, 59, 148, 149, 155, 183,
  246–47, 264, 318, 372
Decision load, 211
Decision-making, 168–69, 246, 276, 281–82,
  289; non-programmable, 262; pace of,
  234, 238, 401
Decisions-in-process. *See* Decision-making
Deep Throat, 267
Dees, Morris, 249
Defense Advanced Research Projects Agency
  (DARPA), 17, 160, 448
Defense industry, 28, 156–57, 260, 296, 297,
  305, 431, 446. *See also* Arms; Military
Defense Intelligence Agency (U.S.), 300
Defense Science, 17
Definitions: data, 18; First Wave, xx; future
  shock, xix; information, 18; knowledge,
  18–19, 409; power, 14, 452, 508–9; power
  triad, 12–13; powershift, 17–18, 34, 44,
  393, 452; Second Wave, xx; Third Wave,
  xx; violence, 13, 40–41

De-industrialization, 25
Deloitte & Touche, 148
Demagogue, 255
DeMaio, Harry B., 522
De-massification: culture, 343–44; economics,
  186, 200; finance, 54, 442; intelligence
  and espionage, 313, 318; Japanese, 123,
  436; markets, xx, 17, 183, 442; media, xx,
  251, 334, 336–37, 341, 344; organizational,
  183, 185–87, 202, 221, 226, 239; political,
  251–52; production, xx, 25, 54, 86–87,
  123, 140, 181, 183, 237–38, 245, 251,
  340, 351, 442, 449; service sector, 54;
  social, 167, 250, 436
Democracy, 11, 243–44, 244–45, 253, 254,
  266, 281, 295, 319, 343, 353, 357,
  368–69, 372–74, 376, 379, 380–81, 383,
  385–87; knowledge problem of, 293;
  mosaic, 251, 253, 264; obsolescence of,
  255. *See also* Mass democracy
Democracy, Second Wave. *See* Mass democracy
Democratic Party (U.S.), 111, 251, 320, 322
Denationalization. *See* Privatization
D'Encausse, Helene Carrere, 494
Deng Xiaoping, xx, 357
Denhart, Robert B., 479
Deniability, *See* Need-Not-to-Know Tactic
Denman, D. R., 481
Denmark, 58, 323, 324
Depression, the Great, 72
Derivatives, 62
Dertouzos, Michael, 154
Descartes, René, 81
Desire, 13, 473, 513; in agrarian societies
  (First Wave), 514; in industrial societies
  (Second Wave), 514; in super-symbolic
  societies (Third Wave), 514
De-skilling, 77
De-synchronization, 183
Determinism, 203, 392, 467
Detroit, 169, 325
D'Eustachio family, 180, 187–88
Deutschebank, 441
Developing economies. *See* Non-industrial societies
Development strategies, 379, 394, 397–412,
  416, 420–21, 466. *See also* Non-
  industrial societies; Slow economies
De-verticalization. *See* Vertical integration
DGSE (Direction Générale de Sécurité
  Extérieur), France, 300
Dick Tracy, 362–63
Dickson, David, 535
DIE (Romania), 308
Digital Equipment Corporation (DEC), 61, 108,
  120, 134–35, 149, 198, 203, 213, 448–49
Dilks, David, 496
Dillingham, Susan, 515
Dilo, 115
DiLorenzo, Thomas J., 486
Diner's Club, 67
Diplomacy, 266, 271, 329, 459
Direct broadcast satellite, 336–38, 342, 435
Direct mail. *See* Marketing
Disaster, 326–27, 346, 380–81
Disease, 8, 14, 275, 325–26, 340. *See also* Health
Diseconomies of scale, 181, 221–22
Dissipative structures, 393
Distribution, 11, 25, 59, 101, 105, 121, 123,
  332, 339, 340; as information system,
  76, 105. *See also* Marketing; Mass
  distribution; Retailing; Sales; Supermarkets

Diversity, social, 167–68. *See also* De-massification
Divestitures, 219, 259. *See also* American Telephone & Telegraph Company (AT&T); Privatization; Takeovers
Divine Right, 468
Division of labor, 299
Diwan, Romesh, 481
Dixon, Norman, 490
DNA, discovery of, 392
Dobrynin, Anatoli, 272, 532
Doctors. *See* Health
Dodd, Alfred, 504
Doddington, George, 154
Doi, Takeo, 499
Dokikai system, 172–73
Donner, Frank J., 497
Donovan, Paul F., 524
Donzelot, Jacques, 479
Dorpalen, Andreas, 492
Double-Channel Tactic, 272–73. *See also* Info-tactics
Dow Jones & Company, Inc., 109
Drake, Sir Francis, 462, 551
Dresden, Germany, 353
Dresdner Bank, 30
Dressler, Fritz R. S., 481
Drexel Burnham Lambert, 47, 49–51. *See also* Milken, Michael
Drexler, Anton, 252
Drexler, K. Eric, 502
Dribble Tactic, 274. *See also* Info-tactics
Dror, Yehezkel, 254, 479, 530
Drugs, 13, 153, 262–63, 266, 373, 374, 447, 450
Drugstores, 104. *See also* Retailing
Dryakhlov, Nikolai, 502
Du Pont de Nemours & Company, E. I., 108, 322
Dubro, Alec, 492
Duke, Benjamin, 499
Duke University, 129
Dumaine, Brian, 522
Duncan, Hugh Dalziel, 501
Duval, Olivier, 518
Duyvendak, J. J., 477
Dvořák, Antonin, 338
Dyslexia, 196
Dyson, Esther, 520–21

EA Falcon (automobile), 205
Eagleburger, Lawrence, 314
East Asia, 405, 437. *See also* Pacific region
East Berlin, 295
East Germany. *See* Germany
Eastern Europe. *See* Central Europe
Eastman Kodak Company, 245
Eastwood, Clint, 451
Ebasco Services, Inc., 88
Eberle, Charles, 215
Eckhart, Meister, 378
Ecological warfare, 311–12
Ecology. *See* Environment and environmentalism
Economics (Samuelson and Nordhaus), 31
Economics, xx, 61, 233–34, 235; concept of value in, 81, 82–83, 153, 158, 187, 230–31; new, 80–83; power in, 31–32
Economies of scale, 52, 181, 221–22, 442
Economist, The, 65, 381

Economy, 4, 21, 27, 65, 67, 69, 83, 91, 107, 235; congruence with political structures, 245, 259–60; de-massification of, 186, 200–201; fast and slow, 397–412, 442–43; hidden subsidies in, 42; knowledge base of, 84; rate of change in, 399; violence in, 35–44
Economy, poverty as goal of. *See* Poverty
Economy, Second Wave. *See* Industrial society
Economy, service sector. *See* Service sector
Economy, super-symbolic. *See* Super-symbolic economy (Third Wave)
Eco-spasm, 386
EDI (Electronic Data Interchange), 90, 120–21, 125, 160–61
Edison, Thomas, 46, 109
Education, xix, 3, 4, 11, 15, 65, 73, 79, 165, 166, 178, 211, 231, 244, 258, 263, 325, 335, 368–69, 371, 374, 375, 395, 406, 409, 428, 429, 433, 435, 444, 447, 450
Edwards, Jon R., 284
Egalitarianism. *See* Equality
Egypt, 118, 296, 314, 316, 328, 333, 393, 402, 411, 424
Ehrlich, Judith Ramsey, 481
E-I. *See* Extra-intelligence
Ekman, Paul, 499
El Salvador, 346
El Sawy, Omar A., 524
Election Watch, 284
Elections, 251, 283, 284–85, 349
Elections, cross-national, 464
Electric Company (TV program), 368
Electrolux (company), 89
Electronic activism, 364–66
Electronic cottage, xx
Electronic countermeasures. *See* Intelligence and espionage
Electronic Data Interchange. *See* EDI
Electronic infrastructure, 369
Electronic mail, 108
Electronic money, 162. *See also* Credit cards; Money
Electronic networks. *See* Networks, electronic
Electronic politics, 365–66
Electronic proletariat, 209–10
Electronic sabotage, 161
Electronic voting, 284–85
Electronics, xx, 71, 79, 132, 153, 195, 235, 359, 395
Elias, Norbert, 504
Elites, 14, 44, 207, 330, 335, 363, 373, 374, 403, 436–37
Elizabeth II (queen of England), 247, 529
Elkind, Peter, 545
Elon, Amos, 492
Ely, Gerald H., 144, 521
Élysée Palace, xxi
Emigré groups, 254
Emmott, Bill, 492
Employee ownership, 48. *See also* Workers
Employment, 50, 69–70, 71–74, 78, 180, 181, 226, 362. *See also* Work
Energy, 71, 88, 119, 209, 379, 404, 411, 418, 450; knowledge as substitute for, 87–88. *See also* Nuclear industry
Engels, Friedrich, 416, 495, 528
Engineering, simultaneous. *See* Simultaneous engineering (SE)
Engineers and engineering, 34, 167, 171, 212, 308, 369, 393, 433, 448, 450

English language, 115, 186, 448
Enlightenment, the, 373, 375, 379
Entertainment, 39, 103
Entertainment, inadvertent content of, 335–36
Entrepreneurs, 28, 49, 226, 398
Environment and environmentalism, 31, 82, 168–69, 176, 245, 248–49, 251, 258, 264, 281, 289, 290–91, 311–12, 322, 334, 346, 374, 377–81, 383, 386, 393, 395, 418, 436, 441, 443, 444, 462, 467, 474, 542; crisis of, 377; eco-blackmail, 248; eco-espionage, 311–12; eco-fascism, 380–81, 386; eco-terrorism, 377; eco-theologues, 378, 381; eco-vandalism, 377; eco-warfare, 311–12; eco-welfare payments, 249; fundamentalism in, 377–81
Environmental Protection Agency (U.S.), 176, 291
Environmental Research Institute of Michigan, 315
Enzensberger, Hans Magnus, 485
Epistemology, 17, 370. *See also* Knowledge
Epstein, Edward Jay, 512
Equality, 201, 213, 415, 474, 475, 547
Equicor (company), 141
Equilibrium and non-equilibrium, 252, 254, 393, 474
Equilibrium theory, 379
Equitable Life, 141
ERDAS, Inc., 316
Erno Laszlo (company), 340
Error, value of, 213–14
Error detection, 415
Eskimos, 280
Espionage. *See* Intelligence and espionage
Espionage, industrial. *See* Business espionage
Espionage in Silicon Valley (Halamka), 155
Esprit program, 137
Ethics, information and, 118, 151
Ethnic networks, 200. *See also* Networks, human
Ethnicity, 249–50, 251, 341, 352, 383, 385, 435, 451, 465; conflict over, 247–48, 249–50, 264, 385, 438, 445, 447, 541–42. *See also* Nationalism; Race and racism
Eudes, Yves, 543
Euphrates River, 311
Eureka 95 project, 132
Euroflex, 180, 188
Europe, xviii, 6–7, 14, 21, 26, 30, 37, 45, 48, 71, 116, 200, 206, 246, 257, 263, 305, 317, 326–27, 333, 337–38, 351, 352, 368, 381–84, 392, 410, 423, 428–29, 437–40, 443–44, 445–46, 450–55, 458, 464; business and economy, 56–57, 58, 64, 70, 74, 89, 120–21, 132–33, 136–38, 173, 181, 218, 223, 226–37, 246, 257, 310, 313, 340, 342–43, 393, 395, 400, 407–8, 411, 426, 432, 435, 441, 443–44, 447, 449, 453–55
Europe, economic power of, 440–43
Europe, knowledge-power of, 443–45
Europe, military power of, 439–40
Europe, role of Germany, 438–45
Europe, strategy of, 441–43, 445, 453–55
Europe, U.S. military withdrawal from, 439, 446
European Bank for Reconstruction and Development, 443
European Community, 7, 136–37, 139, 181, 246, 305, 310, 330, 362, 382, 404, 426, 438–43, 463–64, 469

European Community, obsolete assumptions of, 442
European Community as model, 464
European Community Committee on Science and Technology, 404
European Community Council of Foreign Ministers, 438
European Community Council of Ministers, 137
European Community strategy (Second Wave), 442
European integration as response to system for wealth creation (Third Wave), 438
European Parliament, 383
Europe-Japan alliance, 453–55
Evans, Michael K., 515
Evans, Thomas G., 481
Everhart, Robert B., 499
Existentialism, 444
EXIT (network), 124
Expert systems, 17, 75, 289–90, 427
Experts, xvii, 8, 172, 262, 288–90. *See also* Specialization
Extra-intelligence, 107–8, 123, 127–29, 398, 407–8, 435. *See also* Networks, extra-intelligent
Extremism, 243, 247–48, 250, 253, 260, 374–76, 382–87, 458
Exxon Corporation, 194, 337
Eyck, Erich, 504
Ezoe, Hiromasa, 41

Facsimiles. *See* Fax
Factors of production, 81–82, 84–85, 238, 399
Fads, 166, 335
Fairfield Inn (hotel chain), 156
Falklands/Malvinas war, 303
Falsehood, 18–19, 85
Fam-firms. *See* Family business
Family, xix, 8, 10–11, 36–37, 48, 207, 208, 231–32, 244, 251, 374, 447, 459; economic role of, 189; as work regimen enforcer, 207
Family business, 180–82, 187–89
Fanaticism, 171, 248, 254–55, 264, 318, 355, 374–76, 458, 459–60
Farmers, 52, 97, 280. *See also* Agriculture
Fascism, 379–80, 383–84, 386, 442. *See also* Naziism; Totalitarianism
Fashion, 124, 329, 335, 435, 451
Fast economies, 397–412, 442. *See also* Acceleration; Acceleration effect
Fast foods. *See* Restaurant industry
Fast-cycle company. *See* Acceleration
Favoritism, 188
Fax, 115, 119, 235, 280, 350, 352, 357–58, 362, 363–64
Febvre, Lucien, 504
Federal Aviation Administration (U.S.), 227, 324–25
Federal Bureau of Investigation (FBI), 200, 253, 290
Federal Express Corporation, 61, 75, 398
Federal Reserve Board (U.S.), 426
Federal Statistics Users Council (U.S.), 288
Feedback, 379, 416, 421–22, 528
Feigenbaum, Edward, 499
Feinberg, Mark, 512
Felix, Christopher, 497
Feudalism, 43, 195–96, 381
F4-F (aircraft), 439
Fiat (company), 30
Fiber optics, 131, 364, 407

Field, G. Lowell, 478
Fields, George, 105
Fighter aircraft, 394. See also *names of various types*
Finance, 6, 26–27, 38–39, 45–50, 51–56, 58–59, 62, 64, 67, 75, 81, 86, 89–90, 119, 127, 143–45, 165, 195, 209, 219, 221, 237, 247, 281, 326, 426, 432, 441, 446; de-massification of, 54, 442; liberalization of, 26, 57, 383, 418, 426; of media, 339. See also Banking; Capital; Currency; Money
Financial Times, 30, 80, 135, 205, 218, 226, 284, 316, 350
Fine, Ben, 494
Fingleton, Eamonn, 511
Finn, Judith A., 527
Finney, Martha I., 536
Firestone Tire & Rubber Company, 218
First, Ruth, 478
First Boston, Inc., 144
First Wave (defined), xx
First Wave civilization. See Agrarian society
Fisher, Anne B., 507
Fisher, William, 539
Fitzgerald, Karen, 523
Flanders, 247
Flat Rock, Michigan, 206
Fleischmann's (margarine), 103
Fletcher, Raymond, 490, 494
Flex-firm, 180–203
Flex-time, 183
Flick scandal (Germany), 41–42
Float, 55, 64
Flores, Fernando, 502
Florida, 102, 293
Fluctuations, 474
Foamy (shaving cream), 97
Fomin, Aleksandr, 272
Fonda, Jane, 334
Food and food industry, 43, 52–53, 58, 65–66, 71, 77, 96, 104, 119, 124, 139, 245, 282, 405, 409, 411, 417–18, 528. See also Restaurant industry
Forbes, 27, 53, 400
Force. See Violence
Forced-to-Know Tactic, 273–74. See also Info-tactics
Ford, Daniel, 490
Ford, Franklin L., 486
Ford, Henry, II, 29
Ford, Maggie, 284
Ford Australia (company), 205–6
Ford Motor Company, 38, 75, 77, 121, 176, 224, 460
Foreign aid, 37, 56, 403
Foreign Excellent Trench Coat Company, 314
Foreign exchange. See Currency
Foremost McKesson (company), 122
Forgery. See Masked Source Tactic
Fortune, 28, 156, 280
Fortune 500, 77
Foster, Hal, 499
Foucault, Michel, 499
Fourier, Charles, 417
Fox TV network, 342. See also Media
France, 5, 6, 28, 30, 39, 41, 58, 61, 64, 70, 96, 98, 115, 132, 135, 218, 226, 246, 256, 260, 267, 282, 297, 300–301, 303–5, 308–10, 314–15, 324, 332, 338, 340, 343–44, 362, 439–41, 444, 448, 465
France Telecom (company), 115, 362

Franchising, 187
Franck, Thomas M., 486
Frank, Charles R., Jr., 481
Frankel, Boris, 495
Frankfurt, 58, 117
Frankfurter Zeitung, 297
Franz-Josef, Emperor. See Austro-Hungarian empire
Freches, José, 485
Frederick Atkins Inc., 400
Free information, 330
Free market ideology, 82
Freedom, 368, 371
Freedom of expression, 326, 356, 368–71, 372, 384, 386, 393, 415; economic role of, 410
Freedom of information, 151, 324–26, 370
Freedom of information legislation, 266, 294, 323–24
French Revolution, 357, 370
Friedgut, Theodore H., 495
Friedlander, Saul, 496
Friedman, Alan, 481
Friedman, Milton, 31
Fringe benefits, de-massified, 183
Frolov, I., 495
Front groups. See Masked Source Tactic
Frum, David, 512
F-16 (aircraft), 425
FSX (aircraft), 306, 431
Fuchs, Klaus, 13, 509
Fuchs, Peter, 516
Fugu Plan, 410 n
Fuji Heavy Industries (company), 431
Fujisankei Communications Group, 341
Fujitsu (company), 5, 61, 134, 449
Fuller, Samuel, 448
Fundamentalism, ecological. See Environment and environmentalism
Fundamentalism, religious, 374–76, 382, 385–86, 541–42. See also Religion
Furniture industry, 180
Future shock (defined), xix
Future shock (phenomenon), xix
Future Shock (Toffler), xvii, xix–xx, xxii, 54, 69, 191, 234, 334, 336, 352
Future-consciousness, 395, 444
Futurism, xx, 69, 71
Fuzzy logic, 427
Fyodorov, Valentin, 546

Gabriel, Richard A., 490
Galbraith, John Kenneth, 31, 478–79, 481
Gambling industry, 26
Games, interactive, 361, 365, 368
Gardels, Nathan, 542
Gardner, Howard, 499
Gardner, Martin, 488
Garwood, Darrell, 497
Garzinsky, Joe, 501
Gassman, Bill, 149, 522
Gastonia, North Carolina, 38
Gates, John Warne "Bet a Million," 29
Gatrad, 115
GATT. See General Agreement on Tariffs and Trade
Gatwick Airport, 260
Gay, Verne, 538
GCHQ. See Government Communications Headquarters
GCR. See Groupement de Contrôles Radioélectriques

GenCorp Automotive, 78, 211
Gender, 474, 475, 547
Genentech, 61
General Agreement on Tariffs and Trade
(GATT), 139, 330, 463
General crisis of industrialism, 374
General Electric Company, 28, 45, 88, 125,
159, 205, 225, 308
General Electronics, Ltd., 361
General Foods Corporation, 77, 96, 141
General Mills, 159
General Motors Corporation, 5, 7, 9, 29, 48,
135–36, 138, 162, 210, 218, 224, 281,
288, 337, 460
Generality Tactic, 274. *See also* Info-tactics
Genetics and genetic engineering, xix, 393
Geneva, 80
Genscher, Hans Dietrich, 58
Geopolitics, 445–46
George Washington University, 349
Georgia (U.S.S.R.), 385
Georgia Mafia, 200
Gephardt, Richard A., 507
Geraghty, Tony, 490
Gergen, David, 267, 531
Germany, 6, 26, 30, 42, 58, 61, 96, 98, 117,
132, 135, 139, 160–61, 243, 247,
252–53, 256, 260, 263, 270, 297, 299,
302, 304, 308, 311, 324, 327, 338,
340–41, 343, 353, 362, 378, 380, 383,
386, 438–41, 443–44, 448, 453, 466;
nuclear arms, 440
Germany, national strategy. See *Ost-Strategie*
Giarini, Orio, 80, 482, 515
Gibb, George Sweet, 482
Gilder, George, 361, 526, 541
Gillette Company, 96–99, 101
Gilpin, Robert, 492
Gingrich, Newt, 486
Giscard d'Estaing, Valéry, 439
Glaser, Hermann, 496
Glasgow, 247
Gleichen, Edward, 301
Glenn, Adam, 538
Glenn, Christine, 492
Glenn, Edmund S., 492
Global Gladiators. *See* Chapter 34
Global hyper-competition, 392, 395
Global institutions, 462–65; hierarchy in, 464;
representation in, 465; vertical vs.
horizontal, 463–65
Global issues, 202
Global opinion, 343–46, 357, 469. *See also*
Public opinion
Global "sell," 339–40, 343
Global system, heterogeneous (First Wave),
457–58
Global system, homogeneous (Second Wave),
457
Globalism, 246, 251, 382, 385, 437; conflict
over, 59; as ideology, 344
Globalization, 33, 49, 54, 56–57, 59, 219,
239–40, 251, 253, 306–7, 327, 339–41,
353, 357, 426; financial, 54, 56–57, 58–59
Globalization of media. *See* Media as system
Goals, 196, 198; 452
God, 378–79, 381. *See also* Religion
Goddard Institute for Space Studies, 290
Godson, Roy, 497–98
Goebbels, Josef, 275
Gold, 63, 68

Gold & Stock Telegraph Company, 109
Golden Age myth, 378
Goldin, Dan, 382
Goldman, Sachs, 144
Goldsmith, Sir James, 29
Goldstein, Bernard, 502
Goldwin, Robert A., 479
Golf, 3, 360
Goodman, Danny, 501
Goodwill Games, 334
Goodyear Tires, 48
Gorbachev, Mikhail, xxi, 263, 357, 375, 378,
414, 418, 454, 466, 495, 546
Gore, Al, 291
Gosplan, 147
Gossip, 35, 179, 275
Goulden, Joseph C., 109, 501
Gouldner, Alvin W., 499
Gourevitch, Jean-Paul, 485
Government, 36, 51, 58, 174, 178, 190, 224,
227, 468, 528; and hidden subsidies,
42; information functions of, 295–319,
320–31. *See also* Political system; State
Government Communications Headquarters
(GCHQ), Great Britain, 300, 304–6
Grachev, Andrei, 485, 495
Gralla, P., 519
Grammy Awards, 364
Gramsci, Antonio, 421
Grand Union (company), 98
Great Britain, 5–7, 28–29, 43, 58, 63, 117,
132, 171, 192, 206, 218, 226, 236, 247,
256, 260, 300–301, 303–5, 324, 327, 332,
338–43, 362, 440, 444, 448, 457, 465
Great Neck, New York, 249
Greece, 233
Greed, 26, 30, 43, 51, 418
Green, A. Wigfall, 504
Green Ayatollahs, 380. *See also* Environment
and environmentalism
Green Berets, 462
Green movement, 377–81, 386, 443; and
social democracy, 444. *See also*
Environment and environmentalism
Greenberger, Martin, 486
Greengrass, Paul, 498
Greenpeace movement, 300
Greenspan, Alan, 426, 548
Greenstein, Fred I., 486
Greenstein, Monroe, 121, 519
Gregerman, Ira B., 482
Gregor, A. James, 496
Grolier, Inc., 218
Grolier Encyclopedia, 360
Gromyko, Alexei, 272
Gross, Ronald, 479
Group of Seven (G-7), 58
Groupe Bull (company), 5, 30, 61, 135, 310
Groupe Victoire (company), 30
Groupement de Contrôles Radioélectriques
(GCR), 300
GRU (U.S.S.R.), 300, 309
Gstaad, Switzerland, 374
Guam, 233
Guerrilla warfare, 202, 311–12, 459, 461. *See*
also Military; War
Guetersloh, Germany, 343
Guided Leak Tactic, 266–68, 294, 320. *See also*
Info-tactics
Guider, Elizabeth, 538
Guinness (company), 169

Gurwin, Larry, 482
Gutenberg, Johannes, 413, 546
Guterl, Fred V., 538–39
Gutfreund, John, 55
Guy, Ken, 501
Gwynne, S. C., 482

Habermas, Jurgen, 499
Hachette (company), 218
Haggar Apparel, 400
Haig, Alexander, 275
Haiti, 399, 409
Haitian immigrants, 249
Halamka, John D., 155, 497
Hall, Edward T., 492
Hall, Mildred Reed, 492
Hamilton, Lee, 271
Hammer, Armand, 504
Hammer, Joshua, 538
Hamrin, Carol Lee, 495
Hansen, James T., 290–91
Hansen, Robert H., 499
Hapsburg empire, 247, 529
Haquin, Benedicte, 550
Harant, Gerry, 497
Harper, James D., 302, 534
Harris, Laurence, 494
Harris, Marvin, 492
Hartcher, Peter, 548
Harvard Business Review, 237
Harvard University, 159, 339, 357–58, 434
Havas (company), 260
Havel, Vaclav, 348, 439
Hawaii, 349
Haymarket massacre, 38
HDTV. *See* Television, high-definition
Heald, Tim, 479
Health, 5, 7–8, 73, 213, 245, 263, 288, 291, 325–26, 336, 362, 374
Hearst, William Randolph, 343
Heartland theory, 445, 454
Heart-sea theory, 454
Heathrow Airport, 260
Hebditch, David, 503
Hebrew University (Israel), 254
Hector, Gary, 532
Hedenskog, Bob, 205
Hegel, Georg Wilhelm Friedrich, 421–22
Heilman, Madeline E., 479
Hemingway, Ernest, 95
Hemphill, Charles F., Jr., 501
Hemphill, Robert D., 501
Henderson, Bernard R., 497
Henderson, Nicholas, 487
Henry, Patrick, 357
Herman, Edward S., 482
Herrington, John S., 323
Herrman, Kai, 511
Hersh, Seymour M., 532
Hertz Corp., 108
Hervier, Guy, 520
Hess, Stephen, 487
Hetherington, Henry, 332, 345
Heuvel, Katrina Vanden, 494
Hewitt, David, 210
Hewlett-Packard Company, 75, 187, 197
Hierarchy, 46, 166, 173, 174, 177–78, 182, 192, 196–97, 198, 202–3, 214, 215, 219, 221–23, 224, 261–62, 317, 464
Highbrow business, 21

High-definition television (HDTV). *See* Television, high-definition
High-yield bonds, 49–50, 51, 53, 55
Higley, John, 478
Hill Samuel (bank), 340
Hilton Corp., 108
Hindu fundamentalism, 375. *See also* Fundamentalism, religious
Hinduism, 458. *See also* Religion
Hippie movement, 373–74, 380
Hirohito, Emperor, 384, 509, 543
Hiroshima, 430
Hispanics, 249. *See also* Ethnicity; Minorities; Race and racism
Hitachi (company), 5, 449
Hitler, Adolf, 37, 252–53, 275, 380–81, 383, 386, 438, 475, 496, 530, 542
Hitotsubashi University, 197
Ho Chi Minh City, 364
Hock, Dee, 67, 515
Hodges, Parker, 521
Hoffer, Eric, 488
Hoffman, Lily M., 499
Hofheinz, Roy, Jr., 492
Hogarth, William, 43
Holden, Nigel, 526
Holland. *See* Netherlands
Hollandsworth, Skip, 522
Hollstein, Brian, 154–55, 522
Hollywood, 12, 25, 28, 95, 328–29, 341. *See also* Movies
Hollywood Reporter, The, 336
Holtom, D. C., 489
Holusha, John, 483
Holy Roman Empire, 381
Holy War, 374–75
Home shopping (electronic), 126
Homelessness, 253, 262–63, 293
Homosexual networks, 200. *See also* Networks, human
Honda (company), 76, 197
Hong Kong, 55, 80, 328, 357, 364, 399, 405–6, 431, 461, 466
Hook, Sidney, 504
Hopkins, George, 490
Hopkins, Mark, 540
Hopper, Max, 517–18
Hornstein, Harvey A., 479
Hospital Corporation of America, 141
Hospitals, 3, 15, 73, 75, 122, 166, 282, 288. *See also* Health
Hostages, 170, 320, 375, 462. *See also* Terrorism
Hot deck imputation, 293
Hotels, 64, 75, 156, 227
Hough, Jerry F., 546
Houghton, James R., 201
Housel, Thomas J., 524
Houston, 292
Hout, Thomas M., 237, 527
Hoyt, Edwin P., 492
Hu Yaobang, 356
Hughes Aircraft, 218
Human resources, 153, 157–59, 215–17. *See also* Personnel; Work regimens
Human rights, 151, 345, 386. *See also* Freedom of expression
Human services, 73. *See also* Health
Humint (human intelligence). *See* Intelligence and espionage

Hungarians in Romania, 247. *See also*
    Ethnicity; Minorities
Hungary, 302, 353, 438–39, 441, 458
Huntington, Samuel P., 494
Huppes, Tjerk, 492
Hussein, Saddam, 258, 305
Hutschnecker, A., 478
Hutton Group, E. F., 144
Hyneman, Charles S., 480
HyperCard, 175
Hyper-media, 175–76, 187, 203, 227, 228
Hypersonic aircraft, 407. *See also* Aerospace
    industry

Iacocca, Lee, 25–26, 29, 510
IBM. *See* International Business Machines
    Corporation
Icahn, Carl, 29
ICL (company), 5
Idealism, philosophical, 421
Ideology, 61, 79, 243, 246, 254–55, 292, 340,
    376, 377–81, 382–87, 414, 421, 428,
    444, 452, 529, 542; highbrow, 80–83;
    lowbrow, 79–80
Ifugao tribe (Philippine Islands), 528
Iger, Robert, 337, 538
Illich, Ivan, 379–80, 489, 502, 542
Illiteracy, 253. *See also* Literacy
Imagery, 18
Imagination, 285, 293
Immigration, 249, 254, 293, 325, 382–84, 409
Imperial Hotel (Tokyo), 57
Imperialism, 11, 355, 374, 461
Inc., 226
Indeterminacy, 80. *See also* Chance
Index Group, Inc., 212
Index Medicus (data base), 8
India, 84, 249, 315, 330, 375, 391, 403, 412,
    424
Indiana, 293
Indiana Jones and the Temple of Doom (movie),
    328, 537
Individualism, 199, 547
Indochina War, 267
Indonesia, 391, 411
Industrial civilization. *See* Industrial society
    (Second Wave)
Industrial espionage. *See* Business espionage
Industrial society (Second Wave), xvii–xx, 6,
    9–11, 26–27, 36–37, 43–44, 46, 48, 53,
    56, 59, 60, 71–72, 79–80, 81, 86, 91, 128,
    166, 181, 232, 244–45, 248–51, 340,
    373–75, 378, 379, 386, 391–92, 417;
    innovation in, 398; rate of change in,
    398
Industrialism. *See* Industrial society (Second
    Wave)
Industry and Idleness (art), 43
Industry bias, 421
In-fighting, 168, 169, 171, 182, 268, 292. *See
    also* Info-tactics
Inflation, 52, 67, 218
Info-agenda, 320–31
Info-poor, 363–64, 366–68
Info-rich, 363–64, 366–68
Information (defined), 18. *See also* Knowledge
Information, cross-disciplinary, 81–82, 175–77.
    See also Knowledge
Information, free, 154
Information, freedom of. *See* Freedom of
    information

Information, privatization of, 321
Information, worker access to, 215
Information ethics, 118, 151, 326–27, 331
Information Executive, 283
Information "loan" from consumer, 102–3
Information overload, 168, 200, 289
Information sector, 53, 61, 70, 76, 442, 447.
    See also Knowledge; Mind-work and
    mind-workers; Super-symbolic economy
    (Third Wave)
Information "strike," 216
Information systems, 121, 128, 141–52,
    157–62, 193, 195, 199, 215, 222, 237;
    and distribution, 76, 105. *See also* Chief
    information officers (CIOs); Informa-
    tion technology; Management informa-
    tion systems (MIS)
Information technology, 359, 368–69, 444,
    449; strategic use of, 108, 122, 127,
    444. *See also* Computers; Media;
    Networks, electronic; Telecommunications
Information Technology Requirements Coun-
    cil, 139
Informational polarization, 363–64
Information-sharing, 121, 128, 237
Info-sphere, 427, 448
Info-tactics, 265–77, 280, 287, 293, 318,
    320–21; access, 273; back-channel,
    172, 270–72, 273; big lie, 275; blow-back,
    275; double-channel, 272–73; dribble,
    274; forced-to-know, 273–74; generality,
    274; guided leak, 266–68; masked
    source, 268–70; model of, 268;
    need-not-to-know, 273; need-to-know,
    273; omission, 274; reversal, 275;
    secrecy, 266; tidal wave, 275; timing,
    274; vapor, 275. *See also* Falsehood;
    Knowledge
Info-warriors. *See* Info-tactics
Info-wars, 95–162, 320
Infrastructure, electronic (Third Wave), 107,
    359, 369, 408, 412, 437, 443. *See also*
    Media; Networks, electronic
Infrastructure, Second Wave, 369, 404
In-Inners, 158
Innovation, 32, 49, 54, 133, 155, 179, 213–14,
    225, 235–36, 238, 267, 294, 317, 331,
    332–33, 370, 409, 428, 451; First Wave
    (agrarian), 370; rates of, 397–98; and
    risk, 398; Second Wave (industrial), 370;
    Third Wave (super-symbolic), 370–71
In-Outers, 158
Inscom (Brazil-China project), 316
Insight, 291
Institute, The. *See* Mossad
Institute for Scientific Information, xix
Institute for Social Justice, 347
Institute of Electrical and Electronics
    Engineers (IEEE), 160
Institute of Islamic Culture (Paris), 458. *See
    also* Islam
Instituto de Pesquisas Espaçiais, 315–16
Insurance industry, 30, 41, 45, 49, 54,
    119–20, 141, 209, 213, 289
Integrated Service Data Network (ISDN), 359
Intellectual property, 329–31. *See also*
    Copyright; Patents; Piracy
Intellectuals, xx, 246, 371, 415, 444
Intelligence, competitive. *See* Business
    espionage
Intelligence, world balance of, 304

Intelligence and espionage, 13, 21, 153, 160–61, 171, 186, 253, 269, 272–73, 275–76, 282, 289, 295–319, 321, 327, 331, 403, 428, 459; and "analysis paralysis," 299; bureaucracy in, 299; and civil liberties, 304; consortia, 302, 304; corporate "para-," 313; de-massification of, 313, 318; de-monopolization of, 316; division of labor in, 299; ecological, 311, 312; economic, 304–7; epistemological problems, 317; factory principles in, 299; as major world industry, 300–301; markets, 299; mass production of, 297–99; media, 316; nongovernmental, 301; private sector dependence on, 307; private vendors to, 314; privatization of, 312–16; professionalization of, 296; "resale market" of, 310; Second Wave, 296–99; secret-swapping in, 301–4; self-financing, 309; in space, 298, 315–16; spying on allies, 310; vertical integration in, 314
Intelligence Requirements for the 1990s, 408
Interactive Game Network, 361
Interactive Golf, 360
Interactivity. *See* Media as system
Inter-capitalist conflict, 452, 455. *See also* Global hyper-competition
International Business Machines Corporation (IBM), 5, 14, 61, 71, 98, 108, 112, 125, 131, 133–38, 153, 197, 214, 223, 225, 230, 236, 279, 282, 310, 363, 449, 460
International Harvester Company, 45
International law, 457, 459
International Leadership Center, 246
International Monetary Fund, 404, 437
International Telecommunications Union (ITU), 136
International Telephone & Telegraph Corporation (ITT), 461
Intra-capitalist conflict, 437
Intuition, 178, 182, 199
Inventory, 89, 90, 117, 122, 124, 168, 181, 225, 236, 281, 401
Investment, 46–50, 55–56, 81, 83, 90, 145, 280, 322, 346, 399, 411, 417, 431, 433, 442, 447, 461. *See also* Capital; Finance
I.Q. (intelligence quotient). *See* Management I.Q.
Iran, 170, 263, 271, 314, 320, 355, 374–76, 445, 451, 457, 462
Irangate, 171, 263, 273, 320
Iranian Jewish immigrants, 249–50
Iran-Iraq war, 305, 437
Iraq, 258, 305, 311–12, 314, 316, 424
Iridium system, 412
Irkutsk, 419
Isaacson, Walter, 504
ISDN. *See* Integrated Service Data Network
Ishihara, Shintaro, 425, 453, 492, 548
Ishikawa, Akira, 434
Islam, 374–75, 378, 382, 385, 424, 441, 455–56, 458, 466, 541
Israel, 275, 300, 303, 375, 394
Isuzu (company), 460
Italy, 26, 30, 58, 89, 125, 139, 180–81, 187, 226, 247, 253, 275, 290, 308, 338, 340, 343, 358, 384, 400, 462
Itami, Juzo, 39

ITT. *See* International Telephone & Telegraph Corporation

J. Walter Thompson Company, 339
J. F. Coates, Inc., 161
Jackson, Jane, 154
Jackson, Stanley, 482
Jacques, Martin, 547
Jaguar (aircraft), 439
James, Donald, 495
James, Ron, 542
Jameson, Frederic, 129
Janeway, Elizabeth, 478
Japan, xviii, xxi, 9, 13, 21, 26–27, 41–42, 48, 189, 197, 250, 270, 368, 375, 384–85, 423, 428–31, 433–37, 438, 443–44, 450–55; business and economy, 5–7, 9, 38–39, 57, 61, 64–65, 67, 70, 72, 90, 99, 105, 117, 119–21, 123–27, 131–33, 136, 143, 156, 159, 169, 172–73, 185, 194, 218–19, 223, 236–37, 259–60, 306, 313, 339, 341, 361–62, 392–93, 395, 400, 404–8, 410–11, 440–41, 444, 446–50, 460–61; intelligence and espionage, 270, 296–97, 301, 306, 309–10, 315; military, 296–97, 304, 403, 424–25, 445–46; politics, 41, 246, 256–57, 259–60, 267, 304, 309–10, 324, 330, 384–85, 424–25, 466, 469
Japan, economic power of, 431–33
Japan, knowledge-power of, 433–37
Japan, military power of, 430–31, 454
Japan, national strategy, 436–37, 453–55
Japan, representation in U.S. Congress, 464
Japan Art Association, 436
Japan National Railways, 259
Japan That Can Say "No," The (Morita and Ishihara), 425
Japanese Cabinet Research Office (Naicho), 301
Japanese Defense Academy, 431
Japanese External Trade Organization (JETRO), 306
Japanese Ministry of International Trade and Industry (MITI). *See* MITI
Japanese Ministry of Posts and Telecommunications (MPT), 117, 136, 257–58
Japanese National Police, 309
Japan-Europe alliance, 453–55
Japan–United States alliance, 453–55
Jazz combo, 186
JCB Co., 126
Jenkins, Alan, 493
Jeopardy (TV program), 361, 365
Jepson, Charles, 187, 524
Jerusalem, 56
Jervis B. Webb Company, 236
Jesuits, 346
Jets, 393
Jewish Defense League, 253
Jewish fundamentalists, 375. *See also* Fundamentalism, religious; Jews
Jews, 45, 48, 200, 249–50, 375–76, 386, 409–10, 451, 458. *See also* Anti-Semitism
Jiji Press, 301
Jobs, Steve, 29
Joffe, Josef, 383
John Paul II (pope), 458. *See also* Catholic Church
Johnson, Chalmers, 487
Johnson, Douglas W., 501

Johnson, Josephine, 141, 521
Johnson, Lyndon Baines, 266, 531
Johnson, Paul, 385, 504
Johnson, Tom, 516–17
Johnston, Christopher, 537
Jones, J. P., 482
Jones, Sidney, 286
Josephson, Matthew, 482
Journal of Japanese Trade and Industry, 257
Journal of the American Medical Association, 8
Journalism, 332, 349. *See also* Press
Jouvenel, Bertrand de, 478
Juckett, Harold, 517
Judaism. *See* Jews
Judge, Anthony J. N., 201, 525
Junk bonds, 49–51, 53, 55
Jurgen, Ronald K., 520
Just-in-time delivery, 123, 236, 401
JVC (company), 453

K Mart Corporation, 124, 161
Kabuki, 256
Kahn, Joel S., 480
Kahn, Robert L., 482
Kaiser Aluminum, 145
Kakuma, Takashi, 267
Kaligo, Al, 501
Kamioka, Kazuyoshi, 482
Kanter, Rosabeth Moss, 482
Kaplan, David E., 492
Kaplan, Fred, 490
Kapor, Mitch, 408
Kapuscinski, Ryszard, 505
Karate Kid, The (movie), 451
Kashmir, 375
Kawasaki Heavy Industries, 431
Kazakhstan (U.S.S.R.), 424
KDD (company), 125
Keane, Jack, 533
Keen, Peter G. W., 122, 127, 482
Kehler, Dean, 512–13
Keidanren, 6
Keio University, 90
Kelley, Kathleen, 530
Kelly, John H., 270–71, 532
Kemmerer, Donald L., 477
Kengaku, Kazuo, 38
Kennedy, John F., 272
Kennedy, Marilyn Moats, 480
Kennedy, Paul, 452, 505
Kenwood, A. G., 482
Keohane, Robert O., 478
Keren, Michael, 499
Kernell, Samuel, 261–62, 487
Kerr, Clark, 505
Kerr, Susan, 522
Kets de Vries, Manfred F. R., 485
Keynes, John Maynard, 72, 482
K-Factor. *See* Knowledge
KGB, 269, 272, 296, 300, 302–3, 309
KGB, Line X, 309, 311
Khan, Reza, 374. *See also* Iran
Khomeini, Ruhollah Musavi, 355, 374, 378,
    380, 456–57, 540
Khrushchev, Nikita, 272, 413–14, 546
Kiechel, Walter, III, 524
Kilburn, David, 515
"Killers, The" (short story), 95
Kindaichi, Haruhiko, 499
Kindleberger, Charles P., 482
King, Anthony, 487

King, Dennis, 487
King, Martin Luther, Jr., 366, 541
King, Ralph, Jr., 545
Kingon, Alfred, 533
Kingon International, 533
Kissinger, Henry, 268, 271–73, 314, 532
Kissinger Associates, 314
Kitahara, Yasusada, 501
Klein, Donald F., 77, 515
Klein, Theodore, 149, 522
Knight, Stephen, 480
Knightley, Phillip, 497
Knights of Labor, 38
Knowledge (defined), 18–19, 409
Knowledge, xx, 9, 12–21, 61, 158, 168, 391,
    423, 426, 428, 443, 474. *See also* Power
    triad
Knowledge, control of, 152; allocation of, 73;
    conflict over, 107, 143, 146, 278;
    de-monopolization of, 413; monopoly of,
    7–8, 128, 172, 372–73, 413, 448;
    pre-specification of, 152. *See also*
    Bureaucracy; Censorship; Info-wars
Knowledge, and economy, 83–91, 157, 409;
    assets, 159, 231; as factor of
    production, 9, 84–91; non-finite, 19, 61,
    86, 157, 418–19; as property, 418; as
    substitute for capital, 88–89; as substitute
    for energy, 87–88; as substitute for
    labor, 237; as substitute for raw
    materials, 87–88; as substitute for
    space, 88; as substitute for time, 88; as
    substitute for transportation, 87–88;
    value of, 155. *See also* Super-symbolic
    economy
Knowledge, organization of, 85, 165, 171,
    178, 221, 228, 282, 415, 427;
    abstraction, 62; cross relationships of, 85,
    175–77, 201, 203; free form, 176, 239;
    non-finite, 19, 61, 86, 157, 418–19
Knowledge, in politics: as ammunition, 277; as
    democratic, 20; maldistribution of,
    366, 368, 475; problem in democracy,
    293; redistribution of, 215
Knowledge, processes: circulation, 72, 158;
    "exporting" and "importing," 157–58;
    knowledge load, 211; in revolution, 427;
    transience of, 168
Knowledge about knowledge, 277–79
Knowledge and national power. *See* National
    power, knowledge factor in
Knowledge engineering, 289
Knowles, L.C.A., 482
Knowlton, Evelyn H., 482
Kodak. *See* Eastman Kodak Company
Kogan, Herman, 506
Kohl, Helmut, 263, 327, 439, 531, 549
Kojak (TV program), 348, 540
Komatso (company), 431
Konrad, George, 499, 500
Kontos, Alkis, 478
Koop, C. Everett, 326
Koran, 456
Korean War, 405
Koreatown (Los Angeles), 250
Kornai, Janos, 483
Koschnick, Wolfgang J., 549
Kotaro, Nawa, 520
Kotler, Mindy, 159
Kotz, David M., 483
KPMG Peat Marwick, 202

Krader, Lawrence, 487
Kraemer, Kenneth L., 500
Kraftwerke Union (company), 308
Kramer vs. Kramer (movie), 341
Kraus, Richard Curt, 495
Krauss, Ellis S., 530
Kropotkin, Peter, 478
Kugler, Jacek, 490
Kuiper, Jennifer, 283
Kula, Witold, 505
Kumpe, Ted, 516
Kung! Bushmen, 528
Kurds, 254, 311
Kuwait, 57
Kuzbary, Sam, 153
Kwangju Province, 284
Kyemba, Henry, 487
Kyodo News Service, 301
Kyoei-kai, 229

La Cinq, 338, 343
La Piscine. *See* DGSE (Direction Générale de Sécurité Extérieur)
La Presse, 333
Labor, 37, 84, 88, 91, 238, 399, 409; non-interchangeability of, 250. *See also* Work
Labor, cheap. *See* Cheap labor
Labor costs, 32, 237. *See also* Cheap labor
Labor force. *See* Workers
Labor unions, xxi, 15, 27, 29, 37–38, 40, 45, 48, 52, 70, 73–74, 89, 205, 216, 223, 227–28, 237, 269, 322, 332, 346, 374, 410, 435, 443; representation in global institutions, 465
Labour Party (Great Britain), 344
Lacouture, Jean, 505
Lakatos, Imre, 500
Lamarter, Richard Thomas de, 483
Lamberton, D. M., 500
Lamborghini, Bruno, 226–27, 526
Land, 11, 37, 60, 81, 84, 123, 238, 262
Landau, Robert M., 501
Landier, Hubert, 186
Landsat (satellite), 315–16
Langone, John, 503
Langtry, J. O., 496
Language, xix, 85–86, 115, 118, 247, 344, 357, 359, 367, 393, 436, 448, 509
LANs. *See* Local area networks
Lappen, Alyssa A., 519
Laqueur, Walter, 496–97, 531
LaRouche, Lyndon, 253, 530
Lasers, 100, 460
Lashinsky, Adam, 524
Laski, Harold J., 487
Latin America, 455, 461
Launhardt, Liane, 58
Lavoie, Don, 398, 483
Law and lawyers, 13, 27, 35, 36, 40–41, 43, 51, 90, 102, 104, 139, 154–55, 169, 172, 195, 250, 283, 325, 347, 421, 457, 459; relationship to violence, 40
Law of Acceleration Effect. *See* Acceleration effect
Law of Ubiquity, 363–64, 369
Lawrence Berkeley Laboratory, 160
Lawrence of Arabia (movie), 341
Layoffs. *See* Unemployment
LDCs. *See* Non-industrial societies
LDP. *See* Liberal Democratic Party (Japan)

LDX machine, 235
Le Carré, John, 295
Le Groupe Videotron, Ltd., 361
Le Monde, 382
Le Monde Diplomatique, 132
Le Pen, Jean-Marie, 543
Le Penist movement (France), 383
Le Play, Frederic, 480
Leach, William, 366
Leadbeater, Todd, 509
Leadership, 78, 82, 194, 197–99, 201, 262, 367, 459; judicial function of, 262
Leadership Secrets of Attila the Hun (Roberts), 31
Leaks. *See* Guided Leak Tactic
Learning, 211, 393, 427
Leather industry, 180
Lebanon, 270–71, 468, 473
Lebedoff, David, 487
LeClair, Edward E., Jr., 483
L'eggs (brand), 108
Lehman, John F., Jr., 167, 523
Leipzig, 353
Leisure, 73, 335, 436
Lenin, V. I., 297, 416, 422, 438, 495, 510, 528, 547, 549
Leninism. *See* Socialism and Marxism
Lens, Sidney, 483
Leonard, Gary, 154
Levchenko, Stanislav, 497
Levi, Peter, 489
Levin, Doron P., 483
Levine, Mel, 131, 520
Levinson, Harry, 483
Levite, Ariel, 497
Levitt, Theodore, 339–40
Levy, Jack S., 490
Levy, Steven, 501
Lewin, Ronald, 496
Lewis, Michael, 529
Li Peng, 356
Liberal Democratic Party (Japan), 6, 41, 267, 432
Libertarianism, 374
Libraries, 321
Libya, 253, 303, 327, 382, 424
Lichtheim, George, 495
Liddell Hart, B. H., 490
Lies. *See* Falsehood
Life styles, 167, 251, 255, 352, 444, 450
Lifetime cable network, 8
Lifson, Thomas B., 480
Ligachev, Yegor, 546
Lilliet, Rémy, 537
Lindblom, Charles E., 487
Linguistics, 393. *See also* Language
Lipkin, Richard, 533
Literacy, 84, 207, 362
Literacy, video, 367, 368
Literature, 176, 296, 329, 385, 435–36, 546
Liverpool, 249
Llobera, J. R., 482
Lo Bello, Nino, 489
Loan sharks, 39
Lobbyists, 287–88; electronic, 366
Local area networks (LANs), 108, 160
Localism, 246–47, 251, 264, 385
Localization, 239
Lockerbie (Scotland), 324
Loebl, Eugen, 80, 483, 495, 515
Logic, 17, 62, 85, 285, 290, 368, 370, 427
Logic, fuzzy, 427

Lombardy, 246
London, 6, 58, 62, 90, 134, 168, 267, 328, 342, 407, 432, 450
Long Beach, California, 314
Lop Nor (China), 298
Lord Shang, 290
Los Angeles, 48, 249–50, 292, 333, 346–47, 360, 364, 407
Lotus Development Corporation, 230, 279, 408
Lougheed, A. L., 482
Louis XIII, xxii
Lovins, Amory, 379
Lowbrow business, 21
Ludditism, 373, 379, 443
Lugar, Richard, 349
Lukyanov, Anatoly, xxi
Luskin, Bernard, 360, 541
Lutz, Mark, 481
Lyndon, Neil, 504
Lyon, 246, 249
Lyotard, Jean-François, 500

Ma Bell. *See* American Telephone and Telegraph Company (AT&T)
Macao, 461
MacArthur, Douglas, 297
Maccoby, Michael, 483
Machiavelli, Niccolò, 17, 478
Machismo, 79
Machlup, Fritz, 71, 500
Macintosh, 70
Mack, Toni, 531
Mackenzie, W.J.M., 490
Macmillan, Inc., 342
Macy's (department store), 180
Madrick, Jeff, 483
Madrid, 90
Maeno, Kazuhisa, 530
Mafia, 38, 51, 282, 314
Mafud, Julio, 487
Magazines, 103, 341, 343–44, 351, 363. *See also* Media; Press
Maghreb. *See* North Africa
Magyars, 247
Majority rule, 253
Malaysia, 72, 202, 330, 406
Malone, Thomas W., 526
Management and managers, 3, 5, 11, 27, 31, 51–52, 61, 70, 142, 146, 156–58, 165, 167, 169, 172, 177, 179, 189, 197, 204–5, 210, 221, 231, 239, 335, 342, 371, 398; diversity of, 198–99; middle managers, 71, 172–77, 221, 223; perks, 215–16; Second Wave (industrial), 208–13
Management information systems (MIS), 76, 99, 141–52, 160–61, 174. *See also* Information systems; Information technology
Management I.Q., 77
Management Today, 224
Manchuria, 410
Mandate of Heaven, 469
Mandela, Nelson, 534
Mandl, Alex, 76, 515
Manhattan Project, 323
Manila, 431
Mant, Alistair, 480
Manufacturing, 5, 9, 33, 46, 61, 64, 69–74, 76, 79, 83, 95–106, 121–22, 132, 136–37, 140, 149, 171, 195, 210, 226, 237, 339, 400, 411, 447, 449, 460; knowledge component of, 140; mass (Second Wave), 448, 454

Manufacturing, de-massification. *See* De-massification
Manufacturing Automation Protocol (MAP), 136
Manville Corporation, 169
Mao Tse-tung, 1, 358, 421
Marchand, Marie, 501
Marcom, John, Jr., 538
Marcos, Ferdinand, 14, 348–49
Marenches, Count de, 309, 497
Margiotta, Franklin D., 492
Maritime industry. *See* Shipping industry
Market economies. *See* Capitalism
Marketing, 25, 34, 61, 97, 102–6, 158, 171, 176, 212, 251, 435; research, 158
Markets, 27, 47, 54, 155, 167–68, 179, 214, 219, 239, 352; de-massification of, xx, 17, 183, 442; global, 57, 339–40, 399; and innovation, 397–98
Markets for intelligence and espionage, 299
Markey, Edward J., 133, 520, 541
Markham, Felix, 505
Markoff, John, 515
Marlboros (cigarettes), 398
Marriott Corporation, 156
Martin, Henri-Jean, 504
Martin, Malachi, 489
Marton, Andrew, 512
Marui, 103
Marx, Karl, 34, 61, 371, 414, 416, 421–22, 468, 495, 546
Marx and Marxism. *See* Socialism and Marxism
Marxist Kurdish Workers Party, 311
Maryland, 275
Masao, Kunihiro, 543
Masked Source Tactic, 268–70. *See also* Info-tactics
Mason, June-Collier, 515
Masons, 200, 253
Mass consumption (Second Wave), 244
Mass democracy (Second Wave), 11, 244–45, 248, 250, 253, 373, 376, 442
Mass distribution (Second Wave), 11
Mass education (Second Wave), 11. *See also* Education
Mass media (Second Wave), 244, 351. *See also* Media
Mass movements, 251
Mass production. *See* Production, Second Wave
Mass society. *See* Industrial society (Second Wave)
Massachusetts Institute of Technology (M.I.T.), 154, 225, 278, 434
Masuda, Yuji, 537
Materialism, 80; mechanical, 416
Material-ismo, ideology of, 69–83
Materials, 87–88, 95, 201, 392, 405, 425, 431, 433, 450; de-massified, 405
Matra (company), 260
Matriarchy, 182, 199
Matsushita (company), 86, 229
Mattel Inc., 162
Mattelart, Armand, 483
Matthews, Christopher, 487
Maurras, Charles, 465, 551
Maxwell, Robert, 342, 344, 346, 539
May, Rollo, 478
Mayer, Martin, 483
Mayo Clinic, 336

Mazda Motor Manufacturing (company), 206, 460
Mazlish, Bruce, 505
McCain, John, 283
McCartney, Laton, 483
McCorduck, Pamela, 499
McCreary, Lew, 521
McDonald's Corporation, 73, 77, 108, 340
McFadden, Michael, 531
McFarlane, Robert, 320, 536
McGill, Peter, 523
McGowan, William, 28
MCI Communications Corporation, 28
McKinsey and Company, 226
McLuhan, Marshall, 341, 502
McMillen, Tom, 270
McMurtry, John, 495
McNamara, Robert, 269
McNeill, William H., 505
McQuaid, Kim, 483
Means of production, 216–17, 239, 546
Mechtild of Magdeburg, 378
Media, xvii, xx, 11, 21, 27, 29–30, 48, 51, 56, 97, 132, 167–68, 251–52, 256–57, 279, 291, 316, 320, 326–27, 333–35, 337–39, 343, 345, 369, 382, 415–16, 429, 435, 456, 528; de-massification of, xx, 251, 334, 336–37, 341, 344; and economy, 368; and education, 369; and intelligence and espionage, 316; role of acceleration, 350; state monopoly of, 416; and work skills, 367
Media, cross-national impact, 327, 348–49, 351, 353, 357–58, 382
Media and revolution. *See* Revolution
Media as system, 346, 350, 352–53, 365, 369; bias of, 265, 276; connectivity, 360–62; cross-national, 382; fusion of, 350, 352–53; globalization, 333, 339–46, 360, 364, 457; interactivity, 359–61, 363, 365; mobility, 360–63; ubiquity, 360, 363–64. *See also* Games, interactive
Media barons, 342–44; politics of, 344
Media modes: First Wave, 355–56; Second Wave, 244, 341, 355–56, 358; Third Wave, 355, 357, 359–71
Medical industry, 53, 130. *See also* Health
Medicare, 286. *See also* Health
Medieval era, 118, 351, 378–81
Medievalism, 380–81, 386
Mee, Charles L., Jr., 505
Meetings, 280
Meiji Mutual (company), 120
Meiji Revolution, 434
Melting pot (concept), 250
Melvern, Linda, 503
Melymuka, Kathleen, 521–22
Memorial Day Massacre, 38
Mende, Tibor, 492
Mendelsohn, Andrew, 507
Mendelssohn, Kurt, 503
Mental illness, 262
Mentors, 196. *See also* Vassalage
Mercenaries. *See* Military
Mergers and acquisitions. *See* Takeovers
Merit pay, 166
Merloni, Vittorio, 89–90, 516
Merloni Elettrodomestici (company), 89
Merrill Lynch & Company, 119, 127, 143–45
Messerschmitt (company), 453

Messine, Philippe, 140, 521
Meta-tactics, 277, 278–94, 318. *See also* Info-tactics
Metcalfe, Philip, 505
Metglas, 87
Mexican immigrants, 347, 384
Mexican-Americans, 249
Mexico, 48, 56, 253, 258, 347, 412, 461–62
Meyers, Gerald C., 483
MGM Corporation, 334
Miami, 249
Micro computers. *See* Computers
Middle Core faction (Japan), 259–60
Middle East, 56, 312, 320, 328, 333, 355, 374–75, 424, 455, 464
Middle East, 328
Middle managers. *See* Management and managers
MiG (aircraft), 394
Milan, 90
Milgram, Stanley, 478
Militarism, 375, 442
Military, xxi, 4, 14–15, 17, 37, 42, 165–67, 171, 190, 192–95, 266–67, 272, 283–84, 290–91, 296–97, 300, 304, 312, 315–17, 320, 329, 333, 348–50, 358, 384–85, 393, 402, 413, 428, 430, 432, 434, 437, 439–41, 445–46, 448, 451, 453–54, 459, 462; political role, 349; Second Wave (mass), 446; Third Wave (de-massification of), 446
Military, Europe, 439–40
Military, Japan, 430–31
Military, overseas bases, 402, 406
Military networks, 200. *See also* Networks, human
Military policy, United States, 445–46; obsolete strategy, 445; withdrawal from Asia/Pacific, 431; withdrawal from Europe, 439
Military power (based on knowledge), 17, 394, 425. *See also* Intelligence and espionage
Milken, Michael, 46–53, 55–56, 90, 512–13, 516
Mill, John Stuart, 477
Millar, Fergus, 505
Miller, Abraham H., 492
Miller, John, 315
Miller, Roy Andrew, 492
Miller, William H., 524
Millikin, Roger, 124–25
Millikin & Company, 124
Millis, Walter, 490
Mills, C. Wright, 478, 480
Mills, James, 458
Mind-work and mind-workers, 49, 71, 74–75, 76–83, 158, 206, 212, 280, 409, 414; as "nonproductive," 414, 420–21. *See also* Work; Work regimens
Miniaturization, 87–88
Mining, 37–38, 46
Minitel, 115, 362
Minorities, 45, 252–55; dynamic, 409; pivotal, 252–55. *See also* African-Americans; Ethnicity; Jews; Race and racism; *and names of individual groups*
Mintz, John, 530
Mintzberg, Henry, 480
Mirage (aircraft), 305, 439
Mirapolis, 39
MIS. *See* Management information systems

Mises, Ludwig von, 419, 483
Mis-information. *See* Knowledge (defined)
MI6 (Secret Intelligence Service), Great
    Britain, 300
Miss America Pageant, 97
Missiles, 17, 431. *See also* Strategic Defense
    Initiative (SDI)
MITI (Ministry of International Trade and
    Industry), 6, 124, 434
Mitrad, 115
Mitsubishi (company), 431, 453
Mitsui Research Institute, 407
Mitterand, François, 258, 344
Mobil Corporation, 259
Mobility of media. *See* Media as system
Models, xvii, xxi, 85, 99, 118, 143, 278,
    280–81, 284, 288, 292; conflict over,
    291–92; increase in variables, 289
Modena, Italy, 180
Modernism. *See* Industrial society (Second
    Wave)
Modigliani, Amedeo, 323
Modularization, 239
Mohn, Reinhard, 211, 342–43, 346, 483, 525,
    539
Molly Maguires, 37
Monarchy, 11, 386, 439, 468
Monasteries, 186
Monden, Yasuhiro, 483
Money, 42, 47, 59–60, 62–68, 72, 83, 90–91,
    238, 335, 513, 514; diversification of, 65;
    knowledge content of, 68; laundering,
    42; as system, 43; velocity of, 55. *See also*
    Capital; Wealth
Money, First Wave, 63, 68; preliterate, 68
Money, Second Wave, 26, 63, 68; literacy-
    based, 68; paper, 63; symbolic, 63
Money, Third Wave (super-symbolic), 26,
    64–68, 76, 126, 162, 238; video-based,
    68
Monopolization of information, 128. *See also*
    Knowledge, control of
Monopoly (Goulden), 109
Monopoly, 31, 109, 113, 147, 444, 448
Monopoly, internal. *See* Vertical integration
Montevideo, 152
Montgomery Ward, 259
Moodie, Carol, 481
Moodie, Thomas, 481
Moody, Kavin W., 99, 100, 517
Moody's, 49
Moore, Mary Tyler, 341
Morais, Richard C., 531
Morality, 374, 381, 385, 469, 475–76
More, Sir Thomas, 478
Moreno, Roland, 64
Morgan, John Pierpont (J.P.), 45–48, 50–54,
    60–61, 511
Morgan, Robin, 487
Morgan Stanley, 144
Morgan-Witts, Max, 489
Morinaga (company), 169
Morison, Samuel Eliot, 490
Morita, Akio, 425, 492–93
Morita, Pat, 451
Moritz, Jeffrey, 367–68, 541
Morley, Richard E., 509
Mormons, 200
Moro, R. Ruben, 490
Morocco, 301, 303, 382
Morristown, N.J., 87

Morse, Ronald A., 270
Morse, Samuel F. B., 107–10, 113, 518
Morse code, 110
Mortensen, C. David, 502
Mortimer, Edward, 489
Moscow, xxi, 152, 161, 272–73, 275, 295–97,
    302, 334, 343, 375, 385, 391, 394, 402,
    413, 417–18, 433, 452. *See also* Union of
    Soviet Socialist Republics
Moskal, Brian S., 515, 525
Moskowitz, Milton, 483
Mossad, 301, 303
Mosse, George L., 380, 496
Motion pictures. *See* Movies
Motorola, Inc., 38, 135, 237, 412
Motoshima, Hitoshi, 384
Movies, 12, 15, 28, 39, 66, 131, 280, 328–29,
    335, 337, 341–42, 351–52, 360, 432,
    436, 451. *See also* Entertainment,
    inadvertent content of
Mozart, Wolfgang Amadeus, 120
MTM Enterprises, 341
M-TOPS, 103
MTV, 342, 368
Muck, Christian C., 551
Mudjanto, G., 478
Mueller, Robert K., 483
Multinational corporations, 418, 460–62
Munich, 252
Muqiao, Xue, 495
Murakami, Shigeyoshi, 489
Murder, xi, xxii, 269
Murdoch, Rupert, 341–44, 346, 539
Muroyama, Janet H., 503
Murphy, Thomas Patrick, 489
Murphy Brown (TV program), 335
Murray, Allen, 259
Museums, 95
Musgrave, Alan, 500
Music, 175, 186, 250, 330, 341, 343, 347, 364,
    393, 436
Muslim religion. *See* Fundamentalism,
    religious; Islam
Mutual funds, 54. *See also* Finance
Myers, Gustavus, 505
Myopia, 243
Mysticism, 373–74, 378
Mythology, 12, 13, 378, 509, 529

Nabisco (company), 96, 103, 245
Nachmias, David, 480
Nagao, Teruya, 210–11, 215, 525–26
Nagasaki, 384
Nagel, Jack H., 478
Nagoya (Japan), 214, 249
Naicho, 301
Nakamura, Toshiyuki, 120
Nakdimon, Shlomo, 493
Naniwada, Haruo, 483
Nanocomposites, 405. *See also* Materials
Nanotechnology, 405
Narcotics industry, 459–60, 465. *See also*
    Drugs
NASA, 290, 315
National Academy of Engineering (U.S.), 393
National Association of Manufacturers, 48
National Cash Register (NCR), 98
National College Television, 336, 367
National identity, 382, 384
National power, knowledge factor in, 110–11,
    428, 430, 433–37, 443–45, 448–52

National Reconnaissance Office (U.S.), 300
National Science Foundation (U.S.), 448
National Security Agency (U.S.), 300, 302, 304–7
National Security Council (U.S.), 170, 270–71, 329
National Steel, 224
Nationalism, 243–44, 246, 249, 354, 382–86, 410, 436, 443, 453, 461, 544
Nationalized industry. *See* State ownership and enterprise
Nations, xix, 4, 7, 246, 250; interdependency of, 459. *See also* National power; Nation-state
Nations, supra-, 464. *See also* European Community; Sovereignty
Nation's Business, 180
Nation-state, xx, 7, 11, 135, 226, 248, 426, 457, 465; concept of, 385; conflict with non-state forces, 456–66
NATO, 263, 302, 304, 439, 454
Nature, 377–81, 392
Navarro, Armando, 347
Navarro, Peter, 487
Naylor, R. T., 484
Nazism, 249, 253, 314, 380–81, 383, 440, 443. *See also* Fascism; Totalitarianism
NBC (National Broadcasting Company), 5, 336–37
Need-Not-to-Know Tactic, 273, 314. *See also* Info-tactics
Need-to-Know Tactic, 273. *See also* Info-tactics
Nelson, Joan M., 487
Nelton, Sharon, 524
Neocolonialism, 461
Nepotism, 182, 188
Netherlands, 26, 86, 89, 218, 311, 324, 338, 361
Netmap International, 202
Networks, business, 201–202, 227
Networks, electronic, 54, 58, 90, 107–29, 139, 160, 173, 203, 220, 223, 225, 229, 230, 237, 283, 307, 352, 398, 407–8, 412, 427, 435; strategic use of, 123, 125, 127; vulnerability of, 307. *See also* Networks, extra-intelligent
Networks, extra-intelligent, 115–18, 162, 280, 398, 407–8, 435
Networks, human, 200–201, 459
Networks, intra-intelligent, 113–15; neural, 114, 393
Networks, unintelligent, 113
Networks, value added (VANs), 115–17, 124–25, 359; common carrier, 125; industry-wide, 124–25. *See also* Networks, extra-intelligent
Neuhaus, Richard John, 477
Neural networks. *See* Networks, intra-intelligent
Neustadt, Richard E., 487
New Age movement, 374, 376
New Delhi, 424
New Hampshire, 278–79
New Jersey, 95
"New New Product Development Game, The," 197
New Orleans, Louisiana, 113
New Perspectives Quarterly, 378
New Sovereigns, The (Said and Simmons), 331
New World Symphony, 338
New York, 47, 56, 58, 88, 122, 152, 180, 249, 292, 332–33, 362, 407

New York State Psychiatric Institute, 77
New York Stock Exchange, 47, 432
New York *Sun,* 332
New York Times, The, 215, 350, 426
New Yorkers in Texas, 200
New Zealand, 302
News, 332–33, 335–36, 342, 352, 357, 382. *See also* Media
Newspapers. *See* Press
Newsweek, 183, 337, 352
NHK Spring Company, 90
Nicaragua, 320, 402, 417
Niche markets. *See* Markets
Nicholas II (tsar of Russia), 385
Nicholls, A. J., 505
Nickel, 60, 87
Nickelodeon (cable channel), 368
Nicolis, G., 503
NIEs (newly industrialized economies), 395. *See also* Non-industrial societies
Nietzsche, Friedrich, 478
Nigeria, 270, 382, 409, 411
Nii, H. Penny, 499
Nikkei, 109
Nineteen Eighty-four (Orwell), 359
Nippon Electric Company (NEC), 5, 61, 197, 449
Nippon Life (company), 119
Nippon Telephone and Telegraph Company (NTT), 38, 65, 67, 126, 260
Nissan (company), 431
Nixdorf (company), 135–36, 444
Nixon, Richard M., 267, 271, 493, 505
Nobbe, George, 517
Nobel Prize, xix, 345, 436, 443–44
Noer, Deliar, 500
Nomura Research Institute, 407
Nomura Securities, 119
Nonaka, Ikujiro, 197, 524
Non-determinacy, 203, 467
Non-equilibrium, 393, 474
Non-governmental organizations, role in development, 410. *See also* Civil society
Non-industrial societies, 10, 37, 111, 391, 394–95, 399, 402–3, 405–6, 408–9, 411, 432; Third Wave strategy, 437. *See also* Slow economies
Non-linearity, 152, 252, 474
Non-national corporations, 460–63. *See also* Multi-national corporations
Noonan, John T., Jr., 484
Nordhaus, William D., 31
Noriega, Manuel, 14, 446
Normal, Illinois, 206
Norsk Data (company), 444
North, Oliver, 271
North Africa, 301, 464
North Africans in France, 250, 382
North America, 308
North Korea, 301, 466
North Vietnam, 302
Northcliffe, Lord, 343
Northwest Airlines, Inc., 325
Norton, R. D., 515
Norway, 298, 323, 364, 444
Norwich, John Julius, 505
Nostalgia, 444–45
Novak, William, 510
Novelty, 468
NTSC (TV standard), 131, 138

NTT. *See* Nippon Telephone and Telegraph Company
Nuclear industry, 39, 193, 226, 308–9, 326, 443. *See also* Energy
Nuclear weapons. *See* Arms
Nuer Bushmen, 528
Numeracy, 84
Nunn, Sam, 317
Nurses. *See* Health
Nussbaum, Arthur, 484
Nutrasweet (brand), 152
Nye, Joseph S., 478
Nynex Corporation, 362
Nystrom, Anton, 505

Oaklander, Harold, 222, 526
Occupations. *See* Work; *and names of individual occupations*
Ocean technology (artificial islands), 407
Ockrent, Christine, 497
O'Driscoll, Gerald P., Jr., 484
Office, 209–10, 362; Second Wave (industrial), 208
Ogilvy & Mather, 339
Ohmae, Kenichi, 226, 460, 493, 500, 513, 551
Oil industry, xxi, 27, 46, 56–57, 124, 126, 128, 159, 176, 224, 259, 301, 306, 375, 404, 462
Okhrana, 296
Oklahoma (movie), 28
Okura Hotel (Tokyo), 57
Old boys' networks, 200. *See also* Networks, human
Oldsmobile, 78
O'Leary, Meghan, 522
Olivetti (company), 30, 136, 227
Olmer, Lionel, 306–7, 318, 534
Omission Tactic, 274. *See also* Info-tactics
On the Waterfront (movie), 341
Ong, Walter J., 500
OPEC, 56–57
Opel (automobile), 169
Open Software Foundation (OSF), 135
Open System Interconnection (OSI), 137–38
Oppenheimer, Franz, 487
Optical scanning, 98–101, 398
Optics, 87, 161, 425
Options, 262. *See also* Decision-making
Opus Dei, 200
Order, 468; absence of, 468; socially necessary, 468, 475; surplus, 468, 475
Organization, xix, 21, 26, 61, 78, 166, 168, 177, 184, 220, 393; biological model of, 185, 203; de-massification of, 183, 185–87, 202, 221, 226, 239; informal, 179, 197; machine model of, 173, 185, 203; renewal of, 185; standardization of, 183. *See also* Bureaucracy; Computers
Organizational boundaries, 226; effect of electronic networks, 121
Organizational diversity. *See* Organization
Organizational forms: buro-baronial, 195; checkerboard, 194, 199; commissar, 194–95, 199; networks, 200–202; post-bureaucratic, 190–203; profit center, 185, 203, 220; pulsating, 191–92; self-start, 198; shadow management, 193; skunkworks, 196–97; two-faced, 192–94
Organski, A.F.K., 490

Orwell, George, 209, 350, 359, 485
Osaka, 39, 62, 323
Osaka City Museum of Modern Art, 323
OSF. *See* Open Software Foundation
Osgood, Robert E., 478
OSI. *See* Open System Interconnection
Osterman, Paul, 479
Ost-Strategie, 437–45
O'Toole, Patricia, 484
Ott, James, 531
Out-inners, 158
Out-sourcing. *See* Vertical integration
Ownership. *See* Property

Pace University, 222
Pacepa, Ion, 308, 497
Pachinko (game), 42
Pacific Basin Center Foundation, 256
Pacific Economic Cooperation Conference, 407
Pacific region, 403, 407, 437, 441, 446, 453, 464. *See also names of various countries*
Packaged goods, 96–100
Packaging, 100
Paganism, 374. *See also* New Age; Religion; Secularism
Pahlavi, Mohammad Reza, 355, 374. *See also* Iran
Pakistan, 271, 316, 328, 403, 424
PAL (TV standard), 131, 138
Palazzoli, Mara Selvini, 33, 480
Palestinians, 409
Palmer, John, 493
Pamyat, 385–86
Pan, Lynn, 495
Pan Am Flight 103, 324
Pan American World Airways, 224
Panama, 333, 446, 458
Paperwork, 88, 121, 280
Papua New Guinea, 99
Paribas, 260
Paris, xxi, 6, 55, 81, 90, 116, 246, 310, 325, 440, 458, 461
Parisi, Paula, 538
Park, Jae Kyu, 493
Parker Pen (company), 340
Parliament (Great Britain), 342
Parliaments, cross-national (non-hierarchical), 464–65
Pastism. *See* Nostalgia
Patents, 109, 326, 329, 410, 433, 444, 448
Paternalism, 189
Patriarchy, 20, 182, 199, 381, 509
Pattie, Geoffrey, 267, 531
Paulos, John Allen, 500
Pay-TV, 338. *See also* Television
Peace Institute, Stockholm, 305
Peacock, William P., 484
Pearl Harbor, 297
Pearl River, New York, 65
Pennsylvania, 38
Penny press, 332
Pennzoil Company, 41, 169
Pension funds. *See* Finance
Pentagon, 16, 157, 160, 167, 263, 270–71, 286, 333, 446, 448. *See also* Military
People's Daily, 356
Pepper, Curtis Bill, 519, 545
Pepper, David, 493
Peres, Shimon, 275, 532
Perestroika, 418

Perlmutter, Amos, 487
Permissiveness, 381. *See also* Morality
Perot, H. Ross, 29, 407, 462, 510, 545, 551
Perrault, Gilles, 497
Perry, Roland, 487
Persian Gulf, 316, 437
Personal computers (PCs). *See* Computers
Personnel, 32, 34, 153, 157–59, 215. *See also* Work; Work regimens
Peru, 418, 459
Peterson, DuWayne, 144
Petras, John W., 499
Pfannes, Charles E., 490
Phalon, Richard, 531
Pharaohs, 296
Pharmaceuticals, 5, 331, 404, 410
Phased array radar, 431, 433
Philadelphia, 109
Philippines, 96, 330, 340, 348–49, 402–3, 446, 458
Philips, N. V. (company), 86, 89, 360, 444
Phillips, David Atlee, 497
Phoenicia, 84
Phonepoint (consortium), 362
Photography, 245
Photoreconnaissance. *See* Intelligence and espionage
Physician's Desk Reference, 8
Physics. *See* Science
Physiocrats, 70
Pickens, T. Boone, 29
Pillsbury Company, 77
Pincher, Chapman, 498
Pinochet, Augusto, 40
Pinwill, William, 498
Pipes, Daniel, 489
Piracy, 37, 321, 328–29, 331, 462
Pius X (pope), 46. *See also* Catholic Church
Plainville, Connecticut, 205
Planning, 6, 147, 155, 224, 416; central, 417, 419, 420, 547; knowledge problem in, 419
Plate, Thomas, 498
Playtex, 52
Plaza y Janes (company), 343
PLO (Palestine Liberation Organization), 303
Poe, Robert, 518–19
Poland, xx, 40, 383, 420, 438–39, 441–42, 458
Polanyi, Karl, 484
Police, 4, 35, 38, 42, 153, 166, 200, 253, 263, 332, 335, 347
Police networks, 200. *See also* Networks, human
Polish Ministry of Machine Industry, 302
Politburo. *See* Union of Soviet Socialist Republics (U.S.S.R.)
Political system, xx–xxi, 5, 13, 29, 69, 115, 140, 150, 166, 171, 178, 190, 199, 245, 247–48, 256–64, 336, 341, 344, 372, 387, 427, 432. *See also* Info-agenda; Info-tactics; Media; Meta-tactics
Political system, forces: citizens' groups, 322; corporate influence, 5–6, 25, 41–42, 48, 109, 113, 267; Green movement, 377–81; lobbyists, 287–88. *See also* Political system
Political system, issues: apportionment, 293; conflicts between politicians and bureaucrats, 257, 263; congruence with economic structures, 259–60; info-agenda in, 320–31. *See also* Political system

Political system, processes: communication, 415; feedback, 372; resistance, 256; theater, 25. *See also* Political system
Political system, structures: cross-national influence, 346, 351, 382, 464–65; parties, 251, 415; de-massification of, 251–52; majority rule, 253; rationality of, 276, 546; Second Wave, 11. *See also* Political system
Political system, technologies: and computers, 278, 283–85, 348–50, 365, 369–70, 373, 414, 441; electronic, 365–68; role of media, 332. *See also* Political system
Polling, 280, 285, 398
Pollution. *See* Environment and environmentalism
Polygram Records (company), 360
Pontiac, 78
Ponting, Clive, 488
Pool, Ithiel de Sola, 502
Pool, Robert, 544–45
Pope, Sterett, 536–37
Popkin, Samuel L., 261, 487, 531
Popolizio, John J., 533
Poppel, Harvey L., 502
Popper, K. R., 500
Popular culture, 336, 428, 435, 444, 450–51; ethnicity in, 451. *See also* Culture; Media; Movies
Population, 70, 266, 474
Pornography, 66
Portela, Adolfo, 490
Porter, William J., 271
Portugal, 89, 303
Positive feedback, 252–53. *See also* Feedback
Possony, Stefan T., 495
Post and telecommunications agencies (PTTs), 257, 444. *See also* Divestiture; Networks, electronic
Postal system, 64, 235, 257, 351, 363. *See also* Communications; Satellites
Post-bureaucracy, 166, 180–203
Poster, Mark, 9, 495
Post-mass production. *See* Production
Post-modern civilization. *See* Third Wave civilization
Potter, William, 63, 514
Povejsil, Donald, 181, 524
Poverty, 207, 253, 292, 379, 381, 409, 417
Power (defined), 14, 452, 508–9
Power, xviii–xxi, 3, 7, 10, 11, 473; concentration of, 219, 475; in economics, 31–32; global, 373, 392; and human relations, 12–13, 473; moral basis of, 475–76; nexus, 33–34; nominal, 182, 201; not finite, 33; Second Wave, 49, 51, 53; and social systems, 473–76; transience of, 55, 199
Power, de-massification of, 220. *See also* De-massification
Power, hidden, 182; denial of, 31, 45
Power, national (knowledge factor in). *See* National power, knowledge factor in
Power, national (sources of), 110–11
Power, quality of, 14–16, 43, 423, 452, 470, 529
Power and goals, 452
Power of balance, 423–29 (concept), 431, 435–36, 445, 451
Power triad (defined), 12–13

Power triad, 12–21, 34, 90, 372, 423–29, 431, 433, 440, 451, 454
Power vacuum, 4, 106, 243, 438
Powerlessness, xxi
Power-mosaic, 218–40
Powers, Bruce R., 502
Powers, Richard Gid, 500
Powershift (defined), 17–18, 34, 44, 393, 452
Powershift (phenomenon), 30, 425, 427, 467, 470
Powershifts, in history, 528–29
Praemium Imperiale Awards, 436
Prague, 251, 348, 391
Prediction. *See* Futurism
Preobrazhensky, E. A., 421, 547
Prepaid Card Services Inc., 65
Prescott, John E., 522
Press, 12, 156, 168, 250, 267, 269, 297, 324, 327, 332, 335, 341–42, 344, 348–49, 351–52, 355–57, 363, 435. *See also* Journalism; Media; News
Price, Alfred, 490
Prices, 419
Priestland, Gerald, 493
Prigogine, Ilya, 503
Primitive society, 528
Princeton University, 71, 284
Printing, 245, 413, 427, 456, 546
Prisons, xxi–xxii, 13, 37, 45, 109, 269, 345–46, 348
Privacy, 150–51, 323–26, 359
Privatization, 166, 224, 258–62, 264, 418; of information, 321; of intelligence and espionage, 312–16. *See also* Divestiture; State ownership and enterprise
Procter & Gamble Company, 96, 100, 215
Product differentiation, 237
Product innovation. *See* Innovation
Product standards. *See* Standards
Product systems, 130, 138–40, 239
Production, 11, 59, 82; concept of, 82; de-massification of, xx, 25, 54, 86–87, 123, 140, 181, 183, 237–38, 245, 251, 313, 340, 351, 402, 442, 449; means of, 546; relations of, 546; super-symbolic, 78. *See also* Mass production; System for wealth creation
Production, consumer role. *See* Prosumer
Production, knowledge as factor in, 84–91
Production, Second Wave, 11, 25, 46, 54, 87, 183, 244, 245, 296, 351, 404, 441; ideology of, 69, 79
Production and Distribution of Knowledge in the United States, The (Machlup), 71
Productionism (emphasis on goods), 421
Productivity, 70–71, 79, 82, 223, 229, 370
Products, systemic, 130, 138–40, 239
Professions, 155, 187, 244–45, 352, 474
Profit centers, 171, 185, 189, 203, 220–21, 223, 225, 230. *See also* Organizational forms
Profits, 31, 55, 100, 154, 181, 280, 398, 417, 461
PROFS (network), 108, 223
Progress (concept), 254
Project teams, 191, 212, 237. *See also* Ad-hocracy; Organizational forms
Prométhée (think tank), 81, 516
Proparz system, 194
Property, 210, 286, 417–19
Prosumer, xx, 126, 239; concept, 318

Protectionism, 165, 384, 411, 437, 443, 452–54. *See also* Standards; Trade
Protestant Church, 354–55, 413. *See also* Religion
Prouty, Fletcher L., 498
Provincialism, 435
Proxy wars, 29
Przychodzien, Zdzislaw, 302
Psychologists, 33
PTTs. *See* Post and telecommunications agencies
P-2 Masonic lodge, 253
Public opinion, 332–33, 345. *See also* Global opinion
Public ownership. *See* State ownership and enterprise
Public relations, 25–26, 29, 158. *See also* Polling
Pujol-Davila, José, 493
Pullman rail cars, 46
Pulsating organization, 191–92, 199. *See also* Organizational forms
Pye, Lucian W., 478
Pye, Mary W., 478
Pye, Michael, 484
Pyramids, 118

Qaddafi, Muammar el-, 253
Queen Elizabeth II (ship), 247, 333
Quick Response, 125
Quinney, Richard, 480

Rabcors, 297
Race and racism, 249–51, 253, 347, 366, 385–86, 435, 447, 451, 455, 474–75. *See also* Ethnicity; Minorities
Radac Tailor-Made (bicycle brand), 86
Radint (radar intelligence). *See* Intelligence and espionage
Radio, 337–39, 344, 351–53, 355–57. *See also* Media
Radio City Music Hall, 432
Radio Free Europe, 353
Radio Shack, 283
RAI (Italy), 338
Railroads, 27–28, 45–46, 48, 65, 76, 87, 108–9, 156, 202, 259–60, 404
Rain forest, 249
Rainbow Warrior (ship), 300
Ralph's Supermarkets, 99
Ramsdale, P. A., 502
Rand Corporation, 284
Randomness, xvii, 392, 467–68
Rangel, Carlos, 493
Ranney, Austin, 485
Rationality, 276, 380, 466
Ravenna, 221
Raw materials, 46, 60, 79, 81, 87, 91, 97, 238, 331, 377, 399, 404–5, 409, 466; knowledge as substitute for, 87–88
Raymond, H. Alan, 484
Reading, 103. *See also* Literacy
Reagan, Nancy, 69
Reagan, Ronald, xxi, 69, 170, 256, 258, 263, 273, 303, 320, 329, 349, 536, 541
Real estate, 39, 123, 153, 227, 432
Real time. *See* Time
Recreation, 73
Recruit scandal, 41, 267
Recycling, 239, 377. *See also* Environment and environmentalism

Red Army (U.S.S.R.), 430, 445
Red Brigade, 275
Red Orchestra (spy network), 314
Reddaway, Peter, 495
Reed, Steven R., 488
Regan, Donald T., 69–70, 74, 488
Regional "common markets," 464
Regional disparities, 247
Regional networks, 200
Regionalism, 200, 246, 264, 462
Regulation and deregulation, 29, 56, 71, 111, 128, 325, 435; supra-national, 58
Rehfeld, Barry J., 481
Reich, Robert, 551
Reingold, Edwin M., 493
Relations of production, 546
Relays, 158
Religion, 3, 8, 18, 43, 68, 84, 207, 244, 250, 254, 266, 301, 335, 351, 354–55, 360, 372–76, 378–79, 381–82, 385, 413, 424, 441, 452, 455–60, 462–63, 465–66, 529, 541, 544; and First Wave elites, 373; as mass media, 354–55; as media (First Wave), 354; as media (Second Wave), 354; as vehicle for popular discontent, 355
Religio-politics. See Religion
Religious networks, 200. See also Networks, human
Remote sensing, 298, 312, 315–16
Representation, 465. See also under various categories of Political system
Representation, cross-national, 464. See also Political system, forces; issues; processes; structures; technologies
Republic Steel Corporation, 38
Republican Party (U.S.), 202, 256, 320
Republikaners (Germany), 383
Research and development, 25, 75, 79, 90, 153–55, 165, 235, 258, 407–10, 412, 427–28, 433, 444, 446, 448–49; cross-national, 443; underground, 166
Resources, 404, 405. See also Raw materials
Restaurant industry, 47, 64, 77, 95, 227, 233, 237, 340. See also Food and food industry
Restructure, business, 26–28, 53, 171, 179, 184, 374; financial, 26, 51, 53, 55. See also Organizational forms; Takeovers
Reszler, André, 488
Retailing, 64, 90, 95–105, 121–22, 124, 126, 149, 161, 180, 191, 259, 400
Reveille, Thomas, 496
Reversal Tactic, 275. See also Info-tactics
Reverse engineering, 155
Reversionism, 378
Revlon, Inc., 53, 96
Revolution, 216, 253, 414, 431, 546; Marx's definition, 414; and media, strategies, 347–58; theory of, 546
Rhine River, 311, 378
Rhône-Alpes region, 246
Richelieu, Cardinal, xxii
Richelson, Jeffrey, 498
Rigby, T. H., 495
Right to know, 322–23, 326
Right to Know Network Kansai, 323
Rise and Fall of the Great Powers, The (Kennedy), 452
Risk, 80, 398
Ritual, 186, 397
Rivers, Gayle, 490

Riyadh, 56, 315
Rizzo, Mario J., 484
RJR-Nabisco (company), 218
Roach, John, 545
Robber barons, 28, 45
Robert Bosch GmbH (company), 132
Roberts, John, 533
Robertson, James, 484
Robertson, Jerry, 236
Robertson, Pat, 354
Robots, 9, 71, 78, 226, 237, 398, 433, 443
Rochester, Minnesota, 336
Rochester, New York, 245
Rockefeller, John D., 224
Rodinson, Maxime, 489
Roger & Me (movie), 29
Rogers, William, 271
Roget's Thesaurus, 36
Rohan, Thomas M., 516
Rohlen, Thomas P., 530
Rolls-Royce (company), 236
Romania, 243, 302–3, 308–9, 348–50, 353, 438. See also Ceausescu, Nicolae
Romanticization of the past, 380. See also Golden Age myth; Medievalism; Nostalgia
Rome, 3, 6, 89, 338, 381
Rona, Thomas, 289, 533
Roosevelt, Franklin D., 251, 261
Ropke, Wilhelm, 484
Rosecrance, Richard, 493
Rosenbaum, Ron, 551
Rosenberg, Hans, 480
Rosenbloom, David H., 480
Rosenthal, Stuart, 483
Rositzke, Harry, 498
Rossi, Sergio, 180, 187
Roulet, Jean Remy, 482
Rousseau, Jean-Jacques, 468–69
Rowland, Roland "Tiny," 29
Rubin, Barry, 488
Rueschmeyer, Dietrich, 478
Rumors, 275. See also Gossip
Rushdie, Salman, 254, 456–57, 551
Russell, Bertrand, 478, 508
Russian Orthodox Church, 296, 466. See also Religion
Russian Revolution, 419
Russo-Japanese War, 296
Rustow, Alexander, 479, 528
Rutkowski, Anthony, 518, 546
Ryan, Art, 141, 521

S. Appolinare Nuovo, 221
Saatchi & Saatchi (company), 338–39
Sabotage, 161, 216, 259–60, 283, 365; ecological, 377; electronic, 365–66
Sabre (reservation system), 117
Sachs, Wolfgang, 378–79, 542
Sacramento, California, 145
Sadat, Anwar, 314, 333
Sadler, A. L., 491
Saeed, Syed Mumtaz, 189, 484, 524
Safeway Stores, Inc., 398
Sagan, Eli, 488
Saibu Saison (company), 127
Said, Abdul A., 331, 493
Saigon, 269
St. Louis, Missouri, 113, 117
St.-Gobain (company), 260

Sakharov, Andrei, 345, 544
Salad bowl concept, 250. *See also* Ethnicity;
    Minorities; Race and racism
Salamona, Victor A., 490
Sales, 33, 61, 83, 96–101, 108, 158, 197, 362.
    See also Marketing; Retailing
Salinas de Gortari, Carlos, 258, 531
Salisbury, North Carolina, 205
Salomon Brothers, 55, 144
SALT Treaty, 271
Sam Browne (belts), 380
Sampson, Anthony, 484
Sampson, Geoffrey, 493
Samuelson, Paul A., 31
San Francisco, 88, 312
San Onofre Nuclear Generating Station, 193
Sanders, Ralph, 492
Sandinistas, 402
Sanshu no jingi, 13
São Paulo, 316
Sara Lee, 108, 218
Sarakin, 39
Sardar, Ziauddin, 489
SAS. *See* Special Air Service
Sassoon, Anne Showstack, 495
Satanic Verses, The (Rushdie), 456
Satellites, 49, 89, 113, 131, 280, 289, 298, 300,
    304, 312, 315–16, 327, 333, 338, 342,
    348, 350, 352, 357, 367, 382, 393, 398,
    412, 456, 460
Saudi Arabia, 316, 330
Saudi Center for Remote Sensing, 315
Savalas, Telly, 348
Savannah River, 322
Savas, E. S., 488
Savery, Thomas, 63
Savings and loans. *See* Banking
Savings rate, 432
Scale, 181, 219–21, 392–93, 442
Scali, John, 272
Scandinavia. See *names of individual countries*
Scapegoats, 442. *See also* Anti-Semitism;
    Ethnicity; Race and racism
Schalk, Tom, 154
Schapiro, Mark, 539
Schefer, Ed, 141, 521
Schenker, Jennifer L., 531
Schevill, Ferdinand, 505
Schlereth, Thomas J., 505
Schmerken, Ivy, 523
Schmidt, Robert E., Jr., 522
Schmidt-Hauer, Christian, 505
Schneider, Harold K., 483
Schoenhuber, Franz, 383, 544
Schools. *See* Education
Schultz, Ted, 489
Schumpeter, Joseph A., 80, 484
Schwartz, Tony, 510
Schwarz-Schilling, Christian, 132
Science, xxi, 18, 25, 62, 75, 80, 118, 137, 140,
    165, 208, 239, 252, 258, 309, 329–31,
    360, 370–71, 379, 392, 404, 407–8,
    410–11, 416–17, 427, 433, 443–44,
    448–51, 454
Science, 289, 392
Science fiction, 336, 365–66
Scientific socialism. *See* Socialism and Marxism
Scorsese, Martin, 451
Scotland, 247
Scott, D. R., 500
Scowcroft, Brent, 314

Screenies, 368
Sculley, John, 29, 228–29, 484, 527
SDI. *See* Strategic Defense Initiative
SE. *See* Simultaneous engineering
Search Associates, 159
Sears, Roebuck & Company, 184
Seattle, Washington, 380
SECAM (TV standard), 131, 138
Secession, 243, 247–48, 254, 424
Second Wave (defined), xx
Second Wave society. *See* Industrial society
Secondary enforcement system, 36. *See also*
    Law and lawyers; Police
Secrecy, 13, 120, 150–51, 267, 270, 273,
    278–79, 294–95, 317–20, 323, 326–27,
    370, 428; role of telephone, 110
Secrecy Tactic, 266. *See also* Info-tactics
Secret Intelligence Service (MI6), Great
    Britain, 300
Secret police, 350, 415
Secularism, 373–76, 379, 382, 458, 544; post-,
    458; pre-, 458; as Second Wave
    phenomenon, 373–76, 458. *See also*
    Church and State; Religion
Securitate, 350
Securities, 62, 65. *See also* Derivatives; Finance
Seino Transport (company), 143
Sekigawa, Eiichiro, 531
Self-organization, 197–98, 237
Self-start team. *See* Organizational forms
Selyunin, Vasily, 37, 510
Semiconductors. *See* Computer industry
Semiology, 444
Seneker, Harold, 510
Seniority, 223
Seoul, 38, 276, 284
Serbia, 247, 249
Service Bay Diagnostics System, Ford Motor
    Company, 176
Service sector, 49, 53, 61, 69–70, 74, 76,
    79–80, 155, 442, 447; de-massification
    of, 54; denigration of, 69–83, 421. *See also*
    Material-ismo
Sesame Street (TV program), 367
Seth, Ronald, 498
Seward, Desmond, 505
Sex, xxi, 3, 30, 156, 207, 325, 335, 451
Sexism, 79, 188, 244, 381, 451, 509
Seybold, John W., 481
Shadow management. *See* Organizational
    forms
Shakespeare, William, 45
Shamir, Yitzhak, 275, 532
Shanghai, 310
Shannon, Claude, 18, 502
Sharp, Gene, 491
Shcharansky, Anatoly, 345
Shear, Jeff, 550
Shearson (company), 119, 144
Sheffield, England, 380
Shelbyville, Indiana, 78, 211
Shelf management, 100
Sheller-Globe Corporation, 156
Sherbak, Fiodor, 303
Sheridan, John H., 527
Sherman, Howard, 495
Sherwood, Diane, 536
Shevchenko, Arkady N., 272, 498
Shiites, 457. *See also* Islam
Shimada, Haruo, 90
Shimomura, Mitsuko, 493

Shinto, 375
Shipbuilding, 71
Shipping industry, 37, 43, 48, 87
Shiseido Company, Ltd., 121
Shizuoka University (Japan), 310
Shoe industry, 86
Shultz, George P., 171, 532
Shultz, Richard H., 498
Siberia, 297, 315
Siegel, Richard, 323
Siemens (company), 61, 131, 134–35, 308, 444
Sigint (signals intelligence). *See* Intelligence
    and espionage
Signs, 18
Sik, Ota, 495
Sikata, Kozaburo, 229
Sikhs in Canada, 254
Silicon Valley, 309, 363, 434
Silkwood, Karen, 39, 511
Silver, 63
Simmons, Luiz R., 331, 493
Simon, William, 314
Simulation, 280, 365
Simultaneity, 236
Simultaneous engineering (SE), 236–37
Singapore, 62, 145, 391, 395, 405,
    466
Singer, Benjamin D., 484
Singer, Kurt, 500
Siu, R.G.H., 479
Skills, pre-specification of, 152
Skouras, George, 28
Skunkworks organization. *See* Organizational
    forms
Sky Channel, 342
Sky Television, 338
Slade, M. G., 502
Slavery, 28, 37, 43
Slavs, 466
Sloan, Allan, 512, 513
Slovakia, 247, 458
Slow economies, 397–412, 442. *See also*
    Acceleration; Acceleration effect;
    Non-industrial economies
Sluzba Bezpieczenstwa (SB), Poland,
    302
Small business, 52, 180–81, 226, 228
Small is beautiful. *See* Diseconomies of scale;
    Economies of scale; Scale
Smiley, George (fictional character), 295, 522,
    533–34
Smith, Adam, 301, 484
Smith, Alfred G., 502
Smith, Daniel C., 522
Smith, Gerard C., 271
Smith, Roger, 29
Smith Barney, 181
Smithsonian Institution, 95, 360
Smokestack economy. *See* Industrial society;
    System for wealth creation, Second
    Wave (industrial)
Sobel, Robert, 484
Social Contract, The (Rousseau), 468
Social Democrats (Germany), 443
Social diversity, 249–51. *See also* De-
    massification; Ethnicity
Social indicators, 288
Social justice, 253, 368. *See also*
    Order
Social power, theory of, xx, 12–21
Social Security, 66, 286

Socialism and Marxism, 10, 20–21, 26, 32,
    40–41, 43, 111, 256, 258, 348, 350,
    354–56, 387, 391, 393, 413–22, 458, 466,
    514, 528, 546; knowledge problem of,
    413, 415–22; Lenin on European
    integration and, 438; and pre-cybernetic
    model, 415–16; as "scientific," 417; as
    Second Wave, 415–22
Socialist primitive accumulation, 420–21
Socialist realism, 79, 421
Société Générale de Belgique, 30
Society, de-massification of, 167, 250, 436. *See
    also* De-massification
Society of Competitor Intelligence Profession-
    als, 156
Society of Japanese Aerospace Companies,
    407
Softnomics, 27
Software. *See* Computer industry
Sokaiya, 38
Solidarity movement (Poland), xx, 40, 348
Solis, Michel, 550
Solzhenitsyn, Aleksandr, 544
Sony Corporation, 131, 211, 218, 341, 362,
    425
Sophia University, Japan, 436
Sorge, Richard, 297, 533
Soto, Hernando de, 493
Soule, George, 484
South, 423, 466; fragmentation of, 391, 394
South Africa, 37, 303, 345–46, 418
South America, xxi, 303, 310, 462
South Korea, 38–39, 67, 72, 284, 355, 382,
    391, 395, 400, 405, 431, 466
South Sea Islanders in Japan, 250
South Tyrol, 247
Southeast Asian region, 403, 431. *See also*
    Pacific
Southern California Edison, 193
Southern Poverty Law Center, 249
Sovereignty, 7, 426, 457, 465, 469. *See also*
    Nation-state; Nationalism
Soviet Union. *See* Union of Soviet Socialist
    Republics (U.S.S.R.)
Sowell, Thomas, 500
Space, knowledge as substitute for, 88
Space Media Network, 316
Space program, 393
Spacks, Patricia Meyer, 502
Spain, 30, 338, 342–43, 384, 462
Spanish language, 115, 176, 336
Spatial relations, 91, 123
SPC Software Systems, 175
Special Air Service (SAS), 192–93
Specialization, 167, 172, 177–78, 197, 210,
    262, 449
Speech technology, 119, 129, 153–54, 362
Speed. *See* Acceleration
Speed to market. *See* Acceleration
Spencer, Herbert, 488
Spero, Robert, 530
Sports, 28, 124, 186, 191, 334, 342, 360
SPOT (satellite), 315–16
Spreadsheets, three-dimensional, 279
Sprentnak, Charlene, 486
Sputnik, 434
Spycatcher (Wright), 327
Squatters, xxi
SS-23 (missile), 440
Staaf, Robert, 484
Stadnichenko, A., 485

Stahel, Walter R., 482
Stalin, Josef, 297, 421, 475
Stalk, George, Jr., 527
Standard & Poor's, 49
Standard Oil, 224
Standardization of organization, 183. *See also*
   Bureaucracy; Organization
Standards, 130–40, 152, 239, 362
Standards for standards, 139
Stanford University, 358, 434
Star Wars. *See* Strategic Defense Initiative
   (SDI)
Starr, Chester G., 491
Starr, John Bryan, 496
Starr, Richard, 512
State, 40, 44, 248, 321, 351, 354, 370, 372,
   382, 386, 410, 425, 447, 468, 470; history
   of, 528–29; as machine, 416; monopoly
   of violence, 44; theory of, 528
State ownership and enterprise, 417–19. *See
   also* Privatization
State Street of Boston, 145–46
State University of New York, Stony Brook,
   52
Statistics, validity of, 286–88, 292–93
Steam engine, 63, 209
Steel and steel industry, 27, 37–38, 45–46, 54,
   60, 71, 74, 157, 209, 224, 308–9,
   400–401, 407, 417, 420–21
Steinhoff, Patricia G., 531
Steinke, Ted, 154
Stengers, Isabelle, 503
Stephens, Mitchell, 485
Stephenson, Carl, 506
Sterling, Claire, 493
Stern, 327
Stern, J. P., 380, 505
Stevens, Charles, 39
Stevens, Mark, 485
Stevenson, J. D., 496
Stever, H. Guyford, 503
Stewart, Alex, 105, 485, 517
Stirling, David, 193, 524
Stix, Gary, 523
Stock market. *See* Finance; Securities
Stockholm, 276, 305, 316
Stockman, David A., 286, 488, 533
Stoll, Clifford, 160
Stone, David, 198, 203, 213, 525
Stonehenge, 118
Storage and Transportation General Corpora-
   tion, China, 400–401
Strassman, Paul A., 502
Strategic alliances, 226–27
Strategic Defense Initiative (SDI), 160, 270,
   394, 424, 426
Strategic location, 402–3
Strauss, Howard Jay, 284
Straussman, Jeffrey D., 488
Strausz-Hupe, Robert, 493
Strehlow, T.G.H., 500
Structuralism, 444
Students, 3, 8, 40, 348, 356, 367
Studio, 4, 350
Stulberg, Gordon, 360, 541
Stuttgart, 380
Stuttgarter Zeitung, 453
Submarines, 17, 310, 403–4, 439
Subsistence. *See* Poverty
Sumitomo Warehouse, 123
Sun Microsystems, 134

Sunday Times, The (London), 342
Sun-Tzu, 17, 479
Sununu, John, 278–79, 287, 291, 532
Superconductivity, 404, 433, 443, 450
Supermarkets, 3, 21, 95–105, 152; intelligent,
   104–5. *See also* Marketing; Retailing
Superpowers, 4–5, 424
Superstructure and base, 421
Super-symbolic economy (Third Wave), 10,
   17, 25–75, 86, 91, 118, 128, 147,
   166–67, 190, 245–46, 249, 258, 264, 279,
   293, 307, 321, 324, 335, 359, 370–71,
   392, 395, 398, 401, 414, 418, 420, 426,
   447, 469; dissent in, 371
Supplier coalitions, 230
Supra-national agencies, 246. *See also*
   European Community
Supra-national forces, 250
Supra-nationalism, 58, 264, 383. *See also*
   Globalism; Nationalism
Suter, Keith, 493
Suvorov, Viktor, 498
Swaggert, Jimmy, 354
Sweda (company), 98
Sweden, 89, 202, 254, 324
Swetz, Frank J., 500
Swidler, Leonard, 489
Switzerland, 56, 338
Sydney, 62, 407, 461
Symbols and symbolism, 18, 25
Synthesis, xxii, 81–82, 177, 220, 222, 427
Synthetics, 62. *See also* Investment
Syria, 153, 311–12, 394
Syrians, 394; in West Africa, 409
System Applications Architecture (SAA), 138
System for wealth creation, 9–10, 25–26, 55,
   59, 140, 244, 248; conflict over, 26,
   32–33, 59, 74, 240, 244; pace of, 234
System for wealth creation, First Wave
   (agrarian), 234
System for wealth creation, Second Wave
   (industrial), 234, 351, 365, 395; in
   Central Europe, 438
System for wealth creation, Third Wave
   (super-symbolic), 83, 237, 280–81, 295,
   299–300, 312, 316, 318, 321, 329, 352,
   364, 368, 370, 373, 379, 386, 393,
   395–96, 399–400, 403, 405–6, 411,
   413–14, 417–18, 420, 422, 425, 442,
   460, 465–66, 469, 547; summary, 233–40
System Network Architecture (SNA), 137
Systemic media. *See* Media as system
Systemic products, 239
Systems Control, 302
Szelenyi, Ivan, 500

Taboos, 397
Tafoya, William L., 253, 530
Taipei, 3
Taisei, 407
Taiwan, 328, 330, 348, 357, 391, 395, 405–6,
   466
Takeovers, xviii, 26–27, 29–30, 34, 41, 50,
   52–53, 80, 169, 218–19, 222, 259;
   cross-national, 29–30, 460. *See also*
   Finance; Organizational forms
Takeshita, Noboru, 41, 267, 431, 511, 549
Takeuchi, Hirotaka, 197, 524
Talbott, Strobe, 493
Talk Radio (movie), 352
Tallahassee, Florida, 113

Talman Pty., Ltd., 124
Tanaka, Giichi, 296, 301, 533
Tandem Computers, 166
Tandy Corporation, 400
Tannian, Francis, 484
Tape recorders, 130, 358
Tapie, Bernard, 28
Tapsell, R. F., 506
Tarde, Gabriel, 502
Tashkent, 385
Tate, Paul, 527
Tate, Raymond, 306
Taxes and taxpayers, 26–27, 29, 31, 42, 62, 218, 247, 260, 282, 291, 293, 321, 337, 399, 528
Taxing Woman's Return, A (movie), 39
Taylor, Frederick, 77
Taylor, Maxwell, 269
Taylor, Stanley, 500
Taylorism, 77, 215
Team Bandit, Motorola, 237
Techint (technological intelligence). *See* Intelligence and espionage
Technological espionage, 302, 307–11, 331. *See also* Intelligence and espionage
Technological slowdown, 443
Technology, xx–xxi, 17, 32, 40, 69, 72, 81, 86, 113, 137, 140, 165, 167–68, 179, 181, 208–10, 247–48, 251, 290, 309, 329–30, 332, 373, 377–78, 391–93, 395, 397, 399–400, 402, 404, 406–7, 410, 414, 419, 428, 431, 433, 443, 448–51, 454, 458, 467, 474; Second Wave (industrial), 207–8, 416
Techno-nationalism. *See* Trade
Technophobia. *See* Ludditism
Tefft, Stanton K., 500
Tehran, 168, 320
Teishin-sho. *See* Japanese Ministry of Posts and Telecommunications (MPT)
Telecommunications, 28, 53, 64, 83, 88, 90, 106–29, 135–37, 142–43, 161–62, 190, 201, 223, 235, 257, 321, 326, 351, 359, 362, 407–8, 411–12, 444, 450, 462; maldistribution of, 412; trade, 329. *See also under various categories of* Networks; *and names of individual technologies*
Tele-computers, 361
Tele-5, 343
Telegraph, 107–8, 110, 351. *See also* Telecommunications
Telepanel, Inc., 104
Telephone, 28, 53, 65, 105, 109–11, 113–14, 125, 136, 147, 153, 159, 235, 260, 280, 350–52, 357–58, 361–63, 366, 412. *See also* Telecommunications
Televangelism, 354. *See also* Religion
Television, 3, 8, 28, 53, 97, 132, 139, 152, 162, 251, 266, 333–35, 337–39, 341–44, 348, 350–53, 355–57, 359, 368, 435–36, 451, 456; as de-massified medium (Third Wave), 336–37, 339; as mass medium (Second Wave), 336–37; networks (Second Wave), 337, 361, 368–69. *See also* Media
Television, cable, 333–34, 338–39, 350, 352, 368, 435
Television, direct satellite. *See* Direct broadcast satellite

Television, high-definition (HDTV), 129, 131–33, 337, 359, 435, 453
Television Without Frontiers, 382
Templeman, Martin, 175
Terrorism, 37, 202, 247, 249, 253–54, 273, 275, 320, 324–25, 375, 377, 386, 442, 457, 459–62, 465
Terry, Edith, 529
Texaco, Inc., 41, 169
Texas, 400, 407
Texas Instruments, Inc., 153–54
Textile industry, 37–38, 60, 63, 71, 89, 120, 124–25, 157, 209
TF1, 342
Thailand, 328–29, 395, 406
Thatcher, Margaret, 58, 260, 327
Theater. *See* Arts
Theocracy. *See* Fundamentalism, religious; Religion; Secularism
Third Italy (Italy Numero Tre), 180
Third Wave (defined), xx
Third Wave, The (Toffler), xviii–xx, xxii, 54, 69, 183, 352
Third Wave civilization, xx, 118, 422
Third Wave economy. *See* Super-symbolic economy (Third Wave)
Thomas, Evan, 504
Thomas, Gordon, 489
Thompson, E. P., 506
Thomson, S.A. (company), 132
Thorn/EMI, 132
Three Mile Island, 284, 377
Three T's study, 407
Threshold Test Ban Treaty, 286
Tiananmen Square, 40, 251, 333, 353, 356, 358. *See also* China; Media
Tidal Wave Tactic, 275. *See also* Info-tactics
Time, 274; clocks, 37; in economy, 88, 91, 235, 401; First Wave (agrarian), 207; knowledge as substitute for, 88; real, 64, 88, 398; zones, 47, 54–55. *See also* Timing Tactics
Time, 278
Time bias, 444–45. *See also* Future-consciousness; Nostalgia
Time horizon, xix, 3, 9
Time-Life, 360
Times, The (London), 342
Timing Tactics, 274. *See also* Info-tactics
Timisoara, Romania, 350
Titanium, 404
Tobacco, 63, 398
Todd, Mike, 28
Toffler, Alvin, 480, 485, 507, 540, 546, 548
Toffler, Heidi, xviii, 69, 540, 546
Tokuyama, Jiro, 407, 545
Tokyo, xxi, 39, 55–58, 136, 152, 168, 194, 226, 249, 257, 260, 296–97, 364, 407, 431, 434, 453, 455
Tokyo Stock Exchange, 432
Tolstoi, Alexsei, 385
Toohey, Brian, 498
Tornado (aircraft), 439
Toronto, 55
Torture, 13, 345
Tosches, Nick, 485
Toshiba (company), 65, 166, 310, 363
Toshiba affair, 310
Totalitarianism, 205, 213, 243, 254, 318, 354–55, 359, 370, 376, 387, 469–70
Touraine, Alain, 380, 542

Tourism, 73, 346, 407, 462
Tower, John, 488
Tower Commission, 171
Toxic waste. *See* Environment and environmentalism
Toyoda, Eiji, 485
Toyota (company), 77, 125, 237. *See also* Auto and auto industry
Toys-R-Us, Inc., 100
Trade, 56, 79, 125–26, 131–33, 136–37, 139–40, 152, 165, 282, 304, 306–7, 309, 328–29, 345, 384, 391, 405, 432, 435–36, 441, 447, 450. *See also* Globalization; Markets
Tradegate (network), 124
Tradition and innovation, 397–98
Traditionalism. *See* Agrarian society (First Wave)
Traffic, 252
Training, 73, 78, 193, 206, 213, 225, 258, 335, 447. *See also* Education
Transaction speeds and costs, 222, 234, 239
Transfer pricing, 32, 224
Transience, xix, 228, 427. *See also* Acceleration
Translation, automatic, 115, 129, 362, 448
Transnational corporations. *See* Non-national corporations
Transportation, 87, 103, 105, 116–17, 123, 143, 176, 213, 237, 245, 254, 263, 324–25, 369, 397–98, 401, 407, 410; knowledge as substitute for, 87–88. *See also* Airlines; Auto and auto industry; Railroads; Trucking industry
Trans-Siberian Railroad, 296, 301
Travel. *See* Transportation
Trend projection, xvii
Tribalism, 186, 190, 199, 385, 386, 528
Tripoli, 327
Trucking industry, 105, 116. *See also* Transportation
Trudeau, Garry, 509
Trump, Donald, 25–26, 509–10
Truth, 18–19, 85, 280–81, 287, 290. *See also* Falsehood
TRW, Inc., 382
Tsurumi, Kazuko, 436, 489
Tsurumi, Shunsuke, 493
Tsurumi, Yoshi, 256, 530
Tuck, Jay, 503
Tucker, Robert W., 478
Tujo, J. A., 283, 532
Tunisia, 343
Turf wars. *See* Bureaucracy
Turkey, 311, 374
Turks in Bulgaria, 247. *See also* Ethnicity; Minorities
Turks in Germany, 250, 383. *See also* Ethnicity; Minorities
Turner, Stansfield, 327, 498, 537
Turner, Ted, 169, 333–34, 342, 344, 346, 538
Turtle Talk (newsletter), 146
TV. *See* Television
TV Guide, 103, 342
TV South, 341
Twentieth Century-Fox, 342, 360
Two-faced organization. *See* Organizational forms
Twopenny Dispatch, 332
Tyuratam, 316

Ubiquity, Law of, 363–64, 369
Ubiquity of media. *See* Media as system

Ukraine, 466
UKUSA Security Agreement, 302, 304
Underclass, 366–68
Underground economy, 401, 419
Underground research, 166. *See also* Research and development
Unemployment, 50, 71–74, 222–23, 253, 262, 281, 322, 367, 383, 417, 447; qualitative, 73; quantitative, 72
Union Carbide Corporation, 168
Union of International Associations, 201
Union of Soviet Socialist Republics (U.S.S.R.), xxi, 4, 37, 80, 147, 165–66, 224, 243, 247–48, 263, 270, 272, 275, 326–27, 343, 345, 353, 359, 375, 378, 383, 385, 391, 402–3, 407, 412, 413–14, 416, 417–21, 423, 428–29, 430, 434, 438, 441, 444, 446, 451, 455, 466, 469; intelligence and military, xviii, 161, 194, 219, 271–73, 286, 289, 296–99, 300–307, 309–10, 315–16, 348, 375, 385, 393–94, 402–3, 424–25, 428, 438–40, 445, 453–54
Unisys (company), 135
United Airlines, 169
United Artists, 361
United Kingdom. *See* Great Britain
United Nations, 56, 136, 391, 457, 459, 463; corporate representation in, 463
United Parcel Service (UPS), 75
United Research Company, 210
United States, xviii–xix, 5–9, 21, 153, 200, 249–50, 270, 327, 333, 341–43, 347, 357–58, 366–68, 402, 423, 426, 428–29, 432–36, 443–44, 448–51; business, 25–30, 37–39, 41–42, 46–47, 49, 51–52, 76, 87–89, 95–99, 101, 108–9, 111–12, 117, 120–21, 124–25, 141, 143, 147, 156–57, 172–73, 180–81, 184–85, 188, 190–91, 194–95, 205, 223–24, 226, 235, 245–46, 259, 283, 288, 322–23, 339; business, international, 131–33, 136–38, 218–19, 233, 237, 312–13, 328–29, 361, 392–95, 460–61; economy, 55–56, 63, 66, 69–72, 74, 169, 235, 332, 336–37, 362–63, 373, 393, 395, 399–400, 406–8, 411, 413–14, 432, 440–41, 446–49; intelligence and military, 161, 263, 267, 269–72, 289, 296, 299–300, 302–4, 312–13, 315, 317, 327, 349, 394, 403, 425, 430–32, 437, 439–40, 446; politics, 170, 251, 253, 256, 266–67, 269–71, 275, 283, 287–88, 291, 293, 306, 310, 320, 321–24, 329–30, 349, 354, 384, 438, 464–65, 469
United States, decline theory, 384
United States, economic power of, 446–47
United States, knowledge-power of, 448–51
United States, military power of, 445–46
United States, representation in Japanese Diet, 464
United States, strategy, 445, 447, 452–55
U.S. Bureau of Labor Statistics, 322
U.S. Cabinet, 263, 289
U.S. Census Bureau, 190–91, 286–87, 292–93
U.S. Commerce Department, 286
U.S. Congress, 107, 195, 268, 283, 286–87, 290–91, 293, 317, 320–22, 446, 464. *See also* Parliaments
U.S. Customs Service, 227
U.S. Department of Agriculture, 65

U.S. Department of Commerce, 300, 306, 307, 318
U.S. Department of Defense, 134, 170, 315
U.S. Department of Energy, 291, 300, 322, 323
U.S. Department of Justice, 282
U.S. Department of State, 170, 263, 269, 271–72, 291, 300, 309, 314, 329
U.S. Department of the Treasury, 300
U.S. Department of Transportation, 117
U.S. House Intelligence Committee, 271
U.S. House of Representatives, 131, 270, 293, 324
U.S. Navy, 167. *See also* Military
U.S. Post Office, 227
U.S. Senate, 291, 317, 322
United States Steel Corporation, 45
U.S. Supreme Court, 384
U.S. Telephone, 153
U.S. Trade Representative, Office of, 137, 329
United States–Europe alliance, 453–55
United States–Japan alliance, 453–55
Universalism, 376
Universities, 132, 190, 321, 356, 367, 435
University College, London, 380
University of Alaska, 315
University of California, Berkeley, 3, 49, 358
University of California, Irvine, 9
University of California, San Diego, 261
University of Pennsylvania, 378
University of Toledo, 176
University of Tsukuba, 210
Unix, 134–35
Unpredictability, xxi, 152, 468
UPC (Universal Product Code), 98–101
Urals, 458
Uranium, 87
Urban issues, 11, 386. *See also* Anti-urbanism; Back-to-nature movement
Urban Policy Research Institute, 284
Urban systems, 245, 374
USA Today, 99
User groups, 230
Utopia, 417, 470

Val Vibrata, 180
Value, economic (concept), 81–82, 153, 158, 187, 230–31
Value Added Networks (VANs). *See* Networks, value added
Values, 19, 86, 182; pre-industrial, 380. *See also* Morality
Van den Berg, Jan Hendrik, 501
Vanderbilt, Cornelius "Commodore," 29
VANs (Value Added Networks). *See* Networks, value added
Vapor Tactic, 275. *See also* Info-tactics
Vassalage, 195–96
Vatican. *See* Catholic Church
Vatican Council, 373
VAX, 230
VCRs. *See* Videotape and VCRs
Venice, 281
Venture capital, 411. *See also* Capital
Versailles Treaty, 383
Vertical integration, 106, 224–25, 261, 342; hidden costs of, 225; in espionage, 314
Victorville, California, 347
Video games, 65
Video stores, 66
Videocassette recorders (VCRs). *See* Videotape and VCRs

Videocracy, 350, 353
Videotape and VCRs, 161, 235, 280, 328, 334, 336–37, 341, 347–48, 350, 364, 444
Videotex, 115
Vietnam War, 219, 269, 286, 314, 395, 405, 431
Villegas, José, 365
Violence (defined), 13, 40
Violence, 12–21, 35–44, 90, 423, 470, 474, 528–29; knowledge-intensivity of, 17, 425; state monopoly of, 40. *See also* Law and lawyers; Military; Police; Power triad
Violence, changing nature of. *See* Powershift
Virgin Group (company), 28
Virgin Music (company), 341
Virginia, 400
Visa International, 65, 67, 460; credit card holders, 64
VNET, 108
Voice Control Systems, Inc., 153–54
Voice of America, 353, 358
Volkswagen, 169, 260. *See also* Auto and auto industry
Voluntary Inter-Industry Communications Standard (VICS), 90
Volvo (company), 108
Vorkuta, 37

Waal, Frans de, 479
Waffen-SS, 383
Waldmueller, Annamaria, 549
Walesa, Lech, 348
Walker, James Blaine, 506
Wall Street, 26, 29, 47–51, 53–54, 169, 181, 249, 333, 364, 426, 434. *See also* Finance
Wall Street Journal, 135, 137, 340, 383
Wal-Mart, 101, 124, 161
Walt Disney Company, 145
Walter, Ingo, 493
Wanandi, Jusuf, 493–94
Wandervogel movement, 380
Wang (company), 108
War, 243, 297, 331, 343, 386, 403, 418, 431, 453; consequences of, 395, 405, 466; crimes, 384. *See also* Military
Ward, J. T., 506
Ware, James P., 212, 525
Ware, Willis H., 284
Warehousing, 88, 105, 123, 400–401
Wargames (movie), 282
Warsaw, 302, 391
Warsaw Pact, 295, 439
Washington, D.C., 95, 107, 132, 136, 168, 170, 200, 253, 261, 267, 269–73, 287, 314, 320, 326, 352, 430–31, 434, 453, 455
Washington Post, 268, 349
Washington Shoe Company, 86
WASP, 451
Watergate, 268
Watson, Thomas J., Jr., 214
Wealth, 9, 12–21, 60–68, 71, 79, 85, 423, 425, 430, 433, 448, 470, 474, 528–29; as relational, 227–28. *See also* Capital; Money; Power triad; System for wealth creation
Wealth creation, as cyclical process, 239
Weatherford, Jack, 506
Weaver, Warren, 18, 502
Weber, Herbert, 532
Weber, Max, 480

Weber, Nat, 522
Webster, William, 424
Weimar Republic, 380. *See also* Germany
Weimer, George, 527
Weinberger, Caspar, 270
Weingarten, Robert I., 29, 510
Weir, Ernest T., 224
Weisband, Edward, 486
Weisskopf, Walter A., 80, 515
Welch, David A., 490
Welch, Jack, 28
Welch, Mary-Scott, 480
Welfare, 65, 73, 245
Wells Fargo, 146
Welter, Therese R., 518, 525
Wenburg, John R., 502
Wenceslas Square, 251
Wendt, Lloyd, 506
Wendy's International, Inc., 233, 235–36
Wernick, Murray, 546
West, Nigel, 498
West Berlin, 383. *See also* Germany
West Germany. *See* Germany
West Indians in Britain, 200. *See also*
    Ethnicity; Minorities
Western Europe, 6, 7, 247, 304, 384, 413. *See
    also* European Community
Western Union Corporation, 45, 109, 112–13,
    147
Westinghouse Electric Corporation, 181
Wheel of Fortune (TV program), 361
Wheeler, George, 506
Whistle blowers, 39
White goods industry, 89
White House, xxi, 69, 171, 256, 261, 266–68,
    270, 272–74, 278, 286, 291, 316, 320,
    322, 333, 349, 357, 384
White House Office of Management and
    Budget, 66, 286, 291
White House Science Office, 289
White-collar work. *See* Mind-work and
    mind-workers
Whitehead, Alfred North, 501
Whittemore, Hank, 486
Wholesalers, 96, 121–22
Wiarda, Howard J., 494
Wilcox, A. M., 502
Williams, Jeannie, 510
Wilmot, William W., 502
Wilson, Derek, 506
Wilson, Dick, 496
Wilson, George M., 506
Wing, R. L., 479
Winograd, Terry, 502
Wittfogel, Karl A., 506, 528
Wolferen, Karl van, 488
Women, 37, 45, 97, 188, 509. *See also*
    Patriarchy; Sexism
Woo, Henry K. H., 80, 485, 515
Woodrow Wilson Center for Scholars, 270
Woodstock festival, 380
Woodward, Bob, 498
Woolcom, 124
Work, 9, 71, 76, 90–91, 204–17, 255, 367;
    highbrow, 76–78, 80; interchangeabil-
    ity of, 72; knowledge content of, 212;
    lowbrow, 76, 78, 79; midbrow, 76;
    non-interchangeability of, 73, 212–13,
    216, 239; part-time, xx; Second Wave
    (industrial), 204, 208, 209
Work, home. *See* Electronic cottage

Work regimen, First Wave (agrarian), 206–7
Work regimen, Second Wave (industrial),
    207–8
Work regimen, Third Wave (super-symbolic),
    209–17
Work regimens, 206–217, 335; mismatched,
    209
Workers, 4, 40, 43, 52, 71, 77, 81, 322, 335,
    351–52, 356, 528; autonomy of,
    205–17; mistreated in state enterprise,
    418; participation by, 211, 215, 342;
    power and powerlessness, 212, 215–16
Workers, I.Q. of, 77
Workplace democracy, 211. *See also* Workers,
    participation by
World Bank, 345–46, 437, 463
World Series, 97
World system, heterogeneous (First Wave), 457
World system, homogeneous (Second Wave),
    457
World War I, 269, 374, 417
World War II, 4, 37, 52, 56, 171, 194,
    296–97, 302, 314, 323, 342–43, 375,
    384, 392, 397, 405, 410, 417, 431, 442,
    447–48, 453
World War III, 272, 453
Worldwatch Institute, 378
Woronoff, Jon, 488
WPP (company), 339
Wright, Joseph, 66, 515
Wright, Peter, 327, 498
Wright, Robin, 489
Writing, invention of, 427
Wyden, Peter, 494
WYMIWYG principle, 288

Xenophobia, 382–86
Xerox. *See* Copying machines
Xerox Corporation, 135, 155, 197, 225,
    235
X/Open, 134

Yago, Glenn, 51
Yakuza, 38–39
Yallop, David A., 489
Yamamoto, Takehiko, 310
Yamatoism, 384
Yankee Group (company), 238
Yates, Joanne, 526
Yermoshkin, N., 485
Yoshinaga, Yusuke, 267
Yoshino, M. Y., 480
Young, George K., 494
Youth, 380
Yugoslavia, 243, 247, 343, 438

Zaleznik, Abraham, 485
Zamoshkin, Yu. A., 496
Zenith (company), 30
Zeno of Elea, 19
Zero, invention of, 85
Zhao Ziyang, xx, 356, 546
Zimmerman Telegram, 269
Zionism, 386
Zoom (TV program), 368
Zschau, Ed, 283
Zuboff, Shoshana, 485
Zuchelli, Edmond, 501
Zurich, 56, 168, 364, 374, 432
Zvezdenkov, Valentin, 303
Zygomycosis, 8

ABOUT THE AUTHOR

One of the world's best-known social thinkers, Alvin Toffler is the author of *Future Shock, The Third Wave, Previews and Premises, The Adaptive Corporation,* and other works that are read in more than fifty countries. His ideas have drawn comment from world leaders from Richard Nixon to Mikhail Gorbachev, and have significantly influenced contemporary thought.

At various times a Visiting Professor at Cornell University, a Washington correspondent, and a Visiting Scholar at the Russell Sage Foundation, Toffler earlier spent five years as a factory worker in an auto plant, a steel foundry, and other shops in heavy industry.

His books have won the McKinsey Foundation Book Award for their distinguished contribution to management literature in the United States; the Golden Key Award in China; and the prestigious Prix du Meilleur Livre Étranger in France.

Toffler works in close intellectual partnership with his spouse, Heidi Toffler, who holds an honorary doctorate in law and has been awarded the Medal of the President of the Italian Republic for her own contributions to social thought. He has been named a Fellow of the American Association for the Advancement of Science and an Officier de l'Ordre des Arts et Lettres in France.

BEYOND THE WILD BLUE

Also by Walter J. Boyne

NONFICTION

Clash of Titans: World War II at Sea
Clash of Wings: World War II in the Air
Silver Wings
The Smithsonian Illustrated History of Flight
The Leading Edge
Power Behind the Wheel
Boeing B-52: A Documentary History
Weapons of Desert Storm
The Aircraft Treasures of Silver Hill
Phantom in Combat: A Documentary History
Art in Flight: The Sculpture of John Safer

FICTION

The Wild Blue (with Steven L. Thompson)
Trophy for Eagles
Eagles at War
Air Force Eagles

BEYOND THE WILD BLUE

A HISTORY OF THE UNITED STATES AIR FORCE 1947-1997

by Walter J. Boyne
Colonel, USAF (Ret.)

St. Martin's Press
New York

A Thomas Dunne Book.
An imprint of St. Martin's Press

All photos, except where otherwise noted, are courtesy of the United States Air Force Association.

Design by Interrobang Design Studio

Library of Congress Cataloging-in-Publication Data

Boyne, Walter J.
    Beyond the wild blue :   a history of the U.S. Air Force, 1947–1997
  / by Walter J. Boyne.—1st ed.
        p.   cm.
    "A Thomas Dunne Book."
    ISBN 0-312-15474-7
    1. United States. Air Force—History. 2. Aeronautics, Military—
United States—History. I. Title.
    UG633.B6954   1997
    358.4'00973—dc21   96-53507
                                                                  CIP

First Edition: May 1997

10   9   8   7   6   5   4   3   2   1

This book is respectfully dedicated to all the men and women—and their families—who have served the United States Air Force and its predecessor organizations.

ACKNOWLEDGMENTS

*I*t would be fair to say that millions of men and women have contributed to this history of the United States Air Force—those that served, and those who were family members—for without them, the book could not have been written.

But I've been the beneficiary of much more specific help from people I know and admire, and from strangers who, from a phone or letter request, went to great lengths to dig out the information or photos that I asked for.

First and foremost, I must express my appreciation and pay my respects to a group of leaders whose candor, insight, information, and review of my manuscript were as valuable to me as their service was to their country, which is to say, invaluable. My thanks go to General Joseph E. Ralston, USAF, Vice Chairman of the Joint Chiefs of Staff; General David C. Jones, USAF (Ret.), former Chief of Staff and Chairman of the Joint Chiefs of Staff; General Lew Allen, Jr., USAF (Ret.), former Chief of Staff; General Larry D. Welch, USAF (Ret.), former Chief of Staff; General Merrill A. McPeak, USAF (Ret.), former Chief of Staff; General Michael J. Dugan, USAF (Ret.), former Chief of Staff; General John Michael Loh, former Acting Chief of Staff and the first Commander of the Air Combat Command; General Russell E. Dougherty, USAF (Ret.), former Commander in Chief of the Strategic Air Command; General Robert D. Russ, USAF (Ret.), former Commander, Tactical Air Command; General W. L. Creech, USAF (Ret.), former Commander, Tactical Air Command; General Bernard A. Schriever, USAF (Ret.), former Commander, Air Force Systems Command; General Henry Viccellio, Jr., USAF, Commander, Air Materiel Command; General Robert T. Marsh, USAF (Ret.), former Commander, Air Force Systems Command; General John A. Shaud, USAF (Ret.), former Commander in Chief, Strategic Air Command; General Joseph W. Ashy, USAF (Ret.), former Commander, Air Force Space Command, Commander in Chief of North American Aerospace Command and United States Space Command; Chief Master Sergeant of the Air Force, David J. Campanale, and former Chief Master Sergeant of the Air Force, James McKay. While I am sure that my manuscript, with all its limitations of space and my own limitations as a historian, did not completely satisfy all of these gentlemen, whose inside knowledge of the workings of the Air Force would fill many volumes, I do know that the book could not have been completed without their insight, information, and cooperation.

I am indebted to many others, including the members of the Office of Air Force History. There Dr. George Watson patiently tried to keep me on the correct track, while the inimitable Cargill Hall, with less patience and more invective, provided revealing comments and pointed the direction to more information. Other Air Force historians who were invaluable include Tommy R. Young, Headquarters, Air Mobility Command; Fred Johnsen, Edwards Flight Test Center; John D. Weber, Headquarters, Air Force Materiel Command, SrA. Trisha M. Morgan, Pacific Air Forces, and Thomas Manning, Air Training and Education Command.

The Public Affairs Officers and Information Officers at many levels were of inestimable value. It is remarkable to make a phone call with a specific question, and get not only the correct response, but floods of additional information as was so often the case. Many information and public affairs officers assisted, and I regret that I misplaced a whole list of them, which will surface promptly as soon as this is printed. However, I do have records of help from Lieutenant Colonel K. C. McClain, Air Force General Officer Matters Office, Captain Sam McNiel, Air Force Office of Public Affairs, Major Roger L. Overture, Air Force Institute of Technology; Master Sergeant Catherine A. Segal, Secretary of the Air Force, Public Affairs Office; Sandie Henry, Air Force Special Operations Command, and Amanda Gaylor, of the RAND Corporation. There were many more, some of whom were so efficient that they got me the information before I even had time to get their names.

At the Air Force Association, Pearlie Draughn did her usual inimitable job of ferreting out facts and photos. John Correll offered encouragement and advice, and permitted me to use the AFA Chronology. I also want to thank the Lockheed Martin Company, McDonnell Douglas, Long Beach, and the Boeing Company for assistance with photos and information. Robert F. Dorr, a distinguished author and photographer, was, as usual, very helpful. Henry Snelling did his usual superb job review of the manuscript. My daughter, Molly Boyne, not only typed out many long hours of audio tape from interviews, but compiled the bibliography, for both of which I'm grateful. Wally Meeks made his usual useful suggestions.

At St. Martin's, I've had the good fortune of having the distinguished Tom Dunne as editor, as well as his assistants, Jeremy Katz and Jason Rekulak. As always, I appreciate the efforts of my excellent agent and true gentleman, Jacques de Spoelberch. And I am honored to have the distinguished journalist Hugh Sidey write the Foreword to this book.

CONTENTS

FOREWORD BY HUGH SIDEY   xiii

PREFACE   xvii

1   THE MAN OF INFLUENCE   1

2   THE SORTING-OUT PROCESS: 1943–1949   21

3   THE FIRST CRUCIBLE   51

4   POWER AND PEACE: 1953–1961   95

5   THE MANY FACETS OF WAR   135

6   THE PILLARS OF THE AIR FORCE: FOUR MAJOR COMMANDS   177

7   CHANGE AFTER VIETNAM   211

8   LEADERSHIP, DOCTRINE, AND TECHNOLOGY AFTER VIETNAM   241

9   VICTORY: SPRINGBOARD TO THE FUTURE   281

APPENDIX ONE
Secretaries of the Air Force, Chiefs of Staff of the
Air Force, and Chief Master Sergeants of the Air Force   329

APPENDIX TWO
Commands of the United States Air Force   333

APPENDIX THREE
Guard, Reserve, Air Force Academy, and Civil Air Patrol   339

BIBLIOGRAPHY   343

A CHRONOLOGY OF AEROSPACE POWER SINCE 1903   349

INDEX   425

Beyond the Wild Blue

FOREWORD

*F*or the past fifty years we have been shielded and cradled and awed and inspired by the United States Air Force, which has performed its mission splendidly in times of crisis and tranquillity.

It is startling to read these pages of history so artfully compressed by Walter Boyne and see how intertwined with our lives the Air Force has been in these decades. There may be no other organization in our history which at once has possessed the brute power in war, the coiled strength for peace, the global reach, and the brilliance in research and technology and still held in its collective heart the old devotion to duty and honor. It has not been a flawless journey, as this story notes, nor one without times of confusion and discouragement and clashing ideas. But it has been, in the larger sense, a steady journey upward, a triumph finally of reason and courage.

Long before the birth of the Air Force, the pioneer Army fliers in their Spads and P-26s and P-51s had seized the imagination of my generation. In my tiny corner of Iowa it came from stories my father brought back from the front in World War I, from the lonely drone of a biplane in yellow and blue paint crossing the dusty prairie skies of the 1930s and then the instant and overwhelming arsenal of aircraft devised for World War II. It was a chaotic but glorious incubation for today's Air Force officially birthed by Congress in 1947.

No less impressive than the planes were the men who flew them. They were names that rolled off our tongues as easily as the names of Babe Ruth and Bob Feller—Rickenbacker, Mitchell, Doolittle, Arnold, Spaatz, LeMay. They were more than pilots. They were the godfathers of this remarkable new creation for war and peace. And there were many others, not all of them well known but just as responsible for the ingenious matrix of people and machines. Always colorful, often controversial, these pioneers of air armies had one thought in common: the United States must hold a commanding presence in the skies to keep peace in a troubled world. Today's Air Force remains equal to that challenge, though it is a different age, society, and technology; there are new men and now women, but still the Air Force hears the call of that distant bugle.

In my adult life as chronicler of world events and the use of power, the Air Force drama continued and grew even more intense as the leaders often found their greatest battles were not in the skies but within a political system that too frequently robbed them of the resources needed to meet the responsibilities the country naturally rested on them. I can recall studying the

Life magazine photographs of the Berlin Airlift showing those stub-nosed C-54s lined up like boxcars and used that way, filled with coal and potatoes and medical supplies that kept Berlin alive far behind the iron curtain that came down across Europe. The jet age rushed in on us and there was MiG Alley in Korea and new tactics and a new roll call of aces, new planes that were rakish and festooned with rockets, faster than thought.

When I rewind the history of this half century, I find my memory crowded with the arguments of how to control and use space. I listened to President John Kennedy fret about nuclear warheads clustered on the noses of those monster Soviet missiles and whether we could ever match them before there was a nuclear confrontation. The Air Force fitfully developed the Thor, Atlas, and Minuteman missiles for both real and exaggerated threats, but always there was a lingering doubt, another question whether they were good enough and plentiful enough. In the endless wilderness of space there can be no final answer. The Air Force learned that and lived with it and stayed on guard and kept working.

Once I stood on a Guam tarmac and felt the ground shake as I watched dozens of those droop-winged B-52s scrambling in clusters for the sky like startled buzzards. Air Force Chief of Staff General Curtis LeMay and President Lyndon Johnson, the ultimate arbiter in the use of air power, watched side by side, buffeted by the jet blasts and sound waves. I don't think there was a doubt between them about the heart and will and the capacity of the Air Force to hold the high ground.

There were in my time the flights of the U-2s over Cuba that brought back the photographic proof that the Soviet Union was placing missiles on the island, the moment of truth after months of rumors. The Vietnam War showed us more new planes and weapon systems, and terrorism in Germany prompted President Ronald Reagan to send a flight of F-111s out of England to bomb Libya. In Desert Storm we learned about the squat, homely Warthogs that blasted tanks hunkered down in the sand. I remember President George Bush making a point to me before he unleashed the full fury of that attack about how confident he felt especially after lunching with Air Force Chief General Merrill "Tony" McPeak, who had just returned from flying some F-16 missions over the desert, bringing to the quiet chambers of the White House the smell and feel of that distant land and the breath of war and the calculated confidence of the Air Force.

Everywhere I traveled in these years there were Air Force people on duty, alert and ready and listening to the sounds of an unruly world, established on bases in Europe and Asia and the Middle East, a vast security network stitched together by electronics, airlift, and rescue forces as much as by the awesome firepower of bombers and fighters and missiles. At once a shield and a scepter.

There is a story I carry in my heart about an Air Force plane that bore no weapons, yet it strode the globe as a great symbol of liberty and hope and may have done as much in that cause as any other plane in the Air Force arsenal. Air Force One, then a Boeing 707, landed one rainy night in Paris carrying President Kennedy and his wife, Jacqueline, on their way to the Vienna Summit with Soviet President Nikita Khrushchev. Before the trip the plane had been reconfigured and painted in the cool and elegant blues that have become so familiar on television today. The sun broke through the threatening clouds and limned this small drama, and the gathering of reporters and dignitaries below the ramp fell silent. The message from that plane just then in that distant place was one of beauty and grace inseparable from strength. That same jet flew in a heartbreaking but proud tribute over Arlington Cemetery when John Kennedy was buried, a last salute and an enduring promise that the Air Force would hold the heavens for this nation. A promise kept.

—Hugh Sidey

PREFACE

Writing a history of the fifty glorious years of the United States Air Force is at once a privilege and torment. The privilege lies in reviewing the great accomplishments of the Air Force over its existence as it overcame all difficulties to become the most powerful and proficient force in the world. The torment is in being forced to leave out the tens of thousands of stories that should be told but for which space cannot be found in a single volume.

The best way to tell the story of the Air Force would be to do it in real time, recounting every adventure, every flight, every difficulty, every triumph. The poignant thing about this impossible dream is that the fascinating stories would not be confined to air-to-air combat or masterful leadership or overcoming daunting odds, but would also be found in the motor pools, administrative offices, schools, engine shops, laundries, guardhouses—everywhere. If it had been possible to do, I would have included the story of every unit of every type, past and present, in the Air Force, and with it the story of every member.

This was, of course, impossible, and I've been forced to leave out enormous masses of interesting information, confining my efforts to tracking what seemed to me to be the pivotal points of Air Force history. For every omission, I apologize.

When one contemplates the fifty-year history of the United States Air Force, many things come to mind. First among these are the predecessor services, for the roots of the USAF go back to August 1, 1907, when the U.S. Army Signal Corps established an Aeronautical Division to "take charge of all matters pertaining to military ballooning, air machines, and all kindred subjects." The branches that followed, including the Air Service, the Air Corps, and the Army Air Forces, distinguished themselves in peace and in war, with devoted personnel pushing the technical limits of the aircraft and weapons available to them.

When the United States Air Force was formed on September 18, 1947, few realized the degree of technological change that would occur over the next five decades, one that led to a genuine revolution in warfare. For almost thirty years, the major effort was exerted in improving the "air machines"; for the next twenty years, that effort was continued at a reduced level, while emphasis was placed on "all kindred subjects." The result has been the creation of a new portfolio of weapons, but even more important, new methods of waging war. Combined, these give the United States Air Force of today and of the future a degree of advantage never before contemplated, much less attained—one that goes far beyond the raw energy implicit in super-power status.

This new advantage was a long time in coming and represents the fruits of more than fifty years of a two-part investment in research and technology. The first part of the investment was the money the USAF has plowed into basic and applied research over the years. The second part was the dedicated people who have been brought into the R&D field and allowed to use their full talent.

The deterrent power of the Air Force in its early years depended upon a small stockpile of nuclear weapons and modernized versions of World War II bombers to deliver them. Over time, the number and variety of nuclear weapons grew, as did the types of aircraft and missiles that could carry them. The nuclear power the Strategic Air Command vested in its bombers and missiles created a Pax Americana, one that ultimately brought about victory in the Cold War as the inherent faults of the Communist system caused the Soviet Union to self-destruct.

Yet that nuclear power was unsuitable for use in limited wars, and it was necessary to redirect emphasis to conventional weapons delivered by conventional means. While these were effective, they were not decisive in either the Korean War or the Vietnam War, particularly because they had to be employed with artificial political restraints that vitiated the potential of air power.

The resources that had been poured into research and development began to bear exotic fruit toward the end of the Vietnam conflict, when the first precision-guided weapons proved their worth. In the years that followed, the Air Force saw that it was within the realm of possibility to create not only "smart weapons" but also the equipment essential to provide a new degree of battlefield awareness that would for the first time in history pierce the fog of war. Instead of just seeing "the other side of the hill," the United States Air Force could dominate the battlefield with information gathered from ground-, air-, and spaced-based systems. The preliminary degree of competence in this new concept of warfare was demonstrated in the Persian Gulf War, when the combination of such complementary elements as AWACS, J-STARS, GPS, LANTIRN, FLIR (acronyms that will be explained later), cruise missiles, and a variety of precision-guided munitions were used by highly skilled crews to provide an astounding double victory. The first victory was over the dispirited Iraqi commanders and troops, who quite literally did not understand what had happened to them. The second was over the Soviet Union, whose military leaders *did* understand what had happened, recognized that they could not compete, and elected to permit their country to dissolve.

The illumination of the battlefield with electronic equipment is but the first phase of the information war to be waged in the future. The equipment, strategy, and tactics of this new mode of warfare are highly classified and can only be hinted at. It will, in essence, involve the selective destruction or manipulation of enemy command, control, communications, and intelligence functions to secure a rapid, and relatively bloodless, victory.

Yet despite the revolution in warfare, the success in battle will inevitably devolve upon the same resource that it always has in the past: the people— men and women, officers, airmen, and civilians—who make up the United States Air Force. The USAF has been blessed with excellent leaders, and perhaps even more important, an intelligent and dedicated enlisted force that has always given more than could have been expected of it. In these regards, the USAF is better off than at any point in its history, with well-educated, well-motivated personnel at all levels who are devoted to their work, and who, equipped with the most advanced weapons in history, will be supremely competent to deal with the mental, moral, and physical challenges of the uncertain future.

1
≡

THE MAN OF INFLUENCE

*I*n just fifty years the United States Air Force has grown from a disorganized giant, mired in the jumble of too rapid demobilization after World War II, to the most influential military service in the world today. In the process it has achieved triumphant successes that exceeded even the promise of its evocative song "The Wild Blue Yonder" while overcoming haunting failures of concept, equipment, and personnel.

Fortunately for the United States and the world, the successes have vastly outnumbered the failures in both number and degree. In this decade, the Air Force has been a significant, if not the principal, factor in the remarkable victories of both the Gulf War and the Cold War. Every leader of the United States Air Force, from Secretary to Chief of Staff to squadron commander, would be quick to note that these triumphs were won in concert with the Army and the Navy. No matter how hotly the three services contend for roles and missions, appropriations, media attention, and public support, the serious bickering stops when it comes to battle. The concept of joint operations, so successful in World War II, was not always observed in the intervening years, but was demonstrated admirably in the Persian Gulf War. Nonetheless, while much of what will be said applies equally to its sister services, this book will focus on the United States Air Force.

The Air Force achieved its great successes despite a number of formidable obstacles, foreign and domestic. The first and most immediate of these was the talented, focused, and effective air forces of the Soviet Union, which developed excellent equipment in massive numbers along with the strategy and tactics to use it. The USSR shared its capabilities bountifully with its satellite states, some of which were destined to become fierce opponents of the United States. The threat of the Soviet Union was real, massive, and seemingly never-ending. Soviet nuclear missile capability, exaggerated at first, soon grew to immense proportions. And while the Soviet Union is no more, its missile force, now divided among three of the survivor states, Russia, Ukraine, and Kazakhstan, not only remains but is perhaps more threatening because its control is far less certain.

There were less obvious but equally important hazards at home. The first of these was the continual requirement to cope not only with the vagaries of the Congressional budgeting process but also with the growing restrictions inherent in oversight—a kindly term for micromanagement by both Congress and the Executive Branch. The second was the telling loss of public support, almost two decades in duration, resulting from distaste for the war in Vietnam. For the first time in its history, members of the United States Air Force found themselves publicly vilified for doing what they had been ordered to do. And while the prestige of the USAF has been largely restored today, there lurks a reservoir of antimilitary sentiment still to be found in the media, in academia, and, surprisingly, in the government.

Most remarkably, even while the Air Force struggled to overcome these varied challenges, it created and maintained a unique ability to plan far into the future. The Air Force's reliance on technology was perhaps inherent in the very science of flight itself. More than the Army or the Navy, and more than the services of other nations, including the Soviet Union, the Air Force put its faith in advanced technologies. Fostered from the very start by General of the Air Force Henry H. "Hap" Arnold, and encouraged by succeeding Chiefs of Staff, the Air Force not only made the funds available for research, it granted credibility and opportunity to the military and civilian personnel who pursued technology as a career. The funding was not always constant, for wartime operational considerations invariably drained funds away from research, but the basic idea that research and development was the essential element for the continued success of the Air Force always remained.

Despite every effort to avoid the characteristics and the operating methods of a giant bureaucracy, the very size and age of the Air Force has made it one. Prescience is not normally associated with a huge organization, yet the Air Force has over the years managed to endow its leadership and its operating forces with the ability to anticipate future requirements for equipment and training. The phenomenal result has been that the Air Force, operating under the budget constraints imposed upon all the services, has managed all current crises while doing the necessary research and development to accelerate the technologies necessary for future conflicts.

For forty years the principal task of the United States Air Force was to deter offensive action by the Soviet Union. The USAF accomplished this in part by combining the experience and techniques gained in the employment of air power in World War II with an ever increasing arsenal of atomic weapons, including the intercontinental ballistic missile. The rest of the task was achieved when the Air Force, drawn reluctantly and against its instincts into the space age, responded by capitalizing on the opportunity to create an amazing array of new technologies.

At the same time, the USAF had to respond to other challenges. Some of these were of the monumental size and scope of the Korean and Vietnamese wars, while some were less threatening, like the invasions of Grenada and Panama. In addition, the USAF had to undertake disaster relief at home and abroad, as well as show the flag and project power. And all the while, it had to deal with major social issues ranging from the integration of black personnel into the service, to overcoming civilian distaste for the military during and after the Vietnam War period, to providing equal opportunity for women and minorities.

Despite the multifaceted nature of the Air Force's tasks, it was successful in almost all of them, all the while containing the Soviet Union and making the most vital contributions to winning the Cold War.

In retrospect, the years of the Cold War have a monolithic quality, as if there had been an unchanging confrontation with the Soviet Union which the Air Force steadfastly met with unchanging means. Yet it was not so, for the nature of the threat changed almost annually, forcing a corresponding change in the Air Force's response. In the very early years, at the time of the Berlin Blockade, the Air Force's response was a hollow one, brandishing a nearly empty nuclear arsenal at a gigantic array of Soviet forces. As the years passed, the Soviet Union, through its surrogates, challenged the United States all around the world, in each instance with a minimal involvement of its own troops. Thus it fought the Korean War with North Korean and Chinese forces, supplemented by Soviet equipment, training, and limited personnel. It supported the North Vietnamese in a similar economic manner, letting another country bleed for its own purposes. The same pattern prevailed in the Middle East, in Africa, and ultimately as close as Cuba. With the Soviet Union tugging at the seams of countries all around the world, the U.S. policy of containment, begun by President Truman, was an expensive one.

Yet it was ultimately successful, despite the lack of a decision in Korea and the loss of the war in Vietnam. Over the years, the United States Air Force, both the benefactor and the beneficiary of the American system of free enterprise, was able to build air and missile forces that kept the Soviet Union within the general sphere of influence allotted to it at Yalta.

The Soviet Union was not only contained, it was strained, its military budget consuming it economically and technically. The Soviet advances in military equipment and in space exploration were obtained by investments that matched and often exceeded those of the United States, particularly as a percentage of gross national product. The tremendous expenditures were at the expense of a rational expansion of the USSR's civilian economy. The productive capacity of the Soviet Union, channeled so single-mindedly into its military efforts (for its space program was primarily for military purposes), was unable to develop an industrial base with a technology and a market structure comparable to those of its old Western enemies or of the emerging nations of Asia. The USSR's atrophied civilian industrial base made its military burden increasingly difficult to bear by 1980, and impossible to bear a decade later.

In that critical ten-year period, three separate undertakings by the United States spelled the downfall of the Soviet Union. The first was the buildup of American arms that began in 1980 and reversed the decline in strength that had occurred under the Carter administration. The Soviet economy, already almost exhausted, was strained beyond endurance by the requirement to match the American buildup.

The second undertaking was the dazzling if ultimately unfulfilled prospects of President Ronald Reagan's "Star Wars" program. The grandiose project was obviously beyond the capacity of the Soviet Union to match; the risk that the United States might succeed was too much for Soviet leaders to contemplate.

The third, and conclusive, element was the overwhelming success of our weapons in the Persian Gulf War. The invulnerability of the stealth fighter and the incredible military—and public relations—effect of precision-guided munitions completely disheartened the political and military leaders of the Soviet Union. With their economy imploding under the strain of seventy-four years of corruption and inefficiency, the Soviet leaders were finally compelled to admit that their system had failed, and to abandon—at least temporarily— their historic quest for world domination. Just as Mussolini's corrupt Fascism withered and died almost overnight, so did the Soviet Union and its single political component, the Communist Party, swiftly dissolve into a nightmare of confusion and recrimination.

The Soviet Union, suddenly exposed as a gigantic empty rust belt of industrial and political folly, simply shut down, leaving its people to its own devices, for better or for worse. Its huge military forces, overwhelming in both their conventional and nuclear might, almost instantaneously went from being a threat to the very existence of the world to embarrassing centers of poverty, unable to feed, equip, or clothe their recruits, sometimes unable even to pay their electric bills.

Yet winning the Cold War was only part of the United States Air Force's task during the first fifty years of its existence. Each decade presented a new challenge that it had to handle as a "part-time" job, subsidiary to the principal task of nuclear deterrence. Some of the challenges were internal: adapting to social change, meeting equipment deficiencies, trying each year to do more with less. Other challenges were external, from the sobering experience in

Korea through the demoralizing agony of Vietnam to the exhilaration of winning the Persian Gulf War.

Each challenge was overcome by the men and women of the Air Force, who were simultaneously accomplishing another remarkable feat. Even as they endured the rigors and uncertainties of service life, with its frequent moves, relatively low pay, and often disagreeable jobs, the men and women of the Air Force moved into the mainstream of the American community, and indeed became the United States in microcosm. The old concept of a military base being apart from the community, a self-sufficient entity with its own standards and mores, faded away. USAF personnel increasingly broke away from the frontier outpost outlook that had characterized the military for so many years and instead became active members of their communities, owning homes, working second jobs, sending their children to school, paying taxes, and generally becoming indistinguishable from their civilian neighbors.

One of the most remarkable aspects of this transformation from a parochial group with an essentially garrison mentality into a fundamental part of American society is that it has been rarely perceived and little remarked upon, even by members of the Air Force. People both within and without the Air Force still tend to think of it as a separate social entity, as distinct from being a separate business entity. The fact is that the composition of the Air Force population is essentially identical to the composition of the American populace as a whole, and as such reflects the trends, the biases, the problems, and the potential of that populace.

One of the most interesting questions about the Air Force is how it managed to foresee its equipment and weapons needs as much one or two decades in advance. The successes obtained in World War II might be attributed to a specialized leadership, trained for twenty years with but a single goal, that of establishing air superiority with conventional weapons of the times. The postwar successes, each one perhaps as important as success in battle had been in World War II, resulted from the quick and precise execution of plans that would have been deemed grandiose if they had not succeeded. Among the most remarkable of these for the grandeur of their conception, planning, and execution are the deployment of not one but four intercontinental ballistic missile systems, the establishment of a comprehensive continental radar defense, and the systematic exploitation of the possibilities of space for war and other military purposes.

In the meantime, besides leading the way to victory in the Cold War, the Air Force has, almost off the back of its hand, fought three major and two minor wars, while leading the nation in the process of integrating minorities and women into the service. During the same interval, it has transitioned from a primarily nuclear strike force pitted against a superpower into one capable of responding to regional conflicts with conventional arms, while still maintaining a decisive nuclear capacity.

The answers to the question of the source of the Air Force's general success in operation and in anticipation will be revealed in the following chapters. In essence, the Air Force's success derived from having the right leaders at the right time at the officer level and, perhaps surprisingly but even more importantly, at the noncommissioned officer level. Obtaining those leaders derived from the Air Force's intrinsic ability to attract high-caliber personalities to serve, and from a carefully cultivated culture that allows persons of talent to reach the top. The relationship between officers, noncommissioned officers, and enlisted personnel in the USAF is unique, and stems from a tradition created in the old days when commissioned pilots realized that their lives depended upon noncommissioned crew chiefs—and treated them accordingly. The sense of mutual respect and mutual importance is pervasive in the Air Force today, and is in many ways responsible for the success of the organization.

This is not to say the Air Force has solved all the problems of democracy and is truly egalitarian, for it is not. Nevertheless, the nature of the Air Force organization has always permitted the truly talented to rise to the top, regardless of connections, schooling, or appearance. For the past thirty-five years it has been increasingly easier for truly talented persons to rise to the top regardless of race, and for the last twenty years regardless of sex. The Air Force has always led the nation, including the other services, in the trend toward true equal opportunity, and it has benefited extraordinarily from the practice.

It is said that the Israeli Air Force was born in battle, coming into being as it did in the 1947 struggle for independence. It is not stretching a point to say that the United States Air Force was born in battles, and has remained in battle of one sort or another for its entire existence. The concept of an independent air force was first articulated—prematurely—by Billy Mitchell and others during the 1920s. It was nurtured during World War II, when leaders like General Henry H. Arnold and General Carl "Tooey" Spaatz sometimes conformed operational considerations to the preparation for postwar independence. It was sustained in the demobilization collapse of our military forces after V-J day, and survived the intransigent opposition of the United States Navy. But independence merely meant a new set of wars. The simplest to deal with were actual conflicts, as in Korea, Vietnam, and the Persian Gulf, where the enemy was known and the action required was military. Much more complex were budgetary battles, public relations battles with the Navy, and internal strains as the Air Force bureaucracy grew over time.

Fortunately for the United States, the hand of Providence and good leadership prevailed, and the USAF managed to prevail in each of its battles, learning in the process, and directing its efforts ever to the future.

Many mistakes were made, some trivial, some of immense consequence. Yet the end result of the Air Force's effort was the establishment of a Pax

Americana that deterred World War III and proved to be the carborundum wheel upon which the Soviet Union ground itself to extinction.

The Air Force's achievement was a compound of many elements—people, leadership, equipment, and more. Yet the very basis for its success lay in the commitment it made—and continues to make—to the necessary research and development effort to create the advanced technologies that defined it as a superpower.

Coincidentally, and fortunately, the advances in Air Force capability have characteristics that match two unique demands that have since Vietnam come to be made by the American public. The first of these demands is that we must fight our wars with a minimum number of casualties to our forces. America wants no more Vietnams where our troops are forced to fight and die in unconscionable numbers. The second of these demands is unusual in history, for it is that we must also win our wars with a minimum number of casualties inflicted on the enemy.

These requirements, noble for any nation, may be a reflexive reaction to the years of the Cold War, when the strategies of the Soviet Union and the United States had the appropriate acronym MAD, for mutual assured destruction. Under this doctrine of reciprocal deterrence, it was a given that either side had the ability to inflict unacceptable damage on the other. If the strategy failed, casualties on each side would have been in the tens or hundreds of millions, depending upon how long the madness lasted. Long before the end of the Cold War, it was recognized that the success of the mutual assured destruction concept might prevent global nuclear conflict but would have no effect upon limited wars that were not so threatening as to require the use of nuclear weapons. The war in Vietnam demonstrated this painfully to the United States, which could not find until December 1972 the will to use air power in its fullest measure against North Vietnam. In the preceding eight years of conflict, it had endured—and inflicted—heavy casualties. The public's new requirements were revealed in the victory in the Gulf, where the United Nations casualties, as minimal as they were given the scale of operations, were rightfully resented. Remarkably, there was a similar resentment of the Iraqi casualties, particularly among civilians. Other incidents—friendly-fire losses in the Persian Gulf, the tragic killings in Somalia, the concern about potential losses in Bosnia—all confirm the American public's attitude that wars must be fought with a minimum of bloodshed on both sides.

The demand is without precedent; no military service in history has ever had placed upon it the requirement for victory at minimum cost to both sides. Fortunately, the United States Air Force is, for the first time, in a position to meet the requirement, thanks to a program of technological refinement that extends back more than five decades, and that can be traced to a single driving personality, that of General of the Air Force Henry H. Arnold.

"HAP"

One man, Henry Harley Arnold, did the most to shape the image of the modern United States Air Force. His patient political spadework established trust with the United States Army brass and secured the essential patronage of General George C. Marshall, the Chief of Staff. Among his colleagues, Arnold's career inspired deep friendship—and open hatred, for there were those who disagreed with his views and thought him too political and much too quick to compromise.

Yet it was Arnold's flexibility that laid the groundwork for the modern United States Air Force, and few of his hard-driven subordinates would have agreed that he was too quick to compromise. His focused energy, unrelenting, omnipresent, helped them ensure that the performance of the United States Army Air Forces, locked in the greatest war in history, exceeded all expectations. And, perhaps most important of all, Arnold was willing to depart from his own strengths and past experience to embark the new independent air force upon a course of constant technological change. More of a verbalist than a technician, he did not fully comprehend all of the change he sought, but he knew intuitively that such change was essential. He was Hap Arnold to his friends, the public, and the press, and the free world owes him much.

Arnold rose from an indifferent West Point cadet career to become the first and only five-star General of the Air Force. His roller-coaster rise to the top would see him pioneer, then abandon flying; he would become the youngest colonel in the United States Army by 1917, only to be dropped back to the rank of captain in 1920, in the helter-skelter post–World War 1 curtailment of the armed forces. By hard work, charm, and no little guile, he rose to the rank of major general, becoming Chief of the Air Corps on September 29, 1938. At that moment, Arnold commanded an Air Corps which numbered about 23,000 officers and men, only 2,500 of whom were rated pilots, and about 1,200 mostly obsolete combat aircraft. With thirty-five years of service behind him and retirement looming, Arnold must have felt both satisfaction in his own career and tremendous frustration at the desperately poor condition of the air force he commanded, which lagged behind all the major world powers in the numbers and quality of its aircraft.

Yet the war was imminent, and with it came changes beyond his imagination. Only seven years later, long past the time he would nominally have retired, he wore five stars as his idol General John J. Pershing had done, and commanded more than 2,400,000 troops and an armada of 70,000 planes. More important, he had completely vindicated airpower prophet Billy Mitchell's claims as he closely supervised the air victories in the European and Pacific theaters.

He invested his whole person—including his health—in this effort, and long before V-J day had taken the necessary steps to fulfill his dream of an independent air force.

Arnold was assisted by trusted colleagues, handpicked men who had sacrificed themselves, as he had, to serve in the Air Corps at a time when pay was minimal, prestige nonexistent, and danger ever present, for the fatality rate for fliers was high. The assistance of general officers like Carl "Tooey" Spaatz, Ira C. Eaker, Joseph J. McNarney, Lawrence S. Kuter, George C. Kenney, Lauris Norstad, and Hoyt Vandenberg and of civilians like Assistant Secretary for War for Air Robert A. Lovett and his successor Stuart Symington was invaluable, but it was Arnold who masterminded the effort with political skill and exquisite timing.

Hap was so acutely aware of the importance of timing that early in the war he assigned Major General McNarney to head a committee whose sole purpose was to suppress the tide rising for an independent air force until after the war. Incidents like these cost Arnold in the eyes of fellow officers who wanted an independent air force immediately, but Arnold gladly bartered full alliance with the Army during the war for the Army's postwar support for independence.

His subtle preparations were to have enormous and lasting effect upon the character of the USAF, for it was Arnold—a visionary pragmatist rather than a scientist—who set the Air Force firmly upon the path of research and development. And in a more mysterious, less definable way, it was Arnold who established the culture that permitted the early identification of essential future leaders. From Arnold's era to the present, with very few exceptions, the Air Force has managed to elicit from its ranks the right leaders at the right time, anticipating the ever-changing demands they would be required to meet. Spurred on to do so by Marshall, Arnold began this selection process himself, choosing young officers early in the war for responsible positions and then, as the war drew to its victorious close, taking steps to see that these younger men were given preference over more senior officers in the postwar air force. As salubrious as this was for the nascent United States Air Force, it was the last straw for some senior officers, many of whom had never been in Arnold's camp. They, like Arnold, had endured the dreadful doldrums of the prewar era, with its low pay and lack of promotions. When war came, they were certain they had executed their new wartime responsibilities with admirable efficiency, for Arnold surely would have fired them had they not. But just as the dream of an independent air force was about to be realized, many of them were passed over, given dead-end assignments, or even politely asked to retire. This saddened Arnold, but it was a price he was prepared to pay and it was a tradition in the making.

Arnold's discreet, comprehensive preparations to ensure the emergence of an independent air force were unlike the damn-the-torpedoes working style he used in running the war effort. As such, they indicate a depth and breadth to Arnold's intellect that belie the traditional picture of the reckless airman, intent on the mission and heedless of politics. His plan was a masterful piece of work on its own; that Arnold executed it while building the world's most powerful air force and leading it to victory in World War II is little short of incredible. The smiling, silver-haired general used tact, diplomacy, and well-thought-out public relations in his effort, all talents sneered at by his detractors. Yet he won the trust, affection, and personal commitment of giants like President Franklin Delano Roosevelt and General Marshall not by these traits, but by delivering the goods. Arnold's United States Army Air Forces performed in an outstanding manner, and he personally saw to it that its loyalty to the Army and its dedication to winning the war were unwavering. He never allowed his indirect lobbying efforts for an independent air force to interfere with the resolute prosecution of the war. It was a winning strategy, for by 1943 he had created the climate within the Army, the Congress, and the executive branch that would after the war permit him to realize his dream.

The nickname "Hap" suited his public persona rather better than his supervisory style. He was extremely photogenic, and his genial, confident manner enabled him to get along well socially. A big smile and warm handshake went a long way in the promotion of airpower, and he used them continuously on the prodigious wartime travel circuit that impacted so heavily on his health.

Working for him was something else again. Arnold believed he knew what could be accomplished with air power, and he threw himself into the work of overcoming the manifold deficiencies of the Army Air Forces in the early years of World War II. Enormously energetic, he worked long hours every day, never sparing himself or anyone who worked for him. In 1940 his task seemed impossible: the Air Corps lacked everything, including planes, pilots, ground crew, and bases. There was no training base—less than 1,000 pilots per year were being trained, when the requirement was for 100,000 annually. A modern air force required thousands of skills, ranging from cooks and bakers to navigators and radar observers, but the cadre of regulars to train them simply didn't exist. The industrial base was equally inadequate, despite the infusion of help from prewar purchases of aircraft by the Allies. American aircraft designers were still building to the almost naive specifications of the prewar HIAD—Handbook of Instructions for Aircraft Designers—and blithely ignoring the lessons being taught daily in European skies about the value of armor, self-sealing tanks, and other combat necessities. He overcame each of these difficulties, sometimes by personal intervention, as when he personally saw to it that the vast civilian pilot training scheme was established, sometimes by motivation, as when he induced manufacturers to risk money without a contract in hand, and sometimes by fear, as when he would announce a forthcoming visit to a delinquent subordinate.

Hap was too impatient to be a good administrator, and far too prone to parcel out assignments to the first person—or sometimes, the first few persons—he saw, regardless of their authority, expertise, or ability. He wanted instant results and accepted no excuses for delay or failure. It was remarked of him, in rueful jest, that he was "the most even-tempered man in the Army—always angry."

Most important for the American war effort, Arnold possessed a signal quality that cost him dearly each time he exercised it. Unlike many commanders in foreign air forces, including, oddly enough, the German Luftwaffe, he did not let personal friendship interfere with his evaluation of his subordinates. The Air Corps in which he grew up was so very small that when World War II broke out, not only his friends and colleagues but his rivals and opponents won top positions. Yet no matter who the person was, close friend or rival, Arnold was consistent. He was sparing in praise, but if the person failed to perform to Arnold's expectations, he was relieved without mercy. When he decided that World War I ace Brigadier General Frank O'Driscoll "Monk" Hunter had failed to use his VIII Fighter Command effectively, Arnold insisted that he be replaced. Even his longtime close friend and his coauthor in prewar books on aviation Major General Ira C. Eaker was removed from his Eighth Air Force command position when Arnold felt that he was not extracting the maximum potential from his bomber force. This came as close to breaking Eaker's spirit as anything could, for he had created the Eighth and guided it to the point where it was almost ready to accomplish its task. The incident put a further strain on Arnold's own already troubled heart, adding to the burden of his twelve-hour days, and seven-day weeks. Nonetheless, he met each challenge with the fierce, professional resolution that became the model for air force general officer attitudes.

IMPATIENCE EARNED

Arnold was entitled to be impatient, having paid his dues and more in his long service. He had earned his wings in 1911 with Orville and Wilbur, at the Wright brothers' flying school at Simms Station in Dayton, Ohio. Besides the luster of the association with the Wrights, the school had little to offer, for while its biplanes could go higher than the interurban trolley car that daily sped past the airfield at 45 miles per hour, they could not go as fast.

Instruction began on a crude sawhorse-mounted "simulator" in which the student pilot learned how the controls moved, followed by a series of flights lasting from five to fourteen minutes, depending upon wind and weather and the instructor's nerves. After twenty-eight lessons and a total of three hours and forty-eight minutes in the air, Arnold was considered qualified as a pilot, and thus automatically able to instruct others. It was a time when flying was learned by doing. Arnold initiated the use of goggles after being hit in the eye by a bug; a colleague devised the seat belt after almost being thrown from the airplane.

Arnold knew that flying was dangerous from the start; several Wright exhibition pilots had been killed, and Orville Wright had pointed out to him a man who waited with a wagon each day outside their flying field at Simms Station—the local undertaker in Dayton. The raw statistics were grimmer even than the waiting undertaker. Between 1909 and 1913, there were a total of twenty-four qualified Army aviators; of these eleven were killed while still in training and seven were killed subsequently in crashes.

Assigned to the Signal Corps Aviation School at College Park, Maryland, Arnold, with his almost four hours of flying time, began teaching others. He liked flying. He set several records and won the first MacKay Trophy ever awarded with an unprecedented reconnaissance flight on a triangular course from College Park to Washington Barracks, D.C., then to Fort Myer, Virginia, and back to College Park. The flight exhausted him, for controlling a Wright biplane was a demanding mixture of muscle power and apprehension.

As his knowledge grew, he recognized the danger implicit not in merely being airborne, but in flying the Wright and Curtiss pusher aircraft of the period, which had the engine mounted directly behind the pilot. These aircraft, slow and prone to stall, were literal death traps in a crash, when the engine would tear loose and crush the pilot. (Pushers were banned from the U.S. Army Air Service in 1914, but not until after too many deaths.)

A number of his friends perished in a series of deadly mishaps that followed the same pattern: a stall and a fatal dive directly into the ground. Arnold was at Fort Riley, Kansas, in November 1912, earning a munificent $124 per month and conducting experiments in which he corrected artillery fire by means of a primitive one-way radio. He was flying a Wright Model C with Lieutenant A. L. P. Sands of the Field Artillery perched on the wing alongside him, taking photographs. The Model C differed only slightly in appearance from the original Wright Flyer of 1903, but it was slightly larger, with a 55-horsepower six-cylinder engine and twin chain-driven pusher propellers. The crew of two sat upright on tiny slab wood seats on the wing. Like the earlier Model B, the Model C had an inherent design flaw in the relationship of its center of gravity to the propellers' thrust line. When the aircraft was gliding at low speeds, a sudden application of power would cause the nose to pitch down—exactly the opposite of what a pilot would expect.

Crossing a line of troops at an altitude of about 400 feet, Arnold's biplane suddenly spun in a 360-degree circle and plunged toward the ground. Stall-recovery techniques were still unknown—it was widely believed that Wright's aircraft could not be recovered from a stall—and Arnold was certain that he would be killed. Somehow he managed to pull out at the last instant and land, probably having inadvertently done the correct thing—pushing forward to break the stall and gain speed before pulling back to raise the nose. He was shaken to the core, the photographer still blissfully unaware that anything was wrong.

Arnold assessed the situation and realized that the aircraft he was being asked to fly were intrinsically and unreasonably dangerous. Summoning all of his moral courage, aware that his action would be criticized, he admitted to a fear of flying and requested reassignment. It was granted, and he did not return to aviation until 1916, and then at the specific request of Major William "Billy" Mitchell, Chief of the Signal Corps' Aviation Section. Mitchell was already promoting the concept of an independent air force; in less than ten years his flamboyant demands for such a service would bring him before a court-martial board.

When Arnold returned to flying in 1916, he did so with his customary verve; the airplanes, while still dangerously primitive, were not the deathtraps that the pushers had been, and his love of flight returned. When war came he was promoted to the rank of colonel at the age of thirty-one, the youngest in the Army. Despite his best efforts, he did not see combat, and in the pell-mell postwar reduction in the size of the armed forces, he reverted to the rank of captain in 1920.

Arnold's hallmark of moral courage was put into play on Mitchell's behalf in 1925, when he stoutly defended the outspoken general at his court-martial, despite the fact that Mitchell was certain to be found guilty of the charges against him. Now a major, Arnold spoke out for Mitchell's concept of air power although he knew that doing so would damage his career. He was joined in Mitchell's defense by many of the men to whom he would give important assignments during World War II. When the trial was over, Arnold was sent into exile, commanding a small detachment at the Fort Riley cavalry school, the scene of his near-crash thirteen years before.

The Mitchell trial divided the Air Corps into two groups—those who had defended Mitchell and those who had not. The former group suffered initially, but would band together to endure and then prevail. The trial matured Arnold politically. He recognized that there was not yet sufficient military, public, or Congressional support for the independent air force Mitchell had advocated, and he concentrated on winning friends at every level to acquire that support. In the process he alienated many of his contemporaries, including a man who was his chief rival for the top position in the Air Corps, Frank M. Andrews, of whom more later.

Exile at Fort Riley should have meant the end of Arnold's career, particularly because he continued to lobby covertly for Mitchell's ideas. Although discouraged about his progress—he would remain a major from 1920 to 1931—he turned down the offer of several potentially rewarding civilian jobs in aviation, not wanting to quit while under fire. Even before Mitchell's trial he had been instrumental in forming the nucleus of what became Pan American Airways, and had refused the opportunity to become president of the new line.

Mitchell had been a visionary, but he had imputed to an independent air force a strength that was far beyond the reach of contemporary technology. The aircraft of Mitchell's day lacked every necessary quality to be a war-winning weapon, not possessing the speed, range, bomb load, or defensive capability required for combat. Of equal importance was the totally inadequate defense budget of the time, which would never have permitted an air force to exist as a separate service with its own bases, personnel, and equipment. Arnold believed in air power, but Mitchell's trial had taught him to use politics and low-key diplomacy rather than confrontational methods.

Arnold pursued his career diligently, becoming a true "comeback kid" of the Air Corps. He became Commanding Officer of March Field in 1931, where he later worked both ends of the social spectrum, setting up Civilian Conservation Corps camps and at the same time drawing upon the Hollywood film community for support. In July and August, 1934, he personally led a flight of ten Martin B-10 bombers in a record round-trip flight from Washington D.C. to Fairbanks Alaska, receiving his second McKay Trophy for the achievement.

In February, 1935, already identified as "bomber man," he received an unprecedented peacetime two-jump increase in grade to become a Brigadier General in Command of the 1st Wing of General Headquarters Air Force at March Field. He then moved on to become Assistant to the Chief of the Air Corps, and in March, 1938, was appointed Chief of Air Corps as major general. On June 30, 1941, he became Chief of the Army Air Forces, receiving his third star in December of that year.

Arnold did not spare himself leading the Army Air Forces in World War II, working long hours and sacrificing his health; in the process, he became convinced that the future of an independent Air Force was totally bound with advanced technology.

He continued these tactics despite all the pressures of World War II, never losing sight of his goal. It should be remarked here that the impetus behind this thrust was not careerism, nor the desire for power. Arnold and his airmen recognized that the ultimate effect of air power could never be attained if air forces continued to be controlled by ground commanders. Over the next half century, this would prove to be a lesson strangely hard to learn and extremely easy to forget.

ARNOLD AND RESEARCH AND DEVELOPMENT

One could scarcely imagine two less likely friends than Hap Arnold, the tough, skillful, but not particularly technically inclined airman, and Dr. Theodor von Karman, charming, gentle, professorial, and recognized as the leading research aerodynamicist in the United States. Arnold lived for the most part the austere, almost monastic life of a military leader at war, while von Karman enjoyed academia and had a legendary love of parties where pretty women were abundant. In those days of lesser political correctness, it was said, perhaps apocryphally, that von Karman's progress through a party gathering could be marked by the jumps and surprised squeals of the women he was passing by.

Yet this unlikely combination of stern aviator and convivial theoretician was to have a profoundly beneficial effect upon the Army Air Forces in World War II, and upon the history and culture of the United States Air Force.

An almost prototypical Hungarian, von Karman studied at the Budapest Royal Polytechnic Institute, gaining honors with a degree in mechanical engineering. He went on to pursue his doctorate at Göttingen University, studying under the great Professor Ludwig Prandtl, who would become his colleague, peer, and rival. During World War I he first served as an artillery officer, and then the Austrian Air Service put his knowledge to use in aviation research. He experimented with things as diverse as helicopters (including one powered by four rotary engines driving two counterrotating propellers!), gun synchronizers, and self-sealing fuel tanks. After the war, von Karman became director of the Aachen Aeronautics Institute, where his work earned him a worldwide reputation. There he made contributions to glider design and to the design of the Zeppelin LZ-126, which was awarded to the United States as war reparations and became the ZR-3, the *Los Angeles*—the longest-lived and most successful of all U.S. Navy dirigibles. And, oddly enough, it was this experience with lighter-than-air craft that would be the key to his first interaction with Arnold.

Professor Robert A. Millikan, who headed Cal Tech in Pasadena, was an expert in recruiting eminent scientists. He courted von Karman for several years, and finally managed to persuade him to accept the role of director of the Guggenheim Aeronautical Laboratory at the California Institute of Technology (GALCIT) in Pasadena. Von Karman came to the United States in 1929, in part because of the nascent threat of the Nazis and in part because of the facilities that were made available to him both at Cal Tech and at a lighter-than-air laboratory to be built in Akron. It was an irresistible offer, and one that did well for American aviation.

Von Karman's influence at GALCIT was so great that he enhanced the entire Southern California aviation industry, attracting many graduate students who would go on to become leaders in the industry. He lifted GALCIT beyond the level of his former laboratory at Aachen; the climate he created in his American work elicited a far higher level of performance from his students and colleagues than would otherwise have been possible.

A singular irony in von Karman's work brought him his first contact with Hap Arnold. Von Karman's attention had been fixed on the effects of turbulence, in particular as it related to airship design. Sadly, before his studies were completed and published, two great airships, the U.S. Navy's *Akron* (ZRS-4) and *Macon* (ZRS-5), had crashed as a result of encounters with two very different sorts of turbulence. The *Akron* was christened in 1931 by Mrs. Herbert Hoover before a crowd estimated at 500,000. Only two years later, on April 4, 1933, after seventy-four flights and 1,700 hours in the air, she was caught off the coast of New Jersey in a violent storm that tore her apart, sending her crashing into the Atlantic with a loss of all but three of a crew of seventy-six. One of those dead was the Navy's great champion of both aircraft and airships, the Chief of the Bureau of Aeronautics, Rear Admiral William Moffett.

The *Macon* had been christened by Mrs. William A. Moffett less than a month before, on March 11, 1933, the name honoring the home district of the chairman of the House Committee on Naval Affairs, a man who was later a loyal friend of the Air Force, Congressman Carl Vinson. Like the *Akron*, an aerial aircraft carrier with four Curtiss F9C-2 lightweight fighters aboard, the *Macon* was off the California coast, approaching Point Sur, south of Monterey, and had just recovered the last of her aircraft. A sharp gust of wind suddenly struck the airship and she rolled violently, the top fin of her cruciform tail ripping away, tearing open three of the helium-filled gas bags that kept her aloft. After a gallant forty-minute fight to keep her aloft, she crashed into the sea; only two men of the crew of eighty-one were lost.

Von Karman determined the cause of these accidents through the work of Irving Krick, who explained how an atmospheric disturbance little known at the time, the collision of two powerful air masses, had overwhelmed the airship. Krick became head of a newly formed Cal Tech meteorology department, which caught Hap Arnold's eye and cemented his relationship with von Karman. (Krick would come to prominence during the tension-filled hours before D day, when he and his colleagues made the estimates upon which General Eisenhower decided to launch the invasion.)

Krick also proved to be the key in investigating the disaster with the *Macon*, discovering an even more unfamiliar phenomenon, the hidden turbulence that contributed to the accident.

Arnold had followed these events, attending meetings at Cal Tech on the accident discussions. (This was risky territory for him—Mitchell's court-martial had stemmed from charges he had raised over the 1925 crash of the Navy dirigible *Shenandoah*.) In the course of these meetings, von Karman found him to be sympathetic, particularly when he learned that Arnold had written some children's books (the Bill Bruce series), just as von Karman's father had done. They met again in the fall of 1938 to discuss rockets as a means of assisting heavily laden bombers to take off. Then, in 1939, Arnold showed the prescience that would do so much for the Air Force, asking von Karman to assist in the design of the precedent-breaking 20-foot, 40,000-horsepower wind tunnel at Wright Field. This led to a part-time consultant position—and the beginning of a long and productive relationship that would enter a new and decisive phase in the fall of 1944.

Von Karman relates that he was asked to meet Arnold under mysterious circumstances at La Guardia Field. He was driven to the end of the runway, where Arnold was sitting in an olive-drab staff car. Von Karman entered, and the driver left. Both men were ill. Arnold was exhausted and had already suffered several heart attacks, while von Karman was just recovering from two operations, one for intestinal cancer. Arnold told him in essence that the present war was won, but that he was concerned about the future of air power. He could not mention the atomic bomb, but it scarcely seems possible that von Karman had not had already envisaged that possibility. As the conversation developed, Arnold asked von Karman to come to the Pentagon to head up a group of fellow scientists in order to plan aeronautical research for as far as five decades into the future.

It was a heavy sacrifice, for von Karman enjoyed academic life and was not certain that he could conform to the military culture of the Pentagon. Arnold assured him that he would smooth out any differences; if alterations in style were required, he would see to it that the Pentagon conformed to von Karman.

The scientist agreed, and on November 7, 1944, Arnold formally established the group. Its prestige was heightened soon after, when von Karman was appointed director of the AAF Long Range Development and Research Program, which was ultimately codified, on December 1, 1944, as the AAF Scientific Advisory Group (SAG). The mission of the SAG was to evaluate research and development trends and prepare special studies on scientific and technical matters relevant to airpower.

Of all Arnold's many contributions to the well-being of the future United States Air Force, this was at once the most important—and the most unlikely. It was the initial mechanism that enabled the postwar leaders of the Air Force to survive a catastrophic demobilization and years of inadequate budgets. Thanks to the technology that was generated, the Air Force would be able, time after time, to pull the country's irons out of the recurrent political fires. The amazing victories of the Air Force in the Persian Gulf War were the result of a technological progression begun by von Karman and Arnold.

Von Karman's forte had been pure research, as it had been for most of the extraordinarily talented group he selected to join the SAG, and it would not have been surprising if they had resented the explicit framework for their work that Arnold laid out. They did not, because of his achievements and because of his legendary charm.

Arnold wanted to be sure that the SAG did not place too much emphasis on the results of the last war, but instead looked to the future to see what intensive research programs might develop in the fields of electronics, with emphasis on radar, aerodynamics, propulsion (both jet turbine and rocket), and, of course, the basic sciences.

Arnold kept Marshall's economy concerns in mind and asked the scientists to condition their thinking to a *de minimus* defense budget, in which the effectiveness of the relatively small numbers of personnel in the armed forces had to be multiplied by equipment.

Displaying the flexible thinking that continued to surprise his peers, Arnold asked the SAG to address also the organizational and administrative problems of military-related science, with particular emphasis on the question of what should be the optimum percentage of the budget to be invested in research and development.

Von Karman was practical enough to understand and comply with Arnold's requests. He had the bittersweet pleasure at the close of the war of taking some of his group to his own old haunts in Europe, where they traveled in uniform for safety and convenience, von Karman particularly enjoying his temporary role as a major general. The results of the trip were astounding, as everything from tons of scientific documents to a high-speed wind tunnel was scooped up and sent home.

Von Karman created a report of the trip entitled *Where We Stand*, a comprehensive presentation of the current state of aeronautical knowledge. His conclusions were both startling and far-ranging, and included the imminent arrival of supersonic aircraft, a family of missiles, including both air defense and ballistic, and immeasurably improved navigation and communication devices.

It was but a start. From the trip, and from other studies, the SAG created the multivolume epic *Toward New Horizons*, which included thirty-two reports from twenty-five authors and ranged in subject matter from aerodynamics and aircraft design to explosives and terminal ballistics.

The Scientific Advisory Group was followed by the Scientific Advisory Board (SAB) in 1947, when the Air Research and Development Command was formed. The SAB was so successful that many other government agencies copied it, setting up similar special units of research experts. Ironically, the result was a dilution of the talent available to the SAB, a problem further compounded by the steadily increasing size and importance of the Department of Defense bureaucracy. The SAB's role has been diminished, its original mission now being carried out by "think tanks" like the RAND Corporation MITRE, and other similar civil research and development organizations. Yet had not Arnold not first given emphasis to research and development, and, as will be shown, had not von Karman paved the way with seminal publications, the United States Air Force would not exist as we know it today.

A tremendously important, possibly decisive, problem that neither Arnold nor von Karman could have foreseen was that over the years bureaucratic complexity would develop at a rate commensurate to or exceeding technical capacity. While Arnold could make instant decisions on both R&D and procurement, confident that he would be backed by the War Department and Congress, later Chiefs of Staff of the Air Force found that they had to convince more and more individuals and many more intermediate layers of command. As will be shown later, in time the bureaucracy of the Department of Defense and especially of Congressional staffs became a Sargasso Sea for R&D and procurement, and currently it threatens to stifle both by making them unreasonably costly and lengthy.

Arnold's contribution to research and development in the postwar United States Air Force was as great as the contribution he had made to the Army Air Forces as it fought and won its battles in World War II. In the course of the war he had suffered four heart attacks, and by war's end he was drained, as much a victim of the conflict as any of the men who had fallen in combat. He retired on June 30, 1946, to watch with pleasure as General Spaatz, who succeeded him as Commanding General of the Army Air Forces, carried on with the fight for independence. His work had been widely recognized around the world, and his list of decorations was long, but he was most pleased when on May 27, 1949, President Truman wrote to him that he had just signed a bill making Arnold the first (and to date only) permanent five-star General of the Air Force.

2
≋

THE SORTING-OUT PROCESS: 1943–1949

THE RIGHT SORT OF ALLIES

As impetuous and demanding as Arnold was, he also had the God-given grace to see his own faults and to seek allies who could compensate for them. During World War II, the most important of these was found in an office adjacent to his own where the patrician Robert A. Lovett, Assistant Secretary of War for Air, worked. Lovett favored Arnold and recognized both his strengths and his weaknesses, mitigating the latter when he presented Arnold's ideas to General Marshall.

Marshall had earlier been inoculated with the concept of an independent air force by his prewar friendship with Major General Frank M. Andrews, then Commander of the General Headquarters (GHQ), which constituted what little there was of Air Corps striking power. (It was said that Marshall thought so highly of Andrews that had the latter not died in the crash of his aircraft in May 1943, Marshall might have nominated him to become Supreme Allied Commander in Europe—a position ultimately occupied by General Dwight D. Eisenhower.)

Fellow officers have described Arnold as "smart" and Andrews as "intelligent"; both were wise enough to subordinate their rivalry to the good of the service. Marshall, perhaps convinced by Andrews of the importance of the power of the air force and by Arnold of its willing subordination to the prosecution of the war, transferred his friendship to Arnold and became an ally in the quest for postwar independence. Noted for his reserved, sometimes frigid manner, Marshall approved of Arnold to the unusual degree that, later in the war, he would use the word "affectionately" in signing his letters.

Yet it is probable that without Lovett as a buffer and a facilitator, Arnold's often impulsive manner would have incurred Marshall's wrath.

And just as Lovett smoothed the way for Arnold with Marshall, so did Marshall smooth the way for Arnold with President Franklin Delano Roosevelt, who at first entertained a poor impression of him. Unfounded rumors of Arnold's drinking had almost caused Roosevelt to refuse his promotion to Chief of the Air Corps in 1938. Then, in 1940, Arnold's Congressional testimony had displeased Roosevelt, who later suggested broadly that those who did not "play ball" might well expect an assignment to Guam. Arnold's subsequent performance, particularly at the many summit conferences, eventually smoothed all this over. Marshall made Arnold a Deputy Chief of Staff for Air, remarking that he had tried to make him "as nearly as I could Chief of Staff of the Air without any restraint although he was very subordinate."

When war began, Arnold, just promoted to lieutenant general, became a member of the U.S. Joint Chiefs of Staff and the Anglo-American Combined Chiefs of Staff. This was implicit and unprecedented recognition that the air force was equal to and independent of sea and land power, and was done in part to match the British staffing pattern and in part to ensure that Arnold's views on air power views were not filtered through an Army interpreter.

Arnold made good use of his position, which brought him into contact with the top military and political leaders of the Allied cause, beginning with his invitation to accompany President Roosevelt's party to the historic Atlantic Conference with British Prime Minister Winston Churchill in August 1941. This was the first of an endless series of trips and conferences that would consume Arnold's time—and health—in the course of the war, but would elevate him to the very top rank of military power.

Just as he made good use of his position with the world's leaders, so did he make good use of his staff in laying the administrative groundwork for the postwar air force. In March 1942, the armed forces of the United States were still reeling from the Japanese victories in the Pacific when the War Department issued Circular 59, *War Department Reorganization*. Based largely on early recommendations by Arnold and Spaatz, Circular 59 made the Army Air Forces (AAF) one of three autonomous commands, along with the Army Ground Forces (AGF) and Services of Supply, later the Army Service Forces (AFS).

As heady as the new authority was, the circular's mandate contained a stinger that would cause a flurry of activity in the last years of the war and continuing into the immediate postwar period. The new arrangements set up by Circular 59 were condemned to expire six months after the close of the war—a victim of the wording of the First War Powers Act of December 18, 1941. It thus became imperative for Arnold and his staff to take all the necessary steps to bring about a separate air force as soon as the war had ended. They knew that if the war ended and six months elapsed, their reversion to a mere component of the Army would delay independence, perhaps forever.

More than a year after Circular 59, when the war had obviously taken a turn for the better, another event occurred that enhanced the status of the Army Air Forces and boded well for postwar independence. This was the publication of War Department Field Manual (FM) 100–20, *Command and Employment of Air Power,* July 21, 1943.

Whereas Circular 59 had been the careful expression of academic beliefs on air power and was made possible only because wartime expansion permitted the air force genie to escape from the Army's bureaucratic bottle, FM 100–20 was written with the knowledge—one could almost say swagger—learned in the combat over the North African desert and was not even coordinated with the War Department. FM 100–20 was described with dismay by some members of the Army as the "Army Air Forces 'Declaration of Independence' "—and so it was, for it stated unequivocally that land power and air power were coequal and that the gaining of air superiority was the first requirement for the success of any major land operation.

FM 100–20 went on to say: "The inherent flexibility of air power is its greatest asset. This flexibility makes it possible to employ the whole weight of available air power against selected areas in turn; such concentrated use of the air striking force is a battle-winning factor of first importance. Control of available air power must be centralized and command must be exercised through the Air Force commander if this inherent flexibility and ability to deliver a decisive blow are to be fully exploited. Therefore, the command of air and ground forces in a theater of operations will be vested in the superior commander charged with the actual conduct of operations in the theater, who will exercise command of air forces through the air force commander and command of ground forces through the ground force commander." This doctrine was so welcome to the Army Air Forces that a potentially troublesome element of FM 100–20 was discounted. The manual went on to describe the mission and composition of a strategic air force, a tactical air force, an air defense command, and an air service command; this separation of strategic and tactical air forces would be a bone of contention and a source of both inter-and intraservice rivalry for the next half century.

General Arnold, perhaps wishing to make evident that his apparent sidestepping of the independent air force issue had been practical politics, seized upon FM 100–20 to send a letter to each Army Air Force commander, emphasizing that "the interrelated role of air power must be constantly impressed on all airmen through the medium of command."

Although more than two years of war remained after the issuance of FM 100–20, the creation of an independent air force now seemed inevitable, despite opposition from the Navy. Drawing on wartime experience that clearly showed the efficiency of the unified command of air, land, and sea operations, Arnold now moved toward unification of the armed services as a whole. In February 1944, he increased the pressure by advocating the establishment of a single Secretary of War, with four under secretaries heading the ground forces, naval forces, air forces, and a bureau of war resources. The President would be advised by a single chief of staff and a supreme war council of the four major service commanders, a pattern not unlike that used by the British.

Implicit in this was a red flag to the Navy: the air force was to include "all military aviation except ship borne units operating with the Navy and those artillery-control and 'liaison' units operating with the Army." This was directly opposite to the philosophy of the Navy, which wanted to maintain its own naval and marine air forces, and go on to establish a heavy strategic bomber force of its own.

Arnold's proposal was followed in February by the first formal blueprint for a peacetime air force, known as Initial Postwar Air Force-1 (IPWAF-1), which optimistically called for 105 air groups. The plan, which grew out of a study by Brigadier General Kuter's Post-War Division, was a striking parallel to the famous AWPD-1 of August 1941, in which Kuter had participated as a very young major. AWPD-1 had assessed what would be necessary to defeat Germany and forecast with uncanny accuracy the number of aircraft, crews, missions, and even losses that the war would require.

Kuter was a talented pilot who had flown with Claire Chennault's aerobatic demonstration team as one of the daring young men on "the Flying Trapeze," the ancestors of the famous Thunderbirds. Promoted to the rank of brigadier general at thirty-seven, Kuter was Commanding General of the 1st Bomb Wing in England and later played an important role in the Tunisian campaign. He was thus exactly the sort of leader that Arnold preferred—young, intelligent, widely experienced, and proven in combat. Arnold thought so much of him that when felled by one of his early heart attacks, he sent Kuter to represent him at the Yalta and Malta conferences.

Just as AWPD-1 had ignored costs, so did IPWAF-1—and this was a fatal flaw in the planning, for while the plan naturally emphasized spending on air force requirements and limiting naval and ground forces, it ran counter to General Marshall's concept of what the voters and the economy of the United States would bear in the postwar world, and to the political realities that would define "balanced power" of the U.S. military as a roughly equal division of the total defense budget between Army, Navy, and Air Force.

Marshall wished to revert to a professional peace establishment, slightly larger and better equipped than that which had existed before World War II, and capable of being reinforced quickly from the traditional civilian Army reserves. He was an advocate of Universal Military Training (UMT) to provide the necessary pool of trained personnel for the reserves. As a concept, UMT was not inconsistent with raising a large land army from reserves; however, it was of negative value to an air force, which required career specialists with years of training and experience in order to function.

General Marshall's views are somewhat surprising in retrospect; he was aware of the Manhattan Project, and he had made possible the advances in air power that were proving decisive in the war. Further, he subscribed to the idea that the next war would again be initiated by a surprise attack, and that the United States would have no major allies for at least eighteen months. He mitigated this harsh scenario somewhat by a wistful stipulation that the United States would be aware of the possibility of war by one year, during which emergency measures would be started. Events would soon prove that this too was an incorrect assumption. Indeed, from all of his practical experience, Marshall might have been expected to conclude that while a citizens' army and navy might be practical, a professional air force of large size was essential. Instead, the memories of the totally inadequate defense budget in the years between 1918 and 1941 still weighed too heavily upon him.

His inhibitions about the expense of maintaining a large standing air force were reinforced by the extremely pessimistic forecast from the Special Planning Division of the War Department, which estimated that only $2 billion would be available annually for defense. This restriction effectively crippled the air force, which would then have had to be limited to a total of 120,000 men and sixteen groups.

The AAF reacted strongly, pitting Arnold in the unusual role of contesting with Marshall. A total force of only sixteen groups not only would be inadequate for defensive purposes, it would mean the dissolution of the base of the aviation industry, so that a subsequent buildup would be virtually impossible.

With the uncanny eye for talent that characterized him, Arnold now turned to another rising young two-star, Major General Lauris Norstad, who took over Kuter's post as Assistant Chief of Air Staff, Plans. Norstad had been a top combat air commander in England, North Africa, and Italy and had been promoted to the rank of brigadier general at thirty-six.

Norstad would be guided by one of the grand old men of the AAF, the remarkable Lieutenant General Eaker. Now Deputy Commander and Chief of Air Staff, Eaker, good soldier that he was, had swallowed his resentment at being relieved of command of "his" Eighth Air Force and gone on to do remarkable work as Commander in Chief of the Mediterranean Allied Air Forces. As he had been with the Eighth and in the Med, Eaker was once again deprived of the pleasure of being in at the kill; instead he went to work in the newly built Pentagon, its recently poured concrete walls still sweating, to control planning for the Army Air Forces interim and permanent force structures.

The Army and the Navy were equally concerned about their postwar strengths, and the Secretary of the Navy, James V. Forrestal, moved quickly, proposing legislation to establish the permanent strength of the postwar Navy.

It was the first shot across the bow of an increasingly acrimonious battle that would continue long after the Air Force became an independent service.

The reason for the interservice squabble was obvious. The Navy knew that in any "vote" in a unified service, the Army and its offspring, the independent air force, would ally themselves.

Fortunately for Arnold and his staff, Forrestal's legislative gambit backfired. When President Harry S Truman succeeded Roosevelt on April 12, 1945, no one had gained his confidence more quickly or more fully than the Chief of Staff, General Marshall. Marshall cited Forrestal's request as a typical example of military parochialism and as a perfect argument for postwar unification. Truman then asked all the services to establish their postwar requirements for review.

The AAF was ready; Arnold had tasked his key personnel, Spaatz, Eaker, Norstad, and another young comer, Lieutenant General Hoyt S. Vandenberg, to set a firm goal for the postwar air force. Vandenberg, former commander of the Ninth Air Force, had, like Norstad and Kuter, combined a distinguished combat career with broader tasks, including heading an Air Mission to the Soviet Union under Ambassador Averell Harriman. The three men had something else in common: they were all highly regarded by General Spaatz, whose interpersonal relationships were perhaps less demanding than Arnold's, but who nonetheless expected extremely high levels of performance.

It is worth noting that Arnold and Spaatz might well have just accepted the potential of young officers like Kuter, Norstad, and Vandenberg as a given, without appreciating their importance to the postwar effort. Indeed, it would have been only human for either Arnold or Spaatz to have resented the rapid rise of these young officers and to have instead preferred those with whom they had spent so many long years in the trenches of the prewar Air Corps. Fortunately, both Arnold and Spaatz gladly cooperated with General Marshall's wish to have young officers brought forward. They both had the vision to recognize what would be required, the patience to accept the sometimes bitter censure from their colleagues whom they were forced to pass over, and the courage to prepare the way for their own departure from the scene. These are rare qualities in civil life, and perhaps even rarer in the military.

Thirteen days after Japan agreed to surrender, on August 28, 1945, the planning group under General Eaker established a postwar goal of a seventy-group air force with 550,000 men. (A "group" varied with the type of aircraft. Very Heavy Bombardment [VHB] groups, equipped with Boeing B-29s, had forty-five aircraft and 2,078 men on establishment. A Heavy Bombardment [HB] group of Boeing B-17s or Consolidated B-24s had seventy-two aircraft and 2,261 men. A single-engine-fighter group, with either Republic P-47s or North American P-51s, had 111 to 126 aircraft and 994 men. A troop-carrier group, with Douglas C-47s, had 80 to 110 aircraft and 883 men.) The seventy groups were to be backed up by twenty-seven Air National Guard and thirty-four Air Reserve groups. (The status of Guard and Reserve groups would be an object of controversy for years until the Air Force matured enough to provide them with adequate training, first-rate equipment, and essential missions.)

The seventy-group goal, regarded as barely sufficient by its own air force planners in peacetime, and totally inadequate for war, would remain an elusive target, swamped first by the incredible demobilization that took place immediately after the formal Japanese surrender and then by unrealistically restrictive postwar budgets.

The AAF argued that a standing force of at least seventy groups was essential for a number of reasons, not least of which were the global demands that were now thrust upon the United States as the leading world power. However, the most obvious reason was that in the next war, the United States would not be given time to recover as it had been after the debacle of Pearl Harbor. (This same factor was held to work to the disadvantage of Guard and Reserve units.) There could no longer be a question of the oceans protecting the heartland of the country while an army and an air force was mustered, trained, and equipped.

The seventy-group air force would be a goal that would be reached only temporarily before it was swept away in a series of postwar cost-cutting orgies. But even as Arnold rode out the numbers war with the planners, he was already creating a mind-set, a creative thrust, that would characterize the USAF for the next fifty years, and would, on more than one occasion, be the bliteral savior of the country.

FROM DEMOBILIZATION DEMENTIA TO ORDERLY INDEPENDENCE

The cold recital of administrative events leading to the unification of the services and the establishment of the independent United States Air Force was played out on the shifting sands of the wildest, most expensive and reckless demobilization in history. In the shortest time possible, given physical constraints of transport, the mighty armed services of the United States were reduced to impotence at home and abroad. The Medal of Honor winner who had led the 44th Bomb Group, the Eight Balls, against Ploesti, General Leon W. Johnson, aptly termed the demobilization frenzy a "riot."

Incongruously, the riot occurred just as the United States was recognized for the first time as a superpower (although the term had not yet come into vogue) and its influence and interests were tacitly acknowledged as global. Political and military philosophers from Sun Tzu to Winston Churchill to Colin Powell have always agreed that political policies without military strength are hollow reeds doomed to failure, yet this was exactly the state in which demobilization had left the United States.

The political pressures for demobilization were overwhelming. "Bring the

Boys Home" was the rallying cry, and "points," the credits achieved for length and place of service, were the determining factor. It was a civilian military force, and it wanted out!

At the same time, the armed forces were struggling with the problems implicit in the occupation of the territories of Germany and Japan and in withstanding any encroachment by the Soviet Union outside its designated spheres of influence.

With an incredible naiveté, the United States allowed itself to totally disarm, depending upon its atomic monopoly to maintain its world position. Ironically—and dangerously—the United States possessed almost no such capability. It had very few atomic bombs—only thirteen on June 30, 1947—and its only means of delivery were the B-29s of the famous 509th Bomb Group. The image of a powerfully armed atomic strike force was a myth, pure and simple, for not only were weapons and carriers lacking, but so were the thirty-nine-man technical teams that required two full days to do the intricate assembly and arming of those early weapons.

The situation was actually worse than described above, for a turf-conscious Atomic Energy Commission insisted (in the name of civilian control of the military) on controlling the number and type of bombs as well as all material and manufacture. The Chief of Staff of the Air Force himself had no certain knowledge of the number of bombs available to him for use by his Strategic Air Command.

Demobilization had greater effect on the Navy than the Army, and still greater on the Air Force than the Navy because of the relatively higher degree of technical skills needed. Troops were demobilized purely on the basis of the points they had earned, without regard to their skills or the demand for their services. It was democratic in the extreme, but it was disastrous to the Air Force in particular.

The quantity of equipment was not the problem—there were thousands of everything from trainers to B-29s, with tremendous pipelines of parts to support them. The problem was personnel, for there were simply not enough mechanics to repair the aircraft, or supply clerks to find the parts, or crews to man them.

Unit strengths fell as surely as if they'd been lined up to march over a cliff. The Army Air Forces had 2,253,000 military and 318,514 civilian personnel on strength on V-J day. Four and one-half months later, AAF strength had declined to 888,769 military personnel, a figure that fell to a low of 303,600 in May 1947, when there were about 110,000 civilians still on the rolls.

The gigantic, smoothly functioning machine that had won wars in two theaters ground noisily to a halt, with equipment lost, stolen, scattered, or deteriorating because of lack of maintenance. More than 90 percent of the 350,000 aircraft mechanics departed the service. Where in wartime as many as 50 or 60 percent of the combat aircraft had been ready, the number now averaged about 18 percent, and that only because so many of the airplanes were brand-new and virtually unused. In hard numbers, this meant that of the 25,000 aircraft available, only 4,750 were fit for combat, and these were dispersed around the world.

Most telling was the drop in combat-ready groups. On August 15, 1945, there had been 218 AAF groups of all types, most of them ready to fight. By December 1946, sixteen months later, there were only fifty-two groups remaining in the AAF, and of these only *two* were combat ready.

Arnold and Spaatz had watched the tailspin of their great creation with horror, as much appalled by the lack of proficiency and readiness of the organizations that remained as they were by the lack of personnel. They watched against a backdrop of steadily deteriorating relations with the Soviet Union, whose menacing intentions were evident in the Eastern bloc countries. In March 1946, the old lion Winston Churchill had roared again, this time in Fulton, Missouri, where he used the term "iron curtain," a metaphor previously used by Kaiser Wilhelm, Vladimir Lenin, and an old enemy, Joseph Goebbels, but never so tellingly. Stating, "From Stettin in the Baltic to Trieste in the Adriatic, an iron curtain has descended across the Continent," he went on to note that all the capitals of the ancient states of Central and Eastern Europe, Warsaw, Berlin, Prague, Vienna, Budapest, Belgrade, Bucharest, and Sofia, were subject to Moscow's increasing control. Warrior that he was, what he undoubtedly sensed at that moment in history was that with Britain exhausted, Germany devastated, France a military cipher, and the United States convulsively disarming and its nuclear strike force virtually impotent, Joseph Stalin could have raced across Europe unchallenged. Fortunately, the wounds of the Soviet Union were too recent and Stalin's misapprehensions about U.S. nuclear strength too great, and he missed his opportunity.

The magnitude of what would today be called the "downsizing" of the AAF had not surprised Arnold or Spaatz, but its rate and devastating effect had. Already a dying man, Arnold had increasingly removed himself from the picture after the victories in Europe and the Pacific. On February 15, 1946, Spaatz formally succeeded Arnold, and it fell to Spaatz to undertake the measures necessary to offset the effects of the dangerous demobilization and to prepare for the future independent air force.

Under Spaatz's leadership, the staff had in 1946 built into the old Army Air Forces the structural elements considered necessary for a new air force. The top leaders were bomber men because they had led the most powerful units of World War II. They would be for years to come—and they saw the requirement for a global capability some forty-four years before the motto "Global Reach—Global Power" became the Air Force's watchword.

The new structure, formally established on March 21, 1946, was composed of three new functional organizations, the Strategic Air Command, the Tactical Air Command, and the Air Defense Command. Four support commands included the Air Training Command, Air Materiel Command, Air Proving Ground Command, and Air Transport Command. There were also a number of overseas theater commands, relics of the unified commands, the most important of which were the United States Air Forces in Europe and the Far East Air Forces.

All planning was based on a nominal seventy-group air force, considered by almost all air force planners as the minimum number required to meet its global commitments, serve as a springboard for growth, and, not incidentally, maintain an aviation industry with the capability to build up to previous wartime production levels if necessary.

In a gesture to tradition and for ease in transfer, existing numbered air forces were reassigned into the new commands. The Strategic Air Command (SAC) had been created to fulfill the ideas of several young officers, including Generals LeMay, Vandenberg, and Norstad, to create an atomic strike force. SAC received the one-two punch of the European war, the Eighth and Fifteenth Air Forces.

The Tactical Air Command mission was more disputed; strong elements within the AAF would have preferred to maintain the ground-support force within a larger unit, the Continental Air Command. But General Eisenhower, who had supported air force independence, wanted an air force designated specifically for air-to-ground operations, and Spaatz wanted to please him. There was, besides, the specter of the Army demanding its own tactical aviation and depriving the air force of an important mission. The Third, Ninth, and Twelfth Air Forces were assigned to TAC.

Air Defense Command received the First, Second, Fourth, Tenth, Eleventh, and Fourteenth Air Forces—and had precious little in the way of resources for them.

Then as now, controversy swirled around the personnel given command of the new organizations. General George C. Kenney, who had mesmerized Douglas MacArthur even as he orchestrated the defeat of his Japanese opponents, was named Commander of SAC. Yet Kenney had other interests, including intensive lobbying for an independent air force. SAC was to suffer for his inattention, which might have stemmed from the letdown coming in peacetime work after his brilliant combat career in the Pacific. And it might have been a natural pique; he was senior to Spaatz, but of course had not enjoyed Spaatz's long and close relationship with Arnold. Nonetheless, Kenney would have had to have been more than human not to have felt some resentment at being passed over for the role of Commanding General of the Army Air Forces.

Major General Elwood R. Quesada was given command of TAC. The smiling, personable flier had flown with Spaatz in the 1927 flight of the *Question Mark*, and as the popular leader of the IX Tactical Air Command had been ranked by General Omar Bradley as the fourth most capable American general in the European theater. Here the personality dispute was a raw issue of promotion and turf between Vandenberg and Quesada dating back to their days in Europe. It was a battle that would ultimately leave TAC vitiated and Quesada bitter.

The Air Defense Command was headed by Lieutenant General George E. Stratemeyer, who, in turn, would run into difficulties with Vandenberg during the Korean War.

The level of importance Arnold had attached to research and development can be found in the assignment that came to Major General Curtis E. LeMay. A proven combat leader in both Europe and the Pacific, LeMay was given the job of Deputy Chief of Air Staff, Research and Development. Arnold and Spaatz didn't pick LeMay because of his scientific background—he had no more than the typical commander of the era—but because he would focus powerful energy on the task and imbue it with the importance Arnold knew it deserved.

Spaatz buttressed his new organization plan with the creation of an *Air Board to Review Plans and Policies,* with Arnold's longtime foe, the obstreperous Major General Hugh J. Knerr, as its first secretary-general. Knerr, friend and adviser to Frank Andrews, was a bomber man and had long been a proponent of a separate air force. He was ideally suited for a job that called for independent thinking—he'd been so independent in the past that he was one of the few people ever to have been close to court-martial while on active duty and again after retirement. It was typical of Spaatz that he would nominate a man who had been a thorn in Arnold's side to an important position simply because he felt he was the best man for the job.

It turned out to be a happy choice that boded well for the future, for Knerr set up the Air Board so that it would view the USAF as a business, a viewpoint that would put the Board—and consequently Spaatz—exactly on frequency with the first Secretary of the Air Force, Stuart Symington.

Working entirely within the AAF, depending upon a core of personnel that had been involved in aviation almost from the its beginning (Knerr had actually swept out the Wright brothers' bicycle shop in Dayton), Spaatz and his team (which after August 1947 included the formidable talents of Brigadier General William Fulton "Bozo" McKee) were flexible enough to change the organization of their war-winning service to meet the demands they perceived ahead. Forty years later, another team of officers, victors this time in the Cold War, would undertake the same process.

The leaders of the nascent air force had already identified the Soviet Union as the next potential enemy and were planning how to meet the challenge, not realizing that there was a bigger hazard to an independent air force's survival close to home—the United States Navy.

AN ORGANIZATIONAL STREET FIGHT

At the end of World War II, there were two views on the need for an independent air force: those of the U.S. Navy and those of virtually everyone else. President Truman, General Marshall, General Eisenhower, and most members of the Congress agreed that the results achieved by air power in winning the war justified the existence of a separate, coequal service. In parallel to the obvious requirement for a separate air force was the need for a unity of command, as had been exemplified by the unified commands of World War II. (A unified command is an organization composed of two or more U.S. armed forces; a joint command is an organization that includes an allied force.) Under the pressures of war, the Joint Chiefs of Staff (JCS) had worked together in relative harmony to make unified commands a success. Without that pressure, and subject to the territoriality deriving from competition for the vastly reduced peacetime budgets, few believed that the JCS would still function harmoniously. When the harmony vanished, so would the hope for operating a successful unified command to conduct combat operations.

The Navy was adamantly opposed to both a unified national department of defense and to an independent air force. The Navy believed a unified command, with a single defense chief at the top, would block the access of the Secretary of the Navy to the President. It believed that an independent air force would compete not only for a limited budget, but also for roles and missions, despite AAF disclaimers. They were completely correct in this, for, somewhat euphoric with their success in the war, some AAF leaders, including people as prominent as Lieutenant General Jimmy Doolittle, were openly casting doubt on the future value of aircraft carriers in a world where the only potential enemy had no navy and possessed a huge continental army.

Somewhat hypocritically, given its tendency to deprecate the effectiveness of an air force, the Navy was at the same time lusting for a strategic bombing arm. After the atomic bombs had been dropped on Hiroshima and Nagasaki, this became a naval imperative. It was given tangible expression immediately after the war by the push to create the 65,000-ton super carrier the *United States*, whose size and configuration would have permitted the operation of heavy—i.e., nuclear—bombers.

There was some basic logic in the Navy's argument. The armed forces of the United States had just fought and won the greatest war in history, proving to the Navy's satisfaction that the contemporary organization worked and should not be changed. They relied on what became the popular aphorism "If it ain't broke, don't fix it." The potent counterargument was that air power and nuclear weapons had so altered warfare that it would be foolish to remain tied to World War II concepts.

From 1944 through 1947, there was a veritable storm of special studies, committees, unification bills, and recommendations from senior officers. The conclusions reached were drawn on political lines; those with naval sympathies were against unification, while almost everyone else was for it. An important change in the equation stemmed from the change in administrations. President Roosevelt had been an ardent Navy man, as might be expected from his background, while President Truman came from an Army background. Roosevelt's Presidential cousin Theodore had created the Great White Fleet, and he himself had served as Assistant Secretary of the Navy during World War I. Truman had been an artillery captain, and while all of his experience with aviation had not been positive—his committee had been ruthless in exposing waste and inefficiency in the aircraft industry—he still favored an independent air force and unification.

With the style that would bring him tremendous popularity—but only many years after he left office—President Truman intervened decisively for unification. On December 19, 1945, he called for legislation from the Congress that would combine the War and Navy departments into one single department of national defense, with a coequal, independent air force. His words were cogent: "Air power has been developed to a point where its responsibilities are equal to those of land and sea power, and its contribution to our strategic planning is as great. Parity for air power can be achieved in one department or in three, but not in two. As between one department and three, the former is infinitely to be preferred."

Yet the Navy had not lost anything; it was to retain its carrier and water-based aviation and the Marine Corps. The Army, in turn, would retain aviation integral to its operation, i.e., observation, liaison, and intratheater troop transport.

Truman called for a civilian secretary to administer the new Department of National Defense, with a military Chief of Staff of National Defense, the office to be rotated among the three services. All three requirements were anathema to the Navy.

Despite the support of the President, the naval opposition was too strong, and legislation intended to implement his wishes fell short because of the adamant and expert opposition by the Navy. Vulnerable, the Navy felt a terrible sense of ingratitude, for it had done so much to win the war in the Pacific. Now it was fighting for its life, not least because there was no great enemy naval power to offer an obvious rationale for the Navy's existence.

In a series of standoffs not unlike today's budget battles, the Navy fought for its views with its usual political acumen, exploiting its hold on legislators with large shipyards or naval bases in their states or districts and counting on the loyalty of those members of Congress who had actually served in the Navy.

Eventually, it fell to Major General Norstad, Director of the Army General Staff's Operation Division, and Vice Admiral Forrest P. Sherman, Deputy Chief of Naval Operations, to work out an agreement that had eluded everyone else, including Secretary of War Robert P. Patterson and

Secretary of the Navy James Forrestal. Like Norstad, Sherman had a brilliant war record. A flier since 1922, he had commanded the USS *Wasp* until her loss in 1942; he then became a leader in planning the naval campaigns that ran from the Carolines to Okinawa. Sherman was considered the best naval strategist in the Pacific, and he became Admiral Chester Nimitz's most trusted adviser. It was Sherman who had convinced Nimitz that by 1944 the Navy's carriers had so grown in strength that they could take on and knock out Japanese land-based aviation, a true revolution in air power philosophy. When things became difficult between the services, Nimitz employed Sherman to negotiate with AAF Lieutenant General George C. Kenney and with the Southwest Pacific Commander in Chief, General Douglas MacArthur. Like Norstad, Sherman was a polished and diplomatic negotiator, and most felt that if these two men could not arrive at a solution, no one could.

Sherman and Norstad put the national interest first, and by compromise provided the basis for a draft of the bill for unification. The House and Senate debated the bill from February through July, with continued Navy opposition, but the National Security Act of 1947 finally became law on July 26. President Truman had signed it under poignant circumstances.

Truman's mother was desperately ill, and he sweltered for almost an hour in the Presidential airplane, the Douglas C-54 *Sacred Cow*, at D.C.'s then bucolic National Airport, delaying takeoff until the bill arrived. He signed it, then departed for his home in Independence, Missouri. Sadly, his mother died while he was en route.

The Declaration of Policy of the National Security Act of 1947 provided for the three military services, Army, Navy, and Air Force. All were a part of the National Military Establishment, headed by a Secretary of Defense, who coordinated the departments of the Army, the Navy, and the Air Force, each of which had its own secretary.

The success of the Navy's political infighting was evident in the selection of the former Secretary of the Navy, Forrestal, to become the new Secretary of Defense, and by the careful way that the functions of the Navy were spelled out to include a full range of naval aviation and the Marine Corps. (Forrestal had been Truman's second choice for the position, which he offered first to Secretary of War Robert A. Patterson, who declined.)

The act also created a Joint Chiefs of Staff, a Joint Staff, a Munitions Board, a Research and Development Board, and a War Council.

Within the Department of the Air Force, the United States Air Force was created out of the existing Army Air Forces, which included (still) the Army Air Corps and the Air Force Combat Command.

The act was, on balance, a good effort, for it resolved the major issues of unification and the existence of an independent air force. Yet there were many things to be worked out in relation to the United States Air Force, including its roles and missions, the way it addressed functions that were formerly accomplished by elements of the Army, and, most important, its size and force structure.

President Truman had also signed the short-lived Executive Order 9877, which detailed the function and roles of the three services. There had not been time for his own staff people to discover and correct discrepancies between his Executive Order and the National Security Act of 1947, and these discrepancies were to be the source of controversy for some time. Most of the elements of the Executive Order regarding the Air Force had been provided Truman in draft form by the excellent staff work supervised by Generals Spaatz and Eaker during the prior two years. It hewed closely to the vision of the Air Force that Mitchell, Arnold, and their colleagues had advocated for so long. The specific functions of the Air Force were noted in Section IV of the Executive Order. They are of such fundamental importance to the politics of the time and to the later development of the Air Force that they need to be rendered in full, with their import noted in brackets:

General

The United States Air Force includes all military forces, both combat and service, not otherwise specifically assigned. [This placed a limit on the concessions to the Army and the Navy. The Navy was limited to aircraft for reconnaissance, antisubmarine warfare, the protection of shipping, and air transport essential for naval operations. Included in this were combat, service and training forces, as well as land-based aviation, a crucial loophole.] It is organized, trained and equipped primarily for prompt and sustained air offensive and defensive operations. [This put an irreducible lower limit on the size of the Air Force and served to blunt the most severe of the postwar budget cuts.] The Air Force is responsible for the preparation of air forces necessary for the effective prosecution of the war except as otherwise assigned, and, in accordance with integrated joint mobilization plans, for the expansion of the peacetime components of the Air Force to meet the needs of war. [This set the stage for later unified and joint command operations of which the Air Force would often be a principal component, but would rarely command.]

The specific functions of the United States Air Force are:

1. To organize, train and equip air forces for:
    (a) Air operations, including joint operations.
    (b) Gaining and maintaining general air superiority. [This is the key issue about which all Air Force planning revolved: maintaining general air superiority. It automatically conferred precedence in the event of war.]
    (c) Establishing local air superiority where and as required.
    (d) The strategic air force of the United States and strategic air reconnaissance. [This was a vital element, for the strategic component inevitably involved the nuclear, i.e., war-winning, component.]
    (e) Air lift and support for airborne operations. [This would become key in later arguments with the Army over roles and missions.]

(f) Air support to land forces and naval forces, including support of occupation forces. [Again, critical to later arguments with both the Army and the Navy over the ground support role.]

(g) Air transport for the armed forces, except as provided by the Navy. [An ambiguity that would not be resolved with the formation of the Military Air Transport Service (MATS) on June 1, 1948, but had to wait until the Military Airlift Command (MAC) was created in 1966.]

2. To develop weapons, tactics, technique, organization, and equipment of Air Force combat and service elements, coordinating with the Army and Navy on all aspects of joint concern, including those which pertain to amphibious operations. [The absence of a specific reference to the development of the nuclear mission as an element of joint concern was important here.]

3. To provide, as directed by proper authority, such missions and detachments for service in foreign countries as may be required to support the national policies and interests of the United States.

4. To provide the means for coordination of air defense among all services. [This would prove to be a continuing problem, one never satisfactorily resolved, as the Army would not give up the antiaircraft role, and the Navy could never subordinate fleet defense to air defense.]

5. To assist the Army and Navy in accomplishment of their missions, including the provision of common services and supplies as determined by proper authority. [The danger implicit here was hidden, and applied to all three branches of the military, for it contained the seed of the current—and, in the opinion of many, dangerous—trend toward single-point Department of Defense research and development and procurement for all services. Carried to its logical extreme, the services would be left only with the people who do the fighting—the "spear-chuckers"—while all the functions of R&D, procurement, supply, etc. would be carried out by civilians in the Defense Department.]

The Army, surprisingly supportive through all of the myriad meetings, worked willingly to arrange a series of implementation agreements that facilitated the separation of the Air Force. These ranged in nature from decisions on tactical and strategic missile responsibility (given to the Army and the Air Force, respectively) to intelligence, housekeeping, service and supply, procurement, and administrative functions.

Even though much was still left unresolved, these two documents were sufficient for the launch of the United States Air Force, which came officially into being on September 18, 1947, with the swearing in of the first Secretary of the Air Force, W. Stuart Symington.

Symington was a charismatic individual who had been a highly successful businessman before serving as Assistant Secretary of War for Air. As Secretary of the Air Force, he sat on the National Security Council, where he had great influence on his fellow Missourian President Truman. This friendship gave him a leverage over Secretary of Defense Forrestal, who, in any case, saw his role as a coordinator and facilitator rather than as an authoritative leader. Symington would have a tremendously beneficial impact on the newborn USAF, through the introduction of a cost-control consciousness and his firm and unequivocal backing of the integration policies of the President. The degree of Symington's business sense might be found in the small size of his staff: four officers and eleven civilians. (Symington would later take the ultimate step of a great leader who has somewhere else to go, resigning in 1950 when he determined that the then Secretary of Defense, Louis A. Johnson, had reduced the Air Force budget to unconscionably low levels. Fortunately for the USAF, Symington was elected Senator from Missouri, and in that role was able to continue to foster the Air Force's growth and well-being.)

The first Secretary of the Air Force had a long and pleasant relationship with General Spaatz, the first Chief of Staff. Spaatz, regarded by Eisenhower as the best operational airman in the world, was rather stiff in presentations with Congress, so it evolved that Symington became the point man for the Air Force, his information provided by Spaatz. And because of his confidence in Spaatz, Symington was amenable to his suggestions regarding senior Air Force positions, including that of Spaatz's successor. It was here that Arnold's influence continued, for Spaatz followed in his footsteps in selecting for the future rather than rewarding past performance.

The independent air force, conceived in the 1920s, had experienced an abnormally long gestation period, not coming to term until 1943 and struggling in labor until 1947. The organizational street fight that characterized the birthing process would be maintained in the future, often with more intensity and less decorum. The basis for the continued conflicts lay in the ambiguity caused by the general statements in the National Security Act of 1947 and by the comparative brevity of Executive Order 9877. It would have been unreasonable to expect that such a major change in the American military posture, coming as it did at the conclusion of a great world war and in the midst of a cataclysmic demobilization process, could have been brought into being with every element decided.

The ambiguity in the two enabling documents would in the course of the next year call forth further meetings and agreements to refine the decisions. The results of these meetings impelled President Truman to revoke Executive Order 9877 on April 21, 1948, and issue in its place a much more detailed statement of functions of the armed forces and the Joint Chiefs of Staff. This did not resolve all the turf problems, but it reduced them to a few core issues that would continue to flare up over the years. Some of them could never be resolved.

AFTER INDEPENDENCE

When the Air Force Falcon was finally hatched on September 18, 1947, it immediately became obvious that an immense amount of work had to be done to see that the new service had all the necessary elements to be on a completely equal footing with the Army and Navy.

One of the first and most important changes was to secure a separate promotion list for Air Force personnel, taking them out from under the shadow of the long Army list. Spaatz wanted to build a strong officer corps, one that would want to stay in the service regardless of civil enticements. The Air University was to provide an integrated training system, one that would treat flying and nonflying officers evenhandedly, just as the promotion system would. (It would probably be difficult to convince some nonflying officers that this noble sentiment ever became a reality.)

Spaatz placed equal emphasis on creating a stable enlisted force, one that would attract the best possible candidates by providing extensive training, not only in Air Force specialties but in more general courses. Unfortunately, the essential elements of what today is called "quality of life" were largely overlooked; in many respects, the Air Force remained the Army in its lack of consideration for the living standards, pay scales, and respect due enlisted men.

The most difficult task was to persuade the Army that many of the functions that it had performed for the Army Air Forces—such things as medical, commissary, laundry, and salvage and repair—now had to be duplicated in the Air Force. Such duplication obviously flew in the face of economies of scale, but the strong feeling within the Air Force was that it could never be truly independent unless it operated almost all of its services. It couldn't be done all at once, but it had to be done over time.

In the meantime, the Air Force still had to carry out its mission of defending the country amid the confusion of demobilization and the division of ever tighter budgets with the Army and the Navy.

A CRITICAL TIME

Even as the emerging Air Force sought to resolve the problems of roles and missions with the Navy and administrative and logistic problems with the Army, it was placed in the unpleasant position of being (although almost disarmed) the principal deterrent to the increasing incidence of Soviet aggression.

With the gigantic Soviet Union now several years gone, is difficult to remember the concern it caused in the early postwar years. Joseph Stalin managed to conceal just how near mortal had been the wounds inflicted by Germany. He did not demobilize on anything like the scale that the Western Allies did; instead of turning the mammoth wartime industry of his country to peaceful use and returning his soldiers to the farms, he maintained a war economy.

Stalin, while not the most doctrinaire of his Communist colleagues, must certainly have felt that the tide of Communism was rising. Just as the effects of World War I had brought Communism to all of Russia, so could the effects of World War II create global Communism. Stalin felt that he could almost immediately parlay his political, military, and territorial advantages into the expansion of Communism. Much of the world seemed ripe for the picking; significant gains were being made in China, and the Communist Party was the largest political party in both France and Italy and could bring down the weak coalition governments that faced them at any time they chose.

The great Soviet leader—for as despotically cruel as he had been and would be, Stalin was as essential to the Soviet Union during World War II as Churchill had been to England—believed in his trusted subordinate Vyacheslav Molotov's observation "What happens to Berlin happens to Germany; what happens to Germany happens to Europe." Like all dictators, he needed a foreign enemy against whom he could rally his people, and he fostered a hatred of the Western Alliance. None of the material evidence of America's friendship, from what Churchill called "the most unsordid act," Lend-Lease, to all of the concessions rendered at Yalta, gave Stalin any doubt that the United States was the next enemy.

And it was against that enemy that he gathered information from German scientists and American and British traitors to rush the technological development of his country. He pushed on every front, including the design of an atomic bomb and a masterfully adapted copy of the Boeing B-29 to carry it. Just as American forces had done, Russian teams ransacked German scientific centers for data on jet engines, swept wings, poison gas, and every other military advance of the Germans.

Stalin also accelerated Communist progress politically, from his domination of the division of power in the United Nations to his overt political takeovers backed by the threat of Soviet power. With Communist regimes in all the governments behind the iron curtain, the Soviet Union engineered a coup in Hungary, taking over on June 21, 1947. Similar techniques brought Czechoslovakia to heel on February 29, 1948. Romania came under complete control in December of that year as King Michael was forced to abdicate.

The momentum of the Soviet expansion was accentuated by the obvious political decline of the Western Allies. During the same interval, the Philippines had been granted independence by the United States, while England was divesting herself of India, Pakistan, Burma, Palestine, and other elements of her once vast empire. Other nations, including the Netherlands and France, also looked to the certain loss of their former possessions.

With the exception of the United States, the Western Allies and the former adversary states of Austria, Germany, and Italy were also in critical economic distress. To offset this, in June 1947 the United States announced the European Recovery Program, which was designed to rehabilitate the economies of Western or Southern European countries, including those occupied by the Soviet Union. This became the keystone of the Truman Doctrine, which stated that the United States would help free people fight Communist aggression. Although Truman was really behind the European Recovery Program, for internal U.S. political reasons it was called the Marshall Plan, in honor of George C. Marshall, now Secretary of State.

The Soviet Union refused assistance, and also forced those countries under its dominance to refuse. The $13 billion in assistance that went to the remaining seventeen countries (Austria, Belgium, Denmark, France, Greece, Ireland, Iceland, Italy, Luxembourg, the Netherlands, Norway, Portugal, Sweden, Switzerland, Turkey, the United Kingdom, and West Germany) proved to be vital. The Marshall Plan was a tremendous success, causing a rise in the gross national product of these countries on the order of 15 to 25 percent. It should be remembered that, to his credit, Truman backed the Marshall plan at a time when he was considered a "lame duck," when his standing was so low that his party asked him *not* to campaign for Democratic candidates, when he lacked a majority in both houses of Congress, and when the drive to achieve a budget surplus coincided with increased spending for welfare programs so that the defense budget was kept at about $13–14 billion.

Recognizing the hazards, the new United States Air Force immediately tried to assemble the forces necessary to protect American interests, but it had an embarrassingly long way to go.

The leaders of the postwar Air Force were faced with some contradictory problems. The Air Force was supposed to be the sword and shield of the United States defense policy, yet it had few aircraft and fewer atomic weapons. At the end of 1947, SAC had 319 Boeing B-29s, 230 North American F-51s, and 120 Lockheed F-80s. (The designation "P" for pursuit had changed to "F" for fighter in 1947.) An air-refueling capability was just in the process of being developed, and there would be no operational tankers until late 1948. There were no very-heavy-bomber bases in Europe. As a result, the presumed enemy, the Soviet Union, lay beyond the USAF's practical striking capability unless one-way missions were used. In effect and by default, the strategy of the United States had sunk to the level of a kamikaze attack. (The one-way attack would not disappear from planning for years to come. In 1953, the author's B-50 crew had the mission to attack targets at Tula, a Soviet city near Moscow, and then to turn southwest in the hope that a successful bailout could be made somewhere in the Ukraine, where, we were told, we might encounter "friendly natives." We were not optimistic about the outcome.)

The specter of American economic intervention combined with the successful coups in Czechoslovakia and Hungary to embolden the Soviet Union. Its next step was to begin tightening its hold on Berlin, which lay deep within the Soviet occupation zone of Germany.

THE BERLIN BLOCKADE:
FIRST CHALLENGE FOR THE USAF

The presence of French, British, and American troops in West Berlin was a continual irritant to the Soviet Union, from a social rather than a military standpoint. Because it was political dynamite to expose Soviet soldiers and the citizens of East Berlin to the decadent luxuries common to the armed forces of the Western Allies, the Soviets began to squeeze the Allies out of West Berlin by a gradual application of force in the form of restricted road and rail traffic.

On June 22, 1948—not coincidentally the seventh anniversary of the Nazi invasion of the Soviet Union—the gloves came off, and all barge, rail, and road traffic into West Berlin was halted.

The Soviet Union's ground forces vastly outnumbered those of the Allies, having thirty full-strength army divisions—as many as 400,000 troops, well supported by the capable Soviet tactical air force. The United States had about 60,000 troops in Europe, and of these about 10,000 were in the understrength 1st Cavalry Division.

The USAF was in equally poor shape. The 28th Bomb Group flew into Scampton, in Lincolnshire, on July 17, while on the 18th, the 2d Bomb Group arrived at Lakenheath. On August 8, the 307th Bomb Group, comprising the 270th and 371st Bombardment Squadrons, came to Marham. The B-29s had no atomic bombs at their disposal, but the Soviet Union could not be sure of this. During the third week of July, sixteen F-80s of the 56th Fighter Group at Selfridge AFB, Michigan, set out for Europe. Led by the famous 22.5-victory ace and future in-flight-refueling expert Lieutenant Colonel David Schilling, it flew in stages to Odiham, in Hampshire, and then was transferred to Fürstenfeldbruck, near Munich. It was a token effort, but it was all that the USAF could muster.

The Berlin Blockade proved that committees are not always bad. Lieutenant General Albert Wedemeyer, Deputy Chief of Staff, Operations, and Lieutenant General Henry S. Aurand, Chief of Logistics of the Department of the Army, visited General Lucius D. Clay, the U.S. Military Governor in Occupied Germany, in the spring of 1948. The three men concluded that an airlift was feasible, and so recommended to President Truman. Clay then asked Major General LeMay, now Commander of United States Air Forces in Europe, if the Air Force could supply West Berlin with enough essentials by air to sustain the citizenry until the blockade could be lifted by diplomacy—or other means. LeMay, typically, immediately responded that it could, although preliminary calculations showed that to supply West Berlin at minimum level would require at least 4,500 tons of food, coal, and other supplies a day—far beyond any capability then in Europe.

LeMay immediately brought to bear all his authority and energy to create an initial airlift of 102 Douglas C-47s and two Douglas C-54s, and on June

26, flew in the first 80 tons of supplies, consisting primarily of medicines, flour, and milk. The 60th and 61st Troop Carrier Groups formed the heart of the effort, but C-47s were pulled in from all sides. Two days later, the Royal Air Force began operations with its own fleet of Dakotas (C-47s) and seven squadrons of Avro Yorks, a four-engine sister ship of the Lancaster that had devastated Germany at night during the war.

The initial airlift efforts were not very efficient, being pure improvisation, a tailoring of existing procedures to the mundane task of hauling coal, food, and medical supplies. On July 23, the Military Air Transport System established an Airlift Task Force (ATF) that brought seventy-two C-54s to the task, along with three crews per plane for a twenty-four-hour operation.

The USAF next brought in the world's acknowledged expert in airlift techniques, Major General William H. Tunner, who had made his mark flying the Hump in the massive air supply system of the China-Burma-India theater. After analyzing the situation, Tunner brought about a merger of USAF and RAF operations and organized the airfields, routing, and equipment to provide the maximum efficiency so that the airlift functioned more like a bulk-materials-handling factory than an airline.

Along with a few other miscellaneous types, including (briefly) a Boeing C-97, the giant Douglas C-74, and the workhorse Fairchild C-82, he eventually brought in 319 C-54s, which could carry three times the load of the C-47, and launched them at ninety-second intervals from bases at Celle, Fassberg, Rhein-Main (a base built originally for the giants of another age, the *Graf Zeppelin* and the *Hindenburg*), and Wiesbaden. The aircraft cruised at 170 mph, separated by 500-foot altitude increments and three minutes in time, and landed at either Gatow or Tempelhof, and later at Tegel. All air traffic was strictly controlled, and the ground-controlled approach (GCA) system became increasingly more proficient as time passed. Tunner insisted that all crews land if ceiling and visibility were 400 feet and one mile or better, but threatened court-martial for anyone who went below those minimums.

Efficiency was everything; Tunner reduced ground time to an amazing thirty-minute turnaround, including unloading and refueling. Crews could not leave their planes; refreshments, flight clearances, and weather information were brought directly to them while German civilian crews, many of them women, raced to unload, glad to be helping foil the Reds, happier still to have a job that paid DM 1.20 per hour (about a quarter) and a hot meal.

The results were stunning. Daily airlift totals grew steadily, reaching 2,000 tons per day by July 31 and 5,583 tons per day by September 18, 1948. By October 20, the basic requirement for Berlin was raised from 4,500 tons to 5,620 tons, permitting an increase in rations. By April 15, 1949, 1,398 aircraft brought in 12,940 tons of goods, a figure that convinced the Soviet Union that the blockade was not only broken but had been turned into a smashing political triumph for the Western Allies. When the airlift was finally terminated on September 30, 1949, it had delivered 2,325,000 tons of food, fuel, and supplies to Berlin, a quantity in excess of what would have been routinely brought in by surface traffic during the period. U.S. aircraft had flown 189,963 flights, in 586,827 hours of flying time, for a total distance of 92,061,863 miles—about the distance to the sun.

The $200 million effort had not been without human cost—twelve crashes had claimed thirty-one American lives. The political benefits were incalculable. For the first time since the end of the war, American resolve had halted the Soviet Union in its tracks—with air power and without the use of weapons. Yet had the United States been strong, the blockade would not have been attempted.

THE PRESIDENT'S AIR POLICY COMMISSION

In spite of the cost—and the success—of the Berlin airlift, the Truman administration remained acutely conscious that the American public was focused on reviving the economy. In these times of multitrillion-dollar deficits, it seems strange, but the idea was not only to balance the budget but to create a surplus with which to reduce the deficit caused by the war.

Truman was a believer in air power, and he recognized the hiatus the drastic reductions in spending had caused the U.S. aviation industry. In July 1947, he appointed Thomas K. Finletter to head the President's Air Policy Commission (usually called the Finletter Commission) to provide advice on national aviation policy. (The action was similar to the significant President's Aircraft Board of 1925, which did much to promote the growth of aviation.)

Finletter (later a Secretary of the Air Force) advised that a modern seventy-group air force be developed to counter the foreign (i.e., Soviet) nuclear threat by both defensive means and the threat of offensive action. The commission's report, released in January 1948, said that the military establishment had to be built around air power. Further, it candidly admitted that the Air Force was not capable of fulfilling those duties with its current strength. It recommended a force of more than 12,000 modern aircraft of which at least 700 were to be bombers capable of carrying atomic weapons. The report estimated that it would be 1953 before any aggressor would have nuclear weapons, and also recommended an expansion in naval air strength.

Unfortunately, the Finletter Commission's recommendations ran counter to fiscal realities as perceived by the Truman administration. A limit was put on the fiscal year 1949 budget of $14.4 billion (net)—about one half that projected by the Joint Chiefs of Staff as the absolute minimum necessary. The funds were to be split on an approximately equal basis by the three services.

Secretary Forrestal's health was gradually undermined in part by the disagreements between the Air Force and the Navy over the budget and over roles and missions. After a series of meetings, at Key West, Florida, in March and at Newport, Rhode Island, in August, the strategic issues were parceled out, with strategic air operations awarded to the USAF and control of the sea to the Navy—each service was to assist the other. Unfortunately for the future, no clear mandate was given for missile and space activity. An unexpected but fortunate result of these talks was the creation of the position of Chairman of the Joint Chiefs of Staff.

The strain of the arguments, amplified by the fact that Forrestal himself had insisted that the role of the Secretary of Defense be more that of a coordinator than a decision-maker, took its toll on his mental and physical health. He resigned in March 1949, and was diagnosed as suffering from paranoid delusions, one of them being that he was followed by Israeli agents. On May 22, 1949, he leaped to his death from the nineteenth floor of the Bethesda Naval Hospital. Years later Israel revealed that it had in fact had him followed by its agents.

Forrestal was succeeded by Truman's chief fund-raiser for the 1948 election campaign, Louis A. Johnson. A great table-pounding bear of a man, Johnson was 6 feet 2 inches tall, weighed 250 pounds, and employed intimidation as his principal human relations tool. He alienated every member of Truman's cabinet on many occasions, displaying to them at their meetings the manners of a professional football coach responding to a referee making an adverse call in the Super Bowl.

Yet Johnson harbored his own political ambitions to succeed Truman, and thought these could be furthered by exercising a tight control over military spending. Under his leadership, and against the timid advice of the JCS and his service secretaries, Johnson supported Truman's insistence on keeping proposed defense budgets at a very low level.

The budget dropped to $14.2 billion for fiscal year 1950, reducing the USAF to forty-eight groups rather than seventy. To reach even that modest goal, the USAF had to cut eleven groups from its already too-weak force.

Johnson's economy measures extended to the Navy; in April 1949, he abruptly canceled the USS *United States*, the supercarrier that the Navy wished to use as a step toward a strategic nuclear bombing capability.

He made the decision on the advice of the JCS, but without consulting the Secretary of the Navy, John L. Sullivan, who resigned three days later. The cancellation precipitated what has been called the "Revolt of the Admirals," but what was actually a mutiny. Had some poor enlisted man attempted a similar defiance of order and protocol, he would have been court-martialed without a moment's hesitation. Instead, admirals got away with an unseemly attempt, using crudely bogus anonymous documents, to malign Secretary Symington and the Air Force. Called by Symington "the best hatchet job that I have seen since I've been in town," the documents alleged that the Consolidated-Vultee B-36 did not perform up to specification (future Chief of Naval Operations and then Vice Admiral Arthur W. Radford termed it "the billion-dollar blunder") and that the procurement process was fraudulent, with illegal agreements having been made by Symington and the president of Consolidated-Vultee, Floyd Odlum, often better known as Jacqueline Cochran's husband.

The genesis of the B-36 had been the Air Corps' concern that England might be invaded by Germany, and that the United States would require an intercontinental bomber. Design studies were submitted on April 11, 1941, and Consolidated won the paper competition and was awarded a contract for two prototypes. The war relegated the B-36 to a lower priority, and first flight did not occur until August 8, 1946.

The huge six-pusher-engine B-36 had problems that might be expected in such a precedent-breaking aircraft, but it also proved to be too slow and unable to attain a sufficiently high bombing altitude. Development continued, and on March 26, 1949, the first B-36D flew. It benefited from a spin-off of jet engine technology; four jet engines, two each in nacelles exactly like those used on the inboard wing stations of the new Boeing B-47, were fitted. The new power imparted a speed and altitude capability that enabled the B-36 to earn its nickname "Peacekeeper." It never dropped a bomb in battle, thus exactly fulfilling its mission of deterrence.

House Armed Services hearings, headed by Congressman Carl Vinson, proved that there was not an iota of truth in the allegations contained in the documents being cited by Congressman Carl Van Zandt (a lieutenant commander in the Navy Reserve). The author of the anonymous documents proved to be Cedric Worth, an aide to the Assistant Secretary of the Navy and a former Hollywood script writer, who, by some imaginative twist, was also the person assigned by the Navy to verify the validity of the documents.

The hearings gave both the Air Force and the Navy a chance to present their cases. In essence, the Air Force contended that the B-36 was not invulnerable, but that enough would get through to achieve its mission. The Navy took the tack that it was essential first to win the tactical air battle and obtain air superiority before committing the bomber forces. It also stated that it would be immoral to carry the war to the enemy homeland's population, as an atomic strike would do, although, somewhat inconsistently, it wanted its own capability to do so. The Navy's view was that "we cannot afford our strategic air component over a long term in peacetime, and we should not plan for intercontinental strategic bombing if any other way is possible." The Navy then found itself in the strange position of extolling the virtues of the Boeing B-47 jet bomber, but only because funding for the B-47 was downstream, when another battle could be fought.

Air Force Chief of Staff General Vandenberg showed the B-36 to tremendous advantage in its defense. He rejected the Navy's argument that the Air Force was seeking a cheap and easy way to wage war, saying, "A prime objective of this country must be to find a counterbalance to the potential enemy's masses of ground troops other than equal masses of American and

Allied troops. No such balancing factor exists other than strategic bombing."
He also noted that only four of the Air Force's forty-eight groups would have
B-36s and that the total cost of the B-36 program was less than $1 billion.

The net result of the committee hearings on the surface was that the Air
Force emerged untainted, the B-36 was accepted as a worthwhile weapon
system, and the Navy had egg on its face. At these hearings, the Navy's
staunchest friend, Representative Vinson himself, moved perceptibly toward
the Air Force camp.

Yet the Navy had touched a sensitive nerve. The United States Air Force
was not yet capable of carrying out the type of mission called for by the
Finletter Commission, or, indeed, by its own charter.

Secretary of the Air Force Stuart Symington was dissatisfied with the
defense budgets of 1950 and 1951, and with a becoming courage resigned
in protest. He was succeeded by Thomas K. Finletter, who lacked the leadership qualities Symington possessed in abundance. Finletter was not a "people person" as Symington had been, and had difficulty getting along with his
Chief of Staff, General Vandenberg, among others. He was not interested in
routine details, following larger issues like the newly formed North Atlantic
Treaty Organization (NATO), perhaps because they distanced him from interaction with his staff. Yet it was to be Finletter's lot to be Secretary when
the pressures of war suddenly opened the money floodgates again. In the
meantime, as so often would be the case, the serviceman suffered.

PEOPLE ISSUES

One of the most important considerations of contemporary Air Force
leadership is the improvement in the quality of life of service people. While
never actually defined, the standard for that quality of life is that of middle
America as a whole. To appreciate the change in thinking, we need to understand the baseline of issues regarding the care and welfare of service
members in the new United States Air Force. These are reflected in the
typical public attitude to the military services in the pre–World War II years,
which, sadly enough, ranged from condescension to contempt.

In those days, while an education at West Point or Annapolis was not to
be discounted, and while a person of independent means like George Patton
or Billy Mitchell might be able to imbue service life with a panache not
found at a local country club, service personnel, officer and enlisted alike,
were generally looked down upon by their civilian counterparts. In the case
of officers, the agonizingly slow promotion system, stultifying social life, and
generally hardscrabble nature of living on remote posts was enough to cause
civilians to wonder why anyone would put up with it—if one could do something else. "Genteel poverty" was a term used to describe the threadbare
existence of military families; the niceties of calling cards, being "at home,"
and other such relics of a bygone age served as plaintive substitutes for

vacations, good schools, elective orthodontia for children, and other perks enjoyed by civilians in comparable positions.

In the Air Corps, the pilots at least found that flying was an exhilarating compensation for some of the disagreeable aspects of service life. Flying pay was both an inducement and an issue of contention. Fliers loved it, and showed it off with modestly conspicuous consumption, perhaps buying a secondhand Pontiac instead of a secondhand Chevrolet. Nonfliers, naturally enough, hated the very idea of flying pay, and the economy-minded Congress continually sought to eliminate it. The cruel fact of the matter was that the flying pay would, if used solely for the purpose, buy just enough life insurance to offset the loss of pay inherent in the shorter average life span of pilots. It was actuarially, if not emotionally, sound.

But the public on the whole thought that those who stayed in the service, fliers or not, did so because they didn't consider themselves able to compete "on the outside." The term "lifer," although more common now than then, was used contemptuously to characterize servicemen who stayed in for the dubious reward of a minimal pension. Yet when war came, the spectacular performances turned in by a host of the veterans of the deprived years of the Air Corps should have disabused this idea forever.

The civilian view of their life had a reverse resonance within the service, whose members took a grumpy pride in enduring the hardships and regarded those who opted out as "quitters." When the record-setting Jimmy Doolittle, with a growing family, a doctorate in engineering, and a celebrated flying career, found himself locked in place as a first lieutenant for eleven years, with no assurance of promotion in the near future, he decided to leave the service. He found ready employment that included not only higher pay, but promotion and perquisites. Yet when he returned to duty with the advent of World War II, many senior officers, including General Eisenhower, looked at him askance as one who had "jumped ship" when times were tough. It took many months of typically outstanding Doolittle performance to change their minds.

The public opinion of enlisted men (for women were not yet allowed to make their contribution to the ranks) was equally harsh, although somewhat mitigated by the fact that the Depression had caused such widespread unemployment that any job, even a military one, was coveted. In general, however, fathers' faces did not light up when their daughters reported that they were going to date an enlisted man, nor did mothers' hearts leap when sons told them they had been accepted for enlistment. While James Jones's depiction of Army life in his famous *From Here to Eternity* might not be absolutely accurate in the eyes and minds of the servicemen it portrayed, it was on the mark in terms of public perception of those men.

To the extent possible, the cruel public attitude was mitigated within the services. During peacetime, little privileges such as "Wednesday-afternoon athletics" during which officers and men had time off to exercise—or what-

ever—were common. Officers were careful to maintain a social distance between themselves and enlisted personnel (this gap was narrowest in the Air
Corps), but they did help them as much as they could. There were usually
baseball fields and other similar low-cost sports facilities, and, of course, the
clubs, where beer and liquor were cheap, and drinking was for many a way
of life. (Drinking was a costly factor in service life for decades; only in the
past twenty years have the services emphasized the virtues of temperance by
relating it to performance reports.)

There was not, however, the array of services available to either officers
or enlisted men that is common today; it would not have occurred to a private
in the 1930s Air Corps that the military would provide him any perquisites
such as legal assistance, psychological counseling, job training, or the opportunity for on-base college courses. Even less likely would be the provision of
well-equipped fitness centers, bowling alleys, comfortable theaters, or post
exchanges with an inventory including household items such as refrigerators,
radios, and the like. Most PXs were considered well stocked if they had
anything beyond cigarettes, shaving gear, and shoeshine materials.

When war came, all of the stigma of service life fell away, and civilians
competed to treat servicemen, officers or enlisted, well. If every able person
had to be in service, if there was a war to be won, everything was different.
The sounds of young women curtly refusing to date servicemen was suddenly
drowned out by the music and laughter of slow-moving dances at the USO,
and very often, by wedding bells.

In short, the serviceman in peace and war had everything but adequate
pay, housing, and services. Of food there was plenty, in wastefully gargantuan
amounts, but often poorly prepared by amateur cooks who ladled their sloppy
mixtures into cold and greasy compartmented trays. (Today's mess halls, with
salad bars, diet plates, food kiosks, all immaculately clean and staffed by eager
professionals, would have seemed half Disney, half Orwell at the time.)

In the vast World War II expansion of the military, bases were thrown
up at a staggering rate, all characterized by barren open-bay barracks with
group showers and open rows of toilets, complemented by equally austere
mess halls, administrative offices, classrooms, and supply huts. It was a temporary world of two-by-four pine and slapdash coats of whitewash, intended
to be just good enough to last the war. Larger organizations, like hospitals,
were a series of barrackslike buildings strung together with covered walkways.
Like most wartime construction, the buildings were rarely insulated. The
windows stuck and the heating systems malfunctioned. Elbow grease and
hard paste wax kept buildings clean and glistening, but nothing could make
them comfortable. They were "temps," temporary buildings, all slated for
salvage or replacement in peacetime.

Except, of course, that after the war was over and the services had demobilized, there was no money—nor any apparent reason—to either salvage
or modernize the facilities. Many buildings designated "temporary" in 1941

were still doing business thirty years later, improved with some interior walls and some extra coats of paint perhaps, but still just rectangular pine shacks. It was worse overseas. As late as 1948 in Guam, and in many other places, enlisted personnel still had to make do with open-pit latrines, tents, and open communal washbasins.

Families had suffered during the war, for there was no mechanism to care for them, and no incentive to do so in the pell-mell rush of war. A $10,000 life insurance policy was the only thing available to ease the cold distress brought by the standard War Department telegram notifying parents of a lost son.

In the prewar days, base housing had always been limited. It was intended primarily for relatively senior officers. Junior officers and noncommissioned officers were informally counseled to stay single, while at intervals enlisted personnel were officially counseled to do so. When war came, there was little pressure to expand base housing for families, for personnel rarely stayed for more than a few months at any one place. The wives who followed their husbands from base to base, trying to make a home on the economy, found themselves living in everything from modified chicken coops to two-family-per-room boardinghouses.

Because they were young, and because it was wartime, it was somehow not only endurable but—retrospectively at least—romantic. For many years after the war, the situation eased only slightly. Supply and demand took some of the most outrageous accommodations off the market, but in areas where bases remained at full activity after the war, landlords made a killing for as long as they could.

The fledgling Air Force simply had too much on its hands to begin to attend to such fundamental concerns as making life better for the enlisted troops or improving conditions for families. It would be several years—in many cases till long after the Korean War—before commanders would begin to realize how essential these matters were, and to lobby effectively for reform with Congress. As the years passed, however, the Air Force became increasingly aware that such care was not only important, but essential to survival, and as such, one of the most cost-effective ways to use Air Force resources.

Something that should perhaps have been obvious became recognized only in the late 1970s, when it was demonstrated that budget money spent on improving the quality of life was as important as budget money spent on weapon systems, because of its direct and potent impact on job performance.

Even though the Air Force would be in the vanguard of improving the quality of life of its members, compared to the other services, it had to learn the hard way, following old habits and old routines. Some of the lessons would be taught in the three years of bitter fighting in Korea.

3
≋

THE FIRST CRUCIBLE

*I*n many respects, the United States' bungling, unprepared entrance into the Korean conflict—the wrong war, in the wrong place, at the wrong time, with the wrong enemy, according to the Chairman of the Joint Chiefs of Staff, General Omar Bradley—had many elements of a Greek tragedy. There was hubris on the part of both President Truman and Secretary of State Dean Acheson; there was vision blinded by ambition on the part of Secretary of Defense Louis Johnson; and, for all three, there was an exquisitely painful irony regarding the usually laudable quality of loyalty. To this unhappy mixture must be added the supine acceptance by the Joint Chiefs of Staff and the service secretaries of military budgets that they knew to be inadequate to support the foreign policies of the United States in the face of an increasingly aggressive Soviet Union.

Truman's hubris was certainly human enough, given his triumphant election in which he not only defeated his "man on the wedding cake" opponent, Thomas E. Dewey, but carried the Democrats along to majorities in both houses of Congress. This led to a certain arrogance, unusual for him, expressed by his discounting the counsel of his military experts and preferring instead that of his cronies. His antimilitary bias had deep roots. It began with his inability to qualify physically for a service academy appointment, and was heightened by the traditional disdain a National Guardsman has for regular officers. This attitude was reinforced forever by his experience heading the Special Committee to Investigate the National Defense Program—the Truman Committee—during World War II. The very nature of this task brought Truman into contact with the seamy side of wartime military procurement, coloring his attitude about the service and industry long before Dwight Eisenhower (or, more likely, his speechwriter) coined the term "military-industrial complex" in his farewell address in 1961. As President, Truman undoubtedly saw a parallel in his own military self-education and that of Abraham Lincoln, and became convinced that his judgment was as astute militarily as it was politically. He gave his strongest loyalty downward not to his professional military advisers, but instead to former political cronies like Major General Harry H. Vaughn and to fund-raisers like Johnson. Vaughn, his military aide, had no meaningful military experience, yet was in a position of tremendous influence while serving primarily as a yes-man to corroborate Truman's views.

Nor did upward loyalty work for Truman. Acheson's undoubted loyalty simply reinforced the incompatibility of Truman's foreign policies and his defense budgets, the former expressing a hearty appetite for global interests and support for the United Nations, even as the military was placed on a starvation diet. Misguided loyalty bared its ugly head in other venues as well. It was not in Truman's or the nation's interest when Bradley, the Chairman of the Joint Chiefs of Staff, and the three Chiefs all strongly supported Johnson's defense budgets in public, even though they knew that the low levels of those budgets were destroying the very fabric of the armed services for which they were responsible. It was a time when the heads of the military could better have distinguished themselves by a mass resignation than by a continued service. Truman would undoubtedly have accepted the resignations—if Douglas MacArthur did not intimidate him, Omar Bradley surely would not—but the statement they would have made would have brought them more honor than their past accomplishments in battle.

In Acheson's case, hubris stemmed from his patrician background, the success he had gained as a behind-the-scenes manipulator of White House/State Department intrigues and the inevitable triumphs he scored when brought to a battle of wits with his political enemies. In his aristocratic view, his devotion to Truman was an affecting idiosyncrasy, an illustration of just how superior he was to the hoi polloi of the Congress and the press, for he and almost no one else could see the true merits of the plebeian President from Missouri. To his credit, it must be noted that late in the game his State Department called for the defense of South Korea and for a rearmament policy that should have emanated from the Secretary of Defense.

The opportunistic Johnson's hubris stemmed from humbler roots; he was simply a loose cannon who blew out the decks of the Defense Department and threatened to demolish the entire cabinet. It took but a few weeks of the Korean War to prove just how wrong his eager enforcement of Truman's budget policies had been, for when the North Korean armed forces launched their surprise attack on South Korea on June 25, 1950, the military forces of the United States were caught dangerously unprepared.

Invitations to Trouble

Although the catalog of Communist aggression was impressive, it still had not been enough to arouse the American public or Congress to face up to the cost of an adequate defense force. The administration's naive belief in the deterrent power of the USAF's "air-atomic" (a catchphrase of the time) monopoly prevented it from working for an adequate military budget.

American diplomatic policy had been as remiss as its defensive efforts. The world in general and the North Koreans in particular had been assured repeatedly that the United States did not regard South Korea as a major interest in a series of self-reinforcing disclaimers, each with a different rationale, beginning at the Potsdam Conference during July 1945. Amid the many towering issues of the day, an offhand decision had been made to allow the Soviet Union to disarm Japanese armed forces in Korea down to the 38th parallel, while the United States disarmed them up to that point.

Although it was not until September 8, 1945, that troops of the U.S. 7th Infantry Division entered Korea, the Soviet Union had moved earlier and more rapidly. Within a few days after entering the war, it had sealed off the border, interrupting rail, river, and road traffic permanently between the primarily industrial North and the primarily agricultural South. The thirty-five years of oppressive Japanese occupation had exploited Korea, but had turned it into a viable economic entity. The Soviet division at the 38th parallel created two half-states, neither fully functional.

The Joint Chiefs of Staff, attempting to deal with the disruptions of complete demobilization, and knowing that the services faced a period of declining budgets, had to make hard choices, apportioning forces on the basis of the nation's greatest interest. On September 25, 1947, the JCS provided a memo to the Secretary of Defense, under the signature of JCS Chairman General Eisenhower, advising that there was little strategic interest in keeping the current level of 45,000 (mostly green) troops in Korea. If military action was required to defend South Korea, it was to be provided by means of air power from Japan.

To offset this lack of support, the United States requested the United Nations to arrange to have elections that would unify Korea under one government and end the artificial division that prevented rational development.

Despite opposition to the idea from the Soviet Union, which never welcomed free elections, arrangements were made for a national election on May 10, 1948. The elections were suppressed above the 38th parallel, but in South Korea, the radical Syngman Rhee, seventy-three years old and difficult to handle, was named president of the Republic of Korea on July 20, 1947.

The Soviet Union contested the validity of the election and in the fall of 1948 proclaimed the existence of the People's Republic of North Korea, with the thirty-two-year-old Kim Il Sung (later hailed as "the Great Leader") as premier. As an apparent sop, the Soviet Union proposed a mutual withdrawal of foreign troops, an arrangement exactly to the taste of the United States.

The American troops were pulled out in stages, dropping first to a 7,500-man regimental combat team and then, after a Korean constabulary had been trained, to a small Korean Military Advisory Group (KMAG) of about 500 men. The Korean constabulary was deliberately equipped with only small arms and given no artillery, tanks, or combat aircraft, for the Americans feared that President Rhee would attack the North if he had the military capability to do so.

The Soviet Union had no similar inhibitions and immediately set about training and equipping a formidable North Korean People's Army (NKPA), fully equipped in Soviet style with artillery, tanks, and planes.

The Central Intelligence Agency, still young, but derived from World War II organizations, had said that it did not believe that South Korea could maintain its independence in the face of the withdrawal of U.S. forces. Yet it did not predict that the North Koreans would attack, despite the imbalance of forces and the gravitational tug ordinary economics exerted to unify North and South. North Korea, with a population of about 9 million, was equipped with a formidable offensive force guided by 3,000 Soviet advisers. Nominally democratic South Korea, with a population of about 21 million, had an ill-trained, ill-equipped constabulary of about 50,000 troops, with the 500-man American advisory group. It should have been obvious that North Korea intended to unite the country by force of arms as soon as possible, before South Korea could build its strength.

By the spring of 1949, Truman agreed to internal military pressure that the Republic of Korea army should be built up with U.S. assistance. This decision—foreshadowing the shabby policy of "Vietnamization" more than twenty years later—was another clear indication that the United States had abdicated a serious military role in South Korea, and it was duly noted by the North Koreans.

Two major events should have precipitated a major American defense buildup, but did not. The Nationalist Chinese forces were at last driven from mainland China and Mao Tse-tung announced the People's Republic of China on October 1, 1949, with Chou En-lai as premier. An event not a week earlier was even more ominous: the detection of a Soviet atomic explosion by a just activated Air Force system. When this discovery was announced on September 23, the administration preferred to believe that it was the first Soviet test and that it would still be some time before the USSR had enough bombs stockpiled for a sneak attack. (Despite the lack of a U.S. stockpile of weapons, Truman did not authorize increased production of standard nuclear bombs until October 17, and waited until the following January 31 to authorize research on the hydrogen bomb.)

Yet the possibility lurked that only the most recent test had been observed, that the Soviets had put the bomb into large-scale production even before its test, and that they might, given the pathetic state of U.S. air defenses, send their Tupelov Tu-4s on one-way missions to a dozen or more major American cities. Once again, the fundamental military rule of preparing for what an enemy could do was put aside for the less expensive strategy of preparing for what it was thought it would do.

The two events did trigger a paper from the National Security Council on December 30, 1949, one that was more an admission of weakness than a statement of policy. The paper, NSC 48/2, called for economic assistance to Asian nations to strengthen their resistance to Communist encroachment and explicitly defined the area that the United States would defend militarily as a line that encompassed Japan, the Ryukus, and the Philippines. South Korea was not mentioned. In a further attempt to limit American responsibilities, on January 5, 1950, Truman stated that the Nationalist Chinese forces on Taiwan would get economic but not military assistance.

If the Soviet Union and the North Koreans were not yet aware of the implications of these policies, Dean Acheson made them crystal clear in a speech at the National Press Club on January 12, in which he once again confirmed that the United States would defend only the perimeter specified in the NSC memo, and that other nations would have to rely upon themselves and upon the United Nations for their defense.

Nonetheless, Acheson belatedly recognized the need for a stronger military that would require more than tripling the 1950 defense budget level of about $13 billion. It was too late. Much blood would be shed, and a war would come within a few days and a few miles of being lost because the United States was so terribly unprepared.

MISNOMERS AND MISJUDGMENTS

Three major powers fought two undeclared wars in Korea, and like passengers nervously watching their respective cab drivers brawl, studiously ignored the fact. The Soviet Union, China, and the United States allowed North Korea's army, with Soviet and Chinese "volunteers," to fight against South Korea's army, allied to a United Nations Command made up largely of U.S. troops.

President Truman called it a "police action" to ease his way around the right of Congress to declare war. The United States was able to get a resolution through the UN Security Council accusing North Korea of unprovoked aggression because of an incredible diplomatic blunder by the Soviet Union. The USSR had boycotted the Security Council in objection to Nationalist China's continued representation, and its representative, Jacob Malik, was not present to veto the UN resolution as he otherwise would have done. The resolution laid the groundwork for the later establishment of the United Nations Command that would prosecute the war.

Each side made catastrophic misjudgments. In the first war, the North

Koreans, believing what they had been told, invaded South Korea, confident that the United States would not intervene. They were wrong, and they lost that war. The United States, under the UN banner, pursued the defeated North Koreans to the Chinese border, in the belief that Red China would not intervene. This time the United States was wrong, and it lost the second, larger, war.

And all the while, the United States, the Soviet Union, and Red China remained nominally at peace.

JUNE 25, 1950

At 0400 hours on the morning of June 25, 1950, six columns of North Korean assault troops crashed through token South Korean defenses. A total of 89,000 men, about a third of whom were veterans of the fighting in China, made up seven divisions, a tank brigade equipped with the formidable Soviet T-34 tanks, and two independent infantry regiments trained for special duties. The North Koreans had a reserve force of some 51,000 men grouped in three divisions and their own Border Constabulary. The North Korean Air Force (NKAF) had 162 combat aircraft, including seventy Yakovlev and Lavochkin fighters (near equivalents to the F-51 Mustang) and sixty-two of the excellent Ilyushin Il-10s, an improved version of the historic Shturmovik attack aircraft.

Opposing them were approximately 100,000 South Korean troops in eight understrength divisions; of these, fully one-third were service and support troops, virtually useless for combat. The Americans had intentionally deprived this constabulary of antitank weapons, for the advisory group had considered Korea—like the Ardennes—not to be "tank country." The ROK Air Force had sixteen aircraft: three North American T-6 trainers and thirteen liaison aircraft—five Piper L-4s and eight Vultee (Stinson) L-5s, none fitted with armament.

The North Korean assault was reminiscent of the later days of the Soviet advance through Germany, using tanks, artillery, and infantry in swift-moving combinations that threatened to achieve its objective, the reunification of Korea by military force, within a few weeks. The Republic of Korea forces were badly beaten, and could not have recovered without outside intervention. On June 26, knowing that Seoul would inevitably fall, U.S. Ambassador John J. Muccio ordered all nonessential U.S. embassy personnel and all U.S. dependents in Korea evacuated to Japan.

STATUS OF THE FAR EAST AIR FORCES

In a war full of many ironies, one of the most important was that the budget difficulties which prevented the modernization of the United States Air Force to the degree required left the Far East Air Forces (FEAF) with exactly the right kind of equipment with which to fight the nonnuclear war in which it found itself. Although more modern aircraft in greater numbers would have been welcome, the 365 Lockheed F-80s, thirty-two North American F-82s, twenty-six Douglas B-26s and twenty-two Boeing B-29s that formed the bulk of the combat forces were well suited to slow down and eventually stop the North Korean invaders. The F-82s would be withdrawn relatively early from combat because of their small numbers and lack of spares.

This force would be supplemented by North American F-51s called back into service because of their longer range and ability to operate from the primitive Korean airfields. These included ten pulled back from a flight intended for transfer to the ROK Air Force, thirty withdrawn from storage in the theater, and 145 obtained from stateside Air National Guard units. (There were more than 1,500 F-51s still available in the United States, about half in storage and half assigned to Air National Guard units.) In a retrograde step unusual in wartime, six F-80C squadrons were converted to F-51s, a seemingly innocuous measure until you realize that the pilots were going into combat immediately in an unfamiliar aircraft with totally different flying characteristics, and knew that maintenance was performed by mechanics equally unfamiliar with their mounts.

In addition, FEAF had twenty-five RF-80s and six RB-29s for reconnaissance, along with a number of aircraft dedicated to weather reconnaissance and air/sea rescue.

Another irony, less fortunate, would rear its head almost four months after the war's start, when the MiG-15 was introduced. One of the poorest countries in the world, China, had brought in an advanced aircraft clearly superior to all UN aircraft yet in the war. They were purchased or bartered for from the Soviet Union, which had a history of not giving away war material that extended back to the Spanish Civil War, when Loyalist gold paid for the Ratas and Chatos received from Russia. Nonetheless, China had the swept-wing MiG-15 weeks before the United States was able to offset them with the North American F-86. Further, the Chinese would maintain an establishment of MiG-15s that would dwarf the available strength of F-86s throughout the war.

Although FEAF had been starved for aircraft, men and supplies, it had nonetheless maintained a high standard of training for its assigned tasks. FEAF was the air component of the Far East Command (FEC) commanded by General of the Army Douglas MacArthur. Its primary mission was to maintain an active air defense of Japan, the Ryukyus, the Marianas, and American bases in the Philippines.

FEAF was commanded by Lieutenant General George E. Stratemeyer, a personable commander with wide experience in the field, but one whose tactical air experience was insufficient to gain the complete confidence of the Chief of Staff, General Vandenberg, a professional in that discipline.

The principal component of FEAF was the Fifth Air Force, famous for its wartime exploits under General George Kenney, and trained primarily for the air defense role. The F-51s, F-82s, and F-80s of the Fifth would soon be called on to engage in close air support, for which they were not trained, but in which they would do surpassingly well. The Fifth was commanded by Major General Earle "Pat" Partridge, and was equipped as the following table shows:

Unit	Station	Aircraft
8th Fighter Bomber Wing (FBW)	Itazuke	Lockheed F-80C
68th Fighter All-Weather Squadron (F[AW]S)	Itazuke	North American F-82
49th Fighter Bomber Wing (FBW)	Misawa	Lockheed F-80C
35th Fighter Interceptor Wing (FIW)	Yokota	Lockheed F-80C
339th Fighter All-Weather Squadron (F[AW]S)	Yokota	North American F-82
8th Tactical Reconnaissance Squadron (TRS)	Yokota	Lockheed RF-80A
3d Bombardment Wing (Light) (BWL)	Johnson	Douglas B-26
374th Troop Carrier Wing (TCW)	Tachikawa	Douglas C-54
51s Fighter Interceptor Wing (FIW)	Naha, Okinawa	Lockheed F-80C
4th Fighter All Weather Squadron (F[AW]S)	Naha, Okinawa	North American F-82
31st Photo Recce Squadron° (VLR) (PRS)	Kadena, Okinawa	Boeing RB-29
19th Bombardment Wing (M) (BWM)	Andersen, Guam	Boeing B-29
18th Fighter Bomber Wing (FBW)	Clark, P.I.	Lockheed F-80C
21st Troop Carrier Squadron (TCS)	Clark, P.I.	Douglas C-54
6204th Photo Mapping Flight (PMF)	Clark, P.I.	Boeing RB-17

°Later the 91st SRS

Additional units rounding out FEAF's strength included flights of the 2d and 3d Air Rescue Squadrons (ARS), with SB-29 and SB-17 aircraft; the 512th and 514th Weather Reconnaissance Squadrons (WRS), with Boeing WB-29s; and No. 77 Squadron of the Royal Australian Air Force, equipped with North American F-51s and stationed at Iwakuni.

All in all, it was a great World War II air force with which to prevent World War III. Fortunately, although the equipment was obsolete and the mission dictated by the war was not the one they had trained for, the aircrews were both highly skilled and adaptable. More important, they were ready to fight.

THE AIR FORCE INTERVENES

As the North Korean forces swept south, the NKAF strafed Seoul and Kimpo airports, wiping out the light aircraft of the ROK AF and destroying a U.S. Military Air Transport Service C-54—a sufficient *casus belli* in earlier times. FEAF planning had anticipated a requirement to evacuate Korea in an emergency, and General Partridge, who was commanding in General Stratemeyer's absence, designated Colonel John M. "Jack" Price of the 8th Fighter Bomber Wing to be the air task force commander for the evacuation.

Price gathered a force of his own F-80 and F-82 fighters, ten B-26s of the 8th Bombardment Squadron (Light), twelve C-54s, and three C-47s, and prepared to evacuate personnel from Seoul. He was then ordered to provide combat air patrols over the freighters evacuating personnel by sea from Inchon.

The mission distance ruled out the use of the F-80s as combat air patrol, and Price sent out a call for reinforcements of F-82s and F-51s and made the decision to use the B-26s in the convoy protection role as well.

A series of aerial combats followed that would define the Air Force's role in Korea and permit it to act as both sword and shield for the ground forces. General Partridge told the Fifth Air Force, "No interference with your mission will be tolerated." And none was.

On June 27, a mixed bag of five Communist fighters headed for the transports operating out of Kimpo, including a two-seat Yakolev Yak-11, a Yak-9, and a Lavochkin La-7. All of the aircraft were slower than the Twin-Mustangs, but more maneuverable, and each had formidable armament. In the hands of expert pilots, they could have been tough opponents for the five F-82s from the 68th and 339th F(AW)S that ambushed them.

The Yak-11 tried to pick off the number four F-82, but Lieutenant William G. "Skeeter" Hudson and his radar observer, Lieutenant Carl Fraser, slipped behind him and fired the six .50 caliber machine guns; the first burst knocked pieces off the Yak's tail, and the second took the flap and aileron off as it set fire to the wing. It was the first aerial victory of the Korean War; 975 enemy planes were to follow.

A few moments later, Lieutenants Charles "Chalky" Moran, pilot, and Fred Larkins, radar observer, shot down a Yak-9, and a La-7 was destroyed by Major James W. "Poke" Little, Commander of the 339th, his radar observer, Captain Charles Porter. The eager but inexperienced Yak pilots fled. (Some sources attribute the first victory to Moran, who was lost a few weeks later on a night mission, but official credit has gone to Hudson.)

This first step toward air superiority was reinforced later in the day when eight Il-10s attempted to attack Kimpo; four F-80C jet fighters of the 35th

Fighter Bomber Squadron promptly knocked down four of the Ilyushins, and the remainder turned tail. Two victories were credited to Lieutenant Robert E. Wayne, while Captain Raymond E. Schillereff (the 35th's operations officer) and Lieutenant Robert H. Dewald got one each.

The FEAF fighters provided impeccable protection to the transports operating out of Seoul and the freighters operating out of Inchon. C-54 and C-47 transports flew 851 persons safely to Japan, while another 905 were removed, far less comfortably, by water.

It was a good beginning for the Air Force in a bad war. These opening battles also forecast the essential, decisive element of the Korean War—absolute air superiority—that alone sustained the United Nations forces, twice keeping them from ignominious defeat and ultimately convincing the Communist forces that military victory was impossible. Space limitations prevent detailing each of the 720,980 sorties flown by FEAF during the Korean War, but each one, whether flown by a North American F-86 Sabre in a thrilling dogfight over the Yalu or by an aging Curtiss C-46 Commando limping in to deliver vital cargo to trapped troops, represents a level of proficiency and heroism that nurtured the dramatic changes that the war was going to bring about in the Air Force.

The Korean War was not only a conflict against a competent, determined enemy, it was also the birthing process for the professional Air Force, which would grow in size and strength and carry the United States to the rank of sole superpower. The Korean War was not fought the way the Air Force would have chosen to fight it—nor would most later wars be so fought. The Air Force fought the Korean War according to the dictates of Far East Command and the decisions made in Washington by politicians who were dismayed that the magic "air-atomic" shield was not applicable to "local" conflicts and that a World War II–style battle was in process.

These dictates and decisions often contravened sound air power policy, but the Air Force not only carried out its orders, but accomplished its own larger aims of defeating the enemy in the air and interdicting him on the ground. When at last truce talks began, Lieutenant General Nam Il, chief North Korean delegate to negotiations at Kaesong, said, "I would like to tell you frankly that in fact without direct support of your tactical aerial bombing alone your ground forces would have been completely unable to hold their present positions. It is owing to your strategic air effort of indiscriminate bombing of our area, rather than to your tactical air effort of direct support to the front line, that your ground forces are able to maintain barely and temporarily their present positions." (Nam Il considered the bombing of bridges, railroad yards, electrical power stations, and other such targets as "indiscriminate".)

THE PHASES OF THE WAR

The Korean War was divided on the ground and in the air into five phases that were correlated but not identical. The ground phases consisted of the following:

1. *June 25 to September 14, 1950.* UN forces were driven back into the Pusan (Naktong) perimeter and, severely punished, were several times in danger of being driven into the sea. Even when U.S. forces were reinforced and attempted a counterattack, the NKPA was able to handle them roughly.

2. *September 15 to November 24, 1950.* General MacArthur reversed the course of the war with his magnificent (albeit risky and perhaps even unnecessary) counterstroke at Inchon, coupled with the subsequent breakout of the Eighth Army from the Naktong perimeter. The NKPA, exhausted by battle and depleted by a merciless air interdiction, was driven back across the 38th parallel by UN forces.

On September 27, a decision was made that the UN forces would proceed all the way to the northern borders of North Korea and unify the country politically under the regime of Syngman Rhee. Despite explicit warnings that Communist China regarded Korea as its special sphere of interest, the Joint Chiefs of Staff continued to assume that the North Korean action had not only been sanctioned but masterminded by the Soviet Union. The JCS analysis indicated that the Kremlin would not intervene militarily on behalf of North Korea nor allow Red China to do so. Although General MacArthur normally disagreed with the JCS on practically everything, in this instance he reinforced their stand by stating that China would not intervene with more than a few thousand troops and covert assistance to the North Koreans. He repeated this assurance personally to President Truman at their celebrated (first and last) meeting at Wake Island. The CIA, keeping its Asian forecasting record unblemished, also stated that there would be no intervention to assist the beleaguered North Koreans. The erudite Dean Acheson, who should have known of Korea's two millennia of importance to China as a buffer state, also discounted the risk. Even the first Chinese offensive on October 25 did not register. The wine of the UN victory was too heady for American leaders, who were about to experience a Communist Chinese hangover.

3. *November 25, 1950, to January 24, 1951.* The massive Communist Chinese intervention, begun during the coldest winter in Korea in more than 177 years, caught UN forces completely by surprise and sent them reeling back down the peninsula, suffering heavy losses in the process. The 38th parallel was crossed again on January 1, and Seoul captured for the second time on January 4. Eighth Army Commander, General Walton H. Walker, was killed in a vehicle accident in December, and was replaced by Lieutenant General Matthew Ridgeway, who by sheer force of personality reinvigorated UN troops with the will to resist.

4. *January 25 to November 12, 1951.* Ridgeway adopted a new strategy of attrition that won him acclaim as one of the great combat commanders in history. He no longer had victory and unification as his primary task, but instead negotiation and an armistice. Under his direction, the UN forces fought their way back up the peninsula to a line that ranged beyond the 38th parallel by a few miles. Frequently interrupted armistice talks began at Kaesong on July 10, and were moved to Panmunjom on October 7. The most significant personnel action of the war came on April 11, 1951, when President Truman relieved General MacArthur of all three of his commands— U.S. Far East Command, United Nations Command, and Supreme Commander, Allied Powers. General Ridgeway was named to replace him, and Ridgeway in turn was replaced by Lieutenant General James A. Van Fleet. (Van Fleet would be in command when his own son, Lieutenant James A. Van Fleet, Jr., was lost flying a 13th BS B-26 on a night mission over North Korea.)

5. *November 13, 1951, to July 21, 1953.* As the talks dragged on, there was a long and bitter war consisting of local attacks and counterattacks that caused many casualties but did nothing to assist the peace process. A principal problem was the repatriation of prisoners of war; almost half of the 134,000 Communist prisoners indicated that they did not wish to go back to their homes of origin. The Communists demanded that all POWs be returned, regardless of their personal preferences. A compromise was finally reached that allowed the prisoners who wished to return home to do so within sixty days of signing the armistice; those that did not would be released to do as they wished.

A final large-scale Communist offensive took place in June 1953, but, without air support, suffered a devastating loss of 70,000 troops and ground to a halt. Total casualties in June and July, the last two futile months of a futile war, amounted to more than 160,000 for both sides. The armistice was signed on July 27, 1953, with the battle line becoming the boundary between the two countries.

The UN forces lost 118,515 men killed and 264,591 wounded, with 92,987 captured. U.S. forces lost 33,629 killed and 103,284 wounded. About 3 million South Korean civilians were killed. The Communist armies had about 2 million casualties. A quick calculation shows that there were at least 5.5 million casualties not including civilian wounded, and an incalculable expenditure of treasure, with virtually no change in the boundary or the political status quo.

THE CONDUCT OF THE AIR WAR

All elements of Air Force effort, including air superiority, strategic bombing, reconnaissance, air/sea rescue, cargo (both inter-and intratheater), close air support, and the interdiction of enemy supplies, were constantly adjusted to the exigencies of the ground war, and although frequently praised, were sometimes the subject of criticism, both informed and uninformed.

Praise would have been heightened and criticism diminished if it had been more widely appreciated that the Air Force was fighting its war with aging equipment, inadequate logistics, and a shortage of manpower. And it is rarely acknowledged that the USAF, so strapped for resources in comparison to the demands made on it that General Vandenberg called it "a shoestring Air Force," had a priority higher even than the combat in Korea. This was the creation of a nuclear deterrent force so powerful that it would succeed in preventing a third world war.

Given the limited means available, it is not surprising that many elements of Air Force doctrine, learned at such great expense in World War II, were violated in the conduct of the Korean War, sometimes deliberately, sometimes accidentally, sometimes by *force majeure*. In the main, however, the Air Force attempted to follow its doctrine wherever possible and revised it only when it was demonstrated that conditions had changed.

Analysis of both the phases of the war and the application of Air Force doctrine can often be illustrated by a discussion of how specific types of aircraft were employed.

AIR SUPERIORITY

The United States Air Force was consistently able to follow only one element of its air doctrine, the maintenance of air superiority. It did this throughout the war, without regard to the numerical superiority of the enemy, the surprising relative qualitative superiority of the MiG-15 fighter, or the pervasive advantage the rules of engagement gave to the Chinese Communist forces. The USAF maintained air superiority through the training and élan of its pilots and the loyal, determined support of its aircraft by members of the ground crews. The latter functioned under conditions of extreme climatic and logistics difficulties, with the young airmen enduring the freezing winters and scorching summers with better grace than they endured the shortages of parts and equipment that made their work so much more difficult.

In brief, air superiority, established with very limited means, saved the United Nations from utter defeat on two occasions, permitted the two "comebacks" by UN forces, and, in the end, provided the climate that drove the Communist forces to agree to armistice terms that were, if not satisfactory, at least acceptable. Oddly enough, the actual battle for air superiority was almost independent of the ebb and flow of the fighting on the ground, except when the F-86s were forced to remove themselves to Japanese bases. For the other elements, including strategic and tactical air, the phases of the ground war had more direct influence on operations.

The greatest threat to American air superiority, the Soviet-built MiG-15s, was first seen on November 1, 1950, when they attacked a flight of Mustangs and a T-6; all managed to escape, but it was immediately obvious that the MiGs were superior to any UN aircraft in the theater.

The MiG-15, like the Zero in World War II, should not have been a surprise. First flown on December 30, 1947 (just ninety days after the first flight of the XP-86A), the MiG was built on the brilliance of the Mikoyan-Gurevich OKB (design bureau) and the utterly stupid—if not covertly treasonous—action of the British government in approving the sale of fifty-five Rolls-Royce Nene engines, in batches of ten, fifteen, and thirty. The first of these were promptly reverse-engineered (as interned Boeing B-29s had been) and put into production by Major General V. A. Klimov as the RD-45. The Nene, with its 5,013 pounds of static thrust, was several years in advance of any contemporary Soviet engine, and the developments it inspired ensured the success of not only the MiG-15 but of a whole series of Soviet aircraft.

The MiG-15 was revealed to the world in a flyover at the 1948 Tushino air show, and, despite the usual Soviet secrecy, it was known to be in quantity production—at least 200 per month—and was supplied to satellite nations. In marked contrast, the first order for F-86s called for a total of 221 planes, only enough to outfit the 1st, 4th, and 81st Fighter Interceptor Wings by June 1950, given the unusually high attrition of the early aircraft. A further 333 F-86As were ordered before the pressure from the Korean War spurred increased production of later models.

Smaller and lighter than the F-86A, the MiG performance was marginally superior in all performance aspects. The Soviet Union would learn from combat as the USAF did, and the MiG would be improved over time, just as the F-86 would be. The MiG's greatest advantage was in combat endurance, provided not by its design but by geography and the UN rules of engagement, which forbade attacking the MiGs on their home fields. The American fighters had to fly to the vicinity of the Yalu River to engage the MiGs, a distance that left them with perhaps twenty minutes of fuel for combat. The MiGs could take off from airfields protected by the sanctuary given by the Chinese border, climb to altitude, and be ready for combat with almost full loads of fuel.

The first combat with MiGs came on November 7, 1950, when several swept in to attack the F-80Cs of the 51st Fighter Interceptor Wing escorting B-29s in an attack on Sinuiju. The F-80s of the 25th FIS had made three weapons delivery passes on the flak installations; on the third pass, First Lieutenant Wilbur Creech, in "Jungle Jim Blue" flight, was hit; his throttle jammed at 83 percent power—just about enough to keep the F-80 airborne. He jettisoned his tanks and made his way five feet above the Yalu River toward the China Sea.

Creech had just reached the China Sea when his wingman called, "MiGs are coming in at six o'clock" Above them was the "Top Coat Dog" flight of the 16th FIS, with Lieutenant Russell Brown flying in the number two slot.

The F-80s peeled off and roared down, with the leader overshooting; Brown slowed up and shot down the first MiG. The MiG's were much faster than the F-80s, but in a pattern that would be maintained throughout the war, their pilots had inferior training to their USAF opponents. Brown hammered the enemy out of control with his one unjammed .50 caliber machine gun, becoming the victor in the first jet-versus-jet air combat in history.

There was later some controversy about the number two man breaking off to shoot instead of covering his leader, but when Brown's picture appeared on the cover of *Time* magazine, all controversy ended.

A cry went up for F-86s to be sent to the theater, and on November 8, General Vandenberg ordered the 4th Fighter Interceptor Wing into action. (He also directed that 27th Fighter Escort Wing of F-84s be sent.) The three squadrons of the 4th (334th, 335th, 336th) with a total of forty-nine F-86s were embarked upon the escort carrier USS *Cape Esperance* on November 29, arriving at Yokusuka, Japan, two weeks later with many of the aircraft damaged from salt-air corrosion. The first orientation flight in Korea was flown on December 13.

FIRST KILLS FOR THE SABRE

On December 17, 1950, Lieutenant Colonel Bruce N. Hinton, Commanding Officer of the 336th, led his Baker Flight of four from Kimpo (K-14), the most modern air field in Korea, on a combat air patrol along the Yalu, 430 miles away. They flew to a triangular sliver of land known as "MiG Alley"—6,500 square miles of territory bounded on the north by a Manchurian sanctuary teeming with airfields filled with MiGs, and on the south by the long flight home on nearly empty tanks for the Sabres.

Cruising at Mach .62 to conserve fuel (a technique that was soon abandoned), Hinton sighted a flight of four MiG 15s climbing toward them. The Sabres dove toward the enemy, Hinton damaging the MiG leader and then fastening onto the tail of the number two MiG. A series of long bursts from the F-86's six .50 caliber machine guns—1,500 rounds—smashed into the MiG, which went inverted and dove straight in. It was the first F-86 victory over a MiG; Sabre pilots would down another 791 Soviet fighters before the war was ended.

Two tough hombres in air combat scored in the next encounter. After twenty-three victories in World War II, Lieutenant Colonel John C. Meyer was comfortable commanding the 4th Fighter Interceptor Group and led the first of four flights of F-86 to the Yalu on December 22. (In the Vietnam War, Meyer would be Commander in Chief of the Strategic Air Command and oversee the conduct of Linebacker II, the December 1972 attack on Hanoi and Haiphong.) The CO of the 334th FIS, Lieutenant Colonel Glenn T. Eagleston, who had 18.5 victories in World War II, led the second flight. They arrived in the area cruising at Mach .85, a speed permitting only twenty minutes for the patrol or ten minutes of combat, but giving them the best chance of catching any MiGs they flushed. Meyer's sixteen Sabres attacked a flight of fifteen MiGs and shot six down in a swirling dogfight that ranged from 30,000 feet all the way down to the surface. An F-86 flown by Captain Lawrence V. Bach was shot down in flames. Meyers and Eagleston both scored one of the two victories they each would add to their tallies in Korea. (Bach's aircraft was the second F-86 lost. The first had fallen victim on June 17 to a bomb from a wood-and-fabric Polikarpov Po-2 biplane, the famous nocturnal visitor "Bedcheck Charlie.")

By the end of the year, the 4th had shown that the MiG-15 had met its match; in 234 sorties, eight MiGs had been shot down for the loss of one Sabre in combat. The MiG was conceded to be an excellent aircraft, with only a slight performance edge at high altitudes but with a tremendous advantage of almost 8,000 feet in service ceiling. Cruising at 45,000 feet and above, where the Sabres could not reach them, the MiGs controlled where, when, and if fights would take place.

In 1952, the Communist forces also supplied the MiGs with an excellent ground control intercept system that was at once a tremendous advantage and a drawback. It was a plus for the MiG pilots in that it enabled them to know exactly where their F-86 opponents were, but a minus in that the Communists tended to control the activities of the MiGs from the ground, a fatally incorrect tactical doctrine that would persist through the Vietnam War and beyond.

The American pilots would have bet that the MiG was less maintenance-intensive than the more complicated F-86, which demanded many hours of mechanics' time on the ground for every hour of time in the air. Often as many as 50 percent of the Sabres were grounded for maintenance, many of them AOCP (aircraft out of commission, parts), and the 4th was often hard pressed to get sufficient aircraft for missions.

The F-86 was a more stable gun platform, and its armament of six .50 caliber machine guns was superior to the MiG's battery of cannon, which were originally intended for bomber intercept work. If they could have had their wishes, the Sabre pilots would have preferred to have cannons with a fast rate of fire, for it was difficult to keep a MiG in the gunsight for very long—high speed and G forces made deflection shots difficult—and few pilots got more than one chance to shoot.

The nature of the F-86/MiG-15 contest varied over the long months of the Korean War, primarily because of the varying degrees of resolution with which the enemy elected to fight. Often after a series of severe losses the MiGs would be much more difficult to bring to combat, as if they were assessing their defeats and attempting to come up with solutions. By the end of 1951, the enemy reverted to Spanish Civil War practice, using the battleground over the Yalu as a training ground in which successive groups of pilots would be exposed to combat in six-week cycles.

Competition among the American pilots for victories was fierce, and while few made any but joking allusions to the prospect, the desire to become the first American jet ace was intense. A leading contender was Captain James Jabara of the 334th Fighter Interceptor Squadron, who had scored four victories over the MiGs in his first month in combat in April 1951.

The outspoken Jabara was born in Wichita and trained as an aviation cadet. He flew two tours of combat in Mustangs in Europe and was credited with destroying five and a half enemy planes in the air and four on the ground. On May 7, 1951, Jabara's squadron rotated back to Japan, but he stayed on—looking for the next kill.

It came on May 20, late in the afternoon, when thirty-six Sabres and fifty MiGs engaged in a swirling dogfight. One of Jabara's wing tanks would not jettison, but he plunged into combat anyway, shooting down two MiGs to become the first man in history to shoot down five enemy jets. Official policy concerning aces forced his rotation back to the United States, but he returned in 1953.

The overriding importance of air superiority lay least, oddly enough, in the numbers of MiGs shot down, for the Chinese had MiGs aplenty, and the Soviet Union was turning them out in profusion. Air superiority's great gift was that it permitted the F-80s, F-51s, B-26s, and B-29s to operate, if not with impunity, at least without too much interference of mission—the interdiction of enemy logistics. This interdiction was important at all times, as necessary when the lines were stabilized as when the Communists were advancing. The enemy forces recognized this and made major efforts to reverse the situation by introducing new pilots and new tactics and beginning an airfield construction program. Sheer numbers were heavily in their favor, as China marshaled 445 MiG-15s by 1951; this total would steadily increase throughout the war. The United States had managed to get eighty-nine Sabres to the theater, but only forty-four were in combat with the 4th, and of these perhaps only twenty-two would be ready for action. The poorest of the great powers was demonstrating a ten-or twenty-to-one advantage in first-rate equipment over the richest.

THE HONCHOS ARRIVE

The first of the new Communist programs revealed itself in mid-June 1951. On the 17th, twenty-five MiGs, well and aggressively flown, engaged the Sabres, who promptly shot one down and damaged six others. On the next day, forty MiGs tackled thirty-two Sabres; this time five MiGs went down, but the third F-86 of the war was lost. The third day was worse; four MiGs were damaged in a dogfight, but a Sabre was shot down. American pilots recognized the dramatic change in the enemy pilots' skill level by using the term "honcho" or boss to describe them. The American pilots assumed the newcomers to be veteran aces and instructor pilots from the Soviet Union, this view being validated over time by reports of blond pilots ejecting from damaged MiGs. Less expert pilots were termed "students" and usually provided easy kills.

Apparently gaining confidence despite their losses, the honchos began ranging out from their normal Yalu River fighting area, flying as far south as Pyongyang. The MiGs had a wide variety of markings, from which intelligence officers inferred that the pilots had been seconded from a different unit within the Soviet bloc, and that each pilot had brought his own airplane to war. They also introduced new tactics, including one the Americans named the "Yo-Yo." A formation of MiGs would use their superior altitude capability to orbit over the Sabres, then in pairs make diving attacks that would carry them through the formation and also give them the speed to zoom back up to a height the F-86s could not reach. Later, they would employ what were called "trains," large formations of as many as eighty MiGs in staggered parallel tracks at varying heights, flown down each side of the peninsula. Small units would be dropped off to engage the Sabres patrolling MiG Alley. The two large formations would turn in to join together near Pyongyang, swooping down to attack returning fuel-short Sabres or UN fighter-bombers.

General Stratemeyer had suffered a severe heart attack on May 20, 1951, and Major General Otto P. Weyland was selected to succeed him. Weyland had Vandenberg's complete confidence, for when Weyland commanded the XIX Tactical Air Command in Europe, he protected the Third Army's flank by air, thus earning General George P. Patton's ultimate accolade as "the best damn general in the Air Corps." At the same time, Major General Frank F. Everest was named Commander of the Fifth Air Force.

The new commanders watched the growth in power and aggressiveness of the enemy forces, which they now were forced to credit with the capability of wresting air superiority from the pitifully few F-86s on strength. In these days of sometimes revisionist history, military leaders in the early years of the Cold War are often portrayed as opportunists using a phantom threat from the Soviet Union to back up their wanton budget demands. These views should be analyzed in the light of the F-86 controversy. The leaders of the Air Force were eager for victory in Korea and wanted more than anything to support their ground and air forces fighting there. Yet they considered the threat of an atomic attack by the Soviet Union so genuine that they retained F-86 squadrons for the air defense of the United States instead of sending them to Korea. If the USAF had possessed the 137 to 145 groups that it deemed necessary, instead of the forty the defense budget provided, there would have been adequate forces for both Korean and American air defense.

Fortunately, help was at last on the way, in the form of improved Sabres, creative leadership, and, after anguished deliberation, additional wings of fighters. In the spring of 1953 two more F-86 units would be sent, the 8th and 18th Fighter Bomber Wings. Configured for the ground support role, these Sabres also maintained their interceptor capability.

The first improved Sabre was the F-86E, which featured the all-flying tail pioneered in the Bell X-1 rocket aircraft in which then Captain Charles "Chuck" Yeager broke the sound barrier. (Diehard F-86 fans insist that a Sabre had broken the sound barrier just before Yeager's flight, but that's another story.) The F-86Es were a little slower than the F-86As, but were more maneuverable and easier to maintain. A vastly improved F-86F was put into production at an additional production line in Columbus, Ohio, and was first flown on March 19, 1952. With a more powerful uprated engine, the F model had a new "6-3" wing that was 6 inches wider in chord at the root and 3 inches at the tip, and on which the slats were eliminated and boundary layer fences added. The F-86F reached Korea in the fall of 1952. The Soviet Union was upgrading the MiG as well, and the MiG-15 bis ("bis" indicating a follow-on version) appeared in the Chinese Communist inventory. The F-86F was clearly the superior aircraft, 10 knots faster than the F-86E and able to operate with the MiGs at altitudes above 50,000 feet.

Far more important in both a morale and equipment sense than even new aircraft was the inspiring leadership of Colonel Harrison R. Thyng. A double ace who shot down five airplanes in World War II and five more in Korea, Thyng took over command of the 4th FIW in early November 1951 and soon demonstrated just how vital the qualities of a commander are to his unit. Dismayed by the pilots' frustration with the maintenance on their aircraft and with the even greater anger of the hardworking mechanics, who routinely got the airplanes airborne with patchwork repairs and cannibalized parts, he was outraged at the seemingly insuperable bureaucratic barriers that intervened between the combat area and stateside logistic support. Thyng rebelled and took action on the ground as he had in the air.

From Longstreet at Gettysburg to von Paulus at Stalingrad to Walker in Korea, history is replete with stories of brave military leaders who would risk their lives in combat on a daily basis but would not risk their careers bucking their own superiors. In a stunning gesture defying the established order, Thyng did both, laying his career on the line by going directly to the top, then leaving to lead a patrol to the Yalu. In a message to the Chief of Staff, General Vandenberg, Thyng told him with chilling clarity that he could no longer be responsible for air superiority in the area that had become infamous as MiG Alley. Thyng sent information copies to his direct superiors in the intermediate commands, a gesture that, dependent upon Vandenberg's reaction, ensured either his survival or his removal.

Fortunately for Thyng and the 4th FIW, his message's timing was perfect. On October 22, 1951, Vandenberg had already ordered an additional seventy-five Sabres sent to Korea, which permitted the equipping of an additional wing, the 51st FIW, at Suwon. Only two squadrons of the 51st could be supplied aircraft, but they were all F-86Es and came under the command of Colonel Francis S. Gabreski from the 4th. Gabreski had been the leading American ace in Europe in World War II, with twenty-eight victories; he would score 6.5 more in Korea. The greatest effect of Thyng's message was a massive improvement in the supply of parts and equipment, vastly improving Sabre readiness statistics. This came about in part because of the patriotic enthusiasm of the manufacturers, who supplied the necessary parts without contracts to cover their risk. The joint effort enabled the United States to prevail despite never committing more than six fighter squadrons solely to the single most important factor in the Korean War—the maintenance of air superiority. Despite the odds, those six squadrons of the 4th and 51st FIWs administered an increasingly severe punishment to the Chinese Communist air force over the remaining months of the war, regardless of whether the pilots were honchos or students.

ACE MAKING TIME

At the beginning of 1952, the Communists had lost 339 aircraft; by the armistice, on July 17, 1953, the total had jumped to 954. Of these, 810 were destroyed by F-86s, including no less than 792 MiG-15s.

MiG kills reached their peak when seventy-seven were shot down in June 1953, sixteen being scored on the last day of the month. The eighteen-month-long harvest of MiGs naturally yielded more aces; by the end of the war, thirty-nine F-86 aces had accounted for 305 aircraft. Major William Whisner, who had scored 15.5 victories in World War II in Europe, including six in one day, was the first ace of 1952. Whisner, CO of the 25th FIS of the 51st FIW, raised his score to 5.5 MiGs on February 23, 1952, to become the seventh ace of the Korean War. (Ironically, Whisner, who served his third war in Vietnam, died in an allergic reaction to a bee sting in 1991.)

In the following months, more Sabres with greater capability would allow thirty-two more pilots to achieve five victories. "Gabby" Gabreski became the eighth jet ace on April 1, 1952, and Captain Ivan Kincheloe became the tenth on April 6. Kincheloe went on to become a famous test pilot, only to lose his life flight-testing the Lockheed F-104 on July 28, 1958. The twentieth ace was Major Robinson Risner, who scored eight victories between July 5 and January 21, 1953, those six months representing just 7 percent of the more than eighty-four months he would spend as a prisoner in the Hanoi Hilton during the Vietnam War.

A natural rivalry for the position of top ace developed between Captain Manuel J. Fernandez, Jr., of the 334th FIS and First Lieutenant Joseph McConnell, Jr., of the 16th FIS. Fernandez had started earlier, scoring his 14.5 kills between April 10, 1952, and May 16, 1953. (When the author talked to Fernandez a decade after the war, the ace was convinced that his Hispanic ancestry had worked against him in his fight to become number one.) Scoring sixteen victories between January 14 and May 18, 1953, McConnell survived bailing out over the Yellow Sea and being rescued to emerge as the Rickenbacker of the Korean War. He lost his life in an F-86 accident at Edwards Air Force Base, on August 25, 1954.

James Jabara, now a major, volunteered to fly a second combat tour in Korea, just as he had in Europe; after his return in May 1953, he shot down nine more MiGs, the last on June 15, 1953. His total of fifteen made him the second-ranking ace of the war.

The last ace of the war was Major Stephen J. Bettinger, who scored his fifth victory on July 20, 1953, but was himself shot down and captured, not being released until October 2, 1953. Bettinger had the pleasure of confirming his own fifth victory after he was released. His potential status as an ace had been kept a closely guarded secret while he was a prisoner, in fear of a Communist reprisal.

One Sabre pilot won the Medal of Honor, awarded posthumously. Major George A. Davis was the fifth ace of the war and went on to score fourteen victories, most of them in twos and threes. The leading ace with twelve victories on February 10, 1952, Davis lost his life in a brave attack against a formation of twelve MiGs preparing to attack some F-84 fighter-bombers. Davis destroyed two MiGs and was attacking a third when a fourth enemy fastened on his tail and shot him down.

The war had ended with total UN air superiority, just exactly as its commanders wanted, and just exactly as the ground situation demanded. One reason was the aggressive quality of FEAF's commanders, men like Lieutenant General Glenn O. Barcus, who had assumed command of the Fifth Air Force on June 10, 1952. Unknown to his own superiors, Barcus began flying combat missions, highlighted by a May 1, 1953, attack on Pyongyang. All four F-86 wings participated, the 4th and 51st flying high cover while the 8th and 18th Fighter Bomber Wings worked over the radio station, which had been broadcasting adverse propaganda about the Fifth. Barcus, using a radio frequency known to be monitored by the Communists, announced his presence overhead and promised, "We will be back every time you broadcast filthy lies about the Fifth Air Force."

Despite the MiG-15s' great advantages in number, geography, and rules of engagement, the Sabres had prevailed. While the war was going on, and when it was over, there was a fundamental fact known to the generals, to the aces, to the medal winners, and to the men themselves: none of the successes could have been achieved without the devoted efforts of the noncommissioned officers and men who outdid themselves day after day, month after month, with little reward except the satisfaction of knowing they were appreciated by the men in combat.

AIR TO GROUND: CLOSE SUPPORT AND INTERDICTION

From the earliest days of the war, individual Army commanders and zealous journalists complained that the Air Force did not provide the same degree of close air support to Army units as that provided by the Marine and Navy fliers to Marine units. The messages of gratitude and the praise expressed for Air Force close air support by other army commanders, including Generals Walker and MacArthur, were often overlooked. More important, the relatively higher effectiveness of interdiction efforts compared to close air support, particularly in the last two years of the war, was never fully understood or acknowledged.

The phases of the air-to-ground war closely followed the changing phases of ground operations, each of which placed different types of demands upon the equipment and the aircrews of FEAF. During the first phase, the rapid advance of the North Koreans down the peninsula resulted in an ad hoc air-to-ground campaign, one that demanded every effort from all FEAF's resources, applied in armed reconnaissance missions against the plentiful targets of opportunity. General MacArthur ordered FEAF to attack and destroy all North Korean military targets south of the 38th parallel; no operations north of that line were to be undertaken except in self-defense. The total forces available were two squadrons of Douglas B-26 Invaders, four squadrons of Lockheed F-80s, and two squadrons of North American F-82s.

Initial results were unsatisfactory because of bad weather and a lack of reconnaissance information. On the morning of June 28, in the first of more than 67,000 reconnaissance sorties conducted during the war, Lieutenant (later General) Bryce Poe II made the first USAF jet combat reconnaissance flight ever in his RF-80A. The results cleared the 3d Bombardment Wing (Light), commanded by Colonel Thomas B. Hall, for an attack by twelve B-26s on railroad yards at Munsan. On the way back, strafing targets of opportunity, one B-26 crashed and two were forced down.

The B-26 attacks were supplemented by a morning and afternoon attack by twenty-four F-80s from the 8th FBW, which took full advantage of roads crowded with North Korean vehicles, troops, and artillery.

Still active—though not for long—the North Korean Air Force sent four aircraft to strafe the airfield at Suwon while General MacArthur was there attending a briefing. As the Supreme Commander watched, a flight of four Mustangs that had been slated for service with the ROK AF attacked and shot down all four enemy planes. Second Lieutenant Orrin R. Fox of the 80th FBS destroyed two Ilyushin Il-10s, while Lieutenant Harry T. Sandlin of the 35th FBS nailed a Lavochkin La-7 and First Lieutenant Richard L. Burns of the 35th FBS got an Il-10. Impressed, MacArthur acquiesced to General Stratemeyer's request to attack North Korean air power at its source.

The next day, eighteen B-26s made the first strike north of the 38th parallel, attacking Heijo airfield at Pyongyang, the North Korean capital, destroying hangars, fuel dumps, and barracks and returning to Japan unscathed. Staff Sergeant Nyle S. Mickley, a gunner on one of the 13th BS (L) B-26s, shot down one of the two Yak fighters that had pressed home their attack. Twenty-five more fighters were claimed destroyed on the ground. The success of the B-26s had depended upon surprise; strong North Korean antiaircraft would soon force them to higher altitudes and then to a night bombing role.

As the North Koreans pressed the UN forces back into the Pusan (Naktong) perimeter, the air-to-ground activity intensified with naval aircraft from Task Force 77, B-29s, and the mixed bag of FEAF's ground attack aircraft participating. Extraordinary measures were taken. The F-82Gs, designed as interceptors and operating out of Yakota and Itazuke, did yeoman work strafing and dropping napalm, the pilots flying mission after mission until they were exhausted.

The F-80Cs also operated out of Itazuke, their weight and footprint ruling out flying from the rough airfields remaining in South Korea. With rockets and tip tanks, the Shooting Stars had an operational radius of about 225 miles with about fifteen minutes time over target (TOT). At a maximum radius of 350 miles, the target had to be found on arrival, as there was zero TOT. An interim solution to gain more range was a field modification generated at Misawa by 49th FBW Lieutenants Edward "Rabbit" Johnson and Robert Eckman. They inserted two center sections of a larger (Fletcher) tank in the center of the standard 165-gallon Lockheed tip tank, creating the "Misawa tank" with a 265-gallon capacity. This extended the F-80C time over target to forty-five minutes, but placed dangerously high loads at the wingtips, resulting in some wing failures. The Misawa tanks were also in short supply for several months.

Perhaps the most unusual improvisation was the reversion to Mustangs. The initial effort became famous through the works of Major Dean E. Hess. Ten Mustangs originally intended to be given to the ROK AF were instead manned by U.S. and Korean personnel and moved to Taegu on June 30, to commence "Bout-One" air-to-ground operations against the enemy. A larger-scale but less-well-known effort was Project Dallas, which pulled thirty F-51s from storage and reassigned F-80C pilots from the 18th Fighter Group (most from the 12th Squadron) in the Philippines to fly them. Organized with the "Bout-One" planes and pilots into the 51st Provisional Fighter Squadron at Taegu (K-2), the Mustangs flew their first mission on July 15—the same day the United States scraped the bottom of its air power barrel with 145 National Guard F-51s embarked on the USS *Boxer*. The 40th FIS was also converted from F-80s to F-51s, and moved from Japan to Pohang (K-3) on July 16. A few days later, the 40th, their pilots barely familiar with their mounts, flew more than 220 sorties against a North Korean probe toward Pohang, literally stopping it in its armored tracks.

The National Guard F-51s from the *Boxer* were used to equip the 18th FBG's 67th FBS, the latter commanded by Major Louis J. Sebille, a veteran of sixty-eight combat missions in Martin B-26s in Europe, where he won two Distinguished Flying Crosses and twelve Air Medals. Sebille led his unit out of Ashiya, Japan, to attack an enemy troop concentration on a river near Hamchang. One of his two 500-pound bombs failed to release on his first attack, but he returned for another strafing attack and his aircraft was severely damaged by heavy antiaircraft fire. Sebille knew how vulnerable the Mustang was, but he also knew what a threat the 1,500 well-armed troops were to the Pusan perimeter. Ignoring advice to make an emergency landing at Taegu, he dove to his death on the target. Major Sebille was awarded the Medal of Honor, the first of four posthumously awarded to American airmen in the Korean War.

(Major Charles A. Loring would win his Medal of Honor under strikingly similar circumstances. On November 22, 1952, flying an F-80 from the 80th FBS, Loring was hit after leading a four-plane element against an enemy artillery emplacement. After he was hit Loring turned and deliberately dived into the target, destroying it but killing himself.)

Despite the improvised nature of FEAF's initial response to the invasion, it was effective against the ever-lengthening North Korean supply lines, and the Pusan perimeter held. Standard USAF practices were put into effect as soon as possible, especially in regard to targeting. By mid-July, a joint operations center (JOC) and tactical air control center (TACC) were in place at Taegu, and no less than eighteen tactical air command posts (TACPs) were in the field, controlling strikes. These would be enhanced immeasurably after July 10, when Lieutenant Harold E. Morris demonstrated the utility of the North American T-6 Texan trainer as an airborne controller. The airborne controllers first call signs were Mosquito Able, Mosquito Baker, and Mosquito How, and Mosquitoes became the generic term for the Texans. The Mosquitoes were especially valuable to the F-80Cs, making the most of their short loiter time.

A complex but swift and flexible methodology of calling for and executing a close air support strike was quickly established. A strike request from a TACP would be passed through divisional and corps headquarters to the TACC/JOC, which would clear the fighter-bombers to scramble. They would report in to the airborne controller, who would point out the target. After the attack was made, the fighter-bombers would give a strike report and return to land. Total time from request to landing was often as short as forty minutes.

This grunt-level cooperation was reflected in command operations; General Partridge established his own command post in Taegu, where General Walker's headquarters had been established. One of the first tasks agreed upon was the establishment of PSP (pierced-steel-plank) runways in Korea to permit quick turnaround of F-51 operations. As the F-51 units came on line, they were given the close support work, while the F-80s were interdicting the supply lines.

Long debates raged about the wisdom of using the F-51s in the ground support role, given that their liquid-cooled engines were so vulnerable to ground fire as well as to the dust-laden atmosphere of the airfields. The sole reason that they were used was their availability as "war surplus," a costly economy dictated by the improvidently low peacetime defense budget. The increasingly tired Mustangs were used until 1953, carrying heavy loads of ordnance over a great range, and even operating from Japan when the Communist advances made it necessary.

Some pundits argued against the F-80s, saying that the jet's high speed made it less useful as a ground attack airplane. They were wrong. The high speed was useful in getting to the target with a greater degree of surprise, and the jet was less vulnerable to ground fire than the Mustang. The lethal firepower of the F-80 was demonstrated on July 10, 1950, when yellow-nosed Shooting Stars of the 8th FBS used machine guns and rockets to attack a target of opportunity, destroying 117 trucks and thirty-eight tanks. Tank-busting became a science for the F-80 pilots, who would dive at the T-34s at an angle of 45 to 60 degrees at an airspeed of 400 to 500 mph, aiming where possible at the more vulnerable rear of the tank. The delay fuse on the 5-inch HVAR (high-velocity aircraft rocket) was set so that the rocket would shatter against the armor before exploding, providing a shrapnel effect to kill the tank crew. The F-80 had to break off at least 500 feet above the ground to avoid debris from the target.

During the retreat to the Pusan perimeter, F-80s were given credit for 75 percent of the destruction inflicted by air on the enemy. One important reason was ground crews who worked night and day to keep the airplanes flying, achieving an 84 percent in-commission rate, excellent for a peacetime operation, but brilliant under the conditions at hand.

The long series of extemporaneous responses to North Korean aggression had bled the invaders dry, permitting the defenders at Pusan to build up their strength for a counterattack that coincided with the invasion at Inchon. The North Korean forces could move only at night, and their front lines were wracked as the tempo of close-support sorties built up, almost 7,500 being flown in August. As the North Koreans made a last effort to drive UN forces into the sea in September, Fifth Air Force fighter-bombers and light bombers mounted as many as 683 sorties a day. When the Eighth Army counterattack began driving the North Koreans back, General Walker stated that the Eighth had received excellent air support, and that had it not been for the Fifth Air Force, it would have been forced to evacuate Korea.

THE FIRST MOVE UP THE PENINSULA

The breakout from Pusan coincided with an increase in FEAF strength in the Korean theater obtained by drawing in units then tasked with the air defense of Japan, Okinawa, and the Philippines. The tempo of Fifth Air Force activity picked up in September, with as many as 361 sorties a day flown. Mustangs with napalm proved especially effective against entrenched enemy positions; when the North Koreans broke and ran, they were pounced on by F-80s and B-26s. By September 22, most North Korean tanks had been destroyed and the Communist forces were beginning to reel under the air attack. Enemy morale dropped to the point that on September 23, 200 NKPA troops surrendered to a T-6 Mosquito flown by Lieutenant George A. Nelson, who had dropped a note signed "MacArthur," ordering them to lay down their arms.

Where before the interdiction effort had been to prevent troops and supplies reaching the front, it now was directed at keeping them from getting to the rear. The North Koreans moved primarily at night in their retreat, and B-29s and B-26s worked together, the Superfortresses dropping huge M-26 parachute flares while the Invaders worked over the troops illuminated below.

FEAF's air power, improvised as it had been, had imposed a stunning defeat on enemy forces. Analysis of prisoner interrogations revealed that air power had inflicted losses on the NKPA of 47 percent of personnel, 75 percent of tanks, 81 percent of trucks, and 72 percent of artillery. The inference was drawn by the USAF—if not by MacArthur—that the unending air-ground action had defeated the NKPA—and not the landing at Inchon.

The Fifth Air Force swarmed to South Korea as soon as airfields could be built or improved to the level necessary for operations. The pursuit of the North Koreans turned into a rout, and the fighter-bombers now sometimes found themselves returning with ordnance unexpended for a lack of targets, a condition that changed dramatically with the intervention of the Chinese Communist forces.

Fighting Back Down the Peninsula

In response to the Chinese intervention, General Vandenberg had ordered the Strategic Air Command's 27th Fighter Escort Fighter Wing (FEW) from Bergstrom AFB, Texas, to action. The 27th flew its Republic F-84D and E model Thunderjet fighters to San Diego, where they were too hurriedly embarked on the escort carrier USS *Bataan*. Once again inadequate preventive measures resulted in severe corrosion problems that required a week of work to overcome.

The 27th was sent to Taegu (K-2), where its first mission would be led by Colonel Don Blakeslee. During World War II, he had been a member of the famous RAF No. 121 "Eagle" Squadron, and later he had commanded the famous 4th Fighter Group. In his 1,000 hours of combat and 400 sorties in Europe, Blakeslee had scored fifteen victories. On December 7, 1950, the veteran Blakeslee led a four-aircraft flight on an armed reconnaissance southwest of Pyonyang. Using HVAR rockets and machine guns, the F-84s knocked out locomotives and started raging fires in a marshaling yard—a good effort for a unit trained for escort fighter duties and with no F-84 experience in ground attack work. It was a textbook start for an intensive first month in which the 27th flew 972 combat sorties, of which 275 were ground support. It was also symbolic of the F-84 during the Korean War, during which it would participate in almost every major campaign, complete more than 86,000 sorties, drop more than 50,000 tons of bombs and 5,500 tons of napalm, fire 22,154 rockets, and shoot off literally miles of belted .50 caliber ammunition. A total of 153 Thunderjets were lost, eighteen of them to MiGs. The F-84s managed to shoot nine of the faster MiGs down. Despite this monumental effort, the F-84 garnered far fewer headlines than the more glamorous F-86. Did its pilots and ground crew men mind? Absolutely!

Although the straight-wing F-84s were faster than the P-80s, with a top speed of 613 mph, they were no match for the MiG-15s in air combat at high altitude. If they could lure the MiGs into fighting at 20,000 feet and below, they stood a better chance. In a low-level battle on January 21, 1951, Lieutenant Colonel William Bertram of the 523 FES demonstrated what a good pilot in an F-84 could do, shooting down a MiG-15 in flames. But everyone recognized that the Thunderjets were better suited to the ground support role, where they excelled, like their ancestor the fabled Republic P-47 Thunderbolt. Capable of carrying up to 4,000 pounds of bombs, the heavy (18,000-pound) F-84s sometimes needed a JATO boost to get off the short Korean airfields.

The F-84s had many moments of glory. Early on the morning of January 23, 1951, thirty-three Thunderjets of Colonel Ashley B. Packard's 27th FEW attacked Sinuiju, the North Korean airfield always protected by the flights of MiGs stationed at Antung, a few miles away across the Yalu.

Before the MiGs could be scrambled, the first eight F-84s made a firing pass across Sinuiju, climbing quickly up to 20,000 feet to provide a cover for the successive flights of attacking Thunderjets. Thirty MiGs dove to the defense of Sinuiju, and though faster, could not turn with the F-84s at that altitude. Lieutenant Jacob Kratt quickly shot down two MiGs, and Captains Allen McGuire and William W. Slaughter each claimed another. (McGuire's claim was not confirmed; Kratt would get his third and final victory three days later, destroying a Yak-3.)

Other UN fighter-bombers distinguished themselves in supporting the 3d Marine Division and the 7th Infantry Division as they retreated from the Chosin Reservoir area, saving them from annihilation. For the next month, the disheartened UN forces gave up ground almost as quickly as they had gained it, moving from one designated "stand-fast" line to the next with demoralizing rapidity. Pyongyang fell to the enemy on December 5, Seoul was lost on January 4, and Inchon on the 5th. The pell-mell retreat had forced President Truman to declare a national emergency on December 15.

The Chinese offensive quickly overran many of the UN's airfields, forcing American units to retire to Japan. By February, the Sabres' limited range kept them from reaching farther north than Pyongyang, effectively giving the enemy complete control of MiG Alley. Fortunately, the Communists were not proficient in the use of air power, and despite an immense airfield rehabilitation campaign, were never able to give UN forces the kind of brutal air-to-ground punishment they continued to receive. That punishment would bleed the Chinese offensive dry, as troops, trucks, trains, and supplies were destroyed by the combined efforts of UN fighter-bomber and bomber units.

The constant deprivation of supplies, exacerbated by the requirement to move surviving equipment and troops to secondary roads and land trails to avoid the bombing, vitiated the Chinese offensive. Then the resurgence of the UN forces under General Ridgeway's leadership slowly reversed the course of the war. The continuous retreat was turned into a slow advance by January 6; by March 14, Seoul had been recaptured. In recognition of the vulnerability of the lengthy Communist supply lines, FEAF fighter-bombers were assigned armed reconnaissance areas. Pilots became thoroughly familiar with their own area so that the slightest change would indicate where the targets were.

Ridgeway's emphasis on inflicting the maximum number of casualties on the Chinese, whether in defensive or offensive operations, slowly began to pay off. The Chinese clung to their doctrine, launching no less than six major offensives, before they finally realized that they could no longer hope to overwhelm the UN forces and drive them into the sea. With the realization came a change of objectives on both sides; neither sought victory any longer, and instead each looked for the best deal possible in a face-saving way out. In July, the Great Leader, Marshal Kim Il Sung, responded favorably to Ridgeway's broadcast announcement that the UN was willing to discuss armistice terms. The long series of talks at Panmunjom would ultimately result in an armistice. For the remaining two years of the war, the fighting on the ground was stabilized at a fierce, bloody, but low-order stalemate. The air war would rage on with ever greater intensity, as it was the only means the United Nations had to ensure that the Communists would continue to negotiate.

In the course of the UN forces' struggle to just beyond the 38th parallel in the summer of 1951, the 27th FEW was replaced by the 49th and 136th Fighter Bomber Wings. The experienced 49th, with the 7th, 8th, and 9th FBS, happily gave up their war-weary F-80Cs in exchange for F-84s. The 136th, an Air National Guard unit that had just transitioned from Mustangs into F-84Es, was composed of the 111th and 182d Squadrons from Texas and the 154th from Arkansas. Another Air National Guard F-84 unit, the 116th, arrived in late July with squadrons from Georgia (158th), Florida (159th), and California (196th) and took over the air defense of Japan.

This combined force of Mustangs, Shooting Stars, and Thunderjets would (with the B-26 and B-29 bombers) effectively throttle the enemy—but not the critics of air power. Each battalion commander wanted to see "his" aircraft on "his" front, every hour of the day, especially since (at least anecdotally) Marine air seemed to service the Marine ground troops on that basis. When the front was fluid, on either the advances or the retreats, the very nature of the battle provided a rationale for any absence of local air power, for in a rapidly changing situation it was plausible that aircraft were occupied elsewhere. But when the front settled down to the static fighting of the last two years of the war, when both enemy and UN probes were confined to discrete sections of the line, it seemed irrational not to be able to call in all the air power required, all the time.

The problem lay in the very nature of static warfare. The Communist forces were superb diggers, with deep entrenchments, heavy bunkers with tunnels to connect them to underground storage dumps, and heavily protected, well-concealed artillery and mortar positions. These were so well done that anything less than a direct hit from close air support was not only nonproductive, it was a far more expensive process than conventional artillery fire. Statistical analysis of the first years of fighting had revealed that interdiction far behind the lines yielded greater results, even though lacking the morale-building character of close air support.

Some rough rules of thumb evolved. It was demonstrated that if air power was concentrated on the front line during an offensive, reinforcements would add to the momentum of the attack and allow it to continue. If, however, sufficient forces were dedicated to long-range interdiction, the lack of replacement troops and equipment would gut the attack and it would grind to a halt. The longer the supply line, the more this was true.

The effect of long-range interdiction upon the war became even more evident as the truce talks continued, and the United Nations elected to keep the pressure on the Communist negotiators by the application of air power. Daytime attacks by fighter-bombers forced the enemy to take to the road at night, providing targets for the bombers; working together, they kept pressure on the enemy.

THE LIGHT BOMBERS

The Douglas B-26 Invader—"the little racer" to some of its pilots—has the distinction of having flown the first and the last bombing missions of the Korean War. As noted above, the first was flown on June 28, 1950, led by Captain Harrison Lobdell, Jr., of the 13th BS. The last was flown on the evening of July 27, 1953, when a B-26C of the 34th BS of 17th BW, piloted by First Lieutenant Herbert L. Atkins, used Shoran (short-range navigation) to drop its bombs on Wonson at 8:59 P.M.. It landed at 11:55—five minutes before the cease-fire was to take effect.

In the long, hard thirty-seven months intervening between those two missions, a mere handful of B-26s made life hell for the Communist forces, carrying the war to the North on long solo missions that added miserable weather and rock-filled clouds to the danger of low-level attacks on enemy convoys. The 3d Bombardment Wing and its attached 731st (later 90th) Bombardment Squadron (Light-Night Attack) were based at Iwakuni Air Base on southern Honshu and never in the course of the war had the full complement of seventy-two aircraft on hand. The "rival" B-26 units—the 452nd BG (L) and its successor, the 17th BG (L)—were equally short-handed. (The 452nd was an Air Force Reserve unit that flew its B-26s overseas from George AFB, California.) By the end of the war, B-26s were in such short supply that the Air Force was desperate enough to send older models with flat canopies that could not be flown with standard winter flying equipment and survival equipment. The two units were also short on replacement crews for most of the war.

The effectiveness, inventiveness, and heroism of the B-26 crews can be typified by the actions of Captain John S. Walmsley of the 8th Bombardment Squadron. On the night of September 12, 1951, Walmsley had tested new tactics employing a huge 80-million-candlepower searchlight, illuminating a convoy and destroying sixteen trucks in ten passes. The searchlight gave the B-26s the awesome appearance of an oncoming train dropping out of the sky at 300 mph, terrifying some truck drivers into careening off the road. Two days later, Walmsley was at it again, this time attacking and locating a train. He had run out of ammunition and summoned another B-26 in to finish the train off. Walmsley continued to illuminate the train with his searchlight, and, an ideal target, was shot down and killed. He was posthumously awarded the Medal of Honor. Use of the searchlights was subsequently dropped.

With only a handful of aircraft, the B-26 outfits were routinely assigned to fly thirty-eight missions each night, against all sorts of targets. When the situation demanded, this was raised to forty-eight missions, which could be achieved only by having some of the aircraft fly two missions a night, one as an intruder on armed reconnaissance, and the second in the ground support role. It made for an exhausting evening, for, pleasant as the B-26 was to fly ordinarily, it was a handful to muscle around when pulling out of an attack with the airspeed indicator red-lined at 420 mph.

A single mission was grueling. Flying out of Iwakuni, the B-26s would stage through Taegu airfield, where both fuel and ordnance were often in short supply and the pierced-steel-plank runways played havoc with the tires. At various stages of the war, B-26s also flew out of K-1 (Pusan West), K-8 (Kunsan), and K-16 (Seoul). Takeoffs were made at one-minute intervals with the crews flying alone to assigned areas over the main North Korean supply routes. Targets were difficult to find, and the Communists used guards along the road to warn road traffic of approaching aircraft. Usually trucks would switch off their lights within fifteen to twenty seconds of learning of an intruder. Trains ran without lights and were adept at speeding rapidly from tunnel to tunnel.

The B-26s would try to surprise the enemy, searching for targets while flying at about 2,000 feet above the ground. If flares were carried, they were dropped upwind, about 3,500 feet above the terrain. If there were no flares, the B-26s often dropped their napalm first to light up the area, then tried to block off the convoy's advance and retreat. If the bombs stopped a train or a convoy, strafing attacks would be made until ammunition was exhausted, the pilots sometimes descending to as low as 200 feet to get results.

Mountains were often cloaked in clouds, and the aircrews had to have nerves of steel to descend through the weather into—they hoped—a valley where they could make an attack. It was physically demanding as well, with the noisy pounding of the big R-2600 engines, the constant changes in night adaptation going from full blackness into the blinding light of flares dropped by "Firefly" C-47s, and the ordinary psychic demand of combat, where flak traps set in the valley walls could bring an aircraft down in an instant.

As many as six aircraft might be scheduled to patrol the same area during the night, and timing was crucial. In one incident, a B-26 pilot felt a faint jar as he was breaking away from a run on the target and assumed it was either flak or a bird strike. The next morning, his crew chief found a bomb shackle smeared with the same color paint found on the wingtips of another squadron. A quick check of wingtips in that squadron confirmed just how near a miss it had been.

Despite their age and limited numbers, the B-26s soldiered on, destined to fight yet another war in Vietnam. By the summer of 1952, doubts arose as to the economic return of night intruder missions, and General Barcus redirected their effort in daylight formation raids against hostile communication centers in areas not ordinarily defended by MiGs. Only the most experienced crews remained on night-intruder duty, grouped into the 13th Squadron of the 3d BW and the 37th Squadron of the 17th Wing. Some aircraft were also equipped to do Shoran bombing.

The B-26s flew more than 55,000 sorties in Korea, 44,000 of these at night. One of the great dissatisfactions of the B-26 crews was that they could not get verification of their work, and in the heat of battle could only make rough estimates of the destruction they caused. A compilation of their claims reveals that they destroyed almost 40,000 vehicles, 35,000 railway cars, 406 locomotives (their destruction was more dramatic and thus easier to verify), 168 bridges, and seven enemy aircraft.

HEAVY BOMBERS: THE EARLY DAYS

Although North Korea was industrialized compared to South Korea, the bulk of its war materials originated in the Soviet Union and were supplied through Communist China. Therefore, a strategic campaign against the North had finite limits both as to range of targets and effective payoff. Further, during the two periods of Communist advances, FEAF's B-29s were often placed into the close support role, doing carpet bombing. Nonetheless, the B-29s—and their crews—did a superb job throughout the war, even though many of the aircraft were pulled from mothballed status and many of the crewmen were reservists, their lives disrupted by another tour of combat duty.

FEAF's initial strategic force was the 19th Bomb Group (Medium), based at Andersen Air Base, Guam, and the only B-29 unit outside the control of the Strategic Air Command. The 19th was given orders to move immediately to Kadena, and four aircraft went into action on the afternoon of June 28, primarily as a show of force, hitting rail lines and roads leading to Seoul.

On July 8, 1950, General Stratemeyer established the Far East Air Forces Bomber Command (Provisional), and Major General Emmett "Rosie" O'Donnell, Jr., was dispatched to command it. O'Donnell, who commanded the 14th Bombardment Squadron in the dark days of 1942 in the Philippines and led the first B-29 attack on Tokyo, had gone on to become commander of SAC's Fifteenth Air Force after a distinguished combat career.

O'Donnell was thus uniquely qualified to lead FEAF's Bomber Command, as it was supplemented by units from SAC. The training and discipline of SAC showed to good advantage when the 92nd Bombardment Group (M) at Spokane (later Fairchild) AFB, Washington, and the 22nd Bombardment Group (M) at March AFB, California, were alerted for combat duty in Korea. Nine days and 8,000 miles later, they flew their first combat mission against Wonsan, a tribute to the flyaway kits, the resilience of the aircrews, and SAC theories on mobility. The experience of the move enabled later groups to move even faster. The 98th and 307th Bombardment Groups (M), from Spokane AFB, Washington, and MacDill AFB, Florida, respectively, were summoned to FEAF on August 1. The 98th (stationed at Yokota) flew its first combat mission only six days later, while the 307th (operating from Kadena) took seven.

During the early days of the war, as the initial B-29 effort was directed against delaying the enemy by destroying bridges and railways, a jurisdictional dispute over the selection of targets broke out between MacArthur's GHQ (General Headquarters) Target Group and the professional airmen of the FEAF Target Section. Grudging agreement was given to permit FEAF to select targets, although MacArthur would insist on his organization's designating interdiction targets for the B-29s under certain "special conditions" that he would define.

FEAF conducted a hurried analysis that identified five primary strategic targets in North Korea, including the capital, Pyongyang, plus Wonsan, Hungnam, Chongjin, and Rashin.

The first major effort, three strikes over a five-day period, was against a huge chemical industry site at Hungnam specializing in explosives and would set the precedent for subsequent strategic operations. Forty-seven B-29s used APQ-13 radar sets to bomb the Chosen nitrogen explosives factory complex on the morning of July 30, 1950, destroying 30 percent of it and heavily damaging another 40 percent. On August 1, forty-six B-29s used the Norden bombsight to destroy the Chosen nitrogen fertilizer factory and on August 3, thirty-nine B-29s struck the Bogun chemical plant, using radar bombing. The Hungnam complex was destroyed for all practical purposes for the remainder of the war.

FEAF Bomber Command worked around the clock to sustain the bombing offensive, which soon exceeded World War II records by delivering 30,136 tons of bombs between July 13 and October 31. The tired but true B-29s averaged 8.9 sorties each per month, a tribute to the maintenance personnel, who were operating 8,000 miles from their normal equipment and supplies.

The efficiency of the FEAF missions was enhanced by the use of an airborne commander who preceded the bomber force on weather reconnaissance and then, based on conditions at the target, directed whether the attack would be by radar or visual means and decided whether to use formation or individual bombing techniques. The airborne commander also assessed the effects of the bombing and directed any required changes in technique on the spot.

The pattern of success was repeated against a variety of targets through September, including a controversial attack against the Fusen hydroelectric plant and the naval oil storage areas at Rashin. The latter case was a harbinger of future troubles in Vietnam, for the State Department demanded that Rashin not be a target because of its proximity to the border of the Soviet Union.

During this early period of the war, the enemy was unable to employ fighters against the B-29s, and his antiaircraft defenses were weak, but the B-29 crews faced extreme hazards from the weather, often having to return to Japan for instrument approaches with minimum ceilings and visibility.

The decision to allow UN forces to cross the 38th parallel caused the JCS to halt attacks against strategic targets in North Korea on September 26. During October, Bomber Command facilitated the North Korean rout by hitting troop concentrations, bridges, and other tactical targets, but the advance of UN troops rapidly removed the requirement even for these operations. As a result, a decision was made to return the 92d and 22d Bombardment Groups to the United States.

A NEW BALL GAME

The movement was premature, for when the Chinese Communist forces intervened, FEAF's B-29s had much more fighting to do under conditions far less benign than during the first five months of combat. Necessity again forced FEAF to go back to its first targets, bridges, but this time in a very particular way, and against a new and formidable opponent.

The Communist ground strategy was well conceived. The preliminary offensive, which began on October 25, was limited in strength and raised questions as to the intent of the Chinese, whom some optimists saw as perhaps seeking only to stake out a buffer zone south of the Yalu. The response of the Eighth Army, buoyed by its successful run up from Pusan, was to prepare for a "final" offensive itself.

In the face of the flood of Chinese Communist volunteers he had insisted would not be forthcoming, a chagrined and chastened General MacArthur demanded increased bombing, including incendiary attacks against North Korean arsenals and communications centers, but especially against the "Korean end" of all the bridges across the Yalu. MacArthur was still unaware that the bulk of Chinese forces were already across the Yalu, having filtered in over the previous month. In an un-Solomon-like decision, the JCS authorized the use of bombers against the bridges—but with no violation of Manchurian territory. Bridges from Siberia to Korea were off-limits.

The incendiary attacks were relatively easy and quite effective. The attacks against the bridges were something else, for a number of reasons. First was the strength of the bridges themselves. Built by the earthquake-wary Japanese to withstand natural disasters, they proved able to shake off damage from 500-pound bombs. Then, because they could not violate Chinese airspace, the FEAF bombers had to attack in an east-west direction on an axis parallel to the river and perpendicular to the bridge. Forced by antiaircraft fire to fly at altitudes above 18,000 feet while on the bomb run, they were subject to jet-stream crosswinds in excess of 100 miles per hour. Hitting a pinpoint target—and a 50-foot-wide bridge is less than a pinpoint from 18,000 feet—was stretching the B-29's capability. In addition, they had to endure attacks from Communist aircraft, slow Yaks and swift MiGs, which made use of their sanctuary by climbing to altitude and then making diving passes through the bombers and their escort.

The first major attack came against Sinuiju, on the south shore of the Yalu, directly opposite the Manchurian city of Antung, home base of the MiG 15s. On November 7, 1950, the FEAF attack on Sinuiju was preceded by Fifth Air Force F-80s and F-51s in a flak-suppression attack, during which Lieutenant Brown got the first MiG. Seventy B-29s dropped nearly 600 tons of incendiary bombs on the city, while nine other B-29s dropped their 1,000 pounders on the approaches to the two international bridges.

When the strike photos were interpreted, the bridges were still standing, revealing just how daunting the task of bombing one end of a bridge was. The Chinese were the victors in the battle of the bridges against both B-29s and Navy fighter-bombers. By the end of November, only about half had been cut, and the Chinese proved to be adept at supplementing them with easily repaired pontoon structures. Nature then helped them by freezing the river, reducing the need for bridges.

A dramatic, if imperfect, answer to the destruction of bridges came in the form of updated World War II technology, with the introduction of 12,000-pound Tarzon radio-guided bombs in January 1951. The Tarzons were guided in both range and azimuth to the target by the bombardier and were extremely powerful, able to take out whole sections of any bridge they hit. Unfortunately, they required a high degree of proficiency on the part of the crew and possessed an inherently dangerous feature in that they could not be salvoed safely. Their use was discontinued after eight months; thirty had been dropped, six bridges were destroyed, and one was damaged. True "smart bombs" were still a few years in the future.

REVERSAL OF FORTUNE

When the Chinese Communist forces, 180,000 men in eighteen divisions led by General Lin Piao, intervened, they had played their hand cleverly, allowing the UN forces to move almost to the limits of the North Korean border before springing their trap. The Eighth Army, preparations for its final "Home for Christmas" offensive complete, attacked on November 24, 1950. The Chinese responded on the night of November 25 with a tremendous attack on both the ROK forces and Eighth Army, and followed this with an assault on November 27 against U.S. Marine units.

A week after the Chinese offensive started, the Eighth Army had retreated more than 50 miles; by December, it was dug in below the 38th parallel, 120 miles from its starting point. B-29s were employed in incendiary attacks, including two raids on Pyongyang on January 3 and 5 which destroyed 35 percent of the city.

Brigadier General James E. Briggs took over FEAF Bomber Command on January 10, 1951, when General O'Donnell returned to the United States. Briggs was faced with a tremendous challenge, not only because the MiG-15s were becoming both more numerous and more aggressive, but also because the B-29s' 1944 vintage fire control system, designed to combat 400 mph fighters, made them increasingly dependent upon their escort fighters for protection. Unfortunately, most of the escort fighters available were straight-wing Republic F-84s and F-80s, the latter almost 200 miles slower than the MiGs. Adequate defense budgets would have provided the missing 300 F-86s that would have evened the odds.

With the spring thaw of the Yalu River, destruction of the bridges again became a priority for the B-29s, which in turn became a priority for the MiGs. Employing greater numbers and using new tactics, some MiGs would engage the F-86s in dogfights, while others brushed past the F-84s and F-80s to attack the bombers. The MiGs' armament of one 37mm and two 20mm cannons was lethal, a few hits being enough to bring down a bomber. Sitting on the "perch" high above the bomber formation, they would dive through the escorting fighters to strike the bombers, then pull out before they could be attacked. On April 12, in yet another attack on the railroad bridge at Sinuiju, two B-29s were shot down and six others were badly damaged.

The Red Chinese signaled their further aggressive intentions by building airfields in the recaptured territory. This was a crucial threat, for if they were able to operate their MiGs from the new airfields, the hard-won UN air superiority would be lost, and with it the ground war. Bombing the airfields became an essential—and costly—task for the B-29s.

The week of October 21, 1951, signaled a revolution in the aerial war.

In a series of attacks on airfields and bridges, five B-29s were lost and eight suffered major damage. There were sixty-seven B-29 personnel casualties, including fifth-five dead or missing and twelve wounded. General Vandenberg summed up the situation sadly: "Almost overnight, Communist China has become one of the major air powers of the world." One of the fiercest air battles of the war occurred on October 23, when B-29s attacked a newly constructed airfield at Namsi. Eight B-29s of the 307th BW rendezvoused with fifty-five F-84s of the 49th and 136th FBW acting as escorts. As the B-29s began their run-in, fifty MiGs attacked in classic swooping pursuit, the F-84s performing close escort being unable to intervene. The lead B-29, commanded by Captain Thomas L. Shields, pressed on despite damage and dropped on the target. He bailed his crew out at the coast, but lost his life when his aircraft crashed. Two other B-29s were shot down, and the remainder were damaged. One F-84 was lost, and four MiGs were claimed destroyed, three by B-29 gunners.

The dreary scenario was repeated the next day when eight B-29s of the 98th BW attacked a railway bridge at Sunchon. As many as seventy MiGs attacked the Superfortresses, brushing aside the escort of ten F-84s and sixteen Gloster Meteor F.8s of the Royal Australian Air Force. One B-29 was shot down, but its crewmen were rescued. (The twin-engine F.8 Meteor was an improved model of the Royal Air Force's first jet fighter, comparable to the F-80C in performance. The RAAF used the Meteor primarily for close air support in Korea; it lost forty-eight Meteors while shooting down three MiGs.)

The MiGs reacted strongly again on the 27th, almost a hundred attacking eight 19th BW B-29s. This time, there were sixteen Meteors and thirty-two Thunderjets flying escort, and the MiGs were not as aggressive; only one B-29 was heavily damaged.

Brigadier General Joseph W. Kelly had taken command of FEAF Bomber Command on September 30, 1951, and soon recognized the inevitable: the B-29s were obsolete for daylight operations in the jet age. The Superfortresses flew one more daylight mission in Korea without incident, and then were assigned to night operations, using Shoran bombing techniques, which gave them a temporary respite until the Chinese Communist forces could build up their radar, searchlight, and antiaircraft defenses in critical areas.

For the remainder of the war, the B-29s, their undersurfaces painted black, would continue to hammer the enemy, striking at the few remaining strategic targets when warranted, but concentrating on supply centers and railway junctions.

On March 15, 1952, Brigadier General Wiley D. Ganey assumed command of Bomber Command. He had the benefit of some administrative changes which, for once, resulted in a nominal increase of strength to an average 106 airplanes instead of the authorized ninety-nine. The difference was small but critical, as it permitted an increase in training in the theater.

Ganey also contributed FEAF Bomber Command's share to the "air pressure" tactic designed to ensure that the Communists remained in good faith at the negotiating table. Strongly advocated by FEAF Commander General Otto P. Weyland, it was an air campaign to obtain an armistice. The enemy had come to the conference table knowing the only weapon in his arsenal was a bloody war of attrition in which he was able to inflict an unacceptable level of casualties on UN forces even though he had to sacrifice his own troops in far greater numbers.

The air pressure campaign denied the Communist forces this capability. Called at various times Operation Strangle and Operation Saturate (terms Weyland hated), the combination of bombers, light bombers, and fighter-bombers inflicted enough damage to prevent the enemy from launching an offensive that would bleed the UN forces.

One element of the air pressure campaign began in the summer of 1952 and ran through March 1953, as FEAF and NavFE (Navy Forces, Far East) joined forces in a massive effort to attack the electrical generating facilities at Suiho, Fusen, Chosin, and Kyosen, which serviced Communist industries on both sides of the Yalu. Thirty-one B-29s participated in follow-up attacks on September 12, 1952, on Suiho, placing 2,000-pound armor-piercing bombs on the target for more than two hours and forty minutes. Damage assessment photos indicated that it would take the Communists years to place the systems back in operation.

The final tasks for the B-29s came in the late spring of 1953. Anticipating an armistice that would limit the number of arms allowed to be brought into North Korea, Bomber Command turned to destroying bridges and airfields once again. FEAF was determined not to allow the Communists to bring an air force into North Korea before the armistice was signed. Bomber Command mounted a systematic campaign, neutralizing one airfield after another, returning night after night to reverse the remarkable repair efforts of the enemy. Just seven hours before the cease-fire deadline on armaments movements, a 91st Strategic Reconnaissance Squadron RB-29 toured North Korea and brought back photos to prove that all the airfields they had been concentrating on were unserviceable.

The B-29's performance was remarkable for an aircraft designed in 1940 and built during War II, particularly considering that many of them were mothballed for years in the Arizona desert. During that period, when it seemed the B-29s would never be used again, the men and equipment required to maintain them disappeared. When war came, it was undertaken by a force never greater than an average of 106 aircraft. Headquarters USAF, concerned about the paucity of spares and replacements, sometimes placed arbitrary sortie limits on the B-29s, often as low as twelve per day. Nonetheless, they flew all but twenty-one days out of the three years and one month of the war. In their 21,000 sorties, they dropped 167,100 tons of bombs and claimed sixteen MiGs and seventeen other fighters shot down. Sixteen of the B-29s were shot down over North Korea, but perhaps three times that many were lost or written off in crash landings when they returned to base.

The airplane that had been called "the billion-dollar gamble" proved itself once again.

RECONNAISSANCE

Of all the false economies of the military downsizing that occurred after World War II, none was more costly than the virtual elimination of USAF reconnaissance capability. The art of photographic reconnaissance had been raised to new heights by the USAAF in World War II, then promptly thrown away, the baby with the bathwater, with the cutback of the American military.

When the United States government declared that it would fight in Korea, FEAF did not have a reconnaissance system; it did have two squadrons of aircraft, the RB-29s of the 31st Strategic Reconnaissance Squadron of Kadena, two flights of RB-17s for photo-mapping purposes, and the RF-80As of the 548th Reconnaissance Technical Squadron at Yokota. However, it lacked the personnel, the equipment, and the methods to convert any photos that this ill-assorted collection of aircraft might take into usable intelligence.

And this is the great double-edged sword of budget cuts, which often retain some military hardware while gutting the system that was designed to use it meaningfully. The men who had done such a sterling job of aerial reconnaissance in World War II were discharged or reassigned; the photo labs they had worked with had long since been sold for surplus. Everything had to be reinvented in Korea. In the beginning, the reinvention was done incorrectly, with an irrational administrative setup, inadequate equipment, and ad hoc procedures.

To provide some semblance of a reconnaissance capability, all available resources were pulled in, and by November 1950, the 45th Tactical Reconnaissance Squadron began to receive RF-51s for visual reconnaissance, flying out of Taegu (K2). General Stratemeyer knew that leadership was the key, and he asked that Colonel Karl L. "Pop" Polifka be assigned to the task. Polifka had flown 130 missions in Europe and then commanded the 8th Reconnaissance Squadron, flying Lockheed F-4s in the Pacific. Brigadier General George Goddard, the father of USAF aerial photography, called Polifka the most outstanding reconnaissance pilot of World War II, one who quite literally wrote the book on technique.

In Korea, "Pop" Polifka was almost forty years old, heavyset and absolutely without nerves, still flying the tough missions he did not want to assign to younger men in the 67th Tactical Reconnaissance Wing he commanded. His knowledge and leadership quickly whipped the wing into shape, normalizing the procedures for getting the photo coverage that Fifth Air Force intelligence demanded. Under his guidance, the 67th maintained a periodic surveillance of enemy airfields, did bomb damage assessment, and, just as had been done in World War I, took photos of the front.

On July 1, 1951, he scheduled himself for a dangerous long-range mission into North Korea. On his run-in over the target, his RF-51 was hit by ground fire and he bailed out, only to have his parachute snag on his tail assembly. His loss was a severe setback to the already troubled reconnaissance program.

Polifka's loss in a World War II Mustang symbolized the USAF reconnaissance effort in Korea, which was never given the equipment and the personnel commensurate with the demands placed upon it by the Eighth Army and by the Fifth Air Force. The primary units involved included the 67th Tactical Reconnaissance Wing and the 31st (later the 91st) Strategic Reconnaissance Squadrons. They used a wide variety of aircraft, including North American RF-51s, Lockheed RF-80As and RF-80Cs, RF-86s, RF-26s, a few four-jet North American B-45s, and RB-29s. Each of the aircraft types had limitations which inhibited the performance of the mission.

The RF-80s were red-lined at Mach .8 and thus vulnerable to the MiG-15 and unable to operate in MiG Alley without a heavy F-86 escort. In addition, their cameras had been designed for piston-engine aircraft speeds, so that they had to slow down when taking the required photos. The RF-51s were hopelessly obsolete, and, as Polifka's mission had shown, very vulnerable to ground fire. The RB-26s operated at night, and the artificial illuminating systems they used were not only often defective but had to be operated at a low 3,000-foot altitude where the antiaircraft fire was deadly. The RB-26s eventually reverted to using standard photoflash bombs, which gave good results from higher altitudes. The RB-29s also needed heavy F-86 escort to enter MiG Alley, as did the faster RB-45s. The latter were not useful at night, for opening their bomb bays to drop the photoflash bombs caused an unacceptable buffet. The RF-86s, although fast enough to operate in MiG Alley, had a totally inadequate camera system.

Despite the sorry state of its equipment, USAF reconnaissance in Korea outpaced World War II efforts by a large margin. In April 1945, a record number of 1,300 sorties had been flown in Europe; in May 1952, the 67th Reconnaissance Group, then commanded by Colonel Edwin S. Chickering, flew 2,400 sorties, and it averaged close to 1,800 sorties per month for the year. Even this was not enough, however, for the Eighth Army complained bitterly that only 75 percent of its reconnaissance requirements were met. The F-86s had been able to prevail over superior numbers of MiGs because of the superior training of their pilots. The reconnaissance pilots were faced with a different situation; there was no individual enemy to intimidate, defeat, and thus overcome. Instead, there were simply too many targets to hit and too many square miles of ground to cover. The tight prewar budgets had denied them the capability to do their job, and there was no way that innovation or courage could completely compensate for the equipment they lacked.

KOREAN AIRLIFTERS

The USAF fought the cargo war in Korea with new ideas and, for the most part, old aircraft. Originally called the FEAF Combat Cargo Command (Provisional) and later the 315th Air Division (Combat Cargo), the basic organization for hauling troops and supplies in the Korean theater originated with the master of the Berlin Airlift, Major General William H. Tunner. Tunner simply wanted to bring to a logical conclusion the concepts he had developed in the China-Burma-India theater, flying the Hump, and later amplified in the Berlin relief operation. He believed firmly that the theater air commander should have continuous centralized control over subordinate transport units. With this control established, a single airlift command could meet all commitments, from carrying cargo and dropping parachutists to supplying cutoff units by air or bringing home tired GIs for R&R.

Tunner did not attempt to allocate airlift priorities—he left this to the Joint Airlift Control Organization. Instead, he concentrated on how to best execute the airlift duties he was assigned. By centralizing scheduling—which naturally involved maintenance, crew assignments, and all other aspects of an effective airlift—Tunner was able to accomplish miracles with a small number of aircraft. His fleet averaged about 210 airplanes, and it was made up of a ragtag collection of Douglas C-47s, Curtiss C-46s (many of which had flown the Hump under Tunner), Douglas C-54s, Fairchild C-119s, and small numbers of the huge-for-the-time Douglas C-124s.

The variety of aircraft posed problems for maintenance, parts, supplies, crew coordination, and crew replenishment; it also gave the 315th the flexibility it needed to fight a war under the most primitive conditions. The C-47s—considered "ancient" at the time, but destined to soldier on for another twenty years—were useful in landing supplies at small airfields with limited runway capacity. After ten years of use, the C-46s, great hogs on the ground and not much better in the air, were still reliable, and the 315th pleaded to keep them in service long after the time when they should have been salvaged. The C-54s served as they had in Berlin and everywhere else—completely reliable, lovely to fly, and limited only by their numbers. The C-119s turned out to be a maintenance nightmare, with fragile landing gear and fracture-prone propellers. They were themselves a case study in management—how do you get a decent utilization from aircraft that are regarded as so dangerous to fly that they were forbidden to carry passengers? How do you get aircrews to fly planes that were allowed to drop parachute troops only because it was considered that a paratrooper would know how to bail out quickly in an emergency? The grave limitations of the C-119s precipitated at least two crises in which the 315th Air Division's airlift capability almost collapsed, and with it the Fifth Air Force's logistic support. With all its limitations, the ground-loving C-119 eventually became a useful aircraft. The Douglas C-124, in later years the beloved "Old Shaky," was new on the scene, and went through the usual growing pains of a new aircraft, including massive fuel leaks, lengthy groundings, and reduced operating limitations.

In spite of the limited capabilities of the aircraft on hand, the 315th managed to do a remarkable job, flying more than 200,000 sorties and lifting more than 300,000 medical air-evacuation patients, carrying 2.6 million passengers, and lifting almost 400,000 tons of freight.

Besides these logistic duties, the 315th also participated in combat, dropping both troops and supplies and participating in two of the biggest airborne assault operations of the Korean War. The first took place on October 20, 1950, when the war was scarcely underway. Both General MacArthur and General Tunner were airborne, watching seventy C-119s and forty C-47s pump out 2,860 paratroopers and 300 tons of equipment to drop zones at Sukchon. It was a near-perfect operation and validated Tunner's contention that airlift and paratroopers did not have to train together continuously to be effective. The second operation was at Munsan-ni on March 23, 1951, when seventy-two C-119s and forty-eight C-46s dropped 3,447 paratroopers and 220 tons of equipment, enabling the 187th Regimental Combat Team to assist in closing up the U.S. I Corps drive to the Imjin River.

Despite the fact that the 315th functioned well with its ill-assorted equipment, there were continuous demands by the Army, Navy, Marines, and Air Force for their own dedicated transport capability. These demands might have been blunted if the 315th had been equipped with an all-purpose aircraft that could have handled any of the tasks, from C-47s dropping into tiny fields to C-54s carrying wounded soldiers to Japan to C-124s carrying outsize equipment. The right aircraft for the job, the Lockheed C-130, would fly for the first time a year after the war ended.

AIR/SEA RESCUE

If any one organization typifies the American spirit, it is the Air Rescue Service, which introduced the concept of making rescues even far behind enemy lines. Building upon tactics first used by the Royal Air Force in World War II, the air rescue squadrons quickly established procedures that enabled them ultimately to save 170 U.S. airmen and eighty-four airmen from other UN air forces who had gone down in enemy territory. Operating in flights at various bases and following the front lines as they moved forward or back, the 3d Air Rescue Squadron (later 3d Air Rescue Group) of Detachment F had the usual grab bag of World War II equipment like the converted RB-17s and the Vultee L-5 Sentinel liaison plane plus a pathetically small number of modern aircraft like the Grumman SA-16 Albatross and the Sikorsky H-5 helicopter.

The rugged Albatross made an immediate impression, for it could operate in waves up to 5 feet high, and soon after the war started, it began making saves off the coast of North Korea. Gutsy pilots began landing them close to the enemy coast, ignoring enemy fire to pick up downed aviators. The helicopters were given multiple roles, one of which was immortalized by the *M°A°S°H°* television series, carrying critically wounded soldiers from the front to the mobile Army surgical hospitals. By the war's end, they had carried more than 8,500 wounded to the MASH units. Their primary task was the penetration of enemy territory to pick up downed airmen, but they were also used to pick up agents from behind enemy lines.

September 4, 1950, set the pattern for the Air Rescue Service's future. Captain Robert E. Wayne, who in his F-80 had shot down two Il-10s at Kimpo on July 27, had just made his twelfth strafing pass (not a good idea, he says today) when his F-51 burst into flame from antiaircraft hits. (His 35th FBS had converted to Mustangs in January.) Wayne bailed out, landing in a rice paddy, where he buried himself facing south, hoping to see a helicopter on its way from Pusan while fourteen of his buddies formed a ResCAP (rescue combat air patrol) overhead.

Wayne waited for an hour and fifty minutes before the welcome clopping sound of H-5 helicopter blades came from behind—the chopper had flown wide of his position on the first pass. He jumped up, tore off his flying suit to get at his clean T-shirt, and began waving it. First Lieutenant Paul W. Van Boven had flown to Hanggan-dong, penetrating about 8 miles inland from the coast, to drop his line to the grateful Wayne. This, the first behind-enemy-lines rescue by the Air Rescue Service, was a harbinger of the magnificent efforts that would be undertaken in the Vietnam War.

The immediate success of the rescue efforts brought about an expansion of the organization to new airfields and a moderate amount of additional equipment. The larger Sikorsky H-19 proved immediately useful, for its range of 120 miles gave it a 35-mile advantage over the little H-5. To maximize their utility, the aircraft were spotted at various fields close to hospitals and command posts. When it became evident that the Chinese Communist air force had an aversion to over-water operations, detachments were moved to Chodo, a small island off the coast of North Korea. A communications center there housed the tactical air controller operating under the familiar call sign DENTIST, and the H-5s stationed there were able to work effectively to rescue damaged aircraft returning from missions over North Korea. Speed was of the essence, especially in the winter, when a downed airman could expect to live for only a few minutes in the gelid waters of the Yellow Sea.

The effectiveness of the helicopter operation resulted in many demands being placed on it. Flash floods in July 1952 isolated hundreds of UN troops, who were saved by the helicopters in an intense series of missions that strained the air rescue resources. The helicopter crews usually made the headlines only with the rescue of a famous ace. In September 1952, Major Frederick C. "Boots" Blesse, the leading Sabre ace at the time and a fighter tactician, was saved by an SA-16 after he had run out of fuel after combat in MiG Alley. In April 1953, Captain Joseph C. McConnell, Jr., was saved by an H-19 so that he could go on to become the leading ace of the Korean War.

OTHER FACETS OF THE WAR

Despite the fact that FEAF had begun the war with inadequate resources and had to compete with the nuclear deterrent mission of the stateside Air Force, it grew in strength and proficiency, and in July 1953 it was a much more effective fighting force than when the war began. By the time of the armistice, FEAF had nineteen groups with a total of 1,536 aircraft. It could sustain a daily sortie rate of eighty-five B-26 sorties, 181 F-84 sorties, 171 F-86 fighter-bomber sorties, and 143 F-86 fighter interceptor sorties.

Underlying this offensive strength was a remarkably complex and diverse defensive organization that had grown up in Korea and Japan. The Lockheed F-94Bs night fighters of the 68th and 319th Fighter Interceptor Squadrons operated out of Japan and Korea. The F-94B scored its first victory on January 30, 1953, when Captain Ben L. Fithian and Lieutenant Sam R. Lyons shot down a piston-engine Lavochkin La-9 fighter. The F-94Bs went on to shoot down several jet and "Bedcheck Charlie" aircraft, the latter actually proving more hazardous. The F-94 had to slow down to the point of stall to attack the slow-flying Po-2s and ran the risk of either stalling out or overrunning the target and colliding with it.

A huge apparatus grew up to support the combat units, to include an extensive radar network, sophisticated radio communications, airfield construction, and weather forecasting, along with myriad other support units. General Barcus's directive to keep 75 percent of all aircraft ready for combat forced changes in maintenance procedures and resulted in the development of REMCO (rear echelon maintenance combined operations) maintenance methods. All maintenance personnel above those necessary for ordinary pre- and postflight services were concentrated in REMCOs. Spare parts were also centralized with the REMCO units. There was some initial resistance to the concept—unit commanders liked to keep tabs on their own maintenance and complained about the flying time involved in getting aircraft to and from the REMCO organizations in Japan—but the higher in-commission rates spoke for themselves.

Although FEAF stood shoulder to shoulder with the U.S. Navy and with UN forces in the battle against the Communists, aerial warfare in the Korean War was *not* conducted as a unified command. The primary reason was the decision by the United Nations Command/Far East Command not to have a joint headquarters for most of the war. The activities of the naval and marine units of NavFE were coordinated with FEAF, but not controlled by it. The situation was analogous to that which would prevail in Vietnam, where it was more convenient to designate broad areas of territory to the Navy for general operations than to attempt to have an actual unified command. Coordination was undertaken with good results on specific missions, but the degree of cooperation that had been achieved in joint operations with the USAAF and the RAF in World War II was never matched between FEAF and NavFE.

The Royal Australian Air Force, first flying F-51s and then Gloster Meteors; the South African Air Force, with its F-51s; the Royal Navy, with Supermarine Seafires, Fairey Fireflies, and Hawker Sea Furies; and the Royal Air Force, with its Short Sunderland flying boats, all made important contributions, but they were also coordinated with, rather than controlled by, FEAF. The Royal Thai Air Force and the Royal Hellenic Air Force contributed C-47 units that became a part of the 374th Troop Carrier Wing. Like them, the Republic of Korea Air Force units were controlled by FEAF.

Despite the lack of true unified control, the monumental air effort in Korea resulted in some staggering statistics. Following is a brief tabular distillation of the many months of hard work, danger, injury and death that were the currency of the air effort:

Item	Total UN Effort	Total FEAF Effort	%FEAF
Effort			
Total sorties	1,040,078	720,980	69%
Tons ordnance delivered	698,000	476,000	68%
Aircraft lost	1,986	1,466	74%

Although air power did not win the war for the United Nations, it certainly prevented defeat. In essence, the United Nations was not willing to commit the millions of troops that would have been necessary to win a ground war and relied upon air power to contain the Communist forces. For their part, the enemy realized that without air superiority, it could never win the war through its massive advantage in numbers on the ground. Air power had brought about the tactical stalemate that permitted the armistice to be negotiated.

The effects of the Korean War would be felt throughout the world for many years, not least in the very organizational makeup of the United States Air Force.

4
≋

POWER AND PEACE: 1953–1961

FRIENDLY LEADERS

*F*ortunately for the Air Force, President Eisenhower had a benign view of air power. Despite his Army background, Eisenhower emphasized strategic forces that would respond to enemy challenges by massive retaliation, which led to budget decisions favoring the Air Force and the Nation.

This naturally suited the Air Force Chief of Staff, General Nathan F. Twining, who grasped both the possibilities and the limitations of nuclear weapons, bombers, and ballistic missiles. Twining needed all the help he could get, for it happened that the next two men who occupied the position of Secretary of the Air Force, Harold E. Talbott (February 4, 1953, to August 13, 1955) and Donald A. Quarles (August 15, 1955, to April 30, 1957) were less than powerful leaders. Their performance, however well intentioned, was hampered by external events and by the general shift in power from the service secretaries to the Secretary of Defense.

Distinguished in name and appearance, General Nathan Farragut Twining became the third Chief of Staff on June 30, 1953. Twining was blessed with the kind of quiet, pleasant personality and commonsense style that made people like him without their realizing just how bright he was, qualities that served him well as Chief of Staff and later as the first Chairman of the Joint Chiefs of Staff from the Air Force. He had a remarkable combat career, having commanded the Thirteenth, Fifteenth, Allied Mediterranean, and Twentieth Air Forces. He spent six harrowing days on a raft in the Pacific after his plane ditched. In true Rickenbacker survivor style, Twining, a marksman, defied superstition and provided some of his crew's scant food by shooting an albatross with his pistol.

As Commander of the Twentieth Air Force, he, like some others, opposed dropping the atomic bomb, and he insisted on a written order for its use. Later, he changed his mind, realizing that the deterrent value of nuclear power depended in great measure on the enemy's conviction that the United States would use it if required. Twining was an advocate of the use of nuclear weapons to save the French at Dien Bien Phu and saw to it that tactical nuclear weapons became a part of the Air Force arsenal. Yet his views on the use of atomic power were more sophisticated than most; he believed that it could be used to disarm the enemy completely, rather than destroying him.

He was well prepared to understand the thunderbolt announcement of the explosion of a Soviet thermonuclear device on August 20, 1953, less than a month after the Korean armistice had been signed. In response, the National Security Council issued NSC-162, a paper giving guidance to the Joint Chiefs of Staff on the nature of any war that it now might be expected to fight. The NSC directed that the nation's first line of defense should be an air atomic strike force, one that would deter the Soviet Union from attacking. President Eisenhower announced the NSC policy in his State of the Union message to Congress on January 4, 1954, stating that there would a permanent professional corps of trained officers and men. Air power would be backed up by a mobile strategic reserve that could be deployed to meet local emergencies. Continental air defense was to be upgraded, and industry was to be ready to mobilize to a full wartime status. Funds were to be supplied to meet the additional requirements of the Air Force, while both the Army and the Navy would make reductions in their forces to provide offsetting economies. Eisenhower's policy was called the "New Look," and the Congress provided a defense budget of about $30 billion, divided to give roughly $12 billion to the Air Force, $10 billion to the Navy, and $8 billion to the Army. (The term "New Look" is sometimes attributed to an incongruous derivation from a contemporary phrase for the latest in women's fashions, but actually went back in military history to 1948.)

Five days after Eisenhower's State of the Union address, Secretary of State John Foster Dulles defined the concept of deterrence as "instant, massive retaliation." The capability to inflict such retaliation by a bomber force had long been the goal of General Curtis E. LeMay. An extension of that capability, the creation of the intercontinental ballistic missile (ICBM), was being made simultaneously under the leadership of one of the most famous heroes in Air Force history, General Bernard A. Schriever. Schriever pulled off a managerial coup by fielding no less than three generations of intercontinental ballistic missiles almost simultaneously, a feat in many ways more daunting than the Manhattan Project. In addition, he masterminded the Thor intermediate-range ballistic missile (IRBM) system, instigated the Lockheed

U-2 aircraft, and essentially created the managerial, engineering, and administrative basis for the U.S. space program, for which he is rarely given credit.

The growth of the Strategic Air Command and the successful creation of a retaliatory ICBM fleet were so important in creating the deterrent sword and shield that still defends the free world that they justify going back a moment in time to tell the story. That story is also a demonstration of just how prescient Hap Arnold's emphasis on research and development proved to be.

THE PATH TO TRUE AIR POWER

Even while the Korean War raged, and long before the "New Look" called for it, the U.S. Air Force was firmly focused on the task of making the Strategic Air Command's bomber fleet so powerful that it would deter the Soviet Union from aggression. Hard internal decisions were made relative to the scope of effort to be applied in Korea, the allocation of resources to be spent on air defense, and, perhaps the most contentious of all the problems, the amount to be spent on the Tactical Air Command (TAC). Matters not only of judgment but of personality came into play, for General Vandenberg and Lieutenant General Elwood R. Quesada, TAC Commander, had a thinly veiled hostility of long standing.

Amid all this, USAF leaders were looking to the future, aware that the Soviet Union not only was building a sophisticated bombing force, but also was pushing the development of the intercontinental ballistic missile, against which there was no technically feasible defense. The bomber threat could be met with a sophisticated warning system and an adequate interceptor force, both expensive but achievable. Antiballistic missile weapons were very far in the future. The only way the ICBM threat could be countered was with our own system of ICBMs in such strength that the leaders of the Soviet Union would be deterred from attempting a first strike, knowing that our surviving retaliatory power would still be sufficient to destroy their homeland.

The decisions that put these policies into effect were costly in both economic and psychic terms. For the first time in its history, the United States was going to maintain professional armed forces in peacetime, rather than relying, as it had done in the past, on cadres of professionals upon which to build essentially civilian armed services. The oceans were no longer relevant protection for our shores, and the warning time for crises had dropped from the years provided in World Wars I and II to a matter of minutes. Further, the creation of a system of ICBMs meant the virtual establishment of a second kind of air force, one totally different from anything known in the past. The differences went far beyond the obvious ones of hardware; the missile force structure was made up of personality types new to the Air Force. They were non-aircrew, and even seemingly trivial questions like the creation of a missile badge to rank with the coveted pilot's wings insignia were filled with controversy. The typical "missilier" was very technically oriented and implicitly posed a threat, albeit long-range, to the existence of the flying Air Force.

The ICBM also required a new industry. Although the standards of the American aviation industry were very high, the new requirements for accuracy, reliability, and precision for missile propulsion, navigation, guidance, and weapon systems were an order of magnitude greater. As these requirements were just beginning to be perceived, a basic battle raged as to how the missile force should be divided among the Army, the Navy, and the Air Force and had to be fought out in Congress and the White House.

The introduction of new missiles was only a part of the upsurge in the demand for funds to maintain professional armed services. Personnel costs loomed large in the equation, as did the purchase of new weaponry. Those responsible for the defense budget were thus confronted with huge increases in the projected costs over an indefinite, indeed, unlimited, number of years. As usual, the first approach to dividing the defense budget was met at every level, from the Pentagon to the Congress to the White House, by the time-honored (if inefficient and inequitable) proportionate distribution of funds, raising each service by about the same amount. Over time, however, the Air Force received an increasingly larger share of the pie.

Fortunately, two factors favored the establishment and growth of professional armed forces, including the expensive new missile arms. The first was the general sense of patriotism the populace felt after the triumph of World War II, which was not significantly diluted by the stalemate in Korea. More important, the buildup of the military budget was coincident with an unprecedented period of economic growth in the United States. (The coincidence was so marked that an argument can be made that the growth in the military spending was the engine that drove the economy during this halcyon period of expansion, rather than being a motor driven by economic growth.)

In retrospect, one thing is quite clear. The economy could not have grown, nor the nation have survived, had it not been for the absolute military dominance so quickly established by the Strategic Air Command, a military superiority that was used wisely and justly by the United States. It should be remembered that in all previous history, any nation with a demonstrable military dominance used its strength to increase its territory, whether it was Spain conquering the New World, England extending its empire to every corner of the globe, or the abortive smash-and-grab tactics of Germany and Japan. The nuclear striking power of the Strategic Air Command alone dwarfed the power of every other nation alone or in combination and was vastly greater in both absolute and relative terms than that of any of the great nations of the past. It reflects well upon the United States that this massive superiority in armed might was used only to deter war.

CURTIS LEMAY AND THE STRATEGIC AIR COMMAND

The year 1948 had seen two significant changes of command. The first came on April 30, 1948, when Hoyt Vandenberg succeeded the grand old man, Carl Spaatz, to become the second Air Force Chief of Staff. Vandenberg's tenure would be characterized by crisis, and then by emergency-forced growth. His personal reputation as a leader varied; some thought him the right man at the right time, carefully orchestrating the birth of the independent Air Force, while others were less charitable, believing that he had used politics and his connection with his uncle, the powerful Senator Arthur Vandenberg, to offset certain limitations in his intellect and industry. Given Senator's Vandenberg's political views, which were certainly not rabidly promilitary, this seems unlikely.

The second came on October 19, 1948, when Lieutenant General Curtis E. LeMay became Commander in Chief of the Strategic Air Command. LeMay would hold this position until June 30, 1957—the longest tenure for any military force commander since General Winfield Scott. The USAF and the country were extraordinarily fortunate that, over time, LeMay would be in a position to execute the nuclear strategy conceived of by the brilliant leader and future Chief of Staff General Thomas D. White.

No other U.S. military force commander so imprinted his personality and ideals upon his organization as did LeMay. SAC became LeMay personified—but only after tremendous effort on his part. There were no criticisms of his intellect or industry, nor any suggestion of patronage, but the hard, and often seemingly cold, manner in which he drove SAC gave rise to many stories about him, most of them apocryphal. In 1951, at the age of forty-six, he was confirmed as a full four-star general, the youngest since Ulysses S. Grant. LeMay was "the Iron Eagle" to his admirers, and simply "Iron Ass" to detractors who feared him. Some of his seemingly tough demeanor probably stemmed from a deadened nerve that left his face immobile and unsmiling. In practice, LeMay took better care of his troops than anyone else in the Air Force, and his tenure at SAC was filled with achievements such as improved housing, pay, recreation, promotion, medical care, and other vital personnel requirements. The most important assessment of LeMay was defined by the loyalty and the high morale of the people he commanded.

After his retirement in 1965, LeMay ran as a Vice Presidential candidate in George Wallace's 1968 third-party bid, a move that tarnished his reputation in the eyes of many. One time, later in his life, he was in the company of several other retired four-star generals, including his former aide David C. Jones, himself a former Chief of Staff of the Air Force and Chairman of the Joint Chiefs of Staff. The evening had been mellowed with some drinks, and the conversation took a daring turn—for retired or not, LeMay was still LeMay—to the question of why the general had supported Wallace.

Jones recalls LeMay saying that he had not run because of political ambition—he had none, and knew that Wallace could only lose—but because he feared the direction the country would take if the Democratic candidate won. LeMay told the little group of intimates, friends for many long years, "Don't tell me about George Wallace. I know all about George Wallace. I knew he had no chance of winning. But I ran with him anyway because I thought he could take enough votes away from Humphrey. Humphrey would have been a disaster for this country as President." Always the strategist, LeMay wanted to add enough strength to Wallace's ticket to split the Democratic vote and thus defeat Humphrey. In essence, LeMay was making a last great sacrifice, his political reputation, to serve his country's cause as he saw it.

If his politics offended some, there could be no censure of his military record. No one, friend or foe, doubted for a moment that he made SAC into an elite force, capable of strategic operations on a scale never before conceived and conducted at a level of proficiency that became the standard for the USAF. Inevitably the USAF became a benchmark to which the Army and the Navy, not to mention many foreign armed forces around the world, would aspire. It marks the second phase of USAF professionalism, both in terms of proficiency and in terms of its view of the quality of life within the service. LeMay was a genius at organization, and the Management Control System (MCS) he installed at SAC Headquarters (and which was replicated at lower levels of command) is but one example of his style. The MCS gave LeMay the capability to spot every breakdown or potential breakdown within the SAC system, and because lower-echelon commanders were aware of his system and used it themselves, potential breakdowns were usually detected and corrected before they occurred.

LeMay also had the capacity for choosing good subordinates, delegating authority to them and then letting them do their job. Not all of his choices were popular. His deputy and later successor at SAC, General Thomas S. Power, had a reputation for cold-hearted efficiency that many considered bordering on sadism.

LeMay knew that Power was tough—but he also knew that he got his job done, and that was what counted.

Not a West Pointer, LeMay graduated from Ohio State University in 1927 as a civil engineer before entering Air Corps aviation cadet training. Commissioned a second lieutenant as a pilot in 1929, he labored quietly in the background for years, learning a variety of skills that would benefit him in the future. One of these was navigation, and he later became the proponent of multirated officers, qualified as pilots, radar observers, and bombardiers/navigators.

During World War II, LeMay became one of the all-time great combat commanders, leading from the front to raise standards of professionalism and proficiency in the Eighth Air Force in Europe, and with the XXI Bomber Command in the Pacific. He drove his airmen hard, making them practice formation flying, gunnery, and bombing to a degree many considered fanatic. But his classic "sweat instead of blood" methods saved lives even as they molded forces that would fight hard.

At SAC, he was at war again, this time with the Soviet Union, an enemy he never underestimated. Since the fall of the Soviet Union, it has been shown that LeMay's assessment of their intentions was exactly on the mark, even if intelligence reporting led him occasionally to overestimate their capabilities. LeMay followed the sound military dictum that you should always prepare for what the enemy can do, not what you think he will do. The maxim sounds almost trite, but failure to observe it is costly, as was demonstrated many times during World War II—in Norway and the Low Countries in 1940, by Rommel in North Africa, by the Japanese at Pearl Harbor, the Philippines, and Savo Bay, and by the Germans in the Ardennes in 1944, to name just a few. From the early 1950s on, the Soviet Union *could* have inflicted grievous harm upon the United States and the world. That it did not may be attributed to the fact that it had realistic rather than rogue leaders, hard-bitten survivors of the Soviet competition who were aware of SAC's capability and knew that it would be used to its fullest extent. Neither LeMay nor anyone else could have counted on this, and he flogged SAC continually so that there would never be what script writers term a worst-case scenario.

When LeMay arrived to take over command, he was disappointed but not surprised at what he found—senior Air Force officers were aware that the Strategic Air Command in 1948 was woefully lacking in proficiency, discipline, and professionalism. He went to work immediately to correct things, using on-the-spot leadership to do so.

David Jones, LeMay's aide and pilot at the time, recalled an early incident in which LeMay called him and told him to prepare their command Boeing C-97 for takeoff on a Sunday. When LeMay flew, he flew in the left seat and made all the takeoffs and landings. They landed, without warning, at McDill AFB, Florida. When the startled wing commander, dressed in golf clothes, met him, LeMay said merely, "Execute your war plan." (Their war plan was to load their aircraft up with the specified flyaway kits, fly to England, and fly strike missions from there.)

A Keystone Kops pandemonium followed: squadron commanders could not be found, keys to equipment storerooms were lost, aircraft were not ready. It was, in short, a shambles. LeMay canceled the exercise and flew back to Omaha.

He took no disciplinary action, painfully aware that a similar landing at any other base would produce the same results. Instead he called his staff together and told them what had happened. It was all that was necessary. Six months later he repeated the exercise at Hunter AFB, Georgia, and everything went like clockwork.

Quiet acceptance was not his usual style; he relieved commanders immediately if he found they were not meeting his standards. But he rewarded competence with equal swiftness, once getting into enormous bureaucratic difficulty because he promoted an able young lieutenant to the rank of captain on the spot, illegally ignoring the customary—and cumbersome—Air Force promotion procedure. A mad scramble of communications ensued between SAC and Air Force Headquarters to legalize the promotion retroactively. This was an antecedent if not the inspiration of the controversial, much envied, but highly effective "spot promotion" system that he inaugurated in SAC. Crews were ceaselessly evaluated, and had to meet exacting standards to become "lead" or "select" crews. If all the members of a select crew performed to the highest standards, meeting all their obligations under the intensified SAC training program, having excellent bombing, refueling, and navigation results, they were placed in competition for spot promotions to the next rank. Some exceptional individuals—a relative few—actually had the highest accolade, a "spot on a spot," in other words, a promotion two ranks beyond their normal levels. Needless to say, it was a tremendous incentive program within SAC and the subject of bitter envy outside it.

LeMay's style was to have his best crews set the highest standards, then provide more than adequate training and flying time for other crews to reach those standards of proficiency. He also insisted on scrupulously accurate records and very demanding evaluation procedures, knowing that he had inherited an air force that had reflexively gone from the rigors of war to the pleasures of a really well equipped flying club, one that paid you for belonging. It was a long process, for SAC was expanding rapidly. When the author joined the Strategic Air Command in January 1953, as a green second lieutenant freshly graduated from flying school, he was puzzled by the flying club atmosphere. Flying the big Boeing B-50s was done as a sport, radar bombing, navigation, and gunnery scores were fudged, and the principal occupation seemed to be playing hearts in the briefing room. Then one bright day LeMay's inspection team came in. Heads rolled, rigorous standards were introduced and enforced, and reporting became squeaky clean. Oddly enough, everyone still retaining his head was happier with the new system.

LeMay arrived at SAC Headquarters in Omaha, Nebraska, with a certain knowledge of what he wished to create: an enormous fleet of long-range bombers with sufficient atomic weapons at their disposal to devastate the Soviet Union within the first few days of World War III. LeMay did not wish to judge the margin closely; he wanted overkill on a scale that would terrify his opponents. He knew that he would have to make do with the B-29s on hand and the Boeing B-50s (a B-29 upgraded with larger engines and better systems) just coming into service, in addition to the few squadrons of the controversial B-36s. But he was planning for the future—the Boeing B-47 was showing much promise (as well as many development problems), and the even larger, more capable Boeing B-52 was in the pipeline.

LeMay's management of the jet bomber demonstrates his independent judgment and vision of the future as much as any other facet of his career.

After the B-47 had entered widespread service there was a strong call from both within and outside the Air Force to economize by canceling the B-52 and instead modernizing and improving the B-47. LeMay fought this concept tooth and nail, believing that the B-47 was not sufficiently advanced technologically, and more important, that it was not big enough. He instead insisted on the purchase of the B-52, whose introduction would be accompanied by a phased retirement of the B-47.

His judgment was right on two counts. The B-47's structure proved to have a limited fatigue life because of the metallurgy and metal construction techniques current when it was built. It was also far too small to adapt to the many additions of equipment that have given the B-52 an unprecedented longevity performing an incredible variety of missions. It was first flown in 1952, and current estimates have it in the force structure until the year 2030—almost eighty years. If it does stay in service until then, it will certainly be the longest-lived aerial weapon system in history, and second in seniority overall only to the USS *Constitution*.

LeMay in Action

In both the European and Pacific theaters, LeMay had learned that getting bombs on targets involved far more than a crew, an airplane, and the bombs. Equally important were training, maintenance, morale, health, logistics, pre-and postflight briefings, and a host of other factors. He had also found that training was rarely rigorous enough, and so it was at SAC. When he arrived, practice missions were being flown at "comfortable" altitudes where engines were not taxed and the pressurized cabins worked well. Radar operators helped out in establishing visual bomb runs for bombardiers, while the bombardiers often monitored—and corrected—the radar runs. There was little concern about crew integrity—people flew with those they liked, time hogs (pilots who wanted to build up their flying time to get the coveted Senior Pilot and Command Pilot wings) flew all the time, and shirkers got by putting in their four hours per month for pay purposes.

The changes required in crew training were but the tip of LeMay's problem iceberg. To represent the scope of his predicament, it might be well first to show something of the growth of SAC during his tenure, in terms of size and equipment, and then explore the complications of managing and directing that growth.

The Growth of the Strategic Air Command

LeMay came to SAC, on October 19, 1948, and remained until mid-1957, when he left to become Vice Chief of Staff. On his arrival, he found the following force of 837 combat aircraft:

35   Consolidated B-36 Peacemakers
35   Boeing B-50 Superfortresses
486   Boeing B-29 Superfortresses
131   North American F-51 Mustangs
81   North American F-82 Twin-Mustangs
24   Boeing RB-17 Flying Fortresses
30   Boeing RB-29 Superfortress reconnaissance planes
11   Douglas C-54 Skymasters
4   Beech RC-45 Expeditors

In addition, there was a ragtag collection of support aircraft, including Douglas C-47s and North American B-25s. (For a pilot, one of the great advantages of the period was the unlimited flight time available; pilots were literally begged to take the support aircraft on personal weekend cross-countries, to build proficiency and to "burn up the gasoline," an administrative holdover from World War II when future gas allocations were based on past use.)

LeMay commanded a force of 51,965, including 5,562 officers, 40,038 airmen, and 6,365 civilians. At the time of his departure, SAC personnel had grown fivefold, to 258,703 people, including 34,112 officers, 199,562 airmen, and 25,029 civilians. And he had at his disposal the following fleet of 3,040 aircraft:

22   Consolidated B-36 Peacemakers
380   Boeing B-52 Stratofortresses
1,367   Boeing B-47 Stratojets
176   Boeing RB-47 Stratojets
182   Boeing KC-135 Stratotankers
789   Boeing KC-97 Stratofreighters
51   Douglas C-124 Globemaster IIs
54   North American F-86 Sabres
19   Martin RB-57 Canberras

The growth in numbers from 1948 to 1957 was remarkable, but did not compare with the growth in technology. The B-36 had earned its name, Peacemaker, never having to drop a bomb in anger, but was a 1940 design. A large, complicated aircraft, it was difficult to maintain and had its performance raised from disappointing to marginal for Cold War standards by the addition of four jet engines. It was phased out in 1957.

In gleaming contrast, the Boeing B-47 Stratojet, which was built in greater numbers (2,032) than any other postwar bomber, was the most important multiengine aircraft of the jet age, one that launched not only the B-52 and KC-135 sister ships but the entire fleet of Boeing civilian aircraft from the 707 to the 777. With its swept wings, six jet engines, and almost perfect streamlining, the B-47 had a sensational performance in all respects but range, and this was totally compensated for by in-flight refueling. Compared to the piston-engine aircraft that it replaced, the B-47 was easy to maintain, but it was demanding to fly and unforgiving of mistakes. It was difficult to land, compared to its predecessors, for it was so streamlined that it was slow to decelerate, requiring both an antiskid brake system (known in today's automobiles as ABS) and a brake chute for landing. Go-arounds were difficult because its jet engines were slow to accelerate. A drag chute was fitted for use during the approach, enabling the pilot to maintain a higher power setting to permit faster acceleration. The most dramatic of its challenges could be found on takeoff, when an incorrect response to its roll-due-to-yaw characteristics could turn a simple outboard engine failure into a catastrophe.

The B-47 fleet, in combination with a steady growth in the nuclear weapon stockpile, established SAC as the most powerful military force in the history of the world. The B-47 had a protracted development, entering operations in 1951 on a very small scale. It became the mainstay of SAC, and then was retired in 1967 as an economy measure. Its successor, the B-52, combined the revolutionary advances of the B-47 with the lessons learned in its operation. The most important difference besides its larger size was the use of a thick wing instead of the B-47's very thin wing. The thick wing was easier to construct, stronger, and less fatigue-prone, and it provided room for enormous fuel tanks. As a result of the larger wing and the knowledge gained in operating the Stratojets (as they were almost never called), the B-52 was generally less demanding to fly than a B-47. In a rough automotive comparison, the B-47 was a sports car while the B-52 was a pickup truck.

The improvement in aircraft performance had to be matched by an improvement of onboard equipment. The great fleets that LeMay had commanded in Europe had flown in vast formations to the target and on the formation leader's signal dropped their conventional 500-and 1,000-pound bombs en masse to provide the concentration necessary to damage targets. The B-47s and B-52s flew their missions as single aircraft or in small "cells" of three aircraft. Each one had to be of "lead aircraft" quality. Consequently, hundreds of millions of dollars were devoted to the development of electronic equipment to improve navigation, bombing, and electronic countermeasures. Both aircraft demonstrated their proficiency by winning SAC's annual bombing competition with better results than their piston-engine predecessors. However, the size of the B-52 permitted it to continue development for a much longer period, incorporating equipment that allowed it to completely change its mission's flight regime from dropping nuclear weapons from high altitude to being a low-level penetrator capable of carrying cruise missiles of uncanny precision armed with conventional warheads. The result has been a reduction in fleet size from almost 2,000 bombers in 1961 to about 200 today.

THE TANKERS

All the improvements in bombing capability would have been almost meaningless without the very risky and mostly unsung development of aerial refueling. General Spaatz had seen the need for a refueling capability as far back as 1926, for the need to stretch aircraft range was always present, and the only practical solutions were forward bases and aerial refueling. (In the post–World War II period, research into nuclear-powered aircraft determined that they posed too many problems in terms of weight, radiation hazard, and disaster in the event of an accident.) Forward bases were the only alternative during World War II, despite early Air Corps experiments with aerial refueling. It was left to the British to make the first practical advances with Flight Refueling Ltd.'s trailing-hose system, first patented in 1935, which used a hauling line that trailed behind the tanker and a contact line that trailed behind the receiver. The two aircraft made a crossover maneuver, enabling grapnels on the end of the contact line to engage the hauling line. The receiver then winched both lines in, the contact line was detached, and the hauling line pulled the hose from the tanker. The nozzle of the hose was manually seated in the receptacle, and refueling was begun.

This obviously cumbersome and time-consuming system was followed by a probe-and-drogue system. The tanker reeled out a hose equipped with a funnellike female connector into which the receiver inserted a probe. In SAC, this system was adapted to use by the KB-29, the KB-50, and even two B-47s modified for test.

Both the hose and the probe-and-drogue systems required good weather conditions and took so long to transfer fuel that they were essentially impractical for use with jet aircraft. Boeing proposed a new method called the flying boom, which revolutionized in-flight refueling. (The probe-and-drogue system would prove to be more suitable for refueling fighters and was adapted as standard by TAC on its KB-29 and KB-50 tankers.)

The flying boom consisted of a long telescoping transfer tube with two V-shaped control surfaces, called "ruddervators." The refueling plane flew above and in front of the receiver, which flew in close formation, permitting the boom operator to fly the boom into the receiver's receptacle. With the boom system, fuel could be transferred under high pressure so that refueling times were reduced.

Despite the advantages of the flying-boom system, the disparity in performance between the new jet bombers and the piston-engine tankers (KB-29Ms and KC-97s) greatly compromised the technique. The jet aircraft had to descend to the refueling aircraft's altitude, slow down to almost stalling speed, refuel, and then climb back to its own mission altitude, greatly reducing the net yield of the fuel transfer. The introduction of the Boeing KC-135 Stratotanker, which made its first flight on July 15, 1954, obviated the performance differences and raised in-flight refueling from an arcane art to an industry.

Aerial refueling almost immediately became routine, being adopted first by bombers, then fighters, and later even by cargo planes and helicopters. Well publicized nonstop round-the-world flights informed the public—and the Soviet Union—that aerial refueling conferred almost unlimited range on SAC bombers. Later, aerial refueling permitted the concept of the continuous airborne alert of a portion of the SAC fleet. The full measure of its technically and personally demanding nature is still not generally appreciated. Aerial refueling requires a high level of airmanship, conducted under conditions of imminent danger. Consider the case of the KC-135 and the B-52. The KC-135, cruising at 250 knots indicated and weighing some 300,000 pounds (of which perhaps 150,000 was highly flammable jet fuel), was physically connected, by a tube that averaged about 40 feet long, to the B-52, itself weighing more than 450,000 pounds, flying at the same speed, and perhaps carrying a number of nuclear weapons. Add to this picture of mass and momentum such factors as the dark of night, turbulent weather, and the prospect of combat, and you have all the elements of a genuine white-knuckle drama.

OTHER ELEMENTS OF SAC AVIATION

The requirement for instant mobility had led to the creation of strategic support squadrons, equipped with Douglas C-124s, as an integral element of SAC. These aircraft facilitated the deployment of wings to forward bases. The growth of aerial refueling, combined with budget pressures, resulted in the transfer of the function to the Military Air Transport Service (MATS) in 1961.

The lessons of World War II had also predisposed SAC to require fighter escort units, reaching a peak of 411 Republic RF/F 84 Thunderjets in 1955. Some attempts were made to develop parasite fighters like the unfortunate McDonnell XF-85 Goblin, or the only slightly more practical Republic RF-84K FICON (fighter conveyor), as a means of escorting the B-36s. The in-flight-refueled jet bomber changed the conditions of warfare; B-47s or B-52s penetrating deep within enemy territory individually or in small cells of three aircraft were almost impossible to escort. The fighter escort squadrons were transferred to TAC in 1956.

As some of the support units became obsolete, others were introduced, including North American F-86 fighters to defend SAC bases in Spain, and such exotic aircraft as the Martin RB-57 and Lockheed U-2 reconnaissance planes.

Whatever their function or size of the support units, and regardless of whether they were waxing or waning, they received the full LeMay scrutiny and had to meet LeMay's standards. They were, like the bomber units, most immediately characterized by their equipment. Yet, as LeMay was quick to point out, procuring equipment was but a part of the equation in building a fully capable Air Force.

LESS OBVIOUS ASPECTS

LeMay always insisted that people were the most important factor in building an effective Air Force. His views were echoed by virtually every other Air Force leader, from the first Chief of Staff to the present. In spite of this, for much of the Air Force's existence, circumstances have placed a higher priority on funding weapons with their attendant fuel, spares, and maintenance than on personnel. In effect, the people of the United States Air Force, particularly its enlisted personnel, have subsidized the service by accepting lower pay, inferior living conditions, and inadequate equipment, even as they compensated for other shortages by their own extra effort. Yet this extra measure of service seemed to inoculate the noncommissioned officers and enlisted men of the Air Force with the desire and the ability to take on more responsibility and discharge it with a highly professional competence.

As important as people were to LeMay, was grappling with even greater challenges caused by the rapid progress of technology. For most of the history of military aviation, aircraft procurement had been a relatively simple matter involving the purchase of an airframe from one manufacturer and engines from another. Systems were simple and common to most types. It was almost a rule to create a new aircraft type around a proven engine, and to test new engines in a proven type.

The jet age greatly complicated this process. New aircraft and new engines were often required simultaneously to meet new specifications, and there were many other factors to integrate, including electronic suites, new materials, new methods of flight control, vastly more sophisticated weapons, and the like. And where in the past maintenance had been performed by mechanics largely divided into airframe and engine specialties, a host of new maintenance types emerged to cater to the new equipment.

Bringing an aircraft (missiles were even more demanding) into operational service thus meant the simultaneous management of the procurement, training, maintenance, and logistic processes, among a great many other requirements. For an aircraft as large as the B-52, there were additional considerations, including the building of runways adequate to take the landing weights, hangars large enough to house them (at Castle Air Force Base, California, the first operational B-52 base, the hangars were so large that miniature weather systems, including rain clouds, formed *within* the hangars), new fuel farms for swift refueling, larger munitions storage areas, enormous simulator buildings, and very specialized dollies, tools, and maintenance stands, to name but a few of the unique requirements.

There were massive changes not only in procedures but in processes.

General Henry H. "Hap" Arnold steps out of his staff car to be greeted by the famous designer Jack Northrop.

It was Hap Arnold's vision that led to the establishment of the vitally important Scientific Advisory Board. Here, assembled for its first full meeting in June, 1946, are some of the nation's most distinguished scientists.

The end of one era and the beginning of another. President Harry S. Truman presents the Distinguished Service Medal to General Carl Spaatz, Chief of Staff, USAF.

The exact moment that the USAF officially became an independent service as the first Secretary of the Air Force, Stuart Symington, is sworn in by Chief Justice Fred Vinson on September 18, 1947.

Within days after the North Korean invasion of South Korea, General Hoyt Vandenberg, the second USAF Chief of Staff, flew to the scene of the action.

The North American F-86 Sabre of the 4th Fighter Interceptor Wing taxi out to do battle with the MiG-15s to be found in abundance in "MiG Alley."

A pair of aces. Colonel (and later General and CINCSAC) John C. Meyer, CO of the 4th FIG, congratulates James Jabara on his third MiG kill. Jabara would later go on to be the second-ranking ace of the Korean War.

First Lieutenant Joseph McConnell, Jr., is shown after shooting down his fifth MiG. Portrayed by Alan Ladd in the Hollywood film, *The McConnell Story*, Captain McConnell would lose his life in the crash of a North American F-86D at Edwards Air Force Base, California, in 1954.

Eugene M. Zuckert was a powerfully influential Assistant Secretary of the Air Force to the first Secretary, Stuart Symington, and led the fight for racial integration of the USAF.

The first jets that operated in Korea were the Lockheed P-80 Shooting Stars.

Heavily laden Republic F-84Es of the 49th Fighter Bomber Wing head for targets in North Korea.

Major William T. Whisner, Jr., of the 51st Fighter Interceptor Wing, scored 15.5 victories in World War II and added 5.5 more in Korea. Ironically, Whisner would die in 1989 in a reaction to the sting of an insect.

Air Force Chief of Staff John P. McConnell pins Major General Benjamin O. Davis, Jr.'s third Legion of Merit award. Davis, who led the Tuskegee Airmen in World War II, was the Air Force's first African-American general officer.

Two of the most important men in the United States' ballistic missile program. On the left, Trevor Gardner, Assistant Secretary of the Air Force (Research and Development); on the right is Major General Bernard A. Schriever, who masterminded the development of three ballistic missile systems and one intermediate range system in less than eight years.

Where maintenance was once the fiefdom of the hardworking crew chiefs who "owned" an airplane and were both authorized and competent to do anything from a preflight run-up to an engine change, maintenance systems became industrialized, with successive levels of work being performed on the line, in base shops, and (over time) in various levels of depot maintenance. Some elements of maintenance became so esoteric that building-block units were exchanged rather than repaired when they malfunctioned—a "black box out, black box in" approach. Training naturally became equally rigorous and ever more demanding. SAC flight crews received training at special centers, the 3520th Flying Training Wing (later the 4347th Combat Crew Training Wing [CCTW]) at McConnell AFB, Kansas, for B-47s, the 4017th CCTW at Castle AFB for B-52s, and the 4397th Air Refueling Wing at Randolph AFB.

Huge training centers for each of the specialized tasks were required, and everyone—flight crews, mechanics, specialists—needed almost continuous updating. Where aircraft like the F-80 had flight manuals of less than an inch thickness, with a few maintenance manuals as backup, there now came entire libraries of manuals, the updating of which became a demanding science—configuration control reached out of the factories down to the manuals.

Flight time became so expensive—and the possible hazards so great—that remarkably realistic simulators were provided for additional procedural training. Crews could practice approaches to strange airports, navigation, bombing, and every conceivable emergency situation. Qualified crew members acting as simulator instructors were almost sadistic in the way they would torque up the pressure, adding one malfunction after another to create emergency situations that would have been impossible to attempt in the air. The simulators themselves required dedicated technicians doing specialized maintenance in a climate-controlled environment. Other specialized gear such as test equipment, the calibration equipment for the test equipment, high-altitude physiological training chambers, ejection seats, and personnel equipment had similar needs for their own personnel, who also had to be continuously trained and evaluated.

Underlying all of the requirements was the need for standardization, so that people and equipment could be freely interchanged and anomalies quickly identified.

This brief description merely touches on the scope of the task facing everyone from commanders to mechanics throughout the Air Force. All of these needs and many more had to be met within very short time periods with limited budgets, and with an overwhelming need for secrecy, not only in SAC but in TAC, the Air Defense Command, MATS, and elsewhere. That these needs were met was in large part due to LeMay's SAC management attitude and techniques spilling over to the rest of the USAF even before he became Vice Chief of Staff in 1957 and then Chief of Staff in 1961.

This spread of LeMay's influence was right for the time; his centralist form of management brought the necessary discipline and training that the Air Force required. However, his Air Force–wide influence would be transcended when he became Chief of Staff by the Department of Defense–wide influence of Secretary of Defense Robert Strange McNamara. McNamara would push the pendulum of authoritarian, centrally controlled management to its limits, going far beyond anything LeMay had done and virtually paralyzing the services with paperwork. This phase would, however, set the stage for the third, more liberal and people-oriented management phase of the Air Force that began in the mid-1970s and continues to this day.

All that LeMay had done to field SAC's incredibly powerful bomber force was possible only because of the research and development encouraged by Hap Arnold, which had become part of the fabric of Air Force thinking, and which was made manifest in the establishment of the Air Research and Development Command in 1950. This R&D effort had also laid the foundations for the nation's intercontinental ballistic missile systems, which, as we will see, were under tentative development for an extended period. However, the true incentive for the United States' need for space dominance would come as a total surprise, in the innocuous-sounding yet utterly ominous beeping of the world's first artificial satellite, the Soviet Union's Sputnik I, on October 4, 1957.

LEADERSHIP, R&D, AND MISSILES

The interservice rivalry over the control of air power was but a prelude to the long fight to control the development of missiles. The Army insisted that missiles were a form of artillery and hence within its province; the Air Force disingenuously protested that missiles were nothing more than unpiloted bombers and therefore within its province; the Navy, at odds as usual with both the other services, insisted that naval requirements made it necessary to control all forms of seaborne missiles, whether from ships, submarines, or aircraft. This quarrel differed somewhat from previous situations. In the old days of the "Revolt of the Admirals," the Army and the Air Force were usually allied. In the battle for missile roles and missions, the Army and the Navy most often aligned against the Air Force.

All the normal bureaucratic means to resolve the dispute were tried—existing boards were used; a National Guided Missiles Program was created; committees were formed (one with the classic initials GMIORG for Guided Missiles Interdepartmental Operational Requirements Group); Chrysler's K. T. Keller (whose automotive engineering expertise was exceeded only by his abysmal taste in styling) was appointed as Director of Guided Missiles, i.e., a "Missiles Czar"—but each service stubbornly continued on its own path, refusing more than token coordination or cooperation.

President Eisenhower chose a former president of General Motors,

Charles E. "Engine Charlie" Wilson, to be his Secretary of Defense, the first to come from the automotive world. (Wilson, whose domineering personality and budget-cutting tactics had an adverse effect upon R&D, has been called a Saint John the Baptist presaging the arrival of the Messiah, Robert S. McNamara, in the Department of Defense.) As it had fallen to Louis Johnson to implement President Truman's budget cuts, so did it fall to Wilson to implement President Eisenhower's cuts, which reflected his view that "a sufficiency" of weapons was now the desired standard because Soviet advances had made achieving an overwhelming superiority in the number and size of weapons impossible. To sell the President's ideas, Wilson stated that the military expenditures of the Soviet Union were primarily for defensive purposes—an argument the Communists had refuted at the 1955 Tushino air show, where they had proudly demonstrated three potent bombers, the twinjet Tupelov Tu-16 Badger, the four-jet Myasishchyev M-4 Bison, and the four-turboprop Tupelov Tu-20 Bear.

Aware of the indecision over the question of roles and missions for missiles, Wilson issued a memorandum on November 26, 1956, that addressed a number of issues, including the size of the combat zone in time of war (100 miles behind the line of contact), the limits on Army aircraft (5,000 pounds for fixed-wing and 20,000 pounds for rotary-wing), but most important, assigned departmental responsibility for missile systems among the three services. Wilson established that the Army was given point defense surface-to-air missiles; the Navy and Marine Corps were assigned responsibility for weapon systems to carry out their functions; and the Air Force was to have area defense missiles.

In addition, Wilson allowed the Army to continue development of surface-to-surface missiles with a range of about 200 miles; the Navy was assigned responsibility to employ ship-borne intermediate-range missiles (IRBMs), while the Air Force was confirmed in its operational employment of intercontinental ballistic missiles (ICBMs) and given the joint assignment with the Army of land-based IRBMS. The apportionment was not clean-cut, but it sanctioned the extensive work already undertaken by the Air Force.

Wilson continued the trend of concentrating power in the office of the Secretary of Defense, automatically reducing the influence of the service secretaries. Unfortunately for the Air Force, the two men who occupied the position of Secretary during the critical 1953–1957 era, Harold Talbott and Donald Quarles, while very much committed to the development of the intercontinental ballistic missile, could not stand up to Wilson. Talbott had done an excellent job overseeing the post-Korea expansion of the Air Force to a 137-wing force and worked diligently to improve the lot of the enlisted man, improving pay, housing, and educational opportunities. Unfortunately, his tenure was cut short by a conflict-of-interest controversy. A scientist, Quarles found himself at odds with the Air Force military leadership as well as with Wilson. Both Talbott and Quarles backed the development of the ICBM and of space satellites; sadly, both suffered deep disappointments while serving as Secretary, and both died within two years of leaving office.

It was well that the civilian leadership muddle was compensated for, at least in part, because the United States Army Air Forces had as early as 1946 begun an orderly and systematic missile development program. The most important effort was a study contract for $1.9 million to the Consolidated Vultee Corporation (later unofficially called Convair until the name was made official in 1954) for Project MX-744. A very refined development of the German V-2, Project MX-744 was placed under the leadership of a Belgian émigré, Karel J. Bossert. His rocket featured a thin single-wall pressurized monocoque structure that had to be kept rigid with nitrogen under pressure until fuel was introduced. Unpressurized, it would collapse under its own weight. Bossart also proposed a nose cone that would detach (with its warhead) from the main rocket structure and swiveling rocket engines. Project MX-744 was one of the first victims of the postwar budget cuts and was canceled in 1947, but Convair continued to spend its own money on the project.

Within the USAF, there was an inherent organizational bias against missiles, one freely acknowledged by both Twining and LeMay, and this, coupled with the tendency to hedge development bets, led to a preoccupation with surface-to-surface winged missile types that themselves were never brought to fruition. The aviation industry, which had soared to new heights in World War II, seemed strangely unable to cope with unmanned missiles, most of which fell years behind in their schedules. Among them were the winged, subsonic turbojet missile, the Martin Matador, the rocket-boosted winged supersonic ramjet-powered North American Navajo, and a long-range supersonic turbojet, the Northrop "Boojum." An even greater variety of air-to-surface, surface-to-air, and air-to-air missiles were also under development.

Budget cuts and the Korean War caused a decline in funding for missile research, which was probably not disadvantageous in the long run, for it tended to quickly weed out missiles whose performance seemed doubtful, and those whose development cycle was taking too long. Convair was rewarded for both its engineering skill and its patience on January 23, 1951, with a contract for Project MX-1593. The $500,000 contract called for Convair to outline a vehicle with a maximum over-the-target speed of Mach 6, a range of 5,000 nautical miles carrying an 8,000-pound warhead, and the ability to strike a target with a CEP of 1,500 feet. (CEP stands for circular error probable, a bombing-range term that defines the radius of a circle within which half the weapons targeted for the center of the circle can be expected to land.)

Convair reported that the desired missile was feasible and could either be a ballistic or a glide-rocket type. The ballistic missile would be twice as large as the glide rocket and would require a cluster of five to seven of North

American Aircraft's 120,000-pound-thrust alcohol–liquid-oxygen engines that were decendants of the booster engines used on the Navajo Project. The MX-1593 project was also given the name Atlas, although the Air Force, concerned about roles and missions, continued to call it the XB-65 pilotless bomber for a considerable time.

Many within the Air Force were properly concerned about spending scarce resources on long-range missiles that might not be technically feasible. However, these concerns were soon overshadowed. Reports from the Soviet Union in late 1951 of huge rockets of more than 250,000 pounds of thrust lent urgency to the development of the Atlas.

The principal impediment to proceeding with the Atlas was the size and weight of the warhead, which, on an almost exactly proportionate basis, dictated the size and weight of the rocket required to launch it to the target. (There were many other difficult problems to be solved, including the high heat associated with atmospheric reentry, guidance and control, engine staging, and so on, but these seemed to be more amenable to resolution than the fundamental question of the warhead weight.)

The first experimental hydrogen fusion device was detonated at Eniwetok on November 1, 1952, as a part of "Operation Mike." This device used cryogenic D (deuterium) and T (tritiom), and weighed about 50,000 pounds. It clearly seemed impractical for delivery by bombers, even though SAC immediately began framing requirements for an aircraft that could carry a 25-ton bomb. At a 1953 Scientific Advisory Board meeting in Florida at Patrick Air Force Base, two of the most brilliant scientists of the day, Dr. Edward Teller and Dr. John von Neumann, gave independent presentations which indicated that a "dry" thermonuclear bomb weighing about 1,500 pounds could be built. General Schriever in a recent interview recalled, "I almost came out of my seat in excitement, realizing what this meant for the ICBM."

Then a colonel, Schriever sought confirmation and credibility for this new development. Upon the recommendation of retired Lieutenant General James H. Doolittle, a nuclear weapons panel headed by Dr. von Neumann was established by the Air Force Scientific Advisory Board. The results of this panel's deliberations were more conservative than the original presentations, indicating that a thermonuclear warhead weighing only 3,000 pounds and yielding .5 megaton was possible.

This effectively solved the warhead weight problem, simultaneously reducing the projected weight of the Atlas rocket from 440,000 pounds to 220,000 pounds. Spurred on by this finding, one of the most influential men in the missile program, Trevor Gardner, the Special Assistant for Research and Development to the Secretary of the Air Force, established another committee called the Strategic Missiles Evaluation Group. The committee followed the spirit of Hap Arnold's direction, with von Neumann as chairman, and with stellar members Simon Ramo, Dean Wooldridge, Clark B. Millikan, Hendrik W. Bode, Louis G. Dunn, Lawrence A. Hyland, George B. Kistiakowski, Charles C. Lauritsen, Allen E. Puckett, and Jerome B. Weisner. These men, quite literally the cream of crop of industrial and academic scientists, placed themselves at the service of their country. (It is sad to reflect that in a similar emergency, an equivalent national need, we might not in these liberal days be able to count on an equivalent representation from academia.) Schriever served as the committee's military representative.

After a series of meetings, the "Teapot Committee" (no one seems to be able to recall why it was so called) recommended that the Atlas program be revised to take double advantage of the new lightweight high-yield warheads by reducing the stringent CEP requirements from 1,500 feet to between 2 and 3 nautical miles.

Gardner took the recommendation and ran with it. An impulsive, sharp-tempered, sometimes acerbic man, Gardner was convinced of the imminent danger of the Soviet ballistic missile program and was determined to ramrod a counter to it. Gardner was fortunate in having the backing of Secretary of the Air Force Talbot and Generals Twining and White in a plan that called for $1.5 billion expenditure over the next year to achieve, by July 1958, two launch sites and four operational missiles, and by 1960, twenty launch sites and a hundred missiles.

Designated as Talbott's direct representative in all aspects of the Atlas program, Gardner pressed ahead with a no-holds-barred attitude toward spending. By July 1, 1954, an ARDC field office, called the Western Development Division, was established in Inglewood, California, with now Brigadier General Schriever as commander. It was the best possible appointment.

THE RIGHT MAN IN THE RIGHT PLACE
AT THE RIGHT TIME

Bernard Adolph Schriever was born in Bremen, Germany, in 1910, and was perhaps destined for aviation and space when as a boy he saw the Kaiser's Zeppelins flying over his home, returning from their raids on England. By an unusually provident act of war, the ship upon which his father served was seized in New York harbor in 1916 and its crew interned. Bernard, his mother, and his brother Gerhard came to America in the following year.

Young Bernard's life was difficult, but molded his character and his interests. His father died in an industrial accident in 1918, and his mother supported the family. He worked hard at school and at play, graduating from San Antonio High School with honors. A caddy early in life, Schriever became an expert golfer. He graduated from Texas A&M in 1931 with a degree in architectural engineering; his success in ROTC gave him a chance to become a flier, and he won his wings at Kelly Field, Texas, in June 1933.

The next six years were varied, including flying the airmail for the Army, commanding a Civilian Conservation Corps camp, flying for Northwest Airlines, playing a lot of golf at the professional level, and finally returning for a regular commission when the Air Corps at last began to expand in 1939. During World War II, he flew sixty-three combat missions with the veteran 19th Bombardment Group.

After the war he worked with von Karman, who recognized his talent and made certain that Schriever would carry on the liaison Arnold had established with the scientific community. Schriever's technical expertise led him to push technology to obtain advances in weaponry; his methods were not traditional, and he sometimes experienced opposition within the Air Staff, often with the preeminent pragmatist Curtis LeMay. (It was Schriever who had pushed for the B-47 instead of the B-52.) However, he had the patronage of both Generals Twining and White—necessary to deal with LeMay on an equal basis—and was obviously destined for a leadership position in a technologically advanced Air Force.

In his new assignment as Commander of the Western Development Division, Schriever had been able to handpick his staff. Further, against much opposition, he was permitted a radical new organizational scheme, in which his WDD would retain system responsibility for the Atlas program, employing the Ramo-Wooldridge (later TRW) firm to do the systems engineering and technical direction, with Convair being awarded an airframe and assembly contract. Later, Schriever was made assistant to the Commander of the Air Research and Development Command for Ballistic Missiles, a second hat that enabled him to direct ARDC to assist WDD's efforts, rather than having to solicit help from the ARDC staff. A dotted line is a subtle distinction on the organization chart, but it was a time-saver in developing the ICBM, and Schriever recalls that many seemingly impossible bureaucratic problems were solved by simple telephone calls.

Trevor Gardner had received the backing he wanted for the ICBM with the advent of a report from the President's Technological Advisory Committee in February 1955. Called the Killian Report, after its chairman, James R. Killian, Jr., the president of the Massachusetts Institute of Technology, the report noted the progress in Soviet rocket technology and stressed the vulnerability of the United States to attack. Schriever, Gardner, and von Neumann briefed President Eisenhower and virtually his entire cabinet on the potential of the ICBM. Eisenhower directed that the ICBM program become a nationally supported effort of the highest priority.

With Gardner securing top priority for the ICBM, with separate funding for the Atlas, and under Schriever's leadership, the Western Development Division was well launched. Its furious pace of work began the development not only of the Atlas missile but of what would become the aerospace industry. The new specifications were challenging, and some companies had to be induced to compete for systems unlike any they had ever created. Schriever fostered a competitive climate by subcontracting out every major subsystem to separate contractors and using the WDD as the integrating facility. Schriever never doubted that the Atlas would be a success, but was concerned that the requirement that the missile be fueled and launched in twelve minutes might be difficult to achieve.

The Soviet threat and the momentum of the Atlas program spawned other missiles. A decision was made in May 1955 to develop an intermediate-range ballistic missile (IRBM), the Thor, from the Atlas, and an award was made to the Martin Company in the fall of 1955 to develop the Titan missile as an alternative to the Atlas.

In brief, Schriever found himself at the head of an organization that dwarfed the Manhattan Project in terms of scientific difficulty, spending, number of employees, and, most significant, urgency. For the last year of the Manhattan Project, the United States was confident that neither Germany nor Japan had the capacity to build or deliver an atomic bomb. In striking contrast, there was every reason to believe that the Soviet Union was far more advanced than the United States in rocketry, and its successes with both atomic and hydrogen bombs clearly created an imminent threat. Gardner directed that listening posts to be established in Turkey to monitor Soviet rocket experiments; it would not be long before the hard evidence of their success would be trumpeted to the world by Sputnik.

Schriever's system of concurrent development, production, and operations was risky, but paid off. Within a short time, he was calling on the talents of 18,000 scientists, seventeen prime contractors, 200 subcontractors, and 3,500 suppliers, all employing an estimated 70,000 people, to build the more than 100,000 individual components of the Atlas. Five hundred million dollars was spent on new test facilities. The WDD grew correspondingly, and became the Ballistic Missile Division (BMD) on June 1, 1957. (One spin-off of Schriever's management methods was the growth of what came to be called systems management, an approach to business that was widely adopted in industry.)

Building the Atlas was only part of the task. General Thomas D. White, Vice Chief of Staff, called on the resources of SAC, the Air Training Command (ATC), the Air Materiel Command (AMC), and the Air Research and Development Command to prepare for the advent of the missiles.

The Atlas program was fraught with difficulties and, even after the Killian Report, subject to budget cuts that caused delays in the schedule. There were also the usual development problems. The first launch of an Atlas took place at Cape Canaveral on June 11, 1957; it suffered the classic American first-launch syndrome when an engine failed, sending it into wild maneuvers that called for detonation by the range officer. A second launch suffered the same fate, but the third, on December 17, 1957, was very successful. By then the one-two punch of Sputnik I and Sputnik II in the fall of 1957 had spurred Congressional budget largess again, for it was obvious to everyone that the Russian rocket that orbited a satellite could also propel an ICBM warhead to the United States.

Schriever did his work well. The Strategic Air Command activated its

704th Strategic Missile Wing on January 1, 1958. On September 9, 1959, the first Atlas, a D model, was launched from Vandenberg Air Force Base by a SAC crew. Deployment of the missile was complicated in 1959 when advances in Soviet ICBM capability forced a crash program to place a large part of the Atlas force in huge underground silos, 174 feet deep and 52 feet wide.

By 1963, SAC had thirteen Atlas missile squadrons, with 127 missiles deployed. All of the money, effort, and management expertise had paid off—the Soviet threat had been met. By then the Atlas missile was obsolescent, already overtaken by Titan and Minuteman follow-on missiles. The Atlas force was deactivated during 1965, with many of the missiles going on to serve splendidly as launch vehicles for satellites and other space programs.

Missiles are more difficult to describe than aircraft. The Atlas was produced in a number of models, of which the D is typical. It was 82 feet 6 inches long and 10 feet in diameter and had a launch weight of 260,000 pounds. The D's 10,360-mile range was made possible by its five engines, a LR 89 sustainer rated at 57,000 pounds of thrust, two LR 105 engines each rated at 150,000 pounds of thrust, and two small vernier rockets to provide final "trim" velocity. All five engines were fed the combination of kerosene-like RP-1 fuel and LOX (liquid oxygen) from the two stainless-steel thin-wall pressurized balloon tanks.

The success of the Atlas program alone was an astounding managerial achievement, raised an order of magnitude by the fact that the Thor IRBM and the Titan and Minuteman ICBMs were all being successfully developed in parallel with it.

The Thor was a direct spin-off of the Atlas, with a liberal helping of technology from the rival Army IRBM, the Jupiter. As a result, it had a very successful test program and the shortest interval between contract signing and the IOC (initial operational capability) of only 3.9 years—less time than General Motors was taking to develop and introduce a new-model Chevrolet. With a length of 65 feet, a diameter of 8 feet, and a launch weight of 105,000 pounds, the Thor had a range of 1,976 miles, which made Great Britain the perfect basing point.

The Titan was a far more sophisticated missile than the Atlas, and it was quickly improved with the Titan II. With a rigid rather than a pressurized structure, the Titan used two stages of liquid-fueled rockets to achieve its mission goals. The first stage was an Aerojet LR87-1 engine with two gimbaled chambers rated at 150,000 pounds of thrust each; the second stage was an Aerojet L91-1, rated at 80,000 pounds of thrust, which was ignited in the vacuum of space. A huge vehicle, the Titan was 98 feet long with a 10-foot-diameter first stage and a launch weight of 220,000 pounds. It had a range of 8,000 miles with a huge 4-megaton-yield warhead. The Titan was stored upright in a silo, but had to be lifted to the surface and fueled before firing.

The Titan II was even larger, 103 feet long and 10 feet in diameter and with a launch weight of 330,000 pounds. Its range was over 9,000 miles. It had the significant advantage of being designed for storable fuels and could be launched in position from the bottom of the silo. The LR87-5 engine provided 216,000 pounds of thrust from each of its two chambers, and the second-stage LR91-5 engine put out 100,000 pounds of thrust. The missile could be fired on two minutes' notice.

As advanced as the Titan II was, the Minuteman series was an even more radical and much more satisfactory approach to the problem. Boeing won a hotly fought contest with fourteen competitors to secure the contract, and delivered a three-stage solid-propellant rocket fired from its underground silo. The less complex nature of the Minuteman greatly reduced crew requirements, only two persons being necessary to control a flight of ten silos. Like its predecessors, the Minuteman was continuously refined, resulting in the Minuteman II and III series. Firing was virtually instantaneous.

Each stage of the Minuteman was assigned to a different company, to reduce risk. Thiokol's first stage had 200,000 pounds of thrust, Aerojet's second stage had 60,000 pounds of thrust, and Hercules' third stage had 35,000 pounds of thrust. Launch weight was 64,815 pounds and range was over 6,000 miles.

Every one of the follow-on programs, with their many changes and improvements, confronted Schriever and his rapidly expanding organization with a degree of challenge the same as or greater than the original Atlas had. All four programs were compressed into an amazingly tight schedule, as the following table indicates:

Event	Missile			
	Atlas	Thor	Titan	Minuteman
Contract award	1/55	12/55	12/55	10/58
First launch	6/57	9/57	2/59	2/61
Initial operating capability	9/59	6/58	4/62	11/62

Thus from January 1955 to November 1962, just short of eight years, Schriever's organization guided the United States Air Force and the missile industry to four complete missile systems. Titan and Minuteman had a remarkable longevity, and the first three systems—Atlas, Thor, and Titan—went on to more than pay for their investment through their contribution to the space age as launch vehicles. As early as February 1957, General Schriever announced that about 90 percent of the developments in the ballistic missile program could be applied to advancing in space and to satellites and other vehicles. He viewed ballistic missiles as but a step in a transitional process leading to flights to the moon and beyond, and now sees his contributions to the space program as being even more satisfying than the creation of the ICBM fleet.

There is no governmental or industrial counterpart to Schriever's management feat. In government, the Manhattan Project is most nearly comparable. In industry, one can look to the widespread chaos of Howard Hughes's empires, or to the prairie-fire-swift expansion of Ross Perot's interests, or to the seemingly limitless prospects of Bill Gates software world, and in none of these is there anything near the magnitude of the challenge, the scope of the work, or the rapidity of achievement that can be found in the USAF intermediate and ballistic missile programs. Yet General Schriever, while fully acknowledged within the service and industry for his talents, was never accorded his full measure of fame by the civilian community. This was due in part to his informal manner and modest nature, in part to the security considerations of the time, and in largest part to the fact that the sheer magnitude of the challenges he faced and overcame were beyond most people's ready comprehension.

An aircraft comparison is revealing. During the same time period, the Convair F-102 fighter, admittedly an advanced design, took ten years to go from the establishment of the requirement to the completion of the program, and it cost $2.3 billion. By any measure—scale, scope, importance, technological advance—the ballistic missile and space programs initiated and carried to a successful conclusion by Schriever were far more complex, yet were executed in a shorter period.

One of Schriever's strong backers, General Thomas D. White, a brilliant intellect, had succeeded General Twining as Chief of Staff on July 1, 1957. In November he made a prescient speech at the National Press Club in which he stated, "Whoever has the capability to control the air is in a position to exert control over the land and seas beneath. . . . I feel that in the future whoever has the capability to control space will likewise possess the capability to control the surface of the earth. . . . We airmen who have fought to assure that the United States has the capability to control the air are determined that the United States must win the capability to control space."

White's words were a ringing challenge in the post-Sputnik atmosphere, when the embarrassment of the United States led to spin-control language in the legislation creating the National Aeronautics and Space Act, which President Eisenhower signed in July, 1958. The act provided that activities of the United States in space would be "devoted to peaceful purposes for the benefit of all mankind" in contrast to the ominous, absolutely secret activities of the Soviet Union, which clearly had a military purpose. The act did not abolish military space research and development, and it assigned "those [research and development] activities peculiar to or primarily associated with the development of weapon systems, military operations or the defense of the United States to the Department of Defense." Neil H. McElroy, Secretary of Defense from October 1957 to December 1959, and not a dynamic leader, did have the foresight to assign to the Air Force the responsibility for the development, production, and launching of space boosters. It was a small start to what would become a supremely powerful space presence.

IN THE SHADOW OF SAC BETWEEN KOREA AND VIETNAM

The emphasis given here to the Strategic Air Command is in part because of its importance and in part because the SAC story is also the story of much of the rest of the Air Force. The growth and change in SAC was reflected sooner or later in similar growth and similar change in the major and minor commands.

The physical creation of the bomber and missile fleets was not done in a vacuum; indeed, the Air Force, SAC included, was in a period of continuous turmoil in the years between its involvement in Korea and Vietnam. Fortunately, the rising budget tide lifted all boats. Air Force R&D budgets grew from $62 million in 1950 to $814.8 million in 1959. During the same period, expenditures for aircraft and related equipment grew from $1.2 billion to $7.1 billion, permitting TAC, ADC, and other commands to expand their operations, receive new equipment, and grow—but always in the shadow of SAC. The great support commands without which nothing could be done, Air Training Command, Air Force Logistic Command, and Air Force Systems Command, in all their varying names over time, made it possible for SAC, TAC, and ADC to operate by providing the planning, the training, the equipment, and the maintenance facilities.

SAC's size and prestige received much attention, as did its innovative means of meeting a mounting threat. The war-making qualities that U.S. airmen had demonstrated in World War II and Korea (and would demonstrate again in Vietnam and the Gulf War) were evident in the aggressive, assertive manner in which SAC forces amplified their strength by means of tactics. One common characteristic of these tactics, however, was that they usually came at the expense of the crew members in terms of extra hours at work and extra months away from home.

In 1955, SAC began rotating entire combat wings and their air refueling support to overseas bases in North Africa, England, and later Spain. It was known that the Soviet missile threat was growing and that SAC air bases were a primary target. To offset this, SAC began an alert system, in which one-third of its aircraft were "cocked," i.e, fully armed, fueled, preflighted, and ready to take off, on fifteen minutes' notice. The system was extremely costly to operate and played havoc with the family life of crews, who had to spend days in alert facilities, away from their families, and then many more days flying to meet their training requirements.

There was an added psychic embellishment, one that spoke directly to the insanity of modern war. In times past, warriors would go away to war to chance death while their families waited in relative safety at home. Under the new threat of a missile exchange, the warriors would go away to battle with at least a chance of surviving, very much aware that the families they left behind would be killed by the thermonuclear attack on their base. The instructional films of the period, now dated and so often the butt of jokes, showed the measures to be taken in the event of a nuclear attack—crawling under desks, closing eyes, etc.—and were no comfort to crews who knew too well what the full measure of the carnage would be.

Yet the decisive importance of the alert force was demonstrated during the 1958 Lebanon crisis when President Eisenhower sent 5,000 Marines to Beirut to help quash an internal rebellion. The Soviet Union rattled its sword, attacking the move as "open aggression." In response, Eisenhower put SAC on alert, and within a few hours, 1,100 aircraft were poised ready for takeoff. Soviet rhetoric cooled rapidly, and after a few days the alert was called off.

As the gravity of the Soviet missile threat increased, the alert concept was continuously refined. As noted, SAC had achieved an alert status that required one-third of its crews to be ready to launch within fifteen minutes. In 1961, President John F. Kennedy called for a 50 percent alert, and this was later supplemented by an airborne alert, in which nuclear-armed bombers were kept airborne on station on a continuous basis. The stultifying hours spent in the alert shelters (as they would later be spent in underground missile control rooms) were used by crew members to take correspondence courses for classes at Squadron Officers School, Air Command and Staff College, and the War College, along with civilian courses. The crews studied hard even though they recognized that while the correspondence courses filled a square in their career checklist and demonstrated their seriousness of purpose, in no way did they confer the prestige or, more important, provide the networking to be gained by actual attendance at the schools in question. Thus SAC crew duty actually became a career penalty for many officers.

The monotony was somewhat broken by a continuous flow of new equipment and new concepts. To offset the incredible buildup of the Soviet radar, antiaircraft, and missile defenses into the most sophisticated defense system in history, the B-52 units adopted new low-level tactics. The importance of electronic countermeasures was stressed, and the newest G and H models were designed to carry the AGM-28A Hound Dog cruise missile. This exceedingly sophisticated March 2 cruise missile, which had the capacity to go in at high or low altitudes and later in its life even had a terrain-following feature, remained in service until 1975. The crews loved the idea of suppressing enemy air defenses with the Hound Dog's atomic capability.

The general progress in technology meant that new aircraft would come along at greater intervals and smaller numbers. The gorgeous Convair B-58 Hustler, the world's first supersonic bomber, became operational on August 1, 1960. The delta-wing Hustler could fly at twice the speed of sound and featured an unusual jettisonable pod to carry weapons and fuel. Expensive, difficult to maintain, and cursed by a high accident rate (twenty-six of the 116 built were destroyed in accidents), the Hustler was withdrawn from service in 1970.

No one understood better than the leaders at SAC the value of dramatic flights in improving public relations. From January 16 to 18, 1957, in Operation Power Flite, three SAC B-52Bs flew around the world nonstop, completing the 24,325-mile trip in forty-five hours and nineteen minutes. In June 1958, in Operation Top Sail, two KC-135s broke the speed record for New York to London and return, making the round trip in just under twelve hours. In 1971, a B-58 Hustler flew from New York to Paris in three hours, nineteen minutes, and forty-one seconds, setting a transatlantic record.

Such risky flights were not without their cost. A KC-135 crashed on takeoff during Operation Top Sail, killing its crew. Like many aircraft accidents, the crash was the result of a seemingly innocuous problem, the precession of the aircraft's attitude indicator as a result of acceleration on takeoff. The instrument showed a higher-than-actual climb attitude; unnecessary corrections by the pilot flew the plane into the ground. The B-58 that set the transatlantic record later crashed at the Paris air show, scene of many crashes. Yet there was no doubt that record-setting flights sent messages to the Soviet Union with carbon copies to the Congress and the public.

R&D + POLITICAL FACTORS = CONVERGING CAPABILITIES

The flowering of research and development efforts in the 1950s combined with the changing tide of political strength (fostered by the Defense Reorganization Act of 1958) to alter significantly the nature of the United States Air Force and, for the first time, set the capabilities and missions of the Strategic Air Command and the Tactical Air Command on converging paths. The functions of the two commands would become thoroughly homogenized in the next decade, during the Vietnam War, when SAC bombers conducted close support operations and TAC fighters conducted long-range strategic bombing missions. Yet strategic, budget, and turf considerations would make it necessary for another twenty years to elapse before the logical conclusions of this development were drawn. Only after the dramatic highlights of winning both the Persian Gulf War and the Cold War would TAC and SAC be disestablished, and two new commands—Air Combat Command and Air Mobility Command—be formed.

TECHNOLOGICAL CHANGE IN THE 1950s

The foundation for technological change came with four important breakthroughs: the thermonuclear weapon (especially its smaller versions); improvements in electronics and communications, which raised command and control to a new level; the successful development of the long-range inter-continental ballistic missile; and the concept of space systems, which called for extreme improvements in electronics, especially miniaturization.

Of these the development of the Atlas caused a change in both scientific and budgetary accounting attitudes in weapon development. In the past, re-search and development had been considered an area in which many failures were routine in the process of achieving periodic successes. The urgency of the Atlas program had required that a series of unknown scientific discoveries and technological breakthroughs occur on a rigid schedule. By monumental effort of the best minds in the country, these did occur, with the inadvertent result that on later systems, the "bean-counters" in both the Department of Defense and Congress began to regard such achievements as routine, like obtaining a new muffler for an automobile. The long-term effect of this raised level of expectation would prove to be stultifying to research and develop-ment programs, for failure was no longer considered an option. Congressional and DOD scrutiny virtually demands certainty of success, cost, and schedule. It takes an exceptionally able and brave advocate to guarantee an R&D pro-ject's success in all three areas, so that it will survive the review process.

This sense of "anything is possible" was also fostered by the seemingly endless series of ever more capable aircraft under test at Edwards Air Force Base. The confluence of powerful new jet and rocket engines, advanced aer-odynamics, including swept wings and area-ruled (Coke-bottle–shaped) fu-selages, and new electronics brought forth a series of "X-planes" to lead the world in scientific advances as well as set records. Along with the X-planes came a proliferation of fighter and bomber prototypes to be tested by the most competent professional test pilots in history.

The first, and perhaps most memorable, X-plane achievement had oc-curred earlier, on October 14, 1947, when then Captain Charles "Chuck" Yeager exceeded the speed of sound in the Bell XS-1. The swept-wing Bell X-2, which followed it, was designed to reach speeds at which the problems of aerodynamic heating would come into play. The X-2 had a troublesome early development period, including an explosion while being carried by its Boeing EB-50A mother ship that cost the life of Bell test pilot Jean Ziegler and an observer on board the EB-50A, Frank Wolko. After three years of intensive tests, on July 23, 1956, Captain Frank Everest flew the X-2 to a speed of 1,900.34 mph (Mach 2.87), earning Everest instant identification as "the fastest man alive."

Korean ace Ivan Kincheloe took over X-2 test duties from Everest, setting an altitude record of 126,200 feet on September 7, 1956. Twenty days later, Captain Milburn Apt would fly the Bell X-2 on its thirteenth powered flight, pushing it to and beyond its maximum capabilities. Apt reached a speed of 2,094 mph (Mach 3.196) before the aircraft plunged out of control, carrying him to his death.

The most advanced and perhaps most successful of the X-planes, the

North American X-15, made its first glide flight on March 10, 1959, with the company test pilot, the irrepressible Scott Crossfield, at the controls. Three X-15s were built, and in 199 flights, they set many records, including a peak altitude of 354,200 feet and a speed of 4,534 mph (Mach 6.72). The X-15 also served as a test bed for dozens of experiments to explore the hazards of high-altitude hypersonic flight.

While these and other X-aircraft were tested, the test pilots of Edwards had a field day with new aircraft (year of first flight in parentheses), including the Boeing B-52 (1952), Convair YF-102 (1953), Convair F-106A (1956), Convair B-58 (1956), Douglas B-66 (1954), Lockheed F-104 (1954), Lockheed U-2 (1954), Lockheed C-130 (1954), McDonnell F-101 (1954), North American YF-100 (1953), North American YF-107A (1956), Northrop T-38 (1959), Republic YF-105 (1955) and a host of less well known planes.

These new weapon systems would provide SAC, TAC, and ADC tremendous new capabilities, the latter two commands especially benefiting as they expanded their capabilities despite roller-coaster budgetary changes.

THE DEFENSE REORGANIZATION ACT OF 1958

President Dwight Eisenhower had spent thirty-nine years in the military, rising from West Point cadet to Chief of Staff, and then after retirement being recalled to serve as the first Supreme Allied Commander, Europe, from 1950 to 1952. As a two-term President, he also enjoyed eight years as Commander in Chief, for what might be said to be a total of forty-nine years of combined military service. There is some irony in that it was this quintessential military commander who contributed two vital elements to the basic idea of civilian control over the military. The first of these was his often misconstrued remarks about the military-industrial complex, which have been a rallying cry for the antimilitary over the intervening years.

The second, and far more significant, was his insistence upon the Department of Defense Reorganization Act of 1958. Eisenhower was influenced by a number of factors, the most important of which was his belief that joint and unified commands had worked so well during World War II that some means had to be created to make sure they would be used by the U.S. military in a new emergency. Unremitting interservice rivalry had convinced him that the contemporary DOD arrangement would not ensure this. Disturbed by a series of reports that indicated that the growth of technology had obscured military service roles and made them more competitive than complementary, disgusted by the turf wars indulged in by the members of the Joint Chiefs of Staff, and alarmed by the fact that the Secretary of Defense had been more preoccupied with resolving these turf wars than with initiating military policy, Eisenhower tasked his new Secretary of Defense, Neil H. McElroy, to reform the DOD.

McElroy employed a committee that included the incumbent JCS chairman General Twining and drafted legislation that Congress quickly passed and Eisenhower signed into law on August 6, 1958. In essence, the reorganization placed few limits on the powers of the Secretary of Defense, removing the service secretaries, the Army and Air Force Chiefs of Staff, and the Navy Chief of Naval Operations from the line of operational command. This was an unprecedented departure from American military tradition. The operational chain of command now ran from the President to the Secretary of Defense and through the JCS to the unified and specified commanders. In effect this meant that the Chief of Staff of the Air Force no longer commanded its combat forces, but instead was responsible for their creation, training, and support. When combat forces were to be used in a specific military mission, they were to come under the command of the unified or specified commander, who had full operational control, and who might or might not be an Air Force officer. Reasonably enough, this element of the reorganization has been difficult for many of the succeeding Chiefs and CNOs to accept; for some their lack of acceptance has bordered on denial. The nonoperational line of command flowed from the President to the Secretary of Defense and then to the service secretaries.

Some of the impact of the 1958 act was obscured in its language. Although the original unification act of 1947 had called for three military departments to be separately administered, the 1958 act specified a Department of Defense with three military departments—a subtle but significant difference that handed the keys of the castle to the SecDef. The Secretary of Defense was authorized to establish single agencies to conduct any service or supply activity common to two or more of the services.

This seemingly logical organizational construct paved the way for a loss of control by the military services over several areas of critical *war-making* importance. Only four examples will be given here. The first was the establishment of the control and direction of military research and development in the Director of Defense Research and Engineering in the DOD. This action is now considered by many to be a potentially fatal flaw in the defense establishment, for it removes the military services from the essential decision-making process and places it in the hands of civilian appointees who may or may not have an adequate understanding of future military requirements. The general effect is to circumvent all R&D efforts whose results cannot be guaranteed as to effectiveness, schedule, and cost. Its direct effect is to inhibit managers from attempting projects, no matter what their ultimate value, if they cannot guarantee success—the antithesis of normal R&D philosophy.

A less obvious deficiency came to light during the Vietnam War. In the process of consolidating authority in the DOD, the mission of targeting was removed from the Department of the Air Force and passed to the Defense Intelligence Agency, where it promptly (and naturally) withered and died from a lack of interest—it was no one's rice bowl in that organization. The analysis of enemy logistic capability somehow defaulted to the CIA, so that when the Air Force entered the war in Vietnam, it had very limited tools to assess the enemy's logistic flow for determining interdiction missions.

As another example of good intentions gone awry, the next chapter will show how Eisenhower's desire for a unified command was, under the direction of the Secretary of Defense, carried to such extremes in Vietnam that it forced the abandonment of the air doctrine learned at such great expense in World War II and Korea.

The fourth and most all-embracing deficiency in the Defense Reorganization Act of 1958 was that, in the words of Colonel Harry C. Summers, Jr., USA (Retired), the military had become "merely a logistics and management system to organize, train and equip active duty and reserve forces." The concept of the senior military professional, schooled in warfare, dedicated to a life of service to his country, and using his wisdom to create policy, was abandoned to the hands of competent, well-meaning civilians who are appointed to the role of assistant secretary for this or that as a part of their civil career progress, but who usually do not claim military expertise and cannot be expected to have the ability to craft the long-term goals of the services in planning or to direct them in execution. This policy of political displacement is not followed in industry. Willing and able novices do not substitute for experienced chief surgeons, for large fund managers, for automobile company presidents, or for any position in any progression where experience, specialized education, and long-term devotion are required.

Neither McElroy, who served from October 9, 1957, to December 1, 1959, nor his successor as Secretary of Defense, Thomas S. Gates, Jr., who served from December 2, 1959, to January 20, 1961, had the personality or the tenure in office to make full use of their newly conferred powers, although McElroy did a great service in establishing the Advanced Research Projects Agency (ARPA) within the Department of Defense. ARPA (later DARPA) was chartered to provide unified direction of antimissile programs and outer-space projects. The newly elected President, John F. Kennedy, had originally asked the veteran and admired Robert A. Lovett to be his Secretary of Defense. Lovett, who had done brilliantly in all his work at the Pentagon, including his 1951–1953 stint as Secretary of Defense, demurred because of his age. And while Lovett did not know him personally, a vigorous young man named Robert McNamara had been recommended to him. Lovett passed on the recommendation to Kennedy, saying that what the Pentagon needed was a good administrator rather than a man on horseback who would be intent on making all the decisions. In a career characterized by good calls, Lovett had finally made a bad one. On January 21, 1961, McNamara became Secretary of Defense, and he would use the Defense Reorganization Act of 1958 like a master puppeteer, gathering the strings of control to his office on an ever-increasing basis. He would also be, in the opinion of a great many senior officers of all the services, the absolute worst Secretary of Defense in the nation's history. Extremely bright and able to spot instantaneously the most innocuous error on a briefing chart, he hammered subordinates and assistants alike with his amazing grasp of detail and memory so that he could win arguments even when he was wrong. His insistence on having the last word would lead to major debacles like the attempted procurement of the TFX fighter to serve both the U.S. Navy and U.S. Air Force, and major tragedies like Vietnam, where his philosophy of graduated response would simultaneously nullify air power even as it immured ground power.

Throughout the 1950s, the decline in the power of the office of the Secretary of the Air Force continued undiminished. It was mitigated in part by the conciliatory efforts of James H. Douglas, Jr., who had been Under Secretary for four years before taking office on May 1, 1957. Douglas had managed to soothe relations between his office and the Air Staff and was able to fight the budget cuts demanded by Secretary of Defense Wilson. Douglas's successor, Dudley S. Sharp, served just over a year, from December 11, 1959, to January 20, 1961, and, as a lame duck, was unable to provide vigorous leadership.

Both Douglas and Sharp benefited from their association with the Air Force Chief of Staff, General White. White, an intellectual, was fluent in Chinese, Greek, Italian, Portuguese, Russian, and Spanish. Understated and refined, he understood the implications of nuclear strategy and the impending space age as well as he knew the grass-roots politics of the Pentagon. His successor, General LeMay, would work shoulder to shoulder with the next Secretary of the Air Force, Eugene B. Zuckert, in their joint—and losing—battle with Secretary McNamara.

THE UNDERDOGS: TAC AND ADC

As organizations, the Tactical Air Command and the Air Defense Command (later Aerospace Defense Command) suffered from the roles in which fate had cast them. Although they executed their respective missions with panache, they were, for quite different reasons, always the bridesmaid but never the bride when it came to budget allocation and to their basic wartime roles. The role of SAC, as a specified command, was always well defined, and even when in the Korean and Vietnam wars SAC sent units into combat, the basic integrity of its deterrent mission was preserved. TAC's mission was preparing units for war; when war came those units were assigned to a unified command, such as the Pacific Air Force. ADC units were also seconded to PACAF during the Vietnam War, and when the fighting was over these individual ADC and TAC units came back covered with a glory that did not directly transfer to their parent commands. ADC's principal difficulty, however, was that the threat for which it was created diminished just as ADC came into full flower.

TAC's Mission and Operations

From the start, the mission of the Tactical Air Command was to command, organize, equip, train, and administer the forces assigned and attached to participate in tactical air operations. Like SAC, it was established on March 21, 1946. Unlike SAC, it was soon reduced in status, when in January 1949 it was absorbed into the Continental Air Command. The advent of the Korean War caused it to be reestablished as an active command in August 1950. It built up rapidly during the war, as a host of new responsibilities were added to its mission, including electronic countermeasures, increased airlift capability, and air-ground operations.

After the Korean War, the defense budget had been increased and the technological advances of the previous ten years were being translated into hardware. In an incredibly short period of time, TAC went from its essentially World War II origins to a force equipped with jet fighters and bombers. Tactical nuclear weapons became available, and at about the same time, supersonic fighters. Aerial refueling turned TAC into an ocean-hopping force, and new transports, including the versatile and long-lived Lockheed C-130, came into the inventory. Among the advanced aircraft and missiles were the century-series fighters, including the Lockheed F-104, North American F-100, McDonnell F-101 and RF-101, and Republic F-105. New bombers included the Douglas B-66 and RB-66 and the Martin B-57. The Matador surface-to-surface missile came into use with the 1st and 69th Pilotless Bomber Squadrons, the designation another artless attempt to make the roles and missions more palatable to the Army. About 1,000 Matadors were built; they were succeeded by the Mace, which was retired in 1966.

General Otto P. "Opie" Weyland, fresh from his duties as Commander, FEAF, and just after reorganizing Japan's air defense and aircraft industry, assumed command of TAC on May 1, 1954. Weyland appreciated the new weaponry, but his long experience in limited warfare put him in advance of his time as he advocated the development of the "Composite Air Strike Force" (CASF), an organization that foreshadowed the development of composite units in today's Air Force. The CASF was very mobile and self-contained, with its own fighters, bombers, and transport aircraft. Weyland tested the concept in 1956, during Operation Mobile Baker, which sent fighters, reconnaissance planes, bombers, and tankers from a variety of U.S. bases to Europe.

The first real test of the CASF came on July 15, 1958, with the Lebanon crisis. President Eisenhower ordered the CASF into action, and within twelve hours, it was arriving in at Adana, Turkey. Just over a month later, during the week of August 23, another CASF strike force was sent to reinforce U.S. forces during the Quemoy-Matsu crisis.

TAC used its mobility and its cargo capacity in a succession of humanitarian missions, including delivering medical equipment to Argentina and iron lungs to Japan. Such missions of compassion would become increasingly important in the years to come.

Weyland and his immediate successor, General Frank F. Everest, had maintained TAC's capability and its personality. Under their leadership, TAC remained a freewheeling outfit, mission-oriented but not as concerned with conformity and centralized control as SAC. Yet while TAC's mission had remained much the same, the world of air combat was maturing. The new equipment, and especially the tactical nuclear weapons, demanded a more rigorous environment. It came, in what many veterans of the period describe as the best thing ever to happen to TAC, in the person of General Walter Campbell Sweeney, Jr., who took command on August 1, 1961.

In the phrase of the time, TAC was "SACimcised," for Sweeney was a tough but fair commander who had fought the Pacific war from the battle of Midway on and led the first low-level attack on Tokyo. He became the Commander of SAC's Fifteenth Air Force; in 1954 he led a flight of three B-47s in history's first nonstop jet bomber flight across the Pacific, an event depicted in the Jimmy Stewart film *Strategic Air Command*. In the next few years, TAC's élan and skill would be enhanced by Sweeney's discipline and rigor, enabling its units to operate well under the Pacific Air Command in the tough years to come in Vietnam. Inevitably, however, Sweeney's centralized and authoritarian methods, supercharged by the methods emanating from Mc-Namara's DOD, would be carried to an extreme. Change would come in the 1970s.

THE AIR DEFENSE COMMAND: OPERATIONS AND MISSION

Like TAC, the Air Defense Command did not have the same visibility as SAC, in part because of external events. When the Cold War began, the Soviet threat was limited, but so were ADC's capabilities in terms of aircraft, radar defenses, and weapons. Over the decade of the 1950s, ADC grew strong in all these areas, with new supersonic aircraft being supported by an increasingly sophisticated radar network and equipped with armament of ever-greater lethality.

Even as ADC flourished, the Soviet threat began to shift from bombers to ICBMs. There always remained the possibility that the enemy would launch a bomber attack, in conjunction with, or as a follow-up to, an ICBM attack, but the bomber threat was relatively less terrifying. In January 1958, ADC's name was changed to Aerospace Defense Command, to reflect the dual threat. Unfortunately, any budget conflict within the Air Force began to be resolved with cuts for ADC, and it would diminish in size and importance over time until in 1980 it was inactivated and its assests absorbed by TAC and SAC.

Duty for ADC personnel, officers and enlisted, aircrew and ground crew, was very difficult. Most of the ADC bases were located in the north, and weather conditions were often miserable. The bases had few amenities, and the alert crews had to stay next to their airplanes in drafty hangars and be ready to launch no matter how bad the weather was outside. It was not uncommon in far-northern bases for the snow to be so deep that an aircraft taking off could not be seen until it lifted above snow walls lining the runways. After an intercept—usually of some errant passenger liner—the approach to a landing was often made with the low-fuel warning lights winking red, so that the pilot knew he had only one shot at the snowbound runway. With a minimum ceiling and visibility and frequently gale-force crosswinds, it was enough to make even an expert's palms sweat. It was also enough to make pilots who survived experts.

Other factors impacted adversely on morale. The original ADC equipment—North American F-51s, North American F-82s, and Lockheed F-80Cs—barely had the performance to intercept Tu-4-type aircraft under visual conditions. The first generation of all-weather fighters—the Lockheed F-94 and the Northrop F-89—had a series of problems that took years to resolve. The early airborne radars were difficult to keep in operation, and as the F-94 had no deicing equipment, it was unsuitable for many weather conditions. The F-89 had a very long development process, with several crashes because of structural and engine failures. While both of these aircraft were adequate to meet the Soviet piston-engine threat, their capability against jet bombers was marginal. It was extremely difficult for them to intercept B-47s, especially when the six-jet bomber would turn into them, and even the older B-36 flew at altitudes beyond their reach.

The Air Defense Command recognized the problem and sought to field an array of advanced aircraft and missile weapon systems. The aircraft requirement was to be met by the emerging century series of fighters, which offered promise of extraordinary performance but, as might be expected, suffered teething problems that delayed their entry into service. The medium-range Convair F-102 Delta Dagger—always called the Deuce—entered service first, in mid-1956, and was the first USAF fighter to be designed as a missile carrier. The Deuce, which saw service in thirty-two squadrons, was succeeded by the Convair F-106 Delta Dart—always called the Six—which equipped fourteen squadrons beginning in 1959. The F-106 was fitted with the Hughes MA-1 electronic guidance and fire control system and was designed to operate with the SAGE (Semiautomatic Ground Environment) defense system. The McDonnell F-101B long-range interceptor also entered service in 1959, and eventually equipped seventeen squadrons. The Lockheed F-104 was pressed into small-scale service on two occasions by ADC, but it was not an all-weather fighter by any standards and was clearly an interim measure.

All of the century-series aircraft had the equipment and the performance to intercept incoming bombers, but all were beset by maintenance difficulties that kept too large a percentage of aircraft out of commission. The art of shooting down a bomber had changed considerably, calling for equally new weapons that themselves were beset by development problems. ADC pilots regarded the 2.75-inch-diameter unguided rockets as virtually worthless and derisively called the early Hughes GAR-1 (later AIM-4) Falcon the "sand-seeker" (as opposed to heat-seeker) because it was so unreliable. The most impressive of the missiles was the MB-1 (later AIR-2) Genie, an unguided rocket with a 1.5-kiloton nuclear warhead that had a lethal radius of over 1,000 yards. The 822-pound Genie had a range of about 10 miles and could be fired from a pull-up maneuver that placed even high-flying aircraft in range. In operation, the fire control system (which varied with the aircraft) tracked the target, designated the missiles to be used, instructed the pilot to arm the warhead, fired the missile, then pulled the aircraft into a tight turn to avoid the resulting nuclear blast. The first live Genie was fired by a Northrop F-89J over Yucca Flat, Nevada, on July 19, 1957. Despite the demonstration, aircrews felt a natural apprehension about using a nuclear weapon to explode a bomber carrying nuclear weapons—they could not be sure that they would elude the resulting blast. (It is not generally known that ADC fighters of the period were often launched to unfamiliar civilian airfield dispersal sites with nuclear Genie missiles fully armed and ready to fire. TAC fighters of the period on full alert presented the same hazard. A similar undertaking today would be met with the full fury of environmentalists and homeowners' associations along with full-page headlines in the press.)

While development of a short-range missile system for base defense was left to the Army because of the basic issue of roles and missions, ADC's interceptors were complemented by the Bomarc medium-range interceptor missile. The Bomarc was intended for fixed-base defense of a huge area and was created through the cooperation of Boeing and the Michigan Aeronautical Research Center at the University of Michigan. Fifty-three Bomarc squadrons were initially specified, and thirty-six were ultimately acquired. The Bomarc was the world's first surface-to-air missile with an active homing system. Originally designated the XF-99 (once again maintaining the fiction of "it's just another airplane"), it was subsequently called the IM-99A and later the CIM-10A. Looking like a very sleek airplane, the Bomarc was vertically launched (on thirty seconds' notice from SAGE) by a 50,000-pound-thrust solid-fuel Thiokol rocket motor. In flight, two 12,000-pound-thrust Marquardt ramjets took over to boost it to its cruising height of 65,000 feet and cruise speed of Mach 3. At about 10 miles distance, the Westinghouse DPN-34 radar locked on the target. Conventional or nuclear warheads could be carried. The Bomarc was highly successful against many high-speed drone targets, and 570 were built. Its first flight occurred on September 10, 1952, and it served for twenty years.

Both missiles and aircraft depended upon ground radars to detect incoming bombers, and mammoth amounts of energy and money were spent by the United States and Canada during the decade to create an enormous early warning system. When the Soviet bomber threat was first recognized in 1950, there were no radar warning lines, and World War II radars were pulled out of storage and installed in makeshift buildings in an operation aptly named Lashup. The Ground Observer Corps, which could trace its origins to Great Britain in World War I, was revived and thousands of volunteers vigilantly watched the northern skies to supplement the fragile radar network of forty Lashup stations.

The threat was so great that a decision was made to build the Distant Early Warning (DEW) Line stretching more than 3,000 miles across the 69th parallel, spanning the frozen north from Barter Island, Alaska, to Thule, Greenland. These DEW Line stations called for highly skilled, dedicated technicians who could man them without regard to weather, absence from family, and the almost overpowering boredom. These, like many ADC and related assignments, were truly hardship postings that often created long-term problems, for alcoholic drinks were very inexpensive and often the only apparent anodyne. The DEW Line began test operation in 1953 and was completed by 1955.

Canada was a full partner in the defense effort, and besides supplying nine squadrons of the excellent Avro CF 100 fighter, it cooperated in building the Pinetree Line of aircraft control and warning centers about 1,000 miles farther south than the DEW line. A third line—the Mid-Canada Line—was built across the 55th parallel from Labrador to Hudson Bay. The Mid-Canada Line was to confirm the attack and scramble the interceptors, while the Pinetree Line and permanent radar stations in the United States would guide the interceptors to the bombers. The radar network was further supplemented by the construction of Texas tower sites in the North Atlantic and by the operation of airborne early warning aircraft.

All of this monumental effort—century-series aircraft, supersonic missiles, and extensive radar warning nets—was designed to culminate in the Semiautomatic Ground Environment (SAGE) system. Designed by the Lincoln Laboratory, an organization founded under an agreement by the Air Force with the Massachusetts Institute of Technology, SAGE harnessed giant computers to process the masses of incoming data from the radar sights, Ground Observer Corps, aircraft, and elsewhere. Threats were identified and fighters were designated to intercept the bombers.

ADC had divided the United States into eight air defense regions, each one with a SAGE combat operation center, and thirty-two air defense sectors, each with a SAGE direction center. SAGE installations were elaborate structures of concrete, some designed to withstand nuclear blasts and keep functioning. The first SAGE direction center became operational at McGuire Air Force Base, New Jersey, in 1957, and by 1963 the system, inevitably reduced by budget cuts to twenty-two air defense sectors in the United States and one in Canada, was complete. SAGE was supplemented by the Back-Up Interceptor Control (BUIC) system and would serve until it was replaced by the Joint Surveillance System (JSS) in 1983.

Initially, SAGE's reach for automation exceeded the contemporary level of computer grasp, and controllers were often forced to resort to the manual direction of interceptors, just as controllers had done during the Battle of Britain. The general consensus in the early days of operation was that in the event of an actual attack, the automatic system would be bypassed and directions given manually. Like all such sophisticated systems, it was improved over time and came to serve very efficiently.

Ironically, all of the great ADC effort—fighters, missiles, and SAGE—culminated in an increasingly efficient fighting machine just shortly after the time when the perceived threat of bombers began to decline. Premier Khrushchev had stated that the Soviet Union was emphasizing ICBMs rather than missiles, and it was eventually determined that the USSR indeed had not built as many Bison or Bear aircraft as it could have. General LeMay himself recognized that ICBMs were the major threat, noting that the principal task of the early warning radars was to give SAC sufficient time to scramble its bombers. To ensure that this time—now down to a virtually irreducible fifteen minutes—would be available, two Ballistic Missile Early Warning Sites were begun in 1959, one in Point Clear, Alaska, and the other in Thule, Greenland.

ADC's organizational road was as rocky as its equipment development had been. It became a part of the North American Aerospace Defense Command (NORAD) in 1957, and over time its strength was reduced as its tasks were assigned to Air National Guard and Air Force Reserve units. As previously noted, it was ultimately deactivated in 1980, with its remaining assets divided between TAC and SAC.

Because of the nature of its duties and the placement of its far-flung bases, ADC developed a culture of its own. The isolation and the sense of frustration at flying a mission in which the best possible outcome was that nothing would happen led to discipline and morale problems. The offset, as far as pilots were concerned, was the demanding nature of the flying, for when the word came to scramble, they had to be prepared to go no matter how bad the weather was. This rigor weeded out inferior pilots, and when ADC pilots were assigned to other duties such as close air support, they did exceptionally well, despite a lack of training in the specialty.

CONCLUSION

The United States Air Force had mastered a number of challenges in the eleven years from 1950 to 1961. It became a professional military force in being amidst a technological revolution of unprecedented scope and complexity. Even as its forces were massively expanded, it achieved ever higher levels of proficiency. The great expense and greater lethality of the new weapon systems were recognized, and met with corresponding improvements in procedures, doctrine, and discipline. The combat capability of SAC, TAC, and ADC units was made possible only by a corresponding growth in size and efficiency of supporting commands that will be covered in the following chapters.

5

THE MANY FACETS OF WAR

*I*n his 1960 Presidential campaign, Senator John F. Kennedy railed against the Eisenhower administration for being so dependent upon the concept of massive retaliation that it was incapable of fighting limited wars. Kennedy also charged that an inept Department of Defense policy of "sufficiency" in nuclear arms had created a "missile gap" such that the Soviet Union's ICBM capability now exceeded that of the United States. He made a number of strong recommendations for a new defense posture, including increasing defense appropriations, improving conventional forces as well as their airlift capability, and greatly increasing civil defense measures. After his election, Kennedy tasked the members of his new administration to rectify the problems he had pointed out, work that the new Secretary of Defense, Robert S. McNamara, eagerly embraced.

During the campaign, Kennedy had endorsed the views of retired Army General Maxwell D. Taylor on the strategy of flexible response. The concept had been first articulated in 1954 in *The Realities of American Foreign Policy* by the respected George F. Kennan. As Army Chief of Staff, Taylor had expanded on the idea, and some of his concepts were expressed in Army Field Manual 100-5, even though they were not whole heartedly accepted by the Department of Defense. A glamorous wartime figure who led the 101st Airborne Division into France on D day, he remained prominent after his retirement in July 1959, putting forth his ideas in his well-received book *Uncertain Trumpet*. In essence, Taylor stated that the bomber and missile fleet had become too large and possessed an "overkill" capability. It was now time for the Army and the Navy to build up their forces so that they could react decisively to limited wars. He called for a process, later adopted in modified form by Secretary McNamara, to revise the military budget so that it would show in terms of operational forces how much defense money bought.

In Taylor's view, the policy of massive retaliation had been appropriate only when the Soviet Union did not possess a comparable nuclear power. When the Soviet Union attained a relative parity in nuclear strength, the strategy of massive retaliation became a handicap, reducing conventional forces, like NATO units in Europe, to mere trip wires for setting off a nuclear exchange. Taylor held that unless the United States was willing to unleash a massive attack on the enemy—and suffer the consequent counterattack—a massive retaliation strategy meant that we could not intervene in any limited war the USSR might instigate. In effect, the enemy could nibble away at the rest of the free world, taking one country at a time through intimidation, Sputnik diplomacy, limited brushfire wars, and fomenting of internal revolutions.

His belief that a tenfold "overkill" of nuclear power currently existed was attractive to the Army and the Navy, and they supported his call for finite— and reduced—bomber and missile forces. These would still be sufficient to provide a nuclear deterrent, the all important "air-atomic" shield under which the revitalized conventional Army and Navy forces could handle limited war. Admiral Arleigh "30-Knot" Burke, who had been the Navy's point man in the infamous "Revolt of the Admirals," embraced the argument, for the concept of a finite deterrent capability with its corollary of "controlled retaliation" helped make the case for the Polaris submarine fleet. The banner of the new strategy thus bore a haunting resemblance to the old turf wars.

As might be expected, General White expressed the USAF's disagreement with Taylor's ideas rather eloquently, while General LeMay was more direct. White's superior intellect gave Taylor pause and might in fact have intimidated him. White argued, "Our strategic objective in the event of global war is to eliminate an enemy's war-making capacity in the minimum period of time. In determining the force requirements to do this, we must take into account not only the number, location and vulnerability of the targets, but the reliability, accuracy and warhead yield of our weapons as well as countless operational variables, and the evaluation of the expected enemy defense."

LeMay's view was: "A deterrent force is one that is large enough and efficient enough that no matter what the enemy does, either offensively or defensively, he will still receive a quantity of bombs or explosive force that is more than he is willing to accept." White and LeMay did not agree that the strategic air and missile forces should be reduced to an as yet undefined "finite" limit.

Despite the demonstrated success of the USAF strategy through 1960, Taylor's views would ultimately prevail, especially after Kennedy called him out of retirement in October 1962 to become the Chairman of the Joint Chiefs of Staff. Even before he assumed his new office, Taylor's doctrines provided the most important impetus to the long series of events that propelled the United States into a full-scale military involvement in Vietnam. There "flexible response" became a conveyor belt that ultimately fed 536,100 troops to fight what every thinking American military man had always abhorred: a land war in Asia.

Five American Presidents, from Harry Truman to Richard Nixon, would be involved in the problems of Vietnam. The Kennedy administration's entanglement began on a low-key basis in 1961, a year that was studded with a series of crises that validated Taylor's views that limited warfare would dominate the future. The first erupted in Laos in the spring of 1961, when the new President supported a coalition led by Prince Souvanna Phouma that was resisting a Communist takeover. Following his stated policy of coordinating military and diplomatic action, Kennedy showed the flag with Marine and naval air forces while working with members of the Southeast Asia Treaty Organization (SEATO) to reach an agreement in negotiations at Geneva. The crisis subsided, even if Communist subversion did not; it would continue throughout the Vietnam War.

The second emergency was in the beleaguered nation of Congo, where an emergency airlift, Operation New Tape, had been underway since July 1960. (It would last until January 1964 and be a true testimony to the skill and courage of the men flying the Military Air Transport Service Douglas C-124s, Douglas C-133s, Lockheed C-130s, and Boeing C-135s. It was a long and difficult trip from England or Germany to Elizabethville, with primitive landing fields, few en route navigational facilities, and no weather reporting.) Kennedy made a speech at the United Nations on September 25, 1961, taking note of Communist support of disturbances—called "wars of liberation" by Premier Nikita Khrushchev—in the Congo, Laos, South Vietnam, India, Berlin, and elsewhere, and challenged the Soviet Union to a "peace race" instead of an arms race.

Khrushchev was euphoric because of the repeated Soviet space achievements, stating with his customary diplomatic finesse, "We have bombs stronger than 100 megatons. We placed Gagarin and Titov in orbit, and we can replace them with other loads that can be directed to any place on earth." The Soviet premier, brought up in the hard knocks of the Communist Party and World War II, discounted Kennedy as young, inexperienced, and vulnerable to pressure. Intending to torque up the tension, he announced that he intended to sign a separate peace treaty with the German Democratic Republic (East Germany), believing that this action would force the three Allied powers out of Berlin, as the Berlin Blockade had been intended to do.

Kennedy—a clutch player despite Khrushchev's assessment—was determined not to yield, even though he was aware that NATO forces were inadequate for a conventional war and that if conflict came, he might have to toss Taylor's ideas out the window and resort to nuclear war to defend Europe. The Strategic Air Command accelerated its ground alert, and six wings of B-47s scheduled for inactivation were retained on duty. Thirty-six Air National Guard and Air Force Reserve airlift squadrons were activated and the inactivation scheduled for a number of older tactical fighter and transport units was canceled.

The East German civil populace, particularly its youth, voted with its feet in a 4,000-person-per-week-exodus through Berlin. This drain of the best and the brightest was an intolerable commentary on life in a Soviet satellite and was met with a Soviet solution: the erection of the Berlin Wall.

The tension over Berlin had just begun to subside when President Kennedy was confronted by a new and potentially even more explosive crisis. His administration, somewhat to its embarrassment, had become aware soon after the election that the issue of a missile gap had been a fabrication, and that the United States was qualitatively and quantitatively superior in terms of ICBMs. (The Eisenhower administration had been unable to refute Kennedy's charges during the election without revealing its intelligence sources.) This very superiority, however, had untoward effects in 1962, even as Khrushchev smarted from his rebuff over Berlin.

The so-called missile gap had failed to materialize because the Soviet Union had rightly been dissatisfied with its cumbersome and vulnerable first generation of liquid-fueled ICBMs and had virtually ceased their production, turning instead to medium-range and intermediate-range ballistic missiles (MRBMs and IRBMs). Adequate for deployment in Europe, they offered no threat to the continental United States, which had deployed similar-range Thor missiles in England, Italy, and Turkey. To close its own missile gap and offset its ICBM deficiency, the Soviet Union courted the newly established regime of Fidel Castro in Cuba, with the aim of placing IRBMs there. Thus, in the way of politics, the spurious Kennedy "missile gap" inverted itself to become a genuine crisis in Cuba.

THE CUBAN MISSILE CRISIS

Cuba was extraordinarily attractive to the Soviet Union, for it offered a base within 90 miles of the United States and a conduit for intervention in Central and South America. The United States had been maladroit in its treatment of Fidel Castro's new regime, established in January 1959, and looked on helplessly as the bearded leader turned more and more to Moscow for support. The situation was exacerbated in April 1961 when a newly inaugurated President Kennedy sanctioned the abortive Bay of Pigs invasion by Cuban counterrevolutionaries.

In keeping with its policy of applying pressure at peripheral points all over the globe, the Soviet Union began supplying Cuba with arms at an ever-increasing rate, sweetening the deal with subsidized sugar purchases to maintain the island's economy. When the United States protested the heavy influx of tanks, artillery, antiaircraft guns, SA-2 surface-to-air missiles, and more than fifty MiG-15,-17, and-19 fighters, Khrushchev replied that these were purely defensive weapons. His reply was inadequate, for the Soviet presence represented an incursion on the long-standing Monroe Doctrine, which excluded foreign bases from the Western Hemisphere. The threats to the U.S. naval facility at Guantánamo Bay and to the Panama Canal were intolerable—as was the loss of American prestige.

On October 14, two expert U-2 pilots of the 4080th Strategic Reconnaissance Wing, Majors Richard S. Heyser and Rudolf Anderson, Jr., brought back photographs that proved conclusively that the Soviet Union was building offensive missile sites in the San Cristóbal area. Follow-up flights revealed Ilyushin Il-28 Beagle medium bombers being assembled, and evidence that there were both 1,000-mile-range MRBM and 2,000-mile-range IRBM sites being prepared. Succeeding flights showed that work was proceeding at a feverish pace, and that within two weeks, the Soviet Union would have in place as many as two dozen missiles capable of reaching almost every heavily populated area in the Western Hemisphere.

Aware of the utter gravity of the situation and determined not to have a repeat of the Bay of Pigs fiasco, the President established an Executive Committee of the National Security Council and made his brother Robert, the Attorney General, chairman. Other members included Secretary of Defense McNamara; Secretary of State Dean Rusk and his undersecretary, George Ball; Director of Central Intelligence John McCone; National Security Adviser McGeorge Bundy; and Chairman of the JCS General Taylor.

Normal diplomatic relations with the Soviet Union proceeded as the ExComm, as it was called, met in secret, reviewing all the intelligence data and seeing what it could select to solve the basic problem of getting the Soviet offensive capability out of Cuba without starting World War III.

The full array of flexible response options was considered. The primary proposal by the military was to take out the missiles, bombers, and air defenses in a large-scale attack. Other options included a "surgical" air strike, an invasion by conventional forces, or a blockade. (Historically, "surgical" air strikes have always been a favorite choice of nonfliers. Fliers have been less optimistic, aware that such surgery was difficult to carry out effectively and without collateral damage. Today, with precision-guided munitions, it is a better option.) The blockade—termed a "naval quarantine" because no state of war existed—was finally accepted as a means of applying a carefully calculated degree of power under the shield of America's nuclear capability.

The Strategic Air Command was placed on full alert, with almost seventy B-52s airborne, fully armed, and prepared to fulfill their war mission on an instant's notice. In addition, almost every ounce of existing U.S. strength was mobilized and sent south, to Florida if there was room, or to other Southern states if there was not.

In perhaps the most stirring address of his career, President Kennedy informed the American public of the existence of the Soviet missile threat in a television broadcast on the evening of October 22. He made it clear that the United States was not dealing with Cuba, but with the Soviet Union, and that it was prepared to use the entire weight of its war-making capability to ensure that the missiles were removed. Kennedy announced that the naval quarantine would be lifted only when the Soviet offensive weapons were removed and the missile sites destroyed. The full measure of his determination was revealed when he said, "It shall be the policy of this nation to regard any nuclear missile launched from Cuba against any nation in the Western Hemisphere as an attack by the Soviet Union on the United States, requiring a full retaliatory response upon the Soviet Union."

The first sign of the possibility of a resolution came when Soviet ships bound for Cuba reached the 500-mile boundary line of the quarantine, stopped, then turned around. On October 26, Premier Khrushchev sent a long, lugubrious message to President Kennedy, followed the next day by a shorter, much tougher one that demanded the removal of U.S. missiles from Turkey. Both letters, however, indicated that the Soviet Union recognized the danger of a miscalculation leading to a nuclear exchange, and that it sought a way out. The slight relief in tension was clouded on the 27th, however, when Major Anderson, one of the heroes of the October 14 discovery, was shot down and killed in his Lockheed U-2 by an SA-2 missile.

The possibility of disastrous miscalculation was uppermost in the minds of both American and Soviet leaders as tension built. A considerable degree of private diplomatic activity went on, with the Soviet Union being assured first that the United States did not intend to invade, and second that the missiles in Turkey were going to be removed routinely later in the year. In a formal response to Khrushchev's first letter, Kennedy stated that the United States would guarantee not to invade Cuba if all work was stopped on offensive missile sites immediately, all offensive weapons were removed, and the site destruction was monitored by United Nations observers.

Khrushchev accepted the terms, and the crisis was over, although additional pressure had to be applied to secure the removal of the Il-28s. Secretary of State Rusk made a public statement to the effect that the two nations had stood eyeball to eyeball, and that the Soviet Union had blinked. Red China also took note of the Soviet backdown, which it regarded as cowardly, and relations between the two countries took a turn for the worse in succeeding years.

In later analyses of the crisis, two very unlikely characters found themselves in agreement on the reason for the American success, General LeMay and Premier Khrushchev. Both emphasized the importance of the American nuclear shield, with Khrushchev pointing out, "About 20 percent of all Strategic Air Command planes, carrying atomic and hydrogen bombs, were kept aloft around the clock." LeMay stated that he believed the success of the American efforts was due to SAC's superior strategic nuclear power and President Kennedy's obvious willingness to use it.

Commanding General of the U.S. Far East Air Forces, Lt. General Otto P. "Opie" Weyland, meets with Lt. General Laurence S. Kuter in Japan.

Colonel Harrison B. Thyng is shown receiving five awards—a cluster to his Silver Star, another cluster to his Distinguished Flying Cross, the Legion of Merit, and two more clusters to his Air Medal.

1957 brought a series of promotions to these four gentlemen. From the left, Under Secretary James N. Douglas would become Secretary of the Air Force; Secretary of the Air Force Donald A. Quarles would become Under Secretary of Defense; Chief of Staff General Nathan Twining would become Chairman of the Joint Chiefs of Staff; and Vice Chief of Staff General Thomas D. White would become Chief of Staff.

November 13, 1957: The legendary Commander of the Strategic Air Command, General Curtis E. LeMay, emerges from the Boeing KC-135 tanker, which he has just flown from Buenos Aires to Washington, D.C., in the record-setting time of eleven hours and five minutes. Secretary of the Air Force James Douglas shakes his hand while Air Force Chief of Staff Thomas D. White looks on.

From left: Lieutenant General Archie J. Old, Commander, 15th Air Force; Lieutenant General John P. McConnell, Commander, 2nd Air Force; General Thomas E. Power, Commander, Strategic Air Command; and Lieutenant General Walter C. Sweeney, Jr., Commander, 8th Air Force.

Telling the brass how it is. Captain Joel P. Gordes (left) and Captain Thomas G. Dorsett of the 363rd Tactical Reconnaissance Wing at Shaw Air Force Base, S.C., explain a McDonnell RF-4C mission to (from left) Secretary of the Air Force Robert C. Seamans, General William H. Momyer, Commander, Tactical Air Command, and General John D. Ryan, Chief of Staff, USAF.

The most advanced airplane in the world at the time of its debut in 1956, the super-sonic Consolidated B-58 Hustler bomber provided SAC with a dramatic supplement to the B-52. A high accident rate and soaring maintenance costs forced its withdrawal from service in 1970.

Necessity forced the Air Force to develop some unusual weapon systems. This is a Republic F-84F hooking up as a FICON aircraft to a Consolidated B-36.

The desire to have vertical take-off aircraft raged for a number of years; among the more successful was the Ryan X-13 Vertijet of 1956. The problem of all vertical take-off jets until the advent of the McDonnell Douglas AV-8B Harrier was first the landing, and second, the small payload.

Jack Northrop's jet-flying wing looked like the wave of the future, but an aging design and stability problems kept it from becoming operational.

The author's squadron and their aircraft at Kirtland Air Force Base, circa 1959.

First Lieutenant Bill Creech in the cockpit of his Lockheed F-80C in Korea. Creech would ultimately fly a total of 280 combat missions in Korea and Southeast Asia. *(Courtesy of General W. L. Creech)*

Twenty years ago, no one would have thought that a four-engine transport and heli-copters would be crucial to dominating the battlefield. Yet the Lockheed Martin MC-130P Combat Shadow/Tankers were used with spectacular effect by the 1st Special Operations Wing, refueling Sikorsky MH-53 Pave Low helicopters. *(Courtesy of Robert F. Dorr)*

History is made when Jeanne M. Holm, Director of Women in the Air Force, became the first woman general in Air Force history.

Although it defused the situation and avoided a nuclear exchange, the crisis revealed some deficiencies in the American military machine. As the Tactical Air Command had insisted for years, it had an insufficient number of fighter and cargo aircraft. The Army's general-purpose forces were not adequate for the occasion, and the Navy was desperately short of ships to enforce the quarantine. All of these would be addressed in the months to come, but the success in Cuba had another and more serious result. The members of the ExComm, most particularly Defense Secretary McNamara, National Security Adviser Bundy, and JCS Chairman Taylor, all came away with an inflated sense of their value in the management of the situation, and, more important, of the techniques used to respond to the behavior of the enemy. Their conclusions would be applied in far greater measure in Vietnam, only to result in a long, agonizing, divisive catastrophe.

THE TRAGEDY OF SOUTHEAST ASIA

Many mistakes were made during our involvement in Southeast Asia, but the most egregious mistake of all was Secretary McNamara's basing U.S. strategy for the conflict on the obvious fiction that the war was merely a civil insurrection within South Vietnam. McNamara knew full well that North Vietnam was behind the elaborate problem facing South Vietnam, yet he insisted on this fabrication as a basis for his military policy, for it enabled him to apply his concept of graduated response. In effect, the SecDef planned to educate the North Vietnamese, giving them a logical reason to accede to American policy. The education was simple carrot and stick: concessions for good behavior and varying degrees of punishment for varying degrees of bad behavior. This arrogant philosophy, a by-product of the administration's complete ignorance of the psychology of the North Vietnamese, derived more from Dr. Spock than Clausewitz. McNamara's powers of persuasion were so great that both Presidents Kennedy and Johnson acquiesced in the basic deceit of fighting a war as an insurrection, and thus abandoned traditional military strategy.

Their acceptance is difficult to understand, given that North Vietnam was totally involved in South Vietnam, from deploying regular army troops there to its maintenance of multiple logistic routes through Laos and Cambodia. Everyone was aware of the open, committed support the Soviet Union and China gave North Vietnam. The two giant powers overcame their contemporary mistrust of each other to unite in furnishing equipment, supplies, and training to North Vietnam. It was an excellent investment, for they traded relatively inexpensive military material for the total absorption of the United States into a war disapproved of by its allies, its media, and ultimately a significant and vocal proportion of its population. Nonetheless, McNamara continued to insist to the very end of his tenure that the war was a simple rebellion best handled within the confines of South Vietnam. McNamara was convinced that the North Vietnamese were a mere pawn for Red China, with which he (wisely) wanted to avoid war at all costs. (All through the war, McNamara's interpretation of intelligence data on China was overly pessimistic and did not realistically assess China's means or intentions.) A cursory study of the history of the area would have made it clear that North Vietnam had its own agenda, one that went back to its earliest roots, and that Ho Chi Minh was determined to unite Vietnam for his own regime and not for any other.

As a consequence of this flawed assumption and his acceptance of General Maxwell Taylor's advice, McNamara let the conflict develop into a ground war, with an eventual commitment of more than 500,000 troops—and 56,000 fatalities. Worse, from the point of view of the leaders of the USAF, he forfeited an opportunity to end the war in 1965—and many times thereafter—by the full application of air power. Instead he created a muddled framework of command and control that jettisoned all of the experience gained in the employment of air power in World War II and Korea. (The contention that he forfeited an opportunity to end the war in 1965 might be a matter of debate, were it not for Linebacker II in late December 1972, which proved that it could have been done.)

With the fussy precision of a dedicated executive accountant, McNamara declaimed that the war in Vietnam was to be a laboratory for handling counterinsurgency. McNamara's all-knowing attitude permeated his staff, who came to regard advice from senior military officers as a mere irritant. A rather typical incident captures this attitude of omniscience and contempt for military planners. In early 1965, the North Vietnamese began building surface-to-air missile sites around Hanoi and Haiphong. General William C. Westmoreland, Commander of U.S. Military Assistance Command, Vietnam (COMUSMACV), and Major General Joseph H. Moore, Commander of the 2d Air Division, asked permission to knock them out. Their request was refused, and Assistant Secretary of Defense John T. McNaughton admonished them, "You don't think the North Vietnamese are going to use them! Putting them in is just a political ploy by the Russians to appease Hanoi." McNaughton had a tremendous influence on McNamara's thinking throughout the war. Early on he was an enthusiastic advocate of ground-troop increases and even of bombing the north; by 1966, he had revised his position and become an advocate of abandoning the Vietnamese.

With occasional exceptions, each succeeding year of the war in Southeast Asia transformed the concept of "flexible response" into a rigid belief that warfare was better executed in terms of clever signals, subtle increases of pressure, and "punishment" applied in delicate gradations, rather than in classic military terms of mass, surprise, and selection or the most appropriate objective. Many thousands of miles away from the scene of combat, the leaders in the Department of Defense and in the administration persisted in regarding the enemy as errant schoolboys who could be reformed by a combination of inducements and punishments. Yet it should have been obvious to McNamara and Johnson, of all people, with their massive resources for research and intelligence, that the North Vietnamese and their National Liberation Front auxiliaries were formidable opponents who had been fighting for twenty-five years, battling the tough Japanese and defeating the French.

It should have been seen that the North Vietnamese national psychology did not recognize the size, technological advantage, or national interests of the United States; it recognized only the Vietnamese ability to fight without respite under the most difficult of circumstances. To assume that the North Vietnamese leaders would be sensitive to subtle signals and give up their lifelong tradition of fighting to the threat of "escalation" betrayed an unforgivable intellectual arrogance on the part of the American political leaders. What was presented to the American public as a cool and cautious approach to fighting turned out to be merely a means of training an already capable enemy. The restrictions on bombing and the bombing halts were not perceived by the North Vietnamese as invitations to negotiate, but as weaknesses to be exploited. Unfortunately, the rarefied academic decisions on policy in Vietnam were different from similar decisions in a corporation or a classroom, for they carried with them the weight of daily death in battle of young Americans, as well as the prolongation of suffering and the ultimate sellout of the South Vietnamese government and people.

BACKGROUND TO INVOLVEMENT

The United States had been involved in Indochina at some level since 1945, usually in support of an eventual loser. During the Eisenhower administration, the United States had almost acceded to French requests for direct military support at Dien Bien Phu, where American C-119 Flying Boxcars of the 50th Troop Carrier Squadron were hastily painted in French markings and used to airdrop supplies. The use of a nuclear weapon had been discussed, and preliminary arrangements had been made for conventional bombing by a fleet of ninety-eight Boeing B-29s. Unable to obtain approval from Great Britain and some of Vietnam's neighboring states, the United States declined. Dien Bien Phu fell, and France was ejected from the colony it had exploited for almost a century.

After the fall of Dien Bien Phu, the interim fate of Vietnam was determined at a conference in Geneva, Switzerland, in the summer of 1954, where representatives of France, North and South Vietnam, Cambodia, Laos, Red China, and the Soviet Union hammered out a Korea-like agreement. Secretary of State John Foster Dulles had attended the conference, but left because he felt that the outcome would not be favorable to the United States. A decision was reached to divide the country roughly in half along the 17th parallel, with the northern portion going to the Communist-sponsored Vietminh, led by Ho Chi Minh, and the southern to the Emperor Bao Dai, who was sponsored by the French. As a by-product of the conference, the final dissolution of the French empire in Indochina was ratified by the recognition of Laos and Cambodia as independent sovereign states.

The agreement at Geneva was followed by a mass movement of more than a million refugees from North Vietnam to South Vietnam. The Vietminh soldiers in the South moved to the North, but many thousands were ordered to stay behind to form cadres for local guerrillas who would become known as the Viet Cong. The name comes from "Viet Nam Cong San"—a phrase reportedly coined by South Vietnamese President Ngo Dinh Diem in 1959. Diem did not wish to dignify the Communists with their party title National Front for the Liberation of South Vietnam or National Liberation Front (NLF). The NLF was controlled by the People's Revolutionary Party (PRP) and directed by the Central Committee of the North Vietnamese Communist Party.

Although the United States agreed to observe the Geneva agreement, it was not optimistic, and in September 1954, in a meeting in Manila, it fostered the creation of an Asian counterpart to NATO. The Southeast Asia Treaty Organization (SEATO) included the United States, Great Britain, France, Australia, New Zealand, the Philippines, Pakistan, and Thailand.

U.S. MILITARY INVOLVEMENT

As the French withdrew from Vietnam, the South Vietnamese turned to the United States. A 325-man Military Assistance Advisory Group was in place by 1955, to train the Army of the Republic of Vietnam (ARVN). They found the situation in Vietnam in 1955 had an amazing similarity to the situation in Korea in 1950. Both Korea and Vietnam were peninsulas, bordered on the north by Communist China. Both had been divided artificially in the middle. In both countries, the northern half was Communist and more heavily industrialized, while the southern half was primarily agricultural and governed by only nominally democratic regimes that did not have the full backing of their people. In both instances, the northern army was well trained and well equipped by the Soviet Union, and openly intended to conquer the southern half by force of arms. In both instances the southern army was trained by U.S. forces and badly equipped.

There were many significant differences in the two conflicts besides the temperature contrasts, of which several stand out. In Korea, while the front was sometimes fluid, there was always a front, while the war in South Vietnam was the "war without a front." In Korea, the peninsula was bounded on the west by the Yellow Sea and on the east by the Sea of Japan, both of which were controlled by UN naval forces. Vietnam shared its peninsula with Laos, Cambodia, and Thailand. Although the U.S. Navy could operate off the eastern coast, the North Vietnamese would exploit the unsettled political conditions in the western portion to establish supply routes—the Ho Chi Minh

Trail—through Laos and Cambodia, along with sanctuaries to support an insurgent movement in South Vietnam. U.S. activity began in Laos in 1960, in the form of reconnaissance and covert military action; it would turn into an eight-year interdiction campaign.

Another significant difference in the two situations was the adroit way that the North Vietnamese leaders, particularly Ho Chi Minh and his military leader, General Vo Nguyen Giap, took care to build up a guerrilla movement in the South. The soon-to-be-infamous black-clad Viet Cong, built up from cadres left behind by the Vietminh, were indistinguishable to foreigners from the indigenous population, and over the years they built up a fluid organization that could come together to fight a battle in the city or in the countryside and then quickly disappear. Its techniques of terror were more effective in producing recruits, taxes, foodstuffs, and supplies than were the more conventional techniques of the South Vietnamese. The Viet Cong and the population loyal to the South Vietnamese government were not merely two opposing political parties, Tories and Loyalists, with equal claims on the affection of the people. The Viet Cong would take over a village and terrorize its residents, forcibly recruiting them and threatening death if they did not support the North Vietnamese cause. If they were forced to leave by the arrival of ARVN or U.S. troops, the Viet Cong would do so with the warning that they would return to punish any defectors. The American media never recognized the fundamental terrorist function of the Viet Cong.

FIRST USAF INVOLVEMENT

The initial entrance into Vietnam was utterly innocuous. President Kennedy authorized sending a mobile control and reporting post to Tan Son Nhut Air Base, near Saigon. By October 5, 1961, a detachment of the 507th Tactical Control Group from Shaw AFB, South Carolina, was in operation. On October 11, the President raised the ante, transforming Air Force operations in Vietnam from a purely advisory capacity to a limited combat role by authorizing deployment of a detachment that became known as Farm Gate. Formed by a portion of the 4400th Combat Crew Training Squadron, which had been activated at Eglin AFB on April 14, 1961, the original unit of 155 officers and airmen had four Douglas RB-26s, four Douglas SC-47s, and eight North American T-28s. The B-26s and C-47s had already proved their worth in World War II and Korea, while the T-28 was a trainer masquerading as a fighter-bomber. The troops and the T-28s and SC-47s began arriving at Ben Hoa Air Base in November 1961, with Colonel Benjamin H. King, CO of the 4400th, bringing the first SC-47 in from Hurlburt Field in just over seventy-five hours of flying time. The RB-26s came the next month. All aircraft were in the yellow-and-red South Vietnamese Air Force markings. Their nominal charter was training the South Vietnamese Air Force and "working out tactics and techniques." Operational flights were authorized provided a

Vietnamese was on board for purposes of receiving combat or combat support training. Circumstances and natural disposition soon saw the Farm Gate crews flying combat missions, including reconnaissance, close air support, and surveillance. The C-47 crews provided no direct training to the Vietnamese and instead developed an increasingly higher level of proficiency in bringing supplies to short, rough fields and in air drops.

The 2d ADVON (Advanced Echelon) was established by the Thirteenth Air Force on November 15, 1961, with four numbered detachments, three located in South Vietnam and one in Thailand. It was deactivated on October 8, 1962, and replaced by the 2d Air Division. Brigadier General Rollen H. Anthis was the initial commander for both units, in addition to operating as Chief, Air Force Section, Military Assistance Advisory Group (MAAG).

Farm Gate's main training effort was to teach twenty-five Vietnamese Air Force (VNAF) pilots to fly the T-28s in the newly organized 2d Fighter Squadron, with instruction in bombing, rocket firing, and gunnery. Although somewhat beefed up for their fighter-bomber role, the T-28s would, like the B-26s, prove to be structurally inadequate for the task. Both aircraft were also very vulnerable to the increasingly heavy ground fire they encountered.

The SC-47s were used for psychological warfare and for dropping flares to permit night strikes by the VNAF. These were highly successful, and a directive by McNamara permitted equipping 520 villages with radios to call for help if the Viet Cong attacked. One of the psy-war SC-47s was the second aircraft to be lost in Vietnam, crashing on February 11, 1962, with six Air Force and two Vietnamese crew members killed.

The Farm Gate unit—officially designated Detachment 2, 4400th Combat Training Squadron—was well received by its Vietnamese colleagues, who proved to be apt students. Under the command of Lieutenant Colonel Miles M. Doyle, Farm Gate operations had built up rapidly to 275 officers and men and more than forty aircraft by early 1963 and had been expanded to other South Vietnamese bases. Then attrition and increased enemy defenses took their toll of the aging equipment. Two B-26s were shot down in February 1963, and a wing failed on a third on August 16. All three crews were killed. Unable to obtain reinforcements, by October the unit was down to nine serviceable T-28s and twelve B-26s, the latter operating under flight restrictions intended to avoid wing stress—hardly reassuring when plunging into battle. Once again, the richest country in the world was letting its fliers fight an Asian war with old, inadequate, and dangerous equipment.

The unit was renamed the 1st Air Commando Squadron in mid-1964, and reequipped with the far sturdier if still Korean-war-era Douglas A-1E Skyraider, the formidable "Spad." A second Farm Gate squadron, the 602nd Air Commando Squadron, was organized in October 1964, an indication of the success of the down-and-dirty operations of the unit, despite the miserly way it had been provided resources.

OPERATION MULE TRAIN

As soon as the intervention ice was broken, additional material began to flow at an increasing rate. On January 2, 1962, Lieutenant Colonel Floyd K. Shofner, CO of the 346th Troop Carrier Squadron, brought in the first of sixteen Fairchild C-123 Providers as a part of Operation Mule Train. The first mission was flown the following day. The C-123 had started life as the Chase XC-20G combat glider, designed by Michael Stroukoff, and was transformed into the XC-123 Avitruc by the addition of two Wright R-2800 engines. Fairchild took over development and built 302 for the USAF and twenty-four for Allied countries. In 1966, the C-123K was fitted with a 2, 850-pound-static-thrust General Electric J85 turbojet under each wing. The combination of improved performance and increasing pilot proficiency turned the Provider into an excellent short-field and para-drop aircraft, with a capacity of as many as sixty troops or 8,000 pounds of cargo.

C-123 operations were distinguished by their daring, ingenuity, and high morale. Despite abysmal working conditions—changing engines by the light of jeep headlamps was not uncommon—the relationship between flight crews and maintenance personnel was excellent.

Contact with the enemy's guerrilla forces was difficult to maintain, calling for an increased reconnaissance capability. Aircraft and training were provided to create the VNAF 716th Reconnaissance Squadron. The request for a jet reconnaissance plane, the Lockheed RT-33, had been denied, and McNamara instead authorized a handful of Beech RC-45s, Douglas RC-47s, and North American RT-28s—not exactly fast movers. These were supplemented by a flight of USAF McDonnell RF-101Cs operating out of Don Muang in Bangkok, Thailand.

OPERATION RANCH HAND

The C-123 reached its peak of fame—or notoriety—early in its Vietnamese career by its work as part of Operation Ranch Hand, the painful operation that began as a "limited, three-phased defoliation plan" authorized by Secretary McNamara on November 3, 1961, and ran for nine years. Operation Ranch Hand is a heart-rending example of how good airmen can be forced to do unpleasant work when it is determined that the war effort demands it.

The purpose of the three phases was to defoliate a portion of the Mekong Delta area where the Viet Cong were known to have bases, to destroy manioc groves that the Viet Cong used for food, and to destroy mangrove swamps to which the Viet Cong fled to take refuge.

The British had used defoliants in Malaysia, and this was cited as a precedent in the arguments prepared for President Kennedy's consideration. The full approval of President Ngo Dinh Diem and his government had been received. The risk of charges of biological warfare was recognized and accepted.

The USAF had developed a limited capacity for the work in the course of public service activities. After World War II, a Special Aerial Spray Flight (SASF) had been established at Langley Air Force Base to undertake mosquito-control tasks with aerial spraying. The unit was alerted for duty in Southeast Asia, and six C-123s from TAC were sent to the enormous depot at Olmsted AFB, Pennsylvania, to be equipped with the 1,000-gallon MC-1 spray tank and additional necessary equipment. Somewhat to his surprise, Captain Carl W. Marshall, SASF commander, had no trouble getting volunteers who were willing to fly aircraft without U.S. markings, wear civilian clothes, and be on temporary-duty status (TDU) for extended periods of time. They understood that they would not be acknowledged as USAF members if captured. That there was no shortage of volunteers is a comment on their patriotism—and the powerful appeal of flying a dangerous mission.

After a grueling flight from Pope AFB, the six C-123 spray aircraft arrived in South Vietnam in January 1962 to begin Operation Ranch Hand. Over the next nine years, the unit, expanded over time, would spray more than 20 million gallons of herbicide over almost 6 million acres in South Vietnam. The decision to fight a ground war within South Vietnam changed the use of herbicides from a trial run to a military necessity, for, unlike many experiments in Vietnam, defoliation worked.

In the first year of its use, the number of ambushes dropped dramatically. It was extremely effective in exposing hidden enemy camps and supply dumps, and it was the only means to peer beneath the jungle canopy at the traffic on the Ho Chi Minh trail. In late 1962, the Ranch Hand charter was extended to the destruction of crops that the Viet Cong depended upon, so as to increase their supply difficulties.

Operation Ranch Hand grew in size until it had nineteen UC-123Ks to support the expanded mission. With the strategic hamlet concept in full flower, Army bases ranging in size from large semipermanent fortified establishments to tiny outposts now dotted South Vietnam. The bases were also quite successful, and by 1970 had established control over large areas and prevented the Viet Cong from returning. But almost all the bases were surrounded by the ever-encroaching jungle, and their perimeter fences and minefields had to be kept clear of growth to function. Herbicides kept them clear.

The immediate protests by the North Vietnamese on the use of defoliants were echoed by the Soviet Union and China. By 1965 many civilians in the United States were objecting to their use on humanitarian and environmental grounds. Three years later, President Nguyen Van Thieu of South Vietnam believed that herbicide use had become counterproductive. A 1968 report prepared by a committee appointed by the American ambassador to Vietnam, Ellsworth D. Bunker, indicating that the three principal herbicides, Agents

Blue, Orange, and White, were *not* harmful had an inflammatory reverse effect upon the media, and pressure mounted to stop the practice of defoliation. (Later studies repudiated the report. Eventually, suits against the manufacturers of the herbicides were settled for $180 million, the funds going to some 250,000 claimants. The Veterans Administration also settled claims for 1,800 U.S. veterans. Studies still go on, a recent one showing a link between children born with spinal bifida and their fathers' exposure to Agent Orange. Oddly enough, the people with most exposure to the defoliants, the aircrews, have displayed few symptoms characteristic of Agent Orange poisoning.)

Despite a wistful lingering belief that the herbicides being used in South Vietnam posed no permanent hazard, Secretary of Defense Melvin Laird informed President Nixon on December 22, 1970, that future herbicide use in Vietnam would conform to the standards for herbicide use in the United States. On January 7, 1971, the last Ranch Hand mission was flown.

Once launched, the large-scale ground war had required the use of herbicide to save the lives of troops in the field. The Air Force Ranch Hand units flew their mission with honor, skill, and dedication, often under heavy antiaircraft and small arms fire, and with more intimate exposure to the herbicides than anyone else. The first USAF aircraft lost in the Vietnam War was a Ranch Hand C-123, which crashed on February 2, 1962, killing all three crew members, Captain Fergus C. Groves, Captain Robert D. Larson, and Staff Sergeant Milo B. Coghill.

Time has not dimmed the controversy. A Fairchild UC-123K that had received more battle damage than any of its kind and still flew was brought to the magnificent USAF Museum at Wright Patterson Air Force Base in Dayton, Ohio. There it became the center of a dispute with the local environmentalists, who demanded its removal, decontamination, and destruction, despite the fact that it offered no hazard to anyone. The "compromise" was to have the aircraft cleaned once again, and then totally sealed. It now sits virtually mummified, an eloquent testimony to the basic mistakes that brought about its use in the first place.

AN UNPRODUCTIVE STRUGGLE

From 1962 to 1965, the struggle McNamara chose to wage in Vietnam closely emulated the fate of the Edsel automobile. Both the war and the car had been introduced with a publicity gasconade; both proved to be resounding failures. The crucial difference was that the Edsel was canceled.

McNamara's management style, however difficult, might have been salvageable if he had been willing to use the talents and advice of the men who had fought wars in the past or were engaged in fighting the war in Vietnam. Despite the fact that any operation in Southeast Asia would be undertaken beneath the umbrella of SAC's air-atomic shield, McNamara refused to take the advice of the man who had created that shield: Curtis LeMay. As Air Force Chief of Staff, LeMay had been unable to convince the DOD of the efficacy of an all-out air attack on North Vietnam.

Parenthetically, it is interesting—and sad—to note that as Chief of Staff, LeMay could not influence the Air Force as he had been able to influence the Strategic Air Command when he was its commander. There were a number of reasons, of which the Defense Reorganization Act of 1958 was one: LeMay no longer commanded a combat force. The Air Force was also large, and its bureaucracy in the Pentagon was less cooperative than his staff had been at SAC. The Secretary of the Air Force, the energetic and capable Eugene M. Zuckert, was similarly hamstrung, for despite a good working relationship with LeMay, who kept him fully informed on JCS activities, he was out of the DOD decision loop. In the course of his four years of service, he saw his influence on policy drop to zero. It was an especially bitter pill for Zuckert to swallow, for he had served as an assistant secretary under Stuart Symington, who had enjoyed almost equal influence with the Secretary of Defense.

Despite the best efforts of these two strong men, Zuckert and LeMay together could not stop the flow of power into the hands of McNamara, who used his authority over the DOD budget to withhold funds for projects of which he did not approve, sometimes thwarting the wishes of both the military services and the Congress. In McNamara's view, the day of the heavy bomber had passed; he canceled the B-70 and refused to allow additional B-52s to be built. LeMay was outspoken about McNamara, in one instance comparing him to a hospital administrator who practiced brain surgery on the side.

There is an interesting side note. The centralist, authoritarian management style that LeMay had used so well to bring SAC to its peak of power and that now permeated the rest of the Air Force was amplified by a power of ten by McNamara. The Secretary of Defense carried the style to an extreme, creating a climate of fear and placing a value on reporting rather than on doing. Numbers—whether it be of bodies counted, sorties flown, bombs dropped, or Congressional delegation visits—became the be-all and end-all of the military system McNamara shaped. Report numbers were transformed from black dots on a page into truths that were quantified, defended, and extrapolated from. Whole bureaucracies sprang up to create the numbers, challenge them, defend them, and mold them into new requirements for more numbers. In short, McNamara carried LeMay's methods to an extreme from which a rebound was inevitable. When the rebound came, it proved to be immensely beneficial.

McNamara, Zuckert, and LeMay were still at loggerheads by the fall of 1963, a time of momentous political changes. The most important of these without doubt was the assassination of President Kennedy on November 22. His death had been preceded by that of President Ngo Dinh Diem, who was killed by his own generals on November 2. The junta was led by General Duong Van Minh, who took over as leader. Minh was himself replaced in January by another coup, this one led by Major General Nguyen Khanh. One result of the November coup was the appointment of then Colonel Nguyen Cao Ky to become head of the Vietnamese Air Force. Two years later, Ky, with Major General Nguyen Van Thieu and General Ming, would form a triumvirate to run the country. Ky, a dashing, courageous pilot, was vehemently anti-Communist and much liked by U.S. politicians and airmen alike. Under his leadership, the VNAF grew proficient even as it expanded, a situation that conformed to the official U.S. policy of withdrawing American forces as South Vietnamese forces became capable.

But despite that proficiency, and the increased demands made upon the small U.S. military contingent, the Viet Cong and North Vietnamese were steadily increasing their influence. USAF forces were still suffering from a lack of support and the implicit disadvantage of war-surplus equipment. By February 1964, all Farm Gate B-26s were grounded, two T-28s had been shot down, and two other T-28s had suffered catastrophic wing failures. The 1st Commando Squadron was ultimately forced to borrow nine T-28s from the VNAF to stay operational.

Secretary McNamara's reaction to the growing disaster was to authorize a second Air Commando squadron equipped with Douglas A-1E Skyraiders. However, in May 1964 he ordered that Air Force pilots could no longer fly combat missions, even with Vietnamese observers on board. As an alternative, he authorized expansion of the VNAF by two squadrons and made Douglas A-1H aircraft available for a total of six squadrons.

If at this time the McNamara team had reexamined their basic assumptions and compared them with the known events in South Vietnam, they would have found that as the United States escalated its level of effort, so did the North Vietnamese. Instead of being intimidated and admitting that a small country like North Vietnam could not defeat a large country like the United States, they simply fought harder. In essence, the North Vietnamese had the measure of the American psychology and knew that the public would not support a long war. The American leaders, McNamara chief among them, had no grasp of North Vietnamese psychology and perhaps never attempted to attain one. They believed, almost to the end of their time in office, that their superior gamesmanship would automatically force the North Vietnamese to conform to U.S. wishes. When they finally realized that this was not the case, they changed their position, advocating leaving South Vietnam in the lurch and departing the country.

The North Vietnamese and the Viet Cong responded to increased U.S. pressure as if it were a tonic. The Viet Cong increased their efforts and the North Vietnamese dispatched regular army troops over the Demilitarized Zone (DMZ) to the south. Even as late as 1964, much might have been saved if a reinforced USAF contingent had been directed against the North Vietnamese while the VNAF was left to deal with the Viet Cong. Instead, the USAF was dedicated to counterinsurgency.

The North Vietnamese successes led to the hotly disputed incident in the Gulf of Tonkin on August 2, 1964, when enemy torpedo boats were reported to have attacked the destroyer USS *Maddox*. On August 4, there were two additional attacks reported, against the *Maddox* and the USS *C. Turner Joy*, another destroyer. (Much doubt has since been cast on the truth of these attacks, particularly the second one.) On President Johnson's orders, a retaliatory raid was made on North Vietnamese bases, and on August 7, 1964, the Congress passed the Gulf of Tonkin Resolution, authorizing the President to commit the armed forces to defend South Vietnam's independence and territory. The die was cast.

TIT FOR TAT TAG LINES

The year 1965 saw an abrupt transition for the United States forces in Vietnam. The advisory role was retained and training went on, but the American forces were now there to fight. The number of U.S. military personnel in Southeast Asia in 1964 totaled 23,310. It jumped to 184,314 in 1965 and continued to rise steadily, reaching a peak of 536,134 in 1968. Simultaneously, forces in Thailand had grown from 6,505 to 47,631. During the same time period, the number of USAF aircraft in South Vietnam grew from 84 to 1,085, with an additional 523 planes in Thailand, a full 28 percent of the approximately 6,000 planes in the USAF inventory.

The sugar that made this medicine of massive growth in troop strength go down was an original intent to use U.S. and other Allied forces from Australia, New Zealand, the Philippines, and South Korea to guard enclaves and thus release South Vietnamese troops for combat duty. The good intentions soon gave way to reality as the Allied forces were progressively engaged in combat.

With all pretense of adherence to the Geneva agreement gone, jet aircraft began to arrive—a few Martin RB-57s, thirty-six B-57s, McDonnell RF-101s, small numbers of Convair F-102s, several squadrons of North American F-100s, and a lesser number of Republic F-105s. The numbers were relatively small and the crews were rotated every ninety days, but they clearly presaged the future, as did the first use of SAC tankers to support operations. On June 9, 1964, four KC-135s operating out of Clark Air Force Base (and stylishly nicknamed Yankee Team Tanker Task Force) refueled eight F-100 fighters on their way to strike Pathet Lao antiaircraft defenses on the Plain of Jars in Laos. Yankee Team Tanker Task Force (subsequently renamed Foreign Legion) grew into the "Young Tigers" who kept the air war running with their incredible refueling capabilities.

The Viet Cong reacted predictably to the reinforcements; in a November 1, 1964, mortar attack on Bien Hoa Air Base, they destroyed five B-57s and damaged fifteen others, along with four VNAF Douglas A-1s. Four Americans were killed and seventy-two wounded. This was followed by an attack on an American barracks, the Brink Hotel in the heart of Saigon, this time killing two and wounding seventy-one Americans. These actions served to unite the JCS to recommend U.S. bombing of the infiltration trails in Laos and North Vietnam. However, it was election month, and President Johnson did not wish to jeopardize what proved to be his landslide victory over that redoubtable veteran and friend of the USAF Senator Barry Goldwater of Arizona. (The Senator later always jokingly referred to his 486-to-52 defeat in the electoral college as a "real cliff-hanger.")

The U.S. leadership, if unable to come up with a winning strategy, excelled at dramatic names for operations, which began with the Operation Flaming Dart series of attacks. These were "tit for tat"—a phrase used in the official DOD communications—for the twin February 7, 1965, raids on Pleiku and Tuy Hoa, which destroyed five helicopters and killed eight Americans and wounded more than a hundred others.

Secure in his position, President Johnson ordered the limited Flaming Dart retaliatory strikes against troop concentrations and staging areas in the southern portion of North Vietnam. The Navy attacked first, sending forty-nine aircraft against Dong Hoi; the USAF attacked the following day with F-100s and A-1s striking NVN barracks at Chap Le.

Another portent of the future occurred in February 1965 when B-52s of the 7th and 320th Bomb Wings were deployed to Andersen Air Force Base, Guam. General John P. McConnell, who became Chief of Staff on General LeMay's retirement on February 1, 1965, put forward once again the list of ninety-four targets in North Vietnam against which he wished to conduct a massive air offensive, with the aim of destroying North Vietnam's ability to wage war. This list was substantially the same as the list previously nominated by the JCS and Admiral Ulysses S. Grant Sharp, Commander in Chief, Pacific (CINCPAC), and constituted the heart of North Vietnamese industrial and logistical capability. The targets could have been taken out quickly, with a minimum loss of life, but the suggestion was always overruled.

In its place would come applications of limited force in nondecisive areas with lilting names like Barrel Roll, Steel Tiger, and Tiger Hound in northern, central, and southern Laos, respectively, and Rolling Thunder, which superseded Flaming Dart in Vietnam. Each of these missions put a premium on the skill and daring of the aircrews, whose equipment was often ill-suited to the task and who had to fly under rules of engagement as adverse as the abominable weather conditions. The basic flaw in the design of the missions was that they were striking the wrong end of the North Vietnamese/Viet Cong supply lines, sometimes losing $3 million aircraft in attacks against trucks worth 6,000 rubles and carrying bags of rice. The frustration of Air Force leaders and the men flying the missions was extreme; they understood perfectly well that it was far less risky and far more efficient to sink a ship in

Haiphong harbor carrying 300 trucks with one mission than to have to spend 1,000 missions to try to destroy those same trucks on the Ho Chi Minh Trail. This was hard intelligence, obtained by the pilots who flew north, were shot at, and returned with an acute awareness of the risk versus return. Unfortunately, they were never able to communicate this intelligence to the highest levels in DOD, because the communication lines ran in one direction only: down.

Rolling Thunder

Among the multitude of ironies in the Vietnam War, not least is the fact that tactical aviation, overshadowed for twenty years by the prodigious demands for resources by the Strategic Air Command, now had to bear the brunt of fighting the war, with 50 percent of the fighter units trained and equipped by the Tactical Air Command being permanently assigned to Southeast Asia in 1965. The irony was heightened when SAC bombers, whose leaders were champing at the bit to strike North Vietnam a decisive blow, were instead relegated to bombing Viet Cong base camps and conducting close air support missions in South Vietnam, even as the tactical force went north. The attack against North Vietnam was a tribute to the courage and determination of both the USAF and U.S. naval air; the air attack was conducted relentlessly, regardless of weather or the ever-increasing enemy opposition. Day after day, the attacks went on, never deterred by losses nor by the sickening realization that their effort was not appreciated by the American public, and often not by their own leaders.

Rolling Thunder was a campaign intended to complement the interdiction work in Laos and in South Vietnam. And, as with McNamara's entire Southeast Asia strategy, it was to avoid provoking either China or the USSR, despite the daily evidence that those two countries furnished North Vietnam with almost all its matériel. To ensure that the war remained sanitized, target selection was controlled directly by the White House in a request/approval network that still defies belief. In theory, target requests were to be assessed by the combat wings and forwarded to Seventh Air Force. In practice, the combat wings had no say in the targets. On those few occasions when they were able to nominate targets, the action next went to the Pacific Air Force (PACAF); they then went to CINCPAC, to the Joint Chiefs of Staff, to the Secretary of Defense, and then to the President, who could, if he chose, get advice from the Department of State, the Secretary of Defense, and the National Security Council. The approved target then went back down the same list, five headquarters, before it reached the wings. Even in an age of swift electronic communication, the method took far too long for effective use of tactical air strikes. Instead of getting target lists from the people doing the bombing, most targets were generated at Tuesday luncheons at the White House (from which military men were excluded until 1967), where the President and the Secretary of Defense dictated the choice of targets, tactics, timing, number of aircraft, and ordnance to be used. To say it was ludicrous would be kind; it was an insane way to fight a war, a cold exercise of power for the sake of the exercise, and without regard to the expenditure of life or materiel involved.

The question of unified action by USAF and naval air assets, which President Eisenhower had sought to resolve with the 1958 Defense Reorganization Act, reverted to the same uncooperative setup that had occurred in the Korean War, and for which a similar Band-Aid solution was devised. The Navy insisted that carrier operations, with their inherent rigid requirements for aircraft carriers to position themselves into the wind for both launch and recovery operations, were unable to respond to a centralized control system. Naval air was not the only problem. The command and control confusion was exacerbated because the B-52 bomber and KC-135 tanker force remained under SAC's control, where during the Korean War, the B-29 force had been controlled by FEAF. Targeting request/approval for the bombers was equally complex, and even more vulnerable to the time elapsed in getting a decision, for the Viet Cong were extremely mobile, able to remove themselves from a target area within minutes of notice of an impending attack—which they often had.

Rolling Thunder began on March 2, 1965, when twenty B-57s and twenty-five F-105s struck just north of the DMZ at Xam Bong, blowing up an ammunition dump. By September, almost 4,000 strikes had been made by USAF and Navy aircraft against targets mostly in the south of North Vietnam. These included radar sites, rail lines, marshaling yards, highways and trails, and bridges—the last proving to be a difficult target.

The momentum Rolling Thunder had gained in 1965 was brought to a shuddering stop when President Johnson ordered a bombing halt from December 24, 1965, to the end of January 1966, during which both Christmas and the Buddhist festival of Tet were celebrated. Johnson's intent was to have his opposite number, Ho Chi Minh, interpret the gesture as a signal to negotiate. The Vietnamese used it instead as a time to build up their defenses.

The Rolling Thunder attacks seemed to be successful in terms of destroyed vehicles, burned-out tank farms, and other material losses. A report by Secretary McNamara estimated these to be $150 million for the period February 1965 through October 1966. There were two problems, however. One was that the campaign seemed to encourage rather than deter the North Vietnamese, who simply asked their giant benefactors, China and the USSR, for more oil, more SAMs, more everything. The other was that it was costing the United States $250 *million per month* to sustain the entire interdiction effort by the Air Force and Navy in North and South Vietnam and Laos. Despite this expenditure, Secretary McNamara perceived "no significant impact on the war in South Vietnam."

To McNamara, the answer was obvious: spend more money on increasingly less significant targets. Rolling Thunder sorties rose from 55,000 in 1965 to 110,000 in 1966, while costs rose from $460 million to $1.2 billion as aircraft and munitions became more sophisticated and expensive. The sorties went on until November 1, 1968, when President Johnson halted the bombing of North Vietnam north of the 19th parallel. He also called a halt to his own administration, announcing that he would not run for reelection. This time the bombing halt lasted for *four years*—longer than the entire time the United States was engaged in World War II. As long as this sounds in comparative terms, it was nothing compared to how long it seemed in actual days, weeks, months, and years to the American prisoners of war who, during those four years, continued to be tortured, starved, and killed. During the same long period of the bombing halt, American soldiers in the field continued to be wounded and killed at a rate that reached hundreds per week. Bombing in the North was not resumed until North Vietnamese intransigence at the negotiating table in Paris made it necessary.

Secretary McNamara left office on February 29, 1968, to be succeed by Clark Clifford. A report by one of McNamara's top men, Dr. Alain C. Enthoven, who headed the Office of Systems Analysis in the Pentagon, must have given the new Secretary something to reflect on. Enthoven reported that the gradual escalation of the war to inflict an unbearable attrition on North Vietnam had failed. The war was costing $10 billion per year, and despite more than 500,000 troops, millions of tons of bombs dropped, and an estimated 200,000 enemy troops killed in action, the control of the South Vietnam countryside was about the same as in July 1965. Ironically, it was during this same period that Maxwell Taylor, now in Saigon as the American ambassador, reversed his previous position on fighting a ground war with U.S. troops and instead began to advocate the bombing of the North. When Taylor was forced out of the country by then President Nguyen Cao Ky in 1967, he returned to Washington as a special adviser to President Johnson. He advised sending more troops and bombing the north, thus neatly covering his past positions.

Unfortunately, the situation had changed drastically in North Vietnam. In July 1965, the North Vietnamese air defenses were relatively unsophisticated. By 1968, they had grown into a highly effective network of radar systems, missiles, antiaircraft guns, and interceptors under ground control. The SAMs—surface-to-air missiles—were a new threat.

DEFEATING THE SAM

The North Vietnamese learned to use the new tools of war quickly, increasing their antiaircraft and surface-to-air missile capability and scoring the first SAM kill on July 24, 1965, when a MIGCAP (MiG combat air patrol) McDonnell F-4C was shot down 55 miles northwest of Hanoi. The SA-2 Guideline missile, coupled with the radar system designated "Fansong" in

NATO terminology, seemed like an implacable foe at first, as several aircraft were lost. Its effectiveness was enhanced by the DOD-imposed rules of engagement that, in retrospect, defy belief. SAM sites within 10 miles of Hanoi and Haiphong were off-limits; within 30 miles of Hanoi, SAM sites could be hit only if they were preparing to fire and were not located in a populated area or on a dike of the widespread irrigation system. These became the very places that the North Vietnamese chose to install their weapons. Perhaps the most ludicrous limitation was the prohibition on attacking a site while it was being built, or even of attacking when the operational site was in the radar-surveillance mode. They could be attacked only when they switched to track, i.e., seconds before launching. In the American West of a century ago, a similar rule of engagement would have forbidden the sheriff to draw his weapon until the hammer had dropped on the outlaw's pistol.

But with the courage and determination that Air Force crews would repeatedly demonstrate in Southeast Asia, ways were found to counter the SA-2. Going in low would have been the best solution, but fuel economy, the increasing strength of antiaircraft artillery, and the massive small arms fire ruled this out. Fighter strikes eventually entered the combat area at medium altitudes calculated to best avoid the particular combination of MiGs, SAMs, and antiaircraft defenses around a specific target. If an aircrew were fortunate enough to see a SAM launched or in flight toward them, the best defense was to attack it as if it were an enemy aircraft. Breaking toward the missile and executing a high-G maneuver would cause the stubby-winged SAM to attempt to follow it; the SAM could enter a high-speed stall or break up from the forces involved. With the best of luck it crashed back on those who had fired it.

The most dramatic antidote, however, was the introduction of the Wild Weasel system, created in an emergency seminar chaired by Brigadier General K. C. Dempster. Like most weapons introduced to meet emergencies, the first Wild Weasels were a lash-up. What became the APR-25 RHAW (Radar Homing And Warning) system was installed, along with an IR-133 panoramic receiver to analyze the radar signals and indicate whether they originated from an antiaircraft battery, a ground control intercept radar, or a SAM site. The third element was the APR-26 Launch Warning Receiver, which picked up the increased power of the SA-2 guidance system upon launch. All of these (in their experimental versions) were packed into four aging two-seat North American F-100F fighters. Armament initially varied, but always included the 20mm cannon and 2.75-inch rockets. Later, the AGM-45 Shrike missile, tuned to home in on radar frequencies used by the Fansongs, was introduced. A quick reaction development effort led by Major Garry Willard and a dedicated team of air and ground personnel brought the initial Wild Weasel unit into combat.

By November 21, 1965, the first of seven F-100F Wild Weasel aircraft arrived at Korat Royal Thai Air Force Base, Thailand. The unit became the

6234th TFW (Wild Weasel Detachment), operating as part of the 388th TFW, and its mission became known as Iron Hand strikes. Not surprisingly, given the experimental nature of the work, a Wild Weasel crew was lost before a success was scored. On December 20, Captains John Pitchford and Robert Trier were shot down about 30 miles northeast of Hanoi. Both men ejected. Pitchford was shot while being captured after he landed, and spent more than seven years as a prisoner of war. Trier was killed by his captors, who alleged that he had resisted.

The first Wild Weasel success came soon after, when Captains Al Lamb and Jack Donovan took out a site during a Rolling Thunder strike on the railyard at Yen Bai, some 75 miles northwest of Hanoi.

The men flying the F-100s were the pioneers in the effort; like them, their successors had to be good, for only the very best pilots could handle the Wild Weasel mission. They were complemented by equally skilled electronic warfare officers (EWOs), who had to withstand the stress of high-G maneuvers in a potentially fatal environment while operating the new radar warning systems. (It was the custom of the service at the time to treat non-pilots with hearty denigrating humor; thus the EWOs became GIBs, for guy in back, or Bears, for trained bears. It was terribly unfair, for while a pilot flying the aircraft was used to high-G maneuvers, the EWO was often a navigator or electronic countermeasures officer accustomed to SAC's straight-and-level flying. Yet the success of the mission depended upon the EWOs managing the systems, spotting the SAM site or the SAMs, and ultimately allowing the pilot to position the aircraft to launch his ordnance.)

The F-100s were flown in four-ship flights, often with F-105 escort. The two aircraft were not compatible in terms of their speed capabilities, and the F-100 Weasels, whose motto was "First In—Last Out," were vulnerable to the high density of antiaircraft fire in the area of SAM sites. The effect of the first F-100 Wild Weasel attacks was deadly—but at great cost. Seven attacks took out seven SAM sites, but two aircraft were shot down and five were damaged beyond repair.

Nonetheless it was the proper antidote, and the crews flying the F-100s built up a repertoire of techniques that would benefit the F-105s and F-4s that replaced them. New aircraft were no panacea, however. For example, a group of seven F-105 Wild Weasel aircraft arrived at Takhli RTAFB on Independence Day 1966; thirty-eight days later, all seven aircraft had been shot down. Yet the real reason for Wild Weasel's success was the proficiency built up by the crews in the crucible of a very uneven battle. They established a tradition which would endure through the Persian Gulf War and beyond, the EWOs finding the targets (whose defense techniques became increasingly sophisticated) and the pilots managing to maneuver the aircraft well enough to survive attacks and kill the SAMs.

F-105 Iron Hand flights usually consisted of two F-105G two-place Weasel aircraft, each with a conventional single-seat F-105D on its wing. The

Wild Weasels routinely preceded the attack force into the target area by about five minutes, just far enough in advance that the SAMs would have to be turned on and warming up. When the instruments showed that a SAM site had activated, the Wild Weasel would attack, early in the war with a Shrike, later with a Standard Arm missile. This would be followed by a general attack using conventional weapons from the remainder of the Iron Hand flight.

The intent was as much to keep the SAMs off the air as to destroy them. The North Vietnamese adapted their tactics. They would sometimes alternate having the radar on between supporting SAM sites, to keep track of the F-105s; sometimes they would leave their radar off so as not to present a target, then salvo the SAMs in barrage fire at the strike force. Close cooperation was maintained with antiaircraft artillery and any MiGs that were available.

And just as a shut-down site measured the effectiveness of the Wild Weasel operation, so did the forced alteration in bombing tactics measure the effectiveness of the SAMs. Loss rates per missiles fired were relatively low. In 1965, eleven U.S. aircraft were shot down for 194 SAMs fired—a 5.7 percent rate. It took 3,202 SAMs to shoot down fifty-six aircraft in 1967, a 1.75 percent rate. In 1972, at the relative height of effectiveness of both U.S. countermeasures and SAM proficiency, 4,244 missiles destroyed forty-nine aircraft, for a 1.15 percent rate. But no matter how low the loss rate, the SAMs could not be ignored—they had to be suppressed.

COUNTERING THE MiG THREAT

With memories of the great aces of World War II and Korea firmly in their mind, American fighter pilots, USAF or naval air, wanted most of all to come to grips with enemy MiGs to establish air superiority—and perhaps, just incidentally, to become aces.

The situation proved to be totally different from Korea, however, particularly in end results. The North Vietnamese Air Force was not interested in mixing it up in dogfights except on rare occasions, and the impediments in equipment and rules of engagement kept the USAF, in particular, from running up the scores the pilots wanted.

The most significant lack of equipment was an airborne radar warning and control system (AWACS) type of vehicle to provide coverage in eastern areas of North Vietnam. The Disco Lockheed EC-121Ts (the familiar Super Constellation with a big radar dome and lots of tracking equipment) operating over Laos and the Gulf of Tonkin were invaluable, as was Red Crown, the radar warning and control vessel in the Gulf of Tonkin.

The first American and only all-MiG-21 ace, then Captain and now Brigadier General Steve Ritchie, stated emphatically that every time he was successful he had received good information from either Red Crown or Disco. Navy fighters almost always operated under Red Crown's beneficent eye, and as a result were able to gain the crucial seconds necessary to create and win an encounter with the MiGs.

North Vietnam's greatest advantage lay in its integrated defense system, which provided its MiG fighters with comprehensive information on the air battle. They had the advantage of knowing the customary inbound tracks of the USAF fighters (the radar was assisted by visual guidance made easy by the twin trails of smoke emanating from the F-4s) and could launch their attacks with every advantage.

North Vietnamese defense was aided by American jurisdictional problems. As it had done in Korea, the Navy stoutly refused to participate in a central control system. The Navy's official position did not seem entirely arbitrary. The Commander in Chief, Pacific (CINCPAC), Admiral Ulysses S. Grant Sharp, Jr., was a dedicated supporter of the war who wanted to keep pressure on North Vietnam. However, the official line was that aircraft carriers were less suitable for centralized control because they had the burden of fleet defense. In practical truth, the Navy wished to control its own war.

As a result, just as in Korea, a decision was made to carve out a geographical area for naval air operations to ensure minimum interference. Vietnam was divided into seven segments known as route packages, starting in the south along the 18th parallel, with what the pilots called Pack One. Pack Two, Three, and Four were horizontal east-west slices stacked farther north. At the top of the stack, stretching to the Chinese border, were Pack Five in the west and Pack Six A and Pack Six B, which included Hanoi and Haiphong.

The intensity of enemy opposition increased as the Pack numbers rose, with Packs One through Five known as "the Easy Packs" and Packs Six A and B known as "Downtown"—where the action was.

Little attention was paid to who owned what rights within the Easy Packs, which, prior to President Johnson's termination of Rolling Thunder, were primarily either routine targets of less importance or alternate targets for the strike forces primed to go Downtown.

Pack Six A, including Hanoi, was designated USAF turf, while Six B, including Haiphong, was assigned for Navy targeting. The imaginary line between the two sections of Pack Six were important at the staff and planning level but disappeared for the airborne fighter pilots whenever they needed to cross, or when they could assist their friends on the other side.

The route package system was a clumsy expedient that avoided the issue of centralized control of air assets that presumably had been established for all time during the North African campaign of World War II. The cost was an implicit limitation on the optimum use of the aircraft available.

THE ENEMY DEFENSES

The North Vietnamese Air Force was small. Its pilots had received basic training in the Soviet Union and advanced training in China. In general, they did not compare in skill, aggressiveness, or training with their American counterparts. This was both offset and exacerbated by the integrated air defense system that exercised rigid control over North Vietnamese pilots at every stage of the flight; they were told when to take off, when to engage, when to disengage, and when to return to base. Their excellent Atoll missiles were fired on command from the ground. The downside of this over centralized control for the North Vietnamese was the consequent lack of initiative on the part of pilots accustomed to be told what to do and when to do it.

As with the SAM sites, the skewed rules of engagement put Communist airfields off limits for most of the war. Nothing pained USAF pilots so much as seeing juicy targets sitting on the ground, some with engines running, ready to attack moments later, and being unable to take them out in the classic tactic of aerial warfare, a strafing attack. MiG strength rose from about fifty in 1965 to more than 200 by 1972. Losses were quickly replenished from both Chinese and Soviet stores.

MiG Data

The MiG-17 Fresco was an evolutionary development of the MiG-15 that had been such a dramatic surprise in Korea. USAF and Navy pilots both were shocked to find the relatively unsophisticated MiG-17 to be a formidable adversary at low altitudes, where it often loitered to engage U.S. aircraft returning from a mission low on fuel. Called a "vicious, vicious little beast" by the famed Colonel Robin Olds, it had gun armament similar to the MiG-15's, with two 23mm cannons and one 37mm; later in the war, the AA-2 Atoll missile was carried on outer pylons. The Atoll was a virtual copy of the U.S. AIM-9B Sidewinder heat-seeking missile.

The MiG-19 Farmer (the Chinese designated their version the Shenyang J-6) was reportedly the world's first supersonic production fighter, first exceeding the speed of sound in early 1953. (Fans of the North American Super Sabre dispute this claim on the basis that the YF-100A set an official speed record of 755.149 mph on October 29, 1953.) Heavily armed with three 30mm cannon and an array of missiles, the MiG-19 was a tough customer.

The pride of the North Vietnamese fleet was the delta-wing MiG-21 Fishbed, which played to the McDonnell F-4 as the MiG-15 had to the F-86. The tiny MiG-21 had an empty weight of only 13,500 pounds (the F-4 weighed in empty at about 30,000 pounds) and had a speed in excess of Mach 2. The aircraft's rate of climb and acceleration were excellent, although it did not have as high a sustained turn rate as the Soviets desired.

North Vietnamese ground control tactics used the MiG-21's capabilities perfectly, vectoring them in pairs behind an incoming strike force. The Fishbeds would be positioned behind the formation, accelerate to supersonic speed, fire their heat-seeking Atoll missile, and zoom up and away from the strike force. Their mission was accomplished if they got the F-4s and F-105s to jettison their bomb loads, but on too many occasions, the Atoll scored a victory.

Tactics like these, combined with the general reluctance of the NVAF to participate in dogfights, kept the kill ratio of the USAF at a troublingly low level—between 3.5 and 4 to 1 for the period 1965–1967. During the next year, the ratio fell to 2 to 1. The low kill ratio has been attributed to a number of factors, most important the lack of an AWACS-type aircraft, as previously noted. However, the rules of engagement also required U.S. pilots to have a positive visual identification before firing, and the time required for that put American planes at a severe disadvantage. Until the appearance of the McDonnell F-4E in 1968, the escorting Phantoms had only Sidewinder and Sparrow missiles with which to fight, sometimes supplemented after 1967 by gun pods. The missiles were originally designed for use against bombers. Using them in a dogfight was agonizing, for in a battle where combined head-on speeds could exceed 1,500 mph and where a flick of the stick could re-move a fighter from the sights, the setup, arming, and firing of the missiles took hours-long seconds to accomplish. The tracking and turn capabilities of the missiles were also geared to bombers rather than to nimble fighters, and many a MiG got away that should have fallen to cannon or a specialized-for-fighters missile.

There was another even more important factor that still has repercussions today. The experience of combat made it evident that prewar USAF training was not rigorous enough. Safety considerations and the tendency to train against similar types of aircraft had vitiated the training programs. The so-lution was training programs like the Air Force's famous Red Flag and the Navy's Top Gun that were far more realistic, even at the price of some flying safety considerations.

OPERATION BOLO

The combination of U.S. rules of engagement and the avoidance tactics employed by the North Vietnamese was frustrating to USAF fighter pilots, who wanted to come to grips with the enemy in a classic dogfight. In the relatively few combats that occurred during 1966, nineteen MiGs had been shot down, with the loss of five USAF crews. (The Navy had shot down four and lost four.) The MiG-21s' rear attacks with Atoll missiles were achieving North Vietnamese goals by causing the F-105 formations to jettison their bombs before reaching their targets.

Because the MiG airfields were off-limits, a decision was made by Sev-enth Air Force Commander General William W. "Spike" Momyer to plan a fighter sweep for just after the year-end stand-down. The North Vietnamese Air Force always reacted more strongly after a quiet period, having more aircraft in commission and their tactics refined by training sorties.

The fighter sweep was deliberately designed to appear exactly like a normal F-105 mission, with the standard call signs, designations, and other indicators to show that the mission was just like the many that had preceded it. The difference was that F-4s armed for air-to-air combat would be flying instead of F-105s. The most important deception was the use by the F-4s of ECM pods previously used only by F-105s. Altitudes and airspeeds were flown exactly as if it were the daily strike force.

Operating out of Udorn Royal Thai Air Force Base, on the morning of January 2, the 8th Tactical Fighter Wing, the "Wolfpack," launched Operation Bolo. Led by veteran ace Colonel Robin Olds, who had thirteen aerial and eleven ground victories in Europe during World War II, twenty flights of F-4s and F-105 Wild Weasel aircraft were used to set the trap. Despite some adverse weather, the MiGs reacted exactly as had been hoped, coming up from behind to attack what they presumed to be bomb-laden F-105s. To their surprise, they encountered F-4s, with their tanks already jettisoned and ready to fight. In the space of a few minutes, seven MiGs were shot down, Olds himself getting two of his four victories in Southeast Asia. When the North Vietnamese lost two more MiGs on January 6, and began an immediate stand-down to analyze the situation, the American fighter pilots, if not content, were a little happier.

Operation Bolo illustrates the indisputable fact that the USAF dominated the airspace, north and south, albeit at great cost. The enemy was unable to attack our airfields, our carriers, our front lines, or our most vulnerable asset, the KC-135 tankers that always plied their trade next to—and sometimes in—the combat zone.

The USAF had air superiority, even if not in the overwhelming degree that it might have had if its leaders had not been hobbled by DOD constraints. As will be detailed later, the basic strength of the USAF was demonstrated in a number of ways besides basic combat. One of the most compassionate was the magnificent level of effort of its search and rescue (SAR) service. A less obvious, yet equally important manifestation of inherent organizational strength was the remarkable manner in which support commands like the Air Force Logistic Command (APLC) and the Air Force Systems Command (AFSC) proved their worth with rapid fixes to seemingly insoluble problems, including the vexing requirement for visual identification of enemy fighters.

THE PRINCIPAL FIGHTERS: THUDS AND PHANTOMS

Thuds

The workhorse of the war, the Republic F-105 Thunderjet (affectionately, if sardonically, nicknamed the Thud for the sound it reputedly made when crashing) had originally been designed as a supersonic long-range nuclear strike fighter, capable of carrying bombs of 1 to 20 megatons yield. The name "Thud" was an unfair call, for the F-105 had a sculptural beauty, even after years of modifications had disfigured it with various bumps to hold equipment. Republic, noted for building heavy "ground-loving" fighters, experienced trouble during the development of the aircraft, which flew first on October 22, 1955 (exceeding Mach 1 on its first flight), but did not reach operational status until May 1958. The F-105 was a lovely aircraft to fly, and despite having far too few access panels for ease of maintenance, it had a remarkably high in-commission rate. The first F-105 squadron to deploy to Thailand stayed for five months and racked up 2,231 sorties with an 85 percent availability rate.

Eventually, seven squadrons of F-105s belonging to the 355th (based at Tahkli RTAFB) and the 388th Tactical Fighter Wing (based at Korat RTAFB) bore the brunt of the Rolling Thunder campaign, taking heavy losses in the process. Out of the original 833 production aircraft, some 350 F-105s were lost to combat or other operational causes. Despite their relative lack of maneuverability and the manner in which they were employed, the F-105s managed to shoot down 27.5 MiGs, often off the tail of another F-105 being attacked. (A .5 score means a victory shared with another type of aircraft, probably in this case an F-4.) The attrition rate, combined with a refusal by DOD to reopen the production line, ultimately forced replacement of the Thud by F-4s.

Phantoms

Perhaps the greatest tribute to the USAF aircrews and ground crews is the manner in which they took aircraft designed for one mission and flew and maintained them so artfully that they excelled in many others.

The McDonnell F-4 Phantom II was originally conceived as a naval fleet defense fighter, armed solely with missiles and using a Weapons System Officer to manage its complex fire control system. A huge aircraft, grossing 61,650 pounds on takeoff, the Phantom was propelled at Mach 2.27 speeds by the brute force of its twin afterburning General Electric J79 turbojets, the incredible contribution of Gerhard "Herman the German" Neuman to engine technology.

In a decision almost without precedent, the USAF decided in March 1962 to adopt the Phantom as its standard fighter with absolutely minimum changes from the Navy production version. The original F-110 designation was changed to F-4 when the DOD instituted a tri-service designation system on October 1, 1962.

The big Phantom's in-flight-refueling capability conferred a number of advantages on it—increased range and the ability to take off with less fuel and more bombs and then refuel after takeoff and, thanks to the bravery of the tanker crews, use up most of its fuel in combat, knowing that KC-135s were on station to refuel them for the trip home.

Yet the Phantom's basic USAF requirement was to fly long distances, heavily laden with ordnance, sometimes to engage in dogfights, sometimes to bomb. When the Phantoms made their long journey to the battle arena in North Vietnam, they naturally found the smaller MiG-21s and their older point-interceptor brethren far more maneuverable, with quicker acceleration and a faster turn rate. The F-4's size and weight put it at a disadvantage in the conventional dogfight, as did its lack of an internal gun, for its missiles were originally designed for bomber interception. (SUU-16 gun pods were supplied as an interim answer, but were not entirely satisfactory.) The answer was found in energy maneuverability tactics, which forced a change in dog-fighting from an essentially horizontal plane into a vertical plane. The sheer speed and the power of the Phantom could put it rolling up and down in maneuvers that combated the MiG's greater turning capability. (Energy ma-neuverability is a complex concept; reduced to its essence, it is the proper management of the combined positional and kinetic energy of an aircraft to extract the maximum maneuverability from it.)

The Phantom's greater speed was offset by the requirement for their protective flights, often loaded with ordnance, to cruise at the same speed as the bomb-laden Republic F-105s they were escorting. To cope with an at-tacking MiG flight required the Phantoms to be alerted, jettison their bombs, and accelerate to build an energy margin that would take them above the potential attacker to a point from which a diving attack could be made. All this depended upon early warning—and early warning depended upon radar surveillance, not always available. The lack of coverage forced the rapid de-velopment of the airborne warning and control aircraft, the giant, rotating-dome Boeing E-3Bs that would be so effective in the Gulf War and elsewhere.

But given the slightest warning, the superior ability of American aircrews allowed them to transform their Phantoms into dogfighters, a transformation later enhanced when the F-4E was fitted with an internally mounted 20mm M-61A1 Vulcan multibarrel Gatling gun.

THE INVERSION OF TACTICS

The fundamental fallacy of DOD strategy was never more evident than in the comparative use of F-105s and B-52s. The F-105s daily flew north with bomb loads of 4 or 5 tons, greater than World War II B-17s could carry, but small relative to the need. A "basic package" of F-105s would be sixteen aircraft in four flights of four, with two flights of F-4s positioned fore and aft for fighter cover. The Wild Weasel force would precede the task force on entry and follow it out after the strike. Radar suppression was supplied by Douglas EB-66s orbiting on each side of the target area. The Thuds would drop a tight pattern of perhaps a hundred Mark 117 bombs (750 pounds each) and break off to return.

As will be shown below, while the Thuds were hitting precisely defined and often carefully limited targets in the north with their 75,000 pounds of bombs, three cells of three B-52s might be operating in the south, dropping as much as 560,000 pounds on *suspected* Viet Cong locations. Thus did DOD directives turn basic commonsense tactics upside down.

The most frustrating mission for the F-105s proved to be North Vietnamese bridges, especially the Thanh Hoa (Dragon's Jaw) bridge spanning the Son Ma and the eighteen-span Paul Doumer bridge across the Red River north of Hanoi. The Thanh Hoa bridge seemed indestructible, shrugging off 871 USAF and U.S. Navy air attacks that cost eleven aircraft. The periodic bombing pauses were used to repair it, and in the four years after the November 1, 1968, pause, the bridge was substantially improved as an artery south.

The Paul Doumer, built by the French, was a massive structure 8,467 feet long that rested on eighteen huge concrete piers. The narrow bridge supported a railroad down the center, with roadways on each side. Each day it carried twenty-six trains and hundreds of trucks, funneling an average 6,000 tons of supplies south. A vital artery connecting Hanoi to the rest of the country, the bridge was heavily defended by 300 antiaircraft guns, including radar-directed 85mm flak batteries, and eighty-one SAM sites. All of the MiG interceptors could be quickly scrambled in the event of an attack. The F-105s flew 113 missions against the bridge, losing two aircraft in the process.

A preliminary success came on August 11, 1967, when the bridge was attacked by a flight of twenty F-105s, each fighter carrying two 3,000-pound Mk 118 bombs. The Deputy Commander of the 355th, Colonel Robert H. White, who had won both the Harmon and the Collier trophies along with his astronaut's wings flying the X-15 research airplane, led the flight. The attack was preceded by the usual Wild Weasel and flak suppression unit and brushed through a flight of MiGs that made an unusual Luftwaffe-style head-on attack.

White rolled in for the attack from 13,000 feet, diving through a curtain of flak to release his bombs at 8,000 feet. The rash of explosions obscured the bridge momentarily; when it cleared, three spans were knocked down into the river. Two 105s were damaged, but all returned to base. The resilient North Vietnamese had repaired the bridge by October 3, even as they delivered material by other means, including a ferry. Succeeding bombing attacks also caused damage that was quickly repaired.

It was not until Linebacker I in 1972 that the issue was resolved by F-4s carrying Paveway I laser-guided bombs. Both the Thanh Hoa and Paul Doumer bridges were at last dumped into their respective riverbeds, with no U.S. aircraft destroyed.

The Paveway series of precision-guided munitions were standard bombs

combined with guidance and control kits. In an attack, the target was illuminated by a laser. When the bomb was dropped; a microprocessor fed signals to the bomb's guidance fins to place it on target. These precision-guided
munitions were precursors of weapons to come and a tribute to the AFSC/
AFLC teams that developed them.

BUFFS IN ACTION

The Boeing B-52, SAC's dependable long rifle, was designed to carry
thermonuclear bombs to the heart of the Soviet Union. First flown in 1952,
the Buff (an acronym standing for, in its bowdlerized version, Big Ugly Fat
Fellow) is probably going to be in service well into the twenty-first century
still the most flexible aircraft in military history. Despite its versatility, it will
probably still be engaged in the impromptu role into which it was cast in
Vietnam, dropping massive quantities of conventional ordnance.

B-52 operations began on June 18, 1965, in the first of what were called
the Arc Light strikes, when twenty-seven aircraft from the 7th and 320th
Bombardment Wing flew from Andersen AFB, Guam, to a suspected Viet
Cong base north of Saigon. The enemy base camp was spread out, and previous air attacks had not been effective.

Neither the Air Force nor the Army was optimistic about the effectiveness of the B-52s' performing the same role that artillery had in World War
I, grinding up miles of terrain in the hopes of hitting something. One Air
Force leader termed it "swatting flies with a sledgehammer." The first mission was further tainted when two B-52s collided in midair because of insufficient distance between their planned refueling tracks. Nonetheless,
General William Westmoreland, USMACV Commander, soon became convinced that the B-52 was an indispensable weapon, and Arc Light operations
escalated.

The utility of B-52s was expanded when they began actual close support
operations in November 1965, driving off Viet Cong attackers at Plei Mei in
the Central Highlands. In December, support was provided to the III Marine
Amphibious Force, under the command of Lieutenant General Lewis W.
Walt III. The Marines were and are notoriously demanding about close support efforts, and Walt was delighted by the scope, scale, and accuracy of the
B-52s' effort.

The B-52Fs then being used could carry fifty-one 750-pound bombs,
twenty-seven internally and twenty-four externally. In 1965, a massive program called Big Belly was established to increase the internal capacity of
B-52Ds for 500-pound bombs from twenty-seven to eighty-four, and for 750-
pound bombs from twenty-seven to forty-two. External pylon racks could
carry twenty-four bombs, either 500 or 750 pounds. Maximum bomb load
was thus increased to 54,000 pounds when carrying all 500-pounders and
49,500 pounds when carrying 750-pounders. Fittings for mines and glide

bombs were also installed, and just as a precaution, up to four nuclear gravity bombs could be carried as well.

The B-52s were not bombing typical easily defined targets such as cities or military bases, but rather acres of heavily canopied jungle, so new delivery techniques were needed. Mobile ground radar guidance units were installed to provide Combat Skyspot, a ground-directed bombing system. Radar controllers would direct the B-52s along a course and signal when to drop the bombs. Combat Skyspot was flexible, permitting quick switches in targeting, and was also extremely accurate. The automaton-like nature of the raids on the vast stretches of impenetrable jungle was frustrating, and the overworked crews sardonically referred to themselves as "coconut knockers."

Yet the Viet Cong came to hate the B-52s more than any other weapon, for the first warning of the B-52s presence was the explosions of bombs in a huge corridor. One year after commencing operations, the B-52s were dropping 8,000 tons of bombs per month on Viet Cong targets. Sortie rates rose to 1,800 per month, with aircraft flying out of Andersen and the newly established Royal Thai Naval Air Base at U-Tapao, Thailand. U-Tapao was only two to five hours away from its targets, while aircraft from Andersen faced twelve-hour missions, with at least one refueling in route.

The scale of the logistic effort was massive, as millions of pounds of supplies ranging from food for the guard dogs to bombs for the Viet Cong were trundled across a 12,000-mile pipeline, all scheduled on various milestone charts around the world to keep inventories low—in many ways the system anticipated the modern "just in time" inventory method. The work was demanding for air and ground crews, who worked seventy-two hours a week routinely and eighty-four hours during surge periods. The troops doing the dangerous munitions work were under constant pressure to keep the Big Bellies filled with bombs. The constant heat, the loneliness, and the lack of amenities did nothing to improve their lot. Aircrews were assigned for 179 days of TDY, because a 180-day tour would have had to have been considered a permanent change of station, which was expensive and administratively disruptive. Their life degenerated into an unending cycle of brief, fly, sleep, brief, fly, sleep.

While the B-52 made invaluable contributions throughout during the war, there were two defining missions that stand out, Operation Niagara and Operation Linebacker II. The first of these was early in 1968 at Khe Sanh, where 6,000 Marines and their Vietnamese allies were surrounded by 30,000 North Vietnamese regular soldiers, who hoped to make Khe Sanh for the Americans what Dien Bien Phu had been for the French.

General Westmoreland approved Operation Niagara, which began on January 22, 1968. Even here command and control was difficult, for the Navy and would not agree to subordinate itself to Seventh Air Force for the operation, and the area around the camp had to be divided into small zones, miniature route packages, to avoid interference.

Using Combat Skyspot techniques, six aircraft struck the target every three hours. The B-52s pummeled the North Vietnamese for days, flying 461 missions and 2,701 sorties and dropping 75,631 tons of munitions before the operation ended on March 31. Initially, the B-52 was limited to dropping bombs no closer than 3,300 yards to friendly positions; as the North Vietnamese sappers pushed their trenches forward, the safety zone was dropped to less than 300 yards. This distance may seem like a lot to someone running a race, but to a GI looking out at bombs bursting across a field of barbed wire, it is minuscule. Considering it as the end result of bombs dropped from a bomber flying a course line at 500 mph at 30,000 feet with crosswinds varying as much as 180 degrees in heading and 100 mph in speed throughout the length of the drop, it becomes a remarkable testament to the skill of the bomber and Skyspot crews and the trust of the troops on the ground. In a post-battle assessment, General Westmoreland noted, "The thing that broke their back basically was the fire of the B-52s."

LAOS AND IGLOO WHITE

The sideshow war in Laos was as much a secret war as the war in South Vietnam was a civil insurrection. The DOD tried to pretend that the multibillion-dollar effort to prop up Souvanna Phouma by means of aid, troop training, covert CIA intervention (including running its own airline and using the services of 20,000 Thai troops) and the virtual dedication of Seventh Air Force air assets to the U.S. ambassador in Vientiane simply was not happening.

Yet during the period from 1960 to 1968, American airmen engaged in a life-or-death struggle trying to stop the infiltration of men and material to South Vietnam and support the troops loyal to the central Laotian government. In Laos, as in South Vietnam, the equipment allocated to the task was at first World War II–vintage RB-and B-26s and North American T-28 trainers. And as in Vietnam, as the U.S. effort increased, so did the North Vietnamese response. Over time, the equipment dedicated to warfare in Laos was improved, and by 1968, all of the modern aircraft operating in North and South Vietnam were also at work in Laos, including the deadly Lockheed AC-130 Spectre gunship. The AC-130 had low-light-level television, infrared, radar, and 20mm side-firing Gatling guns. Later versions had 40mm guns and even laser designators. Phantoms were used to provide flak suppression and attack work—extremely nerve-wracking dives into the pitch-black night to deliver bombs that cost just about as much as the trucks they were aimed at. B-52s were brought in to work under Combat Skyspot control. They were once again a success, and a call went up for an expansion of their work, for the quantity of explosive power they could deliver dwarfed that of all the artillery available in the area.

The desperate effort to use the highest-possible technology to sustain the fiction that the war in Southeast Asia was a mere insurrection reached its peak of fantasy in what was first known as the Barrier Concept and was code-named Igloo White.

An original proposal by Professor Roger Fisher of the Harvard Law School to build a 60-mile anti-infiltration barrier across the DMZ and into Laos caught the attention of Assistant Secretary McNaughton. The idea was expanded to become an on-the-ground barrier reaching 180 miles across South Vietnam and Laos—a miniature Great Wall of China—approximately along Route 9 to the Mekong. The concept had been passed to the Jason Committee of the Institute of Defense Analysis, which was serving as Mc-Namara's private Strategic Bombing Survey group. The Jason committee viewed bombing the North as futile and endorsed the concept of an air-supported barrier system that would use electronic sensors to detect enemy activity, which would be countered with air strikes.

The JCS argued against the concept on the basis of its costs and the probable ease with which the enemy might counter it. McNamara ignored the JCS comments and appointed General Alfred Starbird to head Joint Task Force 728 (later given the cover name Defense Communications Planning Group [DCPG]) within the OSD Directorate of Defense Research and Engineering. Thus in a remote-control war can an idea be transmuted by a small committee into a concept for a large committee whose work makes it possible for an even larger committee to turn it into a travesty. The famous aphorism "A camel is a horse designed by a committee" was transcended; what became known as Igloo White was a hydra-headed monster that devoured close to $3 billion, cost many lives, and only marginally disrupted the flow of traffic. The JCS repeatedly attempted to fight the program on the grounds of cost, efficiency, and other more pressing needs, but McNamara had seized the concept as his own and was determined to ramrod it through without regard to advice opposing it. It truly became the McNamara Line.

The DCPG had decided upon a highly advanced air-supported anti-infiltration system consisting of sophisticated air-dropped acoustic and seismic sensors (along with sensors attuned to pick up the ordinary odors of hard-working humans). Read-out aircraft were posted to receive the transmitted signals, which were in turn sent to an enormous central processing facility at Nakhon Phanom (NKP) Royal Thai Air Force Base near the Laotian border. There a huge computerized ground assessment center received, analyzed, and reported enemy logistic flow activity (the grinding of a truck, the pounding feet of rice-bag-laden porters, the acrid scent of urine). This information was relayed to an airborne battlefield command and control center (ABCCC) over Laos, which would then direct attack aircraft to the site. Unfortunately, the North Vietnamese reacted to a limited increase in pressure in Laos exactly as they had to limited increases elsewhere: they fought harder. They seized upon President Johnson's bombing halt to extend their radar control into Laos, moving in SAMs and AAA. For the first time, MiG fighters began making incursions in Laotian airspace; these were quickly checked by Phantoms working with Disco or Red Crown.

By the end of 1968, despite improvements that had been made in slowing the rate of infiltration, there was still a sense of general dissatisfaction, for too many trucks were still getting through. General Momyer pointed out that all previous successful air interdiction campaigns had three components. The first was against the production sources of enemy supplies; the second was the interdiction of movement between the enemy's heartland and his forces in the field; the third was forcing the enemy into active ground warfare so that he would consume his supplies faster than he could replace them. In Laos and in Vietnam, only the second element was being executed.

The JCS once again went on record as advising the closing of North Vietnam's major ports and against continuing Rolling Thunder, since it was not very effective because it was limited to the area south of the 20th parallel.

All of the factors coincided with the initial operational capability of the Igloo White system—which, if it worked as hoped, would be the answer for stopping infiltration. Igloo White was tested in a series of interdiction programs during the dry seasons.

New tactics were used in conjunction with assessments made of intelligence provided by the sensors. Roads would be cut by laser-guided bombs, then land mines powerful enough to destroy heavy vehicular equipment would be emplaced. To inhibit mine clearing, antipersonnel land mines were sown. (McNamara had approved a production schedule of 3.5 million Dragontooth antivehicular mines and 10 million antipersonnel land mines per month.) The results of this effort were then to be monitored by sensors on each side of the mined area, which would determine how many trucks were getting through. A small air force supported Igloo White, including twenty-one Lockheed EC-121 ABCCC planes, eighteen McDonnell F-4Ds, eighteen Douglas A-1Es, twelve Sikorsky CH-3 helicopters, and thirty-four Cessna O-2 Skymasters. Additional aircraft could be called in.

Despite the expenditure of enormous effort and billions of dollars, Igloo White proved to be a spectacular failure for a variety of reasons, the most important being that it was totally the wrong system for existing conditions. North Vietnamese infiltrators streamed down the multiple trails like rain running down a window pane; Igloo White corresponded to a finger placed on the window to halt the runoff. Almost as important was the resilience of the North Vietnamese, who could repair road damage about as fast as bombs could cause it. The North Vietnamese understood immediately what the sensors were for and quickly devised active and passive ways to nullify them or spoof them. They would cover some of the devices with the ubiquitous wicker baskets to mask their sensors; others they would trick by sending a truck back and forth to simulate a convoy. Anything from croaking frogs to thunder could trigger the sensors used to detect vehicles, resulting in traffic reports that made the Ho Chi Minh Trail seem like rush hour on a Los Angeles freeway.

The final obstacle was the geography, climate, and vegetation of the area targeted for Igloo White use. The heavy jungle canopy made it impossible for a FAC (forward air controller) to get visual identification of trucks that the sensors might have picked up, and bad weather often prevented strikes.

Despite brilliant efforts by the almost 5,000 people who tried to make it work, Igloo White was a world-class failure. And in the way of Washington politics, its failure went almost unnoticed because the program was so highly classified. McNamara never had to acknowledge the utter bankruptcy of the scheme he had bullied through over all objections, for in November 1967, he had decamped to become the head of the World Bank.

CAMBODIA

Cambodia had long been a haven for North Vietnamese and Viet Cong, and President Nixon authorized air strikes in early 1969 to destroy the sanctuaries. Under the code name Operation Menu, B-52s made almost 4,000 sorties and dropped almost 110,000 tons of bombs in Cambodia.

On April 30, 1970, the combined factors of the American drawdown and the growth in Communist supply storage areas in the Cambodian sanctuaries caused Nixon to authorize an invasion of Cambodia by both U.S. and ARVN troops. The area of the invasion was limited, and the time of occupation was set at eight weeks. B-52s were again used to bomb.

The military effort was largely successful and reduced the threat to Saigon, but domestic reaction was violent, especially on college campuses, and led to Congressional legislation that forbade future introduction of U.S. ground forces into Thailand, Cambodia, or Laos.

The bombing went on at a reduced rate until August 1973. By 1975, the Communist Khmer Rouge forces of Pol Pot had seized control and begun the genocidal slaughter of 1.5 million of their countrymen.

LINEBACKER II

The abominable term "political air superiority" characterized the gift made by Secretary McNamara to the armed forces of North Vietnam by placing inane restrictions on U.S. air activities in the form of unreasonable rules of engagement. The North Vietnamese retained political air superiority until the enunciation of the Nixon Doctrine by the newly elected President Nixon. Nixon was faced with a dilemma. He had to recognize that after seven years of McNamara's leadership, the war was lost politically no matter what happened in the field. The most vivid example of this anomaly was the Tet offensive, a crushing disaster for the North Vietnamese and the Viet Cong, who had lost 45,000 killed of the 84,000 troops participating. Yet this victory in the field for American and ARVN forces was turned into an agonizing defeat by the U.S. media.

Secretary of Defense Robert S. McNamara (left) confers with General Earle
G. Wheeler (right), USA, Chairman, Joint Chiefs of Staff, and John T.
McNaughton, Assistant Secretary of Defense (International Security Affairs).

In an April, 1965, briefing, Secretary of Defense Robert S. McNamara points to the
notorious Thanh Hoa Bridge, known as "the Dragon's Jaw."

Colonel David "Chappie" James, Jr., after he assumed command of the 7272nd Flying Training Wing at Wheelus, AB, Libya. James went on to become the first African-American four-star general.

One of the great gentlemen of the Air Force, General Russell E. Dougherty, Commander in Chief of the Strategic Air Command, chats with (from left) General George S. Brown, chairman of the Joint Chiefs of Staff, Secretary of Defense James R. Schlesinger, and General David C. Jones, Air Force Chief of Staff.

A veteran of three wars and an eight-victory ace in Korea, Lt. Colonel Robinson Risner was commander of the 67th TFS, flying Republic F-105s, when he was shot down in 1965. Rescued, he was shot down again, this time to remain seven long years in the infamous "Hanoi Hilton." Here, he stands defiant before the enemy camera.

Robinson endured and prevailed, and is here commended by PACAF CINC General Lucius D. Clay, Jr. The joyous welcome homecoming prisoners of war received was perhaps the high point of an otherwise frustrating war.

Despite the DoD-imposed disadvantages of the rules of engagement, the USAF fought well. Here are two of the three USAF aces of that conflict, Captain Charles Debellevue, a Weapons Systems Officer, and Captain Steve Ritchie, pilot.

Older aircraft fought well in South Vietnam against the Viet Cong. Here, a pair of Douglas A-1E Skyraiders attack a Viet Cong barracks near Thanh Minh.

Colonel Robin Olds marks up three victories over MiG-17 aircraft on May 20, 1967. From left: Major Philip P. Combies, First Lieutenant Daniel L. Lafferty, Major John R. Pardo, First Lieutenant Stempen B. Croker, and First Lieutenant Stephen A. Wayne.

Necessity drove technology to reach unbelievable heights. A Lockheed HC-130P tanker refuels a Sikorsky HH-3B helicopter over the Gulf of Tonkin in June, 1970.

Major (later Lieutenant Colonel) Leo K. Thorsness was awarded the Medal of Honor for his courageous actions on April 19, 1967. After silencing a surface-to-air missile site, Thorsness' wingman was shot down. Thorsness circled the crew members to protect them, and in the process shot down one MiG-17 and damaged another. He was later shot down and captured, spending almost six years in Vietnamese prisons.

There was no sweeter sight to a downed air crew man than a Jolly Green Giant helicopter hovering overhead, lowering its jungle-canopy penetrator for the quick ride home. The penetrator, whose bullet shape was transformed into three petal-like supports, could lift three men at the end of its 240-foot hoist cable.

When the battle situation did not permit a landing, the Lockheed C-130s used a Low Altitude Parachute Extraction System (LAPES) to get their cargo where it was needed. Here a Hercules crew delivers a load of supplies to the U.S. Army's 1st Cavalry Division (Airmobile) at An Khe, Vietnam.

General Lew Allen, Jr., served from 1978 to 1982 as Chief of Staff, United States Air Force. A command pilot with four thousand flying hours, General Allen was also highly respected as a scientist in both the military and civil communities.

Nixon had to find a way out, and he found it in the Nixon Doctrine, which promised that the United States would honor its treaty commitments and would provide its nuclear shield to any nation vital to U.S. interests. It would furnish arms and economic assistance, but it expected any threatened nation to provide the manpower for its own defense. Nixon's Secretary of Defense, Melvin Laird, coined the term "Vietnamization," meaning training and arming of South Vietnamese forces to defend themselves, while U.S. forces were systematically and rapidly pulled out. The policy was announced in a speech on Guam on July 25, 1969, without consulting the South Vietnamese government of then President Nguyen Van Thieu. The troops had another phrase for Vietnamization, calling it the "bug-out." Political air superiority now became intolerable, for the North Vietnamese reaction of increased military pressure indicated that they wished to secure a military victory rather than permit the United States to save whatever face remained in a negotiated withdrawal. Much would happen between 1969 and 1972, and eventually, air power would be called upon not to achieve the victory that it might have produced, but to persuade the North Vietnamese to accept a negotiated peace. On March 29, 1972, powerful North Vietnamese mechanized units drove across the DMZ into South Vietnam, in a flagrant violation of the negotiation talks then being conducted. The routed South Vietnamese fell back in disarray, and the task of stopping the advance fell to the South Vietnamese Air Force and to the remaining units of the depleted USAF forces. On May 8, President Nixon recognized the inevitable, called a halt to the peace talks, and authorized Operation Linebacker, which extended the strikes that had been going on since April above the 20th parallel and included the mining of Haiphong and other ports.

The North Vietnamese had immeasurably strengthened their air defenses during the four-year bombing layoff, but the efforts of AFSC and AFLC had provided the USAF with some new weapons too. In November 1968, the McDonnell F-4E had begun to arrive in Southeast Asia. Equipped with more advanced engines, an internal 20mm M-61A1 Vulcan multibarrel cannon, leading-edge maneuvering flaps to improve its dogfighting ability, and (by 1972) TISEO (Target Identification System Electro Optical), a telescope in the leading edge of the left wing, the F-4E was a formidable MiG killer. Electronic warfare capability had been upgraded, and both EB-66s and EC-135s had new jammers to quell enemy electronics. New ways had been found to dispense chaff effectively from F-4s. (Chaff was perhaps the simplest of the jamming devices, being simply sheets of what resembled tinfoil cut into lengths. It jammed certain of the enemy radar frequencies. It had been first used in 1943 in the calamitous Royal Air Force raid on Hamburg.) The electro-optical and laser-guided munitions were available in increased supply, and aircrews had gained familiarity in their use.

Linebacker was an apparent success, for the North Vietnamese returned to the negotiating table. President Nixon ordered a halt to the bombing above the 20th parallel in response, and the enemy as usual interpreted this as a sign of weakness and increased its military pressure. By December 18, the United States was in a desperate position; the North Vietnamese negotiators now obviously believed they would achieve the military victory for which they had been fighting since 1945.

President Nixon then chose to use air power as had been advocated by General LeMay in 1963 and subsequently by Generals McConnell, Earle Wheeler, and John Ryan along with Admiral Sharp. That use was the full application of air power at its highest intensity in all its forms directly against the key political and military targets of the enemy to force a settlement of the war.

Linebacker II had to be conducted during the height of the monsoon season, so it was built around an all-weather force of B-52s, General Dynamic F-111s (which after a disappointing debut were proving to be deadly efficient), F-4s (which had replaced most of the F-105s), Vought A-7s, EB-66s, KC-135s, and naval aircraft. The B-52s were designated to hit airfields, supply depots, and railroad marshaling yards; F-4s, using precision guided munitions, were to hit the Hanoi electrical power plant, Radio Hanoi, and specialized sections of the railyards. F-105 Wild Weasels had their usual dangerous task of SAM suppression. The F-111s were to attack SAM sites, airfields, and marshaling yards, while the A-7s were to attack Yen Bai airfield. These were backed up by KC-135 refuelers, Search and Rescue C-130s and Sikorsky HH-53 Jolly Green Giant helicopters, EC-121s, and a host of others.

The initial attack called for 129 B-52 sorties: forty-two B-52Ds from U-Tapao and fifty-four B-52Gs and thirty-three B-52Ds from Andersen. The second day would have ninety-three sorties and the third ninety-nine; after that, pressure would be applied continuously at the highest level possible. The Andersen Buffs would form the first and third waves over Hanoi, the U-Tapao aircraft the second.

The first takeoff took place at 2:51 P.M. local time at Andersen, on December 18, 1972. Instructions from SAC Headquarters were that the aircraft were *not* to take evasive action from either SAMs or MiGs during the long run in from the initial point (IP) to bombs-away. This rigid—and ultimately costly—requirement was because SAC wanted to make sure that only military targets were hit and to preserve the electronic countermeasure integrity of the three-ship formations.

As soon as the bombers penetrated the target area, SA-2 Guideline missiles filled the sky, their firing signaled by a city-block-square flash on the ground, followed by streaks through the sky that exploded into a huge mushroom-shaped halos of expanding light. As many as forty SAMs were in the air at the same time, often tracking a single cell of three B-52s. The Guidelines were the size of telephone poles, and many passed close enough to B-52 cockpits that a newspaper might have been read in their rockets' glare.

Others hit aircraft, knocking them from the sky. More than 200 SAMs were fired, and three B-52s were lost, two from Andersen and one from U-tapao.

On the second night, six B-52s were shot down out of the ninety-three that were launched, even though permission had been given the second and third waves to take evasive action on their run in from the IP. The heroism was incredible; one pilot on one crew calmly announced that they were going to be hit by a SAM just as they released their bombs. They were, and they were shot down.

The 7 percent loss rate was unacceptable, yet General John J. Meyer, a twenty-six-victory ace in World War II and now Commander in Chief of SAC (CINCSAC), made the tough decision to press on, calling for SAM sites and storage sites to be heavily hit.

His decision was correct, for the enemy had been hurt too, and was running out of SAMs. For three successive days, no B-52s were lost. The MiGs proved to be no threat at all, with two being shot down by B-52 gunners.

Christmas Day saw a stand-down, a pause to get a signal from Hanoi, and to give the crews, particularly the ground crews, much needed rest. The stand-down was a mistake, because it gave the North Vietnamese a respite in which to recover and restock their SAM sites with missiles.

On December 26, entirely new tactics were tried. All Andersen aircraft, seventy-eight B-52s, were to arrive simultaneously over Hanoi, arriving in four waves from four different directions. Three other waves went on to strike Haiphong at the exact same time.

With 110 support aircraft in the air, the attack went off with precision, with only two B-52s being lost despite the heavy increase in SAM firings. In three attacks, the B-52s had established an ascendancy over Hanoi, which at that moment in 1972 had the most heavily defended airspace in the world. All USAF commanders—and all aircrew members—ground their teeth in fury as they recognized what could have been done in 1965 with such ease and with no losses. The argument that had been made time and again—and ignored every time but once—was proved to be correct: air power could dominate North Vietnam and make it comply with U.S. wishes.

The remainder of the eleven raids went off flawlessly, except for the sad, unavoidable loss of two more B-52s. By the eleventh day, the North Vietnamese were out of SAMs, their MiGs were shut down, their radar and communication links disrupted: they were at the mercy of the United States. In the miserable prisons in which they were held, American prisoners of war experienced an unimaginable elation at seeing their brutal captors frightened and suddenly polite.

Pragmatists, the North Vietnamese signaled that they wished to return to the negotiating table in Paris, and the raids were immediately halted. Many observers within and without the U.S. military knew that this was a mistake;

had the raids been continued, the North Vietnamese would have had to accept total military defeat. Instead they secured a victory at the peace tables, one they translated in three years to the full conquest of South Vietnam.

In Linebacker II, SAC had flown 729 sorties, dropped 15,000 tons of bombs, and sustained fifteen losses—less than a 2 percent loss rate. About 1,240 SAMs had been fired. The result of Linebacker II was exactly what had been predicted for the total application of air power in North Vietnam: quick military victory. Had it been applied in the first years of the war, the lives of millions of people would have been spared, hundreds of billions of dollars would have been saved, South Vietnam would not have been ravaged, Cambodia would have not had to endure the Khmer Rouge, and the United States would have not had the ugly experience of the disaffected 1960s and 1970s with the continuing cynicism of the media and the general disaffection of the populace with its government.

6

≋

THE PILLARS OF THE AIR
FORCE: FOUR MAJOR
COMMANDS

*D*uring the Vietnam War, especially the eleven days of Linebacker II, the ferocious capability of fighter, bomber, electronic warfare, tanker, and other combat aircraft was the sharp cutting edge of the United States Air Force's sword.

But the cutting edge of any sword is made lethal only by the reach, heft, balance, and control of the entire weapon and the skill of the person wielding it. During the Vietnam War, the cutting edge of tactical and strategic units' combat capability in the field existed only because of the reach provided by the airlift capability of the Military Airlift Command. The heft of the USAF combat sword was provided by the towering supply support of the Air Force Logistic Command. The balance and control were the result of years of work by the Air Force Systems Command, and the skills of the units wielding the Air Force sword were the product of the Air Training Command.

Over the course of time, the names and sometimes the missions of these organizations have changed, but the twenty-five-year midpoint of the history of the Air Force (which occurred in 1972) is a convenient benchmark to examine them as they have evolved.

THE AIRLIFTERS: ANYTHING, ANYWHERE, ANYTIME

The history of the United States Air Force military airlift units has been one of years of absolute drudgery punctuated by periods of shining glory. Despite being understrength and often using inadequate equipment, military airlift units traditionally have been on call at any time, to fly anywhere in the world in every sort of weather. The "trash haulers," as they ruefully came to call themselves, have been decisive in war and, in a much larger way than is generally recognized, in the preservation of peace. Unfortunately, the ability of the United States Air Force military air transport units to solve problems ranging from the Berlin Airlift and the relief of Israel in the Yom Kippur War to the thousands of compassionate missions flown to people in need is often forgotten—especially during the appropriations process.

The very first demonstration of American military airlift took place at Fort Myer, Virginia, on September 9, 1908, when Lieutenant Frank P. Lahm briefly rode with Orville Wright on the Wright *Military Flyer*. Since then, the story has always been the same, from officers bumming rides from Orville Wright to frantic calls for McDonnell Douglas C-17 support: military airlift is so attractive compared to other means of transport that demand always exceeds supply.

Certain other factors have been consistent throughout the history of military airlift. The first of these has been the desire of expert airlift specialists to keep all airlift assets in a single organization. The first call for organizational unity was made by Brigadier General Augustine W. Robins, Chief of the Air Corps Materiel Division from 1935 to 1939. Opposition to the idea has been just as pervasive, for the desire of most organizations, from the U.S. Army and U.S. Navy down to individual squadrons, has consistently been to maintain their own dedicated airlift capability. In the matter of control, the principal argument over time has been the management of intratheater airlift, including the combat airlift mission, where the transports go in under hostile fire to land or to drop troops and supplies.

Another uniform element in airlift history was the inevitable reduction in airlift resources at the end of every emergency. This has always resulted in a frantic scramble to manage the next crisis on an ad hoc basis, with the concomitant crash program to rebuild airlift capability. An expensive way to do business, it is not confined solely to airlift units. Yet, as will be shown, a contradictory combination of advances in technology and reduced military budgets has served to bring most of these arguments into congruence, if not harmony.

FROM FERRYING AIRCRAFT TO WINNING THE WAR

The first great impetus to military airlift was the requirement to ferry aircraft all over the United States and to the United Kingdom and the Soviet Union. The Air Corps Ferrying Command served for fifty-five weeks and ferried more than 14,000 aircraft before being succeeded by the Air Transport Command (ATC). Created on June 20, 1942, following the recommendations of L. Welch Pogue, then Chairman of the Civil Aeronautics Board, the ATC assumed responsibility for air transportation of personnel, material, and mail for all War Department units, except for those served by Troop Carrier Command units. The most vital function was assigned almost as an afterthought: ATC was responsible for the control, operation, and maintenance of facilities on Army Air Force air routes outside the United States. This was to be the beginning of a vast network of airfields, runways, meteorological stations, radar stations, and other facilities that would serve as the basis for postwar civil and military international air routes.

In four years of war, the ATC delivered 282,437 aircraft and flew 8.1 billion passenger miles along with 2.7 billion ton-miles of freight. By war's end, an ATC aircraft was crossing the Atlantic every thirteen minutes and the Pacific every thirty-seven minutes, twenty-four hours a day. The ATC was started with 11,000 personnel; by August 1945, it employed 41,705 officers, 167,596 airmen, and 104,677 civilians. Among the most important of these—in societal terms—were the pioneering WASPs. Of the 1,830 women who gained admission to the Women's Air Service Pilots, 1,074 graduated as pilots. They delivered 12,652 aircraft in the course of the war. It took until 1979 for the country to come to its senses and grant these brave women the military status they had earned and deserved.

Many lessons were learned in the ATC, including the need to have larger, more reliable aircraft. At the peak of its operations, the ATC had 3,090 aircraft, of which 1,341 were DC-3s. The rest were a mixture of Curtiss C-46s, Consolidated C-87s, and Douglas C-54s. The C-46s were disappointing because of mechanical problems, and the C-87s had the natural disadvantage in cubic capacity of a bomber converted to a transport. The C-54s were a blessing, a remarkable aircraft loved by their air and ground crews and capable of flying great distances with large loads.

Some of the flying performed by the ATC was as dangerous as combat over Europe—a trail of aluminum-spread crash sites punctuated the perilous route over the Himalayan Hump, from China to India. During the war, the command suffered 1,229 accidents, or 5.57 per 100,000 flying hours.

Troop Carrier Command had an equally distinguished record and grew in strength as the war progressed. On D day some 900 aircraft were used; by the time of Operation Market Garden, the abortive September 17, 1944, airborne attack on Arnhem, more than 2,000 C-47s alone were used, along with 600 gliders. Airlift had come along way from Fort Myer.

After the war, the ATC suffered from the same drastic demobilization as the rest of the services, despite a "Dear Tooey" letter from retiring General of the Army Hap Arnold, who advised his successor, General Spaatz, "During times of peace we are apt to retain our combat units and sacrifice the essentials to their successful deployment and immediate operation. We must retain our bases and our means of deployment." His words are as valid today as they were in 1946.

Disturbed by claims of wasteful duplication of Air Force and Navy transport units and spurred by the recommendations of the Finletter Commission, the new Secretary of Defense, James V. Forrestal, literally forced the merger of ATC and the Naval Air Transport Service in June 1948, to create the

Military Air Transport Service. Grumbling, the Navy "loaned" MATS three squadrons and kept most of its transport capability intact for "fleet support."

As related previously, MATS was given an immediate challenge by the 1948 Berlin Airlift, which it met with enormous success, acquitting itself with distinction. It was confirmed there for all time that fewer large transports were more effective than more numerous small ones, and the first great step in that direction was the Douglas C-124 Globemaster II. The C-124 was rarely called the Globemaster—to most it was "Old Shaky" for the orchestrated vibrations that strummed through it from the moment the engines were started until the flight was completed.

The C-124 was huge for the time, with a 174-foot wing that looked thin and quite inadequate to support the cavernous fuselage. Unlike its gallant C-54 predecessor, the C-124 was designed with hauling freight in mind, with clamshell nose-loading doors and a ramp up which tanks, trucks, and other vehicles could be driven. First flown on November 27, 1949, the C-124 would be used by several commands but find its niche with the MATS.

When the Korean War came, the hero of the Berlin Airlift, Major General William H. Tunner, was called upon to organize a Combat Cargo Command (Provisional) for the Far East Air Force. There once again the missions of strategic and tactical airlift converged in a combat role, as indicated in a previous chapter. The Combat Cargo Command made history with its air drops to Marines defending their positions at the Chosin Reservoir, dropping 140 tons of ammunition in two days in late November 1950. When the Marines hacked an airstrip out of the frozen soil, Combat Cargo Command aircraft landed 221 times, bringing in 273 tons of supplies and airlifting out 4,600 wounded.

MATS support grew steadily during the Korean War; early on, it averaged 2.5 tons per day, and by the end of the war the average rose to 106 tons. The combined total of 212,034 MATS sorties, tactical and strategic, delivered more than 391,763 tons of cargo, 2.6 million passengers, and 310,000 medevac patients.

It was an incredible effort, rewarded immediately after the war by another catastrophic drawdown and a continued forced reliance on piston-engine transports. In peacetime, MATS was placed under attack by civil airlines that wanted to carry passengers and freight for the services. Congressman Daniel Flood, a flamboyantly mustachioed Democrat from Pennsylvania, attacked MATS as a "billion-dollar boondoggle" and offered legislation thoughtfully prepared by the Air Transport Association—a lobby for the airlines—to remedy the situation. Flood called for 40 percent of all military passenger traffic and 20 percent of military cargo to be carried by civil airlines. The self-interest of the legislation was exposed almost immediately, for when the Taiwan crisis occurred in 1960, the airlines refused to bid on augmenting MATS service because the emergency had occurred during the profitable tourist season. The lesson was obvious: don't have emergencies during the tourist season.

Fortunately, farsighted Congressmen such as Representative L. Mendel Rivers, a Democrat from South Carolina, became advocates for MATS, particularly its requirement for modern aircraft. The combination of this Congressional backing and the demonstrated ability of MATS to respond to crises in the Middle East, the Far East, and Africa resulted in the first articulation of a national military airlift policy in February 1960. A report entitled "The Role of Military Air Transport in Peace and War" by Secretary of Defense Neil McElroy resulted in nine "Presidentially Approved Courses of Action." The most important of these provisions directed that the Civil Reserve Air Fleet (CRAF) program would augment the military's airlift capability. MATS was required to provide the essential "hard-core" element of air transport. To accede to the demands of the civil carriers, MATS agreed to reduce its regularly scheduled fixed routes (much to the dismay of "space-available" travelers!) and to procure additional airlift through negotiated contracts. Another provision, the closest to the hearts of Air Force leaders, required that MATS begin to modernize its fleet of aircraft. An effective compromise, McElroy's report defined civil and military airlift responsibilities for the next twenty-seven years, until President Ronald Reagan's National Airlift Policy statement of June 1987.

A Congressional subcommittee headed by Representative Rivers directed the Air Force to modernize its airlift. In the 1959 appropriations bill, Public Law 86-601, of July 1, 1960, required that the USAF spend $310.7 million for airlift, including $140 million for Lockheed C-130Es. The C-130 Hercules would set records for production longevity, utility, versatility, and dependability.

The expansion of MATS and the acquisition of modern aircraft coincided with the Kennedy administration's adoption of the concept of "flexible response." Clearly, if highly mobile armed forces were to be used on a moment's notice in any part of the world to stem Communist aggression, a strong MATS was required. Fortunately, the modernization came at a time when airlift technology, profiting by the power of the jet engine, the aerodynamics of jet aircraft, and the relatively new discipline of materials handling, had made it possible to create superlative aircraft with matching ground facilities.

The first foray by MATS into turboprop aircraft had not been happy. The Douglas C-133A Cargomaster, the first USAF turboprop-powered transport, made its initial flight on April 23, 1956. A handsome shoulder-wing aircraft with four Pratt & Whitney T34-P-3 turboprop engines, it could carry 52,000 pounds of cargo over a 4,000-mile route at a 323-mph cruising speed. Fifty aircraft were procured, but they were troubled by a series of enigmatic accidents and, after only ten years of service, by chronic fatigue problems.

Fortunately for MATS, when funds for expansion were made available, a trio of outstanding aircraft were in the wings, all strongly supported by Secretary McNamara. He advocated obtaining ninety-nine Lockheed C-130Es and thirty Boeing C-135s and initiating development of what would become the Lockheed C-141, another stellar performer.

These clearly superior aircraft raised MATS capability to a new level. When the full complement of 284 C-141 StarLifters had entered the fleet by 1968, MATS airlift capability was tripled, literally revolutionizing inter-theater airlift. As a simple comparison of the inherent advantage of a swept-wing jet over a conventional piston-powered aircraft, the venerable Douglas C-124 required ninety-five vibrating flying hours to go from Travis Air Force Base, California, to Saigon and return, carrying a 20,000-pound cargo. The C-124 had a limited daily utilization rate, and thus required thirteen days to make the trip. In contrast, the comfortable C-141, flying above the weather, could carry the same amount of cargo the same distance in thirty-four flying hours. In addition, the C-141 used the innovative 463L materials handling system, which permitted the aircraft to off-load 68,500 pounds of cargo, re-fuel, and reload in less than one hour. Old Shaky drivers could only shake their heads in amazement and hope that their squadron would soon reequip with StarLifters.

AIRLIFT IN VIETNAM

MATS entered the Vietnam war with an obsolete fleet equipped as fol-lows:

Equipment	Number of Squadrons
Boeing C-135 Stratofreighter	3
Lockheed C-130 Hercules	7
Douglas C-133A Cargomaster	3
Douglas C-124 GlobemasterII	21

There were two keys to the strategic and tactical modernization pro-grams. The strategic key, the Lockheed C-141, became operational in April 1965. In terms of sheer performance, the Boeing 707 was 50 mph faster, carried 20,000 pounds more cargo, and flew 500 miles farther, but the C-141 was designed to carry outsized cargo and to work with the 463L system. The result was a superb transport that arrived just in time to support the endless logistic requirements of the Vietnam War.

The tactical key was the Lockheed C-130, which went from strength to strength as it was employed in greater numbers for a wider variety of tasks. Other aircraft were also useful. The C-123, with its short-field capability, was a real workhorse. The de Havilland C-7 Caribou, which had been accepted from the Army only because it was part of the package of assuming the theater airlift responsibility, was also well liked by its crews because it was rugged and simple to maintain. Even the venerable Douglas C-47 did yeoman work, particularly in the dreary task of resettling Vietnamese civilians into protected enclaves. But in the exacting matter of moving tons of equipment over short and medium ranges, too often right into the teeth of enemy flak, there was nothing to compare with the C-130. In terms of efficiency, 100 C-130s could do the work of 1,500 C-47s.

The prototype YC-130 made its first flight at Burbank, California, on August 23, 1954, and the first operational C-130A was delivered to the Air Force on December 8, 1956. The basic design was excellent, and it has been improved over the years as newer models came into service. It is still in production and more than 2,100 have been sold to operators in sixty-five countries. Versatility is the hallmark of the C-130, and its roles include those of personnel and cargo transport, gunship, remote piloted vehicle and drone launcher, search and rescue, tanker, satellite recovery, weather reconnaissance personnel recovery electronic countermeasures, Antarctic delivery, airborne communicator, relay, medical evacuation, maritime patrol, special operations, hurricane hunting, and many more.

The performance of the Hercules was remarkable at the time of its debut, and is still so competitive today that the replacement aircraft for the C-130 seems to be destined to be another, the C-130J. A typical C-130E has a top speed of 384 mph, a service ceiling of 23,000 feet, and a range of 2,420 miles.

And as the C-130 was the right plane for the task, so was General Howell M. Estes, Jr., MATS/MAC Commander from 1964 to 1969, well qualified to meet Vietnam's airlift challenge. With a breadth of experience that ranged from the cavalry to the atomic tests at Eniwetok, Estes drew on the lessons learned in World War II and Korea to establish quick turnaround procedures (called "Quick Stop" and "Quick Change") along with specialized maintenance teams to get aircraft airborne using waivers, one-time flight permits, and even the *bête noire* of maintenance officers, cannibalization of parts from spare aircraft. "Red Ball Express" methods used by General Tunner on the Hump Airlift were revived; MATS guaranteed that important parts and equipment would move to their destination within twenty-four hours of reaching their aerial port of entry (APOE). Estes also established a command post system that formed an integral chain from MATS Headquarters to the lowest field echelons to monitor airlift operations.

MATS was redesignated Military Airlift Command (MAC) in January 1966, an important step that would lead in eight years to establishing a genuine unified control over airlift assets, strategic and tactical. In October 1966, the 834th Air Division was formed under Seventh Air Force at Tan Son Nhut Air Base, Saigon. The 834th's Airlift Control Center (ALCC) used fourteen airlift control elements (ALCE) at fourteen different aerial port locations. In addition, there were forty smaller detachments located throughout the country. The result was a far firmer control of airlift assets and the more rapid movement of troops and freight. The timing was perfect, because in Vietnam the strategic and tactical missions again converged.

STRATEGIC AIRLIFT IN VIETNAM

The war in Vietnam was odd in many ways, none more so than the standard mode of travel of soldiers to the war. In World Wars I and II, soldiers went to war jammed in the holds of freighters for endless days; the average soldier going to Vietnam went in style. No less than 91 percent of the personnel arrived in Southeast Asia aboard commercial jet transports, complete with reclining seats, helpful flight attendants, cocktail service, and, most of all, air-conditioning. All who stepped off the aircraft gasped in disbelief at the humid air smoking from Tan Son Nhut's blistering tarmac. The airliner represented home and comfort; the stinging heat of Vietnam symbolized war with all its loneliness and discomfort.

Yet such was American air superiority that the civil airliners could operate in Saigon with virtual impunity. The Tan Son Nhut flight line was crowded with the airlines of many nations; sometimes an airliner from Honolulu would be parked next to another whose flight had originated in Hanoi.

Commercial airlift also carried about 24 percent of the cargo. The rest was brought in by MAC aircraft, supplemented by Air National Guard and Air Force Reserve units flying venerable Boeing C-97 Stratofreighters, Fairchild C-119 Flying Boxcars, Lockheed C-121 Super Constellations, and, of course, the ubiquitous C-124s. The excellence of their effort influenced in no small way the thinking of President Nixon's Secretary of Defense, Melvin Laird, the proponent for the "Total Force" concept of bringing Guard and Reserve forces to the same level of skill, responsibility, and utilization as the regular Air Force.

Timing is everything, and the C-141 was introduced just in time to provide the capacity to execute President Johnson's decision to begin a massive buildup of American ground forces. Traffic to Southeast Asia grew from a monthly average of 33,779 passengers and 9,123 tons of cargo in 1965 to 65,350 passengers and 42,296 tons of cargo monthly at the height of the buildup in 1967.

At the same time, strategic airlift proved itself capable of combat operations, beginning in 1965 with Operation Blue Light, when 2,952 troops and 4,749 tons of equipment of the 3d Infantry Brigade, 25th Infantry Division was airlifted from Hickam AFB, Hawaii, directly to Pleiku. The movement, conducted by a mixture of C-141s, C-133s, and C-124s, cut days off the planned schedule and was called by General William Westmoreland "the most professional airlift I've seen in all my airborne experience." It was the precursor of even more ambitious efforts that would continue even after the war was long lost.

The next major intervention of strategic airlift into tactical warfare occurred with Operation Eagle Thrust in November 1967. This time MAC carried 10,365 troops of the 101st Airborne Division, along with 5,118 tons of equipment, directly from Fort Campbell, Kentucky, to Bien Hoa Air Base, South Vietnam. The steady stream of C-141s used all of MAC's new tactics, including expedited off-loading that reduced average C-141 ground time at Bien Hoa to an incredible 7.4 minutes. All told, in 1967 MAC strategic airlift carried out tactical missions to transport 141,113 tons of cargo and 345,027 passengers within the Southeast Asian theater.

During the January 1968 Tet offensive, MAC handled a double emergency with Operation Combat Fox. Troops and supplies were airlifted to South Korea from the United States, Japan, and Southeast Asia in response to the USS *Pueblo* crisis and to South Vietnam because of the Tet offensive. The combined effort was more than twice the size of Eagle Thrust.

There were four additional major requirements for strategic airlift in Southeast Asia, three terribly sad and one poignantly heartwarming. The first was during the North Vietnamese Easter offensive in 1972, when TAC made the largest single move in its history to provide air power to stiffen the faltering South Vietnamese forces. The second was rapid withdrawal of American and Allied personnel and equipment after the Paris cease-fire had been signed.

The third was the memorable Operation Homecoming, the repatriation and rehabilitation of the prisoners of war. No one who was there, or who watched on television, will ever forget the expressions on the faces of the men returning to their homeland and to their families after years of torture and neglect. If MAC had existed for no other reason but this one mission, it would have been sufficient. The Military Airlift Command functioned so well in Homecoming that it received the McKay Trophy from the National Aeronautic Association.

The fourth major airlift event was Operation Frequent Wind, the evacuation of American and foreign nationals (as well as loyal South Vietnamese citizens) from Saigon in late April 1975 as the North Vietnamese approached. Operation Babylift, the evacuation of South Vietnamese orphans, was a subset of this mass turmoil, and was marred by tragedy on the very first mission. The new Lockheed C-5A Galaxy had been introduced into the Southeast Asian conflict in May 1972. A C-5A was designated to transport 314 orphans from Tan Son Nhut to Clark Air Base in the Philippines on April 4, 1975. A massive decompression critically damaged the aircraft, causing it to make an emergency forced landing in which 138 adults, children, and babies perished. It was without doubt the nadir of MAC effort in Southeast Asia. The remaining Babylift sorties went off without a hitch, and by May 1975, 1,794 Southeast Asian orphans had been transported to their new American families in the United States.

The versatility, speed, and capacity of the combination of three Lockheed transports—C-130, C-141, and C-5A—drove home the point again that there was no real difference in the missions of tactical and strategic airlift, but it still would take much agonizing to finally cut the cord and combine the two missions.

If final evidence of the capability of strategic airlift to participate in tactical operations were necessary, it came in the fall of 1973. The wind-down in Southeast Asia had been proceeding more or less on schedule when the Yom Kippur War erupted in the Middle East on October 6. A simultaneous attack on Israel by Syria and Egypt caused a massive loss of Israeli material. President Nixon directed that an aerial resupply operation, Operation Nickel Grass, begin on October 13. For thirty-two days, MAC C-141s and the new C-5As carried everything from tanks to missiles directly to Lod International Airport at Tel Aviv, the veritable heart of the battleground. Just a few hundred miles away, a similar stream of Soviet Antonov An-12 and An-22 cargo planes was bringing in similar material to Egypt and Syria. It was an airlift air race, with MAC planes faced with a 6,500-nautical-mile one-way distance, compared to only 1,700 miles for the Soviet aircraft.

MAC won the race handily, the C-5s turning the tide of war by bringing in quantities of vitally needed M-60 and M-48 tanks, 175mm cannons, 155mm howitzers, CH-53 helicopters, and even McDonnell Douglas A-4 fuselages. Israel's prime minister, Golda Meir, described the grateful feelings of her people when she said, "For generations to come, all will be told of the miracle of the immense planes from the United States."

In its first major exercise, the huge Galaxy had carried 50 percent of the cargo while flying only 25 percent of the missions. It was an aircraft whose time had come, despite the controversy that had swamped it almost since the December 22, 1964, announcement by Secretary McNamara that it would be built.

The competition for the contract had been held under the McNamara-inspired Total Package Procurement (TPP) concept. Manufacturers were required to compete for an entire program, including R&D, testing, evaluation, and production, with clearly established price, delivery schedule, and performance commitments. It seemed a marvelous way to "hold the contractor's feet to the fire," but it was impossible to manage in practice. Air Force-dictated changes in requirements, equipment, performance, and, most especially, in the Congressionally driven numbers procured played havoc with the program. There were other typical problems as well—overoptimistic cost estimates on the part of the contractor, a rise in the consumer price index, and an inflexible approach to the TPP contract resulted in a huge cost overrun and an aircraft whose maximum life was only about 25 percent of that forecast. When Lockheed saw that the weight of the aircraft was going to exceed specifications, it offered design changes that would not lower the weight, but would increase performance to meet the specifications. The Air Force, perhaps intimidated by Secretary McNamara's insistence on the matter, was unwilling to buck the DOD interpretation of Total Package Procurement policies and refused. The result was a massive engineering effort to reduce weight by means as primitive as drilling "lightening" holes in wing members. As a result, the C-5A emerged with an estimated 8,000-hour life, rather than the desired 30,000-hour life. The changes to the wing structure, which included a new method of riveting, resulted in fatigue cracks early on. The C-5A became the whipping boy of critics of defense procurement, who used it to symbolize government procurement ineptitude and waste, much as the Boeing 747 in its early days was criticized by airline commentators for being too big, too costly, and designed for a market that did not exist.

Nonetheless, from December 17, 1969, when MAC received its first C-5A, through the many modifications that have led to the present fleet of C-5Bs, the aptly named Galaxy has more than paid its way. With its 222.7-foot wingspan and basic mission weight of 712,000 pounds, the C-5 could cruise at 440 knots for 5,500 miles, and an in-flight-refueling capability gave it unlimited range. Despite the vicissitudes of its development, the C-5 was the right aircraft for military airlift, just as the 747 was the right aircraft for the airlines.

TACTICAL AIRLIFT IN VIETNAM

The efforts begun with Operations Farm Gate and Muletrain were soon extended to a massive tactical airlift system that covered Southeast Asia. Quantitatively, the tonnage handled by the aerial port system grew from 30,000 tons per month in early 1965 to a peak of 209,000 tons per month in March 1968. In 1967, the assistance given by strategic airlift diverted to tactical missions freed up a number of C-130s to be employed as virtual assault transports. The C-130s proved to be so effective in short-field work that they became the basic fixed-wing foundation for General Westmoreland's airmobile tactics against the Viet Cong.

The versatile Hercules could haul entire units, with their complete equipment and thousands of tons of supplies, into forward airstrips for large, long-term search-and-destroy missions. The major offensives conducted in Cambodia in 1970 and Laos in 1971 were possible only because the C-130s could deliver supplies—and especially fuel for the helicopters—to forward sites. The requirement for parachute assault, with all its attendant problems of wind and communications, gave way to fixed-wing and rotary-wing airlift operations.

The tactical airlift capacity served as a mobile fire brigade and permitted a far better utilization of troops. Because the transports could provide quick reinforcement, the defensive garrisons in many areas of this "war without fronts" could be minimized. The C-130s resupply capabilities were tested to the maximum during the December 1967 Khe Sanh airlift. Employed to land amid heavy Communist fire, the C-130s would wend their way down through the clouds into the canyon where Khe Sahn was situated, using a steep approach to minimize the time the North Vietnamese had to fire on them. Later, when the North Vietnamese had approached so close to the Khe Sanh perimeter defenses that it was impossible to land, the C-130s used airdrops and the low-altitude parachute extraction system to deliver critical supplies.

The tactical airlifter's work was hot, hard, and heavy. It was also extremely dangerous. In the eleven years from 1962 to 1973, fifty-three C-130s, fifty-three C-123s, and twenty C-7s were lost in action, with 269 crew members killed or missing in action.

MAC aircraft provided a thousand other services, from ferrying troops to embarkation ports at the end of their tours and bringing in supplies to Montagnard villages to carrying Bob Hope's annual shows. In a way, the variety of duties, from death-defying to pleasure-bringing, was a symbol of MAC's resourcefulness. Blessed with new aircraft, it promptly overworked and undermaintained them to get the job done; blessed with good people, it drove them till they dropped from fatigue, for there were never enough air or ground crews to meet the demands of the war. Yet the airlift job in Southeast Asia was done superbly, and the people who did the work were justly proud.

MAC Search and Rescue in Vietnam

Despite excellent experience gained in Korea in search and rescue techniques, the many years of low budgets had reduced USAF search and rescue capability to the minimum level needed for local-base rescue efforts. The war in Southeast Asia put a strain on resources, so during the first two years of operations in Laos, there was no integral USAF capability and reliance was placed on the men and planes of the CIA airline, Air America. They did excellent work, even though search and rescue for the Air Force was not in their job description.

In South Vietnam, the first USAF air rescue team arrived at Tan Son Nhut on January 10, 1962; it consisted of three officers, three airmen, and no aircraft. Part of the Military Air Transport Command, it received equipment and men slowly. By January 1965 there were helicopter detachments at Ben Hoa and Da Nang in South Vietnam and Udorn, Nakhon Phanom, Takhli, and Korat in Thailand. The fixed-wing aircraft allocated to the task were old Douglas C-54s as airborne command posts and Grumman HU-16 Albatross amphibians. The duty helicopters were the tiny Kaman HH-43B, which had a very limited range.

The requirements for rescue accelerated with the tempo of the war, and Rolling Thunder greatly increased the need. In January 1966, the 3d Aerospace Rescue and Recovery Group at Tan Son Nhut became the primary rescue agency in Southeast Asia, with responsibility for planning, organizing, coordinating, and controlling rescue operations from the Joint Search and Rescue Center at Seventh Air Force.

A basic technique was developed. On receipt of word that an airman was down, a Douglas A-1E Sandy was dispatched to the area to search for the downed pilot. Meanwhile, another Sandy was sent to escort two helicopters to the scene. One helicopter would go in to make the recovery while the other stood by to lend aid if required. Fighters accompanied the formation to act as ResCAP (rescue combat air patrol). When the first A-1E located the survivor, it determined whether he was in a hostile area. If so, the A-1Es and the fighters worked the area over with cannons, rockets, and other ordnance to neutralize it. When it was safe, the helicopter went in to rescue the downed airman.

Over time, both the techniques and the equipment were radically improved. The Sikorsky HH-3E Jolly Green Giants and their successors, the HH-53 Super Jolly Green Giants, were specially tailored for the role, having the range, armor, firepower, and rescue equipment to do an outstanding job. The faithful Lockheed Hercules was adapted as the HC-130, able to fly swiftly over long distances carrying the electronic gear with which to find the downed pilots. To almost everyone's amazement, the HC-130s and HH-3Es were adapted to permit in-flight refueling. Night-rescue equipment was developed, including low-light-level television, night-vision goggles, automatic Doppler navigation systems, terrain avoidance radar, and electronic location finders.

Individual crew members were given instruction on rescue during their survival school training, learning how to use special flares to penetrate the jungle canopy, setting up the special personal codes based on information only the crew member would know (e.g., "What was the name of your father's favorite dog?") that would be used to verify their identity when they were located, and training on escaping on the jungle penetrators let down by cable from the helicopters.

The annals of the search and rescue efforts are studded with achievements, ranging from routine extractions near ground bases in South Vietnam to the sensational recovery of Captain Roger C. Locher after he had spent twenty-three days on the ground evading enemy capture and the gallant, if fruitless, rescue attempt at Son Tay.

Operation Kingpin was planned by the JCS in the summer of 1970, with the aim of rescuing a hundred or more U.S. prisoners of war held at the Son Tay prison 23 miles west of Hanoi. Fifty-six volunteers were selected from the Special Forces and the Rangers; their task was to overwhelm the prison force in a swift assault. Helicopters would be standing by to pick up the rescued prisoners while USAF and Navy aircraft attacked Hanoi to divert attention.

The raid was carried off on the night of November 20–21, with precision and élan; the North Vietnamese forces, including Soviet or Chinese troops there for training, were quickly overcome. Unfortunately, reconnaissance photos had not revealed that massive flooding had caused the POWs to be moved from the prison the previous July 14.

Only one man was injured in the raiding party, and although no prisoners were rescued, the raid had a positive effect on prison life. The morale of the prisoners of war was improved, and the North Vietnamese, suddenly aware of their vulnerability, permitted prison conditions to improve somewhat. The biggest dividend was that many prisoners who had been confined alone or in small groups throughout the country were concentrated together in the prison called the Hanoi Hilton. As atrocious as the conditions were there, the prisoners now had others to encourage them throughout their confinement.

During the years from 1964 to 1973 the search and rescue team functioned superbly, as it saved 3,883 lives, including 2,807 from the U.S. military, 555 allied airmen, and 521 civilians. In the process, forty-five rescue aircraft were destroyed and seventy-one crew members killed.

The very concept of search and rescue is noble, but even this nobility was transcended by the way in which the entire USAF gave a search and rescue effort first priority, breaking off wartime missions to assist, if necessary. The knowledge that no effort or expense would be spared to rescue them gave downed crewmen a sense of hope that enabled them to survive in otherwise desperate situations.

UNITY AT LAST

All the empirical evidence on airlift in the war in Southeast Asia pointed to the inescapable conclusion that centralized control of all airlift assets was essential. On July 29, 1974, Secretary of Defense James R. Schlesinger directed that the Air Force consolidate all military airlift forces under a single manager by the end of the fiscal year 1977, and that this single manager provide airlift for all the armed services, including the Navy and the Marine Corps.

One month later, Air Force Chief of Staff General David C. Jones announced that the Military Airlift Command would be the designated single manager. The Tactical Air Command transferred all of its airlift units, including Air National Guard and Air Force Reserve units, immediately making MAC into the world's largest single airlift organization. The expanded size and the demonstrated importance of the airlift operations in Vietnam and Israel resulted in the Joint Chief's of Staff authorizing MAC to have specified command status, which became effective on February 1, 1977. As such, the MAC commander could now deal directly with the Secretary of Defense and the Joint Chiefs of Staff and have a direct communication link with the National Command Center.

From the verbal orders in 1941 that created the Air Corps Ferry Command to the considered designation of MAC as one of the three specified commands, military airlift had come a long way. The latter part of that journey had been made easier by the research and development undertaken by the Air Force Systems Command and its predecessor organizations.

AIR FORCE RESEARCH AND DEVELOPMENT

Hap Arnold's beloved research and development torch was ignited by Theodor von Karman and then passed to the most appropriate hands, those of Bernard Schriever. Schriever's success with ICBM development and related space programs came because he was a brilliant manager who knew how to get along in the three communities he needed: military, scientific, and industrial. He infused these three sometimes antagonistic groups with a sense of national policy issues and the overall military strategy of the United States, and he saw to it that the interchange among the three elements was not confined to purely technical considerations. As a result, he elicited far more from the scientists and engineers involved than if he had attempted to limit them to their specialized fields. Further, he became a beacon for thousands of young scientists and engineers who valued enormous responsibility early in their careers more than higher salaries. All of these leadership concepts deserve review and emulation today, when top R&D leadership has been moved almost entirely away from the services that use the weapons and into the hands of politically appointed "temps" for whom a position in R&D is only a way station on a career path to higher office.

Schriever became Commander of the Air Research and Development Command (ARDC) in April 1959, and very shortly thereafter he established the Air Force Research Division (AFRD) under Brigadier General Benjamin G. Holzman. The AFRD was dedicated solely to basic research, which Schriever considered vital to the Air Force's overall research program.

ARDC's primary mission was the research and development of weapon systems. Its counterpart command, the Air Materiel Command (AMC), was responsible for the procurement of the weapon systems and their lifetime support in terms of maintenance, spares, and engineering changes. Naturally, ARDC and AMC had a long history of rivalry and overlapping functions that reached back to 1917 with arguments between the Engineering Division and Materiel Division at McCook Field, and with mission conflicts with Fairfield Depot. Over the years, there were various changes in names and functions, and by the 1950s, coordination was enforced by having personnel from both commands man the weapon system project offices (WSPOs). Schriever found the duplication intolerable and suggested that ARDC acquire all of the Air Force's research and development activities, as well as AMC's procurement responsibilities. Despite stiff opposition from AMC and from the Chief of Staff, General White, Schriever persisted.

Time was on his side. Concerned about the Soviet advances in space, the new Kennedy administration offered Secretary of the Air Force Eugene M. Zuckert an incentive to consolidate ARDC and AMC. He was informed by Deputy Secretary of Defense Roswell L. Gilpatrick that if the "Air Force cleaned up its act" (i.e., got its ARDC/AMC conflict resolved), it would be awarded the coveted space mission. Zuckert accepted with alacrity, and General White now saw the merit in Schriever's proposal for ARDC to do some acquisition of its own—that of AMC's role in procurement.

With only two weeks' notice to the affected personnel, on April 1, 1961, ARDC and AMC were redesignated Air Force Systems Command (AFSC) and Air Force Logistics Command (AFLC), respectively. The timing was exquisite, for on April 12, the Soviet Union launched the 5-ton Vostok spacecraft into an orbital flight with Major Yuri Gagarin aboard. American pride twitched like a galvanized frog leg, and the Kennedy administration recognized that funds had to be allocated to recover the nation's position as the leading technological power. Vostok spacecraft would ominously pass over American cities with impunity hundreds of times in the future—at a distance far closer than any enemy ship or aircraft would have been allowed to pass.

Schriever, promoted to full general, assumed command of AFSC and launched it on a course that would be responsible for the remarkable flowering of research and development within the USAF and led directly to the creation of the advanced weaponry and intelligence-gathering systems that won the Persian Gulf War. AFSC also achieved a goal beyond its dreams or its plans by fielding weapon systems that convinced the Soviet Union that it had irrevocably lost the race for supremacy in military arms.

In the reorganization, Schriever suffered one disappointment. AFRD, devoted to basic research, was removed from his command and turned into the Office of Aerospace Research at Air Force Headquarters. But he could look with pride at his newly created divisions that reached across the spectrum of aerospace research, strengthening AFSC's scientific base. They included the Aeronautical Systems Division, Ballistic Systems Division, Space Systems Division, and Electronic Systems Division, all supported by special advisory groups, including civilian think tanks such as MITRE and RAND. Over the following three decades, these units would produce not only the weapon systems to defend the free world, but also many of the principal leaders of the USAF. With his new organization, Schriever had made it possible for individuals known for their engineering and scientific ability rather than their combat record to reach four-star rank, and the Air Force and the country was richer for it.

Secretary Zuckert and Schriever worked well together, perhaps in part because of their differing relationships with Secretary McNamara. The relationship of Zuckert and McNamara is a textbook example of bureaucratic incest. Zuckert had recommended McNamara to succeed him as Assistant Secretary of the Air Force (Management). McNamara had picked Zuckert to be Secretary of the Air Force. Each man obviously admired the other's capabilities. But Zuckert, who had been Stuart Symington's assistant secretary from 1947 to 1952, became intensely frustrated that McNamara's takeover of power had reduced the importance and influence of the office of Secretary of the Air Force. Often driven to the point of resignation, Zuckert could not conceal his antipathy for McNamara, who responded in the most annoying manner: not appearing to notice.

Schriever, who yielded to no man in his dislike of McNamara's methods, nonetheless had the quick wit and the credentials to get along with him on his own terms, i.e., to prove his point by quantitative analysis rather than by the intuitive foresight that was actually Schriever's forte.

It thus happened that Zuckert would claim that his greatest achievement as Secretary of the Air Force was directing Schriever to embark upon Project Forecast, a comprehensive study of long-range technologies for the USAF. Zuckert asked Schriever to determine, via Project Forecast, what the existing state of U.S. air power technology was, what discoveries might occur in the next five to ten years and what they would lead to, and what, in general, science had to offer to help improve the Air Force's ability to do its mission. In effect, Zuckert was asking of Schriever the same thing that Arnold had asked of von Karman: to take an educated look into the future for the benefit of the USAF. Once he had delegated the task, Zuckert then withdrew to let Schriever do things his own way.

With his customary energy and using his familiar network of contacts, Schriever established that Project Forecast would examine the pace of technological advance in the years from 1966 to 1975, relate this change to the planning activities of the Air Force, and see what effect it would have upon USAF weapons.

Ultimately, almost 500 people contributed to Project Forecast, from twenty-eight separate Air Force organizations, thirteen major government organizations including the Army, Navy, and Marines, forty-nine subordinate government agencies, twenty-six colleges and universities, seventy corporations, and ten nonprofit institutions. The most stellar names in government, industry, and academia were included in the panels, which covered six broad subjects, including technology, threat, policy and military considerations, capability, costing, and analysis, evaluation, and synthesis.

It took a man of Schriever's talent to keep a gargantuan committee of this size and scope within bounds. He did so with the assistance of then Major General Charles H. Terhune, Jr., who saw to it that the panels emphasized technologies that had a direct usefulness to national security and a high chance of practical success at a reasonable cost and were, withal, a major advance over presently forecast systems.

The deliberation process on which projects should be nominated for inclusion in the final report went through months of winnowing, filtering, arguing, fighting, and inevitably horse-trading, before its delivery in March 1964.

In the end, a number of technologies met all four of the qualifications outlined above. These included opening significant new areas in aircraft and engine construction through the introduction of high-strength boron filaments and oxide-dispersion strengthened metals. The new materials resulting from this technology made huge cargo transports and vertical takeoff aircraft not only possible but inevitable. A candidate that proved more elusive was the use of liquid hydrogen as a fuel for long-distance reconnaissance planes; the report was closer to the mark with the suggested use of high-pressure oxygen-hydrogen engines for reusable space-launch vehicles. Of the host of promising aerodynamic subjects, the most prominent were reduced-laminar-flow-control and variable-geometry wings.

Other technologies recommended for pursuit included improved nuclear weapons, some with lowered radiation, some with low yields to reduce collateral damage, and some with enhanced radiation, fission-fusion nuclear devices that operated against enemy personnel but did little heat or blast damage to equipment. The last, often termed the "neutron bomb," ran into particularly vehement opposition by groups that somehow saw it as more immoral to kill and not damage material than to kill and damage material.

Perhaps the most important of the recommendations was within the realm of guidance technology. New optical image-matching techniques were developed that promised almost 100 percent accuracy to air-to-ground missiles.

These technologies, sometimes diluted, found their way into weapon systems, from the Lockheed C-5 to the current crop of precision-guided munitions. As valuable as these weapon systems were, their intrinsic importance was vastly overshadowed by the impetus Schriever, AFSC, and the methods of Project Forecast had given to Air Force research and development. Over the next twenty years, from the divisions and laboratories of AFSC and its successor organization, a myriad number of projects would emerge. They would make significant contributions to the magnificent series of spy satellites that gave the United States a measure of intelligence advantage never before possessed by one state over another, one that completely overshadowed the importance of even Ultra and Magic in World War II. Classified until 1995, the Corona spy-satellite program will be discussed at greater length in a later chapter.

Some of the possibilities seen in Project Forecast were adversely affected by the drain of funds to the Vietnam War, but for the most part, its predictions came true. Perhaps more important, it was the vehicle through which Schriever transformed AFSC from a mere merger of two commands into something far larger. He rejuvenated Air Force science by making AFSC the institutional framework in which civilian science and military objectives could be combined. He saw to it that a balance was struck by fostering both basic and applied research and by connecting science to national policy and *practical* military requirements.

By 1962, AFSC had grown in size to employ 26,650 officers and airmen and 37,000 civilians, handling some 54,000 contracts annually, and with a budget of $7 billion at a time when a billion was regarded as real money. AFSC worked closely with the National Aeronautics and Space Administration, supplying the Atlas rockets used for the Project Mercury flights, one of which lifted the spacecraft *Friendship 7* to altitude for Marine Lieutenant Colonel John Glenn's three-orbit flight.

The scope of AFSC's work from its inception was breathtaking. In addition to all the standard feverish activity at the Edwards Air Force Base Flight Test Center, it was engaged in a joint USAF-NASA-Navy test program for the X-15 rocket plane, which Major Robert White flew to a speed of 4,093 mph. It was bringing advanced Atlas, Titan, and Minuteman ICBMs into operational status. The Discoverer series of satellites were being launched, applauded for their ultimate impact on the environment—their real task would remain classified for three more decades. And there was so much more, not all destined for ultimate fulfillment, including the X-20 Dyna-Soar, which anticipated in many ways the space shuttle; the North American RS-70 Mach 3 aircraft; a fantastic "Facet Eye" camera; the completion of the Semiautomatic Ground Environment (SAGE) air defense network; the design and construction of BMEWS, the ballistic missile early warning system; the SPADATS (Space Detection and Tracking System) for monitoring all objects in space from satellites to space junk; and events less worthy of headlines but nonetheless vitally important, such as the creation of the Aerospace Medical Division at Brooks AFB, Texas.

The very complexity of AFSC, the urgency of its mission, and the success Schriever had experienced with the technique in creating the ICBM fleet made him push for concurrent rather than sequential development of the various projects. Strong views against this were voiced at the top, including those of the Director of the Directorate of Defense Research and Engineering (DDR&E), Harold Brown, then the third most powerful man in DOD. Schriever prevailed, and for the most part, concurrency worked. Another element of Schriever's program that met with opposition was the encouragement of federally funded basic research by industry. This proved to be one of the most valuable assets of the AFSC R&D program, but ultimately would be killed because it was an easy political target. Firms could be accused (no doubt justly in some instances) of using government funds to develop products that they would profit from commercially. The result was a progressive reduction of such funding to the point that it jeopardized the research and development effort.

AFSC was an administrative handful. Schriever's initial attempts to control AFSC as he had controlled BMD while creating the ICBM fleet proved to be unworkable because of the increasing demands for reports and briefings from higher levels in DOD. The effect was to create dozens of informal layers of management intended to ensure that the briefings that went to the top were sufficiently inclusive. Schriever's answer was to persuade DOD that AFSC's review methods would be so rigorous that only the critical decisions would have to be made at the top.

The war in Vietnam put a budget ceiling on AFSC's activities for almost a decade and placed a more critical focus on immediate operational problems that had emerged in conflict. An example of this work was the development of the previously mentioned TISEO (target identification system electro-optical), a telescope that gave the pilots a chance to identify hostile aircraft visually at a greater distance. At the same time, the AFSC fostered the "Rivet Haste" modification on the F-4E, which introduced leading-edge slats to provide more maneuverability and a better platform for internally installed cannon. Although immediate requirements like these had priority, long-range work went on for aircraft such as the McDonnell Douglas F-15 and the North American/Rockwell B-1 as well as for missiles such as the AGM-69A SRAM (short-range attack missile) and Maverick AGM-65 television-guided air-to-air "smart weapon," of which more than 100,000 would ultimately be made. Also in the works was the first of what would become known as a "force-multiplying weapon," the AWACS (airborne warning and control system), which would become operational in 1977 as the Boeing E-3A.

With peacetime budget restrictions, risk in weapon system development was feared more than delay. The concurrency concept fell into disfavor, so that development and production were severed and a return was made to traditional "fly-before-buy" methods. Development programs were carefully measured at specified milestones, with special emphasis placed on any critical subsystem development that seemed risky. The delays caused by innumerable reviews added billions to the cost.

For several years after the conclusion of the Vietnam War, funding for AFSC remained relatively constant at about the $7 billion level. By 1982, inflation and expanded needs had pushed it to about $26 billion. While aircraft such as the General Dynamics F-16 Fighting Falcon, the McDonnell Douglas F-15 Eagle, and the resuscitated Rockwell B-1B Lancer and missiles including the LGM-118A Peacekeeper (MX) and advanced medium-range air-to-air missile (AMRAAM) were being developed or brought into use, a tremendous proportion of AFSC effort was devoted to command, control, communications, and intelligence (C^3I), intelligence-gathering satellites, and other smaller, less publicly spectacular programs.

It is a credit to AFSC leadership, from Schriever to the present, that personnel selected for the command remained at a very high level of competence even though the programs were becoming both increasingly specialized and attenuated. Gone were the days when a fleet of ballistic missiles could go from drawing board to launch in four or five years. By the very nature of their complexity and because of the micromanagement of Congress, important programs now required an excruciatingly long time to execute. Because they were usually highly classified, the scientists and engineers working on them were not only denied public recognition for their efforts but were not allowed to publish in the standard journals so that they might enjoy recognition by their peers.

As a single example of the depth and breadth of the work accomplished at AFSC, it is instructive to look at a summary listing of the major work of just one division in the mid-1980s. At the Electronic Systems Division at Hanscom Air Force Base, Massachusetts, no less than 122 *major* programs were underway, ranging from the Boeing E-4 airborne command post, the Milstar satellite communications program, and an upgrade program for the Royal Saudi C^3 system to microwave landing systems (MLS) for airfields. In addition, other programs too classified even to be acknowledged by a public project name were also in progress.

The same depth and breadth of effort were to be found at all the other divisions, as well as at the engineering and flight test centers. The combined results of these concerted efforts would be made manifest in the Persian Gulf War, where all the efforts leading to the use of space in warfare would bring about a decisive conclusion and validate all of AFSC's efforts for the preceding thirty years.

When AFSC and AFLC came into being in April 1961, some observers felt that the Logistic Command had received the short end of the stick. Politically, that might have been the case, but in practical terms, the importance of AFLC grew over the years to overshadow its former stature as AMC. One somewhat ironic reason for this was that the versatility of modern weapon systems—combined with the staggering cost of their replacement— kept aircraft and missiles in service for much longer periods. Unlike the 1950s, when ten new fighters, five new bombers, and four new ballistic missiles were introduced, new weapon systems were now a rare event. Instead, older systems such as the B-52 required AFLC to modify them continuously to keep them in service. Over the years the average age of first-line U.S. fighters, bombers, and missiles grew to twenty, then thirty years—and it keeps on growing. Faced with this unprecedented challenge of maintaining an aging fleet that had long since outlived the manufacturers of many of its components, AFLC managed to keep the USAF ready for combat.

Ultimately, the downsizing of the Air Force had its impact on AFLC and AFSC, which were merged on July 1, 1992, in the Air Force Materiel Command (AFMC). The name and mission changed but the heritage remained the same.

LOGISTICS: ALWAYS VITAL

The World War II organizations that preceded the Air Materiel Command (AMC) and AFLC had a host of names and responsibilities and succeeded in supplying the needs of the United States Army Air Forces on a scale never before achieved in history. The supply organizations and industry worked so well together that by the time of the Japanese surrender, there were huge surpluses of every kind of materiel, including as many as 35,000 first-line aircraft.

The immediate postwar task for AMC was somehow storing and disposing of this vast quantity of materiel without incurring Congressional wrath for wasting funds, or generating accusations of competing with industry. All over the country, huge disposal sites were established, ranging from thousands of acres of western land dotted with endless rows of surplus aircraft down to city-center salvage yards disposing of precious metals. AMC accomplished the task even as it, like the rest of the USAAF, suffered a demobilization meltdown. It had just about completed the work when the Korean War began, and the airplanes it had so laboriously readied for storage would now be hauled out and returned to service. The rehabilitation of stored aircraft was an outstanding success and laid the foundation for today's Military Aerospace Maintenance and Regeneration Center at Davis Monthan Air Force Base in Tucson, Arizona. There aircraft and other materials are still stored for future use while an annual profit is turned on the materials sold.

The advent of the Cold War brought extreme pressures on the science of logistics as practiced in the past. The demand that huge forces of the most sophisticated kind be kept in constant readiness was without precedent in U.S. history. The Eisenhower administration's concept of massive retaliation implicitly recognized that the outcome of a war between the United States and the Soviet Union would be decided in the first ninety days. This new view of warfare—with its attendant ballistic missile systems—made the past logistics concepts largely derived from U.S. Army needs, obsolete. Fortunately, AMC had the capable leadership of General Edwin W. Rawlings, one of the first Air Corps graduates from the Harvard Graduate School of Business Administration, where he received a master's degree in business administration, *cum laude*, in 1939.

Rawlings was to AMC what LeMay was to SAC and Schriever to AFSC. He used his education and experience to place the command on a businesslike basis, adopting a "systems approach," as Schriever had with AFSC. Rawlings made AMC look at logistics as a whole, with a concern not only for acquiring and storing the needed parts and materials but also managing the inventories, improving communications with the field, minimizing and mechanizing record-keeping, making sure that the transport system was swift, and, impelled by the space age, ensuring that new quality-control procedures were applied to both new and old suppliers. Rawlings backed the creation of LOGAIR, an AMC airline that used contractors to fly high-priority cargo in a network that tied AMC depots together with all Air Force bases.

The old Air Corps had been small, and men like LeMay and Rawlings knew each other well on both business and personal levels. In 1954, LeMay told Rawlings that if war came, SAC bombers and tankers would need fast, flexible emergency maintenance service from the very first day. Within two years, Rawlings had established a unique reserve "minute-man" force of 4,000 civilian personnel divided into sixty mobile maintenance teams, ready to leave their assigned jobs on a few hours' notice and deploy to forward bases to repair SAC aircraft. The concept was later extended to ADC, TAC, and MATS.

Every military leader from Sun Tzu on has known the critical importance of military logistics. Yet in times of budgetary crisis, the accountants nonetheless invariably turn to logistic line items for savings. Where deferring procurement of a new aircraft is immediately obvious to all, particularly the Congressman from the district where the aircraft is manufactured, deferring the purchase of spare parts can remain almost unnoticed—until they are needed.

Similarly, the pace of urgently needed modifications can be slowed to save money without its being particularly evident to anyone except those in units flying the unmodified equipment. The result can be a gradual increase in accidents.

The neglect of logistics is felt in other ways: reductions in personnel, freezing of grade levels, and the politically driven use of outside contractors for work best done in-house. All of these methods have been seen in the past and will be seen increasingly in the future.

Having noted this, the fact remains that the logistics effort of the United States Air Force functions at a high level of competence, thanks to the energetic management provided AFLC/AFMC over the years by the top leaders who succeeded Rawlings. These included such stellar general officers as William F. "Bozo" McKee, Samuel E. Anderson, Mark E. Bradley, Thomas P. Gerrity, Bryce Poe II, Henry H. Vicellio, Jr. and many others.

The primary mission of all the commands devoted to logistics—AMC/AFLC/AFMC—has been to see that all Air Force combat units are properly equipped and ready for action at all times, anywhere in the world. This involves procurement of spares and equipment by the billions of dollars each year, along with supply, maintenance, and transportation functions. From being the "supply shack" operation of World War II where canny sergeants rat-holed extra spare parts to keep their own squadrons' airplanes flying, AFLC capitalized on Rawlings's precepts and met the space age head-on with computers to manage inventories, new standards for test and calibration equipment, new manufacturing techniques in the repair facilities, and new methods of materials handling.

At its inception, AFLC was divided into nine air materiel areas (AMAs), huge facilities with as many as 20,000 employees each, which were allocated missions based on both functional tasks and geographic areas of responsibility. (In today's multicultural world, it is interesting to recall that in those early days, members of the San Antonio, Oklahoma City, and Sacramento AMAs proudly referred to their units as "the brown-eyed AMAs" to reflect the high proportion of Hispanic workers.) A combination of economies demanded by the war in Vietnam, improvements in computer control of inventory, and the quicker movement provided by jet aircraft permitted a reduction in the number of AMAs to five—Oklahoma City, Oklahoma; Sacramento, California; San Antonio, Texas; Ogden, Utah; and Warner Robins, Georgia. The end of the Cold War saw further reductions, and ultimately the creation of the current AFMC.

The scope of logistics command work became bewilderingly complex. In 1980, a "typical" year in terms of its having no active combat, AFLC supported 9,000 aircraft and 1,000 strategic missiles. More than 1.5 million items were procured and managed, while 1,800 aircraft and 4,700 engines were overhauled. The demand for technical support varied from the very lowest level—a request for a particular type of sheet-metal screw—to the most esoteric, as in a requirement for inertial guidance systems. As many as 10 million individual requests for service were fulfilled. With assets valued in excess of $70 billion and a total stock fund of $12.7 billion, AFLC was by any standard one of the biggest businesses in the world.

Like the rest of the Air Force, AFLC responded well to pressure. At the time of the Cuban missile crisis, the command distinguished itself by shipping 168,000 tons of freight to Florida bases by air, rail, and convoys of trucks impressed into service from all Air Force bases east of the Mississippi. The effort was so professionally done that almost all the supplies were in place before all of the combat units had assembled.

The Vietnam War placed massive demands on AFLC. Maintenance efforts were now required 10,000 miles from home. Aircraft were literally coming unglued in the moist tropic air, as when the electrical component potting material self-destructed in the McDonnell Douglas F-4s. A new challenge was faced when the Air Force suddenly acquired large numbers of aircraft that had never before been in the inventory, such as the Douglas Skyraider, that had to be upgraded to Air Force standards and spare parts and manuals provided. The familiar task of pulling aircraft out of storage also remained; instead of refurbishing B-29s for Korea, AFLC began restoring B-26s and T-28s for Vietnam.

The command responded to the emergency with Project Bitterwine, a vast expansion system involving twenty-seven bases: ten in South Vietnam, eight in Thailand, three on Taiwan, two in the Philippines, two on Okinawa, and two in Japan. Like some gigantic amoeba splitting, AFLC fought the war by replicating stateside capabilities in bases overseas. As might be expected forced expansion caused its own problems, and emergency situations were met by using new procedures with new acronyms, always the fastest guns out of bureaucratic holsters. Rapid Area Maintenance (RAM) teams were rushed to Vietnam to expedite the removal and repair of battle-damaged aircraft. Rapid Area Transportation Support (RATS, no less) teams were dispatched to expedite deliveries through water and aerial ports. Rapid Area Supply

Support (RASS) teams were rushed to handle the excessive buildup of supplies at bases not equipped to handle it and ensure that accurate inventory and accounting records were kept. These acronyms combined to keep another crucial acronym in check: throughout the Vietnam War, such emergency AFLC support kept the infamous NORS (not operationally ready, supply) for units in the field at the same low level as stateside units. The rate dipped to 2.5 percent—the lowest yet experienced Air Force–wide—and by 1968 reflected new techniques like resupply by airlift, improved computers, a vastly expanded depot repair system, and top-notch management.

The war forced AFLC to improvise, as it did the entire Air Force. One of the most successful programs was the conversion of Korean-vintage Fairchild C-119 Flying Boxcars to gunships for ground support in Vietnam. No one who had ever flown the "ground-loving" C-119 would have imagined that it could have been a success as a ground strafer, but modified with jet pods, armor, and side-firing miniguns, it was a deadly addition to the in-country war.

Nothing affected AFLC's tightly scheduled facility like the sudden discovery of a fatigue problem in an operational aircraft. In the past, the AMAs had responded to similar problems in the B-47 and B-52 in peacetime, but discovery of a potentially catastrophic fatigue problem in the tail of the overworked KC-135s caused an immediate furor. AFLC responded with Project Pacer Fin, carried out at the Oklahoma City AMA, where sixteen KC-135s were put through a modification every day for forty-five days. The AMA worked around the clock and sent teams to Southeast Asia to repair those KC-135s whose mission requirements kept them on station there.

The cost of the Vietnam War caused Secretary McNamara to seek economies, and in 1964 he found some of these with a reduction in the number of air materiel areas to five, with the AMAs at Rome, New York; San Bernardino, California; Mobile, Alabama; and Middletown, Pennsylvania, being closed. One result was a massive migration of functions, along with the associated personnel and equipment to the remaining AMAs.

AFLC had concentrated the preponderance of its efforts on supporting the fighting in Vietnam; with the end of the war, budget cuts forced an immediate contraction. Yet the requirement for supporting nuclear deterrence remained, and in the post-Vietnam period, the command refocused its attention on war readiness. The fall-off in personnel strength (which has always been about 90 percent civilian) was precipitous; in 1957, AFLC had reached a peak of 225,000 persons, military and civilian. Even at the height of the Vietnam War, when the demands for service were both more numerous and more urgent, management decisions had allowed this number to decline to 134,000. It fell further to 90,000 by 1976.

Some of the reduction in force stemmed from increased centralization of common logistic items under the Defense Logistics Agency. The loss in personnel was offset to a degree by the modernization of depot facilities—some of which dated to 1920—improved material-handling equipment, increased use of private contractors, and, advanced data processing.

Like the rest of the Air Force, new life was breathed into AFLC activities with the Reagan administration's expanded defense spending. The modernization of strategic systems and the acquisition of new equipment such as the Rockwell B-1B, Northrop B-2, McDonnell Douglas C-17, and Lockheed F-117 were a challenge that also brought acquisition reform issues to the forefront. Congressional attention was whipped to a new intensity by media coverage of cost overruns, spare parts pricing, and questionable contractor overhead charges.

Congressional reaction was severe and comprehensive; a massive volume of reform legislation was passed, with the inevitable effect of magnifying the micromanagement aspects of Congressional oversight. The President's Blue Ribbon Commission on Defense Management, led by industrialist David Packard, conducted a probing examination that will be explored in the next chapter. Further emphasis on curing the problem was implicit in the Goldwater-Nichols Department of Defense Reorganization Act of 1986.

The external reactions were matched by internal reforms designed to fulfill the multiple recommendations of the Packard Commission, as it came to be known. Amid this *Sturm und Drang* of reaction to vitally needed reforms, AFLC and AFSC nonetheless managed to work together, providing the USAF with the advanced weaponry it would use with such devastating effect in the Persian Gulf War.

AFLC, like AFSC, was vitally affected by the change in focus demanded by the Vietnam War, the subsequent drawdown, and the demands for improvements. The two commands were able to meet the challenge because the Air Force had been foresighted enough to provide its personnel with the necessary training and education. Thus, just as the aircrews were educated to use the most sophisticated computer-controlled weaponry, so were the ground support people prepared to use the modern computer tools just becoming available. The general success of AFSC and AFLC in meeting the twin crises of modern war and modern equipment was made possible by the contributions of the two "school" commands—the Air Training Command and the Air University.

INVESTMENT IN EDUCATION

Education has been the saving grace of the United States Air Force, in terms of capability and its immutable corollary, the retention of qualified personnel. Rarely able to compete in salaries even at the entry level, the Air Force has managed over the years to provide educational opportunities—technical, academic, and professional—that have not only induced people to join and to stay in, but produced the doctrine and the leadership that have made the USAF what it is today. A particular facet of education's contribution has been the creation of the highly professional noncommissioned officer corps, of which more later.

The three principal educating organizations in the history of the USAF have been the Air Training Command (ATC), the Air University Command (AU), and the United States Air Force Academy (USAFA). The ATC and the AU were combined—again—in 1993, to become the Air Training and Education Command. The Air Force Academy is a direct reporting unit (DRU), not connected to a major command and reporting directly to Headquarters USAF.

THE AIR TRAINING COMMAND

Like every other command, ATC has had to face a roller-coaster ride in funding, manning, and bases over the years, but during times of emergencies, the officers guiding ATC were presented with a recurring problem. Just when more instructors were required to build up ATC to meet the demand for more graduates, the combat commands raided ATC units at all levels for experienced personnel—and these, invariably, were the instructors. As a result, ATC has always found itself gearing up for an emergency just when it was itself at minimum strength.

Traditionally, the Air Training Command handled flying training, the Air Force Reserve Officer Training Corps, Officers Candidate School, Officer Training School, the technical training of all the myriad Air Force job specialties, and special schools like the famous survival schools. ATC also had a number of additional missions. One of the most important of these, and directly allied to the basic function of ATC, was the USAF Recruiting Service. Another important unit was the Community College of the Air Force. Added to these were the San Antonio Joint Military Medical Command, a consolidation of Army and Air Force medical facilities, and many subsidiary functions like contracting, real property maintenance, and foreign military training affairs. Of all these fundamentally important tasks, the image of flying training—the "Taj Mahal" at Randolph Field, students crawling into aircraft, formation flyovers—always seemed to epitomize ATC.

PILOT TRAINING

The Air Training Command demonstrated its remarkable flexibility during World War II, when it raised pilot training from a few hundred per year in 1939 to 87,283 in 1944. The boom was made possible in large part by Hap Arnold's foresight in establishing Civilian Pilot Training (CPT) schools that bore the brunt of the training burden throughout the war. Training was cut drastically after the war, with fewer than 400 pilots graduating in 1947. When the Korean War broke out, nine new contract flying schools were established to take up the slack. During the three years of the Korean War, ATC graduated almost 12,000 pilots—about six times the normal peacetime rate. After Korea, and until the defense cutbacks of the 1990s, the number of graduates from pilot training varied from a peacetime high of 6,159 in 1955 to a low of 1,081 in 1979.

Pilot training methods varied over time in the phases of instruction and to reflect phenomenal advances in the trainers. After World War II, primary training was conducted in the ubiquitous North American T-6 Texan, while in advanced training students used the multiengine North American TB-25, an unarmed version of the plane in which Jimmy Doolittle raided Tokyo. Single-engine students flew the North American F-51 (until 1952), the Lockheed F-80, and later the Lockheed T-33.

Variations on this system continued after the war until 1959, when contract training was ended and specialized training for single-or multiengine aircraft was stopped. The advent of jet aircraft caused further changes; by 1961, Consolidated Pilot Training was begun, with preflight, primary, and basic courses combined and instruction provided in Cessna T-37s—the long-lived "Tweety-bird"—and the equally durable T-33s. The Northrop T-38 Talon, a supersonic trainer, was introduced the same year.

The T-37s and T-38s *still* form the backbone of today's much-reduced pilot training system. Preflight screening was long accomplished in the Cessna T-41 Mescalero (a version of the standard civilian Cessna 172), now replaced by the Slingsby T-3 Firefly, imported from Great Britain. The indomitable T-37, first flown on October 12, 1954, still provides training during the basic phase, although it will ultimately be replaced by the winner of the long-contested Joint Primary Aircraft Training System (JPATS), the Raytheon (Beech) Mk II, a variation of the Swiss Pilatus PC-9.

The sleek looks of the T-38 Talon belie the fact that it first flew on April 10, 1959, and for many years provided advanced training for all pilots. A requirement for more specialized training eventually combined with a need to extend the service life of the T-38, and in 1993, a new system, Specialized Undergraduate Pilot Training (SUPT), was put into effect. In the new system, pilots selected for reconnaissance, attack, or fighter aircraft will continue to train in the T-38, while those selected for tankers, bombers, or transport planes will fly the Raytheon (Beech) T-1 Jayhawk. The T-1 is a militarized version of the Beech 400A, itself a variant of the twin-jet Mitsubishi Mu-300 Diamond.

The one constant in pilot training has been the high standards maintained; Air Force pilots receive the finest flight training in the world. Physical qualifications are very strict, and applicants are screened carefully for their flying aptitude. Flying training students are constantly evaluated for their proficiency, a practice that continues after graduation and for as long as the pilot continues to fly.

A Douglas C-124 unloading a Northrop Snark missile—the first operational (albeit briefly) intercontinental cruise missile. *(Courtesy of Harry Gann)*

The first U.S. jet fighter was the Bell XP-59; too slow and underpowered to be used in combat, it was an excellent jet trainer.

The Boeing B-29 distinguished itself in the Pacific in World War II and, after spending years in desert storage areas, came back to do the same in Korea.

The author's favorite aircraft. Perhaps the most important multi-jet aircraft in history, the Boeing B-47 not only had excellent performance for its time, but led to the development of all of Boeing's subsequent lines of bomber, tanker, and passenger aircraft. (*Courtesy of The Boeing Company*)

The North American XB-70 was a Mach 3 bomber that was canceled when it was believed that Soviet missile defenses had made it obsolete.

On the left, a Vought A-7 flanked by a Lockheed Martin (formerly General Dynamics) F-16. *(Courtesy of Eric Hehs)*

One of the most controversial aircraft in history, the Rockwell B-1B has become the principal aircraft of the U.S. bomber fleet.

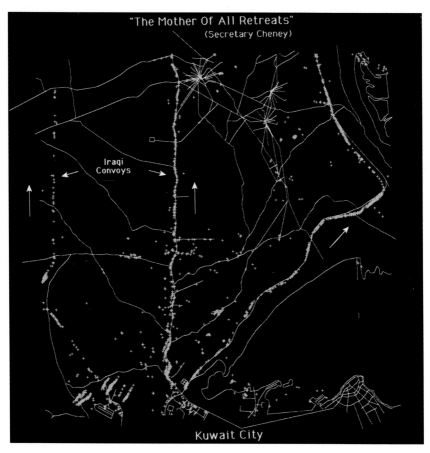

The Joint-STARS radarscopes portrayed thousands of Iraqi vehicles fleeing north from Kuwait City in this manner. Secretary of Defense Dick Cheney characterized it as "The Mother of All Retreats." *(Courtesy of Northrop Grumman)*

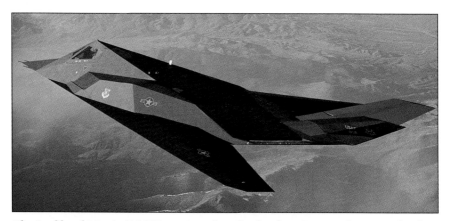

The Lockheed Martin F-117A was introduced to battle in Panama, but proved to be the decisive difference in the Persian Gulf War when it operated unimpeded through the intense Baghdad antiaircraft defenses. *(Courtesy of Lockheed Martin)*

The first team in the Persian Gulf War. Two Lockheed Martin F-16 Fighting Falcons fly on the wings of a three-ship McDonnell Douglas F-15 flight. *(Courtesy of Eric Hehs)*

The most expensive warplane ever built—and worth every penny, according to fans—is the Northrop Grumman B-2, which combines stealth characteristics into a flying wing configuration. *(Courtesy of Northrop Grumman)*

The Convair F-102 Delta Dagger had a long gestation period and an even longer operation career, serving actively from its first flight on October 23, 1953, to its withdrawal from Air National Guard service in 1976. Many were then converted to drones.

The Lockheed Martin F-16 Fighting Falcon is also called the "Electric Jet," "Lawn Dart," "Little Hummer," and (most likely from the enemy's point of view) "Viper."

General Bill Creech was always perfectly turned out, whether meeting with President Ronald Reagan, or in a flight suit. *(Courtesy of W.L. Creech)*

Logistics were extremely important to the Gulf War, and the Lockheed Martin C-5B played an important role. The crew members, sweating in the desert sun, are obviously serious about their tasks. *(Courtesy of Robert F. Dorr)*

The U.S. Army's McDonnell Douglas AH-64 Apache is as lethal as it looks; a fearsome combat weapon, it devastated Iraqi radar stations to which it was guided by USAF Pave Low helicopters. *(Courtesy of Robert F. Dorr)*

The McDonnell Douglas C-17 had a long gestation period, but it will be the mainstay of the airlift fleet for almost the entire twenty-first century. *(Courtesy of McDonnell Douglas)*

With its great success in the Gulf War, the McDonnell Douglas F-15E proved just how much "stretch" there was in the basic design. Originally intended as an air superiority fighter, the improved electronics, navigation, bombing, and communication gear gave the Strike Eagle an entirely new capability. *(Courtesy of McDonnell Douglas)*

OTHER AIRCREW TRAINING

The training programs for other than pilot aircrew members changed over time as aircraft and systems modernized. The traditional disciplines of navigator, bombardier, and radar observer converged, and a new requirement for electronic warfare officers emerged. After thirty-seven years, navigator-bombardier training at Mather AFB, California, ended in 1984, with the responsibility transferred to SAC's Combat Crew Training School at Castle AFB.

Undergraduate navigator training also experienced great variations in the numbers trained. A high point of almost 40,000 was reached in 1944, followed by a precipitous dropoff to only eighteen in 1947. Over the years, the number of navigators graduating ranged from 500 to 5,400, depending upon the needs of the service and the degree of the perceived emergency.

Electronic warfare officers(EWOs) became increasingly important as the years elapsed. Originally confined to bomber crews, EWOs became vital first to aircraft dedicated to electronic warfare, such as the Douglas RB-66, and then to fighters, when the McDonnell Douglas F-4 and the F-105F two-seat fighters appeared. The importance of EWOs grew in direct proportion to the increasing sophistication and strength of enemy defenses.

The requirement for training one of the great combat crew positions, that of gunner, ended in October, 1991 when the Strategic Air Command phased out the tail gunner on the B-52. Gunners had been the backbone of the giant formations of bombers during World War II and had scored additional successes in Korea and even Vietnam. But time and technology finally put an end to a great and honored tradition.

TECHNICAL TRAINING

The methods for providing technical training have varied widely over the years to meet contemporary budget and personnel situations. ATC always preferred to give complete training in residence at established technical training schools, no matter whether in avionics, cryptology, meteorology, supply, or any of the hundreds of other specialties that have been required. Training suffers from the same ratchet effect that airlift, logistics, and all the other disciplines do. In periods of peace, there is little money, and schools are allowed to wither and almost die. When an emergency looms, schools are rapidly expanded, even as instructors are siphoned off to take frontline positions in their specialties. Then, usually just about when the emergency ends, training reaches its peak, with adequate staffs, good recruits, and sufficient time. At the end of the emergency, training is drastically reduced, and the cycle begins again.

The retention problem has similar impact. When the civilian economy is booming, it usually makes economic sense for a first-term airman to leave the service and use the training he or she has received in civil employment. ATC has tried a number of methods to deal with this situation. In "first job" training, a young airman is given just enough theoretical information to enable him or her to learn the skills to perform the mission with extensive "on-the-job" training. New airmen, just out of basic training and perhaps a short course in the specialty, were assigned to mentors on the job who would teach them the task. Unfortunately, were usually too few technicians in the field already. When faced with the alternatives of getting their basic jobs done or training new airmen, the mentors most often chose to do the former.

The results of first job training were unsatisfactory. During 1992—designated the Year of Training by then Air Force Chief of Staff Merrill A. McPeak—an in-depth review of the training process was made. One result of this was the merging of Air Training Command and the Air University Command into the Air Education and Training Command in 1993. Another result was the emphasis placed on resident training and a turn away from on-the-job training.

PROFESSIONAL MILITARY EDUCATION (PME)

Because Professional Military Education (PME) is a prerequisite for advancement, service members understand that failure to be invited to a PME course often portends a career plateau. Competition is keen, and the slots are limited.

The lineage of the Air University can be traced back to February 10, 1921, and the founding of the Air Service School at Langley Field, Virginia. The school was upgraded the following year to the Air Services Field Officers School (i.e., for officers of the rank of major through colonel) and was given the mission of "preparing senior officers for higher Air Service command duty."

An important change occurred in 1926, when the school was redesignated the Air Corps Tactical School (ACTS) and opened to all officers. It then became a military think tank and a hotbed of ideas. It was at the ACTS where firebrands like Claire Chennault became advocates of Billy Mitchell's concept of air superiority, and where other brilliant young officers like future generals Haywood Hansell, Harold L. George, Muir S. Fairchild, Laurence Kuter, and others became proponents of the bomber.

The ACTS set the pattern for the future, for it elicited from its select student body the doctrines, tactics, and strategies of air war that were employed in World War II and subsequently. Its faculty and graduates included future USAF Chiefs of Staff Carl A. Spaatz, Hoyt S. Vandenberg, Nathan F. Twining, Thomas D. White, and Curtis E. LeMay—a very distinguished alumni group.

World War II brought about a suspension of the Tactical School; it was discontinued on October 9, 1942. A series of wartime applied tactical schools replaced it, but it was not until March 12, 1946, that, recognized as a major command, one of the replacement schools, the Army Air Forces School, was redesignated the Air University.

Just as Arnold had insisted on invigorating the research and development process with unfettered thinking, so did the backers of the new Air University insist that it break away from traditionalism and avoid the rigid doctrine and formalized instruction of typical military schools. The first Commander of the Air University, Major General Muir S. Fairchild, insisted, "This is not a post-war school system—it is a prewar school."

The Air University was intended as a single military organization free to concentrate all of its intellect and energies on the leadership, strategies, concepts, and doctrines necessary for winning future wars. The AU has become famous for its ability to continuously revise course content to keep abreast of new technologies. The international scene is closely monitored with classes, lectures, and field trips tailored to keep tabs on events as they develop.

The staff of the AU is made up of the most highly qualified military and civilian instructors available; unlike most similar institutions, the AU encourages a rapid turnover of the faculty to facilitate fresh views. The turnover is possible because the best and brightest of students are tapped to become instructors at the appropriate point in their careers.

The Air University takes its position as the designated keeper of professional military education very seriously, and now has fourteen major subordinate units, including the world-renowned Air University Library. The heart of its PME program for commissioned officers rests on the Squadron Officers School (for company-grade officers), the Air Command and Staff College (for field-grade officers), and the Air War College (for senior officers). There are reciprocal arrangements for similar-level education in other services, including those of our allies, and assignment to these schools was and is hotly coveted.

As important as these schools were in teaching doctrine, and ultimately in synthesizing experience for the creation of doctrine, they nonetheless did not have the overall impact on the Air Force that another branch of the Air University did: the Air Force Institute of Technology.

AFIT: CREATING AN AIR FORCE OF PROFESSIONALS

The tremendous impact that the Air Force Institute of Technology has had stems from the large number of students it has graduated. More than 266,000 personnel, mostly from the Air Force but also from other DOD organizations, have attended AFIT in the last seven decades. Chief of Staff General Charles Gabriel once stated, "The AFIT of today is the Air Force of tomorrow."

The overall goal of AFIT is to maintain itself as a world-class institution higher education in defense science, technology, and management. AFIT ne into being because the large number of technically qualified officers needed by the Air Force could not be attracted because of the low pay and demanding conditions of military service. The alternative was to select qualified applicants who had already chosen the service and provide the education. The result has been the creation of a highly professional corps of career officers.

In essence, the Air Force needed officers with academic attainments to match those of their industrial counterparts, and to obtain them it grew its own. Most of the officers selected for AFIT programs are bright young company-and field-grade officers who avidly desire graduate degrees. It is not an easy choice, for AFIT training, either in residence or at a civilian institution, is demanding, with heavy course loads and an unbending requirement for excellent performance. A "gentleman's C" is a sure ticket to removal and assignment to some less than desirable job.

The mission of AFIT is to support the Air Force through graduate and professional education, research, and consultation. The institute performs two closely related services, graduate-level education and professional continuing education, both drawing on similar academic resources. The graduate-level education is provided to carefully selected officers and Air Force civilian employees to give them the educational background to understand their technological and cultural environments and to analyze and attempt to solve the Air Force's problems. Professional continuing education programs are designed to satisfy specific Air Force and Department of Defense needs for special applications.

The roots of AFIT go back to 1919 and two remarkable men, Colonel Thurman Bane, who could set up a laboratory on one day and fly the Air Service's first helicopter on the next, and First Lieutenant Edwin E. Aldrin, a gifted administrator. Aldrin was also an expert test pilot, and was the father of Apollo 11 astronaut Edwin E. "Buzz" Aldrin, Jr., the second man to step on the moon.

On Bane's instructions, Aldrin did the legwork to establish the Air School of Application at McCook Field, Dayton, Ohio, in 1919, and then became a member of the first graduating class in 1920. In 1926, this became the Air Corps Engineering School, and a year later it was moved to Wright Field. The pressures of war caused a suspension of school activities from shortly after Pearl Harbor until 1944.

In 1946, the Army Air Forces Institute of Technology was established as a part of the Air Materiel Command; this became the Air Force Institute of Technology in 1947. The primary emphasis remained on engineering, but maintenance, logistics, and procurement were also covered.

The Commander, Air University, was authorized by Congress in 1954 to confer degrees upon persons in the AFIT Resident College, and this marked the beginning of a period of rapid growth for the institute. The Resident

College was later subdivided into the School of Engineering, School of Logistics, and School of Business, the last being transferred to civilian institutions in 1960. Full accreditation of AFIT programs at the doctoral level came in 1970.

The constantly changing environment of the modern Air Force has put a premium on training engineers in a broad spectrum of disciplines that range beyond the standard aeronautical, astronautical, computer, electrical, and nuclear engineering fields to esoteric areas like electro-optics, space operations, and the Air Force Test Pilot School program. Graduates of AFIT have made significant contributions to the nation's defense, including the original concept of the Joint Surveillance and Target Attack Radar System (Joint STARS or J-STARS) which was used with such deadly effect in the Persian Gulf War.

Perhaps the most unusual aspect of AFIT is its Civilian Institution Programs (CIP). Each year the CIP directs as many as 3,000 higher education students and 4,000 continuing education students in almost 400 school locations worldwide. The CIP budget of approximately $33 million per year represents about 50 percent of AFIT's entire budget. The CIP vastly expands AFIT's ability to provide schooling possibilities to Air Force personnel and offers advanced degrees in everything from engineering to medicine, dentistry, and law.

AFIT schooling comes with a quid pro quo: students who take advantage of it incur an obligation to remain in service for a specified number of years, depending upon the length of the schooling. The author looks back in gratitude to AFIT, which provided him with both a bachelor's and a master's degree.

OTHER MAJOR COMMANDS

Over the history of the modern USAF, there have been a number of important major commands, including the United States Air Forces in Europe (USAFE), Pacific Air Forces (PACAF), Air Force Communications Command (AFCC), Air Force Space Command (AFSPACECOM), and Air Force Special Operations Command (AFSOC). Each one merits a book of its own; unfortunately, space constraints prohibit telling each one's full story. Short resumes of these commands will be found in Appendix Two.

7

CHANGE AFTER VIETNAM

*I*n the years since Vietnam, the USAF has steadily improved its weaponry, doctrine, and leadership, as well as the quality of its personnel and the quality of life they enjoy. The task has not been easy, for it is engaged in intense competition from industry for the kinds of financial and intellectual resources necessary to field a superior air force. The competition is particularly aggressive for qualified African-Americans, other minority personnel, and women, a situation that will be addressed later in the chapter. For much of the time, the Air Force faced a skeptical public, a hostile press, declining budgets, a long series of external threats, and the daunting and unfamiliar task of achieving dominance in space. As it did so, it retained its nuclear deterrent power, built up its conventional forces, and rallied its allies to new standards of proficiency and performance. It was a demanding, if ultimately rewarding, two decades.

The gradual rise of the Air Force to its present position of eminence can be attributed to many factors. Improvements in doctrine, leadership, and weapons will be addressed in the next chapter. Here we will consider three often overlooked but complementary phenomena that have been the foundation stones of the Air Force's success. The first of these is an enlightened leadership that quite literally inverted traditional management methods. The second is the creation of a superb enlisted corps, led by noncommissioned officers who rose to the challenge of a highly professional, technologically oriented service during a time of profound social turbulence. The NCOs were instrumental in seeing that the entire enlisted force was qualified to handle its far more sophisticated assignments. The third was the belated but welcome exploitation of a huge new pool of talent implicit in bringing women and minorities into the service on an equal opportunity basis. Together these three elements helped shape the Air Force into an instrument that national leaders could use with confidence. The last two phenomena were completely dependent in their execution upon the first, the complete turnaround in Air Force management methods.

THE MANAGEMENT REVOLUTION

General Curtis E. LeMay, the most influential Air Force leader of the postwar period, instilled the discipline and established the highly structured centralized management necessary to create the Strategic Air Command, which provided the nuclear shield for U.S. foreign policy. Secretary of Defense Robert McNamara capitalized on the Defense Reorganization Act of 1958 to lift LeMay's centralist methods to an extreme. His methods trickled downward, inhibiting subordinates at all levels from taking action on their own and creating vast paperwork bureaucracies where any idea had to be "coordinated" with many offices, any one of which could say no, but none of which could give a definitive yes. Decision-making on even minor issues could be made only at the highest levels—and that more often than not meant McNamara himself. As a result there was established a "numbers are everything" reporting mentality that stifled initiative. The momentum McNamara imparted to the process kept the Department of Defense on a centralist course for years after he left.

A far more important effect of this bureaucratic centralism was that it sapped integrity by making the report on a mission more important than the results of a mission. The ability to waffle—what is today called "spin control"—became for some a more important qualification for promotion than the ability to produce. A hierarchy developed in which many rose to the top because they understood the system and knew how to manipulate it; beneath them, too often overlooked for promotion, were the mission-oriented workers who carried out their tasks without regard to their own advancement.

One has only to look at the great ossified bureaucracies around the world to realize how difficult it is to reverse the course of rigid, centralized bureaucratic control. On rare occasions a turnaround occurs. The reversal is usually due to a number of factors and to a large number of people, but there is often a single person who becomes identified with the change of direction. So it was with the Air Force. Identification of the man responsible emerged in the course of a number of in-depth interviews with four-star officers, including Generals David Jones, Larry Welch, Michael Dugan (all three former Chiefs of Staff), Robert Russ (COMTAC), and Michael Loh (COMTAC) and first Commander of the Air Combat Command). All were candid and forthcoming about their own careers in the Air Force and in assessing the contributions of others. Each one, quite independently, and usually in a different context, attributed the remarkable turnaround in Air Force management style, with its consequent increase in proficiency, efficiency, and improved quality of life, to one man: General Wilbur "Bill" Creech. Jones ranks him with Curtis LeMay as one of the two most influential men in his long Air Force experience.

A cynic might think that this was simply "good-old-boyism," praising a popular colleague. Nothing could be further from the truth, for Creech was personally unpopular with many people because of his demanding standards of performance. Those who did not come up to his standards certainly regarded him as being far too critical; some to this day somewhat ironically consider him to have been the spiritual successor to General LeMay.

However, the effect of Creech's work has been specifically acknowledged by a number of other sources, including, as we will see, by the Department of Defense. General Charles Horner, the air commander of the Persian Gulf War, has written at length about how, as a classic fighter pilot, he was at first vehemently opposed to everything Bill Creech stood for, from pressed uniforms and carefully combed hair to minimal drinking and less horseplay at the officers' club. Over time, however, he became not only a convert to Creech's methods but a self-described "Creech clone." Even though Creech had retired long before the war, Horner gives him "number one credit" for the victory of air power in the Gulf War.

Creech's methods worked management miracles in many organizations, creating, despite his admitted rigor, a climate of benign, forward-looking personnel relations throughout the Air Force that is still followed today. This climate—so foreign to anyone who had been dusted off in a McNamara briefing or frosted by a LeMay admonishment—fostered an inventive outlook and engendered an eagerness to create new approaches to old problems.

There were also other practitioners of proactive human relations. Prominent among these was the first man to rise from the ranks of combat crew member to become Commander in Chief of SAC, General Russell Dougherty, who was the complete antithesis of LeMay in personality, always genial and self-proclaimed as the "first nonhero to head SAC." Dougherty's towering intellect is well known in the service and in his retirement career as a prominent businessman and lawyer. As much as Dougherty admired LeMay, he recognized that the authoritarian leadership style had been carried too far. In one of his earliest talks to his commanders, Dougherty told them, "There's nothing in your job description or mine that requires either of us to be an unmitigated son of a bitch." (Dougherty is noted for his erudite and literate presentations to Congress, and his rare use of raw language was to drive home a point.)

When all is said and done, the Air Force that was driven to an absolute and crippling centralism by McNamara was turned around by Bill Creech, who found that many of his brother officers also recognized the problem and were more than willing to adopt his solutions.

"COMMAND MUST BE REASONED"

Many people, unaware of the extent of General Creech's contribution, will question the space devoted here to his career. However, the impact that he had upon the Air Force was both broad and deep, and it is worthwhile to see exactly how it came about.

A distinguished 1949 graduate of that grand old institution the Aviation Cadet program, Creech had a fast-moving career in fighters. In between his 103 combat missions over North Korea and 177 in Vietnam, Creech flew hundreds of aerial demonstration missions with the U.S. Air Force Thunderbirds and their USAFE equivalent, the Skyblazers.

Quality was the underlying principle of Creech's leadership. He created small teams of people who trusted each other and were genuinely concerned about each other's welfare. He added to this the ingredients of leadership and commitment operating from the bottom up. Time and again, he achieved levels of quality and productivity that appear miraculous when compared to the results of prior efforts.

The future General Creech was propelled into management on a larger scale commanding tactical fighter wings at Zweibrucken Air Base, Wiesbaden, Germany, and at Torrejon AB, Spain, during 1970 and 1971. It was at Zweibrucken that Creech's fanatic obsession with quality and productivity first received wide attention as, in nine short months, he turned a new wing and a derelict base into the best unit of its kind in Europe. He was sent immediately to the 401st TFW in Torrejon, which had flunked its last two warfighting inspections. Two wing commanders in a row had been fired. In another nine-month whirlwind of activity, Creech once again proved that his principles worked.

General David Jones, Commander in Chief of U.S. Air Forces in Europe (CINCUSAFE), was impressed. Sensing a kindred soul, he nominated Creech to be his deputy for operations—a major general's slot. Jones had to go to Chief of Staff General John D. "Three Finger Jack" Ryan for permission. Ryan argued against placing a colonel (although Creech was on the promotion list for brigadier general) in a two-star position, but ultimately agreed. Now clearly identified as a comer, Creech received choice assignments as Vice Commander of the Aeronautical Systems Division and later as Commander of the Electronic Systems Division. He applied his management principles in both positions.

Driving himself hard at ESD, Creech, by now a three-star general, suffered a heart attack, which under Air Force policy meant automatic retirement. The Chief of Staff, David Jones, changed the policy. He allowed Creech time to recover, and then assigned him to command what had become the biggest challenge in the Air Force: the Tactical Air Command.

CREECH AT TAC

The magnitude of Creech's assignment was staggering. Promoted to be a four-star general on the day he took over command, he headed an organization that employed 65,000 members of the Air Force and a further 50,000 civilians in more than 150 separate installations around the world. He had a supersonic, nuclear-capable fleet of 3,800 aircraft maintained by a centralized bureaucracy that did not see itself as inefficient nor concern itself that its training sortie rate was dropping an average 8 percent per year, or that its pilots were opting to leave the service in droves after receiving more than $1 million in training. On any given day as many as 1,900 of his fleet of aircraft might have been out of commission. About 220 were certified "hangar queens," unable to fly for three weeks or more because of maintenance or spares deficiencies. A very high abort rate plagued the aircraft that attempted to launch.

Creech received authority to do a large-scale test of his concept of using decentralized, team-based systems. He set about changing TAC, beginning with his familiar tenet that well-trained, well-motivated teams of people, empowered to do their jobs and given a sense of proprietorship, were the most efficient. Creech told his commanders, "Gentlemen, command must be reasoned," and cautioned them against losing their tempers. He also told them that a leader's place was in the air, just as the place of the senior master sergeant on the flight line was in the trenches turning wrenches, not behind a coffee-and-doughnut-laden desk. Aircraft that previously were rotated through an anonymous centralized maintenance procedure now "belonged" to a dedicated crew chief, who had the privilege of painting his name on the side of the fuselage, just as the pilot did. Creech tells a story about one of his routine visits with the troops when he talked to the frontline workers about how things were going. A crew chief shook his hand and told him how much he liked the dedicated crew chief program. Creech asked him why he liked it, and the crew chief asked him a question in return: "General, when was the last time you washed a rental car?"

Some of Creech's attributes worked against him. He didn't have the stentorian voice of a stereotypical great leader. He was fussy in his appearance and demanded that his officers be similarly conscious of their uniforms. His enthusiasm, his leading by example, and most of all his results first commanded respect and then affection. But Creech was tough. If a pilot violated safety regulations, he would be disciplined without a voice being raised—but also without a moment's hesitation. When a hotshot pilot buzzed his hometown of Plano, Texas, Creech fired him. He was lobbied by the pilot's peers and by a petition from the people of Plano. Creech held firm: there was no recourse.

Under his direction, the TAC accident rate dropped from one every 13,000 hours to one every 50,000 hours. During the same interval that the accident rate dropped, the average aircraft sortie rate (flights per aircraft per month) rose from 11 to 21. In plain language this meant Creech had effectively almost doubled the number of aircraft under his command—with no additional procurement.

As hard as he was on safety violations, he was even more rigorous with any violation of personal integrity, which he treated with an instant, severe response. He discovered that a fast-rising brigadier general had lied to him about a safety incident. Creech called the errant BG and told him to resign immediately or face a general court-martial.

Many people—including, at the time, the future General Chuck Horner—thought that Creech went too far, that he was going to snuff out the raucous independence that had characterized fighter pilots since World War I. Creech maintained instead that he was channeling the pilots' energy into a new understanding of their equipment. Pilots in World War I flew $10,000 Spads when the weather was good; his pilots were flying $30 million fighters in all weather. The difference was vast, and Creech knew that pilots had to conform to the new reality.

Despite a reduced budget, Creech had TAC substantially turned around within four years. With typical government myopia, the General Accounting Office was disturbed over the amount of money he was spending on improving the appearance of his installations. The term "Creech brown" had become a joking reference to the number of buildings that had been painted in earth colors as he set about his "Proud Look" campaign, giving every base a sense of pride in its appearance.

In its lengthy investigation, the GAO did find that much money was being spent on "home improvement," but that it was primarily for materials; the airmen *and the officers* were doing most of the work in their off-time. The GAO also found that the new leadership style at TAC had increased productivity by 80 percent. The number of aircraft out for maintenance was cut by 75 percent. Later it was estimated that in a period of four years, Creech's methods had produced equipment availability and combat capability that would have cost more than $12 billion if purchased on the open market.

CREECH'S INFLUENCE ON THE PERSIAN GULF WAR

The profound change of course at TAC was not confined to managerial methods. Creech was a warrior who found TAC's tactics encumbered with what he called "go-low disease"—the perceived need to fly at minimum height to avoid enemy surface-to-air missiles. Creech argued that the buildup in enemy antiaircraft artillery made the go-low approach dangerous, and that new methods were needed. He decreed that taking out SAMs was the first order of business—that the enemy defenses should be nullified and rolled back so that follow-on aircraft would have the flexibility to operate at high or low altitude in hostile territory, depending upon the nature of enemy defenses. Just as in Linebacker II, removal of the SAMs was essential.

The new tactics were drummed into TAC in practice in the rigorous Air Force Red Flag training at Nellis Air Force Base, and with the complementary training functions Creech had devised: Copper Flag for the air defense forces, Green Flag for electronic countermeasures, and Checkered Flag for rapid deployments.

The payoff for the realistic training came in the Persian Gulf War, where USAF casualties were remarkably low. Those coalition partners who stayed with the go-low philosophy suffered heavily as a result of their unwillingness to change tactics.

At the end of the Gulf War, the air commander, General Horner, had an opportunity to review the magnitude of the victory and realized that the USAF had succeeded because it had anticipated the nature of the threat, had trained its pilots to fight on the first day of the conflict, and had provided them with technology and tactics that saved their lives and kept their aircraft at an unprecedented level of operational readiness. He attributed this happy state of events to Bill Creech and three elements of his teachings. The first of these was the critical importance of decentralization in ensuring a maximum flexibility, responsiveness, and feeling of ownership. The second was the absolute necessity of getting leadership and commitment from everyone, regardless of rank or position. The third was the power of planning for quality in every action.

THE SPREAD OF TQM

TAC's turnaround did not go unnoticed; word spread rapidly through the Air Force, and the reins of centralized management were loosened. It was not only more efficient, it was a more pleasant way to work—the quality of life for the airmen improved because their job satisfaction increased.

Perhaps the most important aspect of Creech's methods was that they were exactly in tune with the changes going on in civilian attitudes toward work and the quality of life. Creech was hammering at the frontier-outpost mentality the Air Force had inherited from the Army and driving it into the mainstream of human relations management, at a time when this was absolutely critical. The old methods of the Air Force were not working and probably would not have worked in the post-1970s world. More important, perhaps, they would have left the Air Force unequipped to meet the challenges it would face.

Creech's methods were exactly counter to the ongoing centralist philosophy of the Department of Defense, which like some mythic giant octopus was absorbing as many functions of the services as possible. On December 1, 1982, Deputy Secretary of Defense Frank C. Carlucci signed a DOD memorandum calling for the study of a single defense agency that would "own and operate all DOD installations." All Air Force bases, Army forts, posts, and camps, and Navy stations would be consolidated under a single DOD manager.

Creech met the issue head on, inviting DOD representatives to visit TAC and see what decentralization had accomplished. Robert A. Stone was then Deputy Assistant Secretary of Defense, with the responsibility for all DOD installations worldwide, and was the man behind the memorandum Carlucci had signed. He believed in the efficiency of centralization and wished to reduce costs by bringing all the installations under one set of rules so that procurement, maintenance, repair, and other activities could be standardized.

Stone and his associates were well intentioned. They conducted a full-scale investigation of conditions in TAC and followed Creech's own methods by getting into the field and talking to the people who were doing the work. When they were finished, they reversed their position and asked Creech to help formulate a method for achieving the same success DOD-wide. In early 1984, only a little over a year after his own initial memo on centralizing installations had been signed, Secretary Stone created the DOD-wide Model Installations Program or MIP. After two years of successful tests, on March 26, 1986, DOD issued another memorandum, "Defense-wide Application of the Model Installation Management Approach." The techniques to be used were those Creech had demonstrated in TAC.

Further objective corroboration of Creech's methods came with the President's Blue Ribbon Commission on Defense Management, headed by David Packard, who had made his fame and fortune running Hewlett-Packard in a maverick style. In his foreword, Packard applauded the new methods being used by DOD in managing its installations. It was truly a case where less was more: less management gave more results in installation cost, utilization, and appearance.

Creech began calling his approach Total Quality Management (TQM) in 1981; in 1988 the term was adopted officially by the Department of Defense, and its use was extended to vendors doing business with the military. (The full history of TQM, as well as an in-depth explanation of all its details, may be found in Creech's book *The Five Pillars of TQM: How to Make Total Quality Management Work for You.*)

Creech's influence might well not have been so widespread nor so long-lasting if it had not been institutionalized by the officers who followed him to command positions. Many future leaders who adopted Creech's management precepts were subsequently assigned to organizations outside of TAC. They not only employed his methods in their new positions, but, in turn, they indoctrinated their subordinates in Creech's management philosophy. Individuals often made minor changes, reflecting their own personalities; but for the most part, Creech's ideas became pervasive throughout the USAF.

TQM IMPACT ON THE AIR FORCE'S QUALITY OF LIFE

General Creech's contributions to the Air Force's management revolution have been given special emphasis here because they were fundamental to two other massively important aspects of the Air Force's post-Vietnam turnaround.

First, the Air Force turned to the management methods espoused by Bill Creech at TAC with enthusiasm and relief. The new methods that brought about improvements in proficiency also happened to be attuned to the swift-moving changes in the lives of American civilians. The effect of TQM was to provide the Air Force with more efficiency while it provided Air Force people with a better life, one more nearly comparable in pay, benefits, and prestige to those of their civilian counterparts.

Second, this turnaround also coincided with the maturation of the enlisted forces as a significant managerial element. As we will see below, the enlisted ranks, guided by their noncommissioned officers, changed rapidly over the years and emerged from the trauma of the Vietnam War able to meet the challenges of the modern Air Force.

Before we review the evolution of the Air Force enlisted force from its early days to its present status, it might be salutary—and sobering—to get a snapshot of how the current quality of military life is gauged.

THE BASELINE OF MILITARY QUALITY OF LIFE

The Air Force, like the other services, traditionally placed more emphasis on equipment and readiness than on the quality of life of its members. It now faces a serious crisis in maintaining a quality of life competitive with that of the civilian population. An "all-volunteer force" will have no volunteers if there is not a reasonable parity in military and civil life.

In October 1995, the report of the Defense Science Board task force on "quality of life" was released. It reveals plainly that despite the best efforts of the services, the Congress has not kept its promises. The report emphasizes that preservation and improvement of the quality of life of members of the armed services is not a matter of kindness or generosity. It is instead directly related to the readiness of our military, to the retention of key personnel, to morale.

Conceptually, five basic elements define the quality of life for military services. These include compensation, medical care, housing, personnel tempo, and community or family services. (Personnel tempo is defined as the amount of time a service person is forced to spend away from home compared to the amount of time spent at home. For purposes of the study, field exercises that keep the service person away overnight, even though conducted from a home base, are considered time away.)

As important as they are, compensation and medical care will be given only a brief mention here. They are the subjects of other task forces, whose reports were not completed at the time this was written. Military compensation has traditionally lagged well behind civilian compensation, particularly in times when funds are tight. Military medicine, once greatly admired and one of the chief inducements to make a career of the service, has fallen on even harder times than medicine in the civilian world, and the solemn promise of medical care for retirees has been monumentally diluted. Skyrocketing costs have reduced services everywhere even as noncompetitive salaries drive the most competent professional medical people away from serving even a tour, much less a career, in the military. The inevitable result has been a lowering of standards. The waiting periods to obtain services are long and a variety of fiendish systems have been developed to make getting an appointment much more a matter of sheer dogged persistence than of medical need.

In the three areas covered by the report on quality of life, the basic findings run in sharp opposition to stated Congressional intent and to the policies of current DOD leaders, both military and civilian. Secretary of Defense William J. Perry stated in his 1995 *Report to the President and the Congress,* "Readiness is associated most closely with the morale and espirit de corps of U.S. soldiers, sailors, airmen and Marines. These intangibles are maintained by ensuring the best possible quality of life for people in uniform and their families. Quality of life falls into three general categories: standard of living for Service members; demands made on personnel, especially time away from family; and other ways people are treated while in the Service."

Despite the good intentions of Congress and DOD, a long-term situation has evolved in which reduced budgets and increased commitments have been rationalized only by taking the difference out of the hides of service personnel. In effect the policy of procuring hardware and deferring pay raises has been accepted as a way of doing business.

Here is a brief survey of the three quality-of-life areas covered by the report, along with some relevant quotations.

Housing

Excellent housing facilities and services shall be provided for all military members, their families and eligible civilians. Continual improvement in quality is a measure of excellence, and customers of housing services shall participate in their evaluation.
—Department of Defense Housing Management Manual,
September 1993

The Department of Defense owns or leases about 387,000 homes, which have an average age of thirty-three years. Deferred maintenance, repair, revitalization, and replacement have reached a total of $20 billion. In other words, Congress and the armed services have chosen not to spend the $20 billion known to be necessary to bring housing up to a decent standard. Sixty-four percent of these military homes are rated as "unsuitable" for a variety of reasons. Some 15 percent of military families live in private-sector homes also considered unsuitable. Thus, 79 *percent* of military families are forced to live in housing unsuitable by civilian standards.

The situation is no better for bachelor housing. A $9 billion backlog in repairs and replacement has been amassed, and 62 percent of the 612,000 bachelor housing spaces are considered substandard.

The report notes that "the delivery system [of personnel housing] is so intrinsically flawed that it should be replaced with an entirely new system." The probability of this occurring is small, given that an entirely new system would require Congressional funding at a time when deficit reduction is the political imperative.

Personnel Tempo

The drawdown has caused many Service members to question their long-term commitment and the prospects of a full career. The turbulence of consolidations and base closures has disrupted assignments and family life.
—Secretary of Defense William J. Perry,
November 1994

A direct correlation exists between family separations, spousal support for a military lifestyle, and retention rates. The armed services tend to define "personnel tempo" in a variety of ways. For example, the Navy only credits a unit—not an individual—for time away, and does so only when a deployment is underway for fifty-six days. The Marine Corps uses a ten-day period. Service members, however, define it on a realistic basis: the amount of time they are forced to spend away from home. The task force report also chose to view it in this manner, saying that its yardstick was "1 day away = 1 day away."

In the five years after 1989, the total strength of the Department of Defense decreased by 28 percent. Random samples of service personnel deployments indicate that the average serviceman or servicewoman will be away four times as often in 1995 as in 1989. In other words, as strength has declined, requirements for travel have increased. The results of the increase in the number of days spent away from home are many and varied, and none are good. They range from divorces to the loss of second jobs (a critical necessity for many enlisted personnel) to inability to compete for promotions. As an example of this last problem, technicians from the 429th Electronic Combat Squadron at Cannon Air Force Base, New Mexico, were kept so busy on deployments that they had no time to prepare for the highly competitive promotion exams. The fifty-five staff sergeants of the 429th were among the most highly qualified people in the service in their specialty, that of making sure that the complex electronic suites on their General Dynamic

EF-111 Ravens were in perfect order. (The Ravens did a marvelous job in suppressing enemy electronics in the Gulf War.) Of the fifty-five, *not one* was selected for promotion to technical sergeant, because not one had time to prepare for the examinations. The impact on morale can be imagined.

In the USAF, people with certain skills, such as those required for AWACS or Fairchild A-10 aircraft, deploy as much as 75 percent of the time. These long-term deployments have an inevitable effect upon morale and family integrity; they also adversely affect training, as the tragic friendly-fire shootdown in Iraq of two Blackhawk helicopters by Air Force F-15s under the control of an AWACS demonstrated.

Community and Family Services

Military people stay in service because they like being part of something special. They won't stay long, however, if families aren't treated well.
—General John M. Shalikashvili,
Chairman of the Joint Chiefs of Staff
May 1995

The mores and customs of members of the armed services mirror those of the civilian community. Women are well integrated into all the services, and the phenomenon of the single-parent military family—male and female— all but unknown a generation ago is becoming increasingly common. Almost 65 percent of military spouses work, and in far too many cases, both parents hold down two jobs to make ends meet. This creates a pressing requirement for child care facilities that are safe, affordable, convenient, and of high quality. (It is shocking to note that many service families, unable to sustain a two-parent-four-job employment blitz, are forced to resort to food stamps and other charities. A spouse fighting a war on another continent is unlikely to have his or her morale improved by knowing that only food stamps are keeping the family alive.)

Like housing, funding for child care has fallen steadily behind. Service members have approximately 1 million children under twelve years of age; about half of these are preschool children. The DOD provides child care at 346 locations with spaces for only about 155,000 children. There is a current waiting list of almost 144,000.

All of the services have done a great deal to help themselves, through the use of nonappropriated funds generated from such activities as the base theater and bowling alley and from user fees. However, resolution of the overriding problem of child care can come about only through Congressional action and consistent, sustained funding.

The Defense Science Board came up with recommendations for most of the problem areas it cited; if carried out, they would go a long way to remedy the current shortfall in the quality of military life. Many of the recommendations are within the power of the individual services to act on, and un-

doubtedly they will do so. Unfortunately, many of the more critic
recommendations require legislation and Congressional funding. The prob
ability of this happening is left to the reader's judgment.

In many areas, current Air Force practice was recommended by the
Defense Science Board Report for emulation by other services. This was true
of child care, housing, and, most particularly, education programs. The Community College of the Air Force, of which more later, was singled out for its
exemplary work.

THE RISE OF THE PROFESSIONAL
NONCOMMISSIONED OFFICER CORPS

The foregoing coverage of the DOD report on quality of life is useful as
a background for understanding a significant managerial coup: the creation
of what has been termed the most outstanding corps of noncommissioned
officers of any service in the world—that of the United States Air Force.

The assessment of the quality of the noncommissioned corps comes from
many sources. General Jones recalls that when he was Commander in Chief
of USAFE, he was constantly asked by NATO officers how the USAF
achieved such excellence in its NCO corps. General Robert Russ, former
Commander of TAC, delights in telling the story of the first major exchange
of visits between Soviet and U.S. leaders, initiated by the Chairman of the
Joint Chiefs of Staff, Admiral William J. Crowe, Jr. One of the stops on the
Soviet itinerary was a visit to Russ's headquarters at Langley AFB, Virginia,
by a delegation that included Crowe's counterpart, Soviet Chief of Staff Marshal Sergei F. Akhromeyev.

In a debriefing prior to their departure from the United States, the Soviet
leaders confided to the Admiral Crowe that the one thing that had impressed
them most was not the advanced fighters, nor even the commissaries and
post exchanges bursting with consumer goods. They had expected American
leadership in these areas, and accepted it. But they were totally overwhelmed
by the U.S. noncommissioned officer corps, which had no counterpart in the
Soviet Union. In the Soviet Union and in its successor states, jobs typically
held by noncommissioned officers in this country—crew chiefs, line chiefs,
tank commanders—are always held by officers.

Russ attributes the Soviet assessment of the Air Force NCO corps in
part to a fortuitous choice of the Langley Engine Shop in the tour he provided his guests. The visitors were amared that this multimillion-dollar facility, conducting hundreds of millions of dollars' worth of engine repair each
year, was run by a senior master sergeant. Their astonishment was doubled
when they discovered that the senior master sergeant was a woman. The
Soviets closely questioned the NCO shop manager, convinced that she was
a ringer, a "Potemkin" leader. They were astounded when the shop manager
not only demonstrated a sure knowledge of her job and of the complex pro-

cedures involved in it, but introduced them to the people working for her and explained their jobs as well.

The USAF's requirements for noncommissioned officers and enlisted personnel are somewhat different from those of other U.S. services, particularly the combat arms of the Army and the Marines, where a high turnover in personnel is desirable. It takes young, well-conditioned troops—trigger pullers—to engage in the rough and tumble of conflict, and it is desirable to build up a strong reserve of experienced personnel who can be recalled to duty if necessary. Thus it makes economic sense to bring them in, teach them the trade of ground war, and then replace them with younger troops at the end of their tours.

Air Force personnel are also required to maintain themselves in good physical condition, but other attributes are equally important when it comes to managing the sophisticated systems found in every Air Force discipline. Considerable experience is required for supervisory positions in the fields of jet engines, ICBMs, advanced electronic systems, and modern precision-guided munitions, to name just a few. As the Air Force, like other services, has drawn down, its senior noncommissioned officers have been hard pressed to manage their own assignments and to train new people at the same time. Therefore, retention of experienced people is one of their most important concerns. A first-term airman begins to earn his pay only when he approaches the end of his tour, so it is vital to retain that airman for another enlistment period—more than that if possible—to get a reasonable return on the training investment. A young airman whose name is painted on the side of a $30 million fighter might have civilian technicians—the famous "tech reps"— working under his or her direction who earn twice as much in salary. The demonstrated ability to handle responsibility of this magnitude makes young airmen highly desirable commodities in the civilian job market when the term of enlistment expires. One of the signs of a superior noncommissioned officer supervisor is his or her ability to convince young airmen that their long-term interests are better served by a career in the Air Force than by the plums being dangled by a civilian recruiter.

This would seem an impossible task, given the content of the previously cited Defense Science Board report on quality of life. A brief review of the history of the enlisted force will help put things in perspective, and show how certain fundamental factors, including simple patriotism, maintain their appeal.

BREAKING THE LOGJAM

The demobilization frenzy that had so debilitated the USAAF after World War II ended had its effect upon the enlisted force when the USAF came into being in 1947. The force was "old Army" and top-heavy with rank, for the people who elected to stay in were for the most part those whose seniority gave them an incentive to make a career of the service. Many of them were children of the depression whose motivation was, in the phrase of the time, "three hots and a cot," meaning three hot meals and a place to stay. This was no small matter for those who had come to maturity in the 1930s and, like everyone else, had no idea there would be a postwar economic boom of unprecedented magnitude and longevity.

Over the next several years, the logjam of high-ranking enlisted personnel was exacerbated by regulations that permitted officers who had been separated to enlist at the rank of master sergeant. Thus an outsider, already unhappy at his loss of commissioned status, could come in at the top of the enlisted ranks even though he might not possess the skills or the inclination to execute an NCO's duties with vigor. Another problem was inherent in the high ratio of officers to enlisted in the Air Force compared to other services. Officers were often assigned additional duties that normally could have been done by an NCO.

The advent of the Korean War brought about yet another difficulty. The Air Force again built up rapidly, and many reservists who were recalled elected to stay in service when the war ended in 1953. Many of these reservists, their lives interrupted for a second time, realized that they now had eight or ten years of active duty and that staying another ten or twelve to gain a retirement benefit made sense. This saddled the Air Force with what became known as the "Korean Hump"—an unbalanced rank structure with far too many senior NCOs and a shortage of enlisted personnel in the lower grades, E-1 through E-5.

The excess of senior noncommissioned officers, most of them still many years away from retirement, stagnated the promotion system, stifling the incentive of younger airmen. When promotions were made, the selection was done by local boards, and results were often skewed by the inevitable cronyism. The NCO corps was burdened with yet another problem, the rank of warrant officer, with which the Air Force never really came to grips in defining its place in the grade structure. Warrant officers were usually administrative specialists in a field, e.g., finance, supply, or medicine. They held positions that otherwise would have been held by NCOs and thus helped block the normal progression through the grades.

The promotion stagnation was partially alleviated in 1958 by the creation of two new "supergrades," E-8 for senior master sergeant and E-9 for chief master sergeant. This immediately offered promotion possibilities for master sergeants, and, in domino fashion, for lower ranks. The warrant officer problem was finessed nine months after the supergrades were introduced with a decision to make no further promotions to that rank. Normal attrition lowered their numbers until the last warrant officer was retired in the late 1970s. The problem of officers' performing additional duties in what might ordinarily have been NCO slots was alleviated over the years as the sophistication of Air Force weapon systems increased and there were more officer-level duties to be assigned.

The remainder of the promotion logjam was eventually broken up by two separate events. The first of these was under the impetus of the great friend of the enlisted man Congressman L. Mendel Rivers, a South Carolina Democrat. As chairman of the House Armed Services Committee, he held hearings that resulted in the creation of the Weighted Airman Promotion System (WAPS) in 1970. Under WAPS, promotion was contingent upon objective factors and used clearly defined, weighted criteria such as time in grade and test scores. These criteria were often within the control of the individual airman to manage—for example, if he or she made the effort to take training courses, it helped the score. It also removed the element of cronyism, although there were later charges that the tests had an inherent cultural bias that resulted in low scores by minorities. Work was done to redesign the tests to alleviate this problem.

The second major factor in the final breakup of the promotion logjam shows just how far the Air Force will reach in its search for a catchy acronym. In this case it was an "up-or-out" system for airmen known as TOPCAP, or Total Objective Plan Career Airmen Personnel. TOPCAP initiated a policy of forced attrition. In 1973, the high-year-of-tenure for various ranks was established as follows: an E-4 (senior airman, the equivalent of sergeant) or an E-5 (staff sergeant) had one of twenty years; if not promoted by twenty years, it was necessary to retire. Time requirements for other grades were as follows: E-6 (tech sergeant), twenty-three years; E-7 (master sergeant), twenty-six years; E-8 (senior master sergeant), twenty-eight years; E-9 (chief master sergeant), thirty years.

There were factors adversely affecting enlistment other than promotion. Pay was the most obvious of these; military pay always lagged civilian pay, primarily because lawmakers always turned to a cap on military pay as a means of restraining the federal budget. Only when the gap grew so great that an exodus of officers and enlisted was eminent was some measure of "catch-up" provided.

Salary was only part of the compensation problem. Military people lost out on permanent-change-of-station (PCS) moves because the allowance was never sufficient to cover the expenses of uprooting a household and moving across the country or to another continent. One factor, never quantified in any military pay analysis, was that military people were unable to buy a home and live in it for years, thus building up equity. If they chose to buy, each time they moved they bought in at the current price at whatever interest rate they could obtain. (It was unusual for a military family to buy a home until the 1960s; it became more common during the 1970s and 1980s, but, with the advent of higher home prices and high interest rates, it became more difficult in the 1990s.) Many people at retirement were buying their first home in communities just as their new civilian neighbors, who had never had to move, were making their last mortgage payments.

Tours of temporary duty (TDY) away from home also generally cost money, and, in the case of those who had to make frequent trips, became a significant item in the family budget. TDY trips had another, undemocratic aspect. Officers' quarters were generally of acceptable quality, while for too long enlisted temporary quarters were rough open barracks.

Another factor that had far-reaching effects upon the services, and particularly upon the challenge faced by Air Force noncommissioned officers, was the establishment of the All-Volunteer Force by Congress in 1973. The Air Force and its predecessor organizations had always been volunteer, but for much of the time, the volunteers were motivated as much by the threat of the draft as by the desire to serve. After 1974, it could be presumed that enlisted personnel shared the long-term view of senior NCOs, i.e., that service in the Air Force was a full-time job that served the societal need of protecting the country. In addition, they viewed their job choice as desirable because of the specialized training given in sophisticated trades and the opportunity for gaining additional education.

Yet for the real achievers, another factor was fundamentally important: the Air Force offered the opportunity to obtain far greater responsibility at a much younger age than in civilian life. This is in part a function of the size of the Air Force and of the mobility of its personnel. Jobs turn over more swiftly, and a ready and waiting airman can take over responsibility as it becomes available.

It is difficult to overemphasize the importance of this most intangible of factors. The desire for responsibility is pervasive in the enlisted force, and the psychic return derived from the proper execution of that responsibility is a primary reason that many stay in service. The knowledge an airman has that the aircraft would not have been able to take off on time without his or her expertise is immensely rewarding; it is doubly so when it is acknowledged—usually by no more than a "thumbs-up" sign or a slap on the back—by the airman's peers and superiors. And this sense of reward from responsibilities well discharged is not confined to earth-shaking events. It comes in all jobs at all levels, from a beginning cook who creates a sparkling salad bar to an armorer loading missiles for a strike in the Persian Gulf War. The common denominator is that Air Force leaders at all levels see to it that accomplishments are recognized and appreciated.

The military retirement system was one aspect of service that a noncommissioned officer could use to induce enlisted personnel to remain on duty. The concept of retirement seems remote to a first-termer, but by the end of the second tour, it becomes a real selling point. In today's budget-cutting climate, the military retirement system (already subjected to considerable reductions) is under fire; if it should be significantly altered, it would have an adverse effect upon enlistment rates—and a catastrophic effect upon reenlistments.

As will be shown later in the chapter, the All-Volunteer Force concept helped in another important process: the widespread integration of women and minorities into the work force. Whole pools of previously ignored talent suddenly became available, and the smarter officer and noncommissioned officers were quick to take advantage of it.

CHIEF MASTER SERGEANT OF THE AIR FORCE

The change in the nature of the Air Force's noncommissioned officer corps was a joint product of the growing expertise required by all the systems coming into service and the increased responsibilities these systems demanded. In this context, the term "systems" includes not only weapon systems such as the Minuteman missile, but also the many accounting, inventory, personnel, and other systems that were becoming increasingly sophisticated as they became more automated. The day of the "old soldier", immortalized as Sergeant Bilko or Beetle Bailey's Sarge, a man who had performed the same set of duties for twenty years, was gone. Now new demands were placed upon the intellect and the energy of the noncommissioned officer corps every day. The pressures were welcomed by most, for it provided an opportunity to excel. The bell had tolled for the old-fashioned NCO who preferred to shuffle papers at a desk and wait for happy hour.

The Marines, always aware of the value of the noncommissioned officer, had established the position of Sergeant Major of the Marine Corps in 1957. The United States Army followed suit in July 1965, with the position of Sergeant Major of the Army. Talk of a similar position in the Air Force had been opposed at Headquarters USAF, officially because there were already many channels of communication for the enlisted force. A more gripping reason was voiced unofficially by General John P. McConnell, Chief of Staff, who thought the position would be used as a means of circumventing channels.

As he did on so many occasions, Congressman Rivers stepped into the fray, proposing legislation that mandated a senior enlisted position in all four services. His bill was not passed, but his message was, and on October 24, 1966, General McConnell announced his decision to create the post of Chief Master Sergeant of the Air Force (CMSAF), stating bluntly, "The man selected to fill this job will be used as a representative of the airman force when and where this is appropriate and will serve as a sounding board for ideas and proposals affecting airman matters. It is not intended that he be in the chain of command or on the coordinating staff, but he will have unrestricted access to the Air Staff."

The position description was placed in slightly more cosmetic terms officially. The responsibilities of the CMSAF are "to advise and assist the Chief of Staff and the Secretary of the Air Force in matters concerning enlisted members of the Air Force." These matters were understood to include morale, training, welfare, pay and allowances, discipline, and promotion policies, among others. Traditional duties included representing the enlisted force at official social functions, serving on various enlisted welfare boards, and accompanying the Chief of Staff on visits to bases.

In the finest tradition of the noncommissioned officer corps, each CMSAF has interpreted this guidance broadly, expanding the functions and responsibilities to suit his management style. Far from being a back-door means of circumventing normal channels, the office has become a major relief valve for complaints, often settling things before they ever become an issue, simply because the CMSAF has so much credibility with the enlisted force.

In hindsight, it is easy to see what the Air Force accomplished: it raised the hallowed role of the squadron or wing first sergeant (sometimes called the sergeant major, and always informally the top kick or the first soldier) to a new level, but with the same trappings of confidence and authority. All airmen and officers worth their salt know that, arriving on a base, the number one person to make a friend and confidant of is the first sergeant. No matter what the difficulty—a need for leave, a shortage of housing, a bully in the ranks—the first sergeant could solve the problem legally if possible, by other means if not. When the CMSAF position was created, it inevitably carried with it the cachet and power of the first sergeant in vastly magnified form.

On April 3, 1967, the first Chief Master Sergeant of the Air Force, Paul W. Airey, was sworn in. In 1944, Airey had been shot down and made a prisoner of war on his twentieth combat mission, flying out of Italy as a B-24 radio operator and waist gunner with the Fifteenth Air Force. He might be described as cool under fire; during his parachute descent he tore up his code papers, then lit up a cigarette as he enjoyed the view.

Prison life was tough; over the next year, his weight dropped from its normal 150 pounds to 100, but he survived to be liberated by British forces in May 1945. He remained in service, and in the course of his career, he served as NCOIC of communications at Naha AB, Okinawa, and there received the Legion of Merit for the anticorrosion, antifungus procedures he devised for electronic equipment. He then spent the next half of his career as a first sergeant.

Selected as CMSAF after an intense competition, Airey made an early personal decision that the official responsibilities with which he was charged were merely guidelines; each CMSAF should expand the office to suit his or her special talents. He also made sure that the CMSAF was seen as a spokesperson for the enlisted force, one who was neither a front for the Pentagon nor a lobby for malcontents.

He came to office at a bad time. The Air Force suffered its lowest retention rate in more than ten years in 1967. Airey attributed this not to the unpopularity of the Vietnam War, as most did, but to poor pay, too-numerous remote assignments, an inequitable promotion system, and excellent opportunities for civilian employment. He set about lobbying to change the system, principally by speaking his mind in all the many forums to which he was invited, including testifying before Congress.

Airey's approach has been followed by the eleven Chief Master Sergeants of the Air Force who have followed him. Each has adapted the role of CMSAF to suit his own talents. None has allowed the office to become the out-of-channels conduit that General McConnell feared. The Pentagon, like any large bureaucracy, has its own mores; one of the most important of these is never to allow someone you are working with to be blindsided. Early on, Airey made a practice of networking with the action officers in all the departments concerned with enlisted affairs, and if he knew of trouble brewing—a riot at one of the bases, a Congressional investigation of an enlisted person's complaint, anything—Airey made sure the appropriate action officer knew about it before he told the Chief of Staff. If the Chief happened to call the action officer to inquire what was being done, the action officer could always say, "Right, General, we're working on it, and I'll have a report for you in the morning." Airey's practice has been followed religiously by succeeding CMSAFs, and the result has been an extremely cordial relationship with the Air Staff.

With the passage of time, the prestige and influence of the position of Chief Master Sergeant of the Air Force has grown. All the CMSAFs have been called upon to travel to bases with the Chief of Staff and the Secretary of Defense, who rely increasingly on their advice on enlisted matters. And the CMSAFs have changed with the times. CMSAF Airey began his career with B-24s and Morse code; he carried out his duties at the Pentagon with the aid of a telephone. The tenth Chief Master Sergeant of the Air Force, David Campanale, was not only on the road continuously, he was available on e-mail and had a direct line to his constituents. Campanale, an intense, focused personality with a quick smile and a grasp of all the major Air Force issues, had, like his predecessors, adapted the office of CMSAF to his own personal style. He believed strongly in the chain of command; if he was asked a question, he answered, but was not hesitant to tell the questioner that the information should have been available at squadron or wing level, as applicable. If he found the answers were not available where they should be, he swung into action, having identified a problem.

In 1970, the fabric of the noncommissioned officer corps was further strengthened by the establishment of the position of senior enlisted adviser to commanders. There are now about 230 senior enlisted adviser positions throughout the Air Force, filled by senior NCOs who channel information to and from the enlisted force to the unit commander. (Airey hates the term "senior enlisted adviser" as not being sufficiently military. He would prefer the position to be called "Chief Master Sergeant of the Air Mobility Command" or "Chief Master Sergeant of the 1st Tactical Fighter Wing.")

Initially, the senior enlisted adviser position was opposed by many ranking officers in the field who felt they were establishing a mole in their own office, one whose loyalties would run to the enlisted men below him and to the CMSAF above him. They were entirely wrong, for the senior enlisted advisers feel the same primary loyalty to the Air Force as a general officer does. The position quickly proved itself, and is now regarded as indispensable to the smooth operation of the service.

ENLISTED PROFESSIONAL MILITARY EDUCATION

The opportunity a recruit has for getting further education is one of the most important tools of a recruiter. The Air Force offers a wide spectrum of such opportunities, some general, and some, like the NCO academies, tailored to leadership requirements.

The first NCO academy was established by USAFE in 1950; it was followed by a SAC counterpart in West Drayton, England, in 1952. Other commands quickly followed SAC's example, and NCO academies have become an indispensable part of a noncommissioned officer's career path. In their early days, veteran NCOs sometimes went to great lengths to avoid attendance, feeling that there was something demeaning or at least unmilitary about going back to school midway in a career. No more; attendance at the NCO academies is hotly sought after, for it "adds weight to the WAPS (Weighted Airman Promotion System)." The NCO academies also conferred additional prestige to the senior NCOs who were named to be their commandants.

As the positive results of the command NCO academies became manifest, a decision was made in 1972 to create the Senior NCO Academy at Gunter AFB. The mission of the Senior NCO Academy was to prepare the top three grades in the enlisted force structure to handle the new challenges of the 1970s. The first class graduated on March 3, 1973; among the 120 graduates were three future Chief Master Sergeants of the Air Force, CMS Thomas N. Barnes, CMS James M. McCoy, and CMS Sam E. Parish.

The Senior NCO Academy conducts 280 hours of training for approximately 360 students per class. The typical student is a thirty-nine-year-old senior master sergeant with nineteen years of service and three years of college credit. Graduation from the Senior NCO Academy is a requirement for promotion to chief master sergeant.

Top NCOs are but part of the Air Force's concern for educating the enlisted force. It has always encouraged education, and in 1950, only three years after its formation, it established the Extension Course Institute, which offered correspondence courses that were especially useful to personnel on assignment in remote bases. The results of the ECI courses and attendance at courses taught on the bases were helpful, but more was needed if the enlisted corps was to have a higher representation of college-educated personnel to meet the sophisticated demands of modern technology.

THE COMMUNITY COLLEGE OF THE AIR FORCE

The most directly useful extension of professional military education for enlisted personnel is the Community College of the Air Force (CCAF). The college was created as a direct response to the twin phenomena of the noncommissioned officer corps taking over midlevel managerial positions from officers and the movement of those positions into the high-technology disciplines. (By 1972, more than 70 percent of Air Force jobs were considered to be in high-technology fields.)

To raise the standard of NCO education to the requisite level required a program that would be open to all members of the enlisted force and would provide them with a tangible benefit for participating. Air Force enlisted personnel found it difficult to bring their educational experience, both formal and informal, into a coherent pattern that related directly to their jobs. Civilian schools offered programs providing a wide range of academic course work, but few offered credentialing related to many Air Force specialties, such as munitions or missile maintenance. Air Force personnel also faced the common problems resulting from frequent relocations—credits would be lost in the transfer process, and course work would have to be duplicated to satisfy residency requirements.

After a number of intensive studies, Chief of Staff General John D. Ryan agreed to the establishment of the Community College of the Air Force, which was activated on April 1, 1972, at Randolph AFB, Texas. The CCAF would establish programs that would give credit for enlisted job training and experience and be a center for the accumulation of credit toward a degree.

At the time of its inception, the CCAF drew on the staffs and curriculum of seven major Air Force training schools: the five Air Force Schools of Applied Aerospace Sciences, the USAF School of Health Care, and the USAF Security Service School. The first major task of the CCAF was to implement a two-year program that would broaden the noncommissioned officer as a technician, manager, and citizen.

The Community College of the Air Force grew swiftly, affiliating with other technical and professional schools and becoming accredited on December 12, 1973. By 1980, the Commission on Colleges accredited the CCAF to award the Associate in Applied Science degree.

The expansion was not without problems, particularly that of maintaining a faculty with appropriate credentials. A major step forward was taken in 1994, when the college began registering other service instructors in the Instructor of Technology and Military Science degree program.

By July 1993, it had become the largest multicampus community college in the world, with affiliated schools in thirty states, the District of Columbia, and eight foreign locations and more than 9,000 faculty members. More than 144,000 Associate in Applied Science degrees have been awarded, and annual registration ranges between 375,000 and 515,000.

The most telling statistic, one that directly relates the revolution in Air Force management style to the rise of the noncommissioned officer class, is the percentage of CCAF graduates serving in the top three grades. In December 1994, the latest date for which figures are available, 69.9 percent of all chief master sergeants, 68.9 percent of all senior master sergeants, and 42.2 percent of all master sergeants were graduates of the Community College of the Air Force.

FIFTY YEARS OF PROGRESS

In fifty years, the enlisted force has been transformed from "old Army" into a space-age Air Force team. The process has been possible only because of the dedication, experience, and ability of a phenomenally devoted noncommissioned officer corps. The Air Force has created a class of first-rate executives who have direct access to the enlisted personnel and who lead them by example. There is a poignant patriotism involved in this, one that hearkens to the fundamental basis of this country. The noncommissioned officer corps is smart, and knows that it is underpaid and overworked. Yet the pride and satisfaction it derives from doing a difficult job in an excellent manner, *and being widely recognized for it*, keeps the ranks full.

SOCIAL FACTORS

Amid all these considerations of pay and promotion, the Air Force was rocked, as the nation was, by the events in Vietnam, and by the growth in racial problems. The USAF was caught off guard; it may not always have been perfect in its handling of such critical social questions as the integration of women and minorities into its ranks, but for the most part it had led the way. Early efforts at integration had been highly successful, more so than in any of the other services and certainly much better than in the country as a whole. Therefore the smoldering resentment of the African-American recruit of the 1960s and 1970s came as a surprise.

The path to integration of African-Americans into the Air Force may be best characterized as always superior to that of the civilian community, but uneven in execution. There is no little irony in the fact that integration ultimately came about as a direct result of enforced segregation during World War II. The famous Tuskegee airmen "experiment" resulted in the establishment of the segregated 99th Pursuit Squadron and subsequently the 332d Fighter Group. In these were a body of skilled black airmen and ground personnel who proved their worth in combat against very difficult odds.

Many of the leaders of the U.S. Army Air Forces were not enthusiastic backers of integration, nor entirely approving of the performance of the 332d. General Arnold had insisted that black officers and airmen could only serve in segregated units because of the explosive social issues involved. Generals Spaatz, Eaker, and Vandenberg all commented that the relative difficulty and expense of sustaining segregated units in combat was not an efficient use of resources. What they failed to perceive was that the nature of the Army Air Forces as a service (as was subsequently true in the Air Force) made *segregation itself* the barrier to efficiency.

The barrier was not merely a moral one; it was also a practical one. African-Americans constituted about 7 percent of the Air Force enlisted force and about 0.6 percent of its officer corps. Given the disadvantages then implicit in African-American society in terms of education, cultural bias, and other factors, it was impossible to maintain segregated units with an equitable distribution of ranks and skills. The most prominent unit, the 332d, could not be expanded upon mobilization, because of insufficient resources, nor could it be sustained with replacements if committed to combat. There were some specialties in which there were more qualified African-Americans than there were vacancies, and some specialties in which there were more vacancies than there were African-Americans to fill them.

Five men were most influential in the smooth Air Force preparation for integration. They include the Secretary of the Air Force, Stuart Symington, and his assistant, Eugene Zuckert, and Lieutenant General Idwal H. Edwards, Major General Richard E. Nugent, and Lieutenant Colonel Jack F. Marr.

Based on his business experience, Symington was convinced that integration made sense from both a moral and a cost-efficiency perspective. He was backed in his beliefs by Secretary of Defense James Forrestal and ably supported by Zuckert.

Under Edwards's prompting, a group under the leadership of General Nugent was appointed to study the problem of integration. It transpired that Edwards, Nugent, and Marr all saw the problem in the same light. Segregation was inefficient and could not be made efficient; integration would be efficient and solve the problem of the distribution of talent.

Marr, later described by Zuckert as "the indispensable man" in the integration process, wrote the plan that antedated Truman's order to integrate the service. Marr also stayed on to see his program adopted as a means of carrying out the President's order. His approach to the question of integration was entirely pragmatic: the available pool of talent in the African-American community could not be ignored, and it could not be used efficiently while the practice of segregation continued.

Under Edwards's recommendations, Air Force policy unequivocally endorsed President Truman's Executive Order 9981 and let it be known that ungrudging compliance was expected with both the spirit and the letter of the law. Perhaps the most important facet of Air Force policy was that it made local commanders fully aware of their responsibility for compliance. There could be no passing of the buck—the message was clear.

The result was a quick and uneventful transition of the Air Force from segregated to integrated status. The personnel of the 332d, under the direction of its commander, then Colonel Benjamin O. Davis, Jr., were distributed to other Air Force units. This great American, the first black general officer in the USAF and the son of the first black general in the Army, had first led the 332d to its height of success, and then led the fight for integration.

By June 1952, the personnel of the last all-Negro (in the term of the time) unit in the USAF had been distributed without comment throughout the Air Force. The Air Force had completed its integration process almost before the Army had begun. The Navy made only token efforts during the same period. (The Korean War spurred integration in the Army, when the demand for soldiers overcame the hidebound preference for segregation.)

The black community had watched Air Force performance closely. Indeed, one of the real watchdogs of the civil rights movement, the influential African-American-owned *Pittsburgh Courier*, ran an article on October 22, 1949, with the headline "The Job Is Done—Air Force Completes Integration." The story was a little premature, but is indicative of the appreciative view held at the time by the African-American community. A few years later, the *Courier* ran stories with headlines such as "Tan Fliers Over Korea" and highlighted not only then Captain Daniel "Chappie" James, on his way to becoming the first African-American four-star general, but also First Lieutenant Dayton W. "Rags" Ragland, a 336th Squadron F-86 pilot who shot down a MiG-15 on November 28, 1951.

The Air Force's efforts to enforce policy had mixed effect in communities near bases. The commander of Harlingen Air Force Base, located near Brownsville, Texas, received a letter from a local white church inviting all officers and enlisted personnel of the base, regardless of race or color, to attend any or all church services. This was a precedent-setting event; unhappily it was not matched in all American communities.

Trouble was expected—and found—in the South. The Air Force might have integrated, but the South had not, and assignment to a Southern base could be torture for an African-American serviceman and his family. Travel was difficult. Common carriers like trains or buses were segregated. If a car was used, there could be problems just getting gasoline and oil, and there were few restaurants and fewer hotels where African-Americans were permitted to enter. If a trip had to be made by car, families soon learned to carry their food with them and, if possible, find accommodations at the home of a friend or acquaintance.

Life was bitterly divided: on base, the African-American was treated as a professional; off base, he and his family were subject to all the humiliations of local custom, including separate drinking and rest-room facilities and the requirement to be servile with any white person.

The North was often not much better, particularly in rural areas where one might have thought the great traditions of freedom and independence held sway. The contrary was true; African-Americans were not well treated, and were excluded from service facilities in town even more rudely—and sometimes violently—than they were in the South. African-American airmen at bases in Maine, Michigan, Montana, North Dakota, South Dakota, and elsewhere complained to the National Association for the Advancement of Colored People and to their Congressmen. Pressure was applied on the Air Force to use its economic powers to force local townspeople to alter their attitudes.

The Eisenhower administration was curiously passive in its stance on civil rights, but President John F. Kennedy took the problem to heart, and on July 26, 1962, established the Committee on Equal Opportunity in the Armed Forces, headed by Gerhard A. Gesell. The Gesell Committee, as it was known, found that living conditions off base were intolerable for African-Americans and urged the services to take positive action to change the situation. The Air Force was nonplussed at every level. Local commanders knew that their jurisdiction ended at the boundaries of the base, and that they could jeopardize relations with the townspeople for all their personnel if they attempted to force integration off the base. Yet they also knew the Gesell Committee's analysis was correct. African-Americans were systematically denied housing and entrance to service facilities like barbershops. For dependents, the situation was usually even worse, for the question of integrated schools was perhaps the most inflammatory of all.

It was not until the passage of the Civil Rights Act of 1964 and the Voting Rights Act of 1965 that local base commanders could begin to make their influence felt. The Air Force revised and expanded its AFR 35-78 with the passage of the Civil Rights Act. It would not be until 1969, however, that commanders could instruct their personnel that they could not rent or lease property that was not available to all, regardless of race or color. The regulations had almost immediate effect in every area except the Deep South, where additional efforts were required to overcome the centuries-old viewpoints. In 1970, the regulation was reworded to read, "Commanders will impose off-limits sanctions against all segregating establishments . . . that discriminate against military personnel and their dependents."

It was social engineering, and in his 1968 book *The Essence of Security: Reflections on Office,* Secretary McNamara admitted using the military to attack what he termed "tormenting social problems." Military leaders resisted and resented his tactics at the time, and predictably, Southern politicians saw it as the beginning of a police state. McNamara's policies worked, however, and despite the war in Vietnam, the military continued to lead the country in its efforts at integration.

Perhaps because of this, the Air Force completely misread the trend on racial relations in the country and became complacent until the four-day race riot at Travis Air Force Base, California, May 21 to 24, 1971.

An accumulation of perceived slights precipitated the riot. There were complaints that punishments awarded for the same offense were different for whites and African-Americans and that equal-opportunity housing regulations were not being enforced. The use of the clenched fist salute was forbidden by the base commander. Entertainment facilities were not suited to the taste of young African-Americans. Everything came to a head when a fight broke out in a barracks over the volume of a record player.

After four days, 135 airmen were arrested, including twenty-five whites. Air Force embarrassment was extreme, for the event was played up nationally, and great emphasis was given to the fact that seventy civilian lawmen had to be brought in. There were more than thirty injuries, and one death—from a heart attack.

The Air Force was complacent no longer, nor was the Department of Defense. Education in race relations was made mandatory for all personnel, regardless of rank. Officers now had to be rated on their "Equal Opportunity Participation" on their efficiency reports.

In the years that followed, USAF efforts in the field of race relations have been as sensitive as possible. The linking of personal performance reports to efforts on the behalf of equal opportunity had an immediate salutary effect. Although there is no question that some individuals retain bigoted views, they keep them masked or risk immediate and forceful censure. The Air Force has not been 100 percent successful in its efforts to achieve equality in all aspects of service life. It has not been able to raise the percentage of black pilots significantly, despite extensive efforts to do so. It has not achieved the desired representation of minorities in higher grades, but continues to address the problem. One difficulty is competing for the services of highly qualified minorities in the recruiting process. A well-qualified, well-educated member of a minority will be offered civilian employment at a better salary and with greater benefits than the service can provide. A bright young member of a minority who has entered the service and done well is similarly an attractive potential employee for civilian firms. General Dougherty tells the story of a tremendous push made by Secretary of the Air Force Verne Orr to have more African-American and women generals. Dougherty and others tried to explain to him that minorities who were potential candidates for general were snapped up by industry with salaries and perquisites that the service could not begin to match. Orr would not buy it until he sat down and perused a huge pile of personnel records that proved that fast-track minorities were siphoned off by more attractive opportunities.

WOMEN IN THE AIR FORCE

In 1965, the total number of spaces authorized for women had fallen to 4,700, and these were confined primarily to the clerical, administrative, personnel, information, and medical fields. Some say that the decision to reduce the number of opportunities offered women stemmed from General LeMay, although others deny this. During the 1960s, women were not allowed to serve as flight attendants or in specialty positions in intelligence, weather, equipment maintenance, or control towers—despite the fact that they had served in all of these roles during World War II and into the 1950s.

The turnaround came when then Colonel Jeanne M. Holm was appointed Director, Women in the Air Force, in November 1965. She was to have an enormous influence on the role of women in the Air Force. Her distinguished career began as a Women's Auxiliary Army Corps (WAAC) enlistee in 1942. On July 16, 1971, she became the first woman in the Air Force to rise to the rank of brigadier general, and she was promoted to be a major general on June 1, 1973—again, the first woman to serve in that grade.

During General Holm's tenure as director, WAF strength more than doubled, assignment opportunities were greatly expanded, and uniforms were modernized. As a result of her many initiatives, women were soon allowed to enter almost all but combat positions. The most difficult hurdle, perhaps, was admission of women to flying school, which began in 1975.

The success of the integration of women into the service depended in every instance on the attitudes of the local commanders. Some difficulties occurred because there were a few dinosaurs who opposed the idea of women in the Air Force on principle—but not for long, as they soon discovered that another pool of unlimited talent had been opened. A more subtle problem area was male pride, which often was harder to overcome.

General Dougherty tells a story of some difficulties he encountered when introducing women into the Strategic Air Command's maintenance program. One of his key maintenance people was adamantly opposed to women's working on the flight line because he did not believe they were physically capable of doing the required work—or so he said. One morning he came in with what he thought was an iron-clad argument against their employment. The SAC maintenance manual called for changing alternators on a Boeing KC-135 tanker in one hour. Dougherty's maintenance man crowed that a woman just could not do the job, which required holding the heavy alternator while four bolts were removed, then replacing it with another, holding it in place, and inserting the bolts.

Dougherty asked, "How many electricians do you have on the base?" The man replied, "Probably a hundred and fifty." Dougherty said: "Get them all out on the ramp right now, and we'll see how many of the men can do it." As Dougherty expected, few of the men could do the job without assistance—and positive leadership resolved another impediment to using women in all jobs.

By 1996, women constituted 16 percent of the Air Force, with 11,937 officers and 51,417 enlisted. Over 99 percent of the career fields and positions in the Air Force are open to them. The few closed positions are in accordance with DOD policy, which excludes women from assignments to units whose primary mission is to engage in direct combat on the ground. No career fields are closed to women officers, but they are restricted from certain positions, including certain types of combat helicopters. The chronology included in this book documents the rise of women in the Air Force, but certain key events stand out, the most important of which was the establishment of the All-Volunteer Force in 1973. DOD policies followed which initiated a sex-neutral policy for spouses' entitlements and rescinded previous requirements to involuntarily separate women because of pregnancy and/or parenthood.

The apogee of the service revolution came with changes in the combat exclusion policy that allowed the first large-scale deployment of women to a combat zone in Operation Desert Shield. Of the total of 100,905 Air Force personnel deployed, 12.4 percent were women. The trend toward total equality culminated with a suspension of combat aircraft restriction on women on April 28, 1993; First Lieutenant Jeannie Flynn became the first Air Force woman pilot assigned to an operational fighter aircraft, the McDonnell Douglas F-15E. Lieutenant Flynn's achievement was complemented in 1995 by Lieutenant Colonel Eileen Collins, who became the first Air Force woman to serve as Space Shuttle pilot.

BUILDING ON THE FOUNDATION

The management revolution took full advantage of the potential of the capabilities of its enlisted personnel and exploited the new reserves of talent made available by the full integration of women and minorities into every aspect of Air Force life. This provided a solid foundation for the Air Force's renaissance after Vietnam, when new leaders, new doctrine, and new technology came together over a twenty-year period to produce a service worthy of a superpower.

8

≋

LEADERSHIP, DOCTRINE, AND TECHNOLOGY AFTER VIETNAM

Over the centuries, the armed forces of combatant nations have rebounded from defeat in very different ways. Following the defeat of its armada by England's emerging (but at that time inferior) naval might in 1588, the Spanish navy lapsed into decay. The French, humiliated in the 1871 Franco-Prussian War, so thirsted for revenge that they leaped with élan into the maw of World War I, where they were saved from another disaster by their allies. The German army reacted to its loss in 1918 by viewing it merely as the conclusion of Round One. Two decades later, it began Round Two with confidence, made almost exactly the same mistakes, and lost again.

After enduring the embarrassing—and unnecessary—American defeat in Vietnam, the United States Air Force might have rebounded in any manner, from lapsing into a defeatist lethargy to thirsting militantly for revenge. Fortunately, a combination of good leadership from the top and the clear call for reform from below combined to set the Air Force on a different path, one that led first to space and then to victories in the Persian Gulf and the Cold War.

CONGRESSIONAL HURDLES

Just as the year 1972, the midpoint of the fifty years of Air Force history to date, was a vantage point from which to review the contributions of the major supporting commands, so it provides an excellent perspective for an examination of how the Air Force learned from and adapted to the experience of Vietnam, even as it maintained its awareness of contemporary changes in domestic and international politics. This learning process, still going on today, influences the USAF in matters of policy, leadership, and weapon systems.

The environment was totally different from the days of World War II, when the public, the media, and the Congress vociferously backed the armed forces. In the post-Vietnam period, the USAF had to conduct its fight on many fronts. Its primary mission, from which it never deviated, was the deterrence of aggression by the Communist powers. Secondary fronts arose from year to year—the *Pueblo* and *Mayaguez* incidents, Lebanon, Central America—that had to be dealt with. The third front was the most difficult, however—continually persuading the Congress first to approve and then to sustain procurement of necessary weapon systems. Getting the necessary approval for a needed weapon system had always been difficult; before World War II, for example, the Congress in its wisdom had preferred procuring more of the less capable Douglas B-18s, a twin-engine imitation of a bomber, rather than buying fewer of the far more capable four-engine Boeing B-17s. But in the post-Vietnam environment, every program was given a hard managerial scrub by teams of professional Congressional staffers who often had far more experience in the business—and sometimes even in the particular weapon system—than the Air Force personnel presenting their cases. The staffers recommended to their committees which firms should win or lose in the tough competition among them for budget dollars. Congressmen had a natural penchant to support programs that provided jobs and dollars to their own constituencies, while either opposing procurements that went elsewhere or horse-trading support. It thus became a part of every procurement pitch to show exactly where the program dollars were to be spent and how many jobs would be generated in which Congressional districts. If there were not sufficient dollars being spent in the right district, you can be sure that the contractor would make the necessary adjustments.

A further problem was more sensitive. There have been—and probably always will be—a number of Congressmen whose views make them automatically oppose any military procurement or R&D initiative, irrespective of its merit. To do so is entirely within their right, a part of the healthy democratic process of airing opposing views. However, a succession of elected officials, including Bella Abzug, Les Aspin, Edward Brooke, Ron Dellums, William Proxmire, and Patricia Schroeder, among others, so identified themselves with antimilitary views that their opposition became reflexive. Driving a desired procurement through these intractable Congressional roadblocks takes patient, diligent effort, and consistently strong leadership.

LEADERSHIP AND CHANGE

In the two decades after the Vietnam War, the United States Air Force has had a succession of fifteen Secretaries of the Air Force and ten Chiefs of Staff, including those serving as "acting." Space prohibits a detailed examination of each of their contributions, but in general terms, the Air Force has been fortunate in its leaders, who seemed to have an uncanny adaptability to the requirements of the time, while always managing to keep the vital research and developments efforts going. One remarkable aspect of the leadership chain is the continuity of purpose in pursuing weapon systems through many different tenures of office and over long periods of time. (A list of all Air Force Secretaries and Chiefs of Staff may be found in Appendix 1.) Moreover, most of those leaders had the great good sense to foster the turbulent demand swirling in the ranks for improvements in the weapon systems.

As noted earlier, the Defense Reorganization Act of 1958 put greater power in the hands of the Secretary of Defense, power that was applied vigorously by Secretary McNamara and his successors. The effects of the 1958 reorganization were sometimes shocking. The service secretaries had been moved so far out of the decision-making loop by 1972 that the Secretary of the Navy was not informed about the mining of the harbors of Haiphong and other North Vietnamese ports, and Secretary of the Air Force Robert C. Seamans learned about the air raids on North Vietnam only when he saw them reported on television.

It was obvious that the mission of the Air Force Secretary had changed drastically. In Stuart Symington's day, the Secretary greatly influenced DOD policy; in later years the role was altered to smoothing and streamlining internal Air Force policies and actions. Yet the loss of political power was partially compensated for by the extra time it provided for the Secretary to work within the service. Air Force success has depended upon technology realized under the leadership of its Secretaries who were also scientists, including Seamans, John L. McLucas, Hans Mark, Edward C. Aldridge, and Sheila E. Widnall, the first woman to serve as Air Force Secretary. All of them sustained the emphasis on research and development efforts exemplified by the vision of Hap Arnold, Theodor von Karman, and Bernard Schriever. This R&D effort proved itself in the striking advances of a wide range of weapons, intelligence-gathering systems, and war-gaming techniques that made the United States Air Force ever more powerful even as it exposed the shabby underpinnings of the former Soviet Union.

The American defense industry—one-half of the often-reviled "military-industrial complex"—participated fully in this process, benefiting in some instances from contracts for basic and applied research and in others developing (solely from its own resources) new ideas that were beneficial to the progress of the Air Force. Without the defense industry, the USAF would have been unable to pursue the fertile ideas its R&D had produced. An important interface in this relationship was the "think tanks" such as RAND, MITRE, and others, which were able to gather in a nucleus of scientists and thinkers, pay them at market rates rather than at fixed government salaries, and allow them to give dispassionate advice on research and development.

A LOOK BACK IN TIME

Although it is impossible to recount all of the many achievements and infrequent failures of the Air Force under its successive Secretaries and Chiefs of Staff, it is instructive to look at highlights to see how some of these leaders performed during the period from the middle of the Vietnam War until the end of the Reagan administration. This period reflects the roller-coaster fall and subsequent rise of the Air Force and carries it to the threshold of its greatest triumphs.

Fighting the War: 1965–1969

The two top leaders in Air Force during the period from 1965 to 1969 were not a good match. Secretary of the Air Force Harold Brown was a scientist, an intellectual who was definitely not a "people person." Brown was far more in the mold of Robert McNamara than in that of his Chief of Staff, General John P. McConnell. McConnell was hampered by having to fill General LeMay's shoes, and in his later years of service by an unfortunate drinking problem. Nonetheless, he presided over the buildup of the United States Air Force during the Vietnam War. One of the innovations of his tenure was the USAF modified "Total Force" concept of 1966, which brought U.S. Air Force Reserve and Air National Guard units into daily operations and was subsequently widely adopted by DOD. More important, he fostered the accelerated research and development that attempted to fix the deficiencies in USAF combat aircraft that the war in Vietnam exposed. Major decisions he and his successor as Chief of Staff, General John D. Ryan, made were driven by the Vietnam War, which under President Lyndon Johnson's guns-*and*-butter building of the Great Society was fought entirely from Air Force budgets that had not been increased to bear the additional expenses. McConnell had the bitter duty of reporting on his retirement that he left the Air Force with "less air power than when I became its Chief of Staff four and one-half years ago," one of the last comments that any Chief wishes to make.

Difficult Years: 1969–1973

President Nixon selected the able Robert C. Seamans, Jr., as his Secretary of the Air Force. Seamans and his Chief of Staff, General Ryan, were an excellent match. Both men had pleasant personalities and an unruffled manner of doing business. Seamans was also a scientist and an intellectual, but unlike Harold Brown, he related well to people. Ryan, an experienced combat leader and former Commander in Chief of the Strategic Air Command, was also a man who demanded rigorous honesty of himself and all his colleagues. He displayed his rigor in 1972 when he relieved the Commander of the

Seventh Air Force, General John D. Lavelle, for allegedly violating the rules of engagement and falsifying records to conceal the fact. (Many maintain that Lavelle had been implicitly encouraged by his superiors, including then Secretary of Defense Melvin Laird, to undertake the actions for which he was held accountable, and then, like a good soldier, had to take the fall.)

Seamans and Ryan had to prosecute the Vietnam War with an Air Force whose increasingly obsolete equipment was wearing out and that was running low on some key supplies of spare parts and munitions. Despite their necessary preoccupation with this task, they used their combination of intelligence, compassion, and energy to facilitate a whole series of important USAF projects, including aircraft such as the A-10, B-1, C-5, F-15, and F-111. And in a manner that was a fortunate characteristic of many of the top Air Force leaders, they also gave impetus to the sophisticated electronic warfare devices that would determine the outcome of future wars.

It was the astute Seamans who noted that the Soviet Union did not appear to be conducting its research and development and its production of weapon systems on the basis of what the United States was doing. He observed that instead it was increasing its military spending as its gross national product increased, without regard to the impact on the civilian economy. Further, it was carrying out extensive prototype programs for aircraft and missiles on a scale beyond anything the United States was attempting. He also noted an aspect of the Soviets' activity unusual from the American perspective: they operated at a sustained level of effort in their output of prototypes and production aircraft, and they almost never terminated a program even when it overlapped another in capability. This was in sharp contrast to the United States, where programs were always vulnerable to termination regardless of their technical importance. The volume of production and the type and number of prototypes the Soviet Union was placing into production pointed to a desire to gain the very first-strike capability that the United States had abjured. The importance of this insight was overlooked until the Reagan administration.

Rebuilding from Within: 1973–1976

The Nixon administration brought about remarkable changes in the Department of Defense under the leadership of two Secretaries, Melvin Laird (1969–1973) and James Schlesinger (1973–1975). Many consider Laird, a nine-term Congressman, to be one of the most outstanding Secretaries of Defense in history. He was even-tempered and used his political wiles to mend fences with the JCS even as he superintended the "Vietnamization" process, which phased out American participation in the war. He backed ending the draft and the creation of an All-Volunteer Force. To this end, he directed that the 1966 Air Force concept of using the Air National Guard and the Air Force Reserve in daily operations be followed by other services.

Schlesinger, his successor, followed up on this in 1973 with a call for full integration under the "Total Force" policy, in which members of the National Guard and Reserve were the initial and primary source for augmentation of active forces in emergencies requiring a rapid and substantial buildup. There were many who did not believe that these forces could be brought to meet regular service standards. They were wrong. Air National Guard and Air Force Reserve units so quickly achieved a readiness and proficiency equivalent to regular Air Force standards that General Ryan called their work a . "proud chapter in Air Force history." They have since demonstrated their proficiency on a daily basis, in war and in peace. (The change in twenty years was dramatic. When two future four-star generals, David Jones and Russ Dougherty, were young company-grade officers in a Louisville, Kentucky, airlift reserve unit, they had only single-engine, two-seat North American T-6 trainers to fly. Jones grins now and says, "You can imagine our airlift capability.")

Schlesinger was a much different sort of man from Laird. An academic, he was cold, pedantic, and without Laird's political insight. Yet he was wise enough to look for personable people he could work with—and who could work with Congress. He found one in genial John McLucas, who had succeeded Seamans as Secretary of the Air Force, and another as Air Force Chief of Staff in the hugely popular General George Brown. Brown's star was so ascendant that General Ryan, even before he formally took office, had informed Brown that he would succeed Ryan, and that he had better prepare himself. Despite his meteoric rise, Brown was an unpretentious man who insisted that he not be given the customary military honors upon arrival at a base.

His greatest personal triumph came during the Yom Kippur War in 1973, when on his own, without coordinating with the Secretary of Defense, he allocated two squadrons of McDonnell Douglas F-4s—then the standard USAF fighter—to Israel and began preparations for a massive airlift of munitions. Ironically, Brown would be pilloried as anti-Semitic in November of the following year after a speech at Duke University. An unfortunate choice of words led to calls for his dismissal from his new appointment as Chairman of the Joint Chiefs of Staff.

There is no question that Brown's candor with the press bordered on naiveté. He was caught up again by statements that could be interpreted as anti-Semitic and later in an interview that appeared to criticize the armed forces of the British Empire. Nevertheless, Schlesinger and his successor, Donald Rumsfield, always stood by their man, whose obviously sincere apologies managed to smooth things over. They both valued Brown's experience working with the office of the Secretary of Defense. He had earned it the hard way, working for Robert McNamara for two years and progressing from colonel to major general in the process. His rapport with Congress—something Schlesinger notably lacked—was outstanding, even when under

the pressure of his occasional controversial statements. In 1974, he was selected to become the first Air Force Chairman of the Joint Chiefs of Staff
since Nathan Twining, some thirteen years before. Brown was picked not
because it was the Air Force's turn, but because he was the best man available
for the task.

Of all Brown's many accomplishments, one stands out as most important
to Air Force navigators, bombardiers, and radar observers, for it was he who
forced a change in the regulations that forbade command positions to anyone
but pilots.

When Brown was selected as Chief of Staff, his two principal competitors
had been Generals David C. Jones and John C. Meyer. Meyer, a fighter pilot,
had scored twenty-four victories during World War II and two more in Korea.
As CINCSAC, he had directed the eleven-day campaign against Hanoi and
Haiphong in December 1972. Jones had flown 300 combat hours over North
Korea in B-29s. His competence had been noted early on by Curtis LeMay,
and, like Brown, he had been given assignments that prepared him for the
Air Force's top job, including command of an F-4 wing. It was said of Jones
that he never left an assignment without having improved the organization
he led.

Jones was selected to succeed Brown twice, first as Chief of Staff, and
then in 1978 as Chairman of the Joint Chiefs. Of occasionally fiery temper-
ament, Jones made large numbers of both friends and enemies as he approached his task with intellect and energy. He threw himself on the sword
as an advocate of the B-70 long after Secretary McNamara ruled against it,
believing that with the proper penetration aids, the B-70 could have operated
against the Soviet Union at high speeds and altitudes and greatly compounded the Soviets' defensive problem. Later in his career, when President
Carter canceled the B-1, Jones accepted the cancellation without resigning,
as some had called upon him to do. Jones's response was that his resignation
would not do any good, and, further, that the President had campaigned on
the issue of canceling the B-1 and had been elected, and Jones was not going
to oppose the will of the people.

Jones was an ardent advocate of reforming the Joint Chiefs of Staff and
continued to campaign for reform after he retired. He was instrumental in
the creation of the Goldwater-Nichols Act of 1986, which incorporated many
of the changes he had recommended.

As Chief of Staff, Jones proved to be an innovator in hardware as well
as in organization. He was a zealot for the Airborne Warning and Control
System (AWACS) aircraft. With the head of the Defense Advanced Research
Agency, William J. Perry (later Secretary of Defense under President Clin-
ton), he had the Have Blue stealth program initiated as the first step toward
what became the F-117 stealth fighter.

Like Brown, Jones worked well with Schlesinger, whom he carefully cultivated by adapting himself to the Secretary's special interests, of which or-

nithology was one. He tells an anecdote of the informal way they worked, meeting in civilian clothes on weekends, putting their feet up on the desk, and chatting. One morning Schlesinger asked him, "What would it take to get the Air Force to support a lightweight fighter?" (As we will see below, there was a great debate raging over high-cost fighters such as the McDonnell Douglas F-15E and low-cost fighters such as the proposed General Dynamics F-16 and Northrop F-17.) Jones knew that Schlesinger was not going to offer him any more funds or personnel, but he also knew that it was a chance to expand the force structure, a vitally important consideration, given the declining budget outlook. His reply was, "Four additional wings in the force structure." Schlesinger extended his hand, they shook, and the deal was done. Thus commenced the launch of what became the F-16 Fighting Falcon.

The one incident that Jones remembers with real distaste is the aborted attempt to rescue American hostages being held in Tehran in 1980. In a 1996 interview, Jones said that the biggest mistake in the operation was dividing up responsibility so that every service had a part to play, which resulted in the use of Navy helicopters and crews not experienced in rescue operations. He also faults the inability to rehearse the operation because of the absolute security requirements.

Difficult Years: 1976–1980

When Naval Academy graduate Jimmy Carter was elected President, he came to office convinced that the Pentagon military should be administered by methods somewhere between those of Captain Bligh's handling of the lower elements on the *Bounty* and Admiral Hyman Rickover's treatment of aspirants to nuclear submarine command—in other words, treat them rough. In his election campaign he had promised to make the Pentagon more efficient, halt the B-1 program, and arrange an arms agreement with the Soviet Union.

Carter made little effort to conceal his contempt for the JCS. The JCS, in turn, did not trust Carter or his judgment, an attitude that quickly spread through the military. Carter shook the JCS to its roots with his inquiry as to how quickly the United States could get rid of its nuclear weapons, for he believed that as few as 200 atomic and thermonuclear devices would be a sufficiently large arsenal to deter the Soviet Union. This was essentially similar to the "finite deterrence" straw for which Navy officials had grasped in the 1959 roles and missions dispute, and was now identified as a "countervailing strategy."

The President had selected a soul mate, Harold Brown, to be his Secretary of Defense. Both men were engineers with a clinical approach to problems and, unfortunately, to people. Brown amplified the concept of countervailing strategy by stating that an "essential equivalence" with the Soviet Union would be maintained. He explained this to mean:

(a) That the Soviets would not be able to use nuclear forces to coerce other countries;

(b) That if the Soviets had an advantage in one area of armaments, the United States would have an offsetting advantage in another area;

(c) That the U.S. position would not be perceived as inferior to the Soviet position; and

(d) That nuclear stability would be maintained.

Carter's policy and Brown's explanation of it gave scant comfort to an Air Force bred on the LeMay tradition that it was to maintain an overwhelming nuclear superiority. The Navy was equally dismayed, now that it had become part of the strategic triad with the submarine-launched ballistic missiles (SLBMs). The Army was unhappy because it knew that neither it nor the NATO forces could withstand a conventional attack by the Soviet Union, given the latter's overwhelming superiority in troops, armor, artillery, and aircraft. Since 1991, when the Soviet Union seemed to dissolve like a cube of sugar in a cup of coffee, the sinister threat of its powerful forces has been discounted or forgotten. But during Carter's Presidency, the Soviets had an army of 1.8 million men, 50,000 tanks, 20,000 artillery pieces, and almost 5,000 tactical aircraft—all backing what seemed to be formidable Warsaw pact forces. The survival of NATO forces in Europe depended first upon the American nuclear shield, and second upon its tactical nuclear weapons. Carter's 200-weapon proposal dumbfounded the JCS.

In fact, the size of the nuclear deterrent force was not significantly reduced, but Carter did stop production of the B-1, announcing the substitution of the air-launched cruise missile (ALCM) as the preferred alternative. The ALCM had its origins in the AGM-86 SCAD (subsonic cruise armed decoy) and, at the time of Carter's announcement, was planned as a bargaining chip to be given away at the armament limitation talks.

When George Brown retired as Chairman of the JCS in June 1978, David Jones was named as his successor. (Brown died only five months later, a victim of cancer.) Jones's willingness to accept Carter's decision on the B-1 may have played a part in the appointment, but a more important factor was the President's appreciation of Jones's intelligence and the role he could play in the continuing disarmament negotiations with the Soviet Union. Carter then approved the selection of General Lew Allen, considered by many to be the most gifted scientist in the Air Force, to become the new Chief of Staff. Allen was a missile expert who would be crucial in fostering the development and ultimate acceptance (albeit on a far smaller scale than he had hoped) of the advanced MX missile. Carter would work with Allen and Jones to effect a deal: approval of the MX (later named the Peacekeeper) in exchange for military backing on the disarmament talks (SALT) in progress with the Soviet Union.

Years of Plenty: 1981–1985

President Ronald Reagan campaigned on the requirement to restore the United States' military prowess, and his new Secretary of Defense, Caspar Weinberger, saw to it that every promise was fulfilled. Curiously enough, relations between Weinberger and the JCS were not harmonious at first, even after he had demonstrated his skill at selling the massive budget increases to Congress. Nonetheless, in short order the B-1 program was reintroduced, the MX was approved, Army divisions were brought up to strength, and the Navy was authorized to build to a strength of 600 ships. The secret B-2 stealth program (which had been one of Carter's considerations in canceling the B-1) was still in the "black" (i.e., its budget was a highly classified secret) but received adequate funding. Military spending grew by more than $300 billion in the first four years of the Reagan administration, with about $75 billion earmarked for strategic modernization and another $75 billion for research and development. As welcome as the funds were, they caused concern in the JCS, which feared—correctly—that the funding would not be sustained and that expensive adjustments would have to be made later to programs already under way.

The Reagan program had what appeared to be a huge internal conflict, for it was embarking upon a massive modernization program that was intended to provide the capability to wage a protracted nuclear war and a limited war simultaneously while it was at the same time negotiating with the Soviet Union for strategic arms reduction. General Jones was concerned that the Reagan team conducting the strategic arms limitation talks (START) might carry disarmament to an extreme position that would jeopardize national security. The Chairman, whose relations with Secretary Weinberger were distinctly uncordial, called on all his political skills to bring the dual tracks to convergence. He masterfully orchestrated a compromise that allowed the armament reduction to begin, but at a pace that did not place national security in danger or interfere with modernization of American strategic weapons.

While Jones and Weinberger sparred at the very highest levels on defense policy, the new Secretary of the Air Force, Verne Orr, worked with General Allen and his successor as Chief of Staff, General Charles A. Gabriel. Orr and Gabriel formed an excellent team that continued the modernization of the Air Force and its growth in capability. Both men were extremely personable and passionately concerned about the well-being of the Air Force and its personnel. Orr was not experienced in military aviation, but had full confidence in both Allen and Gabriel and supported them ably.

Leaner Years Again: 1985–1988

Orr was succeeded briefly by Russell A. Rourke, who served only for four months and was then followed by one of the most popular men ever to become Secretary of the Air Force, Edward C. "Pete" Aldridge, Jr. Aldridge was a scientist in the mold of Seamans and McLucas, and his popularity did not impede him from being a coldly calculating deal-maker.

As will be shown, it would fall to Gabriel and his successor, General Larry Welch, to do some of the most farsighted—and in many ways most difficult—planning in Air Force history. They recognized far in advance of others, including other branches of the American armed forces, that the combination of a failing Soviet Union and the inevitable downward revision of military budgets meant that the Air Force would have to be reduced in size. They made a decision to sacrifice force structure for modernization and quality. The success of their efforts will be seen in the next chapter and are still apparent in today's air force.

IT'S A WONDER THAT ANYTHING GETS DONE: THE ADMINISTRATIVE MINEFIELD

In addition to the ordinary problems of running an Air Force alluded to above, there were many other obstacles of varying origins, as the following examples will show.

Political Turmoil

Each President brings his own strategic agenda to his office. This agenda is often the product of campaign promises. These will usually be adhered to initially, no matter how out of tune they might be with reality, as in the cases of President Kennedy's "missile gap" and President Carter's campaign vow to cut $7 billion from the defense budget. To fulfill his agenda, the President will pack his cabinet and make changes in the Chairman of the JCS and in the service chiefs. The Chairman and the chiefs must then balance their loyalties to the good of the service with their sworn duty to the President.

The crucial Presidential cabinet choice is that of a Secretary of Defense who will mirror the President's interests. The power of the SecDef is so great that he can virtually dictate to the service secretaries and the members of the JCS, unless they are prepared to fight for their interests with rigorously researched arguments. This exercise of power goes far beyond the enunciation of policy. It frequently became the practice of successive Secretaries of Defense to go against the advice of their service secretaries and the Joint Chiefs of Staff and make their own decisions on the cancellation or acquisition of certain weapon systems. McNamara started the process with his cancellations of the B-70 and Skybolt, even as he ramrodded through the acquisition of the F-111 and the A-7. Such decisions virtually became a badge of office, as in the case of Secretary Melvin Laird with the Manned Orbiting Laboratory (MOL), Secretary Schlesinger with the lightweight fighter, Secretary Harold Brown with the B-1 and the ALCM, and Secretary Caspar Weinberger with a host of acquisitions.

Adaptation to Policy Changes

The amazing comeback of the Air Force occurred despite changing political climates. Credit must be given first to the great architect of nuclear air power, Curtis LeMay, and only then to the successive Secretaries of the Air Force and Chiefs of Staff who managed to keep their eyes on the technological ball and so create the modern Air Force.

Each succeeding administration coined new terms to reflect its spin on a national defense policy that at its heart remained unchanged. The names changed from "massive retaliation" to "assured destruction" to "flexible and appropriate response," which required an even greater buildup of nuclear power than did "massive retaliation." Later there came changes from "counterforce strategy" to "essential equivalence" to "countervailing strategy," yet all of these variations on a theme were feasible only because they were backed by the tremendous nuclear power that the Strategic Air Command's bombers and missiles represented. The latter were supplemented by the Polaris submarine-launched ballistic missile (SLBM), which completed the essential strategic triad upon which America's security is still based. No American strategy, no matter how it was named, would have been respected by the Soviet Union without first SAC's and then the triad's backing.

Rather than being administrative initiatives, the changes in nomenclature were actually mere reflections of each administration's degree of recognition of the growing strength of the Soviet Union's nuclear force. Massive retaliation was an appropriate strategy only so long as the United States enjoyed an overwhelming nuclear superiority. Soviet strength grew to match or exceed that of the United States in many areas, including "throw weight," the number, size, and sophistication of nuclear weapons at its disposal. Successive American administrations formulated ground rules for slowing down the arms race, sedulously avoiding the impression of attempting to achieve a first-strike capability and trying to negotiate arms limits initially, followed by reductions. As a part of the desire to slow the arms race (and to avoid spending the necessary funds), the United States had virtually no realistic civil defense and turned away from a ballistic missile defense system.

Unfortunately for American strategists—and the American people—the Soviet Union did not respond to these leads, as Secretary Seamans had noted. Just as the North Vietnamese government had done, it interpreted any American concession as a sign of weakness. It signed agreements limiting certain classes of weapons only when it was hopelessly behind in the development of those weapons. It proceeded all the while doing exactly as it wished, building weapons with first-strike capability and supplementing these with a monumental civil defense effort that emphasized the survival of the Communist leadership. The Soviets' capability was immeasurably enhanced by an incredible U.S. government decision in 1972 to sell them the previously restricted Centalign B machines for making the small ball bearings necessary for extremely precise missile-guidance systems. The Soviet Union promptly bought 164 of the machines—twice as many as were in use in the United States—and by 1976 had increased the accuracy of their SS-18 and SS-19 ICBMs to the point that they could destroy an estimated 90 percent of our Minutemen in their silos on a first strike. These are the same missiles and technology that China sought for "commercial space launches."

Technological Attenuation

The development cycle of a weapon in the 1960s, from start to deployment, was about five years. It is now about fifteen, with the result that new weapons systems inevitably must endure review by at least two and perhaps as many as four administrations. The Rockwell B-1 was born only after a twenty-year gestation period that included abortion by the Carter administration and resuscitation by President Reagan. The contract for the McDonnell Douglas C-17 was signed in August 1981; it entered service in late 1995.

The lengthened cycle meant that Air Force leaders had to determine the weapon systems they needed, then defend them through several changes of administration and as many as fifteen annual budgets before having the weapons in hand. When the inevitable changes in the programs occurred—increased costs, lengthened schedules, alterations in performance—they had to be defended anew. Congressional staffers are smart, competitive men and women, patriots who want the United States to have the best weapons at the most favorable cost. However, it is a given that these staffers have the reelection of their member uppermost in their minds. Like gold miners, they pan weapon systems over their life cycles, looking for the glint of political capital. If something glitters it does not matter if it's fool's gold so long as announcing it will get the member favorable attention in the press. Staffers provided Congresswoman Patricia Schroeder's the information for her long and hard campaign against the AWACs as a "billion-dollar boondoggle" (the alliterative term lingers through the years) without regard to the demonstrated need. Conversely, staffers gave Senator John Towers the information necessary to ensure that the General Dynamics F-111 was kept in production long after USAF requirements for it were filled. There are as many more examples as there are weapons systems, and, perhaps, as there are Congressmen.

Changes in Procedures

The very means of doing business has changed drastically over the years. General Larry Welch has commented that when General LeMay was Chief of Staff in the early 1960s, the Air Force did not have a line item for research and development—it had a lump sum that it could allocate as it saw fit. Now R&D items with budgets as low as $100,000 are analyzed separately by DOD and Congress. Further, if LeMay had a program he liked, he had only to confer with perhaps two people in the Department of Defense and four people in Congress—the heads of the four major military committees—to get it approved. Ten years later, General Jones had to deal with as many as five people in DOD and sixteen on the Hill. When General Welch became Chief of Staff in 1986, he found that to push a program forward, he had to deal with at least fifteen key people in DOD and hundreds in Congress.

The number is actually greater, for in the thirty-plus years since General LeMay's tenure, the number of Congressional staffers has multiplied by a factor of thirty, and many of them have to be satisfied before a decision can be obtained. During the same period, the influence of the chairmen of the major military committees has declined. The power that Congressman Rivers or Carl Vinson once had to make a decision on the spot has been greatly eroded.

Technical Complexity

Technical complexity has grown almost as fast as political complexity, and the two are inevitably intertwined. Weapon systems requirements for stealth and precision have reached such exotic levels that successful achievement often depends upon breakthroughs in many sciences, such as metallurgy, electronics, and aerodynamics.

Despite the unpredictable path from conception to successful deployment in the field, weapon systems are scrutinized so that the program advocate has to declare from the outset exactly what a weapon system is going to do, how long it is going to take, and what it is going to cost—all information that is simply unavailable at the time.

This situation has a number of side effects, including a sharp reduction in the number of advocates who are willing to risk their careers to secure a needed weapon system when they know they must promise results that are problematic. Fear of failure makes managers tend to be less willing to make the great leap to the next level of technology, and they become subject to the lure of incrementalism, seeking minor advances in performance because they are safer—politically as well as careerwise—even though they might not meet the ultimate requirement.

In the quarter century after Vietnam, the Air Force overcame these and many other impediments in its march to a demonstration of pure air power in 1991.

THE RISE OF THE PHOENIX: FROM VIETNAM TO THE GULF WAR

Vietnam saw the unprecedented phenomenon of first the American media and then the general public turning against the military services for participating in war that was begun, controlled, lost, and ended by the civilian leadership. After 1972, it could well be argued that the Air Force's mascot should be the phoenix rather than the falcon, for it rose from the cold dead ashes of the Vietnam War to its old place in the hearts of the American public. In the process, it increased its fighting power to an incredible degree with amazing new technologies—and the personnel to match.

LESSONS LEARNED IN COMBAT

The Air Force went from strength to strength in the years after Vietnam, the path made easier by the relatively few fundamental doctrinal changes. The technological focus of the Air Force was adhered to by all its leaders, despite the increasing difficulties imposed by centralized DOD control. The depth and breadth of the Air Force commitment to technology permitted it to endure severe force cutbacks, lean budgets, and a diminishment of its industrial base and still emerge with an air force worthy of the only superpower.

Although the Vietnam War was the low point in United States Air Force history, it nonetheless taught a series of powerful lessons about military operations and, most important, about military operations controlled by the politics of an election-oriented civilian leadership. Despite the speculation of the rabid *Seven Days in May* genre of fiction, the idea of the military taking over political direction as has occurred in other countries in similar situations was never attempted—and probably never contemplated.

Instead, working within the chaos of political change, the Air Force leadership came up with some hard rules that would be difficult to implement but were essential to the future:

1. Air superiority had to be earned immediately; gradualism was the path to disaster.

2. Air superiority, given the expected budget limitations, could be gained only by a huge investment in technology.

3. Significant components of that technology had to be revolutionary rather than evolutionary.

4. In the interim, much existing equipment had to be upgraded by modification rather than replaced.

5. The Vietnam concept of using large numbers of aircraft, each with a relatively low lethality, was wrong, as the Paul Doumer and Than Hoa bridges had conclusively proved.

6. A grinding approach to victory was not politically sustainable. If war came, it had to be fought immediately and won conclusively.

7. The enemy must never be given time to recover after the first attack. Sufficient aircraft and equipment must be available to do the job, and the civilian leaders must be persuaded to abstain from political gimmicks such as bombing halts.

Not listed as a lesson learned because it is beyond the Air Force's purview was the absolute requirement not to undertake any campaign not backed by the will of the American people.

These lessons, among others, became the operative philosophy for the post-Vietnam Air Force. Many additional subsets of lessons learned regarding the requirements for individual weapons, intelligence gathering and air transport of men and supplies supported these fundamentals, materializing in the weapon systems discussed below.

WHAT WEAPONS WERE NEEDED?

The Air Force emerged from the Vietnam War with the certain knowledge that it needed an air superiority fighter, a modern bomber capable of penetrating the Soviet Union, more aircraft with stealth characteristics, an improved ground attack aircraft, improved electronic countermeasures, precision-guided munitions, greatly improved theater airlift capability, and a modern, multiple-warhead intercontinental ballistic missile. All of these had to be tied together with an efficient C^3I system—command control, communications and intelligence.

To obtain these weapons, the Air Force called upon the pool of experienced talent from the Vietnam War and the strong R&D base it had created with so much dedication over the years. These components provided the basis for America's technologically advanced industry to produce two new generations of weapon systems of unprecedented performance—and cost. These systems were overlapped in time with each other and with veterans of the past. Many books have been written about each individual weapon, and only a brief description is possible here.

FIRST-GENERATION WEAPONS

Two key fighters were developed in the first generation. The McDonnell Douglas F-15 Eagle, covered in greater detail below, was the result of hot debate about what a new USAF fighter would be. The General Dynamics (now Lockheed Martin) F-16 Fighting Falcon came as a joint by-product of the revitalized thinking on what a fighter should be and of the F-15's cost. The F-16 (also known as the Viper) was to be a lightweight fighter with less capability than the F-15, but inexpensive enough to be procured in large numbers. After much debate, it was decided that the Air Force was best served by a hi-lo mix—a smaller number of expensive F-15s as the "hi" portion, and a larger number of F-16s as the "lo" portion.

Both the F-15 and the F-16 proved to be superior to any other combat aircraft in their respective classes in the world, and they gave the USAF the capability for establishing air superiority in any theater. They also gave impetus to the Soviet Union, which fielded remarkable competitors in the MiG-29 and Sukhoi Su-27. Other follow-on foreign competitors include the French Rafale and the Eurofighter 2000, the latter a product of a consortium that included the United Kingdom, Germany, Italy, and Spain.

The need for a close air support weapon prompted a competition which was won by the Fairchild A-10 Thunderbolt II—more commonly known as the Warthog for its uncomely appearance. The requirement called for an aircraft that had a large weapon-carrying capability, was uncomplicated and easy to maintain, required a minimum of ground facilities so that it could operate from forward bases, and could withstand extensive battle damage. A single-seat twin-jet aircraft, the A-10 can carry up to 16,000 pounds of ordnance and features a tank-killing 30mm GAU-8/A cannon. It proved itself beyond a shadow of a doubt in the Gulf War.

The Rockwell B-1B Lancer—familiarly known as the Bone to its crews—became the backbone of the long-range bomber fleet after an excruciatingly long development period that began in 1961 and was characterized by terrible acronyms as well as delays. The acronyms included SLAB (Subsonic Low Altitude Bomber), ERSA (Extended Range Strike Aircraft), LAMP (Low Altitude Manned Penetration), AMPSS (Advanced Manned Precision Strike System), and finally AMSA (Advanced Manned Strategic Aircraft—this had originally been the Advanced Strategic Manned Aircraft until it was noticed that ASMA was not exactly a warlike nickname). A total procurement quantity of 244 was planned for what had become the B-1A at the time of contract award in June 1970. The first flight took place on October 26, 1974. The B-1A's variable-geometry wings and blended wing/body configuration made it fast and long-ranged.

The development cost of the B-1A program approached $3 billion, creating a demand for alternatives. These included a stretched General Dynamics FB-111G, a re-engined B-52, and a stand-off cruise missile launcher based on the Boeing 747.

None of these programs met the requirements as well as the B-1A—yet the B-1A was canceled by President Carter. The aircraft was revived by President Reagan as the B-1B, which was similar in appearance to the B-1A but had a reduced radar signature and lacked a low-level supersonic capability. The B-1B is heavier and can deliver nuclear or conventional weapons as well as stand-off missiles. A total of one hundred were delivered to the Air Force.

The Lancer has been controversial over its entire life, primarily because some of its complex electronic equipment did not perform to design specifications but also because of some well-publicized engine problems. The engine anomalies were par for the course for such an advanced aircraft and have been worked out over time. The electronic suite difficulties were in part overcome by superb crew training, but improvements are still planned. Despite this, the last Commander in Chief of the Strategic Air Command, General George L. Butler, stated unequivocally that the B-1B has a higher survivability factor in a penetration role against the Soviet Union without any electronic countermeasures (ECM) than the B-52H has with its ECM fully operational. A series of modifications to enhance the B-1B's conventional arms capability, including improved computers to support precision-guided munitions, makes its employment feasible well into the next century.

The Boeing E-3 Sentry is essentially a 707-320B airframe surmounted by a 30-foot-diameter rotating radome. The AWACS (airborne warning and control system) is capable of all-weather, long-range, high-or low-level surveillance of all air vehicles above all types of terrain. Its Westinghouse radar's look-down capability made it a tremendous advance over all previous airborne radar systems. Its initial task was to track the Soviet warplanes that would have accompanied an invasion of Western Europe. Since then, its role has been expanded to include antidrug patrols and enforcement of the "no-fly" zones imposed in Iraq and Bosnia. The AWACS is continually updated for new tasks, including electronic support measures to locate enemy stealth aircraft. The Sentry retains its capability as a force multiplier, enabling on-scene commanders to allocate forces with precision to the most urgent threats.

The General Dynamics F-111 was one of the most controversial warplanes in history. Deriving from Secretary McNamara's concept of the TFX, a multicapability fighter for use by both the Navy and the Air Force, it served well as a long-range strike fighter, and as the FB-111, as an interim strategic bomber for SAC. However, it reached its peak of utility with its introduction in 1981 as the EF-111A Tactical Jamming System. The high-performance, swing-wing F-111 airframe was combined with the most advanced, most powerful jamming system in the world, derived from the proven ALQ-99 equipment installed on the Grumman EA-6B. Grumman was selected as the contractor to combine the two elements into the EF-111A Raven. The Raven has the ability to loiter for up to four and one-half hours without refueling, yet, after sweeping its wings, it has the speed to keep up with the fastest Air Force fighters, as it demonstrated in the Persian Gulf War.

The temperature of the discussions over the several aircraft involved in the new generation did not rise above that of the fiery arguments over the single new missile, the long-debated MX. Eventually designated the LGM-118A, the Peacekeeper missile was unusual in that there was far more debate about its basing methods than there was about the missile itself. The Peacekeeper is a four-stage ICBM with as many as ten independently targetable reentry systems. It is far more accurate than the Minuteman III, carries more warheads, and has a greater range. SALT talks have placed limits on the number of warheads.

Because of its accuracy, it was conceded to become a prime target for Soviet missiles, and considerable thought was given to elaborate basing plans. One plan called for the missiles to be installed on railroad cars and shuttled around the country on a random basis, to make targeting difficult. Another called for basing the missiles closely together in a "dense pack," so that incoming Soviet missiles would interfere with each other in what became known as "fratricide." The most popular—and expensive—called for the creation (at a cost of $34 billion) of no less than 4,600 missile sites for 200 missiles. Like a pea in a shell game, each missile was to have been shuttled randomly from one spot to another to complicate Soviet target planning. Time and budget finally intervened, and a total of fifty Peacekeepers were finally installed in vacant Minuteman silos—an inadequate compromise in the minds of most.

Second-Generation Weapons

The very unorthodox, very advanced Lockheed F-117A Nighthawk stealth fighter led the second generation. The concept of very-low-observable, or stealth, technology has been with us since World War I, when camouflage and even Cellon, a transparent, celluloid-like covering, were used on aircraft to minimize their visibility. Being "invisible" to radar was another challenge, and was first demonstrated on the German Gotha Go-229 flying-wing jet fighter. USAF interest in the mid-1970s spurred development of prototypes to test how new shapes and materials might reduce a radar signature. One of these was the Lockheed "Have Blue" and another was Northrop's whalelike "Tacit Blue."

As a result of the Have Blue project the Air Force selected Lockheed to build five full-scale development models and fifteen production F-117As. Developed in Lockheed's famous Skunk Works under the direction of the brilliant Ben Rich, the new aircraft provided a study in contrasts. (The distinction between fighter, fighter-bomber, and bomber has become blurred as fighter-sized aircraft like the F-117A aegured bomber-like ranges navigation and bomb-dropping ability.)

The primary task of the Nighthawk is to penetrate enemy territory, unseen by active or passive defenses, and attack high-value targets with precision-guided munitions. A discussion of all the factors pertinent to the design of stealth aircraft is outside the scope of this book, but the F-117A's shape and materials either deflected or absorbed radar signals so that it was virtually invisible to radar. Its engines were hidden within the body so that its infrared signal was minimal. On a mission, it did not operate radar or other electronic equipment that could be picked up by enemy detectors. The shape and configuration necessary to avoid detection by radar or infrared devices resulted in a wedgelike, multifaceted configuration so inherently unstable that it required a full-time fly-by-wire command augmentation system. No mechanical backup system was provided because no pilot could fly the aircraft without computer-controlled stability augmentation. The Air Force originally intended to purchase one hundred of the Nighthawks (also called "the Black Jet" by its crews) but budget limitations reduced this to only fifty-nine. As we shall see, the F-117A operated with a preternatural brilliance in the Gulf War.

Northrop's Tacit Blue was designed as a prototype for a reconnaissance aircraft with a side-looking radar array. Tacit Blue's existence was kept secret even longer than that of the Have Blue series, not being revealed until May 1996. The design was cancelled because its mission could be performed by other means, including unmanned vehicles. Another approach to stealth design was shown in the Northrop B-2 Spirit stealth bomber, which depended more upon composite materials and a smoother, blended shape than the angular faceting of the Nighthawk. About 80 percent of the B-2's airframe weight is made up of composites; titanium and aluminum are used for internal load-bearing structures.

The flying wing was a poignant if coincidental return to tradition for Northrop, which had pioneered the concept with the B-35 and B-49 bombers of the early postwar period. The great designer Jack Northrop lived long enough to learn that his long dream of a production flying-wing aircraft would happen. Although it was remarkably similar in shape and planform to the flying wings of the 1940s, the primary reason for adopting the configuration was its low radar cross section and the convenience the thicker wing shape offered for shielding infrared emissions from engine operation.

The B-2 has been perhaps the most controversial aircraft to enter service in recent years, because of its high program cost. Initial production procurement was capped at twenty aircraft (plus refurbishing the prototype), although funding for an additional twenty aircraft has been proposed.

The McDonnell Douglas C-17A Globemaster III had almost as long a gestation period in all its prior forms as did the B-1. Driven by an urgent airlift requirement that was exacerbated by the wear and tear placed on C-5s and C-141s during the Gulf War, the C-17 became operational in January 1995. The unusual-looking cargo plane is designed for both inter-and intra-theater airlift and can carry outsized cargo, including the M1A2 tank. A total of 120 production aircraft are currently planned, although this figure will undoubtedly grow over time.

The Boeing/Grumman E-8 Joint STARS (Joint Surveillance and Target Attack Radar System) consists of modifing "previously owned" Boeing 707-

300 airframes with the radar and communication equipment necessary for ground surveillance, targeting, and battle management missions. The E-8 uses a Norden side-looking radar that is in a large fairing on the forward fuselage. The radar maintains surveillance over a wide area and is designed to find and track slow-moving ground targets. Fixed targets like tank parks, bridges, and airports are identified in a high-resolution synthetic aperture mode. The system can distinguish between trucks and tanks, so that weapons can be applied against the most valuable targets. J-STARS is in effect an AWACS for the ground war, directing attacks against enemy targets. Prototype E-8s were used with considerable success in the Gulf War.

The final aircraft weapon of this second generation is the most advanced fighter in the world, the Lockheed Martin F-22A/B. The F-22A combines a highly maneuverable airframe at both subsonic and supersonic speeds with low-observable characteristics. Actual performance figures are still classified, but the aircraft is capable of supersonic cruising without the use of afterburner. The twin-engine F-22A (the F-22B is a two-seat version) has a very advanced weapon systems capable of engaging multiple targets. The first of the more than 440 aircraft planned for production will achieve initial operating capability in 2004.

As outstanding as each of the weapon systems of these two closely linked generations is, their cumulative effectiveness would be zero without the network of space systems that provides them unparalleled intelligence, communication, navigation, and meteorological capability. This will be discussed below.

Their usefulness is similarly dependent upon the diverse electronic systems and advanced munitions that have simultaneously been developed for them. The time necessary for the creation of all these modern weapons was purchased by the continued employment of veterans such as the B-52, F-111, SR-71, U-2, and Minuteman III. The usefulness of these weapon systems, every one of which was decried by critics as wasteful folly at one time or another during their procurement cycles, seems unbounded by time or circumstance.

AGING GRACEFULLY

Military aircraft typically fly far fewer hours than their civilian counterparts and are built to different standards that reflect the possibility of harder usage (greater G-forces, for example) but fewer cycles of operation. For most of the history of aviation, military aircraft had an expected service life of perhaps five years in first-line operation, followed by another five in reserve or training applications. In the past thirty years, however, military aircraft life spans have increased dramatically, which is just as well, given that the time required to introduce a new weapon system has also increased.

The current champion combat senior citizen is the Boeing B-52, which first flew in 1952 and ended production in 1962. In 1996, the average age of the eighty-five B-52s still serving in the active inventory over 34 years. Some B-52s are projected to be in service until 2030, when the average age will be something like sixty-seven years, and when their pilots could conceivably be the great-great-grandchildren of the men who first flew them. (The mechanical equivalent would be for a 1929 Keystone bomber to be in frontline service in 1996.) The original average price of about $6 million per B-52 was greeted with outrage and astonishment. However, when one amortizes this over a period of sixty-seven years and several wars, it seems quite a bargain, something to keep in mind for later discussions.

The B-52 survived for a number of reasons. Its excellent performance has been increased by improved engines, and its large size has permitted it to carry a broad range of equipment and munitions for a wide variety of missions. Most important, almost from its inception it has been the beneficiary of continual modification, including rebuilding the wings and fuselage over the years.

The story is the same for the stalwart Boeing KC-135 tanker fleet, which has an average age of 33.7 years and now succors bombers, fighters, and transports with equal care. The KC-135 may well stay in service even longer than the B-52.

Both aircraft have been supplemented over the years. The B-52 had the sleek Convair B-58 as its companion for a time. The Hustler was a supersonic bomber but it could not adapt as well as the B-52 to changing conditions and was retired. The B-52 now shares the major duties of the bomber fleet with the Rockwell B-1B, a youngster averaging only 8.1 years in age. The KC-135 has been assisted by the addition of fifty-nine McDonnell Douglas KC-10s, averaging only about eleven years in age.

Age has had less effect on the transport aircraft than has the routine wear and tear of the demanding task of carrying huge loads to airfields of every description all over the world. The fleet of Lockheed C-141s averages twenty-nine years, but the strain of the accelerated airlift effort of the Gulf War moved them so close to retirement that the necessity for purchasing the C-17 at last became obvious to all. The Lockheed C-5 fleet of eighty-one aircraft averages only 13.8 years, primarily because fifty of the fleet were built over a decade ago. The hardy Lockheed C-130s average 23.3 years and promise to be "hauling trash" for several more decades, almost certainly in company with the highly advanced current model, the C-130J.

The fighter fleet is in comparatively better shape. The F-15, the first-line American air superiority fighter, averages about ten years in age, while its companion, the Lockheed Martin F-16, averages about half that.

Among missiles, the 500 Minuteman IIIs that came into service in the early 1970s have been supplemented by fifty Peacekeeper missiles, which were all in place by 1988. Like the B-52, the Minuteman has benefited from continual modification and updating. Also like the B-52, its purpose will have been perfectly served if it is never used to deliver nuclear weapons.

EVOLVING THE NEW WEAPONS

The program histories of each of these new weapons could fill a library. For the purposes of this book, it is worthwhile to examine how a representative example, the McDonnell Douglas F-15 Eagle, was brought into being.

Its predecessor as the USAF's standard air superiority fighter, the McDonnell Douglas F-4 Phantom II, had started life in 1953 as a proposed naval fleet defense fighter, armed solely with missiles. It evolved into such a highly capable aircraft that Secretary McNamara pressed for its adoption by the USAF in 1962. It became the premier American fighter in Vietnam, serving ably with the Air Force, Navy, and Marines and performing in every role, including air superiority, close air support, reconnaissance, and even as a "fast FAC," a swift-moving forward air control aircraft.

Yet combat revealed deficiencies in the F-4 that the Air Force wished to avoid in a follow-on fighter. Among these were a lack of visibility from the cockpit, the requirement for two men to operate the weapon systems, and the highly visible smoke trails left by the engines. The advantage of having two engines was diminished by the tendency for fire to propagate from one engine to the other. There were also ergonomic problems involving such things as the positioning of the control stick and armament switches. Maintenance was a headache—in some cases the ejection seat had to be removed to replace a radio.

The F-4 was originally armed only with air-to-air missiles, which proved to be a great disappointment. Expectations had been unrealistically high. Because guidance equipment was improved and missile speed was supersonic, their proponents assumed such a very high kill rate for them that guns were omitted from aircraft armament packages. The classic dogfight was considered impossible at supersonic speeds and thus a thing of the past. Ironically, the technology devoted to creating missiles had been aimed at destroying enemy bombers. When it turned out that most air fighting was conducted in dogfights between fighters at subsonic speeds, the missiles proved inadequate. The envelope within which the missiles could be used and the length of time required to prepare them for launch often exceeded practical limits in a dogfight. When elaborate rules of engagement were superimposed on these limitations, the kill ratio of American versus enemy aircraft fell to its lowest point in history.

The young fighter pilot veterans from Vietnam wanted a more agile aircraft that could outmaneuver the nimble MiG-21 as well as its inevitable successors, and they wanted it equipped both with a gun armament and better missiles. Two such young veterans tapped for their fighter experience were future Chief of Staff Larry Welch and future Commander of Air Combat Command Mike Loh.

In the late 1960s, Air Force Pentagon experts were attempting to create a computer simulation of dogfighting and air-to-air combat. Welch's task was to teach them how a fighter pilot makes decisions. After two months, it was obvious to Welch that he was never going to be able to teach a computer programmer about aerial attack. Instead, he took a quick course in FORTRAN programming and with another fighter pilot developed a computer program with variable parameters that was used in designing the F-15 Eagle and subsequent fighters.

Welch's work would augment studies begun in the mid-1960s under the direction of Air Force Secretary Eugene Zuckert to develop the F-X (fighter-experimental). The F-X was to be highly maneuverable even at the expense of sheer speed, and to have superior capabilities for air-to-air combat, ground attack, and all-weather operations. Curiously, the first design studies resulted in a behemoth 60,000-pound clone of the F-111, exactly opposite to then-current thinking as to what a fighter should be.

The situation was saved by an aggressive young Pentagon action officer, Major John R. Boyd, who led the effort to redirect F-X development to a highly maneuverable aircraft optimized for the air superiority role. Boyd was the outspoken advocate of the concept of energy maneuverability that had proved to be the key to the F-4's success in Vietnam. His precepts led to a demand for the F-X to have the capability to outturn and outaccelerate enemy fighters under all conditions encountered in a dogfight.

A massive paper competition under Secretary McNamara's Total Package Procurement (TPP) rules was held among three manufacturers, Fairchild, North American, and McDonnell Douglas. These rules were intensified by a "Demonstration Milestone Chart" that called for the winning design to meet twenty-four individual milestones, ranging from the preliminary design review through first flight, fatigue testing, complete flight testing, and the delivery of the first aircraft to TAC. Each of these milestones had to be met or further funding was delayed—the ultimate combination of contractual stick and carrot.

After 2.5 million man-hours of study by massive teams of USAF military and civilian experts, the McDonnell Douglas entrant was selected as winner by Secretary Seamans on December 23, 1969. Early the next year, another contract was signed with Pratt & Whitney to develop the F100-PW-100 engine to power the F-15 Eagle. (The cost of a TPP procurement to competing contractors was enormous, not only in the colossal dollar outlay, which could be near-ruinous to a smaller company like Fairchild, but in the opportunity costs of projects forgone because the resources were not available. The TPP experiment is a perfect example of bureaucratic bean-counting gone wild, in which the search for perfect numbers overlooks the cost to other elements of the economy and sacrifices the opportunity for progress in other vital areas.)

All of the contractors threw massive resources into the competition. McDonnell Douglas had conducted more than 10,000 hours of very expensive wind tunnel tests, along with extensive use of the then brand-new computer-aided-design equipment. In addition, McDonnell Douglas employed two cockpit air combat simulators to test its design against all possible competitors, with Air Force combat veterans flying the simulators and suggesting improvements in cockpit layout.

In the end, the F-15's world-beating maneuverability depended upon factors as old as the Wright Flyer: a low wing-loading (the relationship of wing area to gross weight) and a high power-to-weight ratio. It made its first flight on July 27, 1973, at McDonnell's St. Louis plant and entered service on November 14, 1974, at Luke AFB, Arizona. In late 1976, the 1st Tactical Fighter Wing at Langley was the first to be operationally combat-ready with the Eagle.

The F-15 encountered some airframe problems in its test program that, while troubling, were susceptible to relatively easy modification. Its engines, at that time the most complex ever used in a fighter, had both operational and maintenance problems that required a much longer time to resolve fully. Despite all this, the F-15 quickly proved that it was the fighter of the future, with a performance that eclipsed that of all existing aircraft of the Soviet Union. Highly maneuverable and equipped with a Hughes multimode pulse Doppler radar, it met all air superiority requirements. The Israeli Air Force would score notable successes with it in 1982, and it would again prove itself in the Persian Gulf War.

Such performance was expensive, and the initial estimate of F-15 unit cost of about $15 million rose through the years to a current $50 million—the result of modifications, inflation, and additional equipment. The F-15 also turned out to be larger than exponents of the lightweight fighter concept preferred. Members of the so-called "fighter Mafia," led by Major Boyd and his colleague Pierre Sprey, a systems analyst with OSD (Office of the Secretary of Defense) sought to raise interest in a smaller aircraft.

The idea of a lightweight fighter brought an instant adverse reaction from Air Force Headquarters. After having made a great effort to sell the F-15, the Air Staff did not wish to provide Congress with a "low-cost rationale" for canceling it. In an effective demonstration of how field-grade action officers can influence future events, Mike Loh saw to it that the nascent movement for a lightweight fighter was caught up by another wave of enthusiasm, that of Deputy Secretary of Defense David Packard's desire to select aircraft by competitive fly-offs. Loh became the program element monitor for what became called the air combat fighter and facilitated the competition between the Northrop YF-17 and the General Dynamics YF-16. Thanks to the presence of Air Force "young Turks," and timely intervention by the Secretary of Defense it thus happened that the successful development of one fighter, the F-15, fostered rather than suppressed the development of another—the F-16.

Each weapon system has a similar history that runs from its initial concept in the minds of planners to its final destination at the smelting pots of the aircraft disposal unit at Davis Monthan AFB. In today's world of protracted development, strung-out production, and long service lives, the interval between concept and salvage may extend for sixty years, or more than three careers for the average airman—or legislator.

The F-15/F-16 saga shows that it takes genuine vision to conceive weapon systems that have to meet specific requirements while operating in an unusually demanding environment over many decades. The vision of a weapon system must be accompanied by diligent management, adroit politicking, and a steadfast adherence to doctrine, again through many changes of leadership and over a long period of time.

The full scope and depth of the task is rarely appreciated. The media, desperately seeking stories about a $600 toilet seat or $25,000 facsimile machines, would find nothing of interest in the magnitude of the problem of creating and fielding a single weapon system or in the fact that at any given moment the Air Force alone may have hundreds of major weapon systems (including munitions and electronic countermeasures) under development. Each of these might have literally tens of thousands of subcomponents, as well as additional thousands of items in support equipment, all of them requiring equivalent care. Every one of these elements has to be designed to criteria that have to be specified in enormous detail to obtain the desired performance, strength, longevity, and capability. (There is a trend away from this sort of specification where commercial items will serve. This is a valid concept when those components already exist, but in many cases they have to be invented for a specialized weapon system—and there is little commercial pressure for such exotic invention.)

Many of the weapon systems have to be designed in anticipation of threats and uses that are not yet fully defined. Personnel have to be trained to manufacture, deliver, use, and maintain them. Most important, American policy and American lives depend upon their being brought to fruition successfully and on time.

Are mistakes made? Yes. In the fabric of the huge society of military and civilian personnel involved in the programs, are there a few miscreants who will take advantage of the system? Yes. Does the vast scope of the endeavor inevitably yield stories that are "newsworthy" for their signs of human failure? Of course. But on the whole, the entire apparatus is carried out with a degree of honesty and success of which any organization, industry or government, could be proud.

As we will see in the next chapter, the Air Force met all of its challenges with skill and panache in so quickly creating the two generations of war-making equipment it knew it required. At the same time, it created the simultaneous advances in the military use of space upon which the proper functioning of these weapon systems demanded.

THE EXPLOITATION OF SPACE

Although there has not yet been a significant groundswell to change the name of the junior service to the United States Aerospace Force, the resources devoted to space and the benefits derived from its exploitation make the change almost certain in the future. The tidal movement toward this new name may be charted in the organizational development that follows.

The initial approach of the Air Force to space was both curious and coincidental, and, not surprisingly, it followed traditional organizational patterns, with responsibilities divided among AFSC, ADC, AFLC, SAC, and the Defense Communications Agency (DCA). The need to create ICBMs put the Air Force in the space business before it could formulate extensive plans for the exploitation of space. That the propulsion and guidance elements of the ICBM could be used for the insertion of satellites into orbit was immediately apparent, but it took time to grasp the full range of possibilities offered by extensive systems of satellites. Further, the technological infrastructure necessary to develop and use satellites as intelligence, communications, navigation, and meteorological networks had yet to be developed. As will be seen, when the technology became available, the USAF created a space superiority that corresponded to older concepts of air superiority.

The earliest concepts on the USAF in space were intuitive. That great thinker General Thomas D. White saw space as a continuum of our atmosphere. He realized that the United States could not dominate all of space. In his view the United States should establish a space superiority to control space activities, just as it had established air superiority to control enemy air actions.

The full economic implications even of this limited strategy were not understood. It soon became obvious that the Soviet Union intended to use space as an extension of its military power. The only certain way to prevent this was a preemptive strike by ICBMs, an act abhorrent to U.S. policy and national character. So it happened that the great Cold War competition between the United States and the Soviet Union went boldly—but blindly—toward a new frontier.

HESITATION IN SPACE POLICY

The Eisenhower and Kennedy administrations both wished to avoid the expense and hazard of an arms race in space. Eisenhower introduced the concept of "freedom of space," which ensured overflight, and saw to it that the first sentence in the 1958 law creating the National Aeronautics and Space Administration (NASA) confirmed this desire: "The Congress declares that it is the policy of the United States that activities in space should be devoted to peaceful purposes for the benefit of mankind." But peaceful purposes embraced space defense support missions such as reconnaissance and communications. (Eisenhower must be given great credit for his courage and foresight in authorizing the Corona program detailed below.)

The law went on to delegate to DOD the responsibility for the use of space for these defensive systems. The Air Force had earlier been given similar responsibilities, a situation confirmed by DOD Directive 5160.22 of September 1, 1970, which provided that "the Air Force will have the responsibility of development, production and deployment of space systems for warning and surveillance of enemy nuclear capabilities, and all launch vehicles, including launch and orbital support operations."

President Kennedy chose the Apollo program as a prestigious but non-threatening means to demonstrate American technological superiority in a way that would not spur an arms race. The Apollo program was wildly successful and restored U.S. international prestige, but it also reinforced the determination of the Soviet Union to seize for military purposes what inevitably was called the "high ground of space." Soviet launch activity surpassed that of the United States in 1971, because Soviet satellites proved less reliable and possessed shorter lives in orbit. By 1973 the Soviets were putting almost five times as many satellites and other space objects into orbit as the Americans. The Soviet Union had no inhibitions about testing antisatellite weapons, conducting tests throughout the late 1970s and early 1980s. Its system proved to have limited capability, in altitude and azimuth.

Unfortunately, the American reaction to the well-trumpeted Soviet space activity was exactly parallel to its handling of events in Vietnam. There American policy was artfully crafted to induce certain positive reactions from the enemy—which never came. The same was true in space. The U.S. thirst for accommodation with the Soviet Union led to a stifling of technological progress in an attempt to avoid destabilizing the quest for arms reduction. The Soviet Union did not reciprocate. Despite this general trend, U.S. satellites became much more reliable than their Soviet counterparts, operating for ten years and more.

In the McNamara era, the accommodation was often accomplished internally by a political variation of "bait and switch" sales tactics, with the switch here coming before the bait. McNamara insisted that military space efforts be consistent with NASA's programs, and then used NASA programs as a reason for canceling Air Force space projects. The first of these was the Boeing X-20 Dyna-Soar, a rocket-boosted vehicle with a single pilot that was to orbit the earth, then return to land at a designated spot. Conceptually a forerunner of the space shuttle, it traced its engineering roots back to German World War II "skip-bomber" concepts originated by Dr. Eugen Saenger.

The Dyna-Soar had been a key element in the Air Force program for developing a manned military patrol capability in space. The hypersonic X-20 was to have tested controlled, maneuverable reentry from orbital flight beginning with its first launch in 1962—the same year in which future Senator John Glenn made his successful orbital flight in the Mercury spacecraft *Friendship 7*. Without detracting an iota from the remarkable work of the Mercury program, the X-20 would have been a far more advanced vehicle than the Mercury spacecraft, and at the very least would have removed the "pilots as monkey" odium from those early orbital flights.

Convinced that the Mercury-Gemini-Apollo programs could accomplish the Dyna-Soar's mission, McNamara canceled the X-20 on December 10, 1963. That was the switch. His simultaneous announcement of the development of a Manned Orbiting Laboratory (MOL) was the bait to allay Congressional and service resentment over the cancellation of Dyna-Soar. As things worked out, the only net gain from the Dyna-Soar was some of the experimental work done on the project that transferred to both the X-15 and Space Shuttle programs.

This shell game of program switches became part of what was known as "paralysis by analysis" within the DOD. Any program not on McNamara's priority list would be so bombarded by questions, demands for briefings, requests for alternatives, and other inquiries that the program officers would be forced to reduce activities on the program just to meet the demands for information. Then, if the programs still progressed, a cancellation was made with the offer of a new program in a similar field. It was a technique that worked well for McNamara and some of his successors, if not for the services or the taxpayers.

The Manned Orbiting Laboratory was a small space station intended to perform a reconnaissance function. In his last year in office, McNamara began to reduce funds for the MOL program, which had a predicted launch date of 1971. As time progressed, the combination of the success of unmanned satellites, funding demands of the Vietnam War, and the Apollo program proved to be too much. Ironically, it fell to an ardent supporter of the MOL, Secretary of Defense Melvin Laird, to cancel the program in June 1969—after $1.37 billion had been spent.

Some of the Air Force's early efforts in space were reactive. The demand for an antidote to a Soviet threat gleefully wielded by Khrushchev, the orbital bomb, led in 1963 to a hurry-up call for an antisatellite capability. The Space Systems Division of AFSC responded in just over a year with Program 437, using an earth-based Thor rocket positioned on a Pacific island to intercept satellites. The guidance systems could place the antisatellite missile within 5 miles of an enemy target satellite, well inside the lethal radius of the missile's nuclear warhead. The system remained operational for ten years before it was ordered deactivated.

In 1961, the Air Force also developed plans for a precursor of President Reagan's Strategic Defense Initiative—"Star Wars"—in the form of a satellite system capable of infrared homing on and destruction of enemy rockets in their initial boost phase. This ballistic missile boost intercept weapon (inevitably known as Bambi) received short shrift from McNamara as being too technically demanding for consideration. Yet it was exactly the sort of revolutionary leap forward that the technology required, and its cancellation illustrates the danger to research and development when practical applications have absolute priority over basic research. McNamara instead preferred to create what he called "technological building blocks" that could be used as the basis for a variety of programs—a space version of what he termed "commonality" in aircraft like the TFX.

Despite these setbacks vitiating announced Air Force space programs, work proceeded on a series of other defense support space programs: missile defense alarm, communications, and meteorological, navigational, and reconnaissance satellites. These highly classified programs would ultimately be supremely successful and demonstrate that space was not a mission in and of itself, but rather a medium in which to exercise the Air Force's traditional role of controlling the combat arena. As that work progressed, there was an increased call for the creation of a space doctrine and the establishment of a space organization. The call would be heeded at successively more important levels.

The first steps toward what became a separate space organization were sponsored by then Colonel Robert T. "Tom" Marsh. In a non-turf-conscious manner that was to be typical of his leadership, Marsh decided there was a requirement for a separate directorate of space within AFSC, and in 1965 he put together a briefing for General McConnell, who approved the idea. Later, as a four-star general commanding AFSC, Marsh again gave up turf by advocating the creation of a separate space command.

By 1977, General Jones, as Chief of Staff, issued a letter on "Air Force Space Policy" in which he included the development of weapon systems and the conduct of military operations in space as among the Air Force's prime responsibilities. The following year, President Carter issued Presidential Directive 37, which, given his generally anti-Pentagon attitude, lent a surprisingly strong Presidential backing to the military aspects of space.

The chill fog of the Cold War obscured the rationale behind the increasing rate of Soviet satellite launches—almost a hundred in 1981. The replacement rate was in fact dictated by the shorter lives of the Soviet satellites, but it could also be inferred that the Soviets were planning frequent replacement as would have to be done in the event of a space war. Soviet professional military journals, normally the most opaque of reading material, openly discussed the military uses of space as a given.

The intensification of Soviet efforts coincided with the increasing U.S. dependence on space systems and the perceived need to take advantage of the imminent arrival of the Space Shuttle. After 1981, with its program of rearmament and the rapid growth of satellite systems discussed below, the Reagan administration set the stage for Air Force Chief of Staff General Lew Allen's June 21, 1982, announcement of the formation of Air Force Space Command (AFSPACECOM), effective September 1, 1983.

Allen crafted AFSPACECOM so that its commander would also be CINCNORAD and CINCADC and have as his deputy the commander of AFSC. This conglomeration of acronyms meant simply that Space Command would have within its jurisdiction the air and missile defense of North America and easy access to the research and development potential of AFSC. Allen also selected a whirlwind of energy as the first SPACECMD commander, pugnacious General James V. Hartinger, a former football star and prototypical fighter pilot. Hartinger was given the mission of managing and operating all assigned space assets, including controlling operational spacecraft and managing DOD space shuttle flights. In addition, he had to centralize and coordinate the management of the blossoming series of highly classified space programs.

In an unselfish move, Secretary of the Air Force Orr and Chief of Staff General Gabriel began to advocate a unified command for space, declaring that no single military organization had authority over military space systems. The need for a clear chain of command from the National Command Authority also called for a unified command. The Army agreed, but the Navy demurred, setting up its own space command and opposing a unified command. It was to no avail, for a new unified U.S. Space Command (USSPACECOM) was established by the DOD on November 23, 1984. It was time, for the lower limits of space were becoming crowded with a galaxy of ever more sophisticated satellites.

In the decade following the formation of USSPACECOM, an intricate organization has grown up to control the interrelated tasks of defending North America, controlling the strategic fleet of missiles and bombers, and integrating the efforts of the three service space commands. The only reasonable way to do this was to endow one commander with a "triple hat." Thus, the Commander in Chief of U.S. Space Command (USCINCSPACE) and the North American Aerospace Defense Command (CINCNORAD) is also Commander of Air Force Space Command (COMAFSPC). USCINCSPACE commands the unified command for directing space control and support operations, including theater missile defense. As CINCNORAD, he is responsible for the air sovereignty of the United States and Canada. As COMAFSPC, he directs satellite control, warning, space launch, and ballistic missile operations. Only the overlap in missions and the close coordination of the several staffs makes management of such a tremendously important aggregation of tasks possible.

The U.S. Strategic Command, which controls the bombers of the Eighth Air Force, the ICBM of the Twentieth Air Force, and the Navy SLBMs, is under the direct control of the JCS and the National Command Authority, which consists of the President and the Secretary of Defense. Again, the efforts of these units are very closely coordinated with those under a single command.

All of the services had other subcomponents devoted to space, but the most advanced, best funded, and most varied were managed by the organizations that came under the umbrella of the Air Force Materiel Command. The number of current space programs managed by AFMC numbers in the hundreds, and ranges from such stalwarts as the Atlas launch vehicle program, in which refurbished Atlas E boosters lift satellites into orbit, to airborne lasers to destroy enemy vehicles in their boost phase, to determining the effects of energy from the sun on Air Force satellites. The array of programs is impressive, not least because each one has survived wire-brush scrubbings by internal Air Force teams, the DOD, and Congress.

TOWARD THE UNKNOWN

All of the American expenditure on all space programs may well have been more than repaid by a single intelligence-gathering program. It began on March 17, 1955—two and one-half years before Sputnik would set the United States upon its scientific ear—with a requirement issued for a strategic reconnaissance satellite. A program called Corona, operated by Air Force and CIA teams working in the National Reconnaissance Office, would tear open many of the secrets of the Soviet Union and China as it mapped 510 million nautical square miles of Communist territory, revealed that there was no missile gap, identified each type and counted each individual submarine, bomber, and fighter, monitored missile site activities in both countries, and provided data in depth on heretofore inaccessible subjects such as atomic weapons storage sites. The scope of this intelligence windfall was unparalleled, being orders of magnitude more important than a combination of the Ultra and Magic intelligence coups of World War II. With admittedly much greater effort, the United States could still have fought and won World War II without either Ultra or Magic. Corona won the greater victory of providing the vital information to win the Cold War while helping to avoid a nuclear conflict.

Masquerading under the code name Discoverer, a cover program operated by the Air Force, Corona was kept absolutely secret for twenty-three years after it had passed out of use. The entire story was unveiled in February

1995, when Vice President Al Gore officially lifted the security classification from the nation's first spy satellite project. The Corona program had operated between 1960 and 1972 and yielded more than 800,000 satellite images.

The CIA provided the project director, Richard Bissel, as well as the funding and the tight security planning necessary to maintain secrecy. Bissell was special assistant for planning and coordination for CIA Director Allen W. Dulles, and was already involved in the equally secret Lockheed U-2 program. Later he would be a prime mover in the Lockheed A-12/SR-71 triumphs. His deputy was the veteran Air Force test pilot Major General Osmond J. Ritland, who had flown more than 200 different aircraft, including British, German, and Japanese combat planes. Their opposite number at the prime contractor, Lockheed, was James W. Plummer, who ran a streamlined management organization patterned after Kelly Johnson's famous Skunk Works.

The heart of the Corona package was the Itek camera used for most of the 130 launches. Resolution early on was about 40 feet; this was improved over the years to less than 10 feet, so that items as small as individual automobiles could be seen and evaluated.

The program lasted from 1956 through 1972 and cost a bargain $850 million. The going was not easy. The first launch, on January 21, 1959, was designated Discoverer 0 and was a failure. The second test was a technical success, although it had been flown without a camera. The next eleven launches were failures, and the pressure on Plummer, Bissell, and Ritland to deliver was extreme. Gary Powers had been shot down in his U-2 on May 1, 1960, and all Soviet overflights were suspended, eliminating the CIA's principal reconnaissance intelligence-gathering mechanism.

Working with a swiftness unfettered by bureaucratic oversight, sometimes making significant contract changes verbally, often over the telephone, the Lockheed and Air Force teams were able to achieve success precisely in the nick of time. On August 10, 1960, Discoverer XIII lifted off for the first completely successful mission. Subsequent Discoverer flights were almost uniformly successful, and aerial recovery of the capsule by specially equipped Fairchild JC-119 and Lockheed NC-130H aircraft became, if not routine, at least predictable. The Corona system provided about 500 times more coverage than the U-2 had been able to do, and without any risk to a pilot.

Although the Corona project was a brilliant success, security prevented the proper acclaim being given to the determined leadership, which had persevered through the bleak months of failure.

There were also many scientific spin-offs from the program. The reentry data gathered from the Corona capsules had direct bearing on the Apollo spacecraft reentry design and materials. The experience was also a key factor in strengthening Lockheed's Space and Missiles Division, which went on to great success in the Polaris, Poseidon, and Trident missile programs, among others. Most important of all, in the great Cold War poker game, Corona served as the mirror in which the United States could read the Soviet Union's cards.

In terms of the involvement of genius, expenditure of resources, resolution of problems, and delivery of results, the Corona program was a paradigm for the ensuing major U.S. space programs, each of which has its own spectacular history. These programs were naturally more sophisticated and faced even greater uncertainties and difficulties than did Corona. Unfortunately for this book, the story of these problems and their resolution is for the most part still classified. The author can only describe what the systems are and what their import is.

MAKING THE UNKNOWN KNOWN

The USAF shares the responsibility for using space to advantage with dozens of other governmental and civilian agencies. The government agencies include the CIA, NASA, the National Reconnaissance Office (NRO), the National Oceanic and Atmospheric Administration (NOAA), and the National Security Agency (NSA). Civilian agencies include INTELSAT, run by the 131-member International Telecommunications Satellite Organization, and Landsat, a privately operated system for monitoring Earth's landmasses and oceans.

Space has provided the venue for a number of military functions. These are supported by a galaxy of satellite systems and their concomitant ground facilities. A brief description of the functions and some of their operating systems follows.

Navigation

The military services in general and the Air Force in particular have reaped enormous benefits from the navigational accuracy conferred by the Navstar Global Positioning System (GPS), operated by the 50th Space Wing located at Falcon Air Force Base, Colorado. A constellation of twenty-four orbiting satellites sends signals to earth to furnish military and civil users with extremely accurate three-dimensional location information, i.e., latitude, longitude, and altitude, plus velocity and time. The service is available twenty-four hours a day, providing continuous real-time information to an unlimited number of users under all weather conditions.

The GPS satellites orbit the earth every twelve hours, emitting continuous navigation signals so accurate that time can be figured to within a millionth of a second, velocity within a fraction of a mile per hour, and location to less than 30 feet. Because of military concern that a potential enemy could make use of GPS accuracy to pinpoint valuable targets like Minuteman silos, the accuracy permitted civilian users was raised to about 300 feet. Demand forced a change in this practice to "differentially corrected" GPS signals, but the military reserved the right to distort the signal for civilian use in times of emergency.

The GPS system achieved fame in the Gulf War when it was used by everything from stealth bombers to B-52s flying the longest combat missions in history to special operation forces navigating in the desert. GPS was essential in establishing precise reference points upon which inertial navigation systems could be calibrated. The demand was so great that many military personnel purchased their own small hand-held GPS units from civilian sources, and British pilots flew their Jaguar fighter-bombers with civilian hand-held versions attached with Velcro to the instrument panels. They were especially valuable during the periods of bad weather.

GPS was also effective in enhancing the accuracy of other attack equipment like the LANTIRN (low-altitude navigation and targeting infrared for night) system. F-16s integrating GPS and LANTIRN were used in the ground attack role against mobile launchers. Other F-16s used GPS for fast-forward air control work, passing back precise coordinates of targets rather than having to lob in a target-marking rocket. A great attraction of the system is that the information is continuously beamed and received passively—there are no emissions to alert the enemy and give away positions.

Use of the system is spreading rapidly, and there is a movement toward having GPS positioning become an essential part of a primary instrument landing system for commercial aircraft.

The first Navstar GPS satellite was launched on February 22, 1978. At the time of the Gulf War, sixteen satellites were available for use. There are currently twenty-four GPS satellites in service, including three spares, each with a design life of seven and one-half years. The GPS satellites are 5 feet wide and 17.5 feet long and weigh 1,860 pounds. They are deployed in a near-circular orbit at an altitude of 10,900 miles. Solar panels generate 700 watts to provide power. The Delta II expendable launch vehicle is used to launch the GPS satellites in orbit. Rockwell International provided the first two series of satellites, and Lockheed-Martin provided the third.

Missile Defense Alarm

The need to track potential incoming missiles has existed since the earliest days of Soviet ICBM success. The concern about attack from the former Soviet Union has diminished, but ballistic and cruise missile technology has proliferated, and the need to track missile firings is as great as ever.

An ideal missile defense would detect launches and destroy the missiles during their boost phase, so that the warheads would fall back on the launcher's territory. Such defenses have been rejected as impractical or too expensive in the past, but the migration of technology to Third World countries makes the concept increasingly attractive. New approaches to this tactic are being developed.

Terminal-area destruction of missiles was demonstrated by the Patriot system during the Gulf War. Initially viewed as an almost 100 percent success story, later analysis indicated that there were drawbacks in the system, of which the random fall of the intercepted missile and warhead on friendly territory was the greatest. Detection of missiles has been more successful. The Defense Support Program (DSP) was first deployed in the 1970s and has since furnished an uninterrupted early warning capability. It is designed to detect and track all ICBMs, IRBMs, space launches, and nuclear detonations, as well as small tactical missiles. The DSP system worked well tracking Scud missile launches during the Gulf War. In 1995 a new method of processing data called ALERT (attack and launch early reporting to theater) was developed. The new method provides improved warning of attack by short-range missiles against U.S. and allied forces overseas.

TRW is the primary contractor for the DSP satellite, which operates in a geosynchronous orbit at about 22,000 miles altitude. Each satellite weighs about 5,000 pounds and is 22 feet in diameter and 32.8 feet high with its solar arrays deployed. The solar arrays generate 1,485 watts of power. Sixteen of a projected total of twenty-four DSP satellites have been launched. A space-based infrared system (SBIRS) will begin to the replace the DPS system after the turn of the century.

The 21st Space Wing, located at Peterson AFB, Colorado, operates DSP satellites and reports warning information to the North American Aerospace Defense Command (NORAD) and U.S. Space Command. Both organizations have early warning centers within the fabled Cheyenne Mountain complex at Colorado Springs. Command and control of the DSP satellites is provided by the 50th Space Wing.

Communications

The first radio message from an aircraft was transmitted in 1910; since then the importance of communications has grown until it is now the most important element in the command, control, and communications arena. Without it, neither command nor control could exist. A number of satellite systems are used to facilitate military traffic for everyone from the national command authorities down to the squadron level. These include the Defense Satellite Communications System (DSCS), the Military Strategic and Tactical Relay (Milstar) system, and the Air Force Satellite Communications (AF-SATCOM) system. The Fleet Satellite Communications system is used both by the Air Force and the Navy.

The DSCS is used for high-priority communications between defense leaders and battlefield commanders and to transmit space operations and early warning data to various users.

At the present time, two Phase II and eight Phase III DSCS satellites orbit Earth at an altitude of more than 23,000 miles. Each satellite uses six super-high-frequency transponder channels to provide worldwide secure voice communications and high-rate data communications. The Phase II DSCS was built by TRW and first launched in 1971. Its cylindrical body is 9 feet in diameter and 13 feet high with its antennas deployed. Solar arrays provide 535 watts of power. The Phase III DSCS was built by Martin Marietta and first launched in 1982. The body is a near-cube 6 by 6 by 7 feet in dimension; the solar arrays unfold to a 38-foot span and generate 1,100 watts. The satellites are unusual in that some have been launched by Titan missiles and some have been placed into orbit by the Space Shuttle.

Two units provide command and control for the DSCS systems, the 3rd Space Operations Squadron at Falcon AFB and the 5th Space Operations Squadron at Onizuka Air Force Station (AFS), California.

As we shall see, the ability to change satellite positions paid dividends during the Gulf War, when a DSCS II satellite was repositioned in geosynchronous orbit above the Indian Ocean, creating excellent communications in an area where they previously had been inadequate.

The Milstar satellite communication system, with Lockheed/Martin as the prime contractor, is under development and will be the most advanced military communications system in history. It will be composed of four satellites in mid-latitude geosynchronous orbits at 22,400 miles altitude, plus a polar adjunct system. The mid-latitude satellites will weigh about 10,000 pounds and have solar panels generating 8,000 watts. The satellites work with terminals on the ground and with mission control. The first Milstar satellite was launched on February 7, 1994, by a Titan IV expendable launch vehicle.

Each Milstar satellite is essentially a switchboard in space, directing traffic from terminal to terminal anywhere on earth, and accessible by Army, Navy, or Air Force terminals. The system works through other satellites, significantly reducing the requirement for ground-controlled switching. The 4th Space Operations Squadron at Falcon AFB provides real-time platform control and communications payload management.

Meteorology

The unsung heroes of the space age satellites are those of the Defense Meteorological Satellite Program (DMSP), which for more than twenty years have been providing continuous real-time information on global weather conditions.

Two DMSP satellites are in polar orbits at all times, at about 450 miles altitude, and survey the entire earth four times a day with both visual and infrared imagery. The data is gathered by tracking stations and analyzed at military weather centers that can determine the location and severity of thunderstorms, hurricanes, and typhoons. The DMSP satellite weighs 1,750 pounds, is 11 feet, 6 inches high, almost 5 feet wide, and a little over 19 feet long. Built by Martin Marietta and launched by a Titan II vehicle, it has a solar array capable of generating 1,000 watts.

Reconnaissance and Surveillance

It is exceedingly difficult to keep a single project, such as the U-2 or the F-117A, in the "black" for an extended period of time. Yet the work of an entire government agency, the National Reconnaissance Office (NRO), was successfully concealed for many years even as it opened enemy skies to constant surveillance. The progenitor of the NRO was first formed by President Eisenhower on August 25, 1960, and was redesignated the National Reconnaissance Office in 1961. The Director of the NRO reports directly to the Secretary of Defense.

The term "reconnaissance" in NRO's title is a euphemism for its basic mission of spying from the sky. The satellite cameras do either reconnaissance, i.e., looking for specific information, or surveillance, i.e., a continual search of general areas for items of interest, as when it is tasked to determine compliance with arms treaties.

The principal mission of spying is augmented by ferret satellites monitoring radar and other electronic emissions, weather satellites, and special top-secret communication links. The constant use of data provided by the NRO satellites, circling the earth twenty-four hours per day, permits an assessment of the degree of military threat in foreign countries at all times and inhibits the use of camouflage and decoys as misinformation. The satellites also yield data useful in diplomatic negotiations. In the Bosnian conflict, for example, the NRO satellites were used to take photos of the notorious concentration camps and mass burial grounds.

The NRO acts essentially as a middleman, receiving instructions as to areas of interest by a committee of the Director of Central Intelligence. NRO does not make its own analysis of its data, leaving this to the using agency. The USAF has used this information for decades to plan and execute both strategic and tactical missions.

The success of the Corona series of satellites already referred to only hints at the extent of surveillance done since 1972. NRO surveillance, besides removing the missile gap myth, pinpointed secret Soviet activities from new ICBMs to the building of a phased-array radar that violated the ABM (antiballistic missile) treaty. NRO satellites were able to identify Chinese CSS-2 IRBMs being deployed in the Saudi Arabian desert, a clear indication of Beijing's expanding interest in arms exportation.

Each advance in computer technology enhances the capabilities of the satellites, which have grown steadily swifter in their processing and transmission of data so that today that they can be extended to nonmilitary uses, including monitoring the environment.

CONVERGENCE

The final decades of the twentieth century would see disparate trends within the USAF converge, against the odds, into a finely honed war-winning mechanism. One trend, maintained resolutely since its invocation by Hap Arnold, was the inexorable demand for improved technology. A second trend, reinforcing the first, was the spread of a culture of enlightened management that obtained the very best results from both the officer and enlisted forces. The third, opposing, trend was the tremendous drawdown after the heady first four years of the Reagan administration, when funds were virtually unlimited. But this drawdown was unlike the catastrophic demobilization after World War II. The severe reduction of almost 40 percent in numbers of aircraft and personnel was carefully managed, so that the resulting "base force" remained extremely capable.

Amid these merging, if partially opposing, trends, the USAF conducted successful operations in smaller emergencies such as Libya, Grenada, Panama, and Bosnia. In addition, it fought a successful war on a much larger scale in the Persian Gulf. The USAF's demonstration of unequaled military prowess in that conflict was demoralizing to the Soviet Union and contributed in large part to its breakup, and to the successful conclusion of the long and bitter Cold War. In the next chapter, these events will be covered to lay the foundation for a look at the Air Force of the twenty-first century.

9

≋

VICTORY: SPRINGBOARD TO THE FUTURE

*T*he United States Air Force entered the last decade of the twentieth century with confidence. For most of its existence, it had been fortunate to have charismatic leaders who were also hardheaded managers able to anticipate changing world conditions. These leaders assessed the genuine and truly awesome threat of the Soviet Union's nuclear striking power and contained it. In doing so, they simultaneously contained adventures by the Communist ground forces.

Mistakes were made in the process. The numbers of bombers, missiles, and warheads fielded over the years have been called excessive—yet they had the desired effect, and a lesser number might not have. It must be remembered that the Air Force was forced to operate under the most difficult policy conceivable, one that was without historic precedent. Its forces had to be able to accept a massive nuclear first strike from the enemy and *then* go on to win the subsequent conflict decisively. Thus, a large quantity of Air Force delivery vehicles and weapons was necessary to ensure that a war-winning force survived. It happened that this was a message the Soviet leaders could understand, one of the few "signals" sent by the United States that was properly interpreted. The massive armament investment also contributed to the breakdown of the Soviet economy as its leadership attempted—in vain—to meet all threats.

The United States probably did invest too much in its air defense efforts over the period by imputing more striking power to Soviet long-range aviation than it possessed. This was the legacy of World War II, when the Battle of Britain and the Eighth Air Force's hard fight over Germany demonstrated the necessity of an extensive air defense system. However, U.S. expenditures on air defense, massive as they were, never approached those of the Soviet Union in either absolute or relative terms.

An argument was made at the time, and could also be made today, that the money could have been better spent. The Air Force often did not have adequate conventional forces, and for the entire period of its existence has been near the breaking point in terms of required air transport capacity. Yet on balance, the task of defending the United States was fulfilled brilliantly, especially if one compares it to the corresponding efforts made by the leaders of Soviet Union, whose mistakes contributed significantly to the ultimate demise of their system.

The success of USAF planning efforts also must be considered in the light of the wildly gyrating budget. The Air Force's budget in 1980 was about $39 billion. It began rising in 1981 to a total of $46 billion and peaked in 1985 at $99.4 billion.

The subsequent fall was significant, the budget slumping to $71.2 billion in 1996.

All the previous figures were in current dollars. In constant Fiscal Year (FY) 1997 dollars, the decline was from an equivalent of $117 billion to $74.5 billion over the decade, or about 37 percent. (Billion-dollar figures are mind-boggling to the average person. It might be of interest to note that the Department of Defense budget as a percentage of the gross domestic product has declined from 6.1 percent in 1986 to 3.8 percent in 1996 and is projected to decline to 2.8 percent by 2002. As the USAF's share of the defense budget is roughly 30 percent, it follows that in 1996, a little over 1 percent of GDP was devoted to the Air Force, and by 2002, this will decline to less than 1 percent. In contrast, entitlements have grown from 10.9 percent of the GDP in 1986 to 12.0 percent in 1996 and will increase to 13.2 percent by 2002.)

Abstract terms like constant dollars and gross domestic product sometimes obscure rather than illuminate the effect of budget reductions, which are felt in the field by the realities of unavailable spare parts, reduced flying time, and shortage, of personnel. In 1987 the Air Force had 7,245 active-duty aircraft; by 1996, this number had been reduced 35 percent to 4,710—about the same number with which the Luftwaffe began World War II. Active-duty personnel have dropped at about the same rate, from 607,000 in 1987 to 388,200 in 1996. Air National Guard (ANG) and Air Force Reserve (AFR) totals have declined during the same period from 263,000 to 181,000. However, ANG and AFR integration into "Total Force" operations has significantly increased Air Force capability over the same time period.

Although the threat of attack from the former Soviet Union has all but disappeared the number of missions assigned to the Air Force has increased—from preparation for smaller conflicts to peace-keeping to nation-building to narcotics control. No one has yet grappled with the frightening notion the states of the former Soviet Union and the Republic of China selling nuclear weapons to any country, association, or individual with the hard cash to buy them. Opinions from think tanks that no rogue nation would have the capability to use an intercontinental missile against a U.S. city until about 2010 are not reassuring. If that estimate is wrong, the United States might lose New York City, Washington, or Los Angeles in an instant.

The declining Air Force budgets have been further strained by the combination of the rising costs of a volunteer force and the upward spiral in the price of weaponry. The leaders coped by creating a smaller, leaner, modernized striking force backed by advanced technology and first-rate personnel. In addition, clear representations have been made to the Department of Defense, Congress, and the Executive Office on just how far air power's shortened blanket will stretch in terms of conducting a certain number of wars, large and small.

The Air Force was able to use the welcome but temporary aberration of greatly increased budgets in the early 1980s to increase force readiness through greater expenditures on the often neglected operation and maintenance funds, creating forward operating bases and increasing training. Then when the reductions appeared inevitable, Generals Gabriel and Welch planned the phased drawdown that traded manpower and older equipment for smaller, more capable forces.

Through all the budget gyrations, the import of Hap Arnold's emphasis on research and development had done far more than create equipment beyond even his imagination. It had created a culture that looked to technology not for a few magic bullets aimed at specific threats, but instead as a renewable source of power to harness for the entire spectrum of offensive and defensive needs. This culture would draw on the lessons learned in Vietnam to create new doctrine. To use the new equipment and the new doctrine effectively, the Air Force, a champion on the comeback trail from Vietnam, would require several tune-up fights before reclaiming its title before the world in the Persian Gulf War.

EVERYTHING COMES TOGETHER

The 1990s saw the convergence of the major elements previously highlighted. A broad research and development program provided Air Force leaders with a portfolio of modern weapons. This would have been far less useful had it not been for the remarkable change in the tenor of Air Force leadership from centralized and authoritarian to decentralized and participative. This change on the one hand encouraged the growth of a superb corps of noncommissioned officers and enlisted personnel who could fulfill the new responsibilities required by the advanced technology, and on the other created within the officer corps a sense of identity and purpose that permitted the full exploitation of the new technology.

A striking example of this phenomenon of total managerial revolution can be found in a publication that came from the very top, the white paper

Global Reach—Global Power, issued in June 1990 by the very effective Secretary of the Air Force Donald R. Rice. In it, Rice, a former president of the RAND Corporation, asserted in measured terms that land-based air power now projected the national image of power and prestige that sea power had done in times past. Rice's paper did not denigrate the Navy or the Army, but instead spoke of the increased requirement for joint operations. But his message was unmistakable. Air power was now endowed with an unprecedented technical capability, one orders of magnitude greater than sea power at its most effective.

Rice pointed out that modern technology provided even cargo carriers with jet-age speed; air refueling enabled fighters, bombers, and cargo planes to fly nonstop to theaters thousands of miles away. The combination of speed and range gave any mixture of these forces an unique flexibility. New space-based navigation and communication equipment enabled Air Force units to use the new precision-guided munitions with an unprecedented accuracy so that the long-touted "surgical strike" became feasible. The combination of these characteristics gave an incredible lethality to air power without the brutal overkill of a nuclear weapon. *Global Reach—Global Power* did not eschew nuclear power—the umbrella of deterrence fashioned by Curtis LeMay was still required. But it did clearly state that air power could now reach anywhere in the world within hours to intervene decisively in any emergency. In essence, Rice maintained that the Air Force could now project dominating power to any point on the globe in *hours,* rather than in the days, weeks, or months that sea power still required. In most emergencies, time and strength are equally critical; x amount of strength in the first hours of a crisis can be worth 10x five days later.

Global Reach—Global Power was a cool, dispassionate representation of contemporary reality. The Air Force, still maintaining the always necessary nuclear shield, already possessed the capacity to execute any other mission that national policy demanded.

In the military services as in business, it is not enough to have new ideas; those ideas must also be adopted and put into use. The change in leadership style that would eventually permit placing the ideas of Rice and his colleagues into practice was also reflected in the way emergencies were met during the 1980s. Even as the Air Force was testing procedures and trying to acclimate to the changing methods of warfare required by the new technologies it had developed, a series of crises had to be mastered.

FIRST TESTS OF THE NEW AIR FORCE

The unfortunately named Operation Urgent Fury, the much-mocked invasion of Grenada on October 25, 1983, has generated such derision through the years that it has become a stock ingredient for stand-up comics. Often cited as a massive overkill, the steroid sledgehammer descending upon a malnourished fly, the intervention was more than justified to protect American lives. To the airmen participating, the antiaircraft fire was real and deadly: almost a dozen helicopters were shot down, and considerable damage was done to the USAF transports that brought in troops and cargo. The greatest outcome of the operation for the Air Force was the realization that ten years after Vietnam, command and control functions still had kinks that needed to be worked out.

The kinks showed up again in a more complex endeavor, the retaliatory strike against terrorists nurtured by the Libyan government. It was the most intense combat operation by the Air Force since 1972. Stephen Decatur had asserted newly found American strength in his attack on Tripoli in 1804; the United States Air Force would reassert that strength in Tripoli in 1986 with Operation El Dorado Canyon.

Disappointing political circumstances dictated that the mission be executed with old equipment, aging General Dynamics F-111F Aardvarks stationed in Great Britain. As had happened so often in the past, the superb skills of the aircrews managed to overcome planning deficiencies and daunting defenses. With sheer courage and superb flying skills, a handful of crews were able to bring off a marginal military success that had excellent political consequences.

STRIKE AGAINST QADDAFI

The persistent terrorist campaign by radical Muslim factions had reached a new height with simultaneous attacks on airports in Vienna and Rome on December 27, 1985. There was an almost immediate flurry of speculation in the media that the United States intended to respond with a chastening military attack on Libya. The inflammatory oratory of dictator Colonel Muammar Qaddafi and the verified existence of terrorist training camps made Libya a reasonable target, even though other nations were almost certainly involved. The situation was brought to a boil by terrorist attacks on a Berlin dance hall and a TWA airliner in April 1986, both of which took American lives.

Planning for a retaliatory raid had begun in January. The assignment to strike selected targets in the Tripoli area on the night of April 14–15, 1986, was given to the 48th Tactical Fighter Wing at Lakenheath, England, which was equipped with General Dynamics F-111 Aardvarks. Six Navy McDonnell Douglas F/A-18 Hornets, six Vought A-7E Corsair IIs, and fourteen Grumman A-6E Intruders from the carriers *America* and *Coral Sea* were to support the USAF mission, while other naval forces engaged in attacks on separate targets in eastern Libya. Most of the crew members going on the mission had never been in combat.

Secretary of the Navy John Lehman (who would have preferred to conduct the operation solely with naval assets) later wrote that only three targets behind the entire iron curtain had more sophisticated air defenses than those of Libya. More than 3,000 Soviet technicians directed the operation of the integrated defense system, which included 500 aircraft, a massive number of surface-to-air missiles, antiaircraft guns, and radar.

It is still galling to record that after the contributions of the United States to Western Europe (combat in World Wars I and II, the Marshall Plan, the containment of the Soviet Union, and the stiffening of NATO, to cite just a few), some of America's longtime allies capitulated to the fear of terrorism. France refused overflight permission (even as it "talked tough" to Qaddafi), while Spain, Italy, and Greece refused the use of their bases. In consequence, the mission had to follow a meandering over-water route around the coastlines of France and Spain. To attack the hazardous target, the crews were forced to spend fourteen hours flying 6,300 miles and refueling in flight eight times. Normal F-111F missions ran two to four hours. The cockpit of the F-111 is fairly commodious, but does not permit a short walk to stretch the legs.

The attack force was followed by many civil and military radars throughout its flight, but only the Italian radar operators went so far as to report the F-111s' passage, alerting counterparts in Malta. The Maltese government promptly warned Libya, removing any remaining vestige of surprise.

The F-111s, most fifteen years old, were tasked with the longest fighter combat mission ever flown in terms of time and distance. Recognizing that the mission duration would put a severe strain on engines and the aging electronic systems, twenty-four F-111s were launched, beginning at 17:36 Zulu (Greenwich Mean Time) on April 14. The aircraft were assessed en route, and the eighteen considered in the best condition were assigned to the attack. The F-111Fs were provided electronic countermeasures support by three of the superb EF-111A Ravens (aka "Spark Vark"), the most effective and sophisticated aircraft of its type.

The unified force hit Libya simultaneously early in the morning of the 15th in a thirteen-minute attack that destroyed five selected targets, including missile sites airfields and other installations. The heavy defensive fire lit up the Libyan sky, a preview of Baghdad a few months later. Two crew members were killed when one F-111 (70-2389) was lost for reasons unknown.

The attack came perilously close to being a failure. Rigorous rules of engagement, designed to minimize civilian casualties, ended up preventing six aircraft from even hitting their targets. Eight other F-111s did not strike their targets because of equipment difficulties. Fortunately, four F-111s hit the targets as planned, giving a preview of the future by using their AN/AVQ-26 Pave Tack infrared and laser targeting system to destroy a line of Ilyushin Il-76 transports, valuable four-engine aircraft corresponding to the Lockheed C-141. Some bombs struck within 50 feet of Qaddafi's residence, including the tent he used as Arab-style living quarters. Being on the receiving, rather than the giving, end of bombs severely shook the Colonel's composure.

If the military results had not been all that was desired, the political fallout proved to be exceptionally worthwhile. Even as the European media discounted the efficacy of the raid, member nations of the European Economic Community began taking much more forceful political and economic action against Libya. The Soviet Union confined itself to the usual propaganda attacks, but did nothing, and even Arab nations gave only pro forma expressions of support. Most important, not only did Libyan terrorist activity go into an immediate decline, that of Syria and Iraq fell off as well. The attack had effectively isolated Qaddafi, which was more than had been hoped for by the mission planners.

OPERATION JUST CAUSE

The changing nature of the world was reflected in the deployment of USAF assets to combat the drug traffic originating in Central and South America. Panama, crucial to U.S. defense needs since the opening of the canal, had become a center for drug traffic under the cruel dictatorship of General Manuel Noriega, a prototypical Central American strongman who had seized power from the legitimate government. A long series of incidents, including the assassination of a U.S.. Marine lieutenant, and the abduction and beating of a Navy lieutenant and his wife prompted President George Bush to order the armed services to intervene so that Noriega—once a protégé of the United States—could be removed from power.

Highly classified preparations for Operation Just Cause, the 1990 invasion of Panama, had been going on for some time. In many ways, the operation would be a test of concepts emerging from the Goldwater-Nichols bill of 1986, which gave theater commanders enhanced control over the forces of all services. Both the planning and the execution would be important dress rehearsals for the team that would just over a year later conduct the Persian Gulf War. Bush had selected a former Congressman, Richard Cheney, to be his Secretary of Defense and teamed him with General Colin Powell, the first black Chairman of the Joint Chiefs of Staff. The Air Force Chief of Staff, General Welch, had anticipated the downsizing of the Air Force and crafted its modernization; now he would see how his efforts would pay off.

As the leaders of Operation Just Cause started their work together, an interesting interpersonal drama began that was to have sudden, explosive impact a year later during Operation Desert Shield, the defensive buildup in Saudi Arabia. A testy Secretary of Defense Cheney, new to his office, was apparently determined to let everyone know who was running the DOD. At his first press conference as Secretary of Defense, Cheney gave General Welch a stern public scolding—before having discussed the matter with him—for his discussions with various Congressmen on the mix of Midgetman (a small, single-warhead ICBM) and MX missiles. The attack was both unprecedented and unwarranted, for Welch had a strong reputation for being loyal and cooperative and had advised DOD officials of his perfectly routine conversations on the Hill. No egotist and a good soldier, Welch retained his composure over the incident, realizing that any protest would be harmful to Air Force interests. Why Cheney acted in such a manner was a subject of debate, but the incident was widely interpreted as a signal of his determination to be regarded as the number one person in DOD. Some even thought that he intended it as a touch of the lash, a calculated insult to the military. Of this, more later.

The real villain in Panama, Noriega, was no stranger to hubris or narcotics. He proclaimed that Panama "is declared to be in a state of war" with the United States on December 15, 1989, and applauded the murderous assaults on U.S. military personnel stationed in the Canal Zone.

Operational secrecy was lost, thanks to a cable television broadcast reporting that Lockheed C-141s destined for Panama were taking off from Pope Air Force Base with the 82d Airborne Division. Nonetheless, the USAF struck just after midnight on December 20, 1989, leading off with a brand-new weapon. Six Lockheed F-117A Nighthawks flew from their secret home base at Tonopah, Nevada, to Panama and back, refueling in flight six times.

It was not recognized at the time, but their assault heralded an entirely new era in warfare, that of stealth aircraft. Two of the F-117s dropped their 2,000-pound bombs at Rio Hato, deliberately striking a large open field next to the barracks of the Panamanian Defense Forces (PDF). The Nighthawks' mission was not to kill Panamanian soldiers, but instead to "stun, disorient, and confuse" them.

(This nicety of judgment was both a forecast of future policy and a reflection of public opinion, which wants wars won with minimal damage to personnel on either side.) Major Gregory Feest of the 37th Tactical Fighter Wing dropped the first bomb—as he would just one year later over Baghdad.

In the first wave of the attack, the Military Airlift Command flew 111 missions, seventy-seven of them by C-141s, twenty-two by C-130s, and eleven by C-5s. A second wave of thirteen C-5s and forty-four C-141s brought reinforcements. The MAC aircraft were refueled by seventeen KC-135As and six KC-10As from SAC. Ten regular Air Force wings participated, as did thirteen Air National Guard and four Air Force Reserve units—the Total Force in action. Seven participating 1st Special Operations Wing Lockheed AC-130H Spectre gunships used their 105mm howitzers and 40mm cannon with devastating effect on PDF vehicles.

Despite the 40 percent drawdown in strength, the modernization program of General Gabriel and Welch had borne fruit, for the F-117As worked with other highly specialized Special Operations unit aircraft to achieve a shock effect. Operation Just Cause used five Sikorsky MH-53J Pave Low helicopters, equipped with nose-mounted FLIR (forward-looking infrared), terrain-following and terrain-avoidance radar, and sophisticated electronic countermeasures equipment. Four Sikorsky MH-60 Pave Hawk helicopters, designed for bringing in or taking out personnel on a clandestine basis, and equipped like the Pave Low aircraft, were also employed, backed up by three Combat Talon I Lockheed MC-130Es. The latter are complex, Rambo-style aircraft, designed to battle their way in and out to conduct in-flight refueling of Special Operations helicopters at night or in adverse weather conditions. Well equipped with electronic countermeasures, the MC-130Es can deliver cargo or the biggest conventional weapon in the U.S. arsenal, the 15,000-pound BLU-82 propane bomb. More conventional HC-130 tankers and AC-130A gunships were also used.

The object of the endeavor, Manuel Noriega, initially gave the invading force the slip by the time-honored but totally unexpected expedient of gaining sanctuary. There was no little irony in Noriega's seeking asylum in the Vatican's diplomatic mission in Panama City, given that Noriega's perhaps limited religious beliefs ran more to the witchcraft of Brazilian Santeria. Noriega surrendered on January 3, 1990, and was flown to Florida in a MC-130E to be arraigned.

With Operation Just Cause, the USAF and its sister services had moved a long way toward a unified conventional war-fighting capability. At the same time, they found a new problem related to modern warfare. NBC had asked permission to land one aircraft at Howard Air Force Base.

The Air Force agreed, anticipating that a Learjet or similar executive aircraft would arrive with half a dozen newspeople. Instead, a chartered Lockheed L-1011 landed, carrying hundreds of media representatives of all sorts, all of whom wanted instant gratification in the form of inside stories. If the Nighthawks were the precursors of the air war in Baghdad, then surely NBC's L-1011 was the precursor of the news carnival in the Persian Gulf.

THE CALM BEFORE THE STORM

Almost surreal political events punctuated the last months of 1989 and the first months of 1990 as the fearsome Soviet Union suddenly began to crumple. Headlines almost weekly depicted some new movement of the Eastern bloc towards democracy, capitalism, and freedom. Hungary declared itself a free republic in October 1989. On November 9, the Berlin Wall was opened and hundreds of thousands of East Germans crossed to the West. On December 1, Presidents George Bush and Mikhail Gorbachev met on stormy seas off Malta to discuss arms limitations and the virtual end of the Cold War. The odious Romanian President Nicolae Ceausescu and his wife were killed on Christmas Day, and a reform government of sorts was established. In valiant Czechoslovakia, where Moscow's domination had been fiercely resented and resisted through the years, Communist leadership was replaced on December 29. The playwright and opposition leader Václav Havel was elected president. Lithuiania declared its independence on March

11, even as the two Germanys began the process of reunification, which ultimately took place at midnight on October 2, 1990.

The USAF continued to hone its new capabilities as it reassigned resources to accommodate these welcome international developments. The Air Force Special Operations Command (AFSOC) came into being on May 22, 1990, with a proud history reaching back through predecessor organizations to clandestine operations in World War II in both Europe and Asia and to full-scale participation in Operation Just Cause. SAC began turning its FB-111s over to TAC, where they were redesignated F-111Gs. General Michael J. Dugan crowned a magnificent Air Force career when he became Chief of Staff on July 1. On July 12, the last of the fifty-nine Lockheed F-117As was delivered. By July 24, world conditions were deemed to have eased to such an extent that the Strategic Air Command ended its "Looking Glass" operations after more than twenty-nine years of continuous airborne alert. More than 275,000 hours had been flown without an accident, and best of all, without any requirement for action, for Looking Glass was the post-attack command and control system (PACCS) designed to take effect if the SAC command post at Offutt Air Force Base, Nebraska, was destroyed in a nuclear attack. Boeing EC-135s conducted the mission, while Boeing E-4s (modified 747s) acted as national emergency airborne command post (NECAP) to provide an airborne link between the National Command Authority and the U.S. military forces. The quiet cessation of this mission seemed to speak volumes for the prospects for peace.

Things changed abruptly when Iraq invaded Kuwait and menaced Saudi Arabia.

OPERATION DESERT SHIELD

Many books have been written about the Persian Gulf War, which proved to be in all respects the perfect arena in which the lean, modernized, highly technological Air Force could demonstrate true Global Reach and Global Power.

Air Force and DOD leaders had made the possibility of war in the Persian Gulf the subject of many exercises. Most of these were aimed at a potential drive by the Soviet Union through Iran to secure Persian Gulf oil, but the possibility of other nations intervening was also considered. As the Soviet threat declined, the new Chairman of the Joint Chiefs of Staff, General Colin Powell, encouraged planning against a possible attack by Iraq on Saudi Arabia, via Kuwait. (When war came, Powell would be very hesitant to conduct operations and actively sought a solution by sanctions or other means that did not involve open warfare.)

The continuing American desire to be able to respond to "limited" emergencies such as an attack on Saudi Arabia had a long history reaching back to 1962, when Strike Command was formed at MacDill Air Force Base, in response to President Kennedy's desire to have more conventional capability. The organization matured over time into the U.S. Readiness Command in 1972, and in 1980 into the Rapid Deployment Joint Task Force. In 1983, U.S. Central Command (CENTCOM) was formed, with the responsibility for the Middle East, Southeast Asia, and Northeast Africa.

CENTCOM was essentially a planning agency with no forces and a staff of about 700 from all four services. In the event of an emergency, the services would be tasked for forces, as required. A man whose father was better known to the American public, General H. Norman Schwarzkopf, was Commander in Chief of Central Command (CINCCENT). (His father had hosted the popular radio show *Gangbusters*.) Lieutenant General Charles A. Horner commanded U.S. Central Command Air Forces (CENTAF). He also commanded the Tactical Air Command's Ninth Air Force at Shaw Air Force Base, South Carolina.

CENTCOM planners had developed Operations Plan 1002-90, which called for a massive deployment of force to Saudi Arabia. In anticipation of this and other requirements, the USAF had prepositioned more than $1 billion of war supplies, from fuel to bombs, in Oman, Diego Garcia, Guam, and on ships in the Indian Ocean. Saudi Arabia had cooperated in regal fashion, building magnificent airfields and other installations for use in an emergency.

As tensions increased, CENTCOM ran the exercise Ivory Justice, in which U.S. tankers would refuel fighters from the United Arab Emirates—a bit of airborne gunboat diplomacy that Iraq's dictator, Saddam Hussein, duly noted but discounted. The Iraqi leader evidently assumed that the United States was still locked in its Vietnam syndrome and would not go to war. He was confident that if it did, the U.S. public could not endure the thousands of casualties that his battle-tested army would inflict upon American forces. In some respects, Hussein had adopted the tactics of Adolf Hitler, who was willing to commit his forces to defensive battles in which the enemy possessed decisive air superiority, counting on his tough troops to hang on and exact a high toll of casualties from the enemy in the process. And despite his oft-demonstrated military incompetence, Hussein must have at least realized that he would not have air superiority. He apparently believed that if the Americans indeed decided to fight, they would do so as they had done in Vietnam. He expected his tough, experienced land armies would inflict enough casualties that the American public would rebel. He was explicit in this in a conversation with the American ambassador, April Glaspie, in which he commented that the United States was a society that "could not accept ten thousand dead in one battle." He knew that *he* could bear his army's casualties without a qualm from his underground bunkers.

IRAQI IRE

When Iraq concluded its debilitating eight-year war against Iran in August 1988, it had expended more than $40 billion and 100,000 lives. One might have thought it would have welcomed a period of peace. Instead, Hussein intended to recoup his country's fortune by the same means by which he had lost it: war. On June 17, 1990, he threatened neighboring Kuwait and the United Arab Emirates, restating his past demands that their oil production be reduced (to raise oil prices) and that they not only forgive Iraq's war debt, but compensate it for the cost of the war against Iran. He also included some Texas-style accusations that the Kuwaitis had stolen $2.4 billion worth of oil by slant drilling and demanded compensation. On June 27, the Organization of Petroleum Exporting Countries (OPEC) agreed to raise the price of oil to $27 a barrel. By June 30, the Kuwaitis had agreed to reduce their oil production, and Hussein assured the leaders of other Arab states that he did not intend to invade Kuwait. Yet Hussein's ultimate objective was obvious; if he invaded Kuwait and then Saudi Arabia, Iraq would control more than 50 percent of the world's supply of crude oil.

At 0100 local time on August 2, 1990, experienced Iraqi units swarmed across the Kuwait border and Iraqi helicopters attacked Kuwait City. The Iraqi Air Force had about 1,000 aircraft; its 550 combat aircraft included MiG-29s, one of the finest fighters in the world. It had opened its war on Iran in the Israeli style with a strike on airfields, but was dilatory in Kuwait, not going into action until 0500 A.M. Several Iraqi helicopters fell to the pitifully few Kuwaiti Mirage interceptors available. It was a harbinger of things to come: the Iraqi Air Force was not spoiling for a fight.

U.S. REACTION

Of all the potential trouble spots in the world, none was more directly a matter of national interest than the oil fields of the Middle East. President Bush was determined to fight rather than relinquish U.S. interests there. The question was how to do it quickly and effectively. With Secretary Cheney and General Powell, he listened to a briefing from Generals Schwarzkopf and Horner on August 4, which detailed a plan based on previous planning exercises and which would become Desert Shield. Horner intended to pack Saudi Arabia with sufficient air power to deter Hussein, while Schwarzkopf followed up with 250,000 troops. The air power reinforcement could begin immediately upon approval and reach the minimum necessary to give Hussein pause within a week, but it would take at least three months to bring in a quarter million troops. Bush agreed to the plan and sent the four men to Saudi Arabia to meet with King Abdul Aziz ibn Fahd in Riyadh.

The king was in a desperate position. He risked alienating the Arab world by allowing American military men—and worse, American military women—

into his country. But he risked his country if he did not, for Hussein already had more than ten divisions in Kuwait, some 200,000 troops, and was massing them on the Saudi border. King Fahd gave approval on August 6 for American aid. Horner remained in Riyadh, bringing in Brigadier General Buster C. Glosson to be director of campaign plans.

At 0900 Greenwich Mean Time, August 8, 1990, a Lockheed C-141B flown by an Air Force Reserve crew from the 459th Military Airlift Wing, Andrews Air Force Base, Maryland, landed, carrying airlift control elements (ALCE). It was followed within a few hours by forty-eight McDonnell Douglas F-15C and D aircraft from the 1st TFW from Langley Air Force Base, Virginia. The great World War II ace David Schilling, the pioneer of transoceanic flights by fighters, must have been looking down with approval on the longest operational fighter deployment in history. The Eagles were serviced six or seven times by tankers on the flight, which took from fourteen to seventeen hours, depending upon the wind. No major mechanical failures were reported after landing, and a little more than a day later the crews were standing combat alert.

The forty-eight Eagles and the competent but small Royal Saudi Arabian Air Force were all that stood between Saddam Hussein and the conquest of Saudi Arabia. Iraqi tanks could cover the 200-mile distance from the Kuwait border to Dhahran in less than a day. At that moment in time, Saddam Hussein still possessed the sixth-largest air force and the fourth-largest army in the world. His forces included 5,530 main battle tanks, 7,500 armored vehicles, 3,500 pieces of artillery, and 1,800 surface-to-surface missiles. The Iraqi air defense was formidable, with as many as 17,000 surface-to-air missiles and about 10,000 antiaircraft guns linked with high-tech equipment. It was indeed a threat to be reckoned with.

OPERATIONAL PLANNING

General Schwarzkopf had called the Air Force Chief of Staff, General Dugan, and requested a plan he could implement if the President wanted "to take some intiative" in December. Thus even while talks were being conducted with King Fahd, operational planning was underway at the Pentagon. There the Directorate of Plans' "Checkmate" team (so called for the war gaming facility created by General David Jones when he was Chief of Staff) initiated planning the air war against Iraq. The group began a very satisfying around-the-clock effort that produced a plan called "Instant Thunder," the name being an implicit repudiation of the failed policy of graduated response that characterized Operation Rolling Thunder in Vietnam. Instant Thunder called for a massive strike at the crucial Iraqi areas—their "centers of gravity"—such as command and control, communications, oil production and distribution, the Iraqi Air Force, Scud missiles and their launchers, and the nuclear, chemical, and biological warfare plants. Every planning effort was made to avoid civilian casualties; when targets were located within highly populated areas, care was taken to assign precision-guided munitions for their destruction.

In brief, the aim of the air campaign was to expel the Iraqi field army from Kuwait. Conceptually, the first task was to prevent any Iraqi disruption of allied air operations. The second was to destroy the Iraqi offensive air threat. Then the target, the Iraqi field army, was to be isolated and reduced by attrition. Finally, the air forces would support the allied ground-force operations.

The U.S. military operation in Saudi Arabia was given the official name Desert Shield, implying the intent to defend Saudi Arabia from harm. The Checkmate unit's plan was passed swiftly up the chain of command, receiving approval from Chief of Staff General Dugan and then from General Schwarzkopf.

Horner was not impressed by the plan, feeling that it lacked the almost infinite number of details that would be required for the massive air attack contemplated. He tasked General Glosson to create an operational plan to include many more targets to be attacked over a much longer period of time. Horner considered that plan to be too optimistic as well, in that projected a collapse of Saddam Hussein's regime after a relatively brief air campaign.

AN EXPLOSION DURING THE BUILDUP

Forces poured into Saudi Arabia at an amazing rate. By September 11, the USAF had 398 fighters in place; by January 17, when Desert Storm started, there were 652. By that date there was an "aluminum bridge" of C-5s and C-141s, which were landing every seven minutes at Dhahran. They, and for the first time in history Civil Reserve Air Fleet (CRAF) aircraft, had flown in more than 125,000 personnel and almost 400 tons of cargo. The CRAF drew on sixteen civilian air lines to provide eighteen long-range passenger aircraft and twenty-one cargo aircraft, with their crews. The military airlift to the Persian Gulf would eclipse all previous airlifts by any standard of measure, reaching the rate of 17 million ton-miles per day, exactly ten times the peak rate of the Berlin Airlift. The total tonnage of the Berlin Airlift was exceeded in the first twenty-two days.

An unheralded but revolutionary change in warfare occurred when the Air Force Space Command positioned satellites of the Defense Satellite Communications System to establish communication links for Desert Shield. With this and the Navstar Global Positioning System, space now cloaked the battlefield with an enveloping power that transcended Iraqi understanding.

There was bathos in Saddam Hussein's response. To this massive display of air and space power, he turned his army to doing what it did best: building field fortifications in the desert sands. Massive defensive positions were constructed along Kuwait's border, even as Kuwait was formally annexed as another province of Iraq. If instead Hussein had flung his army across the border during the first week in August, he could easily have overrun Saudi Arabia and made the response of the United States and the coalition it was forming immensely more difficult. It would not have changed the ultimate outcome, but the war would have been protracted, perhaps going on for years, and infinitely more costly, for he certainly would have destroyed the Saudi Arabian oil fields as he did those of Kuwait.

Fortunately, Hussein hesitated. In the next forty-five days, another 750 American aircraft arrived in Saudi Arabia, even as the ground forces began to build up. Desert Shield, the protection of Saudi Arabia from Hussein, was well underway.

THE BLOWUP

On September 16, 1990, the *Washington Post* printed a headline article quoting Air Force Chief of Staff General Dugan: "The Joint Chiefs of Staff have concluded that U.S. military air power—including a massive bombing campaign against Baghdad that specifically targets Iraqi President Saddam Hussein—is the only effective option to force Iraqi forces from Kuwait if war erupts, according to Air Force Chief of Staff Gen. Michael J. Dugan."

The article went on at great length as Dugan commented on potential targets, and the efficient, decisive results he expected from American air power. He had been quoted correctly, and in the presence of other reporters from the *Los Angeles Times and Aviation Week and Space Technology*, but the inferences drawn from the quotes were often incorrect.

The remarks infuriated Colin Powell and Richard Cheney, who interpreted them as putting too much emphasis on the Air Force and not being in the spirit of joint operations that so characterized Desert Shield. It was unfortunate, for Dugan not only believed in working with the other services, he had directed the Air Force planners to make sure that all planning was done in total cooperation with the Army, Navy, and Marines. Ironically, it was the very ease of manner, articulate presentation, and friendly, outgoing attitude that had carried him to the pinnacle of his profession that now tripped him up. He spoke about Air Force doctrine and what he thought about air power, the reporters were knowledgeable and understood him, but out of the context of his sincere appreciation for joint operations, his words were subject to harsh interpretation.

After having cleared the matter with President Bush, Secretary Cheney summoned General Dugan to his office on the morning of September 17 and demanded his resignation. Dugan understood that protest would hurt the Air Force and accepted the dismissal stoically, a good soldier to the end. It was a bitterly disappointing moment, for Dugan loved the Air Force and had labored to bring it to the peak of proficiency that he knew it now possessed. Then at the moment of truth in the Persian Gulf, he was no longer a player. In a press conference that afternoon with Dugan's written resig-nation in his hands, Cheney ticked off his reasons for the "firing," including "lack of judgment" and "demeaning the contributions of other services."

The Air Force was badly shaken by the popular Dugan's dismissal, com-ing as it did after the rough handling Cheney had given Welch the previous year. Dugan's discharge also coincided with increasing speculation on the potential value of air power in Iraq, especially since Hussein was assiduously digging in his armor and dispersing his aircraft in shelters hardened to sustain a nuclear blast. The whole unfortunate affair was given a poignant grace note by Dugan's farewell letter to the service he loved.

If there was one bright spot in the episode, it was the manner in which the Air Force responded, working cheerfully under Mike Loh as Acting Chief of Staff and then marching smartly off in a new direction under the leadership of General Merrill A. "Tony" McPeak when he took over on November 1, 1990. McPeak had been the alternative candidate when Dugan was selected, so it was naturally assumed that he would be summoned to fill the gap. He was well known to and appreciated by Secretary Rice.

McPeak made his presence known immediately. At a meeting with President Bush and the other Chiefs of Staff at Camp David, most of the other Chiefs were somewhat general in their presentations. McPeak spoke out forthrightly on the tactics to be adopted, what the target list should comprise, what the phases of the air campaign should be, and how long each phase could take. He warned that as many as 200 aircraft would be lost, and estimated that a hundred pilots would be saved by ejection. Of these hundred, fifty would be recovered and fifty would be captured, and he warned Bush that the American public might see captured American aircrews being paraded through the streets of Baghdad. He also warned that there would be collateral damage and civilian casualties. McPeak was conservative in his estimates of how long the actions would take and delib-erately overestimated the number of probable losses, to make sure that he was presenting a rigorous picture. At the end of his remarks he promised, "In any case at the end of thirty days you can kick off the ground cam-paign and it will be a piece of cake because we will have done our job." Bush later asked his National Security Adviser, Brent Scowcroft, "Does McPeak know what he is talking about?" and Scowcroft gave an enthusi-astic affirmative reply.

Early in January 1991, McPeak went out to the Gulf and flew six F-15 sorties, including one sixty-ship mission that used the Italian Tornado aircraft as aggressors in a simulated combat role. He came back impressed with the state of readiness, and was asked by President Bush to lunch at the White House, where the other guests were Scowcroft and Secretary of Defense Cheney. Colin Powell, the Chairman of the Joint Chiefs of Staff, who re-portedly was seeking another thirty-day delay before initiating combat, was absent. When asked by the President what he thought, McPeak responded,

"The only real mistake would be another postponement: these guys are ready to go." Bush indicated his agreement.

During those turbulent times, the effort to provide the necessary tactical air forces in the Gulf War was sustained by General Robert Russ, the TAC Commander, who took a huge workload off General Horner's shoulders and saw to it that forces, supplies, and personnel were funneled into the Gulf at an increasing rate. McPeak attributes a great deal of the success of the war to Russ's preplanning and to the actions he took to achieve Total Force participation by ensuring that Air National Guard and Air Force Reserve forces were used. Russ specifically asked that the 157th TFS of the 169th TFG of the South Carolina Air National Guard be sent because it had done so well in the weapons meets. The entire Air Force wanted to get into the fight, and those regular units that had to remain in the States were discomfited that Guard and Reserve units were sent. Russ also decided to take only two squadrons from each wing, so that the home base had a squadron in place to continue training and have replacement forces available. The net result took a great load off the personnel system and, in typical Russ fashion, caused the well-deserved plaudits to be spread around equitably.

PRESIDENT BUSH: CAUTION, RESOLUTION, THEN SELF-RESTRAINT

President Bush managed the buildup of Desert Shield with caution, loosely weaving a coalition and securing a "hands-off" agreement from President Mikhail Gorbachev of the Soviet Union. He worked carefully with the United Nations to obtain the Security Council resolutions that first condemned Iraq's invasion of Kuwait on August 2 and then progressively placed more pressure through sanctions and embargoes. Finally on November 29, 1990, he received the authorization of UN members to use "all means necessary" to force Iraq to withdraw from Kuwait. By taking his time and avoiding extreme actions, Bush was able to bring a coalition of thirty-eight nations, including several Arab states, into an alliance against Iraq. Israel had to remain out of the coalition, and had to be restrained from taking unilateral action against Saddam's provocations, which would include Scud attacks.

With his cautious approach, Bush, a warrior himself in his youth, also had the self-restraint to leave the prosecution of the war to his military subordinates. The war would not be run from Tuesday luncheon meetings of the sort made infamous by Lyndon Johnson and Robert McNamara, but instead prosecuted by professionals in whom he had confidence.

DESERT SHIELD BECOMES DESERT STORM

Under the leadership of General Glosson, the initial Checkmate planning concept was converted into an extraordinarily detailed operational plan. The original Checkmate paper had envisaged a forced withdrawal of Iraqi forces from Kuwait, but General Powell, who was recognized now as a man determined to avoid open warfare if at all possible, demanded changes that would instead freeze them in place, for ultimate destruction by ground forces.

The growth in the number of aircraft available to the coalition forces, acting as a true unified command, made an expansion of the target list possible. A classical air operation planning system developed in which Schwarzkopf, as CINCCENT, would provide commander's guidance to the CENTAF staff. Each day, they in turn prepared a huge air tasking order (ATO) detailing which aircraft attacked which targets. Routes in and out, refueling, armament, radio frequencies, and all of the other information necessary to execute an air strike were spelled out. It was a mammoth undertaking, one that defined the nature of the unified command and confirmed that the war was not going to be fought like the war in Vietnam. The CENTAF Commander, General Horner, was also the Joint Forces Air Component Commander (JFACC) and thus had operational control over every aircraft that flew. The ATO went out from his headquarters to every element of the coalition forces. (The armed services had come a long way from the days of runners and hand-cranked field phones. Using today's technology, the ATO was distributed electronically by the Air Force Computer-Aided Management System (CAFMS) to most units. However, the lack of an interface with the U.S. Navy computer system required that a floppy disk containing the electronic data be delivered each day.) The degree of control conferred an unstated but implicit control over any possible response by Israel, for without access to the coalition's IFF (identification friend or foe) settings, not even the Israeli Air Force could penetrate the combat area except at prohibitive risk.

During the period of the buildup, the coalition air forces continuously flew missions that simulated the coming offensive. Fighter missions were launched, tankers flew the refueling tracks, electronic countermeasures aircraft conducted operations, AWACS aircraft executed their control functions. Feint after feint was made toward the Kuwaiti and Iraqi borders, testing the enemy integrated air defense systems—and the will of the enemy pilots. By January 15, 1991, the buildup had reached mammoth proportions. The Air Force had 1,133 aircraft in place, including 652 fighters, eighty-seven other combat aircraft (bombers, reconnaissance, electronic warfare, and special operations), and 394 support aircraft (AWACS, tankers, and theater airlift). Navy and coalition aircraft raised the total to 2,614, of which 1,838 were fighters and attack aircraft. Having previously secured the backing of both houses of Congress concurring with the UN resolution that set a date of January 15, 1991, for withdrawal from Kuwait by Iraq, on January 15 President Bush signed the National Security Directive authorizing military action, accepting that all attempts at negotiations with Hussein had failed.

By this time, the air war plan had been elaborated and was divided into four phases. The first one, scheduled to take eight days, called for the establishment of air superiority, the destruction of Iraqi Scuds and any nuclear, biological, or chemical warfare capability, and the disruption of command and control. In the subsequent four-day period, all Iraqi air defenses in the Kuwaiti theater of operations were to be suppressed. This accomplished, the coalition forces would enter phase three, in which emphasis would be shifted to attacking Hussein's field army in Kuwait. When all this was completed, it was expected that the principal emphasis would be concentrated on air support of ground operations until the war was over. Things would work out rather better and far more swiftly than planned.

THE ATTACK BEGINS

Crack elements of the joint Air Force/Army/Navy team began the air war in the early morning of January 17 with three totally different forms of attack: Special Operations helicopters, stealth fighters, and cruise missiles.

The first of the three elements, Task Force Normandy, crossed the border at 2:20 A.M., a full forty minutes in advance of H hour, 3:00 A.M. local Baghdad time. It consisted of two pairs of USAF Sikorsky MH-53J Pave Low helicopters from the 1st Special Operations Wing, each pair providing the navigation and timing for four Army McDonnell Douglas AH-64 Apache attack helicopters of the 101st Aviation Brigade. Their targets were two Iraqi air defense radar sites located 13 and 18 miles behind the border.

The helicopters struck the two targets simultaneously at 0238. The Apache's Hellfire missiles and 70mm rockets were supplemented by the 30mm cannon fire of their M230 chain guns to destroy the radar sites and create a hole in the Iraqi air defense systems. This was the beginning of the payoff for the years of research and development. The MH-53J helicopters were themselves magnificent machines, with a range of 450 miles and a top speed of 196 mph. But in their Pave Low III configuration, they became corsairs of the night, their crews using special night-vision goggles and FLIR (forward-looking infrared). The Pave Low helicopters could maintain exact track of their course by means of their navigation systems, which included the Global Positioning System and inertial guidance and Doppler radar. Their electronic countermeasures suite and their terrain-following and terrain-avoidance radar enabled them to avoid detection by flying close to the surface, sometimes ducking down into the gullies that laced through the desert.

The helicopters gave new and valid meaning to the term "surgical strike." In their swift, slashing attack, they began firing from a range of about 2 miles, aiming first at the radar site's electrical generators, then at the communications facilities, and then at the radar equipment itself. An avalanche of twenty-seven Hellfire laser-guided missiles and nearly one hundred rockets, supplemented by thousands of rounds of 30mm cannon fire, pulverized the installations.

The second element of this overwhelming initial assault was the Lockheed/Martin F-117A stealth fighters, the "Black Jets" of the 37th TFW. Led by Lieutenant Colonel Ralph Getchell, CO of the 415 TFS, ten of the F-117As had departed their remote base at Khamis Mushait (jokingly called Tonopah East because of its resemblance to the stateside base), conducted night in-flight refueling with the customary radio silence, then separated to attack targets deep within Iraq, flying different altitudes and courses. It was a daunting experience; of the sixty-five pilots available to the 37th TFW, only four had ever been in combat before.

The F-117As epitomized the value and the risk of Air Force research and development over the years. Much was riding on their success—and until the war came, no one could say for certain that they would function as designed. And, despite the famous Skunk Work's having produced the F-117As under budget and ahead of schedule, external budget pressures reduced procurement of the Nighthawk to only fifty-nine aircraft.

The Nighthawks were extraordinarily sophisticated aircraft. Despite their awkward, angular appearance, they were pleasant to fly. They had a top speed of 646 mph and an unrefueled mission radius of 656 miles. Packed inside the compact wedge-shaped airframe were the exotic systems that made the aircraft effective. Depending on an inertial guidance system like that of the B-52 to get to the target area, the F-117 pilot then used his FLIR and DLIR (downward-looking infrared) equipment to locate the exact target and track to it. ("Exact" here had a new meaning in bombing terms. Where during World War II "exact" might have meant a square-block area, or in Vietnam a target the size of a bridge, it now meant a specific window or door of a specific building. So demanding were the new standards that if a precision-guided missile did not hit the specified window exactly, and only hit the same building, it was counted as a miss.) The infrared/laser turret next designated the target, and the system released the bomb to home unerringly to the precise spot designated by the laser. The 2,000-pound GBU-10s and the GBU-27 Paveway III laser-guided weapons amazed television audiences around the world as they watched the bombs speed unerringly to their targets. (Subsequent evaluations, including those of the Government Accounting Office, raised questions about the accuracy of precision-guided munitions and their cost relative to conventional weapons. The USAF position is unequivocally that precision-guided weapons are the weapons of the future.)

The importance of the years of research effort at AFSC and the quality control efforts of AFLC were put to the acid test on this first black night of Desert Storm. Any failure of any part of the weapon system—airframe, engines, radar avoidance, navigation, laser, infrared, or bombs—would have negated the F-117s value. A failure in pilot training, maintenance, or mission planning would have had the same effect. If one multiplies the number of parts in each of the components times the number of components in each of the systems times the chance that any one of them might fail, the absolute probability of failure seems very high. Yet there were no failures. The F-117s blasted their targets in a bewildering display of technological superiority, the first notice of their presence being the explosion of their bombs. The stealth fighters took out hardened facilities in Baghdad and in the far reaches of Iraq. Headquarters, airfields, communication and control centers, and air defense sites all fell victim, gutting Iraq's capability to fight back. The invulnerable F-117As pressed their attack hard for the next forty-three days of combat. They were never touched by bullet or SAM, and as far as can be determined, were never even tracked by Iraqi radar. As Lieutenant Colonel Getchell later remarked, his men had been in the right airplane at the right time. The F-117A's success was due to a long train of people, places, and events that led back to the Lockheed Skunk Works, to billions of dollars spent on research and development, and ultimately to Hap Arnold himself.

The third element of this early-morning surprise for Hussein was the cruise missiles, sea-and air-launched. The air-launched missiles came from seven Boeing B-52Gs of the Eighth Air Force. Departing from Barksdale AFB, Louisiana, at 6:36 A.M. on January 16, the Buffs carried AGM-86C cruise missiles armed with a 1,000-pound conventional warhead. They arrived at their launch points after a tiring fifteen-hour flight that included many refuelings. The B-52s, originally designed to fly singly and at high altitude to drop nuclear weapons, now fired thirty-five missiles, thirty-one of which hit their high-value targets. After the launch, the B-52s flew back home against strong headwinds, landing back at Barksdale after a record-setting thirty-five-hour flight. A brilliant representation of Rice's dictum of Global Reach—Global Power, the mission was but a part of an even greater, more elaborate plan that was just unfolding.

The Buff's ALCMs were supplemented by fifty-four TLAMs (Tomahawk land attack missiles) fired from the Navy's battleships *Wisconsin* and *Missouri*, veterans of four wars and now on their last hurrah, and the missile cruisers USS *San Jacinto* and USS *Bunker Hill*.

The combination of these three initial elements—Task Force Normandy, F-117As, and the ALCM and TLAM cruise missiles—opened the way for an avalanche of 650 coalition aircraft, including 400 strike aircraft. They poured through the hole torn in the Iraqi air defense system, their sophisticated mix of weapon systems expanding the gap. Fifty-three of the old faithful F-111s from the 48th TFW hit major airfields, hardened aircraft shelters, and chemical-weapon storage areas with laser-guided missiles. They also used the Durandel runway-cratering bombs to help keep the Iraqi Air Force on the ground, which was where, as things developed, it preferred to be. Nineteen *LANTIRN*-equipped F-15E Strike Eagles went after missile sites and Scud launchers. The Royal Air Force sent Tornadoes in low to hit three airfields, using JP-233 airfield-denial weapons. The RAF would do brilliant work in destroying bridges all through the war, part of the scheme that crippled Iraqi transportation.

Curiously, an unarmed EF-111A Raven electronic counterwarfare plane inflicted the first air-to-air loss on the Iraqi Air Force. Attacked by an Iraqi Dassault Mirage fighter firing missiles, Captain Jim Denton of the 42nd ECS took evasive action in a rolling diving turn. The Mirage pilot tried to follow, but was observed by Captain Brent Brandon, the Raven's EWO, to fly into the ground, blowing up. Shortly thereafter, Captain Steven "Tater" Tate of the 71st Fighter Wing, flying an F-15C, got a more conventional kill, shooting down a Mirage with a Sparrow missile from a 15-mile distance. (The Sparrow, much improved since Vietnam, would prove to be the primary air-to-air weapon of the war, scoring thirty-one victories—two by the Royal Saudi Arabian Air Force—compared to ten by the heat-seeking AIM 9L Sidewinder.) With the AWACS aircraft able to provide positive identification (the most important element lacking in Vietnam), the AIM-7s could be launched from beyond visual range; consequently, most combats were conducted with Sparrows rather than Sidewinders.

In the course of the war, fourteen USAF, fifteen Navy and Marine, and six Army aircraft would be lost in combat for a total of thirty-five. Eight coalition forces aircraft were lost in combat, six of them Tornado low-level attack planes of the RAF. During the period from August 29, 1990, to March 31, 1991, the United States had thirty-seven noncombat losses, including ten from the USAF.

Nothing was more in keeping with this strange, almost bizarre war than the fact that American television commentators were broadcasting from Baghdad during the height of the attack. The American public could see the skies over Baghdad filled with an apparently impenetrable curtain of antiaircraft fire, unaware that U.S. aircraft were flying through the impressive display without any hits being scored. In one of the most incredible real-time confirmations of success in military history, U.S. leaders in the Pentagon and in Riyadh were watching the CNN broadcast from Baghdad when the station went off the air, a victim of a cruise missile.

Never before had there been anything to compare to this attack in the history of air warfare. Pearl Harbor pales in comparison beside it, as does the Nazi May 1940 blitzkrieg. Even the brilliant eleven-day attack on Hanoi and Haiphong in 1972 did not achieve the paralyzing results of this tidal wave of air power. In the first twenty-four hours of the Desert Storm air war, the coalition forces had established air superiority, decapitated Hussein's excellent—until then—command and control system, shut down Iraq's electrical production, and seriously reduced the effectiveness of the many SAM sites and antiaircraft batteries.

The very effectiveness of the attack forced a change in the war plan, for the substantial destruction of the important strategic centers and the integrated defense system took place within the first thirty-six hours. Everything, including the attacks on the field army, was now accelerated. The Iraqi Air Force had been effectively removed from the war; it would be seen again only in isolated sorties, or in the ignominious decampment of 120 aircraft to its former enemy, Iran. After the war, Iran somewhat predictably confiscated the aircraft rather than return them to Saddam.

Despite all this, hard fighting was still to come. Even though now being fired in barrage patterns rather than under radar control, Iraqi antiaircraft batteries put up a tremendous curtain of fire through which coalition aircraft had to fly. The battle-hardened Iraqi soldiers were tough and, not yet having felt the full fury of the coalition air attack, were prepared to inflict heavy casualties in the ground war.

And at the bottom of it all, Hussein remained as before, stubborn and brutal. He demonstrated the latter quality on January 17, when he fired the first two Scuds at Israel. Early the next morning, a fusillade of seven Scuds aimed at Tel Aviv followed. Fortunately, only ten people were injured in this opening act of terrorist warfare. The same morning also saw the first Scud fired at Saudi Arabia. It was destroyed when hit at 17,000 feet altitude by a Patriot missile the very first antimissile missile to be used in combat.

Hussein's purpose was clear: if Israel entered the war, the Arab members of George Bush's coalition would be put in an untenable position and would have to withdraw. Immoral as Hussein's attack was, it was a practical tactical move, for it immediately diverted coalition resources for a campaign-long, 2,500-sortie assault against Scuds and their transporter-erector-launchers, launch sites, storage areas, and production facilities. Two "Scud boxes" were established, one in the west to strike missiles targeted on Israel, and one in the south, where they were targeted against Saudi Arabia. Within these boxes, Scuds were hunted mercilessly by strike aircraft, with at least two A-10s attacking each area twenty-four hours a day.

Reminiscent more of the German V-2 of World War II than of the later ICBMS, the SS-1 Scud was a crude weapon of 1957 vintage, designed and built in the Soviet Union and widely exported. Both Iran and Iraq used it indiscriminately against each other's cities during their eight-year war, each side sorry only that they lacked nuclear warheads. About 38 feet long, with a diameter of 33.5 inches, the Iraqi Scud B had a weight of 14,000 pounds and a range of 175 miles with a 2,205-pound warhead. The MAZ-537 TEL (transporter, erector, and launcher) made the missile highly mobile. With an inertial guidance system that provided only a limited accuracy of about 1.5 miles, the Scud was in fact an indiscriminate "area bomber," as much a terror weapon as a car bomb. Fortunately, the Scud did not hit a vital vulnerable target like a munitions dump or a hospital. If it were fitted with chemical, nuclear, or biological weapons, however, it could be extremely dangerous. The Iraqis had created two improved versions of the weapon, the Al-Husan and the Al-Abbas. By reducing warhead size and substituting fuel, the Iraqis were able to increase the range to about 400 miles.

The coalition intelligence on Iraq had generally been deficient, and nowhere more than in its underestimation of Hussein's Scud capability, where it was off by a factor of five. The Iraqis possessed more than 225 launchers and were as skilled in concealing them as they were in their use. After a launch from a previously surveyed site, the crews could be on their way in just a few minutes to a designated shelter area to hide. The most effective solution against these mobile targets was the patrolling McDonnell Douglas F-15E Strike Eagles. Their long range and high speed could make the best use of their LANTIRN and synthetic aperture radar equipment.

Ultimately it proved impossible to suppress the Scud launches completely, even though a large share of the coalition's resources was devoted to the task. A breakthrough in space-related warfare occurred when the Defense Satellite Communication System satellites, designed for use against ICBMs, proved to be most effective in detecting Scud launches. Another brand-new system, the Boeing/Grumman E-8 Joint STARS aircraft, was still in its experimental test program. Flown by USAF crews and linked to the Army battlefield forces, its radar peered as much as 100 miles into enemy territory, alternating between the Doppler and the synthetic aperture mode to detect transporters on the move or standing still. Lockheed U-2Rs and TR-1As, which flew reconnaissance missions monitoring Iraq before, during, and after the conflict, were also used to detect Scud launches. Immediately after launch, target information was provided to patrolling F-15s as to the TEL's whereabouts, and a warning was dispatched to Patriot missile sites. The Patriot search radar would acquire and track the Scud; as it approached, a salvo of Patriots (usually two) would be launched, guided by the ground-based radar. Sometimes, the Scuds broke up as they reentered the earth's atmosphere, making their tracking and interception more difficult. The Patriot's radar would pick up the incoming missile—or some of its components—guiding the Patriot to a point where its detonation would blow up the Scud. In the first flush of Patriot kills, the general sense was that the Scuds had been mastered. Later analysis showed that although the Patriots had been extraordinarily effective, they did not measure up to the initial impression. The intercepted Scuds still descended upon Israeli or Saudi Arabian territory, the warhead sometimes still intact, and debris from the rest of the missile and the Patriot itself caused damage. (It must be remembered that the Patriots rushed to defend Israel served to keep Israel out of the war during the most crucial period of the Scud assault. The Patriot's political effect might well have been greater than its military effect.)

By chance, one Scud was fired to arrive during the time the appropriate Patriot missile battery was standing down for routine maintenance. The warhead hit a barracks near Dhahran, killing twenty-eight American soldiers and wounding ninety-eight others. In the course of the war, the Scuds killed a total of forty-two people and wounded 450. More casualties were prevented when a group of twenty Scuds being prepared for a mass launch on Israel were discovered and destroyed on February 27.

The air onslaught against the Scuds was effective; fifty had been fired by January 27, but only forty-three more were fired during the remaining thirty-three days of the war. Despite the mammoth effort, the possibility remains to this day that the Scud could be mated with a nuclear, biological, or chemical warhead and do incalculable damage.

With air superiority decisively established, the Iraqi electrical system and C³I (command, control, communications, and intelligence) destroyed, most radar sites incapacitated by SEAD (suppression of enemy air defenses) teams, and the Scud threat muted if not eradicated, more attention was turned to the destruction of the powerful Iraqi army, hunkered down behind their anachronistic desert defenses. The devout Iraqi soldiers believed that death in battle entitled them to an immediate ascent to paradise. Many would make the trip; many more, however, would endure a long hell on earth as coalition aircraft systematically reduced Iraq's mighty army to an inchoate force of starving, frightened soldiers, eager to surrender to anything from a roving Special Operations armored car to an unmanned remotely piloted vehicle.

MORE INTENSE ATTACKS:
GREATER PLANNING PROBLEMS

The massive preparation for Desert Storm yielded results beyond anyone's imagination. One of the results was a huge discontinuity in the planning effort that was supposed to be translated each day into an Air Tasking Order (ATO) to assign the next day's missions. The quick success was welcome, even if it was a case of too much too soon. The forced compression of the four planned bombing phases, the diversion of assets to hunt for Scuds, and unexpectedly bad weather over the target and on the refueling tracks combined with inadequate resources for bomb damage assessment (BDA) to make planning after January 18 very difficult.

Air Force estimates of bomb damage were considered by the national intelligence community to be too high, although they were in fact conservative. Ground force commanders tended to believe the more pessimistic reports, and in a manner that exactly echoed their complaints in World War II, Korea, and Vietnam, demanded more air-to-ground strikes in their own individual areas. Fortunately, General Schwarzkopf took a broader view and relied on the reports furnished him by Horner and Glosson, which in turn were based on the hardest intelligence available: strike camera photos confirmed by the personal observations of the aircrews.

The combination of complicating factors plus the worst weather in fourteen years made the preparation of the ATO so lengthy that mission commanders did not have adequate time to study it or to accommodate the inevitable changes. One result of the changed circumstances was an increase in mission cancellations—456 on January 19 and 431 on the following day. Another was the loss of two F-16s on a mission into the heart of Baghdad that proved the Iraqis could still use their antiaircraft artillery effectively in barrage fire and fire their SAMs ballistically even with their C³I impaired.

Yet the situation soon stabilized, and General Horner was able to direct a well-disciplined, systematic round-the-clock air campaign that would destroy most of the remaining important targets in Iraq, while simultaneously waging a war of savage attrition against Hussein's now immobile army. The B-52s performed the same role they had in Vietnam, dropping huge quantities of weapons upon troop positions, while the strike aircraft, particularly the F-16s and A-10s, sought out and destroyed tanks and artillery.

VERSATILE FORCES = BLOODY ATTRITION

Hussein expressed his frustration in a series of random acts of terror, beginning on January 25, with the destruction of Kuwait's main supertanker loading pier, allowing millions of gallons of crude oil to be dumped into the Persian Gulf and creating an ecological disaster. A precision air strike by F-111Fs, using 2,000-pound GBU-15 (V)-1/B electro-optical bombs, against the pumping station and oil manifolds managed to stop the flow.

No act of vandalism by Hussein could shield his forces from the ferocious aerial attacks. The years of research and development, test and modification had borne fruit; when combined with the sophisticated new munitions, every one of the several types of USAF aircraft proved potent in battle.

The Fairchild A-10, officially named the Thunderbolt II, but invariably called the Warthog because of its starkly functional appearance, became the favorite of the Army troops, for it did a great deal of its work "up close and personal." A-10s fired almost 5,000 Maverick missiles and claimed 4,200 successes—1,000 tanks, 2,000 vehicles, and 1,200 pieces of artillery.

The Lockheed (formerly General Dynamics) F-16 Fighting Falcon was the most numerous USAF fighter in the theater, with 249 on hand. In almost 13,500 sorties, the F-16s attacked every sort of target, from SAM sites to nuclear plants. Ground crews rallied around the aircraft to maintain an unprecedented 92.5 percent in-commission rate, a full five percentage points better than the peacetime average.

The overall effectiveness of some F-16 operations was blunted by a lack of advanced equipment. Some F-16s had the LANTIRN navigation pod but not the targeting pod, and were forced to rely primarily on the standard 2,000-pound Mark 84 "dumb" (i.e., not precision-guided) bomb. Antiaircraft fire forced the F-16s to drop from higher altitudes, degrading their accuracy.

Working in conjunction with the experimental J-STARS aircraft, the multi mission Lockheed (also formerly General Dynamics) F-111s and the deadly accurate Lockheed F-117s turned their attention to hardened aircraft shelters, using laser-guided 2,000-pound bombs. Designed to withstand a nuclear attack, the strongly built shelters served instead to contain the force of the exploding bombs, reducing aircraft and equipment inside to a jumbled mass of rubble. These attacks finished off the Iraqi Air Force: the coalition forces had gone beyond air superiority to air supremacy. As clear confirmation of this, by the second week of the war, KC-135 tankers were permitted to fly into Iraq to refuel the F-117s.

With the hardened shelters destroyed, the F-111s and F-15E Strike Eagles now turned their attention to "tank plinking," a term so chillingly apt that even American tankers disliked it. The J-STARS aircraft were very effective in locating targets and the strike fighters would use up their ammunition before their fuel, saving time and tankers. Iraqi armored vehicles were dug in deeply in the sand but were still betrayed by their heat signature to the infrared sensors of the FLIR pods. The USAF fighters used precision-guided munitions—"smart bombs"—to destroy them at the rate of 100 to 200 per night, "plinking" them like tin cans at a dump site. Iraqi tank crews that formerly took shelter inside their tanks now made sure they bunked down elsewhere. The task was admittedly made more difficult by the Iraqis' extensive use of sophisticated decoys, which mimicked the infrared and radar signatures of the real weapon and required some careful cross-checking by the surveillance aircraft.

The 48th TFW, commanded by Colonel Thomas Lennon, became adept at killing tanks at night. Flying in flights of two or four aircraft, the F-111Fs would patrol the "kill boxes"-60-by-30-mile areas. Each aircraft carried four GBU-12 laser-guided bombs; the 500-pound units had been considered too light to kill tanks, but, dropped from medium altitudes and guided with precision, they were deadly. In just twenty-three days, the F-111s flew 664 successful sorties, taking out tanks, trucks, artillery—anything that radiated enough heat for the Pave Tack infrared pods to pick up. In economic terms, it was a profitable exchange, for the GBU-12 cost about $10,000 versus the open-market price of $1.5 million for a T-72 tank. The F-15Es were equally successful. On one mission, they batted 1.000—two Strike Eagles, each carrying eight GBU-12s, destroyed sixteen armored vehicles.

The ALCM launch by the Barksdale Buffs has already been described. Less well known is the almost simultaneous attack thirteen other of the venerable Boeing B-52Gs made in their first-ever low-level combat mission, a task that had been practiced for years. About 4:00 A.M. Baghdad time, the B-52s, in flights of twos and threes, raced across the Iraqi desert at only a few hundred feet altitude, guided by terrain-avoidance radar, to strike Iraqi air bases with CBU-89 Gator mines and 1,000-pound runway-busting bombs.

The bulk of B-52 activity came later, when more than eighty Buffs were on call for combat duty, flying out of bases in England, Spain, Diego Garcia, Egypt, and Saudi Arabia. Flying in cells of three aircraft, Vietnam-style, they bombed targets every three hours. Each aircraft could carry fifty-one bombs, twenty-seven internally and twelve on each wing pylon, almost always 750-pound M-117s. The cell, flying at altitude, would drop 153 bombs in a swath a mile and a half long and a mile wide, an ear-popping, sinus-shattering symphony of disaster. Because the first warning to the Iraqi troops would be the bombs exploding, the psychological effect was enormous. For twenty-four hours a day, the Iraqi troops were conscious that the next second might see them dead. One Iraqi battalion commander surrendered not because his unit had been under the B-52s' bombs, but because he had seen the devastation wreaked upon another formation exposed to them. The B-52Gs flew 1,624 missions, dropping 25,700 tons of bombs. Perhaps the most amazing facet of the B-52s' performance, and a tribute to the enlisted personnel who maintained them, was their 81 percent in-commission rate—two percentage points better than the peacetime average, and an incredible achievement for a system so large and so old.

FINISHING TOUCHES

As Hussein felt his grip on Kuwait slipping, he began setting fire to the Kuwaiti oil fields, the smoke layering the sky over the battlefield and reducing visibility to 3 miles. As he assessed the effect of this wanton destruction upon the progress of the war, General Horner also made a personal estimate of how future sorties would be allocated. He believed that a total of about 450 sorties would eliminate any remaining Iraqi airfields, complete the destruction of current stocks of Scuds and their production facilities, and eliminate residual electricity and petroleum production. Another 200 sorties would be required to destroy munitions factories, munitions storage sites, and similar military support facilities.

Thus, the major remaining task was the destruction of Iraqi ground forces, especially the elite Republican Guard. He estimated that to do this would require between 17,500 and 20,000 sorties, perhaps even more, depending upon the ability of the Iraqis to resist the unremitting assault.

While the world waited for "G day"—the beginning of the ground attack that Hussein said he wanted to happen more than anyone—Horner accelerated the air assault, doing far more than "prepare the battlefield." By the unremitting ferocity of its attack, the coalition air forces deprived the Iraqi army of its will to fight. With communications destroyed, reinforcement impossible, food and water scarce, and their major strengths, artillery and tanks, being plinked into oblivion day by day, morale fell rapidly. Desertions began, and units were quick to surrender. By the time G day arrived on February 24, 1991, many Iraqi units were at or below the 50 percent point in their nominal combat strength; when morale was factored in, they were even less effective.

By G day, the coalition had 2,790 fixed-wing aircraft in the theater, of which almost 2,000 were "shooters," i.e., strike aircraft. When the ground war was launched, this force intensified close support efforts, with sorties reaching a peak of 3,500 per day on February 27, the day before the fighting stopped. A final example of the close relationship of R&D to the war effort occurred on the same night. The Iraqis had been foresighted in constructing bunkers that would have made Hitler proud, sunk deep in the ground and heavily covered in reinforced concrete. One such command bunker was located at the Al Taji airfield, just north of Baghdad.

Working with Texas Instruments and the Lockheed Missile and Space Company, a quick-reaction Air Force team at Eglin Air Force Base created a bomb tailored to reach deep into the earth after Iraqi leaders. The BLU-113 penetration warhead had been developed in only seventeen days to meet the requirement. Designated the GBU-28-B, the bomb casing of these bunker-busters was machined from 8-inch artillery tubes, filled with 650 pounds of molten tritonal explosive, and fitted with a hardened steel nose cone. Thirty bombs were built, none with any authorizing paperwork. The Paveway III guidance system was modified by Texas Instruments for the new 4,700-pound bombs, which were special-delivered to the F-111Fs of the 48th TFW. Dropped from altitude at supersonic speed to increase their kinetic energy, the bombs had the capability to penetrate 100 feet of earth or 20 feet of concrete. The damage they did sent a clear message to Hussein that there was no longer anywhere to hide.

Did air power win the Gulf War by itself? The answer is no, for the Army, Navy, and Marines rendered glorious service. But the fact remains that the most extensive and successful preparation of the battlefield in history had been accomplished by air power. The Iraqi army, the sword that Hussein hoped the U.S. Army would throw itself upon, was hammered into a shattered mass, incapable of fighting effectively and highly susceptible to surrender. Saddam Hussein himself, his communications reduced to the Revolutionary War standard of runners hand-carrying messages, may never have known the state to which his army had fallen.

The success or the one hundred-hour ground campaign can be attributed to the most effective air campaign in history. If the 111,000-plus sorties of the air campaign had not been planned, flown, and executed as they had been, the ground campaign might have been a hundred days or a hundred weeks, and, instead of being brought to a climax by the great "Hail Mary" flanking movement, might have required a bloody novena of costly frontal battles.

REFLECTIONS ON LESSONS LEARNED

The Air Force had applied much of what it had learned at such bitter experience in Vietnam with satisfying results. Using a new and benign management attitude that permitted leaders to elicit the very best from all personnel, officer and enlisted, it had applied its funds wisely among the varied needs for new equipment, modification of older equipment, training, and the prepositioning of assets. It had adhered to the doctrine it had developed of suppressing and rolling back enemy air defenses to gain air superiority. Reliance was no longer placed upon sheer weight of ordnance and volume of sorties but instead upon the accurate placement of that ordnance. In a curious fashion the pendulum of war had swung away from mass destruction to pinpoint elimination of critical nodes; instead of the doleful mutual deterrence concept of measuring casualties inflicted (and received) in the millions, the point was now to inflict minimum casualties and sustain none, if possible.

To the surprise of no one who had monitored the process, the "Total Force" concept had once again been validated, for of the 54,706 USAF personnel in the theater of war, 12,098 were Air National Guard or Air Force Reserve personnel—more than 22 percent. Nor were these "support troops." Instead, the thirty-seven Guard and twenty-eight Reserve units flew C-130s, KC-135s, A-10s, RF-4Cs, HH-3Es, F-16s, C-141s, and C-5s, all first-line equipment, flying and fighting in the front line. Their excellent performance would point the way to the future of the Air Force, for with declining budgets, the only possible way for the service to retain its striking capability was to transfer even more responsibility to Guard and Reserve units.

Space-age warfare was introduced with the remarkable success of the Global Positioning System, which at the time had sixteen satellites in place, five short of the number needed for complete worldwide coverage and eight short of the ultimate number planned. One of the sixteen suffered a failure that was vital to providing the three-dimensional coverage necessary in desert warfare. Air Force personnel at Falcon AFB's Air Force Space Command developed software that stabilized the satellite, placed it in the right attitude, and made it useful.

The two Defense Satellite Communications System (DSCS) satellites employed in the complex, spaced-based communications network were soon overloaded. Once again AFSPACECOM members stepped in, this time to execute a historic first in space warfare. A DSCS II satellite was being held in reserve over the Pacific, in a stationary orbit 22,300 miles above the earth. Space Command specialists commanded it to start its motor and scooted it westward for several days to a fixed point over the Indian Ocean, where it solved the communications overload. The satellites were exploited by more than thirty ground satellite terminals. These were the basis for an elaborate communications network that integrated the torrential volume of communications flowing over the varied equipment of eight countries. Astute preliminary planning, carried out over a long time span, had resulted in the interoperability of the communications equipment of the forces of the United States, Great Britain, and France.

DOMINATING THE BATTLEFIELD

The post-Vietnam Air Force has moved entirely away from the concept of contests to win air superiority in the mode of the Battle of Britain or the later battles of the Eighth Air Force against Germany. It now wants to win battles over the enemy heartland with such overwhelming superiority that there are few if any USAF casualties while the enemy is completely subdued. Excellent aircraft and intensive training are but a part of the new strategy. There is now an overriding requirement for an electronic supremacy of the battlefield that provides U.S. forces with complete information on enemy strength and intentions while denying the enemy intelligence not only about U.S. forces but even about his own forces. The first demonstration of the efficacy of this concept was provided by the Persian Gulf War.

One of best-known illustrations of this new method of fighting was the remarkable success of the airborne command and control aircraft. These airplanes, the subject of bitter opposition during the period of their procurement because of their great expense, proved to be invaluable. The hard-working Lockheed EC-130E airborne battlefield command and control center (ABCCC) controlled air-to-ground attacks. More familiar because of its huge signature rotating radar dome, the Boeing E-3B Sentry airborne warning and control system (AWACS) controlled the masses of airborne aircraft, including tankers and reconnaissance and strike aircraft. The two experimental E-8 Joint STARS aircraft ferreted out ground targets such as Scud launchers and monitored traffic flow. No battle before had ever been fought with such superb comnand and control facilities—no future battle should ever be fought without this capability.

One of the less well known but vital tasks, the collection and analysis of electronic emissions, was handled with panache by the Boeing RC-135 Rivet Joint aircraft. Using the flight deck crew, electronic warfare officers (EWOs), and airborne intelligence technicians (AITs), the Rivet Joint team used its Elint (electronic intelligence) capability for three main tasks: (1) to provide indications about the location and intention of enemy forces; (2) to broadcast a variety of voice communications, especially combat advisory broadcasts and imminent threat warnings, which warned of SAM launches, assisted in search and rescue, and even helped aircraft on air defense suppression missions; and (3) to operate the data and voice links to ground-based air defenses, providing target information on incoming aircraft or missiles.

Elint is characterized by long hours of work on station and patient analysis of enemy transmissions, punctuated by brief moments of urgency when the vital—often life-or-death—information is transmitted to the appropriate receiver. Three Rivet Joint aircraft of the 55th Strategic Reconnaissance Wing (SRW) were in the theater, providing twenty-four-hour coverage. The Iraqis were well disciplined in their use of electronic equipment before the start of Desert Storm, but the RC-135s were able to ferret out the locations of most of the communication centers.

The RC-135s were complemented by the versatile Lockheed EC-130H Compass Call aircraft, which jammed enemy transmissions with deadly effect. Few Iraqi radios were on the air for more than a few moments until the Compass Call aircraft electronically obliterated their transmissions.

LEADERS WHO WERE WINNERS

The war was started by the ego of one man, Saddam Hussein, but it was ended by a group of men who suppressed their egos for the common good. A great deal of credit must be given to the inner circle of U.S. leaders directing the war who permitted the new command structure envisioned by the Goldwater-Nichols Act to work as intended. The commander, General Schwarzkopf, was allowed operational control of the war without interference.

These U.S. leaders were no strangers to ego—one does not become President, Secretary of Defense, Chairman of the Joint Chiefs, or "even" a three-or four-star general without having acquired a considerable sense of self-worth along the way. Yet every one of them—Bush, Cheney, Powell, Schwarzkopf, McPeak, and Horner, to name only the most obvious—subordinated their egos to the decision-making process. This is not to say that there were not flare-ups, and in the case of one or two individuals, even tantrums. There were, but they did not adversely affect the prosecution of the war. It will be remembered that Secretary Cheney's track record with Generals Welch and Dugan did not indicate any partiality for the Air Force. Therefore, there was considerable comfort and satisfaction from Cheney's oft-quoted postwar comment "The air campaign was decisive."

HARD NUMBERS

The cold statistics of the war give dimension to the role the Air Force played. It flew 59 percent of the total of 109,876 sorties flown and dropped 74 percent of the total U.S. bomb tonnage of 88,500 tons and 90 percent of the U.S. precision-bomb tonnage of 6,520 tons. A formidable enemy force had been shattered so that the ground forces could execute their task with maximum speed and minimum risk.

Yet there were still lessons to be learned. A total of 210,800 gravity "dumb" bombs had been dropped, compared to only 15,500 units of precision-guided munitions. With a declining force structure, it was obvious that this 13.6-to-1 ratio was uneconomic and had to be reversed in future conflicts. Intelligence-gathering prior to, during, and even after the war was inadequate, particularly in regard to bomb damage assessment. As mentioned previously, an equipment mismatch prevented the electronic transmission of the Air Tasking Order to Navy units, an anomaly solved easily enough subsequently. And, despite the brilliant efforts made by MAC and CRAF aircraft, there were simply not enough airlift aircraft of the correct capacity available to meet the need. Had the McDonnell Douglas C-17 been available in quantity, the task would have been much easier. (The number of ships available for sealift was even more deficient, but that's another story.)

Two shortcomings were most evident. The first achieved wide notoriety—casualties due to friendly fire. The public that applauded the technology that put bombs in ventilation shafts was appalled that equivalent means had not been developed to prevent killing our own troops. The second serious deficiency was less obvious, except to those unfortunate enough to suffer from it: the failure to provide the quantity of high-technology search and rescue equipment necessary for a campaign of the magnitude of the Persian Gulf War. Search and rescue is both a moral and a morale issue. The level of funding required to maintain a first-class search and rescue capability compared to the total funds required to field a modern air force is small—therefore no decisions not to have adequate capability based on economy can be justified. Yet when funds are reduced functions such as search and rescue inevitably get cut.

Curiously enough, the greatest effect of the victory in the Gulf War may be in the minds of the American public. General Loh put it in sporting terms, saying that the Gulf War created a new standard in which the U.S. must win quickly, decisively, with overwhelming advantage and few casualties. It must, in short, prevail "by 99 to 1, not 55 to 54 in double overtime."

THE AFTERMATH OF VICTORY: CONTINUED REDUCTION AND TOTAL REORGANIZATION

The U.S. Air Force covered itself with glory during Desert Shield and Desert Storm, and most of its units returned in high spirits to welcoming crowds in the United States. Having done so, it continued the pell-mell process of downsizing and reorganizing to a degree unprecedented for a victorious force. Normally after great victories, armed forces tend to stay the same for years, content that they've solved the problem of warfare. But even before the parades and welcoming parties were over, USAF leaders persisted in the process that would transform the steady ten-year drawdown into a new, better, more effective service.

In the past, the Air Force had brought leaders to the fore who were appropriate to the challenge. General McPeak came to his position as Chief of Staff with a vision for a change in the structure of the Air Force that he says would have been appropriate whether the Air Force was going to build up, draw down, or remain static. McPeak, no stranger to controversy before or after his accession to the top USAF job, had the drive and the personality to handle the dynamics of a revolutionary restructuring of the service he loved. Evidence of his success was found in the quick agreement he obtained on his plan for restructuring the Air Force from Secretary Rice. In a series of late-evening briefings, McPeak convinced Rice of the soundness of his plan, and he obtained essential agreement by Christmas 1990.

McPeak continued the trend of a fighter pilot as Chief of Staff that began with Charles Gabriel. An ROTC graduate, McPeak flew as a solo demonstration pilot with the famed Thunderbirds and accumulated 269 combat missions as a North American F-100D attack pilot and as a high-speed

"Misty" forward air controller (one of the most demanding, hazardous jobs in the war) in Vietnam. His twenty-six assignments, which included twenty-four changes of station over thirty-three years, constituted textbook preparation to become Chief of Staff, for he did everything from flying as a grunt instructor pilot to commanding, in turn, a fighter wing, a numbered air force (the Twelfth), and, finally, PACAF. McPeak has flown over 6,500 hours in more than fifty types of aircraft and achieved combat-mission-ready status in the F-4, F-15, F-16, F-100, F-104, and F-111. He continued flying as Chief of Staff and earn adverse publicity for doing so—four-star generals were not supposed to be flying single-seat fighters. McPeak stoutly maintained that it was the best way to keep his finger on the pulse of the Air Force—and his hand on the stick of a fighter. President Bush, a pilot himself, went out of his way to praise McPeak for flying. McPeak wanted his numbered air force commanders to fly, and posted the monthly hours they flew on a chart.

During his career, McPeak never lost sight of the value of the Air Force as an entity—he did not see it as a fighter pilot's Air Force, but as an organization that functioned well because *all* of its components—cooks, mechanics, air policemen, medics, pilots—were making vital contributions to the best of their abilities. He appreciated technology as well as any of his predecessors, but understood that without realistic, Red Flag–style training such as General Robert Dixon had instigated, the value of technology was diluted.

The decline in strength that Generals Gabriel and Welch had planned for had now materialized. For the ten-year period from 1986 to 1995, the total obligational authority of the budget had declined 34 percent; the active personnel strength declined 27 percent, the total number of aircraft (including Guard and Reserve) declined 20 percent, and base installations declined 24 percent. There was no avoiding the budget cuts; the question was how to manage them. McPeak's view was the same as that put forth by Gabriel and Welch: if the change occurred solely because the Congress reduced funds, outside influences would control the effect of the cuts, but if the Air Force anticipated the problems and took the necessary steps, the Air Force could control the way it was restructured.

Another factor looming in addition to the tremendous reduction in force under way was the superimposition of unified commands like the U.S. Transportation Command (USTRANSCOM), U.S. Strategic Command (USSTRATCOM), and U.S. Space Command (USPACECOM). These commands, intended to coordinate all four military services in accomplishing unified missions, imposed requirements for staffing and equipment that the corresponding USAF commands could not afford to duplicate.

McPeak thus understood that a dissolution of some of the old commands and their reorganization into fewer, leaner new commands was essential—but, he maintains, not as a result of the end of the Cold War nor even as a result of the downsizing, but simply because they needed to be more focused on Air Force operations and the warrior concept. An essential part of his approach was to reduce the overhead, particularly in headquarters. To achieve this, organizations such as Air Divisions, which had historic precedent but whose function had been overtaken by time, were to be eliminated. In a similar way, "staff creep," the inevitable growth of staff at each level of headquarters, had to be eliminated.

McPeak envisioned an "objective Air Force," not the Air Force that existed, and not an Air Force that would ever exist, but one that would represent an ideal to strive far. As subsets of this concept, he talked about "objective numbered air forces, objective wings, and objective squadrons." As a result of his long experience as a commander of every size of unit, from squadron to major air command, McPeak knew how he wanted to reorganize from the start, and he was determined to initiate the process in the first six months that he was Chairman. His goal was to focus the USAF on its principal function, operations, and to ensure that it was instilled with the warrior concept: the Air Force was a fighting outfit, not just pilots and doctors and mathematicians all in the same uniform. It was there to fight.

Throughout the process, McPeak cautioned that when reductions led to mergers of organizations to achieve economies of scale, the real power of the organization was often centralized and moved up an echelon. His view was that of General Creech—organizations had to be decentralized to empower people on the line to do their jobs better. The aim of the restructuring was to flatten organizational charts, reducing the levels of command but at the same time clarifying the roles and responsibilities of support functions.

Realizing that examples were more important than words, McPeak saw to it that the Air Staff was reduced 21 percent, although he now dismisses this as more of a paper change than reality. Yet the biggest hurdle, emotionally and organizationally, was still to come: the disestablishment of the proud Strategic, Tactical, and Military Airlift Commands and the subsequent reorganization of their functions into new commands. Other commands were also affected, and for their members there was the same sense of uncertainty and nostalgia. But for the public at large the loss of SAC, TAC, and MAC was almost sacrilegious.

McPeak also agreed with a concept that had been inherent in the Air Force since its creation, that the division of air power into strategic and tactical elements was a mistake. He often quoted General LeMay, who had proposed in 1957 to combine SAC and TAC into a single Air Offensive Command. LeMay had said, "Whether we choose to recognize it or not, SAC and TAC are bedfellows. . . . They must deter together through their ability to defeat enemy air power together."

The plan put together under McPeak's leadership was draconian. For many years there had been thirteen major air commands, seven operational and six support. The former included the Strategic Air Command, the Tactical Air Command, the Military Airlift Command, U.S. Air Forces in Europe, Pacific Air Forces, the Air Force Space Command, and the Air Force Special

Operations Command. The support commands were the Air Force Systems Command, the Air Force Logistics Command, the Air University, the Air Training Command, the Electronics Security Command, and the Air Force Communications Command.

In the reorganization process, the Air Force Space Command and the Air Force Special Operations Command retained their organizational identities. The first major cut came with the changeover of the Communications Command to three field operating agencies, with a reduction in personnel of more than 40,000. The Electronics Security Command was consolidated and replaced by the new Air Force Intelligence Command, which in turn was redesignated the Air Intelligence Agency on October 1, 1993.

Two of the best known of the support commands, AFSC and AFLC, were combined into the Air Force Materiel Command (AFMC). In addition to the pressing overall need to reduce personnel and consolidate functions, one of the principal reasons for combining the organizations was a fundamental change in the way the Air Force did business. In the rush toward centralization, the Department of Defense has essentially taken over procurement, with an assistant secretary for acquisition making the decisions on all major hardware purchases—in essence, doing work that AFSC formerly did. The services do not like it, and most senior Air Force officers do not consider it judicious to have the decisions on weapons to be used by the force to be made by temporary political appointees. But it is currently a fact of life, and made the creation of AFMC logical.

Even though the Air University and the Air Training Command had often been interrelated in the past, their combination into the Air Education and Training Command was traumatic. McPeak wanted to bring the Air Force Academy under the AETC umbrella, but recognized that it would require too much lobbying effort on his part to do so.

The disestablishment of all the commands involved an awareness of the sensitivities involved. A great deal of preparation went into the process, including soliciting ideas for the changes from the affected commands SAC, TAC, and MAC themselves.

Elements of each unit were combined to form the Air Combat Command (ACC) and the Air Mobility Command (AMC). In the initial planning, ACC received the fighters, bombers, reconnaissance aircraft, intercontinental ballistic missiles, some tacitcal airlift, some tankers, and the C^3I functions. AMC received the strategic airlift, most tactical airlift, some tankers, aeromedical evacuation, and search and rescue. These allocations would change over time; the most important change was to reverse what McPeak calls his greatest mistake in the process, the allocation of ICBM forces to ACC instead of to Space Command. This was rectified about a year later.

Air Mobility Command was given the mission of worldwide strategic deployment. Air Combat Command was given the duty of providing reinforcement forces to the overseas command and is itself able to conduct independent, integrated air operations.

One of the most curious aspects of the great consolidation of these three premier commands was the delicacy with which it was handled and the courtesy with which members of one command treated their opposite numbers in another. In many ways this ran counter to the usual rough-and-ready humor of flying units, where joking insults can usually be expected to fly between bomber and fighter proponents. This was different, and they knew it. Understanding the situation full well, McPeak had to find a way to impose his clearly defined vision of the new Air Force structure and still permit members of the old commands to feel that they were participating in the decisions as to what the new commands would be called, what their missions would be, who would get which assets, what the new identifying insignias would be, and so on. McPeak was extremely sensitive to the heritage issues, and made his staff work hard to ensure that the numbers of the most famous units were preserved, along with their heraldry. After a considerable amount of often heated debate on this subject, the numbers and heraldry of most of the most famous units were saved.

Yet the net effect of a massive change entailing the transformation of three proud and distinguished commands into two new organizations is not measured merely by insignia and thoughtfulness. At every level it is a visceral challenge to humans whose jobs, reputations, promotions, and futures are on the line. It reached out to involve the families, not only because of the stress felt by each service member but because moves were going to be necessary to houses would have to be sold and schools changed, again. This came about during a period when the Air Force, for the first time, was suffering such severe reductions in manning strength that even dedicated members who had done an excellent job were being forced out. Given the commitment necessary to volunteer for service life, and given the lack of similar outside institutions, the uncertainty that racks military members during a downsizing of this magnitude is as great as that which grips the personnel of a civilian company like AT&T or IBM. Many had stayed in the service because it was a stable organization, with a predictable career path and an adequate retirement package if one performed well. Now all that was gone as well-qualified people with outstanding records suddenly found themselves forced to leave.

General Mike Loh was COMTAC at the time, and he recalls the process with a rueful pride, recognizing all the hazards that were attendant to the merger and all the efforts made to make things go smoothly. A "graduate" of the Creech school of quality consciousness, Loh would be the first Commander of the Air Combat Command, where he took the concept of TQM a step further to create a climate of what he called "ACC quality" in every aspect of the organization. But there were many pitfalls before ACC came into existence.

Loh notes that no corporation had ever gone through a simultaneous downsizing and restructuring of the magnitude undertaken by SAC and TAC, which were so different by the nature of their missions. SAC was a designated command i.e. with a defined mission under the control of the National Command Authority, very centralized, and still focused on the role of nuclear deterrence. TAC was far more decentralized, in part as a result of the influence of Generals Creech, O'Malley, and Russ and in part because it was TAC's mission to furnish forces to theater commands for operations.

And there was a genuine rivalry. Just thirty years before, as noted earlier, General Walter Sweeney had come from SAC to "Sacimsize" TAC; now, to mix metaphors, the shoe was on the other foot, and it seemed that TAC would be ascendant. It was now a fighter pilot air force, from the Chief of Staff, McPeak, to the first Commander of ACC, Loh. Even General George L. Butler, CINCSAC, and the last commander of that great organization, had started his career as a fighter pilot, flying F-4s in Vietnam.

McPeak had warned Loh that if too many resources were placed in Air Combat Command, the result would be "Air Combat Command being Snow White, and the seven dwarfs being the other major commands." Both men were determined to come up with a better way to provide balance, including putting the tankers into the Air Mobility Command.

The ACC mission seemed to call for the acquisition of the search and rescue forces. The stateside C-130 units were also shifted to Air Combat Command, on the basis that ACC had to provide that capacity to the theater commands in the event of emergencies. Loh knew that most C-130 units, including regular Air Force, Air National Guard, and Air Force Reserve, had always felt that they were "second-class citizens" in MAC, because their aircraft lacked the glamour and the capability of the C-141s and C-5s. He conscientiously went about the task of emphasizing how important the C-130s were to Air Combat Command because of theater operations. The result was that C-130 unit morale actually rose because of the transfer. Further, Loh took the additional step of seeing to it that people from the C-130 force (and the rescue force) were given positions of greater responsibility throughout ACC.

He adopted the same tactics with the 20th Air Force, which operated the ICBMs under the leadership of Lieutenant General Arlen Dirk Jameson. In SAC, the "missiliers" had always felt that they were not given the same recognition as warriors as were the bomber crews. Loh changed that, pointing out that the 20th Air Force could put its weapons on its targets faster than any other unit in the Air Force. The 20th Air Force was transferred to Space Command, with its ICBMs remaining a component of the U.S. Strategic Command for ICBM forces.

PATCHING UP THE REORGANIZATION

Big events are sometimes best understood in the small vignettes that accompany them. In the case of the gigantic reorganization of SAC, TAC, and MAC—household names for forty-six years—into the new AMC and ACC, a great deal of heat and energy went into the design of the patches the members would wear.

The patch became a symbol of who had won and who had lost the organizational wars. Loh recounts that he had solicited his new command for designs and submitted eight of them to Air Force Headquarters for consideration. McPeak rejected them all, insisting that the ACC combat patch be a duplicate of the old TAC patch, with the words "Air Combat Command" substituted for the words "Tactical Air Command."

The selection was a red flag to former members of SAC. Former SAC members were not mollified that the old SAC patch was slightly modified to become the U.S. Strategic Command patch. The MAC patch soldiered on as the AMC patch. Fortunately, as the new commands began to function, matters like patches and positions were forgotten in the drive to achieve the required proficiency with the new structure.

On June 1, 1992, General McPeak made a whirlwind tour, delivering addresses at Langley Air Force Base, Virginia, Scott Air Force Base, Illinois, and Offutt Air Force Base, Nebraska. His speeches symbolized the activation of Air Combat Command, Air Mobility Command, and U.S. Strategic Command, even as their predecessors, SAC, TAC, and MAC, were deactivated.

In each talk, McPeak made the same points. He congratulated the members and their predecessors for their professionalism and for their great victory in the Cold War. He pointed out how each of the previous commands had done brilliant work in its past endeavors under the command of the greatest names in the Air Force pantheon of heroes. He emphasized that they now carried their heritage on to a new mission in changes that were dictated by events, technology, and the passage of time. He reminded them that the past of each of the deactivated commands had been glorious, and predicted that the future for each of the new commands would be demanding—but equally glorious.

In these and other speeches, McPeak emphasized that the changes should not be regarded as a paring-down of the old Air Force, but instead as the building of a brand-new Air Force from the ground up to meet the challenges of the next century.

The great changes in commands were accompanied by further changes down the administrative hierarchy. The great numbered Air Forces were restructured so that they were no longer management headquarters but tactical echelons with their commanders wearing flight suits (or fatigues) to work each day. Staffs were reduced by 50 percent. The function of a numbered air force commander was changed from a commanding general to that of an inspector general, checking on each of the bases in his unit to test their wartime capability.

Further down the chain of command, wings were restructured so that one man (usually a general officer) would run the base and the wing. Composite units were created so that fighters and tankers (or fighters and airlifters) would no longer be in separate wings but part of the same unit.

McPeak's concept of the composite wing met with philosophical opposition, particularly after an F-16 collided in mid air with a C-130 at Pope Air Force Base, North Carolina. However, the level of resistance on composite wings was nothing compared to the furor created when he introduced a new Air Force uniform that seemed to many to be too similar to the Navy or airline uniforms. McPeak intended the new uniform to symbolize the new Air Force that had emerged from the restructuring: streamlined, clean, and without encumbrances. He was certain that his successors would begin adding insignia to it, and insists that it was well received by the enlisted force, which constitutes some 80 percent of the Air Force, as well as by half of the remaining 20 percent, the officers. Others perceived it as a defamation of the blue suit that had served so well so long.

Nonetheless, McPeak was the man of the hour when the Air Force was at its point of greatest change, and he had the personality, the drive, and the confidence of his superiors to push through the changes he believed in and had crafted. But as General Dougherty has pointed out, after any period of great change, a period of stability is always required, and two people emerged to foster this transition. One was the first female Secretary of the Air Force, Sheila E. Widnall, whose performance has impressed everyone in the service and out. The second was the new Chief of Staff, General Ronald R. Fogleman, the first airlift commander to accede to the post. Dr. Widnall had a distinguished academic career at the Massachusetts Institute of Technology and is internationally known for her work in fluid dynamics, particularly in the areas of aircraft turbulence and the vortices created by helicopter rotors. Like McPeak, Fogleman had flown F-100s and operated as a Fast FAC in Vietnam. After he had served as an F-15 demonstration pilot in many air shows, Fogleman's career path eventually took him to tanker and airlift aircraft. He became Commander in Chief of U.S. Transport Command and Commander of Air Force Air Mobility Command.

Fogleman put his stamp on the Air Force immediately with some very slight but very wise decisions involving compromises on the uniform controversy. Fogleman authorized the U.S. insignia to be worn again, and allowed officers to shift their insignia from the sleeve to the shoulder. He was thus able to satisfy most people with little effort and little expense. It was symbolic for the most part: some of the troops had spoken and Fogleman responded sensibly to their cry.

In the intervening months, Fogleman has made a series of statements on the future of the United States Air Force in light of national requirements, budget realities, and a series of studies prepared both within the Air Force and by the Joint Chiefs of Staff. He has called for the synergistic combination of all the services' capabilities, from the Air Force's stealth aircraft to the Navy's carriers to Army and Marine combat units, to provide deterrence to would-be aggressors of any type.

Fogleman has noted that the United States must transition from its past strategy of annihilation and attrition warfare to a concept which leverages our military capabilities by applying what he terms an "asymmetric force" strategy.

Demonstrated in part during the Persian Gulf War, an asymmetric strategy directly attacks enemy strategic and tactical centers of gravity—targets already defined by commanders in chief while developing war plans for their theater of operations. These centers of gravity include the enemy's leadership elite; command and control; internal security mechanisms; war production capabilities; and its armed forces. They comprise the enemy's ability to wage war effectively.

Asymmetric force strategy compels the enemy to submit to the U.S. will by the shock and surprise of confronting the imminent destruction of its foundations of power. It forces our adversaries to realize that the cost of continuing the conflict will outweigh any conceivable gains. Properly conducted, asymmetric strategy will compel an enemy to do our will with the least cost to the United States in lives and resources—and, given the new precision guided weapons, with the least cost in collateral damage to the enemy civilian population.

Fogleman points out that we have used the concept of asymmetric power to enforce United Nation's sanctions against Iraq. And, once the necessary elements were in place, asymmetric strategy forced such a reduction in the military advantage of the Bosnian Serbs that it led to the peace agreement.

The Chairman of the Joint Chiefs of Staff, General John M. Shalikashvili, approved the publication of *Joint Vision 2010*, which he described as a "conceptual template for how we will channel the vitality of our people and leverage technological opportunities to achieve new levels of effectiveness in joint warfighting."

The JCS document lays out four operational concepts: dominant maneuver, precision engagements, full-dimensional protection and focused logistics. All of these concepts are a vision of the future—and all are dependent upon airpower.

The aim of dominant maneuver is the control of the battlespace while attacking whatever the enemy holds dear. For the Air Force this means "air dominance," a term that transcends "air superiority." Air dominance means that you completely dominate the enemy so that you can fly in his territory with impunity while he cannot fly at all. It *does not* mean a classic battle of attrition in which you inflict more casualties than you receive, nor domination of one field of battle while the enemy dominates another. It means totally destroying the enemy's military capability with few or, if possible, no losses to American forces.

The concept of precision engagement means the ability to apply very lethal forces with great discrimination. Targets must be taken out with a minimum of collateral damage. In the past it has been demonstrated by the stealth fighter and precision-guided munitions. In the future it may well be demonstrated by the B-2 bomber with advanced munitions like the GATS-GAM (Global Positioning System-Aided Targeting System and Global Positioning System-Aided Munitions), or even by the airborne laser, a directed energy weapon designed not only to down theater ballistic missiles, but for many other applications as well.

The third element—full dimensional protection—means denying the enemy the ability to attack at any level, from a bomb-laden truck parked outside a barracks to an ICBM. It means an air and space dominance by the United States that permits us to attack the enemy at all points and denies him any sanctuary at all.

These lofty concepts have to be supported by focused logistics. In the past, transportation was expensive—and scarce—while supplies were cheap. Now the nature of technology makes supplies expensive, while transportation is relatively cheap. Stockpiles can be eliminated and replaced by "just-in-time" inventory methods.

Joint Vision 2010 will demand a great deal of the Air Force, but many of its requirements have been anticipated in a study that Fogelman and Secretary of the Air Force Sheila Widnall elicited from the Scientific Advisory Board. Asking them to follow in the footsteps of Arnold, von Karmann, Schriever, and Zuckert, they called for an independent, futuristic view of how the exponential rate of technological change will shape the Twenty-first Century Air Force. The response was *New World Vistas*, a 2,000-page study in fifteen volumes prepared by individual teams totaling more than 150 people, primarily civilian and military scientists. The future they predict for a time frame ten to twenty years from now is one of awesome power and responsibility.

THE THREAT

In recent years, all of the services have been given additional tasks in peacetime, ranging from peace-keeping and nation building to interdicting drug traffic and assisting Olympic events. Yet the primary purpose of the Air Force, as of all our military services, is to defend the interests of the United States. The size, strength, and capability of the Air Force has to be structured to meet the threats.

For the entire period of the Cold War the threat seemed well defined; the Soviet Union was a powerful nation with aggressive intent. But, it was presumed to have, and in fact did have, rational leaders who were able to temper their aggression to what they perceived as their best interests.

The threats of the future are not so well defined, and it is more difficult to plan what the correct force structure to meet them should be. In the best of all worlds, the twenty-first century would see a rise of reason and international harmony that would make all armed forces unnecessary. In a slightly less utopian situation, the majority of the nations of the earth would be able to join together and pool their resources to ensure that nations less altruistic were controlled.

Neither of these scenarios is likely. Currently, U.S. planning is based largely on the presumption that a major world war is unlikely, but as the sole superpower, the United States will be forced to maintain a reasonably large military force to meet emergency situations around the world. We should all probably be suspicious of this, not because it is not a sound theory, but simply because what is planned for is usually not what occurs.

There are an infinite number of possibilities that must be considered for the future. Ranging from the probable to the far-fetched, they must all be kept in mind.

1. Russia could gather its strength and return to its traditional nationalistic and expansionist agenda, with or without a return of Communism, presenting us with another threat from Eurasia.

2. Russia, while not returning to the same position of strength, could fall into the hands of a radical government whose control of nuclear weapons would be suspect, and which would therefore represent a greater threat even than the above.

3. Russia could ally itself with rogue states like Iran and Iraq, extending its influence and backing their demands with a formidable nuclear force. They might openly supply such states with nuclear weapons to have them operate as surrogates to confront the United States.

4. Or, the above situations could occur in another former state of the Soviet Union, for example, Kazakhstan.

5. The Republic of China could develop an extensive ICBM and SLBM fleet and begin an expansionist policy that would threaten our interests in the Far East. (Many people feel that this is perhaps the greatest threat of all.)

6. Any one of a number of rogue states—Libya, Iraq, Iran, Syria—could over the next twenty years assemble a sufficient arsenal of ICBMs to hold the world in hostage.

7. There might be a federation of fundamentalist Muslim states that would acquire a nuclear arsenal and use it to extend their policies.

8. It is not inconceivable that in a twenty-year period the new leaders of China and the new leaders of Japan might see that their best interest lies in cooperation—the country with the largest population and perhaps

the greatest amount of natural resources allied with the leading technological power of the world. Such a Pan-Asian movement is discounted
now because of the hostility remaining from World War II, but this
hostility could easily be completely overcome in the next twenty years
if it were to become a matter of ending Western dominance in Asia for
all time.

9. The Indian subcontinent is an unknown quantity at present, but it has
the population, the intelligence, and certainly the motivation to emerge
as a major nuclear force, and no one can say what threat it might represent.

Some of these concepts seem far-fetched today, as far-fetched as it might
have seemed in 1971 to say that the Soviet Union would collapse in twenty
years. Whether far-fetched or not, decisions have to be made as to the extent
to which such possibilities will be defended against, and by what means.

THE NEW WORLD VISTAS AIR FORCE

The *New World Vistas* study was based on a number of assumptions
stemming from the changed world conditions since the demise of the Soviet
Union. It assumes that the Air Force will have to be engaged in conflicts at
long distances from the United States against national or terrorist forces. It
assumes that public policy will demand a low casualty rate for U.S. forces. It
will also demand that the enemy forces be completely defeated but with a
minimum of casualties and collateral damage to them. The study anticipates
advances in potential enemy technology as well, to the extent that we might
no longer have a monopoly on stealth aircraft, that directed-energy weapons
(lasers or microwaves) could be used against us, and that our information
system would be attacked. Underlying all these assumptions is the recognition
that costs will be equal in importance to capability, and that the number of
people in the Air Force will be reduced.

The individual volumes of the study range across a wide spectrum of
subjects from munitions to human systems and biotechnology to every aspect
of space technology. The study covers improvements on current weapons,
such as those used to suppress enemy air defenses, and also exotic new concepts such as using directed-energy beams to destroy antiaircraft missiles in
flight and ballistic missiles in their boost phase.

The latter capability must be viewed as the most pressing need of all,
given that there are at present almost forty types of short-or intermediate-
range missiles deployed in dozens of Third World countries around the world.
Given the certainty that longer-range missiles and nuclear warheads have
been or will be sold by the former states of the Soviet Union and or China,
the threat is genuine and near-term. The response to it should be removed
from the realm of *New World Vistas* and thrust firmly into Congress's lap.

The study goes on to enumerate dazzling possibilities including uninhabited (the word a reach from the politically incorrect "unmanned" term) combat aerial vehicles (UCAVs) flown remotely by pilots who never leave the ground; 1,000,000-pound-gross-weight transports, as well as supersonic and stealth transports; and uninhabited reconnaissance aerial vehicles (URAV) that can observe via sensors and synthetic aperture radar from hundreds of miles away, or get down and dirty with overflights that would ferret out signs of chemical or biological agents.

As far out as each volume of *New World Vistas* reaches, the contributors underpin their arguments with fundamental questions of research. The exotic new aircraft suggested by the study are backed up by recommendations as to the improvement of materials, fuels, lubricants, explosives, electronics— all of the elements of the weapon system.

Planning, manning, and controlling exotic systems of the types alluded to above will require almost as great a step forward in personnel selection as it will in technological development. The concept of the well-rounded college student being trained in flying school to step into a cockpit and handle the equipment will be a thing of the past. Anyone operating the systems will have to have a profound familiarity with computers, their language and their methodologies. The fifty-mission crushed hat, the A-2 jacket, and the rows of ribbons will in the Air Force of *New World Vistas* be only poignant symbols of the past, overtaken by the requirements of the computer age and perhaps replaced by less glamorous devices such as pocket protectors, mouse pads, and screen-savers.

THE PROBABLE AIR FORCE OF THE FUTURE

The idealized Air Force of *New World Vistas* is a desirable and perhaps an attainable dream, but in fifty to a hundred years, rather than in ten to thirty. Certainly the research must be launched that will lead to the futuristic capabilities that would fit so perfectly with the concept of attaining dominance with few casualties on either side.

Most Air Force leaders interviewed felt that the Air Force of the future would very closely resemble that of today, simply because the massive funding required to achieve even some of the many research and development goals is not going to be available. In the past twenty years, the most judicious budgeting combined with emphasis placed on modernization and research and development resulted in an Air Force that has a mixed bag of new equipment which sets the standard of the world and aging modified equipment. The replacement of this force with the futuristic systems suggested in *New World Vistas* with the budgets that will probably be available seems highly unlikely.

The Air Force of the first quarter of the next century will be representative of today's ongoing trends: slightly smaller forces, highly trained and armed with high-technology equipment. In simple hardware terms, the Lockheed Martin F-22 fighter, the McDonnell Douglas C-17 transport, and the Joint Advanced Strike Technology (JAST) fighter are the primary systems that need to be acquired to sustain a modern force. The Northrop B-2 will lead the fleet, but the Rockwell B-1B, with its greater numbers, larger payload, and higher speed, will be the primary bomber. The B-52H will remain in service, as will the Lockheed/Martin F-117A. All strike and bomber aircraft will use precision-guided munitions, including highly refined ALCMs. Refueling support will be provided by the existing tanker fleet, possibly supplemented by some tankers modified from civilian airliners. Precision-guided missiles will themselves become an object of intense Congressional interest and scrutiny.

And this seems to be a rational approach until the projected quantities of aircraft are considered. The F-22 procurement, if unchanged, will extend to about 450 aircraft. The number of JAST fighters is undetermined. It now appears that only twenty-one B-2s, including the refitted prototype, will be procured. There are currently eighty-four B-1s and eighty-five B-52s in active service.

Over a twenty-year period, attrition will undoubtedly reduce these numbers slightly. The prospect that this force will be able to defeat, within a two-month period, two enemies in two major regional conflicts (MRCs) on opposite sides of the globe seems marginal indeed. A sustained conflict in even one area would be difficult, for flying large aircraft over great distances into hostile fire will inevitably generate losses.

The prospect is more encouraging for obtaining air supremacy by means of the F-22, in combination with the "information domination" derived from AWACS and Joint STARS aircraft. There are advanced foreign fighters on the horizon, but none of these will be a match for the F-22. They will, however, be more than equal to even improved F-15s, which makes it doubly important to ensure that F-22 procurement is fulfilled despite the inevitable objections to the cost.

The future of the intercontinental ballistic missile force is dependent upon the progress of disarmament negotiations. In the best of all worlds, with all nations pursuing a rational course, it might be that ICBMs and, indeed, all nuclear weapons could be removed from service everywhere. Even if the current nuclear powers agreed to disarm, it seems improbable that proud nations like Iraq, Iran, India, Pakistan, and others, which will have made such costly, determined efforts to obtain nuclear arms over such a long period of time, will agree to give them up just as they obtain them. By the year 2020 there will be more than a dozen and perhaps as many as twenty countries with a nuclear capability. To achieve a nuclear-weapon-free world, every country would have to agree to dispose of its weapons in a way that could absolutely be verified before any other country would give up its own. Given the state of the world, the prospect seems doubtful.

Therefore the United States will probably be forced to continue to depend to a great degree on a nuclear deterrent force as the basis of its political strategy. At lower thresholds of threat, it will have to depend upon a small, aging, but highly proficient Air Force to use precision-guided conventional munitions to ensure that its policies are carried out.

In this process, two other changes loom. The first is a near-term possibility that the extraordinarily adept use of space to extend USAF military capability might be recognized by a name change to the United States Aerospace Force. The second is a far-term look to fifty years in the future. If there is a continued convergence of the missions and the capabilities of the present four services—Army, Navy, Marines, and Air Force—the trend that has given us the unified commands such as U.S. Transportation Command, U.S. Strategic Command, and U.S. Space Command might ultimately lead to a formal unification.

THE AIR FORCE AT FIFTY

All of its members, and all citizens, can look back over the fifty-year history of the United States Air Force with pride in the past and confidence in the future. For almost all of those fifty years, it has been the most incredibly powerful armed force in history, providing the United States with a striking power that dwarfs that of all other countries. Even though its charter is to fight for and defend the United States, much of its efforts through the years has been in compassionate missions, either directly when airlifting supplies to countries stricken by earthquakes or flood, or indirectly by enforcing United Nations sanctions in countries like Iraq or Somalia.

Over those same fifty years, the USAF has grown from a force of piston-engine aircraft, little different from those of World War II, to a force that has truly integrated space warfare into its capabilities. It has been able to do so because its leadership, in the tradition of Hap Arnold and Bernard Schriever, refused to focus on the past but instead resolutely looked to research and development to provide the technologies for the future. In the development of those technologies, the USAF, in the tradition of Curtis LeMay and so many others, never forgot that its task was to fly and fight.

At fifty, the USAF has to face all the problems of contemporary society, including concerns about drugs, sexual harassment, downsizing, child-care, and all the other difficulties faced not only by the United States but by the world in general. Despite a steady downward trend in accidents, the Air Force has been rocked by tragic mishaps, including the shooting down of two Blackhawk helicopters in Iraq, the wanton violation of flying discipline which caused a B-52 to crash, and the loss of the Boeing T-43 carrying Secretary of Commerce Ronald Brown—all inexplicable lapses in discipline and training. To deal with these internal problems of leadership and discipline, the USAF must tread a measured path between "one mistake and you're out" and too broad an interpretation of instructions and regulations.

Discipline must be enforced, equal opportunity must be made available, mission requirements must be met, training must be given, and the quality of life must be preserved, all with diminishing resources. It is a daunting task, one requiring the best leadership at every level.

In the future the USAF will not only have to maintain its standards of equipment, training, and fighting capability, it will also have to muster the resources to induce Congress to see that a viable defense industry is maintained. It used to be that the aircraft industry could be maintained with a handful of contracts doled out to a few industries to keep them in business. Now it is much more complex, for not only do the airframe and engine manufacturers have to be sustained, but also toolmakers and the manufacturers of specialized electronic systems. Many of these industries are essentially irreplaceable if allowed to die out; the disciplines move too swiftly to permit an industry to be "reconstituted," in the catchphrase of the time. Our dependence upon foreign suppliers will have to be closely monitored, for their availability during any future emergency will depend upon the political situation obtaining at that time.

Despite the realities of budgetary limitations and the myriad, formless threats that lie ahead, there is one undying constant that will never change, and that guarantees the success of the Air Force in the future and ensures that it will remain the mainstay of our national defense. That constant is the quality and dedication of the personnel who volunteer to serve in its ranks, to accept the difficulties of service life, and to excel in meeting whatever challenges the future presents. No matter what lies ahead, the people of the United States Air Force will continue to do the planning, improvising, sacrificing, fighting, and, when necessary, dying, necessary to keep our country free.

APPENDIX ONE

SECRETARIES
OF THE AIR FORCE

CHIEFS OF STAFF
OF THE AIR FORCE

CHIEF MASTER SERGEANTS
OF THE AIR FORCE

SECRETARIES OF THE AIR FORCE

Name	Dates in Office	
	From	To
Stuart Symington	September 18, 1947	April 24, 1950
Thomas K. Finletter	April 24, 1950	January 20, 1953
Harold E. Talbott	February 4, 1953	August 13, 1955
Donald A. Quarles	August 15, 1955	April 30, 1957
James H. Douglas, Jr.	May 1, 1957	December 10, 1959
Dudley C. Sharp	December 11, 1959	January 20, 1961
Eugene M. Zuckert	January 24, 1961	September 30, 1965
Harold Brown	October 1, 1965	February 15, 1969
Robert C. Seamans, Jr.	February 15, 1969	May 14, 1973
John L. McLucas (Acting)	May 15, 1973	July 18, 1973
John L. McLucas	July 18, 1973	November 23, 1975
James W. Plummer (Acting)	November 24, 1975	January 1, 1976
Thomas C. Reed	January 2, 1976	April 6, 1977
John C. Stetson	April 6, 1977	May 18, 1979
Hans Mark (Acting)	May 18, 1979	July 26, 1979
Hans Mark	July 26, 1979	February 9, 1981
Verne Orr	February 9, 1981	November 30, 1985
Russell A. Rourke	December 9, 1985	April 7, 1986
Edward C. Aldridge, Jr. (Acting)	April 8, 1986	June 8, 1986
Edward C. Aldridge, Jr.	June 9, 1986	December 16, 1988
James F. McGovern (Acting)	December 16, 1988	April 29, 1989
John J. Welch, Jr. (Acting)	April 29, 1989	May 21, 1989
Donald B. Rice	May 22, 1989	January 20, 1993
Michael B. Donley (Acting)	January 20, 1993	July 13, 1993
Gen. Merrill A. McPeak (Acting)	July 14, 1993	August 5, 1993
Sheila E. Widnall	August 6, 1993	

Chiefs of Staff of the Air Force

Name	Dates in Office	
	From	To
Gen. Carl A. Spaatz	September 26, 1947	April 29, 1948
Gen. Hoyt S. Vandenberg	April 30, 1948	June 29, 1953
Gen. Nathan F. Twining	June 30, 1953	June 30, 1957
Gen. Thomas D. White	July 1, 1957	June 30, 1961
Gen. Curtis E. Lemay	June 30, 1961	January 31, 1965
Gen. John P. McConnell	February 1, 1965	July 31, 1969
Gen. John D. Ryan	August 1, 1969	July 31, 1973
Gen. George S. Brown	August 1, 1973	June 30, 1974
Gen. David C. Jones	July 1, 1974	June 20, 1978
Gen. Lew Allen, Jr.	July 1, 1978	June 30, 1982
Gen. Charles A. Gabriel	July 1, 1982	June 30, 1986
Gen. Larry D. Welch	July 1, 1986	June 30, 1990
Gen. Michael J. Dugan	July 1, 1990	September 17, 1990
Gen. John M. Loh (Acting)	September 18, 1990	October 29, 1990
Gen. Merrill A. McPeak	October 30, 1990	October 25, 1994
Gen. Ronald R. Fogleman	October 26, 1994	

Chief Master Sergeants of the Air Force

Name	Dates in Office	
	From	To
CMSAF Paul W. Airey	April 3, 1967	July 31, 1969
CMSAF Donald L. Harlow	August 1, 1969	September 30, 1971
CMSAF Richard D. Kisling	October 1, 1971	September 30, 1973
CMSAF Thomas N. Barnes	October 1, 1973	July 31, 1977
CMSAF Robert D. Gaylor	August 1, 1977	July 31, 1979
CMSAF James M. McCoy	August 1, 1979	July 31, 1981
CMSAF Arthur L. Andrews	August 1, 1981	July 31, 1983
CMSAF Sam E. Parish	August 1, 1983	June 30, 1986
CMSAF James C. Binnicker	July 1, 1986	July 31, 1990
CMSAF Gary R. Pfingston	August 1, 1990	October 25, 1994
CMSAF David J. Campanale	October 26, 1994	November 4, 1996
CMSAF Eric W. Beaken	November 5, 1996	

APPENDIX TWO

COMMANDS OF THE
UNITED STATES AIR FORCE

AIR FORCE COMBAT COMMAND (ACC)

Air Force Combat Command has its headquarters at Langley Air Force Base, Virginia. Its mission is to organize, train, equip, and maintain combat-ready USAF bombers and USAF combat-coded fighter and attack aircraft based in the continental United States. A lineal descendant of the Strategic Air Command and the Tactical Air Command, ACC provides nuclear-capable forces to the U.S. Strategic Command. As a corollary mission, it monitors and intercepts illegal drug traffic and tests new combat equipment. It supplies aircraft to the five geographic unified commands, the Atlantic, European, Pacific, Southern, and Central Commands. ACC provides air defense forces to the North American Aerospace Defense Command (NORAD) and operates certain air mobility forces in support of the U.S. Transportation Command. It provides fighter, bomber, reconnaissance, combat delivery, battle management, and rescue aircraft, as well as command, control, communications, and intelligence systems.

With a total of approximately 229,000 personnel, ACC operates with four numbered air forces, the 1st at Tyndall AFB, Florida, the 8th at Barksdale AFB, Louisiana, the 9th at Shaw AFB, South Carolina, and the 12th at Davis Monthan AFB, Arizona. ACC has twenty-six wings and one direct reporting unit, the Air Warfare Center. It operates 1,020 aircraft, including Rockwell B-1B, Northrop B-2, and Boeing B-52 bombers; McDonnell Douglas F-15A/C and Lockheed Martin F-16 fighters; Fairchild A-10, McDonnell Douglas F-15E, Lockheed Martin F-111, and Lockheed Martin F-117 attack planes; Boeing KC-135 tankers; Lockheed C-130 and Alenia C-27A combat delivery aircraft; and several other miscellaneous types.

AIR MOBILITY COMMAND (AMC)

Air Mobility Command has its headquarters at Scott Air Force Base, Illinois. Its mission is to provide rapid global airlift and aerial refueling for U.S. armed forces and serve as a component of the U.S. Transportation Command. It provides forces to theater commands as required. In addition, it performs stateside aeromedical evacuation missions and provides operational support aircraft and visual documentation support. Its history extends back through the days of the Military Air Command, Military Air Transport Service, and Air Transport Command. With approximately 123,000 personnel, AMC operates with two numbered air forces, the 15th at Travis AFB, California, and the 21st at McGuire AFB, New Jersey. It has eleven wings and two direct reporting units, the Air Mobility Warfare Center and the Tanker Airlift Control Center. AMC operates 924 aircraft, including the Lockheed Martin C-5, McDonnell Douglas C-17, and Lockheed Martin C-141 mobility aircraft and the McDonnell Douglas KC-10 and Boeing KC-135 tanker aircraft.

Air Force Materiel Command (AFMC)

Air Force Materiel Command has its headquarters at Wright Patterson Air Force Base, Dayton, Ohio. It manages the research, development, test, acquisition, and sustainment of weapon systems and produces and acquires advanced systems. A principal function is the operation of seventeen major centers for development, test, operational support, and specialized support of Air Force equipment and personnel. In addition it operates the USAF Test Pilot School and the USAF School of Aerospace Medicine. It is a lineal descendant of the former Air Force Systems Command and Air Force Logistics Command and of various similar predecessor organizations. With about 115,000 personnel, it operates thirty-nine different types of aircraft. It also supports 10,000 aircraft and 32,000 engines. The command's extensive facilities for research, test, and manufacturing have a capital value approaching $50 billion.

Air Education and Training Command (AETC)

The Air Education and Training Command has its headquarters at Randolph Air Force Base, Texas. It recruits and prepares officers, airmen, and civilian employees for their Air Force duties. It provides international and interservice training and ecucation and medical service training. A descendant of the old Air Training Command and the Air University, it provides continuing education for Air Force personnel throughout their careers. It consists of the 2d Air Force at Kessler AFB, Mississippi, and the 19th Air Force at Randolph AFB, Texas. The educational headquarters is the Air University at Maxwell Field, Alabama. It is also responsible for the Air Force Recruiting Service and the Air Force Security Assistance Training Squadron, all at Randolph AFB, Texas, and the 59th Medical Wing at Lackland AFB, Texas. AETC has ten flying training wings and operates more than 1,500 aircraft, including the Raytheon T-1A, Slingsby T-3, Cessna T-37, Northrop T-38, and Boeing T-43 trainers; the Lockheed C-5, Beechcraft C-12, Learjet C-21, and Lockheed-Martin C-141 transports and Boeing KC-135 tankers; the McDonnell Douglas F-15 and Lockheed Martin F-16 fighters; and many varieties of the Sikorsky MH-53J and HH/MH-60G helicopters, in conjunction with the Bell UH-1.

AIR FORCE SPACE COMMAND (AFSPC)

The Air Force Space Command has its headquarters at Peterson Air Force Base, Colorado. It has six major missions: the operation and test of USAF ICBM forces for the U.S. Strategic Command; operation of missile warning radars, sensors, and satellites; operation of national space launch facilities and operational boosters; operation of worldwide space surveillance radars and optical systems; provision of command and control for DOD satellites; and provision of ballistic missile warning to NORAD and U.S. Space Command. Other responsibilities are broadly based, from serving as lead command for all UH-1 helicopter developments to developing and integrating space support for combat units and providing communications, computer, and base support to NORAD. In addition it supplies range and launch facilities for civil and military space launches. With approximately 20,000 personnel, it has two numbered air forces, the 14th at Vandenberg AFB, California, and the 20th at F. E. Warren AFB, Wyoming. Its primary offensive weapons are fifty Peacekeeper and 530 Minuteman III ICBMs. In addition it operates the Navstar Global Positioning System, the Defense Satellite Communication System, and the Defense Meteorological Satellite Program. Among its other communication responsibilities are the satellite communication NATO III, the Fleet Satellite Communications System, and the UFH follow-on. AFSPC provides the ballistic missile warning systems, including the Ballistic Missile Early Warning System, Pave Paws radars, the Perimeter Acquisistion Radar Attack Characterization System, and many conventional radars. It also is responsible for the space surveillance systems and the satellite command and control system.

AIR FORCE SPECIAL OPERATIONS COMMAND (AFSOC)

The Air Force Special Operations Command has its headquarters at Hurburt Field, Florida. Many believe it will become one of the most important Air Force commands in the future. It is the Air Force component of the U.S. Special Operations Command, a unified command. The AFSOC's mission is to deploy specialized airpower and deliver special operations combat power anywhere, anytime. It is dedicated to unconventional warfare, special reconnaissance, counterterrorism activities, and internal defense support for the unified commands. In addition to the war-oriented aspects of its mission it is also responsible for providing humanitarian assistance and conducting antidrug and psychological warfare operations. With only just over 12,000 personnel, it is divided into one special operations wing and three special operations groups. Its approximate total of 130 aircraft consist of various models of the Lockheed Martin C-130 and the Sikorsky MH-53 and MH-60 helicopters.

AFSOC's motto "Any Time, Any Place" derives from the long history of its predecessor units, which reach back in time to World War II, when the 1st Air Commando Group was formed to support General Orde Windgate and his "chindit" jungle fighters in Burma.

PACIFIC AIR FORCES (PACAF)

The Pacific Air Forces has its headquarters at Hickam Air Force Base, Hawaii. The mission of PACAF is to plan, conduct, and coordinate offensive and defensive air operations in the Pacific and Asian theaters. It organizes, trains, equips, and maintains resources to conduct air operations. Its lineage extends back to the U.S. Army Air Forces in the Far East, and its history has been characterized by the conduct of far-reaching combat operations, often in concert with allied powers.

With a total of about 46,000 personnel, PACAF has four numbered air forces, the 5th at Yokota AB, Japan, the 7th at Osan AB, South Korea, the 11th at Elmendorf AFB, Alaska, and the 13th at Andersen AFB, Guam. It possesses about 320 aircraft, but would be reinforced by units from ACC and AMC in the event of an emergency. Its strength includes the McDonnell Douglas F-15C/D/E, Lockheed Martin F-16C/D, and Fairchild A-10 fighters; the Boeing E-3 AWACS aircraft; the KC-135 tanker; the McDonnell Douglas C-9, Beechcraft C-12, Learjet C-21, Lockheed Martin C-130, and Boeing C-135 transports; and the Bell UH-1 and Sikorsky HH-60 helicopters.

U.S. AIR FORCES IN EUROPE (USAFE)

The U.S. Air Forces in Europe has its headquarters at Ramstein Air Base, Germany. Like command of PACAF, command of USAFE is often a stepping-stone to the position of Air Force Chief of Staff. The mission of USAFE is to plan, conduct, control, coordinate, and support air and space operations to achieve U.S. national and NATO objectives assigned by the Commander in Chief of the U.S. European Command. It also supports U.S. military operations in Europe, the Mediterranean, the Middle East, and Africa. Again like PACAF, it would be reinforced by combat forces from the United States in the event of an emergency. It has three numbered air forces, the 3d at RAF Mildenhall, United Kingdom; the 16th, at Aviano AB, Italy; and the 17th at Sembach Annex, Germany. It has six wings and three regional support groups. With a total personnel of about 32,000, it has about 220 aircraft on hand, including the McDonnell Douglas F-15C/D and Lockheed/Martin F-15C/D fighters; the Fairchild A-10 and McDonnell Douglas F-15E attack aircraft; and about fifty other aircraft of various types. USAFE has also been deeply involved with the North Atlantic Treaty Organization (NATO), which has had profound effect upon the development of the Air Force. Although the subject is too complex to develop here, the NATO Allies for the most part embraced Air Force training, tactical doctrine, and much equipment. The European Central Region was the sizing and defining scenario for Cold War nonstrategic forces. Thus the A-10, F-15, F-16, AWACs, J-STARS, C-17, and others were all defined in the context of support of U.S. policy in conjunction with NATO.

APPENDIX THREE

GUARD, RESERVE, AIR FORCE ACADEMY, AND CIVIL AIR PATROL

AIR NATIONAL GUARD (ANG)

The Air National Guard has its headquarters in Washington, D.C. The lineage of the ANG stretches through the Army National Guard all the way to 1636 and the establishment of the Massachusetts National Guard. The first aviation element of the Guard was established on August 2, 1909, when the Missouri National Guard created a fifteen-man aero-detachment. Guard air units were federalized for the Mexican expedition of 1916 and have participated in all major conflicts since that time. However, it was not until 1920 that aviation units of the National Guard were formally established and recognized, with two units in place by 1921. By World War II there were twenty-nine National Guard observation squadrons; all were called to active duty by October 1941. After World War II, National Guard air units were formed with a much broader span of duties, but were primarily equipped with fighters. By 1949, there were 514 individual ANG units equipped with 2,263 aircraft. But, as one observer of the scene said in 1950, the United States had forty-nine air forces—the USAF and forty-eight Air National Guard air forces, one for each state. Sixty-six ANG units were recalled for the Korean War, in which they served with distinction. The standards of equipment and training for the ANG were continuously improved during the Cold War years, so that it was able to make a substantial contribution to the war effort in Vietnam. One direct result of this performance was the incorporation of the Air National Guard into the "Total Force" policy under which ANG, Reserve, and regular Air Force units all trained on similar equipment to the same standards of proficiency. At the present time, the ANG has eighty-eight wings, assigned to Air Combat Command, Air Education and Training Command, Air Force Special Operations Command, Air Mobility Command, and Pacific Air Forces. It has approximately 1,200 aircraft and provides the USAF 100 percent of the fighter interceptor force, 45 percent of tactical airlift, 43 percent of KC-135 air refueling, 33 percent of fighters, 28 percent of rescue, and 8 percent of strategic airlift. The ANG flies the Lockheed Martin C-5A,

C-141, and C/HC/EC-130 transports; the Boeing KC-135 tanker; the Fairchild A/OA-10A attack aircraft; the Rockwell B-1B bomber; and the McDonnell Douglas F-15s and Lockheed Martin F-16 fighters.

U.S. AIR FORCE RESERVE (USAFR)

The U.S. Air Force Reserve has its headquarters at Robins Air Force Base, Georgia. It traces its origins to the National Defense Act of 1916, which established a Reserve Corps of 2,300 officers and men. It remained a part of the organization of the antecedents of the USAF, and in 1950 it was placed under the Continental Air Command (CONAC). The USAFR became a separate operating agency (SOA) in 1968, and is now a field operating agency It has three numbered air forces, the 4th at McClellan AFB, California; the 10th at Bergstrom Air Reserve Station, Texas; and the 22nd at Dobbins Air Reserve Base, Georgia. There are thirty-seven flying wings operating about 470 aircraft, including the Boeing B-52 H bomber; the Lockheed Martin F-16 fighter; the Fairchild A/OA-10 attack aircraft; the Lockheed Martin C-5A/B, C-141B, and C-130E-H air lifters; the Boeing KC-135 tanker; the Lockheed Martin HC-130H and Sikorsky HH 60G rescue aircraft; and the Lockheed Martin WC-130 H weather and MC-130E special operations aircraft. In its early post–World War II years, the Air Force Reserve was poorly equipped; during the Korean War it had received Curtiss C-46 and Douglas C-47 transports along with Douglas B-26 light bombers. Modernization was slow until after the Vietnam War, when a surplus of equipment made it possible to equip reserve units with Cessna A-37 and Republic F-105 attack aircraft, McDonnell Douglas F-4 and Lockheed Martin F-16 fighters, several versions of the Lockheed Martin C-130 transports, Boeing KC-135 tankers, and Sikorsky H-3 Jolly Green Giant helicopters.

As a part of the Total Force, ten Reserve units participated with distinction in the Persian Gulf War.

U.S. AIR FORCE ACADEMY (USAFA)

The Air Force Academy located at Colorado Springs, Colorado. Its mission is to develop and inspire air and space leaders for the future, to produce dedicated Air Force officers and leaders, and to instill that leadership through academics, military training, athletic conditioning, and spiritual and ethical development. Because of its specialized nature, it is a direct reporting unit (DRU), reporting to Headquarters USAF. Appointment to the Academy is made by Congressional sponsor or by meeting eligibility requirements in other competitive methods. It was established on April 1, 1954, and the first class of 306 cadets entered in July 1955 at a temporary location at Lowry Air Force Base, Colorado. The present complex was completed by August 1958, in time for the first class's graduation in 1959. In 1996, 1,218 cadets entered the program. Over the years, approximately one-third of the cadets leave the program, 75 percent by resignation. About 60 percent of the graduates go on to pilot training. Women entered the Academy as cadets in 1976; almost 3,000 had entered by 1996, with an average graduation rate of about 61 percent. Cadets complete four years of study to obtain a Bachelor of Science degree. The total cadet enrollment is about 4,000, and 1,288 officers, 1, 114 enlisted personnel, and 1,861 civilians are required to operate the Academy. An intensive flying familiarization program is given, using ninety-five aircraft of several different types, including gliders.

THE CIVIL AIR PATROL

The Civil Air Patrol has a long and distinguished tradition that reaches back to its founding on December 1, 1941. During World War II, the CAP allowed private pilots and aviation enthusiasts to use their skills in civil defense efforts. It came under the control and direction of the United States Army Air Forces in 1943, and became a permanent peacetime institution on July 1, 1946, when President Harry S. Truman established it as a federally chartered, benevolent, civilian corporation with Public Law 476. In May, 1948, the CAP became an official auxiliary of the United States Air Force.

The mission of the CAP is aerospace education, cadet training, and emergency services. Its members fly 80 percent of the search and rescue mission hours directed by the Air Force Rescue and Coordination Center at Langley Air Force Base, Virginia.

Since 1985, it has assisted the U.S. Customs Service in its counter-drug efforts by flying air reconnaissance missions along U.S. boundaries, and now works with the Drug Enforcement Administration and the U.S. Forest Service in a similar capacity.

Membership consists of 19,000 cadets and 34,000 adult volunteers organized into fifty-two wings—one for each state, the District of Columbia, and Puerto Rico. The CAP's members operate more than 5,000 privately owned aircraft and 530 CAP aircraft.

BIBLIOGRAPHY

27th Fighter Escort Wing. Yearbook. Texas: Taylor Publishing Company.

Air Force Association. *Foundation Forum: Opportunities and Challenges in Acquisition and Logistics.* Washington, D.C.: Aerospace Education Foundation, 1995.

Air Force Materiel Command: A Legacy in Military Aviation Logistics and R&D. Ohio: Air Force Materiel Command, 1993.

Arnold, Henry H. *Global Mission.* New York: Harper & Brothers, 1949.

Ballard, Jack S., Ray L. Bowers, et al. *The United States Air Force in Southeast Asia, 1961–1973: An Illustrated Account.* Washington, D.C.: Office of Air Force History, 1984.

Bergquist, Mayor Ronald E. *The Role of Airpower in the Iran-Iraq War.* Montgomery, AL: Air University Press, 1988.

Blumenson, Martin, Robert W. Coakley, et al. *Command Decisions.* Washington, D.C.: Office of the Chief of Military History, United States Army, 1960.

Bonds, Ray, ed. *The Vietnam War: The Illustrated History of the Conflict in Southeast Asia.* New York: Salamander Books, 1979.

Bowers, Ray L. *The United States Air Force in Southeast Asia: Tactical Airlift.* Washington, D.C.: Office of Air Force History, 1983.

Boyd, Robert J. *SAC Fighter Planes and Their Operations.* Omaha Headquarters, Strategic Air Command, 1988.

Boyne, Walter J. *Silver Wings, A History of the United States Air Force.* New York: Simon & Schuster, 1993.

———*Clash of Wings, World War II in the Air.* New York: Simon & Schuster, 1994.

———*Gulf War.* Lincolnwood, Illinois: Publications International, 1991.

———*Weapons of Desert Storm.* Lincolnwood, Illinois: Publications International 1991.

Bradley, Omar N., and Clay Blair. *A General's Life*. New York: Simon & Schuster, 1983.

Brennan, Matthew. *Headhunters: Stories from the 1st Squadron, 9th Cavalry, in Vietnam, 1965–1971.*. Novato, Calif.: Presidio Press, 1987.

Bright, Charles D., ed. *Historical Dictionary of the U.S. Air Force*. New York: Greenwood Press, 1992.

Buckingham, William A., Jr. *Operation Ranch Hand: The Air Force and Herbicides in Southeast Asia, 1961–1971*. Washington, D.C.: Office of Air Force History, 1982.

Burnham, Frank A. *Aerial Search: The CAP Story*. Fallbrook, Calif.: Aero Publishers, 1974.

Bush, Vannevar. *Modern Arms and Free Men: A Discussion of the Role of Science in Preserving Democracy*. New York: Simon & Schuster, 1949.

Chant, Christopher. *A Compendium of Armaments and Military Hardware*. London and New York: Routledge & Kegan Paul, 1987.

Chinnery, Philip D. *Life on the Line*. New York: St. Martin's Press, 1988.

————. *Vietnam: The Helicopter War*. Annapolis, Md.: Naval Institute Press, 1991.

Cooling, Benjamin Franklin. *Case Studies in the Development of Close Air Support*. Washington, D.C.: Office of Air Force History, 1990.

Coyne, James P. *Airpower in the Gulf*. Arlington, VA: Air Force Association, 1992.

Davis, Larry. *Wild Weasel: The SAM Suppression Story*. Carrolton, TX: Squadron/Signal Publications, 1993.

Denton, Senator Jeremiah A. *When Hell Was in Session*. Montgomery, AL.: Traditional Press, 1982.

Department of the Air Force. *Vezzano to Desert Storm (History of the Fifteenth Air Force, 1943–1991)*. Washington, D.C.: Department of the Air Force.

The Development of Air Doctrine in the Army Air Arm, 1917–1941. USAF Historical Studies No. 89. Montgomery, Alabama: USAF Historical Division, 1955.

Donald, David, ed., *U.S. Air Force, Air Power Directory*. London: Aerospace Publishing, 1992.

Donnelly, Thomas, Margaret Roth, and Caleb Baker. *Operation Just Cause*. New York: Lexington Books, 1991.

Dorr, Robert F. *Air War Hanoi*. London, New York, and Sydney: Blandford Press, 1988.

————. *Desert Shield, the Buildup: The Complete Story*. Motorbooks International, 1991.

————. *Desert Storm, Air War*. Osceola, WI: Motorbooks International, 1991.

Dorr, Robert F. and Warren Thompson. *The Korean Air War*. Osceola, WI: Motorbooks International, 1994.

Drendel, Lou. *Air War over Southeast Asia: A Pictorial Record*. Vol. 2, *1967–1970*. Carrolton, Texas: Squadron/Signal Publications, Inc., 1983.

————. *. . . And Kill MIGS*. Carrolton, Texas: Squadron/Signal Publications, 1984.

Drendel, Lou. *TAC (A Pictorial History of the USAF Tactical Air Forces, 1970–1977).* Carrolton, Texas: Squadron/Signal Publications, 1978.

———. *THUD.* Carrolton, Texas: Squadron/Signal Publications, 1986.

Drury, Richard S. *My Secret War.* Fallbrook, Calif.: Aero Publishers, Inc., 1979.

Eschmann, Karl J. *Linebacker: The Untold Story of the Air Raids over North Vietnam.* New York: Ballantine Books, 1989.

Flanagan, John F. *Vietnam Above the Treetops.* New York: Praeger, 1992.

Fogleman, General Ronald R. "A New American Way of War." *Aerospace Education Foundation Forum.* Arlington, VA: Aerospace Education Foundation, 1996.

Forrestal, James V. *The Forrestal Diaries.* Walter Millis and E. S. Duffield, eds. New York: Viking, 1951.

Francillon, Rene J. *McDonnell Douglas Aircraft Since 1920.* Vol. 2. Annapolis, Md.: Naval Institute Press, 1979.

Frisbee, John L., ed. *Makers of the United States Air Force.* Washington, D.C.: Office of Air Force History, 1987.

Futrell, Robert Frank. *Ideas, Concepts, Doctrine: A History of Basic Thinking in the United States Air Force, 1907–1964.* Montgomery, Alabama: Air University Press, 1971.

———. *Ideas, Concepts, Doctrine: Basic Thinking in the United States Air Force.* Vol. 1, 1907–1960. Montgomery, Alabama: Air University Press, 1989.

———. *Ideas, Concepts, Doctrine: Basic Thinking in the United States Air Force.* Vol. 2, 1961–1984. Montgomery, Alabama: Air University Press, 1989.

———. *The United States Air Force in Korea, 1950–1953.* Washington, D.C.: Office of Air Force History.

Gansler, Jacques S. *Affording Defense.* Cambridge, Mass.: MIT Press, 1989.

Gantz, Lieutenant Colonel Kenneth F., ed. *The United States Air Force Report on the Ballistic Missile.* New York: Doubleday, 1958.

Gaston, James C. *Planning the American Air War: Four Men and Nine Days in 1941.* Washington, D.C.: National Defense University Press, 1982.

Gorn, Michael H. *Harnessing the Genie: Science and Technology Forecasting for the Air Force, 1944–1986.* Washington, D.C.: Office of Air Force History, 1988.

Gross, Charles Joseph. *Prelude to the Total Force: The Air National Guard, 1943–1969.* Washington, D.C.: Office of Air Force History, 1985.

Gurney, Colonel Gene. *Vietnam: The War in the Air. A Pictorial History of the U.S. Air Forces in the Vietnam War: Air Force, Army, Navy, and Marines.* New York: Crown, 1985.

Halberstadt, Hans. *The Wild Weasels: History of U.S. Air Force SAM Killers, 1965–Today.* Osceola, Wis.: Motorbooks International, 1992.

Hallion, Richard P. *Storm over Iraq.* Washington, D.C.: Smithsonian Institution Press, 1992.

Harrison, Marshall. *A Lonely Kind of War: Forward Air Controller, Vietnam.* Novato, Calif.: Presidio Press, 1989.

Haulman, Dr. Daniel L., and Colonel William C. Stancik, eds. *Air Force*

Victory Credits World War I, World War II, Korea, and Vietnam. Montgomery, AL: United States Air Force Historical Research Center, 1988.

Holley, I. B., Jr. *Ideas and Weapons*. Washington, D.C.: Office of Air Force History, 1983.

Hurley, Colonel Alfred F., and Major Robert C. Ehrhart, eds. *Air Power and Warfare*. Washington, D.C.: Office of Air Force History, 1979.

Kitfield, James. *Prodigal Soldiers*. New York: Simon & Schuster, 1995.

Kohn, Richard H., and Joseph P. Harahan, eds. *USAF Warrior Studies*. Washington, D.C.: Office of Air Force History, 1986.

Kutler, Stanley I. *Encyclopedia of the Vietnam War*. New York: Charles Scribner's Sons, 1996.

Lauer, Colonel Timothy M., and Steven L. Llanso. *Encyclopedia of Modern U.S. Military Weapons*. New York: Berkley Books, 1995.

Lifeline Adrift: The Defense Industrial Base in the 1990s. Arlington, VA: Aerospace Education Foundation, 1991.

Littauer, Raphael, and Norman Uphoff, eds. *The Air War in Indochina*. Boston: Beacon Press, 1972.

Logan, Don. *The 388th Tactical Fighter Wing at Korat Royal Thai Air Force Base, 1972*. Altglen, PA: Schiffer Military/Aviation History, 1995.

Macy, Robert and Melinda. *Destination Baghdad*. Las Vegas: M&M Graphics, 1991.

Manning, Thomas A., Dick J. Bukard, et al. *History of Air Training Command, 1943–1993*. San Antonio, TX: Headquarters, Air Education and Training Command, 1993.

McCarthy, Brigadier General James R., and Lieutenant Colonel George B. Allison. *Linebacker II: A View from the Rock*. Montgomery, AL: Airpower Research Institute, 1979.

McPeak, Merrill A. *Selected Works, 1990–1994*. Montgomery, AL: Air University Press, 1995.

Mesko, Jim. *Airmobile: The Helicopter War in Vietnam*. Carrolton, Texas: Squadron/Signal Publication, Inc., 1984.

Millis, Walter, and E. S. Duffield. *The Forrestal Diaries*. New York: Viking, 1951.

Momyer, General William W. *Air Power in Three Wars: WWII, Korea, Vietnam*. Washington, D.C.: Department of the Air Force.

Moody, Walton S. *Building a Strategic Air Force*. Washington, D.C.: Air Force History and Museums Program, 1996.

Morrocco, John. *Thunder from Above: Air War, 1941–1968*. Boston, Mass.: Boston Publishing, 1984.

Morse, Stan, ed. *Gulf Air War Debrief Described by the Pilots That Fought*. London: Aerospace Publishing, 1991.

Mrozek, Donald J. *The U.S. Air Force After Vietnam: Postwar Challenges and Potential for Responses*. Montgomery, Alabama: Air University Press, 1988.

Murray, Williamson. *Air War in the Persian Gulf*. Baltimore: Nautical & Aviation Publishing Company of America, 1995.

Neufeld, Jacob. *The Development of Ballistic Missiles in the United States Air Force, 1945–1960*. Washington, D.C.: Office of Air Force History, 1990.

Neufeld, Jacob. *Reflections on Research and Development in the United States Air Force.* Washington, D.C.: Center for Air Force History, 1993.

New World Vistas: Air and Space Power for the 21st Century (Summary Volume). Washington, D.C., Department of the Air Force, 1995.

Nordeen, Lon O., Jr. *Air Warfare in the Missile Age.* Washington, D.C.: Smithsonian Institution Press, 1985.

Perry, Mark. *Four Stars.* Boston: Houghton Mifflin, 1989.

Pimlott, John. *Vietnam: The Decisive Battles.* New York: Macmillan, 1990.

Pogue, Forrest C. *George C. Marshall: Ordeal and Hope.* New York: Viking, 1966.

———. *George C. Marshall: Statesman, 1945–1949.* New York: Viking, 1987.

Polmar, Norman, and Timothy Laurer. *Strategic Air Command.* Baltimore: Nautical & Aviation Publishing Company of America, 1970.

Puryear, Edgar F., Jr. *George S. Brown, General, U.S. Air Force: Destined for Stars.* Novato, Calif.: Presidio Press, 1983.

Ravenstein, Charles A. *The Organization and Lineage of the United States Air Force.* Washington, D.C.: Office of Air Force History, 1986.

Reinberg, Linda. *In the Field: The Language of the Vietnam War.* New York and Oxford: Facts on File, 1991.

Ralston, Major General Joseph, W. "Fighter Modernization in the 1990's." *Foundation Forum,* January 31–February 1, 1991.

Rich, Ben R., and Leo Janos. *Skunk Works: A Personal Memoir of My Years at Lockheed.* Boston: Little, Brown, 1994.

Robbins, Christopher. *The Ravens.* New York: Crown, 1987.

Roberts, Michael. *The Illustrated Directory of the United States Air Force.* New York: Crescent Books, 1989.

Schlight, John. *The War in South Vietnam: The Years of the Offensive, 1965–1968.* Washington, D.C.: Office of Air Force History, 1988.

Shapley, Deborah. *Promise and Power: The Life and Times of Robert McNamara.* Boston: Little, Brown, 1993.

Skinner, Michael. *U.S.A.F.E.: A Primer of Modern Air Combat in Europe.* Novato, Calif.: Presidio Press, 1983.

Smith, Barry D. *Air Rescue: Saving Lives Stateside.* London: Osprey Publishing, 1989.

Smith, Harvey H., Donald W. Bernier, et al. *Area Handbook for South Vietnam.* Washington, D.C.: Foreign Areas Studies Division, American University, 1967.

Spector, Ronald H. *Researching the Vietnam Experience.* Washington, D.C.: Analysis Branch, U.S. Army Center of Military History, 1984.

Strategic Air Command History Office. *From Snark to Peacekeeper: A Pictorial History of Strategic Air Command Missiles.* Omaha, NE: Office of the Historian, Headquarters Strategic Air Command, 1990.

Sturm, Thomas A. *The USAF Scientific Advisory Board: Its First Twenty Years, 1944–1964.* Washington, D.C.: Office of Air Force History, 1986.

Summers, Harry G., Jr. *On Strategy: A Critical Analysis of the Vietnam War.* New York: Dell, 1982.

Swanborough, Gordon, and Peter M. Bowers. *United States Military Aircraft Since 1909.* Washington, D.C.: Smithsonian Institution Press, 1989.

Termena, Bernard J., Layne B. Peiffer, and H. P. Carlin. *Logistics: An Illustrated History of AFLC and its Antecedents, 1921–1981.* Dayton, Ohio: Headquarters, Air Force Logistics Command.

Tilford, Earl H., Jr. *Search and Rescue in Southeast Asia, 1961–1975.* Washington, D.C.: Office of Air Force History, 1980.

———. *Setup: What the Air Force Did in Vietnam and Why.* Montgomery, Alabama: Air University Press, 1991.

Tolson, Lieutenant General John J. *Vietnam Studies: Airmobility, 1961–1971.* Washington, D.C.: Department of the Army, 1973.

Trotti, John. *Phantom over Vietnam.* New York: Berkley Books, 1985.

Van Staaveren, Jacob. *Interdiction in Southern Laos, 1960–1968.* Washington, D.C.: Center for Air Force History, 1993.

Venkus, Colonel Robert E. *Raid on Qaddafi.* New York: St. Martin's Press, 1992.

Waddell, Colonel Dewey, and Major Norm Wood, eds. *Air War—Vietnam.* New York: Arno Press, 1978.

Warden, John A., III. *The Air Campaign: Planning for Combat.* Washington, D.C.: National Defense University Press, 1988.

Watson, George M., Jr. *The Office of the Secretary of the Air Force, 1947–1965.* Washington, D.C.: Center for Air Force History, 1993.

Werrell, Kenneth P. *The Evolution of the Cruise Missile.* Montgomery, Alabama: Air University Press, 1985.

Wolf, Richard I. *United States Air Force Basic Documents on Roles and Missions.* Washington, D.C.: Office of Air Force History, 1987.

Wolk, Herman S. *Planning and Organizing the Postwar Air Force, 1943–1947.* Washington, D.C.: Office of Air Force History, 1984.

Woodward, Bob. *The Commanders.* New York: Simon & Schuster, 1991.

Wright, Lieutenant Colonel Monte D., and Lawrence J. Paszek. *Science, Technology, and Warfare.* Proceedings of the Third Military History Symposium, United States Air Force Academy. Washington, D.C.: Office of Air Force History, 1969.

Yarborough, Colonel Tom. *Da Nang Diary: A Forward Air Controller's Year of Combat over Vietnam.* New York: St. Martin's Press, 1990.

Yenne, Bill. *The History of the U.S. Air Force.* New York: Exeter Books, 1984.

A CHRONOLOGY OF AEROSPACE POWER SINCE 1903

Courtesy of the Air Force Magazine

© 1996 The Air Force Association

The Air Force Association
1501 Lee Highway, Arlington, VA 22209-1198

1903–1913

March 23, 1903. First Wright brothers airplane patent, based on their 1902 glider, is filed in America.

August 8, 1903. The Langley gasoline-engine model plane is successfully launched from a catapult on a houseboat.

December 8, 1903. Second and last trial of Langley airplane, piloted by Charles M. Manly, is wrecked in launching from a houseboat on the Potomac River in Washington, D.C.

December 17, 1903. At Kitty Hawk, N. C., Orville Wright achieves the world's first manned, powered, sustained, and controlled flight by a heavier-than-air vehicle. His fourth and longest flight of the day is 852 feet in 59 seconds. Three days earlier, Wilbur Wright achieved the world's

first powered airplane flight—105 feet in 3.5 seconds—but crashed soon after takeoff, and his flight is not regarded as being either sustained or controlled.

January 18, 1905. The Wright brothers open negotiations with the U.S. government to build an airplane for the Army, but nothing comes of this first meeting.

February 5, 1905. T. S. Baldwin takes part in a 10-mile race between his dirigible and an automobile. The dirigible and its pilot win by a three-minute margin.

June 23, 1905. The first flight of the Wright Flyer III is made at Huffman Prairie, outside Dayton, Ohio. The Wright brothers' first fully controllable aircraft is able to turn and bank and remain aloft for up to thirty minutes.

May 22, 1906. After turning down two previous submissions, the U.S. government issues the Wright brothers the first patent on their flying machine.

November 12, 1906. Brazilian Alberto Santos-Dumont sets the first recognized absolute speed record of 25.66 mph in the Santos-Dumont Type 14-bis at Bagatelle, France. However, this speed is slower than speeds posted by the Wright brothers in the United States.

August 1, 1907. The Aeronautical Division of the U.S. Army Signal Corps, forerunner of U.S. Air Force, is established.

October 26, 1907. Henri Farman sets the recognized absolute speed record of 32.74 mph in a Voisin-Farman biplane at Issy-les-Moulineaux, France.

December 23, 1907. The Army's Chief Signal Officer, Brig. Gen. James Allen, issues the first specification for a military airplane.

January 13, 1908. Henri Farman wins the 50,000-franc Deutsch-Archdeacon Prize for the first officially observed 1-kilometer circular flight in Europe.

May 14, 1908. The first passenger flight takes place in the Wright plane at Kitty Hawk in preparation for delivery of a government airplane. Wilbur Wright pilots the machine, with Charles Furnas, an employee, as the first passenger.

May 19, 1908. Signal Corps Lt. Thomas E. Selfridge becomes the first soldier to fly a heavier-than-air machine.

July 4, 1908. Glenn H. Curtiss wins the *Scientific American* trophy with his *June Bug* biplane by flying for more than a mile over Hammondsport, N.Y. Speed for the trip is 39 mph.

August 8, 1908. At Camp d'Auvours, France, Wilbur Wright surpasses French flight records for duration, distance, and altitude.

September 3, 1908. First test flight of an Army flying machine is made at Fort Myer, Va., by Orville Wright.

September 17, 1908. Lt. Thomas E. Selfridge becomes the first person killed in a powered aircraft accident when a Wright Flyer crashes at Fort Myer, Va. Orville Wright, at the controls, suffers serious injuries.

November 13, 1908. Wilbur Wright, in a Wright biplane at Camp d'Auvours, France, and Henri Farman, in a Voisin at Issy, France, concurrently set a world altitude record of 82 feet.

April 24, 1909. Wilbur Wright pilots a Wright biplane at Centocelle, Italy, from which the first aerial motion picture is taken.

July 27, 1909. Orville Wright, with Lt. Frank P. Lahm as passenger, makes the first official test flight of the Army's first airplane at Fort Myer, Va.

August 2, 1909. The Army accepts its first airplane, bought from the Wright brothers for $25,000, plus a $5,000 bonus because the machine exceeds the speed requirement of 40 mph.

August 23, 1909. At the world's first major air meet in Reims, France, Glenn Curtiss becomes the first American to claim the recognized absolute speed record as he flies at 43.385 mph in his Reims Racer biplane.

August 25, 1909. Land for the first Signal Corps airfield is leased at College Park, Md.

October 23, 1909. Lt. Benjamin D. Foulois takes his first flying lesson from Wilbur Wright at College Park, Md.

October 26, 1909. Lt. Frederick E. Humphreys becomes the first Army pilot to solo in the Wright Military Flyer at College Park, Md.

November 3, 1909. Lt. George C. Sweet becomes the first Navy officer to fly, as a passenger in the Wright Military Flyer.

January 19, 1910. Signal Corps Lt. Paul Beck, flying as a passenger with Louis Paulhan in a Farman biplane, drops three 2-pound sandbags in a effort to hit a target at the Los Angeles Flying Meet. This is the first bombing experiment by an Army officer.

March 2, 1910. Benjamin Foulois becomes the first Army officer to fly an Army airplane.

March 19, 1910. Orville Wright opens the first Wright Flying School at Montgomery, Ala., on a site that will later become Maxwell AFB.

May 25, 1910. In Dayton, Ohio, Wilbur and Orville Wright fly together for the first time.

July 10, 1910. Walter Brookins becomes the first airplane pilot to fly at an altitude greater than a mile. He reaches 6,234 feet in a Wright biplane over Atlantic City, N.J.

July 10, 1910. Leon Morane pushes the recognized absolute speed record

to 66.181 mph in a Bleriot monoplane at Reims, France.

August 20, 1910. Army Lt. Jacob Fickel fires a .30 caliber Springfield rifle at the ground while flying as a passenger in a Curtiss biplane over Sheepshead Bay Track near New York City. This is the first time a military firearm has been discharged from an airplane.

September 2, 1910. Blanche Scott becomes the first American woman to solo, flying a Curtiss pusher at the Curtiss company field in Hammondsport, N.Y. She is not granted a pilot's license, however.

October 11, 1910. Former President Theodore Roosevelt becomes the first Chief Executive to fly. He goes aloft as a passenger in a Wright biplane over St. Louis, Mo.

November 7, 1910. Phillip O. Parmalee performs the world's first air cargo mission, flying a bolt of silk from Dayton to Columbus, Ohio.

November 14, 1910. Navy Lt. Eugene Ely, in a Curtiss biplane, takes off from the deck of a modified cruiser, USS *Birmingham*.

January 18, 1911. Navy Lt. Eugene Ely, flying a Curtiss pusher, makes the first landing on a ship. He touches down on a 119-foot-long wooden platform on the stern of the cruiser USS *Pennsylvania*, riding at anchor in San Francisco Bay.

February 1, 1911. The first licensed aircraft manufacturer in the U.S., the Burgess and Curtis Co. (no relation to the company founded by Glenn Curtiss), of Marblehead, Mass., receives authorization from the Wright Co.

March 3, 1911. The first appropria-

tion for Army air operations—$25,000—
is authorized for Fiscal Year 1912.

April 11, 1911. The Army's first permanent flying school is established at College Park, Md.

May 8, 1911. The first Navy airplane, A-1, an amphibian, is ordered from Glenn Curtiss. This date has been officially proclaimed the birthday of naval aviation.

May 12, 1911. Edward Nieuport sets the recognized absolute speed record of 74.415 mph in a Nieuport monoplane at Chalons, France. On June 16, he will push the speed record to 80.814 mph.

September 17–December 10, 1911. Calbraith Perry Rodgers, in the Wright EX biplane *Vin Fiz*, makes the first transcontinental flight, from Sheepshead Bay, N.Y., to Long Beach, Calif. He makes 76 stops and crashes 20 times.

February 22, 1912. Jules Vedrines pushes the recognized absolute speed record past the 100 mph barrier, as he hits 100.22 mph in a Deperdussin racer at Pau, France.

February 23, 1912. First official recognition of the rating "Military Aviator" appears in War Department Bulletin No. 2.

June 5, 1912. Lt. Col. C. B. Winder of the Ohio National Guard becomes the first National Guard pilot. He was taught at the Army Aviation School.

June 14, 1912. Cpl. Vernon Burge becomes the Army's first enlisted pilot.

July 5, 1912. Capt. Charles DeF. Chandler and Lts. T. D. Milling and H. H. Arnold become the first flyers to qualify as "Military Aviators."

November 5, 1912. First artillery adjustments directed from a plane begin at Fort Riley, Kan., by Lts. H. H. Arnold, pilot, and Follett Bradley, observer.

November 27, 1912. The Army Signal Corps purchases the first of three Curtiss-F two-seat biplane flying boats.

December 11, 1912. A French pilot, Roland Garros, sets an altitude record of 18,406 feet in a Morane airplane at Tunis.

February 11, 1913. The first bill for a separate aviation corps, HR 28728, is introduced in Congress by Rep. James Hay of W. Va. It fails to pass.

March 2, 1913. First flight pay is authorized: 35 percent over base pay for officers detailed on aviation duty.

April 27, 1913. Pilot Robert G. Fowler and cameraman R. A. Duhem make the first flight across the Isthmus of Panama. They are arrested by Panamanian authorities upon publication in a newspaper of the story and pictures of the flight.

May 13, 1913. The first flight of the world's first four-engine airplane, the *Russian Knight*, affectionately called "Le Grand," takes place in Russia. The aircraft is designed by Igor I. Sikorsky.

May 30, 1913. The Massachusetts Institute of Technology begins teaching aerodynamics.

June 21, 1913. Eighteen-year-old Georgia "Tiny" Broadwick becomes the first woman to make a parachute jump in the U.S. Her 1,000-foot leap takes place over Los Angeles, Calif.

June 30, 1913. The first Navy aviator

is killed: Ens. W. D. Billingsley is thrown from a seaplane.

July 19, 1913. In the skies over Seattle, Wash., Milton J. Bryant begins a new form of advertising—skywriting.

August 27, 1913. Lt. Petr Nikolaevich Nesterov of the Imperial Russian Army performs history's first inside loop while flying a Nieuport Type IV over Kiev.

November 30, 1913. In late November or early December, the first known aerial combat takes place over Naco, Mexico, between Phil Rader, flying for Gen. Victoriano Huerta, and Dean Ivan Lamb, with Venustiano Carranza. Details are unknown, except that a dozen pistol shots are exchanged.

1914–1923

January 1, 1914. America's first regularly scheduled airline starts operation across Tampa Bay between St. Petersburg and Tampa, Fla., with one Benoist flying boat. It lasts three months.

January 20, 1914. The Navy's aviation unit from Annapolis, Md., arrives at Pensacola, Fla., to set up the first naval air station.

February 24, 1914. In the wake of a rash of accidents, an Army investigative board condemns all pusher-type airplanes.

April 25, 1914. Navy Lt. (j.g). P .N. L. Bellinger, flying a Curtiss AB-3 flying boat from the battleship USS *Mississippi* (BB-23), makes the first U.S. operational air sortie against another country when he searches for sea mines during the Veracruz incident.

May 5, 1914. A patent is issued for hinged inset trailing-edge ailerons.

July 18, 1914. The Aviation Section of the Signal Corps is created by Congress. Sixty officers and students and 260 enlisted men are authorized.

August 25, 1914. Stephan Banic, a coal miner in Greenville, Pa., is issued a patent for a workable parachute design.

August 26, 1914. The first air battle of World War I on the eastern front takes place. Staff Capt. Petr Nikolaevich Nesterov records the first aerial ramming in combat.

December 1–16, 1914. Two-way air-to-ground radio communication is demonstrated in a Burgess-Wright biplane by Army Signal Corps Lts. H. A. Dargue and J. O. Mauborgne over Manila, the Philippines.

January 19-20, 1915. Germany launches the first zeppelin bombing raids on England. One airship, the L.6, turns back, but two others, the L.3 and L.4, drop their bombs on Great Yarmouth and King's Lynn.

March 3, 1915. Congress approves the act establishing the National Advisory Committee for Aeronautics. NACA is to "supervise and direct the scientific study of flight with a view to [its] practical solution." The committee, initially given a budget of $5,000, will evolve into the National Aeronautics and Space Administration.

April 1, 1915. French Lt. Roland Garros shoots down a German Albatros two-seater with a Hotchkiss machine gun fixed on the nose of his Morane-Saulnier Type L monoplane. The airplane's propeller is fitted with wedge-shaped steel deflector plates that protect the blades from damage as the rounds pass through the propeller arc.

November 6, 1915. Navy Lt. Cmdr. Henry C. Mustin makes the first airplane catapult launching from a moving vessel, USS *North Carolina*, in Pensacola Bay, Fla.

December 11, 1915. The first foreign students to enter a U.S. flying training program—four Portuguese Army officers—report to the Signal Corps Aviation School at San Diego, Calif.

March 15, 1916. The 1st Aero Squadron begins operations with Gen. John J. Pershing in a punitive expedition against Mexico and Pancho Villa.

March 21, 1916. The French government authorizes the formation of the Escadrille Américaine. The unit, made up of American volunteer pilots, is later renamed the Lafayette Escadrille.

June 18, 1916. H. Clyde Balsey of the Lafayette Escadrille is shot down near Verdun, France, the first American-born aviator shot down in World War I.

April 30, 1917. During the month, Maj. William "Billy" Mitchell becomes the first American Army officer to fly over the German lines.

November 27, 1917. Brig. Gen. Benjamin D. Foulois takes over as Chief of the Air Service for the American Expeditionary Force (AEF). He replaces Brig. Gen. William L. Kenly.

January 19, 1918. The U.S. School of Aviation Medicine begins operations at Hazelhurst Field, Mineola, N.Y.

January 23, 1918. The first ascent by an AEF balloon is made at the balloon school in Cuperly, France.

February 5, 1918. While flying as a substitute gunner with a French squadron, Lt. Stephen W. Thompson becomes the first American to record an aerial victory while in a U.S. uniform. He shoots down a German Albatros D.III but is credited with only half the victory, sharing the kill with the French pilot.

February 18, 1918. The first American fighter unit proper, the 95th Aero Squadron, arrives in France.

February 28, 1918. Using a radiotelephone, human voice is transmitted from an aircraft to the ground for the first time. The flight took place in San Diego, Calif.

February 28, 1918. Regulation of the airways begins with an order by President Woodrow Wilson requiring licenses for civilian pilots or owners. More than 800 licenses are issued.

March 11, 1918. Lt. Paul Baer becomes the first AEF Air Service member awarded the Distinguished Service Cross.

March 19, 1918. The 94th Aero Squadron makes the first U.S. operational flights across the front lines in France.

April 14, 1918. Lts. Alan Winslow and Douglas Campbell, flying Nieuport 28s of the 94th Aero Squadron, down two German fighters in a 10-minute battle. Lieutenant Winslow is the first pilot in the American sector of the front to down an airplane; Lieutenant Campbell is the first U.S.-trained pilot to score a victory.

April 21, 1918. Rittmeister Manfred von Richthofen, the Red Baron, is shot down in action over France by Capt. A. Roy Brown, a Canadian. The German ace, killed in the battle, had 80 aerial victories.

May 7, 1918. Flying a Nieuport 28, 1st Lt. Edward V. Rickenbacker, who would go on to be the leading American ace of World War I, records his first solo victory, downing a German Pfalz. Flying with the 94th Aero Squadron, he had recorded a half victory, his first, on April 29.

May 15, 1918. The Aviation Section of the Signal Corps begins regular airmail service from Washington, D.C., to New York City.

May 20, 1918. The Division of Military Aeronautics is established, with Maj. Gen. William L. Kenly as director.

May 24, 1918. U.S. Army Air Service organized.

June 12, 1918. The 96th Aero Squadron bombs the Dommary-Baroncourt railway yards in France in the first daylight bombing raid carried out by the AEF.

August 2, 1918. The 135th Corps Observation Squadron makes its first wartime patrol in U.S.-assembled DH-4s powered by American-made Liberty engines.

September 12, 1918. Lt. Frank Luke shoots down his first enemy observation balloon. By the time he is killed seventeen days later, he has shot down nearly 16 balloons and airplanes. In his last mission, near Murvaux, France, he shoots down three observation balloons but comes under attack by eight German pilots and from ground batteries. Severely wounded, he makes a strafing pass on some enemy ground troops before

making a forced landing. Surrounded, he defends himself with his automatic pistol until he is killed by enemy troops. He is posthumously awarded the Medal of Honor for his actions.

September 25, 1918. Capt. Edward V. Rickenbacker of the 94th Aero Squadron attacks seven enemy aircraft, shooting down two of them near Billy, France, and wins the first Medal of Honor given for air activity.

October 6, 1918. 2d Lts. Harold E. Goettler (pilot) and Erwin R. Bleckley (observer) are killed by ground fire while attempting to drop supplies to a battalion of the Army's 77th Division, which had been cut off in the Argonne Forest near Binarville, France. Having been subjected to heavy ground fire on their first attempt, they flew at a lower altitude on the second trip in order to get the packages more precisely on the designated spot. The duo are posthumously awarded the Medal of Honor for their actions.

October 30, 1918. Flying a Spad VII, Capt. Edward V. Rickenbacker, America's Ace of Aces, records his last two aerial victories, an observation balloon and a Fokker DVII, over France. Captain Rickenbacker, who finished the war with 24.33 victories, recorded 12.83 confirmed victories in the month of October alone.

November 7, 1918. Dr. Robert H. Goddard demonstrates tube-launched solid-propellant rockets at Aberdeen Proving Ground, Md.

November 10, 1918. The Air Service records its last two aerial victories of World War I, as Maj. Maxwell Kirby of the 94th Aero Squadron tallies the last solo (and his only) kill, and two crews from the 104th Observation Squadron team up for the other victory.

December 4–22, 1918. Under the command of Maj. Albert D. Smith, four JN-4s fly from San Diego, Calif., to Jacksonville, Fla., to complete the Army's first transcontinental flight. Only Major Smith's plane manages to make the entire trip.

January 24, 1919. Army Air Service pilot 1st Lt. Temple M. Joyce makes 300 consecutive loops in a Morane fighter at Issoudun, France.

May 16–27, 1919. Navy Lt. Cmdr. Albert C. "Putty" Read and a crew of five fly from Trepassey Bay, Newfoundland, to Lisbon, Portugal, via the Azores, in the Curtiss NC-4 flying boat, spending 53 hours, 58 minutes aloft. This is the first crossing of the Atlantic Ocean by air. Two other NCs start the trip but do not complete it.

June 14–15, 1919. Capt. John Alcock and Lt. Arthur Whitten Brown of the United Kingdom make the first nonstop flight across the Atlantic in 16 hours, 12 minutes.

September 1, 1919. Dive bombing is demonstrated at Aberdeen Proving Ground, Md.

October 30, 1919. The reversible-pitch propeller is tested for the first time at McCook Field near Dayton, Ohio.

February 27, 1920. Maj. R. W. "Shorty" Schroeder sets a world altitude record of 33,114 feet in the Packard-LePere LUSAC-11 biplane over McCook Field.

June 4, 1920. The Army reorganization bill is approved, creating an Air Service with 1,514 officers and 16,000 enlisted men.

June 5, 1920. A provision in the Fiscal Year 1921 appropriations bill restricts the Army Air Service to operating from land bases.

February 22, 1921. American transcontinental airmail service begins. The route between San Francisco and Mineola, N.Y., is flown in fourteen segments by pilots flying U.S.-built de Havilland DH-4s. The first flight, made mostly in bad weather, takes 33 hours, 20 minutes.

July 13–21, 1921. In a series of tests off the mouth of the Chesapeake Bay, Army airplanes from Langley Field, Va., sink three ships, including the captured German battleship *Ostfriesland*, demonstrating the vulnerability of naval craft to aerial attack.

September 26, 1921. Sadi Lecointe pushes the recognized absolute speed record past 200 mph, as he hits 205.223 mph in the Nieuport-Delage Sesquiplane at Ville-Sauvage, France.

November 12, 1921. Wesley May, with a five-gallon can of gasoline strapped to his back, climbs from the wing of one aircraft to the wing of another in the first "air-to-air" refueling.

March 20, 1922. USS *Langley* (CV-1), the Navy's first aircraft carrier, is commissioned in Norfolk, Va. The ship is the converted collier *Jupiter*.

September 4, 1922. Lt. James H. Doolittle makes the first transcontinental crossing in an aircraft in a single day—2,163 miles in 21 hours, 20 minutes.

October 17, 1922. The first carrier takeoff in U.S. Navy history is made by Lt. V. C. Griffin in a Vought VE-7SF from USS *Langley* (CV-1), at anchor in the York River in Virginia.

October 18, 1922. Gen. William H. Billy Mitchell becomes the first U.S. military pilot to hold the recognized absolute speed record, as he sets a mark of 222.97 mph in the Curtiss R-6 at Selfridge Field, Mich. This is also the first time the world speed record has been certified outside of France.

May 2–3, 1923. Lt. Oakley G. Kelly and Lt. John A. Macready complete the first nonstop transcontinental flight. The trip from New York to San Diego takes 26 hours, 50 minutes, 3 seconds in a Fokker T-2.

September 4, 1923. First flight of the airship USS *Shenandoah* (ZR-1) is made at NAF Lakehurst, N.J. The airship will make 57 flights in two years before it is destroyed by a storm near Marietta, Ohio.

1924–1933

February 5, 1924. 2d Lt. Joseph C. Morrow, Jr., qualifies as the 24th and last Military Aviator under the rules set up for that rating.

March 4, 1924. The Army Air Service takes on a new mission: aerial icebreaking. Two Martin bombers and two DH-4s bomb the frozen Platte River at North Bend, Neb., for six hours before the ice clears.

April 6–September 28, 1924. The Army Air Service completes the first circumnavigation of the globe. Four crews in Douglas World Cruisers begin the voyage in Seattle, Wash., but only two aircraft (*Chicago* and *New Orleans*) and their crews complete the trip.

September 28, 1923. At Cowes, on the Isle of Wight, off England's southern coast, Navy Lt. David Rittenhouse claims the Schneider Cup for the United States for the first time. Flying a Curtiss CR-3, Lieutenant Rittenhouse wins the prestigious seaplane race with an average speed of 177.37 mph.

October 12–15, 1924. As part of World War I reparations, the German zeppelin LZ-126 is flown from Friedrichshafen, Germany, to NAF Lakehurst, N.J. The Navy will later christen the airship USS *Los Angeles* (ZR-3).

October 28, 1924. Army Air Service airplanes break up cloud formations at 13,000 feet over Bolling Field, D.C., by "blasting" them with electrified sand.

January 24, 1925. The Navy airship USS *Los Angeles* (ZR-3), with 25 scientists and astronomers on board, is used to make observations of a solar eclipse.

February 2, 1925. President Calvin Coolidge signs the Kelly Act, authorizing the air transport of mail under contract. This is the first major legislative step toward the creation of a U.S. airline industry.

July 15, 1925. The Dr. A. Hamilton Rice Expedition, the first group of explorers to use an airplane, returns to the U.S. The expedition, which used a Curtiss Seagull floatplane, discovered the headwaters of the Amazon River.

October 26, 1925. Lt. James H. Doolittle, flying the Curtiss R3C-2 floatplane racer, wins the Schneider Cup race in Baltimore, Md., with an average speed of 232.57 mph. This marked back-to-back wins for the

United States and the only time the Army had competed in a seaplane race. The next day, he sets a world seaplane record of 245.713 mph over a 3-kilometer course.

December 17, 1925. Air power pioneer Billy Mitchell is found guilty of violating the 96th Article of War ("conduct of a nature to bring discredit on the military service") and is sentenced to a five-year suspension of rank, pay, and command. Already demoted from brigadier general, Colonel Mitchell decides instead to resign from the Army.

January 16, 1926. The Daniel Guggenheim Fund for the Promotion of Aeronautics is founded.

March 16, 1926. Dr. Robert H. Goddard launches the world's first liquid-fueled rocket at Auburn, Mass.

July 2, 1926. U.S. Army Air Service becomes U.S. Army Air Corps.

July 2, 1926. Congress establishes the Distinguished Flying Cross (made retroactive to April 6, 1917).

May 20–21, 1927. The first solo nonstop transatlantic flight is completed by Charles A. Lindbergh in the Ryan NYP *Spirit of St. Louis*: New York to Paris in 33 hours, 32 minutes.

September 16, 1927. In a staged publicity event, MGM Studios attempts to make the first nonstop flight across the United States with an animal on board an aircraft. Noted pilot Martin Jensen is chosen to fly Leo, MGM's trademark lion, from San Diego, Calif., to New York City for a promotional tour. Man and beast never arrive, however. After a nationwide search and three days of front-page headlines, Jensen and Leo

are found unhurt in the Arizona desert. A storm had forced Jensen down and the Ryan BI monoplane (which had been fitted with a steel cage for Leo) was heavily damaged on landing.

November 16, 1927. The U.S. Navy's second true aircraft carrier— USS *Saratoga* (CV-3)—is commissioned. The ship will later be deliberately destroyed during a 1946 atomic bomb test.

January 27, 1928. The Navy airship USS *Los Angeles* (ZR-3) lands on the aircraft carrier USS *Saratoga* (CV-3) during a fleet exercise near Newport, R.I., and resumes its patrol after replenishment.

February 15, 1928. President Coolidge signs a bill authorizing acceptance of a new site near San Antonio, Tex., to become the Army Air Corps training center. This center is now Randolph AFB.

March 1–9, 1928. USAAC Lt. Burnie R. Dallas and Beckwith Havens make the first transcontinental flight in an amphibious airplane. Total flight time in the Loening Amphibian is 32 hours, 45 minutes.

March 30, 1928. Italian Maj. Mario de Bernardi pushes the recognized absolute speed record past 300 mph, as he hits 318.624 mph in the Macchi M.52R at Venice, Italy.

April 15–21, 1928. Sir George Hubert Wilkins and Lt. Carl B. Eielson fly from Point Barrow, Alaska, across the Arctic Ocean to Spitsbergen, Norway, in a Lockheed Vega. This first west-to-east trip over the top of the world takes only 21 hours of flying, but the duo are delayed by weather.

May 12, 1928. Lt. Julian S. Dexter of the Air Corps Reserve completes a

3,000-square-mile aerial mapping assignment over the Florida Everglades. The project takes 65 hours of flying, spread over two months.

June 9, 1928. For the third consecutive year, Army Air Corps Lt. Earle E. Partridge wins the distinguished gunnery badge at the Air Corps Machine Gunning Matches at Langley Field, Va.

June 15, 1928. Lts. Karl S. Axtater and Edward H. White, flying in an Air Corps blimp directly over an Illinois Central train, dip down and hand a mailbag to the postal clerk on the train, thus completing the first airplane-to-train transfer.

August 1, 1928. Airmail rates rise to 5 cents for the first ounce and 10 cents for each additional ounce.

September 22, 1928. The number of people whose lives have been saved by parachutes exceeds 100 when Lt. Roger Q. Williams bails out over San Diego, Calif.

October 11–15, 1928. The German *Graf Zeppelin* (LZ-127) makes the first transoceanic voyage by an airship carrying paying passengers. *Graf Zeppelin* travels from Friedrichshafen, Germany, to NAF Lakehurst, N.J., in nearly 112 hours, with 20 passengers and a crew of 37.

November 11, 1928. In a Lockheed Vega, Sir George Hubert Wilkins and Lt. Carl B. Eielson make the first flight over Antarctica.

January 1–7, 1929. *Question Mark*, a Fokker C-2 commanded by Maj. Carl A. "Tooey" Spaatz and including Capt. Ira C. Eaker and Lt. Elwood R. Quesada among its crew, sets an endurance record for a refueled aircraft of 150 hours, 40 minutes, 14 seconds.

January 23–27, 1929. The aircraft carriers USS *Lexington* (CV-2) and USS *Saratoga* (CV-3) participate in fleet exercises for the first time.

February 10–11, 1929. Evelyn Trout sets a women's solo flight endurance record of 17 hours, 21 minutes, 37 seconds in the monoplane *Golden Eagle*.

April 24, 1929. Elinor Smith, seventeen years old, sets a women's solo endurance record of 26 hours, 21 minutes, 32 seconds in a Bellanca CH monoplane at Roosevelt Field, Long Island, N.Y.

May 16, 1929. At the first Academy Award ceremonies in Los Angeles, Calif., the Paramount movie *Wings* wins the Oscar for Best Picture for 1927–28. The World War I flying epic stars Richard Arlen, Buddy Rogers, and Clara Bow. A young Gary Cooper has a minor role.

September 24, 1929. Lt. James H. Doolittle makes the first blind, all-instrument flight at Mitchel Field, N.Y., in a completely covered cockpit (accompanied by check pilot). He took off, flew a short distance, and landed.

September 30, 1929. At Frankfurt, Germany, Fritz von Opel travels just over a mile in the world's first flight of a rocket-powered airplane. The Rak-1 tops 85 mph but crashes.

November 23, 1929. After visiting Dr. Robert H. Goddard, Charles A. Lindbergh arranges a grant of $50,000 from the Daniel Guggenheim Fund for the Promotion of Aeronautics to support Dr. Goddard's work with rockets.

November 29, 1929. Navy Cmdr. Richard E. Byrd, Bernt Balchen,

Army Capt. Ashley McKinley, and Harold June make the first flight over the South Pole. Mr. Balchen is the pilot of the Ford Trimotor *Floyd Bennett*.

December 31, 1929. The Daniel Guggenheim Fund for the Promotion of Aeronautics ends its activities.

April 12, 1930. Led by Capt. Hugh Elmendorf, nineteen pilots of the 95th Pursuit Squadron set an unofficial world record for altitude formation flying over Mather Field, Calif. The P-12 pilots reach 30,000 feet, shattering the old record of 17,000 feet.

May 3, 1930. Laura Ingalls performs 344 consecutive loops. Shortly afterward, she tries again and does 980. In another flight during 1930, she does 714 barrel rolls, setting a pair of records that few people have cared to challenge.

May 15, 1930. Ellen Church, a registered nurse, becomes the world's first airline stewardess as she serves sandwiches on a Boeing Air Transport flight between San Francisco, Calif., and Cheyenne, Wyo. She sits in the jumpseat of the Boeing Model 80A.

October 25, 1930. Transcontinental commercial air service between New York and Los Angeles begins.

March 10, 1931. Air Corps Capt. Ira Eaker attempts to set the transcontinental speed record in the Lockheed Y1C-17, a special version of the civilian Vega. Taking off from Long Beach, Calif., Captain Eaker gets as far as Tolu, Ky., before he has to make a forced landing in a field because of air in the fuel lines. Captain Eaker had traveled 1,740 miles at an average speed of 237 mph, which, if

he had been able to complete the flight, would have shattered the existing coast-to-coast speed mark.

September 4, 1931. Jimmy Doolittle wins the first Bendix Trophy transcontinental race, flying the Laird *Super Solution* from Los Angeles to Cleveland with an average speed of 223.058. Total flying time is 9 hours and 10 minutes. He then flies on to New York to complete a full flight across the continent.

September 29, 1931. Flying in the same aircraft that won the last Schneider Cup seaplane race, Royal Air Force Flt. Lt. George Stainforth pushes the recognized absolute speed record past 400 mph as he hits 407.001 mph in the Supermarine S.6b at Lee-on-Solent, England.

October 3–5, 1931. Americans Clyde "Upside Down" Pangborn and Hugh Herndon, Jr., make the first nonstop transpacific flight from Japan to America, in a Bellanca monoplane. The trip takes 41 hours, 13 minutes.

December 22, 1931. Maj. Gen. Benjamin D. Foulois takes oath as Chief of Air Corps.

August 25, 1932. Amelia Earhart becomes the first woman to complete a nonstop transcontinental flight.

November 19, 1932. National monument to Wilbur and Orville Wright is dedicated at Kitty Hawk, N.C.

April 4, 1933. The Navy dirigible USS *Akron* (ZRS-4) hits the sea during a training flight off the East Coast and breaks up. Of a crew of nearly 80, only three survive. Among the casualties is Rear Adm. William A. Moffett, head of the Navy's Bureau of Aeronautics.

July 15–22, 1933. Famed aviator Wiley Post, flying the Lockheed Vega *Winnie Mae*, becomes the first person to fly around the world solo. The 15,596-mile flight takes 7 days, 18 hours, 49 minutes at an average speed of 134.5 mph.

September 4, 1933. Jimmy Wedell sets a world landplane speed record of 304.98 mph in the Wedell-Williams racer over Glenview, Ill.

December 31, 1933. The prototype Soviet Polikarpov I-16 Mosca is flown for the first time. When the type enters service in 1934, it is the first monoplane fighter to have an enclosed cockpit and fully retractable landing gear.

1934–1939

February 19, 1934. President Franklin D. Roosevelt issues an Executive Order canceling existing airmail contracts because of fraud and collusion. The Army Air Corps is designated to take over airmail operations.

May 1, 1934. Navy Lt. Frank Akers makes a blind landing in a Berliner-Joyce OJ-2 at College Park, Md., in a demonstration of a system intended for aircraft carrier use. In subsequent flights, he makes takeoffs and landings between NAS Anacostia, D.C., and College Park under a hood without assistance.

May 19, 1934. The first flight of the Ant-20 *Maxim Gorki*, at this time the world's largest aircraft, is made in the Soviet Union. The aircraft was designed by Andrei Tupolev.

June 1, 1934. Army Air Corps airmail operations are terminated.

June 18, 1934. Boeing begins company-funded design work on the Model 299, which will become the B-17.

July 18, 1934. Lt. Col. Henry H. Hap Arnold leads a flight of 10 Martin B-10 bombers on a six-day photographic mapping mission to Alaska.

December 31, 1934. Helen Richey, flying a Ford Trimotor from Washington, D.C., to Detroit, Mich., becomes the first woman in the U.S. to pilot an airmail transport aircraft on a regular schedule.

February 12, 1935. The Navy airship USS *Macon* (ZRS-5) crashes off the California coast with two fatalities out of a crew of 83. This loss effectively ends the Navy's rigid airship program.

March 1, 1935. General Headquarters (GHQ) Air Force is created at Langley Field, Va. It is a compromise for those seeking a completely independent Air Force and the War Department's General Staff which wants to retain control of what is thought of as an auxiliary to the ground forces.

March 9, 1935. Future Reichsmarsal Hermann Göring announces the existence of the Luftwaffe in an interview with London *Daily Mail* correspondent Ward Price. This statement implies a gross violation of the Versailles Treaty, which prohibits Germany from having an air force.

March 21, 1935. Company pilot Bill Wheatley, with chief engineer I. M. Mac Laddon as a passenger, makes the first flight of the Consolidated XP3Y-1, the forerunner to the Catalina patrol bomber/rescue aircraft, at NAS Anacostia, D.C. The P-Boat would be produced for more than 10 years and would become the most numerous,

(3,200 + including more than 300 for the USAAF) and quite possibly, the most famous flying boat ever.

August 15, 1935. Famed pilot Wiley Post and humorist Will Rogers are killed in a crash of the hybrid Lockheed Orion-Explorer shortly after takeoff near Point Barrow, Alaska.

September 15, 1935. Alexander P. de Seversky sets a recognized class for record speed over a 3-kilometer course (piston-engined amphibians) of 230.41 mph in a Seversky N3PB at Detroit, Mich. This is the oldest certified aviation record still standing.

November 22, 1935. First transpacific airmail flight, in *China Clipper*, by Capt. Edwin C. Musick, takes place from San Francisco to Honolulu, Midway Island, Wake Island, Guam, and Manila.

December 17, 1935. First flight of the Douglas Sleeper Transport, the first of 10,654 DC-3s and derivatives Douglas will build between 1935 and 1947. The U.S. military uses C-47s in three wars, and some "Gooney Birds" are still in use today. The DC-3 is one of the most famous airplanes of all time.

February 19, 1936. Airpower advocate Billy Mitchell dies in New York City at the age of 57. He is buried in Milwaukee, Wis.

March 5, 1936. Vicker's chief test pilot "Mutt" Summers makes the first flight of the Supermarine Type 300 from Eastleigh Airport in Hampshire, England. The brainchild of designer R. J. Mitchell, this prototype is the first of 18,298 Merlin-powered Spitfires of all marks to be built by 1945.

September 4, 1936. Louise Thaden and Blanche Noyes become the first women to win the Bendix Trophy transcontinental race from New York to Los Angeles in a Beech Model 17 Staggerwing with an average speed of 165.346 mph. Total flying time is 14 hours and 55 minutes.

April 12, 1937. Frank Whittle bench-tests the first practical jet engine in laboratories at Cambridge University, England.

May 6, 1937. The German dirigible *Hindenburg* (LZ-129) burns while mooring at Lakehurst, N.J., killing 36 people.

May 21, 1937. Amelia Earhart and Fred Noonan leave from San Francisco in a Lockheed Electra on a round-the-world flight that ends on July 2, 1937, when they disappear in the Pacific.

July 20, 1937. First shoulder-sleeve insignia authorized for an independent American air unit—for General Headquarters Air Force.

September 1, 1937. Air Corps 1st Lt. Ben Kelsey makes the first flight of the Bell XFM-1 Airacuda multiplace fighter at Buffalo, N.Y. Both the plane and the concept prove to be dismal failures. The Airacuda turns out to be a maintenance nightmare, and the multiplace fighter concept is just not practical.

October 15, 1937. The Boeing XB-15 makes its first flight at Boeing Field in Seattle, Wash., under the control of test pilot Eddie Allen.

February 17, 1938. Six Boeing B-17 Flying Fortresses, under the command of Lt. Col. Robert Olds, leave Miami, Fla., on a goodwill flight to Buenos Aires, Argentina. The return trip to Langley Field, Va., is the longest non-stop flight in Air Corps history.

April 6, 1938. Company pilot James Taylor makes the first flight of the Bell XP-39 Airacobra at Wright Field, near Dayton, Ohio. Nearly 4,800 Lend-Lease P-39s will be used to particularly good effect by Soviet pilots to destroy German tanks.

April 22, 1938. World War I ace Edward V. Rickenbacker buys a majority stake in Eastern Air Lines from North American Aviation for $3.5 million. That sum would roughly cover the cost of a single engine for a Boeing 757 today.

May 15, 1938. U.S. Secretary of the Interior Harold L. Ickes refuses to allow inert helium to be exported to Germany for use in Zeppelins. Secretary Ickes feels that the gas might be diverted to military purposes.

July 10–14, 1938. Howard Hughes, Harry H. P. Conner, Army Lt. Thomas Thurlow, Richard Stoddard, and Ed Lund set a round-the-world flight record of 3 days, 19 hours, 8 minutes, 10 seconds in a Lockheed Model 14 Super Electra passenger aircraft. The crew travels 14,791 miles.

July 17–18, 1938. Ostensibly aiming for California, Douglas "Wrong-Way" Corrigan, flying a Curtiss Robin, lands in Dublin, Ireland, after a nonstop 28-hour flight from Floyd Bennett Field in Brooklyn, N.Y.

August 22, 1938. The Civil Aeronautics Act goes into effect. The Civil Aeronautics Authority will now coordinate all nonmilitary aviation. (The Federal Aviation Act, which created the Federal Aviation Administration, will be passed August 15, 1958.)

September 29, 1938. Brig. Gen. H. H. "Hap" Arnold is named Chief of the Army Air Corps, succeeding Maj.

Gen. Oscar Westover, who was killed in a plane crash September 21.

October 14, 1938. Company test pilot Edward Elliott makes the first flight of the Curtiss XP-40 at Buffalo, N.Y. Almost 14,000 P-40s will be built before production ends in 1944.

December 31, 1938. The Boeing Model 307 Stratoliner, the first passenger plane to have a pressurized cabin, makes its first flight.

January 27, 1939. Lt. Benjamin Kelsey makes the first flight of the Lockheed XP-38 at March Field, Calif. The two leading American aces of all time, Maj. Richard Bong (40 victories) and Maj. Thomas McGuire (38 victories), would fly P-38s.

March 5, 1939. Using a hook trailing from their Stinson Reliant, Norman Rintoul and Victor Yesulantes demonstrate a nonstop airmail system by picking a mail sack off a pole in Coatesville, Pa.

March 30, 1939. Flugkapitan Hans Dieterle sets a world speed record of 463.82 mph in the Heinkel He-100V-8. The flight is made at Oranienburg, Germany.

April 3, 1939. President Roosevelt signs the National Defense Act of 1940, which authorizes a $300 million budget and 6,000 airplanes for the Army Air Corps and increases AAC personnel to 3,203 officers and 45,000 enlisted troops.

April 26, 1939. Flugkapitan Fritz Wendel sets the last recognized absolute speed record before World War II as he pilots the Messerschmitt Bf-209V-1 to a speed of 469.224 mph at Augsburg, Germany.

May 20, 1939. Regularly scheduled

transatlantic passenger and airmail service begins.

June 20, 1939. The German Heinkel He-176, the first aircraft to have a throttle-controlled liquid-fuel rocket engine, makes its first flight at Peenemünde with Flugkapitan Erich Warsitz at the controls.

August 27, 1939. The first jet-powered aircraft, the Heinkel He-178, makes its first flight. Flugkapitan Erich Warsitz is the pilot.

September 1, 1939. At 4:34 A.M., Lt. Bruno Dilley leads three Junkers Ju-87 Stuka dive bombers in an attack against the Dirschau Bridge. The German invasion of Poland, the first act of World War II, begins six minutes later.

October 8, 1939. A Lockheed Hudson crew from the Royal Air Force's No. 224 Squadron shoots down a German Do-18 flying boat. This is the first victory recorded by an American-built aircraft in World War II.

October 13, 1939. Evelyn Pinchert Kilgore becomes the first woman to be issued a Civil Aeronautics Authority instructor's certificate.

December 29, 1939. The prototype Consolidated XB-24 Liberator makes a 17-minute first flight from Lindbergh Field in San Diego, Calif., with company pilot Bill Wheatley at the controls. More than 18,100 B-24s will be built in the next five and a half years, making for the largest military production run in US history.

1940–1945

February 21, 1940. Henry A. H. Boot and John T. Randall, working at the University of Birmingham, England, create the first practical magnetron. The magnetron, a resonant-cavity microwave generator, is vital in the development of airborne radar.

May 16, 1940. President Roosevelt calls for 50,000 airplanes a year.

July 10, 1940. The Luftwaffe attacks British shipping in the English Channel docks in South Wales. These actions are the first in what will become the Battle of Britain.

August 13–October 5, 1940. Against overwhelming odds, Royal Air Force pilots fend off the Luftwaffe during the Battle of Britain and ward off German invasion of the British Isles. The Luftwaffe loses 1,733 aircraft and crews.

September 17, 1940. Adolf Hitler announces that Operation Sea Lion,

the German invasion of Great Britain, "has been postponed indefinitely." This effectively marks the end of the Battle of Britain, although fighting continues.

October 8, 1940. The Royal Air Force announces formation of the first Eagle Squadron, a Fighter Command unit to consist of volunteer pilots from the U.S.

March 21, 1941. The first black flying unit, the 99th Pursuit Squadron, is activated. As part of the 332d Pursuit Squadron, it will become known as the Tuskegee Airmen.

April 11, 1941. With the possibility that the U.S. would be drawn into World War II and that all of Europe could be in Axis hands, the Army Air Corps invites Consolidated and Boeing to submit design studies for a bomber capable of achieving 450 mph at 25,000 feet, a range of 12,000 miles at 275 mph, and a payload of

4,000 pounds of bombs at maximum range. This study results in the Convair B-36.

May 6, 1941. Company test pilot Lowery Brabham makes the first flight of the Republic P-47 Thunderbolt at Farmingdale, Long Island, N.Y. The P-47, the heaviest single-engine fighter ever built in the U.S., will see action in every theater in World War II as both a high-altitude escort fighter and as a low-level fighter-bomber.

June 20, 1941. The Army Air Forces are established, comprising the Office of the Chief of Air Corps and the Air Force Combat Command, with Maj. Gen. H. H. Arnold as Chief.

July 8, 1941. The RAF makes a daylight attack on Wilhelmshaven, Germany, using Boeing Fortress Is. This is the first operational use of the B-17 Flying Fortress.

August 12, 1941. First successful rocket-assisted takeoff of an airplane takes place.

December 1, 1941. Civil Air Patrol is established.

December 7, 1941. Imperial Japanese forces attack Pearl Harbor.

December 8, 1941. The day after the Japanese attack on Pearl Harbor, company test pilot Robert Stanley makes the first flight of the Bell XP-63 Kingcobra, a bigger and more powerful version of the P-39, at Buffalo, N.Y.

December 10, 1941. Five B-17s of the 93d Bomb Squadron, 19th Bomb Group, carry out the first heavy bomb mission of World War II, attacking a Japanese convoy near the Philippines and also sinking the first enemy vessel by U.S. aerial combat bombing.

December 16, 1941. Lt. Boyd "Buzz" Wagner becomes the first American USAAF ace of World War II by shooting down his fifth Japanese plane over the Philippines.

December 20, 1941. The American Volunteer Group (Claire L. Chennault's Flying Tigers), in action over Kunming, China, enters combat for the first time.

February 23, 1942. B-17s attack Rabaul, the first Allied raid on the newly established Japanese base.

February 22, 1942. First American air headquarters in Europe in World War II, U.S. Army Bomber Command, is established in England, with Brig. Gen. Ira C. Eaker commanding.

March 7, 1942. The first five African-American pilots graduate from training at Tuskegee Army Air Field in Alabama. By the end of the war, the "Tuskegee Airmen" would number 950 pilots and open the door to the armed forces for other African-Americans.

March 9, 1942. The War Department is reorganized into three autonomous forces: Army Air Forces, Ground Forces, and Services of Supply.

April 8, 1942. The first flight of supplies takes place over "the Hump"—a 500-mile air route from Assam, India, over the Himalayas, to Kunming, China, where the Chinese continue to resist Japanese forces. By August, Tenth Air Force will be ferrying over 700 tons a month to these troops, who were cut off by the Japanese control of the Burma Road.

April 18, 1942. Sixteen North American B-25s, commanded by Lt. Col. James H. Doolittle, take off from USS *Hornet* (CV-8) and bomb Tokyo. For planning and successfully carrying out this daring raid, Doolittle is promoted to brigadier general and is awarded the Medal of Honor.

May 4–8, 1942. The Battle of the Coral Sea becomes the first naval engagement fought solely by aircraft.

May 26, 1942. Contract test pilot Vance Breese makes the first flight of the Northrop XP-61 Black Widow from Northrop Field in Hawthorne, Calif. The Black Widow is the Army Air Forces' first purpose-designed night fighter.

June 3–4, 1942. In the Battle of Midway, three U.S. carriers destroy four Japanese carriers while losing one of their own, inflicting a major defeat on the Japanese fleet.

June 12, 1942. In the first mission against a European target, 13 B-24s of HALPRO Detachment fly from Egypt against the Ploesti, Romania, oil fields.

July 4, 1942. The first Army Air Forces bomber mission over Western Europe (flown in Douglas A-20s) in World War II is flown against four airdromes in the Netherlands.

July 4, 1942. The Flying Tigers are incorporated into the AAF as the 23d Pursuit Group.

July 7, 1942. A B-18 of 396th Bombardment Squadron sinks a German submarine off Cherry Point, N.C., in first sure kill off the Atlantic coast by aircraft.

August 17, 1942. The first American heavy bomber mission in Western Europe in World War II is flown by B-17s of the 97th Bombardment Group against the Rouen-Sotteville railyards in France.

October 2, 1942. The Bell XP-59A lifts off from Muroc Dry Lake Bed, Calif., with Bell test pilot Robert Stanley at the controls. It is the first flight of a jet airplane in the United States. The next day, Col. Lawrence C. Craigie makes the first flight by a USAAF pilot.

November 2, 1942. NAS Patuxent River, Md., is established as the Navy's test center for aircraft and equipment.

November 8–11, 1942. Army pilots take off from carriers to support the invasion of North Africa. The P-40 pilots then touch down at land bases.

December 1942. The first issue of *Air Force* magazine is published. It succeeds the *Army Air Forces Newsletter*.

December 4, 1942. Ninth Air Force B-24 Liberator crews, based in Egypt, bomb Naples—the first American attacks in Italy.

December 27, 1942. 2d Lt. Richard I. Bong, who would later go on to be America's leading ace of all time and win the Medal of Honor, records his first aerial victory. Bong, who recorded all of his victories while flying the Lockheed P-38, would score more than half of his kills while flying with the 9th Fighter Squadron.

January 5, 1943. Army Air Forces Maj. Gen. Carl A. Spaatz is appointed Commander in Chief of the Allied Air Forces in North Africa.

January 9, 1943. Famed Boeing test

pilot Eddie Allen and Lockheed test pilot Milo Burcham make the first flight of the Lockheed C-69 transport (the military version of the Model 49 Constellation) at Burbank, Calif. Allen was on loan to Lockheed for the occasion.

January 27, 1943. The first American air raid on Germany is made by Eighth Air Force B-17 crews against Wilhelmshaven and other targets in the northwestern part of the country.

February 15, 1943. It is announced that Maj. Gen. Ira C. Eaker will succeed Maj. Gen. Carl A. Spaatz as commander of USAAF's Eighth Air Force.

February 18, 1943. First class of 39 flight nurses graduate from AAF School of Air Evacuation, Bowman Field, Ky.

February 27, 1943. RAF Bomber Command announces that the Allied air forces have made 2,000 sorties in the past 48 hours.

March 2–4, 1943. A Japanese attempt to reinforce Lae, New Guinea, is foiled by aircraft of the Southwest Pacific Air Forces during the Battle of the Bismarck Sea. Modified B-25s are used for the first time in low-level skip-bombing techniques. More than 60 enemy aircraft are destroyed and some 40,000 tons of Japanese shipping are sunk.

March 10, 1943. Fourteenth Air Force is formed under the command of Maj. Gen. Claire L. Chennault.

March 19, 1943. Lt. Gen. H. H. Arnold is promoted to four-star rank, a first for the Army Air Forces.

April 4, 1943. The B-24 *Lady Be Good*, returning from a bombing mission, overshoots its base at Soluch,

Libya, and is not heard from again. In 1959, the wreckage will be found by an oil exploration party 440 miles into the Libyan desert.

April 18, 1943. P-38 pilots from Henderson Field, Guadalcanal, intercept and shoot down two Mitsubishi "Betty" bombers over Bougainville. The aerial ambush kills Japanese Adm. Isoroku Yamamoto, who planned the Pearl Harbor attack.

May 30, 1943. All organized Japanese resistance ceases on Attu in the Aleutian Islands off Alaska. Attu was recaptured by American forces at a fearful cost in-lives; all but 28 members of the Japanese garrison sacrificed themselves.

June 15, 1943. The 58th Bombardment Wing, the Army Air Forces' first B-29 unit, is established at Marietta, Ga.

June 15, 1943. The world's first operational jet bomber, the German Arado Ar-234V-1 Blitz, makes its first flight.

July 2, 1943. Lt. Charles Hall shoots down a German FW-190 over Sicily, becoming the first black U.S. flyer to down an Axis plane.

July 19, 1943. Rome is bombed for the first time. Flying from Benghazi, Libya, 158 B-17 crews and 112 B-24 crews carry out a morning raid. A second attack is staged in the afternoon.

August 1, 1943. Staging from Benghazi, 177 Ninth Air Force B-24s drop 311 tons of bombs from low level on the oil refineries at Ploesti during Operation Tidal Wave. Forty-nine aircraft are lost, and seven others land in Turkey. This is the first large-scale, minimum-altitude attack by AAF heavy bombers on a strongly defended target. It is also the longest major bombing mission to date in terms of distance from base to target. Four officers, Col. Leon W. Johnson, Col. John R. Kane, Maj. John L. Jerstad, and 2d Lt. Lloyd H. Hughes, are awarded the Medal of Honor for their actions. More Air Force Medals of Honor are awarded for this mission than for any other in the service's history.

August 17, 1943. Eighth Air Force bombers attack the Messerschmitt works at Regensburg, Germany, and ball-bearing plants at Schweinfurt in a massive daylight raid. German fighters down 60 of the 376 American aircraft.

August 31, 1943. The Grumman F6F Hellcat goes into operational use with VF-5 off USS *Yorktown* (CV-10) in an attack on Marcus Island, 700 miles south of Japan. Hellcat pilots will account for nearly three-fourths of all Navy air-to-air victories in World War II.

September 12, 1943. German commandos, led by Capt. Otto Skorzeny, help Italian dictator Benito Mussolini break out of a hotel in Gran Sasso where he is being held prisoner. Captain Skorzeny and Il Duce escape in a Fieseler Fi-156 Storch observation plane.

September 27, 1943. P-47s with belly tanks go the whole distance with Eighth Air Force bombers for a raid on Emden, Germany.

October 14, 1943. Eighth Air Force conducts the second raid on the ball-bearing factories at Schweinfurt, Germany. As a result, the Germans will disperse their ball-bearing manufacturing, but the cost of the raid is high;

60 of the 291 B-17s launched do not return, and 138 more are damaged.

October 31, 1943. Over New Georgia in the Solomon Islands, a Chance Vought F4U-2 Corsair aviator accomplishes the Navy's first successful radar-guided interception.

November 22–26; 1943. At the Cairo Conference, Roosevelt and Churchill, along with Chiang Kai-Shek, agree that B-29s will be based in the China-Burma-India theater for strikes on the Japanese home islands.

December 5, 1943. P-51 pilots begin escorting US bombers to European targets. Ninth Air Force begins Operation Crossbow raids against German bases where secret weapons are being developed.

December 24, 1943. First major Eighth Air Force assault on German V-weapon sites is made when 670 B-17s and B-24s bomb the Pas de Calais area of France.

January 8, 1944. Developed in only 143 days, the prototype Lockheed XP-80 Shooting Star, *Lulu Belle*, makes its first flight at Muroc Dry Lake (later Edwards AFB), Calif., with Milo Burcham at the controls. It is the first American fighter to exceed 500 mph in level flight.

January 11, 1944. The first U.S. use of forward-firing rockets is made by Navy TBF-1C Avenger crews against a German submarine.

January 22, 1944. Mediterranean Allied Air Forces fly 1,200 sorties in support of Operation Shingle, the amphibious landings at Anzio, Italy.

February 15, 1944. The Nazi-occupied Abbey of Monte Cassino, Italy, is destroyed by 254 American B-17 crews, B-25 crews, and B-26 crews attacking in two waves. The ruins of the abbey will not be captured by Fifth Army until May 18, 1944.

February 20, 1944. The first mission of "Big Week"—six days of strikes by Eighth Air Force (based in England) and Fifteenth Air Force (based in Italy) against German aircraft plants—is flown.

March 4, 1944. B-17s of the Eighth Air Force conduct the first daylight bombing raid on Berlin.

March 5, 1944. British Brig. Gen. Orde Wingate's Raiders, popularly known as Chindits, land at "Broadway," a site near Indaw, Burma, in a daring night operation. General Wingate will be killed 19 days later in an airplane crash.

March 6, 1944. In the first major USAAF attack on Berlin, 660 heavy bombers unload 1,600 tons of bombs.

March 16, 1944. NACA proposes that a jet-propelled transonic research airplane be developed. This ultimately leads to the Bell X-1.

March 25, 1944. Fifteenth Air Force crews temporarily close the Brenner Pass between Italy and Austria. This mission, against the Aviso viaduct, is the first operational use of the VB-1 Azon (azimuth only) radio-controlled bomb.

April 11, 1944. Led by Royal Air Force Wing Commander R. N. Bateson, six de Havilland Mosquitos of No. 613 Squadron bomb an art gallery at The Hague where population records are kept. These records, many of which were destroyed, were used by the Gestapo to suppress the Dutch resistance.

April 12, 1944. Maj. Richard I. Bong records three aerial kills in a single mission to bring his personal tally to 28, for which he is recognized amid much hoopla as surpassing the total of America's World War I Ace of Aces, Captain Edward Rickenbacker. (Captain Eddie even sent Major Bong a case of scotch.) However, when the Air Force revises its aerial victory credits in the late 1960s, Captain Rickenbacker's long-accepted total of 26 kills is reduced to 24.33, which means that Major Bong actually passed Captain Rickenbacker on April 3, 1944.

May 11, 1944. Operation Strangle (March 19 to May 11) ends. Mediterranean Allied Air Forces' operations against enemy lines of communication in Italy total 50,000 sorties, with 26,000 tons of bombs dropped.

May 21, 1944. Operation Chattanooga Choo-Choo—systematic Allied air attacks on trains in Germany and France—begins.

June 2, 1944. The first shuttle bombing mission, using Russia as the eastern terminus, is flown. Lt. Gen. Ira C. Eaker, head of Mediterranean Allied Air Forces, flies in one of the B-17s.

June 6, 1944. Allied pilots fly approximately 15,000 sorties on D day. It is an effort unprecedented in concentration and size.

June 9, 1944. Allied units begin operations from bases in France.

June 13, 1944. The first German V-1s fired in combat are launched against England. Four of 11 strike London.

June 15, 1944. Forty-seven B-29 crews based in India and staging through Chengdu, China, attack steel mills at Yawata in the first B-29 strike against Japan.

June 19–20, 1944. "The Marianas Turkey Shoot": in two days of fighting, the Japanese lose 476 aircraft. American losses are 130 planes.

June 22, 1944. The GI Bill is signed into law.

July 5, 1944. The Northrop MX-324, the first US rocket-powered airplane, is flown for the first time by company pilot Harry Crosby at Harper Dry Lake, Calif.

July 9, 1944. Part of wrecked and captured Fiesler Fi-103 buzz bombs are delivered to Wright Field, Ohio, for evaluation. Seventeen days later Ford Motor Company finishes building a copy of the Argus pulse jet motor, and by October, Republic is chosen to build copies of the bomb's airframe. The U.S.-built duplicates are called JB-1 Loons.

July 17, 1944. Napalm incendiary bombs are dropped for the first time by American P-38 pilots on a fuel depot at Coutances, near Saint-Lô, France.

July 22, 1944. In the first all-fighter shuttle, Italy-based U.S. P-38 Lightnings and P-51 Mustangs of Fifteenth Air Force attack Nazi airfields at Bacau and Zilistea, northeast of Ploesti. The planes land at Russian bases.

July 27, 1944. The executive committee of the NACA discusses robots and their possibilities for military and other uses.

August 4, 1944. The first Aphrodite mission (a radio-controlled B-17 carrying 20,000 pounds of TNT) is flown against V-2 rocket sites in the Pas de Calais section of France.

August 14, 1944. Capt. Robin Olds records his first victory while flying with the 434th Fighter Squadron in the ETO. He would go on to tally 11 more kills by July 4, 1945. His next aerial victory would come on January 2, 1967, making him the only American ace to record victories in nonconsecutive wars.

August 28, 1944. Eighth Force's 78th Fighter Group claims the destruction of an Me-262, the first jet to be shot down in combat.

September 1, 1944. Company pilot Robert Stanley makes the first flight of the Bell RP-63A Kingcobra, a highly unusual modification to the P-63 that allowed the aircraft to be used as a piloted target. These Pinball aircraft were heavily armored (even the cockpit glazing was extra-thick) and gunnery students would fire frangible bullets made of lead and plastic at these aircraft in flight.

September 8, 1944. The German V-2, the world's first ballistic missile, is first used in combat. Two strike Paris; two more are launched against London.

September 14, 1944. Col. Floyd B. Wood, Maj. Harry Wexler, and Lt. Frank Reckord fly into a hurricane in a Douglas A-20 to gather scientific data.

September 17, 1944. Operation Market Garden begins: 1,546 Allied aircraft and 478 gliders carry parachute and glider troops in an airborne assault between Eindhoven and Arnhem in the Netherlands in an effort to secure a Rhine crossing at Arnhem.

October 24, 1944. Navy Capt. David McCampbell, who will go on to be the Navy's leading ace of all time, sets the U.S. record for aerial victories in a single engagement when he shoots down nine Japanese fighters.

November 1, 1944. A Boeing F-13 (photoreconnaissance B-29) crew makes the first flight over Tokyo since the 1942 Doolittle raid. The first XXI Bomber Command raid will be made on November 24, when 88 B-29s bomb the city.

November 3, 1944. The Japanese start their "Fu-Go Weapon" offensive against the United States. These balloon weapons are carried across the Pacific on the jet stream and release their bomblets over the U.S.

November 10, 1944. Thirty-six B-25s of Fifth Air Force attack a Japanese convoy near Ormoc Bay, Leyte, sinking three ships.

December 15, 1944. Bound for France, famed bandleader Maj. Glenn Miller and two others take off from England in a Noorduyn C-64 Norseman and are never heard from again. Several possible causes for the disappearance have been formulated, but none is ever proved.

December 15, 1944. President Roosevelt signs legislation creating the five-star ranks of General of the Army and Admiral of the Fleet.

December 17, 1944. The 509th Composite Group, assembled to carry out atomic bomb operations, is established at Wendover, Utah.

December 17, 1944. On the forty-first anniversary of the Wright brothers' historic first flight, Maj. Richard I. Bong, America's leading ace of all time, records his fortieth and final aerial victory

December 21, 1944. Gen. H. H. Arnold becomes General of the Army—the first airman to hold five-star rank.

December 26, 1944. Maj. Thomas B. McGuire, Jr., records four aerial victories in a single mission in the Southwest Pacific. These kills bring Major McGuire's victory total to 38, making him the second leading American ace of all time. Major McGuire, a Medal of Honor recipient, is killed in combat 12 days later.

January 20, 1945. Army Air Forces Maj. Gen. Curtis E. LeMay succeeds Brig. Gen. Haywood "Possum" Hansell as commander of XXI Bomber Command in the Mariana Islands.

February 3, 1945. A total of 959 B-17 crews carry out the largest raid to date against Berlin by American bombers.

February 19, 1945. The Marine V Amphibious Corps, with air and sea support, lands on Iwo Jima. The capture of this small spit of volcanic rock has important considerations for the Army Air Forces, as the island's three airfields will be used as emergency landing fields for Marianas-based B-29s and as a base for fighter operations. By March 26, the island will be secured, at a cost of more than 19,000 Japanese and 6,520 American lives.

February 20, 1945. Secretary of War Henry Stimson approves plans to establish a rocket proving ground near White Sands, N. M.

February 25, 1945. B-29 crews begin night incendiary raids on Japan; 334 aircraft drop 1,667 tons of firebombs and destroy 15 square miles of Tokyo.

March 9, 1945. In a change of tactics in order to double bomb loads,

Twentieth Air Force sends more than 300 B-29s from the Marianas against Tokyo in a low-altitude incendiary night raid, destroying about one-fourth of the city.

March 11, 1945. The greatest weight of bombs dropped in a USAAF strategic raid on a single target in Europe falls on Essen, Germany, as 1,079 bomber crews release 4,738 tons of bombs.

March 14, 1945. The first Grand Slam (22,000-pound) bomb is dropped from an Avro Lancaster flown by Royal Air Force Squadron Leader C. C. Calder. Two spans of the Bielefeld railway viaduct in Germany are destroyed.

March 18, 1945. Some 1,250 U.S. bombers, escorted by 670 fighters, deal Berlin its heaviest daylight blow—3,000 tons of bombs on transportation and industrial areas.

March 27, 1945. B-29 crews begin night mining missions around Japan, eventually establishing a complete blockade.

April 9, 1945. The last B-17 rolls off the line at Boeing's Seattle, Wash., plant.

April 10, 1945. The last Luftwaffe wartime sortie over Britain is made by an Arado Ar-234B pilot on a reconnaissance mission out of Norway.

April 10, 1945. Thirty of 50 German Me-262 jet fighters are shot down by U.S. bombers and their P-51 escorts. The German fighters shoot down ten bombers—the largest loss of the war in a single mission to jets.

April 17, 1945. *Flak Bait*, a Martin B-26B Marauder, completes a record 200th bombing mission. The aircraft,

which has now flown more missions over Europe than any other Allied aircraft in World War II, will go on to complete two more missions.

April 23, 1945. Flying Consolidated PB4Y-2 Privateers, Navy crews from VPB-109 launch two Bat missiles against Japanese ships in Balikpapan Harbor, Borneo. This is the first known use of automatic homing missiles during World War II.

May 8, 1945. V-E Day. The war ends in Europe.

June 22, 1945. Okinawa is declared captured by U.S. forces. The price paid to capture this island—16,000 men, 36 ships, and 800 aircraft—is a key consideration in the decision to use the atomic bombs on Japan.

June 26, 1945. B-29 crews begin nighttime raids on Japanese oil refineries.

July 16, 1945. The world's first atomic bomb is successfully detonated at Trinity Site, a desert location near Alamagordo, N.M. The weapon (referred to as "the gadget") is the prototype of the "Fat Man" plutonium bomb and has an explosive yield of 19 kilotons.

August 6, 1945. The "Little Boy" (uranium) atomic bomb is dropped on Hiroshima from the B-29 *Enola Gay*, commanded by Col. Paul W. Tibbets, Jr.

August 6, 1945. Maj. Richard I. Bong, America's all-time leading ace, is killed in a P-80 accident. He had 40 confirmed victories.

August 9, 1945. The "Fat Man" atomic bomb is dropped on Nagasaki from the B-29 *Bockscar*, commanded by Maj. Charles W. Sweeney.

August 14, 1945. Lt. Robert W. Clyde (pilot) and Lt. Bruce K. Leford (radar operator) record the last aerial victory of World War II. Flying a Northrop P-61 nicknamed *Lady in the Dark*, the crew gets behind a Nikajima Oscar, and, in an attempt to escape from its pursuer, the Japanese fighter crashes into the Pacific without a shot being fired.

September 2, 1945. V-J Day. On board USS *Missouri* in Tokyo Bay, Japanese Foreign Minister Mamoru Shigemitsu and Chief of Staff Gen. Yoshijiro Umezu sign instruments of surrender. (*NOTE*: Alternatively, V-J Day is regarded by some to be August 15, the date upon which Emperor Hirohito broadcast his radio message, the Imperial Rescript of Surrender, touching off the celebrations normally associated with V-J Day in allied Nations.)

November 6, 1945. The first landing of a jet-powered aircraft on a carrier is made by Ens. Jake C. West in the Ryan FR-1 Fireball, a fighter propelled by both a turbojet and a reciprocating engine. The landing on USS *Wake Island* (CVE-65) is inadvertent; the plane's piston engine fails, and Ensign West comes in powered only by the turbojet.

November 7, 1945. Royal Air Force Group Capt. Hugh Wilson sets the first postwar recognized absolute speed record and breaks the 600-mph barrier at the same time, as he flies a Gloster Meteor F.4 to a speed of 606.26 mph at Herne Bay, England.

1946–1950

February 4, 1946. The Air Force Association is incorporated.

February 9, 1946. Gen. Carl A. Spaatz is designated Commanding General, Army Air Forces, succeeding Gen. H. H. Arnold.

February 15, 1946. Thirty-five movie stars, studio executives, and reporters board a Lockheed Constellation piloted by Howard Hughes for the inauguration of TWA daily nonstop service between Los Angles, Calif., and New York City. Among the stars are Paulette Goddard, Veronica Lake, and Edward G. Robinson.

February 28, 1946. Maj. William Lien makes the first flight of the Republic XP-84 at Muroc Dry Lake, Calif. The Thunderjet is the Air Force's first postwar fighter and will be used extensively for ground attack missions in the Korean War. Later designated F-84, the Thunderjet is the first fighter to carry a tactical nuclear weapon.

March 21, 1946. Strategic Air Command, Tactical Air Command, and Air Defense Command are activated.

April 24, 1946. The first flights of the Soviet-designed and-built Yak-15 and MiG-9 prototypes are made.

May 4–16, 1946. Five separate recognized class records for altitude with payload in piston-engine aircraft are set by five different USAAF crews flying Boeing B-29A Superfortresses at Harmon Field, Guam. Col. J. B. Warren also sets a separate record for greatest load carried to 2,000 meters. These records still stand.

May 17/19, 1946. Eight separate recognized class records for speed over a closed course (1,000 and 2,000 km) with payload in piston-engine aircraft are set by two different USAAF crews flying Boeing B-29A Superfortresses at Dayton, Ohio. These records still stand.

June 21/28. 1946. Six separate recognized class records for speed over a closed course (5,000 km) with payload in piston engined aircraft are set by two different USAAF crews flying Boeing B-29A Superfortresses at Dayton, Ohio. These records still stand.

June 26, 1946. "Knot" and "nautical mile" are adopted by the Army Air Forces and the Navy as standard aeronautical units of speed and distance.

July 21, 1946. Navy Lt. Cmdr. James Davidson makes the first successful takeoff and landing of a jet-powered aircraft from an aircraft carrier. He is flying a McDonnell FH-1 Phantom from the USS *Franklin D. Roosevelt* (CVB-42).

July 1946. *Air Force* magazine becomes the official journal of the Air Force Association.

August 8, 1946. Almost five years after the prototype was ordered, company test pilots Beryl A. Erickson and G. S. Gus Green and a crew of seven make the first flight of the mammoth Convair XB-36 prototype at Fort Worth, Tex..

August 15, 1947. U.S. Air Forces in Europe is established as a major command.

August 31, 1946. Famed Hollywood stunt pilot Paul Mantz wins the first postwar Bendix Trophy transcontinental race from Los Angeles to Cleveland in a North American P-51 Mustang with an average speed of 435.501 mph. Total flying time is 4 hours and 42 minutes. Col. Leon Gray wins the first Bendix Trophy Jet Division race, flying a Lockheed P-80 Shooting Star over the same course with an average speed of 494.779 mph. Total flying time is 4 hours and 8 minutes.

September 18, 1946. Company pilot Sam Shannon makes the first official flight of the Convair XF-92 at Muroc Dry Lake, Calif. (A short hop had been made on June 9.) The first true delta-winged aircraft, the XF-92 will prove invaluable as a testbed for delta-wing research.

December 9, 1946. Company pilot Chalmers Slick Goodlin makes the first powered flight of the Bell X-1 supersonic research aircraft. He reaches Mach .75 and an altitude of 35,000 feet after being released from a Boeing B-29 mother ship.

March 16, 1947. Company pilots Sam Shannon and Russell R. Rogers make the first flight of the Convair 240 airliner prototype at San Diego, Calif. Versions of the 240 will be used by the Air Force as the T-29 navigator trainer and as the C-131 Samaritan medical evacuation/transport aircraft. One aircraft, the NC-131 variable stability testbed, keeps flying into the 1990s.

June 19, 1947. Col. Albert Boyd sets the recognized absolute speed record, as he flies the Lockheed P-80R to a speed of 623.608 mph at Muroc Dry Lake, Calif.

July 29–30, 1947. Lt. Col. O. F. Lassiter sets a recognized class record for speed over a 10,000-km closed circuit without payload (piston-engine aircraft) of 273.194 mph in a Boeing B-29A Superfortress at Dayton, Ohio. The record still stands.

August 25, 1947. Marine Maj. Marion Carl breaks the recognized absolute speed record set two months previously as he pilots the Douglas D-558-I Skystreak to a speed of 650.8 mph at Muroc Dry Lake, Calif.

September 18, 1947. The U.S. Air Force is established as a separate service, with W. Stuart Symington as its first Secretary. Gen. Carl A. Spaatz, Commanding General of the AAF, becomes the first Chief of Staff on September 26.

October 1, 1947. Company test pilot George S. "Wheaties" Welch, who was one of the few AAF fighter pilots who was able to get airborne during the Pearl Harbor attack, makes the first flight of the North American XP-86 Sabre at Muroc Dry Lake, Calif. The Sabre is the Air Force's first swept-wing fighter.

October 14, 1947. The first supersonic flight is made by Capt. Charles E. Yeager in the rocket-powered Bell XS-1 (later redesignated X-1) over Muroc Dry Lake.

October 21, 1947. The first flight of the Northrop YB-49 flying-wing jet bomber is made. The Air Force's Northrop B-2 stealth bomber bears a family resemblance to this plane when it debuts in 1989.

November 2, 1947. Howard Hughes's wooden H-4 *Hercules* (the "Spruce Goose") makes its first (and only) flight over Los Angeles harbor. Distance traveled is about a mile.

November 23, 1947. The world's largest landplane, the Convair XC-99, the cargo version of the B-36 bomber, makes its first flight at Lindbergh Field in San Diego, Calif., with company test pilots Russell R. Rogers and Beryl A. Erickson at the controls. This aircraft will lift a record 100,000 pound payload on April 15, 1949.

December 17, 1947. The prototype Boeing XB-47 Stratojet bomber makes its first flight from Boeing Field in Seattle, Wash., with company pilots Bob Robbins and Scott Osler at the controls.

December 30, 1947. The Soviet MiG-15 is flown for the first time.

January 30, 1948. Orville Wright dies in his hometown of Dayton, Ohio, at age 76.

February 20, 1948. The first Boeing B-50 Superfortress is delivered to Strategic Air Command (SAC).

April 21, 1948. Secretary of Defense James V. Forrestal assigns the primary responsibility for air defense of the United States to the Air Force.

April 26, 1948. The Air Force announces a policy of racial integration— the first service to do so—well before President Truman's Executive Order on equal opportunity in July 1948.

April 30, 1948. Gen. Hoyt S. Vandenberg is designated to succeed Gen. Carl A. Spaatz as Air Force Chief of Staff.

June 26, 1948. Operation Vittles, the Berlin Airlift, begins with Douglas C-47 crews bringing 80 tons of supplies into the city on the first day. By the time it ends, on September 30, 1949, the Anglo-American airlift will have delivered a total of 2.3 million tons of food, fuel, and supplies to the beleaguered city.

August 16, 1948. Company pilot Fred C. Brethcher makes the first flight of the Northrop XF-89 Scorpion all-weather interceptor at Muroc AFB, Calif.

August 23, 1948. The prototype McDonnell XF-85 Goblin parasite fighter makes its first free flight. It is intended to be carried in the bomb bay of a B-36 for fighter support over a target, but the project will be abandoned a year later when air refueling of fighters proves eminently more practical.

September 15, 1948. Air Force Maj. Richard L. Johnson, flying a North American F-86, recaptures the world speed record for the U.S., streaking over a 3-kilometer course at Muroc AFB, Calif., at 670.981 mph.

October 15, 1948. Maj. Gen. William H. Tunner assumes command of the newly created Combined Airlift Task Force during the Berlin Airlift.

December 7–8, 1948. On the seventh anniversary of the Japanese attack on Pearl Harbor, Hawaii, a 7th Bomb Wing crew flies a Convair B-36B 'Peacemaker' on a 35.5-hour mission from Carswell AFB, Tex., to Hawaii and back. The B-36 is undetected by local air defenses at Pearl Harbor.

December 8, 1948. A six-engine B-36 completes 9,400-mile nonstop flight from Fort Worth, Tex., to Hawaii and back to Fort Worth without refueling.

December 16, 1948. Company pilot Charles Tucker makes the first flight of the Northrop X-4 Bantam at Muroc AFB, Calif. The X-4 is designed to study flight characteristics of small, swept-wing semitailless aircraft at transonic speeds.

December 17, 1948. The 45th anniversary of the first powered flight is commemorated by the donation of the original Wright Flyer to the Smithsonian Institution. The Flyer was displayed in Britain for many years because of a dispute between the Wrights and the Smithsonian.

December 29, 1948. Defense Secretary Forrestal says the U.S. is working on an "earth satellite vehicle program," a project to study the operation of guided rockets beyond Earth's pull of gravity.

December 31, 1948. The 100,000th flight of the Berlin Airlift is made.

January 25, 1949. The U.S. Air Force adopts blue uniforms.

February 4, 1949. The Civil Aeronautics Administration sanctions the use of ground-controlled approach as a "primary aid" for commercial airline crews.

February 26–March 2, 1949. *Lucky Lady II*, a SAC B-50A, is flown on the first nonstop flight around the world. The 23,452-mile flight takes 94 hours, 1 minute and requires four midair refuelings.

March 4, 1949. The U.S. Navy's Martin JRM-2 flying boat *Caroline Mars* carries a record 269 passengers from San Diego to San Francisco, Calif.

March 4, 1949. Crews flying in the Berlin Airlift exceed 1 million tons of cargo hauled.

March 15, 1949. Military Air Transport Service establishes Global Weather Central at Offutt AFB, Neb., for support of SAC.

April 4, 1949. Meeting in Washington, D.C., the foreign ministers of Belgium, Britain, Canada, Denmark, France, Iceland, Italy, Luxembourg, the Netherlands, Norway, and Portugal, along with the U.S. Secretary of State, sign the North Atlantic Treaty.

April 16, 1949. Company test pilot

Tony LeVier and flight test engineer Tony Faulkerson makes the first flight of the YF-94 Starfire prototype from Van Nuys, Calif. The Starfire, actually a modified TP-80, is designed to serve as an interim all-weather interceptor.

May 9, 1949. Republic chief test pilot Carl Bellinger makes the first flight of the XF-91 Thunderceptor jet/rocket hybrid at Muroc AFB, Calif. This unusual aircraft has variable-incidence wings of inverse-taper design (wider at the tips than at the roots).

May 11, 1949. President Harry S. Truman signs a bill providing for a 3,000-mile-long guided-missile test range for the Air Force. The range is subsequently established at Cape Canaveral, Fla.

June 2, 1949. Gen. H. H. Arnold is given the permanent rank of General of the Air Force by a special act of Congress.

August 9, 1949. Navy Lt. J. L. Fruin makes another emergency escape with an ejection seat in the U.S. near Walterboro, S.C. His McDonnell F2H-1 Banshee is traveling at more than 500 knots at the time.

August 10, 1949. President Truman signs the National Security Act Amendments of 1949, renaming the National Military Establishment the Department of Defense.

September 23, 1949. President Truman announces that the Soviet Union has successfully exploded an atomic bomb.

September 30, 1949. The Berlin Airlift, gradually reduced since May 12, 1949, officially ends. Results show 2,343,301.5 tons of supplies carried on 277,264 flights. U.S. planes carried 1,783,826 tons.

October 4, 1949. A Fairchild C-82 Packet crew airdrops an entire field artillery battery by parachute at Fort Bragg, N.C.

November 18, 1949. A crew flying a Douglas C-74 Globemaster I, *The Champ*, lands at RAF Marham, England, after a 23-hour flight from Mobile, Ala. On board are a transatlantic-record 103 passengers and crew.

1950–1953

January 23, 1950. USAF establishes Air Research and Development Command, which in 1961 will be redesignated Air Force Systems Command.

January 31, 1950. President Truman announces that he has directed the Atomic Energy Commission "to continue its work on all forms of atomic-energy weapons, including the so-called hydrogen or super bomb." This is the first confirmation of U.S. H-bomb work.

March 15, 1950. The Joint Chiefs of Staff, in a statement of basic roles

and missions, give the Air Force formal and exclusive responsibility for strategic guided missiles.

April 21, 1950. Piloted by Navy Lt. Cmdr. R. C. Starkey, a Lockheed P2V-3C Neptune weighing 74,668 pounds becomes the heaviest aircraft ever launched from an aircraft carrier. The Neptune is flown off USS *Coral Sea* (CV-43).

April 24, 1950. Thomas K. Finletter becomes Secretary of the Air Force.

June 25, 1950. North Korea attacks South Korea to begin Korean War.

June 27, 1950. President Truman announces he has ordered the USAF to aid South Korea, which has been invaded by North Korean Communist forces.

June 27, 1950. Flying a North American F-82, 1st Lt. William G. Hudson destroys a Yak-11 near Seoul, the first enemy plane shot down in the Korean War.

June 30, 1950. President Truman authorizes General Douglas MacArthur to dispatch air forces against targets in North Korea.

July 1, 1950. Carrier aircraft go into action in Korea with strikes in and around Pyongyang. Also Lt. (j.g.) L. H. Plog and Ensign E. W. Brown each down a Yak-9, the first U.S. Navy kills in air combat in Korea.

September 22, 1950. Air Force Col. David Schilling makes the first nonstop transatlantic flight in a jet aircraft, flying a Republic F-84E from Manston, England, to Limestone (later Loring) AFB, Me., in 10 hours, 1 minute. The trip requires three in-flight refuelings.

November 8, 1950. 1st Lt. Russell J. Brown, Jr., flying a Lockheed F-80 Shooting Star, downs a North Korean MiG-15 in history's first all-jet aerial combat.

April 6, 1951. The Labor Department announces that employment in aircraft and parts plants increased by 100,000 people in the first six months of the Korean War.

May 20, 1951. Capt. James Jabara becomes the Air Force's first Korean War ace. He eventually downs 15 enemy planes in Korea.

June 20, 1951. Company pilot Jean Skip Ziegler makes the first flight of the Bell X-5 at Edwards AFB, Calif. The world's first aircraft to have variable-sweep wings. On the plane's ninth flight, the wings are moved to the full 60-degree sweepback.

August 18, 1951. Col. Keith Compton wins the first USAF jets-only Bendix Trophy transcontinental race, flying from Muroc AFB, Calif., to Detroit, Mich., in a North American F-86A Sabre with an average speed of 553.761 mph. Total flying time is 3 hours, 27 minutes.

August 21, 1951. The Medal of Honor is awarded posthumously to Maj. Louis J. Sebille, USAF, who was killed August 5 near Hamch'ang, Korea. Sebille attacked Red troops in his damaged plane until it crashed. This is the first Air Force Medal of Honor awarded in the Korean War.

September 14, 1951. Flying a night intruder mission, Capt. John A. Walmsley attacks a North Korean supply train near Yangdok, North Korea. His bombs hit an ammunition car, and the train breaks in two. He then makes a strafing attack on the remaining cars, but his guns jam after the first pass. Using the newly installed searchlight in the Douglas B-26 Intruder's nose, he lights the way for another pilot to finish off the train. Captain Walmsley's aircraft is hit by groundfire and crashes. Captain Walmsley will be posthumously awarded the Medal of Honor for his actions.

September 20, 1951. The Air Force makes the first successful recovery of animals from rocket flight when a monkey and 11 mice survive an Aerobee flight to 236,000 feet.

October 2, 1951. Col. Francis S. Gabreski of the 51st Fighter Wing downs a MiG-15, which gives him 6.5 victories in Korea. Since he had 28 victories in World War II, he is the highest-scoring Air Force ace with victories in two wars.

November 30, 1951. Maj. George A. Davis, Jr., becomes another USAF ace of two wars—World War II (7) and Korea (14).

February 1, 1952. The Air Force acquires its first general-purpose computer (a Univac I).

February 10, 1952. Despite being outnumbered 12 to 2, Maj. George A. Davis, Jr., and his wingman attack a formation of MiG-15s over the Sinuiju-Yalu River area of Korea in order to protect a force of U.S. fighter-bombers. Major Davis, who had recorded 7 air-to-air victories in World War II and had added 14 more in Korea, shoots down two of the MiGs (although these are not confirmed kills) before being shot down himself. His wingman manages to escape. For his unselfish action, Major Davis is posthumously awarded the Medal of Honor.

April 15, 1952. The Boeing YB-52 Stratofortress bomber prototype makes its maiden flight from its facility in Seattle, Wash. Company pilot A.M. "Tex" Johnston is at the controls.

June 23–24, 1952. Combined air elements of the Air Force, Navy, and Marines virtually destroy the electrical power potential of North Korea. The two-day attack involves 1,200 sorties and is the largest single air effort since World War II.

July 14, 1952. The Ground Observer Corps begins its round-the-clock sky-watch program as part of a nation-wide air defense effort.

November 1, 1952. The United States tests its first thermonuclear device at Eniwetok in the Marshall Islands. The device, codenamed Mike, has a yield of 10.4 million tons of TNT, 1,000 times more powerful than the bomb dropped on Hiroshima in World War II.

November 22, 1952. While leading a flight of four Lockheed F-80s on a mission to dive-bomb enemy gun positions that are harassing friendly ground troops near Sniper Ridge, North Korea, Maj. Charles J. Loring's aircraft is hit repeatedly as he verifies the position of the enemy guns. His aircraft badly damaged, he turns and deliberately crashes into the gun positions, destroying them completely. For this selfless action, Major Loring is posthumously awarded the Medal of Honor.

January 2, 1953. Cessna Aircraft is declared the winner of the Air Force's primary jet trainer competition. This Cessna, later designated T-37, beats out 14 entries.

January 14, 1953. 1st Lt. Joseph M. McConnell, Jr., who will go on to become the leading American ace in Korea, records his first aerial victory, a MiG-15. Assigned to the 39th Fighter Squadron, he is flying a North American F-86 at the time.

January 26, 1953. Chance Vought Aircraft completes the last F4U Corsair. The Corsair was production for 13 years (and built by two other manufacturers during World War II), and almost 12,700 were built in a number of versions, making for one of the longest and largest production runs in history.

February 4, 1953. Harold E. Talbott becomes Secretary of the Air Force.

March 16, 1953. Republic delivers the 4,000th F-84 Thunderjet to the Air Force. The F-84 has been in production since 1946.

April 7, 1953. The Atomic Energy Commission reveals that it is using QF-80 drone aircraft at the Nevada Proving Ground. The drones are flown directly through atomic bomb blast clouds to collect samples for later examination.

May 12, 1953. Secretary of Defense Charles E. Wilson reveals that projected Air Force strength has been revised downward to 120 wings, instead of the 143 previously planned.

May 18, 1953. Capt. Joseph M. McConnell, Jr., downs three MiG-15 fighters in two separate engagements. These victories give Captain McConnell a total of 16 kills in just five months of action and make him the leading American ace of the Korean War.

May 23, 1953. Company pilot Geoge S. "Wheaties" Welch makes the first flight of the North American YF-100 Super Sabre prototype at the Air Force Flight Test Center at Edwards AFB, Calif. He exceeds Mach 1 on this first flight.

June 8, 1953. Officially activated just a week before, USAF's 3600th Air Demonstration Flight, the Thunderbirds, perform their first aerial demonstration. Flying Republic F-84G Thunderjets, the team flies the show at their home, Luke AFB, Ariz.

June 16, 1953. North American delivers the 1,000th T-28 Trojan tandem-seat trainer to the Air Force.

June 30, 1953. Gen. Nathan F.

Twining becomes Air Force Chief of Staff.

July 16, 1953. Lt. Col. William Barnes pushes the recognized absolute speed record past 700 mph, hitting 715.751 mph in a North American F-86D over the Salton Sea in California.

July 27, 1953. Capt. Ralph S. Parr, a member of the 335th Fighter Interceptor Squadron, flying a North American F-86, records the last aerial victory in the Korean War when he shoots down an Il-2 near Hohadong shortly after midnight. It was his 10th aerial victory.

July 27, 1953. The Korean armistice goes into effect. (It was actually signed the day before.).

July 29, 1953. Two days after the armistice ending the Korean War, the Air Force announces that the Far East Air Force shot down 839 MiG-15 jet fighters, probably destroyed 154 more, and damaged 919 others during the 37 months of war. United Nations air forces lost 110 aircraft in air-to-air combat, 677 to enemy ground fire, and 213 airplanes to "other causes."

August 21, 1953. Flying the Douglas D-558-II Skyrocket, Marine Corps Lt. Col. Marion Carl sets an altitude record of 83,235 feet after being dropped from a Boeing P2B (B-29) flying at 34,000 feet over Edwards AFB, Calif.

September 1, 1953. The first jet-to-jet air refueling takes place between a Boeing KB-47 and a "standard" B-47.

September 11, 1953. A Grumman F6F-5K Hellcat drone is destroyed in the first successful interception test of the N-7 (AIM-9) Sidewinder air-to-air missile at China Lake, Calif. The Naval Ordnance Test Station, which had fashioned the missile basically out of spare parts, conducts the test. More than 150,000 Sidewinders have been produced since.

September 21, 1953. North Korean pilot Lt. Noh Kum Suk defects and flies his MiG-15 to Kimpo AB, South Korea. He is granted asylum and given $100,000.

October 3, 1953. Navy Lt. Cmdr. James B. Verdin establishes a world speed record of 752.94 mph in the Douglas XF4D-1 Skyray over the Salton Sea in California. This is the first time a jet-powered carrier plane has set the speed record.

October 19, 1953. Assistant Secretary of the Air Force Roger Lewis reveals that Boeing B-52 bombers will cost approximately $3.6 million each in production, but the first four aircraft will cost about $20 million each to amortize the design, development, and tooling costs.

October 24, 1953. Company pilot Richard L. Johnson makes the first flight of the Convair XF-102 prototype at Edwards AFB, Calif. Performance of this aircraft is found to be lacking, and the greatly redesigned YF-102A will fly in early 1954. The supersonic Delta Dagger is the USAF's first production delta-winged aircraft, and it will be the first interceptor to become operational armed only with missiles and unguided rockets.

October 29, 1953. Lt. Col. Frank K. Pete Everest, Jr., sets a new world speed record of 755.149 mph in the North American YF-100 prototype over the Salton Sea in California. He breaks the record set just a few weeks earlier by Navy Lt. Cmdr. James B. Verdin.

November 1, 1953. The Air Reserve Personnel Center is established at Lowry AFB, Colo.

November 6, 1953. A Boeing B-47 Stratojet is flown from Limestone (later Loring) AFB, Me., to RAF Brize Norton, England, in 4 hours, 53 minutes to establish a new transatlantic speed record from the continental U.S.

November 20, 1953. NACA test pilot Scott Crossfield becomes the first pilot to exceed Mach 2. His Douglas D-588-II Skyrocket research plane is dropped from a Navy P2B-1S (B-29) at an altitude of 32,000 feet over Edwards AFB.

December 12, 1953. Maj. Charles E. Yeager pilots the rocket-powered Bell X-1A to a speed of Mach 2.435 (approximately 1,650 mph) over Edwards AFB.

1954–1963

February 15, 1954. President Dwight D. Eisenhower nominates Charles A. Lindbergh to be a brigadier general in the Air Force Reserve.

February 24, 1954. President Eisenhower approves the National Security Council's recommendation for construction of the Distant Early Warning (DEW) Line. Operational control of the DEW Line will be transferred from the Air Force to the Royal Canadian Air Force on February 1, 1959.

March 1, 1954. In the Marshall Islands, the U.S. successfully explodes its first deliverable hydrogen bomb.

March 7, 1954. Company test pilot Tony LeVier makes the first flight of the Lockheed XF-104 Starfighter at Edwards AFB, Calif. A first attempt on February 28 was cut short after the aircraft experienced gear retraction problems. Designed as a supersonic air superiority fighter, the F-104 will set a number of records for the U.S., but it will find greater utility for a number of other countries than it will for the USAF.

March 18, 1954. Boeing rolls out the first production B-52A Stratofortress at its plant in Seattle, Wash. Production will continue until 1962.

April 1, 1954. President Eisenhower signs into law a bill creating the U.S. Air Force Academy.

May 25, 1954. A Navy ZPG-2 airship lands at NAS Key West, Fla., after staying aloft for 200.1 hours. Cmdr. M. H. Eppes, the airship captain, is later awarded the Distinguished Flying Cross.

June 22, 1954. The Douglas A4D (A-4) Skyhawk makes its first flight from Edwards AFB with company pilot Robert Rahn at the controls. Some 2,960 aircraft later, "Scooters" will still be flying with the Navy as trainers and with several foreign countries as front-line equipment into the mid-1990s.

July 15, 1954. The Boeing Model 367-80 makes its first flight, with company pilot A. M. "Tex" Johnston in command. The aircraft is the prototype for the Air Force's C/KC-135 series and the progenitor of the 707, which will become the first civilian jetliner to see wide use.

August 23, 1954. Lockheed pilots Stanley Beltz and Roy Wimmer crew the first flight of the YC-130 Hercules at Burbank, Calif. More than 2,100 aircraft later, the C-130 will still be in production at Marietta, Ga., and it is expected to be produced beyond the turn of the century.

August 26, 1954. Maj. Arthur "Kit" Murray reaches a record height of 90,443 feet in the Bell X-1A, which was released from a B-29 over Edwards AFB.

September 24, 1954. Company test pilot Robert C. Little makes the first flight of the McDonnell F-101A Voodoo at Edwards AFB, Calif. The One-oh-Wonder hits Mach 1.2 on its first flight and will go on to fill several roles for a number of Air Force commands.

October 12, 1954. The Cessna XT-37 Tweet trainer is flown for the first time at Wichita, Kan. The T-37 will still be soldiering on nearly 40 years later as the Air Force's primary trainer.

October 27, 1954. Benjamin O. Davis, Jr., son of the first black general officer in the U.S. Army, becomes the first black general officer in the U.S. Air Force. He will retire April 30, 1965, as a lieutenant general.

November 2, 1954. Company test pilot J. F. Coleman, flying in the radial tail-sitting Convair XFY-1, makes a vertical takeoff, changes to horizontal flight, and then returns to vertical for a landing in San Diego, Calif.

November 7, 1954. The Air Force announces plans to build a $15.5 million research laboratory for atomic aircraft engines. To be built in Connecticut, the plant is to be run by Pratt & Whitney and will be finished in 1957.

December 10, 1954. To determine if a pilot can eject from an airplane at supersonic speed and live, Lt. Col. John Paul Stapp, a flight surgeon, rides a rocket sled to 632 mph, decelerates to zero in 125 seconds, and survives more than 35 times the force of gravity.

February 7, 1955. After 131 shows, the Thunderbirds, the Air Force's aerial demonstration team, perform their last show in the Republic F-84G Thunderjet at Webb AFB, Tex. In April, the team will convert to swept-wing F-84F Thunderstreaks.

February 23, 1955. The Army picks Bell Helicopter from a list of 20 competing companies to build its first turbine-powered helicopter. The winning design, designated XH-40, will become the HU-1 (and later still, UH-1) Iroquois, the renowned "Huey."

February 26, 1955. North American Aviation test pilot George Smith becomes the first person to survive ejection from an aircraft flying at supersonic speed. His F-100 Super Sabre is traveling at Mach 1.05 when the controls jam and he is forced to punch out.

July 11, 1955. The first class (306 cadets) is sworn in at the Air Force Academy's temporary location at Lowry AFB, Colo.

August 4, 1955. Company pilot Tony LeVier makes the first official flight of the Lockheed U-2 spyplane at Groom Lake, Nev. An inadvertent hop had been made on July 29.

August 15, 1955. Donald A. Quarles becomes Secretary of the Air Force.

October 22, 1955. Company test pilot Rusty Roth makes the first flight of the Republic YF-105 Thunderchief at Edwards AFB, Calif. The aircraft, commonly known as the Thud (among other things), is the largest

single-engine, single-seat fighter ever built.

November 26, 1955. Secretary of Defense Charles Wilson assigns responsibility for development and operations of land-based intercontinental ballistic missiles to the Air Force.

January 17, 1956. Department of Defense reveals the existence of SAGE, an electronic air defense system.

February 17, 1956. Company test pilot Tony LeVier inadvertently makes the first flight of the Lockheed F-104A Starfighter as the plane skips off the runway during high-speed taxi tests at Edwards AFB, Calif. The first official flight takes place March 4.

March 10, 1956. The recognized absolute speed record passes the 1,000-mph barrier as company pilot Peter Twiss hits 1,132.13 mph in the Fairey Delta 2 research aircraft at Sussex, England.

May 20, 1956. After 91 shows in a little more than a year, the Thunderbirds perform their last demonstration in the Republic F-84F Thunderstreak at Bolling AFB, D.C.

May 21, 1956. An Air Force crew flying Boeing B-52B Stratofortress at 40,000 feet airdrops a live hydrogen bomb over Bikini Atoll in the Pacific. The bomb has a measured blast of 3.75 megatons.

May 28, 1956. Company pilot Pete Girard makes the first flight of the Ryan X-13 Vertijet VTOL research aircraft in hover mode at Edwards AFB, Calif. He had also made the type's first conventional flight on December 10, 1955.

June 30, 1956. The Thunderbirds, the Air Force's aerial demonstration squadron, fly their first show in the supersonic North American F-100 Super Sabre, the type the team would fly for most of the next 13 years.

September 27, 1956. Capt. Milburn Apt, USAF, reaches Mach 3.196 in the Bell X-2, becoming the first pilot to fly three times the speed of sound. Captain Apt is killed, however, when the aircraft tumbles out of control.

October 1, 1956. NASA awards its Distinguished Service Medal to Dr. Richard T. Whitcomb, inventor of the area rule concept, which results in aircraft (such as the Convair F-102) having Coke-bottle-shaped fuselages in order to reduce supersonic drag.

October 26, 1956. Less than 16 months after design work began, and, ironically, the same day that legendary plane-maker Larry Bell dies, company pilot Floyd Carlson makes the first flight of the Bell XH-40 at Fort Worth, Tex. Later redesignated UH-1, the Iroquois, or Huey as it is more popularly known, will go on to be one of the significant helicopters of all time.

November 11, 1956. With company pilot Beryl A. Erickson at the controls, the USAF's first supersonic bomber, the delta-winged Convair B-58 Hustler, capable of flying at speeds of more than 1,000 mph, makes its first flight at Fort Worth, Tex.

December 26, 1956. Company pilot Richard L. Johnson makes the first flight of the first Convair F-106 Delta Dart at Edwards AFB, Calif. The F-106, a substantially redesigned and much improved version of the F-102 interceptor, remains in service until 1988 and is later modified into target drones.

January 18, 1957. Commanded by

Maj. Gen. Archie J. Old, Jr., USAF, three B-52 Stratofortresses complete a 24,325-mile round-the-world nonstop flight in 45 hours, 19 minutes, with an average speed of 534 mph. It is the first globe-circling nonstop flight by a jet aircraft.

April 11, 1957. With company pilot Pete Girard at the controls, the Ryan X-13 Vertijet makes its first full-cycle flight. Girard takes off vertically from the aircraft's mobile trailer, transitions to horizontal flight, performs several maneuvers, and then lands vertically.

May 1, 1957. James H. Douglas, Jr., becomes Secretary of the Air Force.

July 1, 1957. Gen. Thomas D. White becomes Air Force Chief of Staff.

July 1, 1957. Pacific Air Forces established.

July 13, 1957. President Dwight D. Eisenhower becomes the first chief executive to fly in a helicopter as he takes off from the White House lawn in a Bell UH-13J Sioux. Maj. Joseph E. Barrett flies the president a short distance to a military command post at a remote location as part of a military exercise.

July 19, 1957. A Douglas MB-1 Genie aerial rocket is fired from a Northrop F-89J Scorpion, marking the first time in history that an air-to-air rocket with a nuclear warhead is launched and detonated. The test takes place at 20,000 feet over the Nevada Test Site.

July 31, 1957. The DEW Line, a distant early warning radar defense installation extending across the Canadian Arctic, is reported to be fully operational.

August 1, 1957. NORAD, the joint U.S.-Canadian North American Air

Defense Command, is informally established.

August 15, 1957. Gen. Nathan F. Twining becomes Chairman of the Joint Chiefs of Staff, the first USAF officer to serve in this position.

October 4, 1957. The space age begins when the Soviet Union launches Sputnik I, the world's first artificial satellite, into Earth orbit.

November 3, 1957. The first animal in space, a dog named Laika, is carried aboard Sputnik II. The satellite is carried aloft by a modified ICBM.

November 11–13, 1957. Gen. Curtis E. LeMay and crew fly a Boeing KC-135 from Westover AFB, Mass., to Buenos Aires, Argentina, to set a world jet-class record distance in a straight line of 6,322 miles. The crew will set a class speed record on the trip back.

December 6, 1957. The first U.S. attempt to orbit a satellite fails when a Vanguard rocket loses thrust and explodes.

December 12, 1957. Flying a Mc-Donnell F-101A Voodoo, USAF Maj. Adrian Drew sets a world record of 1,207.34 mph at Edwards AFB, Calif.

December 17, 1957. The Convair HGM-16 Atlas intercontinental ballistic missile (ICBM) makes its first successful launch and flight.

January 31, 1958. Explorer I, the first U.S. satellite, is launched by the Army at Cape Canaveral. The satellite, launched on a Jupiter-C rocket, will later play a key role in the discovery of the Van Allen radiation belt.

February 4, 1958. The keel of the world's first nuclear-powered aircraft carrier, USS *Enterprise* (CVN-65), is

laid at the Newport News Shipbuilding and Drydock Co. yards in Virginia.

February 27, 1958. Approval is given to USAF to start research and development on an ICBM program that will later be called Minuteman.

March 6, 1958. The first production Northrop SM-62 Snark intercontinental missile is accepted by the Air Force after four previous successful launchings.

April 8, 1958. An Air Force KC-135 Stratotanker crew flies 10,229.3 miles nonstop and unrefueled from Tokyo to Lajes Field, Azores, in 18 hours, 50 minutes.

May 7, 1958. USAF Maj. Howard C. Johnson sets a world altitude record of 91,243 feet in a Lockheed F-104A Starfighter. Nine days later, USAF Capt. Walter W. Irwin sets a world speed record of 1,404.09 mph, also in an F-104.

May 14, 1958. Trans World Airlines becomes the first air carrier to hire a black stewardess.

May 27, 1958. The first flight of the McDonnell F4H-1 (F-4) Phantom II is made by company pilot Robert Little (who was wearing street shoes at the time) at the company's facility in St. Louis, Mo. On May 20, 1978, McDonnell Douglas will deliver the 5,000th F-4.

June 17, 1958. Boeing and Martin are named prime contractors to develop competitive designs for the Air Force's X-20 Dyna-Soar boost-glide space vehicle. This project, although later canceled, is the first step toward the space shuttle.

July 23, 1958. The Boeing Vertol VZ-2A tilt-wing research aircraft makes the first successful transition from vertical to horizontal flight and vice versa.

July 26, 1958. Capt. Iven C. Kincheloe, Jr., USAF, holder of the world altitude record (126,200 feet, set in the Bell X-2, September 7, 1956), is killed in an F-104 crash.

August 6, 1958. A Department of Defense Reorganization Act removes operational control of combat forces from the individual services and reassigns the missions to unified and specified commands on a geographic or functional basis. The main role of the services becomes to organize, train, and equip forces.

September 1, 1958. A new enlisted supergrade, senior master sergeant (E-8), is created.

September 26, 1958. A Boeing B-52D crew sets a world distance record of 6,233.98 miles and a speed record of 560.75 mph (over a 10,000-meter course) during a two-lap flight from Ellsworth AFB, S.D., to Douglas, Ariz., to Newburg, Ore., and back.

October 1, 1958. The National Aeronautics and Space Administration (NASA) is officially established, replacing NACA.

December 16, 1958. The Pacific Missile Range begins launching operations with the successful flight of the Chrysler PGM-19 Thor missile, the first ballistic missile launched over the Pacific Ocean. It is also the first free-world firing of a ballistic missile under simulated combat conditions.

December 18, 1958. Project Score, an Atlas booster with a communications repeater satellite, is launched into Earth orbit. The satellite carries a Christmas message from President Eisenhower that is broadcast to Earth, the first time a human voice has been heard from space.

January 8, 1959. NASA requests eight Redstone-type launch vehicles from the Army for Project Mercury development flights. Four days later, McDonnell Aircraft Co. is selected to build the Mercury capsules.

January 22, 1959. Air Force Capt. William B. White sets a record for the longest nonstop flight between points in the U.S., as he flies a Republic F-105 Thunderchief 3,850 miles from Eielson AFB, Alaska, to Eglin AFB, Fla., in 5 hours, 27 minutes.

February 6, 1959. USAF successfully launches the first Martin HGM-25A Titan ICBM.

February 28, 1959. USAF successfully launches the Discoverer I satellite into polar orbit from Vandenberg AFB, Calif.

April 2, 1959. Chosen from a field of 110 candidates, seven test pilots—Air Force Capts. L. Gordon Cooper, Jr., Virgil I. "Gus" Grissom, and Donald K. "Deke" Slayton; Navy Lt. Cmdrs. Walter M. Schirra, Jr., and Alan B. Shepard, Jr., and Lt. M. Scott Carpenter; and Marine Lt. Col. John H. Glenn, Jr.—are announced as the Project Mercury astronauts.

April 12, 1959. The Air Force Association's World Congress of Flight is held in Las Vegas, Nev.—the first international air show in U.S. history. Fifty-one foreign nations participate. NBC-TV telecasts an hour-long special, and *Life* magazine gives it five pages of coverage.

April 15, 1959. USAF Capt. George A. Edwards sets a speed record of 816.279 mph in a McDonnell RF-101C Voodoo on a 500-km closed course at Edwards AFB.

April 20, 1959. The prototype Lockheed UGM-27A Polaris sea-launched ballistic missile successfully flies a 500-mile trajectory in a Navy test. Three days later, the Air Force carries out the first flight test of the North American GAM-77 Hound Dog air-launched strategic missile at Eglin AFB.

May 28, 1959. Astrochimps Able and Baker are recovered alive in the Atlantic after their flight to an altitude of 300 miles in the nose cone of a PGM-19 Jupiter missile launched from Cape Canaveral Missile Test Annex, Fla.

June 3, 1959. The first class is graduated from the Air Force Academy.

June 8, 1959. The Post Office enters the missile age, as 3,000 stamped envelopes are carried aboard a Vought RGM-6 Regulus I missile launched from the submarine USS *Barbero* (SSG-317) in the Atlantic. The unarmed missile lands 21 minutes later at the Naval Auxiliary Air Station at Mayport, Fla.

June 8, 1959. After several attempts, North American Aviation pilot Scott Crossfield makes the first nonpowered flight in the X-15.

July 1, 1959. The first experimental reactor (Kiwi-A) in the nuclear space rocket program is operated successfully in a test at Jackass Flats, Nev.

August 7, 1959. First intercontinental relay of voice message by satellite takes place. The voice is that of Maj.

Robert G. Mathis, later USAF Vice Chief of Staff.

August 7, 1959. Two USAF F-100Fs make the first flight by jet fighter aircraft over North Pole.

September 9, 1959. The Atlas missile is fired for the first time by a SAC crew from Vandenberg AFB, Calif., and the missile type is declared operational by the commander in chief SAC. The shot travels about 4,300 miles at 16,000 mph.

September 12, 1959. The Soviet Union launches Luna 2, the first man-made object to reach the moon.

November 16, 1959. Air Force Capt. Joseph W. Kittinger, Jr., after ascending to an altitude of 76,400 feet in *Excelsior I*, an open-gondola balloon (setting three unofficial altitude records on the way), makes the longest free-fall parachute jump in history (64,000 feet) in 2 minutes, 58 seconds at White Sands, N. M.

December 1, 1959. A new enlisted grade E-9, chief master sergeant, is created.

December 11, 1959. Dudley C. Sharp becomes Secretary of the Air Force.

December 15, 1959. Maj. Richard W. Rogers regains the world speed record for the U.S., piloting his Convair F-106 Delta Dart to a speed of 1,525.6 mph at an altitude of 40,550 feet at Edwards AFB, Calif.

December 15, 1959. Maj. Joseph Rogers sets the recognized absolute speed record of 1,525.965 mph in a Convair F-106A at Edwards AFB, Calif.

December 30, 1959. The first U.S.

ballistic-missile-carrying submarine, USS *George Washington* (SSBN-598), is commissioned at Groton, Conn.

January 25, 1960. In what is billed as the "first known kill of a ballistic missile," an Army MIM-23 Hawk antiaircraft missile downs an unarmed MGR-1 Honest John surface-to-surface unguided rocket.

March 22, 1960. The Civil Aeronautics Board reports that slightly more than 10 percent of revenue passenger miles flown in scheduled domestic operations during 1959 were flown by pure jet aircraft.

March 29, 1960. The Naval Weapons Station Annex at Charleston, S. C., opens. It will provide a final assembly capability for UGM-27 Polaris sea-launched ballistic missiles and also a capability for loading them on submarines.

April 1, 1960. The RCA-built TIROS 1 (Television Infrared Observation Satellite), the world's first meteorological satellite, is successfully launched from Cape Canaveral Missile Test Annex atop a Thor launch vehicle.

April 4, 1960. Project Ozma is initiated at the National Radio Astronomy Observatory at Green Bank, W.Va., to listen for possible signal patterns from outer space other than "natural" noise.

April 22, 1960. A federal court of appeals upholds a Federal Aviation Administration order that automatically grounds pilots over 60 years old.

May 1, 1960. Central Intelligence Agency pilot Francis Gary Powers, flying a Lockheed U-2 reconnaissance aircraft, is shot down over the Soviet Union near Sverdlovsk. He is captured and later put on trial for espio-

nage. The incident creates an international furor, and a superpower summit scheduled for later in the month is canceled. In 1962, Mr. Powers will be exchanged for Soviet KGB agent Rudolf Abel.

May 20, 1960. The Air Force launches from Cape Canaveral Missile Test Annex a Convair HGM-16 Atlas ICBM that carries a 1.5-ton payload 9,040 miles to the Indian Ocean. This is the greatest distance ever flown by a U.S. ICBM.

May 21, 1960. The last World War II–era North American B-25 Mitchell is retired from active Air Force service at Eglin AFB.

July 20, 1960. The first underwater launch of a Lockheed UGM-27 Polaris ballistic missile is successfully carried out from USS *George Washington* (SSBN-598) off Cape Canaveral Missile Test Annex.

August 16, 1960. At an altitude of 102,800 feet over Tularosa, N. M., Air Force Capt. Joseph W. Kittinger, Jr., makes the ultimate leap of faith. In the four and a half minutes between stepping out of the balloon's open gondola and opening his parachute, he free-falls 84,700 feet, reaching a speed of 614 mph. Captain Kittinger lands unharmed 13 minutes, 45 seconds after jumping. This the highest jump and longest free fall ever recorded.

September 21, 1960. Tactical Air Command formally accepts the first Republic F-105D Thunderchief all-weather fighter in ceremonies at Nellis AFB, Nev. The aircraft will not officially enter service until the following year, when deliveries to Seymour Johnson AFB, N.C., begin.

October 1, 1960. Ballistic Missile

Early Warning System radar post at Thule, Greenland, begins regular operations, part of chain of three planned installations to warn of air or missile attacks on North America over an Arctic route.

January 12, 1961. A B-58 Hustler piloted by Maj. Henry J. Deutschendorf, Jr., sets six international speed and payload records on a single flight, thus breaking five previous records held by the Soviet Union. On January 14, another B-58 from the same wing breaks three of the records set on January 12.

January 24, 1961. Eugene M. Zuckert becomes Secretary of the Air Force.

January 31, 1961. A chimpanzee named Ham is launched atop a Redstone booster from Cape Canaveral Missile Test Annex in a test of the Mercury manned capsule.

February 1, 1961. The first Boeing LGM-30A Minuteman ICBM is launched from Cape Canaveral Missile Test Annex. It travels 4,600 miles and hits the target area. This is the first time a first-test missile is launched with all systems and stages functioning.

February 3, 1961. SAC's Boeing EC-135 Airborne Command Post begins operations. Dubbed "Looking Glass," the planes and their equipment provide a backup means of controlling manned bombers and launching land-based ICBMs in case a nuclear attack wipes out conventional command-and-control systems.

April 12, 1961. The Soviet Union stuns the world with the first successful manned spaceflight. Cosmonaut Yuri Gagarin is not only history's first

spaceman, he is also the first person to orbit the Earth.

May 5, 1961. Cmdr. Alan B. Shepard, Jr., USN, becomes the first Project Mercury astronaut to cross the space frontier. His flight in *Freedom 7* lasts 15 minutes, 28 seconds, reaches an altitude of 116.5 miles, and ends 303.8 miles downrange.

May 25, 1961. President John F. Kennedy, at a joint session of Congress, declares a national space objective: "I believe that this nation should commit itself to achieving the goal, before this decade is out, of landing a man on the moon and returning him safely to Earth."

June 30, 1961. Gen. Curtis E. LeMay becomes Air Force Chief of Staff.

July 21, 1961. Capt. Virgil I. Grissom becomes the first Air Force astronaut in space. He attains an altitude of 118.3 miles on the second Mercury mission.

August 6–7, 1961. Flying in the Vostok 2 spacecraft, Soviet Air Force Capt. Gherman Titov becomes the first person to orbit the Earth for more than a day. He also becomes the first person to get spacesick.

January 10–11, 1962. Maj. Clyde P. Evely sets a recognized class record for great circle distance without landing (jet aircraft) of 12, 532.28 miles from Kadena AB, Okinawa, to Madrid, Spain, in a Boeing B-52H Stratofortress. The record still stands.

January 12, 1962. Maj. H. J. Deutschendorf, Jr., sets two recognized class records for 2,000-km speed over a closed circuit with payload (jet aircraft) of 1,061.81 mph in a Convair B-

58A Hustler at Edwards AFB, Calif. The records still stand.

February 2, 1962. A C-123 Ranch Hand aircraft crashes while spraying defoliant on a Viet Cong ambush site. It is the first U.S. Air Force plane lost in South Vietnam.

February 20, 1962. Marine Lt. Col. John H. Glenn, Jr., becomes the first U.S. astronaut to orbit the Earth. His *Friendship* 7 flight lasts nearly five hours.

March 5, 1962. Capts. Robert G. Sowers, Robert MacDonald, and John T. Walton, flying in a Convair B-58A Hustler bomber, are the only contestant in the 21st and last Bendix Trophy transcontinental race. The crew completes the Los Angeles to New York course with an average speed of 1214.71 mph and total elapsed time is 2 hours and 56 seconds. This is still the certified speed record over a recognized course between the two cities.

April 30, 1962. Company pilot Lou Schalk makes the first official flight of the Lockheed A-12, the forerunner of the SR-71 high-speed reconnaissance aircraft, at Groom Lake, Nev. Two earlier hops had been made on April 25 and 26.

May 24, 1962. Navy Lt. Cmdr. Scott Carpenter makes the fourth flight of the Mercury space program. The flight is less than perfect, as a number of inflight problems lead to the astronaut's overshooting the recovery ship, the USS *Intrepid* (CVS-11), by more than 250 miles.

July 17, 1962. Maj. Robert White pilots the North American X-15 to an altitude of 314,750 feet, thus making the first spaceflight in a manned aircraft. After the 11-minute fight, Ma-

jor White lands at Edwards AFB, Calif.

September 12, 1962. Navy Lt. Cmdrs. Don Moore and Fred Fanke separately set two recognized class records for altitude with 1,000-and 2,000-kg payloads (piston-engine amphibians) of 29,475 feet and 27,404.93 feet respectively in a Grumman UF-2G Albatross at Floyd Bennett Field, N.Y. Both records still stand.

September 14, 1962. Maj. F. L. Fulton sets a recognized class record for altitude with 5,000-kg payload (jet aircraft) of 85,360.8 feet in a Convair B-58A Hustler at Edwards AFB, Calif. The record still stands.

October 3, 1962. Navy Cmdr. Walter M. Wally Schirra, Jr., makes what is described as a textbook orbital flight during the fifth flight in the Mercury program. He flies in a 100×176 mile orbit, the highest to date, and completes nearly six orbits. He is also the first astronaut to splash down in the Pacific Ocean.

October 14, 1962. An Air Force reconnaissance flight photographs nuclear-armed Soviet missiles in Cuba. Moscow subsequently agrees to remove the missiles under threat of U.S. invasion of Cuba.

October 25, 1962. Coast Guard Cmdr. W. Fenlon sets a recognized class record for great circle distance without landing (piston-engine amphibians) of 3,571.65 miles from Kodiak, Alaska, to Pensacola, Fla., in a Grumman UF-2G Albatross. The record still stands.

November 30, 1962. The first tethered hovering flight is made by the Lockheed XV-4A Hummingbird vertical takeoff and landing airplane at Marietta, Ga.

December 14, 1962. NASA's Mariner II satellite scans the surface of Venus for 35 minutes as it flies past the planet at a distance of 21,642 miles.

January 17, 1963. NASA pilot Joe Walker qualifies for astronaut wings by flying the North American X-15 to an altitude of 271,700 feet or 51.46 miles. He is the 11th man to pass the 50-mile mark.

February 28, 1963. The first Minuteman squadron, the 10th Strategic Missile Squadron (SMS) at Malmstrom AFB, Mont., is declared operational.

March 20, 1963. Capt. Henry E. Erwin, Jr., sets two recognized class records for altitude with 5,000-kg payload (19,747 feet) and greatest payload carried to an altitude of 2,000 meters (12,162.90 pounds) in a Grumman HU-16B Albatross at Eglin AFB, Fla. Both records still stand.

April 11, 1963. The first successful launch of a Boeing LGM-30 Minuteman I ICBM is conducted at Vandenberg AFB, Calif.

May 15, 1963. Maj. L. Gordon Cooper becomes the second Air Force astronaut in space as he makes nearly twenty-two orbits in his spacecraft, *Faith 7*. He is the last American to be launched into space alone, he is the first to spend a complete day in orbit, and because of a failure of the automatic system, he is the first to perform an entirely manual reentry. This is the last Project Mercury space mission.

June 16–19, 1963. Cosmonaut Jr. Lt. Valentina Tereshkova, a former cotton mill worker, becomes the first woman in space. Her Vostok 6 flight lasts nearly three days.

August 22, 1963. NASA pilot Joe Walker achieves an unofficial world altitude record of 354,200 feet in the X-15.

October 17, 1963. The first LGM-30A Minuteman I operational test launch is carried out at Vandenberg AFB, Calif., by a crew from Malmstrom AFB. The shot is a partial success. The reentry vehicle overshoots the target.

October 30, 1963. Navy Lt. James H. Flatley lands a Lockheed KC-130F Hercules on the aircraft carrier USS *Forrestal* (CVA-59) in the Atlantic off Boston, Mass., in a test to see if the Hercules could be used as a Super COD (carrier on-board delivery) aircraft. Lieutenant Flatley and crew will eventually make 21 unarrested full-stop landings and a like number of unassisted takeoffs from the carrier.

November 7, 1963. The Northrop-developed three-parachute landing system for the Apollo command module is successfully tested at White Sands, N. M.

December 17, 1963. With company pilots Leo Sullivan and Hank Dees at the controls, the Lockheed C-141A StarLifter, USAF's first jet-powered transport, makes its first flight at Marietta, Ga., on the sixtieth anniversary of the Wright brothers' first flight.

December 17, 1963. The Thunderbirds, the Air Force's aerial demonstration squadron, fly their 690th and last show in the North American F-100C Super Sabre.

1964–1973

January 8, 1964. The newest Air Force decoration, the Air Force Cross, is posthumously awarded to reconnaissance pilot Maj. Rudolf Anderson, Jr., the only combat casualty of the 1962 Cuban missile crisis.

February 1, 1964. The Boeing 727 passenger liner enters revenue service with Eastern Air Lines.

February 3, 1964. Four airmen locked in a spaceship simulator exhibit no ill effects after exposure to a pure oxygen atmosphere 30 days.

February 29, 1964. President Lyndon B. Johnson announces the existence of the Lockheed A-11 (YF-12A), with a cruising speed of more than Mach 3 at altitudes above 70,000 feet. The plane was ordered as a single-seat reconnaissance aircraft for the CIA in 1960. Only three YF-12A interceptors are built, and the SR-71 program for the Air Force takes precedence.

April 26, 1964. At Norfolk, Va., the Thunderbirds, the Air Force's aerial demonstration team, fly their first show in the Republic F-105B Thunderchief. The team will perform only six shows in the Thud, as it will soon be determined that it is not a suitable show aircraft.

May 11, 1964. The North American XB-70 Valkyrie is rolled out at Palmdale, Calif. Designed to fly at three times the speed of sound and at altitudes above 70,000 feet, the XB-70 is originally planned as a manned bomber, but funding limitations allow for only two aircraft, to be used strictly for testing and research.

August 1964. USAF moves into Southeast Asia in force. B-57s from Clark AB in the Philippines deploy to Bien Hoa in South Vietnam and additional F-100s move to Da Nang on August 5. Eighteen F-105s deploy from Japan to Korat Royal Thai Air Base beginning August 6.

August 2, 1964. The destroyer USS *Maddox* (DD-731) is attacked by North Vietnamese patrol boats in the Gulf of Tonkin. A second incident, involving the *Turner Joy* (DD-951), reportedly occurs two days later. Congress passes the Gulf of Tonkin Resolution on August 7.

August 19, 1964. The Hughes Syncom III satellite is launched by a Thor-Delta launch vehicle. After several weeks of maneuvers, it becomes the world's first geosynchronous satellite.

September 21, 1964. The North American XB-70A Valkyrie makes its first flight, with company pilot Alvin White and USAF pilot Col. Joseph Cotton at the controls.

September 28, 1964. USS *Daniel Webster* (SSBN-626), the first submarine equipped with the Lockheed UGM-27C (A3) Polaris sea-launched ballistic missile, departs Charleston, S. C., on its first patrol.

November 17–26, 1964. C-130s flown by U.S. Air Force in Europe crews deliver Belgian paratroopers to the Congo for a rescue operation credited with saving the lives of nearly 2,000 hostages at Stanleyville threatened by rebels.

December 14, 1964. U.S. Air Force flies the first "Barrel Roll" armed reconnaissance mission in Laos.

December 21, 1964. Company pilots Richard Johnson and Val Prahl make the first flight of the variable-geometry General Dynamics F-111A from Air Force Plant 4 in Fort Worth, Tex. The flight lasts 22 minutes.

December 22, 1964. Lockheed gets approval to start development for the Air Force of the CX-HLS transport, which will become the C-5A. Also on this date, company pilot Bob Gilliland makes the first flight of the Lockheed SR-71A Blackbird strategic reconnaissance aircraft from Palmdale, Calif. He takes the aircraft to an altitude exceeding 45,000 feet and a speed of more than 1,000 mph on the flight.

February 1, 1965. The first Boeing LGM-30F Minuteman II ICBM unit, the 447th Strategic Missile Squadron at Grand Forks AFB, N.D., is activated.

February 1, 1965. Gen. John P. McConnell becomes Air Force Chief of Staff.

February 8, 1965. The Air Force performs its first retaliatory air strike in North Vietnam. A North American F-100 Super Sabre flies cover for attacking South Vietnamese fighter aircraft, suppressing ground fire in the target area.

February 18, 1965. First Air Force jet raids are flown against an enemy concentration in South Vietnam. American Pilots fly Martin B-57 Canberra bombers and North American F-100 fighters against the Viet Cong in South Vietnam, near An Khe.

March 1, 1965. An unarmed Boeing LGM-30B Minuteman I ICBM is successfully launched from an underground silo 10 miles north of Newell, S. D. It is the first time a site other than Vandenberg AFB or Cape Kennedy AFS, Fla., is used for an ICBM launch.

March 2, 1965. Capt. Hayden J. Lockhart, flying an F-100 in a raid against an ammunition dump north of the Vietnamese demilitarized zone, is shot down and becomes the first Air Force pilot to be taken prisoner by the North Vietnamese. He will not be released until February 12, 1973.

March 23, 1965. Air Force Maj. Virgil I. Grissom becomes the first astronaut in the manned spaceflight program to go aloft a second time, as he and Navy Lt. Cmdr. John W. Young are launched on the first Gemini mission, Gemini 3. This three-orbit, 4-hour-and-53-minute shakedown flight is also the first time a spacecraft's orbit is changed in space.

May 1, 1965. Using two Lockheed YF-12As, three Air Force crews set six class and absolute records at Edwards AFB, Calif. Col. Robert Stevens and RSO Lt. Col. Daniel Andre set the recognized absolute speed record with a mark of 2,070.115 mph over the 10.1-mile straight course.

June 3–7, 1965. Air Force Maj. Edward H. White makes the first U.S. spacewalk. The Gemini 4 mission is the first U.S. spaceflight to be controlled from the Manned Spaceflight Center in Houston, Tex., and the crew, which also includes Air Force Maj. James A. McDivitt, stays aloft for a record 62 orbits.

June 18, 1965. SAC B-52s are used for the first time in Vietnam, when 28 aircraft strike Viet Cong targets near Saigon.

July 10, 1965. Capt. Thomas S. Roberts with his backseater Capt. Ronald C. Anderson and Capt. Kenneth E. Holcombe and his backseater Capt. Arthur C. Clark, both flying McDonnell Douglas F-4C Phantom IIs, shoot down two MiG-17s, the first Air Force air-to-air victories of the Vietnam War.

August 11, 1965. Flying in North American F-100D Super Sabres, the Thunderbirds, the Air Force's aerial demonstration squadron, fly their 1,000th show at Waukeegan, Ill.

August 21–29, 1965. The Gemini 5 crew of Air Force Lt. Col. L. Gordon Cooper and Navy Lt. Cmdr. Charles Conrad carry out the U.S.'s first long-duration spaceflight, ending one orbit short of eight full days.

October 1, 1965. Dr. Harold Brown is sworn in as Secretary of the Air Force.

October 18, 1965. New York's Air National Guard 107th Tactical Fighter Group becomes the first tactical guard unit to be deployed in peacetime to the Pacific for a joint-service exercise.

December 15, 1965. In a first for the U.S. space program, the crews of Gemini 6 and Gemini 7 rendezvous in space. Unlike the Soviets who had not managed earlier to get two spacecraft in close proximity to one another in orbit, the Gemini 6 crew of Navy Capt. Walter Schirra and USAF Maj. Tom Stafford maneuver to within 4 inches of Gemini 7.

January 1, 1966. Military airlift units of the Air National Guard (ANG) begin flying about 75 cargo flights a month to Southeast Asia. These flights are in addition to the more than 100 overseas missions a month flown by the ANG in augmenting the Military Airlift Command's global airlift mission.

January 17, 1966. A B-52 loaded with four hydrogen bombs collides with a KC-135 while refueling near Palomares, Spain. Seven of the 11 crew members involved are killed. Three of the four weapons are quickly recovered. The fourth, which falls into the Mediterranean Sea, is not recovered until early spring.

January 23, 1966. The newly renamed (as of January 1) Military Airlift Command completes Operation Blue Light, the airlift of the Army's 3d Brigade, 25th Infantry Division, from Hawaii to Pleiku, South Vietnam, to offset the buildup of Communist forces there. The airlift begins on December 23, 1965, and its 231 C-141 sorties move approximately 3,000 troops and 4,700 tons of equipment.

February 28, 1966. The U.S. space program suffers its first fatalities: the Gemini 9 prime crew of Elliot See and Charles Basset are killed as their Northrop T-38 crashes in St. Louis in bad weather. They were on a trip to inspect their spacecraft at the McDonnell Douglas plant at Lambert Field.

March 4, 1966. A flight of Air Force F-4C Phantoms is attacked by three MiG-17s in the first air-to-air combat of the war over North Vietnam. The MiGs make unsuccesful passes before fleeing to the sanctuary of the Communist capital area.

March 10, 1966. Maj. Bernard F. Fisher, a 1st Air Commando Squadron A-1E pilot, lands on the A Shau airstrip, after it has been overrun by North Vietnamese regulars, to rescue downed A-1E pilot Maj. D. Wayne "Jump" Myers. Major Fisher is later awarded the Medal of Honor for his heroic act.

March 16, 1966. The Gemini 8 crew, Neil Armstrong and USAF Maj.

David R. Scott, successfully carry out the first docking with another vehicle in space.

April 1, 1966. Seventh Air Force, with headquarters at Saigon, is activated as a subcommand of Pacific Air Forces.

April 12, 1966. Strategic Air Command B-52 bombers strike targets in North Vietnam for the first time. They hit a supply route in the Mu Gia Pass, about 85 miles north of the border.

April 26, 1966. Maj. Paul J. Gilmore and 1st Lt. William T. Smith became the first Air Force pilots to destroy a MiG-21. Flying escort for F-105 Thunderchiefs near Hanoi when the flight is attacked, the F-4C pilots down the MiG with an AIM-9 Sidewinder missile.

June 17, 1966. Army Lt. Col. E. L. Nielsen sets a recognized class record for 100-km speed over a closed course (turboprop aircraft) of 293.41 mph in a Grumman OV-1A Mohawk at Peconic River, L.I., N.Y. The record still stands.

October 7, 1966. The Air Force selects the University of Colorado to conduct independent investigations into unidentified flying object (UFO) reports.

November 11, 1966. The Gemini program comes to an end as Navy Cmdr. James Lovell and Air Force Maj. Edwin Buzz Aldrin complete a successful mission on Gemini 12. Astronaut Aldrin makes three spacewalks on the 59-orbit mission.

January 2, 1967. USAF fighter pilots, in the famous MiG Sweep mission, down seven North Vietnamese MiG-21s over the Red River Valley in North Vietnam.

January 2, 1967. By shooting down a MiG-21, Col. Robin Olds becomes the first and only USAF ace with victories in World War II and Vietnam. Flying with Colonel Olds in the backseat of the McDonnell Douglas F-4C was 1st Lt. Charles Clifton.

January 27, 1967. Astronauts USAF Lt. Col. Virgil I. Grissom, Navy Lt. Cmdr. Roger B. Chaffee, and USAF Lt. Col. Edward H. White are killed in a flash fire aboard their Apollo 1 command module during a ground test. The disaster sets the moon-landing effort back two years.

February 24, 1967. USAF Capt. Hilliard A. Wilbanks, a forward air controller, resorts to firing an M16 rifle out the side window of his Cessna O-1 Bird Dog in order to try to cover the retreat of a South Vietnamese Ranger battalion caught in an ambush near Dalat. Severely wounded by ground fire, Captain Hilliard crashes in the battle area, but is rescued by the Rangers. He dies while being evacuated to a hospital. Captain Hilliard is later posthumously awarded the Medal of Honor for his actions.

March 10, 1967. Air Force F-105 Thunderchief and F-4C Phantom II crews bomb the Thai Nguyen steel plant in North Vietnam for the first time. Capt. Merlyn H. Dethlefsen, an F-105 pilot, is later awarded the Medal of Honor for his actions this day in supressing enemy air defenses.

March 10, 1967. Capt. Mac C. Brestel, an F-105 pilot with the 355th Tactical Fighter Squadron, Takhli RTAFB, Thailand, becomes the first Air Force combat crewman to down two MiGs during a single mission.

April 3, 1967. CMSgt Paul W. Airey becomes the first Chief Master Sergeant of the Air Force.

April 19, 1967. Over North Vietnam, Maj. Leo K. Thorsness (along with his electronic warfare officer, Capt. Harold E. Johnson) destroys two enemy SAM sites, then shoots down a MiG-17 before escorting search and rescue helicopters to a downed aircrew. Although the Republic F-105 was very low on fuel, Major Thorsness attacks four MiG-17s in an effort to draw the enemy aircraft away from area. He then lands at a forward air base. Awarded the Medal of Honor for his actions this day, Major Thorsness will not receive his medal until 1973, as on April 30, 1967, he is shot down and spends the next six years as a POW.

May 13, 1967. For the second time, pilots of the 8th Tactical Fighter Wing, Ubon RTAFB, Thailand, shoot down seven MiGs in a single day's action over North Vietnam.

May 20, 1967. Col. Robin Olds (pilot) and backseater 1st Lt. Steven Croaker down two MiG-17s over the Bak Le railyards, giving Olds four aerial victories in Vietnam. He also recorded 12 victories in World War II, making him the only ace to down enemy aircraft in two nonconsecutive wars.

June 1, 1967. Using air refueling, two Sikorsky HH-3E crews complete the first nonstop transatlantic helicopter flight.

August 26, 1967. Badly injured after his North American F-100F is shot down over North Vietnam, Maj. George E. Day is captured and severely tortured. He manages to escape and eventually makes it to the

Demilitarized Zone. After several attempts to signal U.S. aircraft, he is ambushed and recaptured, and is later moved to prison in Hanoi, where he continues to offer maximum resistance to his captors Finally released in 1973, Major Day is awarded the Medal of Honor for his conspicuous gallantry while a POW.

September 9, 1967. Sgt. Duane D. Hackney is presented with the Air Force Cross for bravery in rescuing an Air Force pilot in Vietnam. He is the first living enlisted man to receive the award.

October 3, 1967. Maj. William Knight flies the North American X-15A-2 to the unofficial absolute world speed record of Mach 6.72 (4,534 mph) over Edwards AFB.

October 24, 1967. U.S. planes attack North Vietnam's largest airbase, Phuc Yen, for the first time in a combined Air Force, Navy, and Marine strike. During the attack, the Air Force downs its 69th MiG.

November 8, 1967. While attempting to rescue an Army Reconnaissance team, Capt. Gerald O. Young's Sikorsky HH-3E is shot down in Laos. Badly burned, he gives aid to a crew member who also escaped from the wreckage. After 17 hours of leading enemy forces away from his injured crewman and himself evading capture, the two are rescued. Captain Young is later awarded the Medal of Honor for his actions.

November 9, 1967. While on a flight over Laos, Capt. Lance P. Sijan ejects from his disabled McDonnell Douglas F-4C and successfully evades capture for more than six weeks. He is caught, but manages to escape. Recaptured and tortured, he later contracts pneumonia and dies. For his conspicuous gallantry as a POW, Captain Sijan is posthumously awarded the Medal of Honor.

December 11, 1967. The Aerospatiale-built Concorde supersonic jetliner prototype rolls out at the company's plant in Toulouse, France.

January 12, 1968. The Air Force announces a system for tactical units to carry with them everything they need to operate at "bare" bases equipped only with runways, taxiways, parking areas, and a water supply.

February 29, 1968. Jeanne M. Holm, WAF Director, and Helen O'Day, assigned to Office of the Air Force Chief of Staff, become the first women promoted to colonel.

March 2, 1968. The first of 80 C-5A Galaxy transports rolls out at Lockheed's Marietta, Ga., facility.

March 25, 1968. F-111s fly their first combat mission against military targets in North Vietnam.

March 31, 1968. President Lyndon Johnson announces a partial halt of bombing missions over North Vietnam and proposes peace talks.

May 12, 1968. Lt. Col. Joe M. Jackson, flying an unarmed Fairchild C-123 transport, lands at a forward outpost at Kham Duc, South Vietnam, in a rescue attempt of a combat control team. After a rocket-propelled grenade fired directly at his aircraft proves to be a dud, Colonel Jackson takes off with the CCT on board and lands at Da Nang. He is later awarded the Medal of Honor for his actions.

May 18, 1968. In response to a massive flood, the Air Force airlifts 88.5 tons of food and other supplies to Ethiopia.

June 30, 1968. The world's largest aircraft, the Lockheed C-5A Galaxy, makes its first flight, as company pilots Leo Sullivan and Walt Hensleigh use only 4,500 feet of Dobbins AFB's 10,000-foot runway to get airborne

July 1, 1968. The first WAF in the Air National Guard is sworn in as a result of passage of Public Law 90-130, which allows ANG to enlist women.

August 16, 1968. The first test launch of a Boeing LGM-30G Minuteman III ICBM is carried out from Cape Kennedy AFS.

August 21, 1968. NASA pilot William H. Dana becomes the last pilot to fly into space in the North American X-15 research aircraft. One of seven pilots to earn their astronaut wings in the X-15, Mr. Dana atttains an altitude of 264,000 feet and a speed of Mach 4.71 in the flight over Edwards AFB, Calif.

September 1, 1968. Lt. Col. William A. Jones III leads a rescue mission near Dong Hoi, North Vietnam. Finding the downed pilot, Colonel Jones attacks a nearby gun emplacement. On his second pass, Colonel Jones's aircraft is hit and the cockpit of his Douglas A-1H is set ablaze. He tries to eject, but the extraction system fails. He then returns to base and reports the exact position of the downed pilot (who is rescued the next day) before receiving medical treatment for his burns. Colonel Jones will die in an aircraft accident in the U.S. before he can be presented the Medal of IIonor for his actions the day of the rescue.

October 11–22, 1968. Apollo 7, the

first test mission following the disastrous Apollo 1 fire, is successfully carried out. Navy Capt. Walter M. Schirra, Jr., USAF Maj. Donn F. Eisele, and R. Walter Cunningham stay in Earth orbit for 10 days, 20 hours, 9 minutes.

October 24, 1968. With NASA test pilot William H. Dana at the controls, the North American X-15 makes the type's 199th and final flight, completing 10 years of flight testing. The plane reaches a speed of Mach 5.04 and an altitude of 250,000 feet.

November 26, 1968. While returing to base, 1st Lt. James P. Fleming and four other Bell UH-1F helicopter pilots get an urgent message from an Army Special Forces team pinned down near a riverbank. One helicopter is downed and two others leave the area because of low fuel, but Lieutenant Fleming and another pilot flying in an armed Huey press on with the rescue effort. The first try fails, but not willing to give up, Lieutenant Fleming lands again and is successful in picking the team up. He then lands at his base near Duc Co, South Vietnam, nearly out of fuel. Lieutenant Fleming is later awarded the Medal of Honor for his actions.

November 30, 1968. The Air Force's aerial demonstration squadron, the Thunderbirds, fly their 471st and last show in the North American F-100D Super Sabre. Except for six shows in 1964 when they flew F-105s, the team had been performing in Huns for 13 years.

December 21–27, 1968. Apollo 8 becomes the first manned mission to use the Saturn V booster. Astronauts USAF Col. Frank Borman, Navy Cmdr. James A. Lovell, and USAF

Maj. William Anders become the first humans to orbit the moon.

December 31, 1968. The Soviet Union conducts the first flight of the Tu-144, the world's first supersonic transport.

February 9, 1969. Boeing conducts the first flight of the 747. The jumbo jet, with standard seating for 347 passengers, introduces high passenger volume to the world's airways.

February 15, 1969. Robert C. Seamans, Jr., becomes Secretary of the Air Force.

February 24, 1969. After a North Vietnamese mortar shell rocks their Douglas AC-47 gunship, A1C John L. Levitow, stunned and wounded by shrapnel, flings himself on an activated, smoking magnesium flare, drags himself and the flare to the open cargo door, and tosses it out of the aircraft just before the flare ignites. For saving his fellow crew members and the gunship, Airman Levitow is later awarded the Medal of Honor. He is the only enlisted man to win the CMH in Vietnam and is one of only four enlisted airmen ever to win the award.

February 27, 1969. The aerobics physical fitness program developed by Lt. Col. Kenneth H. Cooper, of Air Force Systems Command's Aerospace Medical Laboratory, is adopted by the Air Force to replace the 5BX program.

March 3–13, 1969. Air Force astronauts Col. James A. McDivitt and Col. David R. Scott, along with civilian Russell L. Schweickart, carry out the first in-space test of the lunar module while in Earth orbit during the Apollo 9 mission. The flight also marks the first time a crew transfer is made between space vehicles using an internal connection.

May 18–26, 1969. In a dress rehearsal for the moon landing, Apollo 10 astronauts Col. Thomas P. Stafford, USAF, and Cmdr. Eugene A. Cernan, USN, fly the lunar module *Snoopy* to within nine miles of the lunar surface. Astronaut Cmdr. John W. Young, USN, remains in orbit aboard *Charlie Brown*, the command module.

June 1, 1969. The Thunderbirds, the Air Force's aerial demonstration squadron, demonstrate McDonnell Douglas F-4E Phantom II for the graduating seniors at the Air Force Academy. The F-4 is the team's sixth show aircraft.

June 4, 1969. The Air Force Air Demonstration Squadron, the Thunderbirds, fly their first show in their new McDonnell Douglas F-4E Phantom IIs.

July 1, 1969. Air Force service numbers are replaced by Social Security account numbers for military personnel.

July 20, 1969. Man sets foot on the moon for the first time. At 10:56 P.M. EDT, Apollo 11 astronaut Neil Armstrong puts his left foot on the lunar surface. He and lunar module pilot Col. Edwin "Buzz" Aldrin, Jr., USAF, spend just under three hours walking on the moon. Command module pilot Lt. Col. Michael Collins, USAF, remains in orbit.

August 1, 1969. Gen. John D. Ryan is appointed Air Force Chief of Staff.

August 1, 1969. CMSgt. Donald L. Harlow becomes Chief Master Sergeant of the Air Force.

October 1969. *Air Force* magazine

cover story "The Forgotten Americans of the Vietnam War" ignites national concern for the prisoners of war and the missing in action. It is reprinted in condensed form as the lead article in the November 1969 issue of *Reader's Digest*, is read in its entirety on the floor of Congress, and is inserted into the *Congressional Record* on six different occasions. This article stirs the conscience of the nation and rallies millions to the cause of the POWs and MIAs. *Air Force* magazine publishes an MIA/POW Action Report from June 1970 until September 1974.

November 3, 1969. The Air Force issues a request for proposal for a new bomber to meet its advanced manned strategic aircraft requirement. Its designation will be B-1.

November 14–24, 1969. Apollo 12 is hit by lightning on liftoff, but Cmdrs. Charles Conrad and Alan Bean make the second manned lunar landing with pinpoint accuracy. The lunar module *Intrepid* touches down 1,000 yards from the Surveyor 3 probe, on the moon since 1967. The all-Navy crew, which also includes Cmdr. Richard F. Gordon, is recovered in the Pacific Ocean by USS *Hornet* (CVS-12).

December 17, 1969. Air Force Secretary Robert Seamans announces the termination of Project Blue Book, the service's program to investigate reports of unidentified flying objects (UFOs).

March 15, 1970. The overseas portion of the Automatic Voice Network (AUTOVON) is completed, making it possible to call any U.S. military installation in the world without leaving one's desk.

March 19, 1970. Air Force Maj. Jerauld Gentry makes the first successful powered flight of the Martin Marietta X-24A lifting-body research aircraft over Edwards AFB.

April 11–17, 1970. Thirteen proves an unlucky number for the Apollo program. An explosion in the service module cripples the spaceship and forces the crew to use the lunar module as a lifeboat to get back to Earth. After a tense four days, the Apollo 13 crew safely splashes down in the Pacific.

May 5, 1970. The Air Force Reserve Officers Training Corps admits women after test programs at Ohio State, Auburn University, Drake University and East Carolina University prove successful.

May 15, 1970. Sgt. John L. Levitow is awarded the Medal of Honor for heroic action on February 24, 1969, over Long Binh Army Post, South Vietnam. He is the first Air Force enlisted recipient of the award since World War II.

June 6, 1970. The first operational Lockheed C-5A Galaxy transport is delivered to the 437th Military Airlift Wing at Charleston, S. C. The debut, made before Rep. L. Mendel Rivers (D–S.C.) and most of the House Armed Services Committee, is less than auspicious: the giant aircraft loses a wheel, and several other tires are punctured on landing.

August 21, 1970. Defense Secretary Melvin Laird announces the "Total Force" policy, leading to much greater reliance by the services on Guard and Reserve units.

August 24, 1970. Two Air Force crews complete the first nonstop transpacific helicopter flight as they land their Sikorsky HH-53Cs at Da Nang AB, South Vietnam, after a 9,000-mile flight from Eglin AFB. The helicopters were refueled in flight during the trip.

November 21, 1970. A special task force of Air Force and Army volunteers makes a daring attempt to rescue American servicemen from the Son Tay prisoner of war camp 20 miles west of Hanoi.

January 27, 1971. Navy Cmdr. D. H. Lilienthal sets a recognized class record for speed over a 15/25-km course (turboprop aircraft) of 501.44 mph in a Lockheed P-3C Orion at NAS Patuxent River, Md. The record still stands.

March 2, 1971. A policy is announced which allows Air Force women who become pregnant to request a waiver to remain on active duty or to be discharged and return to duty within 12 months of discharge.

March 8, 1971. Capt. Marcelite C. Jordan becomes the first woman aircraft maintenance officer after completion of the Aircraft Maintenance Officer's School. She was previously an administrative officer.

July 16, 1971. Jeanne M. Holm becomes the first female general officer in the Air Force.

July 26, 1971. Apollo 15 blasts off with an all–Air Force crew: Col. David R. Scott, Lt. Col. James B. Irwin, and Maj. Alfred M. Worden. The mission is described as the most scientifically important and, potentially, the most perilous lunar trip since the first landing. Millions of viewers throughout the world watch as color TV cameras cover Scott and Irwin as they explore the lunar service using a moon rover vehicle for the first time.

September 3, 1971. President Richard Nixon dedicates the new Air Force Museum building at Wright-Patterson AFB, Dayton, Ohio. A drive to raise private funds for the new museum building had begun in 1960.

October 1, 1971. CMSgt. Richard D. Kisling becomes the third Chief Master Sergant of the Air Force.

October 26–November 4, 1971. Army CWO James K. Church sets one recognized turbine engine helicopter class record for altitude in horizontal flight (36,122 feet), Capt. B. P. Blackwell sets a record for altitude with 1,000-kg payload (31.165 feet), CWO Eugene E. Price sets two records for altitude with 2,000-kg and 5,000-kg payload (31,480 feet and 25,518 feet), and CWO Delbert V. Hunt sets a record for time-to-climb to 9,000 meters (5: 58 minutes), all in the same Sikorsky CH-54B Tarhe at Stratford, Conn. These records still stand.

February 20, 1972. Lt. Col. Edgar Allison sets a recognized class record for great circle distance without landing (turboprop aircraft) of 8,732.09 miles, flying from Ching Chuan Kang AB, Taiwan, to Scott AFB, Ill., in a Lockheed HC-130. The record still stands.

April 1, 1972. The Community College of the Air Force is established.

April 12, 1972. Army Maj. John C. Henderson sets recognized turbine engine helicopter class time-to-climb records to 3,000 meters and 6,000 meters (1: 22 minutes and 2: 59 minutes) in a Sikorsky CH-54B Tarhe at Stratford, Conn. The records still stand.

April 27, 1972. Four Air Force fighter crews, releasing Paveway I "smart bombs," knock down the Thanh Hoa Bridge in North Vietnam. Previously, 871 conventional sorties resulted in only superficial damage to the bridge.

May 10, 1972. Capt. Charles B. DeBellevue (WSO), flying with Capt. Richard S. Ritchie (pilot), in a McDonnell Douglas F-4D, records his first aerial kill. Captain DeBellevue, who would go on to be the leading American ace of the Vietnam War, recorded four of his victories with Captain Ritchie. Both airmen flew with the 555th Tactical Fighter Squadron.

May 10–11, 1972. F-4 Phantoms from the 8th Tactical Fighter Wing drop "smart bombs" on the Paul Doumer Bridge, causing enough damage to keep this mile-long highway and rail crossing at Hanoi out of use. It will not be rebuilt until air attacks on North Vietnam cease in 1973.

June 29, 1972. Capt. Steven L. Bennett attempts to assist a friendly ground unit being overrun near Quang Tri, South Vietnam. Captain Bennett strafes the North Vietnamese regulars with his Rockwell OV-10 Bronco, but is hit by a SAM. Unable to eject because the parachute of his backseater, a Marine artillery spotter, has been shredded by shrapnel, Captain Bennett ditches the aircraft in the Gulf of Tonkin. The observer escapes, but Captain Bennett is trapped and sinks with the wreckage. Captain Bennett is posthumously awarded the Medal of Honor.

July 27, 1972. One month ahead of schedule, company pilot Irv Burrows makes the first flight of the McDonnell Douglas F-15A Eagle air superiority fighter at Edwards AFB, Calif. The F-15 is the first USAF fighter to have a thrust-to-weight ratio greater than 1: 1, which means it can accelerate going straight up.

August 28, 1972. Capt. Richard S. Ritchie, with his backseater, Capt. Charles B. DeBellevue, shoots down his fifth MiG-21 near Hanoi, becoming the Air Force's first ace since the Korean War. Two weeks later, Capt. DeBellevue also shoots down his fifth MiG.

September 9, 1972. Capt. Charles B. DeBellevue (WSO), flying with Capt. John A. Madden, Jr. (pilot) in a McDonnell Douglas F-4D, shoots down two MiG-19s near Hanoi. These were the fifth and sixth victories for Captain DeBellevue, which made him the leading American ace of the war. All of his victories came in a four-month period. Captain Madden would record a third kill two months later.

November 4, 1972. Navy Cmdr. Philip R. Hite sets a recognized class record for distance in a closed circuit (turboprop aircraft) of 6,278.05 miles at NAS Patuxent River, Md., in a Lockheed RP-3D Orion. The record still stands.

December 7–19, 1972. The Apollo 17 mission is the last of the moon landings. It is also the first U.S. manned launch to be conducted at night. Mission commander Navy Cmdr. Eugene A. Cernan and lunar module pilot/geologist Harrison Schmitt spend a record 75 hours on the lunar surface.

December 18, 1972. The U.S. begins Operation Linebacker II, the 11-day bombing of Hanoi and Haiphong. Massive air strikes help persuade

North Vietnam to conclude Paris peace negotiations, which will be finalized January 27, 1973.

December 18, 1972. In a throwback to past aerial combat, SSgt. Samuel O. Turner, the tail gunner on a Boeing B-52D bomber, downs a trailing MiG-21 with a blast of .50 cal. machine guns near Hanoi. Six days later, A1C Albert E. Moore, also a B-52 gunner, shoots down a second MiG-21 after a strike on the Thai Nguyen railyard. These were the only aerial gunner kills of the war.

January 8, 1973. Capt. Paul D. Howman (pilot) and 1st Lt. Lawrence W. Kullman (WSO), flying in a McDonnell Douglas F-4D, record the last USAF victory in the Vietnam War as they shoot down a MiG-21 near Hanoi. It was the duo's only aerial victory.

January 27, 1973. Cease-fire agreements ending the war in Vietnam are signed in Paris.

February 12, 1973. Operation Homecoming, the return of 591 American POWs from North Vietnam, begins.

April 10, 1973. First flight of the Boeing T-43A navigation trainer occurs. The T-43 is developed from the 737-200 civil transport.

May 25–June 22, 1973. An all-Navy crew of Capt. Pete Conrad and Cmdrs. Joseph Kerwin and Paul Weitz salvage the Skylab program, as they repair the space station (which had been damaged on launch) in orbit. Their 28-day, 404-orbit mission is the longest in history to this point.

July 1, 1973. Authorization for the military draft ends.

July 18, 1973. John L. McLucas becomes Secretary of the Air Force.

July 28–September 25, 1973. The Skylab 3 crew of Navy Capt. Alan Bean, Marine Maj. Jack Lousma, and scientist Dr. Owen Garriott perform valuable science experiments and Earth observations during their 59-day, 892-orbit stay on the space station.

August 1, 1973. Gen. George S. Brown becomes Air Force Chief of Staff.

October 1, 1973. CMSgt. Thomas N. Barnes becomes Chief Master Sergeant of the Air Force.

November 10, 1973. The Thunderbirds, the Air Force's aerial demonstration squadron, fly their 518th and last show in the McDonnell Douglas F-4E Phantom II at New Orleans, La.. The team will convert to the Northrop T-38A Talon for the 1974 show season.

November 14, 1973. The U.S. ends its major airlift to Israel. In a 32-day operation during the Yom Kippur War, Military Airlift Command (MAC) airlifts 22,318 tons of supplies.

November 14, 1973. The first production McDonnell Douglas F-15A Eagle is delivered to the Air Force at Luke AFB, Ariz.

November 16, 1973–February 8, 1974. A crew of space rookies, Marine Lt. Col. Gerald Carr, Air Force Lt. Col. William Pogue, a former Thunderbird pilot, and Dr. Edward Gibson form the third and final Skylab crew. At 84 days, this crew, which observes the Comet Kohoutek during the mission, will hold the American space mission duration record until 1995.

1974–1983

January 21, 1974. The General Dynamics YF-16 prototype makes a first, unplanned, flight at Edwards AFB, Calif. Company test pilot Phil Oestricher was conducting high-speed taxi tests and the aircraft lifted off the runway, and rather than risk damage to the aircraft, the pilot elected to lift off and go around to come in for a normal landing. The first official flight is made on February 2, also by Mr. Oestricher.

June 9, 1974. Company pilot Henry E. Hank Chouteau makes the first flight of the Northrop YF-17 at Edwards AFB, Calif. Although the YF-17 would not be selected as the winner of the Air Force's Lightweight Fighter Technology evaluation program, the YF-17 would become the progenitor of the Navy's F/A-18 Hornet.

July 1, 1974. Gen. David C. Jones becomes Air Force Chief of Staff.

September 1, 1974. Maj. James V. Sullivan and Maj. Noel Widdifield set a New York–London speed record of 1,806.964 mph in a Lockheed SR-71A. The trip takes 1 hour, 54 minutes, 55 seconds.

October 24, 1974. The Air Force's Space and Missile Systems Organization carries out a midair launch of a Boeing LGM-30A Minuteman I from the hold of a Lockheed C-5A.

December 23, 1974. Company pilot Charles Bock, Jr., USAF Col. Emil Sturmthal, and flight test engineer Richard Abrams make the first flight of the Rockwell B-1A variable-geometry bomber from Palmdale, Calif.

January 13, 1975. The General Dynamics YF-16 is announced as the winner of the Air Force's Lightweight Fighter Technology evaluation program. The F-16 is also the leading candidate to become the Air Force's new air combat fighter. The YF-17 becomes the predecessor of the Navy's F/A-18 Hornet.

January 16–February 1, 1975. Three USAF pilots set eight recognized class records for time-to-climb (jet aircraft) in the McDonnell Douglas F-15A *Streak Eagle* at Grand Forks AFB, N.D. One of the records, time-to-climb to 20,000 meters (2: 02.94 minutes) set by Maj. Roger J. Smith, still stands.

January 26, 1975. The Force Modernization program, a nine-year effort to replace all Boeing LGM-30B Minuteman Is with either Minuteman IIs (LGM-30F) or Minuteman IIIs (LGM-30G), is completed, as the last 10 LGM-30Gs are turned over to SAC at F. E. Warren AFB, Wyo.

February 1, 1975. Maj. Roger Smith sets a world time-to-climb record to 30,000 meters (98,425 feet) in 3 minutes, 27.8 seconds in the McDonnell Douglas F-15A Streak Eagle.

May 15, 1975. Carrying 175 Marines, Air Force special operations helicopters land on Kho Tang Island, off the Cambodian coast, to begin rescue of the crew of the U.S. merchant ship *Mayaguez*, which had been seized in international waters by the Cambodian navy three days earlier.

June 30, 1975. The last Douglas C-47A Skytrain in routine Air Force use is retired to the U.S. Air Force Museum at Wright-Patterson AFB, Ohio.

July 15–24, 1975. U.S. astronauts Brig. Gen. Thomas P. Stafford, USAF, Vance D. Brand, and Donald K. Slayton rendezvous, dock, and shake hands with Soviet cosmonauts Alexei Leonov and Valeri Kubasov in orbit during the Apollo-Soyuz Test Project.

August 20, 1975. The Viking 1 mission to Mars is launched from Cape Canaveral AFS, Fla., on a Titan III booster. The spacecraft enters Mars orbit on June 19, 1976, and the lander, which takes soil samples and performs rudimentary analysis on them, soft-lands on July 20, 1976.

September 1, 1975. Gen. Daniel "Chappie" James, Jr., USAF, becomes the first black officer to achieve four-star rank in the U.S. military.

October 21, 1975. Fairchild Republic Co.'s A-10A Thunderbolt II makes its first flight. The first combat-ready A-10A wing will be the 354th Tactical Fighter Wing at Myrtle Beach, S.C., which will begin taking delivery of the fighters in March 1977.

November 29, 1975. The first Red Flag exercise at Nellis AFB, Nev., begins a new era of highly realistic training for combat aircrews.

January 2, 1976. Thomas C. Reed becomes Secretary of the Air Force.

May 8, 1976. The Thunderbirds, the Air Force's aerial demonstration squadron, fly the 2,000th show in their 23-year history at Mountain Home AFB, Idaho. The team's Northrop T-38A Talons are sporting a special paint scheme for America's Bicentennial celebration.

July 3, 1976. In an Israeli commando assault on Entebbe airport in Ugnada, the Israelis destroy four MiG-17s and seven MiG-21s on the ground and rescue 105 mostly Israeli and Jewish hostages held by pro-Palestinian terrorists.

July 27–28, 1976. Three different SR-71 pilots (Maj. Adolphus H. Bledsoe, Capt. Robert C. Helt, and Capt. Eldon W. Joersz) set three absolute world flight records over Beale AFB, Calif: altitude in horizontal flight (85,068.997 feet), speed over a straight course (2,193.16 mph), and speed over a closed course (2,092.294 mph). The records are still standing in 1996.

March 24, 1977. Boeing delivers the first basic production version of the E-3A Sentry (AWACS) to Tinker AFB, Okla.

April 6, 1977. John C. Stetson becomes Secretary of the Air Force.

June 30, 1977. President Jimmy Carter, citing the continued ability of the B-52 fleet and the development of cruise missiles, announces he is canceling the B-1A variable-geometry bomber program. Testing of the four B-1A prototypes will continue, however.

August 1, 1977. CMSgt. Robert D. Gaylor becomes Chief Master Sergeant of the Air Force.

August 23, 1977. Cyclist/pilot Bryan Allen wins the $95,000 Kremer Prize for successfully demonstrating sustained, maneuverable, man-powered flight in the MacReady *Gossamer Condor*. Allen pedals the aircraft, which is made of thin aluminum tubes covered with Mylar plastic and braced with stainless steel, over a 1.15-mile course at Shafter Airport, Shafter, Calif.

August 31, 1977. Alexander Fedotov,

flying in the MiG E-266M, a modified MiG-25 Foxbat, sets the recognized absolute record for altitude, reaching 123,523.58 feet at Podmosconvnoe, USSR. This record still stands as of 1996.

October 1, 1977. Volant Oak, the quarterly rotation of six Air Force Reserve and Air National Guard transports to Howard AFB, Panama, for in-place tactical airlift in Central and South America, begins.

December 1, 1977. In total secrecy, company test pilot Bill Park makes the first flight of the Lockheed XST Have Blue demonstrator at Groom Lake, Nev.. Developed in only twenty months, Have Blue is designed as a testbed for stealth technology.

February 22, 1978. The first test satellite in the Air Force's Navstar Global Positioning System is successfully launched into orbit.

March 23, 1978. Capt. Sandra M. Scott becomes the first female aircrew member to pull alert duty in SAC.

July 1, 1978. Gen. Lew Allen, Jr., becomes Air Force Chief of Staff.

August 11–17, 1978. Ben Abruzzo, Maxie Anderson, and Larry Newman complete the first crossing of the Atlantic Ocean by balloon. Flying in the helium-filled *Double Eagle II*, the trio makes the 3,100-mile flight from Presque Isle, Me., to Miserey, France, in 137 hours, 6 minutes.

November 30, 1978. The last Boeing LGM-30G Minuteman III ICBM is delivered to the Air Force at Hill AFB, Utah.

January 6, 1979. The 388th Tactical Fighter Wing at Hill AFB, Utah, receives the first operational General

Dynamics F-16A fighters. The first Air Force Reserve F-16s are delivered to the 419th TFW at Hill on January 28, 1984.

June 12, 1979. Pilot/cyclist Bryan Allen makes the first human-powered flight across the English Channel in the *Gossamer Albatross*.

July 9, 1979. The Voyager 2 space probe, launched in 1977, flies within 399,560 miles of Jupiter's cloud tops. Voyager 2 will pass Neptune in 1989.

July 26, 1979. Hans Mark becomes Secretary of the Air Force.

August 1, 1979. CMSgt. James M. McCoy becomes Chief Master Sergeant of the Air Force.

October 1, 1979. All atmospheric defense assets and missions of Aerospace Defense Command are transferred to Tactical Air Command (TAC). Also on this date, the Aerospace Audiovisual Service becomes the single manager for Air Force combat audiovisual documentation.

March 12–14, 1980. Two B-52 crews fly nonstop around the world in 43 ½ hours, covering 21,256 statute miles, averaging 488 mph, and carrying out sea surveillance/reconnaissance missions.

April 24, 1980. In the middle of an attempt to rescue U.S. citizens held hostage in Iran, mechanical difficulties force several Navy RH-53 helicopter crews to turn back. Later, one of the RH-53s collides with an Air Force HC-130 in a sandstorm at the Desert One refueling site. Eight U.S. servicemen are killed.

May 28, 1980. The Air Force Academy graduates its first female cadets. Ninety-seven women are

commissioned as second lieutenants. Lt. Kathleen Conly graduates eighth in her class.

February 9, 1981. Verne Orr becomes Secretary of the Air Force.

April 12, 1981. The space shuttle orbiter *Columbia*, the world's first reusable manned space vehicle, makes its first flight with astronauts John Young and Navy Capt. Robert Crippen aboard.

June 7, 1981. Eight Israeli Air Force F-16s, escorted by F-15s, attack the Osirak nuclear reactor near Baghdad, Iraq, disabling its core. As a result, the U.S. imposes a temporary embargo on the supply of new F-16s to Israel.

June 18, 1981. In total secrecy, company pilot Hal Farley makes the first flight of the Lockheed F-117A stealth fighter at Tonopah Test Range, Nev. The existence of this aircraft would not be publicly revealed until 1988.

June 26, 1981. The first production Grumman/General Dynamics EF-111A, a specially developed ECM tactical jamming aircraft, makes its first flight.

August 1, 1981. CMSgt. Arthur L. Andrews becomes Chief Master Sergeant of the Air Force.

October 2, 1981. President Ronald Reagan reinstitutes the B-1 bomber program canceled by the Carter administration in 1977.

November 10, 1981. For the first time, U.S. Air Forces in Europe and the German Air Force test a section of the autobahn for emergency landings.

July 1, 1982. U.S. Air Force activates

its first ground-launched cruise missile (GLCM) wing, the 501st Tactical Missile Wing, at Greenham Common in England.

July 1, 1982. Gen. Charles A. Gabriel becomes Air Force Chief of Staff.

September 1, 1982. Air Force Space Command established.

September 1–30, 1982. H. Ross Perot, Jr. and Jay Coburn complete the first circumnavigation of the globe by helicopter. Flying a modified Bell 206L Longranger, the duo average 117 mph during their 246.5 hours of flight time. The trip starts and ends at Fort Worth, Tex.

November 11, 1982. Vance D. Brand, Robert F. Overmyer, Joseph P. Allen IV, and William B. Lenoir lift off in the space shuttle *Columbia*. STS-5 is the first mission to send four astronauts aloft at one time.

February 9, 1983. The first re-winged C-5A makes its first flight at Marietta, Ga. It will be delivered to the Air Force at the end of the month.

February 10, 1983. The Cruise Pact is signed by the U.S. and Canada, allowing testing of U.S. cruise missiles in northern Canada.

March 23, 1983. Flight testing of the Rockwell B-1A resumes at Edwards AFB. This aircraft is modified for the B-1B development effort.

May 9, 1983. A C-141 crew from the 18th Military Airlift Squadron, McGuire AFB, N.J., becomes USAF's first all-female crew to fly a round-trip mission across the Atlantic.

June 17, 1983. The first LGM-118A Peacekeeper (originally MX) ICBM

is test-launched from Vandenberg AFB.

June 18, 1983. The first American woman to go into space, Sally K. Ride, is aboard *Challenger* on the seventh space shuttle mission (STS-7).

July 4, 1983. Flying in their new General Dynamics F-16A Fighting Falcons, the Thunderbirds, the Air Force's aerial demonstration squadron, perform before an estimated crowd of 2 million people at Coney Island, N.Y.

July 22, 1983. Australian Dick Smith, flying a Bell JetRanger, completes the first solo flight around the world in a helicopter. The 35,258-mile trip began August 5, 1982.

August 1, 1983. CMSgt. Sam E. Parish becomes Chief Master Sergeant of the Air Force.

August 30, 1983. Two milestones are recorded on the STS-8 space shuttle mission: The oldest astronaut, William E. Thornton, 54, and the first black astronaut, Lt. Col. Guion S. Bluford, USAF, are sent aloft on the Space Shuttle *Challenger* with three others.

October 25, 1983. Operation Urgent Fury, the rescue of American medical students on the Caribbean island of Grenada, begins. The operation will last until November 2.

November 28, 1983. The ninth space shuttle mission (STS-9) is launched. Mission Commander John W. Young becomes the first person to make six spaceflights, and *Columbia* is the first spacecraft to be launched with a crew of six. The 10-day flight is also the first to use the European Spacelab module.

1984–1989

February 3–11, 1984. Navy Capt. Bruce McCandless becomes the first human satellite as he takes the self-contained Manned Maneuvering Unit (MMU) out for a spin while in Earth orbit on space shuttle mission 41-B.

April 6–13, 1984. The 11th U.S. space shuttle mission (41-C) is a spectacular success as the defective Solar Maximum Mission satellite (Solar Max) is repaired in orbit. After mission specialist George Nelson fails to capture the satellite on his spacewalk, Terry J. Hart uses Challenger's remote manipulator arm to catch Solar Max on the fly. George Nelson and James D. A. van Hoften repair the satellite in the shuttle's payload bay before it is released.

May 22, 1984. The Chiefs of Staff of the Army and the Air Force sign a memorandum of agreement titled "Joint Force Development Process," also known as "The 31 Initiatives."

August 14, 1984. Boeing rolls out the 1,832d and last 727, a 727-252F freighter for Federal Express. The 727 is the only commercial transport to exceed the 1,500 mark in aircraft built.

September 4, 1984. The first production Rockwell B-1B bomber is rolled out at Air Force Plant 42 in Palmdale, Calif.

October 4, 1984. After her pilot husband dies of a heart attack, Elaine Yadwin takes the controls of their Piper Cherokee and manages to land at Dade-Collier Airport in South Florida. She is talked down by ground controllers.

October 5–13, 1984. On the 13th space shuttle mission, *Challenger* lifts off for the first time with a crew of seven. Mission 41-G is the first to have two female astronauts (Sally K. Ride and Kathryn D. Sullivan, who will become the first American woman to make a spacewalk) and the first to have a Canadian astronaut aboard (Marc Garneau). Commander Robert L. Crippen becomes the first to fly on the shuttle four times. Aloft, the crew refuels a satellite in orbit for the first time.

October 18, 1984. Company pilot M. L. Evenson and USAF Lt. Col. L. B. Schroeder make the first flight of the Rockwell B-1B variable-geometry bomber at Palmdale, Calif., and land at Edwards AFB. This is the first of 100 aircraft to be built in the revitalized B-1 bomber program.

December 14, 1984. Grumman pilot Chuck Sewell makes the first flight of the X-29A forward-swept-wing demonstrator at Edwards AFB. The X-29s, two of the most unusual aircraft ever built, are designed to prove the aerodynamic benefits of wings that appear to have been put on backwards.

January 24–27, 1985. The 15th space shuttle mission (51-C) is the first dedicated Department of Defense flight. The *Discovery* crew of Navy Capt. Thomas K. Mattingly (mission commander), Air Force Lt. Col. Loren J. Shriver (pilot), and Air Force mission specialists Lt. Col. Ellison S. Onizuka and Maj. Gary E. Payton, along with Marine Corps Lt. Col. James F. Buchli, deploys a classified payload, believed to be a signals intelligence satellite.

September 13, 1985. The first test of the LTV-Boeing ASM-135A air-launched antisatellite weapon against a target is successfully carried out over-the Western Missile Test Range. Launched from an F-15, the missile destroys a satellite orbiting at a speed of 17,500 mph approximately 290 miles above Earth.

October 25–November 2, 1985. USAF units take part in joint operations against Cubans and Marxists in Grenada.

December 9, 1985. Russell A. Rourke becomes Secretary of the Air Force.

December 16, 1985. After 20 years of operation, the Pioneer 6 satellite becomes the longest-running spacecraft in history. When launched in 1965, the solar-orbiting satellite had a life expectancy of six months.

January 28, 1986. The space shuttle *Challenger* explodes 73 seconds after liftoff, killing all seven astronauts, including schoolteacher Christa McAuliffe. Others on Mission 51-L include Francis R. Scobee, Navy Cmdr. Mike Smith, Judith Resnik, Ronald E. McNair, Air Force Lt. Col. Ellison S. Onizuka, and Gregory Jarvis. The manned space program will be halted for two years while vehicular and management flaws are corrected.

April 15, 1986. In Operation Eldorado Canyon, 18 USAF F-111s flying from RAF Lakenheath in England are joined by carrier-based Navy aircraft in air strikes against Libya in response to state-sponsored terrorism.

April 24–May 7, 1986. Veterans of three wars attend the Air Force Association's "Gathering of Eagles" in Las Vegas, Nev.

June 9, 1986. Edward C. Aldridge, Jr., becomes Secretary of the Air Force.

July 1, 1986. Gen. Larry D. Welch becomes Air Force Chief of Staff.

July 1, 1986. CMSgt. James C. Binnicker becomes Chief Master Sergeant of the Air Force.

October 1, 1986. The Goldwater-Nichols Act gives theater commanders increased control of forces from all services.

December 23, 1986. Richard Rutan and Jeana Yeager complete the first nonstop unrefueled around-the-world trip in their experimental *Voyager*, starting and stopping at Mojave, Calif. The trip sets recognized absolute records for speed around the world, nonstop, nonrefueled (115.65 mph); great circle distance without landing; and distance in a closed circuit without landing (both 24,986.727 miles).

July 4, 1987. Lt. Col. Robert Chamberlain (and crew) sets a dozen recognized class records for speed with payload (jet aircraft) in a Rockwell B-1B at Palmdale, Calif. The brand-new aircraft was on an acceptance flight and flew a 500-mile closed course near Vandenberg AFB, Calif. The records still stand.

July 17–31, 1987. Mike Hance becomes the first pilot to consecutively take off and land in all 50 states and the District of Columbia as he flies his Mooney 252 private plane from Honolulu, Hawaii, to Oshkosh, Wis., via the United States—all the rest of them, obviously.

September 17, 1987. Maj. Brent A. Hedgpeth (and crew) sets nine recognized class records for 5,000-km speed with and without payload (jet aircraft) of 655.09 mph in a Rockwell B-1B at Palmdale, Calif. The records still stand.

September 24, 1987. The Air Force's Thunderbirds fly for a crowd of 5,000 in Beijing. It has been nearly

40 years since a U.S. combat aircraft flew over and landed on Chinese soil.

January 1, 1988. SAC changes missile crew assignment policy to permit mixed male/female crews in Minuteman and Peacekeeper launch facilities.

January 20, 1988. The 100th and final B-1B bomber rolls off the line at Rockwell's plant in Palmdale.

February 10, 1988. The 2,000th F-16 fighter built is accepted by Singapore.

March 3, 1988. The Pioneer 8 solar orbiter, which was launched November 8, 1968, with a six-month life expectancy, is finally declared defunct.

May 23, 1988. The Bell-Boeing V-22 Osprey, the world's first production tiltrotor aircraft, is rolled out at Bell Helicopter Textron's plant in Arlington, Tex.

August 2, 1988. As evidence of thawing superpower relations, U.S. Secretary of Defense Frank C. Carlucci is given the opportunity to inspect the Soviet Tu-160 Blackjack strategic bomber during a visit to Kubinka AB, near Moscow.

September 29, 1988. Launch of the space shuttle *Discovery* ends the long stand-down of the U.S. manned space program in the wake of the *Challenger* disaster.

October 25, 1988. A U.S. Navy S-3 Viking antisubmarine warfare aircraft from the carrier USS *Theodore Roosevelt* (CVN-71) is given a $21 parking ticket after the crew overshoots a runway at a base in southern England and lands on a public road.

November 6, 1988. The Air Force launches its last Martin Marietta Ti-

tan 34D booster from Vandenberg AFB, Calif. It carries a classified payload.

November 7, 1988. The U.S. Postal Service issues a 65-cent commemorative stamp bearing the likeness of Gen. H. H. Hap Arnold in ceremonies at the Arnold Engineering and Development Center at Arnold AFB, Tenn.

November 10, 1988. The Air Force reveals the existence of the Lockheed F-117A stealth fighter, operational since 1983.

November 12, 1988. Soviet cosmonauts Vladimir Titov and Musa Manarov break the world space endurance record as they remain on board the space station Mir ("peace") for their 326th day in orbit.

November 19, 1988. Boeing KC-135R tanker crews from the 19th Air Refueling Wing (Robins AFB, Ga.), 340th ARW (Altus AFB, Okla.), 319th Bomb Wing (Grand Forks AFB, N.D.), and 384th BW (McConnell AFB, Kan.) set 16 class time-to-climb records in flights from Robins AFB. Nine of the records still stand.

November 22, 1988. Northrop and the Air Force roll out the B-2 Stealth bomber at Air Force Plant 42 in Palmdale.

November 30, 1988. The Soviets roll out the An-225 transport, the world's largest airplane.

December 9, 1988. The first Sierra Research/de Havilland Canada E-9A airborne telemetry data relay aircraft is delivered to the Air Force's 475th Weapons Evaluation Group at Tyndall AFB, Fla.

December 29, 1988. The first operational dual-role (air superiority and deep interdiction) McDonnell Douglas F-15E fighter is delivered to the Air Force.

January 4, 1989. Two Libyan MiG-23 Flogger fighters, displaying hostile intentions, are shot down over international waters by an element of U.S. Navy F-14 Tomcats operating from the carrier USS *John F. Kennedy* (CVN-67).

February 14, 1989. The first McDonnell Douglas Delta II space booster is launched from Cape Canaveral AFS. The 128-foot-tall rocket boosts the first operational NS-7 Navstar Block II Global Positioning System satellite into orbit.

February 16, 1989. Northrop completes the 3,806th and final aircraft in the F-5/T-38 series. The milestone aircraft, an F-5E, will later be delivered to Singapore.

March 1, 1989. The first General Dynamics F-16A modified under the Air Force's air defense fighter program is delivered to the Air National Guard's 114th Tactical Fighter Training Squadron at Kingsley Field, Ore.

March 19, 1989. Bell pilot Dorman Canon and Boeing pilot Dick Balzer make the first flight of the Bell-Boeing V-22 Osprey at Bell Helicopter Textron's Flight Research Center in Arlington, Tex.

March 21, 1989. NASA completes the flight test of the Mission Adaptive Wing, a modification to the advanced fighter technology integration (AFTI) F-111 that allows the curvature of the aircraft's leading and trailing edges to be varied in flight. The MAW completes 144.9 hours on 59 flights.

March 30, 1989. Fairchild delivers the first of 10 C-26A operational sup-

port aircraft to the Air National Guard's 147th Fighter Interceptor Group at Ellington ANGB, Tex. The C-26 is the military version of the Metro III commuter aircraft.

April 17, 1989. Lockheed delivers the 50th and last C-5B Galaxy transport to the Air Force in ceremonies at Marietta, Ga.

April 17–18, 1989. Lockheed pilots Jerry Hoyt and Ron Williams set 16 class time-to-climb and altitude records in separate flights in a NASA U-2C at the Dryden Flight Research Facility at Edwards AFB. The 32-year-old aircraft, which was loaned to NASA in 1971, is retired to a museum after the flights. The records still stand.

May 4, 1989. Air Force Maj. Mark C. Lee releases the Magellan probe from the payload bay of the space shuttle orbiter *Atlantis* during the first day of the four-day STS-30 space mission. The 21-foot-tall, 7,604-pound Magellan probe is designed to map Venus with its synthetic aperture radar.

May 22, 1989. Donald B. Rice becomes Secretary of the Air Force.

June 10, 1989. Capt. Jacquelyn S. Parker becomes the first female pilot to graduate from the Air Force Test Pilot School at Edwards AFB.

June 14, 1989. The first Martin Marietta Titan IV heavy-lift space booster is successfully launched from Launch Complex 40 at Cape Canaveral AFS. The booster, nearly 20 stories tall, carries a classified military payload.

July 6, 1989. The nation's highest civilian award, the Presidential Medal of Freedom, is presented to retired

Air Force Gen. James H. Doolittle in White House ceremonies.

July 6, 1989. The 169th and last MGM-31 Pershing 1A intermediate-range ballistic missile is destroyed at the Longhorn Army Ammunition Plant near Karnack, Tex., under the terms of the intermediate nuclear forces (INF) treaty.

July 17, 1989. Northrop chief test pilot Bruce Hinds and Air Force Col. Richard Couch, director of the B-2 Combined Test Force, make the first flight of the Northrop B-2A advanced technology bomber, flying from Air Force Plant 42 in Palmdale, to the Air Force Flight Test Center at Edwards AFB.

August 2, 1989. The Navy successfully carries out the first undersea launch of the Lockheed UGM-133A Trident II (D5) sea-launched ballistic missile. The missile is launched from USS *Tennessee* (SSBN-734) while cruising off Florida.

August 6, 1989. As further evidence of the thaw in U.S.-Soviet relations, two MiG-29 fighters and the giant An-225 transport land and refuel at Elmendorf AFB, Alaska, on their way to an air show in Canada.

August 8–13, 1989. The 30th mission in the U.S. space shuttle program is carried out, as the crew of five service astronauts launches a classified payload from the orbiter *Columbia*. It is the longest military shuttle flight to date.

August 24, 1989. The Voyager 2 space probe completes its grand tour of the solar system as the 1,787-pound vehicle passes within 3,000 miles of Neptune. Voyager 2 was launched in August 1977.

September 14, 1989. The Bell-Boeing V-22 Osprey til-trotor aircraft achieves its first conversion from helicopter mode to airplane mode while in flight.

September 15, 1989. McDonnell Douglas delivers the 500th AH-64 Apache helicopter to the U.S. Army at the company's plant in Mesa, Ariz.

October 1, 1989. Air Force Gen. Hansford T. Johnson, pinning on his fourth star and assuming command of U.S. Transportation Command and MAC, becomes the first Air Force Academy graduate to attain the rank of full general. He is a member of the Academy's first graduating class of 1959.

October 3, 1989. The last of 37 Lockheed U-2R/TR-1A/B high-altitude reconnaissance aircraft is delivered to the Air Force.

October 4, 1989. A crew from the 60th Military Airlift Wing, Travis AFB, Calif., lands a Lockheed C-5B transport at McMurdo Station in Antarctica. This is the first time an aircraft so large has landed on the ice continent. The C-5B, carrying 72 passengers and 168,000 pounds of cargo (including two fully assembled Bell UH-1N helicopters), lands without skis.

October 7, 1989. Wayne Handley sets the recognized U.S. record for longest inverted flat spin with the most rotations (67) in a Pitts Special acrobatic aircraft at Salinas, Calif.

December 3, 1989. Solar Max, the first satellite to be repaired in orbit, is destroyed as it reenters the atmosphere over Sri Lanka.

December 14, 1989. MAC approves a policy change that will allow female aircrew members to serve on C-130 and C-141 airdrop missions.

December 20, 1989. Operation Just Cause begins in Panama. The Air Force plays a major role, ranging from airlift, airdrops, and aerial refueling to bringing Panamanian dictator Manuel Noriega to the U.S. In Just Cause, the Lockheed F-117A stealth fighter is used operationally for the first time.

1990–1995

January 25, 1990. The Lockheed SR-71 Blackbird high-altitude, high-speed reconnaissance aircraft is retired from SAC service in ceremonies at Beale AFB, Calif. SR-71 crews flew more than 65 million miles, half at speeds above Mach 3.

January 31, 1990. Coronet Cove, the Air National Guard's rotational deployments to defend the Panama Canal, ends after more than 11 years. More than 13,000 sorties, totaling 16,959 hours, have been flown since the operation began.

February 21, 1990. The Air Force returns to dual-track pilot training. The team of McDonnell Douglas, Beech, and Quintron is selected over two other teams to provide the Tanker/Transport Training System. This turnkey operation will train pilots going on to fly "heavies" using the T-1A Jayhawk.

March 1, 1990. The Rockwell/MBB X-31A enhanced fighter maneuverability (EFM) demonstrator rolls out at Rockwell's facility at Air Force Plant 42 in Palmdale, Calif. A joint venture between the U.S. and West Germany, the X-31 is designed to prove technologies that will allow close-in aerial combat beyond normal flying parameters.

March 6, 1990. Lt. Col. Ed Yielding (pilot) and Lt. Col. J. T. Vida (reconnaissance systems officer) set four speed records, including a transcontinental mark of 2,112.52 mph (1 hour, 8 minutes, 17 seconds elapsed time) over the 2,404.05-statute-mile course from Oxnard, Calif., to Salisbury, Md., on what was at the time the last Air Force flight of the Lockheed SR-71.

March 26, 1990. Grumman rolls out the first production-standard version of the improved F-14D Tomcat for the U.S. Navy at its plant in Calverton, Long Island, N.Y.

April 2, 1990. Air Force pilot Maj. Erwin "Bud" Jenschke demonstrates in-flight thrust reversing for the first time while flying the McDonnell Douglas NF-15B S/MTD (STOL/Maneuvering Technology Demonstrator) aircraft over Edwards AFB.

April 4, 1990. McDonnell Douglas turns over the last of 60 KC-10A Extender tanker/cargo aircraft to the Air Force at its plant in Long Beach, Calif.

April 5, 1990. The first launch of the Orbital Sciences Corp./Hercules Aerospace Pegasus air-launched space booster, the first all-new booster in two decades, is successfully carried out off the California coast.

April 24, 1990. The space shuttle *Discovery*, with a crew of five, lifts off on the 35th mission in the shuttle program. The next day, astronaut Steven A. Hawley releases the Hubble Space Telescope, an on-orbit observatory with great scientific promise. Although the telescope gathers unprecedented images, it proves to be somewhat myopic (a 2-micron-wide spherical aberration—less than the width of a human hair—is found) and will have to be repaired on a 1993 shuttle flight.

April 25, 1990. Boeing delivers the 200th reengined and upgraded KC-135R tanker to the Air Force. It is delivered to the 340th Air Refueling Group at Altus AFB, Okla.

April 30, 1990. USAF announces that Air Force Special Operations Command, the first new command since 1982, will be established by early summer. This component of the U.S. Special Operations Command will be composed primarily of Twenty-third Air Force assets.

May 4, 1990. The Hughes/Raytheon AIM-120A advanced medium-range air-to-air missile (AMRAAM) passes its "final exam"—demonstration of its ability to achieve multiple kills against multiple targets. There are three direct hits and a lethal near miss in the four-missile vs. four-target test near Eglin AFB.

May 17, 1990. An Air Force crew from McGuire AFB, N.J., lands a Lockheed C-141B transport at Moscow's Sheremetyevo Airport to deliver an inoperative MGM-31 Pershing II missile that will go into a museum in Moscow. The crew then picks up an inoperative Soviet SS-20 for display at the National Air and Space Museum in Washington, D.C.

May 22, 1990. Air Force Special Operations Command is established.

May 22, 1990. Company pilot Larry Walker and Air Force pilot Maj. Erwin Jenschke land the McDonnell Douglas NF-15B S/MTD test bed in a mere 1,650 feet at the Air Force

Flight Test Center at Edwards AFB. Pratt & Whitney two-dimensional, thrust-reversing engine nozzles are the main method of stopping the aircraft.

June 1, 1990. SAC turns over the first pair of General Dynamics FB-111As to TAC. With one internal modification, the aircraft will be redesignated F-111Gs.

June 22, 1990. The Northrop/McDonnell Douglas YF-23A advanced tactical fighter prototype is rolled out in ceremonies at the ATF Combined Test Force Facility at Edwards AFB. It is powered by two Pratt & Whitney YF119-PW-100 engines. Northrop pilot Paul Metz will make the first flight August 27, 1990.

July 1, 1990. Gen. Michael J. Dugan becomes Air Force Chief of Staff.

July 11, 1990. Four Air National Guard F-16 pilots from the 177th Fighter Interceptor Group at Atlantic City IAP, N.J., escort two Soviet MiG-29 fighters and an Il-76 transport in U.S. airspace, flying from Kalamazoo, Mich., to Rockford, Ill., as part of the Soviet Union's first U.S. air show tour.

July 12, 1990. The last of 59 Lockheed F-117A stealth fighters is delivered to the Air Force in ceremonies at the company's Palmdale facility.

July 13, 1990. Alaskan Air Command ceases to exist. The former command now becomes a numbered (Eleventh) Air Force and is made part of Pacific Air Forces.

July 24, 1990. SAC ends "Looking Glass," more than 29 years of continuous airborne alert, as a Boeing EC-135C Airborne Command Post aircraft lands at Offutt AFB, Neb.

August 1, 1990. CMSgt. Gary R. Pfingston becomes Chief Master Sergeant of the Air Force.

August 7, 1990. The U.S. begins Operation Desert Shield, the large-scale movement of U.S. forces to the Middle East in response to Iraq's August 2 invasion of Kuwait and threat to Saudi Arabia.

August 8, 1990. A C-141 carrying Airlift Control Element lands in Dhahran, the first USAF aircraft into the crisis zone. F-15s from 1st Tactical Fighter Wing, Langley AFB, Va., and elements of the 82d Airborne Division, Fort Bragg, N.C., arrive in Saudi Arabia. U.S. AWACS aircraft augment Saudi AWACS aircraft orbiting over Saudi Arabia.

August 17, 1990. The first stage of the Civil Reserve Air Fleet is activated for the first time to increase the availability of airlift to the Middle East.

August 21, 1990. By this date, 1 billion pounds of materiel have arrived in or are en route to Saudi Arabia. Six fighter wings are deployed, and SAC steps up refueling efforts and RC-135 reconnaissance flights in the area. By late August, more than 40,000 reserve components of all services have been called up.

August 23, 1990. The first of two Boeing VC-25A Presidential transport aircraft is delivered to the 89th Military Airlift Wing at Andrews AFB, Md. The new aircraft, a modified 747-200B commercial transport, will replace the VC-137C aircraft currently used as Air Force One.

August 29, 1990. The Lockheed/ Boeing/General Dynamics YF-22A ATF prototype is unveiled in ceremonies at Lockheed Plant 10 in Palm-dale. This aircraft is powered by two General Electric YF120-GE-100 turbofan engines. Lockheed pilot Dave Ferguson makes the first flight of the YF-22 September 29, 1990.

September 6, 1990. The U.S. Postal Service issues a 40-cent postage stamp honoring Lt. Gen. Claire L. Chennault.

September 18, 1990. Gen. John M. Loh becomes Acting Air Force Chief of Staff.

October 11, 1990. Rockwell pilot Ken Dyson makes the first flight of the Rockwell/MBB X-31A enhanced fighter maneuverability (EFM) demonstrator at Air Force Plant 42. The flight lasts 38 minutes.

October 30, 1990. Gen. Merrill A. McPeak becomes Air Force Chief of Staff.

November 9, 1990. Col. (Dr.) Thomas C. Cook, believed to be the Air Force's last World War II combat veteran still serving, retires. He saw action as a B-24 navigator in Europe and transferred to Reserve status in 1948. He returned to active duty in 1976.

December 17, 1990. The Lockheed/ Boeing/General Dynamics YF-22 prototype is flown to an unprecedented 60° angle of attack (AOA) attitude and remains in full control in a test flight over Edwards AFB.

January 7, 1991. Saying that nobody could tell him how much it would cost to keep the program going, Secretary of Defense Dick Cheney announces that he is cancelling the McDonnell Douglas-General Dynamics A-12 Avenger attack aircraft program for default. The A-12 would have been the Navy's first stealth aircraft.

January 16, 1991. At 6:35 A.M. local time, B-52G crews from the 2d Bomb Wing, Barksdale AFB, La., take off to begin what will become the longest bombing mission in history. Carrying 39 AGM-86C air-launched cruise missiles (a conventional version of the nuclear-armed General Dynamics AGM-86B ALCM), the bomber crews fly to the Middle East and launch their missiles against high-priority targets in Iraq.

January 17, 1991. War begins in the Persian Gulf. Operation Desert Shield becomes Operation Desert Storm. More than 1,200 combat sorties are flown, and 106 cruise missiles are launched against targets in Iraq and Kuwait during the first 14 hours of the operation.

January 18, 1991. Eastern Air Lines, one of the oldest U.S. commercial carriers, goes out of business. The airline operated for 64 years.

January 25, 1991. In one of the fastest development and fielding of weapons in modern history, Air Force Systems Command's Armament Division asks the Army to machine 8-inch cannon barrels to the shape of a bomb. On February 24, the first of these Lockheed/Texas Instruments GBU-28/B bombs is tested at Tonopah Test Range, Nev., and penetrates so deeply the weapon is never found. Within five hours of delivery to Saudi Arabia, two of the 4,700-pound weapons are dropped from an F-111 on February 27.

February 6, 1991. Capt. Robert Swain of the 706th Tactical Fighter Group (AFRES), NAS New Orleans, La., shoots down an Iraqi helicopter

in the first air-to-air victory for the Fairchild A-10 Thunderbolt II attack aircraft. He uses the plane's 30mm cannon for the kill.

February 15, 1991. In one of the most unusual air-to-air victories ever, Capt. Tim Bennett and Capt. Dan Bakke of the 4th Tactical Fighter Wing at Seymour Johnson AFB, N.C., shoot down an Iraqi helicopter (probably an Mi-24 Hind) with a GBU-10 2,000-pound laser-guided bomb dropped from their F-15E.

February 22, 1991. Soviet cosmonaut Musa Manarov sets a record for accumulated time in space, amassing his 447th day in orbit. Cosmonaut Manarov is on the 83d day of his Soyuz TM-11 mission, working aboard the space station Mir, when he breaks the record.

February 28, 1991. Iraq surrenders to the U.S.-led coalition. In the 43-day, round-the-clock war, the Air Force flew 59 percent of all sorties with less than 50 percent of the assets, flew more than 50,000 combat sorties, offloaded more than 800 million pounds of fuel, and transported 96,465 passengers and 333 million pounds of cargo.

March 8, 1991. The first Martin Marietta Titan IV heavy-lift space booster to be launched from Vandenberg AFB lifts off. The booster carries a classified payload.

April 6, 1991. Operation Provide Comfort begins, humanitarian air operations to protect and supply Kurds in northern Iraq threatened by Saddam Hussein after the Gulf War, begins.

April 18, 1991. The Air Force carries out the first successful flight test of the Martin Marietta/Boeing MGM-

134A small ICBM. The missile flies 4,000 miles from Vandenberg AFB to its assigned target area in the Army's Kwajalein Missile Range in the Pacific Ocean.

April 23, 1991. Air Force Secretary Donald B. Rice announces that the Lockheed/Boeing/General Dynamics F-22 and the Pratt & Whitney F119 engine are the winners in the Advanced Technical Fighter competition.

May 6, 1991. The U.S. destroys the last of 846 MGM-31 Pershing II missiles prohibited by the INF Treaty. On May 12, the Soviet Union destroys the last of 1,846 SS-20 missiles.

June 6, 1991. The Air Force reveals the existence of the Northrop AGM-137A Triservice Standoff Attack Missile (TSSAM), a stealthy ground attack weapon with a range of less than 600 kilometers.

July 1, 1991. The Warsaw Pact, the military coalition of Soviet Bloc countries, formally disbands.

July 2, 1991. McDonnell Douglas Helicopter Co. announces the first flight of the first production helicopter built without a tail rotor. The MD520N uses a blown-air system for antitorque and directional control.

September 15, 1991. The McDonnell Douglas C-17A transport makes its first flight. The crew of four takes off from the company's plant in Long Beach, Calif., and lands 2 hours, 23 minutes later at the Air Force Flight Test Center at Edwards AFB.

September 27, 1991. Strategic bomber crews stand down from their decades-long, round-the-clock readiness for nuclear war.

November 26, 1991. Clark AB, the Philippines, is officially turned over to the Philippine government, ending nearly 90 years of US occupancy. It was the largest overseas USAF base.

December 17–19, 1991. Four naval aviators set 16 recognized class records for altitude, speed, and time-to-climb with and without payload (turboprop aircraft) in a Grumman E-2C Hawkeye at NAS Patuxent River, Md. The records still stand.

December 19, 1991. Navy Lt. Cmdrs. Eric Hinger and Matt Klunder set a recognized class record for altitude with a 1,000-kg payload (turboprop aircraft) of 41,253.6 feet in a Grumman E-2C Hawkeye at NAS Patuxent River, Md. The record still stands.

December 21, 1991. The first Rockwell new-generation AC-130U gunship is flown for the first time.

December 25, 1991. The Soviet Union ceases to exist.

January 31, 1992. The Navy takes delivery of the last production Grumman A-6 Intruder attack aircraft, closing out 31 years of Intruder production.

February 10, 1992. Operation Provide Hope, the delivery of food and medical supplies to the former Soviet Union, begins.

February 28–29, 1992. Four Air Force crews set recognized class time-to-climb records (jet aircraft) in a Rockwell B-1B at Grand Forks AFB, N.D. Twelve of the records still stand.

April 9, 1992. The Air Force's new variable-stability in-flight simulator test aircraft (VISTA), a modified General Dynamics F-16, designated NF-

16, that will replace the 40-plus-year-old NT-33, is flown for the first time at the General Dynamics facility in Fort Worth, Tex. The flight lasts 53 minutes.

May 12, 1992. Lockheed Aeronautical Systems Co. delivers the 2,000th C-130 Hercules transport in ceremonies at Marietta, Ga. The milestone aircraft, a C-130H, is later delivered to the Air National Guard's 123d Airlift Wing at Standiford Field, Ky.

June 1, 1992. SAC, TAC, and MAC are deactivated. Bomber, fighter, attack, reconnaissance, and electronic combat/electronic warfare aircraft and all ICBMs regroup under Air Combat Command (ACC). Lifter and tanker aircraft regroup under Air Mobility Command (AMC).

June 1, 1992. U.S. Strategic Command is established, with responsibility for planning, targeting, and command of U.S. strategic forces.

July 1, 1992. Air Force Systems Command and Air Force Logistics Command are merged to create Air Force Materiel Command, which is to provide "cradle-to-grave" management of weapon systems.

July 3, 1992. Air Force begins Operation Provide Promise, flying humanitarian relief missions into Croatia and Bosnia-Hercegovina. It is the longest-running air supply effort in history, officially ending January 4, 1996.

August 26, 1992. Air Force begins Operation Southern Watch to enforce a ban on Iraqi aircraft operations south of the 32d parallel.

December 9, 1992. Operation Restore Hope, an international humanitarian operation in Somalia, begins.

More than 28,000 troops are sent to safeguard food, supplies, and aid workers, from armed factions trying to seize power. Thirty-three Air Force active-duty and Reserve units take part in the initial deployment.

December 16/18, 1992. Capts. Pamela A. Melroy and John B. Norton along with company pilots William R. Casey and Charles N. Walls set a number of recognized altitude records with payload (for two different subclasses of jet aircraft) in a McDonnell Douglas C-17A Globemaster III at Edwards AFB, Calif. A class record for greatest load carried to 2,000 meters of 133,422 pounds is also set on the flight. Thirteen of the records still stand.

December 19, 1992. Capt. Jeff Kennedy and crew set a recognized class record for great circle distance without landing (jet aircraft) of 10,083.11 miles in a Boeing KC-135R. The record still stands.

December 19, 1992. An AMC KC-135R crew from the 97th Air Mobility Wing, Altus AFB, Okla., flies more than 8,700 miles from Kadena AB, Japan, to McGuire AFB, N.J., to set an aircraft class record for nonstop unrefueled flight.

December 27, 1992. While flying combat air patrol in Operation Southern Watch, two F-16 pilots from the 363d Fighter Wing, Shaw AFB, S.C., intercept a pair of Iraqi MiG-25s flying in the United Nations–imposed no-fly zone over southern Iraq. One of the pilots, flying an F-16D, fires an AIM-120A AMRAAM and downs one of the MiGs, marking the first use of the AIM-120A in combat and the first USAF F-16 air-to-air victory.

January 13, 1993. USAF Maj. Susan

Helms, flying aboard *Endeavour*, becomes the first U.S. military woman in space.

March 1, 1993. Lockheed Corp. completes acquisition of General Dynamics' Fort Worth Division. The $1.5 billion purchase gives Lockheed control of the F-16 fighter line and increases the corporation's share of the F-22 program to 67.5 percent.

March 9, 1993. A Lockheed SR-71A Blackbird reconnaissance aircraft comes out of retirement to fly its first scientific flight for NASA at the Dryden Flight Research Center at Edwards AFB. The aircraft, fitted with an ultraviolet video camera in the nose bay, is flown to an altitude of approximately 83,000 feet and collects more than 140,000 images of stars and comets.

April 12, 1993. NATO Operation Deny Fight begins, enforcing a ban ordered by the UN Security Council on aircraft operations in the no-fly zone of Bosnia-Hercegovina. The operation ends December 20, 1995.

April 28, 1993. Secretary of Defense Les Aspin lifts the long-standing ban on female pilots flying U.S. combat aircraft, including Army and Marine Corps attack helicopters.

April 29, 1993. German test pilot Karl Lang makes the first demonstration of a high-angle-of-attack, post-stall, 180° turn known as a Herbst maneuver while flying the Rockwell/MBB X-31A EFM demonstrator. The turn is completed in a 475-foot radius.

May 22, 1993. Lt. Cmdr. Kathryn P. Hire, the first woman in the Navy to be assigned to a combat unit, flies her first mission as a tactical crew member on a Lockheed P-3C Update III

maritime patrol aircraft during a bombing exercise. Commander Hire flies with VP-62, a Reserve unit based at NAS Jacksonville, Fla. The first Air Force female combat pilot will be 1st Lt. Jeannie Flynn, who will take her place in an F-15E cockpit later in 1993.

May 25–August 3, 1993. The first successful demonstration of aerobraking (using atmospheric drag to slow a spacecraft) puts the Magellan Venus probe in a lower orbit. The probe suffers no ill effects.

June 14, 1993. The first operational McDonnell Douglas C-17A Globemaster III transport is delivered to the 437th Airlift Wing at Charleston AFB, S. C.

June 17, 1993. Lt. Col. Patricia Fornes becomes the first woman to lead an Air Force ICBM unit. She assumes command of the 740th Missile Squadron at Minot AFB, S. D., a squadron once commanded by her father.

June 29, 1993. The Air Force rolls out the first Boeing OC-135B Open Skies Treaty observation aircraft at Wright-Patterson AFB, Ohio. It is the first of three that will be used by the U.S. to verify foreign compliance with arms treaties.

July 1, 1993. Air Education and Training Command established.

July 1, 1993. Day-to-day control of ICBMs passes to Air Force Space Command.

July 8, 1993. Slingsby Aviation Ltd. rolls out the first T-3A Enhanced Flight Screener for the Air Force at its plant in York, England.

July 30, 1993. The multiaxis thrust-vectoring system installed on the

VISTA NF-16 is employed for the first time in a test at the Air Force Flight Test Center. By September 1993, the aircraft will achieve a transient angle of attack of 110° and a sustained AOA of 80°.

August 5, 1993. The AFTI F-16 completes its 600th mission at the Air Force Flight Test Center. The flight collects data for the AFTI/F-16 Ground Collision Avoidance System test effort.

August 6, 1993. Sheila E. Widnall, associate provost and professor of aeronautics and astronautics at the Massachusetts Institute of Technology, to be Secretary of the Air Force. Dr. Widnall becomes the first female Secretary for any of the armed services. After Senate confirmation, she is sworn in on August 6.

August 11–14, 1993. Global Enterprise, an ACC exercise to train aircrews for long-distance power-projection missions, is carried out from Ellsworth AFB, S.D. Two Rockwell B-1B Lancers are flown to Europe, across the Mediterranean and Red Seas around the Arabian Peninsula, and land at a staging base in southwest Asia. After exchanging crews, the B-1s are flown from southwest Asia, via Japan, over the Aleutians, and then back to South Dakota. Total flight time is 37.3 hours, and the 24-hour first leg is the longest flight ever made by a B-1B crew.

August 17, 1993. The first of 350 early-model Boeing B-52 bombers is cut into five pieces with a 13,000-pound steel guillotine at Davis-Monthan AFB, Ariz. The bombers were destroyed under the terms of the Strategic Arms Reduction Talks II Treaty.

August 18, 1993. McDonnell Douglas's Delta Clipper Experimental (DC-X) subscale single-stage-to-orbit prototype makes a 60-second first flight at the White Sands Missile Range, N. M. The 42-foot-tall vehicle takes off vertically, hovers at about 150 feet, moves laterally approximately 350 feet, and lands tail-down.

August 24/26, 1993. Two mixed Air Force and contractor crews set recognized class time-to-climb and altitude records (jet aircraft) in a McDonnell Douglas C-17A Globemaster III at Long Beach, Calif. All four of the records still stand.

September 10, 1993. Boeing rolls out the 1,000th 747 commercial jetliner in ceremonies at its Seattle, Wash., plant. The milestone aircraft, a 747-400, will be delivered to Singapore Airlines. The first jumbo jet was rolled out in September 1968.

September 15, 1993. Boeing announces that work on the first B-52H bomber to be adapted for conventional warfare missions has been completed at its facility in Wichita, Kan.

October 8, 1993. Capt. Pamela A. Melroy and company pilot Richard M. Cooper set two recognized jet aircraft class records for altitude with a 70,000-kg payload (32,169 feet) and greatest mass carried to a height of 2,000 meters (161,023 pounds) in a McDonnell Douglas C-17A Globemaster III at Edwards AFB, Calif. The records still stand.

December 17, 1993. On the 90th anniversary of the Wright brothers' first sustained flight, the first operational Northrop B-2 stealth bomber, *The Spirit of Missouri*, is delivered to the 509th Bomb Wing at Whiteman AFB, Mo.

February 10, 1994. Lt. Jeannie Flynn, the first female selected for USAF combat pilot training, completes her F-15E training.

February 28, 1994. Air Force F-16s, operating under NATO command, shoot down four Bosnian Serb Super Galeb attack aircraft after twice warning the Serb jets to leave Bosnian airspace. It is NATO's first combat in its 45-year history.

April 7, 1994. Capt. Michael S. Menser (and crew) sets a recognized class record for 10,000-km speed without payload (jet aircraft) of 599.59 mph flying from Grand Forks AFB, N. D., to Monroeville, Ala., to Mullan, Idaho, in a Rockwell B-1B Lancer. At the same time, Capt. R. F. Lewandowski (and crew) sets the recognized record for a different class for 10,000-km speed without payload (jet aircraft) of 594.61 mph over the same course, also in a B-1. Both records still stand.

April 10, 1994. In NATO's first air attacks on ground positions since the Alliance was founded 45 years previously, two Air Force F-16C fighters destroy a Bosnian Serb Army command post with Mk. 82 500-pound bombs.

May 3, 1994. Col. Silas Johnson, Jr., 93rd Wing Commander, flies the last B-52G to the "Boneyard" at Davis Monthan AFB, Ariz., thus removing this series from the active inventory.

June 3, 1994. Maj. Andre A. Gerner and company pilot John D. Burns set a recognized record for STOL aircraft for greatest mass carried to a height of 2,000 meters (44,088 pounds) in a McDonnell Douglas C-17A Globemaster III at Edwards AFB, Calif. The record still stands.

June 24, 1994. The F-117 stealth aircraft is officially named Nighthawk.

June 29, 1994. First visit of a U.S. space shuttle to a space station, the Russian *Mir*.

July 1994. The 184th Bomb Group, Kansas Air National Guard, becomes the first Guard unit to be equipped with the B-1B.

August 2, 1994. During a Global Power mission to Kuwait, two B-52s from the 2d Bomb Wing, Barksdale AFB, La., sets a world record while circumnavigating Earth. Flying 47.2 hours, the bombers set a world record not only for the longest B-52 flight but also for the longest jet aircraft flight in history. Dropping 54 bombs over a range located 25 miles from the Iraqi border, the aircraft demonstrate their global reach and power on the fourth anniversary of the Iraqi invasion of Kuwait.

August 4, 1994. Two B-1Bs (one from the 384th Bomb Group and one from the 184th Bomb Group of the Kansas Air National Guard) complete a 19-hour nonstop Global Power mission to Hawaii. This is the first time the 184th, the first ANG unit to receive the B-1B, flies a Global Power mission.

October 10, 1994. USAF responds to hostile movements in the Persian Gulf area by Iraq's Saddam Hussein by deploying 122 combat aircraft to augment the 67 already in place. Four bombers fly nonstop from bases in the United States to deliver 55,000 pounds of bombs on target, on time, within audible range of Saddam's forces. The Iraqis withdraw northward. Secretary of Defense William Perry later says, "The Air Force really has deterred a war."

October 14, 1994. The first-ever operational C-17 mission lands in the Persian Gulf area, delivering a 5-ton "rolling command post," five vehicles, and assorted supplies for the Army. The 17.2-hour flight was the longest mission to date for a C-17.

October 26, 1994. Gen. Ronald R. Fogleman becomes Air Force Chief of Staff.

October 26, 1994. CMSgt. David J. Campanale becomes Chief Master Sergeant of the Air Force.

November 21–23, 1994. In Project Sapphire, Air Mobility Command C-5s transport more than 1,300 pounds of highly enriched uranium from the former Soviet republic of Kazakhstan to Dover AFB, Del., to protect this large supply of nuclear materials from terrorists, smugglers, and unfriendly governments. From Dover, the uranium is taken to Oak Ridge, Tenn., to await conversion to commercial nuclear fuel.

February 7, 1995. A crew from Whiteman AFB, Mo., makes the first drop of live bombs from the Northrop Grumman B-2A Spirit stealth bomber. The two Mk. 84 bombs were dropped as part of the B-2's first Red Flag exercise at Nellis AFB, Nev.

March 15, 1995. Lockheed Corporation and Martin Marietta complete their merger that was announced the previous August 29. The newly created Lockheed Martin Corporation, with $23 billion in annual sales, becomes the world's largest aerospace and defense contractor.

April 7, 1995. 2d Lt. Kelly Flinn, the first woman to join a bomber crew, begins student pilot training with the 11th Bomb Squadron, 2d Bomb Wing, Barksdale AFB, Louisiana.

April 27, 1995. The Global Positioning System (GPS) satellite constellation is declared to have achieved full operational capability (FOC) by Air Force Space Command.

June 1, 1995. Lockheed Martin and Boeing roll out the stealthy DarkStar Tier III Minus high-altitude unmanned aerial vehicle in ceremonies at Palmdale, Calif.

June 2, 1995. Air Force F-16 pilot Capt. Scott F. O'Grady is shot down over northwest Bosnia on an Operation Deny Flight mission. Rescued after an eight-day ordeal during which he subsisted on bugs and rainwater, Captain O'Grady returns home to a hero's welcome.

June 3, 1995. Two 7th Wing (Dyess AFB, Tex.) B-1Bs land after completing a historic 36-hour, 13-minute, 20,100-mile, nonstop around-the-world flight. This Global Power mission, called Coronet Bat, requires six air refuelings using assets from ACC, AMC, USAFE, PACAF, U.S. Central Command, ANG, and AFRES. To mirror a realistic training scenario for wartime taskings, Coronet Bat incorporates bombing runs over the Pachino Range, Italy; the Torishima Range, near Kadena AB, Japan; and the Utah Test and Training Range.

June 6, 1995. Astronaut Norman Thagard, flying on the Russian Mir space station, set the U.S. record for spaceflight endurance, passing 84 days, 1 hour, and 17 minutes in space. The previous U.S. record-holders were the three astronauts on the third Skylab mission in 1974.

June 22, 1995. Secretary of the Air Force Sheila Widnall announces that Beech Aircraft has been selected to develop and deliver the Joint Primary Aircraft Training System (JPATS) for the Air Force and Navy. The new trainer, a modified version of the Swiss Pilatus PC-9 turboprop traini- ner, will replace the USAF's Cessna T-37Bs and the Navy's Beech T-34Cs.

June 28, 1995. The National Air and Space Museum of the Smithsonian Institution finally puts the *Enola Gay*, the B-29 that dropped the first atomic bomb on Japan, on display. The exhibition program is straightfor- ward and factual. Earlier, amid major controversy, the museum canceled plans to show the *Enola Gay* as a prop in a politicized horror show after Congress and the public—alerted by reports from the Air Force Associa- tion—took strong objection.

July 7–August 5, 1995. The C-17 airlifter, earlier beset by troubles so severe that program cancellation was a possibility, produces outstanding re- sults in a month-long wartime surge test. In November, the Department of Defense says the C-17 has bounced back from its problems and authorizes the Air Force to buy up to 120 of these aircraft.

July 8, 1995. The Minuteman III ICBM achieves 100 million hours of operational duty.

July 29, 1995. Air Combat Com- mand activates the 11th Reconnais- sance Squadron, an unmanned aerial vehicle (UAV) unit, and assigns it to the 57th Operations Group at Nellis AFB, Nev. Equipped with the Tier II Predator—and later Tier II+ and Tier III—types, the 11th RS is tasked to explore the use of remotely piloted aircraft.

August 25, 1995. A 2d Bomb Wing B-52H and its five-member crew set

an aviation world record from Ed- wards AFB, Calif.—flying 5,400 nauti- cal miles, unrefueled, with a payload of 11,000 pounds in 11 hours, 23 minutes with an average speed of 556 mph.

August 30, 1995. U.S. Air Force, Navy, and Marine aircraft lead Opera- tion Deliberate Force, a NATO bombing campaign responding to Bosnian Serb mortar attacks that killed 38 civilians at an outdoor mar- ket in Sarajevo.

September 1, 1995. Officially emerging from mothballed status, the SR-71 is declared operationally capa- ble by Air Combat Command.

September 10, 1995. The *First Lady*, the first production Lockheed C-130 Hercules, is retired in ceremo- nies at Duke Field, Fla. This aircraft, which was first flown on April 7, 1955, had a distinguished career, in- cluding more than 4,500 combat hours in Southeast Asia after it was converted into a gunship. The *First Lady* was later retired to the USAF Armament Museum at Eglin AFB, Fla.

October 1, 1995. Air Combat Com- mand activates the 609th Information Warfare Squadron at Shaw AFB, S. C.

November 2, 1995. Lt. Col. Greg Feest becomes the first pilot to log 1,000 hours of flight time in the Lockheed F-117A Nighthawk stealth fighter.

December 6, 1995. A crew from the 37th Airlift Squadron at Ramstein AB, Germany, marks the beginning of Operation Joint Endeavor by flying their Lockheed C-130E into Tuzla, Bosnia. Operation Joint Endeavor is the ongoing NATO effort to enforce the Bosnian peace treaty signed at Dayton, Ohio.

December 7, 1995. Literally going out in a blaze of glory, the Galileo spacecraft's atmospheric probe separates from the orbiter and plunges into Jupiter's atmosphere. The probe sends a stream of data back to the orbiter and manages to survives 58.5 minutes before it is crushed by the intense pressure. Galileo was launched from the space shuttle in 1989.

December 19, 1995. A federal judge rules in favor of General Dynamics and McDonnell Douglas, establishing that the Navy's A-12 Avenger stealth attack aircraft was canceled for the convenience of the government, rather than default. The A-12 was canceled in 1991.

December 20, 1995. NATO air operation Decisive Endeavor begins to monitor and enforce peace implementation in Bosnia.

January 4, 1996. Sikorsky test pilot Rus Stiles and Boeing test pilot Bob Gradle make the first flight of the Army's YRAH-66 Comanche helicopter prototype at West Palm Beach, Fla. The RAH-66, designed for armed reconnaissance/light attack missions, is the first helicopter to employ stealth technologies.

February 14, 1996. A crew flying the Northrop Grumman E-8A Joint STARS surveillance platform over Bosnia makes the type's 50th mission in support of Operation Joint Endeavor, breaking a sortie record set in Operation Desert Storm in 1991. Despite the E-8's successes in these two operations, Joint STARS is still officially in development.

INDEX

AAF Long Range Development and
Research Program, 17. *See also*
SAG
Abzug, Bella, 242
Acheson, Dean, 51, 52, 55, 61
aerial refueling, 106–7
Aerospace Medical Division, 195
African-Americans and the Air Force,
233–37, 287
Agent Orange, 147–49
Air America (CIA airline), 188
*Air Board to Review Plans and
Policies,* 31
Air Combat Command (ACC), 122,
316, 318, 319
Air Corps Ferrying Command, 178,
190–91
See also Air Transport Command
Air Corps Tactical School (ACTS),
206–7
Air Defense Command (ADC), 29,
30, 31, 124, 127–28, 129–33,
134
Air Force Communication Command
(AFCC), 209

Air Force Computer-Aided
Management System (CAFMS),
298
Air Force Institute of Technology,
207–9
Air Force Intelligence Command, 316
Air Force Logistic Command
(AFLC), 163, 173, 177, 192–97,
197–98, 199–202, 316
Air Force Materiel Command
(AFMC), 316
Air Force NCO (Noncommissioned
Officer) Corps, 223–24, 224–28
Air Force Research Division (AFRD),
191, 192, 318
Air Force Reserve (AFR), 245–46,
282, 297, 310
Air Force Satellite Communications
(AFSATCOM), 276
Air Force Space Command
(AFSPACECOM), 209, 294, 310,
315, 316
Air Force Special Operations
Command (AFSOC), 209, 290,
315–16

Air Force Systems Command
(AFSC), 163, 173, 177, 191, 192,
194, 195, 197, 316
Air Materiel Command (AMC), 30,
116, 191, 197–98
Air Mobility Command (AMC), 122,
316, 318, 319
Air National Guard (ANG), 245–46,
282, 297, 310, 318
Air Proving Ground Command, 30
Air Research and Development
Command, 116, 191–92
Air Training and Education
Command, 203, 316
Air Training Command (ATC), 30,
116, 177, 202–3, 203, 203–4, 205–
6, 316
See also Air Training and
Education Command
Air Transport Association, 180
Air Transport Command (ATC), 30,
178–79
See also Air Corps Ferrying
Command
Air University Command (AU), 202–
3, 207, 316
See also Air Training and
Education Command
Airborne Warning and Control
System (AWACS), 247.
See also aircraft (USA: Boeing):
Boeing E-3A Sentry
aircraft (Chinese)
Shenyang J–6, 161
aircraft (German)
Gotha Go–229 flying-wing (jet
fighter), 259
aircraft (Great Britain/United
Kingdom)
Dakotas (RAF C–47), 42
Fairey Firefly, 94
Gloster Meteor F.8, 86, 94
Hawker Sea Fury, 94
Short Sunderland flying boat, 94

Slingsby T–3 Firefly, 204
aircraft (Iraq)
Dassault Mirage, 302
MiG–29, 292
aircraft (Japan)
Mitsubishi Mu–300 Diamond, 204
Zero, 64
aircraft (Kuwait)
Mirage interceptors, 292
aircraft (Soviet Union)
Antonov An–12 cargo plane, 186
Antonov An–22 cargo plane, 186
Ilyushin Il–10, 56, 59–60, 72
Ilyushin Il–28, 140
Lavochkin La–7, 56, 59, 72
Lavochkin La–9, 93
MiG–15/MiG–15 bis, 57, 63–65, 65–
67, 67–69, 70, 71, 77, 84, 85–86,
89, 139, 159–60, 160–61, 161,
170–71
MiG–17, 139, 161
MiG–19, 139, 161–62
MiG–21 Fishbed, 161, 162–63, 263
Myasishchyev M–4 Bison, 111
Polikarpov Po–2 biplane
("Bedcheck Charlie"), 66, 93
Tupelov Tu–4, 55, 130
Tupelov Tu–16 Badger, 111
Tupelov Tu–20 Bear, 111
Yakovlev Yak–9, 56, 59
Yakovlev Yak–11, 59
aircraft (USA)
Bell X–2, 123
Blackhawk helicopter, 222
CH–53 helicopter, 186
Chase XC–20G combat glider, 147
de Havilland C–7 Caribou, 182–83,
188
Joint Advanced Strike Technology
(JAST) fighter, 326
Kaman HH–43B helicopter, 188
KB–29/KB–29M tanker, 106
KB–50 tanker, 106
KB–97 tanker, 106

Piper L–4 (liaison aircraft), 56
SB–17 aircraft, 58
SB–29 aircraft, 58
Shooting Star, 78
TFX fighter, 127
Vought A–7, 174
Vought A–7E Corsair II, 285
Vultee (Stinson) L–5 (liaison
    aircraft), 56, 91
aircraft (USA: Beech)
Beech RC–45 Expeditor, 104, 147
Raytheon (Beech) Mk II, 204
Raytheon (Beech) T–1 Jauhawk, 204
aircraft (USA: Boeing)
Boeing 707, 182
Boeing 747, 187, 257
Boeing B–17, 26, 242
Boeing B–29 Superfortress, 26, 28,
    40, 41–43, 57, 58, 64, 73, 76, 81–
    83, 84, 85–88, 104, 155, 200, 247
Boeing B–47 Stratojet, 45, 102,
    103, 104, 104–5, 106, 109, 115,
    130, 201
Boeing B–50 Superfortress, 40,
    102, 104
Boeing B–52 Stratofortress, 102,
    103, 104, 105, 107, 109, 122,
    124, 155, 165–67, 167–69, 169,
    174–75, 201, 257, 261, 261–62
Boeing B–52D, 167, 174
Boeing B–52F, 167
Boeing B–52G (Buffs), 174, 301,
    307–8
Boeing B–52H, 257, 326
Boeing C–97 Stratofreighter, 42,
    101, 184
Boeing C–135 Stratofreighter, 182
Boeing E–3A Sentry (AWACS),
    196, 222, 253, 258, 261, 298,
    326
Boeing E–3B Sentry (AWACS),
    165, 311, 326
Boeing E–4, 197, 290
Boeing EC–135, 290

Boeing KC–97 Stratofighter, 104
Boeing KC–135 Stratotanker, 104,
    106–7, 122, 137, 152, 155, 163,
    174, 201, 262, 307, 310
Boeing KC–135A, 288
Boeing RB–17 Flying Fortress, 58,
    88, 104
Boeing RB–29 Superfortress
    reconnaissance plan, 58, 88, 89,
    104
Boeing RB–47 Stratojet, 104
Boeing RC–135 Rivet Joint aircraft,
    311
Boeing T–43, 327
Boeing WB–29, 58
Boeing X–20 Dyna-Soar, 195, 268–
    69
Boeing/Grumman E–8 Joint
    STARS, 260–61, 304, 306, 307,
    311, 326
aircraft (USA: Cessna)
Cessna O–2 Skymaster, 171
Cessna T–37, 204
Cessna T–41 Mescalero, 204
aircraft (USA: Consolidated)
Consolidated B–24, 26
Consolidated B–36 Peacemaker,
    102, 104, 130
Consolidated C–87, 179
Consolidated-Vultee B–36 (B–
    36D), 44–46
aircraft (USA: Convair)
Convair B–58 Hustler, 121–22,
    122, 124
Convair F–102 Delta Dagger
    (Deuce), 130
Convair F–106 Delta Dart (Six)/
    F–106A, 124, 130
Convair YF–102, 124
aircraft (USA: Curtiss)
Curtiss C–46 Commando, 60, 179
Curtiss F9C–2 (lightweight fighter),
    16
Curtiss pusher aircraft, 12

aircraft (USA: Douglas)
Douglas A–1E Skyraider, 146, 151, 171, 189, 200
Douglas B–18, 242
Douglas B–26, 57, 58, 59, 62, 72, 75, 76, 79–81, 85–88, 93, 145, 151–52, 169, 200
Douglas B–66, 124, 128
Douglas C–5A Galaxy, 185–87
Douglas C–5B Galaxy, 187
Douglas C–46, 90, 91, 179
Douglas C–47, 26, 41–42, 59, 60, 90, 91, 94, 104, 179, 183
Douglas C–54 Skymaster, 34, 41–42, 58, 59, 60, 90, 91, 104, 179, 188
Douglas C–74, 42
Douglas C–124 Globemaster II ("Old Shaky"), 90–91, 104, 107, 137, 180, 182, 184
Douglas C–133, 137, 184
Douglas C–133A Cargomaster, 181, 182, 184
Douglas DC–3, 179
Douglas EB–66, 165, 173, 174
Douglas F–15 Eagle, 196, 256–57, 263
Douglas RB–26, 145, 146, 169
Douglas RB–66, 128, 205
Douglas RC–47, 147
Douglas SC–47, 145, 146
McDonnell Douglas A–4, 186
McDonnell Douglas C–17, 202, 253, 262
McDonnell Douglas C–17A Globemaster III, 260
McDonnell Douglas F–4 Phantom II, 205, 246, 263, 264–65
McDonnell Douglas F–15 Eagle, 196, 264
McDonnell Douglas F–15E Strike Eagle, 239, 248, 304, 307
McDonnell Douglas F–105F, 205

aircraft (USA: Fairchild)
Fairchild A–10 Thunderbolt II (Warthog), 222, 245, 306, 310
Fairchild C–82, 42
Fairchild C–119 Flying Boxcars, 90, 91, 143, 184, 201
Fairchild C–123 Provider/C–123K, 147, 147–49, 182, 188
Fairchild JC–119, 273
Fairchild UC–123K, 149
aircraft (USA: General Dynamics/ Lockheed Martin)
General Dynamics F–16 Fighting Falcon, 196, 248, 257, 310, 320
General Dynamics F–111 Aardvarks, 174, 245, 252, 253, 258, 261, 301
General Dynamics F–111F Aardvarks, 285
General Dynamics FB–111, 258, 290
General Dynamics FB–111G, 257, 290
General Dynamics YF–16, 265–66
aircraft (USA: Grumman)
Boeing/Grumman E-8 Joint STARS, 260–61
Grumman A–6E Intruders, 285
Grumman EA–6B, 258
Grumman EF–111A Raven ("Spark Vark"), 258, 286, 301–2
Grumman HU–16 Albatross amphibians, 188
Grumman SA–16 Albatross, 91–92
aircraft (USA: Lockheed/Lockheed Martin)
Combat Talon I Lockheed MC–130, 289
Disco Lockheed EC–121T (Super Constellation), 159, 174
Lockheed A–12/SR–71, 261, 273
Lockheed AC–130 Spectre gunship, 169, 288

Lockheed C–5, 194, 262, 288, 294, 310, 318
Lockheed C–17, 262
Lockheed C–121 Super Constellation, 184
Lockheed C–130 Hercules, 91, 124, 128, 137, 174, 182–83, 186, 188, 189, 262, 288, 310, 318, 320
Lockheed C–130A (YC–130) Hercules, 183
Lockheed C–130E Hercules, 181, 182, 183
Lockheed C–130J Hercules, 183
Lockheed C–141 StarLifter, 182, 184, 185, 186, 262, 286, 288, 294, 310, 318
Lockheed C–141B, 293
Lockheed EC–121 ABCCC, 171, 174
Lockheed EC–130E, 311
Lockheed EC–130H Compass Call, 311
Lockheed (formerly General Dynamics) F–16 Fighting Falcon, 306
Lockheed F–80/F–80C, 40, 41, 57, 58, 59, 59–60, 64, 72, 73, 74, 75, 76, 79, 84, 85, 109, 130, 204
Lockheed F–94/F–94B, 93, 130
Lockheed F–104, 70, 124, 128, 130–31
Lockheed (formerly General Dynamics) F–111, 306, 307
Lockheed F–117, 202, 306–7
Lockheed Have Blue, 259–60
Lockheed NC–130H, 273
Lockheed RF–26, 89
Lockheed RF–80A/RF–80C, 58, 88, 89
Lockheed RF–86, 89, 93
Lockheed RT–33, 147
Lockheed T–33, 204
Lockheed TR–1A, 304

Lockheed U–2 reconnaissance plane, 96–97, 107, 124, 139, 140, 261, 273
Lockheed U–2R, 304
Lockheed Martin F–16, 262
Lockheed Martin F–22A/B, 261, 325–26
Lockheed/Martin F–117A Nighthawk (stealth fighter), 247, 259–60, 288, 290, 299–301, 326
aircraft (USA: McDonnell/McDonnell Douglas)
McDonnell F–4/F–4C/F–D/F–4E Phantom II, 156, 161, 162, 163, 164–65, 171, 173, 196, 200
McDonnell F–101/F–101B, 124, 128, 130
McDonnell RF–101/RF–101C, 128, 147, 152
McDonnell XF–85 Goblin, 107
McDonnell Douglas A–4, 186
McDonnell Douglas AH–64 Apache attack helicopter, 299
McDonnell Douglas C–17, 202, 312, 326
McDonnell Douglas C–17A Globemaster III, 260
McDonnell Douglas F–4, 205
McDonnell Douglas F–15 Eagle, 196, 245
McDonnell Douglas F–15C Eagle, 293, 302
McDonnell Douglas F–15D Eagle, 293
McDonnell Douglas F–15E Eagle, 239
McDonnell Douglas F–105F, 205
McDonnell Douglas F/A–18 Hornets, 285
McDonnell Douglas KC–10/KC–10A, 262, 288
aircraft (USA: Martin)
Martin B–26, 73, 145

aircraft (USA: Martin) (*continued*)
Martin B–57, 128, 152
Martin RB–57 Canberra, 104, 107, 152
aircraft (USA: North American)
North American B–25, 104
North American B–45, 89
North American F–51 (P–51) Mustang, 26, 40, 56, 57, 58, 59, 72–75, 84, 92, 94, 104, 130, 204
North American F–82/F–82G Twin-Mustang, 57, 58, 59, 72, 73, 104, 130
North American F–86/F–86A/F–86E/F–86F Sabre, 57, 60, 64–65, 65–67, 67–69, 70, 77, 93, 104, 107, 161
North American F–100 Wild Weasel, 128, 152, 157, 158–59
North American F–105/F–105D/F–105G, 152, 158, 162–63, 174
North American RS–70 Mach 3, 195
North American RT–28, 147
North American T–6 Texan trainer (Mosquitoe), 56, 74, 76, 204, 246
North American T–28 (trainer), 145, 146, 151, 169, 200
North American TB–25, 204
North American YF–100/YF–100A, 124, 161
North American YF–107A, 124
North American X–15, 123–24
aircraft (USA: Northrop)
Northrop B–2 Spirit (stealth bomber), 202, 250, 260, 326
Northrop F–17, 248
Northrop F–89, 130, 131
Northrop T–38 Talon, 124, 204
Northrop Tacit Blue, 259, 260
Northrop YF–17, 265
aircraft (USA: Republic)
Republic F–84D/F–84E Thunderjet, 76–77, 85, 93, 107

Republic F–105 Thunderjet (Thud), 128, 163–64, 165–67
Republic P–47, 26
Republic RF–84K FICON (fighter conveyor), 107
Republic YF–105, 124
aircraft (USA: Rockwell)
North American/Rockwell B–1, 196
Rockwell B–1A Lancer (canceled by Carter), 196, 245, 247, 248, 249, 252, 253, 257
Rockwell B–1B Lancer (revived by Reagan), 196, 202, 250, 253, 257–58, 262, 326
aircraft (USA: Sikorsky)
Sikorsky CH–3 helicopter, 171
Sikorsky H–5 helicopter, 91–92, 92–93
Sikorsky HH–3E Jolly Green Giant helicopter, 189, 310
Sikorsky HH–53 Jolly Green Giant helicopter, 174, 189
Sikorsky MH–53J Pave Low helicopter, 288, 299
Sikorsky MH–60 Pave Low helicopter, 288–89
Airey, Paul W., 229–30
Airlift Task Force (ATF), 42
airlifts (Vietnam War), 182–84, 184–87, 187–88
Akhromeyev, Sergei F., 223
Akron (U.S. Navy dirigible ZRS–4), 15–16
Aldridge, Edward C. "Pete," Jr., 243, 251
Aldrin, Edwin E., 207
Aldrin, Edwin E. "Buzz," Jr., 207
All-Volunteer Force, 227–28, 239, 245
Allen, Lew, 249, 250, 271
Anderson, Rudolf, Jr., 139, 140
Anderson, Samuel E., 199
Andrews, Frank M., 21, 31
Apt, Milburn, 123

Arnold, Henry Harley "Hap," 2, 6, 7,
    8–19, 21–27, 29, 35, 109, 179,
    191, 207, 243, 322, 327
Aspin, Les, 242
Atkins, Herbert L., 79
Atomic Energy Commission, 28
Aurand, Henry S., 41
Aviation Week, 295
AWPD–1 (1941), 24

Bach, Lawrence V., 65
Ball, George, 139
Bane, Thurman, 207
Bao Dai, Emperor, 143–44
Barcus, Glenn O., 71, 93
Barnes, Thomas N., 231
Berlin blockade, 41–43
    See also Cold War
Bertram, William, 77
Bettinger, Stephen J., 71
Bissel, Richard, 273
Blakeslee, Don, 76
Blesse, Frederick C. "Boots," 92
Bode, Hendrik W., 113
Boyd, John R., 264, 265
Bradley, Mark E., 199
Bradley, Omar, 30, 51, 52
Brandon, Brent, 302
Briggs, James E., 85
Brooke, Edward, 242
Brown, George, 246–47, 249
Brown, Harold, 195, 244, 248–49, 252
Brown, Ronald, 327
Brown, Russell, 64–65, 84
Bundy, McGeorge, 139, 141
Bunker, Ellsworth D., 148
Burke, Arleigh "30–Knot," 136
Burns, Richard L., 72
Bush, George, 287, 289, 292, 295,
    296–97, 297, 298, 312, 314
    See also Desert Storm; Operation
    Desert Shield; Persian Gulf War
Butler, George L., 257, 318

Cambodia, air strikes in, 172
Campanale, David, 230
Carlucci, Frank C., 217
Carter, Jimmy, 247, 248–49, 251,
    253, 270
Cheney, Richard, 287–88, 295, 296,
    312
Chennault, Claire, 24, 206
Chickering, Edwin S., 89
Chief Master Sergeant of the Air
    Force (CMSAF), 228–31
Chou En-lai, 54
Churchill, Winston, 22, 27, 29, 39
CIA (Central Intelligence Agency),
    54, 126, 188, 272–74, 274
Circular 59 *(War Department
    Reorganization),* 22
Civil Reserve Air Fleet (CRAF), 181,
    294
Civilian Pilot Training, 203
Clay, Lucius D., 41
Clifford, Clark, 156
Cochran, Jacqueline, 45
Coghill, Milo B., 149
Cold War, 1–5, 29, 38–40, 137–38,
    242, 252–53, 259, 270–71
    Berlin blockade, 41–43
    Cuban Missile Crisis, 138–41
    missile gap, 135, 138, 251
    SALT (disarmament talks), 249
    START (strategic arms limitation
    talks), 250
    See also Korean War; Vietnam War
Collins, Eileen, 239
Combat Cargo Command, 180
*Command and Employment of Air
    Power* (War Department Field
    Manual [FM] 100–20), 23
Community College of the Air Force
    (CCAF), 232–33
community services (Air Force), 219,
    222–23
    See also compensation; health care;
    housing; personnel tempo

compensation (Air Force), 219–20, 230
See also community or family services; health care; housing; personnel tempo
Creech, Wilbur "Bill," 64, 213, 214–16, 216–17, 217–18, 219, 315
Crossfield, Scott, 124
Crowe, William, Jr., 223
Cuban Missile Crisis, 138–41

Davis, Benjamin O., 235
Davis, George A., 71
Decatur, Stephen, 285
Declaration of Policy of the National Security Act (1947), 34–35
Defense Communications Agency (DCA), 267
Defense Communications System (DSCS), 276–77, 310
Defense Meteorology Satellite Program (DMSP), 277–78
Defense Reorganization Act of 1958, 124–27, 212, 243
Defense Satellite Communications System, 294, 304
Defense Support Program (DSP), 275–76
Dellums, Ron, 242
Demilitarized Zone (DMZ: Vietnam), 151, 170
Dempster, K. C., 157
Denton, Jim, 302
Department of Defense Housing Management Manual, 220
Desert Shield (and Desert Storm)
Scud missiles and launchers, 293, 299, 303–5, 308
search and rescue, 313
statistics, 312–13
Strike Command, 290–91
U.N. Security Council response, 297

U.S. and coalition aircraft losses, 302
U.S. attack (air), 297–99, 299–305, 306–8
U.S. attack (ground), 308–9
U.S. reaction and buildup, 292–93, 294–95, 295–97, 297
U.S. television and, 302
See also aircraft (Iraq); aircraft (Kuwait); Operation Desert Shield; Persian Gulf War
Dewald, Robert H., 60
Dewey, Thomas E., 51
Distant Early Warning, 132
Donovan, Jack, 158
Doolittle, Jimmy, 32, 113, 204
Dougherty, Russell, 213, 237, 238–39, 246, 320
Douglas, James H., Jr., 127
Doyle, Miles M., 146
Dugan, Michael J., 212, 290, 293, 295–97, 312
Dulles, Allen W., 273
Dulles, John Foster, 96, 143
Dunn, Louis G., 113
Duong Van Minh, 151

Eagleston, Glenn T., 65
Eaker, Ira C., 9, 11, 25, 26, 35
Eckman, Robert, 73
Edwards, Idwal H., 234
Eisenhower, Dwight D., 16, 21, 30, 32, 47, 51–52, 53, 95, 96, 110–11, 115, 121, 124–27, 128, 267–68, 278
Enthoven, Dr. Alain C., 156
Essence of Security: Reflections on Office, The (McNamara), 236
Estes, Howell M., Jr., 183
Everest, Frank F., 68, 123, 129
Executive Order 9877, 35, 37
Executive Order 9981, 234–35
Extension Course Institute, 231–32

Fahd, King Abdul Aziz ibn, 292–93, 293
Fairchild, Muir S., 206, 207
family services (Air Force), 219, 222–23
  See also compensation; health care; housing; personnel tempo
Far East Air Force (FEAR), 56–59, 93–94
Feest, Gregory, 288
Fernandez, Manuel J., Jr., 70
Finletter, Thomas K., 43, 46
First War Powers Act (1941), 22
Fisher, Roger, 170
Fithian, Ben L., 93
Five Pillars of TQM: How to Make Total Quality Management Work for You, The (Creech), 218
Fleet Satellite Communications system, 276
Flood, Daniel, 180
Flynn, Jeannie, 239
Fogleman, Ronald R., 320–21
Forrestal, James V., 25–26, 34, 37, 43–44, 179, 234
Fox, Orrin R., 72
Fraser, Carl, 59
From Here to Eternity (Jones), 47

Gabriel, Charles A., 207, 250, 251, 283, 288, 313, 314
Gabreski, Francis S. "Gabby," 69, 70
Gagarin, Yuri, 193
Ganey, Wiley D., 86–87
Gardner, Trevor, 113, 115
Gates, Bill, 119
Gates, Thomas S., 126
George, Harold L., 206
Gerrity, Thomas P., 199
Gesell, Gerhard A., 236
Getchell, Ralph, 301
Gilpatrick, Roswell L., 192
Glaspie, April, 291
Glenn, John, 269

Global Positioning System (GPS), 274–75, 299, 310, 322
Global Reach-Global Power (white paper), 283–84
Glosson, Buster C., 293, 294, 297, 305
Goebbels, Joseph, 29
Goldwater, Barry, 153
Gorbachev, Mikhail, 289
Gore, Al, 273
Grant, Ulysses S., 99
Grenada, invasion of, 284–85
Groves, Fergus C., 149
Guggenheim Aeronautical Laboratory (GALCIT), 15
Gulf of Tonkin Resolution, 152

Hall, Thomas B., 72
Hanoi Hilton (Vietnamese prison), 189–90
Hansell, Haywood, 206
Hartinger, James V., 271
Havel, Václav, 289
health care (Air Force), 219–20
  See also community or family services; compensation; housing; personnel tempo
Hess, Dean E., 73
Heyser, Richard S., 139
HIAD (Handbook of Instructions for Aircraft Designers), 10
Hinton, Bruce N., 65
Ho Chi Minh, 142, 143, 155
Ho Chi Minh trail (Vietnam War), 144–45, 148, 153, 171–72
Holm, Jeanne M., 238
Holzman, Benjamin G., 191
Hoover, Herbert, 15
Hope, Bob, 188
Horner, Charles A. "Chuck," 213, 216–17, 291, 297, 305–6, 308, 312
housing (Air Force), 219, 220–21
  See also community or family

housing (Air Force) (*continued*)
    services; compensation; health
    care; personnel tempo
Hudson, William G. "Skeeter," 59
Hughes, Howard, 119
Humphrey, Hubert H., 100
Hunter, Frank O'Driscoll "Mock,"
    11
Hussein, Saddam, 291, 293, 294–95,
    303
    See also aircraft (Iraq); Desert
    Storm; Operation Desert Shield;
    Persian Gulf War
Hyland, Lawrence A., 113

Igloo White (anti-infiltration barrier:
    Vietnam War), 169–72
Initial Postwar Air Force-1 (IPWAF–
    1), 24
integration
    and the Air Force, 233–37
    and the Korean War, 235
INTELSAT, 274
Iraq-Iran war, 292
    See also Persian Gulf War
Israeli Air Force, 298, 302–3, 306
    See also Desert Storm; Operation
    Desert Shield; Persian Gulf
    War

Jabara, James, 67, 71
James, Daniel "Chappie," 235
Jameson, Arlen Dirk, 318
Johnson, Edward "Rabbit," 73
Johnson, Kelly, 273
Johnson, Leon W., 27
Johnson, Louis A., 37, 44, 51, 52,
    111
Johnson, Lyndon B., 141, 143, 153,
    154–56, 170, 184, 244, 297
Joint Primary Aircraft Training
    System (JPATS), 204

Joint Vision 2010, 321
Jones, David C., 99–100, 101, 212,
    214, 223, 246, 247–48, 249, 250,
    254, 270, 293
Jones, James, 47

Keller, K. T., 110
Kelly, Joseph W., 86
Kennan, George F., 135
Kennedy, John F., 121, 126, 135–38,
    138–41, 141, 143, 145, 147, 150,
    236, 251, 267, 268, 291
Kennedy, Robert, 139
Kenney, George C., 9, 30, 34, 58
Khrushchev, Nikita, 133, 137, 138–
    41, 269
Killian, James R., Jr., 115
Kim Il Sung, 53–54, 78
Kincheloe, Ivan, 70, 123
King, Benjamin H., 145
Kistiakowski, George B., 113–14
Knerr, Hugh J., 31
Korean War, 3, 6
    Air Force intervention, 59–61
    air superiority, 63–65, 65–67, 67–
    70, 70–71
    air war, conduct of, 62–63
    air/sea rescue, 91–93
    beginning of, 51–56
    bombers, 79–81, 81–83, 83–85, 85–
    88
    cargo, movement of, 90–91
    Far East Air Force (FEAR), 56–
    59, 93–94
    ground war, 71–75, 75–79, 83–85
    and integration, 235
    phases of, 61–62
    reconnaissance, 88–90
    statistics, 94
    See also Cold War
Kratt, Jacob, 77
Krick, Irving, 16
Kuter, Laurence S., 9, 24, 26, 206

Kuwait
Hussein's vandalism against, 306
Iraqi invasion of, 291, 292, 306–8
oil fields, setting fire to, 308
See also aircraft (Kuwait); Desert
Storm; Operation Desert Shield;
Persian Gulf War

Lahm, Frank P., 178
Laird, Melvin, 173, 184, 245, 269
Lamb, Al, 158
Landsat, 274
Laos, secret war in, 169
Larkins, Fred, 59
Larson, Robert D., 149
Lauritsen, Charles C., 114
Lavelle, John D., 245
Lehman, John, 285
LeMay, Curtis E., 30, 31, 96, 99–103,
103, 103–5, 107–8, 108–10, 115,
127, 133, 136, 140, 150, 174,
198, 206, 212, 238, 244, 247,
252, 254, 315
Lenin, Vladimir, 29
Lennon, Thomas, 307
Lin Piao, 85
Lincoln, Abraham, 52
Little, James W. "Poke," 59
Lobdell, Harrison, Jr., 79
Locher, Roger C., 189
Loh, Michael, 212, 265, 296, 313, 317–
18, 319
Longstreet, James, 69
Loring, Charles A., 74
Los Angeles (U.S. Navy dirigible ZR-
3), 15
Los Angeles Times newspaper, 295
Lovett, Robert A., 9, 21–22, 126
Lyons, Sam R., 93

MacArthur, Douglas, 30, 34, 52, 57,
61, 62, 72, 76, 82, 91

MacKay Trophy, 12, 14, 185
MacNarney, Joseph J., 9
McCone, John, 139
McConnell, John P., 153, 174, 228,
230, 244, 270
McConnell, Joseph C., Jr., 70, 92–93
McCoy, James M., 231
McElroy, Neil H., 119–20, 124–26,
181
McGuire, Allen, 77
McKee, William Fulton "Bozo," 31,
199
McLucas, John L., 243, 246
McNamara, Robert S., 109, 111, 126,
129, 136, 139, 141, 141–43, 146,
147, 149–52, 155–56, 170, 171,
172, 182, 186, 192–93, 201, 212–
13, 236, 244, 246, 247, 251, 263,
268, 269, 270, 297
McNaughton, John T., 142, 170
Macon (U.S. Navy dirigible ZRS-5),
15–16
McPeak, Merrill A. "Tony," 206, 296–
97, 312, 313–18, 319–20
MAD (mutual assured destruction), 7
Malik, Jacob, 55
Manned Orbiting Laboratory (MOL),
252, 269
Mark, Hans, 243
Marr, Jack F., 234
Marsh, Robert T. "Tom," 270
Marshall, Carl W., 148
Marshall, George C., 8, 9, 10, 21–22,
24–25, 26, 32
Marshall Plan, 40
Martin B-10 bombers, 14
M*A*S*H television series, 92
Mayaguez incident, 242
Meir, Golda, 186
Meyer, John C., 65, 247
Meyer, John J., 175
Mickley, Nyle S., 72
Military Air Transport Command
search and rescue, 188–90

Military Air Transport Service
(MATS), 177–82, 182–84, 184–
87, 187–88
See also Military Airlift Command
Military Airlift Command (MAC),
177, 183–84, 184–87, 187–88,
188–90, 315
See also Military Air Transport
Service
Military Strategic and Tactical
Relay (Milstar) System, 197, 276,
277
Millikan, Clark B., 113
Millikan, Robert A., 15
Milstar satellite communications, 197,
276, 277
Ming, General, 151
missile program, 110–14
BMEWS (ballistic missile early
warning system), 195
intercontinental ballistic missile
(ICBM) system, 96–97, 97–98,
111, 115–20, 123
intermediate-range ballistic missile
(IRBM) system, 96, 111, 116
Polaris/Poseidon/Trident missile
programs, 273–74
Project MX–744 (Convair), 112
Project MX–1593 (Atlas), 112–13,
195
SAM (surface-to-air missile)
deployment (Vietnam), 156–59
See also space program
missiles
AGM–28A Hound Dog cruise
missile, 121
AGM–45 Shrike missile, 157
AGM–69A SRAM (short-range
attack missile), 196
AIM–9B Sidewinder heat-seeking
missile, 161, 162, 302
ALCM cruise missile, 301
Atlas ICBM, 112–13, 115–17, 118,
123

Bomarc medium-range interceptor,
131–32
Hughes GAR–1 (AIR–4) Falcon,
131
Jupiter (Army) IRBM, 117
LGM–118A Peacekeeper (MX),
196, 249, 250
Martin Matador, 112, 128
Maverick AGM–65, 196
MB–1 (AIR–2) Genie, 131
Minuteman ICBM, 117, 118, 195,
253
Minuteman II ICBM, 118, 195,
253
Minuteman III ICBM, 118, 195,
253, 259, 261, 262–63
North American Navajo, 112
Northrop "Boojum," 112
Patriot missile, 304
Peacekeeper (LGM–118A) missile,
259, 262
SA–2 Guideline missile, 174
Scud missiles and launchers, 293,
299, 303–5, 308
Sparrow, 162
Thor IRBM, 96, 116, 117, 118
Titan ICBM, 116, 117, 118, 195,
277
Titan II ICBM, 117–18, 195, 277
Tomahawk land attack missile
(TLAM), 301
missiles (China)
CSS–2 IRBM, 278
missiles (Soviet Union)
AA–2 Atoll missile (MiG
armament), 161, 162–63
Cuban Missile Crisis, 138–41
rocket technology, 113, 115, 116,
121
SA–2 missile, 138, 140, 156–57
SS–18 ICBM, 253
SS–19 ICBM, 253
Mitchell, Billy, 6, 8, 13–14, 16, 35,
46, 206

MITRE (think tank), 18, 192, 243
Moffett, William A., 16
Moffett, Mrs. William A., 16
Momyer, William W. "Spike," 162, 171
Moore, Joseph H., 142
Moran, Charles "Chalky," 59
Morris, Harold E., 74
Muccio, John J., 56

Nam Il, General, 60
NASA (National Aeronautics and Space Administration), 195, 268, 274
National Oceanic and Atmospheric Administration (NOAA), 274
National Reconnaissance Office (NRO), 274, 275, 278
National Security Act (1947), 37
National Security Agency (NSA), 274
Navstar Global Positioning System (GPS), 274–75, 299, 310, 322
NCO (Noncommissioned Officer) Corps, 223–24, 224–28
NCO academy, 231–32
Nelson, George A., 76
New World Vistas, 322, 324–25, 325–27
Ngo Dinh Diem, 144, 147, 150–51
Nguyen Cao Ky, 151
Nguyen Khanh, 151
Nguyen Van Thieu, 148, 173
Nimitz, Chester, 34
Nixon, Richard M., 137, 149, 172, 172–74, 244
Noriega, Manuel, 287–89
Norstad, Lauris, 9, 25, 26, 30, 33–34
North American Aerospace Defense Command (NORAD), 133, 271, 276
North Atlantic Treaty Organization (NATO), 46, 137, 249
North Vietnamese Air Force, 160–61

Northrop, Jack, 260
nuclear weapons, 113, 122, 293, 299
Nugent, Richard E., 234

Odlum, Floyd, 45
O'Donnell, Emmett "Rosie," Jr., 82, 85
Olds, Robin, 161, 163
O'Malley, General, 318
Operation Bolo (Vietnam War), 162–63
Operation Desert Shield (and Desert Storm/Persian Gulf War), 239, 287
  U.S. reaction and buildup, 292–93, 294–95, 295–97, 297
  See also aircraft (Iraq); aircraft (Kuwait); Desert Storm; Persian Gulf War
Operation El Dorado Canyon (raid on Qaddafi), 285, 285–87
Operation Just Cause (Panama invasion), 287–89, 290
Operation Linebacker (Vietnam War), 172–76
Operation Mule Train (Vietnam War), 147
Operation Nickel Grass (Yom Kippur War), 186
Operation Ranch Hand (Vietnam War), 147–49
Operation Rolling Thunder (Vietnam War), 154–56, 171, 293
Operation Urgent Fury (Grenada invasion), 284–85
Orr, Verne, 237, 250

Pacific Air Forces (PACAF), 209
Packard, Ashley B., 77
Packard, David, 202, 218, 265
Panama, invasion of, 287–89, 290
Parish, Sam E., 231

Partridge, General, 59, 74
Patterson, Robert P., 33, 34
Patton, George P., 46, 68
Paulus, Friedrich von, 69
Perry, William J., 220, 221, 247
Pershing, John J., 8
Persian Gulf War, 1, 4, 5, 6, 7, 17,
    122, 192, 202, 216–17, 227, 239,
    257, 258, 262, 277
  AWACS aircraft and, 298
  chemical and biological warfare,
    293, 299
  GBU–28–B bomb, 309
  Iran and, 292, 302–3
  Iraqi desert fortifications, 294–95
  Iraqi forces, 293, 302–3
  Israel and, 298
  friendly fire, 312–13
  Kuwait, Iraqi invasion of, 291, 292,
    306–8
  Kuwaiti oil fields, setting fire to, 308
  Scud missiles and launchers, 293,
    299, 303–5, 308
  search and rescue, 313
  statistics, 312–13
  Strike Command, 290–91
  U.N. Security Council response,
    297
  U.S. and coalition aircraft losses,
    302
  U.S. attack (air), 297–99, 299–305,
    306–8
  U.S. attack (ground), 308–9
  U.S. reaction and buildup, 292–93,
    294–95, 295–97, 297
  U.S. television and, 302
  See also aircraft (Iraq); aircraft
    (Kuwait); Desert Storm;
    Operation Desert Shield
personnel tempo (Air Force), 219,
    221–22
  See also community or family
    services; compensation; health
    care; housing

Phouma, Souvanna, 137, 169
pilot training, 203–4
Pitchford, John, 158
Pittsburgh Courier newspaper, 235
Plummer, James W., 273
Poe, Bryce, II, 72, 199
Pogue, L. Welch, 178
Polifka, Karl L. "Pop," 88–89
Porter, Charles, 59
Powell, Colin, 27, 287, 290, 292, 295,
    296, 298, 312
  See also Desert Storm; Operation
    Desert Shield; Persian Gulf War
Power, Thomas S., 100
Powers, Gary, 273
POWs (Vietnam War), 189–90
Prandtl, Ludwig, 15
Price, John M. "Jack," 59
Professional Military Education
    (PME), 206–7
Project Forecast, 193–94
Project Mercury, 195
Proxmire, William, 242
Puckett, Allen E., 114
Pueblo incident, 242

Qaddafi, Muammar, raid on, 285, 285–
    87
quality of life (in the Air Force), 217–
    18, 219
  community or family services, 219,
    222–23
  compensation, 219–20
  health care, 219–20
  housing, 219, 220–21
  personnel tempo, 219, 221–22
Quarles, Donald A., 95, 111–12
Quesada, Elwood R., 30–31, 97
Question Mark, flight of, 30

race and the Air Force, 233–37
Radford, Arthur W., 44

Ragland, Dayton W. "Rags," 235
Ramo, Simon, 113
RAND Corporation (think tank), 18, 192, 243, 284
Rapid Deployment Joint Task Force, 291
Rawlings, Edwin W., 198–99
Reagan, Ronald, 5, 181, 245, 250, 253
Realities of American Foreign Policy, The (Kennan), 135
Red Crown (radar warning and control vessel), 159
Report to the President and the Congress (Perry), 220
Rhee, Syngman, 53, 61
Rice, Donald R., 284
Ridgeway, Matthew, 61, 62, 78
Risner, Robinson, 70
Ritchie, Steve, 159
Ritland, Osmond J., 273
Rivers, L. Mendel, 181, 226, 228, 254
Robins, Augustine W., 178
rockets (Project MX–1593 Atlas), 112–13, 115–17, 118, 123, 195
    See also missile program; space program
Rommel, Erwin, 101
Roosevelt, Franklin D., 10, 22
Roosevelt, Theodore, 33
Rumsfield, Donald, 246
Rusk, Dean, 139
Russ, Robert, 212, 223, 297
Ryan, John D. "Three Finger Jack," 174, 214, 232, 244, 246

Sacred Cow (Douglas C–54), 34
Saenger, Eugen, 269
SAG (AAF Scientific Advisory Group), 17–18
SAMs (surface-to–air missiles), 156–59, 216–17
Sandlin, Harry T., 72
satellites

antisatellite weapons (Soviet Union), 268
    communications, 276–77
    Corona spy-satellite, 194, 272–74, 278
    Defense Satellite Communications System, 294, 304
    Global Positioning System (GPS), 274–75, 299, 310, 322
    meteorology, 277–78
    Milstar satellite communications, 197, 276, 277
    missile defense alarm, 275–76
    navigation, 274–75
    reconnaissance and surveillance, 278
    SPADATS (Space Detection and Tracking System), 195
    Sputnik (I & II), 110, 116, 272
    See also Manned Orbiting Laboratory
Schlesinger, James R., 190, 245, 252
Schillereff, Raymond E., 60
Schilling, David, 41
Schriever, Bernard A., 96–97, 113, 114–20, 191–92, 193, 195, 243, 322, 327
Schroeder, Patricia, 242, 253
Schwarzkopf, H. Norman, 291, 293–94, 298, 305, 312
    See also Desert Storm; Operation Desert Shield; Persian Gulf War
Scott, Winfield, 99
Scowcroft, Brent, 296
Seamans, Robert C., 243, 244–45
Sebille, Louis J., 73–74
Semiautomatic Ground Environment (SAGE) system, 132–33, 195
Shalikashvili, John M., 222–23, 321
Sharp, Dudley S., 127
Sharp, Ulysses S. Grant, 153, 174
Shenandoah (U.S. Navy dirigible), 16
Sherman, Forrest P., 33–34

Shields, Thomas L., 86
Shofner, Floyd K., 147
Simms Station (Dayton, Ohio), 11
Slaughter, William W., 77
Spaatz, Carl "Tooey," 6, 9, 19, 26, 29, 30, 35, 38, 99, 103, 206
space program, 97, 123, 267, 267–72, 272–74, 274
    Air Force Space Command (AFSPACECOM), 209
    Boeing X–20 Dyna-Soar, 195, 268–69
    governmental and civilian agencies, 274
    Mercury-Gemini-Apollo program, 268, 269
    NASA, 195, 268, 274
    Project Mercury flights, 195
    Soviet achievement, 137
    U.S. Space Command, 271–72
    Vostok spacecraft, 193
    women in, 239
    See also Manned Orbiting Laboratory; missile program; NASA; rockets; satellites; "Star Wars" program
Space Technology, 295
Sprey, Pierre, 265
Stalin, Joseph, 29, 38–39
"Star Wars" program, 4, 270
Starbird, Alfred, 170
Stewart, Jimmy, 129
Stone, Robert A., 218
Strategic Air Command (film), 129
Strategic Air Command (SAC), 29, 30, 40, 82, 98, 99–103, 103, 103–5, 115–17, 120–22, 122, 124, 134, 137–38, 139, 154–56, 205, 252, 290, 315, 318
    aerial refueling, 106–7
    See also Air Combat Command; Air Mobility Command
Stratemeyer, George E., 31, 57, 68, 72, 82, 88

Stroukoff, Michael, 147
Sullivan, John L., 44
Summers, Harry C., Jr., 126
Sun Tzu, 27, 199
Sweeney, Walter Campbell, Jr., 129, 318
Symington, Stuart, 9, 31, 36–37, 44, 46, 234

Tactical Air Command (TAC), 29, 30, 97, 106, 109, 122, 124, 127–28, 128–29, 134, 141, 154–56, 215–16, 290, 315, 318
    See also Air Combat Command; Air Mobility Command
Talbott, Harold E., 95, 111–12, 114
Tate, Steven "Tater," 302
Taylor, Maxwell D., 135–37, 139, 141, 142, 156
Tehran, American hostages in, 248
Teller, Dr. Edward, 113
Terhune, Charles H., Jr., 193
thermonuclear weapons, 113, 122, 293, 299
Thyng, Harrison R., 69–70
Time magazine, 65
TOPCAP (Total Objective Plan Career Airmen Personnel), 226
Total Package Procurement (TPP), 186–87, 264
Total Quality Management (TQM), 217–18, 219
    community or family services, 219, 222–23
    compensation, 219–20
    health care, 219–20
    housing, 219, 220–21
    personnel tempo, 219, 221–22
Toward New Horizons (SAG publication), 18
Trier, Robert, 158
Troop Carrier Command, 179

Truman, Harry S., 19, 26, 32, 33–35, 37, 40, 43–44, 51–52, 61, 62, 77, 111, 137, 234–35
Truman Doctrine, 40
Tse-tung, Mao, 54
Tunner, William H., 42, 90, 91, 180
Tuskegee experiment, 233
Twining, Nathan F., 95, 114, 115, 206, 247

Uncertain Trumpet (Taylor), 135
Universal Military Training (UMT), 24
U.S. Air Force Academy (USAFA), 203
U.S. Air Forces in Europe (USAFE), 209, 315
U.S. Central Command (CENTCOM), 291
U.S. Readiness Command, 291
U.S. Space Command (USSPACECOM), 271–72, 276, 314
U.S. Strategic Command (USSTRATCOM), 314, 318
U.S. Transportation Command (USTRANSCOM), 314
USAF Museum (Wright Patterson Air Force Base), 149
USS *America* (carrier), 285
USS *Bataan* (escort carrier), 76
USS *Boxer*, 73
USS *Cape Esperance* (escort carrier), 65
USS *Constitution*, 103
USS *Coral Sea* (carrier), 285
USS *Maddox* (destroyer), 152
USS *Pueblo* crisis, 185
USS *C. Turner Joy* (destroyer), 152

Van Boven, Paul W., 92–93
Vandenberg, Hoyt S., 9, 26, 30, 31, 45, 46, 57, 63, 65, 69, 76, 86, 97, 99, 206

Van Fleet, James A., 62
Van Fleet, James A., Jr., 62
Van Zandt, Carl, 45
Vaughn, Harry H., 52
Vicellio, Henry H., Jr., 199
Vietnam War, 3, 5, 6, 7
    airlifts in, 182–84, 184–87, 187–88
    American forces as active participants, 152–54, 154–56, 244
    Cambodia, air strikes in, 172
    Demilitarized Zone (DMZ), 151, 170
    early involvement, 137, 141–43, 143–44, 145–46
    Gulf of Tonkin Resolution, 152
    Ho Chi Minh trail, 144–45, 148, 153, 171–72
    Igloo White (anti-infiltration barrier), 169–72
    Operation Bolo, 162–63
    Operation Linebacker (II), 172–76
    Operation Mule Train, 147
    Operation Ranch Hand (defoliants), 147–49
    Operation Rolling Thunder, 154–56, 171, 293
    North Vietnamese Air Force, 160–61
    POWs, 189–90
    SAM deployment, 156–59
    war in Laos, 169
    See also Cold War
Vinson, Carl, 16, 45, 254
Vo Nguyen Giap, 145
von Karman, Theodor, 14–18, 115, 191, 243, 322
von Neumann, Dr. John, 113, 115
Vostok spacecraft (USSR), 193

Walker, Walton H., 61, 69, 72, 74
Wallace, George, 99–100
Walmsley, John S., 80
Walt, Lewis W., III, 167

Washington Post newspaper, 295
Wayne, Robert E., 60, 92
Wedemeyer, Albert, 41
Weighted Airman Promotion System
    (WAPS), 226
Weinberger, Caspar, 250, 252
Weisner, Jerome B., 114
Welch, Larry, 212, 251, 254, 264,
    283, 287–88, 296, 312, 314
Westmoreland, William C., 142, 167,
    168, 169, 184, 187
Weyland, Otto P. "Opie," 68, 87, 128
Wheeler, Earle, 174
Where We Stand (von Karman), 18
Whisner, William, 70
White, Robert H., 166
White, Thomas D., 99, 114, 115, 116,
    119, 136, 191, 206, 267
Widnall, Sheila E., 243, 320, 322
"Wild Blue Yonder, The" (song), 1
Wilhelm, Kaiser, 29
Wilson, Charles E. "Engine Charlie,"
    111, 127
Wolko, Frank, 123

women and the Air Force, 238–39,
    243
Women's Air Service, 179
Women's Auxiliary Army Corps
    (WAAC), 238
Wooldridge, Dean, 113
World War II, air power in, 2–3, 5,
    18–19
Worth, Cedric, 45
Wright, Orville, 11–12, 178
Wright, Wilbur, 11–12
Wright Flyer (pusher aircraft), 12
Wright Model C (pusher aircraft), 12

Yeager, Charles "Chuck," 69, 123
Yom Kippur War, 186, 246
Yorks, Avro, 42

Zeppelin LZ-126, 15
Ziegler, Jean, 123
Zuckert, Eugene B., 127, 150, 192–
    93, 234, 264, 322